CONTEMPORARY MARKETING

17e

David L. Kurtz
University of Arkansas

Australia • Brazil • Japan • Korea • Mexico • Singapore • Spain • United Kingdom • United States

Contemporary Marketing, 17th Edition
David L. Kurtz

Vice President, General Manager, Social Science & Qualitative Business: Erin Joyner
Product Director: Mike Schenk
Sr. Product Manager: Jason Fremder
Sr. Content Developer: Elizabeth Lowry
Sr. Product Assistant: Jamie Mack
Marketing Manager: Jeffrey Tousignant
Content Project Manager: Megan Guiliani
Sr. Media Developer: John Rich
Manufacturing Planner: Ron Montgomery
Production Service: Integra Software Services Pvt. Ltd
Sr. Art Director: Stacy Jenkins Shirley
Intellectual Property
 Analyst: Diane Garrity
 Project Manager: Betsy Hathaway
Cover/Internal Designer: Redhangar Design
Cover Image Background: © ouh_desire/Shutterstock.com
Cover Image (Pizza Sign): © J.D.S/Shutterstock.com
Cover Image (TV): © Stokkete/Shutterstock.com
Cover Image (Pizza on iPhone): © El Nariz/Shutterstock.com
Cover Image (Image on TV):
 © iStockphoto.com /Photolyric
Tablet collage in chapter opener vignette:
 Laurent davoust/iStock/Thinkstock and Wavebreakmediamicrro/Veer
Evolution of a Brand Photo: © Serdar Tibet/Shutterstock.com
Career Readiness: © wavebreakmedia/Shutterstock.com and © Gts/Shutterstock.com
Marketing Success: © ra2studio/Shutterstock.com

© 2016, 2015 Cengage Learning
WCN: 01-100-101

ALL RIGHTS RESERVED. No part of this work covered by the copyright herein may be reproduced, transmitted, stored, or used in any form or by any means graphic, electronic, or mechanical, including but not limited to photocopying, recording, scanning, digitizing, taping, Web distribution, information networks, or information storage and retrieval systems, except as permitted under Section 107 or 108 of the 1976 United States Copyright Act, without the prior written permission of the publisher.

> For product information and technology assistance, contact us at
> **Cengage Learning Customer & Sales Support, 1-800-354-9706**
>
> For permission to use material from this text or product,
> submit all requests online at **www.cengage.com/permissions**
> Further permissions questions can be emailed to
> **permissionrequest@cengage.com**

Unless otherwise noted all items © Cengage Learning®.
Solving an Ethical Controversy: © Lightspring/ Shutterstock.com
Strategic Implications: © alphaspirit/ Shutterstock.com
EOC Case and Video Case: © wongwean/ Shutterstock.com
Part Case: © iStockphoto.com/ amygdala_imagery

Library of Congress Control Number: 2014954370
Student edition ISBN: 978-1-305-07536-8

Cengage Learning
20 Channel Center Street
Boston, MA 02210
USA

Cengage Learning is a leading provider of customized learning solutions with office locations around the globe, including Singapore, the United Kingdom, Australia, Mexico, Brazil, and Japan. Locate your local office at: **www.cengage.com/global**

Cengage Learning products are represented in Canada by Nelson Education, Ltd.

To learn more about Cengage Learning Solutions, visit **www.cengage.com**

Purchase any of our products at your local college store or at our preferred online store **www.cengagebrain.com**

Printed in the United States of America
Print Number: 04   Print Year: 2018

This edition of *Contemporary Marketing* is dedicated to the Cengage Learning sales representatives.

The sales representatives have been crucial in helping get the message out regarding the innovations in *Contemporary Marketing* and acting as my eyes and ears—providing insights that have allowed the author to continually innovate and improve his product.

ABOUT THE AUTHOR

DAVE KURTZ

During **Dave Kurtz's** high school days, no one in Salisbury, Maryland, would have mistaken him for a scholar. In fact, he was a mediocre student, so bad that his father steered him toward higher education by finding him a succession of backbreaking summer jobs. Thankfully, most of them have been erased from his memory, but a few linger, including picking peaches, loading watermelons on trucks headed for market, and working as a pipefitter's helper. Unfortunately, these jobs had zero impact on his academic standing. Worse yet for Dave's ego, he was no better than average as a high school athlete in football and track.

But four years at Davis & Elkins College in Elkins, West Virginia, turned him around. Excellent instructors helped get Dave on a sound academic footing. His grade point average soared—enough to get him accepted by the graduate business school at the University of Arkansas, where he met Gene Boone. Gene and Dave became longtime co-authors; together they produced more than 50 books. In addition to writing, Dave and Gene were involved in several business ventures. Unfortunately, Gene passed away, but Dave continues to carry on the tradition of *Contemporary Marketing*.

Dave wishes you the best of luck in your marketing course. If you have any questions or comments, you can contact Dave at profkurtz@gmail.com.

BRIEF CONTENTS

Preface xxiii

1 Designing Customer-Oriented Marketing Strategies 1

Chapter 1	Marketing: The Art and Science of Satisfying Customers 2
Chapter 2	Strategic Planning in Contemporary Marketing 34
Chapter 3	The Marketing Environment, Ethics, and Social Responsibility 60
Chapter 4	Social Media: Living in the Connected World 98
Chapter 5	E-Business: Managing the Customer Experience 134

2 Understanding Buyers and Markets 169

Chapter 6	Consumer Behavior 170
Chapter 7	Business-to-Business (B2B) Marketing 202
Chapter 8	Global Marketing 238

3 Target Market Selection 271

Chapter 9	Market Segmentation, Targeting, and Positioning 272
Chapter 10	Marketing Research in the Era of Big Data 308
Chapter 11	Relationship Marketing and Customer Relationship Management (CRM) 338

4 Product Decisions 373

| Chapter 12 | Product and Service Strategies 374 |
| Chapter 13 | Developing and Managing Brand and Product Categories 408 |

5 Distribution Decisions 441

| Chapter 14 | Marketing Channels and Supply Chain Management 442 |
| Chapter 15 | Retailers, Wholesalers, and Direct Marketers 478 |

6 Promotional Decisions 513

| Chapter 16 | Integrated Marketing Communications, Advertising, and Public Relations 514 |
| Chapter 17 | Personal Selling and Sales Promotion 554 |

7 Pricing Decisions 591

| Chapter 18 | Pricing Concepts 592 |
| Chapter 19 | Pricing Strategies 624 |

Appendix A Developing an Effective Marketing Plan A-1
Appendix B Financial Analysis in Marketing B-1
Online Appendix Your Career in Marketing (www.cengagebrain.com)
Glossary G-1
Name & Company Index I-1
Subject Index I-23
International Index I-53

CONTENTS

Preface xxiii

Part 1
Designing Customer-Oriented Marketing Strategies

CHAPTER 1 Marketing: The Art and Science of Satisfying Customers 2

OPENING VIGNETTE
Vineyard Vines Markets the Good Life 2

CAREER READINESS
Landing a Job in Social Media Marketing 12

MARKETING SUCCESS
The Weather Channel Expands Its Social Reach 21

SOLVING AN ETHICAL CONTROVERSY
Banning Sugary Drinks 25

Chapter Overview 4

What Is Marketing? 5
 A Definition of Marketing 6 | Today's Global Marketplace 7

Five Eras in the History of Marketing 8
 The Production Era 9 | The Sales Era 9 | The Marketing Era 10 | The Relationship Era 11 | The Social Era 11 | Converting Needs to Wants 11

Avoiding Marketing Myopia 12

Extending the Traditional Boundaries of Marketing 13
 Marketing in Not-For-Profit Organizations 13 | Characteristics of Not-For-Profit Marketing 14

Nontraditional Marketing 15
 Person Marketing 16 | Place Marketing 17 | Cause Marketing 18 | Event Marketing 18 | Organization Marketing 19

From Transaction-Based Marketing to Relationship Marketing 19
 Using Social Marketing to Build Relationships 20 | Converting New Customers to Advocates 20 | Developing Partnerships and Strategic Alliances 22

Costs and Functions of Marketing 23

Ethics and Social Responsibility: Doing Well by Doing Good 24

Strategic Implications of Marketing in the 21st Century 26

Review of Chapter Objectives 27
 Assessment Check: Answers 28 | Marketing Terms You Need to Know 29 | Assurance of Learning Review 29 | Projects and Teamwork Exercises 29 | Critical-Thinking Exercises 30 | Ethics Exercise 30 | Internet Exercises 31

Case 1.1 Kraft Focuses on Brand Building 31

Video Case 1.2 Geoffrey B. Small Is Big on Quality, Customers, Community 32

vii

CHAPTER 2 Strategic Planning in Contemporary Marketing 34

OPENING VIGNETTE
Driving Cultural Change at Yahoo 34

CAREER READINESS
Succeeding in Your First "Real" Job 38

SOLVING AN ETHICAL CONTROVERSY
Can a Team Save Face with Its Fans? 41

MARKETING SUCCESS
Layaway Programs a Big Hit with Shoppers 48

Chapter Overview 36

Marketing Planning: The Basis for Strategy and Tactics 36
Strategic Planning versus Tactical Planning 37 | Planning at Different Organizational Levels 38

Steps in the Marketing Planning Process 39
Defining the Organization's Mission and Objectives 40 | Assessing Organizational Resources and Evaluating Environmental Risks and Opportunities 40 | Formulating, Implementing, and Monitoring a Marketing Strategy 41

Successful Strategies: Tools and Techniques 42
Porter's Five Forces Model 42 | First Mover and Second Mover Strategies 43 | SWOT Analysis 44 | The Strategic Window 45

Elements of a Marketing Strategy 45
The Target Market 46 | Marketing Mix Variables 47 | The Marketing Environment 50

Methods for Marketing Planning 51
Business Portfolio Analysis 51 | The BCG Matrix 52

Strategic Implications of Marketing in the 21st Century 53

Review of Chapter Objectives 53
Assessment Check: Answers 54 | Marketing Terms You Need to Know 55 | Assurance of Learning Review 55 | Projects and Teamwork Exercises 56 | Critical-Thinking Exercises 56 | Ethics Exercise 57 | Internet Exercises 57

Case 2.1 Hotels Target Millennials with New Amenities 57

Video Case 2.2 Nederlander Producing Company Spotlights Customer Rewards 58

CHAPTER 3 The Marketing Environment, Ethics, and Social Responsibility 60

OPENING VIGNETTE
Aflac Leads the Way in Ethics 60

CAREER READINESS
Getting a Job in CSR 75

SOLVING AN ETHICAL CONTROVERSY
Was "Pink Slime" Coverage Fair or Foul? 79

MARKETING SUCCESS
IBM's CSR Initiatives 86

Chapter Overview 62

Environmental Scanning and Environmental Management 63

The Competitive Environment 64
Types of Competition 64 | Developing a Competitive Strategy 65 | Time-Based Competition 66

The Political–Legal Environment 67
Government Regulation 67 | Government Regulatory Agencies 70 | Other Regulatory Forces 71 | Controlling the Political–Legal Environment 71

The Economic Environment 72
Stages in the Business Cycle 72 | The Global Economic Crisis 73 | Inflation and Deflation 73 | Resource Availability 74 | The International Economic Environment 75

The Technological Environment 76
Applying Technology 77

The Social–Cultural Environment 77
Consumerism 78

Ethical Issues in Marketing 81
    Ethics in Marketing Research 82 | Ethics in Product Strategy 83 | Ethics in Distribution 84 | Ethics in Promotion 84 | Ethics in Pricing 85

Social Responsibility in Marketing 85
    Marketing's Responsibilities 86 | Marketing and the Environment 87

Strategic Implications of Marketing in the 21st Century 89

Review of Chapter Objectives 90
    Assessment Check: Answers 91 | Marketing Terms You Need to Know 92 | Assurance of Learning Review 92 | Projects and Teamwork Exercises 92 | Critical-Thinking Exercises 93 | Ethics Exercise 93 | Internet Exercises 93 | Ethics Questionnaire Answers 94

Case 3.1   General Mills and Its CSR Strategies 94

Video Case 3.2   Zappos Employees Do More Than Sell Shoes 95

CHAPTER 4 Social Media: Living in the Connected World 98

OPENING VIGNETTE
LinkedIn Lifts Off 98

MARKETING SUCCESS
Weight Watchers Gets Social 115

SOLVING AN ETHICAL CONTROVERSY
Barnes & Noble Security Breach: Who's to Blame? 122

CAREER READINESS
Job Hunting via Social Media 124

Chapter Overview 100

What Is Social Media? 100
    Social Media Platforms 101 | Social Media Tools 102 | Why Should Marketers Turn to Social Media? 104

How Consumers and Businesses Use Social Media 107
    Consumer Behavior 107 | Business Behavior 108 | Not-For-Profit Organizations 109

Creating a Social Media Marketing Plan 110

Goals and Strategies of a Social Media Marketing Plan 111
    Setting Goals 111 | Targeting the Audience 112 | Developing Strategies and Choosing Tactics 113

Producing Content and Implementing the Plan 115
    Creating Content 116 | Implementing the Plan 116 | Rules of Engagement for Social Media 117

Monitoring, Measuring, and Managing the SMM Campaign 118
    Monitoring and Measuring 118 | Managing 120

Ethical and Legal Issues 121
    Workplace Ethics 121 | Be Honest 121 | Respect Privacy 122 | Be Accountable 123

Careers in Social Media Marketing 123
    Types of Jobs 123 | Tips for Landing a Job in Social Media Marketing 125

Strategic Implications of Marketing in the 21st Century 126

Review of Chapter Objectives 126
    Assessment Check: Answers 127 | Marketing Terms You Need to Know 128 | Assurance of Learning Review 128 | Projects and Teamwork Exercises 129 | Critical-Thinking Exercises 129 | Ethics Exercise 130 | Internet Exercises 130

Case 4.1   Kellogg's Approach to Social Media 130

Video Case 4.2   Zappos Connects with Customers 131

CHAPTER 5 E-Business: Managing the Customer Experience 134

OPENING VIGNETTE
Wayfair Makes a Name for Itself 134

MARKETING SUCCESS
Square Captures Mobile Payment Sector 149

SOLVING AN ETHICAL CONTROVERSY
Fake Online Reviews 153

CAREER READINESS
Tips for Applying for Jobs Online 156

Chapter Overview 136

The Digital World 137

E-Business and E-Marketing 138
 Opportunities of E-Marketing 139 | Web Business Models 141

B2B E-Marketing 142
 Proprietary B2B Transactions 142 | E-Procurement on Open Exchanges 143

B2C E-Marketing 144
 Electronic Storefronts 144 | Benefits of B2C E-Marketing 144 | Online Buyers and Sellers 146

Challenges in E-Business and E-Marketing 147
 Safety of Online Payment 147 | Privacy Issues 148 | Fraud and Scams 149 | Site Design and Customer Service 150 | Channel Conflicts and Copyright Disputes 151

Marketing and Web Communication 151
 Online Communities 152 | Blogs and Podcasts 152 | Promotions on the Web 153

Building an Effective Web Presence 155
 Successful Site Development 155 | Establishing Goals 155 | Implementation and Interest 156 | Pricing and Maintenance 157 | Assessing Site Effectiveness 157

Strategic Implications of Marketing in the 21st Century 159

Review of Chapter Objectives 159
 Assessment Check: Answers 161 | Marketing Terms You Need to Know 162 | Assurance of Learning Review 162 | Projects and Teamwork Exercises 163 | Critical-Thinking Exercises 163 | Ethics Exercise 163 | Internet Exercises 164

Case 5.1 Walgreens Masters E-Commerce 164

Video Case 5.2 Hubway: Boston's Online Bike-Sharing System 165

Scripps Networks Interactive & Food Network Cooking Up Social Media Strategies 168

Part 2
Understanding Buyers and Markets

CHAPTER 6 Consumer Behavior 170

Chapter Overview 172

Interpersonal Determinants of Consumer Behavior 173
 Cultural Influences 173 | Social Influences 176 | Family Influences 180

Contents

OPENING VIGNETTE
Hummus Is the New Salsa 170

MARKETING SUCCESS
Klout Measures Social Media Influence 178

SOLVING AN ETHICAL CONTROVERSY
Should Facial Recognition Technology Fade Away? 187

CAREER READINESS
Avoiding Major Distractions at Work 190

Personal Determinants of Consumer Behavior 182
Needs and Motives 182 | Perceptions 184 | Attitudes 186 | Learning 188 | Self-Concept Theory 189

The Consumer Decision Process 190

Problem or Opportunity Recognition 191
Search 192 | Evaluation of Alternatives 192 | Purchase Decision and Purchase Act 193 | Postpurchase Evaluation 193

Classifying Consumer Problem-Solving Processes 194
Routinized Response Behavior 194 | Limited Problem Solving 194 | Extended Problem Solving 194

Strategic Implications of Marketing in the 21st Century 195

Review of Chapter Objectives 195
Assessment Check: Answers 196 | Marketing Terms You Need to Know 197 | Assurance of Learning Review 197 | Projects and Teamwork Exercises 197 | Critical-Thinking Exercises 198 | Ethics Exercise 198 | Internet Exercises 198

Case 6.1 Amazon Drives Consumer Behavior 199

Video Case 6.2 Ski Butternut Offers Thrills—Not Spills 200

CHAPTER 7 Business-to-Business (B2B) Marketing 202

OPENING VIGNETTE
GE Goes Social for B2B 202

SOLVING AN ETHICAL CONTROVERSY
Making It Difficult for Phone Scammers 207

MARKETING SUCCESS
Foursquare Connects with Business Partners 209

CAREER READINESS
How to Negotiate with Customers 220

Chapter Overview 204

Nature of the Business Market 204
Components of the Business Market 206 | B2B Markets: The Internet Connection 208 | Differences In Foreign Business Markets 208

Segmenting B2B Markets 209
Segmentation by Demographic Characteristics 210 | Segmentation by Customer Type 210 | Segmentation by End-Use Application 211 | Segmentation by Purchase Categories 211

Characteristics of the B2B Market 212
Geographic Market Concentration 212 | Sizes and Numbers of Buyers 212 | The Purchase Decision Process 213 | Buyer–Seller Relationships 213 | Evaluating International Business Markets 213

Business Market Demand 214
Derived Demand 215 | Volatile Demand 215 | Joint Demand 215 | Inelastic Demand 215 | Inventory Adjustments 216

The Make, Buy, or Lease Decision 216
The Rise of Offshoring and Outsourcing 217 | Problems with Offshoring and Outsourcing 217

The Business Buying Process 218
Influences on Purchase Decisions 218 | Model of the Organizational Buying Process 221 | Classifying Business Buying Situations 223 | Analysis Tools 224

The Buying Center Concept 225
Buying Center Roles 225 | International Buying Centers 226

Developing Effective Business-to-Business Marketing Strategies 226
Challenges of Government Markets 226 | Challenges of Institutional Markets 227 | Challenges of International Markets 229

Strategic Implications of Marketing in the 21st Century 230

Review of Chapter Objectives 230
Assessment Check: Answers 231 | Marketing Terms You Need to Know 233 | Assurance of Learning Review 233 | Projects and Teamwork Exercises 233 | Critical-Thinking Exercises 234 | Ethics Exercise 234 | Internet Exercises 234

Case 7.1 B2B Giant Scores Big with Mobile Apps 235

Video Case 7.2 Zappos Offers Insights into Other Businesses 235

CHAPTER 8 Global Marketing 238

OPENING VIGNETTE
Walmart Extends Its Global Reach 238

CAREER READINESS
Tips for International Travel 244

SOLVING AN ETHICAL CONTROVERSY
Who's Responsible for Overseas Working Conditions? 249

MARKETING SUCCESS
McDonald's Thrives in France 257

Chapter Overview 240

The Importance of Global Marketing 241
Service and Retail Exports 242 | Benefits of Going Global 244

The International Marketing Environment 245
International Economic Environment 245 | International Social–Cultural Environment 246 | International Technological Environment 247 | International Political–Legal Environment 248 | Trade Barriers 249 | Dumping 251

Multinational Economic Integration 251
GATT and the World Trade Organization 252 | The NAFTA Accord 252 | The Free Trade Area of the Americas and CAFTA-DR 253 | The European Union 253

Going Global 254

Strategies for Entering Foreign Markets 255
Importing and Exporting 255 | Contractual Agreements 256 | International Direct Investment 257

From Multinational Corporation to Global Marketer 258

Developing an International Marketing Strategy 259
International Product and Promotional Strategies 260 | International Distribution Strategy 261 | Pricing Strategy 261 | Countertrade 262

The United States as a Target for International Marketers 262

Strategic Implications of Marketing in the 21st Century 263

Review of Chapter Objectives 263
Assessment Check: Answers 264 | Marketing Terms You Need to Know 265 | Assurance of Learning Review 265 | Projects and Teamwork Exercises 266 | Critical-Thinking Exercises 266 | Ethics Exercise 266 | Internet Exercises 267

Case 8.1 The NFL Takes Its Brand to London 267

Video Case 8.2 Nederlander Productions Hoof It Around the World 268

Scripps Networks Interactive & Food Network Everyone Eats 270

Contents xiii

Part 3
Target Market Selection

CHAPTER 9 Market Segmentation, Targeting, and Positioning 272

OPENING VIGNETTE
PepsiCo Brands Target Different Markets 272

SOLVING AN ETHICAL CONTROVERSY
Should High-Fructose Corn Syrup Be Banned? 282

MARKETING SUCCESS
Hispanic Consumers Prime Target for Clorox 286

CAREER READINESS
Using Social Media to Reach Target Markets 296

Chapter Overview 274

Types of Markets 275

The Role of Market Segmentation 275
  Criteria for Effective Segmentation 276

Segmenting Consumer Markets 277

Geographic Segmentation 277
  Using Geographic Segmentation 279 | Geographic Information Systems (GISs) 280

Demographic Segmentation 280
  Segmenting by Gender 281 | Segmenting by Age 281 | Segmenting by Ethnic Group 285 | Segmenting by Family Lifecycle Stages 288 | Segmenting by Household Type 288 | Segmenting by Income and Expenditure Patterns 289 | Demographic Segmentation Abroad 290

Psychographic Segmentation 291
  What Is Psychographic Segmentation? 291 | VALS™ 291 | Using Psychographic Segmentation 292

Product-Related Segmentation 292
  Segmenting by Benefits Sought 292 | Segmenting by Usage Rates 293 | Segmenting by Brand Loyalty 293 | Using Multiple Segmentation Bases 294

The Market Segmentation Process 294
  Develop a Relevant Profile for Each Segment 294 | Forecast Market Potential 294 | Forecast Probable Market Share 294 | Select Specific Market Segments 295

Strategies for Reaching Target Markets 295
  Undifferentiated Marketing 295 | Differentiated Marketing 296 | Concentrated Marketing 297 | Micromarketing 297

Selecting and Executing a Strategy 298

Strategic Implications of Marketing in the 21st Century 300

Review of Chapter Objectives 300
  Assessment Check: Answers 301 | Marketing Terms You Need to Know 302 | Assurance of Learning Review 302 | Projects and Teamwork Exercises 303 | Critical-Thinking Exercises 303 | Ethics Exercise 304 | Internet Exercises 304

Case 9.1 Cruise Lines Cater to Travelers' Specific Interests 304

Video Case 9.2 Nederlander Targets Theatergoers Everywhere 305

CHAPTER 10 Marketing Research in the Era of Big Data 308

OPENING VIGNETTE
Netflix Uses Big Data to Develop Content 308

SOLVING AN ETHICAL CONTROVERSY
Who Profits from Your Personal Data? 314

MARKETING SUCCESS
Febreze: From Revolutionary Failure to Best-Selling Success 325

CAREER READINESS
Creating Surveys for Mobile Devices 327

Chapter Overview 310

The Marketing Research Function 311
How Marketing Research Has Evolved 311 | Who Conducts Marketing Research? 311 | Marketing Intelligence 313 | Competitive Intelligence 313 | Data Mining and Predictive Analytics 313 | Key Performance Indicators 314

The Marketing Research Process 315
Define the Problem 316 | Conduct Exploratory Research 316 | Formulate a Hypothesis 317 | Create a Research Design 317 | Collect Data 318 | Interpret and Present Research Data 319

Data Collection in the Marketing Process 319
Secondary Data Collection 320 | Sampling Techniques 322

Primary Research Methods 323
Observation Method 323 | Interpretive Research 325 | Survey Methods 325 | Experimental Method 328

Conducting International Marketing Research 328

Interpretive Research 329
Ethnographic Studies 329

Strategic Implications of Marketing in the 21st Century 330

Review of Chapter Objectives 331
Assessment Check: Answers 332 | Marketing Terms You Need to Know 333 | Assurance of Learning Review 333 | Projects and Teamwork Exercises 333 | Critical-Thinking Exercises 334 | Ethics Exercise 334 | Internet Exercises 334

Case 10.1 Gamification: Game Changer for Marketing Research? 335

Video Case 10.2 GaGa SherBetter Forecasts Hot Sales, Cold Flavors 336

CHAPTER 11 Relationship Marketing and Customer Relationship Management (CRM) 338

OPENING VIGNETTE
Publix's Culture Puts People First 338

MARKETING SUCCESS
Motel 6 Still Growing Strong After 50 343

SOLVING AN ETHICAL CONTROVERSY
Helping the Homeless? 351

CAREER READINESS
Ways to Build Customer Loyalty 354

Chapter Overview 340

The Shift from Transaction-Based Marketing to Relationship Marketing 340
Elements of Relationship Marketing 342 | Internal Marketing 342

Levels of Relationship Marketing 344
Level One: Focus on Price 345 | Level Two: Social Interactions 345 | Level Three: Interdependent Partnership 346

Enhancing Customer Satisfaction 346
Understanding Customer Needs 346 | Obtaining Customer Feedback and Ensuring Satisfaction 347

Building Buyer–Seller Relationships 348
How Marketers Keep Customers 348 | Database Marketing 349 | Customers as Advocates 350

Customer Relationship Management 352
Benefits of CRM 352 | Problems with CRM 353 | Retrieving Lost Customers 353

Contents   xv

Buyer–Seller Relationships in Business-to-Business Markets   355
Choosing Business Partners   356 | Types of Partnerships   356 | Cobranding and Comarketing   356

Improving Buyer–Seller Relationships in Business-to-Business Markets   357
National Account Selling   357 | Business-to-Business Databases   358 | Electronic Data Interchange and Web Services   358

Vendor-Managed Inventory   358
Managing the Supply Chain   358 | Business-to-Business Alliances   359

Evaluating Customer Relationship Programs   360

Sales Forecasting   361
Qualitative Forecasting Techniques   362 | Quantitative Forecasting Techniques   363

Strategic Implications of Marketing in the 21st Century   364

Review of Chapter Objectives   365
Assessment Check: Answers   366 | Marketing Terms You Need to Know   367 | Assurance of Learning Review   368 | Projects and Teamwork Exercises   368 | Critical-Thinking Exercises   368 | Ethics Exercise   369 | Internet Exercises   369

Case 11.1 Teaching Customer Service at the Disney Institute   369

Video Case 11.2 Pepe's Pizzeria Serves Success One Customer at a Time   370

Scripps Networks Interactive & Food Network Scooping Up Consumer Insight   372

Part 4
Product Decisions

CHAPTER 12 Product and Service Strategies   374

OPENING VIGNETTE
Apple's "A" for Innovation   374

MARKETING SUCCESS
Audi Goes Social to Promote Brand   382

SOLVING AN ETHICAL CONTROVERSY
Natural vs. Organic: Who Is Responsible for Knowing the Difference?   387

CAREER READINESS
Email: Think Before You Send   392

Chapter Overview   376

What Is a Product?   376

What Are Goods and Services?   377

Importance of the Service Sector   378

Classifying Goods and Services for Consumer and Business Markets   380
Types of Consumer Products   380 | Classifying Consumer Services   383 | Applying the Consumer Products Classification System   384

Types of Business Products   385

Quality as a Product Strategy   389
Worldwide Quality Programs   390 | Benchmarking   390 | Quality of Services   390

Development of Product Lines   392
Desire to Grow   392 | Enhancing the Company's Market Position   393

The Product Mix 393
Product Mix Width 393 | Product Mix Length 394 | Product Mix Depth 394 | Product Mix Decisions 394

The Product Lifecycle 395
Introductory Stage 395 | Growth Stage 396 | Maturity Stage 397 | Decline Stage 397

Extending the Product Lifecycle 398
Increasing Frequency of Use 398 | Increasing the Number of Users 398 | Finding New Uses 399 | Changing Package Sizes, Labels, or Product Quality 399

Product Deletion Decisions 399

Strategic Implications of Marketing in the 21st Century 400

Review of Chapter Objectives 401
Assessment Check: Answers 402 | Marketing Terms You Need to Know 403 | Assurance of Learning Review 403 | Projects and Teamwork Exercises 403 | Critical-Thinking Exercises 404 | Ethics Exercise 404 | Internet Exercises 405

Case 12.1 Nike Back in the Limelight 405

Video Case 12.2 BoltBus Gives Bus Travel a Jump Start 406

CHAPTER 13 Developing and Managing Brand and Product Categories 408

OPENING VIGNETTE
Under Armour Brand Soars 408

SOLVING AN ETHICAL CONTROVERSY
Who Is Responsible for the Truth of Advertising Claims? 412

MARKETING SUCCESS
Packaging Gives Heinz a Boost 419

CAREER READINESS
How to Be a Team Player 428

Chapter Overview 410

Managing Brands for Competitive Advantage 410
Brand Loyalty 411 | Types of Brands 412 | Brand Equity 414 | The Role of Category and Brand Management 415

Product Identification 416
Brand Names and Brand Marks 416 | Trademarks 417 | Developing Global Brand Names and Trademarks 418 | Packaging 418 | Brand Extensions 421 | Brand Licensing 422

New-Product Planning 423
Product Development Strategies 423 | The Consumer Adoption Process 424 | Adopter Categories 425 | Identifying Early Adopters 426 | Organizing for New-Product Development 427

The New-Product Development Process 429
Screening 430 | Business Analysis 430 | Development 430 | Test Marketing 431 | Commercialization 431

Product Safety and Liability 431

Strategic Implications of Marketing in the 21st Century 432

Review of Chapter Objectives 433
Assessment Check: Answers 434 | Marketing Terms You Need to Know 435 | Assurance of Learning Review 435 | Projects and Teamwork Exercises 435 | Critical-Thinking Exercises 435 | Ethics Exercise 436 | Internet Exercises 436

Case 13.1 Chobani Greek Yogurt Focuses on Tradition 437

Video Case 13.2 At Zappos, Passion Is Paramount 437

Scripps Networks Interactive & Food Network The Line between Content and Commerce 440

Part 5
Distribution Decisions

CHAPTER 14 Marketing Channels and Supply Chain Management 442

OPENING VIGNETTE
Terra Technology Helps Manage Global Supply Chain 442

CAREER READINESS
How to Successfully Close a Sale 447

SOLVING AN ETHICAL CONTROVERSY
Hershey's Takes Responsibility for Its Supply Chain 451

MARKETING SUCCESS
Red Lobster "Seas" Food Differently 460

Chapter Overview 444

The Role of Marketing Channels in Marketing Strategy 444

Types of Marketing Channels 445
Direct Selling 447 | Channels Using Marketing Intermediaries 448 | Dual Distribution 449 | Reverse Channels 449

Channel Strategy Decisions 450
Selection of a Marketing Channel 450 | Determining Distribution Intensity 453 | Who Should Perform Channel Functions? 454

Channel Management and Leadership 455
Channel Conflict 455 | Achieving Channel Cooperation 456

Vertical Marketing Systems 457
Corporate and Administered Systems 457 | Contractual Systems 457

Logistics and Supply Chain Management 459
Radio Frequency Identification 460 | Enterprise Resource Planning 461 | Logistical Cost Control 461

Physical Distribution 462
The Problem of Suboptimization 462 | Customer Service Standards 463 | Transportation 463 | Major Transportation Modes 464 | Freight Forwarders and Supplemental Carriers 467 | Intermodal Coordination 467 | Warehousing 468 | Inventory Control Systems 469 | Order Processing 469 | Protective Packaging and Materials Handling 469

Strategic Implications of Marketing in the 21st Century 470

Review of Chapter Objectives 470
Assessment Check: Answers 471 | Marketing Terms You Need to Know 472 | Assurance of Learning Review 473 | Projects and Teamwork Exercises 473 | Critical-Thinking Exercises 473 | Ethics Exercise 474 | Internet Exercises 474

Case 14.1 Superstorm Sandy Disrupts Global Supply Chain 475

Video Case 14.2 Geoffrey B. Small Keeps Marketing Channels Tight 475

CHAPTER 15 Retailers, Wholesalers, and Direct Marketers 478

OPENING VIGNETTE
Macy's Multi-Level Plan Yields Big Rewards 478

MARKETING SUCCESS
College Towns Help Whole Foods Expand 482

SOLVING AN ETHICAL CONTROVERSY
Who Should Control the Spread of Fake Stores and Counterfeit Products? 489

CAREER READINESS
Tips on Knowing Your Competition 495

Chapter Overview 480

Retailing 480
 Evolution of Retailing 481

Retailing Strategy 481

Selecting a Target Market 483
 Merchandising Strategy 483 | Customer Service Strategy 484 | Pricing Strategy 485 | Location/Distribution Strategy 486 | Promotional Strategy 487 | Store Atmospherics 488

Types of Retailers 490
 Classification of Retailers by Form of Ownership 490 | Classification by Shopping Effort 491 | Classification by Services Provided 491 | Classification by Product Lines 492 | Classification of Retail Transactions by Location 494 | Retail Convergence and Scrambled Merchandising 494

Wholesaling Intermediaries 495
 Functions of Wholesaling Intermediaries 496 | Types of Wholesaling Intermediaries 497 | Retailer-Owned Cooperatives and Buying Offices 502

Direct Marketing and Other Nonstore Retailing 502
 Direct Mail 502 | Direct Selling 503 | Direct-Response Retailing 503 | Telemarketing 503 | Internet Retailing 503 | Automatic Merchandising 504

Strategic Implications of Marketing in the 21st Century 504

Review of Chapter Objectives 505
 Assessment Check: Answers 506 | Marketing Terms You Need to Know 509 | Assurance of Learning Review 507 | Projects and Teamwork Exercises 507 | Critical-Thinking Exercises 508 | Ethics Exercise 508 | Internet Exercises 509

Case 15.1 Costco Plays Catch-Up in Online Sales 509

Video Case 15.2 GaGa SherBetter: Coming to a Market Near You? 510

Scripps Networks Interactive & Food Network Pushing Content into New Channels 512

Part 6
Promotional Decisions

CHAPTER 16 Integrated Marketing Communications, Advertising, and Public Relations 514

Chapter Overview 516

Integrated Marketing Communications 517
 Importance of Teamwork 518 | Role of Databases in Effective IMC Programs 519

Contents   xix

OPENING VIGNETTE
Starbucks Serves Up Successful Marketing "Brew"   514

MARKETING SUCCESS
H&M Integrates Its Beckham Campaign   518

CAREER READINESS
Tips for Career Networking   519

SOLVING AN ETHICAL CONTROVERSY
Fast-Food Advertising Directed to Children   539

The Communication Process   520

Elements of the Promotional Mix   522
Personal Selling 522 | Nonpersonal Selling 522 | Advertising 522 | Product Placement 523 | Sales Promotion 523 | Direct Marketing 523 | Public Relations 523 | Guerrilla Marketing 524 | Advantages and Disadvantages of Types of Promotion 524 | Sponsorships 525

Advertising   526
Types of Advertising 526 | Objectives of Advertising 526

Advertising Strategies   527
Comparative Advertising 527 | Celebrity Testimonials 527 | Retail Advertising 528 | Interactive Advertising 529 | Creating an Advertisement 529 | Translating Advertising Objectives into Advertising Plans 529 | Advertising Messages 530

Advertising Appeals   530
Fear Appeals 530 | Humor in Advertising Messages 530 | Ads Based on Sex 531 | Developing and Preparing Ads 531 | Creating Interactive Ads 532

Media Selection and Scheduling   533
Television 533 | Radio 534 | Newspapers 535 | Magazines 535 | Direct Mail 536 | Outdoor Advertising 536 | Interactive Media 536 | Media Scheduling 537

Public Relations   538
Publicity 538 | Cross-Promotion 538 | Ethics and Promotional Strategies 539

Promotional Mix Effectiveness   540
Nature of the Market 540 | Nature of the Product 540 | Stage in the Product Lifecycle 541 | Price 541 | Funds Available for Promotion 541 | Evaluating Promotional Effectiveness 542 | Measuring Advertising Effectiveness 542 | Media and Message Research 543 | Measuring Public Relations Effectiveness 544 | Evaluating Interactive Media 544

Strategic Implications of Marketing in 21st Century   545

Review of Chapter Objectives   546
Assessment Check: Answers 547 | Marketing Terms You Need to Know 548 | Assurance of Learning Review 549 | Projects and Teamwork Exercises 549 | Critical-Thinking Exercises 549 | Ethics Exercise 550 | Internet Exercises 550

Case 16.1 The Richards Group: A Unique Advertising Group   550

Video Case 16.2 Pepe's Pizzeria Delivers Every Day   551

CHAPTER 17 Personal Selling and Sales Promotion   554

Chapter Overview   556

The Evolution of Personal Selling   557

The Four Sales Channels   557
Over-the-Counter Selling 557 | Field Selling 559 | Telemarketing 560 | Inside Selling 561 | Integrating the Various Selling Channels 561

Trends in Personal Selling   562
Relationship Selling 562 | Consultative Selling 563 | Team Selling 564

Sales Tasks   565
Order Processing 565 | Creative Selling 566 | Missionary Selling 566

xx Contents

OPENING VIGNETTE
Salesforce.com Expands Its Marketing Cloud 554

MARKETING SUCCESS
Successful Cross-Selling Strategies at WellsFargo 564

CAREER READINESS
How to Make a Successful Cold Call 569

SOLVING AN ETHICAL CONTROVERSY
When the Sale Doesn't Benefit the Customer 573

The Sales Process 567
Prospecting and Qualifying 567 | Approach 567 | Presentation 568 | Demonstration 569 | Handling Objections 570 | Closing 570 | Follow-Up 570

Managing the Sales Effort 571
Recruitment and Selection 571 | Training 572 | Organization 573 | Supervision 574 | Motivation 574 | Compensation 575 | Evaluation and Control 576

Ethical Issues in Sales 577
Sales Promotion 578 | Consumer-Oriented Sales Promotions 579 | Trade-Oriented Promotions 581 | Trade Allowances 581 | Point-of-Purchase Advertising 581 | Trade Shows 582 | Dealer Incentives, Contests, and Training Programs 582

Strategic Implications of Marketing in the 21st Century 583

Review of Chapter Objectives 583
Assessment Check: Answers 584 | Marketing Terms You Need to Know 585 | Assurance of Learning Review 586 | Projects and Teamwork Exercises 586 | Critical-Thinking Exercises 586 | Ethics Exercise 587 | Internet Exercises 587

Case 17.1 Shaq Promotes His Personal Brand 587

Video Case 17.2 Hubway Rolls Out Partners and Promotions 588

Scripps Networks Interactive & Food Network Generating Buzz 590

Part 7
Pricing Decisions

CHAPTER 18 Pricing Concepts 592

OPENING VIGNETTE
Dollar General Attracts Shoppers on Price Points, Not Price 592

MARKETING SUCCESS
The Pricey Smell of Success 597

SOLVING AN ETHICAL CONTROVERSY
Differential Pricing for Highway Tolls 605

CAREER READINESS
Getting the Best Car Price 610

Chapter Overview 594

Pricing and the Law 594
Robinson-Patman Act 595 | Unfair-Trade Laws 596 | Fair-Trade Laws 596

Pricing Objectives and the Marketing Mix 597
Profitability Objectives 598 | Volume Objectives 599 | Prestige Objectives 601 | Pricing Objectives of Not-For-Profit Organizations 602

Methods for Determining Prices 603
Price Determination in Economic Theory 604 | Cost and Revenue Curves 605 | The Concept of Elasticity in Pricing Strategy 607 | Practical Problems of Price Theory 609

Price Determination in Practice 609
Alternative Pricing Procedures 609 | Breakeven Analysis 611

The Modified Breakeven Concept 613

Yield Management 614

Contents   xxi

Global Issues in Price Determination 615

Strategic Implications of Marketing in the 21st Century 616

Review of Chapter Objectives 617
- Assessment Check: Answers 618 | Marketing Terms You Need to Know 619 | Assurance of Learning Review 619 | Projects and Teamwork Exercises 620 | Critical-Thinking Exercises 620 | Ethics Exercise 620 | Internet Exercises 621

Case 18.1 ScoreBig: Name Your Price for Live Events 621

Video Case 18.2 Ski Butternut: Great Prices for Winter Fun 622

CHAPTER 19 Pricing Strategies 624

OPENING VIGNETTE
Discounts Reduce Abandoned E-Carts 624

MARKETING SUCCESS
Chili's Serves Everyday Value 630

SOLVING AN ETHICAL CONTROVERSY
Throttling "Unlimited" Data Plans 638

CAREER READINESS
Using Apps for Comparison Shopping 643

Chapter Overview 626

Pricing Strategies 626
- Skimming Pricing Strategy 627 | Penetration Pricing Strategy 628 | Competitive Pricing Strategy 630

Price Quotations 631
- Reductions from List Price 631 | Geographic Considerations 634

Pricing Policies 635
- Psychological Pricing 636 | Price Flexibility 636 | Product-Line Pricing 636 | Promotional Pricing 637

Price–Quality Relationships 639

Competitive Bidding and Negotiated Prices 639
- Negotiating Prices Online 640

The Transfer Pricing Dilemma 641

Global Considerations and Online Pricing 642
- Traditional Global Pricing Strategies 642 | Characteristics of Online Pricing 642 | Bundle Pricing 644

Strategic Implications of Marketing in the 21st Century 645

Review of Chapter Objectives 645
- Assessment Check: Answers 646 | Marketing Terms You Need to Know 647 | Assurance of Learning Review 647 | Projects and Teamwork Exercises 648 | Critical-Thinking Exercises 648 | Ethics Exercise 649 | Internet Exercises 649

Case 19.1 Who Needs the U.S. Penny? 649

Video Case 19.2 BoltBus: Ride for the Right Price 650

Scripps Networks Interactive & Food Network Good, Better, Best 652

Appendix A
   Developing an Effective Marketing Plan   A-1

Appendix B
   Financial Analysis in Marketing   B-1

Online Appendix
   Your Career in Marketing

Glossary   G-1

Name & Company Index   I-1

Subject Index   I-23

International Index   I-53

PREFACE

The *Contemporary Marketing* Resource Package

Since the first edition of this book was published, Boone & Kurtz has exceeded the expectations of instructors, and it quickly became the benchmark for other texts. With its precedent-setting learning materials, *Contemporary Marketing* has continued to improve on its signature package features—equipping students and instructors with the most comprehensive collection of learning tools, teaching materials, and innovative resources available. As expected, the 17th edition continues to serve as the industry benchmark by delivering the most extensive, technologically advanced, user-friendly package on the market.

NEW TO THIS EDITION

Expanding on the social media insights added in the previous edition, the 17th edition features an updated marketing research chapter. Chapter 10, "Marketing Research in the Era of Big Data," discusses how advances in technology continue to impact the collection of consumer and business data. Big data—information that originates in unprecedented volume and speed from the world around us—is changing the way companies collect and use pertinent information as part of their marketing research strategies.

In addition, chapter pedagogy, including opening stories, boxed features, and end-of-chapter cases are new or updated, and business, consumer, and government statistics throughout the text have been researched and refreshed to reflect current trends in marketing and business in both domestic and global settings.

MINDTAP

MindTap is a personalized teaching experience with relevant assignments that guide students to analyze, apply, and improve thinking, allowing you to measure skills and outcomes with ease.

- **Personalize Teaching:** Becomes yours with a Learning Path that is built with key student objectives. Control what students see and when they see it. Use it as is or match to your syllabus exactly—hide, rearrange, add, and create your own content.
- **Guide Students:** A unique Learning Path of relevant readings, multimedia, and activities that move students up the learning taxonomy from basic knowledge and comprehension to analysis and application.
- **Promote Better Outcomes:** Empowers instructors and motivate students with analytics and reports that provide a snapshot of class progress, time in course, engagement, and completion rates.

By combining readings, multimedia, activities, and assessments into a singular Learning Path, MindTap guides students through their course with ease and engagement. Instructors personalize the Learning Path by customizing Cengage Learning resources and adding their own content via apps that integrate into the MindTap framework seamlessly with Learning Management Systems. *Contemporary Marketing* students can also find Basic PowerPoints, videos, quizzes, animated figures, homework, and more.

CHAPTER VIDEO CASES AND SCRIPPS NETWORKS INTERACTIVE & FOOD NETWORK CONTINUING CASE ON DVD (ISBN: 9781305253506)

End-of-chapter video cases for every chapter of the text focus on successful real companies' processes, strategies, and procedures. Real employees explain real marketing situations, bringing key concepts from the chapter to life. The end-of-part videos focus on Scripps Networks Interactive & Food Network's marketing strategies and innovative approach to connecting with consumers through a variety of channels. The written and video cases are divided into seven sections and are tailored to be used at the end of each part of the text.

CERTIFIED TEST BANK POWERED BY COGNERO

Containing more than 3,800 questions, this Test Bank has been thoroughly verified to ensure accuracy—with each question and answer read and reviewed. The Test Bank includes true/false, multiple-choice, essay, and matching questions. Each question in the Test Bank is labeled with text objective, level of difficulty, and A-heads. Each question is also tagged to Interdisciplinary Learning Outcomes, Marketing Disciplinary Learning Outcomes, and Bloom's Taxonomy. The Test Bank is available via Cognero, can be loaded to your SSO account, or PDFs can found on the product support website.

Cengage Learning Testing Powered by Cognero is a flexible, online system that allows you to:

- author, edit, and manage test bank content from multiple Cengage Learning solutions
- create multiple test versions in an instant
- deliver tests from your LMS, your classroom, or wherever you want

Start Right Away!

Cengage Learning Testing Powered by Cognero works on any operating system or browser.

- No special installs or downloads needed
- Create tests from school, home, the coffee shop—anywhere you have Internet access

What Will You Find?

- Simplicity at every step. A desktop-inspired interface features drop-down menus and familiar, intuitive tools that take you through content creation and management with ease.
- Full-featured test generator. Create ideal assessments with your choice of 15 question types (including true/false, multiple choice, opinion scale/likert, and essay). Multi-language support, an equation editor, and unlimited metadata help ensure your tests are complete and compliant.
- Cross-platform capability. Import and export content into other systems.

CONTEMPORARY MARKETING, 17TH EDITION WEBSITE

Our text website is filled with a whole set of useful tools. Instructors will find all the key instructor resources in electronic format: Test Bank, PowerPoint collections, and Instructor's Manual with Media Guide, and Collaborative Learning Exercises.

To access additional course materials and companion resources, please visit www.cengagebrain.com. At the CengageBrain.com home page, search for the ISBN of your title (from the back cover of your book) using the search box at the top of the page. This will take you to the product page where free companion resources can be found.

CUSTOM SOLUTIONS FOR *CONTEMPORARY MARKETING,* 17TH EDITION

Cengage Learning Custom Solutions develops personalized solutions to meet your business education needs. Match your learning materials to your syllabus, and create the perfect learning solution. Consider the following when looking at your customization options for *Contemporary Marketing,* 17th edition:

- Remove chapters you do not cover, or rearrange their order, creating a streamlined and efficient text students will appreciate.
- Add your own material to cover new topics or information, saving you time and providing students with a fully integrated course resource.

Cengage Learning Custom Solutions offers the fastest and easiest way to create unique, customized learning materials delivered the way you want. Our custom solutions also include accessing on-demand cases from leading business case providers such as **Harvard Business School Publishing, Ivey, Darden,** and **NACRA,** and building a tailored text online with our online custom publishing system, which allows you to incorporate your original materials. For more information about custom publishing options, contact your local Cengage Learning representative.

ACKNOWLEDGMENTS

Over the years, *Contemporary Marketing* has benefited from the suggestions of hundreds of marketing instructors. I am most appreciative of their efforts and thoughts.

Reviewers and contributors include the following: Keith Absher, Kerri L. Acheson, Zafar U. Ahmed, Alicia T. Aldridge, M. Wayne Alexander, Bruce Allen, Linda Anglin, Allen Appell, Paul Arsenault, Dub Ashton, Amardeep Assar, Tom F. Badgett, Joe K. Ballenger, Wayne Bascom, Richard D. Becherer, Tom Becker, Richard F. Beltramini, Michael Bernacchi, Daniel W. Biddlecom, Robert Bielski, Carol C. Bienstock, Roger D. Blackwell, David Blanchette, Jocelyn C. Bojack, Barbara Brown, Reginald E. Brown, Michele D. Bunn, Marvin Burnett, Scott Burton, James Camerius, Les Carlson, John Carmichael, Jacob Chacko, Irene Woods Clampet, Robert Collins, Elizabeth Cooper-Martin, Bruce Coscia, Deborah L. Cowles, Howard B. Cox, James Coyle, John E. Crawford, Elizabeth Creyer, Geoff Crosslin, Michael R. Czinkota, Kathy Daruty, Grant Davis, Gilberto de los Santos, William Demkey, Carol W. DeMoranville, Fran DePaul, Gordon Di Paolo, John G. Doering, Curt J. Dommeyer, Jeffrey T. Doutt, Michael Drafke, Sid Dudley, John W. Earnest, Joanne Eckstein, Philip E. Egdorf, Larry T. Eiler, Michael Elliot, Amy Enders, Bob Farris, Lori Feldman, Sandra M. Ferriter, Dale Fodness, Gary T. Ford, Michael Fowler, John Frankel, Edward Friese, Sam Fullerton, Ralph M. Gaedeke, G. P. Gallo, Nimish Gandhi, Debbie Gaspard, Sheryl A. Gatto, Robert Georgen, Don Gibson, David W. Glascoff, Jeffrey L. Goldberg, Robert Googins, James Gould, Donald Granbois, John Grant, Arlene Green, Paul E. Green, William Green, Blaine Greenfield, Matthew Gross, Robert F. Gwinner, Raymond M. Haas, John H. Hallaq, Dana Harris, Cary Hawthorn, E. Paul Hayes, Hoyt Hayes, Joel Haynes, Betty Jean Hebel, Debbora Heflin-Bullock, John (Jack) J. Heinsius, Charlane Held, Sanford B. Helman, Nathan Himelstein, Robert D. Hisrich, Mabre Holder, Ray S. House, Andrew W. Honeycutt, George Housewright, Dr. H. Houston, Donald Howard, John Howe, Michael D. Hutt, Gregory P. Iwaniuk, Don L. James, James Jeck, Tom Jensen, Candida Johnson, David Johnson, Eugene M. Johnson, James C. Johnson, Harold H. Kassarjian, Bernard Katz, Stephen K. Keiser, Michelle Keller, J. Steven Kelly, Marcella Kelly, James H. Kennedy, Charles Keuthan, Maryon King, Stephen C. King, Randall S. Kingsbury, Gail H. Kirby, Donald L. Knight, Linda S. Koffel, Philip Kotler, Kathleen Krentler, Terrence Kroeten, Russell Laczniak, Martha Laham, L. Keith Larimore, Edwin Laube, Ken Lawrence, Francis J. Leary, Jr., Mary Lou Lockerby, Laddie Logan, James Lollar, Paul Londrigan, David L. Loudon, Kent Lundin, Dorothy Maass, Patricia Macro, James C. Makens, Lou Mansfield, Frank Markley, Tom Marshall, Warren Martin, Dennis C. Mathern, James McCormick, Carl McDaniel, Lee McGinnis, Michael McGinnis, James McHugh, Faye McIntyre, Robert M. McMillen, H. Lee Meadow, Norma Mendoza, Mohan Menon, William

E. (Gene) Merkle, John D. Milewicz, Robert D. Miller, Laura M. Milner, Banwari Mittal, Anthony Miyazaki, Harry J. Moak, J. Dale Molander, John F. Monoky, James R. Moore, Jerry W. Moorman, Linda Morable, Thomas M. Moran, Diane Moretz, Eugene Moynihan, Margaret Myers, Mark A. Neckes, Susan Logan Nelson, Colin F. Neuhaus, Robert T. Newcomb, Steven Nichols, Jacqueline Z. Nicholson, Thomas S. O'Connor, Robert O'Keefe, Nita Paden, Sukgoo Pak, George Palz, Eric Panitz, Anurag Pant, Dennis D. Pappas, Constantine Petrides, Barbara Piasta, Dennis D. Pitta, Barbara Pletcher, Carolyn E. Predmore, Arthur E. Prell, George Prough, Warren Purdy, Bill Quain, Salim Qureshi, Rosemary Ramsey, Thomas Read, Thomas C. Reading, Joel Reedy, Gary Edward Reiman, Dominic Rella, Ken Ridgedell, Glen Riecken, Arnold M. Rieger, C. Richard Roberts, Patrick J. Robinson, William C. Rodgers, Fernando Rodriguez, William H. Ronald, Jack J. Rose, Bert Rosenbloom, Barbara Rosenthal, Carol Rowery, Lillian Roy, Ronald S. Rubin, Don Ryktarsyk, Arthur Saltzman, Rafael Santos, Elise T. Sautter, Duane Schecter, Buffie Schmidt, Dennis W. Schneider, Jonathan E. Schroeder, Larry J. Schuetz, Bruce Seaton, Howard Seigelman, Jack Seitz, Steven L. Shapiro, Farouk Shaaban, F. Kelly Shuptrine, Ricardo Singson, Norman Smothers, John Sondey, Carol S. Soroos, James Spiers, Miriam B. Stamps, William Staples, David Starr, Bob Stassen, David Steenstra, Bruce Stern, Robert Stevens, Kermit Swanson, G. Knude Swenson, Cathy Owens Swift, Clint B. Tankersley, Ruth Taylor, Sue Taylor, Donald L. Temple, Vern Terpstra, Nancy J. Thannert, Ann Marie Thompson, Howard A. Thompson, Lars Thording, John E. Timmerman, Frank Titlow, Rex Toh, Dennis H. Tootelian, Fred Trawick, Pam Uhlenkamp, Richard Lee Utecht, Rajiv Vaidyanathan, Toni Valdez, Peter Vanderhagen, Dinoo T. Vanier, Sal Veas, Charles Vitaska, Cortez Walker, Roger Waller, Gayle D. Wasson, Mary M. Weber, Donald Weinrauch, Fred Weinthal, Paul M. Wellen, Susan B. Wessels, Vicki L. West, Elizabeth White, John J. Whithey, Debbora Whitson, David Wiley, William Wilkinson, James Williams, Robert J. Williams, Nicholas C. Williamson, Cecilia Wittmayer, Mary Wolfindarger, Joyce Wood, Van R. Wood, Julian Yudelson, and Robert J. Zimmer.

IN CONCLUSION

I would like to thank my associate Cate Rzasa. Her ability to meet tight deadlines is truly appreciated. Let me conclude by mentioning that the new edition would never have become a reality without the superior efforts of the Cengage Learning editorial, production, and marketing teams. My editors—Jason Fremder, Elizabeth Lowry, and John Rich; my long-serving designer Stacy Shirley; my production editor Megan Guiliani; and my marketing team—Courtney Doyle-Chambers and Chris Walz—all helped to produce another *Contemporary Marketing* winner.

Chapter 1

Marketing: The Art and Science of Satisfying Customers

1. Define marketing and how it creates utility.
2. Contrast marketing activities during the five eras in the history of marketing.
3. Explain the importance of avoiding marketing myopia.
4. Describe the characteristics of not-for-profit marketing.
5. Explain each of the five types of nontraditional marketing.
6. Explain the shift from transaction-based marketing to relationship and social marketing.
7. Identify the eight universal functions of marketing.
8. Demonstrate the relationship between ethical business practices, social responsibility, sustainability, and marketplace success.

VINEYARD VINES MARKETS THE GOOD LIFE

Inspiration came to brothers Shep and Ian Murray, then in their 20s, when they started meeting for lunch and complaining about how they disliked their desk jobs and the business suits and ties that went with them. They decided to go into business for themselves and settled on a product they knew nothing about: neckties. If they sold enough ties, they reasoned, they could stop wearing them.

Today, more than 15 years later, Connecticut-based Vineyard Vines has grown into a multimillion-dollar business. It sells a full line of high-quality clothing for men, women, and children in 30 company stores nationwide, in major retail chains, via catalog and website, and through

licensing partnerships with Major League Baseball, the National Hockey League, and the NFL.

Those familiar with the firm's success credit the Murrays' understanding of their customers' needs and their determination to make customers happy. The brothers say they're interested in dressing people not merely to go to work but rather to "take some fun to work." Their company sells clothes, but also a carefree lifestyle image many people want to adopt.

For instance, one of Shep and Ian's first decisions, when they quit their jobs and began selling ties out of their cars, was to create whimsical designs that reflected the happy summers they spent on Martha's Vineyard while growing up. Thus was born the sporty vacation theme that runs through all their bright pastel designs, featuring lobster pots, sailboats, whales, crabs, and sports paraphernalia such as tennis racquets, golf balls, and hockey sticks. Customers who would rather be sailing, swimming, golfing, or fishing are quickly drawn to the light-hearted images and the lifestyle they conjure up.

The Murrays recognize that, like themselves, most men dislike suits and ties and prefer dressing for work to be as simple as possible. The brothers believe their customers share their desire not so much to impress but to live a comfortable, casual, and enjoyable life. The rapid growth of their firm, fueled largely by word-of-mouth, suggests they are on to something. And among those who have sported Vineyard Vines neckwear are U.S. presidents, New York City mayors, and billionaire investor Warren Buffet.[1]

EVOLUTION OF A

Shep and Ian Murray started their company, Vineyard Vines, as a way to leave their corporate careers behind. Taking a big risk, they quit their day jobs, maxed out their credit cards, and began selling island-inspired ties as a whimsical way to the good life. More than 15 years later, their decision to leave corporate life has paid off, with annual sales topping $100 million in a recent year. Vineyard Vines' marketing strategy is simple yet effective: Market a lifestyle experience to people who want to live the good life the company's brand represents.

- The company's motto is, "Every day should feel this good." How can the marketing team at Vineyard Vines continue to keep this branding approach fresh while attracting new customers and keeping repeat customers?
- Currently more than half of the company's sales are devoted to men's clothing. What strategies can the company use to open up new markets? New licensing partnerships? How can the company use social media to market its products, expand its brand, and capitalize on its laidback image?
- According to recent data, e-commerce accounts for about 30 percent of the company's annual sales. What steps should the company take to increase online sales in both the United States and abroad?

Chapter Overview

"I'll only drink Coke."

"I buy all my clothes at The Gap."

"I like to hang out with my friends at Buffalo Wild Wings."

"I go to Orioles games at Camden Yards."

These words are music to a marketer's ears. They may echo the click of an online purchase, the ping of a cash register, the cheers of fans at a stadium. Customer loyalty is the watchword of 21st-century marketing. Individual consumers and business purchasers have so many goods and services from which to choose—and so many different ways to purchase them—that marketers must continually seek out new and better ways to attract and keep customers. When the world learned that Facebook had assigned two dozen engineers to improve the site's search engine, users and investors were abuzz. A more powerful search engine would mean significantly enhanced capability for Facebook users—and a direct assault on Google, the market leader in search engines and one of Facebook's chief rivals.[2]

The technology revolution continues to change the rules of marketing in the 21st century and will continue to do so in years beyond. The combined power of telecommunications and computer technology creates inexpensive global networks that transfer voice messages, text, graphics, and data within seconds. These sophisticated technologies create new types of products and demand new approaches to marketing existing products. Newspapers are learning this lesson the hard way, as circulation continues to decline around the country, victim in large part to the rising popularity of social media and online websites. On the other hand, e-book readers such as the Amazon Kindle and Apple's iPad are changing the way people read books.[3]

Communications technology also contributes to the globalization of today's marketplace, where businesses manufacture, buy, and sell across national borders. You can bid at eBay on a potential bargain or eat a Big Mac or drink Coca-Cola almost anywhere in the world. Your MP3 player was probably manufactured in China or South Korea; and BMWs are manufactured in South Carolina, Hyundai SUVs are assembled in Alabama, and some Volkswagens are imported from Mexico. Finished products and components routinely cross international borders, but successful global marketing also requires knowledge to tailor products to regional tastes. A chain restaurant in the South might offer grits as an alternative to hash browns on its breakfast menu.

Rapidly changing business landscapes create new challenges for companies, whether they are giant multinational firms or small boutiques, profit-oriented or not-for-profit. Organizations must react quickly to shifts in consumer tastes, competitive offerings, and other market dynamics. Fortunately, information technologies give organizations fast new ways to interact and develop long-term relationships with their customers and suppliers. Such links have become a core element of marketing today.

Every company must serve customer needs—create customer satisfaction—to succeed. We call customer satisfaction an art because it requires imagination and creativity, and a science because it requires technical knowledge, skill, and experience. Marketing strategies are the tools that marketers use to identify and analyze customers'

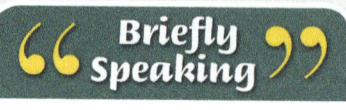
Briefly Speaking

"A lot of companies have chosen to downsize, and maybe that was the right thing for them. We chose a different path. Our belief was that if we kept putting great products in front of customers, they would continue to open their wallets."

—**Steve Jobs**
Late co-founder, Apple Inc.

needs, then show that their company's goods and services can meet those needs. Tomorrow's market leaders will be companies that can make the most of these strategies to create satisfied customers.

This edition of *Contemporary Marketing* focuses on the strategies that allow companies to succeed in today's interactive marketplace. This chapter sets the stage for the entire text, examining the importance of creating satisfaction through customer relationships. Initial sections describe the historical development of marketing and its contributions to society. Later sections introduce the universal functions of marketing and the relationship between ethical business practices and marketplace success. Throughout the chapter—and the entire book—we discuss customer loyalty and the lifetime value of a customer.

WHAT IS MARKETING?

The production and marketing of goods and services, whether it's a new crop of organically grown vegetables or digital cable service, are the essence of business in any society. Like most business disciplines, marketing had its origins in economics. Later, marketing borrowed concepts from areas such as psychology and sociology to explain how people made purchase decisions. Mathematics, anthropology, and other disciplines also contributed to the evolution of marketing. These will be discussed in later chapters.

Economists contributed the concept of **utility**—the want-satisfying power of a good or service. Table 1.1 describes the four basic kinds of utility: form, time, place, and ownership.

Form utility is created when the company converts raw materials and component inputs into finished goods and services. Because of its appearance, gold can serve as a beautiful piece of jewelry, but because it also conducts electricity well and does not corrode, it has many applications in the manufacture of electronic devices such as cell phones and global positioning satellite units. By combining glass, plastic, metals, circuit boards, and other components, Canon makes a digital camera and Sharp produces flat-screen TVs. With fabric and leather, Coach manufactures its high-fashion line of handbags. With a ship and the ocean, a captain and staff, food and entertainment, Royal Caribbean creates a cruise. Although the marketing function focuses on

Define marketing and how it creates utility.

utility Want-satisfying power of a good or service.

TABLE 1.1 Four Types of Utility

Type	Description	Examples	Organizational Function Responsible
Form	Conversion of raw materials and components into finished goods and services	Dinner at Applebee's; Samsung Galaxy phone; Levi jeans	Production*
Time	Availability of goods and services when consumers want them	Dental appointment; digital photographs; 1-800-PetMeds guarantee; UPS Next Day Air delivery	Marketing
Place	Availability of goods and services at convenient locations	Technicians available at an auto repair facility; onsite day care; banks in grocery stores	Marketing
Ownership (possession)	Ability to transfer title to goods or services from marketer to buyer	Retail sales (in exchange for currency, credit, or debit card payment)	Marketing

*Marketing provides inputs related to consumer preferences, but creating form utility is the responsibility of the production function.

PepsiCo's special interactive vending machines allow you to "like" the company's Facebook page and receive a free sample of Pepsi products, connecting the time and place utility of marketing to social media.

"The aim of marketing is to know and understand the customer so well the product or service fits him and sells itself."

—Peter F. Drucker
U.S. management theorist

influencing consumer and audience preferences, the organization's production function creates form utility.

Redbox takes advantage of time and place utility, positioning its kiosks for renting movies and games in high-traffic spots like supermarkets and drug stores around the country. Marketing creates time, place, and ownership utilities. *Time and place utility* occur when consumers find goods and services available when and where they want to purchase them. Vending machines and convenience stores focus on providing place utility for people buying newspapers, snacks, and soft drinks. PepsiCo's recently launched "Like" Vending Machine takes touchscreen and wireless technology even further. The specialized vending machine gives out free samples, but you have to "like" it on Facebook before it dispenses a free can of Pepsi. Consumers can use their smartphones to "like" the Pepsi Facebook page, choose a beverage flavor, and get a free can of Pepsi right away. Or, if they don't have a smartphone handy, the vending machine has a large built-in touchscreen that consumers can use to log into Facebook and "like" Pepsi.[4]

The transfer of title to goods or services at the time of purchase creates *ownership utility*. Signing up for a Sandals tropical vacation or buying a TV creates ownership utility. All organizations must create utility to survive. Designing and marketing want-satisfying goods, services, and ideas are the foundation for the creation of utility. But where does the process start? In the toy industry, manufacturers try to come up with items that children will want to play with—creating utility. But that's not as simple as it sounds. At the Toy Fair held each February in New York, retailers pore through the booths of manufacturers and suppliers, looking for the next Webkinz toys or Lego building blocks—trends that turn into classics and generate millions in revenues over the years. Marketers also look for ways to revive flagging brands and bring them into the digital age. Classic board games such as Monopoly and the Game of Life now have electronic versions that use tablet computers to count money and spin the game wheel—complete with the sound of the old plastic spinner.[5]

But how does an organization create a customer? Most take a three-step approach: identifying needs in the marketplace, finding out which needs the organization can profitably serve, and developing goods and services to convert potential buyers into customers. Marketing specialists are responsible for most of the activities necessary to create the customers the organization wants. These activities include the following:

- identifying customer needs;
- designing products that meet those needs;
- communicating information about those goods and services to prospective buyers;
- making the items available at times and places that meet customers' needs;
- pricing merchandise and services to reflect costs, competition, and customers' ability to buy; and
- providing the necessary service and follow-up to ensure customer satisfaction after the purchase.[6]

A DEFINITION OF MARKETING

The word *marketing* encompasses such a broad scope of activities and ideas that settling on one definition is often difficult. Ask three people to define marketing, and three different definitions are likely to follow. We are exposed to so much advertising and personal selling that most people link marketing only to those activities. But marketing begins long before a product hits the shelf. It involves analyzing customer needs, obtaining the information necessary to design and produce goods or services that match buyer expectations, satisfying customer preferences, and creating and

Chapter 1 Marketing: The Art and Science of Satisfying Customers

maintaining relationships with customers and suppliers. Marketing activities apply to profit-oriented businesses such as Microsoft and Overstock.com as well as to not-for-profit organizations such as the Juvenile Diabetes Research Foundation and the Red Cross. Even government-related agencies such as the U.S. Postal Service engage in marketing activities. Today's definition takes all these factors into account. **Marketing** is the activity, set of institutions, and processes for creating, communicating, delivering, and exchanging offerings that have values for customers, clients, partners, and society at large.[7]

The expanded concept of marketing activities permeates all functions in businesses and not-for-profit organizations. It assumes that organizations conduct their marketing efforts ethically and that these efforts serve the best interests of both society and the organization. The concept also identifies the marketing variables—product, price, promotion, and distribution—that combine to provide customer satisfaction. In addition, it assumes that the organization begins by identifying and analyzing who its potential customers are and what they need. At all points, the concept emphasizes creating and maintaining long-term relationships with customers and suppliers.

marketing The activity, set of institutions, and processes for creating, communicating, delivering, and exchanging offerings that have value for customers, clients, partners, and society at large.

TODAY'S GLOBAL MARKETPLACE

Several factors have forced marketers—and entire nations—to extend their economic views to events outside their own national borders. First, international agreements are negotiated to expand trade among nations. Second, the growth of electronic business and related computer technologies allows previously isolated countries to enter the marketplace for buyers and sellers around the globe. Third, the interdependence of the world's economies is a reality because no nation produces all of the raw materials and finished goods its citizens need or consumes all of its output without exporting some to other countries. Evidence of this interdependence is illustrated by the introduction of the euro as a common currency to facilitate trade among the nations of the European Union and the creation of trade agreements such as the North American Free Trade Agreement (NAFTA) and the World Trade Organization (WTO).

Rising oil prices affect the price that U.S. consumers pay for just about everything—not just gasoline at the pump. Dow Chemical raised the prices of its products up to 20 percent to adjust to

> **Briefly Speaking**
>
> "The Internet is becoming the town square for the global village of tomorrow."
>
> —**Bill Gates**
> *Co-Founder, Microsoft*

FedEx serves its global market by enabling customers in many countries to access the FedEx website in their first language.

its rising cost for energy. The largest U.S. chemical company, Dow, supplies companies in industries from agriculture to health care, all of whom were affected by the price hike. Airlines, too, responded to a near-doubling of the cost of jet fuel. Most carriers now charge customers for redeeming reward miles, and nearly all impose fees for checked baggage on domestic flights.[8]

To remain competitive, companies must continually search for the most efficient manufacturing sites and most lucrative markets for their products. U.S. marketers now find tremendous opportunities serving customers not only in traditional industrialized nations but also in Latin America and emerging economies in central Europe, the Middle East, Asia, and Africa, where rising standards of living create increased customer demand for the latest products. Expanding operations beyond the U.S. market gives domestic companies access to more than 7 billion international customers. China is now the second-largest market in the world—only the United States is larger. And industry observers estimate that Chinese customers purchased 20 million cars in a recent year, so automakers worldwide extended their operations to China.[9] Interestingly, however, signs are mounting that China's increasing prosperity may be reducing its attractiveness as a low-cost labor source. Rising costs already are driving some U.S. manufacturers out of the country, according to the American Chamber of Commerce. Mexico has taken the lead as the lowest-cost country for outsourced production, with India and Vietnam second and third; China stands in sixth place.[10]

Service firms also play a major role in today's global marketplace. Telecommunications firms such as South Africa's MTN, Luxembourg's Millicom International, and Egypt's Global Telecom Holding have carved out new global markets for their products by following the lead of Finnish firm Nokia, among the first high-tech firms to create durable and affordable mobile phones specifically designed for emerging markets. Nokia's mobile-phone business was recently acquired by Microsoft.[11] The opportunities for such telecom innovators will continue to grow as long as electricity-reliant personal computers remain out of reach for millions in the developing world. The United States is also an attractive market for foreign competitors because of its size and the high standard of living American consumers enjoy. Companies such as Nissan, Sony, and Sun Life Financial of Canada operate production, distribution, service, and retail facilities in the United States. Foreign ownership of U.S. companies has also increased. Ben & Jerry's is a well-known firm with a foreign parent (Unilever).

Although many global marketing strategies are almost identical to those used in domestic markets, more and more companies are tailoring their marketing efforts to the needs and preferences of consumers in foreign markets. It is often difficult to standardize a brand name on a global basis. The Japanese, for example, like the names of flowers or girls for their automobiles—names such as Bluebonnet, Violet, and Gloria. Americans, on the other hand, prefer rugged outdoorsy names such as Chevy Tahoe, Jeep Cherokee, and Dodge Challenger.

ASSESSMENT CHECK

1.1 Define marketing, and explain how it creates utility.

1.2 What three factors have forced marketers to embrace a global marketplace?

FIVE ERAS IN THE HISTORY OF MARKETING

2 Contrast marketing activities during the five eras in the history of marketing.

exchange process Activity in which two or more parties give something of value to each other to satisfy perceived needs.

The essence of marketing includes managing customer relationships and the **exchange process**, in which two or more parties give something of value to each other to satisfy perceived needs. Often, people exchange money for tangible goods such as groceries, clothes, a car, or a house. In other situations, they exchange money for intangible services such as a haircut or a college education. Many exchanges involve a combination of goods and services, such as dinner in a restaurant, where dinner represents the good and the wait staff represents the service. People also make exchanges when they donate money or time to a charitable cause such as Habitat for Humanity. Managing customer relationships like these are the essence of successful marketing.

Although marketing has always been a part of business, its importance has varied greatly. Figure 1.1 identifies five eras in the history of marketing: (1) the production era, (2) the sales era, (3) the marketing era, (4) the relationship era, and (5) the social era.

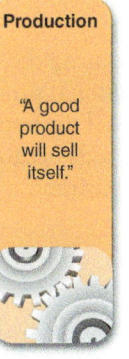

ERA	Production	Sales	Marketing	Relationship	Social
PREVAILING ATTITUDE	"A good product will sell itself."	"Creative advertising and selling will overcome consumers' resistance and persuade them to buy."	"The consumer rules! Find a need and fill it."	"Long-term relationships with customers and other partners lead to success."	"Connecting to consumers via Internet and social media sites is an effective tool."
APPROXIMATE TIME PERIOD	Prior to 1920s	Prior to 1950s	Since 1950s	Since 1990s	Since 2000s

FIGURE 1.1 Five Eras of Marketing History

THE PRODUCTION ERA

Before 1925, most firms—even those operating in highly developed economies in western Europe and North America—focused narrowly on production. Manufacturers stressed production of quality products and then looked for people to purchase them. The prevailing attitude of this era held that a high-quality product would sell itself. This **production orientation** dominated business philosophy for decades; business success often was defined solely in terms of production success.

The production era reached its peak during the early part of the 20th century. Henry Ford's mass-production line exemplifies this orientation. Ford's slogan, "They [customers] can have any color they want, as long as it's black," reflected the prevalent attitude toward marketing. Production shortages and intense consumer demand ruled the day. It is easy to understand how production activities took precedence.

However, building a new product is no guarantee of success, and marketing history is cluttered with the bones of miserable product failures despite major innovations—more than 80 percent of new products fail. Inventing an outstanding new product is not enough, because it must also fill a perceived marketplace need. Otherwise, even the best-engineered, highest-quality product will fail. Even Henry Ford's horseless carriage took a while to catch on. People were afraid of motor vehicles: They spat out exhaust, stirred up dust on dirt roads, got stuck in mud, and tied up horse traffic. Besides, at the speed of seven miles per hour, they caused all kinds of accidents and disruption. It took savvy marketing by some early salespeople—and eventually a widespread perceived need—to change people's minds about the product. Today, most of us could not imagine life without a car and have refined that need to preferences for certain types of vehicles, including SUVs, convertibles, trucks, and hybrids.

production orientation Business philosophy stressing efficiency in producing a quality product, with the attitude toward marketing that "a good product will sell itself."

THE SALES ERA

As production techniques in the United States and Europe became more sophisticated, output grew from the 1920s into the early 1950s. As a result, manufacturers began to increase their emphasis on effective sales forces to find customers for their output. In this era, firms attempted to match their output to the potential number of customers who would want it. Companies with a **sales orientation** assume that customers will resist purchasing nonessential goods and services and that the task of personal selling and advertising is to persuade them to buy.

Although marketing departments began to emerge from the shadows of production and engineering during the sales era, they tended to remain in subordinate positions. Many chief marketing executives held the title of sales manager. But selling is only one component of marketing. As marketing scholar Theodore Levitt once pointed out, "Marketing is as different from selling as chemistry is from alchemy, astronomy from astrology, chess from checkers."

sales orientation Belief that consumers will resist purchasing nonessential goods and services, with the attitude toward marketing that only creative advertising and personal selling can overcome consumers' resistance and persuade them to buy.

THE MARKETING ERA

Personal incomes and consumer demand for products dropped rapidly during the Great Depression of the 1930s, thrusting marketing into a more important role. Organizational survival dictated that managers pay close attention to the markets for their goods and services. This trend ended with the outbreak of World War II, when rationing and shortages of consumer goods became commonplace. The war years, however, created only a pause in an emerging trend in business: a shift in the focus from products and sales to satisfying customer needs.

Emergence of the Marketing Concept

The marketing concept, a crucial change in management philosophy, can be linked to the shift from a **seller's market**—one in which there were more buyers for fewer goods and services—to a **buyer's market**—one in which there were more goods and services than people willing to buy them. When World War II ended, factories stopped manufacturing tanks and ships and started turning out consumer products again, an activity that had, for all practical purposes, stopped in early 1942.

The advent of a strong buyer's market created the need for **consumer orientation** by businesses. Companies had to market goods and services, not just produce and sell them. This realization has been identified as the emergence of the marketing concept. Marketing would no longer be regarded as a supplemental activity performed after completing the production process. Instead, the marketer played a leading role in product planning. *Marketing* and *selling* would no longer be synonymous terms.

Today's fully developed **marketing concept** is a *companywide consumer orientation* with the objective of achieving long-run success. All facets—and all levels, from top to bottom—of the organization must contribute first to assessing and then to satisfying customer wants and needs. From marketing manager to accountant to product designer, every employee plays a role in reaching potential customers. Even during tough economic times, when companies tend to emphasize cutting costs and boosting revenues, the marketing concept focuses on the objective of achieving long-run success instead of short-term profits. Because the firm's survival and growth are built into the marketing concept, companywide consumer orientation should lead to greater long-run profits.

Apple exemplifies the marketing concept in every aspect of its business. Its products are consistently stylish and cutting edge but without overwhelming users with every possible feature. "A defining quality of Apple has been design restraint," says one industry consultant. That hallmark restraint is a characteristic of Apple's late co-founder, Steve Jobs, and is reflected in the work of Apple's designers, managers, and engineers, whose contributions to the company's new products Jobs credited for the company's ability to constantly surprise the marketplace. The release of Apple's iPhone 5, which

---

seller's market A market in which there are more buyers for fewer goods and services.

buyer's market A market in which there are more goods and services than people willing to buy them.

consumer orientation Business philosophy incorporating the marketing concept that emphasizes first determining unmet consumer needs and then designing a system for satisfying them.

marketing concept Companywide consumer orientation with the objective of achieving long-run success.

Apple exemplifies the marketing concept, creating consistently stylish and cutting-edge products. When Apple releases a new product or a new version of an existing product, people line up to purchase the new model.

represented an enhancement of a product designed to anticipate needs many consumers didn't even realize they had, motivated many people to wait in line to purchase the new model. Within three days of its release, the company sold a record-breaking 9 million iPhone 5s and 5c models.[12]

A strong market orientation—the extent to which a company adopts the marketing concept—generally improves market success and overall performance. It also has a positive effect on new-product development and the introduction of innovative products. Companies that implement market-driven strategies are better able to understand their customers' experiences, buying habits, and needs. They can, therefore, design products with advantages and levels of quality compatible with customer requirements.

THE RELATIONSHIP ERA

The fourth era in the history of marketing emerged during the 1990s and continues to grow in importance. Organizations now build on the marketing era's customer orientation by focusing on establishing and maintaining relationships with both customers and suppliers. **Relationship marketing** involves developing long-term, value-added relationships over time with customers and suppliers. Strategic alliances and partnerships among manufacturers, retailers, and suppliers often benefit everyone. In an effort to better engage with its large fan base, NASCAR recently re-launched its digital platform. Collaborating with Livefyre, a leading provider of real-time social software, NASCAR encourages racing fans to have conversations in real time across its website via computer, tablet, or mobile device. Fans also have the option to bring others into their conversations by tagging friends on social media networks such as Facebook and Twitter. According to Livefyre's founder, relationship marketing is all about engaging with and relating to consumers where they spend a lot of their time: online.[13] The concept of relationship marketing, which is the current state of customer-driven marketing, is discussed in detail later in this chapter and in Chapter 11.

relationship marketing Development and maintenance of long-term, cost-effective relationships with individual customers, suppliers, employees, and other partners for mutual benefit.

THE SOCIAL ERA

The social era of marketing is in full swing, thanks to consumers' accessibility to the Internet and the creation of social media sites such as Facebook and Twitter. Building on the relationship era, companies now routinely use the Web and social networking sites to connect to consumers as a way to market goods and services. On a personal level, see the "Career Readiness" feature for suggestions on how to land a social media marketing position.

CONVERTING NEEDS TO WANTS

Every consumer must acquire goods and services on a continuing basis to fill certain needs. Everyone must satisfy the fundamental needs for food, clothing, shelter, and transportation by purchasing items or, in some instances, temporarily using rented property and hired or leased transportation. By focusing on the benefits resulting from these products, effective marketing converts needs to wants. A need for a pair of pants may be converted to a desire for jeans—and, further, a desire for jeans from H&M or Lucky Brand Jeans. The need for food may be converted to a desire for dinner at Macaroni Grill or groceries from Publix. But if the need for transportation isn't converted to a desire for a Ford Focus or Mini Cooper, extra vehicles may sit unsold on a dealer's lot.

Consumers need to communicate. But converting that need to the desire for certain types of communication requires skill. It also requires listening to what consumers want. Consumers' demand for more cell phone and wireless

ASSESSMENT CHECK

2.1 What is the major distinction between the production era and the sales era?

2.2 What is the marketing concept?

2.3 Describe the relationship era of marketing.

> **Briefly Speaking**
>
> "Customers don't always know what they want. The decline in coffee drinking was due to the fact that most of the coffee people bought was stale and they weren't enjoying it. Once they tasted ours and experienced what we call 'the third place,' a gathering place between home and work where they were treated with respect, they found we were filling a need they didn't know they had."
>
> —Howard Schultz
> *Chairman and CEO, Starbucks*

CAREER READINESS
Landing a Job in Social Media Marketing

Are you empathic, enthusiastic about connecting with others, well organized, and tech-savvy? If so, you might have the makings of a social media marketing manager, a dynamic career that's springing up in companies that want to take creative control of their online communication with customers, suppliers, and potential new markets. Here are some ideas for handling the job successfully:

1. Make the most of any customer-service experience you've acquired; it will serve you well in figuring out how to reach people effectively with tools such as Twitter, Facebook, LinkedIn, Pinterest, and YouTube.

2. Take a course to learn about video production and watch a lot of videos online. Online video offers marketers countless opportunities and can be quick and inexpensive to produce. Experience here could be invaluable.

3. Make sure you spend enough time listening to your customers. Listening is the most important communication skill, whether in person or online.

4. Connect with others in your industry. Share what you've learned and learn from the best practices of others in this young and growing field.

5. Keep your company's online presence unique, such as with a distinctive point of view and consistently creative and original content, including contests, blogs, photos, audio, and of course video too.

Sources: Drew Hubbard, "12 Traits of Successful Social Media Managers," *Ragan.com*, accessed January 3, 2014, www.ragan.com; Mikal E. Belicove, "The Daily Dose: Six Must-Have Attributes of Social Media Managers," *Entrepreneur*, accessed January 3, 2014, www.entrepreneur.com/blog/224263; Ed Heil, "8 Attributes of a Qualified Social Media Manager," *StoryTeller*, accessed January 3, 2014, www.storytellermn.com; Kent Lewis, "Why You Should Fire Your Social Media Manager," iMediaConnection.com, accessed January 3, 2014, http://blogs.imediaconnection.com.

---

services seems nearly unlimited, particularly with the surge in social networking sites—providing tremendous opportunities for companies. New products, such as increasingly popular broadband wireless services and the veritable flood of applications now available for smartphones, appear to feed that demand, enabling consumers to use their phones in new ways—for example, checking the weather, monitoring heart rates, finding recipes, and scanning product bar codes to comparison shop.[14]

AVOIDING MARKETING MYOPIA

3 Explain the importance of avoiding marketing myopia.

marketing myopia Management's failure to recognize the scope of its business.

The emergence of the marketing concept has not been without setbacks. One troublesome problem led marketing scholar Theodore Levitt to coin the term **marketing myopia**. According to Levitt, marketing myopia is management's failure to recognize the scope of its business. Product-oriented rather than customer-oriented management endangers future growth. Levitt cites many service industries, such as dry cleaning and electric utilities, as examples of marketing myopia. But many firms have found innovative ways to reach new markets and develop long-term relationships.

For instance, for a long time, Apple has worked to develop greener and more sustainable manufacturing processes and products. Apple's 20-megawatt solar farm and adjacent 10-megawatt fuel-cell farm in North Carolina recently went on line, providing clean power for the company's expansive

TABLE 1.2 Avoiding Marketing Myopia

Company	Myopic Description	Company Motto—Avoiding Myopia
BMW	Automobile	The Ultimate Driving Machine
Sandals Resorts	Resort vacations	The Luxury Included Vacation
MasterCard	Credit card company	There are some things money can't buy. For everything else, there's MasterCard.
Allegra	Antihistamine	Have it All
Bridgestone	Tire manufacturer	Time to perform
UPS	Express package	We ♥ logistics.

data center in what some observers are calling the largest such company-owned facilities in the United States. In addition, the company recently won a patent for a power management system that will work with both a power adapter and a portable solar panel accessory for people using mobile devices.[15] Table 1.2 illustrates how firms in a number of industries have overcome myopic thinking by developing broader marketing-oriented business ideas that focus on consumer need satisfaction.

ASSESSMENT CHECK

3.1 What is marketing myopia?

3.2 Give an example of how a firm can avoid marketing myopia.

EXTENDING THE TRADITIONAL BOUNDARIES OF MARKETING

Today's organizations—both profit-oriented and not-for-profit—recognize universal needs for marketing and its importance to their success. During a television commercial break, viewers might be exposed to an advertisement for a Kia Spectra, an appeal to help feed children in foreign countries, a message by a political candidate, and a commercial for McDonald's—all in the space of about two minutes. Two of these ads are paid for by firms attempting to achieve profitability and other objectives. The appeal for funds to feed children and the political ad are examples of communications by not-for-profit organizations and individuals.

MARKETING IN NOT-FOR-PROFIT ORGANIZATIONS

More than a quarter of all U.S. adults volunteer in one or more of the 2.3 million not-for-profit organizations across the country.[16] In total, these organizations generate hundreds of billions of dollars of revenues each year through contributions and from fund-raising activities. That makes not-for-profit organizations big business.

Not-for-profits operate in both public and private sectors. Federal, state, and local organizations pursue service objectives not keyed to profitability targets. The Federal Trade Commission oversees business activities; a state's department of motor vehicles issues car registrations and driver's licenses; a local school board is responsible for maintaining educational standards for its district. The private sector has an even greater array of not-for-profit organizations, including hospitals, libraries, the American Kennel Club, and the American Lung Association. Regardless of their size or location, all of these organizations need funds to operate. Adopting the marketing concept can make a great difference in their ability to meet their service objectives.

Conner Prairie in Fishers, Indiana, is an open-air re-creation of rural life in 1830s Indiana that features historic areas to explore, including a Lenape Indian camp, the Conner Homestead, a modern museum, and 800 acres of undeveloped land, along with indoor play and learning areas for young children. Costumed staff host events that range from a festive wedding to the experience of slaves seeking freedom through the Underground Railroad. Thousands of families and school groups visit each year.[17]

Some not-for-profits form partnerships with business firms that promote the organization's cause or message. Target Stores funds a facility called Target House, which provides long-term housing for families with children treated at St. Jude Children's Research Hospital. The house has about 100 apartments, plus common areas where families can gather and children can play. Celebrities have also contributed to the house. The Jonas Brothers created a karaoke space for family fun, and Olympic gold-medalist Scott Hamilton donated a family fitness center and an arts-and-crafts room. Other "friends" of the organization include Olympic snowboarder Shaun White and country singer-songwriter Brad Paisley. Sponsors like Procter & Gamble and Dick's Sporting Goods also support the house.[18]

Generally, the alliances formed between not-for-profit organizations and commercial firms and their executives benefit both. The reality of operating with multimillion-dollar budgets requires not-for-profit organizations to maintain a focused business approach. Consider some current examples:

- Share Our Strength's No Kid Hungry campaign receives assistance from food manufacturers and grocery stores in distributing more than 34 million meals to children who need them. A few of the many businesses that support Share Our Strength include Walmart, Arby's, Food Network, American Express, Whole Foods, and Kellogg.[19]
- Corporate Angel Network works with the National Business Aviation Association to use empty seats on corporate jets to provide free transportation for cancer patients traveling to and from their treatments.
- More than $65 million was raised through donations from individuals, companies, and charitable organizations for victims of the recent tornadoes and flooding in the Oklahoma City area. Fundraising was led by the American Red Cross and the Salvation Army.[20]

The diversity of not-for-profit organizations suggests the presence of numerous organizational objectives other than profitability. In addition to their organizational goals, not-for-profit organizations differ from profit-seeking firms in several other ways.

CHARACTERISTICS OF NOT-FOR-PROFIT MARKETING

4 Describe the characteristics of not-for-profit marketing.

bottom line Reference to overall company profitability.

The most obvious distinction between not-for-profit organizations and for-profit firms is the financial **bottom line**, business jargon that refers to the overall profitability of an organization. For-profit organizations measure profitability, and their goal is to generate revenues above and beyond their costs to make money for all stakeholders involved, including employees, shareholders, and the organization itself. Not-for-profit organizations hope to generate as much revenue as possible to support their causes, whether it is feeding children, preserving wilderness areas, or helping single mothers find work. Historically, not-for-profits have had less exact goals and marketing objectives than for-profit firms, but in recent years, many of these groups have recognized that, to succeed, they must develop more cost-effective ways to provide services, and they must compete with other organizations for donors' dollars. Marketing can help them accomplish these tasks. Some groups are finding, for instance, that online social network sites, such as Facebook and Twitter, can bring them increased attention. But they are also using specialized networks devoted to social causes like YourCause.com, and easy payment systems like Rally.org to generate funds.[21]

Chapter 1 Marketing: The Art and Science of Satisfying Customers 15

During October, the National Football League supports Breast Cancer Awareness month with its "A Crucial Catch" campaign, permitting players to wear pink gloves, headbands, or other pink items to show their support for the cause.

Other distinctions exist between for-profit and not-for-profit organizations as well, each of which influences marketing activities. Like profit-seeking firms, not-for-profit organizations may market tangible goods or intangible services. Pink products have long been important in raising both funds for and recognition of National Breast Cancer Awareness month every October. During that month, the National Football League supports the American Cancer Society by permitting its players to wear pink gloves, headbands, or other pink items to signal their support for the cause.[22] While profit-seeking businesses tend to focus their marketing on just one public—their customers—not-for-profit organizations often must market to multiple publics, which complicates decision making about the correct markets to target. Many deal with at least two major publics—their clients and their sponsors—and often many other publics as well. A college or university markets to prospective and current students, parents of students, major donors, alumni, faculty, staff, local businesses, and local government agencies.

A service user of a not-for-profit organization may have less control over the organization's destiny than customers of a profit-seeking firm. Not-for-profit organizations also often possess some degree of monopoly power in a given geographic area. An individual contributor might object to United Way's inclusion of a particular local agency, but that agency will receive a portion of any donor contribution.

ASSESSMENT CHECK

4.1 What is the most obvious distinction between a not-for-profit organization and a commercial organization?

4.2 Why do for-profit and not-for-profit organizations sometimes form alliances?

NONTRADITIONAL MARKETING

As marketing evolved into an organization-wide activity, its application has broadened far beyond its traditional boundaries of for-profit organizations that create and distribute tangible goods and intangible services. In many cases, broader appeals focus on causes, events, individuals, organizations, and places. Table 1.3 lists and describes five major categories of nontraditional marketing:

Explain each of the five types of nontraditional marketing.

5

TABLE 1.3 Categories of Nontraditional Marketing

Type	Brief Description	Examples
Person marketing	Marketing efforts designed to cultivate the attention and preference of a target market toward a person	Athlete Peyton Manning, Denver Broncos quarterback; celebrity Blake Shelton, country singer
Place marketing	Marketing efforts designed to attract visitors to a particular area; improve consumer images of a city, state, or nation; and/or attract new business	California: "Find Yourself Here." Tennessee: "We're Playing Your Song." West Virginia: "Wild and Wonderful."
Cause marketing	Identification and marketing of a social issue, cause, or idea to selected target markets	"Click it or Ticket." "Refill, not landfill."
Event marketing	Marketing of sporting, cultural, and charitable activities to selected target markets	Tokyo 2020 Summer Olympics; American Diabetes Association's Tour de Cure
Organization marketing	Marketing efforts of mutual-benefit organizations, service organizations, and government organizations that seek to influence others to accept their goals, receive their services, or contribute to them in some way	American Red Cross: "Together, we can save a life." March of Dimes: "Working together for stronger, healthier babies." St. Jude Children's Research Hospital: "Finding Cures. Saving Children."

person marketing
Marketing efforts designed to cultivate the attention, interest, and preferences of a target market toward a person (perhaps a political candidate or celebrity).

person marketing, place marketing, cause marketing, event marketing, and organization marketing. These categories can overlap—promotion for an organization may also encompass a cause, or a promotional campaign may focus on both an event and a place.

PERSON MARKETING

Person marketing involves efforts designed to cultivate the attention, interest, and preferences of a target market toward a celebrity or authority figure. Celebrities can be real people or fictional characters. Political candidates engage in person marketing as they promote their candidacy for office. Authors such as Suze Orman of *The Road to Wealth* use person marketing to promote their books. Rachael Ray uses person marketing to promote her *Every Day with Rachael Ray* magazine, where she appears on every cover.

An extension of person marketing is *celebrity endorsements*, in which well-known athletes, entertainers, and experts or authority figures promote products for companies or social causes for not-for-profit organizations. Actresses Olivia Wilde and Emma Stone are spokespersons for Revlon beauty products; Chevrolet recently signed singer/songwriter John Legend to pitch its Impala brand; and "Modern Family" actress Sofia Vergara dances her way through a Miami nightclub in pursuit of a Diet Pepsi.[23] But athletes are the big winners in the celebrity endorsement arena—NBA MVP LeBron James appears in a series of ads touting Samsung's mobile products; New Orleans Saints quarterback Drew Brees is a celebrity spokesperson for Wrangler jeans; and pro golfer Phil Michelson endorses many products, including Rolex watches. And NBA superstar Kobe Bryant was recently named the highest-paid basketball player on *Forbes'* list of the world's highest-paid athletes, ranking third overall with annual earnings of more than $60 million.[24]

> **Briefly Speaking**
>
> "There is only one boss. The customer. And he can fire everybody in the company from the chairman on down simply by spending his money somewhere else."
>
> —**Sam Walton**
> *Founder, Walmart*

PLACE MARKETING

Another category of nontraditional marketing is **place marketing**, which attempts to attract customers to particular areas. Cities, states, regions, and countries publicize their tourist attractions to lure vacation travelers. They also promote themselves as good locations for businesses. Place marketing has become more important in the world economy—not only for tourism but also to recruit business and workers. In an effort to boost the sagging Las Vegas economy, casino operator MGM built a multi-billion-dollar CityCenter complex that includes four 61-story hotel towers, high-end stores, and dozens of bars and restaurants—and, of course, a casino. Interestingly, the tourism enhancements in Las Vegas have started to attract more visitors and turn the economy around, but tourists are gambling less than they used to.[25]

Place marketing can be a showcase for ingenuity. Although commercial space travel remains a somewhat distant possibility, the New Mexico Spaceport Authority has already designed the world's first public launch and landing site for space vehicles. Spaceport America, home to Richard Branson's Virgin Galactic, is located next to the U.S. Army's White Sands Missile Range. Among its objectives, Spaceport America strives to encourage and inspire students in science and math and partners with a science consortium to host an annual student launch. More than 800 students and teachers participated in a recent launch.[26]

Explore Minnesota, a website that promotes the state's almost $12 billion travel and tourism industry, is backed by a strategic plan that details 16 separate programs and tactics to achieve its goals. They include traditional advertising, interactive marketing, partnership and group tour marketing, media relations, meetings and conventions, and the growth area of sports marketing, among others. Primary markets are the north central United States and Canada, Mexico, Japan, the United Kingdom, China, Germany, and Scandinavia.[27]

In another area of the country, West Virginia has a hub for vacationers. For instance, the town of Davis is home to Timberline Four Seasons Resort, which, as its name suggests, offers a wealth of outdoor activities year-round. During the summer, visitors can ride horses, mountain bike, hike, or go whitewater rafting. In the winter, the resort boasts more than 200 inches of snow per year on its Herz Mountain. Timberline is sometimes overlooked by East Coast skiers who travel north and west; however, locals are convinced that their mountain, which recently upgraded the snowmaking capacity for its 37 slopes and trails, is about to be discovered.[28]

place marketing
Marketing efforts to attract people and organizations to a particular geographic area.

The state of Minnesota takes the concept of place marketing seriously in its efforts to attract tourism dollars. Its Explore Minnesota website is just one of 16 separate programs the state uses to promote tourism.

> **Briefly Speaking**
>
> "After all, the chief business of the American people is business."
>
> —Calvin Coolidge
> *Thirtieth President of the United States*

CAUSE MARKETING

A third category of nontraditional marketing, **cause marketing**, refers to the identification and marketing of a social issue, cause, or idea to selected target markets. Cause marketing covers a wide range of issues, including literacy, physical fitness, awareness of childhood obesity, environmental protection, elimination of birth defects, child-abuse prevention, and preventing drunk driving.

As mentioned earlier, an increasingly common marketing practice is for profit-seeking firms to link their products to social causes. Partnering recently with the Boys & Girls Clubs of America, office supply giant Staples sponsored its annual school supplies drive and donated supplies to more than 5,000 communities nationwide. The company has also donated more than $14 million to not-for-profit organizations around the world through its Staples Foundation, corporate charitable giving programs, and other cause marketing efforts.[29]

Surveys show strong support for cause-related marketing by both consumers and company employees. In a recent survey, 92 percent of consumers had a more positive image of companies that support important social causes, and four of five respondents said that they would change brands to support a cause if the price and quality of the two brands remained equal. Cause marketing can help build relationships with customers.

cause marketing
Identification and marketing of a social issue, cause, or idea to selected target markets.

EVENT MARKETING

Event marketing refers to the marketing of sporting, cultural, and charitable activities to selected target markets. It also includes the sponsorship of such events by firms seeking to increase public awareness and bolster their images by linking themselves and their products to the events. Sports sponsorships have gained effectiveness in increasing brand recognition, enhancing image, boosting purchase volume, and increasing popularity with sports fans in demographic segments corresponding to sponsor business goals.

Some people might say that the premier sporting event is baseball's World Series. Others claim it's the Olympics or the World Cup. Still others might argue that it's the Super Bowl, which some consumers claim they watch only to see the debut of commercials. Those commercials are expensive, costing, on average, $4 million for 30 seconds of airtime for a recent Super Bowl.[30] Companies now also feed their commercials to websites and make them available for downloading to personal computers, tablets, and smartphones. Experienced marketers caution that firms planning such a big expenditure should make it part of a larger marketing plan, not just a single shot at fame. For those who prefer the international pageantry of the Olympics, marketers have plenty of plans. The promotion of upcoming Olympics—both summer and winter—begins years in advance. Before the end of each Olympics, hosts of the next games unveil their logo, and the marketing takes off from there. Corporate sponsors like Adidas try to target the next Olympic gold medal winners, draping them in clothing and gear with company logos. The 2014 Winter Olympics in Sochi, Russia, afforded opportunities for hundreds of firms to provide food and drink for hospitality events,

event marketing
Marketing of sporting, cultural, and charitable activities to selected target markets.

Event marketing for the Olympics begins years in advance. Here is the logo for the 2018 Winter Games to be held in PyeongChang, South Korea.

ORGANIZATION MARKETING

Organization marketing attempts to persuade people to accept the goals of, receive the services of, or contribute in some way to an organization. Organization marketing includes mutual-benefit organizations such as Service Employees International Union and the Republican and Democratic political parties; service and cultural organizations such as Purdue University, Baylor College of Medicine, St. Louis's Barnes-Jewish Hospital, and Little Rock's Clinton Presidential Library; and government organizations such as the U.S. Coast Guard, the Newark Police Department, the Sacramento Fire Department, and the U.S. Postal Service. Colleges and universities use organizational marketing to help raise funds. The University of Texas leads all colleges and universities in the sale of licensed merchandise—the school receives more than $10 million a year from these sales.[32]

> **organization marketing** Marketing by mutual-benefit organizations, service organizations, and government organizations intended to persuade others to accept their goals, receive their services, or contribute to them in some way.

ASSESSMENT CHECK

5.1 Identify the five major categories of nontraditional marketing.

5.2 Give an example of a way in which two or more of these categories might overlap.

FROM TRANSACTION-BASED MARKETING TO RELATIONSHIP MARKETING

As marketing progresses through the 21st century, a significant change is taking place in the way companies interact with customers. The traditional view of marketing as a simple exchange process, or **transaction-based marketing**, is being replaced by a different, longer-term approach that emphasizes building relationships with one customer at a time. Traditional marketing strategies focused on attracting customers and closing deals. Today's marketers realize that, although it's important to attract new customers, it's even more important to establish and maintain a relationship with them so they become loyal repeat customers. These efforts must expand to include suppliers and employees as well. Over the long term, this relationship may be translated to the lifetime value of a customer—the revenues and intangible benefits that a customer brings to an organization over an average lifetime, minus the investment the firm has made to attract and keep the customer.

Marketers realize that consumers are becoming more and more sophisticated. They quickly recognize marketing messages and may turn away from them if the messages don't contain information that consumers want and need. So marketers need to develop new techniques to establish and build trusting relationships between companies and their customers. As defined earlier in this chapter, relationship marketing refers to the development, growth, and maintenance of long-term, cost-effective exchange relationships with individual customers, suppliers, employees, and other partners for mutual benefit. It broadens the scope of external marketing relationships to include suppliers, customers, and referral sources. In relationship marketing, the term *customer* takes on a new meaning. Employees serve customers within an organization as well as outside it; individual employees and their departments are customers of and suppliers to one another. They must apply the same high standards of customer satisfaction to intradepartmental relationships as they do to external customer relationships. Relationship marketing recognizes the critical importance of internal marketing to the success of external marketing plans. Programs that improve customer service inside a company also raise productivity and staff morale, resulting in better customer relationships outside the firm.

> **6** Explain the shift from transaction-based marketing to relationship and social marketing.

> **transaction-based marketing** Buyer and seller exchanges characterized by limited communications and little or no ongoing relationships between the parties.

> **" Briefly Speaking "**
> "The best way to get what you want is to help other people get what they want."
> —**Zig Ziglar**
> U.S. motivational speaker

FIGURE 1.2 Converting New Customers to Advocates

(Ladder: New Customer → Regular Purchaser → Loyal Supporter → Advocate)

Relationship marketing gives a company new opportunities to gain a competitive edge by moving customers up a loyalty ladder—from new customers to regular purchasers, then to loyal supporters of the firm and its goods and services, and finally to advocates who not only buy its products but recommend them to others, as shown in Figure 1.2.

Relationship building begins early in marketing. It starts with determining what customers need and want, then developing high-quality products to meet those needs. It continues with excellent customer service during and after purchase. It also includes programs that encourage repeat purchases and foster customer loyalty.

Marketers may try to rebuild damaged relationships or rejuvenate unprofitable customers with these practices as well. Sometimes modifying a product or tailoring customer service to meet the needs of these customers can go a long way toward rebuilding a relationship.

USING SOCIAL MARKETING TO BUILD RELATIONSHIPS

Today's technology allows people to transmit memos, reports, and drawings quickly and inexpensively over phone lines, cables, or wireless devices. People can subscribe to personalized news services that deliver article summaries on specified topics directly to their computers or smartphones. They can communicate via social media, email, voice mail, text messages, videoconferencing, and computer networks; pay bills using online banking services; and use online resources to get information about everything from theater events or restaurant reviews to a local Chevrolet dealer's special sale.

CONVERTING NEW CUSTOMERS TO ADVOCATES

mobile marketing Marketing messages transmitted via wireless technology.

interactive marketing Buyer–seller communications in which the customer controls the amount and type of information received from a marketer through channels such as the Internet and virtual reality kiosks.

social marketing The use of online social media as a communications channel for marketing messages.

As an increasing number of Internet users in the United States use wireless devices such as smartphones or tablets to access the Web and check their email, **mobile marketing**—marketing messages transmitted via wireless technology—has become extremely popular.

Interactive media technologies combine computers and telecommunications resources to create software that users can control. Putting power into the hands of customers allows better communication, which can build relationships. **Interactive marketing** refers to buyer–seller communications in which the customer controls the amount and type of information received from a marketer. This technique provides immediate access to key product information when the consumer wants it, and it is increasingly taking place on social media sites such as Facebook, Twitter, and Pinterest. **Social marketing** is the use of online social media as a communications channel for marketing messages.

Social media is now the top online activity. With almost 1.2 billion monthly active users, it's estimated that if Facebook were a country, it would be the third most populous in the world, right after India.[33] And, after going public with its recent IPO, Twitter announced that its more than 200 million active users post an average of 400 million tweets a day.[34] Over three-fourths of the Fortune 100 companies have joined Twitter, and more than 70 percent use Facebook.[35] The Weather Channel has used social media successfully to strengthen and expand its marketing approach. See "Marketing Success" for more details.

Interactive marketing allows marketers and consumers to customize their communication. Customers may come to companies for information, creating opportunities for one-to-one marketing. They also can tell the company what they like or dislike about a product, and they can just as easily click the exit button and move on to another area. As interactive promotions grow in number and popularity, the challenge is to attract and hold consumer attention.

One small business making good use of social media is Lolly Wolly Doodle, a children's clothing company in Lexington, North Carolina. Founder Brandi Temple started making clothes for her young daughters and realized she made more outfits than her two girls could possibly wear. So she sold the extra outfits on eBay. When her husband lost his job, they decided to move their small retail sales operation from eBay to Facebook, where they currently have more than 930,000 fans.

MARKETING SUCCESS
The Weather Channel Expands Its Social Reach

Background. The Weather Channel (WTC) began as a 24-hour television network delivering up-to-the-minute reporting about rain, sleet, snow, and sunshine.

The Challenge. As new electronic platforms emerged, WTC needed to find new ways to be relevant. How do you market the weather?

The Strategy. WTC expanded its brand through marketing strategies that tap directly into the digital world. Now it operates a cable channel with original reality-show programming, a website highlighting conditions and forecasts for 100,000 locations worldwide plus educational and seasonal features, a radio network with 700 affiliates, a popular mobile app, and a Twitter partnership called Weather Channel Social.

Weather Channel Social offers real-time tweets and forecasts across mobile, broadcast, and Web platforms. Weather.com provides a local Social page with weather-related tweets plus other customer-created content. The iPhone app hosts interactive conversations by users—weather-related and social—while the TV channel integrates real-time tweets into live programming, and viewers can participate. Cities with populations over 100,000 have 200 custom Twitter feeds offering local forecasts with three-hour updates.

The Outcome. "Adding Social to all of our platforms makes our storytelling more complete," says WTC's executive vice president of digital products. During catastrophic Superstorm Sandy, the Weather Channel put its social strategies to good use. Anticipating many people would lose power, the Weather Channel streamed its live, round-the-clock storm coverage online so people could receive updates via mobile devices. The company is in the midst of changing its focus from a cable network viewers watch during weather disasters to a company that forecasts consumer behavior by analyzing when, where, and how often consumers check the weather. It recently changed its name to The Weather Co. to reflect its expanding digital-data business.

Sources: Company website, www.weather.com, accessed January 3, 2014; Katherine Rosman, "Weather Channel Now Also Forecasts What You'll Buy," *The Wall Street Journal*, accessed January 3, 2014, http://online.wsj.com; Doug Henschen, "Big Data Reshapes Weather Channel Predictions," *Information Week*, accessed January 3, 2014, www.informationweek.com; Brian Stelter, "Weather Channel's Parent Company Is Renamed," *The New York Times*, accessed January 3, 2014, www.nytimes.com; Katie Leslie, "Sandy Gives Weather Channel a Chance to Shine," *Denver Post*, accessed January 3, 2014, www.denverpost.com; Amir Efrati, "Today's Weather Channel Forecast: A Chance of Tweets," *The Wall Street Journal*, accessed January 3, 2014, http://blogs.wsj.com.

Temple says the company's followers have provided instant feedback about certain types of clothing and have become unofficial salespeople, posting pictures of their children wearing the company's attractive outfits.[36]

Social media also allows larger exchanges in which consumers communicate with one another using email or social networking sites. These electronic conversations can establish innovative relationships between users and the business, providing customized information based on users' interests and levels of understanding.

The Ford Motor Company uses social media extensively to engage with the public around the globe. The company has created *FordSocial*, which serves as a social hub for consumers, fans, and others to gather information, interact with others, share their questions and stories, and provide feedback and suggestions to the company about its various brands. It hosts *ConnectFord*, an information portal where the company shares articles, videos, and other information that a company might typically share in its PR campaigns. Ford's global head of social media says the site gives bloggers and other journalists a chance to get information directly from Ford, not just through press releases. Ford also hosts separate Facebook and Twitter sites in countries around the world. Its Facebook page in Brazil has more than 1.2 million fans.[37]

The Ford Motor Company uses social media to engage with consumers across the globe through several sites, including *FordSocial*, *ConnectFord*, and separate Facebook and Twitter sites in many countries.

By converting indifferent customers into loyal ones, companies generate repeat sales. The cost of maintaining existing customers is far below the cost of finding new ones, and these loyal customers are profitable. Some of the best repeat customers are those who are also willing to spread the word—create a buzz—about a product. *Buzz marketing* can be very effective in attracting new customers by bridging the gap between a company and its products. Companies as diverse as Microsoft and KFC have tapped customers to create a buzz about their products. Firms that make the most efficient use of buzz marketing warn that it is not a "one-way" approach to building customer relationships.

Buzz can be purely visual, too. "Visual buzz" can be thought of as the tangible expression of an issue or position. To help create jobs in communities with high unemployment throughout America, Starbucks partnered with a financial consortium to launch Create Jobs for USA. Under the program, donors who gave $5 or more received a distinctive red-white-and-blue wristband adorned with the message "Indivisible." Starbucks gave $5 million to seed the project, and the initiative has reached more than $15 million in donations.[38] Effective relationship marketing often relies heavily on information technologies such as computer databases that record customers' tastes, price preferences, and lifestyles. This technology helps companies become one-to-one marketers that gather customer-specific information and provide individually customized goods and services. The firms target their marketing programs to appropriate groups rather than relying on mass-marketing campaigns. Companies that study customer preferences and react accordingly gain distinct competitive advantages.

> **Briefly Speaking**
>
> "There are no traffic jams along the extra mile."
>
> —**Roger Staubach**
> *Businessman, former Dallas Cowboys quarterback, and Heisman Trophy winner*

DEVELOPING PARTNERSHIPS AND STRATEGIC ALLIANCES

Relationship marketing does not apply just to individual consumers and employees. It also affects a wide range of other markets, including business-to-business relationships with the firm's suppliers and distributors as well as other types of corporate partnerships. In the past, companies often have viewed their suppliers as adversaries against whom they must fiercely negotiate prices, playing one off against the other. But this attitude has changed radically as both marketers and their suppliers discover the benefits of collaborative relationships.

The formation of **strategic alliances**—partnerships that create competitive advantages—is also on the rise. Alliances take many forms, including product development partnerships that involve shared costs for research and development and marketing, and vertical alliances in which one company provides a product or component to another firm, which then distributes or sells it under its own brand. Under Armour and Nike pay millions of dollars to outfit college football teams in exchange for the publicity gained from the teams' sometimes outlandish uniforms.[39]

Not-for-profit organizations often use strategic alliances to raise awareness and funds for their causes. Recently, cell service provider Straight Talk Wireless gave more than $1 million to Make-A-Wish Foundation as a result of its "Give a Minute, Help Make-A-Wish" program. Straight Talk donated $1 for every consumer who took a minute to learn about its services at more than 3,000 participating Walmart stores. The charity helps grant wishes for children with life-threatening health conditions.[40]

strategic alliances Partnerships in which two or more companies combine resources and capital to create competitive advantages in a new market.

> **ASSESSMENT CHECK**
>
> 6.1 How does relationship marketing give companies a competitive edge?
>
> 6.2 Why are interactive and social marketing important tools for marketers?
>
> 6.3. What is a strategic alliance?

COSTS AND FUNCTIONS OF MARKETING

Firms must spend money to create time, place, and ownership utilities. Numerous attempts have been made to measure marketing costs in relation to overall product costs, and most estimates have ranged between 40 percent and 60 percent of total costs. On average, half of the costs involved in a product—such as a Subway sandwich, a pair of Gap jeans, or noise-canceling headphones— can be traced directly to marketing. These costs are not associated with wheat, metal, or other raw materials, nor are they associated with baking, welding, or any of the other production functions necessary for creating form utility. What functions does marketing perform, and why are they important in creating customer satisfaction?

As Figure 1.3 reveals, marketing is responsible for the performance of eight universal functions: buying, selling, transporting, storing, standardizing and grading, financing, risk taking, and

7 Identify the eight universal functions of marketing.

FIGURE 1.3 Eight Universal Marketing Functions

1. **Buying** Ensuring that product offerings are available in sufficient quantities to meet customer demands
2. **Selling** Using advertising, personal selling, and sales promotion to match products to customer needs
3. **Transporting** Moving products from their point of production to locations convenient for purchasers
4. **Storing** Warehousing products until needed for sale
5. **Standardizing and Grading** Ensuring that product offerings meet quality and quantity controls of size, weight, and other variables
6. **Financing** Providing credit for channel members (wholesalers and retailers) and consumers
7. **Risk Taking** Dealing with uncertainty about future customer purchases
8. **Securing Marketing Information** Collecting information about consumers, competitors, and channel members for use in making marketing decisions

wholesalers Intermediaries that operate between producers and resellers.

exchange functions Buying and selling.

securing marketing information. Some functions are performed by manufacturers, others by retailers, and still others by marketing intermediaries called **wholesalers**.

Buying and selling represent **exchange functions**. Buying is important to marketing on several levels. Marketers must determine how and why consumers buy certain goods and services. To be successful, they must try to understand consumer behavior. In addition, retailers and other intermediaries must seek out products that will appeal to their customers. Marketers must also anticipate consumer preferences for purchases to be made several months later. Selling is the second half of the exchange process. It involves advertising, personal selling, and sales promotion in an attempt to match the firm's goods and services to consumer needs.

Transporting and storing are physical distribution functions. Transporting involves physically moving goods from the seller to the purchaser. Storing involves warehousing goods until they are needed for sale. Manufacturers, wholesalers, and retailers typically perform these functions.

The final four marketing functions—standardizing and grading, financing, risk taking, and securing marketing information—often are called facilitating functions because they help the marketer perform the exchange and physical distribution functions. Quality and quantity control standards and grades, frequently set by federal or state governments, reduce the need for purchasers to inspect each item. For example, if you request a certain size tire for your automobile, you expect to get it.

Financing is another marketing function because buyers often need access to funds to finance inventories prior to sales. Manufacturers often provide financing for their wholesale and retail customers. Some types of wholesalers perform similar functions for their markets. Finally, retailers frequently allow their customers to buy on credit with either store charge cards or major credit cards.

The seventh function, risk taking, is part of most ventures. Manufacturers create goods and services based on research and their belief that consumers need them. Wholesalers and retailers acquire inventory based on similar expectations of future consumer demand. Entrepreneurial risk takers accommodate these uncertainties about future consumer behavior when they market goods and services.

The final marketing function involves securing marketing information. Marketers gather information about potential customers: who they are, what they buy, where they buy, and how they buy. By collecting and analyzing marketing information, marketers can understand why consumers purchase some goods while passing others by. This information also helps determine what consumers want and need—and how to offer goods and services to satisfy them. So marketing is the direct connection between a firm and its customers, the link that helps build and maintain lasting relationships.

ASSESSMENT CHECK

7.1. Which two marketing functions represent exchange functions?

7.2. Which two functions represent physical distribution functions?

7.3. Which four functions are facilitating functions?

ethics Moral standards of behavior expected by a society.

8 Demonstrate the relationship between ethical business practices, social responsibility, sustainability, and marketplace success.

ETHICS AND SOCIAL RESPONSIBILITY: DOING WELL BY DOING GOOD

Ethics are moral standards of behavior expected by a society. Most companies do their best to abide by an ethical code of conduct, but sometimes organizations and their leaders fall short. Several years ago, the Houston-based energy giant Enron collapsed, taking with it the retirement savings of its employees and wiping out some investors. Similarly, executives from Tyco were convicted of using millions of company dollars for their personal benefit. And chemical manufacturer Monsanto was convicted not only of polluting water sources and soil in a rural Alabama area for decades but of ignoring evidence its own scientists had gathered indicating the extent and severity of the pollution. New ethics issues surface regularly. See the "Solving an Ethical Controversy" feature for a discussion about New York City's recent ban on extra large, sugary drinks.

SOLVING AN ETHICAL CONTROVERSY
Banning Sugary Drinks

In an effort to help reduce obesity rates among its residents, New York City tried to restrict the sale of extra-large sodas and other sugary drinks in restaurants, stadiums, and movie theaters. The proposed ban would have begun in March of 2013. But one day before the ruling was to be enacted, a New York Supreme Court judge ruled that the city could not impose the ban. More recently the state's highest court, the Court of Appeals, ruled that the ban is illegal.

Should cities be allowed to try to prevent consumers from buying extra-large, sugary drinks?

PRO

1. Obesity in this country, particularly among children, is out of control, and any means to make it difficult to purchase sugary drinks will help.
2. By limiting the size of sugary drinks, cities will help consumers reduce their sugar intake, which should help them lose weight.

CON

1. Government should not intervene in consumers' freedom of choice when it comes to what type and size of drinks they can purchase.
2. Limiting the size of drinks for sale could have an adverse affect on small businesses whose profit margins will suffer.

Summary

The fight over extra-large sugary drinks appears to be ongoing. Even though former New York Mayor Michael Bloomberg believed selling smaller-sized drinks would have helped reduce obesity rates and make people healthier in the long run, the case is still in litigation. In July of 2014, San Francisco lawmakers voted to advance a proposal to tax sugary sodas. In November, if voters approve the measure, the tax will become the first of its kind in the nation.

Sources: Laila Kearney, "San Francisco Joins Sugary Drinks Fray with Tax Proposal," *Reuters*, accessed January 5, 2014, www.reuters.com; Michael M. Grynbaum, "New York Soda Ban to Go Before State's Top Court," *The New York Times*, accessed January 5, 2014, www.nytimes.com; Gary Strauss and Rebecca Castagna, "NYC Ban on Large Sugary Drinks Fizzles Again," *USA Today*, accessed January 5, 2014, www.usatoday.com.

Most businesspeople follow ethical practices. More than half of all major corporations now offer ethics training to employees, and most corporate mission statements include pledges to protect the environment, contribute to communities, and improve workers' lives. This book encourages you to follow the highest ethical standards throughout your business and marketing career.

Social responsibility includes marketing philosophies, policies, procedures, and actions whose primary objective is to enhance society and protect the environment through sustainable products and practices. Walmart, for instance, has made great strides in reducing its use of energy in its stores.

Social responsibility often takes the form of philanthropy, making gifts of money or time to humanitarian causes. Many firms, both large and small, include social responsibility programs as part of their overall mission. These programs often produce benefits such as improved customer relationships, increased employee loyalty, marketplace success, and improved financial performance.

social responsibility Marketing philosophies, policies, procedures, and actions that have the enhancement of society's welfare as a primary objective.

sustainable products Products that can be produced, used, and disposed of with minimal impact on the environment.

Sustainable products, those that can be produced, used, and disposed of with minimal impact on the environment, are another goal of socially responsible firms. Many such firms have added annual sustainability reports and a top-level executive position to develop and promote their sustainability efforts. One such company is Colgate-Palmolive, whose global brands include Colgate toothpaste, Speed Stick deodorants, Fabuloso cleaning products, and Science Diet pet foods. According to its recent sustainability report, Colgate has reduced greenhouse gas emissions by 14 percent, reduced the amount of waste sent to landfills by approximately 10 percent, and reduced water consumption by about 30 percent—saving enough water to fill more than 4,700 Olympic-sized swimming pools.[41]

What is the role of marketing in sustainability efforts? Sustainability and social responsibility officers agree that sustainability must permeate the firm's corporate strategy from the top down, so all areas in the firm can align their environmental goals in the same direction for the greatest effectiveness. As IBM notes in its "A Smarter Planet" website, "To be sustainable, organizations must embrace a new objective: optimize operations to minimize environmental impact and improve social outcomes in a manner that also maximizes performance."[42]

Firms stand to gain needed credibility from their efforts to protect the environment by reducing waste and pollution. Not only has the recent economic downturn made it important for them to cut waste and cost as never before, including the costs of damage to the environment, but consumers now are more aware of and ready to support the real need for such drives. Recent research by Accenture suggests that nearly two-thirds of respondents indicated willingness to pay a premium for goods or services that lower greenhouse gas emissions.[43]

Samsung has implemented a Recycling Direct program that helps consumers do their part to make the world greener. Since partnering with qualified take-back and recycling companies around the United States, Samsung has collected and recycled more than 275 million pounds of TVs, digital cameras, cell phones, monitors, and printers that do not find their way into landfills or become toxic waste exported to developing countries.[44]

ASSESSMENT CHECK

8.1 Define ethics.
8.2 What is social responsibility?
8.3 What are sustainable products?

STRATEGIC IMPLICATIONS OF MARKETING IN THE 21ST CENTURY

Unprecedented opportunities have emerged out of electronic commerce and computer technologies in business today. These advances and innovations have allowed organizations to reach new markets, reduce selling and marketing costs, and enhance their relationships with customers and suppliers. Thanks to the Internet and social media tools, business has grown into a global market.

Both profit-seeking and not-for-profit organizations must broaden the scope of their activities to prevent myopic results in their enterprises. If they fail to do so, they lose out on promising opportunities.

Marketers must constantly look for ways to create loyal customers and build long-term relationships with those customers, often on a one-to-one basis. They must be able to anticipate customer needs and satisfy them with innovative goods and services. They must do this faster and better than the competition. And they must conduct their business according to the highest ethical and sustainability standards.

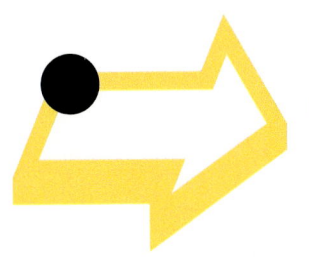

Get online now for additional learning tools to help you master your marketing knowledge—visit **WWW.CENGAGEBRAIN.COM** today!

REVIEW OF CHAPTER OBJECTIVES

1 Define marketing and how it creates utility.

Marketing is the activity, set of institutions, and processes for creating, communicating, delivering, and exchanging offerings that have value for customers, clients, partners, and society at large. Utility is the want-satisfying power of a good or service. Four basic kinds of utility exist: form, time, place, and ownership. Marketing creates time, place, and ownership utilities. Three factors have forced marketers to embrace a global marketplace: expanded international trade agreements, new technologies that have brought previously isolated nations to the marketplace, and greater interdependence of the world's economies.

2 Contrast marketing activities during the five eras in the history of marketing.

During the production era, businesspeople believed that quality products would sell themselves. The sales era emphasized convincing people to buy. The marketing concept emerged during the marketing era, in which there was a companywide focus on consumer orientation with the objective of achieving long-term success. The relationship era focuses on establishing and maintaining relationships between customers and suppliers. Relationship marketing involves long-term, value-added relationships. The social era encourages companies to use the Web and social media sites to connect to consumers as a way to market goods and services.

3 Explain the importance of avoiding marketing myopia.

Marketing myopia is management's failure to recognize a company's scope of business. It focuses marketers too narrowly on products and thus misses potential opportunities to satisfy customers. To avoid it, companies must broadly define their goals so that they focus on fulfilling consumer needs.

4 Describe the characteristics of not-for-profit marketing.

Not-for-profit organizations operate in both public and private sectors. The biggest distinction between not-for-profits and commercial firms is the bottom line—whether the firm is judged by its profitability levels. Not-for-profit organizations may market to multiple publics. A customer or service user of a not-for-profit organization may have less control over the organization's destiny than customers of a profit-seeking firm. In addition, resource contributors to not-for-profits may try to influence the organization's activities. Not-for-profits and for-profits may form alliances that effectively promote each other's causes and services.

5 Explain each of the five types of nontraditional marketing.

Person marketing focuses on efforts to cultivate the attention, interest, and preferences of a target market toward a celebrity or noted figure. Place marketing attempts to attract visitors and businesses to a particular destination. Cause marketing identifies and markets a social issue, cause, or idea. Event marketing promotes sporting, cultural, charitable, or political activities. Organization marketing attempts to influence others to accept an organization's goals or services and contribute to it in some way.

6 Explain the shift from transaction-based marketing to relationship and social marketing.

Relationship marketing represents a dramatic change in the way companies interact with customers. The focus on relationships gives a firm new opportunities to gain a competitive edge by moving customers up a loyalty ladder from new customers to regular purchasers and then to loyal supporters and advocates. Over the long term, this relationship may be translated to the lifetime value of a customer. Interactive technologies and social marketing (via Facebook, Twitter,

7 Identify the eight universal functions of marketing.

Marketing is responsible for eight universal functions, divided into three categories: (1) exchange functions (buying and selling); (2) physical distribution (transporting and storing); and (3) facilitating functions (standardization and grading, financing, risk taking, and securing market information).

8 Demonstrate the relationship between ethical business practices, social responsibility, sustainability, and marketplace success.

Ethics are moral standards of behavior expected by a society. Companies that promote ethical behavior and social responsibility usually produce increased employee loyalty and a better public image. This image often pays off in customer growth, because many buyers want to associate themselves with—and be customers of—such firms. Social responsibility includes marketing philosophies, policies, procedures, and actions whose primary objectives are the enhancement of society and the protection of the environment through sustainable products and practices. These actions also generally promote a firm's public image.

ASSESSMENT CHECK: ANSWERS

1.1 Define marketing, and explain how it creates utility. Marketing is the activity, set of institutions, and processes for creating, communicating, delivering, and exchanging offerings that have value for customers, clients, partners, and society at large. It creates time, place, and ownership utilities.

1.2 What three factors have forced marketers to embrace a global marketplace? International agreements are negotiated to expand trade among nations; the growth of technology is bringing previously isolated countries into the marketplace; and the interdependence of the world's economies is now a reality.

2.1 What is the major distinction between the production era and the sales era? During the production era, businesspeople believed that quality products would sell themselves. But during the sales era, emphasis was placed on selling—persuading people to buy.

2.2 What is the marketing concept? The marketing concept is a companywide consumer orientation with the objective of achieving long-term success.

2.3 Describe the relationship era of marketing. The relationship era focuses on building long-term, value-added relationships over time with customers and suppliers.

3.1 What is marketing myopia? Marketing myopia is management's failure to recognize the scope of a company's business.

3.2 Give an example of how a firm can avoid marketing myopia. A firm can find innovative ways to reach new markets with existing goods and services.

4.1 What is the most obvious distinction between a not-for-profit organization and a commercial organization? The biggest distinction between for-profit and not-for-profit organizations is the bottom line—whether an organization is judged by its profitability.

4.2 Why do for-profit and not-for-profit organizations sometimes form alliances? For-profits and not-for-profits may form alliances to promote each other's causes and offerings. For-profits may do so as part of their social responsibility efforts.

5.1 Identify the five major categories of nontraditional marketing. The five categories of nontraditional marketing are person, place, cause, event, and organization marketing.

5.2 Give an example of a way in which two or more of these categories might overlap. Overlap can occur in many ways. An organization might use a person to promote its cause or event. Two organizations might use one marketing effort to promote an event and a place; for example, Straight Talk Wireless donated money to Make-A-Wish Foundation for all the consumers who stopped by to learn about the cell phone provider in Walmart stores across the country.

6.1 How does relationship marketing give companies a competitive edge? Relationship marketing can move customers up a loyalty ladder, generating repeat sales and long-term relationships.

6.2 Why are interactive and social marketing important tools for marketers? Interactive marketing technologies create direct communication with customers, allow larger exchanges, and put the customer in control. Social marketing media (Facebook and Twitter, for example) let companies show customers they are listening and will respond quickly.

6.3 What is a strategic alliance? A strategic alliance is a partnership formed between two organizations to create a competitive advantage.

7.1 Which two marketing functions represent exchange functions? Buying and selling are exchange functions.

7.2 Which two functions represent physical distribution functions? Transporting and storing are physical distribution functions.

7.3 Which four functions are facilitating functions? The facilitating functions are standardization and grading, financing, risk taking, and securing market information.

8.1 Define ethics. Ethics are moral standards of behavior expected by a society.

8.2 What is social responsibility? Social responsibility involves marketing philosophies, policies, procedures, and actions whose primary objective is the enhancement of society.

8.3 What are sustainable products? Sustainable products are those that can be produced, used, and disposed of with minimal impact on the environment.

MARKETING TERMS YOU NEED TO KNOW

utility 5	consumer orientation 10	cause marketing 18	social marketing 20
marketing 7	marketing concept 10	event marketing 18	strategic alliances 23
exchange process 8	relationship marketing 11	organization marketing 19	wholesalers 24
production orientation 9	marketing myopia 12	transaction-based marketing 19	exchange functions 24
sales orientation 9	bottom line 14		ethics 24
seller's market 10	person marketing 16	mobile marketing 20	social responsibility 25
buyer's market 10	place marketing 17	interactive marketing 20	sustainable products 26

ASSURANCE OF LEARNING REVIEW

1. Identify the four types of utility, and give an example of each.
2. What condition in the marketplace gave rise to the need for a consumer orientation by businesses after World War II?
3. Define relationship marketing, and describe how it fits into the marketing concept.
4. Why do not-for-profit organizations need to engage in marketing efforts?
5. Give an example of how the National Highway Traffic Safety Administration's "Click it or Ticket" campaign could use one or more of the nontraditional marketing techniques to promote the cause in a state that is newly adopting it.
6. What might be some of the benefits of mobile marketing for firms that use it to reach out to consumers?
7. Describe the significance of the shift from transaction-based marketing to relationship marketing. When does relationship building begin?
8. How has social media, such as Twitter and Facebook, changed marketing communications?
9. How do ethics and social responsibility help a firm achieve marketplace success?
10. What motivates firms to develop sustainable products?

PROJECTS AND TEAMWORK EXERCISES

1. Consider each of the following firms and describe how the firm's goods and services can create different types of utility. If necessary, go online to the company's website to learn more about it. You can do this alone or in a team.
   a. American Express, Visa, or MasterCard
   b. Snapfish or other online digital photo services
   c. Sandals Resorts
   d. Amazon.com
   e. Fresh Market grocery stores
2. With a classmate, choose a U.S.-based company whose products you think will do well in certain overseas markets. The company can be anything from a music group to a clothing retailer—anything that interests you. Suggestions include Papa John's Pizza, Zumba, StubHub, Katy Perry, or Bass Pro Shops. Then write a plan for how you would target and communicate with overseas markets.

3. Choose a company that interests you from the following list or select one of your own. Research the company online, through business magazines, or through other sources to identify the scope of its business. Write a brief description of the company's current scope of business. Then describe strategies for avoiding marketing myopia, expanding the company's scope of business over the next ten years.
   a. FedEx
   b. Six Flags
   c. GE
   d. E*Trade
   e. Intel
4. With a classmate, choose one of the following not-for-profit organizations. Then come up with a for-profit firm with which you think your organization could form a strategic alliance. Create a presentation—an ad, a poster, or the like—illustrating and promoting the partnership.
   a. Adopt-A-Pet
   b. The Water Project
   c. Habitat for Humanity
   d. American Diabetes Association
   e. World Wildlife Fund
5. Research one of the following electronics companies, or another of your choosing, and study its efforts to improve the sustainability of its products, particularly their safe disposal. What does the company do well in this area? What could it do better?
   a. Toshiba
   b. Vizio
   c. Microsoft
   d. Nintendo
   e. Samsung

CRITICAL-THINKING EXERCISES

1. How does an organization create a customer?
2. How can marketers use interactive and social marketing to convert needs to wants and ultimately build long-term relationships with customers?
3. Why is utility such an important feature of marketing?
4. What benefits—monetary and nonmonetary—do social responsibility programs bring to a business?
5. Why is determining the lifetime value of a customer an important analysis for a company to make?
6. Why is it important for a firm to establish high ethical standards for sustainability? What role do you think marketers play in implementing these standards?

ETHICS EXERCISE

At a local coffee shop you run into a friend who works for a social media firm that competes with yours. After a brief conversation he remembers an errand he has to run, and he rushes off with a hasty good-bye. As you gather your things to leave a few minutes later, you realize your friend left a file folder on the chair; inside is a report about a client. Your company is very interested in doing some work for this client in the future.

1. Would you take a quick look inside the folder before you return it to your friend? Why or why not?
2. Would you share any information in the report with anyone in your office? Why or why not?
3. When you return the folder to your friend, would you mention the report and offer your own commentary on it? Why or why not?

INTERNET EXERCISES

1. **Marketing terminology.** Like many subjects, marketing appears to have a language of its own. Visit the website of the American Marketing Association. Click on "Resources" and then "AMA Dictionary." Define the following terms: A/B testing, dating, never-out list, and will-call.
   www.ama.org

2. **Event marketing.** The Westminster Kennel Club runs the nation's largest dog show. Go to the event's website. Review the website and prepare a brief report relating what you learned to the material on event marketing in the chapter. Make sure to describe sponsor tie-ins and other joint marketing efforts.
   www.westminsterkennelclub.org

3. **Sustainability.** Johnson & Johnson engages in a major effort to incorporate sustainability into its wide-ranging business activities. Visit the website listed here and read about the firm's recent activities. How does Johnson & Johnson promote sustainability? What are some specific examples?
   www.jnj.com/connect/caring/environment-protection

Note: Internet Web addresses change frequently. If you don't find the exact site listed, you may need to access the organization's home page and search from there or use a search engine such as Google or Bing.

CASE 1.1
Kraft Focuses on Brand Building

Kraft Foods Group launched its own channel on YouTube the first year the video site appeared online. The company had started its own website many years before, offering recipes and cooking tips, and it recently added a Pin-It button so site visitors can link to recipes they've posted on Pinterest. But capitalizing on these new opportunities to communicate and engage with customers is not the only way Kraft Foods hopes to stay connected with its millions of customers.

At the corporate level, the $19 billion company split itself into two business units so each division could focus more carefully on marketing a smaller list of products and building company brands. The two units are (1) the meals and desserts unit, which markets Cool Whip, Jell-O, and Kraft's iconic mac and cheese mix, and (2) the enhancers and snacks division, handling the Planters brand, A1 steak sauce, and Miracle Whip.

The company's attention to customers wouldn't be complete without the addition of new and improved products, of course. Kraft is aware that millennials—those born in the 1980s and 1990s—are starting to move into the kitchen to cook, and they prefer to do things differently than their parents. Millennial men are not afraid or unwilling to cook, for instance; Kraft's vice president of innovation says that younger men see cooking as an adventure and an opportunity for fun. But that doesn't mean millennials, male or female, like spending hours on food preparation or cleanup. So Kraft is updating many of its convenience-food products to make them even easier and more appealing to use, by packaging ingredients in pouches to save measuring and blending, and also by updating flavors in recognition of younger consumers' bolder taste preferences. Consumers can add their own flavor touches and fresh ingredients but without spending the time to cook meals completely from scratch.

The company is also revamping its innovation processes and plans to invest in fewer but more promising new-product ideas, providing new products with more financial and marketing support.

QUESTIONS FOR CRITICAL THINKING

1. Are there more ways Kraft Foods can tailor its structure, its products, or its communication efforts to better satisfy customers? If so, what are they?

2. How do you think splitting the company into two units will help Kraft meet its customers' needs? Can you think of any disadvantages to this split?

Sources: Lorene Yue, "Kraft Foods Group Splits Business into Two Units," *Crain's*, accessed January 4, 2014, www.chicagobusiness.com; Brent Gleeson and Brian Yang, "Successful Content Marketing in Action," *Forbes*, accessed January 4, 2014, www.forbes.com; Jenna Goudreau, "How Kraft Got Its Innovation Groove Back," *Forbes*, accessed January 4, 2014, www.forbes.com; Emily Bryson York, "Kraft Acknowledges Faults, Unveils New Path," *Chicago Tribune*, accessed January 4, 2014, http://articles.chicagotribune.com; Emily Bryson York, "Kraft's New Recipe for Sales: Updating Products for Men, Millennials," *Chicago Tribune*, accessed January 4, 2014, http://articles.chicagotribune.com.

VIDEO CASE 1.2
Geoffrey B. Small Is Big on Quality, Customers, Community

Geoffrey B. Small is a leading avant-garde fashion designer who wants you to think about your clothes—but not the style or color of the outfit you are wearing today, not what a great bargain it was, not the brand name, not which celebrities wear the same design. He wants you to dig deeper than that, thinking about the quality and origin of fabrics you wear, their impact on the environment, and your own view of social responsibility as a consumer. Even if you can't afford his clothes (created in one- or two-of-a-kind, limited editions), you can take away his messages about quality, value, service to the customer and community, and the importance of activism.

Now based in Italy—with easy access to the Paris fashion shows—Small began his career selling jeans at The Gap in Boston. Today, he shrugs off the marketing tactics of the large, name-brand clothing designers and retail outlets, which he believes do little or nothing to create utility for the consumer, because they hide the true cost of the clothes they are selling. "Corporate advertising has made people unaware of what they're really spending their money on, and what things are really costing them," says Small. Cheap fabrics, poor construction, and lack of attention to detail all add up to low prices and nearly disposable garments—costing consumers more money in the long run. "We have to re-educate a lot of consumers because what they think is cheap is not cheap at all," asserts Small. "It's the most expensive."

Small's clothing designs provide form utility by creating the highest-quality garments. Although customers often have to wait months for these hand-made garments, Small believes this is an asset. "Fifty years ago, machine-made products were perfect, new and exciting," explains Small. That's no longer the case. "We don't care how long it takes," he insists. "We don't care what it costs. What we care about is that it's the very, very best it can possibly be"—which is what his customers want. Consumers may view Small's clothes in motion at runway shows or at a select group of exclusive retail shops, or they may communicate with him directly. When they take ownership of a suit or coat, they have a highly individualized piece of clothing that some might call a work of art. "Customers are screaming for something personal and special," Small points out, "something that has a bond between one human being and another."

Small views his relationships with customers as critical to his success, referring to them as the "best and only financial backers" a designer should have. Since his clothes are made to last decades—25 to 30 years—he looks toward developing customer relationships that will survive just as long. "We're in a field where you normally do a lot of marketing," he observes. "I think it's more important to focus on great product, great service, value to the customer, and communicating with the customer honestly." That honest communication—about his products and his beliefs—has built Small a devoted following.

It would be easy for Small to hide in his design studio sketching clothes for a few high-end customers who want the novelty of something edgy and different to wear, which could lead him into the quicksand of marketing myopia. But that's not Small's style. He looks for new ways to satisfy customers without compromising his ideals—in fact, he stitches his ideals right into the fabrics of his clothing. Small is a genuine activist for social causes as well as environmental sustainability, which has proved to be an effective tool for connecting with the people who appreciate his designs. Customers see his activism, and when they make a choice about where to spend their money, they choose his brand. "That's where we want to be positioned," says Small. "We want to do more than just supply clothes. We want to play a role in the community."

Looking forward, Small believes it is his company's responsibility to set an example for other businesses. "The biggest challenge now is not to compromise," he admits, but "to focus on one piece at a time and make it the absolute best it can be."

QUESTIONS FOR CRITICAL THINKING

1. Why is the link between relationship marketing and social responsibility so important to Small's business success?
2. Geoffrey B. Small is an avant-garde designer and unconventional businessperson. What examples does he set, and what might marketers for large corporations learn from his views and practices?

Sources: "The Amazing Geoffrey B. Small Story," company website, accessed January 4, 2014, **www.geoffreybsmall.net/gbsstory.htm**; Geoffrey B. Small, "The Environment of Young Designers," *Not Just a Label*, accessed January 4, 2014, **www.notjustalabel.com**; Claire Ruhlin, "Recycle, Reconstruct, Redesign," *Community*, accessed November 12, 2013, **http://communityathens.blogspot.com**; Eugene Rabkin, "Review: Geoffrey B. Small, Fall/Winter 2012," *StyleZeitgeist*, accessed January 4, 2014, **www.stylezeitgeist.com**.

NOTES

1. Company website, www.vineyardvines.com, accessed January 3, 2014; Kathy Caprino, "What the Vineyard Vines Founders Know About Success That Thousands of Entrepreneurs Don't," *Forbes*, accessed January 3, 2014, www.forbes.com; Bill Cusano, "Story Marketing the Vineyard Vines Way" (blog), http://cusanomarketing.blogspot.com, accessed January 3, 3014; Michael Blanding, "The Brothers Behind Vineyard Vines Talk Ties," *Boston Common*, accessed January 3, 2014, http://bostoncommonmagazine.com; Tom O'Connor, "Success Stories: Totally Prepped," *Connecticut Magazine*, accessed January 3, 2014, www.connecticutmag.com; Jean E. Palmieri, "Vineyard Vines' Roots Run Deep," *Women's Wear Daily*, July 25, 2013.
2. Danny Sullivan, "Google Still World's Most Popular Search Engine by Far, But Share of Unique Searchers Dips Slightly," *searchengineland.com*, accessed January 3, 2014, www.searchengineland.com; Tom Simonite, "Why Facebook's Search Engine Won't Be Anything Like Google's," *MIT Technology Review*, accessed January 3, 2014, www.technologyreview.com.
3. Adrian Covert, "Amazon Kindle Paperwhite Is the Best e-Reader Ever," *CNN Money*, accessed January 3, 2014, www.money.ccn.com; Marguerite Reardon, "Reading Poolside? Which Do You Choose: A Tablet or an e-Reader?" *CNETNews*, accessed January 3, 2014, www.news.cnet.com.
4. Amanda Kooser, "Pepsi Vending Machine Takes Facebook Love, Not Money," *CNET News*, accessed January 4, 2014, www.news.cnet.com.
5. Stephanie Clifford, "Go Directly, Digitally to Jail? Classic Toys Learn New Clicks," *The New York Times*, accessed January 4, 2014, www.nytimes.com.
6. Joseph P. Guiltinan and Gordon W. Paul, *Marketing Management*, 6th ed. (New York: McGraw-Hill), 1996, pp. 3–4.
7. American Marketing Association, "Resource Library," accessed January 4, 2014, www.ama.org.
8. Company website, "Airline Fees," www.airfarewatchdog.com, accessed January 4, 2014.
9. Kenneth Rapoza, "China Official Says Country to Top U.S. Consumer Market by 2015," *Forbes*, accessed January 4, 2014, www.forbes.com; "Automobile Industry Introduction," Plunkett Research, Ltd., accessed January 4, 2014, www.plunkettresearch.com.
10. Peter Coy, "Four Reasons Mexico Is Becoming a Global Manufacturing Power," *Bloomberg Businessweek*, accessed January 4, 2014, www.businessweek.com; "2011 U.S. Manufacturing-Outsourcing Index," *Alixpartners.com*, accessed January 4, 2014, www.alixpartners.com.
11. R. Jai Krishna, "Nokia Deal to Give Microsoft an Edge in Emerging Markets," *The Wall Street Journal*, accessed January 4, 2014, http://blogs.wsj.com.
12. Company website, "First Weekend iPhone Sales Top Nine Million, Sets New Record" (press release), www.apple.com, accessed January 6, 2014.
13. Steve Olenski, "How NASCAR Uses Relationship Marketing," *Forbes*, accessed January 5, 2014, www.forbes.com.
14. Sean Birch, "What Can I Use My New Smartphone for Besides Making Calls?" *Deemable Tech*, accessed January 5, 2014, www.deemable.com.
15. Katie Fehrenbacher, "Apple Now Powering Its Cloud with Solar Panels, Fuel Cells," *gigaom.com*, accessed January 4, 2014, www.gigaom.com; "Apple Invents Power Management System with Solar Panel Option," *Patently Apple*, accessed January 4, 2014, www.patentlyapple.com.
16. Amy S. Blackwood, Katie L. Roeger, and Sarah L. Pettijohn, "The Nonprofit Sector in Brief: Public Charities, Giving, and Volunteering, 2012," *Urban Institute*, accessed January 5, 2014, www.urban.org.
17. Organization website, www.connerprairie.org, accessed January 5, 2014.
18. Organization website, "Target House—Long-Term Patient Stay," www.stjude.org, accessed January 6, 3014.
19. Organization website, www.nokidhungry.org, accessed January 6, 2014.
20. Dana Hertneky, "Oklahoma Tornado Donation Figures Released," *Oklahoma's Own Channel 9*, accessed January 6, 2014, www.news9.com; Suzanne Choney, "How to Help Oklahoma Tornado Victims," *NBC.com*, accessed January 4, 2014, www.usnews.nbcnews.com.
21. Jason Kincaid, "Social Fundraising Platform Piryx Is Reborn as Rally.org with Top Investors in Tow," *Tech Crunch*, accessed January 4, 2014, www.techcrunch.com; organization website, www.yourcause.com, accessed January 5, 2014; organization website, www.rally.org, accessed January 5, 2014.
22. Organization website, "A Crucial Catch: Annual Screening Saves Lives," www.nfl.com, accessed January 5, 2014.
23. Meghan Casserly, "Sofia Vergara Is the Top-Earning Actress on Television…By a Longshot," *Forbes*, accessed January 4, 2014, www.forbes.com; company website, "Chevy Life," www.chevrolet.com, accessed January 6, 2014.
25. Mark J. Miller, "LeBron James Teams with Old Pals Nike and Samsung for NBA Season Opener," *BrandChannel*, accessed January 5, 2014, www.brandchannel.com; Kurt Badenhausen, "The World's Highest-Paid Athletes 2013: Behind the Numbers," *Forbes*, accessed January 5, 2014, www.forbes.com.
25. Adam Nagourney, "Crowds Return to Vegas, But Gamble Less," *The New York Times*, accessed January 7, 2014, www.nytimes.com.
26. Leonard David, "Spaceport America Readies to Welcome Space Tourists," *Space.com*, accessed January 7, 2014, www.space.com.
27. Organization website, www.exploreminnesota.com, accessed January 7, 2014.
28. Company website, www.timberlineresort.com, accessed January 7, 2014.
29. Company website, www.staples.com, accessed January 7, 2014.
30. Bruce Horovitz, "$4M for Super Bowl Ad? Guess Who's Buying," *USA Today*, accessed January 8, 2014, www.usatoday.com.
31. Organization website, "Sochi 2014 Olympic Games Partners," www.sochi2014.com, accessed January 5, 2014.
32. Chris Smith, "College Football's Most Valuable Teams 2013: Texas Longhorns Can't Be Stopped," *Forbes*, accessed January 6, 2014, www.forbes.com; Patrick Beach, "Longhorns Top Sales of College Merchandise for Seventh Straight Year," *Austin American-Statesman*, accessed January 6, 2014, www.statesman.com.
33. Teisha Seabrook, "Facebook Earnings Report for Q3: Huge Increase in Ad-Driven Revenue," *Social Bakers*, accessed January 8, 2014, www.socialbakers.com; "India's Population 2013," www.indiaonlinepages.com, accessed January 8, 2014.
34. Cara Pring, "103 Crazy Social Media Statistics to Kick Off 2014," *The Social Skinny*, accessed January 3, 2014, http://thesocialskinny.com; "Twitter Ends IPO Year on Up Note," *The Wall Street Journal*, accessed January 3, 2014, http://blogs.wsj.com.
35. Sree Sreenivasan, "How the World's Biggest Companies Are Doing Social Media," *cnet.com*, accessed January 3, 2014, http://news.cnet.com.
36. Brian Patrick Eha, "Why Steve Case Is Betting Millions on Lolly Wolly Doodle," *Entrepreneur*, accessed January 3, 2014, www.entrepreneur.com; company website, www.lollywollydoodle.com, accessed January 3, 2014.
37. Company website, "FordSocial," www.social.ford.com, accessed January 3, 2014; Andrew Gothelf, "5 Social Media Lessons to Learn from Ford," *Saleforce Blog*, accessed January 3, 2014, http://blogs.salesforce.com; Ric Dragon, "The Big Brand Theory: Ford Motor Company, Parts I and II," *Social Media Today*, accessed January 3, 2014, www.socialmediatoday.com.
38. Organization website, "Create Jobs for USA One Year Anniversary," press release, http://news.starbucks.com, accessed January 3, 2014.
39. Dave Sheinin, "College Football Uniforms Are Getting More Outrageous, Thanks to Nike, Under Armour," *The Washington Post*, accessed January 3, 2014, www.washingtonpost.com.
40. Organization website, "Straight Talk Wireless Donated over $1 Million to Make-A-Wish," www.wish.org, accessed January 4, 2014.
41. Colgate-Palmolive, "Growing in a Fast-Changing World," *2012 Annual Report*, accessed January 5, 2014, www.colgate-palmolive.com.
42. Company website, "Sustainability on a Smarter Planet," www.ibm.com, accessed January 5, 2014.
43. Company website, www.accenture.com, accessed January 6, 2014.
44. Company website, "Recycling Direct," www.samsung.com, accessed January 7, 2014.

Chapter 2

Strategic Planning in Contemporary Marketing

DRIVING CULTURAL CHANGE AT YAHOO

1. Distinguish between strategic planning and tactical planning.
2. Explain how marketing plans differ at various levels in an organization.
3. Identify the six steps in the marketing planning process.
4. Describe successful planning tools and techniques, including Porter's Five Forces model, first and second mover strategies, SWOT analysis, and the strategic window.
5. Identify the two basic elements of a marketing strategy.
6. Describe the environmental characteristics that influence strategic decisions.
7. Describe the methods for marketing planning, including business portfolio analysis and the BCG matrix.

Yahoo CEO Marissa Mayer has never shied away from hard work. The first female engineer hired at Google, she spent five years heading up search products and later directed the company's local, map, and location services. After Yahoo CEO Scott Thompson left, Mayer was approached by a job recruiter wanting to know if she was ready to take on yet another challenge: running Yahoo.

Yahoo went through four CEOs in five years before its board of directors met with Mayer to discuss her interest in turning the company around. Mayer said yes to taking on the CEO position—at the same time, telling the board she was pregnant. Two weeks after the birth of her son, Mayer returned to work to fine-tune her business strategies.

One of Mayer's first initiatives, called PB&J (process, bureaucracy, and jams), outlined a plan of small changes to make Yahoo more productive. At her initial staff meeting, Mayer encouraged employees to suggest even more changes—a strategy she believes will help shift the company's culture to empowering employees to become involved in the business process. In an email to employees, Mayer said she wanted to make Yahoo "the absolute best place to work."

Mayer continues to make changes and tweak the company's overall vision. She brought on board several senior executives, including a new chief marketing officer, a new chief operating officer, and a new chief financial officer. Some executives came from Google, and some came from other top companies. Mayer also created a new position, executive vice president of people and development, which is Yahoo's dealmaker, overseeing HR, business development, strategy, and mergers and acquisitions.

In less than a year under Mayer, Yahoo made an estimated $1.3 billion in "acqui-hires," buying small companies not necessarily for their products but chiefly for their engineering talent. Yahoo has also focused its efforts on reinventing its mobile strategy, an important component for future success.

Mayer is the youngest CEO of a Fortune 500 company and recently joined Walmart's board of directors. She knows change is difficult, but she is committed to making Yahoo's turnaround a success. Her focused approach has both colleagues and competitors watching.[1]

EVOLUTION OF A BRAND

Yahoo's early success as a Web innovator has not sustained its ongoing business, as other companies such as Google and Facebook took over as the new Internet leaders. Before Mayer, Yahoo's inability to execute a successful business plan resulted in chaos, corporate bureaucracy, and an overall lack of direction. The revolving door in the CEO's office left the company with little or no focus, which had a negative impact on the company's bottom line, employee morale, and product innovation.

- When Marissa Mayer took the helm, revenues in Yahoo's core business were flat—and have remained so. Yet, during her tenure, Yahoo's stock price has more than doubled (largely, analysts say, due to Mayer's strategic acquisitions and distributions of profits to shareholders). How does such a business strategy help foster a financial turnaround at Yahoo?
- Realizing that getting Yahoo back on track would require transforming the corporate culture, Mayer made some sweeping changes, including abolishing the company's long-standing telecommuting policy. Mayer defended the controversial decision by noting that while people may be more productive when working from home, they are more collaborative and innovative when they work together. While change is never easy, it is often necessary. How might a transformed Yahoo culture affect marketing planning?

Chapter Overview

"More and more consumers are purchasing smaller, more fuel-efficient vehicles, such as the Chevrolet Cruze. The market for large trucks and SUVs is dwindling. Are fuel-efficient vehicles the wave of the future? Should we commit to building more of them and feature them prominently in our marketing?"

"Recent marketing research shows that we are not reaching our customer target—consumers in their early to mid-20s. Should we consider another advertising agency?"

planning Process of anticipating future events and conditions and of determining the best way to achieve organizational objectives.

Marketers face strategic questions every day—planning strategy is a critical part of their job. The marketplace changes continually in response to changes in consumer tastes and expectations, technological developments, competitors' actions, economic trends, and political and legal events, as well as product innovations and pressures from suppliers and distributors. Although the causes of these changes often lie outside a marketer's control, effective planning can anticipate many of the changes.

When the price of gas and jet fuel soars, travelers opt to stay closer to home—taking "staycations" instead of booking vacations to exotic, faraway places. This represents an opportunity for places like Ocean City, Maryland, and Branson, Missouri. Local water parks and amusement parks, nearby lakes, indoor playgrounds or gyms, and restaurants can market themselves as potential alternatives. Any destination that promotes itself to potential vacationers within a short drive could find itself adding up the profits.

This chapter provides an important foundation for analyzing all aspects of marketing by demonstrating the importance of gathering reliable information to create an effective plan. These activities provide a structure for a firm to use its unique strengths. Marketing planning identifies the markets a company can best serve as well as the most appropriate mix of approaches to satisfy the customers in those markets. While this chapter focuses on planning, we will examine in greater detail the task of marketing research and decision making in Chapter 10.

> **Briefly Speaking**
>
> "Marketing is too important to be left just to the Marketing Department."
>
> —Philip Almond
> Director, Marketing and Audiences, British Broadcasting Corporation

MARKETING PLANNING: THE BASIS FOR STRATEGY AND TACTICS

Everyone plans. We plan which academic courses we want to take, which movie we want to see, and which outfit to wear to a party. We plan where we want to live and what career we want to pursue. Marketers plan as well. **Planning** is the process of anticipating future events and conditions and determining the best way to achieve organizational objectives. Of course, before marketing planning can even begin, an organization must define its objectives. Planning is a continuous process that includes identifying objectives and then determining the actions through which a firm can attain those objectives. The planning process creates a blueprint for marketers, executives, production staff, and everyone else in the organization to follow for achieving organizational objectives. It also defines checkpoints so that people within the organization can compare actual performance with expectations to indicate whether current activities are moving the organization toward its objectives.

Planning is important for both large and small companies. For years, Richard Branson—founder of the airline Virgin Galactic—dreamed of launching a spaceship designed for commercial travel. The dream required complex design and engineering plans, including the launch of prototypes and rigorous rounds of safety testing. After one of the prototypes became the first privately owned, manned craft to reach space, the company's engineers in New Mexico went to work on a similar craft designed for commercial use, called SpaceShipTwo. If the idea catches on, Branson and Virgin Galactic will have positioned themselves strategically to become the first firm to offer commercial space travel in the near future. More than 650 people have bought tickets (at $250,000 a ticket) for flights on Branson's commercial spacecraft. NBC Universal announced it will broadcast the spacecraft's live launch on its family of networks.[2]

Here on earth—and at the other end of the size spectrum—Shuttleworth, a small firm that manufactures conveyors, had to reevaluate its planning as its core business in electronics began to shrink. The company refocused its efforts on designing and building solar panel conveyors. Its new products have won acclaim, new customers, and a revitalized business.[3]

Marketing planning—implementing planning activities devoted to achieving marketing objectives—establishes the basis for a marketing strategy. Product lines, pricing decisions, selection of appropriate distribution channels, and decisions relating to promotional campaigns all depend on plans formulated within the marketing organization. In today's boundaryless organizations, many planning activities take place over the Internet with *virtual conferences*—teleconferences with computer interfaces. These conferences represent a new way to build relationships among people who are in different geographic locations. Relationships like these are also important for new employees to help ensure their success. See the "Career Readiness" feature for some other tips about making a good impression in your first real job.

An important trend in marketing planning centers on relationship marketing, a firm's effort to develop long-term, cost-effective links with individual customers and suppliers for mutual benefit. Good relationships with customers can arm a firm with vital strategic weapons, and that's as true in business-to-business industries as anywhere else.

Many companies now include relationship-building goals and strategies in their plans. Relationship marketers typically maintain databases to track customer preferences. These marketers may also manipulate product spreadsheets to answer what-if questions related to prices and marketing performance. At Procter & Gamble, the inspiration for new or better products often comes from customers themselves. The company operates in more than 180 countries with 129,000 employees representing about 150 nationalities. Many P&G employees serve as the eyes and ears of the firm, actually spending time in the homes of consumers, observing how they cook and eat meals, when they play, and where they shop. Other employees are trained simply to have conversations with friends and family about their lifestyles and the goods or services they use. Such interaction helps build relationships, and the information helps develop products.[4]

STRATEGIC PLANNING VERSUS TACTICAL PLANNING

Planning often is classified on the basis of its scope or breadth. Some extremely broad plans focus on long-range organizational objectives that will significantly affect the firm for five or more years. Other more targeted plans cover the objectives of individual business units over shorter periods.

Richard Branson's strategic planning has positioned Virgin Galactic to become the first company to offer commercial space travel.

marketing planning Implementing planning activities devoted to achieving marketing objectives.

> **Briefly Speaking**
>
> "The customer experience is the next competitive battleground."
>
> —**Jerry Gregoire**
> *Former Chief Information Officer, Dell Inc.*

1 Distinguish between strategic planning and tactical planning.

CAREER READINESS
Succeeding in Your First "Real" Job

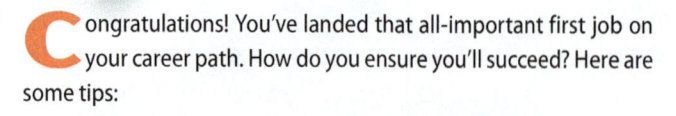

Congratulations! You've landed that all-important first job on your career path. How do you ensure you'll succeed? Here are some tips:

1. Be a keen observer of everything around you. No two organizations are alike, so pay attention to the overall environment, from your new employer's dress code and work ethic to the language your colleagues use. When in doubt, ask questions. And, until you know the ropes, confine your Web surfing to after hours.

2. Remember names. You'll meet a lot of new people in your first few weeks; make an effort to remember their names. Use mnemonics (memory tricks) if you need to, and if you forget a name, apologize and ask again.

3. Monitor your words and actions. You never know who is connected or influential, especially when you're new, so be tactful, be circumspect, and avoid gossip.

4. Spend time with coworkers at all levels. Meetings and team projects are good opportunities to meet helpful peers, invaluable support staff, and potential mentors. If opportunities like these don't readily come your way, volunteer.

5. Be a lifelong learner. The field of marketing is constantly changing. Always be on the lookout to try something new. Be ready to experiment and embrace trends.

Good luck!

Sources: "Best Marketing Career Advice from 10+ Top Marketing Minds," *Coolmarketingstuff.com*, accessed January 10, 2014, www.coolmarketingstuff.com; Dan Schawbel, "My 10 Best Pieces of Career Advice for College Graduates," *DanSchawbel.com*, accessed January 10, 2014, www.danschawbel.com; Brenda Ton, "My Marketing Success Story and Marketing Career Advice," www.brendaton.com, accessed January 10, 2014.

---

strategic planning
Process of determining an organization's primary objectives and adopting courses of action that will achieve these objectives.

tactical planning
Planning that guides the implementation of activities specified in the strategic plan.

Strategic planning can be defined as the process of determining an organization's primary objectives and adopting courses of action that will achieve these objectives. This process includes, of course, allocation of necessary resources. The word *strategy* dates back to a Greek term meaning "the general's art." Strategic planning has a critical impact on a firm's destiny because it provides long-term direction for its decision makers.

Strategic planning is complemented by **tactical planning**, which guides the implementation of activities specified in the strategic plan. Unlike strategic plans, tactical plans typically address shorter-term actions that focus on current and near-future activities that a firm must complete to implement its larger strategies. Sometimes tactical planning requires swift decision making and actions. Disturbances in air travel, like the recent decision by U.S. and other airlines to avoid airspace involved in military conflicts, cause great public concern about safety and security. Such planning requires airlines and other organizations to work together to keep the trust of the flying public on a global basis.[5]

ASSESSMENT CHECK

1.1. Define planning.
1.2. Give an example of strategic planning and tactical planning.

PLANNING AT DIFFERENT ORGANIZATIONAL LEVELS

Planning is a major responsibility for every manager, so managers at all organizational levels devote portions of their workdays to planning. Top management—the board of directors, chief executive officers (CEOs), chief operating officers (COOs), and functional vice presidents, such as chief marketing officers—spend greater proportions of their time planning than do middle-level and supervisory-level managers. Also, top managers usually focus their planning on long-range strategic issues. In contrast, middle-level managers—such as advertising executives,

2 Explain how marketing plans differ at various levels in an organization.

TABLE 2.1 Planning at Different Managerial Levels

Management Level	Type of Planning Emphasized at This Level	Examples
Top Management Board of directors Chief executive officer Chief operating officer Chief financial officer	Strategic planning	Organizationwide objectives; fundamental strategies; long-term plans; total budget
Middle Management General sales manager Team leader Director of marketing research	Tactical planning	Quarterly and semiannual plans; business unit budgets; divisional policies and procedures
Supervisory Management Regional sales manager Supervisor—telemarketing office	Operational planning	Daily and weekly plans; unit budgets; departmental rules and procedures

regional sales managers, and marketing research directors—tend to focus on operational planning, which includes creating and implementing tactical plans for their own business units. Supervisors often develop specific programs to meet goals in their areas of responsibility. Table 2.1 summarizes the types of planning undertaken at various organizational levels.

When it is most effective, the planning process includes input from a wide range of sources: employees, suppliers, and customers. Some marketing experts advocate developing a network of "influencers"—people who have influence over other people's opinions through authority, visibility, or expertise—to provide input and spread the word about company plans and products. Increasingly, companies are investing more resources in social media marketing as its success grows.[6]

> **ASSESSMENT CHECK**
>
> 2.1 How do marketing plans vary at different levels of the organization?
>
> 2.2 Why is it important to get input from others when planning?

STEPS IN THE MARKETING PLANNING PROCESS

The marketing planning process begins at the corporate level with the definition of a firm's mission. It then determines its objectives, assesses its resources, and evaluates environmental risks and opportunities. Guided by this information, marketers within each business unit then formulate a marketing strategy, implement the strategy through operating plans, and gather feedback to monitor and adapt strategies when necessary. Figure 2.1 shows the basic steps in the process.

Identify the six steps in the marketing planning process. **3**

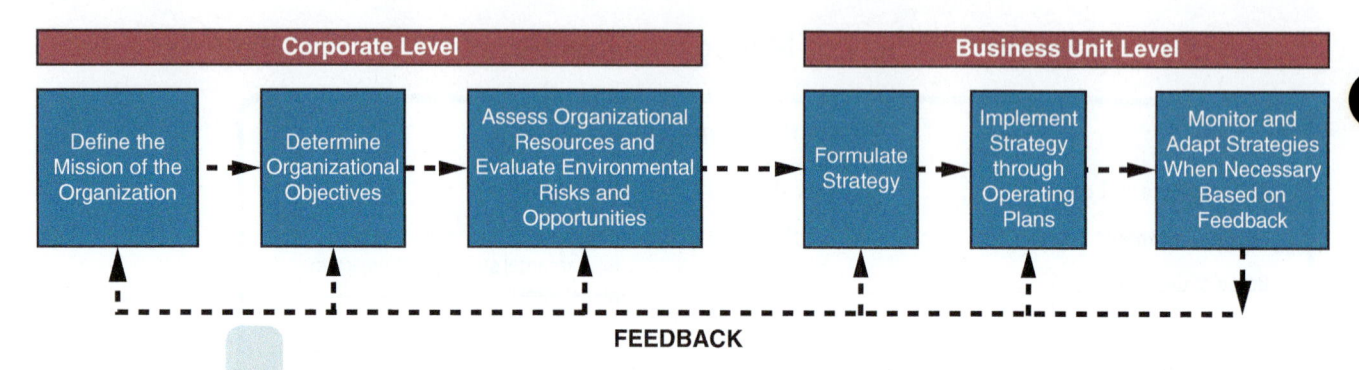

FIGURE 2.1 The Marketing Planning Process

```
Corporate Level                                              Business Unit Level

Define the  →  Determine  →  Assess Organizational  →  Formulate  →  Implement      →  Monitor and
Mission of     Organizational  Resources and            Strategy      Strategy          Adapt Strategies
the            Objectives      Evaluate Environmental                 through           When Necessary
Organization                   Risks and                              Operating         Based on
                               Opportunities                          Plans             Feedback

                                          FEEDBACK
```

DEFINING THE ORGANIZATION'S MISSION AND OBJECTIVES

The planning process begins with defining the firm's **mission**, the essential purpose that differentiates the company from others. The mission statement specifies the organization's overall goals and operational scope and provides general guidelines for future management actions. Adjustments in this statement reflect changing business environments and management philosophies.

Although management guru Peter Drucker cautioned that an effective mission statement should be brief enough "to fit on a T-shirt," organizations typically define themselves with slightly longer statements. But they often condense their mission statement into a catchy slogan such as these:

- Walmart: "Save money. Live better."
- American Cancer Society: "The official sponsor of birthdays."
- Indiana Wesleyan University: "Change Your Life, Change the World."
- Infiniti: "Inspired performance."
- Dunkin' Donuts: "America runs on Dunkin'."

An organization lays out its basic objectives, or goals, in its complete mission statement. These objectives guide development of supporting marketing objectives and plans. Soundly conceived objectives should state specific intentions, such as the following:

- Generate a 15 percent profit over the next 24 months.
- Add 25 new outlets within the next year.
- Improve five products by the end of the year.
- Enter the Chinese market within two years.
- Cut manufacturing costs by 10 percent.
- Reduce waste by 20 percent.

mission Essential purpose that differentiates one company from others.

> **Briefly Speaking**
>
> "For us, our most important stakeholder is not our stockholders, it is our customers. We're in business to serve the needs and desires of our core customer base."
>
> —**John Mackey**
> Co-founder and CEO, Whole Foods Market

ASSESSING ORGANIZATIONAL RESOURCES AND EVALUATING ENVIRONMENTAL RISKS AND OPPORTUNITIES

The third step of the marketing planning process is to assess an organization's strengths, weaknesses, and available opportunities. Organizational resources include the capabilities of the firm's production, marketing, finance, technology, and employees. An organization's planners pinpoint its strengths and weaknesses. Strengths help them set objectives, develop plans for meeting those objectives, and take advantage of marketing opportunities.

Chapter 3 will discuss environmental factors that impact marketing opportunities. Environmental effects can emerge both from within the organization and from the external environment. For example, social media has transformed interpersonal communications as well as communications between companies and their customers.

SOLVING AN ETHICAL CONTROVERSY
Can a Team Save Face with Its Fans?

Thousands of New England Patriots fans purchased tight end Aaron Hernandez's jerseys during his three seasons with the team. When he was arraigned on murder charges, Hernandez was released by the Patriots on the same day. That left some fans wondering what to do with their Hernandez jersey: keep it, sell it online, throw it away? The Patriots Pro Shop came up with another solution—fans could trade the jerseys for a different one. According to the Patriots, roughly 2,500 Hernandez jerseys were returned.

Should team franchises disassociate themselves from a player facing criminal charges?

PRO

1. The seriousness of the charges required the Patriots to consider its mission and principles. Being slow to take action (or taking no action) would elicit public outcry of long standing against the Patriots.
2. Continuing publicity of the investigation and trial would be distracting to the team as it plays out the season in quest of a Super Bowl appearance. Enabling fans to trade in their Hernandez jerseys would help minimize distraction and preserve good will for the team.

CON

1. If Hernandez is found not guilty, fans might be upset that the Patriots disassociated themselves from a player so quickly.
2. The Patriot's Pro Shop lost upwards of $250,000 when more than 2,500 jerseys were traded in over the two-day exchange.

Summary

After Aaron Hernandez was arraigned on murder charges, the New England Patriots released him and initiated the jersey exchange offer. According to owner Robert Kraft, the Patriots' decisions surrounding Hernandez were made based on principle, without regard to financial cost. Kraft also indicated the jerseys would be destroyed, with the shredded material donated for recycling.

Sources: Maria Cramer and John R. Ellement, "Aaron Hernandez Murder Trial to Start in January," *The Boston Globe*, accessed September 22, 2014, **www.bostonglobe.com**; Anthony Riccobono, "Aaron Hernandez Case Update: Two Friends and Fiancee Please Not Guilty; Judge Denies Recusal," *International Business Times*, accessed January 5, 2014, **www.ibtimes.com**; Will Brinson, "Patriots Owner: Team Lost $250K on Aaron Hernandez Jersey Swap," *CBSSports.com*, accessed January 5, 2014, **www.cbssports.com**.

FORMULATING, IMPLEMENTING, AND MONITORING A MARKETING STRATEGY

Once a firm's marketers figure out their company's best opportunities, they can develop a marketing plan designed to meet the overall objectives. A good marketing plan revolves around an efficient, flexible, and adaptable marketing strategy.

A **marketing strategy** is an overall, companywide program for selecting a particular target market and then satisfying consumers in that market through a careful blending of the elements of the marketing mix—product, distribution, promotion, and price—each of which is a component of the overall marketing strategy.

In the two final steps of the planning process, marketers put the marketing strategy into action; then, they monitor performance to ensure that objectives are achieved. Sometimes strategies need to be modified if the product's or company's actual performance is not in line with expected results. For

marketing strategy Overall, companywide program for selecting a particular target market and then satisfying consumers in that market through the marketing mix.

ASSESSMENT CHECK

3.1 Distinguish between an organization's mission and its objectives.

3.2 What is the importance of the final step in the marketing planning process?

> **Briefly Speaking**
>
> "Failure is the opportunity to begin again, more intelligently."
>
> —Henry Ford
> *American industrialist*

4 Describe successful planning tools and techniques, including Porter's Five Forces model, first and second mover strategies, SWOT analysis, and the strategic window.

Porter's Five Forces
Model developed by strategy expert Michael Porter that identifies five competitive forces that influence planning strategies.

When McDonald's started offering high-end coffee drinks, they entered into direct competition with Starbucks and Dunkin' Donuts. The threat of a substitute product can create a need for a company's marketers to find new ways to compete. Now the company is selling its McCafe coffee products in supermarkets.

years, Toronto-based Sun Life Financial, Canada's third-largest insurer, has sold life insurance and annuities for retirement income to individuals and groups in the United States. But when the firm observed that profit margins on individual policies had begun to decline, the company revisited its strategy and discontinued those sales, limiting their target market to groups. As Sun Life CEO put it, "We're changing course and setting a new vision."[7]

Sometimes a marketing strategy backfires. This can happen rapidly in the case of celebrity endorsements, as described in the "Solving an Ethical Controversy" feature.

SUCCESSFUL STRATEGIES: TOOLS AND TECHNIQUES

We can identify a number of successful marketing planning tools and techniques. This section discusses four of them: Porter's Five Forces model, first and second mover strategies, SWOT analysis, and the strategic window. All planning strategies aim to create a sustainable competitive advantage for a firm in which other companies simply cannot provide the same value to their customers—no matter how hard they try.

PORTER'S FIVE FORCES MODEL

A number of years ago, renowned business strategist Michael E. Porter identified five competitive forces that influence planning strategies in a model called **Porter's Five Forces**. Porter later updated his model to include the impact of the Internet on the strategies that businesses use. As illustrated in Figure 2.2, the five forces are potential new entrants, bargaining power of buyers, bargaining power of suppliers, threat of substitute products, and rivalry among competitors.

Potential new entrants sometimes are blocked by the cost or difficulty of entering a market. It is a lot more costly and complicated to begin building aircraft than it is to start up an Internet consulting business. The Internet has reduced the barriers to market entry in many industries. Virtually all businesses now view an Internet presence as a requirement for success. If customers have considerable bargaining power, they can greatly influence a firm's strategy. The Internet can increase a customer's buying power by providing information that might not otherwise be easily accessible, such as alternate suppliers and price comparisons. Firms continue to compete to develop the most effective Internet marketing because they know that customers are savvy users of technology. Microsoft and Google, for example, operate competing online advertising exchanges—AppNexus and DoubleClick—that allow ad sellers and buyers to negotiate in real time.[8]

The number of suppliers available to a manufacturer or retailer affects their bargaining power. If a seafood restaurant in the Midwest has only one supplier of Maine lobsters, that supplier has

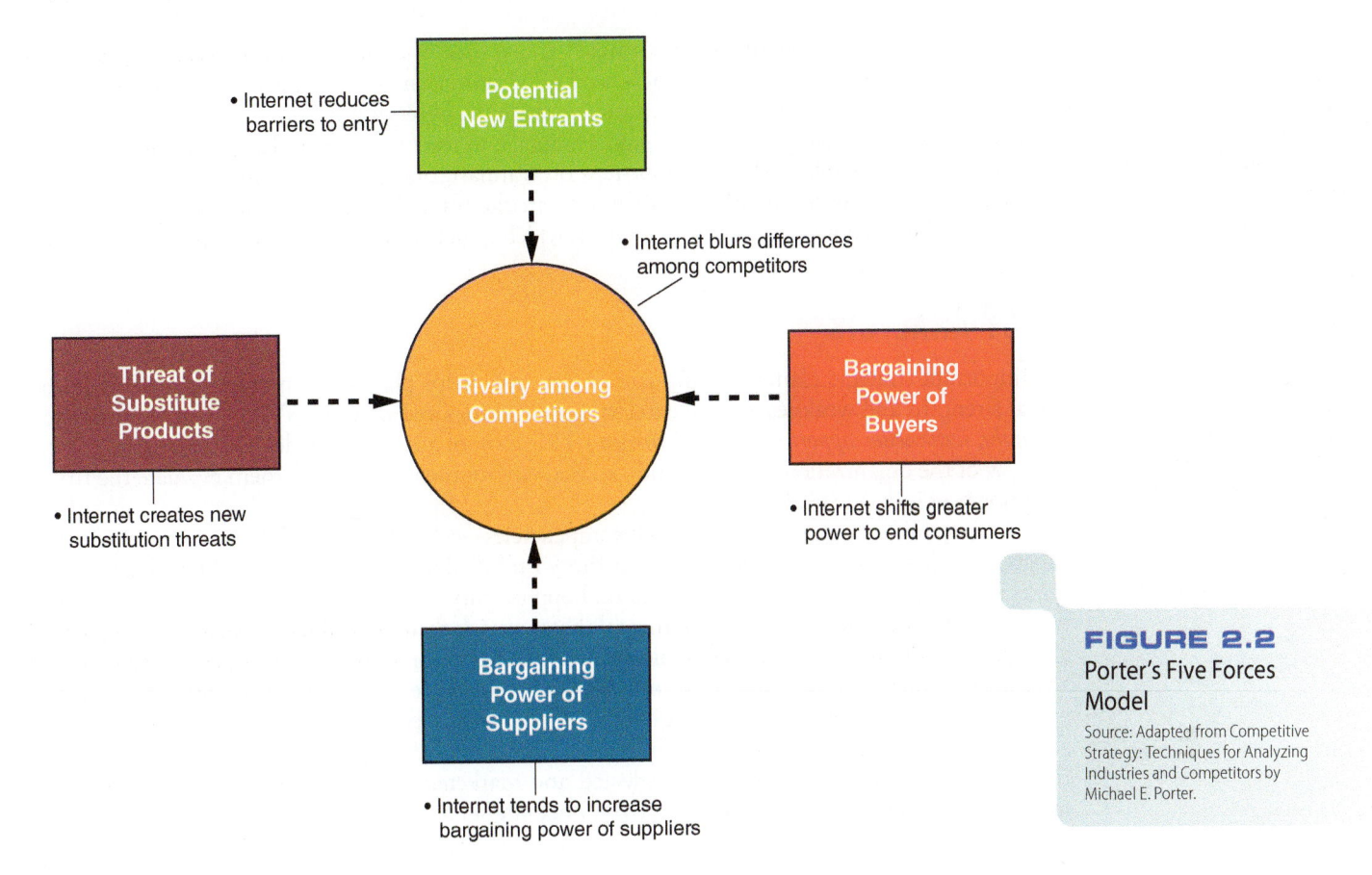

FIGURE 2.2
Porter's Five Forces Model

- Potential New Entrants
  - Internet reduces barriers to entry
- Rivalry among Competitors
  - Internet blurs differences among competitors
- Threat of Substitute Products
  - Internet creates new substitution threats
- Bargaining Power of Buyers
  - Internet shifts greater power to end consumers
- Bargaining Power of Suppliers
  - Internet tends to increase bargaining power of suppliers

Source: Adapted from Competitive Strategy: Techniques for Analyzing Industries and Competitors by Michael E. Porter.

---

significant bargaining power. But seafood restaurants along the coast of Maine have many lobster suppliers, which gives their suppliers less bargaining power.

If customers have the opportunity to replace a company's products with goods or services from a competing firm or industry, the company's marketers may have to find a new market, change prices, or compete in other ways to maintain an advantage. McDonald's made what some considered a bold move when the firm announced the launch of its "McCafe," offering upgraded coffee drinks such as lattes, cappuccinos, and mochas—in direct competition with Starbucks and Dunkin' Donuts. McDonald's recently announced an even bolder move: entering the retail grocery market by testing three new products—packages of McCafe whole beans, ground coffee, and "single-cups"—in supermarkets.[9]

The four previous forces influence the rivalry among competitors. In addition, issues such as cost and differentiation or lack of differentiation of products—along with the Internet—influence the strategies that companies use to stand out from their competitors. With increased availability of information, which tends to level the playing field, rivalry heats up among competitors who try to differentiate themselves from the crowd.

FIRST MOVER AND SECOND MOVER STRATEGIES

Some firms like to adopt a **first mover strategy**, attempting to capture the greatest market share and develop long-term relationships by being the first to enter the market with a good or service, as Virgin Galactic hopes to do by being the first to offer commercial space travel. Being first may also refer to entering new markets with existing products or creating significant innovations that effectively turn an old product into a new one. Naturally, this strategy has its risks—companies that follow can learn from mistakes by first movers. Some well-known first movers include Ford, IBM, Apple, Amazon,

> **Briefly Speaking**
>
> "Innovation is the central issue in economic prosperity."
>
> —Michael Porter
> *U.S. management theorist and writer*

first mover strategy Theory advocating that the company first to offer a product in a marketplace will be the long-term market winner.

second mover strategy Theory that advocates observing closely the innovations of first movers and then improving on them to gain advantage in the marketplace.

SWOT analysis Review that helps planners compare internal organizational strengths and weaknesses with external opportunities and threats.

and MySpace. Each of these firms has stumbled at one time or another, but each is still in business. Ford is making a remarkable comeback, and IBM has risen from the ashes several times.

Other businesses thrive on a **second mover strategy**, observing closely the innovations of first movers and then improving on them to gain advantage in the marketplace. Facebook appeared after MySpace. Target has followed in the footsteps of Walmart. Sometimes first movers are completely replaced by second movers and disappear from the marketplace altogether—as was the case with Pets.com, one of the first online pet accessory retailers, which went bankrupt less than a year after it debuted.

SWOT ANALYSIS

An important strategic planning tool, **SWOT analysis** helps planners compare internal organizational strengths and weaknesses with external opportunities and threats. (SWOT is an acronym for *strengths, weaknesses, opportunities,* and *threats*.) This form of analysis provides managers with a critical view of the organization's internal and external environments and helps them evaluate the firm's fulfillment of its basic mission.

A company's strengths reflect its core competencies—what it does well. Core competencies are capabilities that customers value and competitors find difficult to duplicate. As Figure 2.3 shows, matching an internal strength with an external opportunity produces a situation known as *leverage*. Marketers face a problem when environmental threats attack their organization's weaknesses. Planners anticipate constraints when internal weaknesses or limitations prevent their organization from taking advantage of opportunities. These internal weaknesses can create vulnerabilities for a company—environmental threats to its organizational strength. While the U.S. beverage maker Dr Pepper Snapple Group (DPSG) was under the umbrella of Britain's Cadbury, sales of its once-popular drinks fizzled as distribution networks were neglected and marketers sometimes waited weeks or months for decisions from Cadbury headquarters. But once DPSG achieved a spin-off, it could concentrate

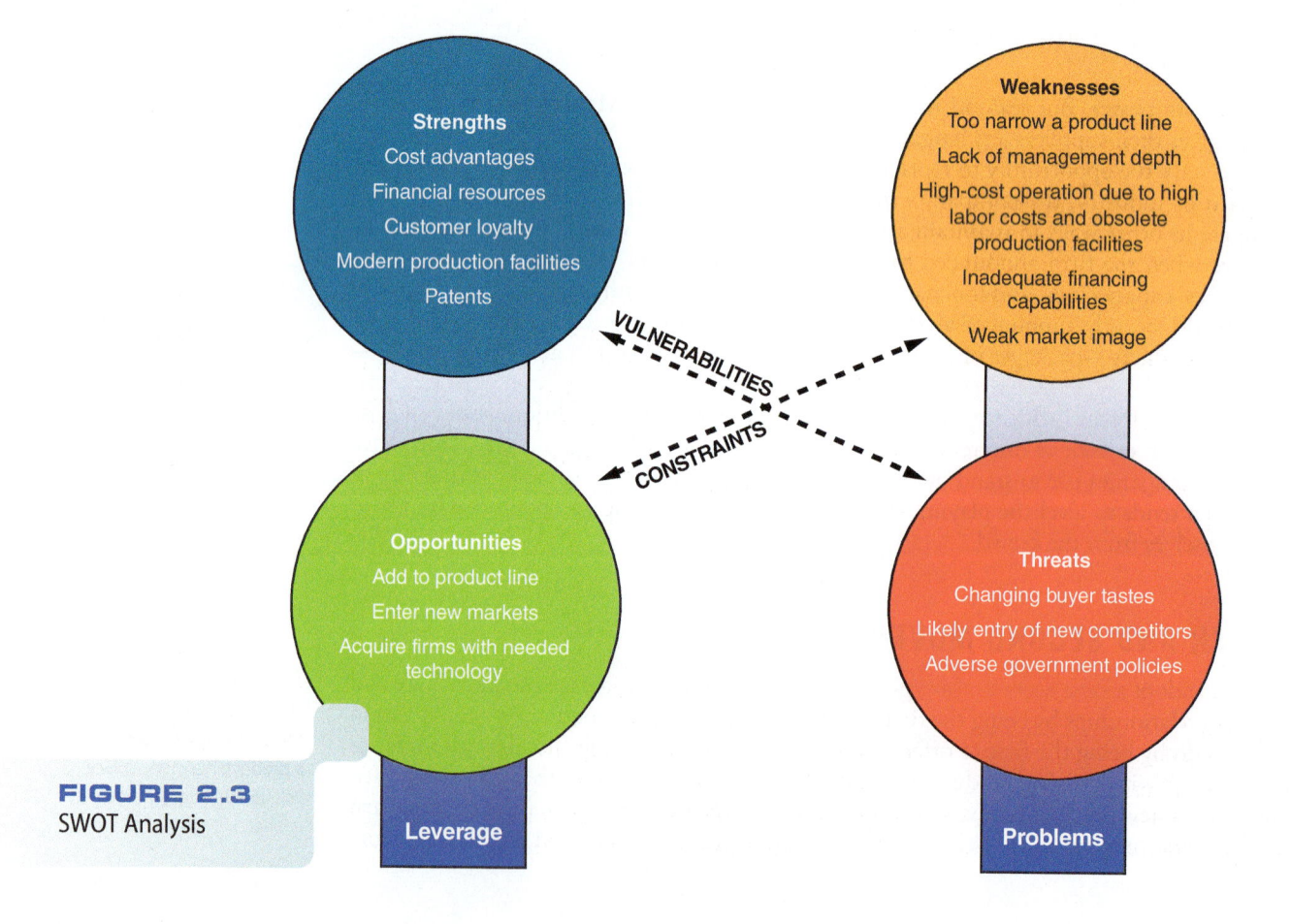

FIGURE 2.3 SWOT Analysis

Strengths
Cost advantages
Financial resources
Customer loyalty
Modern production facilities
Patents

Weaknesses
Too narrow a product line
Lack of management depth
High-cost operation due to high labor costs and obsolete production facilities
Inadequate financing capabilities
Weak market image

Opportunities
Add to product line
Enter new markets
Acquire firms with needed technology

Threats
Changing buyer tastes
Likely entry of new competitors
Adverse government policies

VULNERABILITIES
CONSTRAINTS

Leverage

Problems

on what it does best: making, distributing, and selling its more than 50 brands, which include Dr Pepper, Snapple, 7Up, RC Cola, A&W, and others. Although soda consumption in the United States continues to decline, among the top five contenders only Dr Pepper has seen growth, and A&W is the top-selling root beer. DPSG also recently unseated The Coca-Cola Company as the soft-drink vendor at Chicago's Soldier Field—a spot the Atlanta-based competitor had held for decades.[10]

Even if a company focuses on its core competencies, sometimes it needs to broaden its offerings to maintain a competitive edge. Changes in consumer preferences led Campbell Soup Company to introduce new products outside its core business, soup. Appealing to shoppers who prefer fresh foods, the company recently launched V8 Harvest, a fresh tomato vegetable juice sold in the refrigerated case. Inspired by consumers' preference for bold flavor, Campbell's Pepperidge Farm division looks to re-engage teens who grew up on Goldfish crackers, with baked Goldfish Puffs in bold flavors like buffalo wing and cheddar bacon.[11]

THE STRATEGIC WINDOW

The success of products is also influenced by conditions in the market. Professor Derek Abell has suggested the term **strategic window** to define the limited periods during which the key requirements of a market and the particular competencies of a firm best fit together.[12] The view through a strategic window shows planners a way to relate potential opportunities to company capabilities. Such a view requires a thorough analysis of (1) current and projected external environmental conditions; (2) current and projected internal company capabilities; and (3) how, whether, and when the firm can feasibly reconcile environmental conditions and company capabilities by implementing one or more marketing strategies.

Large and small businesses can make the most of strategic windows. It was a good day for VUDU, a Silicon Valley startup that offers high-definition movie streaming, when the firm attracted the attention of discount retailing giant Walmart. Under Walmart's disc-to-digital service now powered by VUDU, customers can convert their DVDs into a digital library on the cloud using their smartphone, tablet, or other Web-enabled device.[13]

strategic window
Limited periods when key requirements of a market and a firm's particular competencies best fit together.

Small businesses can benefit from the same strategic window if consumers tighten their belts. When this happens, pawn shops and thrift stores often experience an increase in traffic. Instead of donating their gently used, name-brand clothes to a not-for-profit organization such as Goodwill or Purple Heart Veterans, females ages 12 to 24 might take those items to a local consignment shop such as Plato's Closet—and then make a few purchases while there. The franchise operation, with more than 400 stores across the United States and Canada, appeals to consumers who enjoy a bargain.[14]

ASSESSMENT CHECK

4.1 Briefly explain each of Porter's Five Forces.

4.2 What are the benefits and drawbacks of a first mover strategy?

4.3 What are the four components of the SWOT analysis? What is a strategic window?

ELEMENTS OF A MARKETING STRATEGY

Success for a product in the marketplace—whether it is a tangible good, a service, a cause, a person, a place, or an organization—depends on an effective marketing strategy. It's one thing to develop a great product, but if customers don't get the message about it, the product will die. An effective marketing strategy reaches the right buyers at the right time, persuades them to try the product, and develops a strong relationship with them over time. The basic elements of a marketing strategy consist

Identify the two basic elements of a marketing strategy.

Walmart and VUDU made the best of a strategic window when they partnered together. Now Walmart customers can convert their DVDs into a digital library on the cloud using the VUDU service.

of (1) the target market and (2) the marketing mix variables of product, distribution, promotion, and price that combine to satisfy the needs of the target market. The outer circle in Figure 2.4 lists environmental characteristics that provide the framework within which marketing strategies are planned.

THE TARGET MARKET

A customer-driven organization begins its overall strategy with a detailed description of its target market: the group of people toward whom the firm aims its marketing efforts and ultimately its merchandise. Kohl's department stores serve a target market of consumers purchasing for themselves and their families. Other companies, such as Boeing, market most of their products to business buyers such as Delta Airlines and government purchasers. Still other firms provide goods and services to retail and wholesale buyers. In every instance, however, marketers pinpoint their target markets as accurately as possible. Although the concept of dividing markets into specific segments is discussed in more detail in Chapter 9, it's important to understand the idea of targeting a market from the outset.

Although it may be hard to imagine the classic Oreo cookie as anything other than two discs of chocolate with a white cream filling, Kraft Foods (now called Mondelez International) reformulated the favorite to

FIGURE 2.4
Element of a Marketing Strategy and Its Environmental Framework

market it in China. The Chinese version consists of four layers of long, thin biscuits coated in chocolate, which marketers found was more appealing to consumers there. Since the cookie's makeover, Oreo sales in China have grown exponentially, making it the top-selling cookie in China.[15]

Diversity plays an ever-increasing role in targeting markets. According to the U.S. Census Bureau, the rapidly growing Hispanic population in the United States has surpassed African Americans as the largest minority group. The census reports more than 53 million Hispanics in America, or 17 percent of the U.S. population.[16] With this phenomenal growth, marketers would be wise to pay attention to these and other markets—including seniors and children of baby boomers—as they develop goods and services to offer consumers.

Targeting consumers in specific global markets also represents a challenge—and an opportunity. India is an enormous market that is culturally diverse within itself, containing 27 geographical states, numerous languages and religious practices, and a variety of lifestyles. Traditional Indian culture is infused with Western influences. And while nearly half of all Indian citizens earn less than $1 per day, a growing middle class boasts more than 50 million active users of social media. In a recent study, 79 percent of Indian consumers surveyed said they would rather spend time looking for a bargain than pay more to complete a quick purchase. The same sentiment was expressed by middle- and high-income respondents.[17]

MARKETING MIX VARIABLES

After marketers select a target market, they direct their company's activities toward profitably satisfying that segment. Although they must manipulate thousands of variables to reach this goal, marketing decision making can be divided into four strategies: product, distribution, promotion, and pricing strategies. The total package forms the **marketing mix**—the blend of four strategic elements to fit the needs and preferences of a specific target market. While the fourfold classification is useful to study and analyze, remember that the marketing mix can—and should—be an ever-changing combination of variables to achieve success.

Figure 2.4 illustrates that the central focus of the marketing mix variables is the choice of the target market. In addition, decisions about product, distribution, promotion, and price are affected by the environmental factors in the outer circle of the figure. The environmental variables may play a major role in the success of a marketing program, and marketers must consider their probable effects.

marketing mix
Blending of the four strategy elements—product, distribution, promotion, and pricing—to fit the needs and preferences of a specific target market.

Product Strategy

In marketing, the word *product* means more than a good, service, or idea. Product is a broad concept that also encompasses the satisfaction of all consumer needs in relation to a good, service, or idea. So product strategy involves more than just deciding what goods or services the firm should offer to a group of consumers. It also includes decisions about customer service, package design, brand names, trademarks, patents, warranties, the lifecycle of a product, positioning the product in the marketplace, and new-product development.

The "Marketing Success" feature discusses how retailers have brought back layaway programs as a way of providing additional services to their customers.

Distribution Strategy

Marketers develop distribution strategies to ensure that consumers find their products in the proper quantities at the right times and places. Distribution decisions involve modes of transportation, warehousing, inventory control, order processing, and selection of marketing channels. Marketing channels are made up of institutions such as retailers and wholesalers—intermediaries that may be involved in a product's movement from producer to final consumer.

Technology continually opens new channels of distribution in many industries. The Internet has caused the biggest revolution in distribution since the mail-order catalog. Computer software and digital music files are obvious examples, but everything from DVDs to motorcycles to houses can be found on the Web. E-readers such as Amazon's Kindle allow consumers to download and read books and periodicals that were once the domain of the

MARKETING SUCCESS
Layaway Programs a Big Hit with Shoppers

Background. In the past, retailers used layaway programs to offer customers the opportunity to put goods on hold and pay for them on a weekly basis, particularly during the holiday season. This strategy helped customers buy goods they thought could be out of stock as the holidays approached and pay for them in small cash deposits rather than use credit cards and often incur finance charges.

The Challenge. When the economy was booming several years ago, retailers did away with layaway programs because consumers had available credit to purchase goods outright and the programs cost the retailers money, which meant they were not a good investment.

The Strategy. As the recession took hold and consumers felt the pinch of less disposable income and higher credit card fees and interest rates, retailers found sales were lagging. To help increase the bottom line and attract more shoppers into their stores, retailers such as Walmart, Target, Kmart, and Toys "R" Us decided to bring back layaway programs.

The Outcome. Both retailers and consumers win with layaway programs. Retailers get shoppers to buy items they otherwise wouldn't buy, and the programs bring shoppers back in the store to pay off their layaway purchases weekly—perhaps encouraging them to buy more goods on their multiple visits. Consumers benefit from layaway programs because they do not incur credit card debt with these retail purchases. In fact, competition among retailers has heated up for layaway purchases. After touting its free back-to-school layaway plan in commercials, Kmart quickly followed up with ads promoting its no-fee holiday layaway program—more than 100 days before Christmas. Other retailers have waived layaway fees not only for holiday purchases but also for year-round purchases.

Sources: Natalie Zmuda, "105 Days 'til Christmas: Kmart Airs First Holiday Ad Commercial Promoting Layaway Marks Earliest Ever Kickoff to Holiday Marketing," *Advertising Age*, accessed January 11, 2014, www.adage.com; David Gianatasio, "Kmart Ad Turns Schoolyard Taunts of 'Yo Mama' into Compliments," *Adweek*, accessed January 11, 2014, www.adweek.com; Brad Tuttle, "Why Stores and Shoppers Alike Are Embracing Layaway," *Time*, accessed January 11, 2014, http://business.time.com; Oliver St. John and Jayne O'Donnell, "Kmart Follows Toys R Us and Drops Layaway Fees," *USA Today*, accessed January 11, 2014, http://usatoday30.usatoday.com.

printed page. Some publications, such as *Bloomberg Businessweek* and *The Wall Street Journal*, offer both online and print content, with the online version sometimes free (although that is beginning to change). But other publications have abandoned print altogether or were originally established online.

Promotion Strategy

Promotion is the communications link between sellers and buyers. Organizations use varied ways to send messages about their goods, services, and ideas. They may communicate messages directly through salespeople or indirectly through advertisements and promotions. Promotions often offer a product at a reduced price for a limited time, bundle two or more products together, or give away a premium (such as a toy) with purchase. Supermarket chains such as Meijer in the Midwest periodically aim to stimulate sales by disseminating coupons that offer $5 or $10 off a large grocery purchase. Online sites for retailers such as L.L. Bean and Macy's offer free shipping on orders. At back-to-school time, Kohl's department stores offered a "tax relief" discount equal to the applicable sales tax. During a recent promotion to celebrate National Coffee Day, Dunkin' Donuts, Starbucks, and other retailers offered free cups of coffee and deep discounts on packaged coffee and K-cups.[18]

In developing a promotional strategy, marketers blend the various elements of promotion to communicate most effectively with their target market. Many companies use an approach called integrated marketing communications (IMC) to coordinate all promotional activities so that the consumer receives a unified and consistent message. Consumers might receive newsletters, email updates, discount coupons, catalogs, invitations to company-sponsored events, and

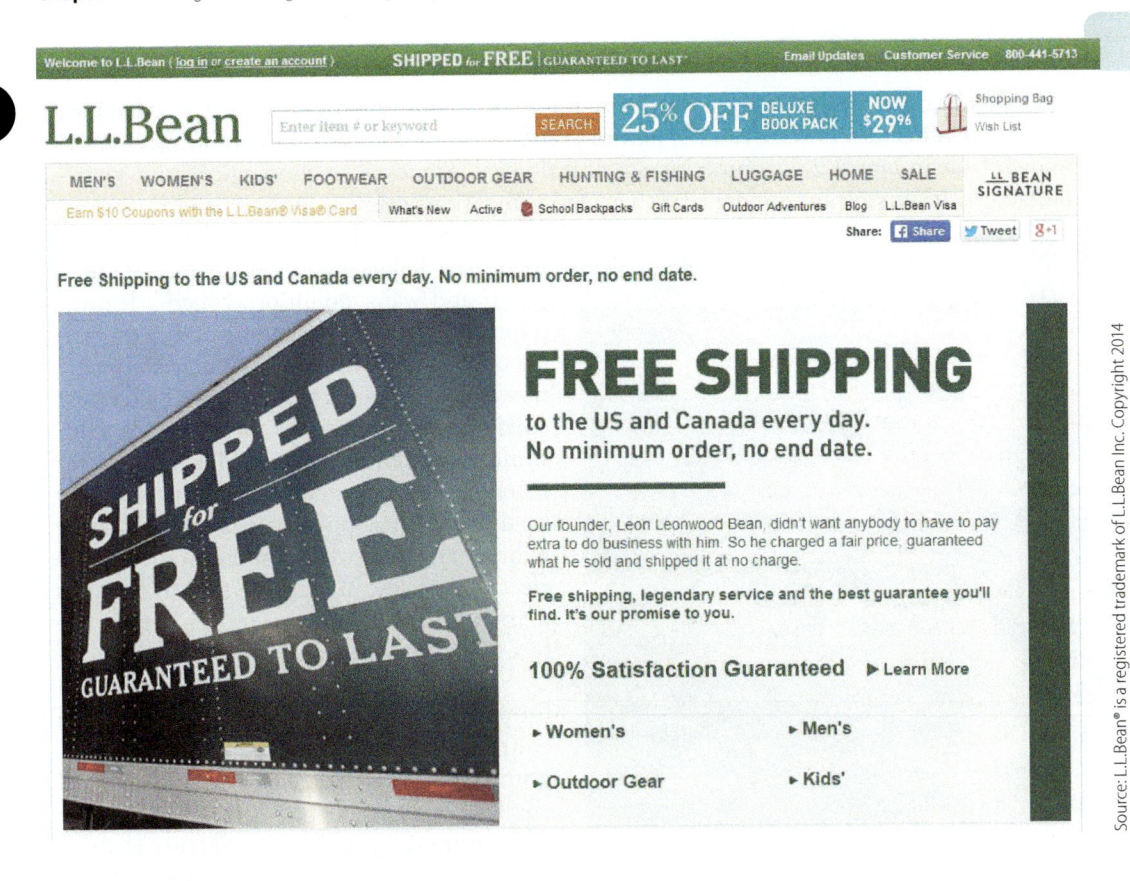

As a promotion strategy to stimulate sales, L.L. Bean offers free shipping on all orders.

any number of other types of marketing communications about a product. Honda dealers mail maintenance and service reminders to their customers. Wendy's places discount coupons in local sales circulars. A political candidate may send volunteer workers through a neighborhood to invite voters to a local reception.

Pricing Strategy

Pricing strategy deals with the methods of setting profitable and justifiable prices. It is closely regulated and subject to considerable public scrutiny. One of the many factors that influence a marketer's pricing strategy is competition. The computer industry has become all too familiar with price cuts by both current competitors and new market entrants. After years of steady growth, the market has become saturated with low-cost computers, driving down profit margins even farther. A good pricing strategy should create value for customers, building and strengthening their relationship with a firm and its products. But sometimes conditions in the external marketing environment cause difficulties in pricing strategies. Political unrest overseas, the soaring price of fuel, or a freeze that destroys crops could all affect the price of goods and services. If the economy is booming, consumers generally have more confidence and are willing to shop more frequently and pay more for discretionary goods. But when the economy slows, consumers look for bargains—they want high quality at low prices. It is a challenge for marketers to strike the right balance to make enough profits to survive and grow. Currently, sales at luxury retailers such as Saks and Abercrombie & Fitch are down. But sales at local dollar stores and larger discount retailers are stronger—sometimes luring shoppers away from traditional giants such as Target and Walmart.[19]

ASSESSMENT CHECK

5.1 What are the two components of every marketing strategy?

5.2 Identify the four strategic elements of the marketing mix.

6 Describe the environmental characteristics that influence strategic decisions.

THE MARKETING ENVIRONMENT

Marketers do not make decisions about target markets and marketing mix variables in a vacuum. They must take into account the dynamic nature of the five dimensions of the marketing environment shown back in Figure 2.4: competitive, political–legal, economic, technological, and social–cultural factors. It's important to note that these five dimensions overlap, interact, and fluctuate.

Concerns about the natural environment have led to new and tighter regulations on air and water pollution, which affect the political–legal environment in which marketers operate. Efforts toward sustainability are now social–cultural factors as well, because consumer awareness is turning into consumer preference. Automobile makers, for instance, have turned public concerns and legal issues into opportunities by developing hybrid cars, autos that run on biodiesel, and electric vehicles. In fact, the race to bring to market the most fuel-efficient vehicles for the future has become extremely competitive.

Businesses are increasingly looking to foreign shores for new growth markets. Of course, these opportunities represent economic, political–legal, and social–cultural challenges as well. The U.S. Department of Commerce provides resources, including contact lists and matching services, for companies trying to enter the market in Romania. Its Gold Key Matching Service helps develop partnerships between U.S. firms and local firms in Romania. The export.gov website reports, "Romania offers significant opportunities to American businesses with products, services, or technologies that either meet growing private demand or contribute to the country's development priorities." For businesses, Romania's attractions include a well-educated workforce with more than 50,000 IT specialists, an expanding economy, and access to the Black Sea and Asia.[20]

Technology continually changes the marketing environment. Marketers are now increasing efforts to get their messages to consumers via smartphone with free mobile apps. For example, Starbucks provides an app that lets customers pay for their coffee with their smartphone. Using the Marriott Mobile App, you can make a hotel reservation, browse city guides, or check your Marriott Rewards account. In the mood for a pizza? Domino's offers mobile apps for both Android phones and iPhones. A Domino's "pizza profile" embedded in the app stores your order information, and a tracker lets you know exactly where your pizza is and how long before it's delivered.[21]

In the competitive environment, some experts have coined the phrase *rule of three*, meaning that in any industry, the three strongest, most efficient companies dominate between 70 and 90 percent of the competitive market. Here are a few examples, all of which are household names:

Cereal manufacturers: General Mills, Kellogg's, Post
Running shoes: Nike, Adidas, Reebok
Supermarkets: Walmart, Kroger, Publix
Pharmaceuticals: Merck, Pfizer, Bristol-Myers Squibb

While it may seem like an uphill battle for the remaining companies in any given industry, they can find a strategy for gaining competitive ground.

The social–cultural environment includes a variety of factors, including prevailing cultural norms. After the

Resale shops such as Plato's Closet appeal to consumers' efforts to help the environment by recycling their gently used clothing.

ASSESSMENT CHECK

6.1 What are the five dimensions of the marketing environment?

6.2 How is concern over the natural environment affecting the other dimensions?

novelty of bidding for auction items on eBay began to wear off for consumers, eBay reshaped itself and introduced the "Buy It Now" option: fixed-price merchandise designed with smartphone users in mind. With the proliferation of pastimes such as Facebook and Twitter, online bidding has lost its appeal, and today the "Buy It Now" option accounts for 85 percent of eBay purchases. The company recently reported annual revenues of more than $6 billion.[22] This new trend also reflects economic factors, including how much consumers are willing and able to spend.

The entire marketing environment provides a framework for all marketing activity. Marketers consider environmental dimensions when they develop strategies for segmenting and targeting markets and when they study consumer and organizational buying behavior.

METHODS FOR MARKETING PLANNING

As growing numbers of companies have discovered the benefits of effective marketing planning, they have developed planning methods to assist in this important function. This section discusses two useful methods: the strategic business unit concept and the market share/market growth matrix.

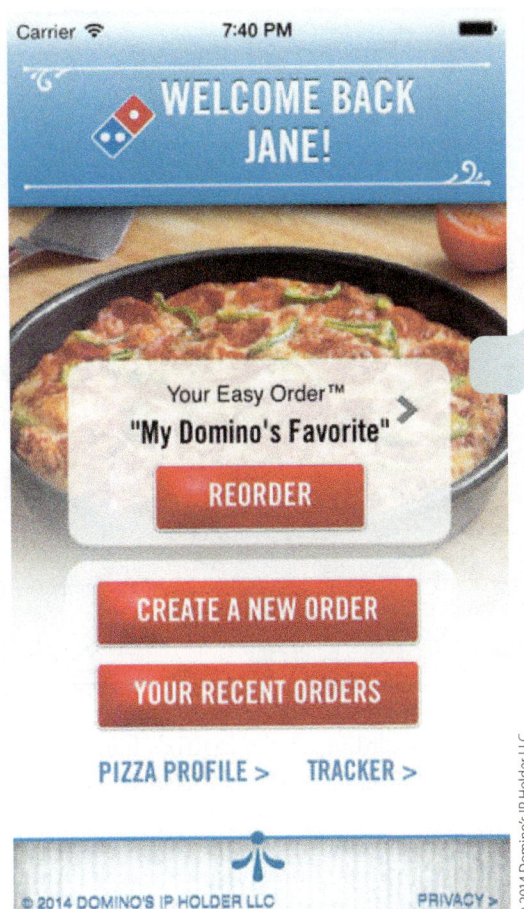

Domino's Pizza has Android, iPhone, and iPad apps that let customers place orders for pizza. The company reports that online and mobile phone orders represent more than one-third of its business.

7 Describe the methods for marketing planning, including business portfolio analysis and the BCG matrix.

BUSINESS PORTFOLIO ANALYSIS

Although a small company may offer only a few items to its customers, a larger organization frequently offers and markets many products to widely diverse markets. Citibank offers a wide range of financial products to businesses and consumers. Nestlé stocks supermarkets with everything from baby food, frozen single-serve entrees, and bottled water to pet food, dietary supplements, and in-home espresso machines. Top managers at these larger firms need a method for spotting product lines that deserve more investment as well as lines that aren't living up to expectations. So they conduct a portfolio analysis, in which they evaluate their company's products and divisions to determine the strongest and weakest. Similar to how securities analysts review their portfolios of stocks and bonds, deciding which to retain and which to sell, marketing planners must assess their products, the regions in which they operate, and other marketing mix variables. This is where the concept of a strategic business unit comes in.

Strategic business units (SBUs) are key business units within diversified firms. Each SBU has its own managers, resources, objectives, and competitors. A division, product line, or single product may define the boundaries of an SBU. Each SBU pursues its own distinct mission and often develops its own plans independently of other units in the organization.

SBUs, also called categories, focus the attention of company managers so that they can respond effectively to changing consumer demand within limited markets. Companies may have to redefine their SBUs as market conditions dictate. IBM was once known as a manufacturer of high-quality clocks. Today, the firm markets everything from computer servers and systems, software, and Internet security to printing paper and toner. Its slogan, "Welcome to the Decade of Smart," conveys the firm's forward-thinking philosophy.[23]

strategic business units (SBUs) Key business units within diversified firms.

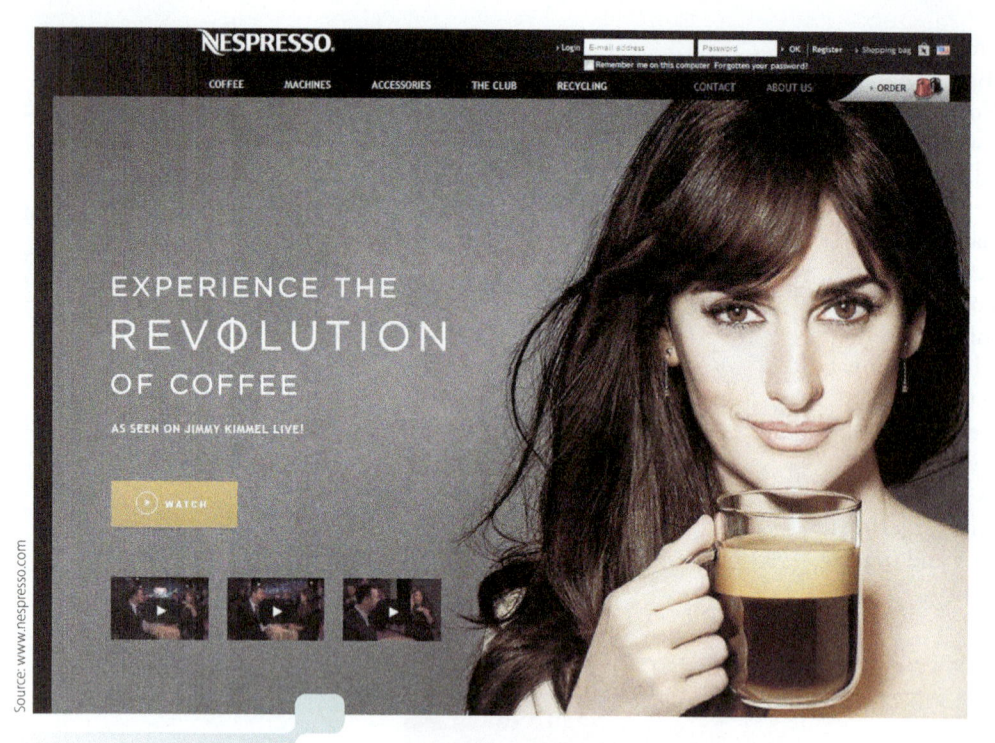

Nespresso, a coffee equipment and beverage retailer, is an SBU of Nestlé, the Swiss global food and beverage company.

FIGURE 2.5 BCG Market Share/Market Growth Matrix

	Relative Market Share	
	High	**Low**
Industry Growth Rate — High	**Stars** Generate considerable income **Strategy:** Invest more funds for future growth	**Question Marks** Have potential to become stars or cash cows **Strategy:** Either invest more funds for growth or consider disinvesting
Industry Growth Rate — Low	**Cash Cows** Generate strong cash flow **Strategy:** Milk profits to finance growth of stars and question marks	**Dogs** Generate little profits **Strategy:** Consider withdrawing

THE BCG MATRIX

To evaluate each of their organization's strategic business units, marketers need some type of portfolio performance framework. A widely used framework was developed by the Boston Consulting Group (BCG). This market share/market growth matrix places SBUs in a four-quadrant chart that plots market share against market growth potential. Market share is the percentage of a market that a firm currently controls (or company sales divided by total market sales). The position of an SBU along the horizontal axis indicates its market share relative to those of competitors in the industry. Its position along the vertical axis indicates the annual growth rate of the market. After plotting all of a firm's business units, planners divide them according to the matrix's four quadrants. Figure 2.5 illustrates this matrix by labeling the four quadrants: stars, cash cows, question marks, and dogs. Firms in each quadrant require a unique marketing strategy.

Stars represent units with high market shares in high-growth markets. These products or businesses are high-growth market leaders. Although they generate considerable income, they need considerable inflows of cash to finance further growth. The Apple iPhone is the top-selling smartphone in the United States, but to maintain that position, Apple continues to offer new models to demanding and tech-savvy consumers.[24]

Cash cows command high market shares in low-growth markets. Marketers for such an SBU want to maintain this status for as long as possible. The business produces strong cash flows, but instead of investing heavily in the unit's own promotions and production capacity, the firm can use this cash to finance the growth of other SBUs with higher growth potentials. For instance, Microsoft uses the profits from sales of its Windows operating system to finance research and development for new Internet-based technologies.[25]

Question marks achieve low market shares in high-growth markets. Marketers must decide whether to continue supporting these products or businesses because question marks typically require considerably more cash than they generate. If a question mark cannot become a star, the firm should pull out of the market and target other markets with greater potential.

JPMorgan Chase recently stopped making student loans, saying the market isn't one that the bank can significantly grow. Industry observers point out that nationally nearly $8 billion in such loans are currently in default—a reality the bank likely took into account when making its decision.[26]

Dogs manage only low market shares in low-growth markets. SBUs in this category promise poor future prospects, and marketers should withdraw from these businesses or product lines

ASSESSMENT CHECK

7.1 What are SBUs?

7.2 Identify the four quadrants in the BCG matrix.

as quickly as possible. In some cases, these products can be sold to other firms, where they are a better fit. Some firms build their entire business on other companies' dogs, purchasing recipes or manufacturing techniques. Blair Candy, an online candy retailer, specializes in hard-to-find brands like Gobstoppers, Necco Wafers, and Zagnut candy bars.[27]

Strategic Implications of Marketing in the 21st Century

As the technological advances of the 21st century speed ahead, planning by marketers has never been more important. They need to plan carefully, accurately, and quickly if their companies are to gain a competitive advantage in today's global marketplace. They need to define their organization's mission and understand the different methods for formulating a successful marketing strategy. They must consider a changing, diverse population and the boundaryless business environment created by the Internet. They must be able to evaluate when it's best to be first to get into a market and when it's best to wait. They need to recognize when they've got a star and when they've got a dog—when to hang on and when to let go. As daunting as this seems, planning can reduce the risk and worry of bringing new goods and services to the marketplace.

Get online now for additional learning tools to help you master your marketing knowledge—visit **WWW.CENGAGEBRAIN.COM** today!

REVIEW OF CHAPTER OBJECTIVES

1 Distinguish between strategic planning and tactical planning.

Strategic planning is the process of identifying an organization's primary objectives and adopting courses of action toward these objectives. In other words, strategic planning focuses on the big picture of which industries are central to a firm's business. Tactical planning guides the implementation of the activities specified in the strategic plan. Once a strategy is set, operational managers devise methods (tactics) to achieve the larger goals.

2 Explain how marketing plans differ at various levels in an organization.

Top management spends more time engaged in strategic planning than middle- and supervisory-level managers, who tend to focus on narrower tactical plans for their units. Supervisory managers are more likely to develop specific plans designed to meet the goals assigned to them—for example, streamlining production processes so that they operate more efficiently.

3 Identify the six steps in the marketing planning process.

The basic steps in the marketing planning process are defining the organization's mission and objectives; assessing organizational resources and evaluating environmental risks and opportunities; and formulating, implementing, and monitoring the marketing strategy.

4 Describe successful planning tools and techniques, including Porter's Five Forces model, first and second mover strategies, SWOT analysis, and the strategic window.

Porter's Five Forces are identified as the five competitive factors that influence planning strategies: potential new entrants, bargaining power of buyers, bargaining power of suppliers, threat of substitute products, and rivalry among competitors. With a first mover strategy, a firm attempts to capture the greatest market share by being first to enter the market; with a second mover strategy, a firm observes the innovations of first movers and then attempts to improve on them to gain advantage. SWOT analysis (strengths, weaknesses, opportunities, and threats) helps planners compare internal organizational strengths and weaknesses with external opportunities and threats. The strategic window identifies the limited periods during which the key requirements of a market and the competencies of a firm best fit together.

5 Identify the two basic elements of a marketing strategy.

Development of a marketing strategy is a two-step process: (1) selecting a target market and (2) designing an effective marketing mix to satisfy the chosen target. The target market is the group of people toward whom a company decides to direct its marketing efforts. The marketing mix blends four strategy elements to fit the needs and preferences of a specific target market: product strategy, distribution strategy, promotion strategy, and pricing strategy.

6 Describe the environmental characteristics that influence strategic decisions.

The five dimensions of the marketing environment are competitive, political–legal, economic, technological, and social–cultural. Marketers must also address growing concern about the natural environment, including new regulations, and increasing cultural diversity in the global marketplace.

7 Describe the methods for marketing planning, including business portfolio analysis and the BCG matrix.

The business portfolio analysis evaluates a company's products and divisions, including strategic business units (SBUs). The SBU focuses the attention of company managers so that they can respond effectively to changing consumer demand within certain markets. The BCG matrix places SBUs in a four-quadrant chart that plots market share against market growth potential. The four quadrants are stars, cash cows, dogs, and question marks.

ASSESSMENT CHECK: ANSWERS

1.1 Define planning. Planning is the process of anticipating future events and conditions and of determining the best way to achieve organizational objectives.

1.2 Give an example of strategic planning and tactical planning. To survive in a challenging environment that includes soaring fuel costs, several airlines have decided to combine as part of their strategic planning. Tactical plans include cutting the number of flights and charging passengers extra for checked baggage.

2.1 How do marketing plans vary at different levels of the organization? Top managers usually focus their planning activities on long-range strategic issues. In contrast, middle-level managers focus on operational planning, which includes creating and implementing tactical plans for their own units. Supervisors develop specific programs to meet the goals in their areas of responsibility.

2.2 Why is it important to get input from others when planning? Input from a variety of sources—other employees, suppliers, or customers—helps ensure that many ideas are considered. Involving those people in planning can also turn them into advocates for the plan.

3.1 Distinguish between an organization's mission and its objectives. The firm's mission is the essential purpose that differentiates the company from others. Its objectives guide development of supporting marketing objectives and plans. Avon's mission is to be "the company for women." One of its objectives might be to convert all its packaging to recycled materials.

3.2 What is the importance of the final step in the marketing planning process? In the final step of the marketing planning process, managers monitor performance to ensure that objectives are achieved.

4.1 Briefly explain each of Porter's Five Forces. Porter's Five Forces are the threats of potential new entrants, which increases competition in a market; bargaining power of buyers, which can depress prices; bargaining power of suppliers, which can increase costs or reduce selection; threat of substitute products, which can lure customers to other products; and rivalry among competitors, which can bring about price wars or divert companies from their main goals.

4.2 What are the benefits and drawbacks of a first mover strategy? The benefits of a first mover strategy include capturing the greatest market share and developing long-term relationships with customers. Disadvantages include the possibility that companies that follow can learn from mistakes by first movers. Procter & Gamble has been a first mover with its line of Swiffer products.

4.3 What are the four components of the SWOT analysis? What is a strategic window? SWOT analysis helps planners compare internal organizational strengths and weaknesses with external opportunities and threats. SWOT is an acronym for *strengths, weaknesses, opportunities,* and *threats.* A strategic window defines the limited periods when key requirements of a market and a firm's particular competencies best fit together.

5.1 What are the two components of every marketing strategy? The basic elements of a marketing strategy are (1) the target market and (2) the marketing mix variables.

5.2 Identify the four strategic elements of the marketing mix. The marketing mix consists of product, distribution, promotion, and pricing strategies.

6.1 What are the five dimensions of the marketing environment? The five dimensions of the marketing environment are competitive, political–legal, economic, technological, and social–cultural factors.

6.2 How is concern over the natural environment affecting the other dimensions? Concerns over the natural environment have led to new and tighter regulations on pollution, which affect the political–legal environment in which marketers operate. Efforts toward sustainability are now social–cultural factors as well, because consumer awareness is turning into consumer preference.

7.1 What are SBUs? Strategic business units (SBUs) are key business units within diversified firms. Each SBU has its own managers, resources, objectives, and competitors.

7.2 Identify the four quadrants in the BCG matrix. The BCG matrix labels SBUs stars, cash cows, question marks, and dogs. Stars are the products with high market shares in high-growth markets; cash cows command high market shares in low-growth markets; question marks achieve low market shares in high-growth markets; and dogs manage only low market shares in low-growth markets.

MARKETING TERMS YOU NEED TO KNOW

planning 36
marketing planning 37
strategic planning 38
tactical planning 38
mission 40
marketing strategy 41
Porter's Five Forces 42
first mover strategy 43
second mover strategy 44
SWOT analysis 44
strategic window 45
marketing mix 47
strategic business units (SBUs) 51

ASSURANCE OF LEARNING REVIEW

1. State whether each of the following illustrates strategic or tactical planning:
   a. Global automakers begin setting up manufacturing plants in China.
   b. Play N Trade Video Games and Dimensions Games Corporation merge.
   c. The Cleveland Browns give up draft picks to obtain QB Johnny Manziel ("Johnny Football").
   d. A regional airline looks for ways to expand to other markets.
2. Imagine you had a chance to interview Google co-founders Larry Page and Sergey Brin. What questions might you ask each about strategic planning for individual divisions and for the firm overall?
3. What is the difference between a firm's mission and its objectives? Why is it important that both are conveyed clearly to employees and to customers?
4. Over which of Porter's Five Forces do consumers have the greatest influence? Over which do they have the least? How might these factors affect a firm's overall marketing strategy?
5. Why is it so important for a firm to identify its core competencies?
6. How might an understanding of diversity help formulate a firm's marketing strategy?
7. Suppose you have been hired as a marketer by an online retailer, such as Wayfair or Amazon, to help develop a new

marketing mix. State one thing you would do to improve the retailer's position through each of the four strategic elements: product, distribution, promotion, and pricing.

8. What is the rule of three? Suppose you worked for a small firm in a large industry, such as a small manufacturer of furniture. How might you actually use the rule of three to enhance your firm's position in the marketplace?

9. What is a portfolio analysis? What purpose does it serve for marketers?

10. How does the BCG matrix help marketers decide which products to offer? According to the matrix, which types of products are most desirable, and why?

PROJECTS AND TEAMWORK EXERCISES

1. Choose one of the following companies, or select another one whose goods and services are familiar to you. On your own or with a classmate, formulate a mission statement for that company. Then create a list of objectives that reflect your company's mission.
    a. Sports Authority
    b. E*TRADE
    c. Sprint
    d. Chipotle

2. Using a first mover strategy, Apple's iPad and iPhone have clearly established the lead in their markets. Research the products of another firm that produces either a tablet or a smartphone to learn about its strategy. How has a second mover strategy benefited the firm? Has the second mover firm been able to catch Apple in sales?

3. When rivals Samsung and Sony each unveiled their new 3D TVs at a major electronics store, some consumers couldn't tell the difference between the two. But the firms' strategies were very different. Sony opted to use outside manufacturing firms to build its TVs, stating that the move would help cut costs and keep the company strong. But Samsung manufactures its own TVs, including its own computer chips. Ultimately, the 3D TV failed, but with different consequences for the two firms.[28] With a classmate, research the two companies and their 3D TVs, evaluating their marketing strategy and the decisions they subsequently made regarding the product. In your opinion, how did the firms' strategies affect their respective outcomes?

4. Select one of the following industries and research which firms might fall into the top three in the industry, creating a rule of three:
    a. online securities trading
    b. upscale hotels
    c. electronics retailing
    d. auto manufacturing

5. On your own or with a classmate, research one of the following large corporations. Select several product lines and classify each in the BCG matrix.
    a. ExxonMobil
    b. Johnson & Johnson
    c. Starwood Hotels & Resorts
    d. DuPont

CRITICAL-THINKING EXERCISES

1. Suppose you are a marketer for a U.S. manufacturer of pet supplies. Two top executives have proposed expanding the company by opening retail stores and marketing pets on-site—puppies, kittens, rabbits, birds, fish, and the like. What are the potential benefits and drawbacks of making a move like this? How would you advise your company to proceed?

2. Netflix has made thousands of streaming videos available to its subscribers. How does this strategy demonstrate a strategic window for the company?

3. Choose one of the following products and describe how it may (or already has) become vulnerable to substitution. Then describe an overall strategy, with two or three tactics, for reducing this vulnerability.
    a. printed copies of periodicals or books
    b. TVs
    c. greeting cards
    d. travel agencies

4. Research the website of one of the following retail firms to identify its target market. Then outline a strategy for expanding that target market.
    a. Forever 21
    b. Target
    c. Penzeys Spices
    d. Nordstrom
    e. Chico's

5. Research a company such as L.L. Bean or Mondelez International (formerly Kraft Foods) that has a number of different successful SBUs. What factors do you think make these units—and this company—successful from a marketing standpoint?

ETHICS EXERCISE

The news media reports a shocking fact from the Centers for Disease Control and Prevention (CDC): Bread is the number-one source of sodium in the average American diet. In fact, most people get twice as much sodium from bread and rolls as they do from a bag of salty snacks such as chips or pretzels.[29] Imagine that you are a marketer for a baking company whose main product lines are bread and rolls. For years, your company has focused on "heart-healthy" as a key claim.

1. You have been assigned to create a new strategy and tactics for your firm's Facebook page. Would you continue to emphasize the heart-healthy message? Would you refer to the CDC study or ignore it?

2. As you review the Facebook site, you note that packaging for your company's bread uses the words "heart-healthy." Would you bring this to the attention of the marketing group responsible for product packaging? Or would you look for a way to obscure the package design online? Defend your answer.

INTERNET EXERCISES

1. **Business portfolio analysis.** Occasionally, companies sell parts of themselves to other firms. One stated motive for such divestitures is that the sold assets are a poor strategic fit for the rest of the company's business portfolios. An example is the sale of a controlling interest in NBC Universal by GE to cable giant Comcast. Using a major search engine, research the sale of NBC Universal. In the context of business portfolio analysis, why did GE decide to sell, and why did Comcast decide to buy NBC Universal?

2. **Mission and objectives.** Visit the corporate website of Under Armour. Define the firm's mission and objectives, and discuss how its brands and activities support both.
www.uabiz.com

3. **SWOT analysis.** Visit the website of an organization whose goods and services interest you—for example, Columbia Sportswear, the new SEC network, Expedia, or Urban Outfitters. Based on your research, create a SWOT analysis for your firm. Outline your own ideas for increasing the firm's strengths and reducing its weaknesses.

Note: Internet Web addresses change frequently. If you don't find the exact site listed, you may need to access the organization's home page and search from there or use a search engine such as Google or Bing.

CASE 2.1
Hotels Target Millennials with New Amenities

Poised to become the largest consumer group in U.S. history, the millennials (born between 1977 and 1994) wield consumer spending power of billions of dollars a year. They differ from baby boomers (born 1946–1964) in many ways, including their preferences when staying at a hotel. Millennials feel "interesting is more important than comfort." They also lack brand loyalty for hotels, making competition for their business fierce.

Hotel chains are therefore hurrying to upgrade their facilities to attract these younger guests in sneakers and baseball caps, who aren't completely at home in quiet lobbies that reek of Olde England. Chains such as Hilton, Starwood, Marriott, and InterContinental have installed sleek and comfortable new lounges with stylish bars, plush furniture, areas for socializing, out-in-the-open power consoles for recharging electronics, and electronic concierge services. They've added state-of-the-art gyms, happy hours, free wine and tea tastings, yoga classes, designer shower heads, check-in kiosks to replace registration desks, and of course Wi-Fi access and high-speed Internet, which one observer described as "almost like air to millennials." And, appealing to millennials' green leanings, they're going eco-friendly. The hotels of Starwood's Element brand are pursuing LEED certification, and Hilton's Home2 Suites eliminated the little bottles of shampoo in favor of less wasteful pumps in the shower.

While baby boomers enjoy the solitude of their rooms after a long day of business or sightseeing, millennials like to visit several restaurants and bars during their travels, so some hotels are introducing multiple eateries and lounges, all designed with different themes to create variety and keep guests from spending their entertainment budgets elsewhere. In New York, TRYP by Wyndham Times Square South partnered with Lobby Friend, a social media app that encourages guests to socialize with each other during their stay. Starwood Hotels and Resorts Worldwide set up a 20-member team to monitor and respond to guests' complaints and suggestions—but not at a desk in the lobby. This team works solely online, constantly monitoring Instagram and Twitter posts by their outspoken guests.

And, of course, hotels are increasing their own online presence, including on Facebook, Twitter, Google+, and YouTube, since the vast majority of travel arrangements are now made online. It's all part of the hotel industry's effort to woo a group whose travel spending has risen rapidly. The business has come a long way from placing chocolates on guests' pillows at night.

QUESTIONS FOR CRITICAL THINKING

1. Hotel chains see millennials as critical to their financial growth. What are some reasons why?
2. How should the hotel industry use social media to connect with younger travelers?

Sources: Brooks Barnes, "But It Doesn't Look Like a Marriott," *The New York Times*, January 11, 2014, www.nytimes.com; Jacqueline Doherty, "On the Rise: The Millennials Are Finally Poised to Start Spending," *Barron's*, accessed January 11, 2014, http://online.barrons.com; Jill Becker, "The Makings of a Modern Hotel," *CNN.com*, accessed January 11, 2014, www.cnn.com; Michelle Groenke, "Millennials Pushing Hotels to Get Up to Speed," *UPI.com*, accessed January 11, 2014, www.upi.com; "Millennials," Social Media on Wyndham's Radar," *Hotel News Now*, accessed January 11, 2014, www.hotelnewsnow.com.

VIDEO CASE 2.2
Nederlander Producing Company Spotlights Customer Rewards

Three to five million people pass through the turnstiles of Nederlander Producing Company theaters each year in New York City. "Why can't they get something for that?" asks James L. Nederlander, president of the company. Nederlander, whose family founded and has run the Nederlander Producing Company for more than 100 years, touches on a central question for every business: How can we serve and reward our customers?

Serving customers, building a relationship with them, and achieving a competitive advantage while doing so requires strategic and tactical planning. Nederlander Producing Company is a third-generation, family-owned company that owns and manages theaters as well as produces and promotes live shows across the United States and the United Kingdom. Nederlander presents diverse acts such as the Bolshoi Ballet, *The Lion King*, and Celine Dion. Strategic planning, which includes identifying Nederlander's primary objectives and figuring out how to attain them, is vital to the company's longevity. One of Nederlander's main objectives is to draw more people toward the performing arts—and keep them there.

Recently, the executive team at Nederlander came up with a new way to do exactly that: Audience Rewards. "When I buy Corn Flakes or a stick of gum, I get points," Nederlander observes. "So why can't our customers get points for buying a theater ticket?" The program functions much like a frequent-flyer plan for theatergoers. Consumers sign up online for free, get a membership number, and start earning points toward rewards, such as free theater tickets, seat upgrades, Broadway merchandise, and even a photo shoot at one of the red-carpet events. The idea is to motivate people to attend the theater more often and try different experiences. It's a tried-and-true tactic with several twists, implemented with digital marketing and the human resources to back it up.

You don't have to see a show to rack up points. You can enter online contests such as "Predictions for Points," in which you predict the 26 Tony Award winners. You automatically get five points for any prediction, but you could win up to 100,000 points if you get them all right. You can answer Audience Rewards trivia questions throughout the year for points as well. And you can score points through Audience Reward partner companies, such as Starwood Hotels, Delta Airlines, United Airlines, Amtrak, Best Buy, and Points.com.

Josh Lesnick, president and CEO of Audience Rewards, notes that large corporations have been eager to become partners in Audience Rewards because "we really bring forward a lifestyle product." For example, a couple who visits New York from Cincinnati may fly on Delta, stay at the Sheraton in Midtown, and buy tickets to see *Wicked*. Then there's the fact that the average annual household income for the Audience Rewards target market hovers around $200,000—and companies such as Starwood and the major airlines want access to those consumers.

Audience Rewards doesn't just benefit theater enthusiasts—it also helps the show go on. Recently, Nederlander ran an Audience Rewards program for the Broadway show *Evita*, in which marketers sent out 5 million emails over 10 days, offering discounts on advance-purchase tickets as well as other perks. The push generated $1 million in presales, allowing the theater producers to strategically reallocate some resources. On a broader scale, the program gives Nederlander and its partners a central platform across which to market different venues and performing arts genres and opens the door to audience development—which circles back to that initial objective of attracting more theatergoers and keeping them in their seats.

As a first-mover strategy, Audience Rewards has already sealed the premier spot in the entertainment rewards arena. Nederlander has a century of connections to theater owners, producers, and presenters (not to mention its own string of theaters and productions) that would be tough for any competitor to break. "It would be hard for someone else to do an arts rewards program," explains Lesnick, "because you have to have the backing of theater companies, and they already back ours."

QUESTIONS FOR CRITICAL THINKING

1. How does the Audience Rewards program support Nederlander's overall strategic plan?

2. It might seem as though Nederlander's first-mover strategy has the entertainment rewards market locked up. But what strategies and tactics could a second-strategy mover use to gain access to theater customers?

Sources: "About Nederlander," accessed January 6, 2014; www.nederlander.com; "About Audience Rewards," www.audiencerewards.com, accessed January 6, 2014; "The Broadway League Names Audience Rewards the Official Patron Loyalty Program for Broadway," *PR Newswire*, accessed January 6, 2014, www.prnewswire.com; "American Airlines Takes the Stage at the Nederlander Organization with New Partnership in New York City," *PR Newswire*, accessed January 6, 2014, www.prnewswire.com.

NOTES

1. Jennifer Saba and Alexei Oreskovic, "Yahoo CEO Mayer Has Advertisers' Attention, But Can She Get Their Dollars?" *Reuters*, accessed January 6, 2014, www.reuters.com; Holly Magister, "How to Sell Your Business to Yahoo," *Forbes*, accessed January 6, 2014, www.forbes.com; Todd Wasserman, "12 Things We Learned about Marissa Mayer in 'Vogue,'" *Mashable.com*, accessed January 6, 2014, http://www.mashable.com; Nanette Fondas, "Marissa Mayer's Potentially Revolutionary Paternity Leave Policy," *Atlantic*, accessed January 5, 2014, www.theatlantic.com; "Marissa Mayer," *Forbes*, accessed January 5, 2014, www.forbes.com; Christopher Tkaczyk, "Marissa Mayer Breaks Her Silence on Yahoo's Policy," *Fortune*, accessed January 5, 2014, http://tech.fortune.cnn.com; Patricia Sellers, "Marissa Mayer: Ready to Rumble at Yahoo," *Fortune*, accessed January 5, 2014, http://postcards.blogs.fortune.cnn.com.

2. Elizabeth Howell, "NBC to Broadcast Virgin Galactic's First Commercial Spaceflight," *Universe Today*, accessed January 5, 2014, www.universetoday.com; Alexandra Wolfe, "Richard Branson on Space Travel," *The Wall Street Journal*, accessed January 5, 2014, http://online.wsj.com; Frank Barrett, "Out of This World! Countdown Is on as Virgin Galactic Prepares for First Space Tourists," *Daily Mail*, accessed January 5, 2014, www.dailymail.uk.

3. Company website, www.shuttleworth.com, accessed January 6, 2014.

4. Company website, www.pg.com, accessed January 6, 2014; *Statisticbrain.com*, accessed January 6, 2014, www.statisticbrain.com.

5. Robert Wall, "U.S. Orders Airlines to Fly at Higher Altitudes over Iraq," *The Wall Street Journal*, accessed August 8, 2014, http://online.wsj.com.

6. Pam Dyer, "Does Social Media Drive ROI? Many Brands Are Still Plagued by This Question," *Social Media Today*, accessed January 6, 2014, http://socialmediatoday.com.

7. Caroline Van Hasselt and Leslie Scism, "Sun Life Revamps Its U.S. Strategy," *The Wall Street Journal*, accessed January 6, 2014, http://online.wsj.com.

8. Company website, www.appnexus.com, accessed January 6, 2014; company website, http://doubleclick.com, accessed January 6, 2014.

9. Roberto A. Ferdman, "McDonald's Is Taking Its Coffee War with Starbucks Straight to Your Kitchen," *Quartz.com*, accessed January 6, 2014, http://qz.com.

10. Shelley DuBois, "The Last Big All-American Soda Company," *Fortune*, accessed January 6, 2014, http://management.fortune.cnn.com; Gregory Karp, "Soldier Field Drops Coke for Dr Pepper Snapple Group," *Chicago Tribune*, accessed January 6, 2014, http://articles.chicagotribune.com; Karen Robinson-Jacobs, "Soft Drink Sales Fizzle Again, Dr Pepper Gains Ground," *Dallas News*, accessed January 6, 2014, www.dallasnews.com; Nanette Byrnes, "Why Dr Pepper Is in the Pink of Health," *Bloomberg Businessweek*, accessed January 6, 2014, www.businessweek.com.

11. E.J. Schultz, "Campbell Eyes 200 New Products from Soup to Sauce," *Advertising Age*, accessed January 6, 2014, www.adage.com.

12. Derek F. Abell, "Strategic Windows," *Journal of Marketing*, 42, no. 3 (July 1978), pp. 21–26, http://www.commerce.uct.ac.za.

13. Chloe Albanesius, "Add Movies to Walmart's 'Disc to Digital' Library from Home," *PC Magazine*, accessed January 6, 2014, www.pcmag.com.

14. Company website, www.platoscloset.com, accessed January 6, 2014.

15. Jeff Beer, "Fortune Cookie: Selling Oreos in China," *HSBC Global Connections*, accessed January 7, 2014, http://globalconnections.hsbc.com.

16. "Hispanic Americans by the Numbers," *Infoplease.com*, accessed January 7, 2014, www.infoplease.com.

17. Namrata Singh, "Indian Consumers Show Both Impulsive and Compulsive Buying Behaviour: Ipsos," *Times of India*, accessed January 7, 2014, http://timesofindia.indiatimes.com.

18. Company website, www.kohls.com, accessed January 6, 2014; Rebecka Schumann, "National Coffee Day 2013: Starbucks, Dunkin' Donuts, and 4 Other Places Where You Can Get a Free Cup of Joe," *International Business Times*, accessed January 6, 2014, www.ibtimes.com.

19. "Bucking the Trend—High-Income Shoppers Visiting Dollar Stores, Reports Mintel," *PR Newswire*, accessed January 5, 2014, www.printthis.clickability.com; Phil Wahba, "Abercrombie & Fitch Same-Store Sales Plummet, Outlook Weak," *Reuters*, accessed January 5, 2014, www.reuters.com; Amy Merrick, 'The End of Saks As We Knew It," *New Yorker*, accessed January 5, 2014, www.newyorker.com.

20. U.S. Department of Commerce, "Doing Business in Romania," http://export.gov, accessed January 6, 2014.

21. Company website, "Marriott Mobile Apps," www.marriott.com, accessed January 6, 2014; Rebecca Borison, "Domino's Earns Consumer Loyalty with Mobile at the Forefront," *Mobile Commerce Daily*, accessed January 6, 2014, www.mobilecommercedaily.com; Kate Taylor, "From Starbucks to Domino's: 6 Tasty Companies with Awesome Mobile Apps," *Entrepreneur*, accessed January 6, 2014, www.entrepreneur.com.

22. Whitson Gordon, "Sometimes It's Better to Ignore Auctions When Selling on eBay," *Lifehacker.com*, accessed January 6, 2014, http://lifehacker.com; Kyle Stock, "An Auction? Most eBay Users Don't Have Time for That," *Bloomberg Businessweek*, accessed January 6, 2014, www.businessweek.com.

23. Ambrose McNevin, "IBM Systems and Technology Group Strategy Revealed," *Datacenter Dynamics*, accessed January 6, 2014, www.datacenterdynamics.com.

24. Company website, "Apple Reports Fourth Quarter Results," press release, www.apple.com, accessed January 6, 2014.

25. Matt Smith, "Meet Microsoft, the World's Best Kept R&D Secret," *TechHive*, accessed January 6, 2014, www.techhive.com.

26. John Carney, "The Student Loan Bubble Is Starting to Burst," *CNBC.com*, accessed January 7, 2014, www.cnbc.com.

27. Company website, www.blaircandy.com, accessed January 6, 2014.

28. "Was 3D TV an Epic Failure? ESPN to End Broadcasts," *Associated Press*, accessed January 6, 2014, www.foxnews.com; Travis Hoium, "Why 3-D TV Has Been an Epic Failure," *Daily Finance*, accessed January 6, 2014, www.dailyfinance.com.

29. Organization website, "Sodium and Food Sources," www.cdc.gov, accessed January 6, 2014.Apple exemplifies the marketing concept, creating consistently stylish and cutting-edge products. When Apple releases a new product or a new version of an existing product, people line up to purchase the new model.

Chapter 3

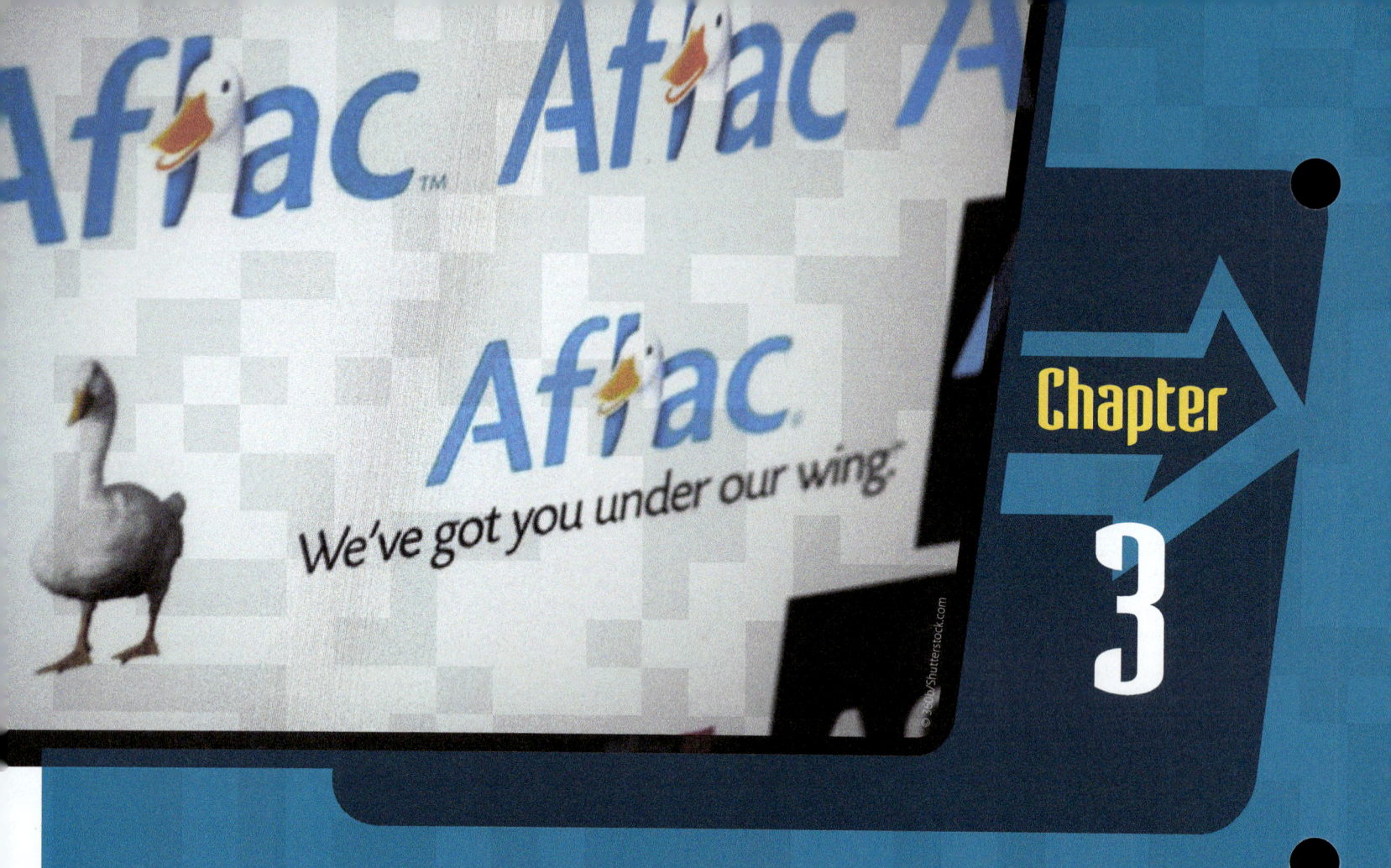

The Marketing Environment, Ethics, and Social Responsibility

1. Identify the five components of the marketing environment.
2. Explain the types of competition marketers face and the steps necessary for developing a competitive strategy.
3. Describe how marketing activities are regulated and how marketers can influence the political–legal environment.
4. Outline the economic factors that affect marketing decisions and consumer buying power.
5. Discuss the impact of the technological environment on a firm's marketing activities.
6. Explain how the social–cultural environment influences marketing.
7. Describe the ethical issues in marketing.
8. Identify the four levels of the social responsibility pyramid.

AFLAC LEADS THE WAY IN ETHICS

Although its representative in TV commercials and other media is an amusing white duck, Aflac Incorporated is a major contender in its industry. With more than 60 million customers, the company is the number-one provider of supplemental life and health insurance in the United States and Japan. Based in Georgia, it was founded by three brothers and is still a family-managed operation, now with almost 8,400 employees. Aflac has also acquired an enviable reputation as a highly ethical company.

Ethisphere Institute, an international organization for the advancement of business ethics, has chosen Aflac as one of the "world's most ethical companies" for seven consecutive years. (Companies in more than 100 countries are nominated every year.) The firm has also been one of *Fortune* magazine's "world's most admired companies" for 12 years, up from second place and ranking first in the industry on several key attributes including people management, quality of management, quality of products/services, and use of corporate assets.

What goes along with being most admired? Being a good employer is a key factor. Aflac has also made *Fortune*'s prestigious list of 100 best companies to work for every year for the last 15 years. Other recognition includes being one of *Black Enterprise* magazine's 40 best companies for diversity for eight years running, and one of *Latina Style* magazine's 50 best companies for Latinas to work for in 13 of the last 15 years. *Computerworld* magazine feels the same, listing the company among its 100 best places to work in IT every year since 1999, and *Training* magazine recognized Aflac for its outstanding workforce development program 10 years in a row.

Women make up more than 50 percent of Aflac's management team (holding positions at the supervisory level or higher), and four in ten employees are minorities. In fact, almost three in ten are minority women, and all employees enjoy benefits such as flexible work schedules and onsite health care. Appropriately for a company in the health insurance business, Aflac offers free mammograms and breast cancer screenings as well. It was the first company to allow shareholders to have input on executive compensation, and its CEO turned down a $2 million bonus several years ago when the company's stock value declined. At Aflac, ethical leadership comes from the top.[1]

EVOLUTION OF A BRAND

For more than a decade, Aflac has been recognized for its ethical approach to business. Using a duck as its spokesperson in various media outlets, Aflac markets its business by reaching out to consumers and educating them about the company's insurance products in a humorous way. In a recent ad campaign, Duck is in physical rehab, recovering from an injury that could plague many consumers who miss work and incur lost wages—without Aflac's supplemental insurance.

- When the actor who gave Duck his original "quack" posted negative tweets about the Japanese earthquake, Aflac took swift action and fired him. Rather than ignore the firing as part of its business strategy, the company collaborated with its marketing partners, including Monster.com, and posted the "quack" opening on its website. How does Aflac's unique approach help build brand identity?
- Duck has a personal Facebook page with close to half a million fans. How can social media play an important role in Aflac's marketing strategies?
- Aflac is a sponsor of college football's annual Heisman Trophy award for the top football player. How does that media exposure help Aflac market its products to consumers of all ages?

Chapter Overview

1. Identify the five components of the marketing environment.

> **Briefly Speaking**
> "Being good is good business."
> —**Anita Roddick**
> Entrepreneur and founder of The Body Shop retail chain

Change is a fact of life for all people, including marketers. Adapting to change in an environment as complex and unpredictable as the world's energy usage is perhaps the supreme challenge. The airline industry was hit hard when the price of oil skyrocketed. In response, airlines such as Delta and United removed their less fuel-efficient aircraft from service and eliminated flights. Despite those moves, high energy costs continue to affect the bottom line—for airlines and the rest of the world. Delta bought an oil refinery to help reduce its jet fuel costs, and the Pennsylvania refinery recently posted its first quarterly profit for the airline.[2]

Although some change may be the result of sudden crises, more often it is the result of a gradual trend in lifestyle, income, population, and other factors. Consumers are increasingly interested in buying "green" products—goods that minimize their impact on the environment. Technology can trigger a sudden change in the marketplace: In a short period of time, it appeared that Internet music downloads had replaced traditional CDs. And within mere months of offering its iPhone, Apple introduced the iPod Touch MP3 player, which borrowed touchscreen technology from the iPhone.

Marketers must anticipate and plan for change. They must set goals to meet the concerns of customers, employees, shareholders, and the general public. Industry competition, legal constraints, the impact of technology on product designs, and social concerns are some of the many important factors that shape the business environment. All potentially have an impact on a firm's goods and services. Decision makers must still consider those influences together with the variables of the marketing mix in developing, and occasionally modifying, marketing plans and strategies that take these environmental factors into consideration.

This chapter begins by describing five forces in marketing's external environment: competitive, political–legal, economic, technological, and social–cultural. Figure 3.1 identifies them as the foundation for making decisions that involve the four marketing mix elements and the target market. These forces provide the frame of reference within which all marketing decisions are made. The second focus of this chapter is marketing ethics and social responsibility. That section describes the nature of marketers' responsibilities both to business and to society at large.

FIGURE 3.1
Elements of the Marketing Mix within an Environmental Framework

ENVIRONMENTAL SCANNING AND ENVIRONMENTAL MANAGEMENT

environmental scanning Process of collecting information about the external marketing environment to identify and interpret potential trends.

Marketers constantly monitor crucial trends and developments in the business environment. **Environmental scanning** is the process of collecting information about the external marketing environment to identify and interpret potential trends. The goal of this process is to analyze the information and decide whether these trends represent significant opportunities or pose major threats to the company. The firm can then determine the best response to a particular environmental change.

In the United States, the Consumer Product Safety Commission (CPSC) is responsible for keeping unsafe products out of the marketplace. For example, it issued a recall of children's books due to choking and laceration hazards. A small rod holding beads on the book's cover can detach and release small parts that present a choking hazard to children. The CPSC also banned drop-side cribs after 150 babies died from injuries suffered when the cribs malfunctioned. The ban led to numerous recalls by crib manufacturers and retailers.[3]

environmental management Attainment of organizational objectives by predicting and influencing the competitive, political–legal, economic, technological, and social–cultural environments.

Environmental scanning is a vital component of effective **environmental management**. Environmental management involves marketers' efforts to achieve organizational objectives by predicting and influencing the competitive, political–legal, economic, technological, and social–cultural environments. In the political–legal environment, managers who seek modifications of regulations, laws, or tariff restrictions may lobby legislators or contribute to political campaigns. Consumer groups lobbying on behalf of credit card users persuaded Congress to create rules regarding credit cards—for example, barring banks from creating minimum interest rates, or "floors"; forbidding card issuers from arbitrarily picking dates with the highest prime rate to apply to interest rates; and prohibiting them from automatically enrolling cardholders in over-the-limit protection.[4]

strategic alliances Partnership in which two or more companies combine resources and capital to create competitive advantages in a new market.

For many domestic and international firms, competing with established industry leaders frequently involves **strategic alliances**—partnerships with other firms in which the partners combine resources and capital to create competitive advantages in a new market. Strategic alliances are especially common in international marketing, in which partnerships with local firms provide regional expertise for a company expanding its operations abroad. Members of such alliances share risks and profits. Alliances are considered essential in a country such as China, where laws require foreign firms doing business there to work with local companies.

Through successful research and development efforts, firms may influence changes in their own technological environments. A research breakthrough may lead to reduced production costs or a technologically superior new product. While changes in the marketing environment may be beyond the control of individual marketers, managers continually seek to predict their impact on marketing decisions and to modify operations to meet changing market needs. Even modest environmental shifts can alter the results of those decisions.

As an issue of safety, the Consumer Product Safety Commission recalled several children's books due to possible safety hazards—the small rod on the book cover could detach and release the colorful beads, which could cause choking.

ASSESSMENT CHECK

1.1 Define environmental scanning.

1.2 How does environmental scanning contribute to environmental management?

THE COMPETITIVE ENVIRONMENT

competitive environment Interactive process that occurs in the marketplace among marketers of directly competitive products, marketers of products that can be substituted for one another, and marketers competing for the consumer's purchasing power.

monopoly Market structure in which a single seller dominates trade in a good or service for which buyers can find no close substitutes.

As organizations vie to satisfy customers, the interactive exchange creates the **competitive environment**. Marketing decisions by individual firms influence consumer responses in the marketplace. They also affect the marketing strategies of competitors. As a consequence, marketers must continually monitor their competitors' marketing activities: their products, distribution channels, prices, and promotional efforts.

Few organizations have **monopoly** positions as the sole supplier of a good or service in the marketplace. Utilities, such as natural gas, electricity, water, and cable TV service, have traditionally accepted considerable regulation from local authorities who controlled marketing-related factors such as rates, service levels, and geographic coverage. In exchange, the utilities gained exclusive rights to serve a particular group of consumers. But the deregulation movement in recent decades has ended total monopoly protection for most utilities. Many shoppers can choose from alternative cable TV and Internet providers, cell phone and traditional telephone carriers, and even gas and electric utilities. Some firms, such as pharmaceutical giants Merck and Pfizer, have *temporary* monopolies provided by patents on new drugs. When the U.S. Food and Drug Administration (FDA) approves a new drug, its manufacturer typically is granted exclusive rights to produce and market the product during the life of the patent. This gives the manufacturer a chance to recoup the millions spent on developing and launching the drug. Once the patent expires, all bets are off, and competitors can flood the market with generic versions of the drug.

antitrust Laws designed to prevent restraints on trade such as business monopolies.

But what about professional sports teams who are part of a league? Is it lawful for their league to operate as a monopoly without violating U.S. **antitrust** laws? Consider the experience of apparel manufacturer American Needle. For 20 years, the company had a contract to make team caps for the National Football League, but it lost the business after the league engaged Reebok as its exclusive provider. American Needle sued the NFL, saying its 32 teams had operated as a monopoly in terms of licensed providers. In a 9-0 ruling, the Supreme Court of the United States ruled that the NFL had violated antitrust laws. The case is still in litigation in the federal courts.[5]

oligopoly Market structure in wjhich relatively few sellers compete and where high start-up costs form barriers to keep out new competitors.

Rather than seeking sole dominance of a market, corporations increasingly prefer to share the pie with just a few rivals. Referred to by economists as an **oligopoly**, this structure of a limited number of sellers in an industry in which high start-up costs form barriers to keep out new competitors deters newcomers from breaking into markets while ensuring that corporations remain innovative. Commercial airplane manufacturers operate within an oligopolistic industry, currently dominated by Europe-based Airbus Industrie and U.S.-based Boeing. After earlier failures at building and marketing commercial airplanes, the Chinese government once again is attempting to enter this exclusive club. With increasing numbers of Chinese air travelers, the government founded the Commercial Aircraft Corporation of China to build fuel-efficient jets domestically, in the hope that China can "buy local" and reduce its dependence on aircraft made in the West. China's "Big Plane" project for the C919 is scheduled to debut its first test flight soon.[6]

TYPES OF COMPETITION

2 Explain the types of competition marketers face and the steps necessary for devel oping a competitive strategy.

Marketers face three types of competition. The most *direct* form occurs among marketers of similar products, as when a competitive gas station such as Marathon opens across the street from a Shell retail outlet. The cell phone market provides consumers with alternative suppliers such as Verizon, AT&T, and T-Mobile.

Costco, which sells everything from home generators to birthday cakes, also takes direct aim at luxury retailers. The largest U.S. warehouse club operator, Costco offers diamond jewelry, billiard tables, and even Suzuki pianos.[7]

A second type of competition is *indirect,* involving products that are easily substituted. In the fast-food industry, pizza competes with chicken, hamburgers, and tacos. In entertainment, a movie could be substituted for a concert or a night at the bowling alley. Six Flags and Universal Studios amusement parks—traditional hot spots for family vacations—now compete with outdoor adventure trips. Many adults in the United States will decide not to make this year's vacation a tranquil week at the beach or a trip to Disney World. Instead, they'll choose to do something more adventurous—thrill-filled experiences such as skydiving, whitewater rafting, or climbing a nearby mountain. So marketers have to find ways to attract consumers to their specific brand as well as to their type of product.

A change such as a price increase or an improvement in a product's attributes can also affect demand for substitute products. As the prices for one type of energy soar, consumers look for cheaper, and more environmentally friendly, alternatives. Growing consumer interest in energy efficiency has led shoppers to look for products that have earned the ENERGY STAR designation. Administered jointly by the U.S. Environmental Protection Agency and the Department of Energy, the program awards the ENERGY STAR credential to appliances, building materials, computers, new homes, tools, and more.[8]

Advances in technology can give rise to other substitute products. Wireless fidelity, or wi-fi, makes the Internet available via radio waves and can be accessed at any number of public "hot spots" in various locations, including airports, coffee shops, hotels, and libraries. The number of registered hot spots continues to grow worldwide, with more than 6 million in existence.[9] While some hosts charge a fee, wi-fi increasingly is offered at no charge.

And as technology continues to advance, industry observers expect wi-fi eventually to be replaced as the wireless standard. The likely successor, LTE (an acronym for long-term evolution), offers enhanced capabilities for numerous applications and boasts a stronger, more secure signal and significantly greater range than does wi-fi. Verizon currently offers LTE in more than 500 markets; AT&T's LTE network spans more than 470 markets.[10]

The final type of competition occurs among all organizations that compete for consumers' purchases. Traditional economic analysis views competition as a battle among companies in the same industry (direct competition) or among substitutable goods and services (indirect competition). But marketers know that *all* firms compete for a limited number of dollars that consumers can or will spend. In this broader sense, competition means that the purchase of a Honda Accord might compete with a Norwegian Cruise Line vacation.

Because the competitive environment often determines the success or failure of a product, marketers must continually assess competitors' marketing strategies. New products, updated features or technology, increased service, and lower prices are variations that marketers look for. When changes occur in the competition, marketers must decide how to respond.

Many hotels offer free wi-fi in their lobbies in an effort to revitalize the space as a social hub for guests and visitors.

DEVELOPING A COMPETITIVE STRATEGY

Marketers at every successful firm must develop an effective strategy for dealing with the competitive environment. One company may compete in a broad range of markets in many areas of the world. Another may specialize in particular market segments, such as those determined by customers' geographic location, age, or income characteristics. Determining a **competitive strategy** involves answering the following three questions:

1. Should we compete?
2. If so, in what markets should we compete?
3. How should we compete?

competitive strategy Methods through which a firm deals with its competitive environment.

Time-based competition allowed for the creation of the electronic boarding pass to expedite the boarding process.

The answer to the first question depends on the firm's resources, objectives, and expected profit potential. A firm may decide not to pursue or continue operating a potentially successful venture that does not mesh with its resources, objectives, or profit expectations. Rupert Murdoch's News Corp., a global media empire, recently completed plans to "demerge" the company's two divisions into separate entities. Publishing assets, including *The Wall Street Journal*, are part of the "new" News Corporation. Broadcasting and film assets, including *Fox News*, are part of 21st Century Fox. The two new companies, as separate entities, will be able to identify and implement cost savings and focus their strategies on their individual markets.[11]

Answering the second question requires marketers to acknowledge their firm's limited resources—sales personnel, advertising budgets, product development capability, and the like. They must allocate these resources to the areas of greatest opportunity. Some companies gain access to new markets or new expertise through acquisitions or mergers. SAP, a leading provider of business management software, bought SuccessFactors, a leader in cloud-based human capital management solutions. The purchase enabled SAP to expand its position in the cloud, strengthen its presence in the growing human capital management market, and gain a greater foothold in social media—an area where SuccessFactors excels.[12]

Answering the third question on the list requires marketers to make product, distribution, promotion, and pricing decisions that give the firm a competitive advantage in the marketplace. Firms can compete on various bases, including product quality, price, and customer service. Family-owned Von Maur is an upscale department store, opened in 1872 in Davenport, Iowa. It now has 29 stores in 13 states across the Midwest and the South, thriving in a competitive retail marketplace on the basis of superlative customer service. Von Maur offers free shipping, free gift-wrapping service, and an interest-free charge account.[13]

TIME-BASED COMPETITION

time-based competition Strategy of developing and distributing goods and services more quickly than competitors.

With increased international competition and rapid changes in technology, a steadily growing number of firms use time as a strategic competitive weapon. **Time-based competition** is the strategy of developing and distributing products more quickly than competitors. Although a video option on cell phones came late to the U.S. market, the new feature has been a big hit, attracting new customers to cell phone providers. The flexibility and responsiveness of time-based competitors enable them to improve product quality, reduce costs, and expand product offerings to satisfy new market segments and enhance customer satisfaction.

In rapidly changing markets, particularly those that involve technology, time-based competition is critical to a firm's success. The Transportation Security Administration (TSA) piloted the use of smartphone technology to move passengers through airports more quickly and to reduce the incidence of fake boarding passes. The innovation—the electronic boarding pass—is now in use on many airlines, including Alaska, Delta, and United. With its encrypted barcode, the boarding pass is transmitted directly to a passenger's cell phone or personal digital assistant (PDA), typically from an airline's mobile app. At check-in, the passenger simply presents the phone or PDA to a TSA officer, who uses a scanner to validate the barcode.[14]

ASSESSMENT CHECK

2.1 Distinguish between direct and indirect competition, and give an example of each.

2.2 What is time-based competition?

THE POLITICAL–LEGAL ENVIRONMENT

Before you play the game, learn the rules! You may find it hard to win a new game without first understanding the rules. Yet some businesspeople exhibit a lack of knowledge about marketing's **political–legal environment**—the laws and their interpretations that require firms to operate under competitive conditions and to protect consumer rights.

The existing U.S. legal framework was constructed piecemeal, often in response to issues that were important when individual laws were enacted. Businesspeople must be diligent to understand the legal system's relationship to their marketing decisions. Numerous laws and regulations affect those decisions, many of them vaguely stated and inconsistently enforced by a multitude of different authorities.

Federal, state, and local regulations affect marketing practices, as do the actions of independent regulatory agencies. These requirements and prohibitions touch on all aspects of marketing decision making: designing, labeling, packaging, distributing, advertising, and promoting goods and services. To cope with the vast, complex, and changing political–legal environment, many large firms maintain in-house legal departments; small firms often seek professional advice from outside attorneys. All marketers, however, should be aware of the major regulations that affect their activities.

> **political–legal environment**
> Component of the marketing environment consisting of laws and their interpretations that require firms to operate under competitive conditions and to protect consumer rights.

GOVERNMENT REGULATION

The history of U.S. government regulation can be divided into four phases. The first phase was the *antimonopoly period* of the late 19th and early 20th centuries. During this era, major laws, such as the Sherman Antitrust Act, Clayton Act, and Federal Trade Commission Act, were passed to maintain a competitive environment by reducing the trend toward increasing concentration of industry power in the hands of a small number of competitors. Laws enacted more than 100 years ago still affect business in the 21st century.

The Microsoft case is a good example of antitrust legislation at work. The U.S. Department of Justice was successful in proving Microsoft guilty of predatory practices designed to crush competition. By bundling its own Internet Explorer browser with its Windows operating system—which runs 90 percent of the world's personal computers—Microsoft grabbed the majority of the market from rival Netscape. It also bullied firms as large as America Online to drop Netscape Navigator in favor of its browser. Microsoft countered that consumers have clearly benefited from the integrated features in Windows and that its bundling decisions were simply efforts to offer customer satisfaction through added value.

The second phase, aimed at *protecting competitors*, emerged during the Great Depression era of the 1930s, when independent merchants felt the need for legal protection against competition from larger chain stores. Among the federal legislation enacted was the Robinson-Patman Act. The third regulatory phase focused on *consumer protection*. The objective of consumer protection underlies most laws, with good examples including the Sherman Act, Federal Trade Commission Act, and Federal Food and Drug Act.

Additional laws have been enacted over the past 45 years. The fourth phase, *industry deregulation*, began in the late 1970s and continues to the present. During this phase, government has sought to increase competition in industries such as telecommunications, utilities, transportation, and financial services by discontinuing many regulations and permitting firms to expand their service offerings to new markets.

The newest regulatory frontier is *cyberspace*. Federal and state regulators are investigating ways to police the Internet and online services. The Federal Trade Commission (FTC), along with private organizations and other government agencies, has created a site, www.onguardonline.gov, where consumers can take quizzes designed to educate them about identity theft, spam (junk email), phishing (luring consumers to provide personal information), and online shopping scams. But cyber crime continues to be an issue. Attacks by malicious software that contain codes capable of stealing account logins, passwords, and other confidential data are on the rise. Numerous state laws as well as the federal Identity Theft Enforcement and Restitution Act enable victims of

> **3** Describe how marketing activities are regulated and how marketers can influence the political–legal environment.

identity theft to seek restitution and make it easier for the government to prosecute phishing and those who threaten to steal or divulge information from a computer.[15]

Privacy and child protection issues are another important—but difficult—enforcement challenge. With the passage of the Children's Online Privacy Protection Act, Congress took the first step in regulating what children are exposed to on the Internet. The primary focus is a set of rules regarding how and when marketers need to get parental permission before obtaining marketing research information from children over the Web. The act was later revised to address the way children use and access the Internet, with additional emphasis on mobile devices and social networking. Finally, the government's Do Not Call Registry, a list to which consumers can add their phone numbers, including cell phones, to avoid telemarketing calls, provides protection for consumers who do not want to be contacted by telemarketers. The law exempts callers representing not-for-profit organizations, companies with which the consumer has an existing relationship, and political candidates. Telemarketing firms must check the list quarterly, with fines of more than $16,000 per occurrence. The government aggressively pursues offenders, resulting in settlements often totaling millions of dollars.[16]

Table 3.1 lists and briefly describes the major federal laws affecting marketing. Legislation covering specific marketing practices, such as product development, packaging, labeling, product warranties, and franchise agreements, is discussed in later chapters.

Marketers must also monitor state and local laws that affect their industries. Many states, for instance, allow hard liquor to be sold only in liquor stores, while others prohibit the sale of alcoholic beverages on Sunday. California's stringent regulations for automobile emissions require special pollution control equipment on cars sold in the state.

TABLE 3.1 Major Federal Laws Affecting Marketing

Date	Law	Description
A. Laws Maintaining a Competitive Environment		
1890	Sherman Antitrust Act	Prohibits restraint of trade and monopolization; identifies a competitive marketing system as a national policy goal.
1914	Clayton Act	Strengthens the Sherman Act by restricting practices such as price discrimination, exclusive dealing, tying contracts, and interlocking boards of directors where the effect "may be to substantially lessen competition or tend to create a monopoly"; amended by the Celler-Kefauver Antimerger Act to prohibit major asset purchases that would decrease competition in an industry.
1914	Federal Trade Commission Act (FTC)	Prohibits unfair methods of competition; establishes the Federal Trade Commission, an administrative agency that investigates business practices and enforces the FTC Act.
1938	Wheeler-Lea Act	Amends the FTC Act to outlaw additional unfair practices; gives the FTC jurisdiction over false and misleading advertising.
1998	Digital Millennium Copyright Act	Protects intellectual property rights by prohibiting copying or downloading of digital files.
B. Laws Regulating Competition		
1936	Robinson-Patman Act	Prohibits price discrimination in sales to wholesalers, retailers, or other producers; prohibits selling at unreasonably low prices to eliminate competition.
1993	North American Free Trade Agreement (NAFTA)	International trade agreement between Canada, Mexico, and the United States designed to facilitate trade by removing tariffs and other trade barriers among the three nations.

(continued)

TABLE 3.1 Major Federal Laws Affecting Marketing (continued)

Date	Law	Description
C. Laws Protecting Consumers		
1906	Federal Food and Drug Act	Prohibits adulteration and misbranding of food and drugs involved in interstate commerce; strengthened by the Food, Drug, and Cosmetic Act (1938) and the Kefauver-Harris Drug Amendment (1962).
1970	National Environmental Policy Act	Establishes the Environmental Protection Agency to deal with various types of pollution and organizations that create pollution.
1971	Public Health Cigarette Smoking Act	Prohibits tobacco advertising on radio and television.
1972	Consumer Product Safety Act	Created the Consumer Product Safety Commission, which has authority to specify safety standards for most products.
1998	Children's Online Privacy Protection Act	Empowers FTC to set rules regarding how and when marketers must obtain parental permission before asking children marketing research questions. Revised in 2013 to address changes in the way children use and access the Internet and widening the definition of children's personal identification to address ways to track a child's activity on line.
1998	Identity Theft and Assumption Deterrence Act	Makes it a federal crime to unlawfully use or transfer another person's identification with the intent to violate the law.
1999	Anti-Cybersquatting Consumer Protection Act	Bans the bad-faith purchase of domain names that are identical or confusingly similar to existing registered trademarks.
2001	Electronic Signature Act	Gives electronic signatures the same legal weight as handwritten signatures.
2005	Real ID Act	Sets minimum standards for state driver's licenses and ID cards and is currently being phased in.
2006	Consumer Telephone Records Act	Prohibits the sale of cell phone records.
2009	Fraud Enforcement and Recovery Act	Expands government's authority to investigate and prosecute mortgage fraud.
2009	Helping Families Save Their Homes Act	Helps homeowners avoid foreclosure and obtain affordable mortgages.
2009	Credit Card Accountability, Responsibility and Disclosure Act	Provides new rules governing credit card rate increases, fees, billing, and other practices.
D. Laws Deregulating Specific Industries		
1978	Airline Deregulation Act	Grants considerable freedom to commercial airlines in setting fares and choosing new routes.
1980	Motor Carrier Act and Staggers Rail Act	Significantly deregulates trucking and railroad industries by permitting them to negotiate rates and services.
1996	Telecommunications Act	Significantly deregulates the telecommunications industry by removing barriers to competition in local and long-distance phone and cable and television markets.
2003	Amendments to the Telemarketing Sales Rule	Created the National Do Not Call Registry prohibiting telemarketing calls to registered telephone numbers. Restricted the number and duration of telemarketing calls generating dead air space with use of automatic dialers; cracked down on unauthorized billing; and required telemarketers to transmit their caller ID information.
2007	Do-Not-Call Improvement Act	Extends Telemarketing Sales Rule; allows registered numbers to remain on Do Not Call list permanently.
2007	Fee Extension Act	Extends Telemarketing Sales Rule; sets annual fees for telemarketers to access the Do Not Call Registry.

GOVERNMENT REGULATORY AGENCIES

Federal, state, and local governments have established regulatory agencies to enforce laws. At the federal level, the FTC wields the broadest powers of any agency to influence marketing activities. The FTC enforces laws regulating unfair business practices and stops false and deceptive advertising. It regulates communication by wire, radio, and television. Other federal regulatory agencies include the Consumer Product Safety Commission, the Federal Power Commission, the Environmental Protection Agency (EPA), the Food and Drug Administration (FDA), and the National Highway Traffic Safety Administration (NHTSA). But regulatory agencies aren't always known for strict oversight or responding in a timely manner. The NHTSA came under fire for not investigating complaints from GM drivers who reported problems with faulty ignition switches that may move out of the "run" position while driving, shutting down the engine and disabling power brakes, power steering, and airbags. After some resistance and more than a decade, GM was compelled to recall more than 2 million cars and pay a $35 million fine to the NHTSA. More than 54 crashes and 15 deaths have been been linked to the defect. GM CEO Mary Barra appeared before Congress to discuss the recall and the plans GM would put in place to reach out to car owners of the recalled vehicles.[17]

The FTC uses several procedures to enforce laws. It may issue a consent order through which a business accused of violations can agree to voluntary compliance without admitting guilt. If a business refuses to comply with an FTC request, the agency can issue a cease-and-desist order, which gives a final demand to stop an illegal practice. Firms often challenge cease-and-desist orders in court. The FTC can require advertisers to provide additional information about products in their advertisements, and it can force firms using deceptive advertising to correct earlier claims with new promotional messages. In some cases, the FTC can require a firm to give refunds to consumers misled by deceptive advertising.

The FTC and U.S. Department of Justice can stop mergers if they believe the proposed acquisition will reduce competition by making it harder for new companies to enter the field. In recent years, these agencies have taken a harder line on proposed mergers, especially in the computer, telecommunications, financial services, and health-care sectors.

Removing regulations also changes the competitive picture considerably. Following deregulation of the telecommunications and utilities industries, suppliers no longer have exclusive rights to operate within a territory. Natural gas utilities traditionally competed with electric companies to supply homeowners and businesses with energy needs. Because of deregulation, they now also compete with other gas companies. The restructuring of the electricity industry by state took hold immediately in the Northeast, ranging from Maine to Virginia and reaching through the Midwest in Ohio, Michigan, and Illinois. Indiana and Vermont abstained, although both states are now taking a look at deregulation in an effort to increase competition. Texas, Arizona, and Oregon also jumped on the bandwagon. But several states delayed deregulation activities, and California actually suspended them altogether. Restructuring caused major headaches for some utilities, leading to shortages, an inability to coordinate service with needs, nonmaintenance of power lines, and lack of funds for operating or decommissioning nuclear power plants. Thus, while deregulation may be designed to promote competition and provide better service and prices for consumers, it doesn't always work as planned.

The latest round of deregulation began with the passage of the Telecommunications Act of 1996 and its 2003 amendment, the Do Not Call law mentioned earlier. The Telecommunications Act removed barriers between local and long-distance phone companies and cable companies. It allowed the so-called Baby Bells—the regional Bell operating companies—to offer long-distance service; at the same time, long-distance companies offered local service. Satellite television providers such as Dish Network and DIRECTV and cable companies such as Comcast can offer phone service, while phone companies can get into the cable business. The change promises huge rewards for competitive winners. Consumers can shop around for the best deals and packages as more companies compete for their business by packaging services at reduced prices.

OTHER REGULATORY FORCES

Public and private consumer interest groups and self-regulatory organizations are also part of the legal environment. Consumer interest organizations have mushroomed since the late 1970s, and today hundreds of groups operate at national, state, and local levels. These organizations seek to protect consumers in as many areas as possible. Citing the need for a standardized credit scoring system, the three major credit-reporting agencies—Equifax, Experian, and TransUnion—collaborated to create VantageScore. But consumer groups and other industry observers have criticized the system for being inconsistent and of questionable value to consumers.[18] The Coalition for Fire-Safe Cigarettes worked state by state to pressure tobacco companies to produce cigarettes that will not smolder and start fires if left unattended. As a result of the coalition's efforts, laws mandating fire-safe cigarettes have been passed in Canada, the District of Columbia, and all 50 states.[19]

Other groups attempt to advance the rights of minorities, senior citizens, and other causes. The power of these groups has also grown. AARP (formerly known as the American Association of Retired Persons) wields political and economic power, particularly as more and more people reach retirement age.[20]

Self-regulatory groups represent industries' attempts to set guidelines for responsible business conduct. The Council of Better Business Bureaus is a national organization devoted to consumer service and business self-regulation. The council's National Advertising Division (NAD) promotes truth and accuracy in advertising. It reviews and advocates voluntary resolution of advertising-related complaints between consumers and businesses. If NAD fails to resolve a complaint, an appeal can be made to the National Advertising Review Board, composed of advertisers, ad agency representatives, and public members. In addition, many individual trade associations set business guidelines and codes of conduct and encourage members' voluntary compliance.

The Direct Marketing Association (DMA) supports consumer rights through its Commitment to Consumer Choice. Under this principle, DMA's more than 3,600 member organizations are required to inform consumers of their right to modify or discontinue receiving solicitations.[21]

As mentioned earlier, regulating the online world poses a challenge. Favoring self-regulation as the best starting point, the FTC sponsored a privacy initiative for consumers, advertisers, online companies, and others as a way to develop voluntary industry privacy guidelines.

CONTROLLING THE POLITICAL–LEGAL ENVIRONMENT

Most marketers comply with laws and regulations. Doing so not only serves their customers but also avoids legal problems that could ultimately damage a firm's image and hurt profits. But smart marketers get ahead of the curve by providing products that will meet customers' future needs while also addressing government goals. Showing remarkable forward thinking, Toyota was one of the first automakers to commit to building hybrid cars. Its efforts were supported by a government tax break for purchasers of the first hybrids. Other manufactures followed Toyota's lead in manufacturing hybrids, and government tax breaks are still available.

Consumer groups and political action committees within industries may try to influence the outcome of proposed legislation or change existing laws by engaging in political lobbying or boycotts. Lobbying groups frequently enlist the support of customers, employees, and suppliers to assist their efforts.

ASSESSMENT CHECK

3.1 Identify the four phases of U.S. government regulation of business. What is the newest frontier?

3.2 Which federal agency wields the broadest regulatory powers for influencing marketing activities?

THE ECONOMIC ENVIRONMENT

4 Outline the economic factors that affect marketing decisions and consumer buying power.

gross domestic product (GDP) Sum of all goods and services produced by a nation in a year.

economic environment Factors that influence consumer buying power and marketing strategies, including stage of the business cycle, inflation and deflation, unemployment, income, and resource availability.

business cycle Pattern of stages in the level of economic activity: prosperity, recession, depression, and recovery.

The overall health of the economy influences how much consumers spend and what they buy. This relationship also works the other way: consumer buying plays an important role in the economy's health. In fact, consumer spending accounts for about 65 percent of the nation's total **gross domestic product (GDP)**, the sum of all goods and services produced by a nation in a year.[22] Because marketing activities are directed toward satisfying consumer wants and needs, marketers must first understand how economic conditions influence the purchasing decisions consumers make.

Marketing's **economic environment** consists of factors that influence consumer buying power and marketing strategies. They include the stage of the business cycle, the global economy, inflation and deflation, unemployment, income, and resource availability.

STAGES IN THE BUSINESS CYCLE

Historically, the economy has tended to follow a cyclical pattern consisting of four stages: prosperity, recession, depression, and recovery. Consumer buying differs in each stage of the **business cycle**, and marketers must adjust their strategies accordingly. In times of prosperity, consumer spending maintains a brisk pace, and buyers are willing to spend more for premium versions of well-known brands. Growth in services such as banking and restaurants usually indicates a strong economy. When economists predict conditions such as low inflation and low unemployment, marketers respond by offering new products, increasing their promotional efforts, and expanding distribution. They might even raise prices to widen profit margins. But high prices for some items, such as energy, can affect businesses and consumers. Skyrocketing gasoline prices have led many consumers to seek other forms of transportation—for example, taking part in bike-sharing programs in major U.S. cities, including Chicago, New York, and Washington, DC. Divvy, the Chicago bike share program, has more than 300 share stations across the Windy City, which are being used by commuters and tourists alike.[23]

During economic slowdowns, consumers focus on more basic, functional products that carry lower price tags. They limit travel, restaurant meals, and entertainment. They skip expensive

High gas prices have led consumers to seek other forms of transportation. In Chicago, commuters and tourists are using the Divvy bike-sharing program to travel around the Windy City.

vacations and cook their own meals. During a recession, marketers consider lowering prices and increasing promotions that include special offers to stimulate demand. They may also launch special value-priced products likely to appeal to cost-conscious buyers.

Consumer spending sinks to its lowest level during a depression. The last true depression in the United States occurred during the 1930s. Although a severe depression could occur again, most experts see it as a slim possibility. Through its monetary and fiscal policies, the federal government attempts to control extreme fluctuations in the business cycle that lead to depression.

In the recovery stage, the economy emerges from recession and consumer purchasing power increases. But while consumers have money to spend, caution often restrains their willingness to buy. A family might buy a new car if no-interest financing is available. A couple might decide to book a trip through a discount travel firm such as Expedia or Travelocity. Companies such as these can make the most of an opportunity and develop loyal customers by offering superior service at lower prices. Recovery still remains a difficult stage for businesses just climbing out of a recession because they must earn profits while trying to gauge uncertain consumer demand. Many cope by holding down costs. Some trim payrolls and close branch offices. Others cut back on business travel budgets, substituting teleconferencing and videoconferencing.

Business cycles, like other aspects of the economy, are complex phenomena that, despite the efforts of government, businesspeople, and others to control them, sometimes have a life of their own. Unforeseen natural disasters, such as the recent spate of tornadoes and flooding across the United States; the threat of terrorist attacks; and the effects of military conflicts all have an impact on business and the economy as a whole. The most effective marketers know how to recognize ways to serve their customers during the best (and worst) of times.

> **Briefly Speaking**
>
> "The Chinese use two brush strokes to write the word 'crisis.' One brush stroke stands for danger; the other for opportunity. In a crisis, be aware of the danger—but recognize the opportunity."
>
> —**John F. Kennedy**
> *35th President of the United States*

THE GLOBAL ECONOMIC CRISIS

Sometimes business cycles take a severe turn and affect consumers and businesses across the globe. That is the case with the recent recession, called the worst economic downturn since the Great Depression of the 1930s. Typically, nations' GDP rates grow—some modestly at 2 percent to 4 percent a year and some, such as India's and China's, near double digits. With the crisis, some economists predicted that the world economy might shrink for the first time in 60 years.

A struggling economy generates its own downward spiral: Fearing worse days ahead, consumers and businesses become cautious about spending money and, as they spend less, demand for many products also drops. Lessened demand forces employers to take extraordinary steps just to stay in business: institute a shortened workweek with reduced salaries or even slash the workforce.

Especially during a recession, marketers look to emphasize value in their offerings. Some slash prices or offer sales to help customers stretch their budget dollars. Retailers that emphasize affordable products, such as Walmart and McDonald's, saw their sales increase. With the severity of a recession, all marketers need to reevaluate their strategies and concentrate on their most promising products.

INFLATION AND DEFLATION

A major constraint on consumer spending, which can occur during any stage of the business cycle, is inflation—rising prices caused by some combination of excess demand and increases in the costs of raw materials, component parts, human resources, or other factors of production. **Inflation** devalues money by reducing the products it can buy through persistent price increases. These rising prices increase marketers' costs, such as expenditures for wages and raw materials, and the resulting higher prices may therefore negatively affect sales. U.S. inflation hit a heart-stopping high of 13.3 percent in 1979. Recently, annual inflation has hovered around 2.0 percent.[24]

inflation Rising prices caused by some combination of excess consumer demand and increases in the costs of one or more factors of production.

If inflation is so bad, is its opposite, *deflation*, better? At first, it might seem so. Falling prices mean that products are more affordable. But deflation can be a long and damaging downward spiral, causing a freefall in business profits, lower returns on most investments, and widespread job layoffs. The last time the United States experienced significant deflation was in the Great Depression of the 1930s.

Unemployment

unemployment
Proportion of people in the economy actively seeking work that do not have jobs.

Unemployment is defined as the proportion of people in the economy who are actively seeking work but do not have jobs. Unemployment rises during recessions and declines in the recovery and prosperity stages of the business cycle. Like inflation, unemployment affects the way consumers behave. Unless safety nets such as unemployment insurance, personal savings, and union benefits effectively offset lost earnings, unemployed people have relatively little money to spend; they buy food, pay the rent or mortgage, and try to keep up with utility bills.

Income

Income is another important determinant of marketing's economic environment because it influences consumer buying power. By studying income statistics and trends, marketers can estimate market potential and plan to target specific market segments. A rise in income represents potential for increasing overall sales. Many marketers are particularly interested in **discretionary income**, the amount of money people have to spend after buying necessities such as food, clothing, and housing. Those whose industry involves the necessities seek to turn those needs into preferences for their goods and services. Emerging from the recent recession, American consumers experienced a slight increase in their net worth and personal income.[25]

discretionary income
Money available to spend after buying necessities such as food, clothing, and housing.

Changes in average earnings powerfully affect discretionary income. Historically, periods of major innovation have been accompanied by dramatic increases in living standards and rising incomes. Automobiles, televisions, telephones, and computers are just a few of the innovations that have changed consumers' lives—and standards of living. The Bureau of Economic Analysis, a division of the U.S. Department of Commerce, tracks personal income and discretionary income in the United States, then determines how much of that income is spent on personal consumption. Marketers can use these figures to plan their approaches to everything from product development to the promotion of their goods and services.

Not only does income affect how much money individuals donate to not-for-profit organizations, but it can also affect the amount of time they're willing to spend on charitable efforts. And some firms have also demonstrated their commitment not only to charities but also to conducting business in a responsible manner. Such activities often fall under the theme of corporate social responsibility (CSR). But charitable giving is not all there is to CSR, as the "Career Readiness" feature shows.

RESOURCE AVAILABILITY

Resources are not unlimited. Shortages, temporary or permanent, can result from several conditions, including political instability, high fuel costs, and the lack of raw materials, component parts, or labor. The global financial crisis, coupled with extreme weather conditions such as drought and typhoons, suggest the possibility of isolated worldwide food shortages.[26]

demarketing Process of reducing consumer demand for a good or service to a level that the firm can supply.

One reaction to a shortage is **demarketing**, the process of reducing consumer demand for a product to a level that the firm can reasonably supply. Oil companies publicize tips for consumers on how to cut gasoline consumption, and utility companies encourage homeowners to install more insulation to reduce heating costs. Volvo's mobile app, Commute Greener!, encourages environmentally friendly commuting. Users can calculate the environmental impact of their trips to and from work or school and can form groups on Facebook to create friendly competition around green commuting.[27] A shortage presents marketers with a unique set of challenges. They may have to allocate limited supplies, a sharply different activity from marketing's traditional objective of expanding sales volume. Shortages may require marketers to decide whether to

CAREER READINESS
Getting a Job in CSR

Are you eager to turn your passion for environmental causes or "green" technology into a career in corporate social responsibility? You can, if you keep some important ideas in mind.

1. *Make sure you know what CSR really is.* While charitable giving still plays a big role in many companies' CSR efforts, and rightly so, it's not the whole story, as this chapter shows. Many CSR experts today feel "it's all about the environment," including problems like climate change and waste reduction.

2. *Be ready to promote your CSR experience.* Don't have any? Volunteer or work a related internship to show your commitment to the field and gain a track record of real accomplishment. It's not enough to say you recycle at home.

3. *Practice your persuasive skills.* Convincing other people within and outside your organization to change their behavior will be a big part of your daily responsibility.

4. *Fine-tune your leadership and communication skills.* These are critical in any field, but particularly in CSR departments that interact with other areas in a company, such as marketing, operations, legal, and human resources.

5. *Cover the basics.* Network with people doing the job, perfect your résumé, study the companies you're interested in, and prepare thoroughly for interviews.

Sources: Logan Harper, "How to Land a Job in Corporate Social Responsibility," *Student Advisor*, accessed January 14, 2014, www.studentadvisor.com; Donna Devaul, "How Can I Get a CSR Job Like Yours?" *GreenBiz.com*, accessed January 14, 2014, www.greenbiz.com; "Landing a CSR Job," *WetFeet.com*, accessed January 14, 2014, www.wetfeet.com; C.B. Bhattacharya, "Corporate Social Responsibility: It's All about Marketing," *Forbes*, accessed January 14, 2014, www.forbes.com; James Epstein-Reeves, "How to Find a CSR Job in a Big Company," *Forbes*, accessed January 14, 2014, www.forbes.com.

---

spread limited supplies over all customers or limit purchases by some customers so that the firm can completely satisfy others.

Marketers have also devised ways to deal with increased demand for fixed amounts of resources. In its annual *Green Book*, the American Council for an Energy-Efficient Economy (ACEEE) gives cars a "green score," rating vehicles on their manufacturers' use of scarce resources and attention to the environment in the production process. The recent winner? The ACEEE rated the hybrid Toyota Prius at the top.[28]

THE INTERNATIONAL ECONOMIC ENVIRONMENT

In today's global economy, marketers must also monitor the economic environment of other nations. Just as in the United States, a recession in Europe or Japan changes consumer and business buying habits. Changes in foreign currency rates compared with the U.S. dollar also affect marketing decisions. Labor costs and other factors affect firms' decisions to shift manufacturing operations overseas, decisions that may result in cutbacks in U.S. jobs and boosts to other nations' workforces. Although U.S. workers worry about the number of jobs sent overseas, some manufacturing remains strong in the United States. While workers in Asia assemble computers, production of computer chips remains in the United States.

As China exports more goods to the world and to the United States in particular, some people voice concern over the widening trade gap. Only recently have broad economic reforms allowed China to play in the global marketplace. Some wonder if China's entry into world markets might help the West economically. They point to China's expanding economy, fueled in part by a growing middle class with vast, untapped marketing potential.[29]

ASSESSMENT CHECK

4.1 Identify and describe briefly the four stages of the business cycle.

4.2 Explain how inflation and income affect consumer buying decisions.

Politics in other countries affects the international economic environment as well. For instance, turmoil in the Middle East continues to affect the oil industry.

The global recession pushed some members of the European Union to the brink of bankruptcy, and the EU and the International Monetary Fund provided financial bailouts for Greece, Ireland, and Portugal. The economies of two other EU members, Spain and Italy, remain sluggish.[30]

THE TECHNOLOGICAL ENVIRONMENT

5 Discuss the impact of the technological environment on a firm's marketing activities.

technological environment Application to marketing of knowledge based on discoveries in science, inventions, and innovations.

The **technological environment** represents the application to marketing of knowledge based on discoveries in science, inventions, and innovations. Technology leads to new goods and services for consumers; it also improves existing products, offers better customer service, and often reduces prices through new, cost-efficient production and distribution methods. Technology can quickly make products obsolete—email, for example, quickly eroded both letter writing and the market for fax machines—but it can just as quickly open new marketing opportunities, sometimes in entirely new industries.

Pets have been wearing RFID—radio-frequency identification—transmitters for years, in case they got lost. Now RFID tags are used in many industries to locate everything from library books to laundry detergent. An RFID tag contains a computer chip with an antenna. A reader scans the tag and transmits the data from the tag to a computer. This innovation means that retailers, manufacturers, and others can locate and track inventory without opening packages. It also means that companies will be able to track consumer behavior in greater detail. Disney unveiled a program called MyMagic+, which will allow visitors to Disney parks to preregister for wristbands embedded with RFID tags. These "MagicBands" will function as room keys, park-entry tickets, Fast Passes, and credit cards. But the use of RFID to track the movement of humans is controversial because of the privacy implications.[31]

Technology can address social concerns. In response to pressure from the World Trade Organization and the U.S. government, automakers used technology to develop more fuel-efficient vehicles and reduce dangerous emissions. Increased use of ethanol made from corn was another solution, but researchers have stepped up efforts to develop biofuels to replace gasoline. One such fuel, cellulosic ethanol, comes from cellulose—grass clippings, wood chips, yard waste—anything organic, even old tires. The biofuel emits significantly less greenhouse gases than gasoline and, if spilled, is less damaging to the environment. Scientists believe advances in technology eventually will make the fuel cost-effective to produce. Meanwhile, several start-up companies are working to create fuel from another organic source: algae. Low cost, fast growing, and carbon neutral, algae shows promise as a source of alternative energy.[32]

Industry, government, colleges and universities, and other not-for-profit institutions all play roles in the development of new technology. Using technology developed by scientists at Argonne National Laboratory, the University of Chicago created a startup company called SmartSignal. The company's patented analytical software monitors machinery and diagnoses problems to head off equipment failures. GE Intelligent Platforms acquired SmartSignal, whose software supports a global clientele.[33]

Another major source of technology is the federal government, including the military. Air bags originated from Air Force ejection seats, digital computers were first designed to calculate artillery trajectories, and the microwave oven is a derivative of military radar systems. Even the Internet was first developed by the U.S. Department of Defense as a secure military communications system. Although the United States has long been the world leader in research, competition from rivals in Europe, Japan, and other Asian countries is intense.

> **Briefly Speaking**
>
> "A lot of things you want to do as part of daily life can now be done over the Internet."
>
> —Marc Andreessen
> *Entrepreneur and venture capitalist*

Chapter 3 The Marketing Environment, Ethics, and Social Responsibility

APPLYING TECHNOLOGY

Marketers monitor the technological environment for a number of reasons. Creative applications of new technologies not only give a firm a definite competitive edge but can also benefit society. Marketers who monitor new technology and successfully apply it may also enhance customer service.

VoIP—Voice over Internet Protocol—has become a viable alternative to traditional telecommunications services provided by telephone companies. Special software transmits phone conversations over the Internet rather than through telephone lines. Globally, VoIP continues to attract growing numbers of users—both consumers and businesses—mainly because of the cost savings. The VoIP business is also growing worldwide, with hundreds of service providers in the United States alone. Skype, now a division of Microsoft, has more than 300 million monthly users.[34]

As convenient as the Internet, cell phones, and wi-fi are for businesspeople and consumers, the networks that facilitate these connections aren't yet compatible with each other. Engineers are working on a new standard that would enable these networks to connect with each other, paving the way for melded services such as video exchanges between a cell phone and a computer. Called the Internet Protocol Multimedia Subsystem (IMS), the new standard attempts to create a common interface so that data can be carried across networks between different devices. The implications for various communications providers are enormous—not only will they find new ways to cooperate, but they will also find new ways to compete.

> **VoIP—Voice over Internet Protocol** A phone connection through a personal computer with any type of broadband Internet connection.

ASSESSMENT CHECK

5.1 What are some of the consumer benefits of technology?

5.2 Why must marketers monitor the technological environment?

THE SOCIAL–CULTURAL ENVIRONMENT

As a nation, the United States is becoming older, more affluent, and more culturally diverse. The birthrate is falling, and subculture populations are rising. People express concerns about the natural environment, buying ecologically friendly products that reduce pollution. They value their time with family and friends, cooking meals at home and exchanging vacation photos over the Internet. Marketers need to track these trends to be in tune with consumers' needs and desires. These aspects of consumer lifestyles help shape marketing's **social–cultural environment**—the relationship between marketing, society, and culture.

To remain competitive, marketers must be sensitive to society's demographic shifts and changing values. These variables affect consumers' reactions to different products and marketing practices. The baby boom generation—the 78 million Americans born between 1946 and 1964—represents a $7 trillion market. As boomers approach and enter retirement, marketers are scrambling to identify their needs and wants. With a longer life expectancy and the hope of more time and money to spend, baby boomers now view retirement much differently than earlier generations did. Marketers already know that boomers feel young at heart and enjoy their leisure time, and they're becoming social media savvy and spend a significant portion of their free time surfing the Web and accessing sites such as Facebook and LinkedIn on their smartphones.[35] Some even launch a second career, starting their own small business. And boomers have a whole new take on the concept of grandparenting. More than past generations, boomer grandparents get actively involved in their grandchildren's daily lives and are more inclined to spend money on them. An estimated 20 percent of all travel involves grandchildren with grandparents, with or without their parents along.

> **6** Explain how the social–cultural environment influences marketing.
>
> **social–cultural environment** Component of the marketing environment consisting of the relationship between the marketer, society, and culture.

Another social–cultural consideration is the increasing importance of cultural diversity. The United States is a mixed society composed of various submarkets, each with its unique values, cultural characteristics, consumer preferences, and purchasing behaviors. In an effort to attract the millions of Hispanic viewers in the United States, satellite and cable TV companies now offer more Spanish-language programming. Spanish-language networks Univision and Telemundo, which once dominated the Hispanic TV market, now face competition from Comcast, Cablevision, Time Warner Cable, DISH Network, and DIRECTV. Traditional media companies are creating networks that target online financial advertising and investment news to Latin American audiences. Nearly 2,500 Hispanic media outlets operate in the United States, with over 100 of the sites online only.[36]

Marketers also need to learn about cultural and societal differences among countries abroad, particularly as business becomes more and more global. Marketing strategies that work in the United States often fail when used in other countries, and vice versa. In many cases, marketers must redesign packages and modify products and advertising messages to suit the tastes and preferences of different cultures. Chapter 8 explores the social–cultural aspects of global marketing.

CONSUMERISM

consumerism Social force within the environment that aids and protects the consumer by exerting legal, moral, and economic pressures on business and government.

Changing societal values have led to **consumerism**, defined as a social force within the environment that aids and protects the consumer by exerting legal, moral, and economic pressures on business and government. Today, everyone—marketers, industry, government, and the public—is acutely aware of the impact of consumerism on the nation's economy and general well-being.

Marketers see a rise in consumer activism. Americans use an estimated 102 billion plastic shopping bags a year—over 500 bags per consumer, most of which end up as solid waste in landfills, clog sewers, or litter waterways. Increasingly, however, retailers are helping to curb the use of plastic bags. Whole Foods discontinued the use of plastic shopping bags throughout its stores in the United States, Canada, and the United Kingdom. They and other retailers, such as CVS and Target, sell reasonably priced, reusable cloth alternatives.[37]

Cultural diversity is an important social–cultural consideration for marketers. There is an increasing number of Spanish-language programs on TV today from satellite and cable TV companies.

Chapter 3 The Marketing Environment, Ethics, and Social Responsibility

But firms cannot always adjust to meet the demands of consumer groups. The choice between pleasing all consumers and remaining profitable defines one of the most difficult dilemmas facing business. This topic is discussed in the "Solving an Ethical Controversy" feature. Given these constraints, what do consumers have the right to expect from the companies from which they buy goods and services? The most frequently quoted answer to this question comes from a speech made by President John F. Kennedy more than 50 years ago. Although Kennedy's list does not amount to a definitive statement, it offers good rules of thumb that explain basic **consumer rights**:

1. *The right to choose freely.* Consumers should be able to choose from among a range of goods and services.
2. *The right to be informed.* Consumers should be provided with enough education and product information to enable them to be responsible buyers.

> **consumer rights** List of legitimate consumer expectations suggested by President John F. Kennedy.

SOLVING AN ETHICAL CONTROVERSY
Was "Pink Slime" Coverage Fair or Foul?

Following a negative comment by a celebrity chef, the U.S. media latched onto a story about boneless lean-beef trimmings, long a standard USDA-approved ingredient in 70 percent of the ground beef consumed in the United States. Dubbing the product "pink slime," reporters and talk-show hosts revealed that it is treated with ammonium hydroxide to kill bacteria, including *E. coli*. Its maker, Beef Products Inc., went on the defensive, backed by the beef industry. The company said the product is safe, nutritious, and 100 percent beef, but many communities insisted it be taken off school-lunch menus immediately. McDonald's and Burger King announced they had stopped using ammonia-treated beef, and Kroger, Safeway, and other grocery chains will stop carrying ground beef that includes it.

Did the media give Beef Products Inc. a fair shake?

PRO 👍
1. People have a right to know what they're eating and how safe it is. The media were doing their job.
2. Lean-beef trimmings are a low-cost ingredient that has allowed the beef industry to quietly increase its profits at consumers' expense.

CON 👎
1. The photo used by many media outlets to illustrate their relentless coverage was not a picture of boneless lean-beef trimmings. Much of the reporting was similarly misleading.
2. The media were simply looking for a sensational story to boost their ratings, whether it was fair or slanted.

Summary
The American Meat Institute posted a YouTube video to educate consumers about beef products, and the USDA announced it would tell school districts which suppliers use the product known as "pink slime" so they could stop buying it if they want to. Beef Products Inc. suspended operations at three plants, affecting hundreds of employees.

Sources: John Sanburn, "One Year Later, the Makers of 'Pink Slime' Are Hanging On, and Fighting Back," *Time*, accessed January 14, 2014, http://business.time.com; P.J. Huffstutter, "Exclusive: Cargill to Change Beef Labeling in Wake of 'Pink Slime' Furor," *Reuters*, accessed January 8, 2014, www.reuters.com; Bryan Gruley and Elizabeth Campbell, "The Sliming of Pink Slime's Creator," *Bloomberg Businessweek*, accessed January 8, 2014, www.businessweek.com; Mickey Meece, "'Pink Slime' Controversy Takes a Toll on Beef Producers," *Forbes*, accessed January 8, 2014, www.forbes.com; "The Facts on Lean Finely Textured Beef," *Beef Is Beef.com*, accessed January 8, 2014, www.beefisbeef.com.

The U.S. government's mobile app for product recalls allows consumers to find information easily from six federal agencies in one location.

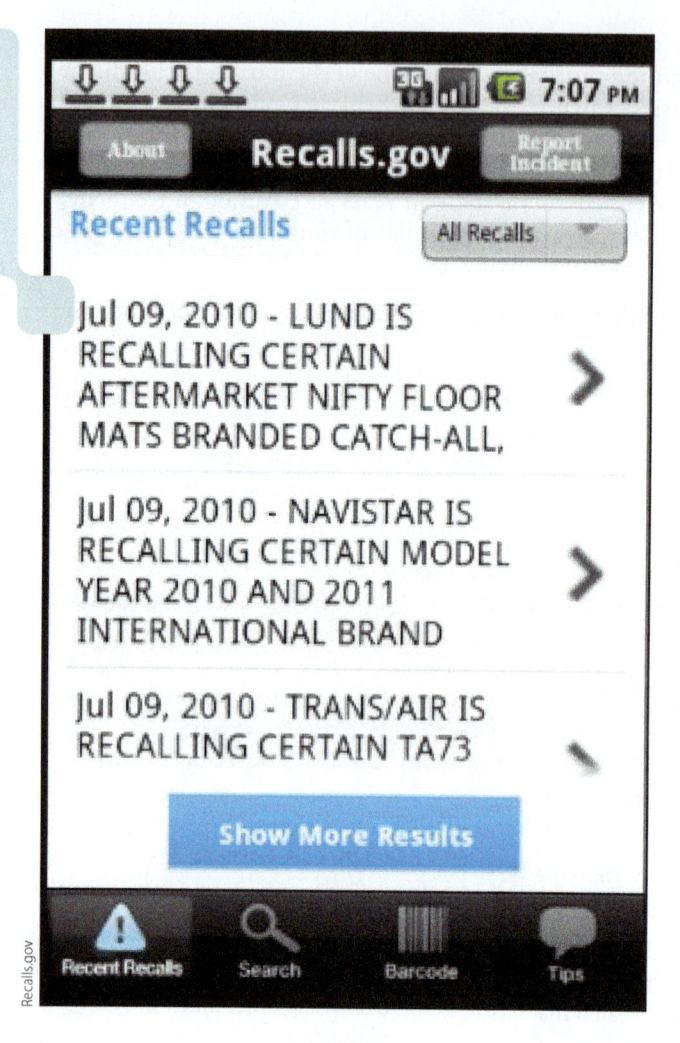

3. *The right to be heard.* Consumers should be able to express their legitimate displeasure to appropriate parties—that is, sellers, consumer assistance groups, and city or state consumer affairs offices.

4. *The right to be safe.* Consumers should be assured that the goods and services they purchase are not injurious with normal use. Goods and services should be designed so that the average consumer can use them safely.

These rights have formed the conceptual framework of much of the legislation enacted during the first five decades of the consumer rights movement. However, the question of how best to guarantee them remains unanswered. Sometimes local, state, or federal authorities step in. In an effort to address obesity, which has become a nationwide health problem, New York became the first city in the United States to require fast-food and casual-dining restaurants to post calorie counts of the items displayed on their menu. The federal government issued a similar mandate to restaurants with at least 20 locations. In response, many restaurants have revamped their menus to include more lower-calorie items.[38]

Consumers' right to safety encompasses a vast range of products, from automobiles to children's toys. Sometimes it seems as though safety recalls are reported in the media too regularly. You might even receive a letter in the mail from a manufacturer informing you of a recall for a part on your refrigerator or car. To streamline the exchange of information among federal agencies and to make it more convenient for consumers to learn about product recalls, the U.S. government has established the website www.Recalls.gov. This website consolidates recall information generated by the six federal agencies empowered to issue recalls, including the Consumer Product Safety Commission, the Food and Drug Administration, and others. The user-friendly site organizes information into broad categories: Boats, Consumer Products, Cosmetics, Environmental Products, Food, Medicine, and Motor Vehicles.[39]

Consumerism, along with the rest of the social–cultural environment for marketing decisions at home and abroad, is expanding in scope and importance. Today, no marketer can initiate a strategic decision without considering the society's norms, values, culture, and demographics. Understanding how these variables affect decisions is so important that some firms have created a new position—typically, manager of public policy research—to study the changing societal environment's future impact on their organizations.

ASSESSMENT CHECK

6.1 Define consumerism.

6.2 Identify the four consumer rights.

ETHICAL ISSUES IN MARKETING

The five environments described so far in this chapter do not completely capture the role that marketing plays in society and the resulting effects and responsibilities of marketing activities. Because marketing is closely connected with various public issues, it invites constant scrutiny. Moreover, because marketing acts as an interface between an organization and the society in which it operates, marketers often carry much of the responsibility for dealing with social issues that affect their firms.

Marketing operates outside the firm. It responds to that outside environment and in turn is acted on by environmental influences. Relationships with employees, suppliers, the government, consumers, and society as a whole frame the social issues marketers must address. The way that marketers deal with these social issues has a significant effect on their firm's eventual success. The diverse social issues that marketers face can be divided into two major categories: marketing ethics and social responsibility. While these two categories certainly overlap, this simple classification system provides a method for studying these issues.

Environmental influences have directed increased attention toward **marketing ethics**, defined as marketers' standards of conduct and moral values. Ethics concern matters of right and wrong. As Figure 3.2 shows, each element of the marketing mix raises its own set of ethical issues. Before any improvements to a firm's marketing program can be made, each element must be evaluated.

Creating an ethics program may be complicated and time consuming, but it's worthwhile. Some firms take their cue from the U.S. Federal Sentencing Guidelines for Organizations, which provides a framework for evaluating misconduct in business activities such as fraud or price fixing. After discovering that courts had resolved similar cases differently, the U.S. Sentencing Commission developed guidelines in 1991 that rely on what legislators call the "stick-and-carrot approach" to corporate ethics: The financial penalties that the courts can impose for wrongdoing are the stick, while the existence of an effective ethics program can reduce the fines the courts can set, which serves as the carrot. Sentencing guidelines act as an incentive for corporations to implement effective ethics compliance programs—if they are hauled into court, the existence of such a program can help reduce penalties.

In some industries, organizations are required by law to maintain corporate-level positions responsible for ethics and legal compliance. Typically, ethics officers are responsible for creating and maintaining an ethical culture within the organization. They ensure that ethical protocols are established and enforced, and they serve as the chief source of information to all stakeholders inside and outside the organization regarding ethics. Figure 3.3 presents a step-by-step framework for building an effective program.

Because ethical behavior is so important to business conduct, some firms and universities have taken an unusual step. They invite convicted corporate criminals to speak to employees and

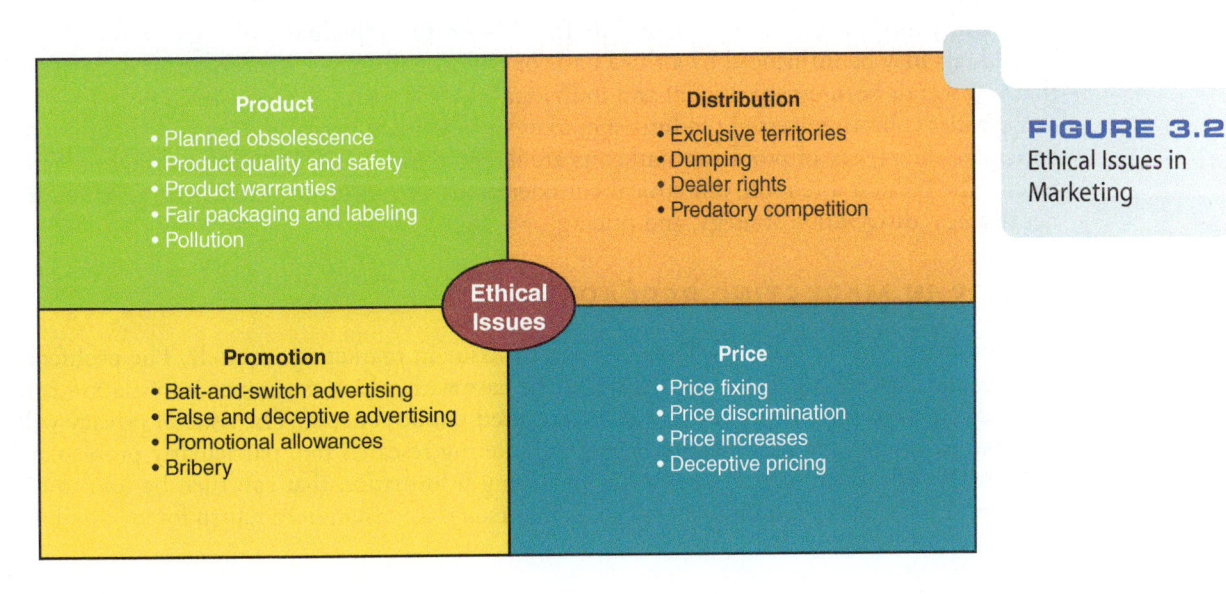

> Describe the ethical issues in marketing. **7**

> **marketing ethics** Marketers' standards of conduct and moral values.

FIGURE 3.2 Ethical Issues in Marketing

Product
- Planned obsolescence
- Product quality and safety
- Product warranties
- Fair packaging and labeling
- Pollution

Distribution
- Exclusive territories
- Dumping
- Dealer rights
- Predatory competition

Promotion
- Bait-and-switch advertising
- False and deceptive advertising
- Promotional allowances
- Bribery

Price
- Price fixing
- Price discrimination
- Price increases
- Deceptive pricing

Ethical Issues

FIGURE 3.3
Ten Steps for Corporations to Improve Standards of Business Ethics

Source: From Ferrell/Fraedrich/Ferrell, *Business Ethics*, 10e. © 2015 Cengage Learning.

1. Appoint a senior-level ethics compliance officer.
2. Set up an ethics code capable of detecting and preventing misconduct.
3. Distribute a written code of ethics to employees, subsidiaries, and associated companies and require all business partners to abide by it.
4. Conduct regular ethics training programs to communicate standards and procedures.
5. Establish systems to monitor misconduct and report grievances.
6. Establish consistent punishment guidelines to enforce standards and codes.
7. Encourage an open-door policy, allowing employees to report cases of misconduct without fear of retaliation.
8. Prohibit employees with a track record of misconduct from holding positions with substantial discretionary authority.
9. Promote ethically aware and responsible managers.
10. Continually monitor effectiveness of all ethics-related programs.

students about their mistakes and the consequences of their actions.

Ensuring ethical practices means promising customers and business partners not to sacrifice quality and fairness for profit. In exchange, organizations hope for increased customer loyalty toward their brands. Yet issues involving marketing ethics are not always clear-cut. The issue of cigarette advertising, for example, has divided the ranks of advertising executives. Is it right for advertisers to promote a product that, while legal, has known health hazards?

For years, charges of unethical conduct plagued the tobacco industry. In the largest civil settlement in U.S. history, tobacco manufacturers agreed to pay $206 billion to 46 states. Four other states—Florida, Minnesota, Mississippi, and Texas—had separate settlements totaling another $40 billion. The settlement freed tobacco companies from state claims for the cost of treating sick smokers. For their part, cigarette makers could no longer advertise on billboards or use cartoon characters in ads, nor could they sell nontobacco merchandise containing tobacco brands or logos. Initially, states used settlement monies to fund tobacco prevention programs, but in recent years nearly all states slashed program funding well below the level recommended by the Centers for Disease Control and Prevention. In a recent year, states collected nearly $26 billion from tobacco taxes and the tobacco settlement but spent less than 2 percent of that revenue on tobacco cessation programs.[40]

People develop standards of ethical behavior based on their own systems of values, which help them deal with ethical questions in their personal lives. However, the workplace may generate serious conflicts when individuals discover that their ethical beliefs are not necessarily in line with those of their employer. For example, employees may think that shopping online during a lunch break using an employer-owned computer is fine, but the company may decide otherwise. The questionnaire in Figure 3.4 highlights other everyday ethical dilemmas. (See page 94 for the answers.)

How can these conflicts be resolved? In addition to individual and organizational ethics, individuals may be influenced by a third basis of ethical authority—a professional code of ethics that transcends both organizational and individual value systems. A professional peer association can exercise collective oversight to limit a marketer's individual behavior. Any code of ethics must anticipate the variety of problems marketers are likely to encounter. Promotional matters tend to receive the greatest attention, but ethical considerations also influence marketing research, product strategy, distribution strategy, and pricing.

ETHICS IN MARKETING RESEARCH

Invasion of personal privacy has become a critical issue in marketing research. The proliferation of databases, the selling of address lists, and the ease with which consumer information can be gathered through Internet technology have increased public concern. The issue of privacy will be explored in greater detail in Chapter 5. One marketing research tool particularly problematic is the promise of cash or gifts in return for marketing information that can then be sold to direct marketers. Consumers commonly disclose their personal information in return for an email newsletter or a favorite magazine.

> **Briefly Speaking**
>
> "There is no such thing as a minor lapse of integrity."
>
> —Tom Peters
> American writer on business management and co-author, *In Search of Excellence*

FIGURE 3.4
Test Your Workplace Ethics

Source: Ethics & Compliance Officer Association, Waltham, Massachusetts; Leadership Group, Wilmette, Illinois; survey sampled a cross-section of workers at large companies and nationwide; used with permission from Ethics & Compliance Officer Association.

Office Technology
1. Is it wrong to use company e-mail for personal reasons?
   ❏ Yes ❏ No
2. Is it wrong to use office equipment to help your children or spouse do schoolwork?
   ❏ Yes ❏ No
3. Is it wrong to play computer games on office equipment during the workday?
   ❏ Yes ❏ No
4. Is it wrong to use office equipment to do Internet shopping?
   ❏ Yes ❏ No
5. Is it unethical to blame an error you made on a technological glitch?
   ❏ Yes ❏ No
6. Is it unethical to visit pornographic Web sites using office equipment?
   ❏ Yes ❏ No

Gifts and Entertainment
7. What's the value at which a gift from a supplier or client becomes troubling?
   ❏ $25 ❏ $50 ❏ $100
8. Is a $50 gift to a boss unacceptable?
   ❏ Yes ❏ No
9. Is a $50 gift from the boss unacceptable?
   ❏ Yes ❏ No
10. Of gifts from suppliers: Is it OK to take a $200 pair of football tickets?
    ❏ Yes ❏ No
11. Is it OK to take a $120 pair of theater tickets?
    ❏ Yes ❏ No
12. Is it OK to take a $100 holiday food basket?
    ❏ Yes ❏ No
13. Is it OK to take a $25 gift certificate?
    ❏ Yes ❏ No
14. Can you accept a $75 prize won at a raffle at a supplier's conference?
    ❏ Yes ❏ No

Truth and Lies
15. Due to on-the-job pressure, have you ever abused or lied about sick days?
    ❏ Yes ❏ No
16. Due to on-the-job pressure, have you ever taken credit for someone else's work or idea?
    ❏ Yes ❏ No

*Ethics questionnaire answers are on page 94.

Privacy issues have mushroomed with the growth of the Internet, with huge consequences to both consumers and marketers. A privacy breach at Target stores recently resulted in data being stolen from more than 110 million customers.[41] In another recent incident, hackers broke into a cloud-based software program used by NASDAQ's board of directors, enabling them to access the stock exchange's computer system.[42] Incidents such as these point to the importance of using encryption programs to safeguard company and consumer data.

Several agencies, including the FTC, offer assistance to Internet consumers. Consumers can go to http://ftc.gov/privacy for information. The Direct Marketing Association also provides services, such as the Mail, Telephone, and Email Preference Services, to help consumers get their names removed from marketers' targeted lists. Registration for the U.S. government's Do Not Call Registry is available at (888) 382–1222 and www.donotcall.gov.

ETHICS IN PRODUCT STRATEGY

Product quality, planned obsolescence, brand similarity, and packaging all raise ethical issues. Some marketers have tried packaging practices that might be considered misleading, deceptive, or unethical. An odd-sized package makes price comparisons difficult. Larger packages take up more shelf space, and consumers notice them. Bottles with concave bottoms give the impression that they contain more liquid than they actually do. Are these packaging practices justified in the name of competition, or are they deceptive? Growing regulatory mandates appear to be narrowing the range of discretion in this area.

How do you evaluate the quality of a product such as a beverage? By flavor or by ingredients? Citing several studies, some consumer advocates say that the ingredients in soft drinks—mainly high sugar content—are linked to obesity in consumers, particularly children. Not surprisingly, the beverage industry disagrees, arguing that lack of exercise and a poor diet in general are greater contributors to weight gain than regular consumption of drinks.

> **Briefly Speaking**
>
> "Character is doing what's right when nobody's looking."
>
> —J. C. Watts Jr.
> Former University of Oklahoma quarterback, politician, founder of JC Watts Companies

ETHICS IN DISTRIBUTION

Two ethical issues influence a firm's decisions regarding distribution strategy:

1. What is the appropriate degree of control over the distribution channel?
2. Should a company distribute its products in marginally profitable outlets that have no alternative source of supply?

The question of channel control typically arises in relationships between manufacturers and franchise dealers. For example, should an automobile dealership, a gas station, or a fast-food outlet be forced to purchase parts, materials, and supplementary services from the parent organization?

The second question concerns marketers' responsibility to serve unsatisfied market segments even if the profit potential is slight. Should marketers build or rent retail stores in low-income areas, serve users of limited amounts of the firm's product, or continue to operate in a declining rural market? These problems are difficult to resolve because often they involve individuals rather than broad segments of the general public. An important first step is to ensure that the firm consistently enforces its channel policies.

ETHICS IN PROMOTION

Promotion raises many ethical questions because it is the most direct link between a firm and its customers. Personal selling has always been a target of criticism—and jokes about untrustworthiness. Used-car dealers, horse traders, and purveyors of quack remedies have been the targets of such barbs in the past. But promotion covers many areas, ranging from advertising to direct marketing, and it is vital for marketers to monitor their ethics in all marketing communications. Truth in advertising—representing accurately a product's benefits and drawbacks, warranties, price, and availability—is the bedrock of ethics in promotion.

Marketing to children has been under close scrutiny for many years because children have not yet developed the skills to receive marketing messages critically. They often believe everything they see and hear. With childhood obesity a serious concern in America, Kellogg Company announced it would change how it advertises its breakfast cereals to children worldwide, focusing solely on products that meet nutrition guidelines. Other organizations, such as General Mills and Quaker Oats, pledged to also emphasize healthy choices.[43] Yet, the Campaign for a Commercial-Free Childhood, a watchdog group, charged that some marketers are increasingly using the Web and social media to target children in promoting the least nutritious products.[44] The federal government recently suggested new nutritional standards for food advertising to children. Critics claim, however, that because the standards are guidelines and not regulations, they aren't enforceable.[45]

Promoting certain products to college students can raise ethical questions as well. College students are a prime market for firms that sell everything from electronics to beer. And although laws prohibit the sale of alcohol to anyone under 21, companies often advertise beer through popular items like hats, shirts, bar signs, and other collectibles. Critics have long claimed this practice supports underage drinking.

Another ethical issue involves paying universities for the use of their logo, team name, or mascot in advertising products to its students. Anheuser-Busch came under fire from colleges and universities across the nation for marketing Bud

Many organizations have modified how they advertise their products to children.

Light on campuses in "Fan Cans" specially designed in their school's colors. Citing concerns about alcohol use and trademark infringement, the schools asked Anheuser-Busch to stop local distribution. The Federal Trade Commission became involved, citing the promotion's appeal to underage drinking. Anheuser-Busch ended up discontinuing the promotion in many campus towns across the United States.[46]

ETHICS IN PRICING

Pricing is probably the most regulated aspect of a firm's marketing strategy. As a result, most unethical price behavior is also illegal. Some aspects of pricing, however, are still open to ethics abuses. For example, should some customers pay more for merchandise if distribution costs are higher in their areas? Do marketers have an obligation to warn vendors and customers of impending changes in price, discount, or return policies?

Some credit card companies target consumers with poor credit ratings and offer them what industry observers call "subprime" or "fee-harvesting" credit cards. Under such an arrangement, the company lures consumers to sign up for the card, promising to improve their credit rating. The cardholder is then charged exorbitant annual fees, leaving them in worse financial shape than before.[47]

While consumers are informed of credit card terms in their agreements, the print often is tiny and the language may be hard to understand. For instance, a credit card issuer might advertise the benefits of its premium card, but the fine print explains that the firm is allowed to substitute a different plan—with a higher interest rate—if the applicant doesn't qualify for the premium card.

The Credit Card Accountability, Responsibility and Disclosure Act, enacted in 2009, curbs abuses in the credit-card industry and ends many questionable practices of credit card companies regarding interest rates, billing cycles, finance charges, and more.[48]

All these concerns must be dealt with in developing a professional ethic for pricing products. The ethical issues involved in pricing for today's highly competitive and increasingly computerized markets are discussed in greater detail in Chapters 18 and 19.

ASSESSMENT CHECK

7.1. Define marketing ethics.
7.2. Identify the five areas in which ethics can be a problem.

SOCIAL RESPONSIBILITY IN MARKETING

Companies can do business in such a way that everyone benefits—customers, the companies themselves, and society as a whole. While ethical business practices are vital to a firm's long-term survival and growth, **social responsibility** raises the bar even higher. In marketing, social responsibility involves accepting an obligation to give equal weight to profits, consumer satisfaction, and social well-being in evaluating a firm's performance. In addition to measuring sales, revenues, and profits, a firm must also consider ways in which it contributes to the overall well-being of its customers and society.

Social responsibility allows a wide range of opportunities for companies to shine. If companies are reluctant, government legislation can mandate socially responsible actions. Government may require firms to take socially responsible actions in matters of environmental policy, deceptive product claims, and other areas. Also, consumers, through their power to repeat or withhold purchases, may force marketers to provide honest and relevant information and fair prices. The four dimensions of social responsibility—economic, legal, ethical, and philanthropic—are shown in Figure 3.5. The first two dimensions have long been recognized, but ethical obligations and the

8 Identify the four levels of the social responsibility pyramid.

social responsibility Marketing philosophies, policies, procedures, and actions that have the enhancement of society's welfare as a primary objective.

FIGURE 3.5
The Four Step Pyramid of Social Responsibility

The Four Step Pyramid of Corporate Social Responsibility from Business Horizons, Vol. 34, 1991, page 92, Freeman & Liedtka, "Corp. Social Responsibility." Reprinted from Business Horizons © 1991 with permission from Elsevier.

Philanthropic
Be a good corporate citizen
- Contribute resources to the community; improve quality of life

Ethical
Be ethical
- Obligation to do what is right, just, and fair
- Avoid harm

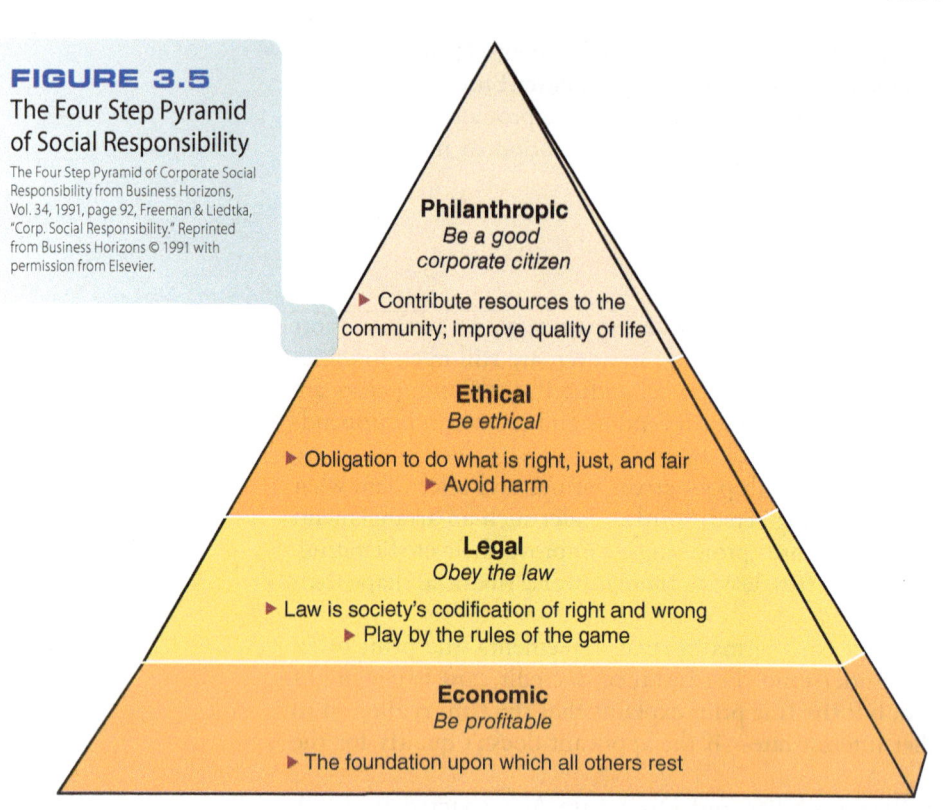

Legal
Obey the law
- Law is society's codification of right and wrong
- Play by the rules of the game

Economic
Be profitable
- The foundation upon which all others rest

need for marketers to be good corporate citizens have increased in importance in recent years. IBM is one company that is committed to being a good corporate citizen. The company has used this facet of corporate responsibility to its advantage in marketing the company's overall focus, as explained in the "Marketing Success" feature.

The locus for socially responsible decisions in organizations has always been an important issue. But who should accept specific accountability for the social effects of marketing decisions? Responses include the district sales manager, the marketing vice president, the firm's CEO, and even the board of directors. Probably the most valid assessment holds that all marketers, regardless of their stations in the organization, remain accountable for the social aspects of their decisions.

MARKETING'S RESPONSIBILITIES

The concept of business's social responsibility has traditionally concerned managers' relationships with customers, employees, and stockholders. In general, managers traditionally have felt responsible for providing quality products at reasonable prices for customers, adequate wages and decent

MARKETING SUCCESS
IBM's CSR Initiatives

Background. IBM is a century-old U.S. firm with more than 430,000 employees operating in almost 170 countries. It holds itself to high standards of corporate social responsibility (CSR), in part because its operations support not only companies around the world but cities, communities, governments, and their infrastructures.

The Challenge. The company believes corporate citizenship "consists of far more than community service" and is constantly looking for ways to make a real difference to all levels of its huge network of stakeholders.

The Strategy. Many of IBM's CSR initiatives rely on sharing the expertise of its own employees. Most efforts are international in scope, such as its Smarter Cities Challenge, which sends IBM experts to 100 cities worldwide to solve local problems in health, education, transportation, and sustainability. The company's participation in Safer Internet Day allows IBMers around the world to help educate communities in dozens of countries, from Finland to Romania, about Internet safety for kids. IBM also lends employees to joint programs such as the World Environment Center's Corporate Sustainability Council of Major Companies.

The Outcome. In addition to paid time they devote to CSR, each year IBM employees supply millions of hours as volunteers in an enormous variety of endeavors.

Sources: Company website, "Responsibility at IBM," www.ibm.com, accessed January 14, 2014; Organization website, "Safer Internet Day 2014," www.saferinternet.org, accessed January 14, 2014; Company press release, "IBM Names Worldwide Recipients of 2013 Smarter Cities Challenge Grants to Improve Urban Life," www-03.ibm.com, accessed January 14, 2014.

working environments for employees, and acceptable profits for stockholders. Only occasionally did the concept extend to relations with the government and rarely with the general public.

Today, corporate responsibility has expanded to cover the entire framework of society. A decision to temporarily delay the installation of a pollution-control device may satisfy the traditional sense of responsibility. Customers would continue to receive an uninterrupted supply of the plant's products, employees would not face layoffs, and stockholders would still receive reasonable returns on their investments. Contemporary business ethics, however, would not accept this choice as socially responsible.

Contemporary marketing decisions must consider their global effect. Some clothing manufacturers and retailers have come under fire for buying from foreign suppliers who force employees, including children, to work long hours in dangerous conditions or pay less than a living wage. In some cases, workers who attempted to form a union have been threatened or fired.[49]

Marketers must also consider the long-term effects of their decisions and the well-being of future generations. Manufacturing processes that damage the environment or that use up natural energy resources are easy targets for criticism.

Marketers can use several methods to help their companies behave in socially responsible ways. Chapter 1 discussed cause marketing as one channel through which firms can promote social causes and at the same time benefit by linking their people and products to worthy undertakings. Socially responsible marketing involves campaigns that encourage people to adopt socially beneficial behaviors such as safe driving, eating more nutritious food, or improving the working conditions of people half a world away. And organizations that sponsor socially responsible programs not only help society but also develop goodwill for an organization, which could help the bottom line in the long run.

One way entire communities can benefit is through socially responsible investing. Many local banks and credit unions are committed to investing in their communities. When consumers purchase certificates of deposit or open money market accounts, the bank or credit union can use the money to finance loans for affordable housing or for small businesses. The U.S. Treasury Department has certified more than 1,000 community development financial institutions that serve neighborhoods. These institutions serve an important purpose: to educate low-income borrowers.[50]

MARKETING AND THE ENVIRONMENT

Many industry and government leaders rank the protection of the environment as the biggest challenge facing today's corporations. Environmental issues such as water pollution, waste disposal, acid rain, depletion of the ozone layer, and global warming affect everyone. They influence all areas of marketing decision making, including product planning and public relations, and they span topics such as planned obsolescence, pollution control, recycling waste materials, and resource conservation.

In creating new-product offerings that respond to consumer demands for convenience by offering extremely short-lived products such as disposable diapers, ballpoint pens, razors, and cameras, marketers occasionally find themselves accused of intentionally offering products with limited durability—in other words, of practicing planned obsolescence. In addition to convenience-oriented items, other products become obsolete when rapid changes in technology create superior alternatives. In the computer industry, changes take place so quickly that lawmakers in several states have proposed legislation to force manufacturers to take back "e-waste"—used computers and other technology products that contain toxic chemicals. For example, manufacturers of printer cartridges include a self-addressed, postage-paid pouch to mail empty cartridges back to the company for reuse.

Public concern about pollution of natural resources such as water and air affects some industries, such as pharmaceuticals or heavy-goods manufacturing, more than others. Still, the marketing system annually generates billions of tons of packaging materials, such as glass, metal, paper, and plastics, that add to the world's growing piles of trash and waste. Recycling such materials, as many manufacturers do, is another important aspect of ecology. Recycling can benefit society by saving natural resources and energy as well as by alleviating a major factor in environmental pollution—waste disposal.

> **Briefly Speaking**
>
> "Success builds character, failure reveals it."
>
> **—Dave Checketts**
> *U.S. businessman*

88   Part 1   Designing Customer-Oriented Marketing Strategies

> Manufacturers of printer cartridges provide receptacles so that businesses can return the empty cartridges for recycling.

As technology advances motivate Americans to ditch their old electronics for newer models, unwanted and outdated electronic waste is the latest trash to overrun landfills. Increasingly, consumers wonder how to dispose of their old computers, monitors, printers, TVs, phones, cameras, and other gadgets, especially since many of the older models contain lead and other hazardous materials requiring special handling. Best Buy, one of the nation's largest electronics retailer, sponsors a recycling program under which customers can drop off a wide variety of unwanted electronics products—even if they weren't bought at Best Buy.[51]

Many companies respond to consumers' growing concern about ecological issues through **green marketing**—production, promotion, and reclamation of environmentally sensitive products. In the green marketing revolution of the early 1990s, marketers were quick to tie their companies and products to ecological themes. Consumers have responded by purchasing more and more of these goods, providing profits and opportunities for growth to the companies that make and sell them. The Sustainability Consortium, an independent organization dedicated to driving sustainability in consumer

green marketing
Production, promotion, and reclamation of environmentally sensitive products.

goods, is working with companies including Cisco, Samsung, Toshiba, and Walmart to create standards to help consumers make green choices in electronics.[52] The Motel 6 chain, Sofitel, and Studio 6 brands—all part of the Accor North America portfolio—committed to PLANET 21, a new companywide sustainability program. Three of Marriott's brands—Courtyard, Residence Inn, and TownPlace Suites—have earned certification by the U.S. Green Building Council.

> Motel 6, Sofitel hotels, and Studio 6 brands—all part of the Accor North America organization—have committed to PLANET 21, a companywide effort to become sustainable.

And Fairmont Hotels & Resorts was recently named one of the top eco-friendly hotel chains by a leading environmental organization.[53]

In partnership with the Natural Resources Defense Council, an environmentalist group, Major League Baseball has identified numerous ways to go green. Its MLB Greening Program is a huge success. Several ballparks, including Busch Stadium in St. Louis, Safeco Field in Seattle, and Kauffman Stadium in Kansas City, employ solar panels to reduce their energy costs. The Cleveland Indians lead the league in harnessing wind power, with a turbine atop Progressive Field. And on Earth Day, the Philadelphia Phillies announced that for each home run hit by a Phillies player at home or away, a tree will be planted as part of the Plant One Million campaign.[54]

ASSESSMENT CHECK

8.1 Identify the four levels of the social responsibility pyramid.

8.2 What are the benefits of green marketing?

> **Briefly Speaking**
>
> "He profits most who serves best."
>
> —**Arthur F. Sheldon**
> *Business educator and early leader of what is now Rotary International*

Strategic Implications of Marketing in the 21st Century

Marketing decisions that businesses make are influenced by changes in the competitive, political–legal, economic, technological, and social–cultural environments. Marketing ethics and social responsibility will continue to play important roles in business transactions in your hometown and around the globe.

As the Internet and the rapid changes in technology that it represents are fully absorbed into the competitive environment, competition is even more intense than before. Much of the competition results from innovations in technology and scientific discoveries. Business in the 21st century is propelled by information technologies but sustained by creative thinking and the willingness of marketers to meet challenges. Marketers face new regulations as the political and legal environment responds to changes in the United States and abroad. As the population ages and the social–cultural environment evolves, marketers will seek to meet the demands for new goods and services for consumers. As always, they will try to anticipate and make the most of every opportunity afforded by the business cycle.

Ethics and social responsibility must underlie everything that marketers do in the 21st century—those who find ways to "do well by doing good" will succeed.

Get online now for additional learning tools to help you master your marketing knowledge—visit **WWW.CENGAGEBRAIN.COM** today!

REVIEW OF CHAPTER OBJECTIVES

1 Identify the five components of the marketing environment.

The five components of the marketing environment are (1) the *competitive environment*—the interactive process that occurs in the marketplace as competing organizations seek to satisfy markets; (2) the *political–legal environment*—the laws and interpretations of laws that require firms to operate under competitive conditions and to protect consumer rights; (3) the *economic environment*—environmental factors resulting from business fluctuations and variations in inflation rates and employment levels; (4) the *technological environment*—application to marketing of knowledge based on discoveries in science, inventions, and innovations; and (5) the *social–cultural environment*—the component of the marketing environment consisting of the relationship between the marketer and society and its culture.

2 Explain the types of competition marketers face and the steps necessary for developing a competitive strategy.

Three types of competition exist: (1) direct competition among marketers of similar products, (2) competition among goods or services that can be substituted for one another, and (3) competition among all organizations that vie for the consumer's purchasing power. To develop a competitive strategy, marketers must answer the following questions: (1) Should we compete? The answer depends on the firm's available resources and objectives as well as its expected profit potential. (2) If so, in what markets should we compete? This question requires marketers to make product, pricing, distribution, and promotional decisions that give their firm a competitive advantage. (3) How should we compete? This question requires marketers to make the technical decisions involved in setting a comprehensive marketing strategy.

3 Describe how marketing activities are regulated and how marketers can influence the political–legal environment.

Marketing activities are influenced by federal, state, and local laws that require firms to operate under competitive conditions and to protect consumer rights. Government regulatory agencies such as the Federal Trade Commission enforce these laws and identify and correct unfair marketing practices. Public and private consumer interest groups and industry self-regulatory groups also affect marketing activities. Marketers may seek to influence public opinion and legislative actions through advertising, political action committees, and political lobbying.

4 Outline the economic factors that affect marketing decisions and consumer buying power.

The primary economic factors are (1) the stage in the business cycle, (2) inflation and deflation, (3) unemployment, (4) income, and (5) resource availability. All are vitally important to marketers because of their effects on consumers' willingness to buy and consumers' perceptions regarding changes in the marketing mix variables.

5 Discuss the impact of the technological environment on a firm's marketing activities.

The technological environment consists of the application to marketing of knowledge based on discoveries in science, inventions, and innovations. This knowledge can provide marketing opportunities: It results in new products and improves existing ones, and it is a frequent source of price reductions through new production methods or materials. Technological applications also pose a threat because they can make existing products obsolete overnight. The technological environment demands that marketers continually adapt to change because its scope of influence reaches into consumers' lifestyles, competitors' offerings, and industrial users' demands.

6 Explain how the social–cultural environment influences marketing.

The social–cultural environment is the relationship between marketing, society, and culture. To remain competitive, marketers must be sensitive to society's demographic shifts and changing values, which affect consumers' reactions to different products and marketing practices. Marketers must consider the increasing importance of cultural diversity, both in the United States and abroad. Changing societal values have led to consumerism, the social force within the environment designed to aid and protect the consumer by exerting legal, moral, and economic pressures on business. Consumer rights include the following: (1) the right to choose freely, (2) the right to be informed, (3) the right to be heard, and (4) the right to be safe.

7 Describe the ethical issues in marketing.

Marketing ethics encompass the marketer's standards of conduct and moral values. Each element of the marketing mix raises its own set of ethical questions. Ethics in product strategy may involve quality and safety, packaging and labeling, and pollution. Ethics in distribution may involve territorial decisions. In promotion, ethical issues include honesty in advertising and promotion to children. Pricing may raise questions about price fixing and discrimination, increases deemed excessive, and deceptive pricing.

8. Identify the four levels of the social responsibility pyramid.

The four levels of social responsibility are: (1) *economic*—to be profitable, the foundation upon which the other three levels of the pyramid rest; (2) *legal*—to obey the law, society's codification of right and wrong; (3) *ethical*—to do what is right, just, and fair and to avoid wrongdoing; and (4) *philanthropic*—to be a good corporate citizen, contributing to the community and improving the quality of life.

ASSESSMENT CHECK: ANSWERS

1.1 Define environmental scanning. Environmental scanning is the process of collecting information about the external marketing environment to identify and interpret potential trends.

1.2 How does environmental scanning contribute to environmental management? Environmental scanning contributes to environmental management by providing current information about the five different environments so marketers can predict and influence changes.

2.1 Distinguish between direct and indirect competition, and give an example of each. Direct competition occurs among marketers of similar products, such as supermarkets or gas stations. Indirect competition involves products that are easily substituted. Fried chicken could compete with pizza or tacos. A baseball game could compete with a trip to a water park.

2.2 What is time-based competition? Time-based competition is the strategy of developing and distributing goods and services more quickly than competitors.

3.1 Identify the four phases of U.S. government regulation of business. What is the newest frontier? The four phases of government regulation of business are the antimonopoly period, protection of competitors, consumer protection, and industry regulation. The newest frontier is cyberspace.

3.2 Which federal agency wields the broadest regulatory powers for influencing marketing activities? The Federal Trade Commission has the broadest regulatory authority.

4.1 Identify and describe briefly the four stages of the business cycle. The four stages of the business cycle are prosperity, recession, depression, and recovery.

4.2 Explain how inflation and income affect consumer buying decisions. Inflation devalues money and therefore may restrict some purchasing, particularly goods and services not considered necessary. Income also influences consumer buying power—the more discretionary income a household has, the more goods and services can be purchased.

5.1 What are some of the consumer benefits of technology? Technology can lead to new or improved goods and services, offer better customer service, and reduce prices.
It can also address social concerns.

5.2 Why must marketers monitor the technological environment? Marketers need to monitor the technological environment to stay current with—and possibly ahead of—competitors. If they don't, they may wind up with obsolete offerings.

6.1 Define consumerism. Consumerism is a social force within the environment that aids and protects the buyer by exerting legal, moral, and economic pressures on business.

6.2 Identify the four consumer rights. As outlined by John F. Kennedy, the four consumer rights are the right to choose freely, the right to be informed, the right to be heard, and the right to be safe.

7.1 Define marketing ethics. Marketing ethics refers to the marketer's standards of conduct and moral values.

7.2 Identify the five areas in which ethics can be a problem. The five areas of ethical concern for marketers are marketing research, product strategy, distribution, promotion, and pricing.

8.1 Identify the four levels of the social responsibility pyramid. The four levels of social responsibility are economic, legal, ethical, and philanthropic.

8.2 What are the benefits of green marketing? Green marketing, which responds to consumers' growing concerns about ecological issues, offers consumers high-quality products without health risks or damage to the environment. Many industries, including appliances, consumer electronics, construction, hospitality, and more, are finding that incorporating green practices rejuvenates their business.

MARKETING TERMS YOU NEED TO KNOW

environmental scanning 63
environmental management 63
strategic alliance 63
competitive environment 64
monopoly 64
antitrust 64
oligopoly 64
competitive strategy 65
time-based competition 66
political–legal environment 67
gross domestic product (GDP) 72
economic environment 72
business cycle 72
inflation 73
unemployment 74
discretionary income 74
demarketing 74
technological environment 76
VoIP (Voice over Internet Protocol) 77
social–cultural environment 77
consumerism 78
consumer rights 79
marketing ethics 81
social responsibility 85
green marketing 88

ASSURANCE OF LEARNING REVIEW

1. Why is environmental scanning an important activity for marketers?
2. What are the three types of competition? Give an example of each.
3. What are the three questions marketers must ask before deciding on a competitive strategy?
4. What is the function of the Federal Trade Commission? The Food and Drug Administration?
5. Describe an industry or firm that you think might be able to weather an economic downturn and explain why.
6. Why do marketers monitor the technological environment?
7. How might marketers make the most of shifts in the social–cultural environment?
8. Describe the importance of consumer rights in today's marketing activities.
9. Why is it worthwhile for a firm to create an ethics program?
10. How can social responsibility benefit a firm as well as the society in which it operates?

PROJECTS AND TEAMWORK EXERCISES

1. With a classmate, choose two companies or brands that compete directly with each other. Select two of the following or choose your own. Then develop a competitive strategy for your firm while your partner develops a strategy for his or hers. Present the two strategies to the class. How are they similar? How are they different?
   a. Walmart and Target
   b. Verizon and AT&T
   c. Sea World and Universal Studios
   d. Visa and MasterCard
   e. Kia and Hyundai
   f. Chili's and Outback Steakhouse
2. Track your own consumer purchasing decisions as they relate to your income. Compare your decisions during the college year and the summer. Do you have a summer job that increases your income? How does that affect your decisions?
3. The U.S. Postal Service essentially enjoys a monopoly on the delivery of most mail. With a classmate, develop a strategy for a business that would compete with the USPS in areas that firms such as UPS and FedEx do not already cover.
4. Choose one of the following products. Working in pairs or small groups, present arguments for and against having the United States impose certain regulations on the advertising of your product. (Note that some products already do have regulations—you can argue for or against them.)
   a. Smokeless tobacco
   b. Firearms
   c. State lottery
   d. Prescription medications
5. With a classmate, research a professional sports team that has threatened to move if locals don't approve subsidies to build a new stadium or arena. Do you think this is a savvy business move on the part of the team's owners? Or, is it an unethical move because area businesses will lose revenues if the team takes its franchise elsewhere?

CRITICAL-THINKING EXERCISES

1. Suppose you and a friend want to start a company that markets frozen vegetarian dinners. What are some of the questions about the competitive environment you would like to have answered before you begin production? How will you determine whom your customers are likely to be? How will you reach them?

2. Emissions standards for motorcycles took effect in 2006 under rules adopted by the Environmental Protection Agency. There were no previous emissions controls for motorcycles at all, but even under the new laws, "dirt" bikes for off-road use will be exempt. The standards add about $75 to the average cost of a motorcycle, according to the EPA, but $250 according to the Motorcycle Industry Council. Why do you think motorcycle makers did not adopt voluntary emissions standards? Should they have done so? Why or why not?

3. The social–cultural environment can have a strong influence on the decisions marketers must make. Animal rights groups have targeted the manufacture and sale of foie gras, a European food delicacy made from goose and duck liver. Activists cite the cruel treatment of these birds, while chefs and restaurant owners claim otherwise. Animal rights groups are pressuring restaurants to stop serving foie gras. Others argue that consumers should be allowed a choice. What aspects of the social–cultural environment are affecting the marketing of foie gras Which of the other components of the marketing environment may come into play, and how?

4. Every year, marketers offer U.S. consumers nearly 400 million rebates—worth about $6 billion. But do consumers like them? Often rebates require more effort than a consumer is willing to make to receive the cash back. Critics of the promotional effort say that marketers know this and are banking on consumers not redeeming them, resulting in extra income for retailers and manufacturers. Do you think rebate programs are ethical? Why or why not?

5. The safe disposal of nuclear waste has been the topic of continuing public debate and an ongoing issue for marketers who work for nuclear power companies. This material is currently stored at 75 sites around the nation. To build a nuclear waste site, the U.S. Department of Energy must apply for and obtain a license. Supporters of such sites argue that they are important to building America's nuclear power capacity, while critics question their safety and usefulness. As a marketer, how would you approach this issue?

ETHICS EXERCISE

Some retail firms protect their inventory against theft by locking their premises after hours even though maintenance and other workers are inside the stores working all night. Employees have charged that they are forbidden to leave the premises during these hours and that during an emergency, such as illness or injury, precious time is lost waiting for a manager to arrive who is authorized to unlock the doors. Although workers could open an emergency exit, in some cases they claim that they will be fired for doing so. Employers assert that managers with keys are on the premises (or minutes away) and that locking employees in ensures their own safety as well as cutting down on costly "shrinkage."

1. Under what circumstances, if any, do you think locking employees in at night is appropriate?

2. If you feel this practice is appropriate, what safeguards do you think should be put into effect? What responsibilities do employers and employees have in such circumstances?

INTERNET EXERCISES

1. **Economic environment.** The U.S. Census Bureau projects what the U.S. population will look like in the next 15 to 25 years. Visit the Census Bureau's website and compare its projections of the U.S. population to current figures. What will the U.S. population look like in the future? How is it different from the current population? List two or three products or industries you feel will benefit from future population trends.
www.census.gov/population/projections/index.html

2. **Fair trade coffee.** Go to the website listed below to learn about so-called fair trade coffee. Prepare a brief report on the subject. How could a coffee manufacturer or retailer integrate fair trade products into its social responsibility efforts.
www.globalexchange.org/campaigns/fairtrade/coffee

3. **Building a brand.** Visit the website for footwear maker Ugg to learn about its efforts at building its brand. How has Ugg answered each of the five questions listed in the chapter concerning the development of a competitive strategy?
www.uggaustralia.com

Note: Internet Web addresses change frequently. If you don't find the exact site listed, you may need to access the organization's home page and search from there or use a search engine such as Google or Bing.

ETHICS QUESTIONNAIRE ANSWERS

Questionnaire is on page 83.

1. 34% said personal email on company computers is wrong.
2. 37% said using office equipment for schoolwork is wrong.
3. 49% said playing computer games at work is wrong.
4. 54% said Internet shopping at work is wrong.
5. 61% said it's unethical to blame your error on technology.
6. 87% said it's unethical to visit pornographic sites at work.
7. 33% said $25 is the amount at which a gift from a supplier or client becomes troubling, while 33% said $50, and 33% said $100.
8. 35% said a $50 gift to the boss is unacceptable.
9. 12% said a $50 gift from the boss is unacceptable.
10. 70% said it's unacceptable to take $200 football tickets.
11. 70% said it's unacceptable to take $120 theater tickets.
12. 35% said it's unacceptable to take a $100 food basket.
13. 45% said it's unacceptable to take a $25 gift certificate.
14. 40% said it's unacceptable to take a $75 raffle prize.
15. 11% reported they lied about sick days.
16. 4% reported they have taken credit for the work or ideas of others.

CASE 3.1
General Mills and Its CSR Strategies

General Mills, headquartered in Minneapolis, is one of the largest food companies in the world. Dedicated to the mission of "nourishing lives," the company produces millions of servings of food every day, from iconic breakfast cereals such as Cheerios to Yoplait dairy products, and from Green Giant vegetables to Häagen-Dazs ice cream. Along the way, General Mills has also donated hundreds of millions of dollars to not-for-profit organizations since the 1950s, including more than $40 million for worldwide hunger relief in a recent year. Its *Global Responsibility Report* outlines a long list of corporate social responsibility goals and achievements.

The report showcases General Mills' commitment to improving health, protecting the environment, and continuing to engage with employees and customers in the workplace and the community. The company's new "sustainable sourcing commitment," for instance, aims to conserve and protect natural resources by promoting environmentally responsible purchasing along the entire length of its supply chain, including its use of raw agricultural inputs and its production processes, packaging, and distribution. General Mills has adopted a goal to source 100 percent of its inputs from responsible and sustainable sources in the near future. It now reports significant progress on ten of its top-priority agricultural commodities, representing more than 50 percent of its annual purchases and including large quantities of certified sustainable palm oil.

The company has also undertaken improvements in the quality of its top products, including adding more healthful ingredients such as whole grains and calcium while reducing less desirable ones such as calories, sugar, sodium, and trans fat. General Mills recently announced that original Cheerios is now made from corn and sugar that have not been genetically modified.

The company has also set goals for reducing its production of solid waste, reducing its use of transportation fuel, and reducing its greenhouse gas emission and use of water. It has even reached many of its social responsibility goals early. For instance, it is ahead of schedule on improving its packaging.

QUESTIONS FOR CRITICAL THINKING

1. Do you think General Mills' rapid progress toward some of its goals means it has set appropriate benchmarks for social responsibility achievement? Or should it set higher ones?

2. How can the company further improve the nutritional quality of some of its sugared cereals such as Lucky Charms and Cocoa Puffs, which one critic likened to "junk food," without risking profit or market share?

Sources: Company website, www.generalmills.com, accessed January 14, 2014; Andrew Adam Newman, "Online, A Cereal Maker Takes an Inclusive Approach," *The New York Times*, accessed January 14, 2014, www.nytimes.com; "General Mills Reports Progress on Global Responsibility Efforts," news release, www.generalmills.com, accessed January 14, 2014; Bruce Horovitz, "Cheerios Drops Genetically Modified Ingredients," *USA Today*, accessed January 2, 2014, www.usatoday.com.

VIDEO CASE 3.2
Zappos Employees Do More Than Sell Shoes

It's hard to imagine not being able to buy a pair of shoes online. It's even harder to imagine not owning a pair of shoes at all. The founders and employees at Zappos (an Amazon company) are familiar with both situations. Co-founder and CEO Tony Hsieh got Zappos off the ground in 1999 when he and other investors realized that nowhere on the Internet could consumers find a real selection of shoes. You know how successful Zappos has become since then, despite subsequent competition—but you might not be aware of the company's efforts to give back to its community, including giving shoes away to children in need.

Zappos engages in social responsibility initiatives because "we feel that it's the right thing to do," explains Shannon Roy, the company's Happiness Hippie (her job title). The company develops relationships with charitable organizations that are similar to those it builds with customers and vendors, looking for ways that employees can interact directly with the community through these organizations. Some of the broad areas in which Zappos offers assistance are poverty and education, cancer research and care, and pets and nature. Specific efforts include partnerships with charitable organizations, such as Goodie Two Shoes, a foundation that provides new shoes and socks to children in crisis or need. Through its Goodie Two Shoes Giveaway each year, the organization teams up with Zappos and other firms to donate and distribute thousands of footwear products to children who need them. "It's giving back to the community," says Roy, who adds that Zappos employees feel driven to participate. "It's part of our being, part of our culture; it's very inherent in what Zappos is all about." Working at Zappos is "grander than the 9 to 5 job. It's doing something for the greater good."

It would be easy for an online retailer such as Zappos to set up shop anywhere and ignore its surroundings. But that's not Zappos. Instead, the firm made a deal to renovate the vacant Las Vegas City Hall for $40 million, bringing about 2,000 employees to downtown Las Vegas—an area that could use an economic and social boost. CEO Hsieh admits that originally he thought about building a "dream corporate campus," much like those of Apple, Google, and Nike. But when the Las Vegas opportunity came along, Hsieh and other Zappos managers thought: "Let's not be like the other companies. Let's not be insular and only care about our employees. We want to help contribute and help build a community and really integrate into a community around our campus." City officials predicted that the economic impact to the downtown area could top $336 million, bolstering real estate, health care, restaurants and hotels, retailers, and other businesses. "I think this is part of what our brand is about," observes Matt Burchard, senior director of marketing, photo, and video. "We've added a core tenet of what we stand for, and that's community."

Burchard notes that Zappos is committed to investing in things beyond its core business, such as the infrastructure of downtown Las Vegas. Recently, The Downtown Project (founded by Hsieh and others) partnered with Venture for America to attract new college graduates for two-year stints to help startup businesses get off the ground in Las Vegas. In addition, The Downtown Project has bought up Las Vegas properties, such as an old Motel 6, a 7-Eleven building, and numerous condominiums for demolition or renovation. The idea is to revitalize the entire area—both economically and socially.

Zappos fulfills the four levels of the social responsibility pyramid: economic, legal, ethical, and philanthropic. The company is stable and profitable, giving it a solid platform from which to launch social responsibility initiatives. It operates with a strong legal and ethical base. When Zappos became the target of a cyber attack that gained access to its internal network (and the accounts of 24 million users), the firm acted quickly, putting nearly every employee to work assisting in its response to the breach. Even though the breach did not reach complete credit card numbers or other critical data, the company notified its customers and reset all of their passwords. Zappos also warned customers to be on the lookout for phishing emails and other scams. Finally, Zappos is generous in its philanthropic efforts, donating money, shoes, and employee time to its various causes. "We don't overanalyze it," says Rob Siefker, director of the customer loyalty team. "We just know who we are and who we want to be. We act on that."

QUESTIONS FOR CRITICAL THINKING

1. Describe how the economic environment may influence Zappos' marketing efforts.

2. Explain how Zappos' move into downtown Las Vegas fulfills the four levels of the social responsibility pyramid.

Sources: Company website, **www.zappos.com**, accessed January 14, 2014; Frank Gruber, "Zappos New Downtown Vegas Office Opens with Rainbows, Unicorns & Llamas," *Tech Cocktail*, accessed January 14, 2014, **http://tech.co**; Benjamin Spillman, "Zappos HQ: Business Brings Money and Presence to Revitalize Downtown," *Las Vegas Review-Journal*, accessed November 25, 2013; Goodie Two Shoes Foundation, **www.goodietwoshoes.org**, accessed January 14, 2014; Joe Schoenmann, "Zappos CEO Buys Motel, Strikes Deal to Bring Young Talent Downtown," *Las Vegas Sun*, accessed January 14, 2014, **www.lasvegassun.com**; "100 Best Companies to Work For," *CNN Money*, accessed January 14, 2014, **http://money.cnn.com**; Andy Greenberg, "Zappos Says Hackers Accessed 24 Million Customers' Account Details," *Forbes*, accessed January 14, 2014, **www.forbes.com**.

NOTES

1. Company website, www.aflac.com, accessed January 14, 2014; Jennifer Rooney, "Ruffled Feathers Behind Him, Aflac CMO Zuna Stays on Course," *Forbes*, accessed January 14, 2014, www.forbes.com; Ruth E. Davila, "Humble Family Man Joey Loudermilk…," *Profile* magazine, accessed January 14, 2014, http://profilemagazine.com; "AFLAC Insurance," Finance Maps of the World, accessed January 14, 2014, http://finance.mapsofworld.com, "World's Most Admired Companies—Fortune," *CNN Money*, accessed January 14, 2014, http://money.cnn.com; "Aflac Makes Ethisphere's Annual World's Most Ethical Companies List," press release, accessed January 14, 2014, http://finance.yahoo.com.
2. Linda Loyd, "Delta-Owned Trainer Refinery Posts Profit," *Philadelphia Inquirer*, accessed January 14, 2014, http://articles.philly.com; "Delta Air Lines: An Airline Buys an Oil Refinery," *The Economist*, accessed January 14, 2014, www.economist.com; "Delta's Oil Refinery Purchase: Should More Airlines Follow Suit?" *Yahoo! News*, accessed January 14, 2014, www.news.yahoo.com; Nancy Trejos, "Airlines Post Losses in Large Part Due to Rising Fuel Costs," *USA Today*, accessed January 14, 2014, http://travel.usatoday.com.
3. U.S. Consumer Product Safety Commission, "Hachette Book Group Recalls Children's Books due to Choking and Laceration Hazards," press release, accessed January 14, 2014, www.cpsc.gov; Holly Lebowitz Rossi, "New Crib Safety Guidelines: What Parents Need to Know," *Parents*, accessed January 14, 2014, www.parents.com.
4. Connie Prater, "What the Credit Card Reform Law Means to You," *CreditCards.com*, accessed January 14, 2014, www.creditcards.com; Odysseas Papadimitriou, "What Does 2012 Have in Store for Your Wallet?" *U.S. News*, accessed January 14, 2014, http://money.usnews.com.
5. Lance Duroni, "NFL Urges Judge to Ditch Hatmaker's Antitrust Suit," *Law 360*, accessed January 14, 2014, www.law360.com; Ashby Jones, "American Needle: High Court Delivers 9-0 Shutout against NFL," *The Wall Street Journal*, accessed January 14, 2014, http://blogs.wsj.com.
6. Jasmine Wang, "Comac Said to Delay Maiden Flight for First Large China Jet," *Bloomberg News*, accessed January 11, 2014, www.bloomberg.com; "China's Challenge for Air Supremacy," *CNN.com*, accessed January 11, 2014, www.cnn.com.
7. Company website, www.costco.com, accessed January 14, 2014.
8. ENERGY STAR website, www.energystar.gov, accessed January 14, 2014.
9. Tammy Parker, "Report: Worldwide Carrier Wi-Fi Hotspots to Number 6.3M by Year's End," *Fierce Wireless Tech*, accessed January 14, 2014, www.fiercewireless.com.
10. Company website, "LTE Information Center," www.verizonwireless.com, accessed January 14, 2014; Company website, www.att.com, accessed January 14, 2014.
11. Company website, "About Us," http://newscorp.com, accessed January 14, 2014; Company website, www.21cf.com, accessed January 14, 2014; Nathan Bell, "Demergers Let Shareholders Multiply by Division," *The Sydney Morning Herald*, accessed January 14, 2014, www.smh.com.au.
12. "SuccessFactors Achieves Exceptional Growth in Cloud HCM," press release, *The Wall Street Journal*, accessed January 14, 2014, http://online.wsj.com; Chris Kanaracus, "SAP Lays Out Cloud Strategy Post–SuccessFactors Deal," *PCWorld*, accessed January 14, 2014, www.pcworld.com; Bob Evans, "Success Factors' Lars Dalgaard: SAP Will Turbocharge Our Innovation," *Forbes*, accessed January 14, 2014, www.forbes.com.
13. Company website, www.vonmaur.com, accessed January 14, 2014.
14. Organization website, "Security Technologies," www.tsa.com, accessed January 14, 2014.
15. Federal Trade Commission website, www.ftc.gov, accessed January 14, 2014.
16. Federal Trade Commission, "Revised Children's Online Privacy Protection Rule Goes into Effect Today," press release, accessed January 15, 2014; "FTC Case against Deceptive Robocallers Leads to Record $30 Million in Civil Penalties," press release, accessed January 15, 2014, www.ftc.gov.
17. Melissa Burden and David Shepardson, "GM Can't Find Nearly 140,000 Recalled Cars for Ignition Switch Defects," *The Detroit News*, accessed August 8, 2014, www.detroitnews.com; Peter Valdes-Dapena and Tal Yellin, "GM: Steps to a Recall Nightmare," *CNNMoney*, accessed August 8, 2014, http://money.cnn.com.
18. Mark P. Cussen, "How Your VantageScore Credit Report Is Calculated," *Forbes*, accessed January 15, 2014, www.forbes.com.
19. Organization website, www.nfpa.org, accessed January 14, 2014.
20. Organization website, www.aarp.org, accessed January 14, 2014.
21. Association website, www.the-dma.org, accessed January 14, 2014.
22. Ylan Q. Mui, "Economy Expands 2.8 Percent in Third Quarter, but Consumer Spending Slows," *The Washington Post*, accessed January 15, 2014, www.washingtonpost.com.
23. Organization website, "About Divvy Bikes," www.divvybikes.com, accessed January 15, 2014; Kate Hinds, "Chicago's Bike Share Program to Become Nation's Biggest by 2014," *WNYC*, accessed January 15, 2014, www.wnyc.org.
24. Bureau of Labor Statistics, "U.S. Annual Inflation Up to 1.2% in November," *TradingEconomics.com*, accessed January 14, 2014, www.tradingeconomics.com.
25. Bureau of Economic Analysis, "Personal Income and Outlays, October 203," accessed January 14, 2014, www.bea.gov.
26. World Hunger Education Service, "2013 World Hunger and Poverty Facts and Statistics," accessed January 14, 2014, www.worldhunger.org.
27. Organization website, www.commutegreener.com, accessed January 14, 2014.
28. Organization website, "New Hybrid Car Scores First Place on Greenest Vehicle List," press release, www.greencars.org, accessed January 14, 2014; Cheryl Jensen, "How Do You Find the Best Green Cars?" *The New York Times*, accessed January 14, 2014, www.nytimes.com.
29. Dominic Barton, "Half a Billion: China's Middle-Class Consumers," *The Diplomat*, accessed January 15, 2014, www.thediplomat.com.
30. Paul Day, "Fragile Spanish Economy Limps Out of Recession," *Reuters*, accessed January 15, 2014, www.reuters.com; Lorenzo Totaro, "Italian Economy Shrinks More Than Initially Estimated," *Bloomberg News*, accessed January 15, 2014, www.bloomberg.com.
31. Brook Barnes, "At Disney Parks, a Bracelet Meant to Build Loyalty (and Sales)," *The New York Times*, accessed January 15, 2014, www.nytimes.com.
32. Chenda Ngak, "Powering the Future: Will Algae Fuel Your Next Car?" *CBS News*, accessed January 15, 2014, www.cbsnews.com.
33. Organization website, www.ge-ip.com, accessed January 14, 2014.
34. Craig Smith, "How Many People Use 300 of the Top Social Media, Apps & Services?" *Digital Marketing Ramblings*, accessed January 15, 2014, http://expandedranblings.com; Organization website, www.skype.com, accessed January 15, 2014.
35. Google and Ipsos, "Reaching Today's Boomers & Seniors Online," *Google: Think Insights*, accessed January 14, 2014, www.google.com.
36. Manny Ruiz, "Top Trends in Hispanic Media," *PR Newswire*, accessed January 14, 2014, http://toolkit.prnewswire.com.
37. Kitt Doucette, "The Plastic Bag Wars," *Rolling Stone*, accessed January 16, 2014, www.rollingstone.com.
38. Clare O'Connor, "How Starbucks Will Profit from Posting Its Calorie Counts," *Forbes*, accessed January 16, 2014, www.forbes.com; Stephanie Strom, "McDonald's Menu to Post Calorie Data," *The New York Times*, accessed January 16, 2014, www.nytimes.com.
39. Organization website, www.recalls.gov, accessed January 14, 2014.
40. Campaign for Tobacco-Free Kids, "Tobacco-Prevention Spending versus State Tobacco Revenues: Fiscal Year 2013," press release, accessed January 16, 2014, www.tobaccofreekids.org.
41. Becky Quick, "Target CEO 'Still Shaken' by the Data Breach, Vows to 'Make It Right,'" *CNBC*, accessed January 13, 2014, www.cnbc.com.
42. Jennifer LeClaire, "Hackers Spied on Board Directors after NASDAQ Breach," *Yahoo! News*, accessed January 16, 2014, http://news.yahoo.com.
43. John Ellett, "Quaker Oats New CMO Justin Lambeth Cooks Up Recipe for Growth," *Forbes*, accessed January 15, 2014, www.forbes.com; "General Mills Reports Progress on Global Responsibility Efforts," press release, accessed January 15, 2014, www.generalmills.com.
44. Anton Troianovski, "Food Marketers Get 'Smarter' about Ads for Kids," *The Wall Street Journal*, accessed January 14, 2014, http://online.wsj.com; Organization website, http://commercialfreechildhood.org, accessed January 15, 2014.
45. Baby Zone, "New Study Suggests Fast Food Companies Should Limit Advertising to Children," *Yahoo Shine*, accessed January 16, 2014, http://shine.yahoo.com; Bruce Levinson, "Does Technology Change the Ethics of Marketing to Children?" *Fast Company*, accessed January 15, 2014, www.fastcompany.com.
46. John Hechinger, "Team-Color Bud Cans Leave Colleges Flat," *The Wall Street Journal*, accessed January 14, 2014, http://online.wsj.com; Jeannie Kever, "Bud

Light Fan Can Promo Losing Its Fizz," *Houston Chronicle*, accessed January 15, 2014, www.chron.com.
47. Jessica Silver-Greenberg and Tara Siegel Bernard, "Lenders Again Dealing Credit to Risky Clients," *The New York Times*, accessed January 16, 2014, www.nytimes.com.
48. Consumer Financial Protection Bureau, "CFPB Finds Card Act Reduced Penalty Fees and Made Credit Card Costs Clearer," press release, accessed January 15, 2014, www.consumerfinance.gov.
49. Organization website, www.laborrights.org, accessed January 14, 2014.
50. Organization website, www.cdfifund.gov, accessed January 14, 2014.
51. Martin Moylan, "Best Buy Sets New High for Recycling Electronics," *Minnesota Public Radio*, accessed January 15, 2014, http://minnesota.publicradio.org; Company website, "Recycle FAQs," www.bestbuy.com, accessed January 14, 2014.
52. Organization website, http://sustainabilityconsortium.org, accessed January 14, 2014.
53. Lo Lankford, "Nine Most Green-Friendly Hotel Chains in the U.S.," *Care 2 Make a Difference*, accessed January 15, 2014, www.care2.com; Leon Kaye, "Motel 6: Sustainability Means We'll No Longer Leave the Light on for You," *Triple Pundit*, accessed January 15, 2014, www.triplepundit.com; "Marriott LEED®s the Way to Green Hotels," press release, accessed January 15, 2014, http://news.marriott.com; Marina Hanes, "How Eco-Friendly Are Fairmont Hotels & Resorts?" *1800Recycling.com*, accessed January 15, 2014, http://1800recycling.com; Company website, www.accor-na.com, accessed January 15, 2014; Company website, www.fairmont.com/corporate-responsibility/environment, accessed January 15, 2014.
54. Organization website, "MLB Greening Program," http://web.mlbcommunity.org, accessed January 14, 2014; Mark Newman, "Clubs Celebrate Earth Day across Baseball," *MLB.com*, accessed January 14, 2014, http://mlb.mlb.com.

Chapter 4

Social Media: Living in the Connected World

1. Explain social media and the differences between social media platforms and social media tools.
2. Describe the ways in which consumers and businesses use social media for their buying decisions.
3. Outline the four key elements of a written social media marketing plan.
4. Discuss the importance of setting goals and developing strategies, including targeting an audience, for a social media marketing initiative.
5. Identify the seven qualities of effective social media content and the rules of engagement with social media.
6. Describe the different means of monitoring, measuring, and managing the social media marketing campaign.
7. Discuss ethical and legal issues encountered by marketers in social media marketing.
8. Explain the different types of positions in social media marketing and how to land an entry-level job.

LINKEDIN LIFTS OFF

When it launched more than ten years ago, LinkedIn was not much more than an online résumé-hosting site that struggled to amass its first million users. Today its popularity as a professional networking and information-sharing resource is soaring, both online and via mobile device.

The Mountain View, Calif., company now boasts more than 300 million members on its user-friendly platform, roughly $500 million a year in revenue from advertising and recruitment applications, and a history of steady and successful innovations in building social media tools for professionals. Page views more than doubled in one recent year, and top-rated posts can generate more than 100,000 views each. LinkedIn's 4,800 employees around the world operate LinkedIn portals in 23 different languages, including Czech, Dutch, French, Italian, Malay, Russian, Spanish, Swedish, and of course English.

As employers face a glut of applicants, they find themselves able to be increasingly choosy about whom they hire. LinkedIn's features allow them to rely more and more on personalized searches among the site's individual members. They can also use the site's vast networks of personal connections and recommendations to filter their candidate pools, and they can advertise, promote themselves, and sponsor content.

Individual users benefit too. They can get insider access to job postings, read insightful posts by hundreds of industry leaders or "top influencers," and pore over company career pages and recruitment ads. They can share content with others, comment about and endorse others, and host video and graphics alongside their customized profiles. Of course they can still build their professional networks by forging new connections and personal introductions with other users on the site.

LinkedIn's top managers aren't sitting back, however. They would like their site to become "the definitive professional publishing platform," which is why they're pushing to offer users more and more content—from recruiting companies, its own stable of invited "top influencers," and other users. In addition, news feeds tailored to users' interests offer current items from thousands of business and news sources; they may soon include sponsored content and videos from advertisers such as Xerox and American Express. LinkedIn hopes that within a matter of months, everyone in the business world will log in each morning to see "what's trending on LinkedIn."[1]

EVOLUTION OF A BRAND

In little more than a decade, LinkedIn has transformed itself. What started out as a handy online resource for jobseekers has become a major player in the social media world—not only for individuals looking to network and find a job but also as a community builder enabling organizations and their marketers to promote their brand, keep tabs on their competitors, and identify best industry practices.

- Using social media can have advantages and disadvantages, as many users have discovered. A recent lawsuit accused LinkedIn of hacking into some users' accounts and using information from their contacts for marketing purposes. The company responded, saying it does not access email accounts without users' permission and suggested that users may not have unchecked certain default settings. Do LinkedIn's explanation and the "buyer beware" nature of the company's response meet your ethical standards? In social media, does privacy matter?
- Chapter 1 described marketing myopia and how organizations can avoid it by gaining a true understanding of the scope of their business. In your opinion, does LinkedIn leadership understand the true scope and long-term potential of their business? What steps might LinkedIn management take to expand their platform even further?

Chapter Overview

Facebook. Twitter. Foursquare. Tumblr. You know what all of these names represent: social media. You may have accounts on most of them—or one, at the very least. You might follow NBA players like LeBron James or Kevin Durant. Maybe you prefer tracking country music star Miranda Lambert or want to keep up with the latest on the stars of the *Hunger Games* trilogy. You can find all of these on various social media. They know it, and so do their sponsors and promoters.

This chapter explores the ways that organizations use social media to market their goods and services. Once the domain of a few adventurous start-ups, now even the largest and most venerable firms—such as Chrysler and General Mills—have established a marketing presence in social media. You can "like" your Chrysler vehicle on Facebook or tweet with General Mills' chief marketing officer. Not-for-profit organizations, such as Crayons to Classrooms and the National Wildlife Federation, are on Facebook as well.

This chapter begins with an overview of the different types of social media, ranging from blogs to social-networking sites, and examines how they work. We look at how consumers use social media—and why. Then we turn to the marketer's point of view: social media marketing. We outline the elements of a formal social media marketing plan as well as the goals and strategies for using social media successfully in marketing in order to connect with customers—including identifying target audiences and the rules of engagement. We discuss the implementation of the plan, along with social media monitoring, measuring, and managing. Next, the chapter addresses the legal and ethical issues surrounding the use of social media, which seems to be growing as rapidly as the technology itself. Finally, we take a look at marketing careers in social media. We conclude that social media represents not just a marketing phenomenon but a marketing era all its own.

WHAT IS SOCIAL MEDIA?

1 Explain social media and the differences between social media platforms and social media tools.

social media Different forms of electronic communication through which users can create online communities to exchange information, ideas, messages, and other content, such as videos or music.

You post a video on YouTube. You tag a friend on Facebook. You create a pinboard of your favorite foods on Pinterest. You start a blog about your motorcycle adventures. These are just a few of the ways you might use social media in your daily life. **Social media** is defined collectively as the different forms of electronic communication (such as networking websites or blogs) through which users can create online communities to exchange information, ideas, messages, and other content, such as videos or music.[2]

Although innovators constantly find new ways to branch out the tree of social media, to date there are several basic forms. These may be divided into two main categories: social media platforms and social media tools. A **social media platform** is a type of software or technology that allows users to build, integrate, or facilitate a community, interaction among users, and user-generated content. The popular blogging site Wordpress is a social media platform, as are social-networking sites Facebook and Foursquare. A **social media tool** enables users to communicate with each other online. Examples include apps, blog postings and comments, and video shares.

The different types of social media often overlap with each other. For example, you can create a forum on LinkedIn to discuss job training, or post a video to your Facebook page. In addition, the media sites themselves cross boundaries; for example, StumbleUpon, a Web search engine that directs users to Web pages based on their interests, has its own Facebook page, Twitter account, and blog.

SOCIAL MEDIA PLATFORMS

Social media platforms act as a home base for an online community. To access the conversations held there, users must become members. Usually this is a matter of typing in a valid email address and creating a password, followed by providing some kind of profile. Some social media platforms require an invitation or sponsor who is already a member. When you join, be sure to learn the site's rules. For example, Facebook strictly regulates where you can run a contest promotion on your timeline as well as how you may choose and contact the winner. If you violate these rules, your firm could be banned from the site.[3]

Social-Networking Sites

Social-networking sites are websites (such as Facebook, Twitter, and LinkedIn) that provide virtual communities for people to share daily activities, post opinions on various topics (ranging from politics to recipes), increase their circle of online friends, and more. Facebook and LinkedIn are two of the most popular social-networking sites. Companies such as Walmart and Target use their Facebook pages to build relationships with consumers. The American Cancer Society, a not-for-profit organization, uses Facebook to promote its annual Relay for Life.[4] Every social network has its own search engine, which allows users to search for topics that interest them. Before launching a social media campaign, marketers may make a list of keywords that relate to the promotion, then use those keywords throughout the campaign—so network users land in the right place on the platform.

When they join, members of social-networking sites typically create an online profile of biographical data—including photos and information such as employment, education, and even relationship status. They invite friends or colleagues to join their social network, and then communicate in a variety of ways—posting on their homepage, sending email or instant messages, or even calling or videoconferencing with chosen members. They can share their likes and dislikes about goods and services as well as links to favorite e-commerce sites.

It's easy to see how quickly information can be disseminated through social media—and the potential for marketers. Web statistics portal Statista estimates that Google alone handles 115 billion online searches each month.[5] Forrester Research reports that American consumers' online retail spending rises each year. Recently, online retail sales totaled more than $230 billion (about 7 percent of overall retail sales). Online retail spending is estimated to hit $370 billion in a couple of years—a number that will account for 10 percent of all retail sales in the United

social media platform A type of software or technology that allows users to build, integrate, or facilitate a community, interaction among users, and user-generated content.

social media tool Software (such as an app or blog) that enables users to communicate with each other online.

social-networking sites A website that provides virtual communities through which people can share information, post opinions, and increase their circle of online friends.

Pinterest is one of many popular social-networking sites that provide virtual communities for people to share activities and post their opinions and interests.

> **Briefly Speaking**
>
> "We think a more open and connected world will help create a stronger economy with more authentic businesses that build better products and services."
>
> —**Mark Zuckerberg**
> *Founder and CEO, Facebook*

States.[6] Media specialists BIA/Kelsey estimate that spending on digital marketing among small and midsize companies will exceed $16 billion by 2016.[7]

SixDegrees.com was the first social-networking site to be launched. Named for the idea of "six degrees of separation" among all people, it lasted from 1997 to 2001. Another social-networking site, Friendster, followed in 2002. While Friendster still exists, it was redesigned as a social gaming site. Friendster members typically are teenagers or young adults who live in Southeast Asia.[8]

Tom Anderson and Chris DeWolfe founded the site MySpace in 2003. MySpace quickly ballooned to blockbuster status, and two years later, News Corporation acquired the site for more than $500 million. Although MySpace was the most-visited social-networking site at the time, Facebook, launched by Mark Zuckerberg in 2004, had already appeared. Facebook outpaced MySpace within a few years and, by 2011, MySpace lost 80 percent of its users. News Corporation subsequently sold MySpace to Specific Media for a fraction of its original purchase price.[9]

Facebook, which boasts more than 1.2 billion monthly users (roughly one-seventh of Earth's population), is now the world's largest online social network.[10] A host of other social networking platforms—Twitter, YouTube, Foursquare, Instagram, LinkedIn, and Pinterest, to name a few—have launched as well. All of these represent opportunities for marketers.

Bookmarking Sites

bookmarking A platform that gives users a place to save, organize, and manage links to websites and other Internet resources.

Bookmarking platforms give you a place to save, organize, and manage links to websites and other resources on the Internet. StumbleUpon is an example; Pinterest combines bookmarking with social networking. Sports teams such as the NHL's Pittsburgh Penguins and football's New York Giants have hopped aboard the Pinterest bandwagon. "What intrigued us initially was that the platform seemed to be dominated by women," says the director of interactive media for the New York Giants. "We certainly thought it was a great way to engage with that demographic and offer a different type of content than can be found on Facebook, Twitter, and Google+."[11]

Social News Sites

social news site A platform where users can post news items to links to outside articles, then vote on which postings get the most prominent display.

People post news items or links to outside articles on a **social news site**, and then vote on which postings get the most prominent display and are viewed by the most readers. Because viewers vote using whatever criteria they want, it would be tricky for a marketer to predict whether a message will get any attention. Digg and Reddit are two top social news sites.

Blogging Sites and Forums

online forums A platform where users post messages and hold conversations on specified topics.

blogging sites A platform where a host or writer posts information or opinions on various topics and followers may respond.

Members hold conversations by posting messages on **online forums**. Some people form special groups on social-networking sites like LinkedIn or Facebook in order to create forums on everything from political causes to recipe exchanges. Blog postings and comments are attached to **blogging sites** and typically focus on specific topics such as favorite travel destinations, support for military veterans, or parenting experiences. Wordpress and Tumblr are popular blogging sites.[12]

Tumblr's functionality and dedicated fan base make it an ideal medium for organizations to market their brands. Fashion brands Calvin Klein, J.Crew, and Ann Taylor use Tumblr to post engaging images and content and draw users to their websites.[13]

Microblogs

microblogs A blog posting that contains only a few words (such as on Twitter).

Through **microblogs**, subscribers receive a steady stream of brief updates from anyone ranging from a high-school friend to a celebrity (like NFL quarterback Cam Newton). Twitter leads the microblogging race. At a limit of 140 characters, tweets by their nature are short—but very effective. Corporate sponsors of MTV's Video Music Awards used Twitter to promote their goods and services before, during, and after the program.[14]

SOCIAL MEDIA TOOLS

Social media tools make the conversation happen. Blog comments, tags, photo and video shares, apps, and other technology items make up the social media toolkit.

Media Sharing

Services such as YouTube and Flickr allow you to upload and share media, including photos and video. Most also let you create a profile or comment on a posting. Some videos have gone viral and made their makers famous.

Marketers realize that a viral video can translate to a jump in demand—and sales—for their products. Nearly a decade after launching a product called Orabrush, its inventor Dr. Robert Wagstaff was still selling only about 10 of the tongue cleaners per month—at $3 each. So Wagstaff hired a freelance marketing consultant to create a funny two-minute video called "How to Tell When Your Breath Stinks." After posting the video on YouTube, the team bought YouTube's Promoted Video Ads service and also put the video on Orabrush's Facebook page. Within six weeks, about 900,000 people had seen the video, and 20 percent of the viewers clicked on the link to the Orabrush website. During those six weeks, Orabrush sold about 10,000 tongue cleaners. Wagstaff now stays in contact with his followers as "Dr. Bob" on Twitter, and Orabrush products are sold by Walgreens, CVS, Target, and other national retailers.[15]

Blog and Microblog Postings

Blogging allows people to communicate in greater detail than microblogging does. Individuals blog about everything from their favorite foods to their pet peeves to the best vacation spots within driving distance. Marketers use blog postings to educate consumers and business customers about new products, to ask for feedback about particular goods and services, to notify the public about social responsibility initiatives, and to manage public relations crises. Many companies designate certain staff members as bloggers, while others hire professional bloggers either in-house or on a consulting basis, because they believe in the power of skilled blogging to influence readers' opinions about their goods and services. On his "Blog Gone Europe," travel writer and TV travel-show host Rick Steves blogs about his personal travel experiences and other observations designed to entice readers to book a tour. The site includes a lively "Graffiti Wall," where travel aficionados post questions and comments.[16]

Microblogging, on the other hand, offers short bursts of news. PepsiCo unveiled a partnership with Twitter through which it offers free downloadable songs to consumers who include a Pepsi hashtag in their tweets and streaming video of live concerts. PepsiCo's Twitter followers may tweet the names of songs they want played—thus influencing concert playlists.[17]

> **Briefly Speaking**
>
> "It's empowering to be asked to look at what's possible, not told how to do it."
>
> —**Jack Dorsey**
> Co-founder and Executive Chairman, Twitter

Apps

Short for *application*, an **app** is a purchased or free software download that links users to a wide range of goods and services, media and text content, social media platforms, search engines, individual businesses, or organizations—just about anything you can think of. It's difficult to determine exactly how many apps exist because new ones are being created at such a rapid rate. But it's estimated that there are currently nearly 1.3 million apps available for Android-powered mobile phones, with thousands introduced each month.[18] Apple's online App Store offers more than 1.4 million apps, with that number also growing every day.[19] And there are apps for computer tablets as well as for the iPad.

Apps allow you to download music, play games, or make dinner reservations; they alert you to news events and weather changes; they make it convenient to buy a pair of shoes online while you're standing on a street corner; they deliver supermarket coupons right to your phone; they allow you to identify stars in the sky and plan your daily schedule. They even allow you to identify your phone's location. Marketers know that potential and existing customers use all kinds of apps, and they want to tap into the opportunities created by this phenomenon. Because there are so many apps for so many platforms and devices, marketers must find ways to identify the apps that will support the goals of their social media marketing efforts. They need to choose the ones that reach and attract their target audience and influence consumers to make decisions in favor of their goods and services.

For example, an app called Booshaka highlights fans who participate the most on an organization's Facebook page, awarding them a little bit of online fame. The Top Fan Pro version of

app Short for *application*, a free or purchased software download that links users to a wide range of goods and services, media and text content, social media platforms, search engines, and the like.

TABLE 4.1 Popular Mobile Apps for Social Media Marketers

App Name	What It Does	How It Helps Marketers
Evernote	A "virtual notepad" to capture your ideas and notes whenever and wherever inspiration strikes.	Keeps you up to date; can be used on computers, notebooks, and other mobile devices.
HootSuite	A social media "dashboard" for posting, monitoring, and measuring social media tools.	Schedule posts and manage multiple Twitter, Facebook, Foursquare, and Google+ accounts.
GoToMeeting	Lets you call in to meetings or presentations remotely, receiving both audio and video on a mobile phone.	Especially good when you're outside the office and don't have wi-fi access.
Eventbrite	Event planners can monitor registrations, track where attendees are coming from, create backend reports, and reconnect with attendees post-event; also allows registrants to access online events they've signed up to attend.	One-stop shop for marketers who plan and coordinate conferences, trade shows, and other events.
Feedly	Aggregates a user's blog subscriptions for reading and sharing.	Good for catching up on blog reading while commuting or out of the office.
Dropbox	Tool for collaboration and file sharing.	Remote access to files at all times, including files too large to transmit via email.

Sources: Radhika Basuthakur, "Social Media Marketing on the Go: 10 Mobile Apps Reviewed," Affilorama, accessed February 6, 2014, www.affilorama.com; Ian Cleary, "5 Tools to Market Your Business Using Mobile Social Media Apps," Razor Social, accessed February 6, 2014, http://222.razorsocial.com; Rachel Sprung, "11 Apps Every Marketer Should Download," HubSpot, accessed February 6, 2014, http://blog.hubspot.com.

the app rewards the top fans with perks. Need to locate a wi-fi area in a hurry? An app called WiFi Finder features more than 550,000 free and paid wi-fi sites in 144 countries around the world. If you're shopping in a brick-and-mortar store and want to access product information, visit the Snaptell app. Just snap a photo of the cover of any book, DVD, or video game, and within seconds you'll receive a rating and description of the product along with links to Google, YouTube, Wikipedia, IMDb (Amazon's Internet movie database), Barnes & Noble, and other sites.[20] Table 4.1 provides several examples of popular apps for social media marketers—and what they do.

QR Codes

QR codes Short for "quick response," a two-dimensional barcode that can be read by some mobile phones with cameras.

Short for "quick response," **QR codes** are two-dimensional barcodes that can be read by some mobile phones with cameras (often, a dedicated QR code reader is necessary as well). The codes look like small black-and-white squares with patterns and appear in various ads. Once a mobile phone snaps a picture and "reads" the code, the information contained in the code is shared with the user—it might lead to a video, give details about a product, or offer a coupon.

The ever-increasing number of mobile apps can help companies connect with their customers. The Booshaka app allows marketers to recognize the consumers (or fans) who actively participate on their organization's Facebook page.

WHY SHOULD MARKETERS TURN TO SOCIAL MEDIA?

Despite its relatively brief existence, social media has quickly grown to be an important tool for marketers to build relationships with customers, strengthen brands, launch new products, enter new markets, and boost sales. Once considered the domain of teens and young adults, sites such as YouTube and Facebook report that their user base is now much broader. More than 70 percent of adults use social media sites, and the 45–54 age group is the fastest-growing demographic on Facebook, with 46 percent of Facebook users age 45 or older.[21]

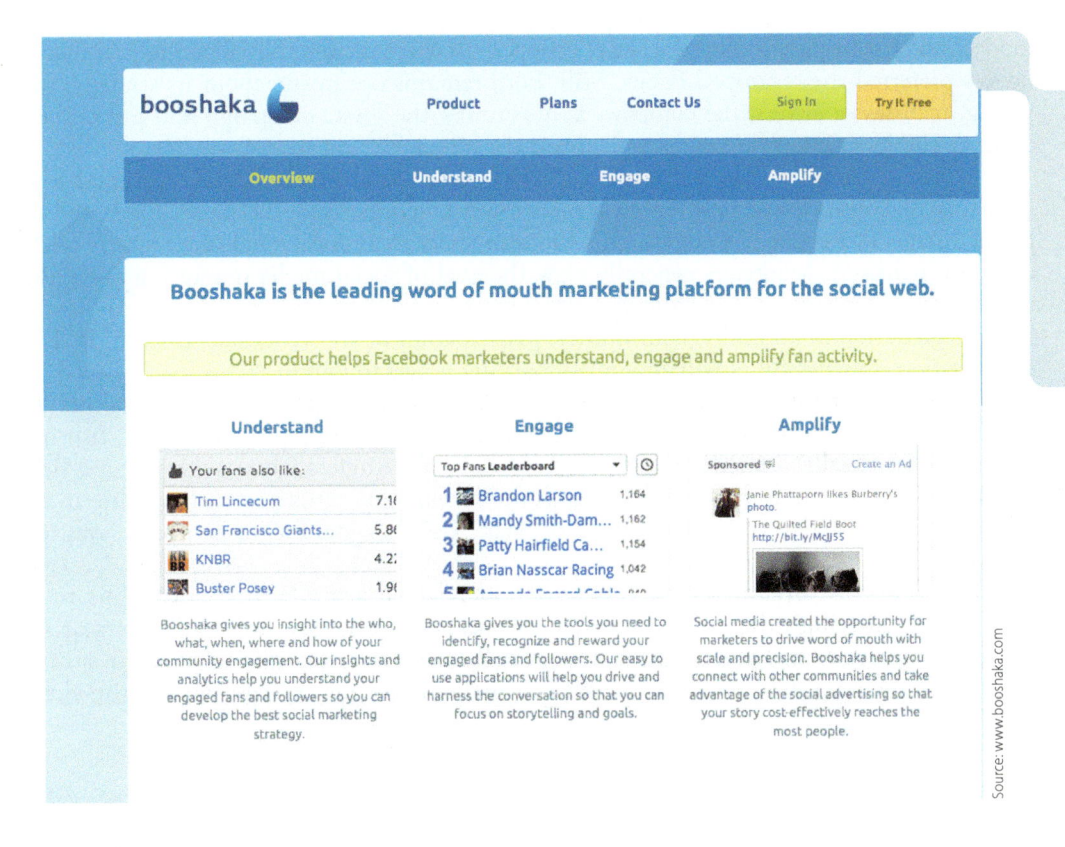

Many different apps help companies connect with their customers. Booshaka is an app that helps marketers track customer engagement and activity on social media sites.

Source: www.booshaka.com

Studies show that consumers are connecting with retailers, restaurants, travel and entertainment firms, financial companies, and other businesses via social media.[22] The messages conveyed via social media, whether from friends and family or from organizations that interest us, wield substantial power. Here are a few more reasons companies to turn to social media for part of their overall marketing strategy:

- In a recent survey of marketers, 74 percent said they regarded Facebook as important to their lead-generation strategy.
- An estimated 4 billion people use a mobile device to access social media sites.
- Social media generates nearly twice the marketing leads that trade shows, telemarketing, and direct mail do.
- Twitter boasts almost 300 million active users per month.
- More than two-thirds of Google+ users are male.
- Three in five Google+ users log in every day.
- More than 5 million photos are uploaded on Instagram per day.
- L.L. Bean is the most popular brand on Pinterest with more than 5.5 million followers.
- YouTube claims more than 1 billion unique visitors each month.[23]

This doesn't mean every social media effort is successful. When Ford prepared to launch the Ford Fiesta, the carmaker recruited 100 influential bloggers and gave them each a Fiesta to drive for a specified period of time. For the most part, the bloggers liked the car and generated buzz about the "Fiesta Movement" campaign. While the campaign put Ford on the social media map, neither the bloggers nor Ford took into account that the company's more popular subcompact—the Focus—was undergoing a major design overhaul and wasn't yet available. Thus, while Ford sold

social media marketing (SMM) The use of social media portals to create a positive influence on consumers or business customers toward an organization's brand, products, public image, or website.

more than 69,000 Fiestas that year, sales dropped off dramatically the following year, because car buyers preferred the revamped Focus. Still, Ford remains optimistic about its strategy: targeting young, tech-savvy buyers, the company is re-running the Fiesta campaign and put out a call for another 100 blogging influentials to field-test the Fiesta.[24]

Effective **social media marketing (SMM)** uses social media portals to create a positive influence on consumers or business customers toward an organization's brand, goods and services, public image, or website. Of course, this can also apply to an individual like a sports celebrity or entertainment star. Marketers generally view the goal of social media marketing as developing a conversation with potential customers—resulting in a purchase, subscription to an email newsletter, registration in an online community, participation in an event, and so forth. If the online conversation is successful, it will go viral—sparking others to join in.

Outdoor sporting goods retailer Cabela's uses its Facebook page to help roll out its "Fish for Millions" promotion. Fish and game commissions in 19 states helped by tagging fish in public waters with specially created tags provided by Cabela's. Anglers who caught tagged fish stood to win up to $2 million in prizes ranging from Cabela's gift cards and merchandise to a Chevy Silverado pickup and two Ranger 520Z bass boats. Cabela's goal for the campaign was to spread the word about its brand.[25]

Not-for-profit organizations also create social media marketing campaigns to expand their reach. Although the organization is 100 years old, Big Brothers Big Sisters of America recently launched its "Start Something Web Series" to highlight individual success stories. Videos were posted on its YouTube channel, which then spread via website shares and Facebook postings.[26]

> **Briefly Speaking**
>
> "The hardest thing for marketers is to turn over the brand experience to the community and let them define it."
>
> —Eric Erwin
> *Executive Vice President and CMO, Wilton Products*

To spread the word about its brand, Cabela's used its Facebook page to roll out its "Fish for Millions" promotion.

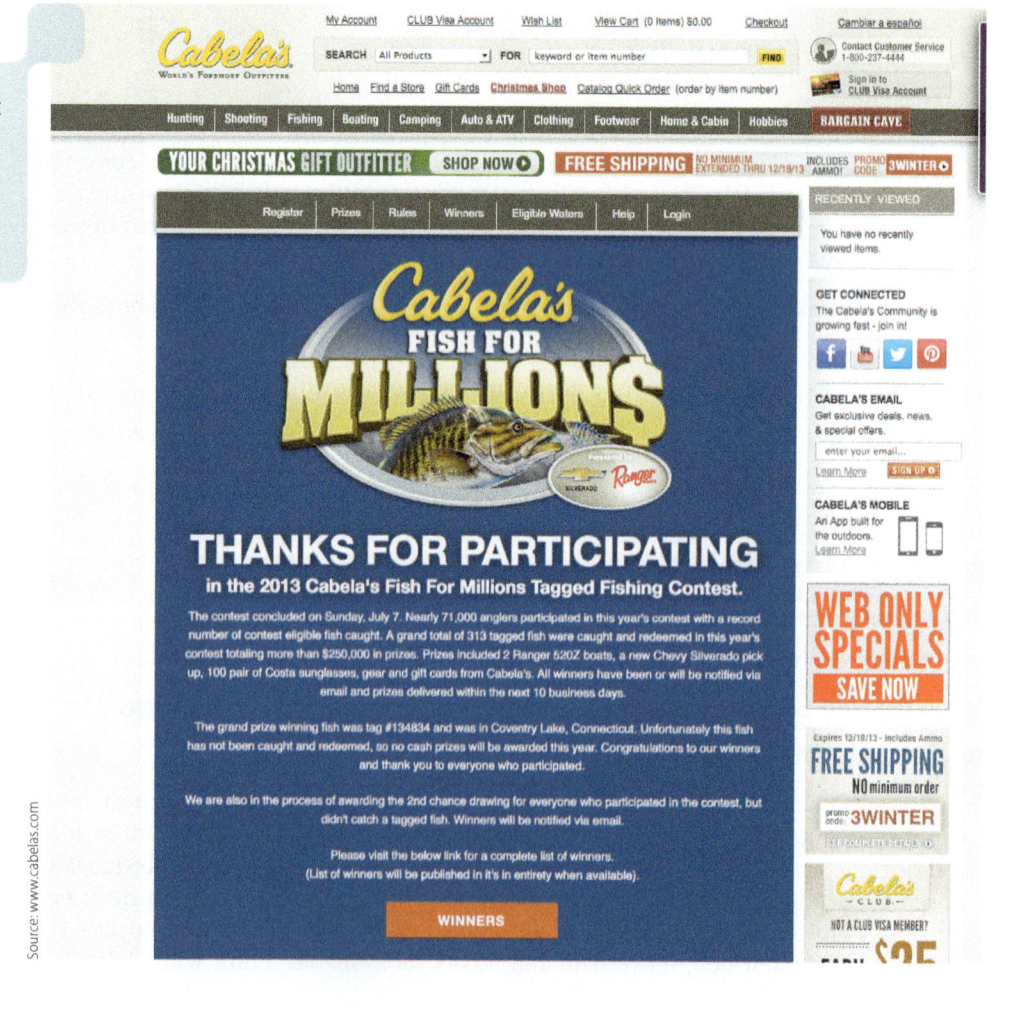

Source: www.cabelas.com

Social media marketing contains three essential features:

1. *It creates a buzz.* Buzz is the engine that drives social media marketing. Buzz carries the marketing message from one user to the next until it becomes viral, spreading as far and as rapidly as possible. The message doesn't have to be related directly to a firm's goods or services, but it must be compelling and memorable.

2. *It creates ways for customers or fans to engage in conversations with each other and the organization.* Social-networking sites, blogs, and forums promote these conversations.

3. *It allows customers to promote the firm's messages themselves.* Social-networking sites such as Facebook and Twitter enable customers to easily become a firm's promoter.

ASSESSMENT CHECK

1.1 What are social-networking sites?
1.2 Define social media marketing.

HOW CONSUMERS AND BUSINESSES USE SOCIAL MEDIA

For businesses to be successful at using social media to reach their customers, they need to understand how consumers—and other businesses—use social media to decide whether to buy certain goods and services. Figure 4.1 shows the top 10 social-networking sites and forums by U.S. market share of visits, with Facebook, YouTube, and Twitter leading the pack.

> Describe the ways in which consumers and businesses use social media for their buying decisions.

CONSUMER BEHAVIOR

Studies show an overall link between social media and trends in consumer behavior. For example, 91 percent of consumers have visited a brick-and-mortar store because of an online experience. Nearly 90 percent research a product using online search engines. And more than 60 percent of consumers make an in-store purchase after researching online.[27]

According to one recent report conducted by comScore and Group M Search, roughly half of online consumers use a combination of search engines and social media in making purchase decisions. Fifty-eight percent of consumers start with search engines such as Google or Bing, while 24 percent go straight to social media. Here's the twist: 46 percent of consumers who start with social media then turn to search engines.

Shoppers who start with search engines do so because these provide the most information about products and companies. Search engines also help with comparison shopping, particularly when it comes to price. More than 86 percent surveyed say that search engines are extremely important to their buying decisions.[28] Figure 4.2 shows the top five search engines by estimated unique monthly visitors—Google heads the list. Marketers can use this kind of insight to develop social media marketing campaigns that incorporate—or start consumers at—search engines.

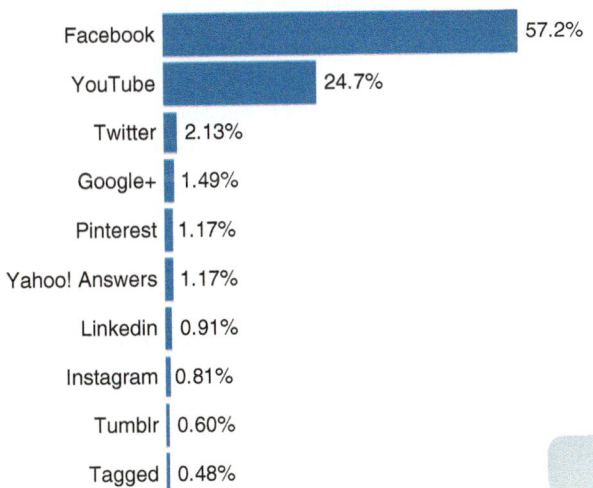

Site	Share
Facebook	57.2%
YouTube	24.7%
Twitter	2.13%
Google+	1.49%
Pinterest	1.17%
Yahoo! Answers	1.17%
LinkedIn	0.91%
Instagram	0.81%
Tumblr	0.60%
Tagged	0.48%

FIGURE 4.1
Top Ten Social-Networking Websites and Forums by U.S. Market Share (Visits)

Source: "Top 10 Social-Networking Websites & Forums," *Marketing Charts*, accessed January 19, 2014, http://www.marketingcharts.com. Data provided by Experian Marketing Services.

Consumers rely on the communities created by social media for their buying decisions in the following ways:

- *To learn about new goods and services.* In the study discussed above, 28 percent of respondents said that sites like YouTube, Facebook, and Twitter helped steer them toward new brands and products.

- *To conduct research and share information.* Consumers visit blogs and social-networking sites to delve further into a topic—whether it's an industry, a company, a brand, or a specific product. Reviews or rankings by fellow consumers, along with other shared information, can carry a lot of weight in certain purchase decisions. For example, according to one survey, more than 40 percent of American consumers turn to social media—including YouTube, Facebook, and Twitter—for information about health care. They share opinions about everything from doctors to drugs to insurance companies. "The power of social media for health organizations is in listening and engaging with consumers on their terms," says one health industries leader. "Social media has created a new customer-service access point where consumers expect an immediate response."[29]

- *To make final purchase decisions.* Another study found that 72 percent of consumers regard online reviews as a primary driver of their decision to buy.[30] If they've learned about the product and conducted more research about it online, engaging with the company as well as other consumers via social media, they become part of the community that the product's marketers want to create. Consumers may purchase the product and then share their response to it through social media, widening the circle even more.

> **Briefly Speaking**
>
> "If you're a brand marketer looking at this as a creative way of just getting that one-time transaction done, you're not recognizing the power of social media and how consumers are playing in the marketing space."
>
> —**Chris Perry**
> *President of Digital Communications, Weber Shandwick*

Some experts contend that social media can shift the way consumers behave within entire industries. A study conducted by marketing research firm The Hartman Group concluded that communication via social media has altered the way American consumers eat—how they plan their meals, what they buy and where, and how they cook. Nearly half of American consumers get their information about food—menus and recipes, diet trends, nutritional data, and so forth—from social media sites. "Consumers used to rely on mom and family traditions for meal planning, but now search online for what to cook, without ever tasting or smelling," observes Hartman Group CEO Laurie Demeritt.[31] This doesn't mean food companies should abandon other forms of marketing in favor of social media marketing; it does suggest that, even though consumers can't smell or taste food online, they do rely on social media for a wide range of choices.

FIGURE 4.2
Top Five Search Engines by Unique Monthly Visitors (estimated)

Source: "Top 15 Most Popular Search Engines," *EBizMBA*, accessed August 15, 2014, www.ebizmba.com.

1 | Google
1.1 billion—Estimated Unique Monthly Visitors

2 | bing
350 million—Estimated Unique Monthly Visitors

3 | Yahoo! Search
300 million—Estimated Unique Monthly Visitors

4 | Ask
245 million—Estimated Unique Monthly Visitors

5 | Aol Search
125 million—Estimated Unique Monthly Visitors

BUSINESS BEHAVIOR

Like consumers, businesses also use social media to build relationships, including partnerships with other companies. More than 93 percent of business-to-business (B2B) firms surveyed in a recent study use social media to market their businesses.[32] However, only about 56 percent say that they have been able to develop a "loyal fan base" among business customers via social media. Perhaps this is because the nature of relationships between B2B marketers and their customers is different from that of firms that market products to consumers. Businesses buy a wide range of goods and services from each other, ranging from communications networks to electricity to delivery trucks, and each purchase must benefit a firm's overall strategy rather than simply satisfying a need or want. In addition, once a relationship between firms is established, it can be more difficult to alter than a relationship between a consumer and the manufacturer of, say, a breakfast cereal.

Still, B2B marketers report that they are achieving significant results with social media efforts, using an average of six social media platforms:

- Almost 70 percent say they are able to gather relevant marketplace insights.
- Nearly 60 percent have recently seen improved search rankings.
- More than 56 percent have formed new business partnerships.[33]

Some B2B firms have turned the field of social media marketing into a business enterprise of its own, helping companies leverage social media to their competitive advantage. Social Media Explorer is a company that teaches firms how to participate in social media marketing and offers information products as well. The firm shows companies how to make it easier for visitors to follow them on Twitter or Facebook and showcases guest writers on its blog to help build trust among potential business customers.[34]

NOT-FOR-PROFIT ORGANIZATIONS

Not-for-profit organizations use social media to market themselves to individuals as well as to other organizations. They might promote a fundraising auction or road race on Twitter; ask for donations on Facebook; or blog about a cause in an appeal to potential business partners. They use social media to connect with the general public, the business community, and each other.

Best Friends Animal Society helps find permanent homes (called "forever homes") for dogs and cats, some of which have been designated "unadoptable" by others. Its Invisible Dogs Campaign is a grassroots movement that employs user-generated content created through the iPhone or Android app named My Dog ID. The app lets people take photos of themselves and then applies facial recognition to find their perfect dog match. In addition to being entertaining, the app prompts people to share their photo matches with friends on Twitter, Facebook,

Best Friends Animal Society pictures pets that need a home on its Facebook page, offering to cover travel expenses if the featured pets are adopted the week they are shown on the website.

and Best Friends' "Dog Wall." This gets dog lovers involved with the cause and allows them to spread the word about dogs in need.[35]

Other not-for-profits turn to social media for the following purposes:

- To generate donations or other types of funding
- To spur action, such as signing an online petition or emailing government officials or legislators
- To promote an event for fundraising or educational purposes
- To educate the public about a situation or cause
- To encourage and showcase partnerships with other organizations

Visitors to the Special Olympics home page can click a button to donate, or if they prefer, go to the organization's blog. They can read about partnerships with companies, such as Procter & Gamble, The Coca-Cola Company, and Mattel. Visitors may follow the organization on Facebook, YouTube, and Twitter as well as subscribe to the newsletter. At the Facebook page, fans may post comments and "meet" the athletes. They'll also find ways to volunteer.[36] The entire social media effort is designed to educate and engage followers whether it's through a one-time donation, a long-term volunteer commitment, or increased awareness of the organization and its activities.

ASSESSMENT CHECK

2.1 Why do online shoppers often begin with search engines?

2.2 Why might B2B firms have a difficult time developing a loyal fan base via social media marketing?

CREATING A SOCIAL MEDIA MARKETING PLAN

3 Outline the four key elements of a written social media marketing plan.

social media marketing plan A formal document that identifies and describes goals and strategies, targeted audience, budget, and implementation methods, as well as tactics for monitoring, measuring, and managing the SMM effort.

Like every other type of marketing, effective social media marketing requires setting goals and developing strategies to reach a target audience. The **social media marketing plan** identifies and describes all three of these variables, the tactics required to implement the plan, the budget and expected returns, and the methods for monitoring and measuring the campaign's effectiveness.

A social media marketing plan contains many of the same elements found in a traditional marketing plan or business plan. The formal plan is important because it documents in writing the firm's goals and strategies for the SMM initiative, its budget and expected returns, as well as the company's chosen methods for monitoring, measuring, and managing the effort. A well-written plan contains clear, concise prose that covers the salient points and answers anticipated questions. Although the format and length of SMM plans may vary from firm to firm (or even from project to project), most contain the following information:

- *An executive summary.* This is a paragraph or two explaining the *who, what, when, where, how,* and *why* of the plan. An effective summary gives compelling reasons why the plan should be adopted—for example, to remain competitive in a particular market. Most marketers write the executive summary last, even though it appears first in the plan.

- *A brief overview.* The overview briefly describes the overall market conditions, the firm's current position in social media, and any other factors that the social media marketing effort will address.

- *Analysis of the competition.* The plan examines competitors' presence in social media, including which platforms and tools they select and an evaluation of their overall effectiveness.

- *The body of the plan.* The remaining sections of the SMM plan cover the following: statement of goals and strategies, target audience, budget (including human resource needs) and expected returns, as well as methods for implementing, monitoring, measuring, and managing the SMM campaign.

ASSESSMENT CHECK

3.1 What function does the SMM plan serve?

3.2 What are the main characteristics of an effective executive summary?

The following sections describe in detail the steps in creating the plan for a social media marketing campaign. As marketers develop goals and strategies, decide on methods of implementation, and consider how to monitor, measure, and manage a social media marketing initiative, they keep in mind the elements of the formal document they will produce.

GOALS AND STRATEGIES OF A SOCIAL MEDIA MARKETING PLAN

Before embarking on a social media marketing campaign, social media marketers need to understand two major distinctions between traditional marketing and SMM. First, traditional marketing seeks to control the content and message received by an audience. But SMM actively solicits the audience's participation in the message, and more often than not, the audience creates its own message—that's the nature of interactivity. Second, successful social media marketing efforts require the audience's trust. It may take a while to build this trust—and, in fact, some parts of the SMM effort may be directed toward trust building—but without credibility, the two-way conversation between company and consumer can't occur. The audience will cease to participate, and the effort will fail.

We can break the process of developing a social media marketing campaign into six basic phases, keeping in mind that they actually represent a cycle: set goals, target the audience, develop strategies, produce content, implement the plan, monitor, and measure.[37] Figure 4.3 illustrates the cycle of social media marketing.

Marketers must also keep in mind the importance of listening throughout all phases of the campaign. Because the basis for social media is conversation, smart marketers use social media to listen to what is being said about their own company and its products, competitors, consumer likes and dislikes, consumer wish lists or problems they would like solved, even the overall hopes and fears of the general public—are people worried about the economy or feeling optimistic? Marketers may use social media to tap conversations with or about their intended audience—blog posts, tweets, social news, and the like. Social media also is helpful for connecting with **influencers**—individuals with the capability of affecting the opinions and actions of others. If you want to stay current on upcoming fashion trends, follow stylist Rachel Zoe's Facebook page. Oprah Winfrey, Lady Gaga, and Steven Spielberg made *Forbes'* recent list of the top 10 most influential celebrities.[38] You can find all of them on various forms of social media.

4 Discuss the importance of setting goals and developing strategies, including targeting an audience, for a social media marketing initiative.

influencers Individuals with the capability of affecting the opinions or actions of others.

Briefly Speaking

"Ultimately, brands need to have a role in society. The best way to have a role in society is to understand how people are talking about things in real time."

—Jean-Philippe Maheu
CEO, Publicis Modem

SETTING GOALS

A successful social media marketing campaign starts with clear goals. Marketers should ask themselves: "What do we want to accomplish through this campaign?" Examples of social media marketing goals include:

- Creating or building brand awareness
- Reaching new customers

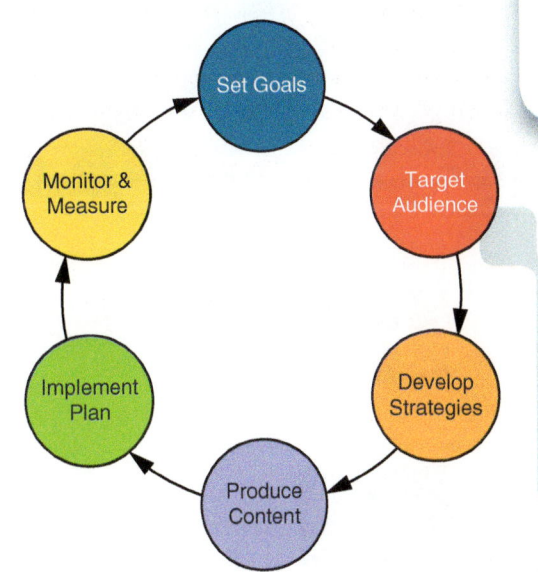

FIGURE 4.3
Cycle of Social Media Marketing

Source: Based on Ron Jones, "6 Steps in Developing a Social Media Strategy," *Clickz.com*, accessed February 6, 2014, www.clickz.com.

- Strengthening relationships with existing customers
- Increasing customer satisfaction
- Launching new products
- Stimulating demand
- Generating sales leads
- Integrating social media with other marketing efforts such as public relations or promotion
- Acquiring an existing business or account
- Managing a crisis

Once goals are established, marketers are better able to develop strategies and choose the right platforms or outlets for their messages. Clear goals also help everyone involved in the campaign to aim their efforts in the right direction. In the aftermath of the BP oil spill off the Gulf Coast, the Louisiana Tourism Coastal Coalition had one major goal: to reduce losses resulting from the spill and rebuild tourism along the Louisiana coast. Collaborating with the Internet consulting firm WSI, the coalition launched a social media campaign that included postings on Facebook, Twitter, YouTube, and Flickr. Taking its social media strategy one step further after the oil spill, the coalition hosts the Visit Louisiana Coast website that highlights the various travel opportunities along the Gulf Coast via Facebook, Twitter, Flickr, YouTube, and a travel blog.[39]

Goals should also be flexible. Conditions in the marketing environment may change, and marketers should be able to adapt their goals without scrapping an entire plan. Upon measuring the results of a campaign, marketers may determine that a change is necessary. A social media effort might be so successful that a firm wants to expand its goals. Unexpected customers may appear, in which case marketers could tweak the message or add another type of social media to the mix in order to serve them. A new social-networking site could pop up and attract visitors at a high rate—leading marketers to reevaluate not only their choice of platforms but also their immediate goals. A company might decide to return to its roots to reconnect with customers.

Taking a page from founder Sam Walton's playbook, which emphasized the importance of retail as a local business, Walmart refocused some of its marketing goals to target local communities. The company chose local social media as its strategy to connect with consumers on a grassroots level. "We are just barely starting to see the potential that [local social marketing] offers us," Walmart CMO Stephen Quinn explains. "We're going to have to absolutely become a part of those communities and know what's going on in that community."[40]

Visit Louisiana Coast is just one of the several social media strategies used by the Louisiana Tourism Coastal Coalition to market tourism to the Gulf Coast.

TARGETING THE AUDIENCE

"Who are we trying to reach?" This is the first question marketers ask when they begin to develop strategies for any marketing effort—including one involving social media. Social media efforts customize marketers' approach to targeted audiences more than many types of traditional marketing because they are interactive. A television commercial for the latest Volkswagen Beetle could reach school-age children, parents of large families, teenagers with limited money for a new car, young professionals who prefer a sport model, and many others not in the market for a Beetle. But visitors who follow the model on Pinterest can view or pin pictures of road trips and decorated cars, or reminisce about VW Beetle advertisements through the years.[41] The social media effort targets interested consumers much more specifically than a television commercial.

How do social media marketers arrive at a target audience? It depends on the goal of the marketing effort. If it's to create brand awareness, the audience will be broader than for strengthening relationships with existing customers. Marketers narrow this target further by determining which social media will be best suited to certain types of consumers. People who want to learn more about a product and its features are more apt to search out this information on Facebook or Google+, while those interested in a promotional event more likely will follow Twitter. Although Chapter 9 discusses the concept of market segmentation and targeting in detail, here we examine ways for marketers to target their audience for social media campaigns.

In order to pinpoint the audience for social media marketing, firms gather information on the following:

- *Demographics.* This refers to features of the group (or groups) within the larger population that the firm wants to reach. Characteristics include age, gender, geographic location, income, ethnicity, marital status, and so forth.

- *What the group (or organization) needs or wants.* Marketers identify what their potential customers need or want—say, gluten-free foods or sports apparel—and determine if and how the firm's products could satisfy this. If the company decides that a particular group of people represents a good match for its products, marketers then begin to develop strategies for engaging the group through social media.

- *Which of the firm's products and social media will meet the needs and wants of particular groups of people.* Marketers not only identify a target group, they also pinpoint which of their goods and services will best serve that group, and begin to determine which social media should deliver the messages that will spark interest and interaction.

Developing the best strategies for social media marketing requires a thorough understanding of the target audience in order to influence their behavior—whether it's to make an immediate purchase, spread the word, sign an online petition, participate in a survey, or visit a brick-and-mortar store.

Vintage Plantations, maker of handcrafted chocolates, invites website visitors to participate in its Cocoa Cultures blog and forum, which the company aims at "aficionados of pure chocolate." The chocolate maker identifies its customers as consumers who not only prefer to eat the highest-grade chocolate but also care about its origins: "We make chocolate in cooperation only with entities willing to follow the Rainforest Alliance Guidelines, and we train them to achieve very high standards of quality." Consumers are encouraged to join Cocoa Cultures to learn more about the chocolate, spread the word, and purchase Rainforest Alliance–certified goods produced by Vintage Plantations and others.[42]

DEVELOPING STRATEGIES AND CHOOSING TACTICS

Every strategy in an effective social media marketing campaign traces back to the campaign's goals and ultimately links to a firm's overall strategic goals. Once marketers answer the question of who they are trying to reach by targeting their audience, they ask a second vital question in social media marketing: "How do we engage the audience in a conversation?" Then they develop strategies for developing and delivering the content that will drive the interaction. They decide:

- *Which social media platforms to use, and how to combine them to reach and engage with the audience.* Recently, cable provider Comcast introduced a pilot program in Houston—the Web equivalent of a public access channel called "Houston's Voice." Viewers can watch video on demand, post comments, and even submit their own video footage. It's "a mix between

> **Briefly Speaking**
>
> "Quit counting fans, followers, and blog subscribers like bottle caps. Think, instead, about what you're hoping to achieve with and through the community that actually cares about what you're doing."
>
> —Amber Naslund
> *Social media strategist*

YouTube, Facebook, and Yelp," says a Comcast spokesperson. People can log in at the site or through Facebook, Twitter, and YouTube.[43]

- *Which social media tools should deliver the campaign's content, and how best to link them with the selected social media platforms.* There's an app for just about everything, and tools like QR codes are gaining popularity as well. Consumers who scan QR codes generally expect a coupon or a deal on products.

- *Who will participate in the conversation on behalf of the company (staff members, professional bloggers, celebrities, and other influencers).* Marketers looking for a list of top influencers in a particular industry can browse those compiled online by SocMetrics for fields ranging from advertising and design to politics and public relations.[44]

- *How to make it easy for potential customers to locate and participate in the conversation.* One way to do this is to create a specific landing page for a marketing campaign instead of directing consumers to the company's home page first. This works especially well for larger companies that are marketing many products. For its "Begin with Ben" campaign, Uncle Ben's rice launched its "Ben's Beginners Cooking Contest" for children and their parents as a way to get kids interested in cooking healthful meals. Contestants uploaded their entries in the form of cooking video clips and consumers voted for their favorites on the "Ben's Beginners" website.[45]

Once strategic decisions are made, marketers zoom in on specific tactics like recruiting specific influencers, setting up a photo or naming contest, offering coupons or discounts, highlighting loyal customers or fans, sending out regular updates, and the like. The "Marketing Success" feature describes how Weight Watchers used social networking and celebrities to connect with consumers and increase revenues.

Savored, a company that offers online reservations and discounts to restaurants in New York City, had a simple goal for its most recent social media marketing effort: to sign up new members and collect email addresses for further marketing. The company decided to launch a Facebook campaign with Wildfire, a Web app that lets businesses create their own interactive promotions, publish them on social networks, and view the real-time results along with analytics to interpret the data. With Wildfire, one of Savored's designers created an ad for a sweepstakes in which consumers had a chance to win $100 each week for a year at any Savored restaurant. To enter, all participants had to do was "like" Savored's Facebook page and register with their email addresses. Within a couple of months, more than 12,000 people had entered the sweepstakes; 4,000 were non-members, and more than 500 of those diners signed up for Savored's service. Thus, Savored achieved its goal with its targeted audience. Just as important, the Facebook exposure broadened Savored's potential customer base. "There are a billion people on Facebook," noted the firm's vice president, "so there are always new eyeballs to reach."[46]

For its "Begin with Ben" campaign, Uncle Ben's rice launched its "Ben's Beginners Cooking Contest" for children and their parents as a way to get kids interested in cooking healthful meals.

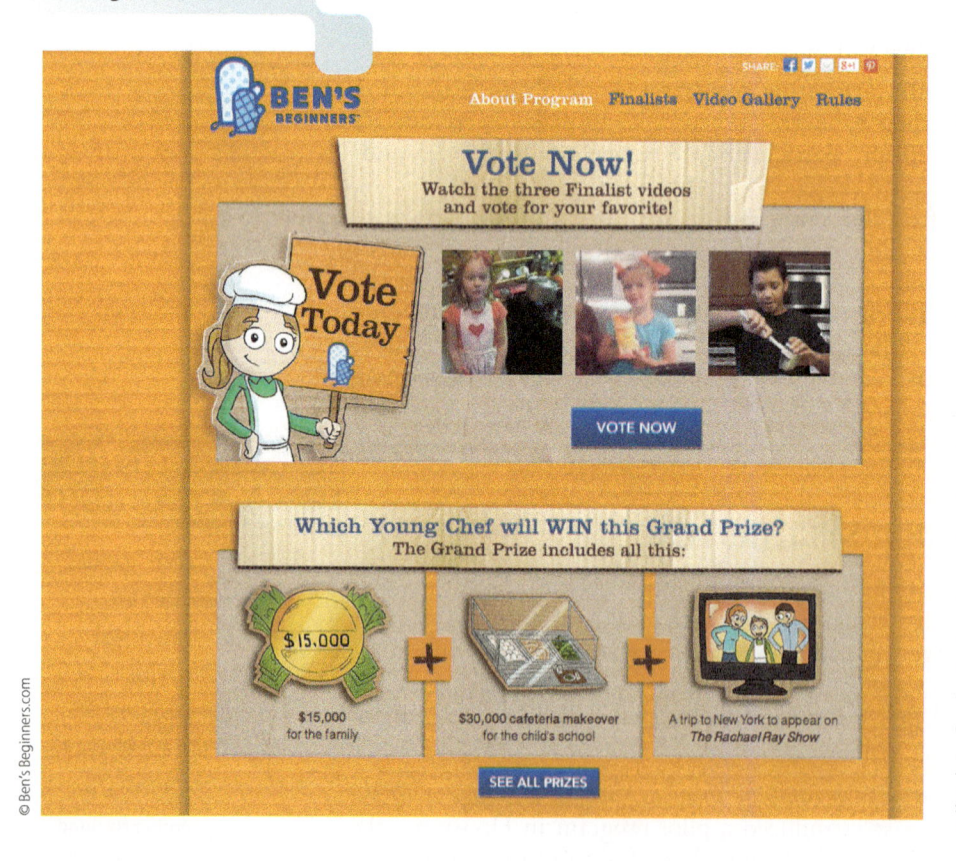

MARKETING SUCCESS
Weight Watchers Gets Social

Background. Weight Watchers' approach has always included a strong social element, with members meeting regularly with weight counselors and other members to discuss progress in losing weight and developing healthier lifestyles.

The Challenge. Over the past several years, revenues were flat and the company looked for ways to increase sales. Because of its "community-centric" approach, Weight Watchers focused its strategies on social networking to attract new members and retain existing ones.

The Strategy. The company connects with followers through Weightwatchers.com, Facebook, Twitter, online community groups, blogs, and mobile apps. It provides recipes, weekly workout challenges, inspirational quotes, dining out tips, and the like. The company has more than 1.6 million Facebook fans, and its Twitter followers number more than 250,000.

The Outcome. According to Weight Watchers, Oscar-winning actress and company spokesperson Jennifer Hudson—who lost 80 pounds on the plan—brought in record traffic. Former NBA star Charles Barkley, who shed more than 50 pounds, leads Weight Watchers' "Lose like a man" initiative, sometimes even appearing in ads wearing a dress. After giving birth to her second child, entertainer Jessica Simpson heads up the company's new "Mom's Initiative," targeting the legions of mothers seeking to return to their pre-pregnancy weight. And a recent study by Baylor College of Medicine—funded in part by Weight Watchers—found that dieters who used the Weight Watchers' tools lost significantly more weight than did those who diet on their own.

Sources: Company website, www.weightwatchers.com, accessed August 15, 2014; "Jennifer Hudson Shows off Her Slender Figure in Skin-Tight Leggings and Tank Top as She Promotes Black Nativity," *Mail Online*, accessed January 17, 2014, http://www.dailymail.uk; Melissa Healy, "Trying to Lose Weight? Don't Go It Alone, Study Says," *Los Angeles Times*, accessed January 17, 2014, http://articles.latimes.com; Andrew M. Seaman, "Weight Watchers Better Than Self-Help for Weight Loss," *Reuters*, accessed January 17, 2014, http://www.reuters.com; Patrick Coffee, "Weight Watchers Rebrands Spokesperson Jessica Simpson," *Media Bistro*, accessed January 17, 2014, http://www.mediabistro.com; "Weight Watchers' Famous Faces," *CNN Money*, accessed January 17, 2014, http://money.cnn.com.

ASSESSMENT CHECK

4.1 Identify the two main distinctions between traditional marketing and a SMM campaign.

4.2 In order to target an audience, what three types of information do marketers gather?

4.3 What vital question do marketers ask when developing strategies for a SMM plan?

PRODUCING CONTENT AND IMPLEMENTING THE PLAN

Identify the seven qualities of effective social media content and the rules of engagement with social media.

Marketers create content and implement the SMM plan with the firm's goals and strategies in mind. The idea is to reach the targeted audience and engage them with the company's brand. For companies that manage to build followers on social media, this is a huge branding opportunity.

CREATING CONTENT

SMM content differs from traditional marketing in that it is, by definition, a two-way street. In order for SMM to succeed, the content of its messages must engage the target audience in the conversation. According to the Content Marketing Institute (CMI), more than nine out of ten organizations already use some type of content marketing (usually in a combination of traditional and social media marketing), and 65 percent report that they had increased their content marketing from the previous year.[47] **Content marketing** involves creating and distributing relevant and targeted material to attract and engage an audience, with the goal of driving them to a desired action.

Content for an effective SMM campaign has the following qualities:

- *A strong brand focus.* Every communication includes current messages relevant to the brand. The Make-A-Wish Foundation shares video wishes on its YouTube channel, publishes every granted wish on its website, and shares similar content on Facebook and Twitter.[48]

- *A focus on the audience rather than the organization.* While it's important to maintain a strong brand identity and meet marketing goals, SMM content focuses on its audience rather than promoting the company outright. Some of the most successful SMM campaigns have transpired via stories about consumers and user-generated content.

- *Targeted keywords.* Good keywords are those the targeted audience will most likely search with when looking for information about goods and services. Marketers may obtain outside research on this or research it themselves.

- *Relevant information.* This is more than a list of product features or specifications. Content may include problem-solving tips, answers to frequently asked questions, community polls, guest writers, interviews, statistics, case studies, and so forth.

- *Shareworthy text and images.* Marketers can turn customers into storytellers by encouraging them to post images related to the brand. In fact, Dunkin' Donuts recently used such shareworthy content from fans to create a recent TV advertising campaign. Marketers pored over tens of thousands of Facebook and Twitter posts from fans who would appear in TV commercials based on the fans' actual social content.[49]

- *Invitations to generate content via posts, shares, discussions, reviews, or other forms of dialogue with the organization as well as with fellow customers.* At its Kraft Recipes website, Kraft Foods Group invites consumers to join the community page where they can exchange and review recipes and menus, ask questions about ingredients, and post photos and tips for substitutions or short cuts using Kraft Foods products. Cooks may log on or share through Facebook, YouTube, and Pinterest.[50]

- *Promotions that offer discounts, gifts, or other special deals in exchange for participation.* To launch a gardening app called Sprout It, Web developers invited their fans to snap a picture of their backyard and post it to Instagram or Twitter. The grand prize: a professional garden makeover.[51]

IMPLEMENTING THE PLAN

Like traditional marketing plans, the social media marketing plan requires a timeline for implementation. Marketers may decide to create separate schedules for the rollout onto each social media platform. In addition, the SMM plan builds in a specified time period for engaging with the public, offering special promotions, and the like. Finally, the timeline includes managing, monitoring, and measuring the success of the effort.

As the marketing effort is launched, someone representing the firm must stand watch to respond to customers who comment on blog posts, review products, ask questions, post videos and photos, or enter contests. The good thing about social media is that it operates around the clock; the bad thing is that marketers never have down time. However, they can use software products such as HootSuite, a social media management system (or dashboard) to manage multiple social profiles, schedule messages and tweets, track brand mentions, and analyze social traffic.[52]

---

content marketing
Creating and distributing relevant and targeted material to attract and engage an audience, with the goal of driving them to a desired action.

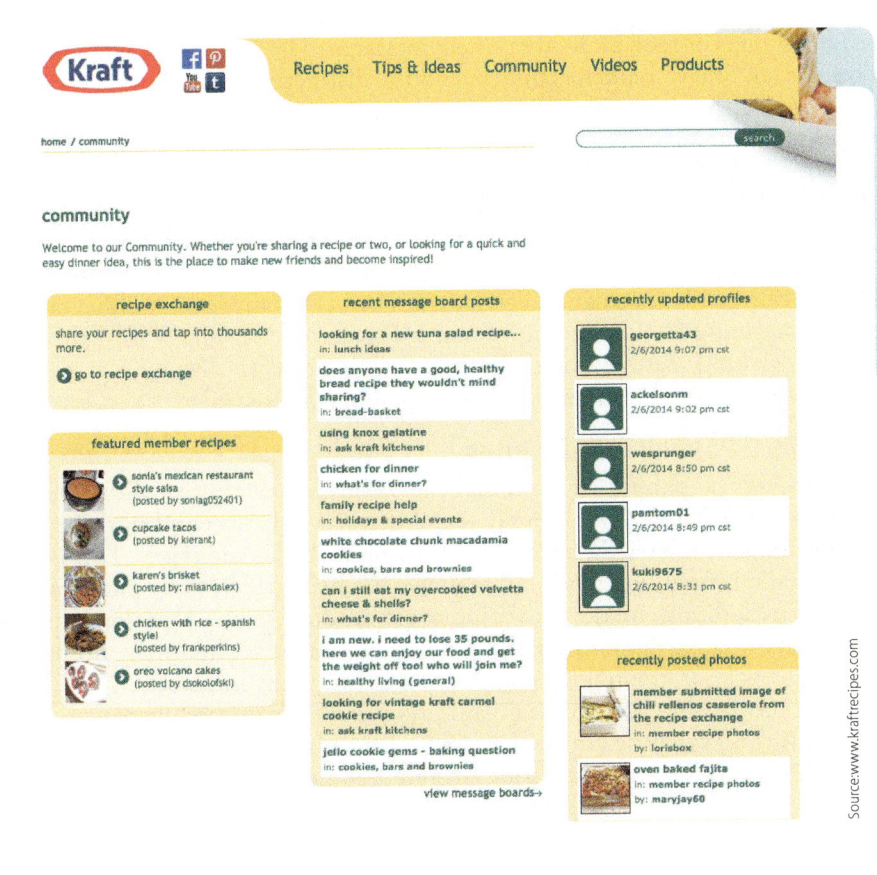

Kraft Foods Group invites consumers to join its community page where they can exchange and review menus and post photos and tips about using Kraft food products.

Another app called Post Planner enables marketers to post with pictures or video and has a version that allows companies to customize the app name and send visitors who click on it to the company's website instead of to an application. Various apps allow firms to add newsletter sign-ups to their pages. Constant Contact is one of these apps. It doesn't allow for maximum customization, but marketers may add text to discuss their newsletter as well as an image. Horsefeathers Restaurant in North Conway, New Hampshire, which features pub fare, uses Constant Contact for its newsletter. The restaurant also runs a blog and maintains Facebook and Twitter accounts.[53]

Experts recommend that marketers refrain from scheduling content more than a week away because information can change, consumer responses may shift, and events might occur that would change the content. As long as marketers have enough time to make last-minute changes, scheduling the rollout of content should be a relatively smooth process.

RULES OF ENGAGEMENT FOR SOCIAL MEDIA

Marketers who use social media to reach their targeted audience are entering into conversations with customers, and they must respect the conventions of personal interaction if they want to build successful relationships. The rules of engagement for social media are meant to make the exchange a positive one for all parties.

Follow Rules and Guidelines
Social-networking sites often have strict rules about advertising, and some have rules governing membership. Marketers shouldn't try to sidestep these in an effort to get marketing messages to users—it will backfire and may result in a ban from any presence on the site.

Use Social Media Channels as They Were Intended
Each social media channel has an intended use by its community. Marketers should be aware of these functions and stay within those parameters. For example, LinkedIn members can join

discussion groups or send each other direct messages. The same thing goes for Facebook, Twitter, and other sites. Smart marketers understand the distinction and tailor their postings accordingly. Businesses also should avoid creating social medial profiles for the sole purpose of marketing. Most people do not care to see unwanted product messages on the personal blogs they read or the forums in which they participate. Failure to follow these conventions may result in posts being hidden or unfollowed—or outright public criticism.

Starbucks stumbled in the UK when it attempted to increase brand recognition and capitalize on the holiday season with the hashtag #SpreadTheCheer. The campaign launch unfortunately coincided with news that the coffee giant had paid only $13.8 million taxes in Great Britain despite a staggering $4.9 billion in revenues. Thereafter, consumers used the hashtag to criticize Starbucks. Making matters worse, the tweets were displayed live on a giant screen at London's Natural History Museum, where Starbucks sponsors the ice rink.[54]

Think Before Posting—or Deleting

Before hitting that "publish" button, marketers must be certain that the content they are making public is exactly what they want to say—and that it will be received in the intended manner. It's always a good idea to ask, "What could go wrong with this message?" This is particularly true if the organization is multinational and messages are being received by potential customers around the world. In addition, marketers should avoid sending spam. A person who follows a page or group doesn't necessarily want regular promotional messages and may ultimately decide to stop following the page or group if the company sends too many messages.

Social media strategists advise organizations *not* to delete comments, no matter how painful or unflattering they may be (unless they are profane, obscene, or illegal). Instead, they recommend that marketers weather legitimate criticism and deal directly with an online crisis instead of trying to avoid it. When Volkswagen deleted negative Facebook comments related to Greenpeace's accusations that the carmaker used "its huge political muscle to lobby against environmental laws," a firestorm ensued. Tens of thousands of Greenpeace supporters took Volkswagen to task for not addressing the issue publicly. Greenpeace even created, "VW: The Dark Side," a parody of the automaker's popular "Star Wars" TV commercial, and the parody went viral. Ultimately, Volkswagen agreed to support European environmental laws. However, social media experts observed that the crisis could have died down much sooner if Volkswagen had responded immediately and offered to continue any discussions at its own website.[55]

social media monitoring The process of tracking, measuring, and evaluating a firm's social media marketing initiatives.

social media analytics Tools that help marketers trace, measure, and interpret data related to social media marketing initiatives.

ASSESSMENT CHECK

5.1 What is content marketing?

5.2 What is the one major drawback to social media as it pertains to scheduling?

5.3 What is the function of rules of engagement in social media marketing?

MONITORING, MEASURING, AND MANAGING THE SMM CAMPAIGN

> **6** Describe the different means of monitoring, measuring, and managing the social media marketing campaign.

It's one thing to launch a social media marketing campaign, but without tracking its course, the campaign may sink or run aground. The role of **social media monitoring** is to track, measure, and evaluate a firm's social media marketing initiatives. Marketers must also manage their company's SMM efforts by making changes when necessary.

MONITORING AND MEASURING

One of the greatest challenges faced by social media marketers is monitoring the progress of an SMM effort, partly because its reach can stretch far beyond the capabilities of the company. But various **social media analytics** tools help marketers track (find and follow social content), measure, and interpret data related to SMM initiatives. For example, the company Klout provides social media analytics that measure users' influence across 10 different social networks,

TABLE 4.2 Social Media Monitoring and Analytics Tools

Product Name	What It Does
Cyfe	Creates dashboards and tracks social accounts.
Google Analytics	Inspects user traffic, including what percentage comes from social media links.
Simply Measured	Provides competitive analysis for social impact, analytics for Facebook and Twitter, and a complete suite of monitoring and reporting tools.
Social Mention	Supplies real-time social media search and analysis and alerts.
Social Report	Monitors as many as five projects at once, analyzing audience growth, engagement, reach, and activity. Delivers directly to your inbox.
Sum All	Connects your social media analytics with other areas of the business, enabling marketers to calculate ROI.
Tweriod	Analyzes when followers are online and identifies the best time to send Tweets for maximum exposure.
Viralheat	Aggregates social media traffic into a single stream; has dashboard capability and supports up to seven social media accounts.

Sources: Kristi Hines, "4 Tools That Improve Your Social Media Analytics," *Social Media Examiner*, accessed January 17, 2014, www.socialmediaexaminer.com; Breanna Jacobs, "25 Awesome Social Media Tools Your Brand Should Be Using," *Social Media Strategic Summit*, accessed January 17, 2014, http://socialmediastrategicsummit.com; Ian Barker, "Best Social Media Analytics Tools: 8 of the Best to Use," *TechRadar*, accessed January 17, 2014, www.techradar.com.

giving them a score from 1 to 100 (see the "Marketing Success" feature in Chapter 6 for more information about Klout).[56] Table 4.2 gives some examples of different types of social media analytics tools.

Monitoring and measuring help marketers understand what their customers need and want, ultimately making adjustments to SMM or product offerings to satisfy those customers. Marketers select monitoring tools based on the needs of their own firms. Social media analytics software, such as Trendrr and Brandwatch, are all designed to help companies monitor the cyber conversations about their brands and about their competitors. Trendrr tracks the popularity and awareness of trends, especially in television. Brandwatch offers solutions that monitor its business customers' reputations as well as their competitors; answers customer complaints and questions on the Web; supports its customers' online communities; promotes goods and services; prevents and handles negative news coverage or other public relations crises; and provides market research.[57]

Firms also calculate the **return on investment (ROI)** of their social media marketing initiatives, using reach (the percentage of people in a target market who are exposed to the marketing effort at least once) and frequency (the number of times an individual is exposed to the marketing material during the campaign) as variables. Expenses (such as employee time spent answering customer tweets or Facebook questions) are weighed against savings (employees not having to make in-person calls to customers). Although not all marketers agree on the validity of measuring SMM campaigns this way, companies do concede that they look for quantitative ways like this to evaluate the efficiency of the marketing effort.

Effective monitoring gives marketers a clearer picture of an organization's influence via social media. Recent analytics show that 98 percent of not-for-profit organizations maintain a presence on Facebook, and 74 percent are on Twitter. UNICEF, which generates hundreds of millions of dollars in revenues each year to benefit the world's children, is one nonprofit organization that has figured out how to leverage the power of social media. It understands that Facebook is the place to develop deeper and longer conversations with its nearly 4 million followers, while Twitter gives access to "live coverage" of events around the world. UNICEF also maintains accounts on

return on investment (ROI) The rate of revenues received for every dollar spent on an expense.

UNICEF maintains a presence on several social media platforms around the world.

> **Briefly Speaking**
>
> "For us [social media] doesn't have to be an exact science. If people are talking about Our brand in a favorable way, that's good enough."
>
> —Adam Broitman
> VP of Global Digital Marketing,
> MasterCard

YouTube, Scribd, and MySpace. In addition to English, its Facebook, Twitter, and YouTube pages are available in Arabic, Chinese, and French.[58]

Measuring the success of a social media marketing plan includes such factors as share of voice (number of conversations about the company versus competitors and overall market), awareness of the company or brand, level of engagement by the targeted audience, influence created, and popularity among target audience members. Of course, every marketer aims for success—but not every campaign meets its goals. This is where competent management of social media efforts becomes important to businesses.

MANAGING

Managing a social media marketing campaign—or a company's overall social media efforts—requires skill, expertise, and understanding of the company's brand, its competitors, and the social media environment. This means maintaining a grasp on the success or failure of previous strategies, knowledge of the benefits and drawbacks of the different social media platforms and tools, and an ability to interpret data without losing sight of the overall goal. It also means being flexible enough to change tactics when necessary to avert or minimize a crisis.

Southwest Airlines relies on social media for much of its communication with consumers. The airline's Twitter feed has more than 1.6 million followers, and nearly three times that many people "like" its Facebook page. The company's Nuts About Southwest blog sets the standard for dialogue with the public. The social media team at Southwest uses social media management tools, such as CoTweet for Twitter and Facebook, which enable them to monitor key words and other aspects of SMM campaigns.[59]

Southwest's organizational culture seems to be a natural fit for social media. The airline believes in embracing all forms of media, maintaining transparency in its communications, and "being real" in social media conversations with customers.

The effects of social media exposure can also turn against a company quickly, as another airline recently discovered. Air travelers recognize that sometimes airlines misplace people's luggage. However, when British Airways was slow to respond after luggage went missing on a business trip, a disgruntled flyer took action. To complain about the airline's customer service, a Chicago business owner paid $1,000 for a promoted tweet, targeting the airline's 50,000 New York and United Kingdom followers with a complaint about his lost luggage. The matter escalated when the airline took eight hours to respond to the tweet, saying only that it checks tweets from 9 to 5 Monday through Friday. Ultimately, the missing luggage was located—but not before the incident engaged thousands of British Airways followers as well as the media. As the airline likely learned, timeliness and transparency are vital approaches for a firm involved in managing a potential social media crisis.[60]

> **ASSESSMENT CHECK**
>
> 6.1 What is the function of social media monitoring?
>
> 6.2 Identify the two vital approaches for a firm as it manages a potential social media crisis.

ETHICAL AND LEGAL ISSUES

Social media marketers face ethical and legal issues such as privacy and accountability as part of their job. As rapidly as the various social media evolve and expand, so too will new ethical situations arise. Firms will have to stay apprised of new threats as well as the solutions to problems. Marketers who maintain an educated and cautious approach to these issues—laced with common sense—will be best prepared to meet challenges head on.

Discuss ethical and legal issues encountered by marketers in social media marketing. **7**

WORKPLACE ETHICS

Recent studies have begun to examine correlations between social media use (particularly during the work day) and ethical behavior. This has led companies to begin instituting formal policies about social networking in the workplace.

Many companies are now drafting written policies for the use of social media, by individuals in the workplace as well as by groups such as the marketing department for company purposes. Well-written social media policies have the following qualities:

- Consistent with a firm's organizational culture and values
- Explain why employees should take certain steps or actions (or avoid them)
- Broad enough to cover the major points, but brief enough to fit onto two pages
- Linked to other relevant company policies and guidelines[61]

BE HONEST

Social media messages travel at lightning speed around the world; potentially millions of people may view a message in a matter of seconds or minutes. This means that postings, ads, comments, and even images come under intense scrutiny—and must be checked for accuracy, fair and realistic claims or promises, balance and objectivity, and potential for misinterpretation. Honesty is

SOLVING AN ETHICAL CONTROVERSY
Barnes & Noble Security Breach: Who's to Blame?

Barnes & Noble recently announced more than 60 stores suffered a security breach when hackers broke into keypads where customers swipe their credit and debit cards, and enter personal ID numbers, or PINs. As a result of the breach, hackers stole financial information and PINs for thousands of customers who shop at the retail chain.

Should Barnes & Noble be responsible for keeping consumer data secure?

PRO

1. The company should take every precaution to ensure its security measures provide the best defense against the theft of personal data.
2. With hackers becoming more sophisticated in their efforts to steal information, a multi-prong security approach should be used, even if it means hiring outside firms to ensure the system is safe.

CON

1. Let the buyer beware. Identity thieves continue to be aggressive when trying to find out personal data, including PINs and passwords.
2. Because they have no input on business security measures, shoppers should avoid using keypads at the checkout and ask the cashier to swipe their credit/debit card directly into the register.

Summary

Once the breach was discovered, Barnes & Noble officials acknowledged the attack and suggested consumers change their PINs and check bank and/or credit card statements for unauthorized transactions. To be safe, consumers should select PINs that cannot be guessed easily by others and sign up for mobile alerts from banks and credit card companies about unusual transactions in their accounts.

Sources: Glenn G. Lammi, "Will California's New Data Breach Notification Duty Stimulate Class Action Litigation?" *Forbes*, accessed January 17, 2014, www.forbes.com; Ethan P. Schulman, Jeffrey Poston, Jennifer S. Romano, and Robin B. Campbell, "Data Breach Class Action against Barnes & Noble Dismissed for Lack of Standing," *E-Discovery Law Insights*, accessed January 17, 2014, www.ediscoverylawinsights.com; Bureau of National Affairs, "Barnes & Noble Customers Lack Standing to Bring Data Breach Litigation, Court Rules," accessed January 17, 2014, www.bna.com; Jeffrey Benzing, "Data Breach Complaint against Barnes & Noble Dismissed," *Main Justice*, accessed January 17, 2014, www.mainjustice.com.

---

the best policy when marketing via social media; transparent communications help develop trust among followers and may ultimately contribute to strengthening a firm's brand.

RESPECT PRIVACY

Although marketers try to gather as much information as possible about a targeted audience, they must not distribute any personal information without consent. Because social media is interactive by its nature, marketers must be vigilant about confidentiality and not letting personal information or other data accidentally slip into unauthorized hands. Violation of these practices and other privacy laws and guidelines could destroy a company's reputation and cost millions of dollars.

Almost immediately after Sony revealed a breach of its PlayStation Network customers' personal data, the first lawsuit was filed, alleging that the firm took too long to notify people, failing to allow customers to make an informed decision as to whether to change credit-card numbers, close the exposed accounts, check their credit reports, or take other actions. Although Sony temporarily turned off its PlayStation Network and Music Unlimited service and hired an outside security firm to investigate the unauthorized intrusion, the company's reputation was damaged, and claims are likely to be very costly. The UK Information Commissioner's Office fined Sony 250,000 British pounds (more than $415,000) after an investigation revealed the breach could have been avoided had Sony's software been up to date.[62]

In the quickly changing social media world, organizations need to be nimble when dealing with security measures that affect them and their customers. The "Solving an Ethical Controversy" feature discusses a security breach that posed challenges for Barnes & Nobles and its customers.

BE ACCOUNTABLE

Mistakes happen. When they do, smart social media marketers take action to solve the problem or resolve the issue. First, they acknowledge the problem and take responsibility for it. Second, they communicate with the right people, via the most relevant channel(s), and promise to take steps necessary to correct the situation. Third, they implement the agreed-upon changes or make other concessions and evaluate ways to avoid similar problems in the future. While it's important for businesses to be accountable for their actions, they must do so in a realistic manner, making changes that are relevant to the situation.

> **ASSESSMENT CHECK**
>
> 7.1 How does the interactivity of social media cause potential privacy issues?
>
> 7.2 Identify the three positive steps that firms take when they make a mistake related to social media marketing.

CAREERS IN SOCIAL MEDIA MARKETING

As more and more businesses engage in social media marketing, many people are now seeking careers in the field—either with companies looking to boost their social media presence or with firms that specialize in assisting these companies with their marketing efforts. People are also developing successful careers in social media itself, with firms like Facebook, Twitter, Pinterest, and others. Figure 4.4 shows a breakdown of overall social media job titles in the United States.

Even if you aren't looking for a position specifically in social media marketing, it's likely that you will undertake at least some portion of your job hunt through social media. See the "Career Readiness" feature for some suggestions on using social media to find a job.

8 Explain the different types of positions in social media marketing and how to land an entry-level job.

TYPES OF JOBS

Job titles vary from company to company, but here is a sampling of the different types of positions in social media marketing and the individual's responsibilities:

- *Social media marketing manager (or digital marketing manager).* Oversees all of the company's social media functions, ranging from blogging copywriter to social media strategist.
- *Social media strategist.* Primary decision maker who runs the firm's social media program.

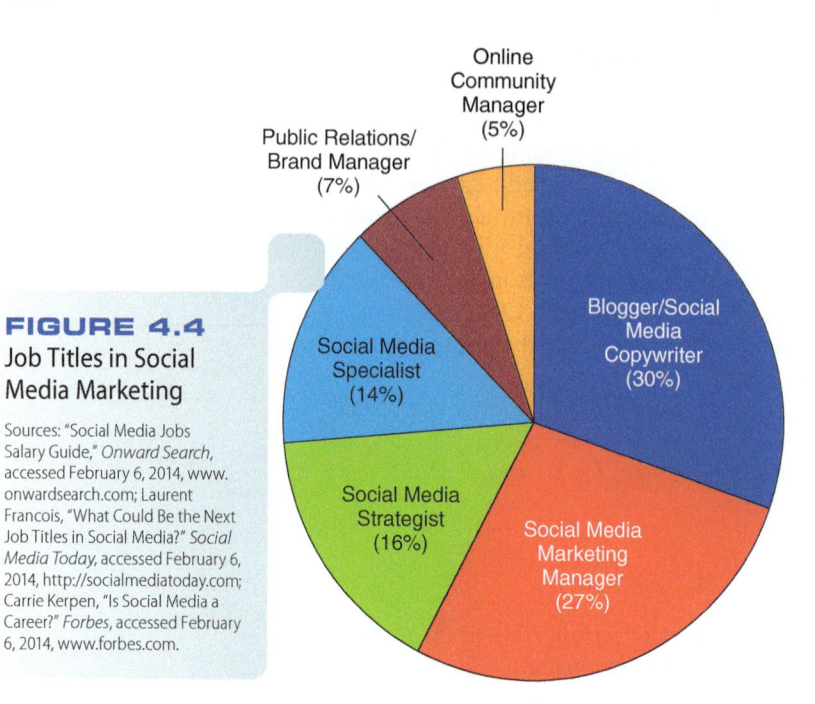

FIGURE 4.4
Job Titles in Social Media Marketing

Sources: "Social Media Jobs Salary Guide," *Onward Search*, accessed February 6, 2014, www.onwardsearch.com; Laurent Francois, "What Could Be the Next Job Titles in Social Media?" *Social Media Today*, accessed February 6, 2014, http://socialmediatoday.com; Carrie Kerpen, "Is Social Media a Career?" *Forbes*, accessed February 6, 2014, www.forbes.com.

Pie chart:
- Blogger/Social Media Copywriter (30%)
- Social Media Marketing Manager (27%)
- Social Media Strategist (16%)
- Social Media Specialist (14%)
- Public Relations/Brand Manager (7%)
- Online Community Manager (5%)

- *Brand manager.* Manages a brand and its public relations over social media sites.
- *Online community manager.* Manages external engagement with customers in social media channels (such as Facebook, Twitter, blogs, or community forums).
- *Influencer relations.* Serves as liaison between a company and those considered to be influencers within the social media community.
- *Social media specialist.* Descriptions vary by company size and needs, but typically handles a variety of tasks, from overseeing blog copy to implementing a company's entire social media program.
- *Social media analytics.* Armed with a background in marketing research or Web analytics, measures the results of a social media marketing effort.

CAREER READINESS
Job Hunting via Social Media

Ninety percent of companies now use social media for recruitment. How can you use social media to succeed in the job market? Here are some tips.

1. Know what each social media site does best.
2. While Facebook is mostly social, recruiters routinely check applicants' walls. Post responsibly, segregate your friend groups appropriately, and monitor friends' posts and tags about you. Delete anything that could be perceived as unprofessional.
3. Use LinkedIn to actively build your professional network. Be strategic in building your profile: to elicit the most visits, include as many of your industry's keywords as possible.
4. Be proactive on LinkedIn. Find people who work for companies of interest and identify links in your network who can introduce you to them.
5. Use LinkedIn, Facebook, and Twitter to let your network know you're looking for a job.
6. Post a professional-looking head shot on your LinkedIn and Facebook pages.
7. If you connect your LinkedIn account to your blog or Twitter feed, remember that you've just given potential employers access to all those additional posts.
8. Use Twitter to follow the companies and industries you're targeting in your search.
9. Proofread every post. Even in the cyberworld, prospective employers give candidates bad marks for poor communication skills.
10. Always be professional when you post. In a recent CareerBuilder survey of hiring managers, more than one-third said they browse candidates' social media profiles to evaluate their character. The rule about social media remains: Don't post anything you wouldn't want to read in tomorrow's news.

Sources: Alexis Grant, "10 Smart Ways to Use Social Media in Your Job Search," *U.S. News & World Report*, accessed February 7, 2014, http://money.usnews.com; Trudy Steinfeld, Social Media: Must-Have Strategies in Your Job Search," *Forbes*, accessed February 7, 2014, www.forbes.com; Christina Jedra, "5 Ways to Use the Internet to Score Your Dream Job," *USA Today*, accessed February 7, 2014, www.usatoday.com; "How to Improve Your Job Search by Using Social Media," *Social Media Today*, accessed February 7, 2014, http://socialmediatoday.com; Jacquelyn Smith, "How Social Media Can Help (or Hurt) You in Your Job Search," *Forbes*, accessed February 7, 2014, www.forbes.com.

- *Social media design.* Oversees the look and feel of an online community, Facebook page, or other branded content. Typically has a graphic-design background.
- *Social media developer.* Provides the programming to build and assemble the features for social tools, such as blogs and communities.
- *Content programmer.* Creates content and generates discussions about topics related to the company's social media presence such as product releases and lifestyle conversations.
- *Blogger or copywriter.* Writes blogs and other social media copy.

Social media marketing jobs offer a wide range in salaries (depending on level, company size, geographic location, and so forth). A survey of chief marketing officers in major corporations revealed that their organizations allocate, on average, more than 10 percent of their marketing budget to social media, and that number is expected to rise steadily in the next several years—potentially creating more jobs.[63]

TIPS FOR LANDING A JOB IN SOCIAL MEDIA MARKETING

If you are just starting out from college, chances are you may be looking for an entry-level job in social media marketing. Here are some suggestions for beginning your career in this field:

- *Land an internship.* Internships—paid or not—are a good way to gain experience in your chosen field. You might have a chance to contribute to a blog or learn some of the skills necessary to begin programming features for social tools.
- *Take online courses that teach social media marketing skills.* Taking online courses demonstrates your willingness and ability to learn prior to landing your first job. Examples include "4 Hour Social Media Strategy Course" from Brazen Careerist and "Inbound Marketing University" from Hubspot. You may include this as professional training on your résumé.
- *Highlight your own online social profile.* Update your Facebook, LinkedIn, YouTube, and Twitter accounts (along with any others) to be sure they are professional and polished. Potential employers do look at these—in fact, you may invite them to do so.
- *Point out your personality.* Tell employers about the characteristics that make you an individual. When building a team, employers often look for traits such as a sense of humor, creativity, passion for the business, and communication skills.[64]

> **Briefly Speaking**
>
> "Yes, we know you're a ninja on Twitter, Facebook, and Foursquare, and Mashable is your homepage—but tell us something we don't know. Impress us."
>
> —Dave Brown
> *Director of Digital Strategy at MKG, an Experiential Marketing Agency*

ASSESSMENT CHECK

8.1 Why is it likely that more jobs in social media marketing will be created in the near future?

8.2 Why do experts recommend taking online courses that teach social media marketing skills?

Strategic Implications of Marketing in the 21st Century

When a new medium of communication emerges, marketers must pay attention. In a short span of time, social media has rooted itself in our global culture. Thus, companies are figuring out how to use this new mode of communication—which creates a two-way conversation—with potential and existing customers.

Despite false starts and various pitfalls, marketers are quickly learning the benefits of using social media to reach their targeted audiences. According to one survey, 89 percent of marketers say that the number-one benefit of social media marketing is generating more exposure for their business; 75 percent report that the greatest benefit is increasing traffic; and 69 percent say it's providing insight into the marketplace.

On the downside, sometimes social media marketing campaigns don't work the way marketers intended, and they must adapt accordingly by making changes or dropping the initiative all together. Social media still takes up a lot of time during the workday—62 percent of surveyed marketers say they spend six or more hours each week on it. Nearly 17 percent reported spending 20 or more hours a week on social media activities.[65]

Despite these numbers, the various social media platforms, tools, and services continue to expand at a rapid rate. This opens up opportunities for firms to adopt social media for their competitive advantage and allows people to build careers in social media marketing. Industry experts anticipate significant growth for social media sites. Thus, marketers will be on constant watch for new developments and ways they can harness the power of social media to reach and engage their customers.

Get online now for additional learning tools to help you master your marketing knowledge—visit **WWW.CENGAGEBRAIN.COM** today!

REVIEW OF CHAPTER OBJECTIVES

1 Explain social media and the differences between social media platforms and social media tools.

Social media is defined collectively as the different forms of electronic communication through which users can create online communities to exchange information, ideas, messages, and other content such as videos and music. A social media platform is a type of software or technology that allows users to build, integrate, or facilitate a community, provide interaction among users, and generate user-authored content. Social-networking sites and bookmarking sites are social media platforms. Social media tools enable users to communicate with each other online. Examples include apps and QR codes.

2 Describe the ways in which consumers and businesses use social media for their buying decisions.

Consumers use social media to learn about new goods and services, conduct research and share information, and make final purchase decisions. Businesses use social media to gather relevant market insights, improve search rankings, and form new business partnerships.

3 Outline the four key elements of a written social media marketing plan.

The formal social media marketing plan contains (1) an executive summary explaining the "who, what, when, where, how, and why" of the plan; (2) a brief overview of market conditions and other factors; (3) a competitive analysis; and (4) a body including goals and strategies, target audience, budget with expected returns, and methods for implementing and managing the effort.

4 Discuss the importance of setting goals and developing strategies, including targeting an audience, for a social media marketing initiative.

Clear goals help marketers set the SMM campaign in the right direction. Flexible goals enable firms to adapt to changing circumstances. Social media marketing efforts customize their approach to targeted audiences more than any other type of marketing because they are interactive, so it is important for marketers to link the targeted audience with the goals of the initiative. Once these decisions are made, marketers must develop strategies, such as which media platforms and tools to use, who will participate, and how to make it easy for customers to participate in the conversation—all within the parameters of the plan's goals.

5 Identify the seven qualities of effective social media content and the rules of engagement with social media.

Effective content has the following qualities: a strong brand focus; emphasis on the audience instead of the organization; targeted keywords; relevant information; shareworthy text and images; invitations to the audience to generate its own content; and offers for discounts or deals. The rules of engagement include: follow site-specific rules and guidelines; use social media channels as they were intended; and think before posting—or deleting.

6 Describe the different means of monitoring, measuring, and managing the social media marketing campaign.

Marketers often use social media analytics tools to help them track, measure, and interpret data related to the SMM effort. They calculate the return on investment (ROI) of the marketing campaign, typically measuring success in terms of share of voice, awareness of company or brand, level of audience engagement, influence created, and popularity. Marketers follow keywords and use tools, such as Trendrr and Brandwatch, to measure and manage specific activities. Flexibility and quick response are also vital to the management of SMM.

7 Discuss ethical and legal issues encountered by marketers in social media marketing.

Social media marketers face ethical and legal issues in their marketing efforts, as well as workplace ethics by employees. Social media marketing efforts should be honest, respect privacy (for example, when collecting data from users), and accountable. When mistakes happen, marketers must acknowledge the problems and take responsibility for fixing them.

8 Explain the different types of positions in social media marketing and how to land an entry-level job.

SMM jobs include: social media marketing manager, social media strategist, brand manager, online community manager, influencer relations, social media analytics, social media design, content programmer, and blogger or copywriter. Candidates for entry-level positions in SMM may: land an internship; take online courses; highlight their social profiles; and point out their personality to prospective employers.

ASSESSMENT CHECK: ANSWERS

1.1 What are social-networking sites? Social-networking sites are the websites that provide virtual communities for people to share daily activities, post opinions on various topics, and increase their circle of friends.

1.2 Define social media marketing. SMM uses the social media portals to create a positive influence on consumers or business customers toward an organization's brand, products, public image, or website.

2.1 Why do online shoppers often begin with search engines? Search engines provide the greatest amount of information about products and companies.

2.2 Why might B2B firms have a difficult time developing a loyal fan base via social media marketing? The nature of the relationships between B2B marketers and their customers is different from that of marketers and consumers. Each business must benefit a firm's overall strategy instead of the needs or wants of an individual, and once a relationship between firms is established, it can be more difficult to alter.

3.1 What function does the SMM plan serve? The SMM plan documents in writing the goals, strategies, target audience, budget, tactics for implementation, and methods for monitoring and managing the campaign's effectiveness.

3.2 What are the main characteristics of an effective executive summary? An effective executive summary explains the *who*, *what*, *when*, *where*, *how*, and *why* of the plan and provides compelling reasons why the plan should be adopted.

4.1 Identify the two main distinctions between traditional marketing and a SMM campaign. While traditional marketing seeks to control the content and message received by an audience, SMM activity solicits the audience's participation in the message. Successful SMM efforts require the audience's trust, whereas traditional marketing may or may not.

4.2 In order to target an audience, what three types of information do marketers gather? Marketers collect information on demographics, what the group needs or wants, and which of the firm's products and social media will meet those needs.

4.3 What vital question do marketers ask when developing strategies for an SMM plan? Marketers ask "How do we engage the audience in a conversation?"

5.1 What is content marketing? Content marketing involves creating and distributing relevant and targeted material to attract and engage an audience, with the goal of driving them to a desired action.

5.2 What is the one major drawback to social media as it pertains to scheduling? Because social media operates around the clock, marketers rarely have down time.

5.3 What is the function of rules of engagement in social media marketing? The rules of engagement for social media are meant to make the exchange between marketers and their target audience a positive one.

6.1 What is the function of social media monitoring? The role of social media monitoring is to track, measure, and evaluate a firm's social media marketing initiatives.

6.2 Identify the two vital approaches for a firm as it manages a potential social media crisis. Timeliness and transparency are vital approaches for a firm involved in managing a potential social media crisis.

7.1 How does the interactivity of social media cause potential privacy issues? Marketers are collecting personal data about users that could possibly slip into unauthorized hands.

7.2 Identify the three positive steps that firms take when they make a mistake related to social media marketing. Marketers acknowledge the problem and take responsibility for it; communicate with the right people via relevant channels; and implement agreed-upon changes.

8.1 Why is it likely that more jobs in social media marketing will be created in the near future? Businesses are increasingly engaging in social media marketing, potentially creating more jobs in this field in the coming years.

8.2 Why do experts recommend taking online courses that teach social media marketing skills? Taking these courses demonstrates willingness and the ability to learn prior to landing the job, and teaches skills that may not be taught in a traditional college curriculum.

MARKETING TERMS YOU NEED TO KNOW

social media 100
social media platform 101
social media tool 101
social-networking site 101
bookmarking site 102
social news site 102
online forum 102
blogging site 102
microblog 102
app 103
QR code 104
social media marketing (SMM) 106
social media marketing plan 110
influencers 111
content marketing 116
social media monitoring 118
social media analytics 118
return on investment (ROI) 119

ASSURANCE OF LEARNING REVIEW

1. Briefly describe the marketing uses for each of the social media platforms and social media tools.
2. What are the three essential features of social media marketing?
3. For what purposes do not-for-profit organizations turn to social media marketing?
4. Why is it important for the goals of a social media marketing campaign to be both clear and flexible?

Chapter 4 Social Media: Living in the Connected World

5. How do social media marketers select a target audience?
6. Who might participate in the social media interaction on behalf of a company? What strengths could each of these people contribute to the conversation?
7. Why must SMM content focus on the audience rather than the organization?
8. What is the purpose of monitoring and measuring the SMM campaign?
9. What are the four main features of a well-written corporate social media policy? Why should companies write such policies?
10. As you scan the list of types of positions in social media marketing, choose two for which you think you would be best suited. Explain the reasons for your choice.

PROJECTS AND TEAMWORK EXERCISES

1. For a week, keep a log on your social media use as a consumer. Which sites and tools do you frequent? Why? How much time do you spend on each one daily? Weekly? Do you interact with social media marketing efforts? Create a profile of yourself as a consumer, describing preferences, influencers, and any other factors that are relevant to your online interaction with SMM.
2. With a classmate, select a television commercial or print ad for a product, such as an upcoming concert or theater production, a hybrid vehicle, a clothing retailer, pet food, or a line of low-fat snacks. Create a poster or brief PowerPoint presentation showing how you would transform this from a traditional marketing effort into social media marketing. Customize your plan for the targeted audience.
3. With a classmate, choose one of the following brands (or select your own):
   a. Cinnamon Toast Crunch cereal
   b. REI clothing
   c. Bose headphones
   d. *Sports Illustrated*
   e. IHOP restaurants

   Create one item of content for a social media marketing effort for your brand, such as a blog or forum, a digital slide show, a short video, or an online contest. No matter which social media platform you choose, be sure to target your audience and invite them to interact.
4. Research a recent social media marketing crisis like the one described in the chapter between a Chicago business owner and British Airways (use a few keywords on a search engine to find examples). Describe the situation and how the company handled it. Was the company's response effective? Why or why not? If not, how would you have handled the situation?
5. Choose one of the social media marketing positions described in this chapter and research online several actual job descriptions for this position (or one like it). You may visit a job site such as CareerBuilder, Indeed, or LinkedIn—or log on to the website of a company that interests you and click on its careers section to look for SMM postings. When you have thoroughly familiarized yourself with the job description, list your current strengths and weaknesses as they relate to the job description—and your strategies for landing a job like this.

CRITICAL-THINKING EXERCISES

1. Choose one of the following and describe how you think social media marketing could help strengthen its brand:
   a. J.Crew
   b. Canon copiers
   c. Great Wolf Lodge resorts
   d. Nivea for Men skin care
   e. Rock band Thirty Seconds to Mars
2. Log on to the Facebook, Tumblr, or Pinterest page of a company that you like or follow. What are people saying about the company, its goods and services, problems they would like solved, or new products they would like to see? How do they describe their experiences and their general views as consumers?
3. When designing a social media marketing plan, marketers must be sure to select and use channels as they were intended—or risk difficulties. For each of the following, state your choice of channel type (social-networking site, microblog, bookmarking site, and so forth) and explain why.
   a. Discussion of product attributes
   b. Opinion survey
   c. Exchange of ideas for saving energy
   d. Personal stories
   e. Video contest featuring pets
4. Do you agree that companies should have formal, written policies regarding the use of social media by employees in the workplace? Why or why not?
5. How do you view the future of social media—and social media marketing? Write a description citing three or four trends or developments you think may evolve over the next decade.

ETHICS EXERCISE

The Ethics Resource Center recently conducted a study to explore the relationship between workplace ethics and social media. The report noted that active social networkers find themselves at higher risk for observing misconduct on the job. According to the findings:

- 72 percent of social networkers observed misconduct by others in the workplace during the previous 12 months (compared with 54 percent of other workers)
- 56 percent of social networkers experienced retaliation after reporting an incident (compared with 18 percent of other workers)
- 42 percent of social networkers felt pressure to compromise their own standards (compared with 11 percent of other workers)[66]

Consider these findings in light of your own experiences in the workplace or college setting.

1. Do these findings surprise you? Why or why not? How might you apply what you have learned about social media and social media marketing from this chapter to your own workplace ethics?
2. Using concepts from this chapter, outline the major points of a social media policy for your college or employer.

INTERNET EXERCISES

1. **Visit the app store.** Using your computer or smartphone, visit an app store (Apple, Google, Amazon, Samsung, or the like) and browse through the various apps available. Which appeal to you and which do not? Why? Write a thumbnail review for four apps (two positive and two negative) explaining your viewpoint as a consumer.

2. **Emphasize the local.** Some large companies are refocusing part of their social media marketing goals and strategies to target local communities and customers. Log on to the website of one of the following firms (or choose your own) to learn more about how the company is using social media marketing to connect with local consumers:

   www.walmart.com

   www.bk.com

   www.starwoodhotels.com

   www.cinemark.com

3. **Familiarize yourself with a new social media platform or tool.** You are probably already a social media user—now it's time to learn about a social media platform or tool with which you are not yet familiar. Choose a social media platform in which you are *not* a member, or a social media tool that you have *not* yet used. Learn as much as you can about your selection from its home page, online reviews, and news articles. Create a presentation outlining the features, benefits, and drawbacks of your choice—including your own view of its effectiveness as a vehicle for social media marketing.

CASE 4.1
Kellogg's Approach to Social Media

It's easy to assume all companies have jumped wholeheartedly into every avenue of social media with innovative marketing messages and reaped untold rewards. However, even a successful marketer like Kellogg's might take a try-it-and-see approach, preferring to find, and focus on, what works best. Kellogg's has several popular Facebook pages for top products like Pop-Tarts, Frosted Flakes, and Nutri-Grain. These host daily marketing messages along with product updates, customer questions, quotations, links to the company's Instagram feeds, and apps that offer chances to win event tickets, scholarships, and other prizes. The Pop-Tarts' Facebook page boasts almost 5 million fans.

The company launched a mobile app for its Special K brand that offers an array of ways to manage weight loss goals, with customized programs, meal plans with recipes, and an electronic journal and shopping lists. Virtual badges serve as rewards, and users can check their progress online as well as on their iPhone or Android device. Kellogg's recently announced a new line of products, Special K Nourish, and is using social media in a unique way—the new brand is sending out tweets to followers with suggestions on how to eat healthier meals and snacks. The suggestions are based on a partnership with Food Network personality and registered dietitian nutritionist Ellie Krieger.

Kellogg's is also expanding its use of digital data, collected through retailers' shopper loyalty cards, to track what its competitors are doing and refine its marketing messages. Its own loyalty program, Kellogg's Family Rewards, lets customers enter product codes online to qualify for discounts and prizes. The rewards program continues to provide Kellogg's with useful insights on consumer buying behavior and allows the company to target its social media strategies.

QUESTIONS FOR CRITICAL THINKING

1. In what additional ways can Kellogg's capitalize on the popularity of social media to market its products?
2. What changes do you think Kellogg's could profitably make in its current social media strategy?

Sources: Company website, www.kelloggs.com, accessed February 6, 2014; John Gaffney, "Kellogg's Energizes Special K Brand," *Brand Innovators*, accessed February 6, 2014, http://brand-innovators.com; "Kellogg Consumer Loyalty Plan Yields Data Insights," *Consumer Goods Technology*, accessed February 6, 2014, http://consumergoods.edgl.com; Pat Lenius, "Analysis of Retail Digital Media Activity Helps Kellogg Better Shape Strategies," *CPG Matters*, accessed February 6, 2014, www.cpgmatters.com; Lauren Johnson, "Kellogg Co. Builds on 2012 Marketing Strategy with Mobile," *Mobile Marketer*, accessed February 6, 2014, www.mobilemarketer.com; Kate Kaye, "Kellogg Cracks the Code on Loyalty," *Ad Age*, accessed February 6, 2014, http://adage.com; David Moth, "How Kellogg's Uses Facebook, Twitter, Pinterest and Google+," *Econsultancy*, accessed February 6, 2014, http://econsultancy.com.

VIDEO CASE 4.2
Zappos Connects with Customers

Zappos, an Amazon company, proudly displays its marketing slogan on the side of every box that contains a shipment of shoes, clothes, and handbags: "Powered by service." But the company could just as easily adopt a slogan that says, "Connected with customers." That's because communication—connecting with customers—is an integral part of the company's core values and its reputation for customer service. Recently, social media marketing has become a strong component of Zappos' drive to connect. "Social media is really a communication tool," observes Robert Richman, product manager at Zappos. "We want to be available to people wherever they are." Rob Siefker, director of the customer loyalty team at Zappos, explains the company's view of social media further. "When people feel marketed to, they know there's a reason for it. But when they feel there's a connection, and it's something more human, I think that's more powerful—and that's our approach." Zappos uses social-networking sites Facebook and Twitter to interact rapidly with customers, choosing these outlets because that's where the people are. "If people are gathering at a site, we want to be there and be open to conversation," says Robert Richman. "If someone is reaching out to us, we want to be there to respond. It's not so much a strategy for reaching them as engaging them in conversation—about anything." It's a two-way street: Through these conversations, not only does Zappos learn about its customers' needs and preferences, but consumers also learn something about the retailer and its employees.

On Facebook and Twitter, the customer loyalty team can monitor any product or service issues that customers might be having. If a customer posts a complaint about slow delivery or mistakes in a shipment, the team acts quickly to correct the situation. If a customer praises the company for any reason—fast delivery time, great selection, friendly customer representatives—the team is able to thank that person directly. A customer might ask if Zappos plans to carry a certain line of shoes for an upcoming season or just post a comment like, "Once again, you exceeded my expectations!" Either way, Zappos staff members are on hand to reply immediately. Zappos also posts videos and other images of events and products for consumers to watch and comment upon.

Siefker observes that people sometimes don't expect to interact with companies on Twitter—they reserve it for quick messages to friends. But microblogging renders the company more personal or human. Siefker believes that tweeting with consumers helps them realize that Zappos is staffed by friendly, quirky, and intelligent workers. "I think that Twitter and other social media have enabled us to get closer to people on a personal level, and that's very valuable for us," he notes. Twitter also serves another marketing purpose for Zappos: discovery. Zappos offers approximately 136,000 different products for sale, but consumers might not be aware of everything that is available to them. So Zappos marketers created a TweetWall to inform consumers of what their fellow customers are tweeting about. Visitors can browse the TweetWall image gallery, view product tweets from others, and add their own comments as well. "It creates a fun way to see what may be trending or what may just be the odd item we carry that's a fun conversation starter," explains Alice Han, creator of the TweetWall.

At its website, consumers may sign up for various blogs ranging from "More Than Shoes" to "Fashion Culture" to "Wedding Blog." In fact, there are about 20 blogs to which fans may subscribe. Consumers might follow blogs on their favorite brands, such as Lilypond (handbags and luggage made from recycled and sustainable materials) and Wildfox Jewelry (an American line of jewelry inspired by fairy tales, daydreams, and vintage designs). Of course, they are encouraged to comment on any or all of the postings.

Unlike other firms, Zappos does not have a formal policy for employee tweeting or other social media. Instead, its rules are based on the company's corporate culture and core values. The customer loyalty team receives no directive other than to interact with people and help them whenever possible—and have fun. "We don't want to overcomplicate it," explains Siefker. "We train our employees, we empower them, and we trust them."

QUESTIONS FOR CRITICAL THINKING

1. In your view, does Zappos use social media effectively to strengthen its brand? Why or why not?
2. Zappos does not have a formal policy about social networking in the workplace. What are the benefits of this decision? What might be the drawbacks?

Sources: Company website, www.zappos.com, accessed February 6, 2014; company Facebook page, www.facebook.com/zappos, accessed February 6, 2014; Aziz Bawany, "Educate and Engage Your Customer through Social Media: The Zappos Strategy," *Scoop.it!*, accessed February 6, 2014, http://blog.scoop.it; Paul Chaney, "Zappos TweetWall Focuses on Real-Time Product Discovery," *Social Commerce Today*, accessed February 6, 2014, http://socialcommercetoday.com; "Zappos Sticks to Its Values in Communicating Customer Database Breach," *Holtz*, accessed February 6, 2014, http://holtz.com/blog.

NOTES

1. Company website, "About," http://press.linkedin.com, accessed August 15, 2014; Craig Smith, "By the Numbers: 110 Amazing LinkedIn Statistics," Digital Marketing Ramblings, accessed August 15, 2014, http://expandedramblings.com; Liz Klimas, "If You Have a LinkedIn Account, You Should Probably Know about These Accusations," *The Blaze*, accessed January 17, 2014, www.theblaze.com; Leslie Kaufman, "LinkedIn Builds Its Publishing Presence," *The New York Times*, accessed January 17, 2014, www.nytimes.com; Ken Yeung, "LinkedIn Is 10 Years Old Today," *The Next Web*, accessed January 17, 2014, http://thenextweb.com; Ilya Pozin, "200 Million Users? LinkedIn Is Just Getting Started," *Forbes*, accessed January 17, 2014, www.forbes.com; Evelyn M. Rusli, "LinkedIn: The Ugly Duckling of Social Media," *The Wall Street Journal*, accessed January 17, 2014 http://online.wsj.com.
2. *Merriam-Webster Online Dictionary*, accessed January 17, 2014, www.merriam-webster.com.
3. Emeric Ernoult, "How to Run a Facebook Timeline Promotion: 6 Tips for Success," *Social Media Examiner*, accessed January 18, 2014, www.socialmediaexaminer.com; "Five Ways to Get Banned from Facebook," *NewsCore*, accessed January 18, 2014, www.myfoxtwincities.com.
4. Organization website, www.relayforlife.org, accessed February 6, 2014.
5. Company website, "Google Handles 115 Billion Searches a Month," www.statista.com, accessed January 18, 2014.
6. Lauren Indvik, "Forrester: U.S. Online Retail Sales to Hit $370 Billion by 2017," *Mashable*, accessed January 18, 2014, http://mashable.com.
7. Ashley Zeckman, "Tips & Tools for Organizing, Implementing, & Monitoring Social Content Marketing," *TopRank*, accessed January 17, 2014, www.toprankblog.com.
8. Organization website, www.friendster.com, accessed February 6, 2014.
9. Chris Casacchia, "Specific Media Seeks $50M for Myspace Push," *Orange County Business Journal*, accessed January 18, 2014, http://www.ocbj.com.
10. "Facebook," *Statistic Brain*, accessed January 18, 2014, www.statisticbrain.com.
11. Sam Laird, "Pinsanity: How Sports Teams Are Winning on Pinterest," *Mashable*, accessed January 17, 2014, http://mashable.com.
12. Brandon Widder, "Best Free Blogging Sites," *Digital Trends*, accessed January 18, 2014, www.digitaltrends.com.
13. Albert Costill, "Top 21 Brands Getting the Most Out of Tumblr," *Search Engine Journal*, accessed January 19, 2014, www.searchenginejournal.com.
14. Cotton Delo, "Twitter Teams with Viacom to Sell Its Ads to VMA Sponsors," *Advertising Age*, accessed January 19, 2014, www.adage.com.
15. Company website, http://www2.orabrush.com, accessed January 19, 2014; https://twitter.com/Orabrush, accessed January 19, 2014.
16. "Rick Steves' Europe through the Back Door," blog, accessed January 19, 2014, http://blog.ricksteves.com.
17. James Johnson, "Pepsi's New Campaign Gives Away Song Downloads via Twitter," *Blog Herald*, accessed January 18, 2014, www.blogherald.com.
18. *AppBrain.com*, accessed August 15, www.appbrain.com.
19. "App Store Metrics," Pocket Gamer, accessed August 15, 2014, www.pocketgamer.biz.
20. Company website, www.booshaka.com, accessed February 6, 2014; Debbie Hemley, "26 Mobile Apps to Improve Your Business and Networking," *Social Media Examiner*, accessed February 6, 2014, www.socialmediaexaminer.com.
21. Shea Bennett, "Social Media Stats 2014," Media Bistro, accessed August 15, 2014, www.mediabistro.com; Joanna Brenner, "Social Networking," Pew Internet, accessed August 15, 2014, www.pewinternet.org.
22. Steve Olenski, "Are Brands Wielding More Influence in Social Media Than We Thought?" *Forbes*, accessed January 20, 2014, www.forbes.com.
23. Hannah Clark, "These 5 Brands Are Killing It on Pinterest," Hootsuite, accessed August 15, 2014, http://blog.hootsuite.com; Jonathan Bernstein, "Social Media in 2013: By the Numbers," *Social Media Today*, accessed January 20, 2014, http://socialmediatoday.com.
24. Stephen Edelstein, "Ford Relaunches Fiesta Movement Social Media Marketing Campaign," *Digital Trends*, accessed January 20, 2014, www.digitaltrends.com.
25. Company website, www.cabelas.com, accessed January 20, 2014; Pennsylvania Fish and Boat Commission, "2013 'Fish for Millions' Contest Nets Some Big Winners," press release, accessed June 27, 2013, www.fish.state.pa.us.
26. Organization website, www.bbbs.org, accessed January 20, 201.
27. Matthew Peneycad, "Unignorable Facts about How Social Media Influences Purchase Behaviour," *Social Media Today*, accessed January 20, 2014, http://socialmediatoday.com.

28. Company website, "The Virtuous Circle: The Role of Search and Social Media in the Purchase Pathway," http://groupmnext.com, accessed January 21, 2014.
29. "24 Outstanding Statistics & Figures on How Social Media Has Impacted the Health Care Industry," *Med City News*, accessed January 21, 2014, http://medcitynews.com; Miranda Miller, "33% of U.S. Consumers Use Social Media for Health Care Info," *Search Engine Watch*, accessed January 21, 2014, http://searchenginewatch.com.
30. Matthew Peneycad, "Influencing Purchase Decisions with Online Reviews and How to Get More of Them," *Social Media Today*, accessed January 21, 2014, http://socialmediatoday.com.
31. Caroline Scott-Thomas, "Social Media Has Changed How Americans Eat, Says Hartman Report," *Food Navigator*, accessed January 21, 2014, www.foodnavigator-usa.com.
32. Sara Rancero-Menendez, "Marketers Are Putting Their Money and Confidence in Social Media," *Mashable*, accessed January 21, 2014, http://mashable.com.
33. "B2B Content Marketing: 2014 Benchmarks, Budgets, and Trends–North America," *Content Marketing Institute*, accessed January 21, 2014, www.contentmarketinginstitute.com; Phil Mershon, "How B2B Marketers Use Social Media: New Research," *Social Media Examiner*, accessed January 22, 2014, www.socialmediaexaminer.com.
34. Company website, www.socialmediaexplorer.com, accessed January 22, 2014.
35. Organization website, http://bestfriends.org, accessed February 6, 2014.
36. Organization website, www.specialolympics.org, accessed January 22, 2014.
37. Ron Jones, "6 Steps in Developing a Social Media Strategy," *Clickz.com*, accessed February 6, 2014, www.clickz.com.
38. "The World's Most Powerful Celebrities," *Forbes*, accessed January 22, 2014, www.forbes.com.
39. Organization website, http://visitlouisianacoast.com, accessed February 6, 2014; "WSI Uses Social Media to Help Louisiana Tourism Coastal Coalition (LTCC) Increase Tourism after BP Oil Spill Disaster," press release, accessed February 6, 2014, http://www.wsidigitalmarketing.com.
40. Christopher Heine, "Walmart's Social Is Getting 10X ROI and Tens of Thousands of Daily Interactions," *Adweek*, accessed January 22, 2014, www.adweek.com.
41. Company website, www.vw.com, accessed January 22, 2014.
42. Company website, www.vintageplantations.com, accessed January 21, 2014.
43. Houston's Voice website, http://houstonsvoice.com, accessed January 21, 2014; Chris Moran, "Houston Gets Its Own Internet Channel," www.chron.com, accessed January 21, 2014.
44. Company website, http://socmetrics.com, accessed January 22, 2014.
45. Company website, www.bensbeginnerscontest.com, accessed January 22, 2014; Stuart Elliott, "Brand Seeks to Make Child's Play of Cooking," *The New York Times*, accessed January 22, 2014, www.nytimes.com.
46. Issie Lapowsky, "Turning 'Likes' into Loot with Facebook Promotions," *Inc.*, accessed January 24, 2014, www.inc.com.
47. "New Research Shows 92 Percent of Nonprofits Use Content Marketing," press release, accessed January 24, 2014, http://www.prnewswire.com.
48. Organization website, http://wish.org, accessed January 24, 2014.
49. "Dunkin' Donuts' New #mydunkin Advertising Campaign Puts Real Fans' Social Media Content in the Spotlight," press release, accessed January 24, 2014, www.marketwatch.com.
50. Kraft Recipes Community website, www.kraftrecipes.com, accessed January 24, 2014.
51. Jenna Dobkin, "3 Top Influencer Marketing Campaigns of 2013 and Lessons Every Marketer Can Learn from Them," *Social Media Today*, accessed January 24, 2014, http://socialmediatoday.com; "Sprout It—Backyard Takeover Contest," *Chris Loves Julia*, blog, accessed January 25, 2014, www.chrislovesjulia.com; Dan Eaton, "Sprout It Gardening App Debuts in Partnership with Scotts," *Columbus Biz Insider*, accessed January 25, 2014, http://www.bizjournals.com.
52. Company website, http://hootsuite.com, accessed January 25, 2014.
53. Company website, www.postplanner.com, accessed January 25, 2014; Company website, www.horsefeathers.com, accessed January 25, 2014.
54. Michael Scotty, "Starbucks' Twitter Campaign Goes Horribly Wrong," *Local Surge Media*, accessed January 25, 2014, www.localsurgemedia.com.
55. Organization website, www.greenpeace.org, "Greenpeace Takes on Europe's Biggest Carmaker… and Wins!", blogpost, accessed January 25, 2014; Tia Fisher, "What We Can Learn from the Crisis: Volkswagen vs. Greenpeace," *Social Media Today*, accessed January 25, 2014, http://socialmediatoday.com.
56. Company website, http://klout.com, accessed January 25, 2014.
57. Breanna Jacobs, "25 Awesome Social Media Tools Your Brand Should Be Using," *Social Media Strategies Summit*, accessed January 25, 2014, http://socialmediastrategysummit.com.
58. Organization website, www.unicef.org, "UNICEF Social Media," accessed January 25, 2014; Ann Marie van den Hurk, "Non-profits Should Not Forget Online Platforms When Reaching Out to Potential Donors," accessed January 25, 2014, kentucky.com; Aine Creedon, "Infographic: Social Media's Impact on Giving in 2012," *Nonprofit Quarterly*, accessed January 25, 2014, www.nonprofitquarterly.com.
59. Southwest Airlines Twitter page, http://twitter.com/SouthwestAir, accessed February 6, 2014; Southwest Airlines Facebook page, http://www.facebook.com/Southwest, accessed February 6, 2014.
60. Burson-Marsteller Europe, Middle East & Africa, "Social Media Crisis: What's Your Excuse for Ignoring the Danger?" blog, accessed January 25, 2014, http://burson-marsteller.eu; "British Airlines vs @HVSVN I CAN HAZ MY LUGGAGE PLZ?" *Viral in Nature*, accessed January 24, 2014, http://wwwviralinnature.com; Victor Luckerson, "Man Spends More Than $1,000 to Call Out British Airways on Twitter," *Time*, accessed January 24, 2014, http://business.time.com.
61. Carol Rozwell, "Why Social Media Policies Should Focus on the Dos Rather Than the Don'ts," *Forbes*, accessed January 25, 2014, www.forbes.com.
62. Saroj Kar, "PSN Breach amid the Largest of Past Years," *Silicon Angle*, accessed January 26, 2014, http://siliconangle.com; Lisa Vaas, "Sony to Pay £250,000 Fine for Play Network Breach," *Naked Security*, accessed January 25, 2014, http://nakedsecurity.com.
63. Company website, "Garnter Survey Reveals Digital Marketing Budgets Will Increase by 10 Percent in 2014," press release, www.gartner.com, accessed August 15, 2014.
64. Whitney Parker, "5 Stellar Strategies to Land Your First Social Media Job," *Brazen Careerist*, accessed January 25, 2014, http://blog.brazencareerist.com.
65. Michael A. Stelzner, "2013 Social Media Marketing Industry Report," *Social Media Examiner*, accessed January 25, 2014, www.socialmediaexaminer.com.
66. Sharlyn Lauby, "Ethics and Social Media: Where Should You Draw the Line?" *Mashable*, accessed January 25, 2014, http://mashable.com.

Chapter 5

E-Business: Managing the Customer Experience

1. Describe the growth of Internet use worldwide.
2. Explain e-business, e-marketing, and the opportunities e-marketing presents.
3. Distinguish between a corporate website and a marketing website.
4. List the six major forms of business-to-business e-marketing.
5. Explain business-to-consumer (B2C) e-marketing.
6. Describe online buyers and sellers.
7. Describe the challenges associated with online marketing and e-business.
8. Discuss how marketers use the communication function of the Web as part of their online marketing strategies.
9. Describe the process of developing successful e-business websites and how to assess their effectiveness.

WAYFAIR MAKES A NAME FOR ITSELF

When two college friends looking for a new venture stumbled upon a website that sold only birdhouses, and then other sites selling only beanbag chairs, meat slicers, grandfather clocks, and porch swings, they realized they had found a promising place to invest their business expertise and capital. So Niraj Shah and Steve Conine grouped about 200 such niche sites together in a company they called CSN Stores and ran it successfully for almost 10 years. The company grew into a hugely successful enterprise, applying target marketing, Web analytics, and flawless execution to highly specialized sites in about 25 different product categories. It soon became the largest U.S. online-only retailer of home decor goods.

The only problem? Nobody had ever heard of it.

Recently Shah and Conine decided to rebrand their company, eliminating all the individual, anonymous sites and uniting the entire product stream under a new name, Wayfair.com. Their enterprise has a virtual inventory of about 7 million items, employs 1,300 people, and has revenues of over $900 million annually. It is one of the biggest privately owned e-commerce websites and has been posting double-digit growth for several years.

The founders' goal now is to develop their new brand and create some customer loyalty. Online sales in the $20 billion U.S. furniture and home decorating market are small, accounting for only about 8 percent annually, but Wayfair intends to become a destination website, particularly for its target market of women between 30 and 45 with annual household incomes of between $50,000 and $150,000. These customers are looking for ways to make their homes feel special but lack the budget for interior decorators and customized designs. Wayfair's immense inventory, and its ability to control prices by shipping from manufacturers' warehouses as often as possible, lend the newly designed site the means to increase its name recognition as well as its appeal.

One strategy that seems to be working is the flash sale, a time-sensitive offering of selected merchandise at steep discounts, which Wayfair hosts at its Daily Fair website. Flash-sale customers are looking for entertainment as much as merchandise, and Wayfair's target market is no exception. The sense of urgency that characterizes flash sales should also help drive more mobile traffic to the site, achieving another one of Wayfair's brand-recognition goals.[1]

EVOLUTION OF A BRAND

With little media fanfare, Wayfair.com has become of one of the biggest e-commerce success stories of the past few years. The company's co-founders used their business savvy and online retail experience to create "the ultimate home store" website with more than 7 million products from 12,000 suppliers. They have succeeded in part by focusing on their e-commerce target market: women in their 30s and 40s with modest incomes who can't live without stylish home furnishings.

- Although Wayfair is close to the $950 million mark in annual sales, the Boston-based company has received little national media attention. What marketing strategies could help the website reach a broader audience?
- The co-founders say they built their e-commerce business while embracing the concept of change. With such strong revenues, the company is likely to go public in the near future. How would taking the company public change its approach to doing business with its 12,000 suppliers? How would an IPO impact Wayfair's customer base?
- How can the company continue to use mobile marketing and social media strategies to increase its e-commerce presence?

Chapter Overview

e-business Conducting online transactions with customers by collecting and analyzing business information, carrying out the exchanges, and maintaining online relationships with customers.

During the past decade, marketing has become the cutting-edge tool for success on the Internet. Profit-seeking organizations are not the only benefactors of the Internet; organizations of all kinds are emphasizing marketing's role in achieving set goals. Colleges and universities, charities, museums, symphony orchestras, and hospitals now employ the marketing concept discussed in Chapter 1: providing customers the goods and services they want to buy when they want to buy them. Contemporary marketing continues to perform its function of bringing buyers and sellers together; it just does it faster and more efficiently than ever before. With just a few clicks of a mouse, the Internet revolutionizes every aspect of life. New terms have emerged, such as *shopping blog*, *RSS*, and *big data*; and old words have new meanings never imagined a few years ago: *Web*, *surfer* and *server*, *banner* and *browser*, *tweet* and *Twitter*, *online* and *offline*.

Electronic business, or **e-business**, refers to conducting business via the Internet and has turned virtual reality into reality. With a computer and Internet access, a virtual marketplace is open 24/7 to provide almost anything anywhere to anyone, including clothes, food, entertainment, medicine, and information. You can pay your cell phone bill, make travel reservations, do research for a term paper, apply for a job, or buy a used car—perhaps at a lower price than you could in person.

Internet marketers can reach individual consumers or target organizations worldwide through a vast array of computer and communications technologies. In a few short years, hundreds of thousands of companies large and small have been connected to electronic marketing channels. The size and scope of e-business is difficult to estimate. For instance, in a recent year, an estimated 180 million online shoppers in the United States bought more than $252 billion in goods. Although e-commerce is about 10 percent of total retail sales, industry observers say online retail sales will continue to grow.[2]

E-business is much more than just buying and selling goods and services. Some surveys suggest that the Web is the number-one medium for new-product information, eclipsing catalogs, print ads, and trade shows. The Internet allows retailers and vendors to exchange vital information, improving the overall functioning of supply and distribution, lowering costs, and increasing profits. Moreover, an increasing number of Americans now get some of their news and information from blogs (online journals) rather than from traditional media such as television and newspapers. Consequently, a growing number of businesses use blogs to put human faces on their organizations and communicate directly with customers.

This chapter examines the current status and potential of e-business and e-marketing. We begin by describing the growth of Internet use throughout the world. Next, we explore the scope of e-business and outline how marketers use the Internet to succeed, and then distinguish different types of Web business models. This discussion is followed by a review of the major types of B2B marketing online.

We then explore the types of goods and services

> ## Briefly Speaking
> "In 6,000 years of storytelling, [people have] gone from depicting hunting on cave walls to depicting Shakespeare on Facebook walls."
>
> —**Joe Sabia**
> *Digital artist and consultant*

most often traded in B2C marketing on the Internet, along with a profile of online buyers and sellers. We then describe some of the challenges associated with marketing on the Web, followed by a discussion of how marketers use the communication function of the Internet. We conclude the chapter by examining how to build an effective Web presence.

THE DIGITAL WORLD

In the past decade, the number of Internet users in the United States and worldwide has grown dramatically. Today, over 270 million people—more than 86 percent of the U.S. population—have access to the Internet at home, school, work, or public access sites. The number of Internet users worldwide totals more than 2.8 billion.[3] The map in Figure 5.1 shows the number of Internet users and Internet penetration for each of the world's continents and regions. *Internet penetration* is the percentage of a region's population who use the Internet.

Asia leads the world in the sheer number of users and the speed of growth in Internet use. Among individual countries with the highest number of Internet users, China ranks first, with almost one-quarter of the world's Internet users. The next three countries are the United States, India, and Japan.[4] China's Internet audience has grown by more than 2,000 percent since 2000; the United States' audience rose about 157 percent for the same period.[5] South Korea has the fastest Internet service in the world, followed by Japan, Hong Kong, Netherlands, and Switzerland. South Korea's Internet speed is more than two times faster than that in the United States, which recently ranked eighth in the world for Internet speed.[6]

What do people do online? Let's look at the two countries with the most Internet users—the United States and China. In the United States, Internet usage is mostly about communication, information, and purchases. Nearly all American users say they use email and use a search engine for information; almost 85 percent get news or look for maps or driving directions. About four-fifths search for health or medical news or check the weather. More than three-quarters look for information about items they're interested in buying or go online just to pass the time or to have fun.[7] Among U.S. users under the age of 24, more than half check their Facebook pages when they wake up; over a quarter of those said that they check their Facebook pages on their mobile phones even before they get out of bed. The fastest growing U.S. demographic group on Twitter is people 55 and older.[8] In China, where the average age of Internet users is 25, instant messaging and using search engines

1 Describe the growth of Internet use worldwide.

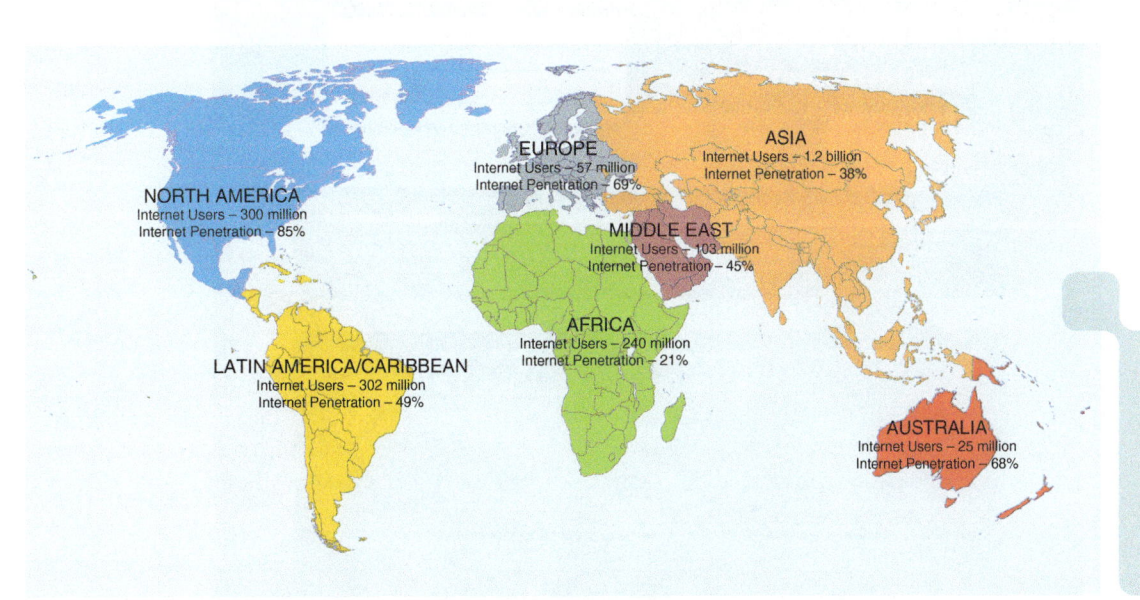

FIGURE 5.1
Number of Internet Users and Internet Penetration Rate (by Region)

Source: Data from "Internet Usage Statistics," accessed August 15, 2014, www.internetworldstats.com.

NORTH AMERICA
Internet Users – 300 million
Internet Penetration – 85%

EUROPE
Internet Users – 57 million
Internet Penetration – 69%

ASIA
Internet Users – 1.2 billion
Internet Penetration – 38%

MIDDLE EAST
Internet Users – 103 million
Internet Penetration – 45%

AFRICA
Internet Users – 240 million
Internet Penetration – 21%

LATIN AMERICA/CARIBBEAN
Internet Users – 302 million
Internet Penetration – 49%

AUSTRALIA
Internet Users – 25 million
Internet Penetration – 68%

are the most popular activities, followed by downloading music, blogging, viewing videos, online gaming, and other modes of social networking. After a relatively slow start, online purchase transactions in China have jumped significantly, helped by the spread of local online payment systems.⁹

So where is e-business going, and how can marketers capitalize on the digital links with consumers? In spite of the past success and future potential of the Internet, issues and concerns relating to e-business remain. Some highly touted e-business applications have proven less than successful, cost savings and profits have occasionally been elusive, and many privacy and security issues still linger. Nevertheless, the benefits and potential of e-business outweigh the concerns and problems.

ASSESSMENT CHECK

1.1 How would you describe the growth of Internet use worldwide?

1.2 What do most U.S. consumers do online?

E-BUSINESS AND E-MARKETING

2 Explain e-business, e-marketing, and the opportunities e-marketing presents.

Today, *e-business* describes the wide range of business activities taking place via Internet applications such as email and virtual shopping carts. E-business can be divided into the following five broad categories: (1) *e-tailing*, or virtual storefronts on websites; (2) business-to-business (B2B) transactions; (3) electronic data interchanges (EDI), the business-to-business exchange of data; (4) email, instant messaging, blogs, podcasts, vlogs (video blogs), and other Web-enabled communication tools and their use as media for reaching prospective and existing customers; and (5) the gathering and use of demographic, product, and other information through Web contacts.

The component of e-business of particular interest to marketers is *electronic marketing*, or **e-marketing**, the strategic process of creating, distributing, promoting, and pricing goods and services to a target market over the Internet or through digital tools such as smartphones and tablets. E-marketing is the means by which e-business is achieved. It encompasses activities such as the following:

e-marketing Strategic process of creating, distributing, promoting, and pricing goods and services to a target market over the Internet or through digital tools.

- viewing your favorite band's latest videos on YouTube
- ordering a meal from your favorite local takeout restaurant

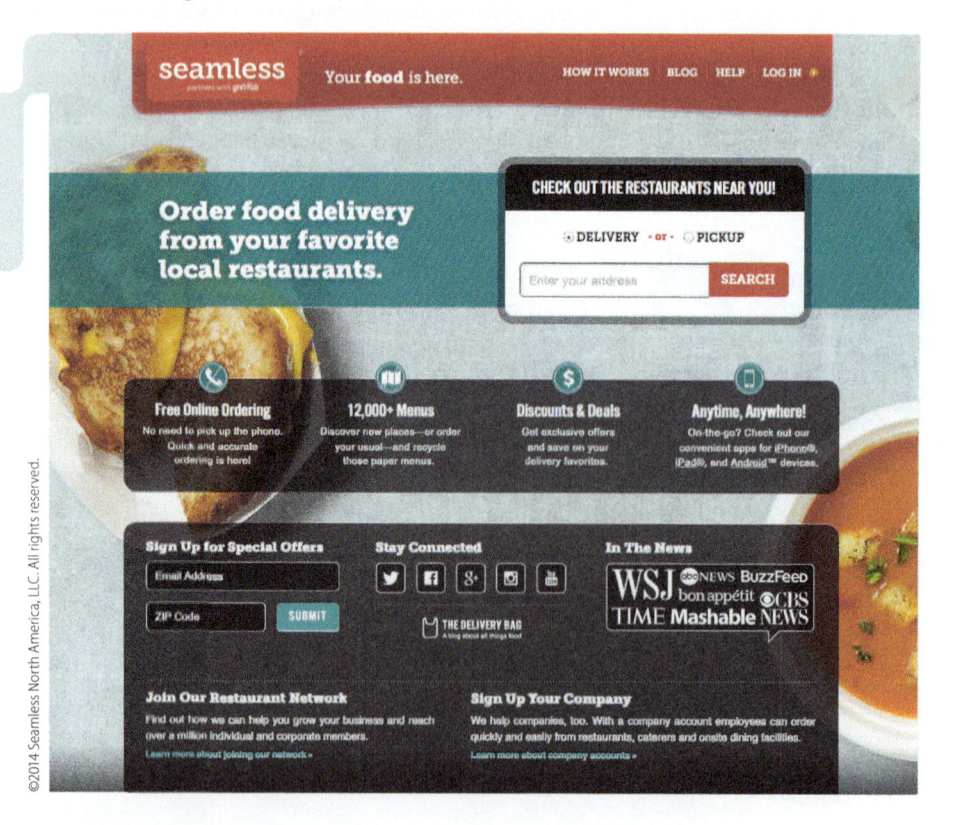

Ordering a meal from a takeout website such as Seamless.com is an example of e-marketing.

- researching digital cameras on CNET.com and then placing an order on Newegg.com
- accessing research site LexisNexis through your college's network, allowing you to work on a paper, and then checking apartment rentals online

The application of these electronic tools to contemporary marketing has the potential to greatly reduce costs and increase customer satisfaction by increasing the speed and efficiency of marketing interactions. Just as e-business is a major function of the Internet, e-marketing is an integral component of e-business.

A closely related but somewhat narrower term than e-marketing is *online marketing*. While electronic marketing can encompass digital technologies ranging from video streaming to interactive store kiosks that do not involve computers, online marketing refers to marketing activities that connect buyers and sellers electronically through interactive computer systems.

OPPORTUNITIES OF E-MARKETING

E-marketing offers countless opportunities to reach consumers. This radical departure from traditional brick-and-mortar operations provides the following benefits to contemporary marketers (summarized in Table 5.1).

- *Global reach.* The Internet eliminates the geographic protections and limitations of local business and gives smaller firms a wider audience. Independent filmmakers often have a difficult time forging relationships with traditional distributors who buy the rights to films and promote them as they see fit. As a result, independent films sometimes have a limited audience. But the Internet is allowing filmmakers to organize their own screenings, send messages to interested online communities, and sell their films directly through their websites.[10]

- *Personalization.* Road Runner Sports, which caters to running and walking enthusiasts, remembers customers' recent shoe purchases and alerts them when their favorite shoes are about to be discontinued. Its website also has a shoe-finder questionnaire to help customers find their perfect pair of shoes.[11]

TABLE 5.1 E-Marketing Capabilities

Capability	Description	Example
Global reach	The ability to reach anyone connected to the Internet anywhere in the world.	Independent filmmakers use the Internet to generate audiences and sales for their films.
Personalization	The ability to create products to meet customer specifications.	Polyvore.com has a feature that allows buyers to mix and match items to complete outfits to suit their individual tastes.
Interactive marketing	Buyer–seller communications through channels such as the Internet and interactive kiosks.	Dell maintains an IdeaStorm site where users share ideas, information, and product feedback.
Right-time marketing	The ability to provide a product at the exact time needed.	United Airlines website lets customers make advance reservations, check in online, check flight status, and sign up for the carrier's rewards program.
Integrated marketing	Coordination of all promotional activities to produce a unified, customer-focused promotional message.	Sony uses the slogan "make.believe" in both online and offline promotions.

An effective online presence can improve the performance of traditional marketing operations. Kitchen supply retailer Sur La Table advertises its in-store cooking classes on its website.

interactive marketing Buyer–seller communications in which the customer controls the amount and type of information received from a marketer through channels such as the Internet and virtual reality kiosks.

> **Briefly Speaking**
>
> "Almost overnight, the Internet's gone from a technical wonder to a business must."
>
> —Bill Schrader
> *CEO of PSINet*

- *Interactive marketing.* Using a concept called **interactive marketing**, McDonald's recently partnered with Microsoft's Xbox division to give away millions of Xbox prizes in a holiday promotional campaign. People who purchase any Premium McWrap, selected Quarter Pounder sandwiches, or medium-sized fries will receive a game piece with an instant Win message. Players can enter the code found on the game label to redeem prizes using their smartphone, tablet, or computer. With more than 140 million total game pieces, McDonald's and Microsoft hope to capitalize on the popularity of Xbox One, the latest entertainment system coveted by video gamers.[12]

- *Right-time marketing.* Online retailers, such as Westelm.com and REI.com, can provide products when and where customers want them.

- *Integrated marketing.* The Internet enables the coordination of all promotional activities and communication to create a unified, customer-oriented promotional message.

In addition to the benefits listed here, an effective online presence can improve the performance of traditional marketing operations. Recent surveys of consumers found that, whether they purchase online or in person, more than two-thirds of shoppers do online product research before buying. In one recent survey, 79 percent of online shoppers said research would continue to be a critical factor in their purchasing decisions.[13] The Internet continues to be a powerful force in shaping consumer behavior, even if it is seldom the only avenue most consumers pursue in their search for product information. Meanwhile, with online sales growing by well over 10 percent each year while retail stores remain flat, brick-and-mortar stores are fighting back with options that online sellers can't deliver. Macy's department stores offer visitor services for travelers, including coat and package check and language assistance. Kitchen supply retailer

Chapter 5 E-Business: Managing the Customer Experience   141

ASSESSMENT CHECK

2.1 Define e-marketing.

2.2 Explain the difference between e-business and e-marketing.

2.3 What are the major benefits of e-marketing?

Sur La Table offers in-store cooking classes and demonstrations; participants receive a 10 percent coupon to use in the store or on the company's website up to seven days after the class.[14]

WEB BUSINESS MODELS

The vast majority of businesses today have websites. They may offer general information, electronic shopping, and promotions such as games, contests, and online coupons. Type in the firm's Internet address, and the website's home page appears on your computer screen.

Two types of company websites exist. Many firms have established **corporate websites** to increase their visibility, promote their offerings, and provide information to interested parties. Rather than sell goods and services directly, these sites attempt to build customer goodwill and assist channel members in their marketing efforts. For example, Wendy's website offers menus and nutritional information, a store locator, and videos and other types of promotions.[15] In addition to using the Web to communicate product information and build relationships with customers, many companies also use their corporate websites for a variety of other purposes, including disseminating financial information to investors; giving prospective employees the opportunity to apply online for jobs; and providing a communication channel for customers and other interested parties via email, blogs, and online forums.

Although **marketing websites** often include information about company history, products, locations, employment opportunities, and financial information, their goal is to increase purchases by visitors. For instance, the Argo Tea website contains all of the information traditionally found on a corporate website, but it also includes an online store selling everything from various types of loose-leaf teas and bottled tea drinks to mugs, stylish teapots, and electronic gift cards.

> **3** Distinguish between a corporate website and a marketing website.
>
> **corporate websites** Site designed to increase a firm's visibility, promote its offerings, and provide information to interested parties.
>
> **marketing websites** Site whose main purpose is to increase purchases by visitors.

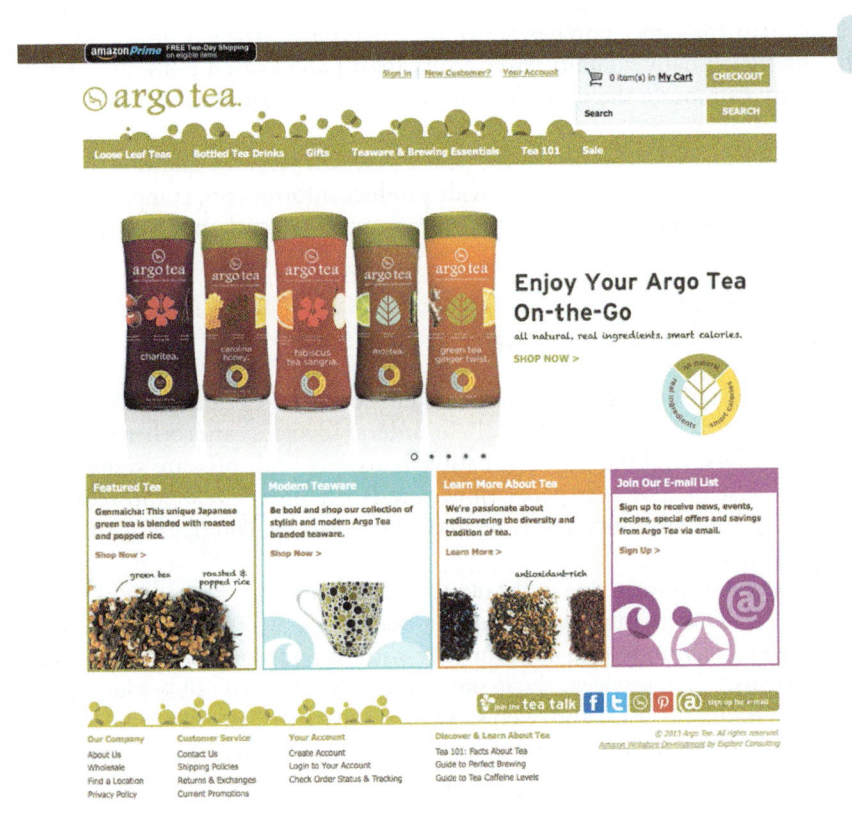

Argo Tea sells tea and food items in its stores. On its website, the company sells everything from loose-leaf teas to bottled tea drinks, tea mugs, teapots, and gift cards.

© Argo Tea

Many marketing websites try to engage consumers in interactions that will move them closer to a demonstration, trial visit, purchase, or other marketing outcome. Some marketing websites, such as Sony.com, are quite complex. Visitors can compare the company's different models of digital cameras and other products, selecting five at a time for detailed feature comparisons as well as finding product registration and support, checking out weekly deals, signing up for news and promotions, and locating a Sony dealer.[16] But not all products lend themselves to sales on the Internet. Complex products or those requiring demonstration or trials may be better sold in person. And some companies have relationships with partners, such as dealers and franchisees, who sell their products. We discuss these relationships later in the chapter.

> **ASSESSMENT CHECK**
>
> 3.1. Explain the difference between a corporate website and a marketing website.
> 3.2. Why would companies *not* sell products on their websites?

B2B E-MARKETING

> **4** List the six major forms of business-to-business e-marketing.

FedEx's website is not designed to be flashy. Although it contains some graphics and a link to view videos on how to pack and ship packages, its main purpose is not entertainment. Instead, it provides a lot of practical information to help the firm's customers. The site enables customers to check rates, compare services, schedule package pickups and deliveries, track shipments, and order shipping supplies. This information is vital to FedEx's customers, most of whom are businesses. Customers access the site thousands of times a day.

business-to-business (B2B) e-marketing Use of the Internet for business transactions between organizations.

Business-to-business (B2B) e-marketing is the use of the Internet for business transactions between organizations. Although most people are familiar with online firms such as Amazon and eBay, the number of consumer transactions is dwarfed by their B2B counterparts. By some estimates, B2B e-commerce revenues are more than double that of consumer transactions.[17]

In addition to generating sales revenue, B2B e-marketing also provides detailed product descriptions whenever needed. Payments and other information are exchanged on the Web, and B2B e-marketing can slash order-processing expenses. Business-to-business transactions, which typically involve more steps than consumer purchases, can be much more efficient on the Internet. Orders placed over the Internet usually contain fewer errors than handwritten ones, and when mistakes occur, the technology can locate them quickly. So the Internet is an attractive option for business buying and selling.

B2B e-marketing activity has become more varied in recent years. In addition to using the Web to conduct individual sales transactions and provide product information, companies use tools such as *electronic data interchange* (EDI), Web services, extranets, private exchanges, electronic exchanges, and e-procurement.

PROPRIETARY B2B TRANSACTIONS

One of the oldest applications of technology to business transactions is EDI, computer-to-computer exchanges of price quotations, purchase orders, invoices, and other sales information between buyers and sellers. EDI requires compatible hardware and software systems to exchange data over a network. Use of EDI cuts paper flow, speeds the order cycle, and reduces errors. In addition, by receiving daily inventory status reports from vendors, companies can set production schedules to match demand.

Early EDI systems were limited due to the requirement that all parties had to use the same computer operating system. That changed with the introduction of *Web services*—Internet-based systems that allow parties to communicate electronically with one another regardless of the computer operating system they use. Web services rely on open-source XML (Extensible Markup Language, a formatting language) standards. EDI and Web services are discussed further in Chapter 11.

The Internet also offers an efficient way for businesses to collaborate with vendors, partners, and customers through *extranets*, secure networks used for e-marketing and accessible through the firm's website by external customers, suppliers, or other authorized users. Extranets go beyond ordering and fulfillment processes by giving selected outsiders access to internal information. Like other forms of e-marketing, extranets provide additional benefits such as enhanced relationships with business partners. *Intranets* are secure internal networks that help companies share information among employees, no matter how many or how widespread they are. The office-supply firm Staples has thousands of employees in 26 countries. In-store devices connect them to the company's intranet, The Hub, where they can exchange information and find job-related software. The Hub also carries customer success stories and best practices from various Staples stores, as well as video updates on company news. The Hub has twice been named one of the ten best-designed intranets by the Nielsen Norman Group, a usability consulting agency.[18]

> **Briefly Speaking**
>
> "Five years ago, we thought of the Web as a new medium, not a new economy."
>
> **—Clement Mok**
> *Award-winning interactive designer and author*

Security and access authorization remain critical issues, and most companies create virtual private networks that protect information traveling over public communications media. These networks control who uses a company's resources and what users can access. Also, they cost considerably less than leasing dedicated lines.

The next generation of extranets is the *private exchange*, a secure website where a company and its suppliers share all types of data related to e-marketing, from product design through order delivery. A private exchange is more collaborative than a typical extranet, so this type of arrangement is sometimes called *c-business*. The participants can use it to collaborate on product ideas, production scheduling, distribution, order tracking, and any other functions a business wants to include. For example, Walmart has a private exchange it calls Retail Link. The system permits Walmart employees to access detailed sales and inventory information. Suppliers such as Procter & Gamble and Nestlé, in turn, can look up Walmart sales data and forecasts to manage their own inventory and logistics, helping them better meet the needs of the world's largest retailer and its millions of customers worldwide.

E-PROCUREMENT ON OPEN EXCHANGES

In the early stages of B2B transactions, marketers believed all types of products would be traded online. Entrepreneurs created electronic exchanges to bring buyers and sellers together in one electronic marketplace and cater to a specific industry's needs, but the performance of these sites was disappointing. Many suppliers weren't happy with the pressure to come in with the lowest bid each time, and buyers preferred to cultivate long-term relationships with their suppliers, even if those suppliers sometimes charged slightly more. Purchasing agents simply didn't see enough benefits from electronic exchanges to abandon suppliers they knew.

Evolving from electronic exchanges is **e-procurement**, Web-based systems that enable all types of organizations to improve the efficiency of their bidding and purchasing processes. Royal Dutch/Shell Group, a group of energy companies with operations in 140 countries, purchases millions of dollars of parts, components, supplies, and services every day. The firm replaced its network of more than 100 purchasing systems with a streamlined new system to unify procurement and reduce costs.[19]

E-procurement also benefits the public sector. The Scottish government awarded an £18.5 million ($30 million) contract to Amor Group, a Scottish IT services company recently acquired by Lockheed Martin. Amor Group manages the government's eProcurement Scotland Service, or ePS. This online procurement service already has 50,000 registered users whose purchases are entirely electronic, from requisition to payment.[20] The state of Virginia maintains a website called eVa for its Web-based purchasing system. The site allows state and local agencies and government offices, as well as the state's colleges and universities, to invite bids, receive quotes, and place orders.[21]

e-procurement Use of the Internet by organizations to solicit bids and purchase goods and services from suppliers.

ASSESSMENT CHECK

4.1 What is B2B e-marketing? How large is it relative to consumer e-marketing?

4.2 Define EDI and Web services.

4.3 Briefly explain how e-procurement works.

B2C E-MARKETING

5 Explain business-to-consumer (B2C) e-marketing.

business-to-consumer (B2C) e-marketing Selling directly to consumers over the Internet.

One area of e-business that consistently grabs news headlines is Internet shopping. Known as **business-to-consumer (B2C) e-marketing**, it is selling directly to consumers over the Internet. Driven by convenience and improved security for transmitting credit card numbers and other financial information, online retail sales—sometimes called *e-tailing*—have grown rapidly in recent years. During a recent holiday shopping period, Internet shopping sales hit $46.5 billion, marking a 10 percent increase from the previous year's holiday totals. Shopping on the Monday after Thanksgiving—known as "Cyber Monday"—recently totaled more than $2.2 billion.[22]

With more than 56 percent of all U.S. adults owning smartphones, mobile retail is taking off, currently making up about 15 percent of online sales. Over 92 percent of the top 100 brands now have mobile-commerce websites or applications that usually can be downloaded onto smartphones or tablet devices for free. Those brands include Disney, IBM, Samsung, Coca-Cola, BMW, and GE.[23]

Most people think of the Web as a giant cybermall of retail stores selling millions of goods online. However, service providers are also important participants in e-marketing, including providers of financial services. Brick-and-mortar banks such as PNC and brokerage firms such as Charles Schwab have greatly expanded their online services. In addition, many new online service providers are rapidly attracting customers who want to do more of their own banking and investment trading at whatever time and day suits them. And where would individual buyers and sellers be without online classified ads?

ELECTRONIC STOREFRONTS

electronic storefronts Company websites that sell products to customers.

Virtually all major retailers have staked their claims in cyberspace by setting up **electronic storefronts**, websites where they offer items for sale to consumers. Clothing retailer American Eagle sees e-retailing as a "significant growth opportunity" for all its brands and has been enjoying double-digit increases in website sales from year to year. The company's attractive website offers a store locator and wish list feature, gift card purchasing, a feedback link, and the opportunity to sign up for sales and other promotions. Clothing is organized by category—tops, bottoms, accessories, footwear, and so on—and the site has separate sections for sales and clearance items as well as for new arrivals and Web exclusives.[24]

electronic shopping cart File that holds items the online shopper has chosen to buy.

Generally, online retailers—such as Gap.com and LLBean.com—provide an online catalog where visitors click on items they want to buy. These items are placed in a file called an **electronic shopping cart** or *shopping bag*. When the shopper indicates that he or she wants to complete the transaction, the items in the electronic shopping cart are listed on the screen, along with the total amount due, so the customer can review the whole order and make changes before paying.

One factor having a significant influence on the growth of online shopping is the increased capability of smartphones, such as the iPhone and Android-powered phones. But tablet devices such as the iPad are emerging as the next mobile shopping tool. More than one-third of U.S. adults own tablet devices, and they prefer to use their tablets for shopping. For one thing, tablets have larger screens than smartphones and are now almost equally portable. Also, apps for tablet devices are far more versatile, permitting page flipping, scrolling, and other "real-world" conveniences. Retailers like tablet apps because they can emphasize features of their products rather than merely comparing prices. Ralph Lauren, Amazon, eBay, and other companies—both brick-and-mortar and Internet-based—have launched their own tablet apps.[25]

BENEFITS OF B2C E-MARKETING

Many consumers prefer shopping online to the time needed to drive to a store and select purchases. Why do consumers shop online? Three main reasons are most often cited in consumer surveys: competitive pricing, access and convenience, and personalized service.

Competitive Pricing

Many of the best deals on products, such as airfares and hotels, can be found on the Internet. Kayak.com is just one of several sites that offer packages with combinations of flight, hotel, and car rental, plus special sales and last-minute flight specials at attractive prices organized by city and date of travel.[26] Though most airlines now charge passengers for checked baggage, most offer reduced rates with branded credit cards.[27] The bookseller Barnes & Noble's website offers member discounts and benefits, including free express shipping on orders and 40 percent off hardcover bestsellers.[28]

The Web is an ideal method for savvy shoppers to compare prices from dozens—even hundreds—of sellers. Online shoppers can compare features and prices at their leisure. Say, for instance, you're in the market for a new computer monitor. **Bots (shopbots)**—short for *robots*—aid consumers in comparison shopping. Bots are search programs that check hundreds of sites, gather and assemble information, and bring it back to the sender. For instance, at PriceGrabber.com, you can specify the type and size of monitor you're looking for, and the website displays a list of the highest-ranked monitors, along with the e-tailer offering the best price on each item and estimated shipping expenses. The website even ranks the e-marketers by customer experience and tells you whether a particular model is in stock.

bots (shopbots) Software program that allows online shoppers to compare the price of a particular product offered by several online retailers.

Access and Convenience

A second important factor in prompting online purchases is shopper convenience. Cybershoppers can order goods and services from around the world at any hour of the day or night. Most e-marketers allow customers to register their credit card and shipping information for quick use in making future purchases. Customers are required to select a user name and password for security. Later, when they place another order, registered customers are asked to type in their password. E-marketers typically send an email message confirming an order and the amount charged to the buyer's credit card. Another email is sent once the product is shipped, along with a tracking number, which the customer can use to follow the order through the delivery process. A service provided by *Elle* magazine's British website is the ability to use online photos to conduct visual matches for desired shopping items. In other words, using a digital picture of what you want—say, a pair of shoes—you can locate similar items for sale online. The Google Shopping website showcases everything from washing machines to clothing to watches. Shoppers can create short lists on the shopping site to organize their ideas as they shop. Google Shopper, a smartphone app, allows subscribers to scan the cover art of books and electronic products such as DVDs or games to find those products—or simply say the name of a product to find it. This app also allows subscribers to see nearby offers, find local stores, scan barcodes of products for more information, and check out online prices. Google Offers lists participating restaurants in the subscriber's local area.[29]

Personalized Service

Although online shopping transactions often operate with little or no human interaction, successful B2C e-marketing companies know how important personalization is to the quality of the shopping experience. Customer satisfaction is greatly influenced by the marketer's ability to offer service tailored to many customers. But each person expects a certain level of customer service. Consequently, most leading online retailers offer customized features on their websites.

The early years of e-business saw Web marketers casting their nets wide in an effort to land as many buyers as possible. Today, the emphasis has turned toward creating loyal customers likely to make repeat purchases. How does personalized marketing work online? Say you buy a product at Amazon and register with the site. The site welcomes you back for your next purchase by name. Using special software that analyzes your previous purchases, it also suggests several other products you might like. You even have the option of receiving periodic emails from Amazon.com informing you of new products. And the company now offers Amazon Prime, a membership program that includes expedited free shipping for a yearly fee. Many other leading e-marketers have adopted similar types of personalized marketing.

The Google Shopping website offers convenience to online shoppers and features a wide range of products.

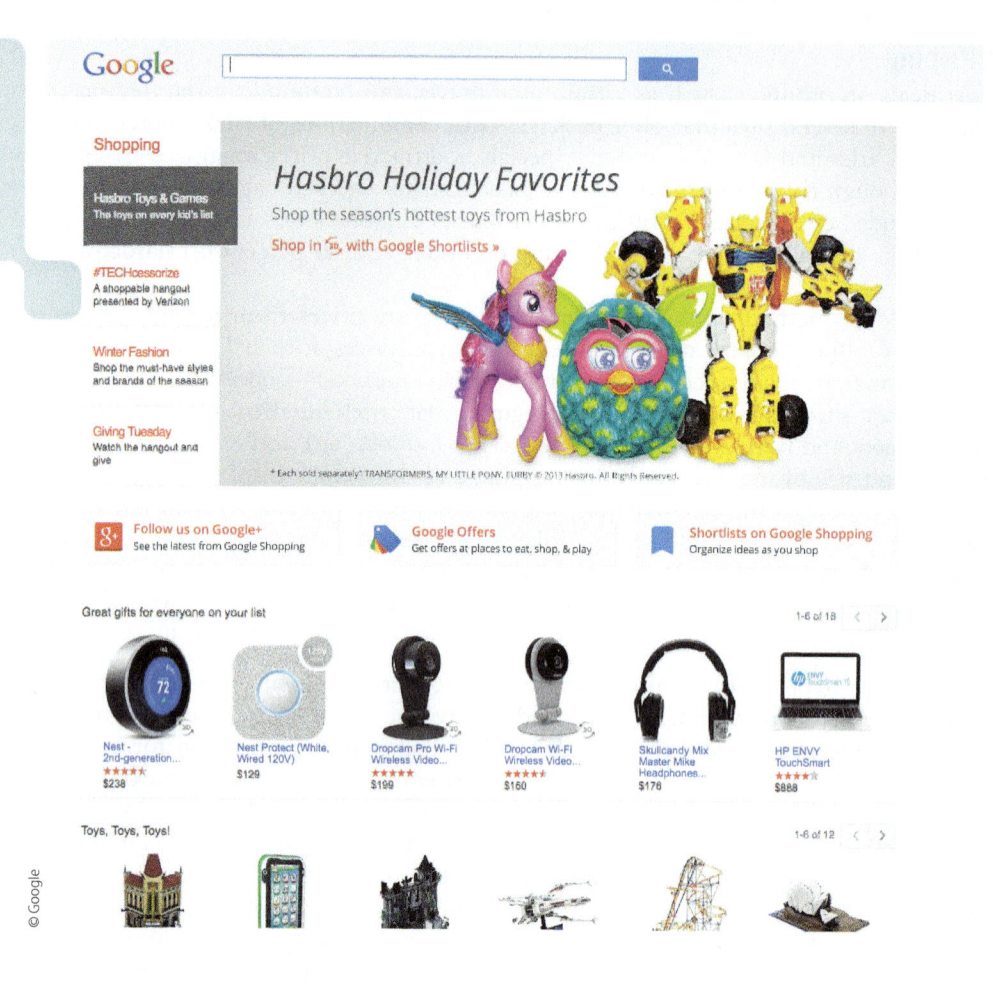

ASSESSMENT CHECK

5.1 What is B2C e-marketing?

5.2 Explain the difference between a shopping website and an informational website.

5.3 Discuss the benefits of B2C e-marketing.

Some websites offer customized products to match individual consumer requirements. For instance, Nike offers online shoppers the opportunity to customize a running shoe, personalizing features such as the outsole, the amount of cushioning, and the width. The personalized shoe costs about $10 more than buying a product off store shelves. Some sites provide demonstrations and other product videos, and some, such as Nordstrom, offer 3D (three-dimensional) product images and allow shopping by cost and by feature.

ONLINE BUYERS AND SELLERS

6 Describe online buyers and sellers.

Recent research paints a picture of the characteristics of online users and buyers (see Figure 5.2). Women make up more than 60 percent of people who shop online. Male and female shoppers under age 45 spend more time online. The typical Internet user is likely to be between 18 and 64 years of age. More than half of all users make at least one purchase online each month, and more than six in ten research products online before buying them in a store. Half of all shoppers spend three quarters of total shopping time doing product research. Many online shoppers are loyal and buy mostly from a single site; Amazon and eBay are the most popular. A broader range of Internet users now purchase products online compared with a few years ago and more than half of them use their mobile devices for purchases.[30]

Realizing that customers would have little or no opportunity to rely on many of the sense modes—smelling the freshness of direct-from-the-oven bread, touching the soft fabric of a new cashmere sweater, or squeezing fruit to assess its ripeness—early online sellers focused on offering products consumers were familiar with and tended to buy frequently, such as books and music. Other popular early online offerings included computer hardware and software and airline tickets.

Women's apparel, consumer electronics, and video games top the list of top products sold online. Sales of health and beauty products have increased, with tools showing a decline.[31]

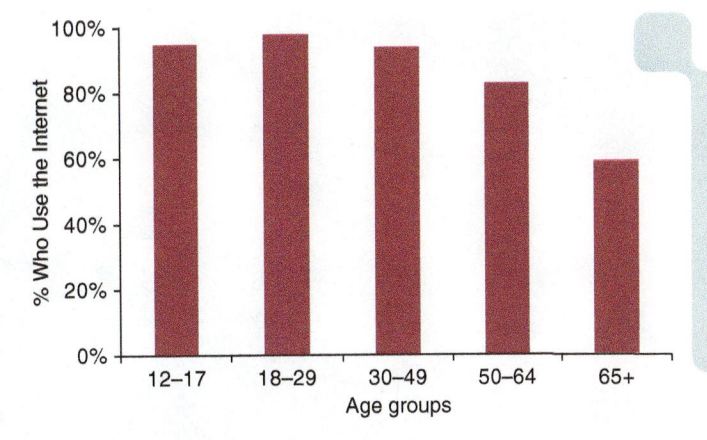

FIGURE 5.2
Characteristics of U.S. Internet Users

Source: Pew Research Center, "Internet User Demographics, Teens and Adults, September 2013," accessed February 14, 2014, www.pewinternet.org.

Thanks to retailers' efforts, consumers' online shopping experiences have been steadily improving in quality and convenience. Many Facebook users utilize the social networking site to click through to the websites of their favorite retailers. The result? Retailers advertising on Facebook see click-through rates almost four times higher than in the past, with increasing returns on their advertising dollars.[32]

ASSESSMENT CHECK

6.1 Who shops online? Are the characteristics of online shoppers changing?

6.2 What are some of the capabilities e-marketers might add to their websites in the future?

CHALLENGES IN E-BUSINESS AND E-MARKETING

For all their advantages, e-business and e-marketing face some problems and challenges. Some of the most significant include developing safe online payment systems, protecting consumer privacy, preventing fraud and scams, improving site design and customer service, and reducing potential channel conflicts and copyright disputes.

> Describe the challenges associated with online marketing and e-business.

SAFETY OF ONLINE PAYMENT

In response to consumer concerns about the safety of sending credit card numbers over the Internet, companies have developed secure payment systems. Internet browsers, such as Microsoft Internet Explorer, contain sophisticated encryption systems to protect sensitive information. **Encryption** is the process of encoding data for security purposes. When such a system is active, users see a special icon that indicates they are at a protected website.

To further increase consumer security, most companies involved in e-business—including all major credit card companies—use **Secure Sockets Layer (SSL)** technology to encrypt information and provide authentication. SSL consists of a public key and a private key. The public key is used to encrypt information and the private key is used to decipher it. When a browser points to a domain with an SSL certificate, the technology authenticates the server and the visitor and establishes an encryption method and a unique session key. Both parties can then begin a secure session that guarantees message privacy and integrity. Symantec is now one of the leading providers of SSL technology used by many Fortune 500 companies.[33]

Many online shoppers are switching to payment services such as PayPal, Bill Me Later, and WU Pay (formerly eBillme). Such services tend to speed checkout and make shopping more secure. They ensure that fewer merchants actually see the shopper's personal information and thus make

encryption The process of encoding data for security purposes.

Secure Sockets Layer (SSL) Technology that secures a website by encrypting information and providing authentication.

Square, a mobile payment system, allows shoppers to make secure credit card purchases by swiping their card through a small device that plugs into a smartphone or tablet.

it less vulnerable to hackers. These services benefit e-marketers, too, because they incur minimal marketing costs that then allow them to charge merchants lower transaction fees than credit card companies.[34] Square is one of the latest entries in the mobile payment services market; see the "Marketing Success" feature for the story.

PRIVACY ISSUES

Marketing research indicates privacy as one of the top concerns of many Internet users. Recently, the European Commission adopted regulations that will require companies such as Google and Facebook to get specific consent to use consumers' personal data. The Federal Trade Commission has explored instituting a Do Not Track option, similar to the Do Not Call option to stop phone sales calls.[35]

More recently, **electronic signatures** have become a way to enter into legal contract policies online. With an e-signature, an individual obtains a form of electronic identification and installs it in his or her Web browser. Signing the contract involves looking up and verifying the buyer's identity with this software.

Thanks to *cookies* and *spyware*—software used to automatically collect data from Internet browsers—online companies can track their customers' shopping and viewing habits. Amazon, for instance, has long employed sophisticated data collection systems to track customer preferences, and Google and other search engines gather users' search terms as a way to better target the ads that provide their revenue. This technology can be a double-edged sword, giving companies the potential both to make visits to the website more convenient and to invade computer users' privacy.

Most consumers want assurances that any information they provide won't be sold to others without their permission. In response to these concerns, online merchants take steps to protect consumer information. For example, many Internet companies have signed on with Internet privacy organizations such as TRUSTe. By displaying the TRUSTe logo on their websites, they indicate their promise to disclose how they collect personal data and what they do with the information. Prominently displaying a privacy policy is an effective way to build customers' trust.

Companies, too, are concerned about the privacy of their data, and with good reason. Hackers recently launched a massive cyber attack on Target, stealing login information, emails, and encrypted passwords for up to 110 million of its customers. Despite repeated warnings, many Internet users often use the same password on different websites. With hackers accessing user passwords, they may be able to log into other sites with the stolen passwords.[36]

electronic signatures Electronic identification that allows legal contracts such as home mortgages and insurance policies to be executed online.

MARKETING SUCCESS
Square Captures Mobile Payment Sector

Background Square is a mobile payment system that allows shoppers to make credit card purchases by swiping a small white plastic device that plugs into a smartphone or tablet. Merchants using the system pay Square a 2.75 percent transaction fee.

The Challenge With no mass-media marketing budget, Square needed to show businesses how easy it is to use the service and also create the same trust evoked by financial giants such as Chase, Visa, and Citibank.

The Strategy Square's co-founder and CEO Jack Dorsey knew Square should be "something that never gets in the way of our users doing what they want to do," which meant design and ease of use had to come first.

Outcome By creating a simple and well-designed customer experience, the company attracted 1 million customers with little more than word of mouth. Many users are small businesses, from cabbies to purveyors of handmade or luxury goods and services, who love its "transparency and simplicity." Square processes more than $20 billion in payments per year and has attracted over $100 million in outside investments. Next it will add inventory data for its customers. If growth continues, analysts predict it will go public.

Sources: Austin Carr, "Jack Dorsey and Other Square Insiders Respond to All the Haters," *Fast Company*, accessed August 15, 2014, www.fastcompany.com; Alex Wilhelm, "Putting Square's $5 Billion Valuation into Context," *TechCrunch*, accessed February 17, 2014, http://techcrunch.com; Douglas MacMillian, "Square Exploring 2014 IPO with Banks," *The Wall Street Journal*, accessed February 14, 2014, http://blogs.wsj.com; Gerry Shih, "Burnished by Starbucks, Upstart Square Battles Payment Giants," *Reuters*, accessed February 14, 2014, http://www.reuters.com; Larry Magid, "Square and Starbucks Lead Transition to Mobile Payment," *Forbes*, accessed February 14, 2014, www.forbes.com.

To prevent intrusions, companies install combinations of hardware and software called *firewalls* to keep unauthorized users from tapping into private corporate data. A **firewall** is an electronic barrier between a company's internal network and the Internet that limits access into and out of the network. However, an impenetrable firewall is difficult to find. A determined and skilled hacker often can gain access, so it is important for firms to test their websites and networks for vulnerabilities and back up critical data in case an intruder breaches security measures.

firewall Electronic barrier between a company's internal network and the Internet that limits access into and out of the network.

phishing High-tech scam that uses authentic-looking email or pop-up messages to get unsuspecting victims to reveal personal information.

FRAUD AND SCAMS

Fraud is another impediment to the growth of e-business and e-marketing. The FBI and the National White Collar Crime Center have formed a partnership called the Internet Crime Complaint Center (IC3) to receive and refer criminal complaints about cyber fraud and other Internet crime.[37] CSO Security and Risk, the U.S. Secret Service, and other security organizations conduct an annual cyber security survey. The most recent results suggest that although more attacks come from outside organizations, insider attacks are the most costly. Defenses against outside attacks and leaks are becoming more effective. According to the CERT program at Carnegie Mellon, it is a much more challenging problem to defend against insiders stealing classified information to which they have authorized access or against technically sophisticated users who want to disrupt operations.[38]

One type of Internet fraud is called **phishing**. It is a high-tech scam that uses email or pop-up messages that claim to be from familiar businesses or organizations such as banks, Internet service providers, or even government agencies. The message usually asks the reader to "update" or "validate" account information, often stating that some dire consequence will occur if the reader doesn't respond. The purpose of phishing is to get unsuspecting victims to disclose personal information such as credit card numbers, bank account numbers, Social Security numbers, or computer passwords. Phishing is also commonly used to distribute viruses and malicious spyware programs to computer

> **Briefly Speaking**
>
> "Privacy is implied. Privacy is not up for discussion."
>
> —Mikko Hypponen
> *Cybercrime expert*

vishing Scam that collects personal information through voice response systems; stands for *voice phishing*.

smishing Scam that collects personal information through cell phone text messages; stands for *SMS (short message service) phishing*

users. In **vishing**, which stands for voice phishing, an email or VoIP phone call requests the user to make a phone call to a voice response system that asks for the caller's credit card number. The latest spin on phishing is **smishing** (derived from SMS, or select message service), a scam delivered via text message—60 percent of U.S. adults who send or receive texts have received scams via mobile devices.[39]

Payment fraud is another problem for many e-marketers. Orders are placed online and paid for using a credit card, and the retailer ships the merchandise. Then the cardholder asks the credit card issuer for a chargeback to the e-tailer, claiming he or she never made the purchase or never received the merchandise. Some claims are legitimate, but many involve fraud. Because an online purchase doesn't require a customer's signature or credit card imprint, the merchant—not the card issuer—bears the liability in most fraud cases.

SITE DESIGN AND CUSTOMER SERVICE

For firms to attract and keep customers, e-marketers must meet buyers' expectations. For instance, customers want to find products easily and have questions answered quickly. However, websites are not always well designed and easy to use. Competition and customer expectations will also drive more sites to include three-dimensional product photos and video demonstrations, because industry experts estimate better site design can quadruple the number of shoppers who actually buy what they put in their shopping carts. Product reviews, shopping information, pop-up discount offers, and instant chats for customer questions are other features that can help online retailers to close sales.[40]

Another challenge to successful e-business is merchandise delivery and returns. Retailers sometimes have trouble making deliveries to on-the-go consumers. And consumers don't want to wait for packages to be delivered. Also, if customers aren't satisfied with products, then they have to arrange for pickup or send packages back themselves. Retailers are addressing these issues. Most have systems on their websites that allow customers to track orders from placement to delivery. E-marketers have also worked hard on a process known as *reverse logistics*. Detailed directions on how to return merchandise, including preprinted shipping labels, are included in orders. Some, such as Nordstrom and Zappos, even pay the shipping cost for returns.

Many of the so-called "pure-play" dot-com retailers—those without traditional stores or catalogs—didn't survive for very long. They had no history of selling and satisfying customers.

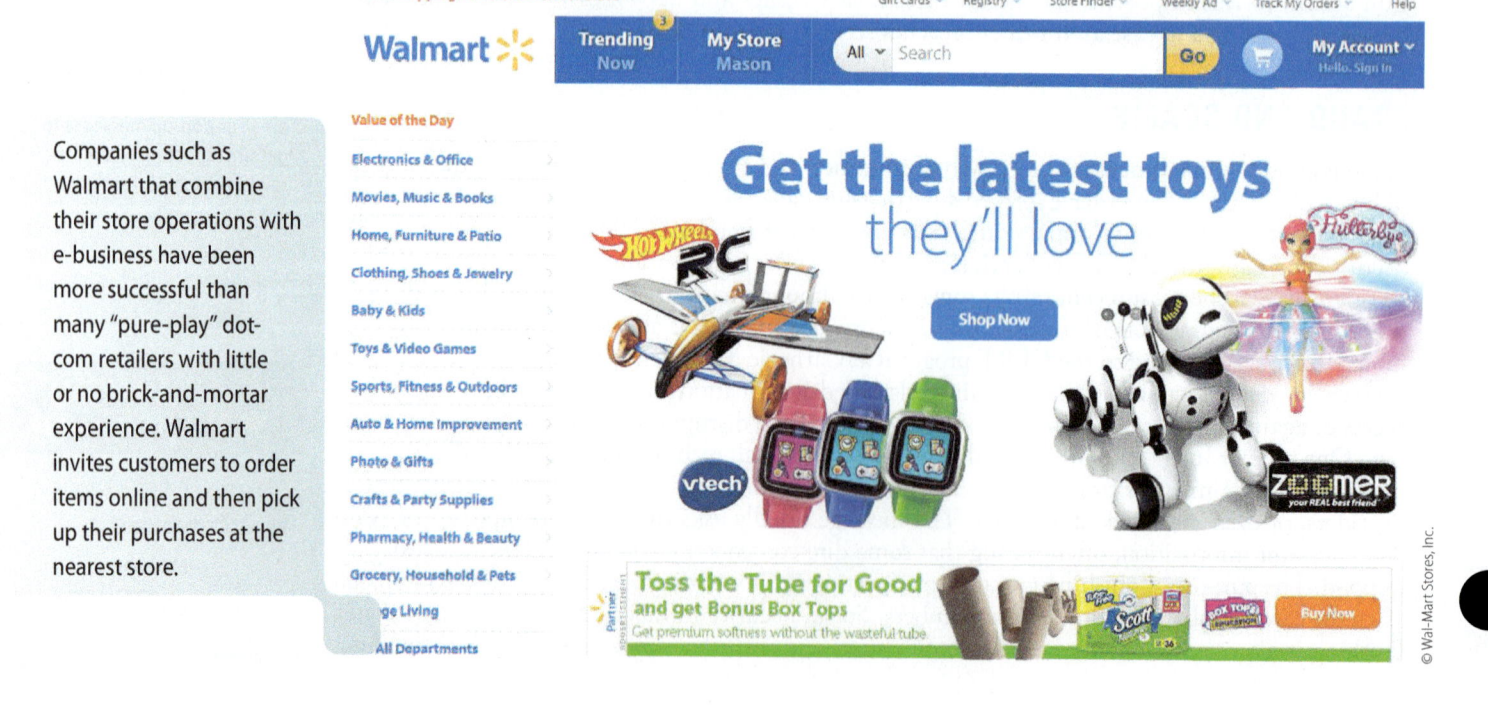

Companies such as Walmart that combine their store operations with e-business have been more successful than many "pure-play" dot-com retailers with little or no brick-and-mortar experience. Walmart invites customers to order items online and then pick up their purchases at the nearest store.

Because of expertise in all parts of retailing, companies such as REI that combine their store and catalog operations with e-business generally have been more successful than those with little or no retail experience. The exception to that rule is Amazon, which now ranks first as the top online retailer. Staples, Apple, and Walmart—all with traditional brick-and-mortar stores—come in second, third, and fourth on the most recent list.[41]

The same lesson also applies to other service industries. To be successful at e-business, firms must establish and maintain competitive standards for customer service. When it began offering customers the opportunity to check flight schedules and purchase tickets online, Southwest Airlines worked hard to make sure its website had the same high service standards the airline is known for. Southwest.com has proved very popular and profitable for the airline.

CHANNEL CONFLICTS AND COPYRIGHT DISPUTES

Companies spend time and money nurturing relationships with their partners. But when a manufacturer uses the Internet to sell directly to customers, it can compete with its usual partners. Retailers often have their own websites, so they don't want their suppliers competing with them for sales. As e-business broadens its reach, producers must decide whether these relationships are more important than the potential of selling directly on the Web. Conflicts between producers, wholesalers, and retailers are called **channel conflicts**.

> **channel conflicts**
> Conflicts among manufacturers, wholesalers, and retailers.

Mattel, well known for producing toys such as Barbie, Cabbage Patch dolls, and Matchbox cars, sells most of its products in toy stores and toy departments of other retailers such as Target and Walmart. The company wants an Internet presence, but it would cut the retailers out of this important source of revenue if it sold toys online to consumers. Mattel cannot afford to lose the goodwill and purchasing power of major retailers such as Toys "R" Us, so the company limits online offerings to specialty products, including pricey American Girl dolls.

Another conflict arises in the area of copyright law, usually when a site hosts content to which someone else holds the rights. Over the last several years, Google has scanned more than 20 million books from libraries around the world to make them searchable online. The Authors Guild filed a copyright infringement suit to stop the project, and the suit was recently dismissed by a U.S. circuit judge in New York, saying Google's scanning of the books and making "snippets" available online constitutes fair use under U.S. copyright law. The ruling is being appealed by the Authors Guild.[42]

ASSESSMENT CHECK

7.1 What are the major challenges to growth in e-business and e-marketing?

7.2 Describe phishing, vishing, and smishing.

7.3 Explain how e-marketing can create channel conflicts and copyright disputes.

MARKETING AND WEB COMMUNICATION

There are four main functions of the Internet: e-business, entertainment, information, and communication. Even though e-business is growing rapidly, communication remains the most popular Web function. One survey estimates that 200 billion emails are sent *every day*.[43] Contemporary marketers also use the communication function of the Internet to advance their organizational objectives.

Companies have long used email to communicate with customers, suppliers, and other partners. Most companies have links on their websites that allow visitors to send email directly to the most appropriate person or division within the company. For instance, if you have a question concerning an online order from Williams-Sonoma, you can click on a link on the retailer's website and send an email to a customer service representative. Many online retailers have gone even

> **8** Discuss how marketers use the communication function of the Web as part of their online marketing strategies.

spam Popular name for junk email.

further by offering their customers live help. Using a form of instant messaging, live help provides a real-time communication channel between customers and customer service representatives.

Firms also use email to inform customers about events such as new products and special promotions. While using email in this manner can be quite cost effective, companies have to be careful. A growing number of customers consider such emails to be **spam**, the popular name for junk email. A recent study found as much as 70 percent of all email is spam.[44] It is no wonder many Internet users employ *spam filters* that automatically eliminate junk email from their in-boxes.

ONLINE COMMUNITIES

In addition to email, many firms use social media (the topic of Chapter 4), Internet forums, blogs, and podcasts to appeal to people with common interests. All these sites take advantage of the communication power of the Internet. Members congregate online and exchange views and information on topics of interest. These communities may be organized for commercial or noncommercial purposes.

Online communities can take several forms, but all offer specific advantages to users and organizations alike. Online forums, for instance, are Internet discussion groups. Users log in and participate by sending comments and questions or receiving information from other forum members. Forums may operate as blogs, as libraries for storing information, or even as a type of classified ad directory. Firms often use forums to ask questions and exchange information with customers. Communities such as these are built on trust. They thrive on shared information but can be undercut by false or misleading posts. See the "Solving an Ethical Controversy" feature for a discussion of fake customer reviews.

Online communities are not limited to consumers. They also facilitate business-to-business marketing. Using the Internet to build communities helps companies find other organizations, including suppliers, distributors, and competitors, that may be interested in forming an alliance. Marketers wanting to expand internationally frequently seek advice from other members of their online community.

> **Briefly Speaking**
>
> "I think it's fair to say that personal computers have become the most empowering tool we've ever created. They're tools of communication, they're tools of creativity, and they can be shaped by their user."
>
> —**Bill Gates**
> *Co-founder of Microsoft*

BLOGS AND PODCASTS

blog Short for *Web log*, an online journal for an individual or organization.

wiki Web page that anyone can edit.

podcast Online audio or video file that can be downloaded to other digital devices.

Another popular online communication method is the **blog**. Short for *Web log*, the term *blog* describes a Web page that is a publicly accessible journal for an individual or organization. Typically updated daily or even more frequently, these hybrid diary-guide sites are read regularly by almost 30 percent of American Internet users. Using *RSS (Really Simple Syndication)* software, readers continually are kept up-to-date on new material posted on their favorite blogs whenever they are online. Unlike email and instant messaging, most blogs let readers post comments and ask questions aimed at the author, called a *blogger*. Some blogs also incorporate **wikis**. A wiki is a Web page anyone can edit so a reader can, in addition to asking questions or posting comments, actually make changes to the Web page. **Podcasts** are another emerging technology. Anyone from bloggers to traditional media sources can prepare an audio or video recording and then post it to a website from which it can be downloaded to any digital device that can play the file.

Given the growing interest in blogs and podcasts, it hasn't taken long for marketers to incorporate them into their e-business strategies. Of particular interest to marketers are blogs that focus on new-technology products, because they can prove effective at quickly forming public opinion. To try to reduce the damage from rumors and misinformation, some companies have decided to treat bloggers as members of the press and acknowledge their ability to spread news and influence. Other firms set up their own blogs. Many companies allow, and even encourage, employees to start their own blogs, believing employee blogs can serve useful functions. With 400,000 employees in 170 countries, IBM was one of the earliest companies to encourage its employees to start blogs and engage in other types of social networking. The company claims that these blogs help to resolve differences among cultures and social divides and hopes that the blogs will foster "virtual societies" among its employees.[45]

SOLVING AN ETHICAL CONTROVERSY
Fake Online Reviews

Some companies offer product rebates for glowing online reviews posted by customers; others hire people to write essentially fake reviews, comments, and blogs about goods and services they haven't used, in hopes of not only increasing sales but also boosting their ranking in search engine results. Regulators are trying to crack down on "deceitful hyping." The FTC has expressed concern, and critics worry that customers making high-stakes decisions could be misled by the practice. But others defend it, saying it is little different from other marketing strategies.

Are paid online reviews a legitimate marketing strategy?

PRO

1. One company that gave customers a rebate for posting Amazon reviews of its leather Kindle case only hinted that it would prefer a five-star score. Customers got the product they wanted for just shipping charges, sales increased, and no one was harmed.

2. Giving free items in exchange for a review merely provides an incentive for customers to voice their honest opinion for others' benefit, which many would not otherwise take time to do.

CON

1. Fake reviews don't accurately represent the good or service and are simply unethical as a marketing strategy.

2. Misleading "customer" comments create an atmosphere of mistrust in the online community, and "if consumers don't trust the content, then there is no value for anyone," says a Yelp spokesperson.

Summary

It's estimated that as many as 30 percent of online reviews may be fake. The state of New York recently fined 19 companies more than $350,000 for commissioning fake user reviews on several sites in an effort to bolster their marketing. Researchers are working on software algorithms that can help detect fake reviews, often with as much as 90 percent accuracy, compared to humans' scores of about 50 percent. All things considered, the old adage, "Let the buyer beware," still applies.

Sources: Christopher Calnan, "Bazaarvoice Tool Aims to Expose Fake Product Reviews Online," *TechFlash*, accessed February 14, 2014, www.bizjournals.com; Max Nisen, "Fake Reviews Are Becoming an Even Bigger Problem for Businesses," *Business Insider*, accessed February 10, 2014, www.businessinsider.com; Brad Tuttle, "How Computer Geeks Aim to Put a Stop to Fake Online Reviews," *Time*, accessed February 10, 2014, http://moneyland.time.com; Cheryl Conner, "Online Reputation: New Methods Emerge for Quashing Fake, Defamatory Reviews," *Forbes*, accessed February 10, 2014, www.forbes.com; Erik Sherman, "Fake Online Reviews Not Likely to Stop after Fines," *Money Watch*, accessed February 10, 2014, www.cbsnews.com.

Some companies have strict policies about the content of employee blogs, and some employees have even been disciplined over what their employers thought was improper blogging. However, most companies today still have no official policies regarding employee blogs.

PROMOTIONS ON THE WEB

Rather than rely completely on their websites to attract buyers, companies frequently expand their reach in the marketplace by placing ads on sites their prospective customers are likely to visit. **Banner ads**, the most common form of Internet advertising, are typically small,

banner ads Strip message placed in high-visibility areas of frequently visited websites.

A popular form of online communication, blogs are public Web pages authored by individuals or organizations that let readers post comments and ask questions about online content. IBM was one of the first companies to encourage the use of blogs both internally and as an external marketing tool.

pop-up ads Separate window that pops up with an advertising message.

pre-roll video ads Brief marketing message that appears before expected video content.

search marketing Paying search engines, such as Google, a fee to make sure the company's listing appears toward the top of the search results. Also called *search engine optimization (SEO)*.

strip messages placed in high-visibility areas of frequently visited websites. **Pop-up ads** are separate windows that pop up with an advertising message. The effectiveness of pop-up ads, however, is questionable. First, scam artists use pop-ups. Second, many Internet users simply hate pop-up ads—even those from legitimate companies. Consequently, most ISPs now offer software that blocks pop-up ads. Google and Microsoft also offer free pop-up ad-blocking software.

Pre-roll video ads, marketing messages that play before an online video, are very popular. Although users have shown some resistance, YouTube is one of the few sites to let viewers opt out of watching. SpotXchange, which sells pre-roll video advertising, launched a service called SkipIt that, for a small fee, allows viewers to opt out of viewing the ads.[46] Another type of online advertising is **search marketing** or search engine optimization (SEO). This is considered one of the most effective forms of Web-based advertising. Companies pay search engines fees to have their websites or ads pop up after a user enters certain words into the search engine, or to make sure their firm's listing appears toward the top of the search results. Google and other search engines include "Sponsored Links" on the right side of the search results page. A user who clicks on one of the sites listed under Sponsored Links is taken to that site, and the company pays the search engine a small fee. Google and Microsoft, among others, have made major investments in improving their search marketing services and capabilities.

Another way companies use the Web to promote their products is through online coupons. For instance, customers can visit a company's website to learn about items on sale and then print a discount coupon redeemable at participating retailers.

ASSESSMENT CHECK

8.1 What are online communities? Explain how online communities can help companies market their products and improve customer service.

8.2 What are blogs, wikis, and podcasts?

8.3 Explain the differences between a banner ad, a pop-up ad, a pre-roll video ad, and search marketing (also called search engine optimization).

BUILDING AN EFFECTIVE WEB PRESENCE

An e-business website can serve many purposes. It can broaden customer bases, provide immediate access to current catalogs, accept and process orders, and offer personalized customer service. As technology becomes increasingly easy to use, anyone with Internet access can open an account and place a simple website on the Internet. How people or organizations use their sites to achieve their goals determines whether their sites will succeed. Figure 5.3 lists some key questions to consider in developing a website, and the "Career Readiness" feature introduces some ideas for making the best use of company websites where jobs are posted. Find out how to be the applicant who stands out in the crowd.

> **9** Describe the process of developing successful e-business websites and how to assess their effectiveness.

SUCCESSFUL SITE DEVELOPMENT

Most Web experts agree: It is easier to build a bad website than a good one. When judging websites, success means different things to different businesses. One firm might be satisfied by maintaining a popular site that conveys company information or reinforces name recognition—just as a billboard or magazine ad does—without requiring any immediate sales activity. Websites such as those of the *Los Angeles Times* and *USA Today* draw many visitors who want the latest news, and Yahoo, Google, and ESPN.com are successful because they attract heavy traffic. Besides enhancing their brands, popular websites such as these add to their success by selling advertising space to other businesses.

Internet merchants need to attract customers who conduct business on the spot. Entrepreneurs are wise to clearly define their business goals, perhaps by creating a community of enthusiasts to build up sales in advance and to pay due attention to tried-and-true marketing tools that can complement Internet efforts, including television advertising. Listening to consumers is as important as talking to them via a company website or blog.

ESTABLISHING GOALS

What is the company's goal for its website? Answering this question is the first and most important step in the website development process. For the broadband telephone service provider Vonage, the primary objective is to sign up new customers. So the website designers put a link called "Sign Up" prominently in the upper portion of the home page.

Objectives for the website also determine the scope of the project. If the company's goal is to sell merchandise online, the site must incorporate a way for customers to place orders and ask questions about products, as well as links to the company's databases to track inventory and deliveries. The plan should include not only the appearance of the website but also the company's behind-the-scenes resources for making the website deliver on its promises.

Other key decisions include whether to create and maintain a site in-house or to contract with outside designers. Some companies prefer to retain control over content and design by producing their own sites. However, because acquiring the expertise to develop websites can be very time-consuming, hiring specialists may be more cost effective. Naming the website is another important early step in the planning process. A domain name should reflect the company and its products and be easy to remember. However, with millions of domain names already registered, the search for a unique, memorable, and easily spelled name can be difficult.

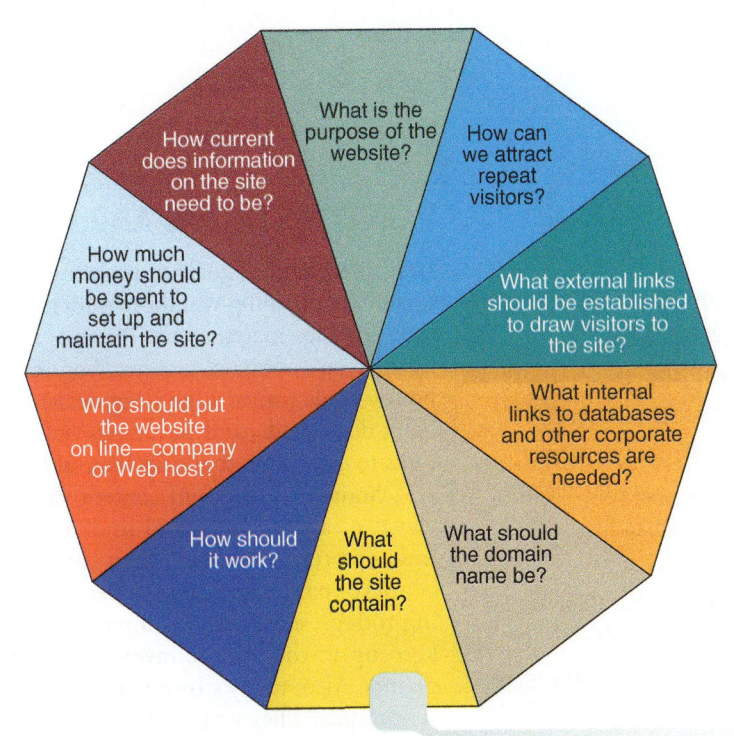

FIGURE 5.3 Questions to Consider in Developing a Website

- What is the purpose of the website?
- How can we attract repeat visitors?
- What external links should be established to draw visitors to the site?
- What internal links to databases and other corporate resources are needed?
- What should the domain name be?
- What should the site contain?
- How should it work?
- Who should put the website on line—company or Web host?
- How much money should be spent to set up and maintain the site?
- How current does information on the site need to be?

CAREER READINESS
Tips for Applying for Jobs Online

Firms such as Starbucks and Procter & Gamble attract millions of online job applications a year, and they're forced to use screening software to eliminate thousands of applications that are never read. How can you make yours stand out in the crowd?

1. Be prepared to supply links to your blog or social networking account, especially if applying to a tech firm. Your "Web presence" says more about you than your résumé can.

2. Fill your résumé with key words applicable to the job, such as "portfolio analysis" or "social media marketing expertise."

3. Recognize that an online application is a one-size-fits-all document that might not fit you. Avoid answering questions about your salary, for instance. Type "$100" and keep going.

4. Write "To be discussed" for the name of your current boss, especially if you are unemployed, and answer, "Available upon strong mutual interest" to a request for references. Many advisors say these questions are premature until the interview.

5. If the application asks for a current job description, write "Please see résumé."

6. Finally, use your personal network to link your way to someone inside the firm where you're applying. A personal contact can still be the best way to land that all-important interview.

Sources: Susan Adams, "How to Make Them Respond When You Apply for a Job Online," *Forbes*, accessed February 16, 2014, www.forbes.com; Rachel Emma Silverman, "No More Résumés, Say Some Firms," *The Wall Street Journal*, accessed February 10, 2014, http://onlinewsj.com; Lauren Weber, "Your Résumé vs. Oblivion," *The Wall Street Journal*, accessed February 10, 2014, http://onlinewsj.com.

IMPLEMENTATION AND INTEREST

Implementing the goals of the site is the next stage, and content is one of the most important factors in determining whether visitors return to a site. People obviously are more inclined to visit a site that provides material that interests them. Many e-business websites try to distinguish themselves by offering additional features. For example, Amazon's website lures traffic to the site with daily and hourly deals (called Lightning deals), a separate clothing store, garden supplies, music, movie, and book downloads, and numerous online community forums on a variety of topics. Many sites offer links to other sites that may interest visitors.

Standards for good content vary for every site, but available resources should be relevant to viewers; easy to access and understand; updated regularly; and written or displayed in a compelling, entertaining way. When the World Wide Web was a novelty, a page with a picture and a couple of paragraphs of text seemed entertaining. But such "brochureware" falls far short of meeting today's standards for interactivity, including the ability to accept customer data and orders, keep up-to-the-minute inventory records, and respond quickly to customer questions and complaints. Also, today's Internet users are less patient about figuring out how to make a site do what it promises. They won't wait ten minutes for a video clip to download or click through five different pages to complete a purchase. Revamping a site can help maintain interest and keep users on the site longer. Facebook recently rolled out a new design for its home page that is more than just cosmetic. The changes are meant to improve site navigation and gather useful links and information in one part of the site.[47]

> **Briefly Speaking**
>
> "If the Starbucks secret is a smile when you get your latte... ours is that the Web site adapts to the individual's taste."
>
> —Reed Hastings
> *Founder and CEO, Netflix*

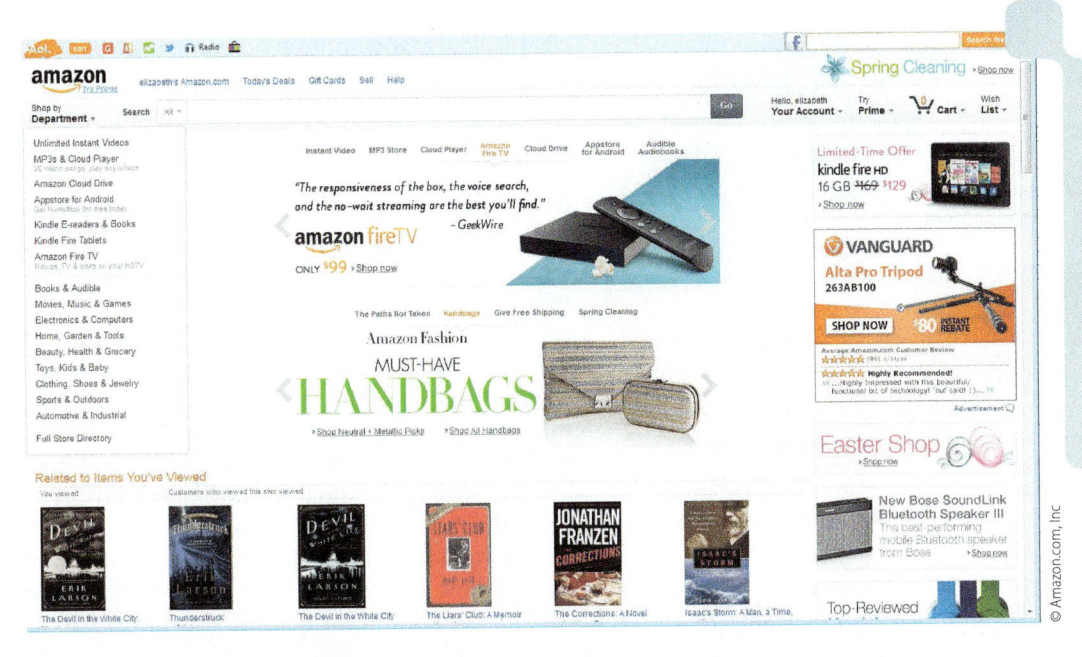

Websites such as the one for Amazon are successful because they attract heavy traffic and offer shoppers a variety of products and deals as well as opportunities to join in discussions on a variety of topics via community forums.

After making content decisions and designing the site, the next step is connecting to the Internet by placing the required computer files on a server. Companies can have their own dedicated Web servers or contract to place their websites on servers at Internet Service Providers (ISPs) or other host companies. Most small businesses lack the necessary expertise to set up and run their own servers; they are better off outsourcing to meet their hosting and maintenance needs. They also need to draw business to their site. This usually requires a listing with the major search engines, such as Google, Bing, and Yahoo.

PRICING AND MAINTENANCE

As with any technological investment, website costs are an important consideration. The highly variable cost of a website includes not only development expenses but also the cost of placing the site on a Web server, maintaining and updating it, and promoting it. A reasonably tech-savvy employee with off-the-shelf software can create a simple piece of brochureware for a few hundred dollars. A website that can handle e-business will cost at least $10,000. Creating it requires understanding how to link the website to the company's other information systems.

Although developing a commercial website with interactive features can cost tens of thousands of dollars, putting it online can cost as little as $30 a month for a spot on the server of a Web host such as Yahoo, and Web hosts such as Just Host and iPage deliver a huge audience.[48]

It's also important for a website to stay current. Visitors don't return to a site if they know that the information never changes or that claims about inventory or product selection are not relevant or current.[49] Consequently, updating design and content is another major expense. In addition, site maintenance should include running occasional searches to test that links to the company's website are still active.

ASSESSING SITE EFFECTIVENESS

How does a company gauge the return from investing in a website? Measuring the effectiveness of a website is tricky, and the appropriate process often depends on the purpose of the website. Figure 5.4 lists some measures of effectiveness. Profitability is relatively easy to measure in companies that generate revenues directly from online product orders, advertising, or subscription sales. Southwest Airlines generates more than 81 percent of its bookings online at Southwest.com. However, what's not

FIGURE 5.4
Measures of Website Effectiveness

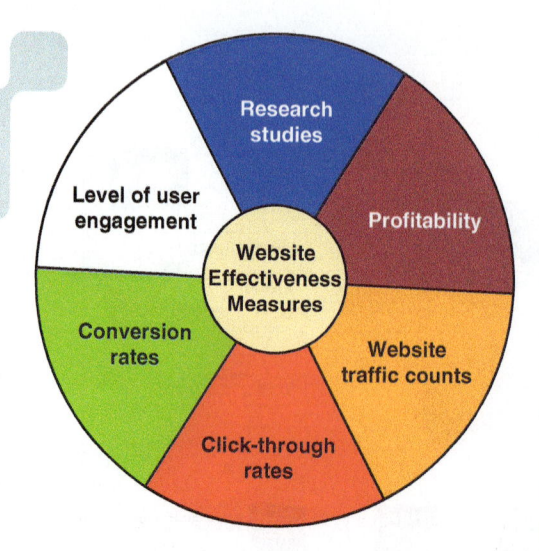

Website Effectiveness Measures: Research studies, Profitability, Website traffic counts, Click-through rates, Conversion rates, Level of user engagement

Web-to-store shoppers Consumers who use the Internet as a tool when shopping at brick-and-mortar retailers.

click-through rates Percentage of people presented with a banner ad who click on it.

conversion rate Percentage of visitors to a website who make a purchase.

engagement Amount of time users spend on sites.

clear is how many of those tickets Southwest would have sold through other channels if Southwest.com did not exist. Also, evidence exists that so-called **Web-to-store shoppers**—a group that favors the Internet primarily as a research tool and time-saving device for retail purchases made in stores—are a significant consumer niche.

For many companies, revenue is not a major website objective. Most company websites are classified as corporate websites, not shopping sites, meaning that firms use their sites to showcase their products and to offer information about their organizations. For such companies, online success is measured by increased brand awareness and brand loyalty, which presumably translates into greater profitability through offline transactions.

Some standards guide efforts to collect and analyze traditional consumer purchase data, such as how many Ohio residents purchased new Jeeps the previous year, watched *The Voice* on NBC, or tried Starbucks Dark Roast coffee. Still, the Internet presents several challenges for marketers. Although information sources are getting better, it is difficult to be sure how many people use the Internet, how often, and what they actually do online. Some Web pages display counters that measure the number of visits. However, the counters can't tell whether someone has spent time on the page or skipped over it on the way to another site, or whether that person is a first-time or repeat viewer.

Advertisers typically measure the success of their ads in terms of **click-through rates**, meaning the percentage of people presented with an online ad who click on it, thereby linking to a website or a pop-up page of information related to the ad. The average click-through rate in the United States is about 0.10 percent of those viewing an ad. This rate is much lower than 1.4 percent response rate for direct-mail advertisements. Low click-through rates have made Web advertising less attractive than when it was new and people were clicking on just about anything online. Selling advertising has therefore become a less reliable source of e-business revenue.

As e-business continues its popularity, new models for measuring its effectiveness are being developed. A basic measurement is the **conversion rate**, the percentage of visitors to a website who make purchases. A conversion rate of 3 percent is average by today's standards. A company can use its advertising cost, site traffic, and conversion rate data to find out the cost to win each customer. E-businesses try to boost their conversion rates by ensuring their sites download quickly, are easy to use, and deliver on their promises. Many are turning to one of several firms that help companies improve the performance of their websites. Nielsen/Net Ratings developed a new way to rate websites that measures **engagement**, or how much time users spend on sites, rather than counting how many pages of a site they view. Google Analytics is a tool for tracking the number of visitors to a site, which pages they visit, where they come from, and whether they buy, among other statistics.[50]

Webtrends' Mobile Analytics offers similar measurements of consumer wireless activity. A recent version of its software, Webtrends Analytics 10, aims to integrate analytics from mobile, social, and Web channels. It can analyze marketing data from Facebook pages, iTunes Connect, and other media platforms.[51]

ASSESSMENT CHECK

9.1 What are the basic questions a company should ask itself when planning a website?

9.2 How does the type of website affect measures of effectiveness?

9.3 Explain the difference between click-through rate, conversion rate, and engagement.

Strategic Implications of Marketing in the 21st Century

The future is bright for marketers who continue to take advantage of the tremendous potential of e-business and e-marketing. Online channels, such as podcasts, that seem cutting edge today will be eclipsed within the next decade by newer technologies, some of which haven't even been invented yet. First and foremost, e-business empowers consumers. For instance, already a significant percentage of car buyers show up at a dealership armed with information on dealer costs and option packages—information they obtained online. And the percentage of informed buyers is only going to increase. This trend isn't about being market led or customer focused; it is about consumer control. Some argue that the Internet represents the ultimate triumph of consumerism.

Since the end of World War II, there has been a fundamental shift in the retailing paradigm from Main Street to malls to superstores. Each time the framework shifted, a new group of leaders emerged. The old leaders often missed the early warning signs because they were easy to ignore. When the first Walmart and Home Depot stores appeared, how many people really understood what impact these large retailers would have on the marketing environment? Similarly, marketers must understand the potential impact of the Web. Initially, some experts predicted the death of traditional retailing. This hasn't happened and probably will never happen. Rather, a marketing evolution for organizations has occurred, one that embraces Internet technologies as essential parts of their marketing strategies. E-business is fueled by information; marketers who effectively use the wealth of data available will survive—and thrive—in cyberspace.

Get online now for additional learning tools to help you master your marketing knowledge—visit **WWW.CENGAGEBRAIN.COM** today!

REVIEW OF CHAPTER OBJECTIVES

1 Describe the growth of Internet use worldwide.

The number of Internet users worldwide has reached more than 2.8 billion. Among individual countries with the highest number of Internet users, China is first with almost a quarter of its population online, followed by the United States, India, and Japan.

2 Explain e-business, e-marketing, and the opportunities e-marketing presents.

E-business involves targeting customers by collecting and analyzing business information, conducting customer transactions, and maintaining online relationships with customers by means of computer networks such as the Internet. E-marketing is the strategic process of creating, distributing, promoting, and pricing goods and services to a target market over the Internet or through digital tools. The capabilities and benefits of e-business and e-marketing include the elimination of geographical boundaries, personalized marketing, interactive marketing, right-time marketing, and integrated marketing.

3 Distinguish between a corporate website and a marketing website.

The vast majority of businesses have websites. Generally, these sites can be classified as either corporate websites or marketing websites. Corporate websites are designed to increase the firms' visibility, promote their offerings, and provide information to interested parties. Marketing websites are also designed to communicate information and build customer relationships, but the main purpose of marketing websites is to increase purchases by site visitors.

4 List the six major forms of business-to-business e-marketing.

B2B e-marketing is the process of selling goods and services from one business to another through online transactions. B2B e-marketing includes product information; ordering, invoicing, and payment processes; and customer service. In a B2B context, e-business uses Internet technology to conduct transactions between two organizations via electronic data interchange, Web services, extranets, private exchanges, electronic exchanges, and e-procurement.

5 Explain business-to-consumer (B2C) e-marketing.

Business-to-consumer (B2C) e-marketing is maturing. B2C uses the Internet to connect companies directly with consumers. E-tailing and electronic storefronts are the major forms of B2C online sales channels. B2C websites are either shopping sites or informational sites. Products can be purchased on shopping sites; informational sites provide product information along with links to sellers. Benefits of B2C e-marketing include competitive prices, increased access and convenience, and personalized service.

6 Describe online buyers and sellers.

Today's typical Internet user is from 18 to 64 years of age. Women now outnumber men online. During a recent year, the top products sold online included women's apparel, consumer electronics, and health and beauty products.

7 Describe the challenges associated with online marketing and e-business.

One of the challenges to e-business is developing safe online payment methods. Most firms involved in e-business use Secure Sockets Layer technology to encrypt information and provide authentication. The growth of e-business has also been hampered by consumer security and privacy concerns and fraud. In addition, poor website design and service, unreliability of delivery and returns, and lack of retail expertise has limited e-business success. The Internet can also generate conflict among manufacturers, wholesalers, and retailers and present another avenue for copyright disputes.

8 Discuss how marketers use the communication function of the Web as part of their online marketing strategies.

Communication remains the most popular function of the Internet. Companies have long used email to communicate with customers, suppliers, and other partners. Online communities are groups of people who share common interests. Companies use online communities such as forums to communicate with and obtain feedback from customers and other partners. Blogs are online journals that have gained popularity in recent years. Wikis are Web pages anyone can edit, and podcasts are audio and video files that can be downloaded from the Web to any digital device. Web-based promotions include advertising on other websites using banner ads and pop-up ads, pre-roll video ads, and search marketing (also known as search engine optimization). Banner ads are strip messages placed in high-visibility areas of frequently visited websites. A pop-up ad is a separate window that pops up with an advertising message. Pre-roll video ads appear before a selected video. Search marketing is an arrangement by which a firm pays a search engine such as Google a fee to make sure the firm's listing appears toward the top of the search results.

9 Describe the process of developing successful e-business websites and how to assess their effectiveness.

Businesses establish websites to expand their customer bases, increase buyer awareness of their products, improve consumer communications, and provide better service. Before designing a website, a company's decision makers must first determine what they want to achieve with the site.

Other important decisions include who should create, host, and manage the site; how to promote it; and how much funding to allocate. Successful websites contain informative, up-to-date, and visually appealing content. Sites should also download quickly and be easy to use. Finally, management must develop ways of assessing how well a site accomplishes its objectives. Common methods of measuring the effectiveness of websites include profitability, click-through rates, conversion rates, and engagement.

ASSESSMENT CHECK: ANSWERS

1.1 How would you describe the growth of Internet use worldwide? Worldwide, the number of Internet users has reached more than 2.8 billion. Among individual countries with the highest number of Internet users, China is first with almost one-quarter of the population online. The next three countries are the United States, India, and Japan. Growth in Asia has been rapid.

1.2 What do most U.S. consumers do online? Nearly all U.S. consumers say they use email; almost 85 percent get news, search for health or medical news, look for information about items they're interested in buying, or go online just to pass the time or to have fun.

2.1 Define e-marketing. E-marketing is the strategic process of creating, distributing, promoting, and pricing goods and services to a target market over the Internet.

2.2 Explain the difference between e-business and e-marketing. E-business involves a wide range of activities that take place via the Internet. It is divided into five broad categories: (1) e-tailing; (2) business-to-business transactions; (3) electronic data interchanges; (4) email, instant messaging, blogs, podcasts, and other Web-enabled communication; and (5) gathering and use of information through Web contacts. E-marketing transfers the traditional marketing functions of creating, distributing, promoting, and pricing goods and services to the Internet or through digital tools.

2.3 What are the major benefits of e-marketing? The major benefits of e-business include the elimination of geographical boundaries, personalized marketing, interactive marketing, right-time marketing, and integrated marketing.

3.1 Explain the difference between a corporate website and a marketing website. A corporate website is designed to increase a firm's visibility, promote its offerings, and provide information for interested parties. A marketing website generally includes the same information found on a corporate website but is also designed to increase sales by site visitors.

3.2 Why would companies *not* sell products on their websites? Their products might not lend themselves to online sales, or the firms may have relationships with partners, such as dealers or franchisees, that sell their products instead.

4.1 What is B2B e-marketing? How large is it relative to consumer e-marketing? B2B e-marketing is the use of the Internet for business transactions between organizations. By some estimates, B2B e-commerce revenues are more than double that of consumer transactions.

4.2 Define EDI and Web services. An EDI is a computer-to-computer exchange of invoices, purchase orders, price quotations, and other sales information between buyers and sellers. All parties must use the same computer operating system. Web services consist of Internet-based systems that allow parties to communicate and exchange data regardless of the computer operating system they use.

4.3 Briefly explain how e-procurement works. E-procurement systems are Web-based systems that enable all types of organizations to improve the efficiency of their bidding and purchasing processes.

5.1 What is B2C e-marketing? B2C e-marketing uses the Internet to connect companies directly with consumers either through shopping sites or through informational sites.

5.2 Explain the difference between a shopping website and an informational website. Consumers can purchase products on shopping sites, while informational sites provide product information along with links to sellers. However, consumers cannot actually purchase products on informational sites.

5.3 Discuss the benefits of B2C e-marketing. Benefits of B2C e-marketing include competitive prices, increased access and convenience, and personalized service.

6.1 Who shops online? Are the characteristics of online shoppers changing? The typical Internet user now is likely to be between 18 and 64 years of age. Men used to shop more frequently online than women did, but today women shoppers outnumber men.

6.2 What are some of the capabilities e-marketers might add to their websites in the future? E-marketers need to update their offerings at their websites at an increasing rate, speed the checkout process, add video segments to their online product catalogs, implement advanced and easy-to-use search and navigation technologies, and initiate network-type conversations with and among their customers.

7.1 What are the major challenges to growth in e-business and e-marketing? The major challenges include developing safe online payment, privacy concerns, and fraud and scams. In addition, poor site design and customer service, unreliability of delivery and returns, and lack of retail expertise have limited e-business success.

7.2 Describe phishing, vishing, and smishing. Phishing is a scam that uses email or pop-up messages that claim to be from familiar banks, Internet service providers, or other organizations asking for personal information. The purpose of phishing is to get unsuspecting victims to disclose personal information such as credit card numbers. Vishing is the voice equivalent of phishing, and consists of a voice message or email telling the user to make a phone call designed to elicit credit card information. Smishing is the text-message equivalent of phishing and consists of a spam text message delivered to a cell phone asking the user to reply to the message with personal information.

7.3 Explain how e-marketing can create channel conflicts and copyright disputes. The Internet can generate conflict among manufacturers, wholesalers, and retailers—so-called channel conflicts. For instance, a channel conflict could be created when a manufacturer sells its products online and competes with its retail partners. Copyright disputes usually arise when a site hosts content to which someone else holds the rights.

8.1 What are online communities? Explain how online communities can help companies market their products and improve customer service. Online communities can take several forms and include Internet discussion groups and social media sites (discussed in Chapter 4). Users log in and participate by sending comments and questions or receiving information from other forum members. Companies use online communities to ask questions and exchange information with customers.

8.2 What are blogs, wikis, and podcasts? A blog, short for *Web log*, is a Web page that serves as a publicly accessible journal for an individual or organization. A wiki is a Web page anyone can edit. A podcast is an audio or video file that can be downloaded from a website to a digital device. Companies use blogs, wikis, and podcasts as tools to build and maintain customer relationships.

8.3 Explain the differences between a banner ad, a pop-up ad, a pre-roll video ad, and search marketing. Banner ads are strip messages placed in high-visibility areas of frequently visited websites. A pop-up ad is a separate window that pops up with an advertising message. Pre-roll video ads are brief marketing messages that appear before expected video content. Search marketing is an arrangement by which a firm pays a search engine—such as Google—a fee to make sure the firm's listing appears toward the top of the search results.

9.1 What are the basic questions a company should ask itself when planning a website? The first question deals with the purpose of the website. The second deals with whether the firm should develop the site itself or outsource it to a specialized firm. The third question is determining the name of the site.

9.2 How does the type of website affect measures of effectiveness? For a shopping site, profitability is an important measure of effectiveness, though profitability can be difficult to measure given the tendencies of Web-to-store shoppers. For company websites, online success is measured by increased brand awareness and loyalty, which presumably translate into greater profitability through offline transactions.

9.3 Explain the difference between click-through rate, conversion rate, and engagement. The click-through rate is the percentage of viewers who, when presented with a banner ad, click on it. The conversion rate is the percentage of visitors to a website who actually make purchases. Engagement measures how long a user spends on a site instead of how many pages he or she views.

MARKETING TERMS YOU NEED TO KNOW

- e-business 136
- e-marketing 138
- interactive marketing 140
- corporate website 141
- marketing website 141
- business-to-business (B2B) e-marketing 142
- e-procurement 143
- business-to-consumer (B2C) e-marketing 144
- electronic storefronts 144
- electronic shopping cart 144
- bots (shopbots) 145
- encryption 147
- Secure Sockets Layer (SSL) 147
- electronic signatures 148
- firewall 149
- phishing 149
- vishing 150
- smishing 150
- channel conflicts 151
- spam 152
- blog 152
- wiki 152
- podcast 152
- banner ads 153
- pop-up ads 154
- pre-roll video ads 154
- search marketing 154
- Web-to-store shoppers 158
- click-through rate 158
- conversion rate 158
- engagement 158

ASSURANCE OF LEARNING REVIEW

1. List the five e-business categories.
2. Explain how a Web presence can improve the performance of traditional brick-and-mortar operations.
3. Describe the type and purpose of information found on a corporate website.
4. Which is larger, B2B or B2C e-marketing?
5. How is wireless access changing e-marketing?
6. List the reasons consumers give for why they shop online.
7. Describe how firms can alleviate some of the privacy concerns of online shoppers.

8. What is purchase fraud?
9. How can companies benefit from blogs and avoid their downsides?
10. Describe the issues that go into developing a successful website. How does the purpose of the website affect its implementation and cost?

PROJECTS AND TEAMWORK EXERCISES

1. In small teams, research the benefits of purchasing the following products online:
   a. tablet computers
   b. hotel rooms in Orlando
   c. movie tickets
   d. auto insurance
2. Assume your team is assigned to develop the website for a large online clothing retailer that also has traditional retail stores. Research the characteristics of Web users and online shoppers. What features would you want to incorporate into your website?
3. How can marketers use the concept of community to add value to their products? Give a real-world example of each type of community discussed in the chapter.
4. Working with a small group, assume your group designs e-business websites. Identify a local company that operates with little or no online presence. Outline a proposal that explains to the firm the benefits of either going online or significantly expanding its online presence. Sketch out what the firm's website should look like and the functions it should perform.
5. Working with a partner, identify and visit ten different e-business websites. These can be either B2C or B2B sites. Which of these sites, in your opinion, have the highest and lowest conversion rates? Explain your choices and suggest some ways in which the conversion rates of all ten sites could be improved.

CRITICAL-THINKING EXERCISES

1. Who are typical online buyers and sellers? What are some of the strategic implications of these facts to online marketers?
2. Some marketers argue that search marketing is a more effective means of using the Web to advertise than traditional pop-up or banner ads. Research the concept of search marketing. What are some of the benefits of using search marketing?
3. Assume you work for a U.S. company that markets its products throughout the world. Its current online presence outside the United States is limited. Outline some steps the company should take to expand its online presence internationally.
4. Visa offers a service called Verified by Visa. The purpose is to reduce Internet-related fraud. (MasterCard and American Express have similar services.) Research "Verified by Visa" and prepare a report summarizing the program and how it protects both buyers and sellers.
5. One factor that appears to impede growth in online sales is consumers' fear of receiving unsolicited email after a purchase is made. Given that fear, should companies continue to use email to communicate with customers? If so, how?

ETHICS EXERCISE

One of the lingering obstacles to e-business revolves around privacy concerns. Virtually all websites collect user data. Internet service providers, for example, can track where users go on the Web and store that information. Search engines keep detailed data on users' Internet searches. Those arguing that additional privacy laws and regulations are needed claim that users never know exactly what information is collected, nor when it is collected. Moreover, there is no means for determining whether websites follow their own privacy policies.

On the other hand, some say current laws and regulations are adequate because they make it illegal for firms to misrepresent their privacy policies or fail to disclose the type of information collected. Furthermore, there is no evidence that Internet companies are quietly passing on specific customer information to outside parties.

Aside from the strictly legal issues, Web privacy raises a number of ethical issues as well.

Assume your company collects and stores personal information about its online customers. The company's privacy policy allows the company to give limited amounts of that information to "selected" third parties.

1. Is this policy, in your opinion, appropriate and adequate? What ethical issues does your company's policy raise?
2. How would you change the privacy policy to reflect your ethical concerns?
3. From strictly an economic perspective, is the company's existing policy adequate and appropriate?

INTERNET EXERCISES

1. **Online shopping.** Assume you're in the market for a tablet computer. Visit at least two of the websites listed below and review shopping suggestions and model ratings. Next, list your top two models and, using a shopping site such as Shopping.com (www.shopping.com), search for online retailers offering the best combination of price, user ratings, shipping, and other relevant criteria. Prepare a report summarizing your experience. What did this exercise teach you about the benefits and challenges of online retailing?

   www.pcmag.com

   www.tabletpccomparison.net

   www.pcworld.com

   www.cnet.com

2. **Marketing uses of social networking.** Choose two online retailers and two manufacturers. Go to each website. Compare and contrast how all four firms use blogs and/or podcasts to market their products. Which, in your opinion, uses these online strategies most effectively?

3. **Search marketing.** Visit the website listed below. Prepare a brief report outlining how to optimize the use of search marketing. Be sure to include a discussion on measuring the effectiveness of search marketing.

   www.toprankblog.com/2009/03/charting-search-engine-optimization

   Note: Internet Web addresses change frequently. If you don't find the exact site listed, you may need to access the organization's home page and search from there or use a search engine such as Google or Bing.

CASE 5.1
Walgreens Masters E-Commerce

With recent acquisitions of drugstore.com and beauty.com, Walgreens has put the business community on notice that the company is much more than a century-old, brick-and-mortar retailer. The company believes consumers want choices, and it has implemented e-commerce and mobile strategies that will keep the brand in consumers' decision-making process. Walgreens first stepped into e-commerce over a decade ago when it started walgreens.com, which recently ranked as one of the top retail sites on the Web with an estimated 12 million visits each week to the site. The company's mobile shopping app allows consumers to track medication schedules, receive reminders, and order refills by scanning the barcode on prescription bottles with their smartphones. The company says more than 40 percent of Walgreens' online prescription refills come from mobile devices.

When consumers switched to digital cameras, many retailers got out of the one-hour photo-processing business. Not Walgreens. With its QuickPrint function, the mobile app allows customers to take photos on their smartphones, find a local Walgreens, send images to the store for printing, and pick up the prints typically within an hour. The company believes the photo option provides additional revenues because so many pictures "live" on people's smartphones. Walgreens also has agreements with several mobile photo-sharing companies to allow their subscribers to "print to Walgreens."

Walgreens learned that customers who are reached through multiple channels are three times as valuable to the company's bottom line as those customers reached through only one channel. With more than 8,200 stores in the United States and two-thirds of the population living within three miles of a store location, Walgreens believes its multifaceted approach will continue to appeal to consumers of all ages. The company recently announced the creation of a new digital division that combines e-commerce, corporate marketing, and customer loyalty and insights.

QUESTIONS FOR CRITICAL THINKING

1. According to a recent Nielsen survey, there has been a significant increase in the number of consumers 65 years and older using smartphones. How can Walgreens take advantage of this demographic as the company expands its online retail presence?

2. Walgreens took a majority stake in Alliance Boots, a European pharmacy retailer, for more than $6 billion. What effects will this partnership have on the company's e-commerce strategies?

Sources: Cynthia Koons and Makiko Kitamura, "Walgreen Stays in U.S. as It Buys Rest of Alliance Boots," *Bloomberg*, accessed August 15, 2014, www.bloomberg.com; Artemis Berry, "Talking with Walgreens President of E-commerce Sona Chawla," *Shop.org*, accessed February 17, 2014, http://blog.shop.org; Thad Rueter, "Walgreens Promotes Its e-Commerce Chief to Lead a New Digital Division," *Internet Retailer*, accessed February 17, 2014, www.internetretailer.com; Brigid Sweeney, "Walgreen's Mobile Strategy Is A) Huge or B) Not So Much," *Crain's Chicago Business*, accessed February 14, 2014, www.chicagobusiness.com; Michael Johnsen, "The 'What, Where and When' of e-Commerce," *Drug Store News*, accessed February 14, 2014, http://www.drugstorenews.com; Brian Quinton, "Walgreens Powers Multi-Touch Strategy with Mobile, Social and Ecommerce," *Chief Marketer*, accessed February 14, 2014, http://chiefmarketer.com; Lauren Johnson, "Passbook Vaulted Walgreens App to No. 8 in Free App Store Day after Launch," *Mobile Commerce Daily*, accessed February 10, 2014, http://www.mobilecommercedaily.com; Brian Dolan, "Walgreens App Adds Pill Reminders, Rx Transfer," *Mobile Health News*, accessed February 10, 2014, http://mobilehealthnews.com; Sarah Perez, "App Developers Can Now 'Print to Walgreens'; Company Outed as Aviary's Strategic Investor," *Tech Crunch*, accessed February 10, 2014, http://techcrunch.com; Mark Scott, "Walgreen to Take Stake in Alliance Boots for $6.7 Billion," *The New York Times*, accessed February 7, 2014, http://dealbook.nytimes.com.

VIDEO CASE 5.2
Hubway: Boston's Online Bike-Sharing System

If you've ever lived in a major city, you know that getting around can be a challenge. Traffic jams, overflowing parking lots, crammed subway cars, drivers who plow through puddles that spray water on pedestrians—all of these may be enough to make you pack your bags and head for the suburbs. A company in Boston is trying to change that, using a fleet of bicycles and the Internet. Hubway (sponsored by New Balance and operated by Alta Bicycle Share) is Boston's recently established bike-sharing system that features more than 100 stations, 1,000 bicycles, and an interactive component that allows urban consumers to borrow a bike at one location with the swipe of a credit card—and return it to another destination. On a Hubway bike, you can pedal to the gym or the grocery store; commute to work; or visit a friend across town. You can grab an available bike spur of the moment by swiping your credit card at one of the kiosk stations, giving you a 24-hour or 3-day membership. Or you can sign up for an annual membership online; within a week, Hubway will mail you a station key with a printed code. The cost of membership includes unlimited rides that are less than 30 minutes, with additional fees for longer rides.

Hubway operates entirely in the realm of e-commerce, marketing to consumers and conducting transactions completely online. "There is no store or counter to get a key," says Hubway's Brogan Graham, who bears the title of Hype Master. "You put in your information online and we mail you a key." The touchscreens at the bike stations are solar-powered, offering access 24/7, meaning that bike riders may rent a bike at any time without the assistance of another human being. General Manager Scott Mullen points to the efficiency of this operating system, as opposed to the "unwieldiness" of staffing each station with a Hubway representative, which he claims "would be a 1.0 solution to a 2.0 problem." Customer service does exist, however. If you cruise into a station with a flat tire or broken chain, you just hit the red "mechanic" button, which will secure the bike without letting someone else unwittingly take it out on the road. A Hubway mechanic will retrieve the bike and repair it. An app called Spot Cycle identifies the locations of different stations, including whether or not bikes are available at a specific station.

Hubway relies on the communication function of the Internet to provide current information to its customers. Consumers get station updates and marketing messages through social media sites such as Facebook and Twitter; for example, if a station's Internet connection isn't working properly, Hubway will alert consumers via social media—including an estimated time for the station to go live. On its Facebook page, some Hubway members post suggestions for improvement (such as which stations need more bikes on a regular basis), while others receive kudos for bicycling achievements (such as the first member to reach 250,000 rides). "We leverage the Internet," says Scott Mullen.

Hubway's typical customers tend to be those who are the most tech savvy about swiping credit cards at kiosks, using touchscreens, and maximizing services via the company's website and social media accounts. But its marketers emphasize that Hubway's system is easy to use. Most people need only to "use the system once to understand it because it is so intuitive," remarks Marketing Director Mary McLaughlin.

Whether we're talking about e-commerce or traditional commerce, the numbers don't lie. Hubway began with a goal of attracting 3,000 members and launching 100,000 rides during its first year of business. In fact, the company hit the 100,000-ride target in less than 11 weeks and topped 250,000 trips in 6 months. On one sample day, more than 2,500 station-to-station rides were recorded. By year's end, 3,700 members had signed on. With this kind of success, Hubway planned expansion into more Boston neighborhoods, as well as adjacent towns such as Cambridge and Brookline—with the near-term goal of doubling the number of stations and increasing the number of bikes. Riding is "cool and fun," says Graham. "It's a great way to explore a new city."

QUESTIONS FOR CRITICAL THINKING

1. What are the benefits of e-marketing for Hubway? What are the potential drawbacks?

2. Thus far, Hubway has essentially engaged in business-to-consumer (B2C) e-marketing. Cite two or three ways in which Hubway might branch out into business-to-business (B2B) e-marketing.

Sources: Company website, www.thehubway.com, accessed February 14, 2014; Martine Powers, "Hubway Tests Out Winter Service in Cambridge," *The Boston Globe*, accessed February 14, 2014, www.bostonglobe.com; Eric Moskowitz, "Hubway Bike-Sharing Program Is on a Roll," *Boston.com*, accessed February 14, 2014, http://articles.boston.com; Jonathan Simmons, "On Biking: Learning to Love Hubway," *Boston.com*, accessed February 14, 2014, http://articles.boston.com.

NOTES

1. Abram Brown, "How Wayfair Sells Nearly $1 Billion Worth of Sofas, Patio Chairs, and Cat Playgrounds," *Forbes*, accessed August 15, 2014, www.forbes.com; Curt Woodward, "$2B Wayfair Valuation a Big Statement in Winner-Take-All E-Commerce," *Xconomy*, accessed February 17, 2014, www.xconomy.com; Hayley Peterson, "Home Goods E-Retailer Wayfair's Sales Set to Hit $1 Billion after an Explosive Year," *Business Insider*, accessed February 14, 2014, www.businessinsider.com; Dennis Keohane, "Wayfair—How Is One of the Quietest Companies in Boston Also Potentially Its Biggest?" *Venture Fizz*, accessed February 14, 2014, http://venturefizz.com; J.J. Colao, "Flash Sales Work: Wayfair, the $600 Million Ecommerce Behemoth, Launches Daily Fair," *Forbes*, accessed February 14, 2014, www.forbes.com; Kasey Wehrum, "Special Report: Wayfair's Road to $1 Billion," *Inc.*, accessed February 10, 2014, www.inc.com; J.J. Colao, "An E-Commerce Giant Reveals Its Strange Strategy: Sending Customers to Competitors," *Forbes*, accessed February 10, 2014, www.forbes.com; Craig Giammona, "Wayfair.com Wants You to Say Its Name," *CNNMoney*, accessed February 10, 2014, http://tech.fortune.cnn.com.
2. "E-commerce Speeds Up, Hits Record High Share of Retail Sales," *Market Watch*, accessed August 15, 2014, http://blog.marketwatch.com.
3. Internet World Stats, accessed August 15, 2014, www.internetworldstats.com.
4. "Top 20 Countries with the Highest Number of Internet Users," *Internet World Statistics*, accessed February 14, 2014, www.internetworldstats.com; Andrea Peterson, "China Has Almost Twice As Many Internet Users As the U.S. Has People," *The Washington Post*, January 31, 2014, www.washingtonpost.com.
5. "Top 20 Countries with the Highest Number of Internet Users."
6. Taylor Soper, "Here Are the 10 Countries Where You'll Find the World's Fastest Internet," *Geekwire*, January 28, 2014, www.geekwire.com.
7. "What Internet Users Do Online: Trend Data," *Pew Internet*, accessed February 14, 2014, www.pewinternet.org.
8. "The Top 20 Valuable Facebook Statistics—Updated December 2013," *Zephoria*, accessed February 14, 2014, http://zephoria.com; Jeff Bullas, "46 Amazing Social Media Facts in 2013," accessed February 14, 2014, www.jeffbullas.com.
9. "Internet Usage in China—Statistics and Trends" (infographic), *Go Globe*, accessed February 14, 2014, www.go-globe.com.
10. "VOD Options for Independent Films and Series," *Douglashorn.com*, accessed February 12, 2014, http://douglashorn.com.
11. Company website, www.roadrunnersports.com, accessed February 17, 2014.
12. Company website, "McDonald's USA to Offer Thousands of New Xbox One Entertainment Systems," (press release), http://news.mcdonalds.com, accessed February 10, 2014; Brett Molina, "Sales of Xbox One Top 2 Million," *USA Today*, accessed February 10, 2014, www.usatoday.com.
13. Don Davis, "Online Consumers Rely on the Web for Product Research," *Internet Retailer*, accessed February 10, 2014, www.internetretailer.com.
14. Company website, www1.macys.com, accessed February 14, 2014; company website, www.surlatable.com, accessed February 10, 2014.
15. Company website, www.wendys.com, accessed February 14, 2014.
16. Company website, http://store.sony.com, accessed February 14, 2014.
17. "Mobile Sales and e-Commerce Take Off in B2B Market," *Supply&Demand Chain Executive*, accessed February 14, 2014, www.sdcexec.com.
18. Jakob Nielsen, "10 Best Intranets of 2012," *Jakob Nielsen's Alertbox*, accessed February 10, 2014, www.useit.com; Kelly Kass, "Staples Intranet Is a Two-Time Winner—Here's Why," *HR Communication*, accessed February 10, 2014, www.hrcommunication.com.
19. "SAP Customer Success Story: Royal Dutch/Shell Group," accessed February 14, 2014, www.sap.com.
20. Company website, www.amorgroup.com, accessed February 14, 2014; Antony Savvas, "Scottish Government Awards £18.5m E-Procurement Support Contract," *ComputerWorld UK*, accessed February 14, 2014, www.computerworlduk.com.
21. State website, www.eva.virginia.gov, accessed February 17, 2014.
22. Maria Ajit Thomas, "Shopper Trak: Discounts Drive U.S. Holiday Retail Growth," *Reuters*, accessed February 14, 2014, www.reuters.com; Adobe Digital Index, "Shopping in a Digital World: Cyber Monday Blows Past $2B in Online Sales," *CMO.com*, accessed February 14, 2014, www.cmo.com.
23. Greg Sterling, "Pew: 61 Percent in US Now Have Smartphones," *Marketing Land*, accessed December 9, 2013, http://marketingland.com; "150% Increase in Mobile Online Shopping Black Friday Through Cyber Monday," *Dark Reading*, December 4, 2013, www.darkreading.com; John Koetsier, "Apps and Brands: What the World's Top 100 Brands Are Doing on Google Play, iOS, and Amazon," *Venture Beat*, November 21, 2013, http://venturebeat.com.
24. Company website, www.ae.com, accessed February 14, 2014.
25. Stephen Shankland, "Tablets Outdo Phones When Closing Holiday-Shopping Deals," *CNET*, November 29, 2013, http://news.cnet.com; Kathryn Zickhur, "For the First Time, a Third of American Adults Own Tablet Computers," *Pew Internet*, June 10, 2013, www.pewinternet.org.
26. Stacy Rapacon, "23 Best Travel Sites to Save You Money," *Kiplinger*, accessed February 10, 2014, www.kiplinger.com.
27. Ann Carrns, "Cards That Help Save on Airline Baggage Fees," *The New York Times*, accessed February 10, 2014, http://bucks.blogs.nytimes.com.
28. Company website, www.barnesandnoble.com, accessed February 10, 2014.
29. Company website, www.googleshopping.com, accessed February 10, 2014.
30. Cheryl Conner, "Fifty Essential Mobile Marketing Facts," *Forbes*, accessed February 10, 2014, www.forbes.com; company website, "Men versus Women, Online Shopping," (infographic), http://visual.ly, accessed February 10, 2014.
31. "Top Selling Internet Items," *Statistic Brain*, accessed February 14, 2014, www.statisticbrain.com.
32. John Koetsier, "One Social Network You've Never Heard of Drives 20% of All Social Commerce," *Venture Beat*, accessed February 14, 2014, http://venturebeat.com; Mark Walsh, "Study: Facebook Delivering 152% ROI for Retailers in 2013," *Media Post*, accessed February 14, 2014, www.mediapost.com.
33. Company website, www.symantec.com, accessed February 10, 2014.
34. Company website, www.westernunion.com, accessed February 14, 2014; company website, www.paypal.com, accessed February 14, 2014.

35. Anne Flaherty, "Study Finds Online Privacy Concerns on the Rise," *Yahoo News*, accessed February 10, 2014, http://news.yahoo.com; government website, www.ftc.org, accessed February 10, 2014.
36. Anthony Wing Kosner, "Actually Two Attacks in One, Target Breach Affected 70 to 110 Million Customers," *Forbes*, accessed August 15, 2014, www.forbes.com.
37. Government website, www.ic3.gov, accessed February 14, 2014.
38. Carnegie Mellon University, "2012 CyberSecurity Watch Survey: How Bad Is the Insider Threat?" (pdf), accessed February 10, 2014, http://resources.sei.cmu.edu/asset_files/Presentation/2013_017_101_57766.pdf.
39. Susan Johnston, "How to Protect Yourself from SMiShing and Vishing," *US News*, accessed February 14, 2014, http://money.usnews.com.
40. Mark Brohan, "Big Design Changes Drive Growth Online at Under Armour," *Internet Retailer*, accessed February 10, 2014, www.internetretailer.com.
41. "Top 500 List," *Internet Retailer*, accessed February 13, 2014, www.internetretailer.com.
42. Jim Milliot, "Authors Guild Hits Back at Google Ruling," *Publishers Weekly*, accessed August 15, 2014, www.publishersweekly.com.
43. Email vs Snail Mail: Breaking Down the Winner," *Integrator Café*, accessed February 10, 2014, http://relidy.com.
44. Kurt Wagner, "More than 70% of Email Is Spam," *Mashable*, accessed February 13, 2014, http://mashable.com.
45. Susanne Gargiulo, "The Global Workforce: Challenge or Asset?" *CNN.com*, accessed December 12, 2013, http://edition.cnn.com.
46. Company website, "SkipIt Because Now You Can," www.skipit.com, accessed February 10, 2014.
47. Sarah Kessler, "Facebook Timeline Changed the Way We See Brand Pages: Here's How," *Mashable Business*, accessed December 12, 2013, http://mashable.com.
48. "2014 Best Web Hosting Reviews: Product Comparisons," *Top Ten Reviews*, accessed February 14, 2014, http://web-hosting-review.toptenreviews.com.
49. Heather Chaet, "Is Your Business's Website Out of Date? 7 Ways to Know If It Needs Revamping," *Small Business Online Community*, accessed February 10, 2014, https://smallbusinessonlinecommunity.bankofamerica.com.
50. Kevin Gold, "What Is the Average Conversion Rate? A 2013 Update," *Search Marketing Standard*, accessed February 14, 2014, www.searchmarketingstandard.com; Meghan Peters, "How To: Get Started with Google Analytics," *Mashable Business*, accessed February 14, 2014, http://mashable.com.
51. Company website, http://webtrends.com, accessed February 14, 2014.

Scripps Networks Interactive & Food Network

PART 1
Designing Customer-Oriented Marketing Strategies

Cooking Up Social Media Strategies

Food, cooking, and social media seem like natural ingredients to stir together in the same stew pot. The portfolio of Scripps Networks Interactive—a leading developer of lifestyle content for media platforms—includes well-known television brands Food Network, Cooking Channel, HGTV, DIY Network, Travel Channel, and Great American Country (GAC). The food category of Food Network and Cooking Channel specifically brings consumers mouth-watering programming as well as online video, social media, and e-commerce opportunities. With 2,200 employees based in Knoxville, Tennessee, Scripps generates about $2.5 billion in revenue each year on content viewed around the world. These numbers aren't chicken feed—they reflect an understanding of the target market and careful strategic planning. "We have an audience that knows us for ideas and inspirations around food and cooking," says Susie Fogelson, senior vice president, marketing, creative services, and public relations for Food Network and the Cooking Channel. Identifying this group of people helps Scripps and Food Network—one of its major brands—design content and develop a customer-driven marketing strategy to attract loyal viewers. "At Scripps we are constantly evolving and iterating how we deliver content," says Chris Powell, executive vice president of human resources. For Food Network, this involves three variables of the marketing mix: product strategy, distribution strategy, and promotion strategy, all designed to engage viewers who want to be inspired and educated about food.

By its very nature, social media lends itself to relationship building. Scripps marketers understand this and tailor the marketing strategy for Food Network and its other brands to use social media effectively. "Social media gives us a really great place to identify who our brand advocates and brand fans are and then message them" with relevant content, says Jonah Spegman, director of digital media and database marketing for Scripps. "Our brands are intrinsically social," he adds. Viewers love to talk about favorite dishes they've made themselves or enjoyed at restaurants—and they do it on Facebook, Twitter, Pinterest, YouTube, and Tumblr. When viewers are talking at these sites, Scripps and Food Network want to be there. "Wherever consumers are, we want to be," says Powell.

Despite what appears to be a connection between culinary entertainment and social media, Scripps hasn't taken a first-mover strategy of adopting specific social-media sites or tools. Instead, the firm prefers a second-mover strategy. "You need to wait and adopt technology at the right time," observes Rich Ma, manager of digital marketing. "See what consumers are gravitating toward." For example, Facebook and Twitter are already considered well-established social media outlets, whereas Pinterest has soared during the last year. "It's important to be a market leader in those established places," says Ma. In addition, companies must learn how to leverage the technology, instead of jumping in without a plan.

Fogelson agrees with the importance of planning. "We have this enormous audience with this enormous demand to really feed the appetites of people who are looking for ideas and inspiration around cooking," she says. To serve this huge audience, Scripps and Food Network have begun to key in on what Fogelson refers to as the "tent poles"—the shows that have a certain focus (and target market) also have related shows and marketing wrapped around them. Such shows include *Food Network Star* and *Great Food Truck Race*. Marketers link these shows to the social sites to interact with fans, get feedback, create exchanges, and spark enthusiasm for other shows. In addition, marketers for all of Scripps' branded networks share the data they gather about social media marketing. If one network has success with Pinterest but not with Twitter, marketers will exchange the information. "All of the networks are experimenting and sharing the knowledge," says Jeffrey Kissinger, vice president of digital marketing and database marketing at Scripps. "Everyone is experimenting and trying, and we're always learning from each other." In addition, with competition for viewers an ongoing issue in the entertainment industry, Scripps and Food Network integrate this into their strategic planning. "The strategy going forward is to be as well known for entertainment in the digital and social space as we are for inspiring people to love food and cooking," says Fogelson.

Social media marketing brings with it a certain amount of social responsibility—and because of its global reach and interactive nature, it raises certain ethical issues, not the least of which is privacy. For example, Scripps and Food Network must ensure that any data they collect about consumers via interactive exchanges doesn't fall into unauthorized hands. But they respect the significance of their relationship with viewers and treat it like the gift of a good meal. "There's something special there, that you can have a relationship and communicate with your audience—and always be on," says Fogelson. "But that is a tremendous responsibility as much as it is an opportunity. So we're all asking a lot of questions about how to do it right."

QUESTIONS FOR CRITICAL THINKING

1. What steps could Scripps and Food Network take to avoid marketing myopia? Create a company motto for them reflecting your ideas.
2. Identify three trends in the social-cultural environment that you believe should be factors in strategic marketing planning for Scripps and Food Network.
3. How might Scripps and Food Network contribute to the highest level of the social responsibility pyramid—philanthropy?
4. What strategies might Scripps and Food Network use to become as well known for entertainment in digital and social media as they are for educating and inspiring people about food and cooking?

Part 2
Understanding Buyers and Markets

6 Consumer Behavior

7 Business-to-Business (B2B) Marketing

8 Global Marketing

Chapter 6

Consumer Behavior

1. Describe consumer behavior and its role in marketing decisions.
2. Describe the three interpersonal determinants of consumer behavior.
3. Explain the five personal determinants of consumer behavior.
4. Distinguish between high-involvement and low-involvement purchase decisions.
5. Outline the six steps in the consumer decision process.
6. Differentiate among routinized response behavior, limited problem solving, and extended problem solving by consumers.

HUMMUS IS THE NEW SALSA

The chickpea may not seem very glamorous, but this humble legume is poised to take over the gigantic snack market in the United States and even bring new hope to the nation's farmers.

Mashed chickpeas are the main ingredient in hummus, a spreadable vegetable paste flavored with olive oil, lemon, and garlic that's growing in popularity across the country. Savvy marketing efforts by Sabra, a joint venture of PepsiCo and the Strauss Group, have lifted it to the top position in the $530 million refrigerated-spreads category with more than half of the market share. Sabra representatives first handed out millions of hummus samples. It was the right move—tasting the once-unfamiliar product seems to have persuaded many consumers to give it a try at home. Sabra followed up by using PepsiCo's marketing muscle to get grocers to stock its brand of the flavored spread.

Sabra is credited with growing the refrigerated-spreads category almost 40 percent over the last few years. The company sees itself at the first stage of a three-step customer acceptance process, which begins with getting people to adopt hummus as a dip. An imaginative television campaign was recently unveiled to remind consumers to "dip life to the fullest." The next stage is popularizing hummus as a spread by itself on toast or as a substitute for mayonnaise in sandwiches. Finally, Sabra hopes hummus will be popular as a side dish, the way it's traditionally consumed in the Middle Eastern region where it originated. Acceptance is only a matter of time, says Sabra's CEO. At the moment, U.S. consumers in the Northeastern states lead the way, buying about twice as much hummus as those in the West.

To introduce the product to younger people who might then consume it for many years, Sabra has developed single-size packages handy for snacks and lunchboxes, and it is pushing the product as a vegetarian entry for school cafeteria menus. The company also has made an additional $86 million investment in its Virginia facilities, including a research and development lab. Along with finding ways to increase farmers' chickpea yields and to persuade tobacco farmers to trade their declining profits for chickpea revenue, the lab will explore new hummus flavors. Already successful are roasted red pepper and spinach-artichoke varieties as well as Tuscan garden, jalapeño, and olive tapenade.[1]

EVOLUTION OF A BRAND

With archeologists uncovering evidence of chickpeas in digs dating back 10,000 years, it's clear that hummus (or some variation thereof) has served as a staple of the Middle Eastern diet for a long time. In recent years, the immigration of Middle Easterners to the United States has helped introduce their unique cuisine to this country. As a result, the timing was right for PepsiCo to launch Sabra hummus, and the tasty dish has grown in popularity. Today, the Sabra brand commands an estimated 60 percent share of the market. Volunteers recruited by Sabra helped introduce the product in the United States, traveling by food truck to many of the nation's cities and distributing samples of the taste treat.

- The distinctive texture and flavor of hummus represents a new taste experience for most Americans. What must marketers do to move consumers toward the decision to buy Sabra hummus?
- What is behind Sabra's strategy in targeting younger consumers? Do you think the strategy makes sense? Why?
- To produce hummus in the United States, Sabra needs a ready supply of chickpeas. If the company succeeds in persuading local tobacco farmers to grow chickpeas instead of tobacco, how might a reduced tobacco crop change the social landscape in this country?

Chapter Overview

Why do you call for Papa John's Pizza whenever you have a craving for extra cheese and pepperoni? Why does your roommate stock Fuze in the fridge? Why does your best friend drive five miles out of the way to work out at Planet Fitness—when the campus fitness center is much closer? The answers to these questions aren't obvious, and they directly affect every aspect of marketing strategy, including the development of a product, the level at which it is priced, and the way it is promoted. Developing a marketing strategy requires an understanding of the process by which individual consumers buy goods and services for their own use and organizational buyers purchase business products for their organizations.

> **Briefly Speaking**
>
> "Know what your customers want most and what your company does best. Focus on where those two meet."
>
> —Kevin Stirtz
> *Web marketing consultant*

1 Describe consumer behavior and its role in marketing decisions.

consumer behavior Process through which buyers make purchase decisions.

A variety of influences affect both individuals buying items for themselves and businesspeople purchasing products for their firms. This chapter focuses on individual purchasing behavior, which applies to all consumers. **Consumer behavior** is the process through which the ultimate buyer makes purchase decisions from toothbrushes to automobiles to vacations. Chapter 7 will shift the focus to business buying decisions.

The study of consumer behavior builds on an understanding of human behavior in general. In their efforts to understand why and how consumers make buying decisions, marketers borrow extensively from the sciences of psychology and sociology. The work of psychologist Kurt Lewin, for example, provides a useful classification scheme for influences on buying behavior. Lewin's proposition is

$$B = f(P, E)$$

This statement means that behavior (B) is a function (f) of the interactions of personal influences (P) and pressures exerted by outside environmental forces (E).

The statement usually is rewritten to apply to consumer behavior as follows:

$$B = f(I, P)$$

Consumer behavior (B) is a function (f) of the interactions of interpersonal influences (I)—such as culture, friends, classmates, coworkers, and relatives—and personal factors (P) such as attitudes, learning, and perception. In other words, inputs from others and an individual's psychological makeup affect his or her purchasing behavior. Before looking at how consumers make purchase decisions, we first consider how both interpersonal and personal factors affect consumers.

ASSESSMENT CHECK

1.1 Why is the study of consumer behavior important to marketers?

1.2 Describe Kurt Lewin's proposition.

INTERPERSONAL DETERMINANTS OF CONSUMER BEHAVIOR

You don't live in a bubble—and you don't make purchase decisions there. You might not be aware of it, but every buying decision you make is influenced by a variety of external and internal factors. Consumers often decide to buy goods and services based on what they believe others expect of them. They may want to project positive images to peers or satisfy the expectations of family members. They may buy a certain book because someone they respect recommended it. Or they may make reservations at a particular restaurant based on a good review in the newspaper. They may buy a home in a neighborhood they think will impress their family and friends. Students may even choose which college or university to attend based on where their parents went, how the school is ranked for certain features, or on their friends' impression of the school. Marketers recognize three broad categories of interpersonal influences on consumer behavior: cultural, social, and family influences.

> **2** Describe the three interpersonal determinants of consumer behavior.

CULTURAL INFLUENCES

Culture can be defined as the values, beliefs, preferences, and tastes handed down from one generation to the next. Culture is the broadest environmental determinant of consumer behavior. Marketers need to understand their role in consumer decision making, both in the United States and abroad. They also must monitor trends in cultural values as well as recognize changes in these values. As attention to the environment becomes more prevalent in the United States and other cultures, marketers are responding to this change by offering products that either contain environmentally friendly components or are made with energy-saving processes. Utah homebuilder Garbett Homes now focuses its marketing messages on potential homebuyers' desire for energy-efficient features by positioning itself as Utah's "greenest" builder. The firm is constructing medium-sized, affordable solar- and thermal-powered homes called the Solaris Collection. All of these homes are built to the 100-percent ENERGY STAR specification, which decreases monthly energy bills for their owners.[2]

> **culture** Values, beliefs, preferences, and tastes handed down from one generation to the next.

Marketing strategies and business practices that work in one country may be offensive or ineffective in another. Marketers may even need to vary strategies from one area of a country to another. This is especially true in the United States, where the population continues to diversify at a rapid rate. When you insert your bank card into an ATM, the first screen often prompts you for your language preference for the transaction. Depending on where you live, you may choose between Spanish and English or French and English.

Core Values in U.S. Culture

Some cultural values change over time, but basic core values do not. The work ethic and the desire to accumulate wealth are two core values in American society. Even though the typical family structure and family members' roles have shifted over the years, American culture still emphasizes the importance of family and home life. This value is strengthened during times of upheaval such as natural disasters—hurricanes, floods, wildfires, or tornadoes. Other core values include the importance of education, individualism, freedom, youth, health, volunteerism, and efficiency. You can probably recognize yourself in some of these core values. Each of these values influences consumer behavior, including your own. Focusing on the core values of family and health, Stouffer's launched a joint marketing campaign called "Let's Fix Dinner," which encouraged families to eat dinner together. Marketing messages emphasized the benefits of families dining together at home, including a study that found children who eat five or more meals a week with their family are "more likely to think their parents are proud of them." The campaign featured Stouffer's prepared frozen meals and side dishes.[3]

Values that change over time also have their effects. As technology rapidly changes the way people exchange information, consumers adopt values that include communicating with anyone, anytime, anywhere in the world. The generation that includes older teens and young adults in their 20s is the most adept at learning and using rapidly changing communications technology, including smartphones. They regularly communicate via Facebook, Twitter, and other social media.

> **" Briefly Speaking "**
>
> "Seventy to 90 percent of decisions not to repeat a purchase of anything are not about product or price. They are about some dimension of service."
>
> —**Barry Gibbons**
> *Former CEO, Burger King*

Stouffer's "Let's Fix Dinner" marketing campaign emphasizes the core values of family and health as an important aspect of American culture.

subcultures Groups with their own distinct modes of behavior.

Marketers recognize this, and in anticipation of more consumers adopting new communications technology, they are increasing their allocation of resources to reach consumers in this way. McDonald's is testing a mobile app in the United States and Australia that permits customers to use a smartphone or tablet to order and pay for their food, and then pick up their order in person at a store or drive-thru window. Using a McDonald's mobile app introduced earlier, customers can find restaurants, access nutritional information, and search for jobs.[4]

International Perspective on Cultural Influences

Cultural differences are particularly important for international marketers. Marketing strategies that prove successful in one country often cannot extend to other international markets due to cultural variations. Europe is a good example, with many different languages and a wide range of lifestyles and product preferences. Even though the continent is becoming a single economic unit as a result of the expansion of the European Union and the widespread use of the euro as currency, cultural divisions continue to define multiple markets.

While Domino's has been a known quantity in the United States for years, now its business has gone global with the opening of its 10,000th store in Istanbul, Turkey. Nearly half of its stores are outside the United States and soon, management predicts, overseas stores will outstrip U.S. units.

What's behind this global success? According to the company's CEO, pizza ingredients—for the most part—are common products used in many parts of the world. And it is relatively easy to change some of the pizza ingredients to tailor the product to a specific market, such as adding fish in Asia or curry in India.[5]

Subcultures

Cultures are not homogeneous groups with universal values, even though core values tend to dominate. Each culture includes numerous **subcultures**—groups with their own distinct modes of behavior. Understanding the differences among subcultures can help marketers develop more effective marketing strategies.

The United States, like many nations, is composed of significant subcultures that differ by ethnicity, nationality, age, rural versus urban location, religion, and geographic distribution. The southwestern lifestyle emphasizes casual dress, outdoor entertaining, and active recreation. Orthodox Jews purchase and consume only kosher foods. Younger consumers are quicker to use new technology than older consumers. Immigrants from various nations often seek out spices, vegetables, and meats that are considered tasty or popular in their homelands. Understanding these and other differences among subcultures contributes to successful marketing of goods and services.

America's population is aging. According to the U.S. Census Bureau, by the year 2050, the U.S. population will total about 458 million, up from over 318 million today. By the year 2030, nearly one in five residents will be age 65 or older.[6]

America's population is also becoming more diverse. Collectively, the three largest and fastest-growing U.S. ethnic subcultures—Hispanics, African Americans, and Asians—are expected to become the majority by the year 2060. The Hispanic population, which constituted nearly 17 percent of the U.S. population in the last census, is expected to more than double by 2060 and account for nearly one in three U.S. residents. African Americans represented 12.3 percent of the U.S. population in the last census, totaling nearly 16 million in a recent year. By 2060, the African American population is expected to reach nearly 62 million, or 14.7 percent of the population, and Asians will account for 8 percent.[7] Figure 6.1 shows the current makeup of U.S. society by race.

Marketers need to be sensitive to these shifts in population and to the differences in shopping patterns and buying habits of the members of different subcultures. Businesses must develop marketing messages that consider the needs of these different types of consumers. For example, members of one subculture might be attracted to bargain offers while those of another might be offended by them. As important as differences in national origin may be, the differences in acculturation, or the degree to which newcomers have adapted to U.S. culture, plays a vital role in consumer behavior. Marketers should not assume that all Hispanics understand or speak Spanish or the same dialect of Spanish. In addition, Asians come from a variety of countries, speak a wide range of languages, and eat different foods.

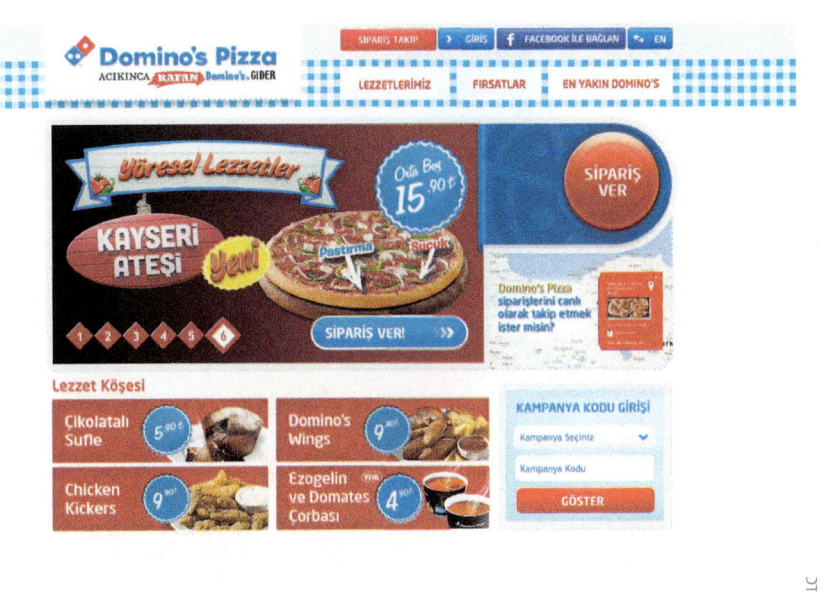

One thing that marketers must do is actually find where consumers of different subcultures live. After a record low attributed to a sluggish economy and weak housing market, the U.S. Census Bureau is now reporting a modest uptick in Americans' relocation to different regions of the country.[8]

Domino's has been successful in the global market because it tailors its products to local tastes. The company recently opened its 10,000th store in Istanbul, Turkey.

Hispanic American Consumers

Marketers face several challenges in appealing to Hispanic consumers. The 53 million Hispanics in the United States are not a homogeneous group. They—or their parents and grandparents—come from a wide range of countries, each with its own culture. More than 33 million are from Mexico; nearly 5 million are Puerto Rican, while about 2 million are Cuban. More than 1 million each are Dominican or Guatemalan. Colombia, Ecuador, Honduras, Nicaragua, Peru, Spain, Venezuela, and other nations are also represented in the United States.[9] Many distinct segments exist within the broad classification of Hispanic. More than three-fourths of the Hispanic population—and consumers—are distributed across California, Texas, Florida, New York, Illinois, Arizona, New Jersey, Colorado, New Mexico, and Georgia.[10]

As the Hispanic population begins to include the second, third, and fourth generations, the attitudes and values of these consumers are likely to shift toward those of their age group and region. Still, it is important for marketers to be aware of subtle cultural differences in preferences in goods and services as well as media. A recent survey revealed that native-born Hispanics are more likely than Hispanics who are foreign-born to surf the Internet and to use cell phones. The survey also found that native-born Hispanics are more likely to use apps on their cell phone.[11] This information could have a huge impact on marketers who are trying to determine where and how to deliver their messages to this market. In addition, marketers should consider that Hispanics control more disposable income than any other minority group—currently estimated at $1.2 trillion.[12]

African American Consumers

The continuously growing African American market offers a tremendous opportunity for marketers who understand its buying patterns. The African American population stands at

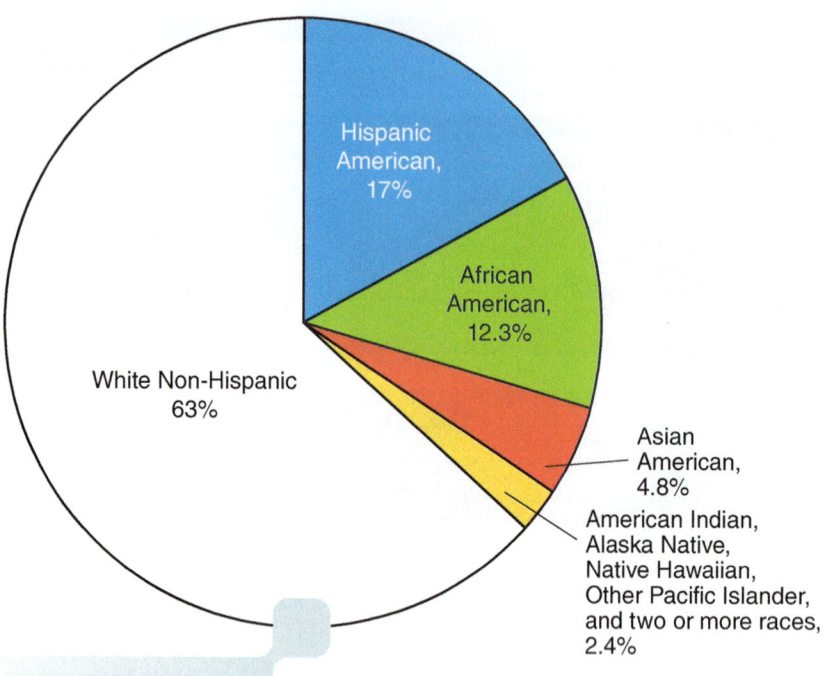

FIGURE 6.1 Ethnic and Racial Minorities as a Percentage of the Total U.S. Population

Note: Percentages do not total to 100 percent due to overlap of some racial and ethnic categories.

Source: U.S. Census Bureau data quoted in Hope Yen, "Census: White Majority in U.S. Gone by 2043," Associated Press, accessed February 17, 2014, http://usnews.nbcnews.com.

- White Non-Hispanic 63%
- Hispanic American, 17%
- African American, 12.3%
- Asian American, 4.8%
- American Indian, Alaska Native, Native Hawaiian, Other Pacific Islander, and two or more races, 2.4%

43 million people, with more than $1 trillion in buying power. A couple of trends that marketers should consider include the following:

- Seventy-one percent of African American consumers own a smartphone.
- Annually on average, African American consumers take 156 shopping trips, compared to 146 trips for the overall market. They also buy nine times more ethnic beauty and grooming products than the overall market.
- Eighty-one percent of African American consumers find advertising using black media more relevant to them.[13]

Despite these trends, as with any other subculture, marketers must avoid approaching all African American consumers in the same way; they must consider demographic factors such as income, age, language, and educational level. Most African Americans are descended from families who have lived in the United States for many generations, but some are recent immigrants and are members of every economic group.

Asian American Consumers

Marketing to Asian Americans presents many of the same challenges as reaching Hispanics. Like Hispanics, the country's more than 18 million Asian Americans are spread among culturally diverse groups, many retaining their own languages. The Asian American subculture consists of more than two dozen ethnic groups, including Chinese, Filipinos, Indians, Japanese, Koreans, and Vietnamese. Each group brings its own language, religion, and value system to purchasing decisions. Asian American consumers wield more than $718 billion in buying power, with an average household income of nearly $68,000 in a recent year—nearly twice that of a Hispanic consumer. Fifty percent of Asian Americans have graduated from college, with 20 percent of them ages 25 or older holding advanced degrees.[14] Marketers might keep the following trends in mind:

- Eighty-seven percent of Asian Americans use the Internet; 80 percent have broadband access at home.
- Ninety percent of Asian Americans have a cell phone; nearly three-fourths have laptops.[15]

Sorabol Korean BBQ & Asian Noodles is the first Korean fast-food chain in the United States. Its mission is to make Korean food mainstream for all U.S. consumers, not just Asian Americans. While some restaurants are trying hard to add Asian items to their menus, Sorabol has actually "Americanized" its menu to appeal to a broader range of consumers while retaining a distinctly Asian foundation. Diners can order traditional *kabi* (barbecued short ribs) or *dak guyee* (barbecued chicken), stir-fried entrees or appetizers, or one of many noodle dishes. In Korean culture, noodles are a symbol of long life and are served in a variety of ways. Noodles are a popular breakfast dish as well, because they are considered to be a healthy start to the day. Sorabol locates its restaurants in high-traffic retail locations, in financial districts, and on campuses. The restaurant chain seeks to offer an alternative to burgers and fries, making fast food "a pleasurable dining experience full of culture and flavor."[16]

SOCIAL INFLUENCES

As a consumer, you belong to a number of social groups. Your earliest group experience came from membership in a family. As you began to grow, you might have joined a group of friends in elementary school or in the neighborhood. Later, you might have played on a soccer team, sang in a chorus, or volunteered in the community. By the time you became an adult, you had already been a member of many social groups—as you are now.

Group membership influences an individual consumer's purchase decisions and behavior in both overt and subtle ways. Every group establishes certain norms of behavior. Norms are the values, attitudes, and behaviors a group deems appropriate for its members. Group members are expected to comply with these norms. Members of such diverse groups as the Harley Owners Group (H.O.G.) and the local swim club tend to adopt their organization's norms of behavior. Norms can even affect nonmembers. Individuals who aspire to membership in a group may adopt its standards of behavior and values.

With more than $718 billion in buying power, Asian Americans are an important consumer segment for marketers.

Differences in group status and roles also can affect buying behavior. Status is the relative position of any individual member in a group; roles define behavior that members of a group expect of individuals who hold specific positions within that group. Some groups (such as the American Medical Association) define formal roles, and others (such as a book club among friends) impose informal expectations. Both types of groups supply each member with both status and roles; in doing so, they influence that person's activities, including his or her purchasing behavior. Communities have regulations governing pet ownership—especially rules about cleaning up after pets. One company considers these rules an opportunity to create a competitive advantage for itself. Like other pet care businesses, Tampa-based DogSmith offers a full range of dog-care services, from boarding to training to daily "park romps." But DogSmith goes the extra mile—it also offers customers pet waste cleanup service for their yard.[17] Customers who have limited time for this necessary task of pet ownership—or who simply prefer to pay someone else to do it—appreciate the extra service.

People often make purchases designed to reflect their status within a particular group, particularly when the purchase is considered expensive by society. In the past few years, affluent consumers have spent money on home renovations and exotic trips. Loyal customers of Apple products are willing to pay top dollar for the latest gadgets, apps, and upgrades, not only because of their high quality, but because of the status they reflect.

As the economy fluctuates, affluent shoppers actually achieve status by joining warehouse clubs or shopping at discount stores and consignment shops. Searching for the best value becomes the new norm and status symbol. These consumers are willing to spend more on fresh or organic produce, often found at upscale grocery markets, and they like to tout the health and environmental benefits of these foods. Over the past several years, as the economy has dipped and adjusted itself, a new norm has emerged for most U.S. consumers, regardless of their economic standing—restrained spending and an emphasis on value. In fact, a certain amount of frugality has become chic.

The Asch Phenomenon

Groups influence people's purchase decisions more than they realize. Most people adhere in varying degrees to the general expectations of any group they consider important, often without conscious awareness. The surprising impact of groups and group norms on individual behavior has been called the Asch phenomenon, named after social psychologist S. E. Asch, who first documented

Regardless of a U.S. consumer's economic standing, restrained spending and an emphasis on value found in warehouse clubs like Sam's Club have become the norm in our economy.

reference groups
People or institutions whose opinions are valued and to whom a person looks for guidance in his or her own behavior, values, and conduct, such as a spouse, family, friends, or celebrities.

characteristics of individual behavior. Through his research, Asch found that individuals conformed to majority rule, even if it went against their beliefs. The Asch phenomenon can be a big factor in many purchase decisions, from major choices such as buying a car to deciding whether to buy a pair of shoes on sale. One company that promises to measure individuals' social media influence is called Klout; see the "Marketing Success" feature.

Reference Groups

Discussion of the Asch phenomenon raises the subject of **reference groups**—groups whose value structures and standards influence a person's behavior. Consumers usually try to coordinate their purchase behavior with their perceptions of the values of their reference groups. The extent of

MARKETING SUCCESS
Klout Measures Social Media Influence

Background. The number of people posting, linking, and tweeting on a daily if not hourly basis offers marketers a potentially powerful new tool for leveraging word-of-mouth about their goods and services.

The Challenge. How do companies know who wields the most influence when it comes to product endorsements or recommendations? Is Bill Gates more credible than Kobe Bryant? Marketers are searching for ways to identify and partner with the Web's most powerful individuals.

The Strategy. A San Francisco company called Klout tracks what is in effect your "social credit score" by analyzing your online influence and the power of your network. The company tracks re-tweets and Facebook "likes" to derive an influence score for what it says is more than 620 million people.

The Outcome. Nike, Disney, HP, and Audi were among Klout's first customers. The company puts these firms in touch with relevant influencers who have signed up with it, and then it's up to the marketers to offer deals they hope will persuade their influencers to generate the appropriate online buzz. The company launched a business portal to be used by major brands to better understand their online audiences. Klout was recently acquired by Lithium Technologies, which makes tools companies can use to provide customer service on social networks.

Sources: Company website, http://klout.com, accessed September 3, 2014; Steve Kovach, "Social Influence Measurement Site Klout Is About to Be Sold for At Least $100 Million," *Business Insider*, accessed February 18, 2014, www.businessinsider.com; "Why Your Klout Score Matters," *Social Media Today*, accessed February 18, 2014, http://socialmediatoday.com; "How Can You Amplify Your Klout Score?" *Social Media Today*, accessed February 18, 2014, http://socialmediatoday.com; Natalie Robehmed, "The Marketing Magic of Klout Perks," *Forbes*, accessed February 17, 2014, www.forbes.com; Miriam Slozberg, "How the Klout Score Is Calculated," *DashBurst*, accessed February 17, 2014, http://dashburst.com; JP Mangalindan, "Klout Launches Business Portal, Is Gunning for Brands," *CNNMoney*, accessed February 17, 2014, http://techfortune.cnn.com.

reference-group influence varies widely among individuals. Strong influence by a group on a member's purchase requires two conditions:

1. The purchased product must be one that others can see and identify.
2. The purchased item must be conspicuous; it must stand out as something unusual, a brand or product that not everyone owns.

Reference group influence would significantly affect the decision to buy a luxury home in an upscale neighborhood but probably wouldn't have an impact on the decision to buy a loaf of bread, unless that loaf of bread was purchased at a gourmet bakery. Reference-group influence can create what some marketers call "elastic consumers"—consumers who make decisions to save or splurge in the same economy. During a slow economy, a consumer might purchase generic brands at the supermarket but because of reference group influence, might spend those savings on designer jeans or a flat-screen TV. Banking on the fact that grandparents like to show off their grandchildren to friends—and are willing to spend the money to do so, even if they skimp on themselves—some retailers offer premium-priced apparel for babies and small children. At Hanna Andersson, a Portland, Oregon retailer, for example, one-piece sleepers for babies retail at $34; a fleece hoodie, $52. Keeping in mind that babies and toddlers outgrow clothing quickly, these tags translate to luxury prices.[18] Children are especially vulnerable to the influence of reference groups. They often base their buying decisions on outside forces such as what they see on television and the Internet (including social networking sites) or the opinion of friends. Understanding this phenomenon, marketers sometimes take a step back so that older children, preteens, and teens can shop—even if they don't have their own money to spend. More retailers now welcome teens who browse but don't buy. These retailers know they are still developing loyal customers—the teens will return when they have their own or their parents' money.

In addition, marketers are recognizing the power of the Internet as a tool for reaching children and teens—not just to market new or existing goods and services, but to learn more about reference groups and upcoming trends. Ninety-five percent of consumers ages 12 to 17 are online, visiting social networking sites, getting information, and forming opinions from these interactions. They download music, play games, and participate in interactive marketing online. Although they will shop online, a recent survey found that three-fourths of teens preferred to shop at brick-and-mortar stores.[19]

> Even though most 12 to 17 year olds are online, visiting social sites, gathering information, and forming opinions, fewer than a third of them are making online purchases. They prefer to do their shopping at brick-and-mortar stores.

Social Classes

W. Lloyd Warner's research identified six classes within the social structures of both small and large U.S. cities: the upper-upper, lower-upper, upper-middle, and lower-middle classes, followed by the working class and lower class. Class rankings are determined by occupation, income, education, family background, and residence location. Note that income is not always a primary factor; pipe fitters paid at union scale earn more than many college professors, but their purchase behavior may be quite different. Still, the ability to make certain purchases, such as a private jet or an ocean-view home, is an important factor in determining class.

Family characteristics, such as the occupations and incomes of one or both parents, have been the primary influences on social class. People in one social class may aspire to a higher class and therefore exhibit buying behavior common to that class rather than to their own. Middle-class consumers often buy items they associate with the upper classes. Marketers of certain luxury goods appeal to these consumers. Coach, Tiffany, and Bloomingdale's—all traditionally associated with high-end luxury goods—now offer their items in price ranges and locations attractive to middle-class consumers. Saks Fifth Avenue, one of the nation's most well-known luxury retailers, recently unveiled a private-label collection of men's clothing priced less than some of its premier brands. The new collection features Italian wool suits for under $1,200 and dress shirts for $195—but the retailer's marketers consider that a bargain when compared to the typical $8,000 price tag for its designer suits.[20]

Marketers use language in their marketing messages designed to appeal to certain social classes—or to those who aspire to them. Here are a few examples:

- Maserati: "The key to an extraordinary life is quite literally a key."
- Bermuda Tourism: "So much more."
- Dreams Resorts: "The Dreams Experience makes for an incredible vacation. The privileges of unlimited luxury make it even better."[21]

Opinion Leaders

In nearly every reference group, a few members act as **opinion leaders**. These trendsetters are likely to purchase new products before others in the group and then share their experiences and opinions via word-of-mouth. As others in the group decide whether to try the same products, they are influenced by the reports of opinion leaders. Generalized opinion leaders are rare; instead, individuals tend to act as opinion leaders for specific goods or services based on their knowledge of and interest in those products. Their interest motivates them to seek out information from mass media, manufacturers, and other sources and, in turn, transmit this information to associates through interpersonal communications. Opinion leaders are found within all segments of the population.

Information about goods and services may flow from the Internet, television, or other mass media to opinion leaders, and then from opinion leaders to others. Sometimes information flows directly from media sources to all consumers. In still other instances, a multistep flow carries information from mass media to opinion leaders and then on to other opinion leaders before dissemination to the general public.

Some opinion leaders influence purchases by others through their own actions. Self-made billionaire Tory Burch is one such influencer. Building a multi-billion dollar fashion empire in less than a decade, Burch influences women around the world and their choice of clothing and accessories. Recently named to Forbes list of the World's 100 Most Powerful Women, Burch is also leveraging her experience and success through her foundation, an organization dedicated to empowering female entrepreneurs worldwide.[22]

FAMILY INFLUENCES

Most people are members of at least two families during their lifetimes—the ones they are born into and those they eventually form later in life. The family group is perhaps the most important determinant of consumer behavior because of the close, continuing interactions among family members. Like other groups, each family typically has norms of expected behavior and different roles and status relationships for its members.

According to the U.S. Census Bureau, the structure of families has changed greatly over the last century. Today, only about half of all households are headed by married couples. Many couples are separated or divorced, so single heads of households are more common. In addition, there has been an increase in households headed by same-sex couples. Women are having fewer children, giving birth later in life, and spacing their children farther apart. More women are choosing to live alone,

---

opinion leaders Trendsetters who purchase new products before others in a group and then influence others in their purchases.

Fashion designer Tory Burch has become an influencer, not only for fashion, but also for business and philanthropy.

with or without children, and more senior citizens are living alone or without younger generations present in their homes. Still, to target a market for goods and services, marketers find it useful to describe the role of each spouse in a household in terms of the following four categories:

1. Autonomic role is seen when the partners independently make equal numbers of decisions. Personal-care items would fall into the category of purchase decisions each would make for himself or herself.

2. Husband-dominant role occurs when the husband usually makes certain purchase decisions. Buying a generator or woodstove for the home is a typical example.

3. Wife-dominant role has the wife making certain buying decisions. Children's clothing is a typical wife-dominant purchase.

4. Syncratic role refers to joint decisions. The purchase of a house follows a syncratic pattern.

Categories 2 and 3 have changed dramatically over the years. The increasing occurrence of the two-income family means that women have a greater role in making large family purchases, such as vacations and automobiles. Studies show that women take the lead in choosing entertainment, such as movies and restaurants. Women also now outspend men in the purchase of electronics. Conversely, as more highly educated women begin to achieve earning parity with their spouses, men are appearing more frequently at the grocery store. A research firm recently coined the term "manfluencer" to describe the growing group of men who are responsible for at least half the grocery shopping in their households.[23] Men also are taking a more active role in child care. Both of these shifts in family life mean that marketers must consider both genders as potential consumers when creating their marketing messages. For example, as the number of women car buyers begins to equal that of men in the United States, marketers need to take note that the two groups buy differently: Men are inclined to value ruggedness and exterior style while women tend to focus on safety and affordability.[24]

Studies of family decision making also have shown that households with two wage earners are more likely than others to make joint purchasing decisions. Members of two-income households often shop in the evening and on weekends because of the number of hours spent at the workplace. Shifting family roles have created new markets for a variety of products. Goods and services that save time, promote family togetherness, emphasize safety, or encourage health and fitness appeal to the family values and influences of today.

Children and Teenagers in Family Purchases

Children and teenagers represent a huge market—nearly 54 million strong—and they influence what their parents buy, from cereal to automobiles. These consumers are bombarded with messages from a variety of media. They are presented with a wide array of choices. Young people now wield $1.2 trillion of their own spending power.[25] They also have significant influence over the goods and services their families purchase. According to a recent study, purchase decisions in families are becoming increasingly collaborative, with three of five parent respondents saying they even consider their children's point of view when buying a car.[26]

As teenagers influence their parents to make large purchases, they also influence the type of purchases their parents make, such as fuel-efficient cars that are cheaper to fill with gas.

> **Briefly Speaking**
>
> "There is a spiritual aspect to our lives—when we give we receive—when a business does something good for somebody, that somebody feels good about them!"
>
> —**Ben Cohen**
> Co-Founder, Ben & Jerry's Ice Cream

ASSESSMENT CHECK

2.1. List the interpersonal determinants of consumer behavior.

2.2. What is a subculture?

2.3. Describe the Asch phenomenon.

PERSONAL DETERMINANTS OF CONSUMER BEHAVIOR

> **3** Explain the five personal determinants of consumer behavior.

Consumer behavior is affected by a number of internal, personal factors in addition to interpersonal ones. Each individual brings unique needs, motives, perceptions, attitudes, learned responses, and self-concepts to buying decisions. This section looks at how these factors influence consumer behavior.

NEEDS AND MOTIVES

need Imbalance between a consumer's actual and desired states.

Individual purchase behavior is driven by the motivation to fill a perceived need. A **need** is an imbalance between the consumer's actual and desired states. A person who recognizes or feels a significant or urgent need then seeks to correct the imbalance. Marketers attempt to arouse this sense of urgency by making a need "felt" and then influencing consumers' motivation to satisfy their needs by purchasing specific products.

motive Inner state that directs a person toward the goal of satisfying a need.

Motives are inner states that direct a person toward the goal of satisfying a need. The individual takes action to reduce the state of tension and return to a condition of equilibrium.

Maslow's Hierarchy of Needs

Psychologist Abraham H. Maslow developed a theory that characterized needs and arranged them into a hierarchy. Maslow identified five levels of needs, beginning with physiological needs and progressing to the need for self-actualization. According to Maslow, a person must at least partially satisfy lower-level needs before higher needs can affect behavior. In developed countries, where relatively large per-capita incomes allow most people to satisfy the basic needs on the hierarchy, higher-order needs may be more important to consumer behavior. Table 6.1 illustrates products and marketing themes designed to satisfy needs at each level.

Physiological Needs

Needs at the most basic level concern essential requirements for survival, such as food, water, shelter, and clothing. Pur promotes its water filtration system with the slogan, "Your water should be Pur." Its ads emphasize the need for clean water: "When you realize how often water touches your family's life, you discover just how important healthy, great-tasting water is."

Safety Needs

Second-level needs include financial or lifestyle security, protection from physical harm, and avoidance of the unexpected. To gratify these needs, consumers may buy life insurance, alarm systems, or retirement plans. In one of its ads Fidelity asks, "Will you be ready for retirement?" The answer to the question is, "Turn here. Fidelity Investments."

Social/Belongingness Needs

Satisfaction of physiological and safety needs leads a person to attend to third-level needs—the desire to be accepted by people and groups important to that individual. To satisfy this need, people may join organizations or programs to buy goods or services that make them feel part of a group. Chase offers its Blueprint program, "a new set of free features only for Chase customers."

Esteem Needs

People have a universal desire for a sense of accomplishment and achievement. They also wish to gain the respect of others and even exceed others' performance once lower-order needs are satisfied. Pandora's marketing encourages consumers to buy its pieces because "Life has its moments… make them unforgettable."

Self-Actualization Needs

The top rung of Maslow's ladder of human needs represents people's desire to realize their full potential and find fulfillment by expressing their unique talents and capabilities. Companies that run exotic adventure trips aim to satisfy consumers' needs for self-actualization. Not-for-profit

TABLE 6.1 Marketing Strategies Based on Maslow's Hierarchy of Needs

Needs	Products	Marketing Themes
Physiological	Food, water, medicines, vitamins, exercise equipment and gym memberships, health care and cleaning products, sleep aids and mattresses, food for pets	Fresh Express salads: "Consistently, deliciously, fresh." GNC vitamins and supplements: "Live well." Colgate Total: "#1 recommended by dentists and hygienists."
Safety	Health and life insurance, computer antivirus software, smoke and carbon monoxide detectors, antibacterial cleaners, business protection, auto safety features	Progressive Insurance: "Helping you save money. That's Progressive." Blue Cross Blue Shield Association: "The Power of Blue." Better Business Bureau: "Start with trust."
Belongingness	Cosmetics, food, entertainment, fashion, appliances and home furnishings, clubs and organizations, cars	Avon Walk for Breast Cancer: "The more of us who walk, the more of us survive." Lowe's: "Never Stop Improving." Lee: "Get what fits." Payless shoes: "Save now. Feel good." Olay: "Love the skin you're in." Ford: "Drive one."
Esteem	Fashion, jewelry, gourmet foods, electronics, cosmetics, luxury cars, credit cards, investments, sports and hobbies, travel, spas	Rolex watches: "It Doesn't Just Tell Time. It Tells History." Lincoln automobiles: "Travel well." L'Oréal Paris: "Because you're worth it."
Self-actualization	Education, cultural events, sports and hobbies, motivational seminars, technology, travel, investments	University of Phoenix: "I'm a Phoenix." Tony Robbins: "Unleash the power within." Canyon Ranch: "The power of possibility."

organizations that invite paying volunteers to assist in such projects as archaeological digs or building homes for the needy appeal to these needs as well. Four Seasons Hotels and Resorts advertises one of its African locations by showing two guests riding elephants through the mist. "It's said they never forget," reads the tag line. "Neither will you."

Maslow believed that a satisfied need no longer has to be met. Once the physiological needs are met, the individual moves on to pursue satisfaction of higher-order needs. Consumers periodically are motivated by the need to relieve thirst and hunger, but their interests soon return to focus on satisfaction of safety, social, and other needs in the hierarchy. Some people may not progress through the hierarchy; they may fixate on a certain level. For example, consumers who live through an economic downturn may always be motivated to save money in order to avoid financial insecurity—a second-level need. Marketers who understand this can create opportunities for their firms by offering money-saving goods and services.

Critics have pointed out a variety of flaws in Maslow's reasoning: Some needs can relate to more than one level; individuals may progress through the needs hierarchy in a different order; and some individuals bypass social and esteem needs and are motivated by self-actualization

People have a universal desire for a sense of accomplishment and achievement and wish to gain the respect of others. Pandora's marketing encourages consumers to buy its pieces because "Life has its moments… make them unforgettable."

needs. However, the hierarchy of needs can offer an effective guideline for marketers who want to study consumer behavior.

PERCEPTIONS

perception Meaning that a person attributes to incoming stimuli gathered through the five senses.

Perception is the meaning that a person attributes to incoming stimuli gathered through the five senses—sight, hearing, touch, taste, and smell. Certainly a buyer's behavior is influenced by his or her perceptions of a good or service. Researchers now recognize that people's perceptions depend as much on what they want to perceive as on the actual stimuli. For this reason, Neiman Marcus and Target are perceived differently, as are Godiva chocolates and M&Ms. A person's perception of an object or event results from the interaction of two types of factors:

1. *stimulus factors*—characteristics of the physical object such as size, color, weight, and shape
2. *individual factors*—unique characteristics of the individual, including not only sensory processes but also experiences with similar inputs and basic motivations and expectations.

Perceptual Screens

The average American consumer is constantly bombarded with marketing messages. A typical supermarket now carries 30,000 different packages, each serving as a miniature billboard vying to attract consumers' attention. More than 6,000 commercials are aired on network TV each week. As marketers compete for attention—and dollars—they get more creative about where they place their messages. Consumers might find a carton of eggs stamped with the name of a television show, or takeout cartons emblazoned with the name of a major airline. Old-fashioned billboards—once thought to be obsolete—have made a comeback with 3D elements and large digital advertising screens.

perceptual screens Mental filtering processes through which all inputs must pass.

The problem with many messages is they create clutter in the minds of consumers, causing them to ignore many promotional messages. People respond selectively to messages that break through their **perceptual screens**—the mental filtering processes through which all inputs must pass. Marketers use techniques such as doubling the size of an ad, using certain colors or graphics, or developing unique packaging to elicit positive responses from consumers. Color is so compelling that its use on product packaging and logos often is the result of a long and careful selection process. Red grabs the attention, and orange has been shown to stimulate appetite. Blue is associated with water, and so it is used on many cleaning products. Green connotes low-fat or healthful food products. The psychological concept of closure also helps marketers create messages that stand out. Closure is the human tendency to perceive a complete picture from an incomplete stimulus. Advertisements that allow consumers to do this often succeed in breaking through perceptual screens.

Creative marketers compete for the attention of consumers through the use of 3D billboards.

Marketers have become more creative in an effort to break through the barrier of clutter. Increasingly, billboards incorporate one or more life-sized mannequins into the message. Emergency dispatchers frequently receive calls from worried motorists reporting what appears to be a dangerous situation. If the goal is to get people's attention, these billboards achieve their objective.[27]

Word-of-mouth is probably the oldest marketing technique in existence. It is also one of the most effective. If one satisfied customer tells a friend, relative, neighbor, or coworker about a positive experience with a product, that message quite often breaks through the listener's perceptual screen because trust between the two already exists.

On the other end of the scale lie newer, high-tech marketing tools. These include virtual

The successful "Pure Michigan" campaign features traditional TV, radio, and magazine ads, along with billboards and ads wrapped around buses.

Source: www.michigan.gov

reality (in which a consumer can test-drive a car or tour a resort) and social media such as Facebook, Twitter, and LinkedIn. While investment in these new tools is increasingly rapidly, it is interesting to note that the old methods remain strong—with modification—as in the case of the billboard. Although some marketers predicted the certain demise of the traditional 30-second television commercial, that prediction has not come true.[28] Travel Michigan's "Pure Michigan" campaign includes TV and radio ads along with images of engaging Michigan scenes on Facebook, Twitter, and the Pure Michigan website. In regional markets like Chicago, the campaign employs billboards and "wrapped" buses. Michigan's tourism office recently reported the "Pure Michigan" campaign yielded a return of $5.76 for every campaign dollar spent.[29]

With selective perception at work screening competing messages, it is easy to see the importance of marketers' efforts in developing brand loyalty. Satisfied customers are less likely to seek information about competing products. Even when competitive advertising is forced on them, they are less apt than others to look beyond their perceptual filters at those appeals. Loyal customers simply tune out information that does not agree with their existing beliefs and expectations.

Subliminal Perception

More than 50 years ago, a New Jersey movie theater tried to boost concession sales by flashing the words "Eat Popcorn" and "Drink Coca-Cola" between frames of actress Kim Novak's image in the movie *Picnic*. The messages flashed on the screen every five seconds for a duration of one three-hundredth of a second each time. Researchers reported that these messages, though too short to be recognizable at the conscious level, resulted in a 58 percent increase in popcorn sales and an 18 percent increase in Coke sales. After the findings were published, advertising agencies and consumer protection groups became intensely interested in **subliminal perception**—the subconscious receipt of incoming information.

Subliminal advertising is aimed at the subconscious level of awareness to circumvent the audience's perceptual screens. The goal of the original research was to induce consumer purchases while keeping consumers unaware of the source of the motivation to buy. All later attempts to duplicate the test findings were unsuccessful. Although subliminal advertising is considered manipulative, it is exceedingly unlikely to induce purchasing except by people already inclined to buy. There are three reasons for this:

1. Strong stimulus factors are required just to get a prospective customer's attention.

2. Only a very short message can be transmitted.

3. Individuals vary greatly in their thresholds of consciousness. Messages transmitted at the threshold of consciousness for one person will not be perceived at all by some people and will be all too apparent to others. The subliminally exposed message "Drink Coca-Cola" may go unseen by some viewers, while others may read it as "Drink Pepsi-Cola," "Drink Cocoa," or even "Drive Slowly."

Regardless of the findings about subliminal advertising, neuroscientists know that thoughts and emotions, including those a person may not be consciously aware of, play a vital role in decision making, and marketers looking for ways to elicit emotions that motivate people toward a purchase. Neuromarketing already has taken some concrete forms. Firms like Yahoo, Hyundai, and Microsoft are using EEGs and MRIs—which measure brain activity—to study consumers' responses to certain

subliminal perception
Subconscious receipt of incoming information.

stimuli associated with their products. Researchers at Frito-Lay used brain imaging to analyze the packaging for its potato chips. They discovered that shiny packages triggered activity in the area of the brain associated with guilt feelings, but matte-beige packaging did not. This finding helped Frito-Lay choose the matte-finish packaging.[30]

Facial recognition technology offers yet another way of identifying and targeting specific consumers. See the "Solving an Ethical Controversy" feature for some of the issues it may raise.

ATTITUDES

Perception of incoming stimuli is greatly affected by attitudes. In fact, a consumer's decision to purchase an item is strongly based on his or her attitudes about the product, store, or salesperson. **Attitudes** are a person's enduring favorable or unfavorable evaluations, emotions, or action tendencies toward some object or idea. As they form over time through individual experiences and group contacts, attitudes become highly resistant to change. New fees, a reduction in service hours, or a change in location can be difficult for customers to accept. Because favorable attitudes likely affect brand preferences, marketers are interested in determining consumer attitudes toward their offerings. Numerous attitude-scaling devices have been developed for this purpose.

attitudes Person's enduring favorable or unfavorable evaluations, emotions, or action tendencies toward some object or idea.

Attitude Components

An attitude has cognitive, affective, and behavioral components. The cognitive component refers to the individual's information and knowledge about an object or concept. The affective component deals with feelings or emotional reactions. The behavioral component involves tendencies to act in a certain manner. In deciding whether to shop at a specific retailer for a laptop computer, a consumer might gather information about what the store offers from advertising, visits to the store, and input from family, friends, and coworkers—the cognitive component. The consumer also might receive affective input by listening to others about their shopping experiences at this store. Affective input might cause the consumer to make a judgment about people who shop at the store and whether those people represent a group with which the consumer wants to be associated. Finally, the consumer might decide to buy his or her new laptop at that store—the behavioral component. All three components maintain a relatively stable and balanced relationship to one another. Together, they form an overall attitude about an object or idea.

Changing Consumer Attitudes

A favorable consumer attitude is vital to the success of a marketing effort. Marketers can approach this in one of two ways:

1. By attempting to produce consumer attitudes that will lead to the purchase of an existing product
2. By evaluating existing consumer attitudes and creating or modifying products to appeal to these attitudes

It's always easier to create and maintain a positive attitude toward a product than it is to change an unfavorable one to favorable. But if consumers view a product unfavorably, all is not lost. The seller might redesign the product, offer new or desired options, or enhance service. Sometimes an attitude isn't unfavorable, but consumers just don't feel a need for the product—they aren't motivated to make the purchase. Marketers must find a way to change shoppers' attitude to include the desire to buy. For example, although most consumers don't necessarily have a negative attitude toward sweet potatoes, they might not have a strong enough positive attitude to cause them to add sweet potatoes to their grocery list. In order to boost sales, marketers for the North Carolina Sweet Potato Commission recently began to provide more information about sweet potatoes, including their high content of vitamins, antioxidants, and dietary fiber. This information addressed the

> **Briefly Speaking**
>
> "If you do build a great experience, customers tell each other about that. Word of mouth is very powerful."
>
> —Jeff Bezos
> Founder and CEO, Amazon

SOLVING AN ETHICAL CONTROVERSY
Should Facial Recognition Technology Fade Away?

It's already a commonplace marketing strategy to put cookies on users' computers that allow companies to identify their likes and dislikes in order to target online ads to these preferences. Now a parallel strategy is about to roll out that uses facial recognition technology to identify people as males or females in specific age brackets. The first users are expected to be bars, clubs, and restaurants that want to monitor the mix of customers, but other marketers see many opportunities. Facial-recognition mechanisms at store entrances can help ensure customers see only digital and mobile ads that matter to them, but privacy advocates are concerned about potential misuse of the technology, such as lack of an opt-in or opt-out feature.

Is it acceptable for companies to use facial recognition technology without telling customers?

PRO
1. Identifying customers lets marketers pinpoint their ads so people won't see advertising that doesn't relate to or interest them.
2. People who see messages about the right product at the right time are more likely to buy, benefitting everyone.

CON
1. Facial recognition technology is yet another way for companies to amass personal data about people without their consent.
2. Unless there are industry standards, including an opt-out feature like Facebook had to add when its facial-recognition photo-tagging function angered users, companies will make up their own rules.

Summary
Some casinos already use facial recognition for security purposes, but privacy advocates believe unchecked use of the technology could infringe on individual rights and give companies excess power. The worst outcome, say some, would link store cameras to social networks. So, instead of pitching ads based on a customer being, say, a woman in her 20s, a retailer could scan her online profile to mine her friends network.

Sources: Natasha Singer, "Never Forgetting a Face," *The New York Times*, accessed September 3, 2014, www.nytimes.com; Mike Krumboltz, "No Special Characters Required: Password App Uses Facial Recognition," *Yahoo News*, accessed February 16, 2014, http://news.yahoo.com; Jim Stenman, "Embracing Big Brother: How Facial Recognition Could Help Fight Crime, "*CNN*, accessed February 16, 2014, www.cnn.com; Martin Kaste, "A Look into Facebook's Potential to Recognize Anybody's Face, "*NPR*, accessed February 14, 2014, www.npr.org.

---

cognitive component of consumers' attitude toward sweet potatoes, pushing it enough toward the positive that shoppers began to buy them more often.[31]

Modifying the Components of Attitude

Attitudes frequently change in response to inconsistencies among the three components. The most common inconsistencies result when new information changes the cognitive or affective components of an attitude. Marketers can modify attitudes by providing evidence of product benefits and by correcting misconceptions. Marketers may also change attitudes by engaging buyers in new behavior. Free samples might change attitudes by getting consumers to try a product.

Good-looking cakes and pastries in a bakery window might influence a hungry person to stop in and buy a pastry or other dessert item as a response to that cue.

learning Knowledge or skill acquired as a result of experience, which changes consumer behavior.

shaping Process of applying a series of rewards and reinforcements to permit more complex behavior to evolve.

Sometimes new technologies can encourage consumers to change their attitudes. Consumers who sign up to receive Internet coupons for goods and services might be more likely to try these products without knowing a lot about them. Personalized shopping alerts from firms such as Amazon.com might encourage consumers to purchase a new book or CD by making shoppers feel as though the retailer cares about their individual reading or listening preferences.

LEARNING

Marketing is concerned as seriously with the process by which consumer decisions change over time as with the current status of those decisions. Learning, in a marketing context, refers to immediate or expected changes in consumer behavior as a result of experience. The learning process includes the component of drive, which is any strong stimulus that impels action. Fear, pride, greed, jealousy, hunger, thirst, comfort, and rivalry are examples of drives. Learning also relies on a cue—any object or signal in the environment that determines the nature of the consumer's response to a drive. Cues include a flashing neon sign in the window of a bakery (a cue for a hungry person) and a commercial for a business franchise (a cue for someone who wants more money). A response is the individual's reaction to a set of cues and drives. The hungry person might duck into the bakery to buy a pastry, while the person who wants to earn more money might investigate owning a company franchise.

Reinforcement is the reduction in drive that results from a proper response. As a response becomes more rewarding, it creates a stronger bond between the drive and the purchase of the product, likely increasing future purchases by the consumer. Reinforcement is the rationale that underlies frequent-buyer programs that reward repeat purchasers for their loyalty. These programs may offer rewards for premiums or discounts, frequent-flyer miles, and the like. However, so many companies now offer these programs that marketers must find ways to differentiate them. Firms that don't offer the programs quickly learn that consumers will bypass their products and move on to those of competitors.

Customization is the latest trend toward attracting reward card users. Chase Sapphire card users can choose points or cash rewards that never expire. In addition, they have access to live customer-service representatives around the clock, personal concierge services, and premier travel services that include booking any flights with points they choose without being subject to blackout dates.[32]

Applying Learning Theory to Marketing Decisions

Learning theory has some important implications for marketing strategists, particularly those involved with consumer packaged goods. Marketers must find a way to develop a desired outcome such as repeat purchase behavior gradually over time. Shaping is the process of applying a series of rewards and reinforcements to permit more complex behavior to evolve.

Both promotional strategy and the product itself play a role in the shaping process. Marketers want to motivate consumers to become regular buyers of certain merchandise. Their first step in getting consumers to try the product might be to offer a free sample that includes a substantial discount coupon for the next purchase. This example uses a cue as a shaping procedure. If the item performs well, the purchase response is reinforced and followed by another inducement—the coupon. A sample works well because it allows the consumer to try the product at no risk. Supermarket shoppers have the opportunity to sample products on a regular basis—crackers, cheese, appetizers, salad dressings, cookies, and the like. A display is often set up near the aisle where the item is sold, staffed by a person who dispenses the sample along with a coupon for a future purchase.

The second step is to entice the consumer to buy the item with little financial risk. The discount coupon enclosed with the free sample prompts this action. Suppose the package that the consumer purchases has another, smaller discount coupon enclosed. Again, satisfactory product performance and the second coupon provide reinforcement.

The third step is to motivate the person to buy the item again at a moderate cost. A discount coupon accomplishes this objective, but this time the purchased package includes no additional coupon. The only reinforcement comes from satisfactory product performance.

The final test comes when the consumer decides whether to buy the item at its true price without a discount coupon. Satisfaction with product performance provides continuing reinforcement. Repeat purchase behavior literally is shaped by effective application of learning theory within a marketing strategy context.

SELF-CONCEPT THEORY

Our **self-concept**—our multifaceted view of ourselves—plays an important role in our consumer behavior. Perhaps you see yourself as a creative person, someone who thinks outside the box. You pride yourself on keeping up with the latest trends—in fact you like to think of yourself as a trendsetter, ahead of the wave. You might express this self-concept by wearing a certain watch, like a Shinola crafted in Detroit. Shinola watches, designed and built in the Motor City, refute the notion that manufacturing in America is extinct.[33]

Perhaps your self-concept lets you see yourself as a talented multitasker, but if you find that you're often distracted at work, see the "Career Readiness" feature for some tips on regaining your focus.

The concept of self emerges from an interaction of many of the influences—both personal and interpersonal—that affects buying behavior. A person's needs, motives, perceptions, attitudes, and learning lie at the core of his or her conception of self. In addition, family, social, and cultural influences affect self-concept.

A person's self-concept has four components: real self, self-image, looking-glass self, and ideal self. The real self is an objective view of the total person. The self-image, the way an individual views himself or herself, may distort the objective view. The looking-glass self, the way an individual thinks others see him or her, also may differ substantially from self-image because people often choose to project different images to others than their perceptions of their real selves. The ideal self serves as a personal set of objectives, because it is the image to which the individual aspires.

When making purchasing decisions, consumers will likely choose products that move them closer to their ideal self-images. For example,

self-concept Person's multifaceted picture of himself or herself.

Consumers might express the self-concept theory by wearing a certain brand of watch, such as a Shinola timepiece crafted in the city of Detroit.

CAREER READINESS
Avoiding Major Distractions at Work

Phone calls, emails, and visitors are part of every workday, but they can distract you from work. Here are some tips for getting your focus back.

1. Set a realistic schedule that prioritizes the week's tasks—including responding to emails—by deadline and importance. Now you have specific goals to focus on in orderly fashion. Update this schedule at the beginning or end of each week.

2. Check email just three times a day—morning, lunch, and close of business—and turn your email application off in between. If you can train yourself to check only twice a day, even better.

3. While office environments with an open floor plan are said to encourage collaboration, they can also be distracting. Don't hesitate to tell people you're busy or have a deadline. If you are polite, they'll understand. If they insist, invite them to walk with you while you grab lunch or head back to your office.

4. Let family members use the office number to reach you in an emergency, leaving you free to shut your personal phone off at work so personal calls don't interrupt you.

5. Your computer offers multiple distractions. For starters, leave Facebook, Twitter, Pinterest, and the rest for off-hours. Need more help staying focused? Take a look at software apps like Dark Room or Q10, which help users get work done.

Sources: "The Biggest Office Interruptions Are…" *The Wall Street Journal*, accessed February 17, 2014, http://online.wsj.com; "Office Distractions Come from Other Workers," *Scribbs Howard News Service*, accessed February 17, 2014, www.standard.net; Alex Cocilova, "Get Back to Work! Great Software for Reducing Distractions," *PC World*, accessed February 17, 2014, www.pcworld.com; Jacquelyn Smith, "How to Avoid Distractions in the Workplace," *Forbes*, accessed February 17, 2014, www.forbes.com.

ASSESSMENT CHECK

3.1. Identify the personal determinants of consumer behavior.
3.2. What are the human needs categorized by Abraham Maslow?
3.3. How do perception and learning differ?

suppose your ideal self-image is one of a trendsetter, but you generally have a hard time wearing anything other than conventional clothes. You might buy a cap or T-shirt from a retailer you don't ordinarily frequent in an effort to break out of the box and bring you closer to your ideal self-image. Social network media such as Facebook appeal to people's ideal self-image—users are often likely to post pictures and entries that paint themselves in a flattering light.

THE CONSUMER DECISION PROCESS

4 Distinguish between high-involvement and low-involvement purchase decisions.

high-involvement purchase decisions Purchases with high levels of potential social or economic consequences.

Although we might not be aware of it, as consumers, we complete a step-by-step process in making purchasing decisions. The time and effort devoted to a particular purchasing decision depend on how important it is.

Purchases with high levels of potential social or economic consequences are said to be **high-involvement purchase decisions**. Buying a car or deciding where to go to college are examples of high-involvement decisions. Routine purchases that pose little risk are **low-involvement purchase decisions**. Buying a loaf of bread or a pint of ice cream at the corner grocery store is a good example.

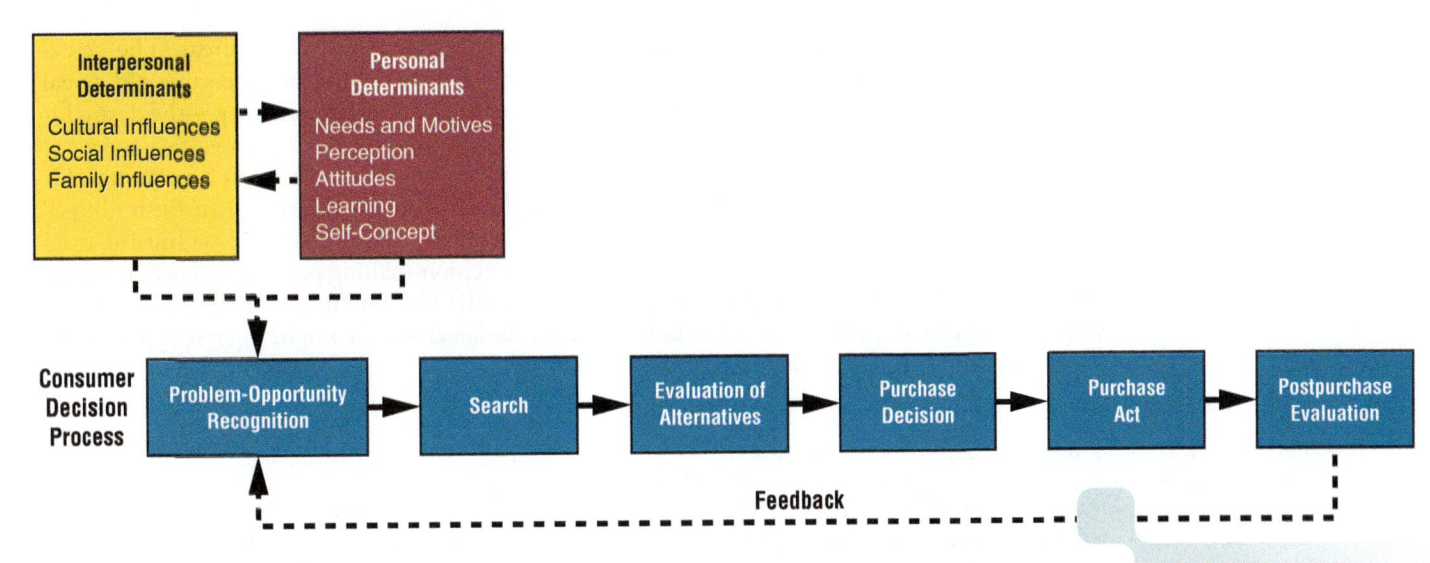

FIGURE 6.2
Integrated Model of the Consumer Decision Process

Source: Roger Blackwell, Paul W. Miniard, and James F. Engel, *Consumer Behavior*, 10th ed. (Mason, OH: South-Western, 2006).

Consumers generally invest more time and effort in buying decisions for high-involvement products than in those for low-involvement products. A home buyer will visit a number of listings, compare asking prices, apply for a mortgage, and have the selected house inspected before signing the final papers. Few buyers invest that much effort in choosing a brand of orange juice at the supermarket. Believe it or not, they will still go through the steps of the consumer decision process—but on a more compressed scale.

Figure 6.2 shows the six steps in the consumer decision process. First, the consumer recognizes a problem or unmet need, searches for appropriate goods or services, and evaluates the alternatives before making a purchase decision. The next step is the actual purchase. After buying the item, the consumer evaluates whether he or she made the right choice. Much of marketing involves steering consumers through the decision process in the direction of a specific product.

Consumers apply the decision process in solving problems and taking advantage of opportunities. Such decisions permit them to correct differences between their actual and desired states. Feedback from each decision serves as additional experience in helping guide subsequent decisions.

low-involvement purchase decisions
Routine purchases that pose little risk to the consumer.

ASSESSMENT CHECK

4.1. Differentiate between high-involvement decisions and low-involvement decisions.

4.2. Categorize each of the following as a high- or low-involvement product: toothpaste, laptop, apartment rental, cup of coffee, and cell phone service.

PROBLEM OR OPPORTUNITY RECOGNITION

During the first stage in the decision process, the consumer becomes aware of a gap between the existing situation and a desired situation. You have experienced this yourself. Perhaps you open the refrigerator door and find a slice of cheese and a cup of yogurt. You are really hungry for a sandwich. By identifying the problem—not enough food in the refrigerator—you can resolve it with a trip to the grocery store. Sometimes the problem is more specific. You might have a full refrigerator, but no mustard or mayonnaise for sandwiches. This problem requires a solution as well.

Outline the six steps in the consumer decision process.

Suppose you are unhappy with a particular purchase, say, a brand of cereal. The cereal might be too sweet or too crunchy. Or maybe you just want a change from the same old cereal every morning. This is the recognition of another type of problem or opportunity—the desire for change.

What if you just got a raise at work? You might decide to splurge on dinner at a restaurant. Or you might want to try a gourmet, prepared take-home dinner from the supermarket. Both dinners are more expensive than the groceries you have always bought, but now they are within financial reach. The marketer's main task during this phase of the decision-making process is to help prospective buyers identify and recognize potential problems or needs. This task may take the form of advertising, promotions, or personal sales assistance. A supermarket employee might suggest appetizers or desserts to accompany a gourmet take-home dinner.

SEARCH

During the second step in the decision process, a consumer gathers information about the attainment of a desired state. This search identifies different ways to solve the problem. A high-involvement purchase might mean conducting an extensive search for information, whereas a low-involvement purchase might require much less research.

The search may cover internal or external sources of information. An internal search is simply a mental review: Is there past experience with the product? Was it good or bad? An external search involves gathering information from all kinds of outside sources—for instance, family, friends, coworkers or classmates, advertisements or salespeople, online reviews, and consumer magazines. Because conducting an external search requires time and effort, it usually is done for high-involvement purchases.

The search identifies alternative brands or models for consideration and possible purchase. The collection of alternatives a consumer actually considers in making a purchase decision is known in marketing as the **evoked set**. In some cases, consumers already know which brands merit further consideration; in others, consumers make external searches to develop such information. The number of brands that are included in the evoked set may vary with the situation and the person. An immediate need, such as filling a nearly empty gas tank, might limit the evoked set. A driver with half a tank of gas, with more time to make a decision, might expand the evoked set to choose from a broader range of options that include lower prices or certain brands.

Consumers now choose among more alternative products than ever before. This variety can confuse and complicate the analysis that narrows the range of choices. Instead of comparing one or two brands, a consumer often faces a wide array of brands and sub-brands. Products that once included only regular and decaffeinated coffee now are available in many different forms—flavored coffee, latte, mocha, cappuccino, espresso, and iced coffee, to name a few. Researchers have conducted studies showing that too many choices—and resulting decisions—can cause anxiety and stress.[34]

Recognizing this, and wanting to help consumers find their way through the maze of choices, some firms have set up online sites where shoppers can compare products. The Biz Rate website allows shoppers to compare everything from shoes to GPS devices to living room furniture and sunglasses. They can compare features, prices, and reviews of all the products listed.[35]

EVALUATION OF ALTERNATIVES

The third step in the consumer decision process is to evaluate the evoked set of options. Actually, it is difficult to completely separate the second and third steps because some evaluation takes place as the search progresses; consumers accept, distort, or reject information as they receive it. Knowing that you are looking for a new pair of boots, your roommate might tell you about this great online site for shoes she visited recently. You don't particularly like her taste in shoes or boots, so you reject the information, even though the site might have a pair of boots that you would have bought.

---

evoked set Number of alternatives a consumer actually considers in making a purchase decision.

The outcome of the evaluation stage is the choice of a brand or product within the evoked set, or possibly a decision to keep looking for alternatives. To complete this analysis, the consumer must develop a set of evaluative criteria to guide the selection. **Evaluative criteria** are the features a consumer considers in choosing among alternatives. These criteria can either be objective facts (a vehicle's fuel economy) or subjective impressions (a favorable view of K-Swiss athletic shoes). Common criteria include price, brand name, and country of origin. Evaluative criteria can vary with the consumer's age, income level, social class, and culture; what's important to a senior citizen might not matter at all to a college student. When it comes to dining out, an affluent senior citizen might look for a restaurant with an upscale atmosphere and high-quality food; a budget-conscious college student might choose a place that's inexpensive and fast to accommodate study hours or class.

Marketers attempt to influence the outcome of this stage in three ways. First, they try to educate consumers about attributes they view as important in evaluating a particular class of goods. They also identify which evaluative criteria are important to an individual and attempt to show why a specific brand fulfills those criteria. Finally, they try to induce a customer to expand the evoked set to include their product.

> **evaluative criteria** Features a consumer considers in choosing among alternatives.

> **Briefly Speaking**
> "Life is the sum of all your choices."
> —**Albert Camus**
> *French author, journalist, and philosopher*

PURCHASE DECISION AND PURCHASE ACT

The search and alternative evaluation stages of the decision process result in the purchase decision and the actual purchase. At this stage, the consumer has evaluated each alternative in the evoked set based on his or her personal set of evaluative criteria and narrowed the alternatives down to one.

The consumer then decides where—or from whom—to make the purchase. Sometimes this decision is part of the evaluation; perhaps one seller is offering a better price or better warranty than another. The purchase may be made online or in person at a retail store. The delivery options also might influence the decision of where to purchase an item.

POSTPURCHASE EVALUATION

The purchase act produces one of two results. The buyer feels either satisfaction at the removal of the discrepancy between the existing and desired states or dissatisfaction with the purchase. Consumers are generally satisfied if purchases meet—or exceed—their expectations.

Sometimes, however, consumers experience post-purchase anxiety called **cognitive dissonance**. This anxiety results from an imbalance among a person's knowledge, beliefs, and attitudes. You might experience some dissonance about your purchase of a TV if you can't figure out how to use it, if it doesn't have the features you thought it had, or if you see an ad the next week for the same model at a discount.

Dissonance is likely to increase (1) as the dollar value of a purchase increases, (2) when the rejected alternatives have desirable features that the chosen alternatives do not provide, and (3) when the purchase decision has a major effect on the buyer. In other words, dissonance is more likely with high-involvement purchases than with those that require low involvement. If you buy a diet soda and don't like the flavor, you can toss it and buy a different one. But if you have spent more than $400 on a TV and aren't satisfied with it, you will most likely experience dissonance. You might try to reduce the dissonance by focusing on good reviews about your choice. Or you might show a friend all the neat features on your TV—without pointing out anything you find dissatisfactory.

Marketers can help buyers reduce cognitive dissonance by providing information that supports the chosen item. Automobile dealers recognize the possibility of "buyer's remorse" and often follow up purchases with letters or telephone calls offering personal attention to any customer questions or potential problems. Advertisements that stress customer satisfaction also help reduce cognitive dissonance.

A final method of dealing with cognitive dissonance is to change products. The consumer may ultimately decide that one of the rejected alternatives would have been the best choice,

> **cognitive dissonance** Imbalance among knowledge, beliefs, and attitudes that occurs after an action or decision, such as a purchase.

> **ASSESSMENT CHECK**
>
> 5.1. List the steps in the consumer decision process.
> 5.2. What is meant by the term *evoked set*?
> 5.3. What are evaluative criteria?

and vow to purchase that item in the future. Marketers may capitalize on this with advertising campaigns that focus on the benefits of their products or with tag lines that say something like, "If you're unhappy with them, try us." Making a different choice isn't always an option, particularly if the item requires a large investment in time and money. If you decide you aren't happy with your TV, you could try selling it, perhaps on a website like eBay or Craigslist, before purchasing another one.

CLASSIFYING CONSUMER PROBLEM-SOLVING PROCESSES

> **6** Differentiate among routinized response behavior, limited problem solving, and extended problem solving by consumers.

As mentioned earlier, the consumer decision processes for different products requires varying amounts of problem-solving efforts. Marketers recognize three categories of problem-solving behavior: routinized response, limited problem solving, and extended problem solving. The classification of a particular purchase within this framework clearly influences the consumer decision process.

ROUTINIZED RESPONSE BEHAVIOR

Consumers make many purchases routinely by choosing a preferred brand or one of a limited group of acceptable brands. This type of rapid consumer problem solving is referred to as routinized response behavior. A routine purchase of the same brand of dog food or the renewal of a magazine subscription are examples. The consumer has already set evaluative criteria and identified available options. External search is limited in such cases, which characterize extremely low-involvement products.

LIMITED PROBLEM SOLVING

Consider the situation in which the consumer previously set evaluative criteria for a particular kind of purchase but then encounters a new, unknown brand. The introduction of a new shampoo is an example of a limited problem-solving situation. The consumer knows the evaluative criteria for the product but has not applied these criteria to assess the new brand. Such situations demand moderate amounts of time and effort for external searches. Limited problem solving is affected by the number of evaluative criteria and brands, the extent of external search, and the process for determining preferences. Consumers making purchase decisions in this product category will likely feel involvement in the middle of the range.

> **ASSESSMENT CHECK**
>
> 6.1. What is routinized response behavior?
> 6.2. What does limited problem solving require?
> 6.3. Give an example of an extended problem-solving situation.

EXTENDED PROBLEM SOLVING

Extended problem solving results when brands are difficult to categorize or evaluate. The first step is to compare one item with similar ones. The consumer needs to understand the product features before evaluating alternatives. Most extended problem-solving efforts involve lengthy external searches. High-involvement purchase decisions—cars, homes, and colleges—usually requires extended problem solving.

Strategic Implications of Marketing in the 21st Century

Marketers who plan to succeed with today's consumers need to understand how their potential market behaves. Cultural influences play a big role in marketers' relationships with consumers, particularly as firms conduct business on a global scale but also as they try to reach diverse populations in the United States. In addition, family characteristics are changing—more women are in the workforce, more senior citizens are living alone—and this forecasts a change in the way family units make purchasing decisions. One of the biggest shifts in family spending involves the amount of power that children and teens wield in the marketplace.

These young consumers are more and more involved, in some cases know more about certain products—such as electronics—than their parents do, and very often influence purchase decisions. This holds true even with high-involvement purchases such as autos and computers.

Marketers constantly work toward changing or modifying components of consumers' attitudes about their products to gain a favorable attitude and purchase decision. Finally, they refine their understanding of the consumer decision process and use their knowledge to design effective marketing strategies.

Get online now for additional learning tools to help you master your marketing knowledge—visit **WWW.CENGAGEBRAIN.COM** today!

REVIEW OF CHAPTER OBJECTIVES

1. Describe consumer behavior and its role in marketing decisions.

Consumer behavior refers to the buyer behavior of individual consumers. Consumer behavior plays a huge role in marketing decisions, including what goods and services to offer, to whom, and where. If marketers can understand the factors that influence consumers, they can develop and offer the right products to those consumers.

2. Describe the three interpersonal determinants of consumer behavior.

Cultural influences, such as the general work ethic or the desire to accumulate wealth, come from society. Core values may vary from culture to culture. Social or group influences include social class, opinion leaders, and reference groups with which consumers may want to be affiliated. Family influences may come from spouses, parents, grandparents, or children.

3. Explain the five personal determinants of consumer behavior.

A need is an imbalance between a consumer's actual and desired states, and a motive is the inner state that directs a person toward the goal of satisfying a need. Perception is the meaning that a person attributes to incoming stimuli gathered through the five senses. Attitudes are a person's enduring favorable or unfavorable evaluations, emotions, or action tendencies toward something. Learning refers to immediate or expected changes in consumer behavior as a result of experience. In self-concept theory, a person's view of himself or herself plays a role in purchasing behavior. In purchasing goods and services, people will likely choose products that move them closer to their ideal self-images.

4 Distinguish between high-involvement and low-involvement purchase decisions.

Purchases with high levels of potential social or economic consequences are called high-involvement purchase decisions. Examples include buying a new car or home. Routine purchases that pose little risk to the consumer are called low-involvement purchase decisions. Choosing a candy bar or a magazine are examples.

5 Outline the six steps in the consumer decision process.

The consumer decision process consists of six steps: problem or opportunity recognition, search, alternative evaluation, purchase decision, purchase act, and post-purchase evaluation. The time involved in each stage of the decision process is determined by the nature of the individual purchases.

6 Differentiate among routinized response behavior, limited problem solving, and extended problem solving by consumers.

Routinized response behavior refers to repeat purchases made of the same brand or limited group of items. Limited problem solving occurs when a consumer previously set criteria for a purchase but then encounters a new brand or model. Extended problem solving results when brands are difficult to categorize or evaluate. High-involvement purchase decisions usually require extended problem solving.

ASSESSMENT CHECK: ANSWERS

1.1 Why is the study of consumer behavior important to marketers? If marketers can understand the behavior of consumers, they can offer the right products to consumers who want them.

1.2 Describe Kurt Lewin's proposition. Kurt Lewin proposed that behavior (*B*) is the function (*f*) of the interactions of personal influences (*P*) and pressures exerted by outside environmental forces (*E*). This research sheds light on how consumers make purchase decisions.

2.1 List the interpersonal determinants of consumer behavior. The interpersonal determinants of consumer behavior are cultural, social, and family influences.

2.2 What is a subculture? A subculture is a group within a culture that has its own distinct mode of behavior.

2.3 Describe the Asch phenomenon. The Asch phenomenon is the impact of groups and group norms on individual behavior.

3.1 Identify the personal determinants of consumer behavior. The personal determinants of consumer behavior are needs and motives, perceptions, attitudes, learning, and self-concept theory.

3.2 What are the human needs categorized by Abraham Maslow? The human needs categorized by Abraham Maslow are physiological, safety, social/belongingness, esteem, and self-actualization.

3.3 How do perception and learning differ? Perception is the meaning that a person attributes to incoming stimuli. Learning refers to immediate or expected changes in behavior as a result of experience.

4.1 Differentiate between high-involvement decisions and low-involvement decisions. High-involvement decisions have high levels of potential social or economic consequences, such as selecting an Internet service provider. Low-involvement decisions pose little financial, social, or emotional risk to the buyer, such as purchasing a magazine or gallon of milk.

4.2 Categorize each of the following as a high- or low-involvement product: toothpaste, laptop computer, apartment rental, cup of coffee, and cell-phone service. High-involvement products are the laptop computer, apartment rental, and cell-phone service. Low-involvement products are the toothpaste and cup of coffee.

5.1 List the steps in the consumer decision process. The steps in the consumer decision process are problem or opportunity recognition, search, evaluation of alternatives, purchase decision, purchase act, and post-purchase evaluation.

5.2 What is meant by the term *evoked set*? The evoked set is the number of alternatives a consumer actually considers in making a purchase decision.

5.3 What are evaluative criteria? Evaluative criteria are the features a consumer considers in choosing among alternatives.

6.1 What is routinized response behavior? Routinized response behavior is the repeated purchase of the same brand or limited group of products.

6.2 What does limited problem solving require? Limited problem solving requires a moderate amount of a consumer's time and effort.

6.3 Give an example of an extended problem-solving situation. An extended problem-solving situation might involve purchases like a car or a college education.

MARKETING TERMS YOU NEED TO KNOW

consumer behavior **172**
culture **173**
subcultures **174**
reference groups **178**
opinion leaders **180**
need **182**

motive **182**
perception **184**
perceptual screens **184**
subliminal perception **185**
attitudes **186**
learning **188**

shaping **188**
self-concept **189**
high-involvement purchase decisions **190**
low-involvement purchase decisions **191**

evoked set **192**
evaluative criteria **193**
cognitive dissonance **193**

ASSURANCE OF LEARNING REVIEW

1. What are core values? Describe what you think are three core values of American society. Do you consider these your core values as well?
2. Why is the concept of acculturation important to marketers who want to target such groups as Hispanic, Asian, or African American consumers?
3. Describe a purchase that a consumer might make that would reflect his or her status within a particular group. If that person's status increased, how might the purchase selection change?
4. What are the four role categories that describe each spouse in a household? Which role has changed the most in recent years, and why?
5. According to Maslow, what is the difference between needs and motives? How can marketers make use of these two concepts to lead consumers toward purchases?
6. What are the two factors that interact to create a person's perception of an object? How is this important for marketers?
7. What are the three reasons that subliminal perception is unlikely to result in a purchase? Despite these findings, what role is neuroscience now playing in the creation of marketing messages?
8. What are the components of attitude? Explain the two ways in which marketers can try to change consumer attitudes toward their products.
9. What is learning as it relates to marketing? Explain the four steps in the learning process and give examples as they relate to marketing.
10. For each of the following consumer decisions, what steps might marketers take to transform them from a limited problem-solving situation for a consumer to a routinized response situation?
    a. Buying a gym membership
    b. Renewing a magazine subscription
    c. Making a haircut appointment
    d. Filling a prescription at a pharmacy
    e. Taking the car in for an oil change

PROJECTS AND TEAMWORK EXERCISES

1. Choose a person whom you believe to be a true opinion leader. It might be a media celebrity, a political leader, a sports figure, or someone in another category entirely. Research ways in which the person has possibly shaped consumer attitudes toward various goods and services. Present your findings in class.
2. Consider your own participation in family purchases. How much influence did you have on your family's decisions as a child? As a teenager? Over what types of products did you have an influence—or not? Compare your answers with those of classmates.
3. One major trend in consumer spending that is likely to last for the next several years is a focus on value. Dollar stores and discount supermarkets have been profitable, and their popularity shows no sign of abating.[36] While consumers search for bargains, manufacturers and retailers of luxury goods are struggling to change consumer attitudes toward their products. On your own or with a classmate, choose one of the following luxury brands (or select one of your own) and create an advertisement for the product that seeks to change consumer attitudes about your product and show it would make a good purchase.
    a. Jaguar automobiles
    b. Louis Vuitton leather goods
    c. TAG Heuer watches
    d. Four Seasons Hotels and Resorts
    e. FlightOptions jet ownership
4. Consider a purchase decision involving a new smartphone, a fitness membership, or an Internet cable provider. Develop an evoked set of three alternatives for your purchase decision.

Then create a list of evaluative criteria that you would use to choose among the alternatives. Research your alternatives in more detail—online, at a store, and the like. Finally, make your purchase decision. Describe to the class how you made your decision—and why.

5. Choose a partner and select a low-involvement, routinized consumer product such as toothpaste, a bottle of salad dressing, fabric softener, or kitchen trash bags. Create an ad you think could stimulate consumers to change their preferred brand to your pick.

CRITICAL-THINKING EXERCISES

1. Describe a group to which you belong—it might be a team, a club, or your roommates. Outline the norms of the group, the major roles that different members play, and your own status within the group. Have you ever sought to change your status? Why or why not?

2. What are the two conditions that must exist for a consumer to be influenced by a reference group? Have you ever made a purchase based on reference group influence? If so, what was the purchase and how did you come to the decision to make it? If not, why not?

3. Marketers point out that the five levels in Maslow's hierarchy of needs are sometimes combined or even bypassed by consumers making purchase decisions. Explain how each of the following could fulfill more than one need:

    a. A donation to the Red Cross to help tornado victims
    b. A retirement investment account
    c. Axe body wash
    d. Dinner at an upscale restaurant

4. What are some of the ways marketers can break through consumers' perceptual screens? If you were a marketer for a line of designer dog clothing, what method might you use?

5. Suppose you are employed by a large electronics retailer, and a customer comes to you with cognitive dissonance over the purchase of an expensive computer system from your store the previous week. How would you work with the customer to help eliminate the dissonance?

ETHICS EXERCISE

Marketers of online news content are struggling to change consumer attitudes about whether or not it is fair to charge for this content. While consumers are already willing to pay for movies, music, and games, they don't want to pay for news—whether it is from online versions of newspapers and magazines or online feeds of radio and talk shows. Yet these news formats are created by paid professionals and can be expensive to produce. Increasingly, daily newspapers in the United States have begun creating "pay walls" that require readers, after a while, to pay for a digital subscription.[37]

1. Express your own view. Is it ethical for marketers of online news content to begin charging consumers for their services? If so, under what circumstances? If not, why or why not?

2. Go online to research different news sources—those that are free (such as the headlines offered on Yahoo) and those for which there is a charge (such as online magazine or newspaper subscriptions). Is there a difference in features or the extent of services offered?

3. Based on your research and your knowledge of consumer behavior, what steps do you think news marketers might take to change consumer attitudes about whether news should be offered for free?

INTERNET EXERCISES

1. **Marketing to children.** Advertising and other marketing efforts directed toward children have long been controversial. Visit the website of Children's Advertising Review Unit (CARU)—an organization created by the advertising industry to address issues associated with marketing to children. What is the purpose of CARU? What are the major issues regarding marketing to children? What have been some of its recent actions? Why have some prominent marketers, such as The Coca-Cola Company, decided to end advertising aimed at children? In your opinion, can industry self-regulation ever be an effective substitute for government regulation?
www.caru.org

2. **Consumer decision making.** Assume you're in the market for both a new cell phone and cell phone provider. Follow the beginning stages in the consumer decision model described in the chapter—recognition of problem or opportunity, search, and evaluation of alternatives. Use the Internet to aid in your consumer decision process. Prepare a report summarizing your experience. Compare and contrast your experience with an actual consumer purchase decision you recently made.

3. **Marketing strategies and Maslow's hierarchy of needs.** Visit the websites listed here. Review the marketing strategies shown in each site. Which level of Maslow's hierarchy of needs does each site emphasize? Be prepared to defend your answers.

www.michelinman.com
www.starbucks.com
http://shop.nordstrom.com
www.hollandamerica.com
www.unilever.com

Note: Internet Web addresses change frequently. If you don't find the exact site listed, you may need to access the organization's home page and search from there or use a search engine such as Google or Bing.

CASE 6.1
Amazon Drives Consumer Behavior

A recent study of digital consumers by GroupM Next reveals that 17 percent of people who use digital media on their pathway to purchase products are visiting Amazon.com as part of the process. This is true whether customers purchase online or in a store, and it includes shoppers from all demographic groups. Sometimes they begin their journey at Amazon, sometimes they end there, and in about 6 percent of cases, Amazon is the only destination they choose. In behavioral terms, this means Amazon has become a research destination as well as a retail site, a place where many digitally savvy shoppers go to search, compare, price, and analyze before making their buying decision. Convenience weighs heavily in their behavior, says GroupM; Amazon lets shoppers bypass crowds and salespeople.

Price has always been in Amazon's favor. With its increasingly wide product variety, offering everything from books to housewares, clothing, and music, consumers' odds of finding just what they want get better all the time. Digital agency Hawkeye has discovered another reason so many Amazon visitors become customers: Amazon Prime, the program that offers free or upgraded shipping, free video streaming, and selected free Kindle titles for an annual fee.

Hawkeye's recent survey shows Amazon Prime in a very comfortable first place for consumer awareness, participation, and favorability among top U.S. brand experiences (runners-up include McDonald's Happy Meals and Starbucks Rewards). At $99 a year ($49 for college students), Amazon Prime has soared in popularity and is estimated to have signed on more than 10 million subscribers since its introduction only a few years ago.

Two behavioral factors seem to account for Amazon Prime's success and its contribution to Amazon's overall dominance in online retail. First, subscribers know they'll get free shipping, so many eventually stop shopping anywhere else. Second, customers want to get their money's worth from their fee, so they'll buy from Amazon even when they could shop somewhere else, spending an average of $1,200 at the site each year. That's about twice what non-Prime customers spend.

QUESTIONS FOR CRITICAL THINKING

1. One observer explained Amazon Prime's success by saying that when something is free, people don't think it is valuable. Do you agree? Why or why not?

2. How else can Amazon leverage its growing popularity as a shoppers' research site to generate more sales?

Sources: Brett Molina, "Amazon Raises Price of Prime Membership to $99," *USA Today*, accessed May 12, 2014, **www.usatoday.com**; corporate website, "Join Amazon Student," **www.amazon.com**, accessed March 18, 2014; Laurie Sullivan, "Emerging Behaviors Drive Purchase Path; Amazon Always in Mix," *Online Media Daily*, accessed February 18, 2014, **www.mediapost.com**; "GroupM Next Study Illuminates the Evolving Role of Digital in the Consumer Journey," *Business Wire*, accessed February 18, 2014, **http://finance.yahoo.com**; Karen Flynn, "Amazon Prime Leads Brand Experiences," *Researchscape*, accessed February 18, 2014, **www.researchscape.com**; Brad Tuttle, "Amazon Prime: Bigger, More Powerful, More Profitable than Anyone Imagined," *Time*, accessed February 18, 2014, **http://business.time.com**.

VIDEO CASE 6.2
Ski Butternut Offers Thrills—Not Spills

"Ski Butternut is a true family mountain," says Matt Sawyer, director of marketing for the ski and snowboarding resort nestled in the Berkshire Mountains of western Massachusetts. Smaller than the peaks of Colorado or even the crags of the Green Mountains of Vermont and White Mountains of New Hampshire, Butternut is what Sawyer refers to as a "soft mountain"—one that beginners can enjoy while they grow comfortable on skis or snowboards. In fact, through extensive surveying and data collecting (as well as 50 years of experience), Ski Butternut has been able to identify exactly who its customers are—and what they want when they come to a mountain like Butternut. A number of factors influence consumers' decision to try Butternut, ranging from interpersonal to personal determinants. The mountain's marketers, including Matt Sawyer and advertising consultant Ed Brooks, use various methods to tease out these factors in an effort to attract and keep customers. Cultural influences, such as the desire for quality recreation and leisure time, is one factor that drives people to a mountain resort; but there are plenty of such mountains scattered around New England and upstate New York. How does Ski Butternut compete? First, it focuses on families and the core value of spending time together. Matt Sawyer observes that Butternut's typical customers are families with young children, and "by capturing them early, we get to have them for a long time." Second, it reaches out to other subgroups, including senior citizens and those in the teen-to-25 age range. Senior citizens may want to perpetuate the image of themselves as physically active while enjoying membership in a group, while high school and college students want the thrills of challenging terrain. Other target groups for Ski Butternut include beginning skiers and those who race. Beginners aspire to be part of the skiing population, while racers aspire to reach achievement goals. Third, via social media, Ski Butternut engages customers and develops programs designed to keep them coming back for more.

Through more than 1,000 surveys across ski areas in the region as well as out west (and on its own mountain), Ski Butternut has amassed a comprehensive database that helps pinpoint who its customers are and what they want. "Ski Butternut believes in knowing as much as we can about our guests," explains Matt Sawyer. For example, Ski Butternut collects data during the equipment rental process. When a guest rents a pair of skis or a snowboard, that person provides standard information, such as name, address, and phone number. But the guest is also asked questions about age and ability to ski or snowboard, as well as the names of other winter resorts he or she has visited. The mountain compiles both individual and family profiles. In fact, says Sawyer, the average family skiing at Butternut has two children and one parent on the mountain. (Ski Butternut offers day care for the youngest ski bunnies.) All of this information helps Matt Sawyer, Ed Brooks, and others devise strategies designed to compete with other mountains in the region, such as beginner ski programs and three distinct racing programs—each targeted for a different level of interest in competition.

While the data show that first-time skiers generally keep their allegiance to the mountain on which they learn for about seven visits, Sawyer notes that the toughest group to capture is the teen-to-25 age range. A decade ago, this group (along with younger kids) was drifting off to other mountains that had more challenging terrain. So Ski Butternut built a terrain park—with a half pipe, jumps, and other obstacles—to lure them back. Sawyer points out with pride that Butternut is now the preeminent terrain park in the region covering southern New England and New York.

Another strategy for reaching this group is price discounts. Deciding where to spend recreation dollars falls in the high-involvement category for most of this group, with limited problem solving. Ski Butternut decided to offer them an incentive—$20 off ticket prices on weekends and holidays (virtually unheard of in the industry). They marketed the offer mostly through social media—and the students "came in car loads," recalls Sawyer. With this group in mind, the company also recently updated its Web and mobile sites.

Looking for ways to draw consumers to the mountains for different reasons and at different times of the year, Ski Butternut also hosts weddings and banquets during the spring, summer, and fall. Thus, the ideal Butternut customers will get married on the mountain in the fall, honeymoon on the slopes during the winter, and return with their children for years after.

QUESTIONS FOR CRITICAL THINKING

1. Describe the social influences that might affect the decisions that consumers make about where to spend their winter recreation time and dollars.

2. The evaluatiton of alternatives is an important step in the buying decision for consumers who are considering whether to visit Butternut or some other mountain. What would be some of the evaluative criteria in this decision, and why?

Sources: Company website, www.skibutternut.com, accessed February 16, 2014; "New Website and Mobile Site for Ski Butternut," press release, accessed February 16, 2014, www.skibutternut.com; Toby Hill, "Seasonal Spotlight: Ski Butternut," *MA Finds*, December 8, 2013, www.massvacation.com; Jeanette DeForge, "Skiing Areas Spending Millions to Upgrade Snowmaking," *The Republican*, December 4, 2013, www.masslive.com.

NOTES

1. Chuck Kent, "Post-Cultural Branding: How Sabra Sells So Much Hummus in the U.S.," *Branding*, accessed February 18, 2014, www.brandingmagazine.com; Duane Stanford, "Pepsi, Others Bet Hummus Can Be the Next Salsa," *Bloomberg Businessweek*, accessed February 18, 2014, www.businessweek.com; Jane Wells, "Sabra Wants You to Say: Please, Pass the Hummus," *CNBC*, accessed February 18, 2014, www.cnbc.com; David Larter, "Q&A: Hummus Giant Digs Deeper into Virginia," *Richmond Biz Sense*, accessed February 18, 2014, www.richmondbizsense.com; David Kesmodel and Owen Fletcher, "Hummus Is Conquering America," *The Wall Street Journal*, accessed February 18, 2014, http://online.wsj.com.
2. Company website, www.garbetthomes.com, accessed February 14, 2014.
3. Company website, www.stouffers.com, accessed February 14, 2014; Organization website, www.casacolumbia.org, accessed February 14, 2014.
4. "McDonald's Testing Mobile App in Australia," *Mobile Payments Today*, accessed February 15, 2014, www.mobilepaymentstoday.com; Leslie Patton, "McDonald's Testing Mobile Order App for U.S. Stores," *Bloomberg Businessweek*, September 10, 2013, www.bloomberg.com.
5. Dale Buss, "Domino's Global Growth Feeds Pizza Chain's Rising Success," *Forbes*, accessed February 17, 2014, www.forbes.com.
6. U.S. Population Clock Projection website, www.census.gov, accessed September 3, 2014; Jennifer M. Ortman and Christine E. Guarneri, "United States Population Projections: 2000 to 2050," accessed February 16, 2014, www.census.gov; U.S. Department of Health and Human Services Administration on Aging, "Aging Statistics," accessed February 16, 2014, www.aoa.gov.
7. U.S. Census Bureau, "U.S. Census Bureau Projections Show a Slower Growing, Older, More Diverse Nation a Half Century from Now," press release, accessed February 16, 2014, www.census.gov.
8. "Census Bureau Reports National Mover Rate Increases after a Record Low in 2011," press release, accessed December 20, 2013, http://www.census.gov; U.S. Census Bureau, "Geographic Mobility/Migration: 2012 to 2013," November 15, 2013, http://www.census.gov.
9. Mark Hugo Lopez, Ana Gonzalez-Barrera, and Danielle Cuddington, "Diverse Origins: The Nation's 14 Largest Hispanic-Origin Groups," Pew Research Hispanic Trends Project, June 19, 2013, http://www.pewhispanic.org.
10. College Board Advocacy and Policy Center, "78.3% of All Latinos in the U.S. Live in Ten States," accessed February 14, 2014, http://completionagenda.collegeboard.org.
11. "Hispanics & Mobile Phones," *Latino Briefs Digest*, accessed February 14, 2014, http://ucanr.edu.
12. Elena Etcharren, "Why CPG Marketers Need to Reach Hispanic Shoppers," *CMO*, accessed February 14, 2014, www.cmo.com.
13. "African-American Consumers Are More Relevant Than Ever," *Nielsen.com*, press release, accessed February 18, 2014, www.nielsen.com.
14. Organization website, "14 Important Statistics about Asian Americans," www.asian-nation.org, accessed February 15, 2014; Gracie Zheng, "Nielsen Highlights the Buying Power of Asian Americans," *V3con*, accessed February 15, 2014, http://v3con.com.
15. Company website, "State of the Asian American Consumer," accessed February 18, 2014, www.nielsen.com.
16. Restaurant website, www.sorabolrestaurants.com, accessed February 15, 2014.
17. Company website, http://www.dogsmith.com, accessed February 18, 2014.
18. Company website, http://hannaandersson.com, accessed February 18, 2014.
19. Mary Madden, Amanda Lenhart, Maeve Duggan, Sandra Cortesi, Urs Gasser, "Teens and Technology," Pew Research Center, accessed February 16, 2014, www.pewinternet.org; Vahe Habeshian, "Social Media Becomes Less Important to Teens," *MarketingProfs.com*, accessed February 16, 2014, www.marketingprofs.com.
20. Jean E. Palmieri, "Saks Fifth Avenue Revamping Men's Private Label," *Women's Wear Daily*, accessed February 15, 2014, www.wwd.com.
21. Tourism website for Bermuda, "Bermuda: So Much More," www.gotobermuda.com, accessed February 15, 2014; company website, www.dreamresorts.com, accessed February 14, 2014; advertisement for Maserati, *Conde Nast Traveler*, December 2013.
22. Moira Forbes, "Billionaire Tory Burch's Seven Lessons for Entrepreneurs," *Forbes*, accessed February 18, 2014, www.forbes.com; Laura M. Holson, "What Does Tory Burch Want?" *The New York Times*, accessed February 18, 2014, www.nytimes.com.
23. David Koeppel, "Supermarket Bromance: More Men Are Shopping," *Money*, accessed February 18, 2014, http://money.msn.com.
24. Sue Mead, "Women Flex Their Car Buying Muscles," *Boston.com*, accessed February 15, 2014, http://www.boston.com; Catherine Green, "Gender Divide on the Car Lot: Women Shop Safety, Men Shop Style," *Los Angeles Times*, accessed February 15, 2014, www.latimes.com.
25. "Kids Spending and Influencing Power: $1.2 Trillion Says Leading Ad Firm," *Center for Digital Democracy*, accessed February 18, 2014, www.democraticmedia.org.
26. Martha C. White, "American Families Increasingly Let Kids Make Buying Decisions," *Time*, April 11, 2013, http://business.time.com.
27. Company website, "Mannequin Installers," accessed February 15, 2014, www.lvmannequins.com.
28. "The Second Coming of the 30-Second Spot," *Social Media Week*, accessed February 18, 2014, http://socialmediaweek.org.
29. "Pure Michigan Starts Fall Campaign," *CBS Detroit*, accessed February 18, 2014, http://detroit.cbs.local.com; Melissa Anders, "Pure Michigan Campaign Helped Attract More Out-of-State Visitors This Fourth of July, Hotels Say," *mlive*, accessed February 18, 2014, http://www.mlive.com.
30. Brett Casella, "Neuromarketing 101: What Is Neuromarketing and How Are Companies Using It?" *impactbnd.com*, accessed February 18, 2014, http://www.impactbnd.com.
31. North Carolina Sweet Potatoes website, www.ncsweetpotatoes.com, accessed February 18, 2014.
32. Company website, https://creditcards.chase.com, accessed February 18, 2014.
33. Company website, www.shinola.com, accessed February 18, 2014; Joann Muller, "In Bankrupt Detroit, Shinola Puts Its Faith in American Manufacturing," *Forbes*, accessed February 18, 2014, www.forbes.com.
34. Carolyn Cutrone, "Cutting Down on Choice Is the Best Way to Make Better Decisions," *Business Insider*, accessed February 18, 2014, www.businessinsider.com.
35. Company website, http://www.bizrate.com, accessed February 18, 2014.
36. Ashley Lutz, "Budget-Conscious Consumers Are Abandoning Wal-Mart for Dollar Stores," *Business Insider*, accessed February 14, 2014, www.businessinsider.com.
37. Ryan Chittum, "Lessons from *The Dallas Morning News's* Failed Paywall," *Columbia Journalism Review*, accessed February 18, 2014, www.cjr.org.

Chapter 7

Business-to-Business (B2B) Marketing

1. Explain the four components of the business-to-business (B2B) market.
2. Describe the major approaches to segmenting business-to-business (B2B) markets.
3. Identify the major characteristics of the business market and its demand.
4. Discuss the decision to make, buy, or lease goods and services.
5. Describe the major influences on business buying behavior.
6. Outline the eight steps in the organizational buying process.
7. Describe the three organizational buying situations.
8. Explain the buying center concept.
9. Discuss the challenges and strategies for marketing to government, institutional, and international buyers.

GE GOES SOCIAL FOR B2B

GE knows that more than 90 percent of B2B buyers report using social media in their decision processes. In fact, the company has developed an enviable reputation in its industry for its forward-thinking and successful use of social media and a growing list of mobile apps to find and generate new corporate business. GE's B2B marketing arm uses popular sites such as LinkedIn, where it hosts several targeted groups; Facebook, where its page has garnered more than 1.3 million "likes"; and Twitter, where it has more than 260,000 followers. The company uses multiple social channels for its goods and services to engage with its B2B partners and consumers. With these digital and social media efforts, GE builds on the high standards it sets for the B2B customer experience in the industries in which it operates, which are as diverse as aviation, energy, media, health care technology, and financial services.

GE wants to deliver content it considers "micro-relevant," which means it reaches just the right customers rather than the biggest audience, and it delivers content that's specific to their needs. Its mobile apps allow restaurants to estimate the energy savings they can reap with more energy-efficient lighting, for instance, or let railroads monitor their tracks and gather diagnostics on their locomotives. Another app helps manage gas turbines and electric transformers, while another allows health care professionals to review x-rays images using wi-fi technology.

The company is so enthusiastic about using social media to reach its B2B customers that it has even embraced the possibilities offered by Pinterest, the rapidly growing scrapbook-like website that's especially popular with women ages 20 through 40. Some B2B marketers feel Pinterest has little to offer them, but GE is finding that its sample posts—selected inspirational words from Thomas Edison (the company's founder)—have drawn considerable Pinterest traffic (more than 23,000 followers and growing).

Despite the social media initiatives the company has already undertaken, GE believes it has only scratched the surface of mobile and social media marketing, especially for its B2B customers. Look for more to come.[1]

EVOLUTION OF A BRAND

When we think of social networking sites, we usually imagine ourselves posting status updates or photos to share with family and friends. But companies such as GE recognize the potential for B2B outreach, given how many buyers rely on social media when making purchasing decisions. GE has wholeheartedly committed itself to social media, availing itself of social networking sites ranging from LinkedIn and Facebook to Pinterest. Its Mobile App Store lists B2B applications, such as order tracking, order status, price, and availability. Its "Ecomagination" website features ideas that combine inventiveness and environmental consciousness. The company reaches the many industries it serves by focusing on specific customers and providing them with specific content.

- Linda Boff, the company's executive director for global brand marketing, says, "We use the mantra 'business is social' increasingly at GE. Social is accessible no matter how big your company is." How does this type of marketing improve GE's B2B outreach?
- One possible future innovation in social networking is the mobile-friendly corporate website. How might such a website help GE reach its business customers even more directly?

Chapter Overview

business-to-business (B2B) marketing
Organizational sales and purchases of goods and services to support production of other products, to facilitate daily company operations, or for resale.

We are all aware of the consumer marketplace. As consumers, we're involved in purchasing needed items almost every day. In addition, we can't help noticing the barrage of marketing messages aimed at us through various media. But the business-to-business marketplace is, in fact, significantly larger. U.S. companies pay more than $300 billion each year just for office and maintenance supplies. Government agencies contribute to the business-to-business market even further; for example, the Department of Defense budget request for one recent year was almost $500 billion.[2] U.S. business-to-business commerce conducted over the Internet now totals over $550 billion.[3]

Whether through face-to-face transactions, via telephone, or over the Internet, each day business marketers deal with complex purchasing decisions involving multiple decision makers. They range from simple reorders of previously purchased items to complex buys for which materials are imported from all over the world. They often involve the steady building of relationships between companies and customers as well as the ability to respond to changing circumstances in existing markets. Customer satisfaction and customer loyalty are major factors in the development of these long-term relationships.

This chapter discusses buying behavior in the business or organizational market. **Business-to-business (B2B) marketing** deals with organizational sales and purchases of goods and services to support production of other products, to facilitate daily company operations, or for resale. But you ask, "How do I go about distinguishing between consumer purchases and B2B transactions?" Actually, it's pretty simple. Just ask yourself two questions: (1) Who is buying the good or service? and (2) Why is the purchase being made?

Consumer buying involves purchases made by individuals. We purchase items for our own use and enjoyment—and not for resale. By contrast, B2B purchases are made by businesses, government, and marketing intermediaries to be resold, combined with other items to create a finished product for resale, or used up in the operations of the organization. So ask yourself the two questions—"Who is buying?" and "Why?"—and you have the answer.

NATURE OF THE BUSINESS MARKET

Firms usually sell fewer standardized products to organizational buyers than to ultimate consumers. Although you might purchase a cell phone for your personal use, a company generally has to purchase an entire communications system from a supplier such as AT&T, whose OneNet Service offers digital voice and Internet technology in a single business network.[4] Purchases like this require greater customization, more decision making, and usually more decision makers. So the buying and selling process becomes more complex, often involving teams and taking an average of 6 to 36 months to make decisions. Because of the complexity of the purchases, customer service is extremely important to B2B buyers. Advertising plays a much smaller role in the business market than in the consumer market, although social media strategies have become commonplace in business marketing. Business marketers advertise primarily to announce new products,

TABLE 7.1 Comparing Business-to-Business Marketing and Consumer Marketing

	Business-to-Business Marketing	Consumer Marketing
Product	Relatively technical in nature; exact form often variable; accompanying services very important	Standardized form; service important but less than for business products
Promotion	Emphasis on personal selling	Emphasis on advertising
Distribution	Relatively short, direct channels to market	Product passes through a number of intermediate links en route to consumer
Customer Relations	Relatively enduring and complex	Comparatively infrequent contact; relationship of relatively short duration
Decision-Making Process	Diverse group of organization members makes decision	Individual or household unit makes decision
Price	Competitive bidding for unique items; list prices for standard items	List prices

to build brand awareness, and to attract potential customers who would then deal directly with a salesperson. Personal selling plays a much bigger role in business markets than in consumer markets, distribution channels are shorter, customer relationships tend to last longer, and purchase decisions can involve multiple decision makers. Table 7.1 compares the marketing practices commonly used in both B2B and consumer marketing.

Like final consumers, an organization purchases products to fill needs. However, its primary need—meeting the demands of its own customers—is similar from firm to firm. A manufacturer buys raw materials, such as wood pulp, fabric, or grain, to create the company's product. A wholesaler or retailer buys the manufactured products—paper, clothing, or cereal—to resell. Mattel buys everything from plastic to paints to produce its toys; FAO Schwartz buys finished toys to sell to the public. Passenger airlines buy or lease aircraft from Boeing and Airbus. Wilson Sporting Goods supplies the National Football League with its official game ball, "The Duke." Institutional purchasers such as government agencies and not-for-profit organizations also buy products to meet the needs of their employees, whether it is global positioning system (GPS) mapping devices or meals ready to eat (MREs) for troops in the field.

Companies also buy services from other businesses. A firm may purchase legal and accounting services, office-cleaning services, call-center services, or recruiting services. Jan-Pro is a commercial cleaning service company that has been in business since 1991. The chain has more than 100 master franchise offices throughout the United States, Canada, and nine other countries, and more than 10,000 individual franchise operations in the United States alone.[5]

Environmental, organizational, and interpersonal factors are among the many influences in B2B markets. Budget, cost, and profit considerations all play parts in business buying decisions. In addition, the business buying process typically involves complex interactions among many people. An organization's goals must also be considered in the B2B buying process. Later sections of the chapter will explore these topics in greater detail.

Some firms focus entirely on business markets. For instance, DuPont sells materials, such as polymers, coatings, and color technologies, to manufacturers that use them in various products. Caterpillar makes construction and mining equipment, diesel and natural gas engines, and industrial gas turbines. SAP America provides collaborative business software that allows companies to work with customers and business partners using databases and other applications from every major software vendor. Other firms sell to both consumer and business markets. Knoll makes award-winning office furniture as well as stylish furniture for the home, and Intel's digital and wireless computer technology is found in business computing systems and personal computers. Note also that marketing strategies developed in consumer marketing often are appropriate for the business sector. Final consumers

Knoll Furniture sells office and home furniture to both the business and consumer markets.

1 Explain the four components of the business-to-business (B2B) market.

commercial market Individuals and firms that acquire products to support, directly or indirectly, production of other goods and services.

trade industries Retailers or wholesalers that purchase products for resale to others.

resellers Marketing intermediaries that operate in the trade sector.

often are the end users of products sold into the business market and, as explained later in the chapter, can influence the buying decision.

The B2B market is diverse. Transactions can range from orders as small as a box of paper clips or a printer cartridge for a home-based business to transactions as large as thousands of parts for an automobile manufacturer or massive turbine generators for an electric power plant. As mentioned earlier, businesses are also big purchasers of services such as telecommunications, computer consulting, and transportation services. See the "Solving an Ethical Controversy" feature for a discussion of one of the problems companies face in their increasing reliance on mobile phones.

Four major categories define the business market: (1) the commercial market, (2) trade industries, (3) government organizations, and (4) institutions.

COMPONENTS OF THE BUSINESS MARKET

The **commercial market** is the largest segment of the business market. It includes all individuals and firms that acquire products to support, directly or indirectly, production of other goods and services. When Dell buys computer chips from Intel, that transaction takes place in the commercial market. It's the same when Pepperidge Farm purchases wheat to mill into flour for an ingredient in its baked goods and a plant supervisor orders light bulbs and cleaning supplies for a factory in Tennessee. Some products aid in the production of other items (for example, screens for smartphones). Others are physically used up in the production of a good or service (the wheat). Still others contribute to the firm's day-to-day operations (the maintenance supplies). The commercial market includes manufacturers, farmers, and other members of resource-producing industries; construction contractors; and providers of services such as transportation, public utilities, financing, insurance, and real-estate brokerage.

The second segment of the organizational market, **trade industries**, includes retailers and wholesalers, known as **resellers**, who operate in this sector. Most resale products, such as clothing, appliances, sports equipment, and automobile parts, are finished goods that buyers sell to final consumers. ACCO Brands supplies paper clips, ring binders, vinyl envelopes, sheet protectors, and fasteners to Office Depot.[6] In other cases, the buyers may complete some processing or repackaging before reselling the products. A retail meat market may purchase a side of beef and then cut individual pieces for its customers. Lumber dealers and carpet retailers may purchase in bulk and then provide quantities and sizes to meet customers' specifications. In addition to resale products, trade industries buy computers, display shelves, and other products needed to operate their businesses. All of these goods—as well as maintenance items and specialized services such as scanner installation, newspaper inserts, and radio advertising—represent organizational purchases.

The government category of the business market includes domestic units of government—federal, state, and local—as well as foreign governments. This important market segment makes a wide variety of purchases, ranging from highways to military uniforms to Internet services. The primary motivation of government purchasing is to provide some form of public

SOLVING AN ETHICAL CONTROVERSY
Making It Difficult for Phone Scammers

Phone spoofing allows callers to subvert caller ID by hiding behind someone else's number. Although the Federal Trade Commission (FTC) and Federal Communications Commission (FCC) both prohibit telemarketers from using phone spoofing services, which are inexpensive and legal, scammers increasingly use them for illegal purposes. Criminals can perpetrate identify theft under cover of a legitimate business's phone number and gain access to mobile voice mailboxes, obtaining just enough personal information about the owner to enter the victim's online bank and credit card accounts and raid them for sensitive information. They can then call the bank to transfer cash or trigger the issuance of duplicate credit cards. Most major mobile carriers offer customers password protection for voice mail, making it more difficult for fraudsters to get in.

Should mobile phone carriers be required to make it harder for crooks to use phone spoofing?

PRO
1. Privacy advocates find it "alarming that virtually anyone can get access to your payment and purchase information." Phone carriers can easily make this crime more difficult.
2. Businesses are especially at risk because banks often don't reimburse them for financial losses from online accounts. U.S. and European losses can total more than $1 billion a year.

CON
1. Business and individual mobile users want ready access to their information. Mandating an extra step such as password verification reduces the convenience of the voice mail service for them.
2. Business owners should be savvy enough to use all available tools, such as the password option, to protect themselves from possible fraud.

Summary
Both the FTC and the FCC are considering new and stronger rules against phone spoofing, and Congress passed the Truth in Caller ID Act several years ago. But businesses should be aware that any type of mobile communications is a growth area for spoofing.

Sources: Federal Communications Commission, "Caller ID and Spoofing," accessed February 18, 2014, www.fcc.gov; Bill McGinty, "How to Protect Your Cell Number from Being 'Spoofed,'" wcnc.com, accessed February 18, 2014, www.wcnc.com; Emily Patterson, "Scammers Impersonate Police with Spoofed Caller ID," *Better Business Bureau*, accessed February 16, 2014, www.bbb.org; David Lazarus, "When Caller ID Gets Spoofed," *Los Angeles Times*, accessed February 10, 2014, http://articles.latimes.com; Kevin Hunt, "Who Stole My Phone Number?" *The Courant*, accessed February 10, 2014, http://articles.courant.com.

---

benefit, such as national defense or pollution control. But government agencies have also become creative when it comes to selling; local police departments and state and federal agencies sell unclaimed shipments, confiscated goods, and seized real estate property on Internet auction sites. Lucky bidders might be able to buy a custom yacht for their business, a sausage grinder for their restaurant, or an auto transmission for their delivery truck through an Internet auction.[7]

Institutions, both public and private, are the fourth component of the business market. This category includes a wide range of organizations, such as hospitals, churches, skilled care and rehabilitation centers, colleges and universities, museums, and not-for-profit agencies. Some institutions,

Considered a reseller, Illinois-based Edward Don & Company designs, sells, and installs food-service equipment for hotels, restaurants, and other institutions nationwide.

such as public higher education, must rigidly follow standardized purchasing procedures, but others have less formal buying practices. Business-to-business marketers often benefit by setting up separate divisions to sell to institutional buyers.

B2B MARKETS: THE INTERNET CONNECTION

Although consumers' use of Internet markets receives the bulk of public attention, about 91 percent of all Internet sales are B2B transactions.[8] Many business-to-business marketers have set up private portals that allow their customers to buy needed items. Service and customized pages are accessed through passwords provided by B2B marketers. Online auctions and virtual marketplaces offer other ways for buyers and vendors to connect with each other over the Internet. See the "Marketing Success" feature for the innovative way the online service Foursquare is connecting with new business customers.

During the early Internet boom, start-up companies rushed to connect buyers and sellers without considering basic marketing principles such as targeting their customers and making sure to fulfill their needs. As a result, many of these companies failed. But the companies that survived—and new firms that have learned lessons from others' mistakes—have established a much stronger marketing presence. For instance, they recognize that their business customers have a lot at stake and expect greater value and utility from the goods and services they purchase as well as streamlined marketing communications, delivered through social media, email, blogs, and podcasts.[9] Another way for marketers to connect with each other online is through affiliate marketing. The Internet also opens up foreign markets to sellers. One such firm, which began as a cotton exchange called The Seam, survived the Internet boom and bust and is now bringing together global buyers of commodities such as cotton, peanuts, and grain.[10]

DIFFERENCES IN FOREIGN BUSINESS MARKETS

When The Seam first moved into other countries, its marketers had to consider that foreign business markets might differ due to variations in government regulations and cultural practices. Some business products need modifications to succeed in foreign markets. In Australia, Japan, and Great Britain, for instance, motorists drive on the left side of the road. American-made automobiles must be modified to accommodate such differences.

MARKETING SUCCESS
Foursquare Connects with Business Partners

Background. Foursquare, the free online service that helps users find out where friends are and what they're doing, has grown to include more than 50 million people worldwide. More than 2 million businesses have registered on its Merchant Platform, which allows them to offer custom deals and rewards, called "Specials," to Foursquare users who "check in" with the business.

The Challenge. Its developers have been looking for even more ways to expand the services Foursquare can offer to businesses, especially retailers that depend on foot traffic to drive sales volume. At the same time, it wants to improve users' experience of "exploring the real world" and let them tell friends even more about what they're doing.

The Strategy. Foursquare has partnered with third-party companies such as MovieTickets.com, ESPN, and SongKick to launch its Events platform. This application provides users with information about events such as movies, sporting events, and concerts that take place near them when they check in with local businesses.

The Outcome. Foursquare has high hopes for its Events strategy and expects customers to share information about events the same way they now share news about specials. The company is already working on developing partnerships with other third parties and has been in discussions with tech companies such as Yahoo and Apple to share data. The company recently announced it was opening up ad space for advertisers of all sizes. By going to Foursquare's ads dashboard, small businesses can now create their own promotions to attract Foursquare users.

Sources: Company website, www.foursquare.com/business, accessed September 9, 2014; Matthew Panzarino, "Why Do People Keep Giving Foursquare Money?" *Tech Crunch*, accessed February 18, 2014, http://techcrunch.com; Anthony Ha, "Foursquare Raises $35M More, Says It Has 45M Registered Users," *Tech Crunch*, accessed February 18, 2014, http://techcrunch.com; Austin Carr, "Foursquare Opens Ad Platform to 1.5 Million Merchants," *Fast Company*, accessed February 18, 2014, www.fastcompany.com; Ingrid Lunden, "With an Eye to More Revenue, Foursquare Opens Ads Platform to All Small Businesses," *Tech Crunch*, accessed February 18, 2014, http://techcrunch.com; Austin Carr, "Why Yahoo and Apple Want Foursquare's Data," *Fast Company*, accessed February 18, 2014, www.fastcompany.com.

Business marketers must be willing to adapt to local customs and business practices when operating abroad. They should also research cultural preferences. Factors as deceptively simple as the time of a meeting and forms of address for associates can make a difference. A company even needs to consider what ink colors to use for documents because colors can have different meanings in different countries.

ASSESSMENT CHECK

1.1 Define B2B marketing.
1.2 What is the commercial market?

SEGMENTING B2B MARKETS

Business-to-business markets include wide varieties of customers, so marketers must identify the different market segments they serve. By applying market segmentation concepts to groups of business customers, a firm's marketers can develop a strategy that best suits a particular segment's needs. The overall process of segmenting business markets divides markets based on different criteria, usually organizational characteristics and product applications. Among the major ways to segment business markets are demographics (size), customer type, end-use application, and purchasing situation.

2 Describe the major approaches to segmenting business-to-business (B2B) markets.

SEGMENTATION BY DEMOGRAPHIC CHARACTERISTICS

As in consumer markets, demographic characteristics define useful segmentation criteria for business markets. For example, firms can be grouped by size, based on sales revenues or number of employees. Marketers may develop one strategy to reach Fortune 500 corporations with complex purchasing procedures and another strategy for small firms in which one or two people make the decisions. According to one study, many firms actually increase their outreach to small and midsize businesses. For the past several years, American Express has sponsored Small Business Saturday, an opportunity for consumers to "shop small" and patronize local small businesses over the Thanksgiving weekend, the traditional start of the holiday shopping season. American Express estimates $5.7 billion was spent at independent merchants on a recent Small Business Saturday, with more than 3 million "likes" on a Facebook page dedicated to the promotion.[11]

SEGMENTATION BY CUSTOMER TYPE

Another useful segmentation approach classifies prospects according to type of customer. Marketers can apply this concept in several ways. They can group customers by broad categories—manufacturer, service provider, government agency, not-for-profit organization, wholesaler, or retailer—and by industry. These groups may be further divided using other segmentation approaches discussed in this section.

customer-based segmentation Dividing a business-to-business market into homogeneous groups based on buyers' product specifications.

Customer-based segmentation is a related approach often used in the business-to-business marketplace. Organizational buyers tend to have much more precise—and complex—requirements for goods and services than ultimate consumers do. As a result, business products often fit narrower market segments than consumer products, which leads some firms to design business goods and services to meet detailed buyer specifications. Pasadena-based Tetra Tech provides various environmental services, including technology development, design, engineering, and pollution remediation for organizations around the world. Because the company's customers include government agencies as well as private firms—and because customers' needs are different—Tetra Tech has 14,000 employees and 330 offices worldwide that offer a range of programs to suit each type of customer. For instance, the firm provides consulting services for utilities, helps communities clean up polluted water sources, and even conducts programs to clear public and private sites of unexploded military supplies.[12]

North American Industry Classification System (NAICS)

In the 1930s, the U.S. government set up a uniform system for subdividing the business marketplace into detailed segments. The Standard Industrial Classification (SIC) system standardized efforts to collect and report information on U.S. industrial activity.

SIC codes divided firms into broad industry categories: agriculture, forestry, and fishing; mining and construction; manufacturing; transportation, communication, electric, gas, and sanitary services; wholesale trade; retail trade; finance, insurance, and real-estate services; public administration; and nonclassifiable establishments. The system assigned each major category within these classifications its own two-digit number. Three-digit and four-digit numbers further subdivided each industry into smaller segments.

North American Industry Classification System (NAICS) Classification used by NAFTA countries to categorize the business marketplace into detailed market segments.

For roughly 70 years, B2B marketers used SIC codes as a tool for segmenting markets and identifying new customers. The system, however, became outdated with implementation of the North American Free Trade Agreement. Each NAFTA member—the United States, Canada, and Mexico—had its own system for measuring business activity. NAFTA required a joint classification system that would allow marketers to compare business sectors among the member nations. In effect, marketers required a segmentation tool they could use across borders. The **North American Industry Classification System (NAICS)** replaced the SIC and provides more detail than previously available. The NAICS created new service sectors to better reflect the economy of the 21st century. They include information; health care and social assistance; and professional, scientific, and technical services.

Table 7.2 demonstrates the NAICS system for wholesale home furnishings. The NAICS uses six digits, compared with the four digits used in the SIC. The first five digits are fixed among the members of NAFTA. The sixth digit can vary among U.S., Canadian, and Mexican data. In short, the sixth digit accounts for specific data needs of each nation.[13]

TABLE 7.2 NAICS Classification for Home Furnishing Merchant Wholesalers

42	Wholesale Trade
423	Merchant Wholesalers, Durable Goods
4232	Furniture and Home Furnishing Merchant Wholesalers
42322	Home Furnishing Merchant Wholesalers
423220	Home Furnishing Merchant Wholesalers in the U.S. Industry

Source: NAICS, U.S. Census Bureau, **www.census.gov**, accessed February 19, 2014.

SEGMENTATION BY END-USE APPLICATION

A third basis for segmentation, **end-use application segmentation**, focuses on the precise way in which a business purchaser will use a product. For example, a printing equipment manufacturer may serve markets ranging from a local utility to a bicycle manufacturer to the U.S. Department of Defense. Each end use of the equipment may dictate unique specifications for performance, design, and price. Praxair, a supplier of industrial gases, for example, might segment its markets according to user. Steel and glass manufacturers might buy hydrogen and oxygen; food and beverage manufacturers need carbon dioxide. Praxair also sells krypton, a rare gas, to companies that produce lasers, lighting, and thermal windows. Many small and medium-sized companies also segment markets according to end-use application. Instead of competing in markets dominated by large firms, they concentrate on specific end-use market segments. The approximately 30 companies that manufacture wooden baseball bats for Major League Baseball focus on specific end users who are very different from the youth, high school, and college players who use aluminum bats.

end-use application segmentation The division of a business-to-business market based on how industrial purchasers will use the product.

SEGMENTATION BY PURCHASE CATEGORIES

Firms have different structures for their purchasing functions, and B2B marketers must adapt their strategies according to those organizational buyer characteristics. Some companies designate centralized purchasing departments to serve the entire firm. Others allow each unit to handle its own buying. A supplier may deal with one purchasing agent or several decision makers at various levels. Each of these structures results in different buying behavior.

When the buying situation is important to marketers, they typically consider whether the customer has made previous purchases or this is the customer's first order, offering special rates or programs for valued clients. Verizon Wireless offers government customers cell phone discounts as either credits or reimbursements.[14]

Increasingly, businesses that have developed **customer relationship management (CRM)** systems—strategies and tools that reorient an entire organization to focus on satisfying customers—can segment customers in terms of the stage of the relationship between the business and the customer. A B2B company, for example, might develop different strategies for newly acquired customers than it would for existing customers to which it hopes to sell new products. Similarly, building loyalty among satisfied customers requires a different approach than developing programs to "save" at-risk customer relationships. CRM will be covered in more depth in Chapter 11.

customer relationship management (CRM) Combination of strategies and tools that drives relationship programs, reorienting the entire organization to a concentrated focus on satisfying customers.

ASSESSMENT CHECK

2.1 What are the four major ways marketers segment business markets?

2.2 What is the NAICS?

CHARACTERISTICS OF THE B2B MARKET

> **3** Identify the major characteristics of the business market and its demand.

Businesses that serve both B2B and consumer markets must understand the needs of their customers. However, several characteristics distinguish the business market from the consumer market:

1. Geographic market concentration
2. The sizes and numbers of buyers
3. The purchase decision process
4. Buyer–seller relationships

The next sections consider how these traits influence business-to-business marketing.

GEOGRAPHIC MARKET CONCENTRATION

The U.S. business market is more geographically concentrated than the consumer market. Manufacturers converge in certain regions of the country, making these areas prime targets for business marketers. For example, the Midwestern states of Indiana, Wisconsin, Iowa, Michigan, and Ohio lead the nation in manufacturing concentration. The South, the Southwest, and the Pacific Northwest have also gained strength in recent years.[15]

Certain industries locate in particular areas to be close to customers. Firms may locate sales offices and distribution centers in these areas to provide more attentive service. For instance, the Washington, DC, area is favored by companies that sell to the federal government.

In the automobile industry, suppliers of components and assemblies frequently build plants close to their customers. Volkswagen's supplier park near its Chattanooga assembly plant is home to more than 17 different vendors. The campus, which has generated more than 2,500 jobs, allows suppliers to produce or assemble products close to the plant, reducing costs, controlling parts inventory, and increasing flexibility. The facility also includes the VW Training Academy, launched in partnership with Chattanooga State Community College. The academy combines classroom and lab instruction with hands-on training and recently graduated its first class of apprentices.[16] As Internet-based technology continues to expand, allowing companies to transact business even with distant suppliers, business markets may become less geographically concentrated. Much of government purchasing, for example, is now conducted through the Internet.

> **Briefly Speaking**
>
> "Don't be afraid to get creative and experiment with your marketing."
>
> —Mark Volpe
> *Chief Marketing Officer, HubSpot*

SIZES AND NUMBERS OF BUYERS

In addition to geographic concentration, the business market features a limited number of buyers. Marketers can draw on a wealth of statistical information to estimate the sizes and characteristics of business markets. The federal government is the largest single source of such statistics. It conducts an Annual Survey of Manufactures (ASM) and a Census of Retailing and Wholesaling, which provide detailed information on business establishments, output, and employment. Many government units and trade organizations also operate websites that contain helpful information.

Many buyers in limited-buyer markets are large organizations. A few large buyers, such as McDonald's, Wendy's, and Burger King, dominate the fast-food industry. These chains have the power to name the price they will pay cattle farmers for meat and can dictate living conditions and standards of labor on ranches.

Trade associations and business publications provide additional information on the business market. Private firms such as Dun & Bradstreet publish detailed reports on individual companies. These data are a useful starting point for analyzing a business market. Finding data in such a source requires an understanding of the NAICS, which identifies much of the available statistical information.

Having an enormous number of business customers with varying needs can pose quite a logistical challenge to a firm.

THE PURCHASE DECISION PROCESS

To market effectively to other organizations, businesses must understand the dynamics of the organizational purchase process. Suppliers who serve business-to-business markets must work with multiple buyers, especially when selling to larger customers. Decision makers at several levels may influence final orders, and the overall process is more formal and professional than the consumer purchasing process. Purchasers typically require a longer time frame because B2B involves more complex decisions. Suppliers must evaluate customer needs and develop proposals that meet technical requirements and specifications. Also, buyers need time to analyze competing proposals. Often, decisions require more than one round of bidding and negotiation, especially for complicated purchases.

BUYER–SELLER RELATIONSHIPS

An especially important characteristic of B2B marketing is the relationship between buyers and sellers. These relationships often are more complex than consumer relationships, and they require superior communication among the organizations' personnel. Satisfying one major customer may mean the difference of millions of dollars to a firm.

Relationship marketing involves developing long-term, value-added customer relationships. A primary goal of business-to-business relationships is to provide advantages that no other vendor can provide—lower price, quicker delivery, better quality and reliability, customized product features, more favorable financing terms, and so on. For the business marketer, providing these advantages means expanding the company's external relationships to include suppliers, distributors, and other organizational partners. Based in suburban Chicago, CDW, for instance, relies on various vendors to meet its own business, government, and education customers' technology needs with hardware, software, networking, and data storage. It has developed a CDW Supplier Diversity Program to increase and improve relationships with small-business suppliers owned by minorities, women, and veterans, and thus must manage its supplier as well as its customer relationships successfully.[17]

Close cooperation, whether through informal contacts or under terms specified in contractual partnerships and strategic alliances, enables companies to meet buyers' needs for quality products and customer service. This holds true both during and after the purchase process. Tetra Tech EC is a wholly owned subsidiary of Tetra Tech, mentioned earlier in the chapter. Tetra Tech EC has implemented formal Client Service Quality and Shared Vision programs, designed to engage customers in continuous communication leading to customer satisfaction.

Relationships between for-profit and not-for-profit organizations are also as important as those between two commercial organizations. Walmart is a longtime corporate sponsor of Children's Miracle Network, an international organization that helps improve children's health and welfare by raising funds for state-of-the-art care, cutting-edge research, and education. In one recent year, Walmart and Sam's Club raised and donated more than $40 million to 170 children's hospitals in the network.[18]

> **Briefly Speaking**
>
> "Every great business is built on friendship."
>
> —**J.C. Penney**
> *Founder, J.C. Penney Company*

EVALUATING INTERNATIONAL BUSINESS MARKETS

Business purchasing patterns differ from one country to the next. Researching these markets poses a particular problem for B2B marketers. Of course, as explained earlier, the NAICS has corrected this problem in the NAFTA countries.

In addition to assessing quantitative data such as the size of the potential market, companies must also carefully weigh its qualitative features. This process includes considering cultural values, work styles, and the best ways to enter overseas markets in general. The Coca-Cola Company, based in Atlanta, Georgia, has a presence in 200 countries worldwide. The company manages the sometimes volatile variations in culture and politics in Eurasia and Africa with a structure of locally based business units in five areas: Turkey and Central Asia; Middle East and North Africa; Russia, Ukraine, and Belarus; Central, East, and West Africa; and South Africa. A functional team in Istanbul manages finance, marketing, and strategy, working with each business unit to devise a

In a limited-buyer market such as fast food, a few large buyers, such as McDonald's, Wendy's, and Burger King, are the major customers.

global sourcing Purchasing goods and services from suppliers worldwide.

strategic plan for that unit's market. For example, the business unit in Turkey developed a special marketing campaign for the Muslim holy month of Ramadan. The campaign proved so successful that the company expanded it to other Muslim countries where Coca-Cola is sold.[19]

In today's international marketplace, companies often practice **global sourcing**, purchasing goods and services from suppliers worldwide. This practice can result in substantial cost savings, although product quality must be carefully monitored. India, Indonesia, and Estonia are the world's top destinations for outsourcing. Singapore, Bulgaria, China, the Philippines, Lithuania, Thailand, Malaysia, Sri Lanka, and Vietnam are also high on the list. South and Central American countries such as Chile, Argentina, and Costa Rica are also in the top 30.[20]

Global sourcing requires companies to adopt a new mindset; some must even reorganize their operations. Among other considerations, businesses sourcing from various multinational locations should streamline the purchase process and minimize price differences due to labor costs, tariffs, taxes, and currency fluctuations.

ASSESSMENT CHECK

3.1 Why is geographic segmentation important in the B2B market?

3.2 In what ways is the buyer–seller relationship important in B2B marketing?

3.3 What is global sourcing?

BUSINESS MARKET DEMAND

The previous section's discussion of business market characteristics demonstrates considerable differences between marketing techniques for consumer and business products. Demand characteristics also differ in these markets. In business markets, the major categories of demand include derived demand, volatile demand, joint demand, inelastic demand, and inventory adjustments. Figure 7.1 summarizes these different categories of business market demand.

DERIVED DEMAND

Derived demand refers to the linkage between demand for a company's output and its purchases of resources, such as machinery, components, supplies, and raw materials. The demand for computer microprocessor chips is *derived* from the demand for personal computers. If more businesses and individuals buy new computers, the demand for chips increases; if fewer computers are sold, the demand for chips decreases. Sales of PCs have dropped more than 15 percent over the past few years, as consumers have become more interested in mobile technology using tablets and smartphones. PC chipmakers such as Intel have had to switch their focus to developing processors for mobile devices.[21]

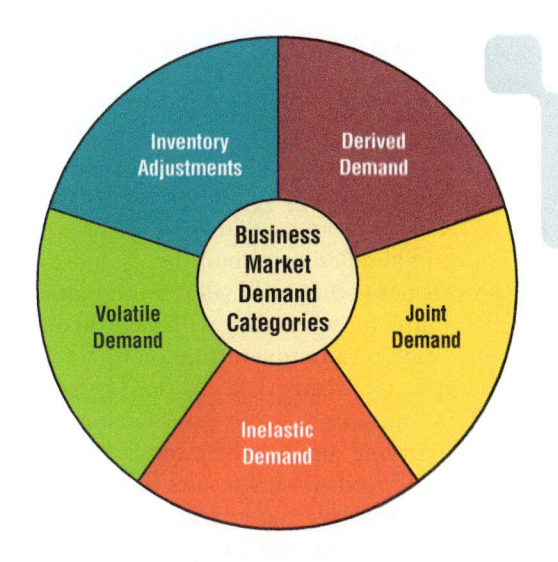

FIGURE 7.1 Categories of Business Market Demand

derived demand Demand for a resource that results from demand for the goods and services produced by that resource.

Organizational buyers purchase two general categories of business products: capital items and expense items. Derived demand ultimately affects both. Capital items are long-lived business assets that must be depreciated over time. *Depreciation* is an accounting term that refers to charging a portion of a capital item's cost as a deduction against the company's annual revenue for purposes of determining its net income. Examples of capital items include major installations such as new manufacturing plants, office buildings, and computer systems.

Expense items, in contrast, are items consumed within short time periods. Accountants charge the cost of such products against income in the year of purchase. Examples of expense items include the supplies necessary to operate the business, ranging from copy paper to machine lubricants.

VOLATILE DEMAND

Derived demand creates volatility in business market demand. Assume the sales volume for a gasoline retailer is increasing at an annual rate of 5 percent. Now suppose the demand for this gasoline brand slows to a 3 percent annual increase. This slowdown might persuade the firm to keep its current gasoline pumps and replace them only when market conditions improve. In this way, even modest shifts in consumer demand for a gasoline brand would greatly affect the pump manufacturer.

JOINT DEMAND

Another important influence on business market demand is **joint demand**, which results when the demand for one business product is related to the demand for another business product used in combination with the first item. Both lumber and concrete are required to build most homes. If the lumber supply falls, the drop in housing construction will most likely affect the demand for concrete. Another example is the joint demand for electrical power and large turbine engines. If consumers decide to conserve power, demand for new power plants drops, as does the demand for components and replacement parts for turbines.

joint demand Demand for a product that depends on the demand for another product used in combination with it.

INELASTIC DEMAND

Inelastic demand means that demand throughout an industry will not change significantly due to a price change. If the price of lumber drops, a construction firm will not necessarily buy more lumber from its suppliers unless another factor—such as lowered mortgage interest rates—causes more consumers to purchase new homes.

inelastic demand Demand that, throughout an industry, will not change significantly due to a price change.

INVENTORY ADJUSTMENTS

Adjustments in inventory and inventory policies can also affect business demand. Assume manufacturers in a particular industry consider a 60-day supply of raw materials as the optimal inventory level. Now suppose economic conditions or other factors induce these firms to increase their inventories to a 90-day supply. The change will bombard the raw-materials supplier with new orders.

Furthermore, **just-in-time (JIT)** inventory policies seek to boost efficiency by cutting inventories to absolute minimum levels and by requiring vendors to deliver inputs as the production process needs them. JIT allows companies to better predict which supplies they will require and the timing for when they will need them, markedly reducing their costs for production and storage. Widespread implementation of JIT has had a substantial impact on organizations' purchasing behavior. Firms that practice JIT tend to order from relatively few suppliers. In some cases, JIT may lead to **sole sourcing** for some items—that is, buying a firm's entire stock of a product from just one supplier. Electronic data interchange (EDI) and quick-response inventory policies have produced similar results in the trade industries. The latest inventory trend, **just-in-time II (JIT II)**, leads vendors to place representatives at the customer's facility to work as part of an integrated, on-site customer–supplier team. Suppliers plan and order in consultation with the customer. This streamlining of the inventory process improves control of the flow of goods.

Although inventory adjustments are critical in manufacturing processes, they are equally vital to wholesalers and retailers. Limited Brands, which owns Victoria's Secret and Bath & Body Works, recently upgraded its technology infrastructure and distribution centers. With a large variety of products, Victoria's Secret and Bath & Body Works benefited from improved inventory management, which sped up the process of keeping popular items in stock and removing those that didn't sell.[22]

just-in-time (JIT) Inventory practices that seek to boost efficiency by cutting inventories to absolute minimum levels. With JIT II, suppliers' representatives work at the customer's facility.

sole sourcing Purchasing a firm's entire stock of an item from just one vendor.

ASSESSMENT CHECK

3.4 How does derived demand create volatile demand?

3.5 Give an example of joint demand.

3.6 How might JIT II strengthen marketing relationships?

THE MAKE, BUY, OR LEASE DECISION

4 Discuss the decision to make, buy, or lease goods and services.

Before a company can decide what to buy, it should decide whether to buy at all. Organizational buyers must figure out the best way to acquire needed products. In fact, a firm considering the acquisition of a finished good, component part, or service has three basic options:

1. Make the good or provide the service in-house.

2. Purchase it from another organization.

3. Lease it from another organization.

If the company has the capability to do so, manufacturing the product itself may be the best route. It may save a great deal of money if its own manufacturing division does not incur costs for overhead that an outside vendor would otherwise charge.

On the other hand, most firms cannot make all the business goods they need. Often it would be too costly to maintain the necessary equipment and supplies. As a result, purchasing from an outside vendor is the most common choice. Xerox manufactures more than 50 types of color printers to meet nearly any business need—from affordable color laser printers to high-performance ink-jet printers. Its wide array of products, coupled with its track record of supplying businesses for more than a century, has made it a leader in the B2B printer market.[23] Companies can also look outside their own plants for goods and services formerly produced in-house, a practice called *outsourcing*, which the next section will describe in more detail.

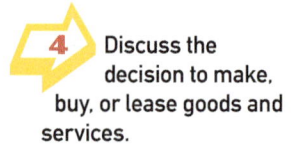

In some cases, however, a company may choose to lease inputs. This option spreads out costs compared with lump-sum costs for up-front purchases. The company pays for the use of equipment for a certain time period. A small business may lease a copier for a few years and make monthly payments. At the end of the lease term, the firm can buy the machine at a prearranged price or replace it with a different model under a new lease. This option can provide useful flexibility for a growing business, allowing it to easily upgrade as its needs change.

Companies can also lease sophisticated computer systems and heavy equipment. For example, some airlines prefer to lease airplanes rather than buy them outright because short-term leases allow them to adapt quickly to changes in passenger demand.

THE RISE OF OFFSHORING AND OUTSOURCING

Chances are, if you dial a call center for a firm such as Dell, GE, or American Express, your call may be answered by someone in India. In recent years, a firestorm has been ignited by the movement of U.S. jobs to lower-cost overseas locations, a business practice referred to as **offshoring**. This relocation of business processes to a lower-cost location can involve production offshoring or services offshoring. China continues to be the preferred destination for production offshoring, while India is still the dominant player in services offshoring.

Some U.S.-based firms want to remain closer to home but take advantage of the benefits of locating some of their operations overseas. Mexico and Canada are attractive locations for these **nearshoring** operations. In today's highly competitive marketplace, firms look outside the United States to improve efficiency and cut costs on just about everything, including customer service, human resources, accounting, information technology, manufacturing, and distribution. **Outsourcing**, using outside vendors to produce goods and services formerly produced in-house, is a trend that continues to rise. Businesses outsource for several reasons: (1) they need to reduce costs to remain competitive, (2) they need to improve the quality and speed of software maintenance and development, and (3) outsourcing has begun to offer greater value than ever before.

Outsourcing allows firms to concentrate their resources on their core business. It also allows access to specialized talent or expertise that does not exist within the firm. The most frequently outsourced business functions include information technology (IT) and human resources, along with other white-collar service jobs, such as accounting, drug research, technical research and development (R&D), and film animation. Although most outsourcing is done by North American companies, the practice is rapidly becoming commonplace in Asia, Europe, and Central America.

China has led the way in offshore manufacturing, making two-thirds of the world's copiers, microwaves, DVD players, shoes, and virtually all of the world's toys. The size of its manufacturing workforce in the Guangdong province is estimated to rival that of the entire United States. In recent years, however, China's very success and the resulting rise of an increasingly wealthy middle class have pushed up its labor and management costs and have helped shift many companies to suppliers in Vietnam and India, where such costs are still low.[24]

Outsourcing can be a smart strategy if a company chooses a vendor that can provide high-quality products and perhaps at a lower cost than could be achieved by the company itself. This priority allows the outsourcer to focus on its core competencies. Successful outsourcing requires companies to carefully oversee contracts and manage relationships. Some vendors now provide performance guarantees to assure their customers they will receive high-quality services that meet their needs.

offshoring Movement of high-cost jobs from one country to lower-cost overseas locations.

nearshoring Moving jobs to vendors in countries close to the business's home country.

outsourcing Using outside vendors to provide goods and services formerly produced in-house.

PROBLEMS WITH OFFSHORING AND OUTSOURCING

Offshoring and outsourcing are not without their downsides. Many companies discover their cost savings are less than vendors sometimes promise. Also, companies that sign multiyear contracts may find their savings drop after a year or two. When proprietary technology is an issue, outsourcing raises security concerns. Similarly, if companies are protective of customer data and relationships they may think twice about entrusting functions such as customer service to outside sources.

In some cases, outsourcing and offshoring can reduce a company's ability to respond quickly to the marketplace, or they can slow efforts in bringing new products to market. Suppliers that fail to deliver goods promptly or provide required services can adversely affect a company's reputation with its customers.

Outsourcing and offshoring are controversial topics with unions, especially in the auto industry, as the percentage of component parts made in-house has steadily dropped. These practices can create conflicts between nonunion outside workers and in-house union employees, who fear job loss. Management initiatives to outsource jobs can lead to strikes and plant shutdowns. Even if they do not lead to disruption in the workplace, outsourcing and offshoring can have a negative impact on employee morale and loyalty.

> **ASSESSMENT CHECK**
>
> 4.1 Identify two potential benefits of outsourcing.
>
> 4.2 Identify two potential problems with outsourcing.

THE BUSINESS BUYING PROCESS

5 Describe the major influences on business buying behavior.

Suppose that MyMap Inc., a hypothetical manufacturer of GPS devices for automakers, decides to upgrade its manufacturing facility with $5 million in new automated assembly equipment. Before approaching equipment suppliers, the company must analyze its needs, determine goals the project should accomplish, develop technical specifications for the equipment, and set a budget. Once it receives vendors' proposals, it must evaluate them and select the best one. But what does *best* mean in this context? The lowest price or the best warranty and service contract? Who in the company is responsible for such decisions?

The business buying process is more complex than the consumer decision process. Business buying takes place within a formal organization's budget, cost, and profit considerations. Furthermore, B2B and institutional buying decisions usually involve many people with complex interactions among individuals and organizational goals. To understand organizational buying behavior, business marketers require knowledge of influences on the purchase decision process, the stages in the organizational buying model, types of business buying situations, and techniques for purchase decision analysis.

INFLUENCES ON PURCHASE DECISIONS

B2B buying decisions react to various influences, some external to the firm and others related to internal structure and personnel. In addition to product-specific factors such as purchase price, installation, operating and maintenance costs, and vendor service, companies must consider broader environmental, organizational, and interpersonal influences.

Environmental Factors

Environmental conditions, such as economic, political, regulatory, competitive, and technological considerations, influence business buying decisions. MyMap may wish to defer purchases of the new equipment in times of slowing economic activity. During a slowdown, sales to auto companies might drop because consumers hesitate to spend money on a new car. The company would look at the derived demand for its products, possible changes in its sources of materials, employment trends, and similar factors before committing to such a large capital expenditure.

Environmental factors can also include natural disasters, such as Superstorm Sandy, which affected more than ten states, caused more than $65 billion in damages and economic losses, and severely damaged or destroyed more than 200,000 businesses. One such company was IceStone, a countertop manufacturer in Brooklyn, New York. With more than five feet of salt water in its factory, the company lost several hundred thousand dollars' worth of equipment, and the CEO thought about closing the business. Instead, he and his 38 employees cleaned up and renovated the factory and existing inventory, fixed the damaged equipment, and were back making countertops six months later.[25]

Political, regulatory, and competitive factors also come into play in influencing purchase decisions. Passage of a privacy law that restricted GPS tracking would affect demand, as would competition from smartphones and other devices containing map features. Finally, technology plays a role in purchase decisions. When GPS systems were first introduced, many customers bought separate units to install in their cars. But as more new cars come factory-equipped with the units, the market for standalone boxes naturally decreases.

Organizational Factors

Successful business-to-business marketers understand their customers' organizational structures, policies, and purchasing systems. A company with a centralized procurement function operates differently from one that delegates purchasing decisions to divisional or geographic units. Trying to sell to the local store when head office merchandisers make all the decisions would clearly waste salespeople's time. Buying behavior also differs among firms. For example, centralized buying tends to emphasize long-term relationships, whereas decentralized buying focuses more on short-term results. Personal selling skills and user preferences carry more weight in decentralized purchasing situations than in centralized buying.

How many suppliers should a company patronize? Because purchasing operations spend more than half of each dollar their companies earn, consolidating vendor relationships can lead to large cost savings. However, a fine line separates maximizing buying power from relying too heavily on a few suppliers. Many companies engage in **multiple sourcing**—purchasing from several vendors. Spreading orders ensures against shortages if one vendor cannot deliver on schedule. However, dealing with many sellers can be counterproductive and take too much time. Each company must set its own criteria for this decision.

multiple sourcing Purchasing from several vendors.

Interpersonal Influences

Many people may influence B2B purchases, and considerable time may be spent obtaining the input and approval of various organization members. Both group and individual forces are at work here. When committees handle buying, they must spend time to gain majority or unanimous approval. Also, each buyer brings to the decision process individual preferences, experiences, and biases. See the "Career Readiness" feature for some tips on negotiating with these individual buyers.

Business marketers should know who in an organization will influence buying decisions for their products and should know each of their priorities. To choose a supplier for an industrial press, for example, a purchasing manager and representatives of the company's production, engineering,

Environmental factors include natural disasters, such as Superstorm Sandy, which devastated homes and businesses along the U.S. East Coast.

> "Think like a customer."
> —Paul Gillin
> *Author and B2B social media strategist*

and quality control departments may be involved in deciding on a supplier. Each of these principals may have a different point of view that the vendor's marketers must understand.

To effectively address the concerns of all people involved in the buying decision, sales personnel must be well versed in the technical features of their products. They must also interact well with employees of the various departments involved in the purchase decision. Sales representatives for medical products—traditionally called "detailers"—frequently visit hospitals and doctors' offices to discuss the advantages of their products and leave samples with clinical staff.

The Role of Merchandisers and Category Advisors

Many large organizations attempt to make their purchases through systematic procedures employing professional buyers. In the trade industries, these buyers, often referred to as **merchandisers**, secure needed products at the best possible prices. Macy's has buyers for shoes and clothing that will ultimately be sold to consumers. Chrysler has buyers for components that will be incorporated into its cars and trucks. A firm's purchasing or merchandising unit devotes all of its time and effort in determining needs, locating and evaluating alternative suppliers, and making purchase decisions.

Purchase decisions for capital items vary significantly from those for expense items. Firms often buy expense items routinely with little delay. Capital items, however, involve major fund commitments and usually undergo considerable review.

One way a firm may attempt to streamline the buying process is through **systems integration**, or centralization of the procurement function. One company may designate a lead division to handle all purchasing. Another firm may choose to designate a major supplier as the systems integrator.

merchandisers Trade sector buyers who secure needed products at the best possible prices.

systems integration Centralization of the procurement function within an internal division or as a service of an external supplier.

Career Readiness
How to Negotiate with Customers

In a business situation, there will be occasions when you'll need to rely on your negotiating skills to interact with customers. Here are some tried-and-true tips.

1. Do your homework first. Before you begin a negotiation, you should already have a good general idea what the customer's needs and wants are and what other options they have for meeting these.

2. Listen. Now it pays to be a bit of a detective and simply listen while the other party tells you what you need to know to close the deal.

3. Read body language. Don't overlook the importance of what people tell you with their gestures, position, and eye contact.

4. Agree in advance about what you are negotiating. Don't assume the negotiation is all about price. Customers may want to negotiate a better deal on service, an earlier delivery date, more add-on features, replacement parts, and the like.

5. Believe in the value of what you're selling.

6. Avoid the word "between." If you propose a range, you give the other party the ability to choose the lower price or later delivery date, giving up ground when you don't need to.

7. Don't commit anything to writing until the negotiation is over.

Sources: Ed Brodow, "Ten Tips for Negotiating in 2014," *Brodow.com*, accessed February 13, 2014, www.brodow.com; Mark Hunter, "6 Sales Negotiation Tips You MUST Know," *TheSalesHunter.com*, accessed February 13, 2014, http://thesaleshunter.com; Mike Hofman, "5 Things You Should Never Say While Negotiating," *Inc.*, accessed February 13, 2014, www.inc.com; Erik Sherman, "5 Negotiation Tips from Steve Jobs," *Time*, accessed February 12, 2014, http://business.time.com; blog Staff, "5 Tips for Closing the Deal," *Harvard Law School Daily Blog*, accessed February 12, 2014, www.pon.harvard.edu.

Chapter 7 Business-to-Business (B2B) Marketing

This vendor then assumes responsibility for dealing with all of the suppliers for a project and for presenting the entire package to the buyer. In trade industries, this vendor is sometimes called a **category advisor or category captain**.

A business marketer may set up a sales organization to serve national accounts that deal solely with buyers at corporate headquarters. A separate field sales organization may serve buyers at regional production facilities.

Corporate buyers often use the Internet to identify sources of supplies. They view online catalogs and websites to compare vendors' offerings and obtain product information. Some use Internet exchanges to extend their supplier networks.

category advisor or category captain Trade industry vendor who develops a comprehensive procurement plan for a retail buyer.

> **ASSESSMENT CHECK**
>
> 5.1 Identify the three major factors that influence purchase decisions.
>
> 5.2 What are the advantages and disadvantages of multiple sourcing?

MODEL OF THE ORGANIZATIONAL BUYING PROCESS

An organizational buying situation takes place through a sequence of activities. Figure 7.2 illustrates an eight-stage model of an organizational buying process. Although not every buying situation requires all these steps, this figure provides a good overview of the whole process.

> **6** Outline the eight steps in the organizational buying process.

Stage 1: Anticipate or Recognize a Problem/Need/Opportunity and a General Solution

Both consumer and business purchase decisions begin when the recognition of problems, needs, or opportunities triggers the buying process. Perhaps a firm's computer system has become outdated or an account representative demonstrates a new service that could improve the company's performance. Companies may decide to hire an outside marketing specialist when their sales stagnate.

The problem may be as simple as needing to provide a good cup of coffee to a firm's employees. The founders of Massachusetts-based Keurig Incorporated, which supplies millions of individually brewed cups of coffee to U.S. homes and offices each day, started by asking themselves, "Why do we brew coffee a pot at a time when we drink it a cup at a time?"[26]

Stage 2: Determine the Characteristics and Quantity of a Needed Good or Service

The coffee problem described in stage 1 translated into a service opportunity for Keurig. The small firm was able to offer a coffee system that would brew one perfect cup of coffee at a time, according to the preferences of each employee. After finding success in the offices of many accounting, law, and medical practices, the company developed a single-cup brewer for home use. This model has a unique full-color touch screen that allows coffee lovers to readily customize each cup's temperature and strength. Keurig's Vue V1200 commercial brewer, intended for office use, has radio frequency identification technology (RFID), which further ensures the quality of the final brew.[27]

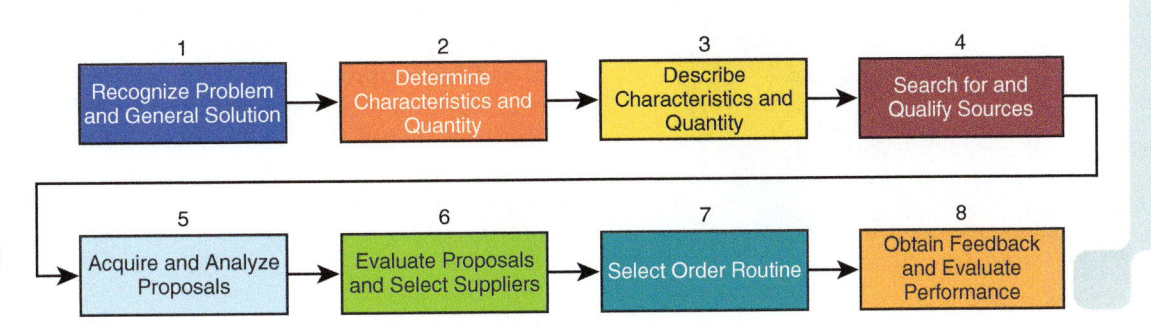

FIGURE 7.2
Stages in the B2B Buying Process

1. Recognize Problem and General Solution
2. Determine Characteristics and Quantity
3. Describe Characteristics and Quantity
4. Search for and Qualify Sources
5. Acquire and Analyze Proposals
6. Evaluate Proposals and Select Suppliers
7. Select Order Routine
8. Obtain Feedback and Evaluate Performance

Source: Based on Michael D. Hutt and Thomas W. Speh, *Business Marketing Management: B2B*, 11th ed. (Mason, OH: South-Western, 2013).

Stage 3: Describe Characteristics and the Quantity of a Needed Good or Service

After determining the characteristics and quantity of needed products, B2B buyers must translate these ideas into detailed specifications. Customers told Keurig they wanted a foolproof, individual coffee maker. The Keurig system supplies a plastic K-Cup® or partially recyclable Vue pack™ individual portion pack, containing ground coffee that the coffee lover simply places in the proper coffee maker—no measuring of water or coffee is required. Out comes the perfect cup of coffee. Firms could easily base the quantity requirements of the Keurig system on the number of coffee-drinking employees they have or the amount of space they occupy.

Stage 4: Search for and Qualify Potential Sources

Both consumers and businesses search for good suppliers of desired products. The choice of a supplier may be relatively straightforward—because there was no other machine like it, its early adopters had no trouble selecting the Keurig coffee system. Other searches may involve more complex decision making. A company that wants to buy a group life policy, for example, must weigh the varying provisions and programs of many different vendors.

Stage 5: Acquire and Analyze Proposals

The next step is to acquire and analyze suppliers' proposals, often submitted in writing. If the buyer is a government or public agency, this stage of the purchase process may involve competitive bidding. During this process, each marketer must develop its bid, including a price that will satisfy the criteria determined by the customer's problem, need, or opportunity. While competitive bidding is less common in the business sector, a company may follow the practice to purchase nonstandard materials, complex products, or products made to its own specifications.

Stage 6: Evaluate Proposals and Select Suppliers

Next in the buying process, buyers must compare vendors' proposals and choose the one that seems best suited to their needs. Proposals for sophisticated equipment, such as a large computer networking system, can include considerable differences among product offerings, and the final choice may involve trade-offs.

Price is not the only criterion for the selection of a vendor. Relationship factors such as communication and trust may also be important to the buyer. Other issues include reliability, delivery record, time from order to delivery, quality, and order accuracy. These are particularly important in the package delivery business. UPS equips its drivers worldwide with a handheld computer that expedites uploading of package-tracking information and hence delivery to customers. This mobile device, called the Delivery Information Acquisition Device or DIAD V, is half the size and weight of the previous generation of package trackers. It also has a color camera for proof of delivery, is sturdier, and can store more information. The DIAD V is the first to use Qualcomm's Gobi Radio Technology, which allows the device to switch instantly to another cellular carrier if the signal is lost.[28]

> **Briefly Speaking**
>
> "Spend a lot of time talking to your customers face to face. You'd be amazed how many companies don't listen to their customers."
>
> —**Ross Perot**
> *Founder, Electronic Data Systems*

Relationship factors such as reliability, on-time delivery, and order accuracy are important in the vendor-selection process. UPS equips its drivers with handheld computers that expedite the package delivery process to customers around the world.

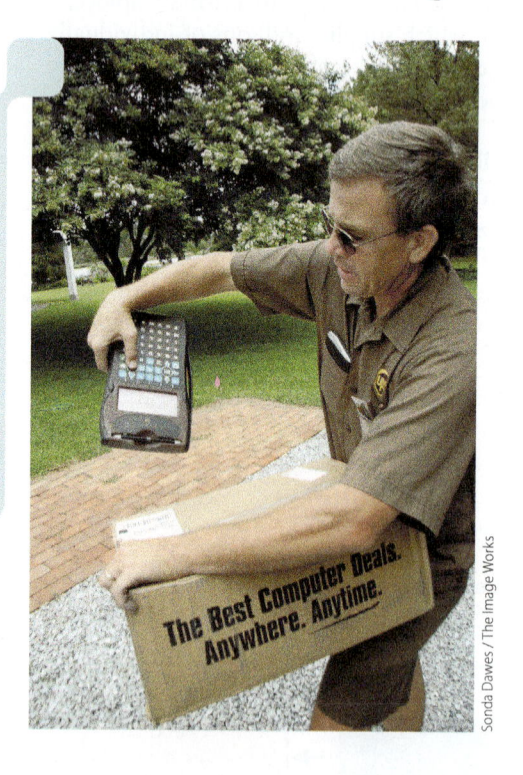

Stage 7: Select an Order Routine

Once a supplier has been chosen, buyer and vendor must work out the best way to process future purchases. Ordering routines can vary considerably. Most orders will, however, include product descriptions, quantities, prices, delivery terms, and payment terms. Today, companies have a variety of options for submitting orders: written documents, phone calls, faxes, or electronic data interchange (EDI).

Stage 8: Obtain Feedback and Evaluate Performance

At the final stage, buyers measure vendors' performances. Sometimes this judgment may involve a formal evaluation of each supplier's product quality, delivery performance, prices, technical knowledge, and overall responsiveness to customer needs. At other times, vendors may be measured according to whether they have lowered the customer's costs or reduced its employees' workloads. In general, bigger firms are more likely to use formal evaluation procedures, while smaller companies lean toward informal evaluations. Regardless of the method used, buyers should tell vendors how they will be evaluated.

Sometimes firms rely on independent organizations to gather quality feedback and summarize results. J.D. Power and Associates conducts research and provides information to various firms so they can improve the quality of their goods and services.

> **ASSESSMENT CHECK**
>
> 6.1 Why does the organizational buying process contain more steps than the consumer buying process?
>
> 6.2 List the steps in the organizational buying process.

CLASSIFYING BUSINESS BUYING SITUATIONS

As discussed earlier, business buying behavior responds to many purchasing influences, such as environmental, organizational, and interpersonal factors. This buying behavior also involves the degree of effort the purchase decision demands and the levels within the organization where it is made. Like consumer behavior, marketers can classify B2B buying situations into three general categories, ranging from least to most complex: (1) straight rebuying, (2) modified rebuying, and (3) new-task buying. Business buying situations may also involve reciprocity. The following sections look at each type of purchase.

Describe the three organizational buying situations. **7**

Straight Rebuying

The simplest buying situation is a **straight rebuy**—a recurring purchase decision in which a customer reorders a product that has satisfied its needs in the past. The buyer already likes the product and terms of sale, so the purchase requires no new information. The buyer sees little reason to assess competing options and so follows a routine repurchase format. A straight rebuy is the business market equivalent of routinized response behavior in the consumer market. Purchases of low-cost items such as paper clips and pens for an office are typical examples of straight rebuys. Reorders of K-cups from Keurig would also be straight rebuys. Marketers who maintain good relationships with customers by providing high-quality products, superior service, and prompt delivery can go a long way toward ensuring straight rebuys.

straight rebuy Recurring purchase decision in which a customer repurchases a good or service that has performed satisfactorily in the past.

Modified Rebuying

In a **modified rebuy**, a purchaser is willing to reevaluate available options. Buyers may see some advantage in looking at alternative offerings within their established purchasing guidelines. They might take this step if their current supplier has let a rebuy situation deteriorate because of poor service or delivery performance. Price, quality, and innovation differences can also provoke modified rebuys. Modified rebuys resemble limited problem solving in consumer markets.

modified rebuy Situation in which a purchaser is willing to reevaluate available options for repurchasing a good or service.

B2B marketers want to induce current customers to make straight rebuys by responding to all of their needs. Competitors, on the other hand, try to lure those buyers away by raising issues that will persuade them to reconsider their decisions. For example, other coffee suppliers now produce single-serving coffee "pods" that work with Keurig's coffee brewing machines and cost less.

New-Task Buying

new-task buying First-time or unique purchase situation that requires considerable effort by decision makers.

The most complex category of business buying is **new-task buying**—first-time or unique purchase situations that require considerable effort by the decision makers. Kaiser Permanente, an Oakland, California–based health maintenance organization with more than 9 million members, purchased an electronics health records system for its 37 hospitals and 600 medical offices at a cost of $4 billion. The system took more than five years to become fully operational. The database system is used by doctors and other health care professionals for everything from scheduling appointments to ordering lab results and contains the health care records of all of its members.[29] The consumer market equivalent of new-task buying is extended problem solving.

A new-task buy often requires a purchaser to carefully consider alternative offerings and vendors. A company entering a new field must seek suppliers of component parts that it has never before purchased. This new-task buying would require several stages, each yielding a decision of some sort. These decisions would include developing product requirements, searching out potential suppliers, and evaluating proposals. Information requirements and decision makers can complete the entire buying process, or they may change from stage to stage.

Reciprocity

reciprocity Buying from suppliers who are also customers.

Reciprocity—a practice of buying from suppliers who are also customers—is a controversial practice in a number of procurement situations. An office equipment manufacturer may favor a particular supplier of component parts if the supplier has recently made a major purchase of the manufacturer's products. Reciprocal arrangements traditionally have been common in industries featuring homogeneous products with similar prices, such as the chemical, paint, petroleum, rubber, and steel industries.

Reciprocity suggests close links among participants in the organizational marketplace. It can add to the complexity of B2B buying behavior for new suppliers trying to compete with preferred vendors. Although buyers and sellers enter into reciprocal agreements in the United States, both the Department of Justice and the Federal Trade Commission view them as attempts to reduce competition. Outside the United States, however, governments may take more favorable views of reciprocity. In Japan, close ties between suppliers and customers are common.

ANALYSIS TOOLS

value analysis Systematic study of the components of a purchase to determine the most cost-effective approach.

vendor analysis Assessment of supplier performance in categories such as price, back orders, timely delivery, and attention to special requests.

Two tools that help professional buyers improve purchase decisions are value analysis and vendor analysis. **Value analysis** examines each component of a purchase in an attempt to either delete the item or replace it with a more cost-effective substitute. Airplane designers have long recognized the need to make planes as lightweight as possible. Value analysis supports using a composite material such as Kevlar in airplane construction because it weighs less than the metals it replaces. The resulting fuel savings are significant for buyers in this marketplace.

Vendor analysis carries out an ongoing evaluation of a supplier's performance in categories such as price, back orders, delivery times, liability insurance, and attention to special requests. In some cases, vendor analysis is a formal process. Some buyers use a checklist to assess a vendor's performance. A checklist quickly highlights vendors and potential vendors that do not satisfy the purchaser's buying requirements.

ASSESSMENT CHECK

7.1 What are the four classifications of business buying situations?

7.2 Differentiate between value analysis and vendor analysis.

THE BUYING CENTER CONCEPT

The buying center concept provides a model for understanding B2B buying behavior. A company's **buying center** encompasses everyone involved in any aspect of its buying activity. A buying center may include the architect who designs a new research laboratory, the scientist who works in the facility, the purchasing manager who screens contractor proposals, the chief executive officer who makes the final decision, and the vice president of research who signs the formal contracts for the project. Buying center participants in any purchase seek to satisfy personal needs, such as participation or status, as well as organizational needs. A buying center is not part of a firm's formal organizational structure. It is an informal group whose composition and size vary among purchase situations and firms.

buying center Participants in an organizational buying decision.

BUYING CENTER ROLES

Buying center participants play different roles in the purchasing decision process. **Users** are the people who will actually use the good or service. Their influence on the purchase decision may range from negligible to extremely important. Users sometimes initiate purchase actions by requesting products, and they may also help develop product specifications. Users often influence the purchase of office equipment.

users Individual or group that actually uses a business good or service.

Gatekeepers control the information that all buying center members will review. They may exert this control by distributing printed product data or advertisements or by deciding which salespeople may speak to which individuals in the buying center. A purchasing agent might allow some salespeople to see the engineers responsible for developing specifications but deny others the same privilege. The office manager for a medical group may decide whether to accept and pass along sales literature from a pharmaceutical detailer.

gatekeepers Person who controls the information that all buying center members will review.

Influencers affect the buying decision by supplying information to guide evaluation of alternatives or by setting buying specifications. Influencers typically are technical staff such as engineers or quality-control specialists. Sometimes a buying organization hires outside consultants, such as architects, who influence its buying decisions.

influencers Typically, technical staff who affect the buying decision by supplying information to guide evaluation of alternatives or by setting buying specifications.

The **decider** chooses a good or service, although another person may have the formal authority to do so. The identity of the decider is the most difficult role for salespeople to pinpoint. A firm's buyer may have the formal authority to buy, but the firm's chief executive officer may actually make the buying decision. Alternatively, a decider might be a design engineer who develops specifications that only one vendor can meet.

decider Person who chooses a good or service, although another person may have the formal authority to complete the sale.

The **buyer** has the formal authority to select a supplier and to implement the procedures for securing the good or service. The buyer often surrenders this power to more influential members of the organization, though. The purchasing manager often fills the buyer's role and executes the details associated with a purchase order.

buyer Person who has the formal authority to select a supplier and to implement the procedures for securing a good or service.

B2B marketers face the task of determining the specific role and the relative decision-making influence of each buying center participant. Salespeople can then tailor their presentations and information to the precise role an individual plays at each step of the purchase process. Business marketers have found their initial—and in many cases, most extensive—contacts with a firm's purchasing department often fail to reach the buying center participants who have the greatest influence, because these people may not work in that department at all.

Consider the selection of meeting and convention sites for trade or professional associations. The primary decision maker could be an association board or an executive committee, usually with input from the executive director or a meeting planner; these individuals might choose meeting locations, sometimes with input from members; finally, the association's annual meeting committee or program committee might make the meeting location selection. Because officers change periodically, centers of control may change frequently. As a result, destination marketers and hotel operators must constantly assess how an association makes its decisions on conference locations.

INTERNATIONAL BUYING CENTERS

Two distinct characteristics differentiate international buying centers from domestic ones. First, marketers may have trouble identifying members of foreign buying centers because of cultural differences in decision-making methods. Second, a buying center in a foreign company often includes more participants than U.S. companies involve. International buying centers typically employ from 1 to 50 people, with 15 to 20 participants commonplace in the United States. Global B2B marketers must recognize and accommodate this greater diversity of decision makers.

International buying centers can change in response to political and economic trends. Many European firms once maintained separate facilities in each European nation to avoid tariffs and customs delays. When the European Union lowered trade barriers among member nations, however, many companies closed distant branches and consolidated their buying centers. The Netherlands has been one of the beneficiaries of this trend.

> **ASSESSMENT CHECK**
>
> 8.1 Identify the five roles of people in a buying center decision.
>
> 8.2 What are some of the problems that U.S. marketers face in dealing with international buying centers?

DEVELOPING EFFECTIVE BUSINESS-TO-BUSINESS MARKETING STRATEGIES

9 Discuss the challenges and strategies for marketing to government, institutional, and international buyers.

A business marketer must develop a marketing strategy based on a particular organization's buying behavior and on the buying situation. Clearly, many variables affect organizational purchasing decisions. This section examines three market segments whose decisions present unique challenges to B2B marketers: units of government, institutions, and international markets. Finally, it summarizes key differences between consumer and business marketing strategies.

CHALLENGES OF GOVERNMENT MARKETS

Government agencies—federal, state, and local—together make up the largest customer group in the United States. More than 90,000 government units buy a wide variety of products, including office supplies, furniture, concrete, vehicles, grease, military aircraft, fuel, and chicken, to name just a few.[30]

To compete effectively, business marketers must understand the unique challenges of selling to government units. One challenge results because government purchases typically involve dozens of interested parties who specify, evaluate, or use the purchased goods and services. These parties may or may not work within the government agency that officially handles a purchase.

Government purchases are also influenced by social goals, such as "Buy American" provisions and minority subcontracting programs. Government entities such as the U.S. Postal Service strive to maintain diversity in their suppliers by making a special effort to purchase goods and services from small firms and companies owned by minorities and women. The Postal Service has developed a Supplier Diversity Corporate Plan to show its commitment to ensuring "a continued focus on—and improvement in—our relationships with small, minority-owned, and women-owned businesses."[31] The government also relies on its prime suppliers to subcontract to minority businesses.

Contractual guidelines create another important influence in selling to government markets. The government buys products under two basic types of contracts: fixed-price contracts, in which seller and buyer agree to a set price before finalizing the contract, and cost-reimbursement contracts, in which the government pays the vendor for allowable costs, including profits, incurred during performance of the contract. Each type of contract has advantages and disadvantages for B2B marketers. Although the fixed-price contract offers more profit potential than the alternative, it also carries greater risks from unforeseen expenses, price hikes, and changing political and economic conditions.

Government Purchasing Procedures

Many U.S. government purchases go through the General Services Administration (GSA), a central management agency involved in areas such as procurement, property management, and information resources management. The GSA buys goods and services for its own use and for use by other government agencies. In its role as, essentially, the federal government's business manager, it purchases billions of dollars' worth of products. The Defense Logistics Agency (DLA) serves the same function for the Department of Defense.

By law, most federal purchases must be awarded on the basis of bids, or written sales proposals, from vendors. As part of this process, government buyers develop specifications—detailed descriptions of needed items—for prospective bidders. U.S. government purchases must comply with the Federal Acquisition Regulation (FAR), an approximately 30,000-page set of standards originally designed to cut red tape in government purchasing. FAR standards have been further complicated by numerous exceptions issued by various government agencies. Because they provide services to various federal government agencies such as the Department of Energy, Environmental Protection Agency, and Department of Defense, large environmental engineering firms, such as MACTEC, Tetra Tech, and Weston Solutions, typically have procurement and contract specialists on staff. These specialists stay current with FAR standards and conduct internal quality-assurance and quality-control programs to make sure the standards are followed by their companies.

State and local government purchasing procedures resemble federal procedures. Most states and many large cities have created buying offices similar to the GSA. Detailed specifications and open bidding are common at this level as well. Many state purchasing regulations give preference to in-state bidders.

Government spending patterns may differ from those in private industry. Because the federal government's fiscal year runs from October 1 through September 30, many agencies spend much of their procurement budgets in the fourth quarter, from July 1 to September 30. They hoard their funds throughout the year to cover unexpected expenditures, and if they encounter no such problems, they find themselves with money to spend in late summer. Companies understand this system and keep their eyes on government bulletins so that they can bid on the listed agency purchases, which often involve large amounts of money.

Online with the Federal Government

Like their colleagues in the private sector, government procurement professionals are streamlining purchasing procedures with new technology. Rather than paging through piles of paper catalogs and submitting typed purchase orders, government buyers now prefer online catalogs that help them compare competing product offerings. In fact, vendors find doing business with the government almost impossible unless they embrace electronic commerce.

Vendors can sell products to the federal government through three electronic options. Websites provide a convenient method of exchanging information for both parties. Government buyers locate and order products, paying with a federally issued credit card, and the vendors deliver the items within about a week. Another route is through government-sponsored electronic ordering systems, which help standardize the buying process. GSA Advantage! allows federal employees to order more than 37 million goods and services directly over the Internet at the preferred government price.[32] The Phoenix Opportunity System, set up by the Department of Commerce, provides a similar service for minority-owned companies. The U.S. Treasury is increasing electronic check payments to speed up the settling of vendor invoices.

Despite these advances, many government agencies remain less sophisticated than private-sector businesses. The Pentagon, for instance, is still coping with procurement procedures that were developed over the past 50 years. However, it is introducing a streamlined approach to defense contracting that reduces the time necessary to develop specifications and select suppliers.

CHALLENGES OF INSTITUTIONAL MARKETS

Institutions constitute another important market. Institutional buyers include a wide variety of organizations, such as schools, hospitals, libraries, foundations, clinics, churches, and not-for-profit agencies.

Institutional markets are characterized by widely diverse buying practices. Some institutional purchasers behave like government purchasers because laws and political considerations determine their buying procedures. Many of these institutions, such as schools, may even be managed by government units.

Buying practices can differ among institutions of the same type. In a small hospital, the chief dietitian may approve all food purchases, while in a larger medical facility, food purchases may go through a committee consisting of the dietitian and a business manager, purchasing agent, and cook. Other hospitals may belong to buying groups, perhaps health maintenance organizations or local hospital cooperatives. Still others may contract with outside firms to prepare and serve all meals.

Within a single institution, multiple buying influences may affect decisions. Many institutions, staffed by professionals such as physicians, nurses, researchers, and instructors, may also employ purchasing managers or even entire purchasing departments. Conflicts may arise among these decision makers. Professional employees may prefer to make their own purchase decisions and resent giving up control to the purchasing staff. This conflict can force a business marketer to cultivate both professionals and purchasers. A detailer for a pharmaceutical firm must convince physicians of the value to patients of a certain drug while simultaneously convincing the hospital's purchasing department that the firm offers competitive prices, good delivery schedules, and prompt service.

Group purchasing is an important factor in institutional markets because many organizations join cooperative associations to pool purchases for quantity discounts. Universities may join

GSA Advantage! is a program that allows federal employees to purchase goods and services directly via the Web at preferred government prices.

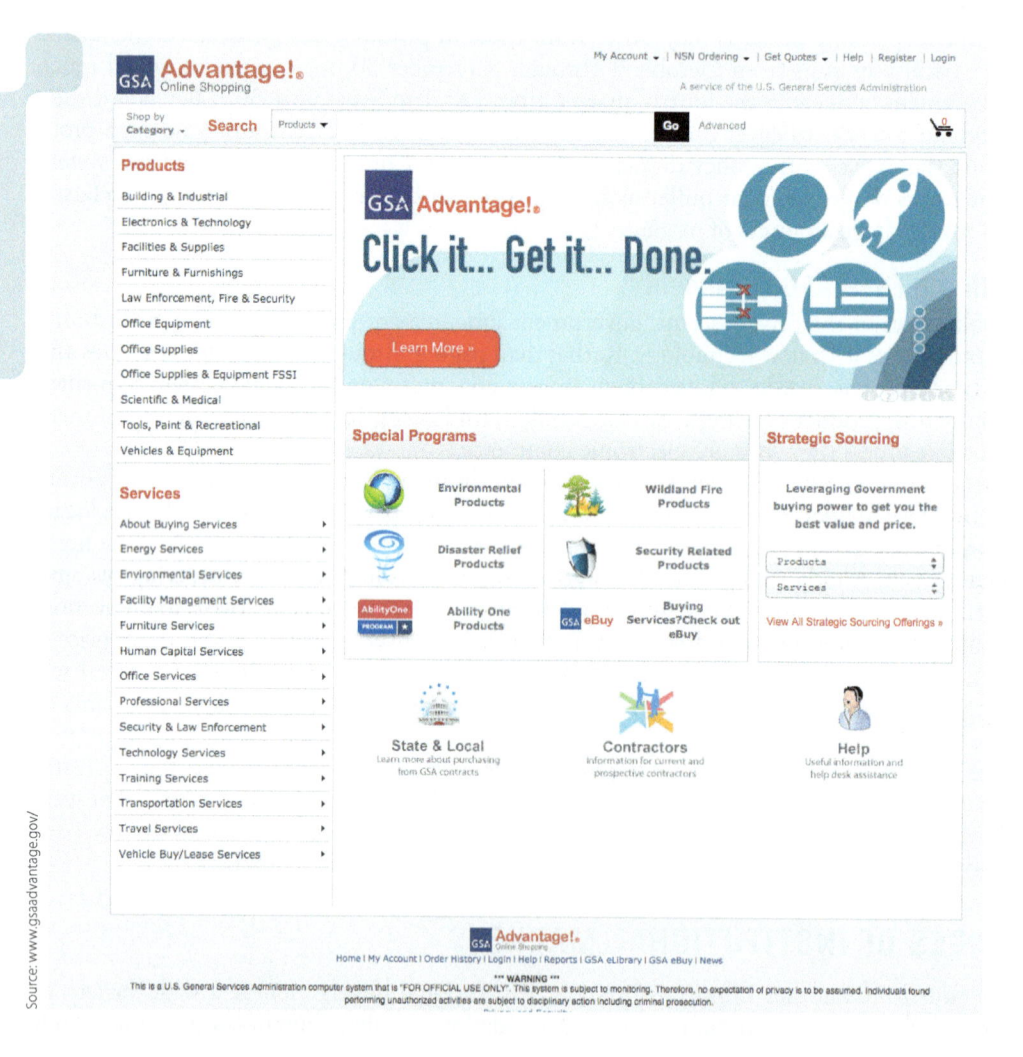

the Education and Institutional Cooperative Purchasing; hospitals may belong to regional associations; and chains of for-profit hospitals such as HCA Healthcare can negotiate quantity discounts. Central headquarters staff usually handles purchasing for all members of such a chain.

Diverse practices in institutional markets pose special challenges for B2B marketers. They must maintain flexibility in developing strategies for dealing with a range of customers, from large cooperative associations and chains to midsize purchasing departments and institutions to individuals. Buying centers can work with varying members, priorities, and levels of expertise. Discounts and effective distribution functions play important roles in obtaining—and keeping—institutions as customers.

Buying practices can differ among institutions of the same type. In a small medical practice, a physician, in collaboration with office staff, approves purchases, while in a larger facility, such as a hospital, purchases may go through a committee or a separate purchasing group.

CHALLENGES OF INTERNATIONAL MARKETS

To sell successfully in international markets, business marketers must consider buyers' attitudes and cultural patterns within areas where they operate. In Asian markets, a firm must maintain a local presence to sell products. Personal relationships are also important to business deals in Asia. Companies that want to expand globally often need to establish joint ventures with local partners. International marketers must also be poised to respond to shifts in cultural values.

Local industries, economic conditions, geographic characteristics, and legal restrictions must also be considered in international marketing. In Spain many local industries specialize in food and wine, whereas Germany supports a large automobile industry. Therefore, a maker of forklift trucks might market smaller vehicles to Spanish companies than to German firms, which require bigger, heavier trucks.

Remanufacturing—efforts to restore worn-out products to like-new condition—can be an important marketing strategy in a nation that cannot afford to buy new products. Developing countries often purchase remanufactured factory machinery, which costs 35 percent to 60 percent less than new equipment.

Foreign governments represent another important business market. In many countries, government- or state-owned companies dominate certain industries, such as construction and other infrastructure sales. Additional examples include airport and highway construction, telephone system equipment, and computer networking equipment. Sales to a foreign government can involve an array of regulations. Many governments, like that of the United States, limit foreign participation in their defense programs. Joint ventures and countertrade are common, as are local content laws, which mandate domestic production of a certain percentage of a business product's components.

remanufacturing
Efforts to restore older products to like-new condition.

ASSESSMENT CHECK

9.1 What are some influences on government purchases?

9.2 Why is group purchasing important in institutional purchases?

9.3 What special factors influence international buying decisions?

Strategic Implications of Marketing in the 21st Century

To develop marketing strategies for the B2B sector, marketers must first understand the buying practices that govern the segment they are targeting, whether it is the commercial market, trade industries, government, or institutions. Similarly, when selling to a specific organization, strategies must take into account the many factors that influence purchasing. B2B marketers must identify people who play the various roles in the buying decision and understand how these members interact with one another, other members of their own organizations, and outside vendors. Marketers must be careful to direct their marketing efforts to their organization, to broader environmental influences, and to individuals who operate within the constraints of the firm's buying center.

Get online now for additional learning tools to help you master your marketing knowledge—visit **WWW.CENGAGEBRAIN.COM** today!

REVIEW OF CHAPTER OBJECTIVES

1 Explain the four components of the business-to-business (B2B) market.

The B2B market is divided into four segments: the commercial market, trade industries, governments, and institutions. The commercial market consists of individuals and firms that acquire products to be used, directly or indirectly, to produce other goods and services. Trade industries are organizations, such as retailers and wholesalers, that purchase for resale to others. The primary purpose of government purchasing at federal, state, and local levels is to provide some form of public benefit. The fourth segment, institutions, includes a diverse array of organizations, such as hospitals, schools, museums, and not-for-profit agencies.

2 Describe the major approaches to segmenting business-to-business (B2B) markets.

Business markets can be segmented by (1) demographics, (2) customer type, (3) end-use application, and (4) purchasing situation. The North American Industry Classification System (NAICS), instituted after the passage of NAFTA, further classifies types of customers by the use of six-digit codes.

3 Identify the major characteristics of the business market and its demand.

The major characteristics of the business market are geographic concentration, size and number of buyers, purchase decision procedures, and buyer–seller relationships. The major categories of demand are derived demand, volatile demand, joint demand, inelastic demand, and inventory adjustments.

4 Discuss the decision to make, buy, or lease goods and services.

Before a company can decide what to buy, it must decide whether to buy at all. A firm has three options: (1) make the good or service in-house, (2) purchase it from another organization, or (3) lease it from another organization. Companies may outsource goods or services formerly produced in-house to other companies either within their own home country or to firms in other nations. The shift of high-cost jobs from the home country to lower-cost locations is known as *offshoring*. If a company moves production to a country close to its own borders, it uses a *nearshoring* strategy. Each option has its benefits and drawbacks, including cost and quality control.

5 Describe the major influences on business buying behavior.

B2B buying behavior tends to be more complex than individual consumer behavior. More people and time are involved, and buyers often seek several alternative supply sources. The systematic nature of organizational buying is reflected in the use of purchasing managers to direct such efforts. Major organizational purchases may require elaborate and lengthy decision-making processes involving many people. Purchase decisions typically depend on combinations of factors such as price, service, certainty of supply, and product efficiency.

6 Outline the eight steps in the organizational buying process.

The organizational buying process consists of eight general stages: (1) anticipate or recognize a problem/need/opportunity and a general solution, (2) determine characteristics and quantity of needed good or service, (3) describe characteristics and quantity of needed good or service, (4) search for and qualify potential sources, (5) acquire and analyze proposals, (6) evaluate proposals and select supplier(s), (7) select an order routine, and (8) obtain feedback and evaluate performance.

7 Describe the three organizational buying situations.

Organizational buying situations differ. A straight rebuy is a recurring purchase decision in which a customer stays with an item that has performed satisfactorily. In a modified rebuy, a purchaser is willing to reevaluate available options. New-task buying refers to first-time or unique purchase situations that require considerable effort on the part of the decision makers. Reciprocity involves buying from suppliers who are also customers.

8 Explain the buying center concept.

The buying center includes everyone who is involved in some way in an organizational buying action. There are five buying center roles: users, gatekeepers, influencers, deciders, and buyers.

9 Discuss the challenges and strategies for marketing to government, institutional, and international buyers.

A government purchase typically involves dozens of interested parties. Social goals and programs influence government purchases. Many U.S. government purchases involve complex contractual guidelines and often require detailed specifications and a bidding process. Institutional markets are challenging because of their diverse buying influences and practices. Group purchasing is an important factor because many institutions join cooperative associations to get quantity discounts. An institutional marketer must be flexible enough to develop strategies for dealing with a range of customers. Discounts and effective distribution play an important role. An effective international business marketer must be aware of foreign attitudes and cultural patterns. Other important factors include economic conditions, geographic characteristics, legal restrictions, and local industries.

ASSESSMENT CHECK: ANSWERS

1.1 Define B2B marketing. Business-to-business, or B2B, marketing deals with organizational purchases of goods and services to support production of other products, to facilitate daily company operations, or for resale.

1.2 What is the commercial market? The commercial market consists of individuals and firms that acquire products to be used, directly or indirectly, to produce other goods and services.

2.1 What are the four major ways marketers segment business markets? Business markets can be segmented by (1) demographics, (2) customer type, (3) end-use application, and (4) purchasing situation.

2.2 What is the NAICS? The North American Industry Classification System (NAICS) is a unified system for Mexico, Canada, and the United States to classify B2B market segments and analyze trade.

3.1 Why is geographic segmentation important in the B2B market? Certain industries locate in particular areas to be close to customers. Firms may choose to locate sales offices and distribution centers in these areas to provide more attentive service. For example, the Washington, DC, area is favored by companies that sell to the federal government.

3.2 In what ways is the buyer–seller relationship important in B2B marketing? Buyer–seller relationships often are more complex than consumer relationships, and they require superior communication among the organizations' personnel. Satisfying one major customer could mean millions of dollars to a firm.

3.3 What is global sourcing? Global sourcing involves contracting to purchase goods and services from suppliers worldwide.

3.4 How does derived demand create volatile demand? Business demand often is derived from consumer demand. Even modest shifts in consumer demand can produce disproportionate—and volatile—shifts in business demand.

3.5 Give an example of joint demand. Both lumber and concrete are required to build most homes. If the lumber supply falls, the drop in housing construction will most likely affect the demand for concrete.

3.6 How might JIT II strengthen marketing relationships? Under JIT II, suppliers place representatives at the customer's facility to work as part of an integrated, on-site customer–supplier team. Suppliers plan and take orders in consultation with the customer. This streamlining of the inventory process improves control of the flow of goods.

4.1 Identify two potential benefits of outsourcing. Outsourcing allows firms to concentrate their resources on their core business. It also allows access to specialized talent or expertise that does not exist within the firm.

4.2 Identify two potential problems with outsourcing. Many companies discover that their cost savings are less than vendors sometimes promise. Also, companies that sign multiyear contracts may find that their savings drop after a year or two.

5.1 Identify the three major factors that influence purchase decisions. In addition to product-specific factors such as purchase price, installation, operating and maintenance costs, and vendor service, companies must consider broader environmental, organizational, and interpersonal influences.

5.2 What are the advantages and disadvantages of multiple sourcing? Spreading orders ensures against shortages if one vendor cannot deliver on schedule. However, dealing with many sellers can be counterproductive and take too much time.

6.1 Why does the organizational buying process contain more steps than the consumer buying process? The additional steps arise because business purchasing introduces new complexities that do not affect consumers.

6.2 List the steps in the organizational buying process. The steps in organizational buying are (1) anticipate or recognize a problem/need/opportunity and a general solution, (2) determine characteristics and quantity of a needed good or service, (3) describe characteristics and quantity of needed good or service, (4) search for and qualify potential sources, (5) acquire and analyze proposals, (6) evaluate proposals and select supplier(s), (7) select an order routine, and (8) obtain feedback and evaluate performance.

7.1 What are the four classifications of business buying situations? The four classifications of business buying are (1) straight rebuying, (2) modified rebuying, (3) new-task buying, and (4) reciprocity.

7.2 Differentiate between value analysis and vendor analysis. Value analysis examines each component of a purchase in an attempt either to delete the item or replace it with a more cost-effective substitute. Vendor analysis carries out an ongoing evaluation of a supplier's performance in categories such as price, backorders, delivery times, liability insurance, and attention to special requests.

8.1 Identify the five roles of people in a buying center decision. There are five buying center roles: users (those who use the product), gatekeepers (those who control the flow of information), influencers (those who provide technical information or specifications), deciders (those who actually choose the product), and buyers (those who have the formal authority to purchase).

8.2 What are some of the problems that U.S. marketers face in dealing with international buying centers? International buying centers pose several problems. First, there may be cultural differences in decision-making methods. Second, a buying center in a foreign company typically includes more participants than is common in the United States. Third, international buying centers can change in response to political and economic conditions.

9.1 What are some influences on government purchases? Social goals and programs often influence government purchases.

9.2 Why is group purchasing important in institutional purchases? Group purchasing is an important factor because many institutions join cooperative associations to get quantity discounts.

9.3 What special factors influence international buying decisions? An effective international business marketer must be aware of foreign attitudes and cultural patterns. Other important factors include economic conditions, geographic characteristics, legal restrictions, and local industries.

Chapter 7 Business-to-Business (B2B) Marketing

MARKETING TERMS YOU NEED TO KNOW

business-to-business (B2B) marketing 204
commercial market 206
trade industries 206
resellers 206
customer-based segmentation 210
North American Industry Classification System (NAICS) 210
end-use application segmentation 211
customer relationship management (CRM) 211
global sourcing 214
derived demand 215
joint demand 215
inelastic demand 215
just-in-time (JIT)/ JIT II 216
sole sourcing 216
offshoring 217
nearshoring 217
outsourcing 217
multiple sourcing 219
merchandisers 220
systems integration 220
category advisor/category captain 221
straight rebuy 223
modified rebuy 223
new-task buying 224
reciprocity 224
value analysis 224
vendor analysis 224
buying center 225
users 225
gatekeepers 225
influencers 225
decider 225
buyer 225
remanufacturing 229

ASSURANCE OF LEARNING REVIEW

1. Which is the largest segment of the business market? What role does the Internet play in the B2B market? What role do resellers play in the B2B market?
2. How is customer-based segmentation beneficial to B2B marketers? Describe segmentation by purchasing situation.
3. How do the sizes and numbers of buyers affect B2B marketers? Why are buyer–seller relationships so important in B2B marketing?
4. Give an example of each type of demand.
5. For what reasons might a firm choose an option other than making a good or service in-house? Why is outsourcing on the rise? How is offshoring different from outsourcing?
6. What are some of the environmental factors that may influence buying decisions? Identify organizational factors that may influence buying decisions. Describe the role of the professional buyer.
7. Why are there more steps in the organizational buying process than in the consumer buying process? Explain why feedback between buyers and sellers is important to the marketing relationship.
8. Give an example of a straight rebuy and a modified rebuy. Why is new-task buying more complex than the first two buying situations?
9. What buying center participant is a marketer likely to encounter first? In the buying center, who has the formal authority to make a purchase?
10. Describe some of the factors that characterize U.S. government purchases. Why are institutional markets particularly challenging?

PROJECTS AND TEAMWORK EXERCISES

1. As a team or individually, choose a commercial product—such as computer chips, flour, paint, or equipment—and research and analyze its foreign-market potential. Report your findings to the class.
2. In pairs, select a business product in one of two categories—capital or expense—and determine how derived demand will affect the sales of the product. Create a chart showing your findings.
3. Imagine you and your teammates are buyers for a firm such as Applebee's, Dick's Sporting Goods, Hilton Hotels, or another company you like. Map out a logical buying process for a new-task purchase for your organization.
4. Form a team to conduct a hypothetical team-selling effort for the packaging of products manufactured by a food company such as General Mills. Have each team member cover a certain concern such as package design, delivery, and payment schedules. Present your marketing effort to the class.
5. Conduct research into the U.S. government's purchasing process. Select a federal agency or department such as the Environmental Protection Agency, the National Aeronautics and Space Administration or the Department of Health and Human Services. What types of purchases does the agency make? What is the range of contract amounts? Who are the typical suppliers? What type of process is involved in buying?

CRITICAL-THINKING EXERCISES

1. Imagine you are a wholesaler for dairy products such as milk and cheese, which are produced by a cooperative of small farmers. Describe what steps you would take to build relationships with both the producers (farmers) and retailers (supermarkets).
2. Describe an industry that might be segmented by geographic concentration. Then identify some of the types of firms that might be involved in that industry. Keep in mind that these companies might be involved in other industries as well.
3. Imagine you are in charge of making the decision to lease or buy a fleet of trucks for the moving company for which you work. What factors would influence your decision and why?
4. Do you think online selling to the federal government benefits marketers? What might be some of the drawbacks to this type of selling?

ETHICS EXERCISE

Suppose you work for a well-known local restaurant, and a friend of yours is an account representative for a supplier of restaurant equipment. You know the restaurant owner is considering upgrading some of the kitchen equipment. Although you have no purchasing authority, your friend has asked you to arrange a meeting with the restaurant owner. You have heard unflattering rumors about this supplier's customer service.

1. Would you arrange the meeting between your friend and your boss?
2. Would you mention the customer service rumors either to your friend or your boss?
3. Would you try to influence the purchase decision in either direction?

INTERNET EXERCISES

1. **Marketing to airlines.** Boeing and Airbus are major manufacturers of commercial aircraft. Visit the websites of both firms. After you review the websites, prepare a report that compares and contrasts the marketing strategies employed by both firms.

   www.boeing.com/commercial

   www.airbus.com

2. **Marketing to small businesses.** According to some experts, there are important differences between marketing to large businesses and marketing to small businesses. Go to the websites listed here and review the material. Prepare a summary you can use in a class discussion on the topic.

   http://www.inc.com/marla-tabaka/5-surprising-secrets-for-selling-to-corporate-clients.html

   http://smallbusiness.foxbusiness.com/marketing-sales/2013/10/02/here-is-your-sizzle-for-b2b-marketing/

   http://smallbiztrends.com/2007/02/five-mistakes-when-selling-to-small-business-owners.html

3. **Selling to the federal government.** The General Services Administration (GSA) purchases billions of dollars' worth of goods and services for various federal agencies. Visit the GSA's website to learn more about selling to the federal government. What products does the GSA purchase? Who may sell products to the federal government? What are the requirements to become a federal government vendor?

   www.gsa.gov/portal/category/100000

Note: Internet Web addresses change frequently. If you don't find the exact site listed, you may need to access the organization's home page and search from there or use a search engine such as Google or Bing.

CASE 7.1
B2B Giant Scores Big with Mobile Apps

W.W. Grainger has such a good handle on who its more than 2 million business customers are that it recently redesigned its website to cater to two specific types: buyers in the field, using any of Grainger's more than 1.2 million maintenance and repair products, and purchasing agents, placing orders for Grainger products from corporate headquarters. Customers who need a product right now in the field can enter their ZIP code to find out whether one of Grainger's more than 360 U.S. branches is nearby and has the required item. (The company has 709 branches worldwide.) If so, they can pick it up, often the same day. Purchasing agents take a longer view of their inventory, and they like Grainger's ability to recognize them online, tell them what they've ordered in the past, and help them check the status of their current orders. Both types of customers benefit from Grainger's mobile apps, which includes a new app for the iPad. The new app provides real-time product availability, detailed product pages to provide customers with key information to help select an item that fits their needs, and a single-page checkout that includes customer information. Field workers can request purchasing approval for needed items, while purchasing agents can approve the requests without logging on to Grainger's website, even if they're away from their desks. Anyone ordering from the website can also use the handy *click to chat* or *click to call* buttons to directly connect with a Grainger customer service rep for help. In fact, the website alerts Grainger's staff when a customer is having a problem with an order, so a customer service employee can step in with a chat or invitation to offer immediate help.

Grainger's successful development of its e-commerce division has enabled it to grow its online business more than twice as fast as its base operations, increasing it 23 percent in one recent year to help the company reach more than $9 billion in annual revenues. Many of Grainger's customers are in government offices or schools; in heavy or light manufacturing operations; or in retail, wholesale, fleet maintenance, or asset management.

"We're giving our customers more control," the company's vice president of global e-commerce says. "Our platform enables customers to manage purchasing and spending better."

QUESTIONS FOR CRITICAL THINKING

1. Why is it important for W.W. Grainger to understand exactly who its B2B customers are?
2. In what other ways can Grainger provide a good customer experience via its mobile apps and company website?

Sources: Company website, http://pressroom.grainger.com, accessed September 9, 2014; "Hot 100 E-Retailers of 2013," *Internet Retailer*, accessed February 17, 2014, www.internetretailer.com; "Grainger Modifies Structure, Pulick Leaving for CEO Job," *Chicago Business Journal*, accessed February 17, 2014, www.bizjournals.com; Stefany Moore, "How Grainger Tackles the B2B Challenges of Selling Online," *Internet Retailer*, accessed February 17, 2014, www.internetretailer.com; "Grainger Unveils New B2B E-Commerce Platform and iPad App" (press release), *The Electrical Distributor Magazine*, accessed February 17, 2014, www.tedmag.com; Tracey Schelmetic, "How E-commerce Can Reinvent Your Industrial Supply Model," *Industry Market Trends*, accessed February 10, 2014, http://news.thomasnet.com.

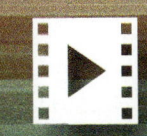

VIDEO CASE 7.2
Zappos Offers Insights to Other Businesses

How many firms throw open their doors to the business community, essentially offering access to trade secrets so other companies can learn and grow? Zappos does this—in fact, the online shoe retailer has created an entire division devoted to the effort, called Zappos Insights. Based on the company's core value of open and honest communication, Zappos conducts business-to-business marketing in an unusual way: giving away

information for free. Zappos, an Amazon company, is well known among other businesses for two things it does extremely well: providing top-notch customer service and building a culture that spreads happiness. Zappos' focus on customer service was born of necessity. When it started in the late 1990s, the company didn't have any money to market the novel idea of online shoe selling. So its founders sank everything they had into customer service, including the idea of free shipping both ways. As the company built its business and its reputation, it also created a culture in which people liked to work. "It's an environment where people are in service to each other," explains Robert Richman, product manager for Zappos Insights. Zappos' expertise in customer service has become a product itself, as Zappos Insights offers training to other firms in how to do what it does so well.

Access to the Zappos culture starts for free, with a tour of the company and information available to everyone online. From there, businesses can join Zappos Insights and pay for various levels of training, such as a two-day onsite boot camp at Zappos or a customized program conducted at an individual company's location. Membership benefits include training modules on leadership development, techniques for keeping team members engaged and empowered, and strategies for delivering Zappos' signature "WOW" service to customers. At a one-day seminar, a business owner or executive learns applications for tenets such as "culture drives success," "getting the culture right," "getting the right people on board," "creating a fun physical environment creates energy," and "communication is everything, and everything is communication." These aren't just taglines. They are organizational values that Zappos has proved to be successful.

Zappos segments its B2B customers by sifting through the data it has collected on companies that request the free portion of its program and determining what kind of business they do (customer type) as well as how they might use Zappos training to further their business (end-use application). In essence, explains Richman, it's about "offering a lot of free value and then seeing who wants to go deeper." In fact, Zappos Insights doesn't advertise or send direct email; for the most part, companies come to them. They may be as varied as Google, Eli Lilly, and Intuit—but they all want one thing: a culture driven by customer service. Why isn't Zappos worried about sharing its methods? "Culture can't be duplicated because it's based on people," says Richman. "So because of that, it's completely different when transferred from company to company."

The decision for an organization to pay for an in-depth membership to Zappos Insights requires consideration of certain factors, such as price (there are several levels) and availability (businesses can attend workshops and seminars at Zappos, or have Zappos come to them). The buying situation itself varies as well. As a client enters into a new relationship with Zappos Insights, it's a new-task purchase. Managers are involved not only in the purchase but probably in the experience itself. If a company continues its membership, adding services, upgrading, or renewing, it becomes a modified rebuy. Reciprocity also occurs, as some of Zappos' vendors are enrolled in the Zappos Insights program.

When you think about strategies for businesses marketing to each other, you might not necessarily consider the strategy of delivering happiness. But Zappos Insights places the concept of happiness in the business environment at the top of its list. The training programs offered by Zappos Insights "play into the larger vision of delivering happiness, because we are essentially training the people who are responsible for hundreds of thousands of other people," says Richman. "We've seen the trickle effect." As Zappos trains companies to build places where employees like to work, all those employees deliver better experiences to their customers. "It's a rising tide that raises all boats," Richman muses. "If we create stronger cultures, everybody in business will have better relationships."

QUESTIONS FOR CRITICAL THINKING

1. Describe the buyer–seller relationship between Zappos Insights and its business clients.
2. How would you classify the business market demand for Zappos Insights training? Explain your answer.

Sources: Company website, www.zapposinsights.com, accessed September 9, 2014; Katherine Gustafson, "Want to Be Like Zappos? Get Insights Directly from the Company," *Intuit Small Business Blog*, accessed February 18, 2014, http://blog.intuit.com; James La Barrie, "Defining Service and Culture: The Zappos Model," *Beyond Marketing: Amaze the Customer* (blog), accessed February 17, 2014, http://blog.amazethecustomer.com.

NOTES

1. Corporate website, www.ge.com, accessed September 9, 2014; GE Mobile App, "Centricity Radiology Mobile Access," *iTunes App Store*, accessed February 10, 2014, www.apple.com/itunes; Kate Maddox, "Study: Social Media Influences B2B Tech Purchases," *BtoB* magazine, accessed February 10, 2014, http://www.btobonline.com; Eric Melin, "How Are B2B Marketers Finding Success?" (infographic), *Social Media Today*, accessed February 8, 2014, http://socialmediatoday.com; Kate Maddox, "BtoB's Best Marketers: Linda Boff, General Electric Company," *BtoB* magazine, accessed February 8, 2014, http://www.btobonline.com; Christopher Heine, "GE Gets 30% Better Returns Through Smart Content Marketing," *Adweek*, accessed February 8, 2014, www.adweek.com; David Moth, "How General Electric Uses Facebook, Twitter, Pinterest and Google+," *econsultancy*, accessed February 8, 2014, http://econsultancy.com.
2. U.S. Department of Defense, "DOD Releases Fiscal 2015 Budget Proposal" (press release), accessed September 9, 2014, www.defense.gov.
3. "Study: Global Independent Research Firm Finds E-Commerce and Mobile Sales Offer Significant New Opportunities," *Globe News Wire*, accessed February 12, 2014, http://globenewswire.com.
4. "Bundled Offers: Simplify Billing and Save Money: AT&T OneNet Service," company website, AT&T, accessed February 8, 2014, www.business.att.com.
5. Company website, www.jan-pro.com, accessed February 14, 2014.

6. Company website, www.accobrands.com, accessed February 14, 2014.
7. Company website, "Federal Government Rates," www.bid4assets.com, accessed February 10, 2014.
8. U.S. Census Bureau, "E-Stats," p. 2, accessed February 10, 2014, www.census.gov/estats.
9. Tim Asimos, "How to Measure the Effectiveness of Your B2B Online Marketing Program," *Business 2 Community*, accessed February 14, 2014, www.business2community.com.
10. Company website, www.theseam.com, accessed February 18, 2014.
11. Patrick Clark, "Small Business Saturday's $5.7 Billion Shopping Spree," *Bloomberg Businessweek*, accessed February 12, 2014, www.businessweek.com.
12. Company website, www.tetratech.com, accessed September 9, 2014.
13. U.S. Census Bureau, "North American Industry Classification System (NAICS)," accessed February 12, 2014, www.census.gov.
14. Company website http://business.verizonwireless.com, accessed February 10, 2014.
15. Michael B. Sauter, Alexander E.M. Hess, and Thomas C. Frohlich, "Ten States Where Manufacturing Matters," *24/7 Wall Street*, accessed February 12, 2014, http://247wallst.com.
16. Company website, "Study Shows Volkswagen Factory Created 12,400 Jobs" (press release) and "Volkswagen Chattanooga Celebrates Inaugural Graduation of Automation Mechatronic Apprentices" (press release), http://media.vw.com, accessed February 12, 2014.
17. Company website, "Meeting the Diverse Needs of Our Customers," www.aboutcdw.com, accessed February 14, 2014.
18. Company website, "Walmart and Sam's Club Help the 1 in 10 North American Kids Treated by Children's Miracle Network Hospitals, Raising $40 Million During Six-Week Fundraising Campaign" (press release), http://news.walmart.com, accessed February 14, 2014.
19. Company website, "Our Company: Senior Operations Leadership," https://cms.coca-colacompany.com, accessed February 14, 2014; William J. Holstein, "How Coca-Cola Manages 90 Emerging Markets," *strategy+business*, accessed February 10, 2014, www.strategy-business.com.
20. "Top Outsourcing Countries," *Sourcing Line*, accessed February 15, 2014, www.sourcingline.com.
21. Mark Hachman, "IDC: PC's Decline Is Far Worse Than Expected," *PC World*, December 2, 2013, www.pcworld.com.
22. "Good Inventory Planning and Global Expansion Will Drive Limited Brands' Growth," *Trefis*, accessed February 12, 2014, www.trefis.com;
23. Company website, "Xerox at a Glance," www.xerox.com, accessed February 18, 2014.
24. Jon Springer, "Vietnam's Stock Market Year in Review, Bull Market Ahead," *Forbes*, accessed February 18, 2014, www.forbes.com; Vietnam Outsourcing Portal, "Why Vietnam?" accessed February 18, 2014, www.vietnamoutsourcing.org.
25. Patrick Clark, "What Happened to Small Businesses Walloped by Hurricane Sandy?" *Bloomberg Businessweek*, accessed February 10, 2014, www.businessweek.com, accessed February 10, 2014; Nick Leiber, "A Flooded Manufacturer Rebounds after Hurricane Sandy" (photo essay), *Bloomberg Businessweek*, accessed February 10, 2014, http://images.businessweek.com; Elizabeth MacDonald, "Superstorm Sandy: One Year Later," *Fox Business*, accessed February 10, 2014, www.foxbusiness.com.
26. Company website, "The Keurig Story," www.keurig.com, accessed February 12, 2014.
27. Company website, "The Keurig Vue Commercial Brewing System," www.keurig.com, accessed February 12, 2014.
28. Company website, "UPS Deploys Next High-Tech Mobile Computer to Drivers," http://pressroom.ups.com, accessed February 12, 2014; Larry Dignan, "UPS Upgrades Driver Handhelds; Utilizes Gobi," *ZDNet*, accessed February 12, 2014, www.zdnet.com.
29. Company website, "Connectivity," http://share.kaiserpermanente.org, accessed February 19, 2014; Devin Leonard and John Tozzi, "Why Don't More Hospitals Use Electronic Health Records?" *Bloomberg Businessweek*, accessed February 19, 2014, www.businessweek.com.
30. Table: Government Units by State, 2012 Census of Governments. *American FactFinder*, U.S. Census Bureau, accessed February 12, 2014, http://factfinder2.census.gov.
31. Organizational website, "Supplier Diversity Corporate Plan," http://about.usps.com, accessed February 12, 2014.
32. Organizational website, "GSA Advantage!" https://www.gsaadvantage.gov, accessed February 14, 2014.

Chapter 8

Global Marketing

WALMART EXTENDS ITS GLOBAL REACH

1. Describe the importance of global marketing from the perspectives of individual firms and the country as a whole.
2. Identify the five major components of the environment for global marketing.
3. Outline the basic functions of GATT, WTO, NAFTA, FTAA, CAFTA-DR, and the European Union.
4. Identify the six alternative strategies for entering foreign markets.
5. Differentiate between a global marketing strategy and a multidomestic marketing strategy.
6. Describe the five alternative marketing mix strategies used in global marketing.
7. Explain the attractiveness of the United States as a target market for foreign marketers.

Even as growth in its huge U.S. market slows, Walmart is finding new global markets to help offset any decline in its total revenues. With some U.S. locations on the rebound and others nearing saturation, Walmart has more than 4,900 stores across the country, including Supercenters and Sam's Club outlets.

Although domestic revenues are still substantial, contributing more than 65 percent of Walmart's total financial picture, international revenues have been growing at a much faster pace. Walmart has been averaging an impressive 15 percent revenue growth overseas, as the $473 billion retailer has expanded to Africa, Europe, Asia, and Latin America. The company now operates more than 6,100 stores selling food and general merchandise in 27 countries and e-commerce websites in 10 countries.

Cultural and legal differences have occasionally forced Walmart to leave a new global market, such as Germany and South Korea. Competitors like Tesco and Carrefour have encountered similar setbacks in markets as varied as Russia, Thailand, and Algeria. Walmart is counting on its longstanding advantages of price leadership and its supply chain expertise to help maintain its healthy global growth in Chile, Brazil, Mexico, South Africa, and China, among others. Many of these areas offer huge untapped markets where shoppers enjoying newfound middle-class prosperity are eager to embrace Walmart's signature everyday low prices and enormous assortment of goods.

Walmart is taking extra care in some markets, too. After finding itself with a few locations in poorly managed malls in China, the company slowed expansion there in order to research new store locations carefully. But its major stake in Yihaodian, a Chinese e-commerce site, has paid off, helping to increase the company's global e-commerce sales by almost 40 percent in a recent fiscal quarter.

At the moment, Walmart stores in South Africa are visited mainly by wealthier customers, but the company is primed for an influx of middle-class food shoppers there and in Latin America. In Brazil everyday low pricing is a novelty the company plans to capitalize on, and it's looking to open more Supercenters in Canada where food sales continue to grow.[1]

EVOLUTION OF A BRAND

Even though Walmart ranks as the world's largest retailer, achieving success overseas isn't a guarantee. The company's global profitability has yet to match that of the company overall. As a result, the company has dialed back its presence in some key markets, closing about 50 underperforming sites in Brazil and China, where it operates hundreds of stores.

- Strategies that work domestically don't always transfer well to overseas destinations, as Walmart management has found. Hiring local managers, the company discovered, is important because they understand the culture and grasp how to market to specific consumer preferences. Why does culture play such a key role in global expansion?
- Walmart has also found that a well-defined real estate strategy may be even more critical overseas than it is in the United States. Besides conducting extensive research, what else can Walmart do to ensure successful location choices?

Chapter Overview

exporting Marketing domestically produced goods and services in foreign countries.

importing Purchasing foreign goods and services.

related party trade Trade by U.S. companies with their subsidiaries overseas as well as trade by U.S. subsidiaries of foreign-owned firms with their parent companies.

Global trade now accounts for more than 20 percent of the U.S. gross domestic product (GDP), compared with 10 percent 30 years ago. Figure 8.1 shows the top ten nations with which the United States trades. Those ten countries account for more than 69 percent of U.S. imports and 62 percent of U.S. exports.[2]

Global trade can be divided into two categories: **exporting**, marketing domestically produced goods and services abroad, and **importing**, purchasing foreign goods and services. Global trade is vital to a country and its marketers for several reasons. It expands markets, makes production and distribution economies possible, allows companies to explore growth opportunities in other nations, and makes them less dependent on economic conditions in their home nations. Many also find that global marketing and trade can help them meet customer demand, reduce costs, and provide valuable information on potential markets around the world.

For North American marketers, trade with foreign markets is especially important because the U.S. and Canadian economies represent a mature market for many products. Outside North America, however, it is a different story. Economies in many parts of sub-Saharan Africa, Asia, Latin America, central Europe, and the Middle East are growing rapidly. This opens up new markets for U.S. products as consumers in these areas have more money to spend and as the need for American goods and services by foreign companies expands.

Global trade also builds employment. In a recent year, the United Nations estimated that 82,000 transnational corporations were in operation, employing about 69 million workers directly and through subsidiaries.[3] Many of these companies and their subsidiaries represent **related party trade**, which includes trade by U.S. companies with their subsidiaries overseas as well as trade by U.S. subsidiaries of foreign-owned firms with their parent companies. According to the U.S. Department of Commerce, related party trade in a recent year accounted for more than 40 percent of total goods traded.[4] Because importing and exporting of so many goods and services play such an important role in the U.S. economy, your future job might very well involve global marketing, either here in the United States or overseas.

FIGURE 8.1
Top U.S. Trading Partners—Total Trade Including Exports and Imports

Source: Data from U.S. Census Bureau, "Top Trading Partners—December 2013," accessed February 20, 2014, www.census.gov.

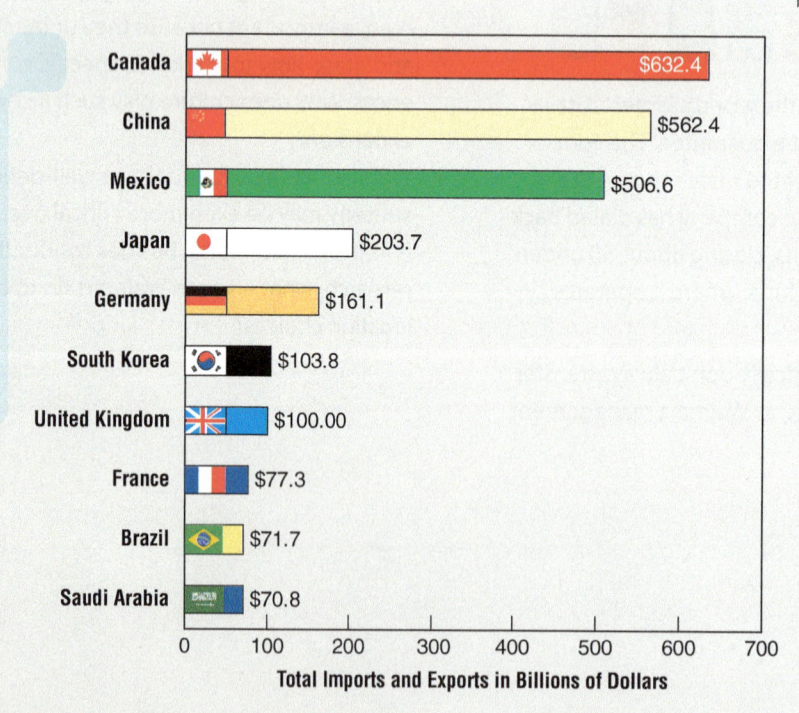

Country	Total Imports and Exports (Billions of Dollars)
Canada	$632.4
China	$562.4
Mexico	$506.6
Japan	$203.7
Germany	$161.1
South Korea	$103.8
United Kingdom	$100.00
France	$77.3
Brazil	$71.7
Saudi Arabia	$70.8

Global marketers carefully evaluate the marketing concepts described in other chapters. However, transactions that cross national borders involve additional considerations. For example, different laws, varying levels of technological capability, economic conditions, cultural and business norms, and consumer preferences often require new strategies. Companies that want to market their products worldwide must reconsider each of the marketing variables—product, distribution, promotion, and price—in terms of the global marketplace. To succeed in global marketing, today's marketers answer questions such as these:

- How do our products fit into a foreign market?
- How can we turn potential threats into opportunities?
- Which strategic alternatives will work in global markets?

Many of the answers to these questions can be found by studying techniques used by successful global marketers. This chapter first considers the importance and characteristics of foreign markets. It then examines the international marketing environment, the trend toward multinational economic integration, and the steps that most firms take to enter the global marketplace. Next, the importance of developing a global marketing mix is discussed. The chapter closes with a look at the United States as a target market for foreign marketers.

THE IMPORTANCE OF GLOBAL MARKETING

As the list of the world's ten largest public corporations shown in Table 8.1 reveals, less than half of these companies are headquartered in the United States. For most companies—large and small—global marketing is rapidly becoming a necessity. The demand for foreign products in the fast-growing economies of the Pacific Rim and other Asian nations offers one example of the benefits of thinking globally. U.S. exports to China, Indonesia, and Vietnam continue to rise.[5] This increase is due to a weak American dollar as well as to Asian consumers' belief that American goods are higher quality than those made in their own countries. International marketers recognize that the slogan "Made in the USA" yields tremendous selling power.

Over the past decade, U.S. goods and services exports have nearly doubled.[6] In a recent year, the United States exported more than $1.5 trillion in goods and services, making it the world's second-largest exporter behind China.[7] Among the leading U.S. firms in revenues generated from exports are Boeing, Intel, Motorola, and Caterpillar.

As discussed in the opening story in this chapter, Walmart currently ranks as the world's largest retailer and largest private employer. With 2.2 million employees, its annual sales are more than double those of Target, Sears, and Costco combined. If Walmart were a country, industry observers estimate its gross domestic product would be the 25th-largest in the world. Walmart's goods represent 15 percent of all U.S. imports from China. The retail giant imports more from China than do Taiwan and Russia combined. Walmart allocates billions of dollars in expansion efforts in Africa, China, Central America, Japan, and South America.[8]

The rapid globalization of business and the boundless nature of the Internet have made it possible for every marketer to become an international marketer. While it isn't easy to be a successful

1 Describe the importance of global marketing from the perspectives of individual firms and the country as a whole.

TABLE 8.1 World's Ten Largest Public Companies (Ranked by Annual Sales)

Rank	Company	Country	Industry	Sales (US $ billion)
1	Walmart Stores	United States	Retailing	476.8
2	Royal Dutch Shell	Netherlands	Oil and gas operations	451.4
3	Sinopec-China Petroleum	China	Oil and gas operations	445.3
4	ExxonMobil	United States	Oil and gas operations	394.0
5	BP	United Kingdom	Oil and gas operations	379.2
6	PetroChina	China	Oil and gas operations	328.5
7	Volkswagen	Germany	Consumer durable	261.5
8	Toyota Motor	Japan	Consumer durable	255.6
9	Total	France	Oil and gas operations	227.9
10	Chevron	United States	Oil and gas operations	211.8

Source: Data from "The Global 2000," Forbes, accessed September 14, 2014, www.forbes.com.

marketer on the Web, and larger firms have the advantage of more resources and wider distribution systems, smaller companies can build websites for as little as a few hundred dollars and can bring products to market quickly. Coverity, a San Francisco-based developer of tools that help companies uncover bugs in their software, has seen rapid growth since its founding little more than a decade ago. Small companies like Coverity succeed by being nimble and identifying the unmet needs of prospective customers.[9]

Just as some firms depend on foreign and Internet sales, others rely on purchasing raw materials abroad as input for their domestic manufacturing operations. A North Carolina furniture manufacturer may depend on purchases of South and Central American teak, while 21st century furniture retailers take advantage of increased Chinese-made styling and quality and their traditionally low prices. Among the top U.S. imports are crude oil, machines, engines, and pumps, consumer electronics, and passenger cars.[10]

SERVICE AND RETAIL EXPORTS

The United States has seen great shifts in the sources of its annual production over the years. In the 1800s, more than 90 percent of Americans worked in farming; today, less than 1.5 percent do. Likewise, manufactured goods no longer account for the lion's share of U.S. production output; today, only about 10 percent of the workforce works in manufacturing. Despite these shifts in the work population, the United States continues to produce record volumes of agricultural and manufactured goods.

The service industry has seen steady growth, with about 80 percent of Americans now working in services. Nearly four of every five dollars in the nation's gross domestic product comes from services such as banking, entertainment, business and technical services, retailing, and communications.[11] These figures represent a profound change from a largely manufacturing economy to a largely service economy. Still, manufacturers as diverse as General Motors and Procter & Gamble strive to serve growing markets, such as China. GM sells its Buick, Chevrolet, Cadillac, and Opel brands in China—more than 3 million cars in a recent year and more than it sold in the United States. GM recently unveiled plans to build the Cadillac in a plant in Shanghai. With numerous leading brands in China, P&G recently launched a $1 billion investment campaign in the country. Plans include construction of a plant in Guangzhou, where Pampers are manufactured.[12]

Procter & Gamble is the leading consumer products marketer in China.

In addition to agricultural products and manufactured goods, the United States is the world's largest exporter of services and retailing. Of the more than $632 billion in annual U.S. service exports, one-fifth of it comes from travel and tourism—money spent by foreign nationals visiting the United States.[13] With rising disposable income and appreciating currency, China is the world's largest source of tourists. In a recent year, more than 100 million Chinese tourists spent more than $120 billion on travel outside their country.[14]

Profitable U.S. service exports include business and technical services, such as engineering, financial, computing, legal services, insurance, and entertainment. The financial services industry, already a major presence outside North America, is expanding globally via the Internet. Today, even the most novice Web users visit finance websites to pay bills, do their banking, or trade stocks online. According to a recent Pew Research Center study, 51 percent of American adults use online banking services (and 32 percent do their banking by mobile phone).[15] A glance at the increasing number of foreign companies listed on the New York Stock Exchange illustrates the importance of global financial services. A number of global service exporters are household names in the United States: American Express, AT&T, Citigroup, Disney, and Allstate Insurance. Many earn a substantial percentage of their revenues from international sales. Others are smaller firms, such as the many software firms that have found overseas markets receptive to their products. Still others are nonprofit organizations, such as the U.S. Postal Service, which is attempting to increase overall revenues by operating a worldwide delivery service. The USPS competes with for-profit firms like UPS and Federal Express.

The entertainment industry is another major service exporter. Movies, TV shows, and music groups often travel to the ends of the earth to entertain their audiences. Almost a century of exposure to U.S.-made films, television programs and, more recently, music video clips has made international viewers more familiar with American culture and geography than that of any other nation on earth.

Americans show a growing appetite for imported entertainment as well. Recently, more than 10 million U.S. viewers tuned in to their local PBS station to watch the premiere episode of *Downton Abbey's* new season. Chronicling the life of British aristocracy around the time of World War I, the series holds the viewership record for PBS, whose audiences generally average 2 million.[16]

> **Briefly Speaking**
>
> "Globalization is a fact of economic life."
>
> —**Carlos Salinas de Gortari**
> *Mexican economist and president of Mexico, 1988–1994*

U.S. retailers, ranging from Foot Locker and Abercrombie & Fitch to Office Depot and Costco, have opened stores around the world. Pottery Barn, founded in 1949 in Manhattan, offers a full range of upscale furnishings for the home. In addition to locations throughout the United States and Canada, the retailer operates stores in Australia, Dubai, and Kuwait.[17]

BENEFITS OF GOING GLOBAL

Besides generating additional revenue, firms expand operations outside their home country to gain other benefits, including new insights into consumer behavior, alternative distribution strategies, and advance notice of new products. By setting up foreign offices and production facilities, marketers may encounter new products, new approaches to distribution, or clever new promotions that they may apply successfully in their domestic market or in other international markets. Often these ventures require firms to send employees abroad on special assignments; see the "Career Readiness" feature for some tips for successful international business travel.

Global marketers typically are well positioned to compete effectively with foreign competitors. A major key to achieving success in foreign markets is the ability to adapt products to local preferences and culture. Restaurants like McDonald's succeed outside the United States by paying attention to local tastes and modifying their menu. Similarly, Yum! Brands, parent of KFC, Pizza Hut, and Taco Bell, has seen success in India by catering to local tastes. The company's aggressive overseas

CAREER READINESS
Tips for International Travel

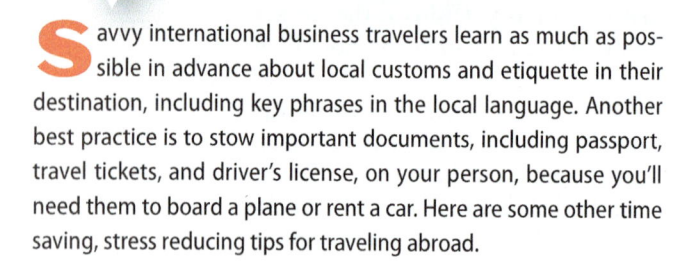

Savvy international business travelers learn as much as possible in advance about local customs and etiquette in their destination, including key phrases in the local language. Another best practice is to stow important documents, including passport, travel tickets, and driver's license, on your person, because you'll need them to board a plane or rent a car. Here are some other time saving, stress reducing tips for traveling abroad.

1. Make sure you have the right voltage converters for the countries you'll visit (check http://voltageconverters.com). Don't count on borrowing or buying these when you arrive; bring your own.

2. Keep must-have items like toiletries and the chargers and adaptors for your electronics in your carry-on luggage at all times so that they're ready when you are.

3. Keep your laptop with you at all times while in transit, and back up work regularly to protect against computer crashes or theft.

4. Make sure your mobile phone will operate overseas. You may need a special SIM card, even if your phone uses GSM technology (a radio frequency accepted across the globe).

5. Charge all your devices the night before your trip. Having your electronics at maximum charge provides flexibility.

6. For the best exchange rate, get your cash from ATMs. Other sources—hotel front desks and airport currency exchanges—give a less attractive rate, and will charge a fee.

7. Track the details of your trip on an app like Evernote. It's accessible no matter where your busy career takes you.

Sources: Sienna Kossman, "10 Tips for Efficient Business Travel," *US News & World Report*, accessed February 20, 2014, http://money.usnews.com; Mandi Woodruff, "Experienced Business Travelers Reveal Their Favorite Travel Tips," *Business Insider*, accessed February 20, 2014, www.businessinsider.com; Arianne Cohen, "Expert Business Travel Tips," *Bloomberg Businessweek*, accessed February 20, 2014, www.businessweek.com; Larry Olmsted, "10 Expert Tips for Leisure and Business Travel, Part I," *Forbes*, accessed February 20, 2014, www.forbes.com.

expansion strategy includes operating nearly 300 KFC stores in India, along with its other leading brands Pizza Hut and Taco Bell.[18]

Subway has more than 42,600 stores in 108 countries. After opening its first overseas Subway (in 1984 in Bahrain), the company targeted ten markets for further expansion, primarily Australia, New Zealand, Japan, and countries in Europe. When other regions—such as Russia—showed strong growth, the company added them to the list. Subway is now well on its way to achieving its goal of opening 1,000 stores in Russia. But tastes differ around the globe. While all Subways feature the same basic menu, cultural and religious preferences often help shape the fare. For example, a sandwich prepared with beef or pork in the United States is likely to use lamb, chicken, or turkey instead in Muslim or Hindu countries. In India, vegetarian sandwiches are another popular choice. And while the type of bread may vary, there's one thing Subway customers can count on: It's baked on-site, daily.[19]

KFC is a leading brand in India. Yum! Brands repeats its Chinese success by catering to local tastes in India.

Because companies must perform the marketing functions of buying, selling, transporting, storing, standardizing and grading, financing, risk taking, and obtaining market information in both domestic and global markets, some may question the wisdom of treating global marketing as a distinct subject. As this chapter will explain, there are similarities and differences that influence strategies for both domestic and global marketing.

ASSESSMENT CHECK

1.1 Define importing and exporting.
1.2 What is the largest category of exports from the United States?
1.3 What must global marketers do effectively to reach foreign markets?

THE INTERNATIONAL MARKETING ENVIRONMENT

As in domestic markets, the environmental factors discussed in Chapter 3 have a powerful influence on the development of a firm's global marketing strategy. Marketers must pay close attention to changing demand patterns as well as economic, social–cultural, political–legal, technological, and competitive influences when they venture abroad.

2 Identify the five major components of the environment for global marketing.

INTERNATIONAL ECONOMIC ENVIRONMENT

A nation's size, per-capita income, and stage of economic development determine its prospects as a host for international business expansion. Nations with low per-capita incomes may be poor markets for expensive industrial machinery but good ones for agricultural hand tools. These nations cannot afford the technical equipment that powers an industrialized society. Wealthier countries may offer prime markets for many U.S. industries, particularly those producing consumer goods and services and advanced industrial products.

Although the U.S. per-capita GDP of $52,800 ranks way above China's $9,800 and India's $4,000, these nations have far larger populations and thus more potential human capital to develop in the future.[20] Their ability to import technology and foreign capital, as well as to train scientists and engineers and invest in research and development, ensures that their growth will be rapid and their income gaps with the United States will close quickly. Most recently, India's GDP rose 5.4 percent, and China's increased 7.5 percent, but the United States' GDP grew only about 2 percent.[21]

Infrastructure—the underlying foundation for modern life and efficient marketing that includes transportation, communications, banking, utilities, and public services—is another important economic factor to consider when planning to enter a foreign market. An inadequate infrastructure may constrain marketers' plans to manufacture, promote, and distribute goods and services in a particular country. People living in countries blessed by navigable waters often rely on them as inexpensive, relatively efficient alternatives to highways, rail lines, and air transportation. Thai farmers use their nation's myriad rivers to transport their crops. Their boats even become retail outlets in so-called floating markets, like the one located outside Bangkok. Often the population in rural areas begins to shift to where the infrastructure is more developed. This change is happening in both China and India, with suburbs springing up around some of India's largest cities. Although both countries' populations continue to grow, India is expected to begin to overtake China around the year 2028, when both countries' populations are projected to stand at 1.45 billion.[22] Marketers expect developing economies to have substandard utility and communications networks. China encountered numerous problems in establishing a 21st century communications industry infrastructure. The Chinese government's answer was to bypass the need for landline telephone connections by leapfrogging technologies and moving directly to cell phones.

Changes in exchange rates can also complicate international marketing. An **exchange rate** is the price of one nation's currency in terms of another country's currency. Fluctuations in exchange rates can make a nation's currency more or less valuable compared with those of other nations. In today's global economy, imbalances in trade, dependence on fossil fuels, and other conditions affect the currencies of many countries, not just one or two. The rising cost of energy and raw materials, stricter business standards, higher labor costs, and a faltering U.S. dollar contributed to price increases for most goods produced in China.[23]

At the beginning of the 21st century, most members of the European Union (EU) switched to the euro as the replacement for their national currencies. The long-range idea is that switching to a single currency will strengthen Europe's competitiveness in the global marketplace. Russian and many eastern European currencies are considered *soft currencies* that cannot be readily converted into such hard currencies as the dollar, euro, or Japanese yen.

INTERNATIONAL SOCIAL–CULTURAL ENVIRONMENT

Before entering a foreign country, marketers should study all aspects of its culture, including language, education, religious attitudes, and social values. The French love to debate and are comfortable with frequent eye contact. In China, humility is a prized virtue, colors have special significance, and it is insulting to be late. Swedes value consensus and do not use humor in negotiations. Navigating these rules that are commonly understood among the citizens of a foreign country takes time, patience, and a willingness to learn about other cultures.

Language plays an important role in global marketing. Table 8.2 lists the world's ten most frequently spoken languages. Marketers must make sure not only to use the appropriate language or languages for a country but also to ensure the message is correctly translated and conveys the intended meaning.

Firms that rely on call centers located in India and staffed by Indian nationals have discovered an occasional language gap. But these employees do speak English, the worldwide language of commerce. Despite some glitches, the call centers, along with other outsourced operations, are booming—creating jobs and a new middle class in India. The country's economy has benefited

---

infrastructure A nation's basic system of transportation networks, communications systems, and energy facilities.

exchange rate Price of one nation's currency in terms of another country's currency.

> **Briefly Speaking**
>
> "International business has always existed in some form. But because of advances in technology and travel, we can do business with India as well as Indiana. In fact, it might even be cheaper to do business with India than Indiana…. There are new cross-cultural markets you can expand into. You've got to know how to work well with other cultures."
>
> —**Dean Foster**
> *U.S. business consultant and author*

TABLE 8.2 The World's Most Frequently Spoken Languages

Rank	Language	Number of Speakers (in millions)
1	Mandarin (Chinese)	1,917
2	Spanish	406
3	English	335
4	Hindi	260
5	Arabic	223
6	Portuguese	202
7	Bengali	193
8	Russian	162
9	Japanese	122
10	Javanese	84

Source: Data from "Most Widely Spoken Languages in the World," accessed September 14, 2014, www.infoplease.com.

hugely from the influx of foreign direct investment that came after the country loosened restrictions on foreign ownership. India now boasts the fastest-growing market for wireless services; mobile-phone sales tripled in a recent two-year period. And IBM recently opened seven offices in India in one year. Big Blue has more workers in India than in any other country, including the United States.[24]

INTERNATIONAL TECHNOLOGICAL ENVIRONMENT

More than any innovation since the telephone, Internet technology has made it possible for both large and small firms to connect to the entire world. The Internet transcends political, economic, and cultural barriers, reaching every corner of the globe. It has made it possible for marketers to add new business channels. It also helps developing nations compete with industrialized nations. However, a huge gap still exists between the regions with the greatest Internet usage and those with the least. Asia, Europe, and North America together account for about 76 percent of the world's total Internet usage. Latin America and the Caribbean follow with more than 10 percent, while Africa accounts for 9 percent, the Middle East 4 percent, and Oceania/Australia 1 percent. Despite those numbers, usage in Africa jumped more than 3,600 percent since 2000, and usage in the Middle East grew more than 2,600 percent.[25]

Technology presents challenges for global marketers that extend beyond the Internet and other telecommunications innovations. A major issue involving food marketers is genetic reengineering. Although U.S. grocery shelves are filled with foods grown with genetically modified organisms (GMOs), most Americans are unaware they are eating GMO foods because no

Technology presents challenges to global marketers worldwide. Here protesters set up demonstrations against the cultivation of GMO crops.

labeling disclosures are required. Worldwide, many nations—including Australia, Austria, Bulgaria, France, Germany, Greece, Hungary, India, Ireland, Japan, Luxembourg, Mexico, New Zealand, and Switzerland—have banned the cultivation of some or all GMO crops. However, in Europe the European Court of Justice has yet to issue a ruling that would ban GMOs throughout the European Union. With soaring food prices and global grain shortages, governments the world over are rethinking their position on foods made from crops that are engineered to resist pests and drought.[26] This complex issue affects almost every marketer in the global food industry.

INTERNATIONAL POLITICAL–LEGAL ENVIRONMENT

Global marketers must continually stay abreast of laws and trade regulations in each country in which they compete. Political conditions often influence international marketing as well. Political unrest in places such as the Middle East, Africa, Eastern Europe, Spain, Greece, and South America sometimes results in acts of violence, such as destruction of a firm's property or even deaths from bombings or other violent acts. As a result, many Western firms have set up internal **political risk assessment (PRA)** units or turned to outside consulting services to evaluate the political risks of the marketplaces in which they operate.

political risk assessment (PRA) Units within a firm that evaluate the political risks of the marketplaces in which they operate as well as proposed new marketplaces.

The political environment also involves labor conditions in different countries. For decades, Chinese laborers have suffered workplace abuses, including forced labor, withholding of pay, and other unfair practices. While recently enacted labor laws give workers more rights, violations still exist.[27] See the "Solving an Ethical Controversy" feature for a further discussion.

The legal environment for U.S. firms operating abroad results from three forces: (1) international law, (2) U.S. law, and (3) legal requirements of host nations. International law emerges from treaties, conventions, and agreements among nations. The United States has many **friendship, commerce, and navigation (FCN) treaties** with other governments. These agreements set terms for various aspects of commercial relations with other countries, such as the right to conduct business in the treaty partner's domestic market. Other international business agreements concern worldwide standards for various products, patents, trademarks, reciprocal tax treaties, export control, international air travel, and international communications. Since the 1990s, Europe has pushed for mandatory **ISO (International Organization for Standardization) certification**—internationally recognized standards that ensure a company's goods, services, and operations meet established quality levels. The organization has two sets of standards: the ISO 9000 series of standards sets requirements for quality in goods and services, and the ISO 14000 series sets standards for operations that minimize harm to the environment. Today, many U.S. companies follow these certification standards as well. Currently, organizations in 164 countries participate in both series.[28] The International Monetary Fund (IMF), another major player in the international legal environment, lends foreign exchange to nations that require it to conduct international trade. These agreements facilitate the entire process of world marketing.

friendship, commerce, and navigation (FCN) treaties International agreements that deal with many aspects of commercial relations among nations.

ISO (International Organization for Standardization) certification Internationally recognized standards that ensure a company's goods, services, and operations meet established quality levels and its operations minimize harm to the environment.

The second dimension of the international legal environment, U.S. law, includes various trade regulations, tax laws, and import and export requirements affecting international marketing. One important law, the Export Trading Company Act of 1982, exempts companies from antitrust regulations so they can form export groups that offer a variety of products to foreign buyers. The law seeks to make it easier for foreign buyers to connect with U.S. exporters.

Another important law is the Foreign Corrupt Practices Act, which makes it illegal for Americans to bribe a foreign official in an attempt to solicit new or repeat sales abroad. This act has had a major impact on international marketing and mandates that adequate accounting controls be installed to monitor internal compliance. Violations can result in a $1 million fine for the firm and a $10,000 fine and five-year imprisonment for the individuals involved. This law has been controversial, mainly because it fails to clearly define what constitutes bribery. The 1988 Trade Act amended the law to include more specific statements of prohibited practices.

Finally, legal requirements of host nations affect foreign marketers. Despite China's many advances in recent years—and even as it attempts to build a modern economy—the Chinese government continues to censor the Internet. More than 618 million Chinese currently use the Internet—more than the entire population of the United States—and an active group of Chinese "hacktivists" works to outwit the government's firewall and help fellow citizens gain unfettered access.[29]

SOLVING AN ETHICAL CONTROVERSY
Who's Responsible for Overseas Working Conditions?

The *New York Times* published a front-page story about abusive, unsafe working and living conditions endured by poorly paid employees building iPads and iPhones in Chinese factories operated by Foxconn Technology. Foxconn employs 1.6 million people and manufactures about 40 percent of consumer electronics worldwide for Amazon, IBM, Dell, Hewlett-Packard, Lenovo, Nintendo, Nokia, Sony, Toshiba, and Samsung, as well as Apple. Apple says it conducts rigorous audits of all its suppliers and requires them to correct abuses when found. Critics say consumers would be horrified if they knew what really went into producing their sleek electronic devices.

Should foreign companies be responsible for unsafe working conditions in China?

PRO
1. If customers of Foxconn Technology and other manufacturers threatened to take their profitable business elsewhere, conditions would quickly improve.
2. Apple and other firms must act responsibly wherever they do business.

CON
1. What U.S. consumers may frown on is often necessary or accepted business practice in other countries.
2. Foreign customers of companies like Foxconn have no right to dictate how its factories should be run.

Summary

Apple's audits reveal that more than half its suppliers regularly violate its code of conduct, but its efforts to enforce standards must also accommodate customers' constant desire for innovative new products. Meanwhile, Foxconn has made progress on improving safety and other working conditions in its Chinese plants—but more improvement is needed.

Sources: Lorraine Luk, "Foxconn Still Exceeds Working Hours," *The Wall Street Journal*, accessed February 20, 2014, http://blogs.wsj.com; Vindu Goel, "Foxconn Audit Finds a Workweek Still Too Long," *The New York Times*, accessed February 20, 2014, www.nytimes.com; "Foxconn Faces Challenge Reducing Work Hours, Monitor Says," *Bloomberg.com*, accessed February 18, 2014, www.bloomberg.com; Fair Labor Association, "Fair Labor Association Verifies Ongoing Progress at Apple Supplier Foxconn," press release, accessed February 18, 2014, www.fairlabor.org; Gordon G. Chang, "Is Foxconn Fleeing China? Sure Looks Like It," *Forbes*, accessed February 18, 2014, www.forbes.com.

TRADE BARRIERS

Assorted trade barriers also affect global marketing. These barriers fall into two major categories: **tariffs**—taxes levied on imported products—and administrative, or nontariff, barriers. Some tariffs impose set taxes per pound, gallon, or unit; others are calculated according to the value of the imported item. Administrative barriers are more subtle than tariffs and take a variety of forms, such as customs barriers, quotas on imports, unnecessarily restrictive standards for imports, and export subsidies. Because the GATT and WTO agreements (discussed later in the chapter) eliminated tariffs on many products, countries frequently use nontariff barriers to boost exports and control the flows of imported products.

The United States and other nations continually negotiate tariffs and other trade agreements. A recent trade agreement between the United States and South Korea eliminated numerous tariffs on U.S. exports to South Korea and wiped out nontariff barriers to U.S. goods and services, creating protections for exporters, investors, and holders of intellectual property rights in the United States.

tariffs Tax levied against imported goods.

The elimination of the tariffs alone is expected to generate an estimated $10 billion to $12 billion in U.S. GDP and create new opportunities with South Korea.[30]

Tariffs

revenue tariffs Taxes designed to raise funds for the importing government.

protective tariffs Taxes designed to raise the retail price of an imported product to match or exceed that of a similar domestic product.

Tariffs can be classified as either revenue or protective tariffs. **Revenue tariffs** are designed to raise funds for the importing government. For years, most U.S. government revenue came from this source. **Protective tariffs**, usually higher than revenue tariffs, are designed to raise the retail price of an imported product to match or exceed that of a similar domestic product. Some countries use tariffs in a selective manner to discourage certain consumption practices and thereby reduce access to their local markets. For example, the United States has tariffs on luxury items, such as Rolex watches and Russian caviar. In 1988, the United States passed the Omnibus Trade and Competitiveness Act to remedy what it perceived as unfair international trade conditions. Under the so-called Super 301 provisions of the law, the United States can single out countries that unfairly impede trade with U.S. domestic businesses. If these countries do not open their markets within 18 months, the law requires retaliation in the form of U.S. tariffs or quotas on the offenders' imports into this country.

Governments sometimes use tariffs to retaliate for real or perceived threats by a trading partner. After the passage of the North American Free Trade Agreement, or NAFTA (discussed later in this chapter), Mexico and the United States engaged in a dispute regarding Mexican truckers operating on U.S. highways. In response, Mexico announced punitive tariffs on 99 U.S.-made goods. The tariffs affected $2.4 billion in U.S. exports and ranged from produce and toiletries to sunglasses and curtain rods. After years of negotiation, Mexico lifted the tariffs.[31]

Other Trade Barriers

In addition to direct taxes on imported products, governments may erect a number of other barriers, ranging from special permits and detailed inspection requirements to quotas on foreign-made items in an effort to stem the flow of imported goods—or halt them altogether. In one of the longest-running trade disputes, European shoppers paid about twice as much for bananas as did North Americans. Through a series of import license controls, Europe had limited the importation of bananas from Latin American countries in an effort to protect producers in former European colonies in Africa and the Caribbean, who pay no tariff. The World Trade Organization ruled that the European tariffs on imported bananas unfairly discriminated against Latin American banana growers. After 16 years of wrangling, the European Union reached an agreement with Latin American growers, which will make them subject to lower tariffs and likely lower the cost of bananas in Europe.[32]

import quotas Trade restrictions limiting the number of units of certain goods that can enter a country for resale.

Other forms of trade restrictions include import quotas and embargoes. **Import quotas** limit the number of product units in certain categories that can cross a country's border for resale. The quota is supposed to protect domestic industry and employment and preserve foreign exchange, but it doesn't always work that way. Import quotas on sugar traditionally help protect U.S. farmers who grow sugar beets. But in a recent year, historic rains and flooding in the Midwest and unusually low temperatures in Florida disrupted domestic sugar production and threatened to create a shortage. These conditions led the U.S. government to temporarily relax import restrictions on sugar.[33]

embargo Complete ban on the import of specified products.

The ultimate quota is the **embargo**—a complete ban on the import of a product. As an example, in 1960, the United States instituted an embargo against Cuba in protest of Fidel Castro's dictatorship and the expropriation of property and disregard for human rights. Not only do the sanctions prohibit Cuban exports—cigars and sugar are the island's best-known products—from entering the United States, but they also apply to companies that profit from property that Cuba's communist government expropriated from Americans following the Cuban Revolution. As another example, some years ago, the discovery of mad cow disease and the potential for contaminated beef resulted in embargoes in many countries, including South Korea. More recently, South Korea again banned some beef imports from the United States after discovering meat containing zilpaterol, a cattle feed additive, might still be in the supply chain.[34]

subsidies Government financial support of a private industry.

Other trade barriers include **subsidies**. China has long subsidized the cost of many products, such as gasoline, to boost consumption. After Chinese wireless carriers subsidized the cost of 3G (third-generation) mobile phones, they saw sales skyrocket.[35] Some nations also limit foreign ownership in the business sectors. Yet another way to block international trade is to create so many regulatory barriers that it is almost impossible to reach target markets. China has a maze of regulations controlling trade, and while the government continues to lift the barriers, experienced businesspeople agree that it's important to have personal connections, or *guanxi*, to help navigate the bureaucratic challenges.

Foreign trade can also be regulated by exchange control through a central bank or government agency. **Exchange control** means that firms that gain foreign exchange by exporting must sell foreign currencies to the central bank or other foreign agency, and importers must buy foreign currencies from the same organization. The exchange control authority can then allocate, expand, or restrict foreign exchange according to existing national policy.

DUMPING

The practice of selling a product in a foreign market at a price lower than it commands in the producer's domestic market is called **dumping**. Critics of free trade often argue that foreign governments give substantial support to their own exporting companies. Government support may permit these firms to extend their export markets by offering lower prices abroad. In retaliation for this interference with free trade, the United States adds import tariffs to products that foreign firms dump on U.S. markets to bring their prices in line with those of domestically produced products. However, businesses often complain that charges of dumping must undergo a lengthy investigative and bureaucratic procedure before the government assesses import duties. U.S. firms claiming that dumping threatens to hurt their business can file a complaint with the U.S. International Trade Commission (ITC), which—on average—rejects about half the claims it receives.

The European Union recently accused China of selling Chinese-made glass for solar panels in Europe at below cost. This dumping of goods permitted Chinese exporters to expand their market share in Europe fivefold in three years' time. The EU imposed a steep anti-dumping tariff on the Chinese companies.[36]

> Due to the embargo on goods from Cuba, cigars exported from Cuba are prohibited in the U.S. Cigars are still rolled by hand in the Little Havana section of Miami.

exchange control Method used to regulate international trade among importing organizations by controlling access to foreign currencies.

dumping Controversial practice of selling a product in a foreign market at a price lower than what it receives in the producer's domestic market.

free-trade area Region in which participating nations agree to the free trade of goods among themselves, abolishing tariffs and trade restrictions.

ASSESSMENT CHECK

2.1 What are the three criteria that determine a nation's prospects as a host for international business expansion?

2.2 What is an FCN treaty?

2.3 What are the two major categories of trade barriers?

MULTINATIONAL ECONOMIC INTEGRATION

A noticeable trend toward multinational economic integration has developed over the seven decades since the end of World War II. Multinational economic integration can be set up in several ways. The simplest approach is to establish a **free-trade area** in which participating nations agree to the

> Outline the basic functions of GATT, WTO, NAFTA, FTAA, CAFTA-DR, and the European Union.

3

customs union Establishment of a free-trade area plus a uniform tariff for trade with nonmember unions.

common market Extension of a customs union by seeking to reconcile all government regulations affecting trade.

free trade of goods among themselves, abolishing tariffs and trade restrictions. A **customs union** establishes a free-trade area plus a uniform tariff for trade with nonmember nations, and a **common market** extends a customs union by seeking to reconcile all government regulations affecting trade. Despite the many factors in its favor, not everyone is enthusiastic about free trade. For more than a decade, Americans have lost jobs when employers outsourced their work to countries like Mexico, where wages are lower. Now, workers in Mexico face the same outsourcing threat as their employers begin outsourcing work to China, where wages are even lower. Although productivity and innovation are said to grow more quickly with free trade, workers often find themselves working longer and for reduced pay as operations move overseas. Many firms view the change as a way to offer superior service.

GATT AND THE WORLD TRADE ORGANIZATION

General Agreement on Tariffs and Trade (GATT) International trade accord that has helped reduce world tariffs.

The **General Agreement on Tariffs and Trade (GATT)**, a trade accord that has sponsored several rounds of major tariff negotiations, substantially reducing worldwide tariff levels, has existed for six decades. In 1994, a seven-year series of GATT conferences, the Uruguay Round, culminated in one of the biggest victories for free trade in decades. The Uruguay Round reduced average tariffs by one-third, or more than $700 billion. Among its major victories:

- Reduced farm subsidies, which opened vast new markets for U.S. exports
- Increased protection for patents, copyrights, and trademarks
- Included services under international trading rules, creating opportunities for U.S. financial, legal, and accounting firms
- Phased out import quotas on textiles and clothing from developing nations, a move that cost textile workers thousands of jobs when their employers moved many of these domestic jobs to lower-wage countries, but benefited U.S. retailers and consumers

World Trade Organization (WTO) Organization that replaces GATT, overseeing GATT agreements, making binding decisions in mediating disputes, and reducing trade barriers.

A key outcome of the GATT talks was the establishment of the **World Trade Organization (WTO)**, a 159-member organization that succeeds GATT. The WTO oversees GATT agreements, serves as a forum for trade negotiations, and mediates trade disputes. It also monitors national trade policies and works to reduce trade barriers throughout the world. Unlike GATT, WTO decisions are binding. Countries that seek to become members of the WTO must participate in rigorous rounds of negotiations that can last several years. Russia holds the record for waiting the longest: Having applied for membership in 1993, its application was approved in 2011.[37]

To date, the WTO has made slow progress toward its major policy initiatives: liberalizing world financial services, telecommunications, and maritime markets. Trade officials have not agreed on the direction for the WTO. Big differences between developed and developing nations create a major roadblock to its progress, and its activities thus far have focused more on dispute resolution through its Dispute Settlement Body than on reducing trade barriers. But the WTO also provides important technical assistance and training for the governments of developing countries.[38]

THE NAFTA ACCORD

North American Free Trade Agreement (NAFTA) Accord removing trade barriers among Canada, Mexico, and the United States.

More than a decade after the passage of the **North American Free Trade Agreement (NAFTA)**—an agreement between the United States, Canada, and Mexico that removes trade restrictions among the three nations—negotiations among the nations continue. The three countries insist they will not create a trade bloc similar to the European Union; that is, they will not focus on political integration but instead on economic cooperation. NAFTA is particularly important to U.S. marketers because Canada and Mexico are two of its largest trading partners.

NAFTA is a complex issue, and from time to time groups in one or more of the three countries chafe under the agreement. In Mexico, farm workers have charged that NAFTA puts their industry at a disadvantage. In Canada, some observers claim NAFTA has compromised their country's oil reserves. In the United States, critics argue that U.S. workers lose jobs to cheap labor south of

THE FREE TRADE AREA OF THE AMERICAS AND CAFTA-DR

NAFTA was the first step toward creating a **Free Trade Area of the Americas (FTAA)**, stretching the length of the entire Western Hemisphere, from Alaska's Bering Strait to Cape Horn at South America's southern tip. The FTAA encompasses 34 countries, and has a population of 800 million and combined gross domestic product of more than $11 trillion. As proposed, the FTAA would be the largest free-trade zone on earth and would offer low or nonexistent tariffs; streamlined customs; and no quotas, subsidies, or other barriers to trade. However, implementation of the FTAA still has many hurdles to overcome as countries wrangle for conditions most favorable to them.[40]

As FTAA negotiations continued, the United States entered into an agreement with the Dominican Republic and Central American nations known as the **Central American Free Trade Agreement-DR (CAFTA-DR)**. Some of its provisions took effect immediately, while others will phase in over the next two decades. Supporters of the agreement say it will help American workers, farmers, and small businesses thrive and grow; critics worry that more American agricultural and manufacturing jobs will be lost. However, both sides agree that CAFTA's economic impact is likely to be relatively small compared with NAFTA.[41]

THE EUROPEAN UNION

The best-known example of a multinational economic community is the **European Union (EU)**. As Figure 8.2 shows, 28 countries make up the EU: Austria, Belgium, Bulgaria, Croatia, Cyprus, the Czech Republic, Denmark, Estonia, Finland, France, Germany, Greece, Hungary, Ireland, Italy, Latvia, Lithuania, Luxembourg, Malta, the Netherlands, Poland, Portugal, Romania, Slovakia,

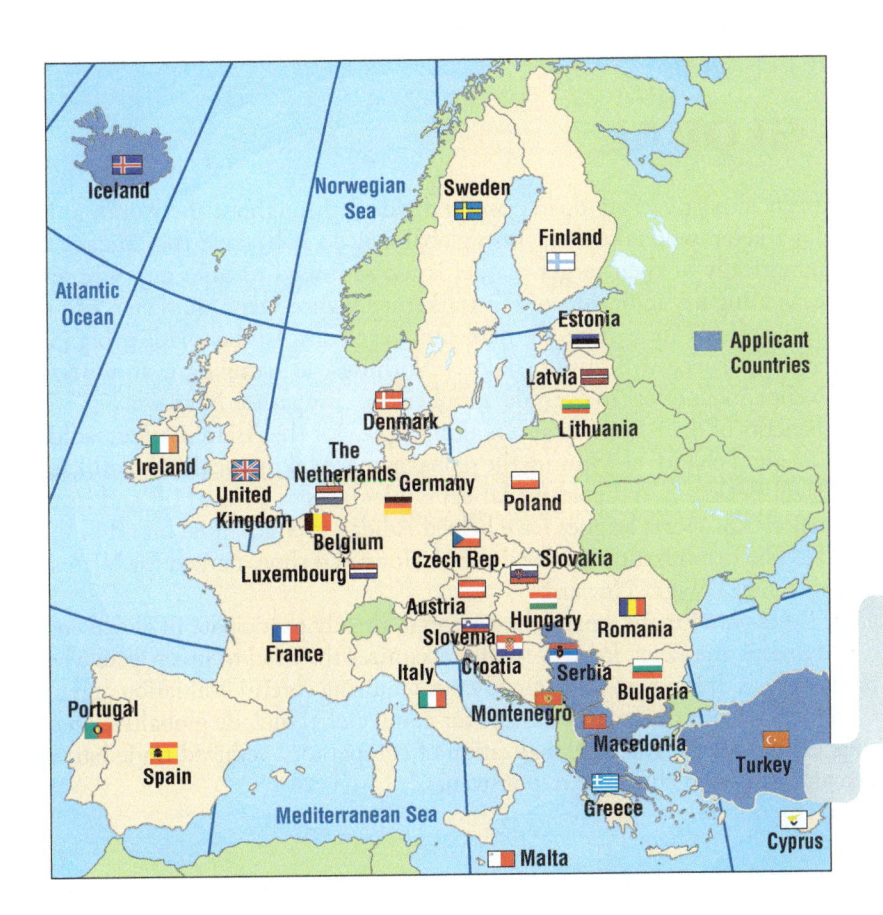

> **Briefly Speaking**
>
> "NAFTA recognizes the reality of today's economy—globalization and technology. Our future is not in competing at the low-level wage job; it is in creating high-wage, new technology jobs based on our skills and our productivity."
>
> —John F. Kerry
> U.S. Secretary of State

Free Trade Area of the Americas (FTAA) Proposed free-trade area stretching the length of the entire Western Hemisphere and designed to extend free trade benefits to additional nations in North, Central, and South America.

Central American Free Trade Agreement-DR (CAFTA-DR) Trade agreement among the United States, Central American nations, and the Dominican Republic.

European Union (EU) Customs union that is moving in the direction of an economic union by adopting a common currency, removing trade restrictions, and permitting free flow of goods and workers throughout the member nations.

FIGURE 8.2
The 28 Members of the European Union

Slovenia, Spain, Sweden, and the United Kingdom. Currently five countries—Iceland, Macedonia, Montenegro, Serbia, and Turkey—are candidates for membership. With a total population of more than 505 million people, the EU forms a huge common market.[42]

The goal of the EU, headquartered in Belgium, is eventually to remove all barriers to free trade among its members, making it as simple and painless to ship products between Finland and Hungary as it is between New Mexico and Ohio. Also involved is the standardization of currencies and regulations that businesses must meet. Introduced in 1999, the EU's euro is the common currency in 17 member-countries, with eight other EU countries planning to phase it in over time. Only Denmark, Sweden, and the United Kingdom have declined to use the euro.[43]

In addition to simplifying transactions among members, the EU looks to strengthen its position in the world as a political and economic power. Its recently ratified Treaty of Lisbon is designed to further streamline operations and enables the EU to enter into international agreements as a political entity.

In some ways, the EU is making definite progress toward its economic goals. It is drafting standardized eco-labels to certify that products are manufactured according to certain environmental standards, as well as creating guidelines governing marketers' uses of customer information. Marketers can also protect some trademarks throughout the entire EU with a single application and registration process through the Community Trademark (CTM), which simplifies doing business and eliminates having to register with each member-country. Yet marketers still face challenges when selling their products in the EU. Customs taxes differ, and no uniform postal system exists. Using one toll-free phone number for several countries will not work, either, because each country has its own telephone system for codes and numbers. Mexico negotiated a trade agreement with the EU that makes it easier for European companies to set up operations in Mexico. The agreement gives EU companies the same privileges enjoyed by the United States and Canada and brings new investors to Mexico.

ASSESSMENT CHECK

3.1 What is the World Trade Organization?

3.2 What countries are parties to the NAFTA accord?

3.3 What is the goal of the European Union?

GOING GLOBAL

Globalization affects almost every industry and individual throughout the world, at least in some way. Traditional marketers who take their firms global may do so because they already have a strong market share domestically or their target market is too saturated to offer any substantial growth. Sometimes, by evaluating key indicators of the marketing environment, marketers can move toward globalization at an optimal time. The German footwear firm Adidas made a big jump into the global market after its successful "Impossible Is Nothing" ad campaign, announcing it would purchase rival Reebok in an effort to overtake number-one competitor Nike.

Using the benefits of the EU while also making a play for the Asian market, Adidas marketers believe they have a good chance at winning the global game. Making deals with athletes like British soccer legend David Beckham and gold-medal heptathlete Jessica Ennis-Hill and issuing licensing agreements to major U.S. sports leagues have helped Adidas strengthen its brand in major markets around the world. The firm recently unveiled the D Howard 4 shoe, named for NBA superstar and Houston Rockets center Dwight Howard.[44]

Most large firms—and many smaller businesses—already participate in global commerce, and virtually every domestic marketer, large or small, recognizes the need to investigate whether to market its products overseas. It is not an easy step to take, requiring careful evaluation and preparation of a strategy. Common reasons that marketers cite for going global include globalization of customers, new customers in emerging markets, globalization of competitors, reduced trade barriers, advances in technology, and enhanced customer responsiveness.

STRATEGIES FOR ENTERING FOREIGN MARKETS

Successful global marketing starts at the top. Without the enthusiasm and support of senior managers, an initiative is likely to fail. Once marketers have researched and identified markets for expansion and won the support of leadership, they may choose from three basic strategies for entering foreign markets: importing and exporting; contractual agreements, such as franchising, licensing, and subcontracting; and international direct investment. As Figure 8.3 shows, the level of risk and the firm's degree of control over international marketing increase with greater involvement. Firms often use more than one of these entry strategies.

> Identify the six alternative strategies for entering foreign markets.

IMPORTING AND EXPORTING

An importer is a firm that brings in goods produced abroad to sell domestically or to be used as components in its products. In making import decisions, the marketer must assess local demand for the product, taking into consideration factors such as the following:

- Ability of the supplier to maintain agreed-to quality levels
- Flexibility in filling orders that might vary considerably from one order to the next
- Response time in filling orders
- Total costs—including import fees, packaging, and transportation—in comparison with costs of domestic suppliers

Exporting, another basic form of global marketing, involves a continuous effort in marketing a firm's merchandise to customers in other countries. Many firms export their products as the first step in reaching foreign markets. Furniture manufacturer IKEA has built an entire exporting strategy around its modular furniture. Because IKEA's furniture is lightweight, packs flat, and comes in components that customers can assemble, the firm can ship its goods almost anywhere in the world at a lower cost than manufacturers of traditional furniture.[45]

First-time exporters can reach foreign customers through one or more of three alternatives: export trading companies, export management companies, or offset agreements. An export trading company (ETC) buys products from domestic producers and resells them abroad. While manufacturers lose control over marketing and distribution to an ETC, it helps them export through a relatively simple and inexpensive channel, in the process providing feedback about the overseas market potential of their products.

The second option, an export-management company (EMC), provides the first-time exporter with expertise in locating foreign buyers, handling necessary paperwork, and ensuring that its goods meet local labeling and testing laws. However, the manufacturer retains more control over the export process when it deals with an EMC than if it were to sell the goods outright to an export-trading company. Smaller firms can get assistance with administrative needs, such as financing and preparation of proposals and contracts from large EMC contractors.

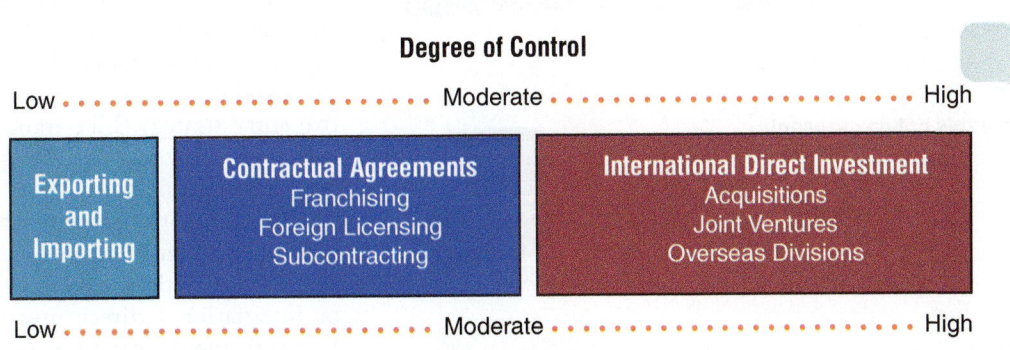

Degree of Control

Low ················· Moderate ················· High

| Exporting and Importing | Contractual Agreements
Franchising
Foreign Licensing
Subcontracting | International Direct Investment
Acquisitions
Joint Ventures
Overseas Divisions |

Low ················· Moderate ················· High

Degree of Risk

FIGURE 8.3
Levels of Involvement in Global Marketing

franchise Contractual arrangement in which a wholesaler or retailer agrees to meet the operating requirements of a manufacturer or other franchiser.

foreign licensing Agreement that grants foreign marketers the right to distribute a firm's merchandise or to use its trademark, patent, or process in a specified geographic area.

The final option, entering a foreign market under an offset agreement, teams a small firm with a major international company. The smaller firm essentially serves as a subcontractor on a large foreign project. This entry strategy provides new exporters with international experience, supported by the assistance of the primary contractor, in such areas as international transaction documentation and financing.

CONTRACTUAL AGREEMENTS

As a firm gains sophistication in global marketing, it may enter contractual agreements that provide several flexible alternatives to exporting. Both large and small firms can benefit from these methods. Franchising and foreign licensing, for example, are good ways to take services abroad. Subcontracting agreements may involve either production facilities or services.

Franchising

A **franchise** is a contractual arrangement in which a wholesaler or retailer (the franchisee) agrees to meet the operating requirements of a manufacturer or other franchiser. The franchisee receives the right to sell the products and use the franchiser's name as well as a variety of marketing, management, and other services. Fast-food companies like McDonald's have been active franchisers around the world.

One advantage of franchising is risk reduction by offering a proven concept. Standardized operations typically reduce costs, increase operating efficiencies, and provide greater international recognizability. However, the success of an international franchise depends on its willingness to balance standard practices with local customer preferences. McDonald's, Pizza Hut, and Domino's are expanding into India with special menus that feature lamb, chicken, and vegetarian items, in deference to Hindu and Muslim customers who do not eat beef and pork. McDonald's adapted with great success in France, where palates are notoriously finicky, although the process took time. See the "Marketing Success" feature for the story.

Furniture manufacturer IKEA has built its entire exporting strategy around modular furniture, which is lightweight, packs flat, and is easy to ship.

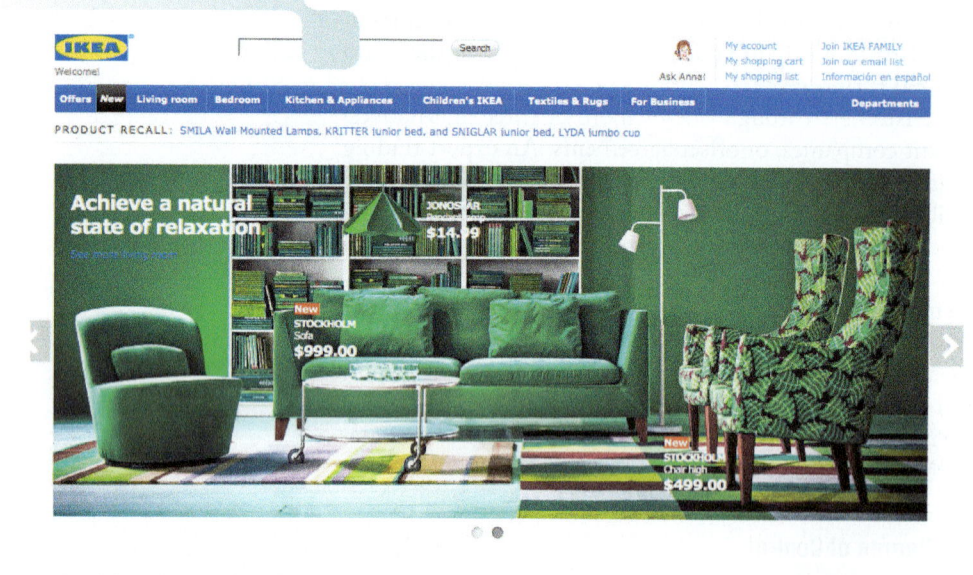

Foreign Licensing

A second method of going global through the use of contractual agreements is **foreign licensing**. Such an agreement grants foreign marketers the right to distribute a firm's merchandise or to use its trademark, patent, or process in a specified geographic area. These arrangements usually set certain time limits, after which agreements are revised or renewed.

Licensing offers several advantages over exporting, including access to local partners' marketing information and distribution channels and protection from various legal barriers. Because licensing does not require capital outlays, many firms, both small and large, regard it as an attractive entry strategy. Like franchising, licensing allows a firm to quickly enter a foreign market with a known product. The arrangement may also provide entry into a market that government restrictions close to imports or international direct investment. Entertainment software producer Electronic Arts entered into a ten-year

Source: http://www.ikea.com/us/en/

MARKETING SUCCESS
McDonald's Thrives in France

Background. McDonald's is the world's largest restaurant chain, operating in 119 countries with 1.8 million employees and opening hundreds of new locations every year. For many, it has long represented U.S. culture abroad, tailoring basic burgers, salads, and fries to local tastes.

The Challenge. McDonald's opened its first French restaurant in 1979, followed by a franchise expansion where, for many years, "what we did above all was offer people a slice of America." But the French love quality in their cuisine, mostly eat at home, rarely snack, and like to take their time at the table. McDonald's needed to determine how to better satisfy preferences in France.

The Strategy. The company changed its recipes, incorporating French-style ingredients and dishes and even introducing the McBaguette. Customers can order through their smartphone or at order kiosks in the restaurants, making it possible for McDonald's to affordably provide table service instead of counter service and allow customers to linger over coffee and dessert. Its French stores are spacious and tasteful, including McCafés with plush seating, and the kitchens rely on fresh, locally sourced ingredients.

The Outcome. France is now McDonald's second-largest market (after the United States), with more than 1,300 restaurants and a 30-unit annual growth rate. French customers typically spend about 4 times as much per visit as U.S. patrons do.

Sources: Company website, **www.aboutmcdonalds.com**, accessed September 14, 2014; Rob Wile, "The True Story of How McDonald's Conquered France," *Business Insider*, accessed September 14, 2014, **www.businessinsider.com**; company website, "McDonald's Europe: A Quick Snapshot," **www.mcdpressoffice.eu**, accessed September 14, 2014; Jeff Morganteen, "Le Big Mac? Mais Oui!" *CNBC*, accessed February 20, 2014, **www.cnbc.com**; "PayPal to Provide Online, In-Store and Mobile Payments for McDonald's France," *Bobsguide.com*, accessed February 17, 2014, **www.bobsguide.com**; Matt Goulding, "Why the French Secretly Love the Golden Arches," *Slate.com*, accessed February 17, 2014, **www.slate.com**; Carol Matlack, "McDonald's Offers France a High-Calorie McBaguette," *Bloomberg Businessweek*, accessed February 15, 2014, **www.businessweek.com**.

---

licensing agreement with Disney to develop *Star Wars* games. Disney's recent investment in the *Star Wars* brand offers flexibility for Electronic Arts to create a broad array of *Star Wars*–themed games.[46]

Subcontracting

A third strategy for going global through contractual agreements is **subcontracting**, in which the production of goods or services is assigned to local companies. Using local subcontractors can prevent mistakes involving local culture and regulations. Manufacturers might subcontract with a local company to produce their goods or use a foreign distributor to handle their products abroad or provide customer service. Manufacturing within the country can provide protection from import duties and may be a lower-cost alternative that makes it possible for the product to compete with local offerings. It can also have a downside if local suppliers don't make the grade or if a manufacturer imposes an unrealistically tight timeframe on a supplier to deliver the product, leading to long hours or sweatshop conditions in the factory.

subcontracting
Contractual agreements that assign the production of goods or services to local or smaller firms.

INTERNATIONAL DIRECT INVESTMENT

Another strategy for entering global markets is international direct investment in foreign firms, production, and marketing facilities. As the world's largest economy, the United States has significant foreign direct investment inflows and outflows. U.S. direct investment abroad is nearly $3.7 trillion, with its greatest presence in Canada, the Netherlands, and the United Kingdom. On the other hand, foreign direct investment in the United States in a recent year totaled $3.9 trillion and originated chiefly through investors in Australia, Canada, Europe, Japan, and South Korea.[47]

Although high levels of involvement and high risk potential are characteristics of investments in foreign countries, firms choosing this method often have a competitive advantage. Direct investment can take several forms. A company can acquire an existing firm in a country where it wants to do business, or it can set up an independent division outside its borders with responsibility for production and marketing in a country or geographic region. Asian firms, particularly Chinese, have been seeking to purchase U.S. businesses, mostly in industries involving natural resources, such as oil, natural gas, metals, and coal. However, they have been making inroads in industrial, technology, and finance companies as well. China's Meidu Holding Company recently acquired U.S.-based Woodbine Acquisition, an oil and gas development company.[48]

Companies may also engage in international marketing by forming joint ventures in which they share the risks, costs, and management of the foreign operation with one or more partners. These partnerships join the investing companies with nationals of the host countries. While some companies choose to open their own facilities overseas, others share with their partners. Because India puts limits on foreign direct investment, Gap recently announced it signed a letter of intent to form a partnership with Indian conglomerate Arvind Brands to open retail stores in India.[49]

Although joint ventures offer many advantages, foreign investors have encountered problems in several areas throughout the world, especially in developing economies. Lower trade barriers, new technologies, lower transport costs, and vastly improved access to information mean that many more partnerships will be involved in international trade.

ASSESSMENT CHECK

4.1 What are the three basic strategies for entering foreign markets?
4.2 What is a franchise?
4.3 What is international direct investment?

FROM MULTINATIONAL CORPORATION TO GLOBAL MARKETER

A multinational corporation is a firm with significant operations and marketing activities outside its home country. Examples of multinationals include General Electric, Siemens, and Mitsubishi in heavy electrical equipment, and Timex, Seiko, and Citizen in watches. Since they first became a force in international business in the 1960s, multinationals have evolved in some important ways. First, these companies are no longer exclusively U.S. based. Today, it is as likely for a multinational to be based in Japan, Germany, or Great Britain. Second, multinationals no longer think of their foreign operations as mere outsourcing appendages that carry out the design, production, and engineering ideas conceived at home. Instead, they encourage constant exchanges of ideas, capital, and technologies among all the multinational operations.

Multinationals often employ huge foreign workforces relative to their American staffs. More than half of all Ford and IBM personnel are located outside the United States. These workforces are no longer seen merely as sources of cheap labor; on the contrary, many multinationals center technically complex activities in locations throughout the world. Texas Instruments does much of its research, development, design, and manufacturing in East Asia. U.S. multinationals often bring product innovations from their foreign facilities back to the States.

Multinationals have become global corporations that reflect the interdependence of world economies, the growth of international competition, and the globalization of world markets. However, many people worry that this globalization means that U.S. dominance in many markets will decline and disappear. Sixty percent of households in Hong Kong get their television services through ultra-high-speed broadband connections that turn their TVs into computers, a concept still catching on slowly in the United States. European and Asian consumers now use smart cards with embedded memory chips instead of traditional credit cards or cash for retail purchases. Chile has emerged as a top destination in South America for multinational firms seeking to expand their global business by outsourcing some functions. Swiss engineering and technology giant ABB chose Chile as the site of its first remote service center. The center provides real-time monitoring, diagnostics, and technical assistance for a number of ABB's businesses.[50]

> **Briefly Speaking**
>
> "Learn Chinese. There's going to be a lot of action in China."
>
> —**Lakshmi Narayanan**
> *Vice chairman, Cognizant Technologies*

ASSESSMENT CHECK

4.4. What is a multinational corporation?
4.5. What are two ways in which multinationals have changed since the 1960s?

DEVELOPING AN INTERNATIONAL MARKETING STRATEGY

In developing a marketing mix, international marketers may choose between two alternative approaches: a global marketing strategy or a multidomestic marketing strategy. A **global marketing strategy** defines a standard marketing mix and implements it with minimal modifications in all foreign markets. This approach brings the advantage of economies of scale to production and marketing activities. Marketers at Procter & Gamble devised a global marketing strategy for Pringles potato chips by selling the same formulation in every country, meeting 80 percent of worldwide demand with only six flavors of Pringles and one package design. Such a standardized approach saves money because it allows large-scale production runs and reinforces the brand's image. Pringles' strong global performance figured heavily in Kellogg's decision to acquire the brand from P&G. Under Kellogg's ownership, Pringles has expanded its reach with new flavors—such as Sweet Paprika for Germany, Roast Chicken and Herbs for France and the UK, and Cheddar Cheese in Arab countries.[51]

A global marketing perspective can effectively market some goods and services to segments in many nations that share cultures and languages. This approach works especially well for products with strong, universal appeal such as Nike, luxury items like Rolex watches, and high-tech brands such as Microsoft. Global advertising outlets such as international editions of popular consumer and business magazines and international transmissions of TV channels like Fox, CNN, MTV, and the CNBC financial network help marketers deliver a single message to millions of global viewers.

A global marketing strategy also can be highly effective for luxury products that target upscale consumers everywhere. Marketers of diamonds and luxury watches, for instance, typically use advertising with little or no copy—just a picture of a beautiful diamond or watch with the name discreetly displayed on the page.

But a global strategy doesn't always work, as Domino's discovered after it opened stores in Asia during the late 1990s. With its "30-minutes-or-it's-free" policy, the pizza purveyor had long been

> Differentiate between a global marketing strategy and a multidomestic marketing strategy.
>
> **global marketing strategy** Standardized marketing mix with minimal modifications that a firm uses in all of its domestic and foreign markets.

Under Kellogg's ownership, Pringles brand now uses a multidomestic marketing strategy to customize its offerings in other countries such as Germany.

multidomestic marketing strategy
Application of market segmentation to foreign markets by tailoring the firm's marketing mix to match specific target markets in each nation.

known for the fastest pizzas rather than the best-tasting ones. Apparently for Asians, the 30-minute guarantee wasn't attractive enough to offset how the food tasted, and Domino's ended up closing more than 50 stores in Hong Kong, Indonesia, Singapore, and Thailand from 1997 to 2001. Further spurred by lawsuits involving delivery drivers and car crashes, Domino's conducted research and learned that for many customers, speed doesn't equate to quality. Domino's dropped the 30-minute guarantee and recent campaigns focus on quality, not speed.[52]

A major benefit of a global marketing strategy is its low cost to implement. Most firms, however, find it necessary to practice market segmentation outside their home markets and tailor their marketing mixes to fit the unique needs of customers in specific countries. This **multidomestic marketing strategy** assumes that differences between market characteristics and competitive situations in certain nations require firms to customize their marketing decisions to effectively reach individual marketplaces. Many marketing experts believe that most products demand multidomestic marketing strategies to give them realistic global marketing appeal. Cultural, geographic, language, and other differences simply make it difficult to send the same message to many countries. Specific situations may allow marketers to standardize some parts of the marketing process but customize others.

ASSESSMENT CHECK

5.1 What is the difference between a global marketing strategy and a multidomestic marketing strategy?

INTERNATIONAL PRODUCT AND PROMOTIONAL STRATEGIES

6 Describe the five alternative marketing mix strategies used in global marketing.

Global marketers can choose from among five strategies for selecting the most appropriate product and promotion strategy for a specific foreign market: straight extension, promotion adaptation, product adaptation, dual adaptation, and product invention. As Figure 8.4 indicates, the strategies center on whether to extend a domestic product and promotional strategy into international markets or adapt one or both to meet the target market's unique requirements.

An organization may follow a one-product, one-message straight extension strategy as part of a global marketing strategy. This strategy permits economies of scale in production and marketing. Also, successful implementation creates universal recognition of a product for consumers from country to country. ONE, the advocacy organization cofounded by rock musician Bono, works to eradicate poverty and preventable disease, particularly in Africa. With a presence on Facebook, LinkedIn, and Twitter, its multilingual website is carried in French, German, and English.[53]

Other strategies call for product adaptation, promotion adaptation, or both. Marketers in the greeting-card industry adapt their product and messaging to cultural differences. For example, Russians are unlikely to send a card to a man on his 40th birthday. The reason: A common superstition in Russia that says big parties for a man celebrating that particular milestone attract "the Death." In Japan, where the parent–child relationship is formal, cards intended for a parent are also formal and express less sentimentality. And most cultures outside of the United States don't resonate to images of Santa Claus.[54]

Finally, a firm may select product invention to take advantage of unique foreign market opportunities. To match user needs in developing nations, an appliance manufacturer might introduce a hand-powered washing machine, even though such products became obsolete in industrialized countries years ago. Although Chapter 13 discusses the idea of branding in greater detail, it is important to note here the value of a company's recognizable name, image, product, or even slogan around the world.

FIGURE 8.4 Alternative International Product and Promotional Strategies

		Product Strategy		
		Same Product	**Product Adaptation**	**New Product**
Promotion Strategy	**Same Promotion**	Straight Extension: General Mills Cheerios, Coca-Cola, Mars Snickers candy bar	Product Adaptation: Campbell's soup, Exxon gasoline	Product Invention: Nonelectric sewing machines, Manually operated washing machines
	Different Promotion	Promotion Adaptation: Bicycles/motorcycles, Outboard motors	Dual Adaptation: Coffee, Some clothing	

An improved distribution network and edgy ad campaigns have helped boost sales for the Fiat 500 Abarth.

INTERNATIONAL DISTRIBUTION STRATEGY

Distribution is a vital aspect of overseas marketing. Marketers must set up proper channels and anticipate extensive physical distribution problems. Foreign markets may offer poor transportation systems and warehousing facilities—or none at all. Global marketers must adapt promptly and efficiently to these situations to profit from overseas sales.

A distribution decision involves two steps. First, the firm must decide on a method of entering the foreign market. Second, it must determine how to distribute the product within the foreign market through that entry channel. After Chrysler Group introduced the Fiat 500 in the United States, sales were flat—a phenomenon that management attributed to an insufficient distribution network. The following year, the automaker launched its Fiat 500 Abarth with an edgy campaign featuring a supermodel and sales have surpassed sales expectations. Chrysler recently created a unique ad for the car that appeared in *ESPN The Magazine's* "Body Issue"—a Fiat 500 Abarth Cabrio constructed from over a dozen artists, models, and contortionists.[55]

PRICING STRATEGY

Pricing can critically affect the success of an overall marketing strategy for foreign markets. Considerable competitive, economic, political, and legal constraints often limit pricing decisions. Global marketers can succeed if they thoroughly understand these requirements.

Companies must adapt their pricing strategies to local markets and alter them when conditions change. In India, Unilever's partner Hindustan Lever offers "penny packets" of shampoo to lower-income consumers who typically cannot afford to buy an entire bottle of shampoo. Although local firms follow the same practice, Hindustan Lever wants to develop loyalty among these consumers so that when they move up the income scale, they will be more apt to buy the firm's higher-priced products as well.

An important development in pricing strategy for international marketing has been the emergence of commodity marketing organizations that seek to control prices through collective action. The Organization of Petroleum Exporting Countries (OPEC) is a good example of this kind of collective export organization.

COUNTERTRADE

countertrade Form of exporting whereby goods and services are bartered rather than sold for cash.

In a growing number of nations, the only way a marketer can gain access to foreign markets is through **countertrade**—a form of exporting in which a firm barters products rather than selling them for cash. Less-developed nations sometimes impose countertrade requirements when they lack sufficient foreign currency to attain goods and services they want or need from exporting countries. These nations allow sellers to exchange their products only for domestic products as a way to control their balance-of-trade problems.

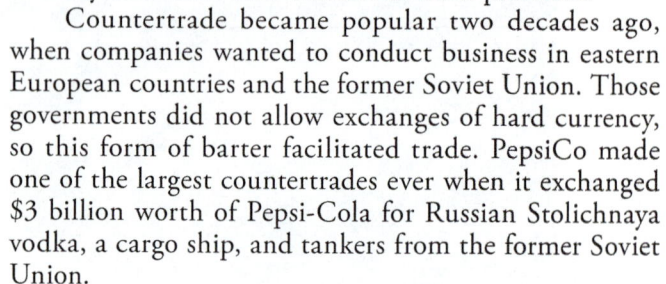

Countertrade became popular two decades ago, when companies wanted to conduct business in eastern European countries and the former Soviet Union. Those governments did not allow exchanges of hard currency, so this form of barter facilitated trade. PepsiCo made one of the largest countertrades ever when it exchanged $3 billion worth of Pepsi-Cola for Russian Stolichnaya vodka, a cargo ship, and tankers from the former Soviet Union.

ASSESSMENT CHECK

6.1 What are the five strategies for selecting the most appropriate product and promotional strategy for a specific foreign market?

6.2 What is countertrade?

THE UNITED STATES AS A TARGET FOR INTERNATIONAL MARKETERS

7 Explain the attractiveness of the United States as a target market for foreign marketers.

Foreign marketers regard America as an inviting target. It offers a large population of more than 316 million people. In addition, U.S. consumers have a high level of discretionary income, with a GDP per capita estimated at $52,800 and a median gross family income of about $53,046.[56] Risks to foreign marketers are also low due to the United States' political stability, generally favorable attitude toward foreign investment, and growing economy.

For South Korean consumer electronics giant LG Electronics, the United States is a hugely profitable market. Since establishing a North American headquarters in the United States, total sales topped $53 billion in a recent year. LG markets a broad array of home appliances as well as consumer electronics products, including Blu-ray players, cell phones, computers, TVs, and other digital media.[57] Among the best-known industries in which foreign manufacturers have established U.S. production facilities is automobiles. Most of the world's leading auto companies have invested heavily in assembly facilities in the United States: BMW in South Carolina; Honda in Alabama, California, Florida, Georgia, Indiana, North Carolina, Ohio, and South Carolina; Hyundai in Alabama, California, and Michigan; Kia in Georgia; Mercedes-Benz in Alabama; Nissan in Mississippi and Tennessee; Toyota in Alabama, Arizona, Arkansas, California, Indiana, Kentucky, Michigan, Mississippi, Missouri, New York, North Carolina, Tennessee, Texas, and West Virginia; and Volkswagen in Tennessee.[58]

As we discussed earlier, foreign investment continues to grow in the United States. Increasingly, foreign multinationals will invest in U.S. assets as they seek to produce goods locally and control distribution channels.

ASSESSMENT CHECK

7.1. What characteristics of the United States make it an inviting target for foreign marketers?

7.2. Why would U.S. automobile manufacturing be a target for foreign companies?

Strategic Implications of Marketing in the 21st Century

The first 15 years of the new century have marked a new era of truly global marketing, in which the world's marketplaces are accessible to nearly every firm. Marketers in both small, localized firms and giant businesses need to re-evaluate the strengths and weaknesses of their current marketing practices and realign their plans to meet the new demands of this era.

Marketers are the pioneers in bringing new technologies to developing nations. Their successes and failures will determine the direction global marketing will take and the speed with which it will be embraced. Actions of international marketers will influence every component of the marketing environment: competitive, economic, social–cultural, political–legal, and technological.

The greatest competitive advantages will belong to marketers who capitalize on the similarities of their target markets and adapt to the differences. In some instances, the actions of marketers today help determine the rules and regulations of tomorrow. Marketers need flexible and broad views of an increasingly complex customer. Goods and services will likely become more customized as they are introduced in foreign markets, yet some recognizable brands seem to remain universally popular just as they are. New and better products in developing markets will create and maintain relationships for the future.

Get online now for additional learning tools to help you master your marketing knowledge—visit WWW.CENGAGEBRAIN.COM today!

REVIEW OF CHAPTER OBJECTIVES

1 Describe the importance of global marketing from the perspectives of individual firms and the country as a whole.

Global marketing expands a company's market, allows firms to grow, and makes them less dependent on their own country's economy for success. For the nation, global trade provides a source of needed raw materials and other products not available domestically in sufficient amounts, opens up new markets to serve with domestic output, and converts countries and their citizens into partners in the search for high-quality products at the lowest possible prices. Companies find that global marketing and international trade can help them meet customer demand, reduce certain costs, provide information on markets around the world, and increase employment.

2 Identify the five major components of the environment for global marketing.

The major components of the international environment are economic, social–cultural, technological, political–legal, and competitive. A country's infrastructure also plays an important role in determining how effective marketers will be in manufacturing, promoting, and distributing their goods and services.

3 Outline the basic functions of GATT, WTO, NAFTA, FTAA, CAFTA-DR, and the European Union.

The General Agreement on Tariffs and Trade is an accord that has substantially reduced tariffs. The World Trade Organization oversees GATT agreements, mediates disputes, and tries to reduce trade barriers throughout the world. The North American Free Trade Agreement removes trade restrictions among Canada, Mexico, and the United States. The proposed Free Trade Area of the Americas seeks to create a free-trade area covering the entire Western Hemisphere. As another step in that direction, the United States has made an agreement with the Dominican Republic and Central American nations known as the Central American Free Trade Agreement–DR (CAFTA-DR). The European Union is a customs union whose goal is to remove all barriers to free trade among its members.

4 Identify the six alternative strategies for entering foreign markets.

Several strategies are available to marketers, including exporting, importing, franchising, foreign licensing, subcontracting, and direct investment. This progression moves from the least to the most involvement by a firm.

5 Differentiate between a global marketing strategy and a multidomestic marketing strategy.

A global marketing strategy defines a standard marketing mix and implements it with minimal modifications in all foreign markets. A multidomestic marketing strategy requires firms to customize their marketing decisions to reach individual marketplaces.

6 Describe the five alternative marketing mix strategies used in global marketing.

Product and promotional strategies include the following: straight extension, promotion adaptation, product adaptation, dual adaptation, and product invention. Marketers may also choose among distribution, pricing, and countertrade strategies.

7 Explain the attractiveness of the United States as a target market for foreign marketers.

The United States has a large population, high levels of discretionary income, political stability, a favorable attitude toward foreign investment, and a steadily growing economy.

ASSESSMENT CHECK: ANSWERS

1.1 Define importing and exporting. Importing involves purchasing foreign goods and services. Exporting refers to marketing domestically produced goods and services abroad.

1.2 What is the largest category of exports from the United States? The largest category of exports from the United States is services.

1.3 What must global marketers do effectively to reach foreign markets? Global marketers must adapt their goods and services to local preferences.

2.1 What are the three criteria that determine a nation's prospects as a host for international business expansion? A nation's size, per-capita income, and stage of economic development determine its prospects as a host for international business expansion.

2.2 What is an FCN treaty? FCN stands for friendship, commerce, and navigation. These treaties set terms for various aspects of commercial relations with other countries.

2.3 What are the two major categories of trade barriers? The two categories of trade barriers are tariffs and nontariffs.

3.1 What is the World Trade Organization? The World Trade Organization (WTO) oversees GATT agreements and mediates disputes. It also continues efforts to reduce trade barriers around the world.

3.2 What countries are parties to the NAFTA accord? The United States, Canada, and Mexico are members of NAFTA.

3.3 What is the goal of the European Union? The European Union (EU) seeks to remove all barriers to free trade among its members and strengthen its position in the world as an economic and political power.

4.1 What are the three basic strategies for entering foreign markets? The three basic strategies are importing and exporting, contractual agreements, and international direct investment.

4.2 What is a franchise? A franchise is a contractual agreement in which a wholesaler or retailer (the franchisee) agrees to meet the operating requirements of a manufacturer or other franchiser.

4.3 What is international direct investment? International direct investment is direct investment in foreign firms, production, and marketing facilities.

4.4 What is a multinational corporation? A multinational corporation is a firm with significant operations and marketing activities outside the home country.

4.5 What are two ways in which multinationals have changed since the 1960s? Two ways these firms have changed are that they are no longer exclusively U.S. based, and they no longer think of their foreign operations as mere outsourcing appendages.

5.1 What is the difference between a global marketing strategy and a multidomestic marketing strategy? A global marketing strategy defines a marketing mix and implements it with minimal modifications in all foreign markets. A multidomestic marketing strategy requires that firms customize their marketing decisions to reach individual marketplaces.

6.1 What are the five strategies for selecting the most appropriate product and promotion strategy for a specific foreign market? The five strategies are straight extension, promotion adaptation, product adaptation, dual adaptation, and product invention.

6.2 What is countertrade? Countertrade is a form of exporting in which a firm barters products rather than selling them for cash.

7.1 What characteristics of the United States make it an inviting target for foreign marketers? The characteristics making the United States an attractive target for foreign marketers are a large population to sell products to and high levels of discretionary income that make purchases possible. In addition, it has low risks to foreign marketers due to a stable political environment, favorable attitude toward foreign investment, and a growing economy.

7.2 Why would U.S. automobile manufacturing be a target for foreign companies? Because the United States has a large population and high income levels, foreign car manufacturers find the country an attractive and lucrative market. The size and weight of cars make them bulky to transport long distances, so firms might find local manufacturing a profitable alternative to exporting.

MARKETING TERMS YOU NEED TO KNOW

exporting 240
importing 240
related party trade 240
infrastructure 246
exchange rate 246
political risk assessment (PRA) 248
friendship, commerce, and navigation (FCN) treaties 248
ISO (International Organization for Standardization) certification 248
tariffs 249
revenue tariffs 250
protective tariffs 250
import quotas 250
embargo 250
subsidies 250
exchange control 251
dumping 251
free-trade area 251
customs union 252
common market 252
General Agreement on Tariffs and Trade (GATT) 252
World Trade Organization (WTO) 252
North American Free Trade Agreement (NAFTA) 252
Free Trade Area of the Americas (FTAA) 253
Central American Free Trade Agreement-DR (CAFTA-DR) 253
European Union (EU) 253
franchise 256
foreign licensing 256
subcontracting 257
global marketing strategy 259
multidomestic marketing strategy 260
countertrade 262

ASSURANCE OF LEARNING REVIEW

1. What are the benefits to firms that decide to engage in global marketing?
2. Why is a nation's infrastructure an important factor for global marketers to consider?
3. What are the two different classifications of tariff? What is each designed to do?
4. How does an import quota restrict trade?
5. What are two major victories achieved by the Uruguay Round of GATT conferences?
6. Why has the progress of the WTO been slow?
7. What are the three alternatives for first-time exporters to reach foreign customers?
8. Define and describe the different types of contractual agreements that provide flexible alternatives to exporting.
9. In what conditions is a global marketing strategy generally most successful?
10. What type of nation benefits most from countertrade? Why?

PROJECTS AND TEAMWORK EXERCISES

1. Imagine you and a classmate are marketers for one of the following companies: Trader Joe's, Ace Hardware, or Menard's. Choose one of the following markets into which your company could expand: Mexico, India, or China. Research the country's infrastructure, social–cultural environment, technological environment, and any possible trade barriers your firm might encounter. Then present your findings to the class, with a conclusion on whether or not you think the expansion would be beneficial.

2. Assume you are a marketer for Weight Watchers International, a global company that operates in more than 20 countries. With a classmate, identify a country that Weight Watchers has not yet reached and write a brief plan for entering that country's market. Then create a print ad for that market (you can write the ad copy in English). It may be helpful to visit Weight Watchers' website or Facebook page for some ideas.

3. The 2016 Summer Olympics take place in Rio de Janeiro, Brazil. By yourself or with a classmate, identify a company that might benefit from promoting its goods or services at the Rio Olympics. In a presentation, describe which strategy you would use: straight extension, product or promotion adaptation, dual adaptation, or product invention.

4. Suppose you work for a firm that is getting ready to introduce its brand of headphones to the Chinese marketplace. With a classmate, decide which strategies your firm could use most effectively for entering this market. Present your ideas either in writing or to the class.

5. Chinese automaker Geely (pronounced *jeely*) announced plans to enter the U.S. market over the next few years. With a classmate, research Geely to find out more about its cars, then create an ad for the firm, targeting U.S. consumers.

CRITICAL-THINKING EXERCISES

1. Few elements in the global marketing environment are more difficult to overcome than the unexpected, such as natural disasters or outbreaks of disease such as the avian flu. Travel may be curtailed or halted by law, by a breakdown in infrastructure, or simply by fear on the part of consumers. Suppose you work for a firm that has resorts on several continents. As a marketer, what kinds of contingency plans might you recommend for your firm in the event of an unexpected disaster?

2. Zippo lighters have been around for more than 80 years. But as the number of smokers in the United States continues to decline, Zippo has spent the last half-century scouting the world for new markets. Today, Zippo is a status symbol among Chinese consumers, who prefer U.S. products. Recently, Zippo also broadened its product line to include watches, writing instruments, and items for outdoor enthusiasts. Can you think of other product lines that would be logical extensions for Zippo? And if Zippo decided to introduce additional product lines, which would work better: a global marketing strategy or a multidomestic strategy? Explain the reasons for your choice.

3. Do you agree with the goals and ideas of the proposed FTAA? Why or why not?

4. Do you agree with countertrade as a legitimate form of conducting business? Why or why not? Describe a countertrade agreement that Microsoft might make in another country.

5. Foreign investment continues to grow in the United States. Do you think this is a positive trend for U.S. businesses and consumers? Why or why not?

ETHICS EXERCISE

Cheap—and illegal—copies of pirated popular movies, video games, and music often are available for sale in Asia within days of their worldwide release. The entertainment industry has so far had little success in stopping the flow of these copies into consumers' hands. Do you think multinational economic communities should be more effective at combating piracy? Why or why not? What actions could they take?

INTERNET EXERCISES

1. **Chinese currency policy.** Critics contend that the Chinese government pursues policies that keep the value of the Chinese currency artificially low relative to other currencies such as the U.S. dollar and the euro. Using Google News and other online news sources, research the current state of Chinese currency policy. Why would the Chinese government engage in such efforts? What impact do these efforts have on global trade? Assume you work for a U.S.-based firm that engages in extensive trading operations with China. What impact would a major revaluation of the Chinese currency have on your firm?

   http://news.google.com

2. **Global marketing strategies.** Samsung—the electronics company based in South Korea—has been quite successful over the past ten years at marketing its products worldwide. Visit the Samsung website and note two or three elements of the firm's global marketing strategy. Next visit the websites of two other global electronics companies, such as Sony or Philips. Compare and contrast the marketing strategies used by all three companies.

   www.samsung.com
   www.philips.com
   www.sony.com

3. **World statistics.** The *CIA World Factbook* contains a wide range of information and statistics on individual countries. Go to www.cia.gov, select "World Factbook," and then "Guide to Country Comparisons." Next, click on the relevant section to obtain the top five countries in each of the following:
   a. Per-capita GDP
   b. Real growth rate in GDP
   c. Inflation rate
   d. Exports
   e. Population growth rate

Note: Internet Web addresses change frequently. If you don't find the exact site listed, you may need to access the organization's home page and search from there or use a search engine such as Google or Bing.

CASE 8.1
The NFL Takes Its Brand to London

More than a hundred million U.S. viewers watch the NFL Super Bowl every year. That's one of every three people in the country, making Super Bowl Sunday practically a national holiday. While the NFL is pleased with that number, recent leveling off of the Super Bowl audience suggests that the most popular U.S. sport might be nearing market saturation. Where does professional football go from here?

The answer might well be to London.

The NFL has already increased its broadcast offerings to include not only Sundays and Monday nights but Thursdays as well. Its television and live audiences have grown steadily, but the $9 billion organization remains the only major U.S. sports league still operating exclusively in the United States.

A European venture called NFL Europe ran in Germany for several years, with enthusiastic audiences, but the league eventually failed. It was soon followed by a new and entirely different effort: one regular-season NFL game a year at London's storied Wembley Stadium. These games have proved so successful with British audiences that the NFL recently announced it was increasing the number to three.

The question for many U.S. football fans now is, will the NFL try to create a London-based football franchise? There's no doubt the NFL is asking itself this very question, and while London offers many logistical advantages, success in the British market is by no means certain. Soccer is wildly popular in England, where it is known as football; hotly contested matches are frequent and well attended, and broadcasts are widely watched. With soccer entrenched, will the NFL attract enough new fans of American style football to justify an English team, especially if season tickets cost thousands of pounds?

It's not just profits that are at stake. Soccer is known as the world's most popular sport, and that's a title the NFL would dearly like to share.

QUESTIONS FOR CRITICAL THINKING

1. What accounts for the popularity of the NFL games in London? Do the British really like American-style football, or is it just a novelty? How might the NFL answer this critical question if it plans a British league?

2. Do you think a sports franchise as American as NFL football could become truly global? Why or why not? What obstacles do you think the NFL would have to overcome?

Sources: Josh Katzowitz, "NFL Announces Trio of Dates of Next Year's London Games," *CBS Sports*, accessed February 20, 2014, www.cbssports.com; Allen Adamson, "The NFL Has Long Known That Content—No, Audience—Is King," *Forbes*, accessed February 20, 2014, www.forbes.com; Chris Murphy, "Global Touchdown: Why the NFL Loves London," *CNN*, accessed February 20, 2014, http://edition.cnn.com; Ryan Alfieri, "How Popular Can the NFL Become?" *Bleacher Report*, accessed February 20, 2014, http://bleacherreport.com; Will Imbo, "NFL Chief Marketing Officer Mark Waller Shares His Thoughts on European Expansion," *SB Nation*, accessed February 20, 2014, www.sbnation.com.

VIDEO CASE 8.2
Nederlander Productions Hoof It Around the World

Many people would assert that New York's Broadway is the hub of the musical theater universe. Some would argue that the West End in London holds that title Nederlander Producing Company has a firm foothold in both cities. Founded in Detroit in 1912 by David T. Nederlander, the company is in its third generation as a family-owned, family-run company that produces shows as well as owns and manages theaters here and abroad. "When you think about the musical format expanding around the world, that really doesn't happen unless you've succeeded on Broadway," says Nick Scandalios, executive vice president of the Nederlander Organization. "Broadway is the global imprimatur, it's the *Good Housekeeping* seal of approval." But it works both ways, as evidenced by the recent revival of Evita that made its way from London's Adelphi Theatre (owned by Nederlander) to New York.

Nederlander entered the international market through direct investment by purchasing theaters in London. It now owns three prestigious locations: Adelphi Theatre, Aldwych Theatre, and Dominion Theatre. According to Scandalios, Nederlander is one of the few successful theater production companies in the United Kingdom that is American. Depending on the theme of the show, its target audience, and its performers, a straight product extension might work. But variables, such as language differences and the contractual availability of performers, make production adaptation the more likely strategy for moving a show from one country to another, even if it's only from New York to England. For example, slight variations in word use or interpretation could make a joke or lyric soar or flop. For this and other reasons, it took Nederlander and co-lead producer Scott Sanders about six years and $10 million to bring a new production of the hit musical Evita from London back to New York. This process included everything from discussions with creators Andrew Lloyd Webber and Tim Rice to the hiring of new performers.

In the meantime, the Nederlander Organization also set its sights much farther afield on countries like China and Turkey. Recently, Nederlander Worldwide Entertainment signed a global strategic partnership agreement with the China Arts and Entertainment Group (CAEG) to endorse and promote Chinese cultural products to the world. While Nederlander recognizes the huge market in China and CAEG's exportation of more than 630 shows internationally over the past decade (along with its purchase of 30 theaters throughout China), CAEG is looking for Nederlander's help with more sophisticated management and new channels of distribution. Nederlander will help CAEG get its productions into overseas markets, while CAEG will help Nederlander enter the Chinese market.

In Turkey, Nederlander Worldwide has partnered with the Zorlu Property Group to create and develop a performing arts center complex in Istanbul. The new center contains two theaters, one seating 2,300 customers and the other seating 770—making it the largest multipurpose performing arts center in Turkey's capital city. The center hosts concerts, dance performances, and Broadway musicals, along with other types of entertainment. "Istanbul is home to thousands of years of history with a rich cultural tradition, and it's an honor for us to work with Zorlu Property Group," says Robert Nederlander, Jr., president and CEO of Nederlander Worldwide Entertainment. Zorlu officials say their goal is to make Istanbul an international cultural center, noting that when tourists visit such major cities as New York, London, or Paris, they often like to take in a concert or theater production. With the addition of the center in Istanbul—and the marketing clout of Nederlander—they hope to put Istanbul on the global theater map.

All of these projects need audiences, and the only way to put people in those theater seats is to sell tickets. One future goal for Nederlander is to connect ticket purchasing globally—so a traveler from the United States can buy a ticket to a show in London, Istanbul, or Beijing before departing from U.S. soil. If seats are sold out? It'll be easy to book another show with a keyboard click.

QUESTIONS FOR CRITICAL THINKING

1. How might Nederlander benefit from expanding its business throughout the European Union (outside the United Kingdom)? What might be the drawbacks?
2. Nederlander has already engaged in some product and promotional adaptations to bring shows from London to New York and vice versa. What additional adaptations might the firm have to make for the Turkish and Chinese markets?

Sources: Company website, www.nederlander.org/london, accessed February 15, 2014; Nederlander Worldwide Entertainment, "Push Chinese Performing Arts Products to Broadway Together," accessed February 15, 2014, www.nederlanderworld.com; Nederlander Worldwide Entertainment, "The Zorlu Center for Performing Arts," accessed February 12, 2014, www.zorlucenterpsm.com.

Chapter 8 Global Marketing

NOTES

1. Company website, www.walmart.com, accessed September 14, 2014; "Walmart Releases 2014 Annual Shareholders' Meeting Proxy and Annual Report," http://news.walmart.com, accessed September 14, 2014; Mark Brohan, "Wal-Mart Grows Global e-Commerce 40% in Q3," *Internet Retailer*, accessed February 20, 2014, www.internetretailer.com; Phil Wahba and Siddharth Cavale, "Wal-Mart Taps Insider to Head International Division," *Reuters*, accessed February 20, 2014, www.reuters.com; Jon Springer, "Diverse Opportunities for Walmart International," *Supermarket News*, accessed February 20, 2014, http://supermarketnews.com; "A Snapshot of Walmart's International Business and How It Can Boost Growth," *Trefis*, accessed February 18, 2014, www.trefis.com; Walter Loeb, "Successful Global Growers: What We Can Learn from Walmart, Carrefour, Tesco, Metro," *Forbes*, accessed February 18, 2014, www.forbes.com; "Wal-Mart's Slow U.S. Growth Needs International Muscle to Drive Earnings," *Forbes*, accessed February 18, 2014, www.forbes.com.
2. U.S. Census Bureau, "Top Trading Partners—Total Trade, Exports, Imports, YTD through December 2013," accessed February 20, 2014, www.census.gov.
3. United Nations Conference on Trade and Development, *World Investment Report 2012*, accessed February 18, 2014, www.unctad.org.
4. "U.S. Goods Trade: Imports & Exports by Related-Parties 2012," *U.S. Census Bureau News*, accessed February 20, 2014, www.census.gov.
5. U.S. Census Bureau, "Top Trading Partners—Total Trade, Exports, Imports, YTD through December 2013," accessed February 20, 2014, www.census.gov; U.S. Census Bureau, "Trade in Goods with Indonesia," accessed February 20, 2014; U.S, www.census.gov. Census Bureau, "Trade in Goods with Vietnam," accessed February 20, 2014, www.census.gov.
6. U.S. Census Bureau, *Statistical Abstract of the United States*, "U.S. Trade in Goods and Services, 1960–2012," accessed February 20, 2014, www.census.gov.
7. U.S. Census Bureau, "Foreign Trade—U.S. Top Trading Partners," accessed February 20, 2014, www.census.gov; "China Eclipses U.S. as Biggest Trading Nation," *Bloomberg News*, accessed February 20, 2014, www.bloomberg.com.
8. Company website, www.walmartstores.com, accessed February 20, 2014; "Infographic of the Day: Walmart Dwarfs Entire Industries and Nations," *Fast Company*, accessed February 20, 2014, www.fastcodesign.com.
9. Company website, http://www.coverity.com, accessed January 4, 2014.
10. Organization website, "World's Richest Countries," www.worldsrichestcountries.com, accessed February 18, 2014.
11. Bureau of Labor Statistics, "Employment by Major Industry Sector," accessed February 18, 2014, www.bls.gov; Central Intelligence Agency, *World Factbook*, accessed February 18, 2014, www.cia.gov.
12. Chris Woodyard, "Volkswagen Likely to Outsell GM in China," *USA Today*, accessed February 20, 2014, www.usatoday.com; Barrett J. Brunsman, "P&G Dominates List of Power Brands in China," *Cincinnati Business Courier*, accessed February 20, 2014, www.bizjournals.com; Colum Murphy, "GM to Build Cadillac Plant in China," *The Wall Street Journal*, accessed February 18, 2014, http://online.wsj.com; "P&G to Build New Pampers Production Plant in Southern China," *RiteSiteAsia*, accessed February 14, 2014, http://ritesiteasia.en.
13. U.S. Department of Commerce, "U.S. International Trade in Goods and Services December 2013," accessed February 20, 2014, www.bea.gov.
14. Wolfgang Georg Arlt, "China Outbound Tourism: More than 100 Million Border Crossings in 12 Months," *Forbes*, accessed September 14, 2014, www.forbes.com.
15. Susannah Fox, "51% of U.S. Adults Bank Online," *Pew Internet*, accessed February 16, 2014, www.pewinternet.org.
16. Brian Stelter, "'Downton Abbey' Premiere Breaks Ratings Record," *CNN*, accessed February 20, 2014, www.cnn.com.
17. Company website, www.potterybarn.com, accessed February 12, 2014.
18. Jennifer Booton, "Move over China, Yum Brands Setting Its Sights on India," *FOX Business*, accessed February 20, 2014, www.foxbusiness.com.
19. Company website, www.subway.com, accessed September 14, 2014; Carol Tice, "The American Fast Food the World Loves: Top Global Brands," *Forbes*, accessed February 20, 2014, www.forbes.com.
20. Central Intelligence Agency, *The World Factbook*, accessed January 4, 2014, www.cia.gov.
21. Ibid.
22. Jason Overdorf, "India's Population to Overtake China's Sooner Than Expected," *Global Post*, accessed February 20, 2014, www.globalpost.com.
23. Mary Amiti and Mark Choi, "Consumer Goods from China Are Getting More Expensive," *Liberty Street Economics*, accessed February 20, 2014, http://libertystreeteconomics.newyorkfed.org.
24. Darryl K. Taft, "IBM Continues India Expansion with New Punjab Office," *eWeek*, accessed February 20, 2014, www.eweek.com.
25. "Internet Usage Statistics," *Internet World Stats*, accessed September 14, 2014, www.internetworldstats.com.
26. Case Adams, "Many Countries Ban GMO Crops, Require GE Food Labels," *Real Natural*, accessed February 20, 2014, www.realnatural.org.
27. Vindu Goel, "Foxconn Audit Finds a Workweek Still Too Long," *The New York Times*, accessed February 20, 2014, www.nytimes.com.
28. International Organization for Standardization website, accessed September 14, 2014, www.iso.org.
29. Kaylene Hong, "China's Internet Population Hit 618 Million at the End of 2013, with 81% Connecting via Mobile," *The Next Web*, accessed September 14, 2014, http://thenextweb.com; "Anonymous' Hackers Take on the Great Firewall," *China Digital Times*, accessed February 18, 2014, http://chinadigitaltimes.net.
30. Office of the U.S. Trade Representative, "New Opportunities for U.S. Exporters under the U.S.–Korea Trade Agreement," press release, accessed February 18, 2014, www.ustr.gov.
31. Elizabeth Williamson, "U.S., Mexico in Truck Deal," *The Wall Street Journal*, accessed February 20, 2014, http://online.wsj.com.
32. "Banana War Ends after 20 Years," *BBC News*, accessed February 18, 2014, http://www.bbc.co.uk.
33. Dave Wilkins, "USDA Relaxes Sugar Quotas," *Capital Press*, accessed February 20, 2014, www.capitalpress.com.
34. Jane Chung and Theopolis Waters, "South Korean Suspends Some U.S. Beef Imports over Feed Additive," *Reuters*, accessed February 20, 2014, www.reuters.com.
35. Jeremy Wagstaff and Lee Chyen Yee, "For the Mobile Internet, Tomorrow Belongs to Asia," *Reuters*, accessed February 20, 2014, http://mobile.reuters.com.
36. Ian Clover, "EU Imposes Maximum 42.1% Anti-Dumping Tariff on Chinese Solar Glass Exporters," *PV Magazine*, accessed February 20, 2014, www.pv-magazine.com.
37. World Trade Organization website, www.wto.org, accessed February 15, 2014.
38. Ibid.
39. Organization website, "North Americans Are Better Off after 15 Years of NAFTA," www.naftanow.org, accessed February 20, 2014.
40. Public Citizen Globalization and Trade Website, "Free Trade Area of the Americas," http://www.citizen.org, accessed February 18, 2014.
41. CAFTA Intelligence Center website, www.caftaintelligencecenter.com, accessed February 19, 2014.
42. European Union website, www.europa.eu, accessed February 18, 2014.
43. Ibid.
44. Company website, www.adidas.com, accessed February 20, 2014; Ben Golliver, "Adidas Unveils 'D Howard 4' Signature Shoe for Rockets' Dwight Howard," *Sports Illustrated*, accessed February 20, 2014, http://si.nba.com.
45. Company website, www.ikea.com, accessed February 20, 2014.
46. "EA Holding Star Wars License for a Decade," *MMO Game News*, accessed February 18, 2014, www.news.mmosite.com.
47. U.S. Department of Commerce, Bureau of Economic Analysis, "U.S. Direct Investment Abroad: Trends and Current Issues," accessed February 18, 2014, www.fas.org; White House, "New Report: Foreign Direct Investment in the United States," press release, accessed February 18, 2014, www.whitehouse.gov.
48. "Meidu Holding Co Ltd to Acquire Woodbine Acquisition LLC," *Reuters*, accessed February 18, 2014, www.reuters.com.
49. Susan Berfield, "Can All-American Gap Succeed in India?" *Bloomberg Businessweek*, accessed September 14, 2014, www.businessweek.com.
50. Corporate website, "ABB in Chile," www.abb.com, accessed February 20, 2014; Nneka Etoniru, "Chile 2013 Blog: FDI in Chile Breaking Records," Americas Society/Council of the Americas, accessed February 20, 2014, www.as-coa.org.
51. "Pringles Secures Its Market Share with New Flavors," *Yahoo Finance*, accessed February 18, 2014, http://finance.yahoo.com.
52. Maureen Morrison, "Pizza in 30 Minutes…or More? Domino's Touts Slower Delivery," *Advertising Age*, accessed February 20, 2014, www.adage.com.
53. Organization website, "About ONE," www.one.org, accessed February 20, 2014.
54. Robert Bridge, "10 Things to Know about Moscow," *Walking Tours of Moscow*, accessed February 20, 2014, http://waytomoscow.com.
55. Jason Siu, "Fiat 500 Abarth Recreated with Women, Body Paint," *AutoGuide.com*, accessed February 18, 2014, www.autoguide.com.
56. Central Intelligence Agency, *The World Factbook*, www.cia.gov, accessed September 14, 2014; U.S. Bureau of the Census, "People: Quick Facts," www.census.gov, accessed September 14, 2014.
57. Steve Smith, "LG Reports Improved Annual Sales, Profitability," *Twice*, accessed September 14, 2014, www.twice.com.
58. Company website, www.bmwusa.com, accessed February 20, 2014; company website, www.daimler.com, accessed February 20, 2014; company website, http://world.honda.com, accessed February 20, 2014; company website, www.hyundaiusa.com, accessed February 20, 2014; company website, www.kia.com, accessed February 20, 2014; company website, "Toyota in Action," www.toyota.com, accessed February 20, 2014; "Where Are Nissan Cars Built? A Nissan Car FAQ," *CarsDirect.com*, www.carsdirect.com, accessed February 20, 2014; company website, "About Chattanooga," www.volkswagengroupamerica.com, accessed February 20, 2014.

Scripps Networks Interactive & Food Network

PART 2
Understanding Buyers and Markets

Everyone Eats

Scripps Networks Interactive has engineered a huge success based on the single behavior shared by all consumers: everyone eats. In fact, it's so obvious that marketers could easily overlook it when trying to identify consumer behaviors and influences. But Scripps has built an empire of food-related networks and shows, including its flagship Food Network.

Although everyone eats, the challenge to marketers is figuring out what people eat, when they eat, how they eat, and with whom. "Food behavior is very situational," observes Sergei Kuharsky, senior vice president and general manager of licensing and merchandising at Scripps. This means that sometimes people actually behave differently from what they *say* they do, or change their behavior based on certain conditions. Food choices might depend on how they feel, who they're with, what options are available, and so forth. Of course, food choices depend on other influences as well—cultural (vegetarianism or buying local), social (aspiring to fine foods or restaurants), and family (the husband or wife makes menu decisions). To make sense of all of this, Scripps relies on consumer interactions with social media. "It's easy for us to know what our viewers value because we talk to them all the time," says Kuharsky. "Word-of-mouth is the best advertising in the world, and it's also the best recommendation in the world. Social is really people reaching out to people they trust, to find things that they like."

Since food is universal among consumers, the trick is to narrow the experience enough to actually target a demographic and decision makers. "The beauty of Food Network is that it plays in multiple demographics," says Laura Galietta, senior vice president of ad sales and marketing. The company's main demographic is the 25 to 54 age group, but Galietta points out that Food Network is also very popular among other demographic groups. The network's core viewers are those women who are decision makers in their households. So the marketers' strategy is to reach upscale women with credit cards and the authority to decide what to buy. Since these consumers are also avid users of social media, Scripps and Food Network play to that strength.

Social media helps Scripps and Food Network marketers tap into viewers' perceptions and attitudes. "You can get a read so much more quickly through social media," says Susie Fogelson, senior vice president for marketing, creative services, and public relations. "You need a reliable sample to be able to glean true results, but it gives you a sense of what people are thinking about." Fogelson acknowledges that consumers who actually take the time and effort to engage in conversations online are often the "small, fiery group." But they do provide valuable information. "I think social media is the greatest gift to a marketer and also a tremendous responsibility."

In addition to marketing to consumers, Scripps and its branded networks market to other businesses. These organizations generally fall into one (or more) of three categories: advertising partners, affiliate partners, and new business partners. Advertisers understand the value of Scripps brands and their broad reach; they advertise because it makes sense for these viewers to see their products. "We have an expertise and authority that our advertisers want to latch on to," says Galietta. The partner relationship goes further, according to Galietta. A partner understands the deeper meaning that Scripps' brands have in people's everyday lives, and that working with Scripps will help them tap into that. These B2B partnerships generally function for mutual benefit. For example, retailer Kohl's sells Food Network–branded stainless steel cookware and other products that consumers may buy after being inspired by their favorite cooking shows. Entwine Wine is a partnership between Food Network and the California-based Wente Vineyards to offer a collection of fine wines that are also affordable to consumers looking for the perfect food and wine pairings.

Scripps' business partners also understand the value of being part of a hit show like *Food Network Star*, on which they promote their products and messages. These firms then promote their relationship with Food Network at their own websites, Facebook pages, and the like. Food Network and Buitoni ran a sweepstakes on Twitter, during which viewers could Tweet to win free pasta after watching the show. "People want to know more," explains Galietta. "They want to know what happens after the show ends, and they want to be part of it." Scripps and Food Network accomplish this through social media.

Scripps and its branded networks have successfully leveraged the universal appeal of food. "We position the Scripps portfolio as brands for life," remarks Galietta. "We have great brands, we inspire people to act, and the TV commercials are informational. Viewers take that information and go online to find out more—and then they act." Action is the endgame for marketers, whether it's on the part of consumers or business partners.

QUESTIONS FOR CRITICAL THINKING

1. Scripps identifies its core audience as upscale women who are decision makers. Give at least one example each of cultural, social, and family influences that might sway their viewing and purchasing choices as related to Food Network.

2. What marketing efforts might Scripps and Food Network make to change the attitude of men who are not viewers, so that they become viewers of Food Network?

3. How would you segment Food Network's business partners? Give an example of each segment you cite.

4. In addition to the free-pasta sweepstakes, describe how Buitoni might leverage its relationship with Food Network via social media.

Sources: Company website, www.foodnetwork.com, accessed September 14, 2014; company website, www.kohls.com, accessed September 14, 2014; company website, www.entwine-wines.com, accessed September 14, 2014.

Part 3
Target Market Selection

9 Market Segmentation, Targeting, and Positioning

10 Marketing Research in the Era of Big Data

11 Relationship Marketing and Customer Relationship Management (CRM)

Chapter 9

Market Segmentation, Targeting, and Positioning

PEPSICO BRANDS TARGET DIFFERENT MARKETS

1. Identify the two essential components of a market.
2. Outline the role of market segmentation in developing a marketing strategy.
3. Describe the four components necessary for effective segmentation.
4. Explain the geographic approach to segmenting consumer markets.
5. Discuss the demographic approach to segmenting consumer markets.
6. Outline the psychographic approach to segmenting consumer markets.
7. Describe product-related segmentation.
8. Identify the four steps in the market segmentation process.
9. Discuss four basic strategies for reaching target markets.
10. Explain the four types of positioning strategies and the reasons for positioning and repositioning products.

What's wrong with plain water? If you're looking for a healthy drink, not much. But from a beverage company's standpoint, it's very hard to differentiate your bottled water from your competitor's. PepsiCo, however, isn't too worried.

Carbonated soft drinks account for almost 25 percent of the entire U.S. beverage market and have long been a guaranteed profit maker for beverage companies. But with soft drink sales now declining in the United States and other industrialized markets, PepsiCo is relying on the great diversity of its portfolio of beverage products to maintain its competitive advantage. The $13 billion company earns only about a quarter of its revenue from its carbonated soft drinks. By comparison, The Coca-Cola Company depends on Coke for about 60 percent of its U.S. revenue.

PepsiCo has a strong lead in bottled water, juices, and sports drinks, some of the fastest-growing beverage categories. Demand is being driven by health-conscious consumers' increasing desire for products that are better for them than heavily sugared drinks.

PepsiCo offers something for almost every thirsty market segment. Aquafina is its bottled water brand, and for those who prefer added fruit flavor, vitamins, and herbal extracts, PepsiCo offers SoBe Lifewater. Naked Juice, Dole, Tropicana, and Ocean Spray offer fruit juices, while Brisk, Lipton, Tazo, and Pure Leaf are PepsiCo's tea brands. Prefer coffee drinks? PepsiCo has Starbucks ready-to-drink coffee beverages for you. Mountain Dew and Sierra Mist are non-cola soft drinks, and Sierra Mist is caffeine free. And for energy-drink lovers, there's Gatorade in many flavors and varieties.

Among its newer products, PepsiCo includes a new Mountain Dew-flavored breakfast drink called Kickstart, a "sparkling juice" beverage with added caffeine and vitamins that it hopes will appeal to young, active customers who aren't already making tea or coffee part of their morning routine. Another new PepsiCo product, patented but yet to be marketed, is expected to be a four-ounce protein shot aimed at women, which one industry observer predicts will create wholly new market segment, combining energy and protein drinks in one.[1]

EVOLUTION OF A BRAND

PepsiCo's market segmentation strategy in its beverage business has helped shield the company from the financial effects of the declining carbonated soft drink sales in the United States and other developed markets. Of the 22 PepsiCo brands that top the billion dollar sales mark annually, 12 of them are beverages.

- PepsiCo is the market leader in the fast-growing beverage segments of bottled water, juices, and sport drinks in the United States. How can the company continue to grow this business while trying to enter other domestic beverage markets?
- The Coca-Cola Company has strengthened its grip on emerging beverage markets such as China, Russia, and India. What kind of strategy should PepsiCo put in place to expand its presence in global markets?
- PepsiCo recently introduced a premium bottled water called "Qua" (short for *Aqua*) in the United States. Although the new brand is still in the test-market phase, how can PepsiCo target various demographic groups with this new product in an effort to compete with the likes of high-priced Fiji Water and Smartwater?

Chapter Overview

market Group of people with sufficient purchasing power, authority, and willingness to buy.

target market Specific group of people a firm believes is most likely to buy its goods and services.

Each of us is unique. We come from different backgrounds, live in different households, and have different interests and goals. You and your best friend may shop at different stores, listen to different music, play different sports, and take different courses in college. Suppose you like country music, but your best friend prefers rock. Marketers for all kinds of music-related products, ranging from digital songs to live concerts, want to capture your interest as well as that of your friends. Do you play an instrument or sing? Or are you a fan who goes to clubs and downloads music? Marketers at Reebok, for example, look at customers and potential customers to figure out what their characteristics are, whether they can identify certain subgroups, and how they can best offer products to meet their needs. Your interests and needs, your lifestyle and income, the town where you live, and your age all contribute to the likelihood that you will listen to and buy certain types of music—say, Bruno Mars or the score to *Wicked*. All of these factors make up a market. A **market** is composed of people with sufficient purchasing power, authority, and willingness to buy. Marketers must use their expertise to understand the market for a good or service, whether it's a new athletic shoe for marathon runners or a vacation package at Disney World.

Many markets include consumers with different lifestyles, backgrounds, and income levels. Nearly everyone buys toothpaste, but that does not mean every consumer has the same lifestyle, background, or income. So it is unusual for a single marketing mix strategy to attract all sectors of a market. By identifying, evaluating, and selecting a target market to pursue, such as consumers who prefer toothpaste made with all-natural ingredients or those who want an extra-whitening formula—marketers develop more efficient and effective marketing strategies. On the other hand, some products, such as luxury sports cars and fly-fishing supplies, are intended for more specific markets. In either case, the **target market** for a product is the segment of consumers most likely to purchase a particular item.

Marketing now takes place on a global basis more than ever, incorporating many target markets. To identify those markets, marketers must determine useful ways for segmenting different populations and communicating with them successfully. This chapter discusses useful ways to accomplish this objective, explaining the steps of the market segmentation process and surveying strategies for reaching target markets. Finally, it looks at the role of positioning in developing a marketing strategy.

TYPES OF MARKETS

Products usually are classified as either consumer products or business products. **Consumer products** are bought by ultimate consumers for personal use—for example, cell phones, sports tickets, or fashion magazines. **Business products** are goods and services purchased for use either directly or indirectly in the production of other goods and services for resale. Most goods and services purchased by individual consumers, such as tablets and restaurant meals, are considered consumer products. Rubber and raw cotton are examples of items generally purchased by manufacturers and therefore classified as business products. B.F. Goodrich buys rubber to manufacture tires; textile manufacturers such as Burlington Industries convert raw cotton into cloth.

However, in many cases, a single product can serve different uses. Tires purchased for the family car constitute consumer products, but tires purchased by Ford Motor Company to be mounted on its Ford Fusion are business products because they become part of another product destined for resale. Or a product that was once a business product might be modified for consumer use, and vice versa. A line of professional cookware sold to restaurants—a business product—could be adapted by its manufacturer to become a line of cookware for home use—a consumer product. If you want to determine the classification of an item, just think about who is going to buy the product, who will use it, and how or why the product will be used. The bottle of mouthwash you buy at the supermarket is a consumer product, but if a big hotel chain purchases large quantities of the same mouthwash from a wholesaler, it becomes a business product.

> **1** Identify the two essential components of a market.
>
> **consumer products** Products bought by ultimate consumers for personal use.
>
> **business products** Goods and services purchased for use either directly or indirectly in the production of other goods and services for resale.

ASSESSMENT CHECK

1.1 Define target market.
1.2 Distinguish between a consumer product and a business product.

THE ROLE OF MARKET SEGMENTATION

There are more than 7 billion people in the world today; of those, over 319 million live in the United States.[2] In today's business world, too many variables exist in consumer needs, preferences, and purchasing power to attract all consumers with a single marketing mix. That's not to say that firms must actually change products to meet the needs of different market segments—although they often do—but they must attempt to identify the factors that affect purchase decisions and then group consumers according to the presence or absence of these factors. Finally, they adjust marketing strategies to meet the needs of each group.

Consider motor vehicles. Unlike a century ago, when Henry Ford pronounced that customers could order any color of car they liked—as long as it was black—today there is a make, model, and color for every taste and budget. But auto manufacturers need to adjust their messages for different markets. And savvy marketers look toward markets that show growth, such as the U.S. Hispanic population—now the largest ethnic group in the country—and aging baby boomers, whose needs for goods and services are changing.

The division of the total market into smaller, relatively homogeneous groups is called **market segmentation**. Both profit-oriented and not-for-profit organizations practice market segmentation.

> **2** Outline the role of market segmentation in developing a marketing strategy.
>
> **market segmentation** Division of the total market into smaller, relatively homogeneous groups.

ASSESSMENT CHECK

2.1 Define market segmentation.
2.2 Describe the role of market segmentation.

CRITERIA FOR EFFECTIVE SEGMENTATION

3 Describe the four components necessary for effective segmentation.

Segmentation doesn't automatically guarantee success in the marketing arena; instead, it is a tool for marketers to use. Its effectiveness depends on four basic requirements.

First, the market segment must present measurable purchasing power and size. With jobs, incomes, and decision-making power, female consumers represent a hefty amount of purchasing power, over $7 trillion, or more than 60 percent of the nation's wealth.[3] Women control or influence the purchase of more than 85 percent of all consumer goods, including items such as stocks and bonds for investment, personal computers, and family vehicles.[4] With this information in mind, car manufacturers and dealers now market directly to women. In addition, websites such as AskPatty.com offer advice to women on making car purchases—and certify "female-friendly" dealers and automotive centers that provide the kind of service that builds loyalty among female consumers.[5]

Second, marketers must find a way to promote and serve the market segment effectively. Because women now wield purchasing power in the technology market, marketers need to find different ways to appeal to them. Some companies have taken this advice to heart. T-Mobile and Microsoft have created ads featuring working moms.

Third, marketers must then identify segments large enough to give them good profit potential. Because women significantly influence 80 to 90 percent of home purchases, homebuilders have turned their marketing efforts to them. The Nebraska-based Design Basics, the largest home-plan design company in the country, now focuses on designs aimed at women. Its guidelines include improving storage options, creating multipurpose rooms, and emphasizing the practicality of the back-door entry—with space for muddy boots and school backpacks, car keys, mail, and a cell-phone charger. The firm's Livability at a Glance division features color-coded layouts showing areas for entertaining (yellow), de-stressing (blue), storing (orange), and flexible living (green). The company also publishes *Her Home*

Nebraska's Design Basics publishes *Her Home*, a digital magazine that targets content to women about home design, construction ideas, and other products.

digital magazine twice a year, which focuses on women's perspectives on design, construction, and products for the home.[6]

Fourth, the firm must aim for segments that match its marketing capabilities. Targeting a large number of small markets can be an expensive, complex, and inefficient strategy, so smaller firms may decide to stick with a particular niche, or target market. But Harley-Davidson, once thought to be the exclusive domain of men, has experienced a surge in purchases by women, who are the fastest-growing segment of the motorcycle business and currently account for nearly one in four motorcyclists. So Harley-Davidson runs targeted ads in women's magazines, hosts annual "garage party" events throughout the United States geared specifically to women, and hosts a website for women motorcyclists.[7]

SEGMENTING CONSUMER MARKETS

Market segmentation attempts to isolate the traits that distinguish a certain group of consumers from the overall market. An understanding of the group's characteristics—such as age, gender, geographic location, income, and buying patterns—plays a vital role in developing a successful marketing strategy. In most cases, marketers seek to pinpoint a number of factors affecting buying behavior in the target segment. Marketers in the travel industry consider employment trends, changes in income levels and buying patterns, age, lifestyle, and other factors when promoting their goods and services. To boost attendance at its theme parks, Disney World advertises to "empty nesters" and groups of friends instead of focusing entirely on families with young children. Marketers rarely identify totally homogeneous segments, in which all potential customers are alike; they almost always encounter some differences among members of a target group but must be careful to ensure their segments accurately reflect consumers.

In the next sections, we discuss the four common bases for segmenting consumer markets: geographic segmentation, demographic segmentation, psychographic segmentation, and product-related segmentation. These segmentation approaches offer important guidance for marketing strategies, provided they identify significant differences in buying behavior.

ASSESSMENT CHECK

3.1 Identify the four criteria for effective segmentation.

3.2 Give an example of a market segment that meets these criteria.

GEOGRAPHIC SEGMENTATION

Marketers have long practiced **geographic segmentation**—dividing an overall market into homogeneous groups based on their locations. Geographic location does not ensure all consumers in a location will make the same buying decisions, but this segmentation approach helps identify some general patterns.

The more than 319 million people living in the United States are not scattered evenly across the country. For instance, many are concentrated in major metropolitan areas; New York is the largest U.S. city, with about 8.3 million residents, but the metropolitan area surrounding it includes more than 20 million people. Los Angeles ranks second, with 3.9 million, and a surrounding area of over 15 million.[8] Figure 9.1 shows populations of the ten largest cities in the United States and the ten states with the largest populations. California tops the list with more than 38.3 million residents. Wyoming is the least-populous state, with 583,000. In addition to total population, marketers need to look at the fastest growing states to plan their strategies for the future. Texas gained the most in population since the most recent census, followed by California, Florida, Georgia, and North Carolina.[9]

A look at the worldwide population distribution illustrates why so many firms pursue customers around the globe. China has the most citizens, with more than 1.3 billion people. India is second with over 1.2 billion. The United States is third with over 319 million, and Indonesia is fourth with

> **4** Explain the geographic approach to segmenting consumer markets.
>
> **geographic segmentation** Division of an overall market into homogeneous groups based on their locations.

FIGURE 9.1
The Ten Largest Cities and Ten Most Populous States in the United States

Sources: "Top 50 Cities in the U.S. by Population and Rank," *Info Please*, accessed March 12, 2014, www.infoplease.com; U.S. Census Bureau, "National and State Population Estimates: July 2013," accessed March 12, 2014, www.census.gov.

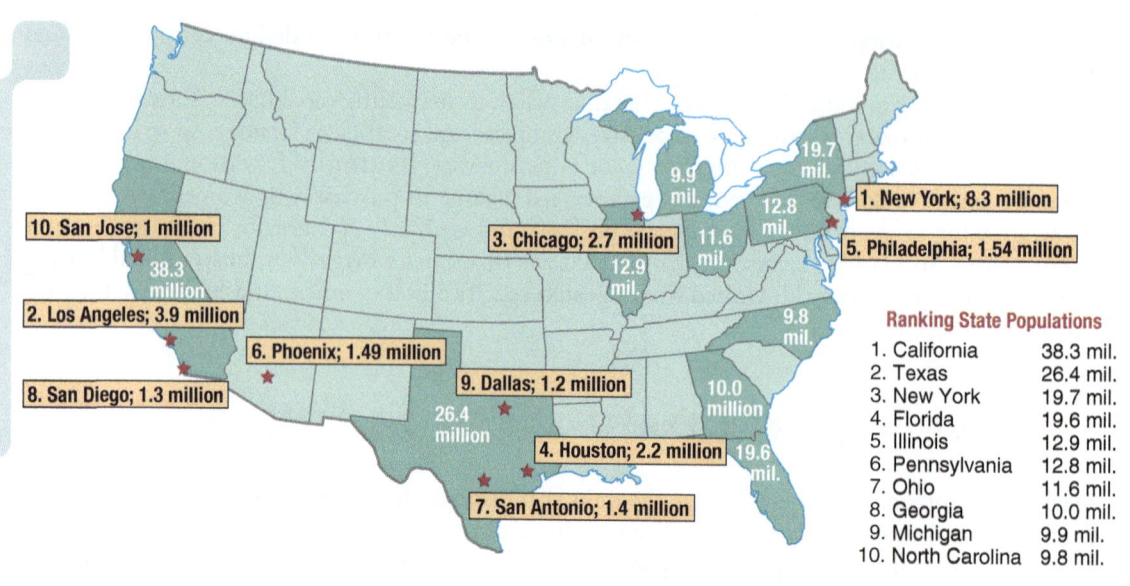

Cities:
1. New York; 8.3 million
2. Los Angeles; 3.9 million
3. Chicago; 2.7 million
4. Houston; 2.2 million
5. Philadelphia; 1.54 million
6. Phoenix; 1.49 million
7. San Antonio; 1.4 million
8. San Diego; 1.3 million
9. Dallas; 1.2 million
10. San Jose; 1 million

Ranking State Populations
1. California — 38.3 mil.
2. Texas — 26.4 mil.
3. New York — 19.7 mil.
4. Florida — 19.6 mil.
5. Illinois — 12.9 mil.
6. Pennsylvania — 12.8 mil.
7. Ohio — 11.6 mil.
8. Georgia — 10.0 mil.
9. Michigan — 9.9 mil.
10. North Carolina — 9.8 mil.

over 254 million. Japan is a distant tenth with over 127 million.[10] As in the United States, much of the world's population lives in urban environments. The two largest cities in the world are Shanghai, China, with 23.9 million and Mumbai, India, with 20.5 million. The two largest metropolitan areas are Tokyo, Japan, with 37.2 million, and Jakarta, Indonesia, with over 26.7 million.[11]

Population size alone, however, may not be reason enough for a business to expand into a specific country. Businesses also need to look at a wide variety of economic variables. Some businesses may decide to combine their marketing efforts for countries that share similar population and product-use patterns instead of treating each country as an independent segment. This grouping is taking place with greater frequency throughout the European Union as the currency and trade laws of the member nations become more unified.

While population numbers indicate the overall size of a market, other geographic indicators such as job growth give useful guidance to marketers, depending on the type of products they sell. Automobile manufacturers might segment geographic regions by household income, because it is an important factor in the purchase of a new car.

Geographic areas also vary in population migration patterns. Job transfer and retirement are two circumstances that cause people to move. Major natural disasters may affect population migration, as in the case of Hurricane Katrina, which devastated New Orleans. It's also important for marketers to observe who is moving where: People who leave the East Coast aren't necessarily jumping to the West Coast, and vice versa. New Yorkers tend to gravitate to the South or to Connecticut or New Jersey. Californians often move to other western states instead of coming farther east. In a recent annual survey by Allied Van Lines, it appears that a stable business environment has people on the move. Texas is the top state drawing more people, while New York and Illinois are losing the most residents to other states.[12]

The move from urban to suburban areas after World War II created a need to redefine the urban marketplace. This trend radically changed cities' traditional patterns of retailing and led to decline in many downtown shopping areas. Subsequently, traditional city boundaries become almost meaningless for marketing purposes. However, marketers now observe a trend toward the revitalization of some downtown urban areas.

In an effort to respond to these changes, the government now classifies urban data using the following categories:

- The category of **core based statistical area (CBSA)** refers collectively to metropolitan and micropolitan statistical areas. Each CBSA must contain at least one urban area with a population of 10,000 or more. Each metropolitan statistical area must have at least one urbanized area of 50,000 or more inhabitants. Each micropolitan statistical area must have at least one urban cluster with a population of at least 10,000 but less than 50,000. There are 381 metropolitan and 536 micropolitan statistical areas in the United States.[13]

- A **metropolitan statistical area (MSA)** is a freestanding urban area with a population in the urban center of at least 50,000 and a total metropolitan statistical area population of 100,000

> "We built this company from the customer back, not from the company out."
> —Lou Gerstner
> *Former CEO of IBM*

core based statistical area (CBSA) Collective term for metropolitan and micropolitan statistical areas.

metropolitan statistical area (MSA) Freestanding urban area with a population in the urban center of at least 50,000 and a total MSA population of 100,000 or more.

or more. Buyers in metropolitan statistical areas exhibit social and economic homogeneity and usually border on non-urbanized counties. Examples include Little Rock, Arkansas; Kalamazoo–Battle Creek, Michigan; and Rochester, New York. Figure 9.2 identifies the ten largest metropolitan areas in the United States.

- A **micropolitan statistical area** has at least one town of 10,000 to 49,999 people—it can have several such towns—and proportionally few of its residents commuting outside the area. Recently, the government counted 536 such areas in the continental United States. Examples of micropolitan statistical areas include Corning, New York; Kalispell, Montana; Kahului-Wailuku, Hawaii; and Key West, Florida.

- The category of **consolidated metropolitan statistical area (CMSA)** includes the country's 25 or so urban giants, such as Detroit–Ann Arbor–Flint, Michigan; Los Angeles–Riverside–Orange County, California; and Philadelphia–Wilmington–Atlantic City. (Note that, in the third example, three states are involved: Pennsylvania, Delaware, and New Jersey.) A CMSA must include two or more primary metropolitan statistical areas, discussed next.

- A **primary metropolitan statistical area (PMSA)** is an urbanized county or set of counties with social and economic ties to nearby areas. PMSAs are identified within areas of 1-million-plus populations. Olympia, Washington, is part of the Seattle–Tacoma–Bremerton PMSA; Bridgeport, Connecticut, is part of the New York–northern New Jersey–Long Island PMSA; and Riverside–San Bernardino, California, is a PMSA within the Los Angeles–Riverside–Orange County PMSA.[14]

micropolitan statistical area Area with at least one town of 10,000 to 49,999 people with proportionally few of its residents commuting to outside the area.

consolidated metropolitan statistical area (CMSA) Urban area that includes two or more PMSAs.

primary metropolitan statistical area (PMSA) Urbanized county or set of counties with social and economic ties to nearby areas.

USING GEOGRAPHIC SEGMENTATION

Demand for some categories of goods and services can vary according to geographic region, and marketers must be aware of how these regions differ. Marketers of major brands are particularly interested in defining their **core regions**, the locations where they get 40 to 80 percent of their sales.

Residence location *within* a geographic area is an important segmentation variable. City dwellers often rely on public transportation and may get along fine without automobiles, whereas those who live in the suburbs or rural areas depend on their own cars and trucks. Also, those who live in the suburbs spend more on lawn and garden care products than city dwellers. A recent survey found that, on average, 63 percent of Americans drink coffee daily with more than a third of the population drinking a gourmet coffee beverage each day. Seattle and Portland, Oregon, top the list in coffee consumption. Marketers can use this information to determine where their products are most likely to be successful.[15]

Geographic segmentation provides useful distinctions when regional preferences or needs exist. A consumer may not want to invest in a snow blower or flood insurance but may *have* to because of the location of his or her home. But it's important for marketers not to stop at geographic location as a segmentation method because distinctions among consumers also exist within a geographic location. Consider those who relocate from one region to another for work or family reasons. They may bring with them their preferences from other parts of the country. Using multiple segmentation variables is probably a much better strategy for targeting a specific market.

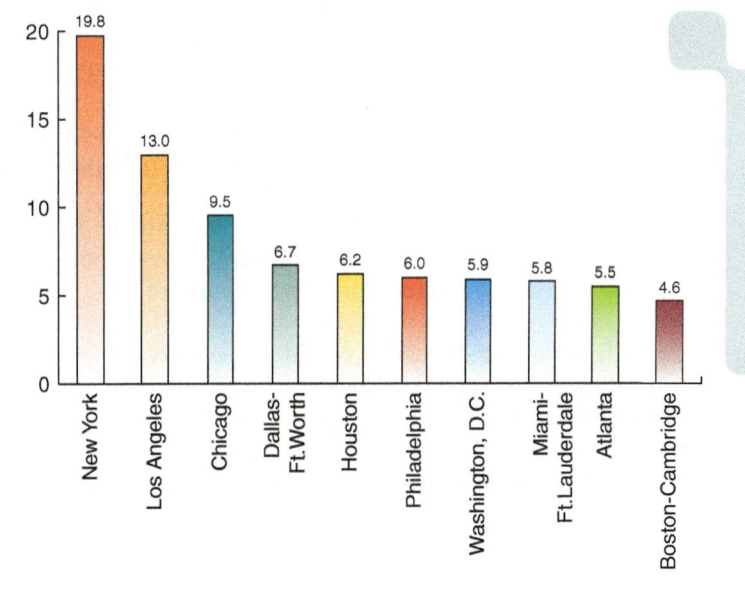

core regions Region from which most major brands get 40 to 80 percent of their sales.

FIGURE 9.2
The Ten Largest Metropolitan Areas in the United States

Source: Company website, "Metropolitan Areas: Assessing Competitive Position and Change," http://proximityone.com, accessed March 12, 2014.

Metropolitan Area	Value
New York	19.8
Los Angeles	13.0
Chicago	9.5
Dallas-Ft. Worth	6.7
Houston	6.2
Philadelphia	6.0
Washington, D.C.	5.9
Miami-Ft. Lauderdale	5.8
Atlanta	5.5
Boston-Cambridge	4.6

GEOGRAPHIC INFORMATION SYSTEMS (GISs)

geographic information systems (GISs) Software packages that assemble, store, manipulate, and display data by their location.

Once used mainly by the military, **geographic information systems (GISs)** are computer systems that assemble, store, manipulate, and display data by their location. GISs simplify the job of analyzing marketing information by relating data to location. The result is a geographic map overlaid with digital data about consumers in a particular area. A growing number of companies benefit from using a GIS to locate new outlets, assign sales territories, plan distribution centers, and map out the most efficient delivery routes. Google Earth is a recent application of GIS technology that allows computer users to view different parts of the country up close. Users simply type in an address and zoom into it, whether it's a house, a theme park, a school, or a store.

In Richmond, Virginia, local Outback Steakhouses tested the power of geographic networking by using a Foursquare check-in marketing campaign.

GISs have become more mobile and more social as people increasingly turn to applications such as Foursquare and Around Me to locate restaurants, movies, and stores. In Richmond, Virginia, Outback Steakhouse ran a promotion in which consumers were encouraged to check in via Foursquare when they went to the local Outback restaurants. Called "Laps for Apps," the campaign, tied in to Outback-sponsored NASCAR driver Ryan Newman, awarded laps to consumers each time they went back and forth from their houses to the restaurant, accruing a lap for each round trip. After consumers make a second check-in to Outback, they were given free appetizers with their next purchase. Over a three-week period, more than 675 consumers checked in to Outback via Foursquare. Based on the positive results in Richmond, the company may take the location-based marketing campaign national.[16]

demographic segmentation Division of an overall market into homogeneous groups based on variables such as gender, age, income, occupation, education, sexual orientation, household size, and stage in the family lifecycle; also called *socioeconomic segmentation*.

ASSESSMENT CHECK

4.1 Under what circumstances are marketers most likely to use geographic segmentation?

4.2 What are the five main categories for classifying urban data?

5 Discuss the demographic approach to segmenting consumer markets.

DEMOGRAPHIC SEGMENTATION

The most common method of market segmentation—**demographic segmentation**—defines consumer groups according to demographic variables such as gender, age, income, occupation, education, household size, sexual orientation, and stage in the family lifecycle. This approach is also called *socioeconomic segmentation*. Marketers review vast quantities of available data to complete a plan for demographic segmentation. One of the primary sources for demographic data in the United States is the Census Bureau. Marketers can obtain many of the Census Bureau's statistics online at www.census.gov.

The following discussion considers the most commonly used demographic variables. Keep in mind, however, that while demographic segmentation is helpful, it can also lead to stereotyping—a preconception about a group of people—which can alienate a potential market or cause marketers to miss a potential market altogether. The idea is to use segmentation as a starting point, not as an endpoint. Demographic segmentation can help marketers communicate effectively with their target markets.

SEGMENTING BY GENDER

Gender is an obvious variable that helps define the markets for certain products, but segmenting by gender can be tricky. In some cases, the segmenting is obvious—lipstick for women, facial shaving products for men. However, in recent years, the lines have increasingly blurred. Some men wear earrings and use skin-care products, once both the province of women. Some of today's women purchase power tools and pickup trucks, once considered traditionally male purchases. So marketers of cars and trucks, power tools, jewelry, and skin-care products have had to change the way they segment their markets. Dove, well known for its skin-care products for women, created an entire line of men's skin-care products called Dove Men+Care. Some companies successfully market the same, or similar, products to both men and women. Visa markets its small-business credit card services to firms owned by both men and women.

As purchasing power in many households has shifted toward women, marketers learned that female consumers who regularly use the Internet make most of the decisions about retail items. Based on this information, Yahoo launched Shine, a site specifically for women. The site offers content in various areas ranging from entertainment to finance and provides opportunities for advertisers to reach a targeted female audience. Kellogg's, Olay, and Purina are among the brands that advertise on the site.[17]

SEGMENTING BY AGE

Age is another variable marketers use to segment their markets. As with gender, age seems an easy distinction to make—baby food for babies, retirement communities for seniors. But the distinctions become blurred as consumers' roles and needs change and as age distribution shifts and changes in each group take place. St. Joseph's baby aspirin is no longer marketed just to parents for their infants; now, it is also marketed to adults to help prevent heart disease.

School-Age Children

School-age children—and those even younger—exert considerable influence over family purchases, as marketers are keenly aware, particularly in the area of food. Children as young as two make choices about what they want to eat, play with, and wear. The food industry reportedly spends $10 billion each year marketing to children. Its advertisements for products such as breakfast cereals, snack foods, and beverages are designed to attract the attention of children under the age of 12—who in turn persuade their families to purchase them. With childhood obesity on the rise, nutritionists and pediatricians are concerned about the nutritional value of foods marketed to children. In fact, a recent study by the American Academy of Pediatrics revealed that the advertising of junk food plays a key role in childhood obesity.[18] See the "Solving an Ethical Controversy" feature for a discussion of the role of high-fructose corn syrup, a high-calorie ingredient whose use in a wide variety of foods concerns many.

Tweens and Teens

Tweens—sometimes also called *preteens*—and teens are a rapidly growing market. This group is 71 million strong and packs a wallop when it comes to spending—some researchers estimate as much as $200 billion. But they also influence billions of dollars' worth of purchases made by their families. Although members of this group don't fall into a single category—they reflect the diversity of the U.S. population in general—the most popular purchases include candy and snacks, soft drinks, clothing, music, and electronics. If marketers could characterize this group with one word, it would likely be *interactive*. They grew up with the Internet, and they expect to be actively involved in their own entertainment. They might prefer to determine the outcome of a video game than to see who won a football game on TV. Even the TV shows they watch, such as *The Voice*, provide opportunities for input. They are completely comfortable in a digital world, and many cannot imagine life without their smartphones and iPads. When they want to communicate with friends or parents they send text messages. They expect a vast array of choices in programming, media alternatives, and interactive experiences. The big challenge for marketers is keeping up with them—let alone staying a step ahead. Phone companies and car companies have increased their spending on advertising to older teens, while snacks, clothing, and video games claim the attention of the younger set.[19]

SOLVING AN ETHICAL CONTROVERSY
Should High-Fructose Corn Syrup Be Banned?

High-fructose corn syrup is a common ingredient in many processed foods and drinks U.S. consumers buy and eat every day, from soda to baked goods and even yogurt. Made from corn kernels blended into a thick syrup, the ingredient is cheaper than sugar but high in calories, with either little or no nutritional value (depending on whom you ask). It is blamed for a wide variety of health problems (including childhood obesity) and environmental impacts.

Should high-fructose corn syrup be banned from foods and soft drinks?

PRO

1. Long-term consumption leads to high levels of body fat and cholesterol, which can contribute to obesity, diabetes, and heart disease.
2. High-fructose corn syrup requires the cultivation of corn as a monoculture, depleting the soil of nutrients while flooding soil and groundwater with pesticides.

CON

1. High-fructose corn syrup helps baked, canned, and frozen goods look better and stay fresh and moist longer.
2. Even calories, in moderation, have their place in a balanced diet. Consumers should be able to make their own choices about what they eat.

Summary

Given the wide use of the ingredient, a ban seems unlikely for now. As always, consumers should educate themselves to make wise decisions about what they buy and eat.

Sources: "Drinking Your Way to Obesity?" *Kfit Health*, accessed March 13, 2104, www.kidfitnessandhealth.com; company website, "5 Reasons High Fructose Corn Syrup Will Kill You," accessed March 13, 2014, http://drhyman.com; Jennifer K. Nelson, "High-Fructose Corn Syrup: Any Health Concerns?" *Mayoclinic.org*, accessed March 13, 2014, www.mayoclinic.org; Marin Gazzaniga, "Sickeningly Sweet: The Effects of High-Fructose Corn Syrup," *MSN Health Living*, accessed March 13, 2014, http://healthyliving.msn.com; Nanci Heilmich, "Study: Kids Get More Added Sugar from Foods Than Drinks," *USA Today*, accessed March 13, 2014, http://yourlife.usatoday.com.

Some companies have expanded their product lines to include specific offerings to tweens and teens. Lululemon Athletica, which specializes in athletic wear for women, launched Ivivva, a website that features athletic and dance clothing for girls.[20]

Generation X

The group born between 1968 and 1979, now generally in their mid-30s to late 40s, are often referred to as *generation X*. This group of an estimated 50 million faced some economic and career challenges as they began their adult lives and started families: Housing costs were high and debt associated with college loans and credit cards was soaring. But their financial squeeze has eased somewhat as they are in their prime earning years. This group is very family oriented—not defining themselves by their careers as much as previous generations—well educated, and optimistic. Like their younger counterparts, gen Xers are comfortable with the Internet; even if they make a purchase at a retail store, they are likely to have researched their choices online. But like their elders, they were raised on television—so the TV is still an important marketing tool.[21]

As this generation matures, they are growing more concerned about social issues and protecting the natural environment, both of which they view as affecting the well-being of their children.

As a result, they are turning to goods and services that support certain causes. Singer-songwriter Jack Johnson, in his mid-30s, recorded an album using solar energy. He requires his concert promoters to recycle and launched an online social networking site, All At Once, where fans can support environmental not-for-profit organizations. Johnson, a member of generation X, appeals both to his own age group and older teens.[22]

Baby Boomers

Baby boomers—those born between 1946 and 1964—are a popular segment to target because of their numbers and income levels. Approximately 78 million people were born during this period in the United States.[23] The values of this age group were influenced both by the Vietnam War era and the career-driven era that followed. They also came of age with early television and with TV commercials serving as a backdrop to most of their lives. They tried new breakfast cereals, ate TV dinners, and recall when cigarettes were advertised on television.

Not surprisingly, baby boomers are a lucrative segment for many marketers. Baby boomers wield spending power estimated at over $7 trillion, which is why businesses try to woo this group.[24] Subgroups within this generation complicate segmentation and targeting strategies. Some boomers put off having children until their 40s, while others their age have already become grandparents. Boomers tend to value health and quality of life—a fact not lost on marketers for products like organic foods, financial investments, travel, and fitness. But boomers are also quick to embrace new technology, even as they age. According to a recent Pew Research Center study, 83 percent of baby boomers use the Internet. In addition, about 60 percent of all boomers use at least one social-networking site.[25]

The motorcycle industry has boomers clearly in its sights. As a group, baby boomers are significantly more physically active than their counterparts in previous generations. However, boomers are beginning to experience the wide range of health problems that typically come with age—arthritis, back pain, chronic joint and muscle issues, and more—making it difficult for them to continue to ride their two-wheelers. With baby boomers making up more than 40 percent of the motorcycling population, several manufacturers have introduced trikes—that is, three-wheeled motorcycles. The trikes even include luxury features, such as GPS navigation, cruise control, and stereo speakers.[26]

Seniors

As baby boomers age and Americans continue to live longer, the median age of the U.S. population has dramatically increased. Today, more than 40 million people are now over age 65. With discretionary income and rates of home ownership higher than those of other age groups, they also account for a major proportion of new-car sales and travel dollars spent. Many marketers have found that seniors are a group worth targeting. Although many seniors live on modest, fixed incomes, those who are well off financially have both time and money to spend on leisure activities and luxury items.

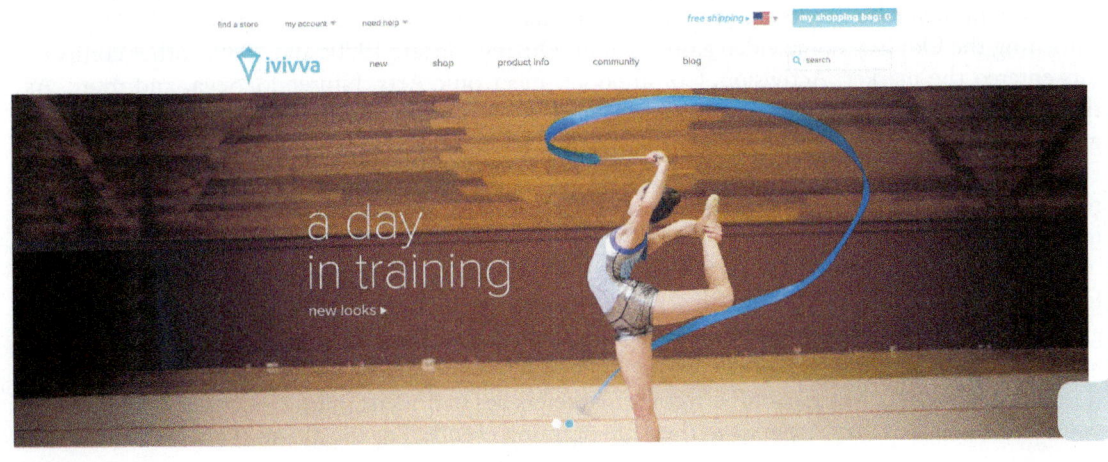

Some companies have expanded their product lines to include specific offerings to tweens and teens. The Ivivva website is targeted specifically to girls.

Other important characteristics of this group include the following:

- Families experienced economic hardship during this group's childhood.
- They built the suburbs.
- They value hard work.
- They like to associate with people who have similar views and backgrounds.
- They are concerned with personal safety.
- They spend money conservatively but have reached a level of financial comfort where they like to indulge in some luxury.
- They are not likely to be the first to try new products.[27]

Understanding just a few of these characteristics helps marketers develop goods and services and create marketing messages that will reach this group. Road Scholar, a branch of Elderhostel, is a not-for-profit organization that has been offering educational travel for seniors since 1975. Its "Adventures in Lifelong Learning" currently comprise 5,500 educational tours in every state and 150 countries. Instead of guides, the tours are run by instructors who are experts in their fields and by local educators. Lectures and field trips are included, and the Road Scholar Travel Assistance Plan, included in the cost of the programs, ensures that anyone with a medical emergency will be cared for. Participants pay tuition rather than fees, and the program is supported by donations.[28]

The Millennials

cohort effect Tendency of members of a generation to be influenced and bound together by events occurring during their key formative years—roughly ages 17 to 22.

Marketers can learn from a sociological concept called the **cohort effect**, the tendency of members of a generation with common characteristics—such as an interest in sustainability—to be influenced and bound together by significant events occurring during their key formative years, roughly ages 17 to 22. These events help define the core values of the age group that eventually shape consumer preferences and behavior. For seniors, the events would be World War II and the Korean War, because many were in this age bracket at that time. Later groups were influenced by the Cold War and the civil rights movement. For older baby boomers, it would be the Vietnam War, the military draft, and the women's movement.

A current cohort—generally consisting of those born during the late 1970s to the early 1990s—may be the most cohesive to date. Marketers have called this group by several names: *the millennials*, *generation Y*, *generation next*, and *echo boomers*. Others called it the *9-11 generation* because its members were in their formative years during the terrorist attacks of September 11, 2001.

But something else happened during the millennials' formative years to shape its preferences and behaviors: While they were coming of age, so too were video games and other types of technology.

The early versions of video games were developed during the 1950s and 1960s and were displayed on oscilloscopes, mainframe computers, and television screens. Atari and Magnavox were the first commercial entrants on the scene, with Atari introducing its Pong game and Magnavox launching the Odyssey home video game system. During the late 1970s and 1980s, other competitors entered the market: Activision, Commodore, Electronic Arts, Nintendo, Sega, and more. As the technology improved, the games and systems became more sophisticated, with 3D, realistic graphics, and handheld consoles. The industry has continued to evolve, with the introduction of PlayStation, the Nintendo DS, Microsoft's Xbox, and the Wii. Today, more consumers of all ages regularly play video games—at home, on their mobile devices, on the beach, anywhere—than go to the movies.

Members of the millennial generation are highly visual and are generally comfortable with all forms of technology. They gravitate to activities that provide constant entertainment and immediate gratification. They get their information from social media such as Facebook and Twitter as opposed to traditional media, and they prefer texting to emails.

The significance of the cohort effect for marketers lies in understanding the general characteristics of millennials as they responds to their life-defining events. The social and economic influences

Members of the millennial cohort are highly visual, comfortable with technology, gravitate toward activities that provide constant entertainment and instant gratification, and prefer communicating via texts rather than emails.

this generation experiences help form members' long-term beliefs and goals in life—and can have a lasting effect on their buying habits and the product choices they make.[29]

SEGMENTING BY ETHNIC GROUP

According to the Census Bureau, America's racial and ethnic makeup is constantly changing. The three largest and fastest-growing racial/ethnic groups are Hispanics, African Americans, and Asian Americans. From a marketer's perspective, it is important to note that spending by these groups is rising at a faster pace than for U.S. households in general.

Hispanics and African Americans

Hispanics and African Americans are currently the largest racial/ethnic minority groups in the United States, with Hispanics surpassing African Americans at over 54 million, according to the most recent census data. In fact, the Census Bureau revealed that, although whites will still be a majority for some time to come, for the first time, there were more minority births than white births in the United States.[30] The Hispanic population is growing much faster than the African American population.[31] The population growth has created *majority-minority counties*—that is, places where more than half the population is a single racial or ethnic group other than non-Hispanic white. Majority-minority counties exist in several states.[32] Although U.S. Hispanics' disposable income is still significantly less than that of non-Hispanic whites, a recent study found that Hispanic buying power is rising at a rate nearly triple that of the national average—an important insight for marketers. One estimate puts the buying power of the Hispanic community at more than $1.5 trillion.[33] See the "Marketing Success" feature to learn how Clorox is using a multi-pronged targeted approach to reach these consumers.

Many marketers have focused their efforts on the Hispanic population in the United States. Procter & Gamble, The Coca-Cola Company, and Walmart are among the largest advertisers to target this group of consumers. Still, many companies find it a challenge to reach Hispanic consumers and turn them into customers. The Captura Group conducts online marketing research geared to help companies connect with Hispanic consumers. Based in San Diego, California, Captura provides marketing solutions in both English and Spanish. Among Captura Group's clients are PayPal, Allstate, Ford, and Kellogg.[34]

MARKETING SUCCESS
Hispanic Consumers Prime Target for Clorox

Background. Clorox Company earns revenues of more than $6 billion a year from sales in over 100 countries. In the U.S. market, the buying power of the Hispanic market is expected to soon grow to more than $1.5 trillion.

The Challenge. Hispanic consumers are younger, on average, than the median market age. Heavy users of the Internet and mobile phones, they are influenced by technology and media. They make fewer shopping trips than non-Hispanics but spend more each time, and they often retain the strong family ties and Spanish language of their home cultures. Clorox needed to reach them in a carefully targeted way.

The Strategy. Clorox joined Vme, the Spanish-language network, in a marketing campaign to champion germ prevention, including flu shots, hand washing, and disinfection accomplished with Clorox cleaning products. The company also introduced a marketing and advertising platform called Clorox Fragancia that airs on Telemundo and Univision and includes radio, digital, and direct mail strategies, all in Spanish. It also worked with a medical doctor to offer a Spanish website about health and health training and launched the Hispanic Nurses Network, a family resource that includes a Facebook page.

The Outcome. With these and other media efforts, Clorox is well positioned to reach the growing Hispanic market.

Sources: Jack Neff, "Why New Clorox CEO Won't Mimic Alma Mater P&G's Marketing Cuts," *Advertising Age*, accessed September 25, 2014; http://adage.com; Michelle Saettler, "General Mills, Clorox Target Hispanic Mobile Shoppers via Bilingual Promotions App," *Mobile Marketer*, accessed September 25, 2014; www.mobilemarketer.com; Kristen Cloud, "Clorox Identifies Four Mega Trends for Hispanic Consumers," *The Shelby Report*, accessed March 13, 2014, www.theshelbyreport.com; "Content Marketing: How P&G, Clorox and Tampico Engage Hispanic Audiences," *Portada*, accessed March 13, 2014, www.portada-online.com; Tiffany Hsu, "Clorox Launches New Products, Campaign on Latino Cleaning Habits," *Los Angeles Times*, accessed March 13, 2014, http://articles.latimes.com; "Nielsen: Hispanic Consumers' Buying Power to Grow 50% by 2015" *Drug Store News*, accessed March 8, 2014, www.drugstorenews.com; Laurel Wentz, "Clorox Fragancia Launch Targets U.S. Hispanic Consumers," *Advertising Age Hispanic*, accessed March 8, 2014, http://adage.com; Alaric Dearment, "Growing Hispanic Consumer Power Increases Need for Outreach from Retailers, Suppliers," *Drug Store News*, accessed March 8, 2014, www.drugstorenews.com; Allison Cerra, "Clorox, NAHN Introduce Hispanic Nurses Network," *Drug Store News*, accessed March 8, 2014, www.drugstorenews.com; Michael D. Hernandez, "Big Brands Target Hispanic Consumers," *USA Today*, March 8, 2014, www.usatoday.com.

> **Briefly Speaking**
>
> "Immigration is the sincerest form of flattery."
>
> —**Jack Paar**
> Host of *The Tonight Show*, 1957–1962

Like Hispanics, who originate from various countries, the more than 45 million African Americans in the United States—who make up more than 14 percent of the population—do not comprise a single category. Instead, they represent broad diversity ranging from country of origin to income, age, education, and geographic location. Studies show that affluent African Americans are creating a significant impact on the consumer economy. The number of African American households earning $75,000 or more continues to grow. This group now has an estimated $1.1 trillion in buying power.[35]

This growing segment represents an opportunity for advertisers, few of whom currently target African Americans in national campaigns. In an effort to reach out to African American women and celebrate their beauty, global giant Procter & Gamble started the "My Black is Beautiful" initiative. The marketing campaign's goal is to help African American women improve their self-images and to promote loyalty to P&G brands in hair care, cosmetics, and oral care.[36]

Asian Americans

Although Asian Americans make up a smaller segment than either the African American or Hispanic populations, with almost 19 million in the United States, they have been the fastest-growing segment of the population since 2000. The Census Bureau estimates this group will grow to almost 23 million by the year 2020, more than 5 percent of the U.S. population.[37] Asian Americans are an attractive target for marketers because they also have the fastest-growing income.

The Asian American population is concentrated in fewer geographic areas than other ethnic markets. Half of Asian Americans live in California, New York, and Texas. The population is diverse, however, because it represents numerous cultures, and its members speak a wide variety of languages, including Bengali, Cantonese, Hawaiian, Hindi, Hmong, Japanese, Korean, Laotian, Mandarin, Tamil, Telugu, Thai, Urdu, and Vietnamese. As a result, demographics differ widely by Asian group. For example, the median household income for Asian Indians in a recent year totaled nearly $97,000, while median income for Bangladeshi Americans during the same period was about $45,000.[38]

Native Americans

Another important minority group is Native Americans, whose current population numbers over 5.2 million, or 2 percent of the total U.S. population, including both American Indians and Alaska natives. In addition to tribes located in the continental United States, such as Cherokee, Apache, Navaho, Pueblo, and Iroquois, the Census Bureau includes Alaska native tribes such as Aleut and Eskimo. The Native American population increased 26.7 percent between the 2000 and 2010 censuses, faster than the U.S. population in general, which grew 9.7 percent during the same period.[39]

In addition to population growth, Native American businesses are growing. In a recent year, almost 237,000 nonfarm Native American firms operated in the United States, with $34.4 billion in receipts. Almost a third operated in the construction, maintenance and repair, retail, and services industries.[40] Reservation-based casinos and related gaming activities make up a multi-billion-dollar industry.

American Indian Business Leaders is "the only American Indian non-profit organization solely dedicated to empowering business students in the United States." This organization's goal is to increase the number of Native American and Native Alaskan businesspeople and entrepreneurs by providing business and leadership education opportunities.[41]

People of Mixed Race

U.S. residents completing census forms now have the option of identifying themselves as belonging to more than one racial category. According to the Census Bureau, about 9 million U.S. residents classify themselves this way, and their numbers are growing.[42] Marketers need to be aware of this change. On one hand, it benefits marketers by making racial statistics more accurate; on the other hand, marketers may find it difficult to compare the new statistics with data from earlier censuses. In some cases, people of mixed race prefer to emphasize one part of their heritage over another; in other cases, they prefer not to make a choice. Recent estimates place about 45 percent of the U.S. mixed-race population under the age of 25, and these consumers are having their own families.[43] Forward-thinking marketers should keep tabs on this group, identifying their needs and preferences.

Asian Americans, the fastest growing segment of the U.S. population, are an attractive target for marketers because they also have the fastest rising income. Jeremy Lin, who is very popular in this highly desired market, has quickly become the most recognizable Asian American in the NBA and communicates with his global fan base via his official website.

family lifecycle
Process of family formation and dissolution.

SEGMENTING BY FAMILY LIFECYCLE STAGES

Still another form of demographic segmentation employs the stages of the **family lifecycle**—the process of family formation and dissolution. The underlying theme of this segmentation approach is that life stage, not age per se, is the primary determinant of many consumer purchases. As people move from one life stage to another, they become potential consumers for different types of goods and services.

An unmarried person setting up an apartment for the first time is likely a good prospect for inexpensive furniture and small home appliances. This consumer must probably budget carefully, ruling out expenditures on luxury items. Alternatively, a young single person still living at home will probably have more money to spend on products, such as a car, entertainment, and clothing. As couples marry, their consumer profiles change. Couples without children are frequent buyers of personalized gifts, furniture, and homes. Eating out and travel may also be part of their lifestyles.

The birth or adoption of a first child changes any consumer's profile considerably; parents must buy cribs, changing tables, baby clothes, baby food, car seats, and similar products. Parents usually spend less on the children who follow because they have already bought many essential items for the first child. Today, the average woman gives birth to fewer children than she did a century ago and usually waits until she is older to have them. Although the average age for American women to have their first child is 25, many women wait much longer, often into their 30s and even 40s. This means that, if they work outside the home, older women are likely more established financially with more money to spend. However, if a woman chooses to stay home after the birth of a child, income can drop dramatically.

Families typically spend the most during the years their children are growing—on everything including housing, food, clothing, braces, and college. Thus, they often look to obtain value wherever they can. Marketers can create satisfied and loyal customers among this group by giving them the best value possible.

Once children are on their own—or at least off to college—married couples enter the "empty nest" stage. Empty nesters may have the disposable incomes necessary to purchase premium products once college tuitions and mortgages are paid off. They may travel more, eat out more often, redecorate the house, or go back to school themselves. They may treat themselves to a new and more luxurious car or buy a vacation home. In later years, empty nesters may decide to sell their homes and become customers for retirement or assisted-living communities. They may require home-care services or more health care products as well. However, some older adults report they have not saved enough for retirement. People currently in this stage of life now say they would advise younger adults to address issues of a lifetime income, the cost of health care, and less reliance on Social Security benefits for income. Whether to meet expenses or for intellectual stimulation, many retired adults return to work at least part time—as consultants in their field of expertise, starting their own businesses, or working as Walmart greeters.[44]

One trend noted by researchers in the past decade is an increase in the number of grown children, or "boomerangs," who return home to live with their parents. A recent study found that three out of ten young adults are boomerangs, some of them bringing along pets or families of their own.[45] Another trend is the growing number of grandparents who care for grandchildren on a regular basis—making them customers all over again for baby and child products, such as toys, food, and safety devices.[46]

> **Briefly Speaking**
>
> "Diversity: The art of thinking independently together."
>
> —**Malcolm S. Forbes**
> *American publisher, Forbes magazine*

SEGMENTING BY HOUSEHOLD TYPE

The first U.S. census in 1790 found an average household size of 5.8 people. Today, that number is below three, due in part to a declining birth rate.[47] Sociologists attribute the decline to couples' reluctance to take on the added expense of a child.[48] The U.S. Department of Commerce cites several other reasons for the trend toward smaller households: lower fertility rates (including the decision to have fewer children or no children at all), young people's tendency to postpone marriage, the frequency of divorce, and the ability and desire of many people to live alone.

Today's U.S. households embody a wide range of diversity. They include households with a married couple and their children; households blended through divorce or loss of a spouse and remarriage;

those headed by a single parent, same-sex parents, or grandparents; couples without children; groups of friends; and single-person households.

Couples without children may be young or old. If they are seniors, their children already may have grown and are living on their own. Some older couples choose to live together without marriage because they prefer to keep their finances separate and because they could lose valuable health or pension benefits if they married. Younger couples without children are considered attractive to marketers, because they often have high levels of income to spend. These couples typically eat out often, take expensive vacations, and buy luxury cars.

Same-sex couples and other LGBT community members who share households—with or without children—are on the rise. More than 2 million U.S. children are raised by LGBT parents. Recent estimates put the buying power of the LGBT community at more than $830 billion annually. Even as the social conversation over same-sex marriage and civil unions continues, marketers recognize these consumers as important customers. Companies such as Apple, Jet Blue, and JCPenney target LGBT consumers in their marketing efforts.[49]

People live alone for various reasons—sometimes by choice and sometimes by necessity, such as divorce or widowhood. In response, marketers have modified their messages and their products to meet the needs of single-person households. Food industry manufacturers are downsizing products, offering more single-serving foods, ranging from soup to macaroni and cheese.

Marketers have modified their messages and their products to meet the needs of single-person households, offering items such as single-serving foods.

SEGMENTING BY INCOME AND EXPENDITURE PATTERNS

Part of the earlier definition of *market* described people with purchasing power. Not surprisingly, then, a common basis for segmenting the consumer market is income. Marketers often target geographic areas known for the high incomes of their residents. Or they might consider age or household type when determining potential buying power.

ENGEL'S LAWS

How do expenditure patterns vary with income? Over a century ago, Ernst Engel, a German statistician, published what became known as **Engel's laws**—three general statements based on his studies of the impact of household income changes on consumer spending behavior. According to Engel, as household income increases, the following will take place:

1. A smaller percentage of expenditures goes for food.
2. The percentage spent on housing, household operations, and clothing remains constant.
3. The percentage spent on other items (such as recreation and education) increases.

Are Engel's laws still valid? Recent studies say yes, with a few exceptions. Researchers note a steady decline in the percentage of total income spent on food, beverages, and tobacco as

Engel's laws Three observations about the impact of household income on consumer spending behavior: as household income increases, a smaller percentage of expenditures goes for food; the percentage spent on housing, household operations, and clothing remains constant; and the percentage spent on other items (such as recreation and education) increases.

income increases. Although high-income families spend greater absolute amounts on food items, their purchases represent declining percentages of their total expenditures compared with food expenditures of low-income families.[50] In addition, the overall percentage of income spent on food has declined over the last century.[51] But as food prices become inflated, consumers change how they shop—they may spend the same to buy fewer items, spend more to buy the same items, or try to spend less and buy as many items as possible within the new budget. Marketers note that consumers are more selective, on the alert for bargains at the supermarket. One other recent finding splits the food dollar according to meals cooked and eaten at home versus meals eaten out at restaurants. Over the years, the proportion of food U.S. consumers ate away from home gradually increased, to nearly half their food dollar. However, with the belt-tightening that accompanies a slow economy, the restaurant industry saw a sustained dip in sales over the past few years. Currently, U.S. consumers reportedly spend about 40 percent of their food dollar on meals eaten away from home.[52]

The second law remains partly accurate. However, the percentage of fixed expenditures for housing and household operations has increased over the past 30 years. And the percentage spent on clothing rises with increased income. Also, expenditures may vary from region to region. In general, residents of the Northeast and West spend more on housing than people who live in the Midwest and South.

The third law remains true, with the exception of medical and personal-care costs, which appear to decline as a percentage of increased income.

Engel's laws can help marketers target markets at all income levels. Regardless of the economic environment, consumers still buy luxury goods and services. One reason is some companies now offer their luxury products at different price levels. Mercedes-Benz has its lower-priced C-class models, while Tiffany sells a $125 sterling silver heart pendant with chain. Both of these firms continue to offer their higher-priced items but have broadened their market by serving other consumers.

DEMOGRAPHIC SEGMENTATION ABROAD

Marketers often face a difficult task in obtaining the data necessary for demographic segmentation abroad. Many countries do not have scheduled census programs. Germany skipped counting from 1970 to 1987, and France conducts a census about every seven years. By contrast, Japan and Canada conduct censuses every five years; however, the mid-decade assessments are not as complete as the end-of-decade counts.

Also, some foreign data include demographic divisions not found in the U.S. census. Canada collects information on religious affiliation, for instance. On the other hand, some of the standard segmentation data for U.S. markets are not available abroad. Many nations do not collect income data. Great Britain, Japan, Spain, France, and Italy are examples. Similarly, family lifecycle data are difficult to apply in global demographic segmentation efforts. Ireland acknowledges only three marital statuses—single, married, and widowed—while Latin American nations and Sweden count their unmarried cohabitants.

One source of global demographic information is the International Programs Center (IPC) at the U.S. Census Bureau. The IPC provides a searchable online database of population statistics for many countries on the Census Bureau's Web page. Another source is the United Nations, which sponsors national statistical offices that collect demographic data on various countries.

In addition, private marketing research firms can supplement government data. Firms such as Boston Consulting Group gather data on income of consumers around the world, focusing in particular on millionaire households. Although the global recession caused it to decline, worldwide wealth is on the rebound. The United States remains the country with the most millionaire households, with more than 7 million.[53]

ASSESSMENT CHECK

5.1 What is demographic segmentation?

5.2 What are the major categories of demographic segmentation?

PSYCHOGRAPHIC SEGMENTATION

Marketers have traditionally referred to geographic and demographic characteristics as the primary bases for dividing consumers into homogeneous market segments. Still, they have long recognized the need for fuller, more lifelike portraits of consumers in developing their marketing programs. As a result, psychographic segmentation can be a useful tool for gaining sharper insight into consumer purchasing behavior.

> Outline the psychographic approach to segmenting consumer markets.

WHAT IS PSYCHOGRAPHIC SEGMENTATION?

Psychographic segmentation divides a population into groups with similar values and lifestyles. Lifestyle refers to a person's mode of living and describes how an individual operates on a daily basis. Consumers' lifestyles are composites of their individual psychological profiles, including their needs, motives, perceptions, and attitudes. A lifestyle also bears the mark of many other influences, such as family, job, social activities, and culture.

The most common method for developing psychographic profiles of a population is to conduct a large-scale survey asking consumers to agree or disagree with a collection of several hundred AIO statements. These **AIO statements** describe various activities, interests, and opinions. The resulting data allow researchers to develop lifestyle profiles. Marketers can then develop a separate marketing strategy that closely fits the psychographic makeup for each lifestyle segment.

Marketing researchers have conducted psychographic studies on hundreds of goods and services, such as beer and air travel. Hospitals and other health care providers use such studies to assess consumer behavior and attitudes toward health care in general, to learn the needs of consumers in particular marketplaces, and to determine how consumers perceive individual institutions. Many businesses turn to psychographic research to learn what consumers in various demographic and geographic segments want and need.

psychographic segmentation Division of a population into groups having similar attitudes, values, and lifestyles.

AIO statements Items on lifestyle surveys that describe various activities, interests, and respondents' opinions.

VALS Segmentation system that divides consumers into eight psychographic categories: innovators, thinkers, achievers, experiencers, believers, strivers, makers, and survivors.

VALS™

Over a quarter-century ago, the research and consulting firm SRI International developed a psychographic segmentation system it called VALS, an acronym for *VAlues and LifeStyles*. Initially, VALS categorized consumers by their social values—how they felt about issues such as legalization of marijuana or abortion, for example. Today, VALS is owned and managed by Strategic Business Insights, (SBI), an SRI spin-off that has revised the system to link it more closely with consumer buying behavior. The revised VALS system categorizes consumers by characteristics that correlate with purchase behavior. It is based on two key concepts: resources and self-motivation. **VALS** divides consumers into eight psychographic categories: innovators, thinkers, achievers, experiencers, believers, strivers, makers, and survivors. Figure 9.3 details the profiles for these categories and their relationships.

The VALS framework in the figure displays differences in resources as

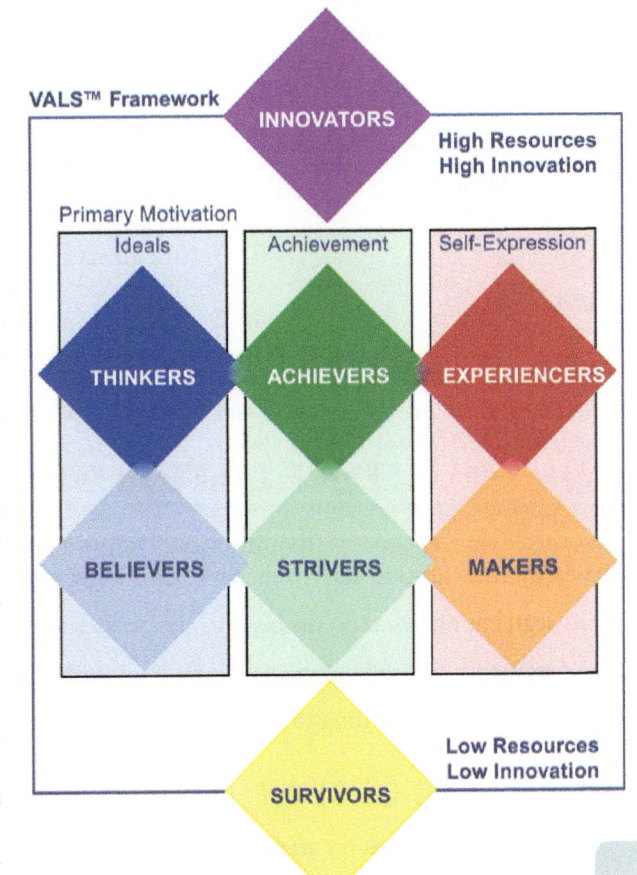

FIGURE 9.3
The VALS™ Framework

Source: Strategic Business Insights, "About VALS," www.strategicbusinessinsights.com/vals, accessed January 15, 2014.

vertical distances, and primary motivation is represented horizontally. The resource dimension measures income, education, self-confidence, health, eagerness to buy, and energy level. Primary motivations divide consumers into three groups: principle-motivated consumers who have a set of ideals and morals they live by; achievement-motivated consumers, influenced by symbols of success; and action-motivated consumers who seek physical activity, variety, and adventure.

SBI has created several specialized segmentation systems based on this approach. GeoVALS™, for instance, estimates the percentage of each VALS type in a U.S. residential ZIP code. Marketers can identify ZIP codes with the highest concentrations of the segment they want to reach, they can use the information to choose locations for retail outlets, and they can tailor marketing messages for a local audience. Japan-VALS™ segments the Japanese marketplace with an emphasis on early adopters of new ideas and products. U.K.-VALS™ segments the United Kingdom marketplace into six separate groups of consumers, which helps marketers make smarter choices for strategic planning. SBI is developing several other systems for countries in South American and the Caribbean.[54]

USING PSYCHOGRAPHIC SEGMENTATION

No one suggests that psychographic segmentation is an exact science, but it does help marketers quantify aspects of consumers' personalities and lifestyles to create goods and services for a target market. Psychographic profile systems such as those of SBI can paint useful pictures of the overall psychological motivations of consumers. These profiles produce much richer descriptions of potential target markets than other techniques can achieve. The enhanced detail aids in matching a company's image and product offerings with the types of consumers who use its products.

Identifying which psychographic segments are most prevalent in certain markets helps marketers plan and promote more effectively. Often, segments overlap; however, in a recent study of mobile phone users, consumer-research firm Experian Simmons discovered five distinct segments, which they named basic planners, mobile professionals, pragmatic adopters, social connectors, and mobirati. Mobile phones have become so prevalent that the user population is large enough to be studied—and segmented.[55]

Psychographic segmentation is a good supplement to segmentation by demographic or geographic variables. For example, marketers may have access to each consumer type's media preferences in network television, cable television, Internet use, radio format, magazines, and newspapers. Psychographic studies may then refine the picture of segment characteristics to give a more elaborate lifestyle profile of the consumers in the firm's target market. A psychographic study could help marketers of goods and services in Baltimore, Des Moines, or Seattle predict what kinds of products consumers in those cities would be drawn to and eliminate those that are not attractive.

ASSESSMENT CHECK

6.1 What is psychographic segmentation?

6.2 Name the eight psychographic categories of the U.S. VALS framework.

PRODUCT-RELATED SEGMENTATION

7 Describe product-related segmentation.

product-related segmentation Division of a population into homogeneous groups based on their relationships to a product.

Product-related segmentation involves dividing a consumer population into homogeneous groups based on their relationships to the product. This segmentation approach can take several forms:

1. segmenting based on the benefits people seek when they buy a product
2. segmenting based on usage rates for a product
3. segmenting according to consumers' brand loyalty toward a product

SEGMENTING BY BENEFITS SOUGHT

This approach focuses on attributes people seek and benefits they expect to receive from a good or service. It groups consumers into segments based on what they want a product to do for them. Consumers who drink Starbucks premium coffees are not just looking for a dose of caffeine. They are willing to pay extra to savor a pleasant experience, one that makes them feel pampered and appreciated. Women who work out at Curves want to look their best and feel healthy. Pet owners who feed their cats and dogs Science Diet believe they are giving their animals a great-tasting, healthful pet food. Case 9.1 at the end of this chapter outlines how cruise-ship companies offer cruises designed for travelers with specific types of interests.

Even if a business offers only one product line, however, marketers must remember to consider product benefits. Two people may buy the same product for very different reasons. A box of Arm & Hammer baking soda could end up being used as a refrigerator freshener, a toothpaste substitute, an antacid, or a deodorizer for a cat's litter box.

SEGMENTING BY USAGE RATES

Marketers may also segment a total market by grouping people according to the amounts of a product they buy and use. Markets can be divided into heavy-, moderate-, and light-user segments. The **80/20 principle** holds that a big percentage of a product's revenues—maybe 80 percent—comes from a relatively small, loyal percentage of total customers, perhaps 20 percent. The 80/20 principle is sometimes referred to as *Pareto's law*. Although the percentages need not exactly equal these figures, the general principle holds true: Relatively few heavy users of a product can account for the bulk of its consumption.

Depending on their goals, marketers may target heavy, moderate, or light users as well as nonusers. A company may attempt to lure heavy users of another product away from their regular brands to try a new brand. Nonusers and light users may be attractive prospects because other companies are ignoring them. Usage rates can also be linked to other segmentation methods such as demographic and psychographic segmentation.

80/20 principle
Generally accepted rule that 80 percent of a product's revenues come from 20 percent of its customers.

SEGMENTING BY BRAND LOYALTY

A third product-related segmentation method groups consumers according to the strength of the brand loyalty they feel toward a product. A classic example of brand loyalty segmentation is the frequent-purchase program—it might be frequent flyer, frequent stay, or frequent purchase of books or gasoline. Other companies attempt to segment their market by developing brand loyalty over a period of time, through consumers' stages of life. Disney has a collection of toddler and children's shoes featuring their many animated characters. K-Swiss offers sneakers for infants and toddlers: tiny replicas of the famous tennis shoes for adults. Marketers for these companies are intent on creating brand loyalty for their shoes at the earliest stages of life.[56]

Companies spar for loyalty on just about every front. In recent years, fast-food chains such as McDonald's and Burger King started offering breakfast menus. In order to win its own share of early-morning customers, Taco Bell joined with Cinnabon, Tropicana, Seattle's Best, and other brands to offer breakfast

Segmenting by benefits focuses on the attributes that people seek and the benefits they expect to receive from a good or service. This ad focuses on the healthy benefits of Science Diet dog food for puppies.

menu items in test markets around the country. The new breakfast menu, including waffle tacos, a breakfast "crunchwrap," and an "A.M." version of Mountain Dew (a mixture of orange juice and Mountain Dew), has gone national.[57]

USING MULTIPLE SEGMENTATION BASES

Segmentation can help marketers increase their accuracy in reaching the right markets. Like other marketing tools, segmentation is probably best used in a flexible manner—for instance, combining geographic and demographic segmentation techniques or dovetailing product-related segmentation with segmentation by income and expenditure patterns. An important point to keep in mind is that segmentation is a tool to help marketers get to know their potential customers better and ultimately satisfy their needs with the appropriate goods and services.

> **ASSESSMENT CHECK**
>
> 7.1 List the three approaches to product-related segmentation.
>
> 7.2 What is the 80/20 principle?

THE MARKET SEGMENTATION PROCESS

8 Identify the four steps in the market segmentation process.

To this point, the chapter has discussed various bases on which companies segment markets. But how do marketers decide which segmentation base—or bases—to use? Firms may use a management-driven method, in which segments are predefined by managers based on their observation of the behavioral and demographic characteristics of likely users. Or they may use a market-driven method, in which segments are defined by asking customers for the attributes important to them. Then, marketers follow a four-stage process.

DEVELOP A RELEVANT PROFILE FOR EACH SEGMENT

After identifying promising segments, marketers should understand the customers in each one. This in-depth analysis of customers helps managers accurately match buyers' needs with the firm's marketing offers. The process must identify characteristics that both explain the similarities among customers within each segment and account for differences among segments.

The task at this stage is to develop a profile of the typical customer in each segment. Such a profile might include information about lifestyle patterns, attitudes toward product attributes and brands, product-use habits, geographic locations, and demographic characteristics.

FORECAST MARKET POTENTIAL

In the second stage, market segmentation and market opportunity analysis combine to produce a forecast of market potential within each segment. Market potential sets the upper limit on the demand competing firms can expect from a segment. Multiplying by market share determines a single firm's maximum sales potential. This step should define a preliminary "go" or "no-go" decision from management because the total sales potential in each segment must justify resources devoted to further analysis. For example, in deciding whether to market a new product to teens, electronics firms need to determine the demand for the product and the disposable income of that group.

FORECAST PROBABLE MARKET SHARE

Once market potential has been estimated, a firm must forecast its probable market share. Competitors' positions in targeted segments must be analyzed, and a specific marketing strategy must be designed to reach these segments. These two activities may be performed simultaneously.

> **"Briefly Speaking"**
>
> "You read a book from beginning to end. You run a business the opposite way. You start with the end, and then you do everything you must to reach it."
>
> —Harold S. Geneen
> American businessman

Moreover, by settling on a marketing strategy and tactics, a firm determines the expected level of resources it must commit—that is, the costs it will incur to tap the potential demand in each segment.

Apple's iPhone took the marketplace by storm, followed by the iPad, and analysts believe these two products helped boost sales of the iMac computer as well. Recently Apple introduced the iPhone 6 and iPhone 6 Plus. Over the first three days after introducing the new product, Apple sold 10 million units, a record for the technology giant.[58]

SELECT SPECIFIC MARKET SEGMENTS

The information, analysis, and forecasts accumulated throughout the entire market segmentation decision process allow management to assess the potential for achieving company goals and to justify committing resources in developing one or more segments. Demand forecasts, together with cost projections, determine the profits and the return on investment the company can expect from each segment. Marketing strategy and tactics must be designed to reinforce the firm's image, yet keep within its unique organizational capabilities.

At this point in the analysis, marketers weigh more than monetary costs and benefits; they also consider many difficult-to-measure but critical organizational and environmental factors. The firm may lack experienced personnel to launch a successful attack on an attractive market segment. Similarly, a firm with 60 percent of the market faces possible legal problems with the Federal Trade Commission if it increases its market concentration. This assessment of both financial and nonfinancial factors is a difficult but vital step in the decision process.

> **ASSESSMENT CHECK**
>
> 8.1 Identify the four stages of market segmentation.
>
> 8.2 Why is forecasting important to market segmentation?

STRATEGIES FOR REACHING TARGET MARKETS

Marketers spend a lot of time and effort developing strategies that will best match their firm's product offerings to the needs of particular target markets. An appropriate match is vital to the firm's marketing success. Marketers have identified four basic strategies for achieving consumer satisfaction: undifferentiated marketing, differentiated marketing, concentrated marketing, and micromarketing. Social media is rapidly becoming a profitable means of reaching audiences in all these strategies; see the "Career Readiness" feature for some ways to do so successfully.

Discuss four basic strategies for reaching target markets.

UNDIFFERENTIATED MARKETING

A firm may produce only one product or product line and promote it to all customers with a single marketing mix; such a firm is said to practice **undifferentiated marketing**, sometimes called *mass marketing*. Undifferentiated marketing was much more common in the past than it is today.

While undifferentiated marketing is efficient from a production viewpoint, the strategy also brings inherent dangers. A firm that attempts to satisfy everyone in the market with one standard product may suffer if competitors offer specialized alternatives to smaller segments of the total market and better satisfy individual segments. In fact, firms that implement strategies of differentiated marketing, concentrated marketing, or micromarketing may capture enough small segments of the market to defeat another competitor's strategy of undifferentiated marketing. The golden arches of McDonald's have always stood for quick, inexpensive meals. Consumers could count on the same food and same dining experience at every McDonald's they visited. But McDonald's marketers are

undifferentiated marketing Strategy that focuses on producing a single product and marketing it to all customers; also called *mass marketing*.

CAREER READINESS
Using Social Media to Reach Target Markets

Social media allows for more precise targeting of consumer and other markets than ever before. How can *you* make the most of it? Here are some tips.

1. Know your target market and its most important segments. How does your audience use your product, and what unsolved problems do they face?

2. Join the online communities where your target audience gathers, including Facebook, LinkedIn, Twitter, Google+, and Pinterest, and subscribe to influential blogs.

3. Understand how these sites and their users differ from each other. All social media sites are not alike.

4. Start by spending some time listening, so you can learn about users' concerns, problems, and preferences. Learn and follow the social conventions of each community as well.

5. Start chiming in with helpful tips and advice that revolve around your market, not your product. Help users solve problems rather than pitching your good or service.

6. Ensure your brand is visible on social media early and often by publishing product content and engaging in frequent conversations.

7. If you add additional tools, such as widgets or apps, make sure they're easy to use and require minimal effort.

8. Consider using audio and video. Approximately 100 hours of video are uploaded to YouTube every minute of the day.

Sources: Organizational website, "Fun Facts," www.iacpsocialmedia.org, accessed September 25, 2014; Susan Gunelius, "7P's of Social Media Marketing That Drive Results," *Forbes*, accessed March 13, 2014, www.forbes.com; Erin Richards-Kunkel, "6 Common Social Media Myths (Debunked)! *Business 2 Community*, March 8, 2014, www.business2community.com; Roxane Divol, David Edelman, and Hugo Sarrazin, "Demystifying Social Media," *McKinsey Quarterly*, accessed March 8, 2014, www.mckinseyquarterly.com; Anton Koekemoer, "Using Twitter, Facebook, and LinkedIn to Reach Your Target Audience," *Memeburn.com*, accessed March 8, 2014, http://memeburn.com; Phil Mershon, "5 Social Media Tips for Finding and Engaging Your Target Audience: New Research," *Social Media Examiner*, accessed March 8, 2014, www.socialmediaexaminer.com.

---

changing the firm's strategy somewhat in response to a trend that says consumers want a little luxury with fast food and a more varied dining experience from restaurant to restaurant. Some stores feature updated color schemes and new decor, flat-screen TVs, free wi-fi, and lounge seating. The company has also introduced new products, such as Chicken McWraps and Fruit & Nut Oatmeal, and has extended operating hours at some stores.[59]

DIFFERENTIATED MARKETING

differentiated marketing Strategy that focuses on producing several products and pricing, promoting, and distributing them with different marketing mixes designed to satisfy smaller segments.

Firms that promote numerous products with differing marketing mixes designed to satisfy smaller segments are said to practice **differentiated marketing**. By providing increased satisfaction for each of many target markets, a company can produce more sales by following a differentiated marketing strategy than undifferentiated marketing would generate. Oscar Mayer, a marketer of a variety of meat products, practices differentiated marketing. It increased its sales by introducing Lunchables, aimed at children. The original Lunchables were so successful that Oscar Mayer introduced more choices in the line, including snack versions. In general, however, differentiated marketing also raises costs. Production costs usually rise because additional products and variations require shorter production runs and increased setup times. Inventory costs rise because more products require added storage space and increased efforts for record keeping. Promotional costs also rise because each segment demands a unique promotional mix.

Despite higher marketing costs, however, an organization may be forced to practice differentiated marketing to diversify and reach new customers. The travel industry now recognizes the need to target smaller groups of travelers with specialized interests. History buffs can attend special events at Colonial Williamsburg or at George Washington's estate, Mount Vernon.[60] The Sierra Club and other environmental organizations—in addition to commercial travel operators—offer hikes, kayaking expeditions, and bird-watching trips for outdoor enthusiasts.[61] Luxury travel company Tauck now offers a series of guided, all-inclusive trips called Tauck Bridges, designed with traveling families or grandparents and their grandchildren in mind.[62]

CONCENTRATED MARKETING

Rather than trying to market its products separately to several segments, a firm may opt for a concentrated marketing strategy. With **concentrated marketing** (also known as **niche marketing**), a firm focuses its efforts on profitably satisfying a single market segment. This approach can appeal to a small firm lacking the financial resources of its competitors and to a company offering highly specialized goods and services. American Express, a large firm with many financial products, recently introduced two new credit cards designed for very specific markets: The Knot, for engaged couples, and The Nest, for newlyweds.

Peanut Butter & Co. appeals to the world's peanut butter lovers with its proprietary brand of gourmet, natural peanut butter flavors including Smooth Operator, Crunch Time, and Dark Chocolate Dreams. Its Mighty Maple is intended for pancake fans, and The Bee's Knees can replace a humdrum jar of honey. Fans visiting the flagship store in New York City can sample favorites such as "ants on a log" or grilled peanut butter, banana, honey, and bacon sandwiches; or they can shop for their favorite blends online.[63]

But along with its benefits, concentrated marketing has its dangers. Because the strategy ties a firm's growth to a specific segment, sales can suffer if new competitors appeal successfully to the same target. If another firm targets peanut butter lovers in the same manner, Peanut Butter & Co. may face enhanced competition. In addition, errors in forecasting market potential or customer buying habits can lead to severe problems, particularly if the firm has spent substantially on product development and promotion. If more people—children in particular—continue to develop peanut allergies, sales of Peanut Butter & Co.'s products may begin to decline. Anticipating this, the company could begin to diversify product offerings to include non-allergenic foods.

concentrated marketing (niche marketing) Focusing marketing efforts on satisfying a single market segment.

MICROMARKETING

The fourth targeting strategy, still more narrowly focused than concentrated marketing, is **micromarketing**—targeting potential customers at a very basic level, such as by ZIP code, specific occupation, or lifestyle. Ultimately, micromarketing can even target individuals. A salesperson at

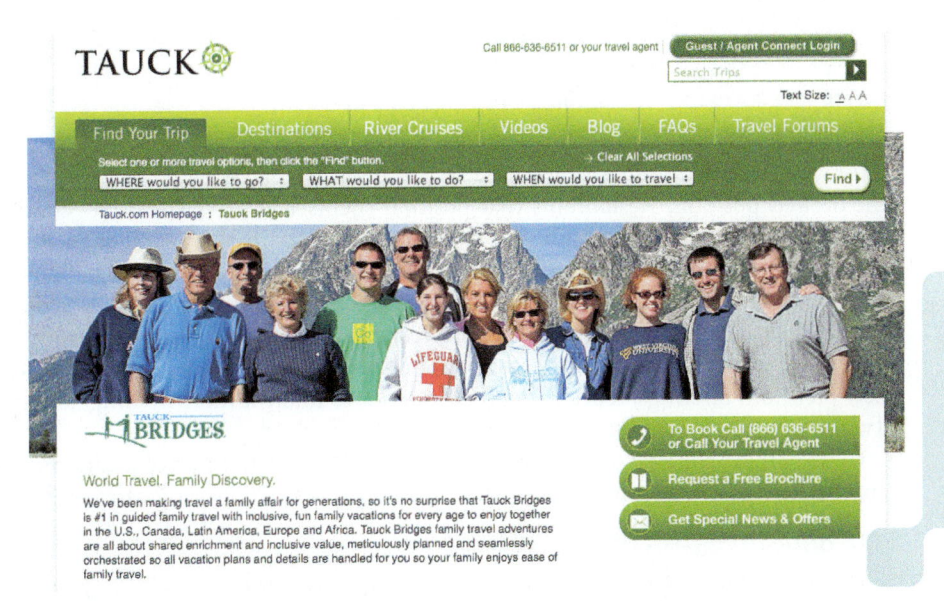

micromarketing Targeting potential customers at very narrow, basic levels, such as by ZIP code, specific occupation, or lifestyle—possibly even individuals themselves.

Upscale travel operator Tauck offers guided, all-inclusive trips designed for extended families or grandparents traveling with their grandchildren.

> **ASSESSMENT CHECK**
>
> 9.1 Explain the difference between undifferentiated and differentiated marketing strategies.
>
> 9.2 What are the benefits of concentrated marketing?

your favorite clothing boutique may contact you when certain merchandise she thinks you might like arrives at the store. The Internet allows marketers to make micromarketing even more effective: By tracking specific demographic and personal information, marketers can send email directly to individual consumers most likely to buy their products.

When a shopper visits Amazon, the website welcomes the shopper by name and recommend products that shopper might be interested in buying, given previous purchases. Amazon also sends out emails recommending specific products similar to items shoppers have already purchased.

But micromarketing, like niche marketing, can become too much of a good thing if companies spend too much time, effort, and marketing dollars to unearth a market too small and specialized to be profitable. In addition, micromarketing may cause a company to lose sight of other, larger markets. So it's important for marketers to assess the situation and pursue the most profitable markets.

SELECTING AND EXECUTING A STRATEGY

10 Explain the four types of positioning strategies and the reasons for positioning and repositioning products.

> **Briefly Speaking**
>
> "Increasingly, the mass market is turning into a mass of niches."
>
> —**Chris Anderson**
> Former editor-in-chief, Wired magazine, and author of The Long Tail

positioning Placing a product at a certain point or location within a market in the minds of prospective buyers.

Although most organizations adopt some form of differentiated marketing, no single choice suits all firms. Any of the alternatives may prove most effective in a particular situation. The basic determinants of a market-specific strategy are (1) company resources, (2) product homogeneity, (3) stage in the product life cycle, and (4) competitors' strategies.

A firm with limited resources may have to choose a concentrated marketing strategy. Small firms may be forced to select small target markets because of limitations in their sales force and advertising budgets. On the other hand, an undifferentiated marketing strategy suits a firm selling items perceived by consumers as relatively homogeneous. Marketers of grain, for example, sell standardized grades of generic products rather than individual brand names. Some petroleum companies implement undifferentiated marketing to distribute their gasoline to the mass market.

The firm's strategy may also change as its product progresses through the stages of the lifecycle. During the early stages, undifferentiated marketing might effectively support the company's effort to build initial demand for the item. In the later stages, however, competitive pressures may force modifications in products and in the development of marketing strategies aimed at segments of the total market.

The strategies of competitors also affect the choice of a segmentation approach. A firm may encounter obstacles to undifferentiated marketing if its competitors actively cultivate smaller segments. In such instances, competition usually forces each firm to adopt a differentiated marketing strategy.

Having chosen a strategy for reaching their firm's target market, marketers must then decide how best to position the product. The concept of **positioning** seeks to put a product in a certain position, or place, in the minds of prospective buyers. Marketers use a positioning strategy to distinguish their firm's offerings from those of competitors and to create promotions that communicate the desired position. Restaurants that position themselves as "fast-casual" continue to outperform most other categories of restaurants. Top menu choices in this segment include Mexican, bakery café, pizzas, Asian, chicken, and hamburgers. Analysts believe fast-casual restaurants provide consumers with the chance to sit down to a dinner priced lower than what is offered at an upscale restaurant yet of higher quality than a fast-food restaurant. Fast-casual provides good value in the minds of many consumers. Many fast-casual restaurants currently are trying to upgrade their menu with new premium offerings, redesigning their interior to make it more inviting, and using Facebook and Twitter to attract even more customers.[64]

To achieve the goal of positioning, marketers follow a number of positioning strategies. Possible approaches include positioning a product according to the following categories:

1. *Attributes*—eBay, "Buy it. Sell it. Love it."

2. *Price/quality*—Omega watches, "We measure the 100th of a second that separates winning from taking part."

Restaurants that position themselves as "fast-casual," such as Chipotle, continue to outperform most other categories of restaurants.

3. *Competitors*—Walmart, "Save money. Live better."
4. *Application*—Blue Cross Blue Shield health insurance, "Experience. Wellness. Everywhere."
5. *Product user*—Crane's stationery, "for the writer somewhere in each of us."
6. *Product class*—BMW, the "ultimate driving machine."

Whatever strategy they choose, marketers want to emphasize a product's unique advantages and differentiate it from competitors' options. A **positioning map** provides a valuable tool in helping managers position products by graphically illustrating consumers' perceptions of competing products within an industry. Marketers can create a competitive positioning map from information solicited from consumers or from their accumulated knowledge about a market. A positioning map might present two different characteristics—price and perceived quality—and show how consumers view a product and its major competitors based on these traits. The hypothetical positioning map in Figure 9.4 compares selected retailers based on possible perceptions of the prices and quality of their offerings.

Sometimes changes in the competitive environment force marketers to **reposition** a product—changing the position it holds in the minds of prospective buyers relative to the positions of competing products. Repositioning may even be necessary for already successful products or firms to gain greater market share. After publishing multivolume print editions for 244 years, Encyclopaedia Britannica is now only available online. The company updates the online edition, which is far bigger than any print version, every twenty minutes.[65]

FIGURE 9.4
Hypothetical Positioning Map for Selected Retailers

positioning map Tool that helps marketers place products in a market by graphically illustrating consumers' perceptions of competing products within an industry.

reposition Changing the position of a product within the minds of prospective buyers relative to the positions of competing products.

ASSESSMENT CHECK

10.1 What are the four determinants of a market-specific strategy?

10.2 What is the role of positioning in a marketing strategy?

Strategic Implications of Marketing in the 21st Century

To remain competitive, today's marketers must accurately identify potential customers. They can use various methods to accomplish this, including segmenting markets by gender and geographic location. The trick is to figure out the best combination of methods for segmentation to identify the most lucrative, long-lasting potential markets. Marketers must also remain flexible, responding to markets as they change—for instance, following a generation as it ages or reaching out to new generations by revamping or repositioning products.

The greatest competitive advantage will belong to firms that pinpoint and serve markets without segmenting them to the point at which they are too small or specialized to garner profits. Marketers who reach and communicate with the right customers have a greater chance of attracting and keeping those customers than marketers who search for the wrong buyers in the wrong place.

Get online now for additional learning tools to help you master your marketing knowledge—visit **WWW.CENGAGEBRAIN.COM** today!

REVIEW OF CHAPTER OBJECTIVES

1 Identify the two essential components of a market.

A market consists of people and organizations with the necessary purchasing power, willingness, and authority to buy. Consumer products are purchased by the ultimate consumer for personal use. Business products are purchased for use directly or indirectly in the production of other goods and services. Certain products may fall into both categories.

2 Outline the role of market segmentation in developing a marketing strategy.

Market segmentation is the process of dividing a total market into several homogeneous groups. It is used in identifying a target market for a good or service. Segmentation is the key to deciding a marketing strategy.

3 Describe the four components necessary for effective segmentation.

Effective segmentation depends on these four basic requirements: (1) the segment must have measurable purchasing power and size, (2) marketers can find a way to promote to and serve the market, (3) marketers must identify segments large enough for profit potential, and (4) the firm can target a number of segments that match its marketing capabilities.

4 Explain the geographic approach to segmenting consumer markets.

Geographic segmentation divides the overall market into homogeneous groups according to population locations.

Chapter 9 Market Segmentation, Targeting, and Positioning

5 Discuss the demographic approach to segmenting consumer markets.

Demographic segmentation classifies the market into groups based on characteristics such as age, gender, and income level.

6 Outline the psychographic approach to segmenting consumer markets.

Psychographic segmentation uses behavioral profiles developed from analyses of consumers' activities, opinions, interests, and lifestyles to identify market segments.

7 Describe product-related segmentation.

Product-related segmentation can take three basic forms: segmenting based on the benefits people seek when buying a product, segmenting based on usage rates for a product, and segmenting according to consumers' brand loyalty toward a product.

8 Identify the four steps in the market segmentation process.

Market segmentation is the division of markets into relatively homogeneous groups. Segmentation follows a four-step sequence: (1) developing user profiles (2) forecasting the overall market potential, (3) estimating market share, and (4) selecting specific market segments.

9 Discuss four basic strategies for reaching target markets.

Four strategies are (1) undifferentiated marketing—uses a single marketing mix; (2) differentiated marketing—produces numerous products, each with its own mix; (3) concentrated marketing—directs all the firm's marketing resources toward a small segment; and (4) micromarketing—targets potential customers at basic levels, such as ZIP code or occupation.

10 Explain the four types of positioning strategies and the reasons for positioning and repositioning products.

Positioning strategies include positioning a good or service according to attributes, price/quality, competitors, application, product use, and product class. Positioning helps distinguish a firm's products from those of competitors and provides a basis for marketing communications. Repositioning a product—changing the position it holds in consumers' minds—may be necessary to gain greater market share.

ASSESSMENT CHECK: ANSWERS

1.1 Define target market. A target market is the specific segment of consumers most likely to purchase a particular product.

1.2 Distinguish between a consumer product and a business product. A consumer product is purchased by the ultimate buyer for personal use. A business product is purchased for use directly or indirectly in the production of other goods and services.

2.1 Define market segmentation. Market segmentation is the process of dividing a total market into several homogeneous groups.

2.2 Describe the role of market segmentation. The role of market segmentation is to identify the factors that affect purchase decisions and then group consumers according to the presence or absence of these factors.

3.1 Identify the four criteria for effective segmentation. The four criteria for effective segmentation are: (1) the market segment must present measurable purchasing power and size, (2) marketers must find a way to promote effectively and serve the market segment, (3) marketers must identify segments sufficiently large to give them good profit potential, and (4) the firm must aim for segments that match its marketing capabilities.

3.2 Give an example of a market segment that meets these criteria. Examples might include women, teenagers, Hispanics, empty nesters, and NASCAR enthusiasts.

4.1 Under what circumstances are marketers most likely to use geographic segmentation? Marketers usually use geographic segmentation when regional preferences exist and when demand for categories of goods and services varies according to geographic region.

4.2 What are the five main categories for classifying urban data? The five categories are core based statistical area (CBSA), metropolitan statistical area (MSA), micropolitan statistical area, consolidated metropolitan statistical area (CMSA), and primary metropolitan statistical area (PMSA).

5.1 What is demographic segmentation? Demographic segmentation defines consumer groups according to demographic variables such as gender, age, income, occupation, household, and family lifecycle.

5.2 What are the major categories of demographic segmentation? The major categories of demographic segmentation are gender, age, ethnic group, family lifecycle, household type, income, and expenditure patterns.

6.1 What is psychographic segmentation? Psychographic segmentation divides a population into groups with similar values and lifestyles.

6.2 Name the eight psychographic categories of the U.S. VALS framework. The eight categories are innovators, thinkers, achievers, experiencers, believers, strivers, makers, and survivors.

7.1 List the three approaches to product-related segmentation. The three approaches are segmenting by benefits sought, segmenting by usage rates, and segmenting by brand loyalty.

7.2 What is the 80/20 principle? The 80/20 principle states that a big percentage (80 percent) of a product's revenues comes from a relatively small number (20 percent) of loyal customers.

8.1 Identify the four stages of market segmentation. The four stages are developing user profiles, forecasting the overall market potential, estimating market share, and selecting specific market segments.

8.2 Why is forecasting important to market segmentation? Forecasting is important because it can define a preliminary "go" or "no-go" decision based on sales potential. It can help a firm avoid a disastrous move or point out opportunities.

9.1 Explain the difference between undifferentiated and differentiated marketing strategies. Undifferentiated marketing promotes a single product line to all customers with a single marketing mix. Differentiated marketing promotes numerous products with different marketing mixes designed to satisfy smaller segments.

9.2 What are the benefits of concentrated marketing? Concentrated marketing can allow a firm to focus on a single market segment, which is especially appealing to smaller firms and those that offer highly specialized goods and services.

10.1 What are the four determinants of a market-specific strategy? The four determinants are company resources, product homogeneity, stage in the product lifecycle, and competitors' strategies.

10.2 What is the role of positioning in a marketing strategy? Positioning places a product in a certain position in the minds of prospective buyers so marketers can create messages that distinguish their offerings from those of competitors.

MARKETING TERMS YOU NEED TO KNOW

market 274
target market 274
consumer products 275
business products 275
market segmentation 275
geographic segmentation 277
core based statistical area (CBSA) 278
metropolitan statistical area (MSA) 278
micropolitan statistical area 279
consolidated metropolitan statistical area (CMSA) 279
primary metropolitan statistical area (PMSA) 279
core regions 279
geographic information systems (GISs) 280
demographic segmentation 280
cohort effect 284
family lifecycle 288
Engel's laws 289
psychographic segmentation 291
AIO statements 291
VALS 291
product-related segmentation 292
80/20 principle 293
undifferentiated marketing 295
differentiated marketing 296
concentrated marketing (niche marketing) 297
micromarketing 297
positioning 298
positioning map 299
repositioning 299

ASSURANCE OF LEARNING REVIEW

1. Classify each of the following as a business product or a consumer product:
    a. Detroit Tigers ticket
    b. bottle of body lotion
    c. fleet of delivery trucks
    d. bulk order of rice
    e. digital camera
    f. GE jet engine

2. What are core regions? Why do marketers try to identify these regions?

3. What is the cohort effect? How would you classify your generation?

4. What is the fastest-growing racial/ethnic minority group in the United States? What types of things do marketers need to know about this group to sell successfully to these consumers?

5. How is segmentation by family lifecycle and household type useful to marketers? Briefly describe your own family in these terms, identifying characteristics that might be helpful to marketers for a firm selling "smart" TVs.
6. What are AIO statements? How are they used by marketers?
7. Identify a branded product to which you are loyal, and explain why you are loyal to this item. What factors might cause your loyalty to change?
8. Choose another branded product. Create a relevant profile for the marketing segment this product serves.
9. What are the six categories generally used to position a product?
10. How does a positioning map work? What are its benefits?

PROJECTS AND TEAMWORK EXERCISES

1. On your own or with a partner, choose one of the following consumer products and think about how it could be used as a business product. Then create a business advertisement for your product.
   a. lawn care products
   b. microwave oven
   c. golf balls
   d. bottled water
   e. electric car
   f. vacuum cleaner
2. With a classmate, choose one of the following products you believe is generally targeted for either men or women and create an advertisement for the product aimed at the opposite gender.
   a. barbecue grill and accessories
   b. hunting or fishing supplies
   c. nail salon
   d. SUV
   e. online video game
   f. massage
3. Create a chart showing how your family's income and expenditure patterns have changed over the years as the family lifecycle changed. You don't need exact figures, just the general picture. If possible, ask other family members for additional information.
4. With a classmate, choose a product and come up with a slogan representing each of the six positioning approaches for the product.
5. On your own or with a classmate, select one of the following products. Visit the firm's website to see how the product is positioned, then create an advertisement showing how you think marketers could reposition the product to gain greater market share.
   a. Gatorade
   b. Dove soap
   c. Barilla pasta
   d. Fiskars scissors
   e. Hallmark cards

CRITICAL-THINKING EXERCISES

1. Create a profile of yourself as part of a market segment. Include the following:
   a. geographic location
   b. gender and age
   c. household type
   d. income and spending habits
2. Select one of the following products and explain how you would use segmentation by income and expenditure patterns to determine your targeted market.
   a. Busch Gardens theme parks
   b. GoPro video camera
   c. Healthy Choice frozen entrées
   d. Land Rover Evoque
3. How do you think the Internet has affected differentiated marketing techniques?
4. Choose one of the following products and describe a marketing approach that segments the target market by benefits sought:
   a. Kryptonite bicycle lock
   b. A private college or university
   c. Andersen windows and doors
   d. Coke Zero
   e. Edy's Grand Ice Cream
5. Visit the website of a large company, such as Kraft Foods, Samsung, or Campbell Soup. Look for ways the firm practices differentiated marketing. How do you think this approach benefits the firm?

ETHICS EXERCISE

Marketers are making a new pitch to men—at the risk of political incorrectness. Marketers for firms such as Unilever and Kmart were frustrated in their attempt to reach young male consumers with their messages. After searching for clues about what this crowd likes, these firms created marketing campaigns designed to grab their attention—perhaps at the expense of other consumers. Some advertising is designed to appeal to "bad boy" attitudes, lowbrow humor, and sex.

1. What are some of the pitfalls of this kind of segmentation?
2. Do you think these ads will be successful in the long run? Why or why not?
3. Should marketers be concerned about offending one market segment when trying to reach another? Why or why not?

INTERNET EXERCISES

1. **Psychographic segmentation.** Visit the websites of Caterpillar, Marriott Hotels, and Dr Pepper. How does each firm employ psychographic segmentation (such as the VALS approach) to the marketing of its products? Is there a relationship between the use of psychographic segmentation and the types of products sold by each firm?

   www.cat.com
   www.marriott.com
   www.drpepper.com

2. **Market segmentation.** Go to the website of Siemens. How does Siemens segment its markets, such as geographical, product related, demographic, or brand loyalty? Does the firm use more than one method of product segmentation? Why or why not?
   www.siemens.com/entry/cc/en

3. **Target market.** Visit the website of Philips. What strategy or strategies does the firm employ for reaching its target markets? Does it rely more on undifferentiated or differentiated marketing?
   www.usa.philips.com

Note: Internet Web addresses change frequently. If you don't find the exact site listed, you may need to access the organization's home page and search from there or use a search engine such as Google or Bing.

CASE 9.1
Cruise Lines Cater to Travelers' Specific Interests

The typical cruise ship passenger may not actually exist. While the core target market for cruise vacations is 35 or older, with a passport and household income of at least $60,000 who is likely to have cruised at least once before, that description now covers more than 30 percent of the U.S. population. That's why cruise marketers no longer think in terms of an "average" customer. So many different specialty cruises are springing up to appeal to different market segments that almost anyone can find themselves in a target group.

What's your passion? Whether you like to cook, quilt, tango, snorkel, listen to jazz, play baseball, garden, watch movies, gaze at Impressionist art, explore investment strategies, hold a family reunion, or engage in a host of other pursuits, there's a themed cruise for you, with specific on-board and on-shore activities, workshops, and seminars hosted by skilled instructors. Even if you're attending a business meeting or conference rather than enjoying a vacation, you may well find yourself cruising for the occasion. Business managers find that meetings on cruise ships can save as much as a third of the cost of land-based gatherings, once all cost factors such as meals, lodging, travel, and audio-visual equipment are taken into account. Besides, says the co-founder of a company that plans such events, cruising "excites people."

Passengers do fall into a number of traditional demographic categories that cruise marketers find useful. Analyzing factors such as country of origin, language, economic status, and psychographics, marketers have devised distinct market segments. "Explorers" are well-to-do repeat customers, a small group that's profitable but challenging to please. "Admirals" are older and loyal; they appreciate a traditional experience. "Marines" are young professionals on the lookout for a better experience each time; they're eager to parasail, surf, and rock climb. "Little Mermaids" are upper-middle-class families in search of a memorable vacation, while "Escapers" just want to get away from the daily grind without worries or complications. Finally, "Souvenirs" are in search of the best deal; price is their priority.

Marketers even have a term for those whose interest and income make them unlikely to become cruise customers. They are "Adrift."

QUESTIONS FOR CRITICAL THINKING

1. Is segmenting customers as "Explorers," "Admirals," and the like a useful marketing tool? Why or why not?
2. Which segments of the cruise market are most likely to be influenced by social media? Why?

Sources: Organization website, *Theme Cruise Finder*, www.themecruisefinder.com, accessed March 13, 2014; organization website, *Cruise Market Watch*, www.cruisemarketwatch.com, accessed March 13, 2014; Fran Golden, "Theme Cruises," *USA Today*, accessed March 13, 2014 www.usatoday.com, "CLIA's 2013 North America Cruise Industry Update," *Cruising.org*, accessed March 13, 2014, www.cruising.org; company website, http://landrykling.com, accessed March 13, 2014.

VIDEO CASE 9.2
Nederlander Targets Theatergoers Everywhere

For marketers to send effective messages to customers, they need to know who those customers are—and what they want. Nederlander Producing Company has been in the theater business for a century, but its owners aren't looking backward. Instead they're focused forward, on the most advanced ways to identify and serve their audiences. "Everything we do along the food chain of the theater industry is about enhancing the customers' feeling when they experience a Broadway show," says Nick Scandalios, executive vice president of the Nederlander Organization. To do this, the company goes to great lengths to target exactly who those customers are.

Nederlander segments its audiences in a few ways: geographic, demographic, and psychographic. The company also engages in some product-related segmentation by building brand loyalty to its stable of theaters, productions, and concerts. Since Broadway is located in New York City, it's natural for Nederlander to market to consumers living within the tri-state area of New York, New Jersey, and Connecticut. But Nederlander also owns theaters and produces shows in Chicago, Detroit, Los Angeles, San Diego, Tucson, and Raleigh, among other cities—so the company markets to consumers living around those areas as well. Then there are the tourists who live elsewhere but travel to any of those cities—Nederlander makes sure to communicate with them too. Thus, the geographic range extends nationwide. "Nederlander was the first such company to develop a one-on-one digital interaction with all of the people who go to all of the Nederlander houses across the country, called Broadway Direct," says Scott Sanders, co-lead producer of the revival of the Broadway hit musical *Evita*. "There are over 2.5 million people on that list. It's a very valuable list, these are very targeted theatergoers."

Broadway Direct also helps Nederlander and its partners segment their audiences by demographics and psychographics. For example, by tapping the digital list, says Sanders, "we sold more than $500,000 to those customers, all at full price." These are consumers who can afford premium seats and performances and are willing to pay for them. They are people who enjoy the theater and make it part of their entertainment lifestyle. All of the data gathered by Broadway Direct creates user profiles that the company relies on for everything from deciding which shows to invest in or host, to which consumers will most likely attend each show. "The more we know about audience purchasing habits, the better we can become at serving them with the shows we think they'd find most interesting," notes Sean Free, vice president of sales and tracking at Nederlander.

The company doesn't stop with an initial communication blast to more than 2.5 million theatergoers. Instead, it follows up with what Free calls retargeting, which further identifies audience members by their preferences. Each Broadway Direct newsletter contains opportunities for consumers to click on different options for content. "We put these people in specific buckets," explains Free. For example, as *Evita* approached its launch, Broadway Direct sent theatergoers an online newsletter containing feature articles, video, audio, a sweepstakes, and, of course, a "Buy Tickets" button. Consumers had a seven-day window to purchase tickets at a lower price, after which the price would go up. Those who clicked the button but didn't follow through with a purchase received a follow-up email from Broadway Direct a few days later, reminding them of the opportunity. Free estimates that the second email generated an additional 15 to 20 percent in sales.

Nederlander also carefully positions its offerings to differentiate itself not only from other theater productions but also from other types of entertainment on which consumers might spend their dollars. "We thought it was important to position *Evita* as an important event because it was the first time in 30 years the show had been on Broadway," notes Free. "So this was going to be a big deal." Nederlander and its partners treated it as such. When they landed Ricky Martin for the lead role of Che, they immediately contacted Martin's fan club and marketing team to launch a presale for Martin's fan base. These might not be regular theatergoers, but they wanted to see Martin on stage. Then Nederlander marketers followed up with a presale to its Audience Rewards customers, who are members of the company's loyalty program. "Loyalty is key for any venue or any show," acknowledges Free. "People want to come back to see shows and they should be rewarded for that." An excited audience crammed the theater in New York to see the premiere of *Evita*. On opening night, Ricky Martin and the cast got a standing ovation.

QUESTIONS FOR CRITICAL THINKING

1. How does Nederlander achieve the three major criteria for effective market segmentation?

2. Where would you place *Evita's* audience members on the VALS™ framework? Explain your choice. How might Nederlander use this framework to identify audiences for future shows?

Sources: Company website, www.nederlander.com, accessed March 14, 2014; "Evita Broadway Premiere: A Star-Studded Opening Night for Ricky Martin," *International Business Times*, accessed March 14, 2014, www.ibtimes.com; "Ricky Martin Receives Standing Ovation at 'Evita' Broadway Opening Night," *Pink*, accessed March 14, 2014, www.pinkisthenewblog.com.

NOTES

1. PepsiCo Inc. Annual Income Statement 2013," *Market Watch*, accessed September 25, 2014, www.marketwatch.com; Candice Choi, "PepsiCo's First Premium Water to Make Appearance," *Associated Press*, accessed September 25, 2014, http://bigstory.ap.org; Mario Squicciarini, "Pepsi: The Beverage Stock That's So Much More Than Beverages," *Seeking Alpha*, accessed March 13, 2014, http://seekingalpha.com; "Can PepsiCo's Diversification Help It Outperform Coca-Cola?" *Trefis*, accessed March 13, 2014, www.trefis.com; Sean Sullivan, "Pepsi's Secret Billion Dollar Product," *Motley Fool*, accessed March 13, 2014, http://beta-fool.com; "Water Gives Coke, Pepsi a Way Out of Soda Slump," *CNNMoney*, accessed March 13, 2014, http://money.msn.com; Aimee Picchi, "Can Mountain Dew Break Into Breakfast?" *CNNMoney*, accessed March 13, 2014, http://money.msn.com; Mike Esterl, "Is This the End of the Soft-Drink Era?" *The Wall Street Journal*, accessed March 13, 2014, http://online.wsj.com.
2. U.S. Census Bureau, "U.S. and World Population Clock," accessed September 25, 2014, www.census.gov.
3. Company website, "Fifth Annual 'What Women Want' Survey Results," www.gingerminneapolis.com, accessed March 12, 2014; "What Women Want: Insights into $7 Trillion Women's Purchasing Power," *PR Newswire*, accessed March 12, 2014, www.prnewswire.com.
4. Ibid.
5. Company website, www.askpatty.com, accessed March 12, 2014.
6. Company website, www.designbasics.com, accessed March 12, 2014; Mary Umberger, "Designing with Her Outlook," *Chicago Tribune*, accessed March 12, 2014, http://articles.chicagotribune.com.
7. Company website, www.harley-davidson.com, accessed March 12, 2014; Rick Barrett, "In Quest to Expand Market, Harley-Davidson Reaches Out to Women," *Milwaukee Journal Sentinel*, accessed March 12, 2014, www.jsonline.com.
8. "Top 50 Cities in the U.S. by Population and Rank," *Infoplease.com*, accessed September 25, 2014, www.infoplease.com; Joel Kotkin and Wendell Cox, "The World's Fastest Growing Megacities," *Forbes*, accessed March 12, 2014, www.forbes.com.
9. U.S. Census Bureau, "National and State Population Estimates: July 1, 2013," accessed March 12, 2104, www.census.gov.
10. "Top Ten Countries with the Highest Population," *Internet World Stats*, accessed September 25, 2014, www.internetworldstats.com.
11. Organization website, "Shanghai Population, 2014, and Mumbai Population, 2014," http://worldpopulationreview.com, accessed September 25, 2014.
12. "Allied Van Lines: 46th Annual Magnet States Report Puts Texas on Top Again," *PR Newswire*, accessed March 12, 2014, www.prnewswire.com.
13. U.S. Census Bureau, "Metropolitan and Micropolitan Statistical Areas," accessed March 12, 2014, www.census.gov.
14. U.S. Census Bureau, "Census 2010 Geographic Definitions," accessed March 12, 2014, www.census.gov.
15. Karen Fernau, "Coffee Grinds Fuel for Nation," *USA Today*, accessed March 12, 2014, www.usatoday.com; organization website, "2013 National Coffee Drinking Trends," accessed March 12, 2014, www.ncausa.org; Lyz Pfister, "Coffee Culture in America: Top 4 Cities for a Cup of Joe," *Nerd Wallet*, accessed March 12, 2014, www.nerdwallet.com.
16. Lauren Johnson, "Outback Steakhouse Local Foursquare Campaign Netted 678 Check-ins," *Mobile Marketer*, accessed March 12, 2014, www.mobilemarketer.com.
17. Company website, "About Us," http://shine.yahoo.com, accessed March 12, 2014.
18. Organization website, "Familiarity with Television Fast-Food Ads Linked to Obesity," www.aap.org, accessed March 12, 2014.
19. Taryn Luna, "Generation Y a Tough Target for Marketers" *The Boston Globe*, accessed March 12, 2014, www.bostonglobe.com.
20. Company website, www.ivivva.com, accessed March 12, 2014; Sheila Shayon, "Lululemon's Little Sister Tests the Waters in America," *Brand Channel*, accessed March 12, 2014, www.brandchannel.com.
21. Gavin O'Malley, "Gen X Proves Boon to Marketers" *Online Media Daily*, accessed March 12, 2014, www.mediapost.com.
22. Jack Johnson website, http://jackjohnsonmusic.com, accessed March 12, 2014.
23. Brian Conlin, "Marketing to Baby Boomers Online: Where and How to Reach Them" *Vocus Marketing Cloud*, accessed March 12, 2014, www.vocus.com.
24. "Don't Ignore Boomers—The Most Valuable Generation," *Nielsen Wire*, accessed March 13, 2014, www.nielsen.com; Steve Olenski, "Advertisers Marketing to Baby Boomers Just Got an Additional Thirty Eight Million Prospects," *Business 2 Community*, accessed March 13, 2014, www.business2community.com.
25. "Trend Data: Demographics of Internet Users," *Pew Internet*, accessed March 13, 2014, http://pewinternet.org; Andrea Coombes, "Boomers Dive into Social Media," *MarketWatch*, accessed March 13, 2014, www.marketwatch.com.
26. Tony Bizjak, "Adult Tricycles Could Be the Next Boom for Boomer Cyclists" *WPTV.com*, accessed March 13, 2014, www.wptv.com.
27. U.S.Census Bureau," Older Americans Month: May 2013," accessed March 13, 2014, www.census.gov; Katie Moran, "The Overlooked: Social Media Marketing for Senior Citizens," *Forbes*, accessed March 12, 2014, www.forbes.com.
28. Organization website, "Why Road Scholar?" www.roadscholar.org, accessed March 13, 2014.
29. Luna, "Generation Y a Tough Market for Marketers."
30. Jens Manuel Krogstad, "11 Facts for National Hispanic Heritage Month," *Pew Research*, accessed September 25, 2014, www.pewresearch.org; Jeffrey S. Passel, Gretchen Livingston, and D'Vera Cohn, "Explaining Why Minority Births Now Outnumber White Births," *Pew Research Social & Demographic Trends*, accessed March 13, 2014, www.pewsocialtrends.org.
31. "Hispanics Were Not the Fastest-Growing Minority Group Last Year," *Marketing Charts*, accessed March 13, 2014, www.marketingcharts.com.
32. Emily Badger, "6 More U.S. Counties Are Now Majority–Minority" *The Atlantic Cities*, accessed March 13, 2014, www.theatlanticcities.com.
33. "Hispanic Americans by the Numbers" *Info Please*, accessed March 13, 2014, www.infoplease.com; company website, "Latinas Are a Driving Force behind Hispanic Purchasing Power in the U.S" *Nielsen Newswire*, accessed March 13, 2014, www.nielsen.com.
34. Company website, www.capturagroup.com, accessed March 13, 2014.
35. "Interesting Facts about the African American Population," *Black Demographics*, accessed September 25, 2014, http://blackdemographics.com; David Lazarus, "Black Buying Power Hits $1.1 Trillion. What Does That Mean?" *Marketplace*, accessed September 25, 2014, www.marketplace.com.

36. Josh Pichler, "'My Black Is Beautiful' Effort Aims to Improve Lives," *USA Today*, accessed March 13, 2014, www.usatoday.com; organization website, www.myblackisbeautiful.com, accessed March 13, 2014; Jack Neff, "My Black Is Beautiful," *Advertising Age*, accessed March 13, 2014, http://adage.com.
37. "Asians Fastest-Growing Race or Ethnic Group in 2012, Census Bureau Reports," *U.S. Census Bureau*, accessed March 13, 2014, www.census.gov.
38. U.S. Census Bureau, "Profile America, Facts for Features: Asian/Pacific American Heritage Month: May 2014," accessed September 25, 2014, www.census.gov.
39. U.S. Census Bureau, "Profile America, Facts for Features: American Indian and Alaska Native Heritage Month: November 2013," accessed March 13, 2014, www.census.gov.
40. U.S. Census Bureau, "Profile America, Facts for Features: American Indian and Alaska Native Heritage Month"; U.S. Census Bureau, "Census Bureau Reports American Indian– and Alaska Native–Owned Businesses Generated $34 Billion in Receipts in 2007" (press release), accessed March 13, 2014, www.census.gov.
41. Organization website, www.aibl.org, accessed March 13, 2014.
42. Nicholas A. Jones and Jungmiwha Bullock, "The Two or More Races Population" *2010 Census Briefs*, accessed March 13, 2014, www.census.gov.
43. U.S. Census Bureau, "Table 12: Resident Population Projections by Race, Hispanic Origin Status, and Age: 2010 and 2015," accessed March 13, 2014, www.census.gov.
44. Allison Linn, "Plan on Working Past Age 65? You'll Have Company" *NBC News*, accessed March 13, 2014, www.cnbc.com.
45. Les Christie, "Boomerang Kids: Nothing Wrong with Living at Home" *CNNMoney*, accessed March 13, 2014, http://money.cnn.com.
46. Amy Hoak, "Study: More Grandparents Raising Grandkids" *MarketWatch*, accessed March 13, 2014, http://blogs.marketwatch.com.
47. U.S. Census Bureau, "Average Household Size by Age," accessed March 13, 2014, http://factfinder2.census.gov.
48. Annalyn Kurtz, "Baby Bust: U.S. Births at Record Low" *CNNMoney*, accessed March 13, 2014, http://money.cnn.com.
49. Phillip Zonkel and Zen Vuong, "Anheuser-Busch, JetBlue among Companies Targeting Advertising toward LGBT Consumers," *Press-Telegram*, accessed September 25, 2014, www.presstelegram.com; Susan Donaldson James, "2 Million Kids Raised by Gay Couples Are at Risk," *ABC News*, accessed March 13, 2014, http://abcnews.go.com.
50. Aylin Kumcu and Phil Kaufman, "Food Spending Adjustments During Recessionary Times" *Amber Waves*, accessed March 13, 2014, www.ers.usda.gov.
51. U.S. Department of Agriculture, Food CPI and Expenditures: Table 7, accessed March 13, 2014, www.ers.usda.gov.
52. "Consumer Expenditures—2013," *Bureau of Labor Statistics*, accessed September 25, 2014, www.bls.gov.
53. "Global Wealth 2014: Riding a Wave of Growth," Boston Consulting Group, accessed September 25, 2014, www.bcgperspectives.com.
54. Company website, "About VALS™," www.strategicbusinessinsights.com, accessed March 13, 2014.
55. Helen Leggatt, "Experian Segments Mobile Users by Behavior/Attitudes," *BizReport*, accessed March 13, 2014, www.bizreport.com.
56. Company website, www.disneystore.com, accessed March 13, 2014; company website, www.kswiss.com, accessed March 13, 2014.
57. Bruce Horovitz, "Taco Bell Tests Breakfast Biscuit Taco," *USA Today*, accessed September 25, 2014, www.usatoday.com.
58. David Goldman, "Apple Sells 10 Million iPhone 6 and iPhone 6 Pluses," *CNN Money*, September 22, 2014, http://money.cnn.com.
59. Chris Nichols, "Burger Giants Roll Out Remodels, But Are You Noticing?" *Yahoo Finance*, accessed March 13, 2014, http://finance.yahoo.com.
60. Organization website, www.mountvernon.org, accessed March 13, 2014.
61. Organization website, www.sierraclub.org, accessed March 13, 2014.
62. Company website, www.tauck.com, accessed March 13, 2014.
63. Company website, http://ilovepeanutbutter.com, accessed March 13, 2014.
64. Tiffany Hsu, "Chipotle, Panera, Fast-Casual Chains Continue Restaurant Reign" *Los Angeles Times*, accessed March 13, 2014, http://articles.latimes.com.
65. Company website, www.britannica.com, accessed March 13, 2014; Judy Keen, "Encyclopaedia Britannica Turns a Page, Ends Print Edition," *USA Today*, accessed March 13, 2014, www.usatoday.com.

Chapter 10

Marketing Research in the Era of Big Data

1. Describe the development of the marketing research function and its major activities.
2. Explain the six steps in the marketing research process.
3. Distinguish between primary and secondary data sources.
4. Explain probability and nonprobability sampling techniques.
5. Describe the three principal methods marketing researchers use to collect primary data.
6. Explain the challenges of conducting marketing research in global markets.

Netflix used to be the company that sent you DVDs of last year's movies in little red mailing envelopes. Now it's earned multiple Emmy nominations for three original entertainment series that never aired on television.

With a $3 billion budget for content, 10 percent of which is reserved for original programming, Netflix has the potential to transform the way consumers view entertainment—and the way companies produce and provide it. The proof? The company knew "House of Cards," its streamed political drama, would be a hit even before audiences had seen it.

Netflix has inked profitable new deals with television networks that let viewers stream broadcast favorites like "Breaking Bad" one season after broadcast instead of the traditional four years. Its enthusiastic plunge into

NETFLIX USES BIG DATA TO DEVELOP CONTENT

original programming has brought the company's masterful command of big data the most attention. Netflix has made expert use of its huge and complex database, which steadily captures the likes, dislikes, habits, searches, and preferences of its more than 50 million streaming customers. Those viewers watch a billion hours of entertainment every month, consuming one-third of North America's Internet data traffic, and Netflix closely monitors their content choices, viewing behavior, and even the type of device on which they watch. It then translates that data, some 30 million pieces a day, into closely guarded algorithms. That's how the company knew political dramas such as "House of Cards" would be successful with its audiences.

U.S. viewers now watch more movies online (via legal outlets, mainly Netflix) than on Blu-Ray disks or DVDs. This format shift seems likely to give Netflix more market power and strengthen the reliability of its unparalleled database and algorithms. Some worry that post-viewing ratings have become irrelevant. Netflix, however, can already claim that its recommendations make up 60 percent of what streaming subscribers opt to watch, and that this kind of influence will allow it to greatly reduce its marketing costs and develop better-targeted programming.[1]

EVOLUTION OF A BRAND

Technological advances enabled Netflix to take the old principle "Know your audience" to new heights—almost overnight. For marketers, understanding the customer mindset is a critical and ongoing task: What are their buying preferences, and what factors influence those preferences? How do customers make purchase decisions? What's behind customer loyalty?

The ever-growing power and capabilities of the Internet have made it possible for companies like Netflix to quickly collect mountains of data about their customers (seemingly with minimal effort). However, the challenge lies in managing and analyzing that data and then making sound marketing decisions from it. By leveraging the power of the Internet and social media tools to better understand its customer base, Netflix has seen huge profitability gains. What's more, it has been able to transform itself from an enterprise whose main line of business was providing a service to one that develops and delivers products customers want.

- By using the Internet to track huge volumes of customers' viewing and search habits, Netflix has been able to predict a great deal about its customers, including how they watch programming. How else might the company use this information?
- For decades, companies have conducted research to understand their customers and make marketing decisions. However, capturing and analyzing big data is a relatively recent trend made possible, in part, because of faster computers that can complete ever-greater numbers of computations and the emergence of social media, smartphones, and hundreds of thousands of apps. Analyzing all of the data now available in a 21st century world has become a huge marketing challenge. Even if marketers can conduct the data analysis, do you think it is necessarily more accurate than traditional, more subjective methods?
- Assuming all organizations already use some kind of research to better understand their customers, is there any point at which marketing research activities using big data could be seen as inappropriate or unethical?

Chapter Overview

marketing research Process of collecting and using information for marketing decision making.

big data Fueled by 21st century technological advances, the vast and unprecedented volume, speed, and array of data available for informed decision making.

marketing intelligence Sum total of information related to a firm's markets, which a firm gathers in order to better understand their customers, target customer segments, and develop long-term customer relationships.

Collecting and managing information about what customers need and want is a challenging task for any marketer. **Marketing research** is the process of collecting and using information for marketing decision making. Traditionally, data comes from a variety of sources, such as:

- Well-planned studies designed to elicit specific information
- Sales force reports, accounting records, and published reports
- Controlled experiments and computer simulations

Increasingly, however, the technological advances of the last two decades—the Internet, smartphones, social media, and more—have given rise to what's been called **big data**: data that originates in unprecedented volume and at unprecedented speed from the world around us. These advances make it possible for anyone—from a student entrepreneur running a fledgling business from her dorm room to the global marketing department of a Fortune 500 firm—to gather and analyze data from customers, prospects, visitors to a website or Facebook page, smartphone users, GPS tracking data, and many other sources. The volume, speed, and sheer variety of big data are bringing about great changes in the way organizations learn about their customers. And while the purpose and principles of marketing research have not changed, the speed and volume—and the possibilities—are greatly increased.

Big data has the potential to increase revenue, create new revenue streams, improve return on investment, and build commanding market share. The greatest challenge for marketers is being able to manage and analyze all of this data—more than 2.5 *quintillion* bytes of data created every day.[2]

This chapter describes the marketing research function. Regardless of how it is collected, marketers use research to amass marketing intelligence for their firm. **Marketing intelligence** refers to the sum total of information related to a firm's markets, which a firm gathers in order to better understand its customers, target customer segments, and develop long-term customer relationships—all keys to profitability. Information collected through marketing research underlies much of the material on market segmentation discussed in the previous chapter. This chapter also describes how technology drives most facets of marketing research today, from gathering and analyzing to decision making and planning. Although the presence of big data has the potential to affect virtually every facet of life, this chapter focuses on marketers' use of big data.

> **Briefly Speaking**
>
> "Test fast, fail fast, adjust fast."
>
> —**Tom Peters**
> American writer on business management, co-author, *In Search of Excellence*

THE MARKETING RESEARCH FUNCTION

Before looking at how marketing research is conducted, we must first examine its historical development, the people and organizations it involves, and the activities it entails. Because an underlying purpose of research is to find out more about consumers, research is clearly central to effective customer satisfaction and customer relationship programs.

> **1** Describe the development of the marketing research function and its major activities.

HOW MARKETING RESEARCH HAS EVOLVED

Advertising pioneer N. W. Ayer conducted the first organized marketing research project in 1879. Most early research gathered little more than written testimonials from purchasers of firms' products. Research methods became more sophisticated during the 1930s as the development of statistical techniques led to refinements in sampling procedures and greater accuracy in research findings.

Computer technology significantly changed the complexion of marketing research. Besides accelerating the pace and broadening the base of data collection, computers help marketers make informed decisions about problems and opportunities. Simulations, for example, allow marketers to evaluate alternatives by posing what-if questions. Marketing researchers at many consumer goods firms simulate product introductions through computer programs to determine whether to risk real-world product launches or even to subject products to test marketing.

As computers became smaller but also faster and more powerful, they created reams of data. However, marketers found the data difficult to use and not always relevant or easily accessed. These business challenges led to development of the **marketing information system (MIS)**, a planned, computer-based system that provides decision makers with a continuous flow of information relevant to their areas of responsibility. A component of an organization's overall management information system, an MIS serves as a company's "nerve center," monitoring the market environment—both inside and outside the organization—and providing instantaneous information. Marketers use the MIS to store, classify, and analyze the data, and retrieve it as needed.

Test kitchens provide marketers with important data by allowing companies to introduce new products on a small scale and avoid risking a real-world product launch that consumers might not like.

Armed with the raw data from their marketing information system, marketers use a **marketing decision support system (MDSS)** to make informed decisions. An MDSS organizes MIS data in ways that allow users to model different scenarios and evaluate them before making marketing decisions. For example, an MIS might provide a list of product sales from the previous day. A manager could use an MDSS to transform this raw data into graphs illustrating sales trends or reports estimating the impact of specific decisions, such as raising prices or expanding into new regions.

marketing information system (MIS) Planned, computer-based system designed to provide managers with a continuous flow of information relevant to their specific decisions and areas of responsibility.

marketing decision support system (MDSS) Marketing information system component that links a decision maker with relevant databases and analysis tools.

WHO CONDUCTS MARKETING RESEARCH?

The size and organizational form of the marketing research function is usually tied to the structure of the company. Some firms organize research units to support different product lines, brands, or geographic areas. Others organize their research functions according to the types of research they need to perform, such as sales analysis, new-product development, advertising evaluation, or sales forecasting.

> **Briefly Speaking**
>
> "It is not a brave new world we are facing as researchers, but it is a more demanding one. As our tools grow in number and sophistication, we need better trained researchers to understand them and to be able to explain the results we derive from them."
>
> —**Stephen Needel**
> *Marketing researcher and managing partner, Advanced Simulations*

Many firms outsource their research needs and depend on independent marketing research firms. These independent organizations might specialize in handling just part of a larger study such as conducting consumer interviews. Firms can also contract out entire research studies.

Marketers usually decide whether to conduct a study internally or through an outside organization based on cost. Another major consideration is the reliability and accuracy of the information collected by an outside organization. Because collecting marketing data is what these external firms do full time, the information they gather often is more thorough and accurate than that collected by less experienced in-house staff. Often an outside marketing research company can provide technical assistance and expertise not available within the company's marketing unit. Interaction with outside consultants also ensures that a researcher does not conduct a study only to validate a favorite viewpoint or preferred option.

Data Analysis Companies

The use of big data has created new companies that collect and analyze data and sell their proprietary software to all types of businesses. Generally called data brokers, data resellers, or data partners, these firms work with other businesses to fine-tune marketing strategies in real time. National retailers like Brooks Brothers, Neiman Marcus, and Sur La Table work with a data company called eCommera. Using eCommera's software, these retailers automatically track and visualize large volumes of sales data, using this information to adjust their marketing strategies to meet customer demand.[3]

Marketing research companies range in size from sole proprietorships to national and international firms such as Nielsen Company and IRI Worldwide. They can be classified as syndicated services, full-service suppliers, or limited-service suppliers depending on the types of services they offer to clients. Some full-service organizations are also willing to take on limited-service activities.

An organization that regularly provides a standardized set of data to all customers is called a **syndicated service**. Mediamark Research, for example, operates a syndicated product research service based on personal interviews with adults regarding their exposure to advertising media. Clients include advertisers, advertising agencies, magazines, newspapers, broadcasters, and cable TV networks.

Another syndicated service provider is J.D. Power and Associates, a global marketing information firm headquartered in California that specializes in surveying customer satisfaction, product quality, and buyer behavior. It serves clients in a wide range of industries, including automotive, financial services, health care, insurance, telecommunications, and travel and leisure.[4]

An organization that contracts with clients to conduct complete marketing research projects is called a **full-service research supplier**. Detroit-based Morspace Inc. provides quantitative and qualitative research to clients in the automotive, financial services, retail, and technology, supporting clients' strategies in brand management, product development, and customer satisfaction.[5] A full-service supplier becomes the client's marketing research arm, performing all of the steps in the marketing research process (discussed later in this chapter).

A marketing research firm that specializes in a limited number of activities, such as performing data processing or conducting field interviews, is called a **limited-service research supplier**. Quick Test/Heakin specializes in data collection in shopping malls. The company's employees conduct more than 2 million interviews a year.[6] The firm also prepares studies to help clients develop advertising strategies and to track awareness and interest. Syndicated services also can be considered a type of limited-service research supplier.

---

syndicated service Organization that provides standardized data on a periodic basis to its subscribers.

full-service research supplier Marketing research organization that offers all aspects of the marketing research process.

limited-service research supplier Marketing research firm that specializes in a limited number of research activities, such as conducting field interviews or performing data processing.

Considered a syndicated marketing service, J.D. Powers and Associates is a global marketing firm that focuses on surveying customer satisfaction for its clients.

MARKETING INTELLIGENCE

Marketing intelligence is the process of gathering information and analyzing it to improve business strategy, tactics, and daily operations. Using advanced software tools, marketers gather information from within and outside the organization. The information is typically expressed as **metrics**—that is, quantifiable measurements that are compared against organizational objectives to gauge overall performance. Marketing intelligence can thus tell the firm how its own sales operation is doing or how its top competitors are performing. For marketers, common metrics in marketing intelligence could include sales revenues, profitability, customer churn rate, and more.

metrics Quantifiable measurements that are compared against organizational objectives to gauge overall performance.

The key is not only gathering the information but also organizing it into a form that management can make sense of and use for decision making and strategizing. Software can help users collect, aggregate, and create reports with outside information available on the Web from such databases as, say, Dun & Bradstreet. SmartOrg is one firm that specializes in helping firms such as Ford and Hewlett-Packard identify and manage information. Ford managers use SmartOrg software in the production-line decision-making process. The software also supported the creation of new businesses within Hewlett-Packard, many of them considered innovations that changed an existing market.[7]

COMPETITIVE INTELLIGENCE

Competitive intelligence is a form of business intelligence that focuses on finding information about competitors using published sources, interviews, observations by salespeople and suppliers in the industry, government agencies, public filings such as patent applications, and other secondary sources, including the Internet and social media sites. It aims to uncover a competitor's specific advantages, such as new-product launches, innovative features in existing goods or services, or original marketing or promotional strategies. Even a competitor's advertising can provide clues. Marketers use competitive intelligence to make better decisions that strengthen their own competitive strategy in turn.

DATA MINING AND PREDICTIVE ANALYTICS

Data mining is a technique in which a user employs special software to search through computerized data files to detect patterns. It focuses on identifying relationships not obvious to marketers—in a sense, answering questions that marketing researchers may not even have thought to ask. The data is stored in a huge database called a *data warehouse*. Software for the marketing decision support system often is associated with the data warehouse and is used to mine data. Once marketers identify patterns and connections, they use this intelligence to check the effectiveness of different strategy options.

data mining Technique in which a user employs special software to search through computerized data files to detect patterns.

Data mining is an efficient way to sort through huge amounts of data and to make sense of that data. It helps marketers create customer profiles, pinpoint reasons for customer loyalty or the lack thereof, analyze potential returns on changes in pricing or promotion, and forecast sales. (Sales forecasting will be discussed in Chapter 11.) Data mining offers considerable advantages in retailing, the hotel industry, banking, utilities, and many other areas, and it holds the promise of providing answers to many specific strategic questions.

Predictive analytics refers to the use of marketing intelligence data to model scenarios and create forecasts. Marketers in many industries use predictive analytics to set strategy and direction. Using data captured through data mining, predictive analytics allows marketers to focus their efforts on customer targets with the greatest likelihood of purchasing the company's product or service, thereby assuring that the company operates more efficiently and more profitably.

predictive analytics Use of business intelligence data to model scenarios and create forecasts.

The data mining made possible in the big-data world drives concerns about the amount of personal data that companies like Facebook and Google are able to gather, and the uses to which it may be put in the absence of any U.S. regulations governing such use. Indeed, some uses of data mining remain controversial. Pharmacies in the United States are required by law to maintain records of doctors' prescriptions, and many sell those records to data-mining companies. After Vermont passed a law banning pharmaceutical firms from using the data to target physicians, the industry sued. Pharmaceutical companies called the law unconstitutional, claiming it hinders them from identifying their prospects. A ruling by the U.S. Supreme Court overturning Vermont's law has led other states to carefully consider how to word similar legislation to resist a court challenge and still maintain consumer privacy.[8] Situations like these generate questions about ethical behavior, as discussed in the "Solving an Ethical Controversy" feature.

KEY PERFORMANCE INDICATORS

key performance indicator Quantifiable measurement, articulated in advance, that reflects an organization's goals and is critical to its success.

Marketers use key performance indicators, or KPIs, to measure the success of a marketing initiative or strategy. A **key performance indicator** is a quantifiable measurement, articulated in advance, that reflects an organization's goals and is critical to its success. For most firms, customer satisfaction is a key performance indicator. Austin, Texas–based Bazaarvoice charges a monthly fee for such wide-ranging activities as designing and managing a firm's customer feedback area on its website to moderating online discussion groups and analyzing comments.[9] Some marketers have gained

SOLVING AN ETHICAL CONTROVERSY
Who Profits from Your Personal Data?

Facebook makes billions in advertising each year by targeting ads to its users based on information they voluntarily post about themselves. Google makes more than 10 times as much with ads targeted to users based on their Gmail and Web searches. Other organizations use personal information gleaned online to turn people down for jobs, insurance coverage, or loans and credit, sometimes based on information about others with similar profiles, rather than on accurate data about the individuals themselves.

Should online companies be allowed to profit from using your personal data?

PRO
1. Privacy is a subjective concept; not everyone objects to the use of data they voluntarily provide, and those who do can leave it offline.
2. Knowing consumers' likes and dislikes lets companies efficiently target their marketing to present only the messages those users will welcome.

CON
1. No laws limit what online companies and data aggregators can do with the information they collect, so they do as they please without regard to individuals' privacy.
2. The possibilities for abuse and theft of the collected data are too great.

Summary
Nearly 70 percent of respondents in a recent survey believed people have a right to know what an online company knows about them, and some advocate the passage of a corresponding law to that effect.

Sources: Laura Secorun Palet, "Privacy or Profit? These Firms Want to Help You Sell Your Data," *NPR*, accessed October 3, 2014, www.npr.org; "Should Companies Profit by Selling Customers' Data?" *The Wall Street Journal*, accessed March 12, 2014, http://online.wsj.com; Adam Tanner, "One Easy Way to Stop Target and Other Companies from Selling Your Data," *Forbes*, accessed March 12, 2014, www.forbes.com; Doug Walp, "Facebook Users Should Be Wary of Company's Data Mining," *The Daily Athenaeum*, accessed March 11, 2014, www.thedaonline.com; Lori Andrews, "Facebook Is Using You," *The New York Times*, accessed March 11, 2014, www.nytimes.com.

Chapter 10 Marketing Research in the Era of Big Data   315

A national study recently reported that Virgin America had the best on-time performance among airlines.

valuable insights by tracking the dissatisfaction that led customers to abandon certain products for those of competitors. Often, customer defections are only partial; customers may remain somewhat satisfied with a business but not completely satisfied. Such attitudes could lead them to take their business elsewhere. Studying the underlying causes of customer defections, even partial defections, can be useful for identifying problem areas that need attention.

In the airline industry, on-time performance is a critical measure of success because it is one criterion on which the flying public bases its purchase decisions. The annual "Airline Quality Rating" survey scores specific carriers, and the airline industry in general, on such measures as on-time performance, baggage handling, diverted and cancelled flights, overbooking, and number of customer complaints. The national study, a joint effort by faculty at Purdue and Wichita State universities, recently reported that Virgin America had the best on-time performance, while American Eagle captured the "most improved" designation.[10]

Some organizations conduct their own measurement programs through online polls and surveys. Kohl's shoppers find a URL on the bottom of their receipt. Accessing the URL brings up a customer satisfaction survey that offers respondents a chance to participate in a sweepstakes.[11]

ASSESSMENT CHECK

1.1. Identify the different classifications of marketing research suppliers, and explain how they differ from one another.
1.2. Distinguish between data mining and predictive analytics.
1.3. Describe the process of collecting marketing and competitive intelligence.
1.4. What is a key performance indicator?

THE MARKETING RESEARCH PROCESS

Businesses rely on marketing research to provide the information they need to make effective decisions. The chances of making good decisions improve when the right information is provided at the right time during decision making.

2 Explain the six steps in the marketing research process.

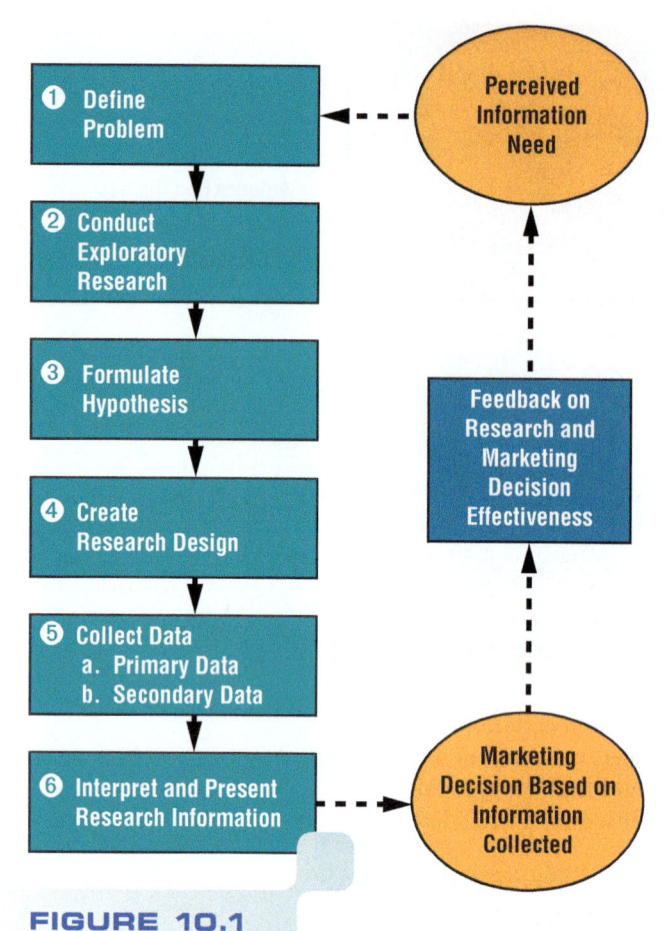

While the era of big data represents a game changer for marketers due to its increased volume, speed, and variety, the principles and process of marketing research have stood the test of time. Marketing researchers follow a six-step process as shown in Figure 10.1. They begin by defining the problem, conduct exploratory research, and then formulate a hypothesis to be tested. Next, they create a design for the research study and collect needed data. Finally, researchers interpret and present the research information.

FIGURE 10.1
The Marketing Research Process

1. Define Problem
2. Conduct Exploratory Research
3. Formulate Hypothesis
4. Create Research Design
5. Collect Data
   a. Primary Data
   b. Secondary Data
6. Interpret and Present Research Information

Perceived Information Need

Feedback on Research and Marketing Decision Effectiveness

Marketing Decision Based on Information Collected

DEFINE THE PROBLEM

A popular anecdote advises that well-defined problems are half solved. A well-defined problem permits researchers to focus on securing the exact information needed for the solution. Clearly defining the question that researchers need to answer increases the speed and accuracy of the research process.

Researchers must carefully avoid confusing symptoms of a problem with the problem itself. A symptom merely alerts marketers that a problem exists. For example, suppose that a maker of frozen pizzas sees its market share drop from 8 to 5 percent in six months. The loss of market share is a symptom of a problem the company must solve. To define the problem, the firm must look for the underlying causes of its market share loss.

A logical starting point in identifying the problem might be to evaluate the firm's target market and marketing mix elements. Suppose, for example, a firm has recently changed its promotional strategies. Research might then seek to answer the question, "What must we do to improve the effectiveness of our marketing mix?" The firm's marketers might also look at possible environmental changes. Perhaps a new competitor entered the firm's market. Decision makers will need information to help answer the question, "What must we do to distinguish our company from the new competitor?"

When marketers at Target came up with what they called the "PFresh" concept—adding grocery departments in Target stores—the company first tested the concept for two years in two locations. After the company implemented PFresh at just 108 U.S. stores and saw sales rise above $4.5 million, it expanded more broadly. Today, nearly 1,300 Target stores include a grocery department—broadening the retailer's product categories and reducing its reliance on purchase of discretionary items.[12]

CONDUCT EXPLORATORY RESEARCH

Once a firm has defined the question it wants to answer, researchers can begin exploratory research. **Exploratory research** seeks to discover the cause of a specific problem by discussing the problem with informed sources both inside and outside the firm and by examining data from other information sources. Talking with customers, suppliers, and retailers is one way for marketers at a restaurant chain like Chili's or Outback Steakhouse to do this. Company executives might also ask for input from the sales force or look for overall market clues. Exploratory research can include an evaluation of company records, such as sales and profit analyses, and available competitive data. Exploratory research yields plentiful results when marketers monitor the company's Facebook page along with its presence on such social media sites as YouTube, Twitter, Instagram, Trip Advisor, Pinterest, and others. Marketing researchers often refer to internal data collection as situation analysis. The term *informal investigation* is often used for exploratory interviews with informed people outside the researchers' firms.

exploratory research Process of discussing a marketing problem with informed sources both within and outside the firm and examining information from secondary sources.

Using Internal Data

Marketers can find valuable data in their firm's own internal records. Typical sources of internal data are sales records, financial statements, and marketing cost analyses. Marketers analyze sales performance records to gain an overall view of company efficiency and to find clues to potential problems. Prepared from company invoices or a computer database system, this **sales analysis** can provide important details to management. The study typically compares actual and expected sales based on a detailed sales forecast by territory, product, customer, and salesperson.

Once the sales quota—the level of expected sales to which actual results are compared—has been established, it is a simple process to compare actual results with expected performance. Randa Luggage is a global designer and licensed distributor of upscale luggage brands such as Tommy Bahama, Perry Ellis, and Nautica. The New Jersey–based firm installed a centralized software system to track the comings and goings of the millions of items it distributes annually. Reports trigger restocking and inventory decisions and provide information for financial statements and reporting.[13]

Sales analysis may also separate transactions by customer type, product, sales method (Internet, mail, telephone, or personal contact), type of order (cash or credit), and order size. Sales analysis is one of the least expensive and most important sources of marketing information available to a firm.

Accounting data, as summarized in the firm's financial statements, can be another good tool for identifying financial issues that influence marketing. Using ratio analysis, researchers can compare performance in current and previous years against industry benchmarks. These exercises may hint at possible problems, but a more detailed analysis would be required to reveal specific causes of indicated variations.

A third source of internal information is *marketing cost analysis*—evaluation of expenses for tasks, such as selling, warehousing, advertising, and delivery, to determine the profitability of particular customers, territories, or product lines. Firms often examine the allocation of costs to products, customers, and territories. Marketing decision makers then evaluate the profitability of particular customers and territories on the basis of the sales produced and the costs incurred in generating those sales. Sometimes internal data can provide remarkably detailed customer profiles.

FORMULATE A HYPOTHESIS

After defining the problem and conducting an exploratory investigation, the marketer needs to formulate a **hypothesis**—a tentative explanation for some specific event. A hypothesis is a statement about the relationship among variables that carries clear implications for testing this relationship. It sets the stage for more in-depth research by further clarifying what researchers need to test. For example, suppose Hallmark experienced an uptick in sales of gifts and greeting cards. To test its hypothesis that the increase is related to a recent companywide program to enhance customer service, Hallmark might invite customers to participate in an online survey that asks about the quality of service on their recent visit to a Hallmark Gold Crown store.

Not all studies test specific hypotheses. However, a carefully designed study can benefit from the rigor introduced by developing a hypothesis before beginning data collection and analysis.

CREATE A RESEARCH DESIGN

To test hypotheses and find solutions to marketing problems, a marketer creates a **research design**, a master plan or model for conducting marketing research. In planning a research project, marketers must be sure the study will measure what they intend to measure. A second important research design consideration is the selection of respondents. Marketing researchers use sampling techniques (discussed later in the chapter) to determine which consumers to include in their studies.

Test kitchens and willing palates are indispensable in the fast-food business. At McDonald's test kitchen, the team reviews approximately 1,800 new ideas a year. After input

> **Briefly Speaking**
>
> "The early days of social [media] are over and we're finding that people are using social data in very sophisticated ways to make better decisions."
>
> —**Rob Bailey**
> CEO, Datasift

sales analysis In-depth evaluation of a firm's sales.

hypothesis Tentative explanation for a specific event.

research design Master plan for conducting market research.

318 Part 3 Target Market Selection

> **ASSESSMENT CHECK**
>
> 2.1. Name the six steps in the marketing research process.
>
> 2.2. What is the goal of exploratory research?

from the firm's business research and marketing teams about where McDonald's seeks to increase its business, the company's four chefs and suppliers' chefs get together for brainstorming. About 30 ideas each year get a closer look, and about half of those are presented to the fast-food chain's management team. Between three and five new concepts are actually launched in a given year.[14]

3 Distinguish between primary and secondary data sources.

secondary data Previously published information.

primary data Information collected for a specific investigation.

COLLECT DATA

Marketing researchers gather data that can be classified as secondary or primary. **Secondary data** is information from previously published or compiled sources. Census data is an example. **Primary data** refers to information collected for the first time specifically for a marketing research study. An example of primary data is statistics collected from a survey that asks current customers about their preferences for product improvements. Global research firm Ipsos collects primary data in the Americas, Asia, Europe, and the Middle East. With offices in 86 countries, the Paris-based firm conducts thousands of projects and focus groups and more than 35 million interviews with 4.5 million panelists in a year—all under the corporate slogan "Nobody's unpredictable."[15]

The era of big data has blurred how data is classified. For example, suppose you're a marketer for a small chain of restaurants with an enthusiastic customer base. When you monitor the Internet

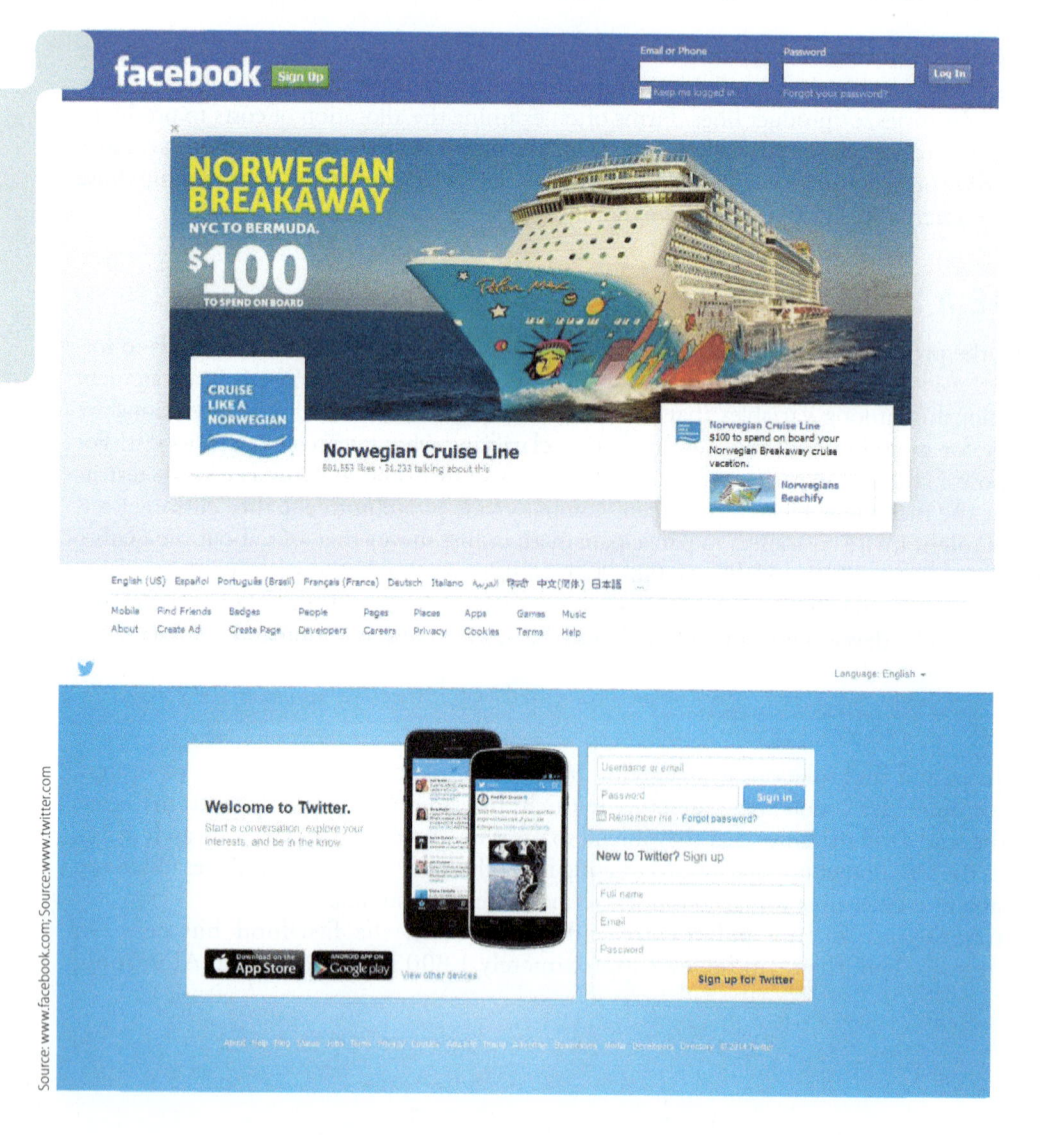

Companies soliciting input from their customers via social media sites are collecting primary data that will help guide their marketing strategies.

for mentions of your restaurant, the data you find can be thought of as secondary data. But if you solicit input from your company's Twitter and Facebook followers, their feedback can be regarded as primary data—because you solicited it (presumably for a specific purpose, but possibly for the general purpose of staying abreast of what consumers are saying about your restaurants). As the world adjusts to the changes brought by big data, how we define data also will evolve.

Secondary data offers two important advantages: (1) Such data is almost always less expensive to gather than primary data, and (2) researchers usually spend less time to locate and use secondary data. A research study that requires primary data may take three to four months to complete, while a researcher often can gather secondary data in a matter of days, or even hours, given the rapid pace of social media.

Secondary data has limitations that primary data does not. First, unless updated regularly, published information becomes obsolete. A marketer analyzing the population of various areas may discover that even the most recent census figures already are out of date because of rapid growth and changing demographics. Second, published data collected for an unrelated purpose may not be completely relevant to the marketer's specific needs. For example, census data does not reveal the brand preferences of consumers.

Although research to gather primary data can cost more and take longer, the results can provide richer, more detailed information than secondary data offers. The choice between secondary and primary data is tied to cost, applicability, and effectiveness. Many marketing research projects combine secondary and primary data to fully answer marketing questions. This chapter examines specific methods for collecting both secondary and primary data in later sections.

> **Briefly Speaking**
>
> "It is important to understand quantitative hard facts as well as qualitative soft facts. Both are driving the business at the point of sale."
>
> **—Karsten Kamin**
> *International account director,*
> *The Coca-Cola Company,*
> *Germany*

INTERPRET AND PRESENT RESEARCH DATA

The final step in the marketing research process is to interpret the findings and present them to decision makers in a format that allows managers to make effective judgments. Possible differences in interpretations of research results may occur between marketing researchers and their audiences due to differing backgrounds, levels of knowledge, and experience. Both oral and written reports should be presented in a manner designed to minimize such misinterpretations.

The era of big data presents many challenges to marketers at this stage of the process. The sheer volume of data that has become increasingly available presents a significant challenge to analysis. Companies are discovering that in order to make stunning predictions based on the data, they need expensive, complex software programs that allow them to harness the power of their database (as Netflix did) or create complicated algorithms that can accurately predict the future.

Particularly with the speed at which data can now be accumulated, marketing researchers and research users must cooperate at every stage in the research process. Too many studies go unused because management fears that the results are of little use, once they hear lengthy discussions of research limitations or unfamiliar terminology. Marketing researchers must remember to direct their reports toward management and not to other researchers. They should spell out their conclusions in clear and concise terms that can be put into action. Reports should confine technical details of the research methods to an appendix, if they are included at all. By presenting research results to all key executives at a single sitting, researchers can ensure that everyone will understand the findings. Decision makers can then quickly reach consensus on what the results mean and what actions need to be taken.

DATA COLLECTION IN THE MARKETING PROCESS

An essential component of marketing research, data collection is both challenging and time consuming. Marketers must decide not only what data to collect but how to collect it. In the era of big data, marketers' options abound. This section discusses the most commonly used methods by which marketing researchers find both secondary and primary data.

SECONDARY DATA COLLECTION

> **Briefly Speaking**
>
> "What is research but a blind date with knowledge?"
>
> —**Will Harvey**
> American entrepreneur and founder of consumer virtual world Internet companies

Secondary data comes from many sources. The overwhelming quantity of secondary data available at little or no cost challenges researchers to select only data relevant to the problem or issue studied.

Secondary data consists of two types: internal and external data. Internal data, as discussed earlier, includes sales records, product performance reviews, sales force activity reports, and marketing cost reports. External data comes from a variety of sources, including government records, syndicated research services, and industry publications. Computerized databases provide access to vast amounts of data from both inside and outside an organization. The following sections on government data, private data, and online sources focus on databases and other external data sources available to marketing researchers.

Government Data

The U.S. government is a leading source of marketing data. Conducting a periodic census of housing, population, business, manufacturing, agriculture, minerals, and governments, the U.S. Census Bureau provides the most frequently used government statistics. The Census Bureau also conducts a census of population every ten years.

The U.S. Census of Population

The U.S. Census of Population contains a wealth of valuable information for marketers. It breaks down the U.S. population of more than 319 million people by very small geographic areas, making it possible to determine population traits by city block or census tract in large cities. It also divides the populations of nonmetropolitan areas into census tracts, which are important for marketing analysis because they highlight small groups of about 1,500 to 8,000 people with similar traits. Census data, collected every ten years since 1790 as required by the U.S. Constitution, allows the government to allocate states' seats in the U.S. House of Representatives.

Implementation problems during the most recent census caused the bureau to abandon plans to conduct a paperless census. Workers were able to use handheld computers to verify addresses but had to collect census data with pen and paper from those who did not respond to the mailed survey. Plans for the 2020 census call for the use of online surveys, handheld devices, and data storage on the cloud.[16]

Marketers, such as local retailers and shopping center developers, can readily access census data to gather vital information about customers in an immediate neighborhood without spending time or money to conduct comprehensive surveys. Marketing researchers have found even more valuable resources in TIGER (Topographically Integrated Geographic Encoding and Referencing), the government's computerized mapping database. This system overlays topographic features, such as railroads, highways, and rivers, with census data such as household income figures. The data set is downloadable and covers all 50 states, the District of Columbia, and Puerto Rico.[17]

Marketers often use other federal government information, such as the following:

- *Catalog of U.S. Government Publications* published annually and available online
- *Survey of Current Business* updated monthly by the Bureau of Economic Analysis
- *County and City Data Book* typically published every three years and available online, providing data on all states, counties, and cities of more than 25,000 residents

Plans for conducting the 2020 U.S. Census include use of handheld devices, online surveys, and data storage on the cloud.

Electronic systems that scan UPC bar codes speed purchase decisions and allow consumers to check a price before committing to the purchase.

Private Data

Many private organizations provide information for marketing decision makers. A trade association may be an excellent source of data on activities in a particular industry. Gale's *Encyclopedia of Associations*, available in many libraries, can help marketers track down trade associations that may have pertinent data. Also, the advertising industry continuously collects data on audiences reached by various media.

Business and trade magazines also publish a wide range of valuable data. *Ulrich's Periodicals Directory*, another common library reference, can point researchers in the direction of trade publications that conduct and publish industry-specific research. Because few libraries carry specialized trade journals, the best way to gather data from them is either directly from the publishers or through online periodical databases, such as ProQuest's ABI/Inform, available at many libraries. Most trade publications maintain Web home pages that allow archival searches. Larger libraries can often provide directories and other publications that can help researchers find secondary data.

Several national firms offer information to businesses by subscription. GfK Roper Reports Worldwide provides continuing data on consumer attitudes, life stages, lifestyle, and buying behavior for more than 30 developed and developing countries. Wright Investors produces research reports and quality ratings on 31,000 companies from over 60 countries.

Electronic systems that scan UPC (Universal Product Code) barcodes speed purchase transactions and provide data used for inventory control, ordering, and delivery. Scanning technology is widely used by grocers and other retailers, and marketing research companies, such as Nielsen and IRI Worldwide, store this data in commercially available databases. These scanner-based information services track consumer purchases of a wide variety of products using UPC barcodes. Retailers can use this information to target customers with the right merchandise at the right time.

Techniques that rely on radio frequency identification (RFID) technology (tags that use a tiny chip with identification information that can be read by a scanner using radio waves) are in growing use. American Apparel, a chain of U.S.-made clothing with an online operation as well as retail stores in the Americas, Asia, Australia, and Europe, tested RFID tags for stocking and inventory replenishment in its New York City store. The company found the tags reduced internal shrinkage by as much as 75 percent in some stores and enabled customers to find more items in the right size and color on the selling floor, increasing sales and freeing salespeople from restocking chores so they could spend more time helping shoppers. In addition, inventory counts that once occupied several salespeople for an entire day were more accurately handled by two people in a few hours. Based on this experience, American Apparel installed the RFID technology in all its stores.[18]

Techniques that rely on RFID technology are growing in use to track and monitor various types of inventory.

Online Sources of Secondary Data

Internet tools sometime simplify the hunt for secondary data. Hundreds of databases and other sources of information are available online. A well-designed, Internet-based marketing research project can cost less yet yield faster results than offline research.

The Internet has spurred the growth of research aggregators—companies that acquire, catalog, reformat, segment, and then resell premium research reports that have already been published. Aggregators put valuable data within reach of marketers who lack the time or the budget to commission customized research. Because Web technology makes their databases easy to search, aggregators like Datamonitor and eMarketer can compile detailed, specialized reports quickly and cost-effectively.[19]

Social networking sites also yield valuable marketing information, including secondary private data. Google Analytics measures online sales; tracks email, social media, and ad campaigns; and benchmarks key measures against competitors. YouTube Analytics gives video uploading account holders an array of statistics, graphs, and maps about the audiences they attract, far more specific than just the number of views it used to collect.[20] Recently Twitter generated more than $70 million licensing its data—users' tweets—to other companies. These companies then sold access to Twitter's big data to social analytics firms and consumer companies.[21]

In this era of big data, marketers must continue to carefully evaluate the validity of any information they find on the Internet or social media sites. People without in-depth knowledge of a subject may post information. Similarly, Web pages might contain information gathered using questionable research methods. The phrase *caveat emptor* ("let the buyer beware") should guide evaluation of secondary data on the Internet.

ASSESSMENT CHECK

3.1. Distinguish between primary and secondary data.

3.2. What are the major methods of collecting secondary data?

SAMPLING TECHNIQUES

4 Explain probability and nonprobability sampling techniques.

Before undertaking a study to gather primary data, researchers must first identify which participants to include in the study. **Sampling** is the process of selecting survey respondents or research participants. Sampling is important because, if a study fails to involve consumers who accurately reflect the target market, the research is likely to yield misleading conclusions.

The total group of people the researcher wants to study is called the **population** or **universe**. For a political campaign study, the population would be all eligible voters. For research about a new lipstick line, it might be all women in a certain age bracket. The sample is a representative group

sampling Process of selecting survey respondents or research participants.

chosen from this population. Researchers rarely gather information from a study's total population, resulting in a census. Unless the total population is small, the costs of a census are simply too high. Sometimes limitations can reduce the size of the sample. Online surveys, for instance, often draw large but self-selected, rather than random, groups of respondents who don't usually represent the total population. Vague questions and surveys that are too long further reduce the number of respondents and can skew results even further.

Samples can be classified as either probability samples or nonprobability samples. A **probability sample** is one that gives every member of the population a known chance of being selected. Types of probability samples include simple random samples, stratified samples, and cluster samples.

In a **simple random sample**, every member of the relevant universe has an equal opportunity of selection. The military draft lottery of the Vietnam era and earlier is an example. The days of the year were drawn and set into an array. The placement of a person's birthday in this list determined his likelihood of being called for service. In a **stratified sample**, randomly selected subsamples of different groups are represented in the total sample. Stratified samples provide efficient, representative groups that are relatively homogeneous for a certain characteristic for such studies as opinion polls in which groups of individuals share various divergent viewpoints. In a **cluster sample**, researchers select a sample of subgroups (or clusters) from which they draw respondents. Each cluster reflects the diversity of the whole population being sampled. This cost-efficient type of probability sample is widely used when the entire population cannot be listed or enumerated.

In contrast, a **nonprobability sample** relies on personal judgment somewhere in the selection process. In other words, researchers decide which particular groups to study. Types of nonprobability samples are convenience samples and quota samples. A **convenience sample** is a nonprobability sample selected from among readily available respondents; this sample often is called an *accidental sample* because those included just happen to be in the place where the study is being conducted. TV call-in opinion polls are a good example. Marketing researchers sometimes use convenience samples in exploratory research but not in definitive studies. A **quota sample** is a nonprobability sample divided to maintain the proportion of certain characteristics among different segments or groups seen in the population as a whole. Each field worker is assigned a quota that specifies the number and characteristics of the people to contact. A quota sample differs from a stratified sample in which researchers select subsamples by some random process; in a quota sample, participants are handpicked.

> **population (universe)** Total group that researchers want to study.
>
> **probability sample** Sample that gives every member of the population a known chance of being selected.
>
> **simple random sample** Basic type of probability sample in which every individual in the relevant universe has an equal opportunity of being selected.
>
> **stratified sample** Probability sample constructed to represent randomly selected subsamples of different groups within the total sample; each subgroup is relatively homogeneous for a certain characteristic.
>
> **cluster sample** Probability sample in which researchers select a sample of subgroups (or clusters) from which they draw respondents; each cluster reflects the diversity of the whole population sampled.
>
> **nonprobability sample** Sample that involves personal judgment somewhere in the selection process.

ASSESSMENT CHECK

4.1. What is sampling?
4.2. Explain the different types of probability samples.
4.3. Identify the types of nonprobability samples.

PRIMARY RESEARCH METHODS

Marketers use a variety of methods for conducting primary research. The principal methods for collecting primary data are observation, surveys, and controlled experiments. The choice among these methods depends on the issues under study and the decisions that marketers need to make. In some cases, researchers may decide to combine techniques during the research process.

> **5** Describe the three principal methods marketing researchers use to collect primary data.
>
> **convenience sample** Nonprobability sample selected from among readily available respondents.

OBSERVATION METHOD

Marketers trying to understand how consumers behave in certain situations find observation a useful technique. In observational studies, researchers view the overt actions of the subjects they're studying. Observation tactics may be as simple as counting the number of cars passing by a potential site for a fast-food restaurant or checking the license plates at a shopping center near a state line to determine where shoppers live.

quota sample
Nonprobability sample divided to maintain the proportion of certain characteristics among different segments or groups.

One of the first documented observational studies occurred during the early years of the 20th century by Charles C. Parlin, an ad salesman for *The Saturday Evening Post*. Parlin was trying to persuade the Campbell Soup Company to advertise in *The Saturday Evening Post*. The company resisted, believing the *Post* reached primarily working-class readers, who they thought preferred to make their own soup. Campbell Soup marketers were targeting higher-income people who could afford to pay for the convenience of soup in a can. To prove Campbell wrong, Parlin began counting soup cans in the garbage collected from different Philadelphia neighborhoods. His research revealed that working-class families bought more canned soup than did wealthy households, who had servants to cook for them. Campbell Soup soon became a regular *Post* client.

It is interesting to note that garbage remains a good source of information for marketing researchers even today. Before cutbacks in food service, some airlines studied the leftovers from onboard meals to determine what to serve passengers on future flights.

Technology offers increasingly sophisticated ways for observing consumer behavior. The television industry relies on data from people meters, electronic remote-control devices that record the TV viewing habits of individual household members to measure the popularity of TV shows. Traditional people meters require each viewer to press a button each time he or she turns on the TV, changes channels, or leaves the room.

Communications technology will also change the way consumers respond to advertising. Internet users are more willing than ever to use real money for purchases that arise during their social gaming and social-networking sessions. For instance, in Diablo III, a video game from Blizzard Entertainment, players can sell virtual items they discover while playing the game—or buy the loot they can't find while they play.[22]

Videotaping consumers in action is also a marketing research observation technique. Cookware manufacturers may videotape consumers cooking in their own kitchens to evaluate how they use their pots and pans. A toothbrush manufacturer asked marketing research firm E-Lab to videotape consumers brushing their teeth and using mouthwash in its quest to develop products that would leave behind the sensation of cleanliness and freshness. Procter & Gamble used observations of customers doing their housecleaning to save its Febreze product from failure. See the "Marketing Success" feature for the story.

In an effort to understand what makes younger consumers tick, a trend-forecasting firm called TRU (for *Teenage Research Unlimited*) gathers the reflections of teens in 40 markets across five continents. This primary data is used to create the firm's annual TRU Study report, a "living, breathing" document of teen insights.[23]

Communications technology is changing the way consumers respond to advertising. Gamers can buy or sell items they discover while playing Diablo III.

MARKETING SUCCESS
Febreze: From Revolutionary Failure to Best-Selling Success

Background. After Procter & Gamble (P&G) spent millions creating an inexpensive but revolutionary product to eliminate household odors, it expected the product, Febreze, to be a huge success. But sales started low and fell from there.

The Challenge. P&G had begun marketing Febreze by assuming people would change their housecleaning routines to incorporate its use. It soon became apparent, however, that people didn't use it because they didn't recognize the odors that Febreze could eliminate from their homes. P&G needed to find a new marketing strategy or risk an expensive failure.

The Strategy. It took a little more research, including watching people use the product, for P&G to realize that it could market Febreze, reformulated with perfume, as a way for users to reward themselves with a fresh scent after completing their cleaning routine. A revamped marketing campaign delivered the reward message, rather than urging consumers to take what they perceived as an extra cleaning step to eliminate odors they didn't acknowledge.

The Outcome. Sales doubled within two months and soared to more than $200 million a year later. Febreze is now one of the best-selling products in the world. The spray and its many spinoff products account for more than $1 billion a year in P&G's sales.

Sources: Ellen Byron, "Febreze Joins P&G's $1 Billion Club," *The Wall Street Journal*, accessed March 12, 2014, http://online.wsj.com; Charles Duhigg, "How Companies Learn Your Secrets," *New York Times Magazine*, accessed March 12, 2014, www.nytimes.com; Julia O'Malley, "Would You Pay for a Whiff of Alaskan Springtime?" *Anchorage Daily News*, accessed March 12, 2014, www.adn.com.

INTERPRETIVE RESEARCH

Another type of primary research is **interpretive research**, a method in which a researcher observes a customer or group of customers in their natural setting and interprets their behavior based on an understanding of the social and cultural characteristics of that setting. We discuss interpretive research in more detail later.

> **interpretive research** Observational research method developed by social anthropologists in which customers are observed in their natural setting and their behavior is interpreted based on an understanding of social and cultural characteristics; also known as *ethnography*, or "going native."

SURVEY METHODS

Observation alone cannot supply all of the information researchers desire: They must ask questions to get information on attitudes, motives, and opinions. It is also difficult to get exact demographic information, such as income levels, from observation. To discover this information, researchers can use either interviews or questionnaires. South Bend, Indiana–based Press Ganey provides research on trends in the health care industry, relying on the data it gathers from the perspectives of millions of survey respondents.[24]

Telephone Interviews

Telephone interviews are a quick and inexpensive method for obtaining a small quantity of relatively impersonal information. Simple, clearly worded questions are easy for interviewers to pose over the phone and are effective at drawing appropriate responses. To maximize responses and save costs, some researchers use computerized dialing and digitally synthesized voices that interview respondents.

However, phone surveys have several drawbacks. Most important, many people refuse to take part in them. Their reasons include lack of time, the nuisance factor, negative associations of phone surveys with telemarketing, and poorly designed surveys or questions that are difficult to understand. The National Do Not Call Registry, which regulates telemarketing, allows calls made for research purposes.[25]

Personal Interviews

One way of obtaining detailed information about consumers is the personal interview, because the interviewer can establish rapport with respondents and explain confusing or vague questions. In addition to contacting respondents at their homes or workplaces, marketing research firms can conduct interviews in rented space in shopping centers where they gain wide access to potential buyers of the merchandise they are studying. Downtown retail districts and airports provide other valuable locations for marketing researchers.

Focus Groups

Marketers also gather research information through the technique of focus-group interviews. A **focus group** brings together 8 to 12 individuals in one location to discuss a subject of interest. Unlike other interview techniques that elicit information through a question-and-answer format, focus groups usually encourage a general discussion of a predetermined topic. Focus groups can provide quick and relatively inexpensive insight into consumer attitudes and motivations.

In a focus group, the leader, or moderator, typically begins by explaining the purpose of the meeting and suggesting an opening topic. The moderator's main purpose, however, is to stimulate interaction among group members to encourage their discussion of numerous points. The moderator may occasionally interject questions to direct the group's discussion. The moderator's job is difficult, requiring preparation and group-facilitation skills.

Focus-group sessions often last one or two hours. Researchers usually record the discussion on tape, and observers frequently watch through a one-way mirror. Focus groups are a particularly valuable tool for exploratory research, developing new product ideas, and preliminary testing of alternative marketing strategies. They can also aid in the development of well-structured questionnaires for larger scale research.

Researchers have devised ways to cultivate the focus-group environment on the Internet. Experienced moderators are able to elicit valuable qualitative information online in a chat room setting at a fraction of the cost of running a traditional focus-group session. Online focus groups can be both cost- and time-efficient, with immediate results in the form of discussion transcripts. The convenience of online conversations also improves attendance, particularly among those who are otherwise difficult to include, such as professionals and frequent travelers, and the problem of peer pressure is virtually eliminated. Some drawbacks include the lack of ability to see body language and nonverbal cues, the difficulty of testing any products in which taste or smell is relevant, and the potential for samples to be nonrepresentative, because respondents must have Internet access and be somewhat tech savvy.

Surveys

Although personal interviews can provide very detailed information, cost considerations usually prevent their use in a large-scale study. An efficient, cost-effective alternative to one-on-one interviews is a survey. Delivered to many individuals by mail or online, surveys can provide anonymity that may encourage respondents to give candid answers. They can also help marketers track consumer attitudes through ongoing research and sometimes provide demographic data that may be helpful in market segmentation.

Mail questionnaires have some limitations. Response rates are typically much lower than for personal interviews. Because researchers must wait for respondents to complete and return questionnaires, mail surveys usually take a considerably longer time to conduct. Unless they gather additional information from nonrespondents through other means, researchers must worry about possible bias in the results stemming from differences between respondents and nonrespondents.

The growing number of Internet users has spurred the growth of online surveys. Using the Web speeds the survey process, increases sample sizes, ignores geographic boundaries, and dramatically reduces costs. A proliferation of Web-based survey tools streamlines the survey task: Armed with a user-friendly tool like Survey Monkey, SurveyGizmo, or Zoomerang, even a novice can build, deliver, tabulate, and analyze a survey. While a standard research project can take up to eight weeks to complete, a thorough online project may take two weeks or less. The ease of answering online may even encourage higher response rates. All of that said, the significant

---

focus group Small group of individuals brought together to discuss a specific topic.

> **Briefly Speaking**
>
> "Sometimes, a great shopper insight is more valuable than a great product."
>
> —Jeff Swearingen
> *Group Vice-President/Sales and Shopper Marketing, Frito-Lay*

challenge remains designing a survey instrument that yields the information marketers can use to make productive decisions. For some tips on creating surveys for mobile devices, see the "Career Readiness" feature.

Other Internet-Based Methods

Businesses and other organizations are increasingly including questionnaires on their Web pages to solicit information about consumer demographics, attitudes, and comments and suggestions for improving goods and services or improving marketing messages. Online polling is also increasingly popular. Worldwide, consumers spend more than 20 percent of their day online, recently surpassing the amount of time they spend watching TV. Facebook has the largest number of unique users—more than 829 million daily active users worldwide, with more than 152 million of them in the United States alone.[26] While companies have struggled for ways to measure the impact of social media, more tools than ever exist for tracking which ones drive traffic to any particular site or sites and, thus, which would be the best sites for posting polls or questionnaires.

At present, no industrywide standards define techniques for measuring Web use. Some sites ask users to register before accessing the pages; others keep track of the number of "hits"—the number of times visitors access a page. Marketers have tried to place a value on how long a site visit lasts—its "stickiness" as a means of measuring effectiveness. Others use "cookies"—the electronic identifiers deposited on viewers' computers—to track click-through behavior, the paths users take as they move through the site. However, because some consumers change their Internet service providers frequently and special software is available to detect and remove them, cookies have lost some of their effectiveness.

Research suggests that most marketing executives are unsure of the return they are getting for their online marketing efforts—and even how to measure it. Some observers believe the traditional measure of ROI, or return on investment, must evolve into other, more measurable, results, such

CAREER READINESS
Creating Surveys for Mobile Devices

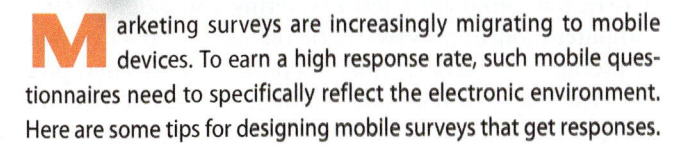

Marketing surveys are increasingly migrating to mobile devices. To earn a high response rate, such mobile questionnaires need to specifically reflect the electronic environment. Here are some tips for designing mobile surveys that get responses.

1. Design the survey with the mobile environment in mind. Consider the smartphone's smaller screen, for instance, and choose larger type and colors with good contrast.

2. Limit your use of images. Some email clients block them, and they slow down loading time on mobile devices.

3. Keep your survey short and simple. Try to reduce the amount of scrolling up and down respondents have to do for each question, and limit yourself to no more than 12 questions.

4. Offer an incentive. It doesn't have to be big, but incentives have been shown to draw five times as many responses.

5. Make sure you don't require respondents to navigate to a separate browser or interrupt whatever task they may be doing.

6. Where possible, try to offer the choice to complete the survey on a computer. Completing a survey on a mobile device can take as much as 50 percent longer.

Sources: Stacy Sherwood, "6 Tips for Designing an Effective Mobile Survey," *qSample.com*, accessed March 13, 2014, http://blog.qsample.com; "Basics of Survey and Question Design," *Howto.gov*, accessed March 13, 2014, www.howto.gov; Marni Zapin, "Should You Make Your Survey Mobile-Friendly? Yes!" *Survey Gizmo*, accessed March 13, 2014, www.surveygizmo.com.

Companies post questionnaires and opinion polls on Web pages to solicit consumer information and other marketing data.

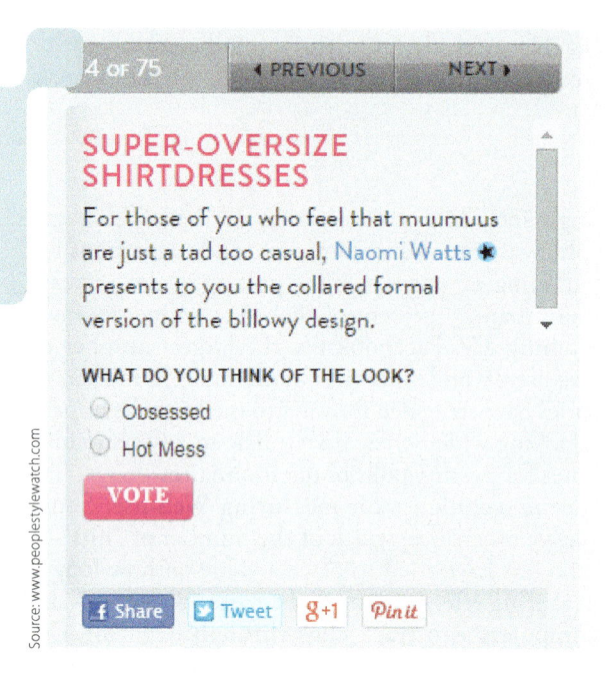

as the sales success rate, the ability to build self-moderating customer service programs within social networks, or the creation of brand advocates, perhaps tracked with click-through sales or promotional codes. Others look to turn the often intangible effects of social media into new measures, such as user time spent interacting with others, degree of user involvement, and level of user attention.

Certainly observing consumers online, where users spend more time than with any other medium including TV, offers marketers the opportunity to monitor the buying decision process, understand what turns a browser into a buyer, see how shoppers compare product features, and grasp the relative impacts on purchase decisions of marketing and price. Details like these help advertisers grow increasingly accurate about where they place their messages.

EXPERIMENTAL METHOD

controlled experiment Scientific investigation in which a researcher manipulates a test group and compares the results with those of a control group that did not receive the experimental controls or manipulations.

test marketing Marketing research technique that involves introducing a new product in a specific area and then measuring its degree of success.

The third and least used method for collecting primary data is the **controlled experiment**. A marketing research experiment is a scientific investigation in which a researcher controls or manipulates a test group (or groups) and compares the results with those of a control group that did not receive the experimental controls or manipulations.

The most common use of this method by marketers is **test marketing**, or introducing a new product in a specific area and then observing its degree of success. Up to this point, a product development team may have gathered feedback from focus groups. Other information may have come from shoppers' evaluations of competing products. Test marketing is the first stage at which the product performs in a real-life environment. Some firms omit test marketing and move directly from product development to full-scale production, citing three problems with test marketing: (1) It is expensive; (2) competitors quickly learn about the new product and may develop competing products; and (3) some products are not well suited to test marketing.

Companies that decide to skip the test-marketing process can choose several other options. A firm may simulate a test-marketing campaign through computer-modeling software. By plugging in data on similar products, it can develop a sales projection for a new product. Another firm may offer an item in just one region of the United States or in another country, adjusting promotions and advertising based on local results before going to other geographic regions. Another option may be to limit a product's introduction to only one retail chain to carefully control and evaluate promotions and results.

ASSESSMENT CHECK

5.1. What are the principal methods for collecting primary data?

5.2. Identify the different types of survey methods.

CONDUCTING INTERNATIONAL MARKETING RESEARCH

6 Explain the challenges of conducting marketing research in global markets.

As corporations expand globally, they need to gather more knowledge about consumers in other countries. Although marketing researchers follow the same basic steps for international studies as for domestic ones, they often face some very different challenges.

U.S. organizations can tap many secondary resources as they research global markets. One major information source is the U.S. government, which offers a wealth of information through its dedicated website, Export.gov. Here, marketers can find marketing research, business leads, and other data on international trade and intellectual property protection drawn from sources across the U.S. government. The site's treasure-trove of international marketing research is organized by country (more than 130 nations) and by industry. Personalized counseling and customized research are available (the latter for a fee), as well as guidance on improving international business strategy, targeting markets overseas, evaluating international business partners, and increasing brand awareness around the world. U.S. trade show organizers can get help attracting foreign visitors.[27]

When conducting international studies, companies must be prepared to deal with both language issues—communicating their message in the most effective way—and cultural issues, or capturing local citizens' interests while avoiding missteps that could unintentionally offend them. Companies also need to take a good look at a country's business environment, including political and economic conditions, trade regulations affecting research studies and data collection, and the potential for short- and long-term growth. Many marketers recommend tapping local researchers to investigate foreign markets.

Businesses may need to adjust their data collection methods for primary research in other countries, because some methods do not easily transfer across national frontiers. Face-to-face interviewing, for instance, remains the most common method for conducting primary research outside the United States.

While mail surveys are a common data collection method in developed countries, they are useless in many other nations because of low literacy rates, unreliable mail service, and a lack of address lists. Telephone interviews also may not be suitable in other countries, especially those where many people do not have phones. Focus groups can be difficult to arrange because of cultural and social factors. To help with such challenges, a growing number of international research firms offer experience in conducting global studies.

ASSESSMENT CHECK

6.1. What are some U.S. organizations that can serve as sources of international secondary marketing data?

6.2. What is the most common method of primary data collection outside the United States?

INTERPRETIVE RESEARCH

As mentioned earlier, interpretive research is a method that observes a customer or group of customers in their natural settings and then interprets their behavior based on an understanding of social and cultural characteristics of that setting.

Interpretive research has attracted considerable interest in recent years. Developed by social anthropologists as a method for explaining behavior that operates below the level of conscious thought, interpretive research can provide insights into consumer behavior and the ways in which consumers interact with brands.

ETHNOGRAPHIC STUDIES

In interpretive research, the researcher first spends an extensive amount of time studying the culture, and for that reason, the studies are often called *ethnographic* studies. The word *ethnographic* means that a researcher takes a cultural perspective of the population being studied. For that reason, interpretive research is often used to examine consumer behavior within a foreign culture where language, ideals, values, and expectations are subject to different cultural influences. After experiencing a number of product failures in low-income markets in Latin America, Procter & Gamble began an "immersion research" program called "Living It," in which the company's managers and executives spent time with low-income families around the world, living in their homes to develop a better understanding of their needs and desires. P&G's subsequent sales suggest that the effort was worthwhile. Among the mistakes the firm corrected was a low-sudsing detergent it introduced in Mexico, unaware that

Ethnographic studies capture consumers interacting with products in their environment.

most of its customers there were manual laborers who associated suds with cleaning power.[28]

Interpretive research focuses on understanding the meaning of a product or the consumption experience in a consumer's life. Its methods capture consumers interacting with products in their environment—capturing what they actually do, not what they say they do. Typically, subjects are filmed in specific situations, such as socializing with friends in a bar for research into beverage consumption, or for extended periods of time for paid participants. Paid participants may be followed by a videographer who records their day-to-day movements and interactions, or they may film themselves. Some companies even pay consumers to wear mini video cameras attached to visors and linked to a sound recorder. These systems record consumer behavior while participants are shopping or doing chores.

An iPhone app called EthOS (Ethnographic Observation System) allows ethnographic researchers to take photos, notes, and audio and video clips of subjects while conducting their studies. Users can organize the material by theme and send it to their email account to review later.[29]

ASSESSMENT CHECK

6.3. How is interpretive research typically conducted?
6.4. When should ethnographic research be employed?

STRATEGIC IMPLICATIONS OF MARKETING IN THE 21ST CENTURY

Marketing research can help an organization develop effective marketing strategies. Most new products eventually fail to attract enough buyers to remain viable. Why? A major reason is the seller's failure to understand market needs.

Consider, for example, the hundreds of dot-com companies that went under. A characteristic shared by all of those failing businesses is that virtually none of them was founded on sound marketing research. Very few used marketing research techniques to evaluate sales potential, and even fewer studied consumer responses after the ventures were initiated. While research might not have prevented every dot-com meltdown, it may have helped a few of those businesses survive.

Marketing research ideally matches new products to potential customers. Marketers also conduct research to analyze sales of their own and competitors' products, gauge the performance of existing products, guide the development of promotional campaigns and product enhancements, and develop and refine products. All of these activities enable marketers to fine-tune their marketing strategies and reach customers more effectively and efficiently.

Marketing researchers have at their disposal a broad range of techniques with which to collect both quantitative and qualitative data on customers, their lifestyles, behaviors, attitudes, and perceptions. In the era of big data, vast amounts of data are available to be collected, accessed, interpreted, and applied to improve all aspects of business operations. Because of customer relationship management technology, that information is no longer generalized to profile groups of customers—it can be analyzed to help marketers understand every customer.

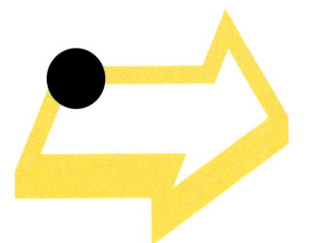

Get online now for additional learning tools to help you master your marketing knowledge—visit **WWW.CENGAGEBRAIN.COM** today!

REVIEW OF CHAPTER OBJECTIVES

1 Describe the development of the marketing research function and its major activities.

Advertising pioneer N. W. Ayer conducted the first organized marketing research project in 1879. In the 20th century, most early marketing research consisted chiefly of written testimonials from a product's users. Today, the most common marketing research activities are (1) determining market potential, market share, and market characteristics and (2) conducting sales analyses and competitive product studies.

Computer technology figures heavily in marketing research activities. A marketing information system (MIS) provides a continuous flow of information relevant to a firm's specific decision-making needs and areas of responsibility. A marketing decision support system (MDSS) links decision makers with databases and analysis tools. Data mining is the process of searching through consumer information files or data warehouses to detect patterns that guide marketing decision making. Business intelligence is the gathering and analysis of information to improve business strategy, tactics, and daily operations. Competitive intelligence focuses on finding and analyzing information about competitors. Predictive analytics is the use of business intelligence data to model scenarios and create forecasts.

2 Explain the six steps in the marketing research process.

The marketing research process can be divided into six specific steps: (1) defining the problem, (2) conducting exploratory research, (3) formulating hypotheses, (4) creating a research design, (5) collecting data, and (6) interpreting and presenting the research information. A clearly defined problem focuses on the researcher's search for relevant decision-oriented information. Exploratory research refers to information gained outside the firm. Hypotheses, tentative explanations of specific events, allow researchers to set out specific research designs—the series of decisions that, taken together, comprise master plans or models for conducting the investigations. The data collection phase of the marketing research process can involve either or both primary (original) and secondary (previously published) data. After the data is collected, researchers must interpret and present them in a way that is meaningful to management.

3 Distinguish between primary and secondary data sources.

Primary data can be collected by the firm's own researchers or by independent marketing research companies. Three principal methods of primary data collection are observation, surveying, and experimentation. Secondary data can be classified as either internal or external. Sources of internal data include sales records, product evaluation, sales force reports, and records of marketing costs. Sources of external data include the government and private sources such as business magazines. Both external and internal data can also be obtained from computer databases.

4 Explain probability and nonprobability sampling techniques.

Samples can be categorized as either probability samples or nonprobability samples. A probability sample is one in which every member of the population has a known chance of being selected. Probability samples include simple random samples, in which every item in the relevant universe has an equal opportunity to be selected; stratified samples, in which randomly selected subsamples of different groups are represented in the total sample; and cluster samples, in which geographic areas are selected from which respondents are drawn. A nonprobability sample is arbitrary and does not allow application of standard statistical tests. Nonprobability sampling techniques include convenience samples, in which readily available respondents are picked, and quota samples, divided so that different segments or groups are represented in the total sample.

5 Describe the three principal methods marketing researchers use to collect primary data.

Observation data is gathered by observing consumers via devices like people meters or videotape. Survey data can be collected through telephone interviews, personal interviews, focus groups, surveys (either mail or online), or other online methods. Telephone interviews give the researcher a fast and inexpensive way to get small amounts of information but generally not detailed or personal information. Personal interviews are costly but allow researchers to elicit detailed information from respondents. Surveys are a means of conducting large-scale studies at a reasonable cost; their main disadvantage is potentially inadequate response rates (although online surveys can capture feedback quickly and economically). Focus groups elicit detailed, qualitative information that provides insight not only into behavior but also into consumer attitudes and perceptions. The experimental method creates verifiable statistical data through the use of test and control groups to reveal actual benefits from perceived benefits.

6 Explain the challenges of conducting marketing research in global markets.

Many resources are available to help U.S. organizations research global markets. Government resources include the Department of Commerce, state trade offices, small-business development centers, and foreign embassies. Private companies, such as marketing research firms and companies that distribute research from other sources, are another resource. Electronic networks offer online international trade forums, in which marketers can establish global contacts.

ASSESSMENT CHECK: ANSWERS

1.1 Identify the different classifications of marketing research suppliers, and explain how they differ from one another. Marketing research suppliers can be classified as syndicated services, which regularly send standardized data sets to all customers; full-service suppliers, which contract to conduct complete marketing research projects; or limited-service suppliers, which specialize in selected research activities.

1.2 Distinguish between data mining and predictive analytics. Data mining is a technique in which a user employs special software to search through computerized data files to detect patterns. It focuses on identifying relationships not obvious to marketers. Predictive analytics is the use of business intelligence data to model scenarios and create forecasts. Using data captured through data mining, predictive analytics allows marketers to focus their efforts on customer targets that maximize the company's profitability.

1.3 Describe the process of collecting marketing and competitive intelligence. Marketing intelligence is the process of gathering information and analyzing it to improve business strategy, tactics, and daily operations. Competitive intelligence focuses on finding information about competitors using published sources, interviews, observations by salespeople and suppliers in the industry, government agencies, public filings such as patent applications, and other secondary methods including the Internet.

1.4 What is a key performance indicator? A key performance indicator is a quantifiable measurement, articulated in advance, that reflects an organization's goals and is critical to its success.

2.1 Name the six steps in the marketing research process. The marketing research process can be divided into six specific steps: (1) defining the problem, (2) conducting exploratory research, (3) formulating hypotheses, (4) creating a research design, (5) collecting data, and (6) interpreting and presenting the research information.

2.2 What is the goal of exploratory research? Exploratory research seeks to discover the cause of a specific problem by discussing the problem with informed sources within and outside the firm and examining data from other information sources.

3.1 Distinguish between primary and secondary data. Primary data are original; secondary data have been previously published.

3.2 What are the major methods of collecting secondary data? Sources of internal data include sales records, product evaluations, sales force reports, and records of marketing costs.

4.1 What is sampling? Sampling is the process of selecting representative survey respondents or research participants from the total universe of possible participants.

4.2 Explain the different types of probability samples. Types of probability samples include simple random samples, stratified samples, and cluster samples.

4.3 Identify the types of nonprobability samples. Nonprobability samples are convenience samples and quota samples.

5.1 What are the principal methods for collecting primary data? The principal methods for collecting primary data are observation, surveys, and controlled experiments.

5.2 Identify the different types of survey methods. Different survey methods may include telephone interviews, personal interviews, focus groups, mail and online surveys, online polling, and other Internet-based methods.

6.1 What are some U.S. organizations that can serve as sources of international secondary marketing data? The Departments of Commerce and State offer reports and guides to many countries. Other sources include state trade offices, small-business development centers, and U.S. embassies in various nations.

6.2 What is the most common method of primary data collection outside the United States? Face-to-face interviewing remains the most common method for conducting primary research outside the United States.

6.3 How is interpretive research typically conducted? Interpretive research observes a customer or group of customers in their natural setting and interprets their behavior based on social and cultural characteristics of that setting.

6.4 When should ethnographic research be employed? Ethnographic research is used to look at the consumer behavior of different groups of people.

MARKETING TERMS YOU NEED TO KNOW

- marketing research 310
- big data 310
- marketing intelligence 310
- marketing information system (MIS) 311
- marketing decision support system (MDSS) 311
- syndicated service 312
- full-service research supplier 312
- limited-service research supplier 312
- metrics 313
- data mining 313
- predictive analytics 313
- key performance indicator 314
- exploratory research 316
- sales analysis 317
- hypothesis 317
- research design 317
- secondary data 318
- primary data 318
- sampling 322
- population (universe) 323
- probability sample 323
- simple random sample 323
- stratified sample 323
- cluster sample 323
- nonprobability sample 323
- convenience sample 323
- quota sample 324
- interpretive research 325
- focus group 326
- controlled experiment 328
- test marketing 328

ASSURANCE OF LEARNING REVIEW

1. Outline the development and current status of the marketing research function.
2. What are the differences between full-service and limited-service research suppliers?
3. How does the era of big data present opportunities and challenges to marketing researchers?
4. How do the activities of data mining and predictive analytics work together?
5. List and explain the steps in the marketing research process. Trace a hypothetical study through the stages in this process.
6. Distinguish between primary and secondary data. When should researchers collect each type of data?
7. What is sampling? Explain the differences between probability and nonprobability samples and identify the various types of each.
8. Distinguish among surveys, experiments, and observational methods of primary data collection. Cite examples of each method.
9. Define and give an example of each of the methods of gathering survey data. Under what circumstances should researchers choose a specific approach?
10. Describe the experimental method of collecting primary data and indicate when researchers should use it.

PROJECTS AND TEAMWORK EXERCISES

1. Nielsen Company offers data collected by optical scanners from the United Kingdom, France, Germany, Belgium, the Netherlands, Austria, Italy, and Finland. This scanner data tracks sales products with UPC barcodes in those nations. In small teams, imagine you are Nielsen clients in the United States. Teams might represent a retail chain, an Internet company, and another videogame manufacturer. Discuss the types of marketing questions these data might help you answer. Share your list with other teams.
2. Sandwich maker Subway opened its first overseas store in 1984, in the Middle East. Today, it has nearly 43,000 stores in 108 countries. Discuss some of the challenges Subway might face in conducting marketing research in potential new international markets. What types of research would you recommend the company use in choosing new countries for expansion?
3. Working alone or with a partner, choose a new-product idea or a variation on an existing product that you think would appeal to your classmates, such as single-serve hummus and chips or an energy drink in a new flavor. Then, devise a test marketing plan for it. Determine where you will test your product and which variables you will assess, such as price and promotional activities. Be prepared to present your plan to the class and include a description of the information you hope your test market will provide.
4. Interpretive research offers marketing researchers many possibilities, including the opportunity to improve product features such as packaging for food or over-the-counter medication that is difficult for seniors or the disabled to open. List some other ways in which you think this observation method can help make existing product offerings more appealing or more useful to specific users. What kind of products would you choose, and how would you test them?

5. McDonald's conducts extensive marketing research for all its new products, including new menu items for its overseas stores. Because of cultural and other differences and preferences, the company cannot always extrapolate its results from one country to another. For instance, Croque McDo fried ham-and-cheese sandwiches are unlikely to be as popular in the United States as they are in France, which invented the *croque monsieur* sandwich on which the McDonald's product is based. Can you think of any other kinds of firms that share this limitation on global applications of their research? In contrast, what sorts of questions *could* multinational firms answer on a global basis? Explain.

CRITICAL-THINKING EXERCISES

1. Some companies are broadening their markets by updating classic products to appeal to younger people's tastes and preferences. What primary and secondary marketing information would you want to have if you were planning to reinvigorate an established brand in each of the following categories? Where and how would you obtain the information?

   a. fabric softener
   b. gourmet pet food
   c. whole wheat pasta
   d. electrical appliances

2. Marketers sometimes collect primary information by using so-called mystery shoppers who visit stores anonymously (as if they were customers) and note such critical factors as store appearance and ambiance, items in stock, and quality of service including waiting time and courtesy of employees. Prepare a list of data you would want to obtain from a mystery shopper surveying a chain of electronics stores in your area. Devise a format for gathering the information that combines your need to compile the data electronically and the researcher's need to remain undetected while visiting the stores.

3. Customer loyalty is an important aspect of building a brand, but sales are only one measure of customer loyalty. Suppose you are a marketer for the goods or services below. For each, list the types of data you would want to collect to gauge customer loyalty, and the method you would use to gather it.

   a. athletic shoes
   b. bottled water
   c. over-the-counter cold and flu medication
   d. self-service car wash
   e. travel agency that specializes in adventure vacations

4. The Internet provides ready access to secondary information but is also a portal to an almost limitless store of primary information via social-networking sites, message boards, chat rooms, questionnaires, and website registration forms. What are some specific drawbacks of each of these methods for obtaining primary information from customers?

ETHICS EXERCISE

Consumer groups sometimes object to marketers' methods of collecting primary data from customers. They disagree with such means as product registration forms; certain types of games, contests, or product offers; and "cookies" and demographic questionnaires on company websites. Marketers believe these tools offer them an easy way to collect data. Most strictly control the use of such data and never link identifying information with consumers' financial or demographic profiles. However, the possibility of abuse or error always exists.

Research the code of ethics of the American Marketing Association (AMA). Especially note the guidelines for use of the Internet in marketing research.

1. Check the websites of a few large consumer products companies. How effective do you think these sites are at informing visitors about the use of "cookies" on the sites? Do you think marketers could or should improve their protection of visitors' privacy? If so, how?

2. Do you think the AMA's code of ethics would be violated if marketers compiled a mailing list from information provided on warranty and product registration cards and then used the list to send customers new-product information? Why or why not? Does your opinion change if the company also sends list members special discount offers and private sale notices?

INTERNET EXERCISES

1. **Focus groups.** Visit the websites listed below. Each discusses the proper way to organize and conduct a focus group. After reviewing the material, prepare a brief report on the subject.

   www.businessweek.com/stories/2009-10-08/how-to-conduct-a-focus-group

   http://managementhelp.org/businessresearch/focus-groups.htm

   www.ehow.com/how_4393027_conduct-focus-group.html

2. **Marketing research firm services.** Nielsen is one of the world's largest marketing research firms. Go to the firm's U.S. website. Assume you run a small online retailer. What types of marketing research services could a firm like Nielsen provide to your company? What are some of the benefits?

   http://en-us.nielsen.com

3. **Data analysis.** The U.S. government publishes vast amounts of data about the nation each year. Visit the website shown below. Collect the following data by state: per-capita income, percent of population living in urban areas, median age, percent of population with college degrees. Analyze the relationships between income and urban population, age, and education.

   www.census.gov

Note: Internet Web addresses change frequently. If you don't find the exact site listed, you may need to access the organization's home page and search from there or use a search engine such as Google or Bing.

CASE 10.1
Gamification: Game Changer for Marketing Research?

There's no stopping a good idea. As millions of avid fans enjoy online games such as Farmville, businesses are responding with similar games on corporate websites, but their purpose isn't to amass virtual goods or defeat alien armies. Rather, these games are designed to build customer relationships, reward loyalty, and, not incidentally, gather marketing research data. Samsung Nation rewards users who post comments on the company's website, answer other users' questions, and link to Samsung.com from their Twitter accounts. Although a television set was offered as the top prize, players reaching higher levels in Samsung Nation enjoy only virtual rewards such as colored badges and titles like "Connoisseur." They also spend more time on the company's site, share more product information, and let Samsung track their online behavior. The CEO of Badgeville, a start-up that designs corporate games like Samsung's, says his client companies "use gamification to measure and influence user behavior to meet their business goals." Increased site activity impresses potential customers; positive user comments can increase sales with lower marketing costs; and peer reviews are seen as highly trustworthy. For marketers, who also get to swell their customer databases, gamification is a win–win strategy.

Corporate games attract some unexpected demographic groups, like women in their late 30s who don't fit the typical gamer profile. That boosts companies' confidence that the data they're gathering accurately reflects their target segments. Sears, Groupon, the USA Network, Warner Brothers, and Verizon Wireless have adopted gaming techniques to draw more users to their websites and extend the time they spend there. Badgeville's CEO says some companies track hundreds of actions by millions of people.

Gamification is even growing within firms. Global consulting giant Deloitte runs a game app called "Who, What, Where" on its internal social network Yammer. Employees are rewarded with status and virtual badges for sharing information with colleagues, nurturing client relationships, and completing training. Says one 25-year-old employee who values the program's visibility with upper management, success in the game "could be the difference between being known as an up-and-comer or not."

QUESTIONS FOR CRITICAL THINKING

1. Critics say marketing games manipulate customers into giving away an increasing amount of personal information without the real thrill of game playing. Do you agree? Why or why not?

2. Banks say they are cautious about adopting gamification techniques because of concerns about keeping the collected data secure. Are they right? Why or why not?

Sources: Kyle Turco, "Gamification Case Study: Badgeville," *Technology Advice*, accessed March 13, 2014, http://technologyadvice.com; Etienne Do, "Marketing Gamification: How Samsung Used 5 Game Mechanics to Promote the Galaxy S4," *MakeYourLifeaGame.com*, blog, accessed March 13, 2014, http://makeyourlifeagame.com; Rajat Paharia, "This Is Not a Game: Why Gamification Is Becoming a Multi-Billion Dollar Way to Motivate People," *Pando Daily*, accessed March 13, 2014, http://pando.com; Brandon Workman, "Gamification: Companies of All Sizes Are Using This Strategy to Win Customers and Pummel Competitors," *Business Insider*, accessed March 13, 2014, www.businessinsider.com; "10 Great Gamified Sites and Apps," *Enterprise Apps Today*, accessed March 13, 2014, www.enterpriseappstoday.com.

VIDEO CASE 10.2
GaGa SherBetter Forecasts Hot Sales, Cold Flavors

It's a blazing hot day, and all you can think about is the cold, sweet sensation of ice cream on your tongue. Or maybe you prefer the tangy, icy taste of sherbet. GaGa SherBetter is both—or neither, depending on how your taste buds react to the tart flavor and smooth texture of this frozen confection. Less than a decade ago, Jim King decided to whip up a few batches of his grandmother GaGa's lemon sherbet to see if anyone outside his family liked it. He peddled the sherbet to grocery stores in Rhode Island before stopping at Munroe Dairy, where the owner fed it to his dog—who lapped up the lemon dessert. "I'll take 500 pints," said Munroe's owner. Although this wasn't the most scientific way to test a market, the purchase put King and his wife Michelle in business—and they've churned out thousands of pints ever since. Despite the fact the product line has expanded from one flavor to seven (along with six novelty bar flavors), consumers still aren't quite sure what GaGa SherBetter is—which is a challenge for the Kings from a marketing standpoint. SherBetter is the Kings' own name for the product, meaning "sherbet but better." At only 160 calories and 4 grams of fat per serving, GaGa is lighter than ice cream, but it packs a creamy punch in the mouth. They've positioned their product as the best of both: SherBetter. GaGa product cartons feature a tagline that spells it out: "Smooth as ice cream, fresh like sherbet."

Michelle King, now marketing director for the company, acknowledges, "We haven't had a very scientific approach to marketing research. We've called upon our own resources, our family and friends, and done a little bit of focus-group research." They have conducted taste tests that confirm consumers' preference for GaGa over other products. At one taste test of nine frozen dessert products, Gaga ranked first or second with every participant.

The Kings also rely heavily on sampling at markets and events to get the word out among consumers and the products onto store shelves. Giving away the product "is the biggest way to increase sales," says CEO Jim King. If they are in a store, not only do people buy GaGa that day, they tend to return for more later on, trying new flavors like key lime or toasted coconut. The Kings track sales from these efforts to help forecast future potential sales and consumer preferences.

From the beginning, the Kings knew they couldn't compete with ice cream giants like Breyers. Sherbet accounts for only 4 percent of total ice cream sales, trimming the market even further. They targeted the higher-end ice cream makers, such as Ben & Jerry's and Häagen-Dazs, but their product didn't fit there either. "The mistake we made was mis-marketing the product, trying to market it as something it's not, because we thought it would be more appealing to consumers," admits Michelle King. Finally, they hired a company to conduct some marketing research and received the advice they'd intuited all along: "Be true to ourselves."

The Kings would advise other young start-ups to conduct focus groups and other marketing research "right out of the gate" instead of waiting as they did. They continue to do the best they can with a tight budget, making the most of free marketing such as sampling and social media. But they believe that all consumers need to do is try a spoonful of GaGa, and they'll become loyal followers. The dessert gets sweet reviews in the press and blogs, and it has made its way to some regional and national chains like Shaw's, Wegmans, and Whole Foods. As for the name, the Kings trademarked it long before Lady Gaga ever hit the stage. There's no research on what Jim's grandmother would have thought about that.

QUESTIONS FOR CRITICAL THINKING

1. How would you define the major problem faced by GaGa that a marketing research program could resolve? How has this problem affected the marketing of the company's products? How might marketing research help?

2. Identify the methods of collecting primary data, and give an example of how GaGa might implement each method.

Sources: Company website, www.gonegaga.net, accessed March 13, 2014; "GaGa's Rainbow SherBetter," *On Second Scoop*, accessed March 13, 2014, www.onsecondscoop.com; Judi Atkins Bridges, "Summer Market Blackberries," *AL.com*, accessed March 13, 2014, http://blog.al.com; Curt Nickisch, "GaGa's for Lady Gaga? Coincidental Celebrity Lifts Local Brands," *NPR (Boston)*, accessed March 13, 2014, www.wbur.org.

NOTES

1. Jessica Derschowitz, "Adam Sandler to Make Four Movies for Netflix," *CBS News*, accessed October 3, 2014, www.cbsnews.com; Lacey Rose, "Netflix's Original Content VP on Development Plans, Pilots, Late-Night and Rival HBO," *The Hollywood Reporter*, accessed October 3, 2014, www.hollywoodreporter.com; Dawn C. Chmielewski, "Netflix Executive Upends Hollywood," *Los Angeles Times*, accessed March 12, 2014, www.latimes.com; Rob Toledo, "Tech Tuesday: Netflix and Big Data," The Best of Netflix, accessed March 12, 2014, http://thebestofnetflix.com; "8 Marketers Doing Big Data Right," *Mashable*, accessed March 12, 2014, http://mashable.com; Kosha Gada, "Netflix and the Culture of Creation," *Forbes*, accessed March 12, 2014, www.forbes.com; David Carr, "Giving Viewers What They Want," *The New York Times*, accessed March 12, 2014, www.nytimes.com; Andrew Leonard, "How Netflix Is Turning Viewers into Puppets," *Salon*, accessed March 12, 2014, www.salon.com; Alexis Madrigal, "Netflix Built Its Microgenres by Staring into the American Soul," *NPR*, accessed March 12, 2014, www.npr.org.
2. Company website, "What Is Big Data?" www.-01.ibm.com, accessed March 12, 2014.
3. Mohana Ravindranath, "Brooks Brothers, National Retailers Analyze 'Big Data' from Sales to Adjust Marketing," *The Washington Post*, accessed March 12, 2014, www.washingtonpost.com.
4. Company website, www.jdpower.com, accessed March 12, 2014.
5. Company website, www.brain-research.com, accessed March 12, 2014.
6. Company website, www.quicktest.com, accessed March 12, 2014.
7. Company website, http://smartorg.com, accessed March 12, 2014.
8. Joan Biskupic, "Court Strikes Law Restricting Sale of Prescription Information," *USA Today*, accessed March 12, 2014, http://usatoday30.usatoday.com.
9. Company website, www.bazaarvoice.com, accessed March 12, 2014.
10. Brent D. Bowen and Dean E. Headley, "Airline Quality Rating 2013," accessed March 12, 2014, http://docs.lib.purdue.edu.
11. Company website, www.kohls.com, accessed March 12, 2014.
12. Company website, "Fact Card Q2: Stores and Distribution Centers," www.target.com, accessed October 3, 2014; Thomas Lee, "Target's Complicated Relationship with PFresh," *Star-Tribune*, accessed March 12, 2014, www.startribune.com; "Target PFresh Remodeling Program Nears Completion," *Retailing Today*, accessed March 12, 2014, http://retailingtoday.com.
13. Company website, "About Us," www.randaluggage.com, accessed March 12, 2014.
14. Kim Bhasin, "Go Inside the Secret Test Kitchen Where McDonald's Invents New Menu Items," *Business Insider*, accessed March 12, 2014, www.dailyfinance.com.
15. Company website, www.ipsos.com, accessed March 12, 2014.
16. Reid Davenport, "2020 Census Is Counting on Technology," *Federal Computer Week*, accessed March 12, 2014, http://fcw.com.
17. Government website, "TIGER Products," www.census.gov, accessed March 12, 2014.
18. "American Apparel Implements RFID Tool from Impinj," *Retail Customer Experience*, accessed March 12, 2014, www.retailcustomerexperience.com.
19. Company website, www.datamonitor.com, accessed March 12, 2014.
20. *YouTube Analytics*, accessed March 13, 2014, https://support.google.com.
21. Victor Luckerson, "Twitter Has a Massive Plan to Conquer Your Data," *Time*, accessed October 3, 2014, http://time.com.
22. "How to Make Money Playing Video Games," Gamercity.com, accessed March 13, 2014, http://gamercity.co.uk.
23. Company website, www.tru-insight.com, accessed October 3, 2014.
24. Company website, www.pressganey.com, accessed March 13, 2014.
25. National Do Not Call Registry website, www.donotcall.gov, accessed March 13, 2014.
26. Craig Smith, "By the Numbers: 155 Amazing Facebook User & Demographic Statistics," *Digital Marketing Ramblings*, accessed October 3, 2014, http://expandedramblings.com.
27. Government website, http://export.gov, accessed March 13, 2014.
28. Company website, "Can P&G Win with $2-a-Day Consumers?" press release, http://news.pg.com, accessed March 13, 2014.
29. Company website, "EthOS App," https://itunes.apple.com, accessed March 13, 2014; Stefani Relles, "Ethnography? There's an App for That!" *21st Century Scholar*, accessed March 13, 2014, http://21stcenturyscholar.com.

Chapter 11

Relationship Marketing and Customer Relationship Management (CRM)

1. Contrast transaction-based marketing with relationship marketing.
2. Explain the four basic elements of relationship marketing.
3. Identify the three levels of relationship marketing.
4. Explain how firms can enhance customer satisfaction.
5. Describe how companies build buyer–seller relationships.
6. Explain customer relationship management (CRM) and the role of technology in building customer relationships.
7. Describe the buyer–seller relationship in business-to-business marketing and the four types of business partnerships.
8. Describe the six key elements of business-to-business marketing.
9. Describe the six techniques used to evaluate relationship marketing programs.
10. Identify the two major types of sales forecasting methods.

PUBLIX'S CULTURE PUTS PEOPLE FIRST

Publix, a $28.9 billion chain of almost 1,100 stores in Florida, Georgia, Alabama, South Carolina, and Tennessee, is not just one of the largest supermarket companies in the United States. It is also the most profitable, and the largest U.S. company of any kind that is employee owned. That last characteristic may be one of the best reasons for its more than 80 years of success, because it means everyone, from baggers to cashiers to managers, is responsible for ensuring that customers are happy enough to keep coming back.

Consistently named one of *Fortune* magazine's 100 Best Companies to Work For, Publix has more than 168,500 employees, called "associates," and many have been with the company for years. They share in the company's profits in several ways, including distributions of company stock and dividends, as well as a profit-based bonus pool given out several times a year at each store. A typical store manager with a 20-year career can earn a six-figure salary, own $300,000 worth of stock, and receive $30,000 in dividends. It's a goal available to almost everyone, via advancement charts displayed in every store and a policy of promoting employees mostly from within. And plenty of associates can demonstrate how well it works: One Florida store manager began by bagging groceries in his teens, while a distribution center manager who started as a railcar worker now oversees 800 people.

Although Publix works to keep its prices low, it doesn't claim to beat low-price giant Walmart at its own game. Instead the company bases its appeal on clean, well-stocked stores that are safe and convenient, amenities such as free short-term supplies of some generic prescription drugs, a house brand of organic foods, a cooking school, and, most important, people trained to go out of their way to help customers. Clerks routinely ask, "Can we help you with anything?" Associates retrieve items for shoppers instead of just saying which aisle the items are in. Baggers are always on hand to carry packages out. Even the company president stops to pick up trash off the floor. Publix associates are not just workers; they're shareholders with an 80 percent stake in the company, and their store's success is their success.

Despite inroads by Walmart, Kroger, and Trader Joe's, Publix remains successful, with employees who have the best incentive to do everything they can for their customers.[1]

EVOLUTION OF A BRAND

Lakeland, Florida–based Publix Super Markets takes its commitment to cultivating relationships very seriously. Its customer-friendly approach is grounded in the philosophy of treating its 168,500 associates as an integral part of the company's success. Publix has made *Fortune's* 100 Best Companies to Work For list every year since its inception.

- On its careers website page, Publix offers job seekers several tips about how to brush up on interviewing skills and ten "don'ts" when it comes to preparing résumés. How does this attention to hiring the best candidate for the job underscore the company's commitment to maintaining its positive business image?
- Publix has expanded its business to the Raleigh, North Carolina, area, which is crowded with other national supermarket competitors. What strategies should Publix use to attract and retain new customers there?
- Over the past two decades, Publix has scored the highest in customer satisfaction among other supermarkets in a national survey. What steps does the company need to take to keep this customer satisfaction rating intact?

Chapter Overview

transaction-based marketing Buyer and seller exchanges characterized by limited communications and little or no ongoing relationship between the parties.

relationship marketing Development, growth, and maintenance of long-term, cost-effective relationships with individual customers, suppliers, employees, and other partners for mutual benefit.

Marketing revolves around relationships with customers and all the business processes involved in identifying and satisfying them. The shift from **transaction-based marketing**, which focuses on short-term, one-time exchanges, to customer-focused relationship marketing is one of the most important trends in marketing today. Companies know they cannot prosper simply by identifying and attracting new customers; to succeed, they must build loyal, mutually beneficial relationships with both new and existing customers, suppliers, distributors, and employees. This strategy benefits the bottom line because retaining customers costs much less than acquiring new ones. Building and managing long-term relationships between buyers and sellers are the hallmarks of relationship marketing. **Relationship marketing** is the development, growth, and maintenance of cost-effective, high-value relationships with individual customers, suppliers, distributors, retailers, and other partners for mutual benefit over time.

Relationship marketing is based on promises: the promise of low prices, the promise of high quality, the promise of prompt delivery, the promise of superior service. A network of promises—within the organization, between the organization and its supply chain, and between buyer and seller—determines whether or not a relationship will grow. A firm is responsible for keeping or exceeding the agreements it makes, with the ultimate goal of achieving customer satisfaction.

This chapter examines the reasons organizations are moving toward relationship marketing and customer relationship management, explores the impact this move has on producers of goods and services and their customers, looks at ways to evaluate customer relationship programs; and discusses the various forecasting techniques critical to implementing an effective marketing plan.

THE SHIFT FROM TRANSACTION-BASED MARKETING TO RELATIONSHIP MARKETING

1 Contrast transaction-based marketing with relationship marketing.

Since the Industrial Revolution, most manufacturers have run production-oriented operations. They have focused on making products and then promoting them to customers in the hope of selling enough to cover costs and earn profits. The emphasis has been on individual sales or transactions. In transaction-based marketing, buyer and seller exchanges are characterized by limited communications and little or no ongoing relationship. The primary goal is to entice a buyer to make a purchase through inducements such as low price, convenience, or packaging.

Some marketing exchanges remain largely transaction based. In residential real estate sales, for example, the primary goal of the agent is to make a sale and collect a commission. While the agent may seek to maintain the appearance of an ongoing buyer–seller relationship, in most cases, the possibility of future transactions is fairly limited. The best an agent can hope for is to represent the seller again in a subsequent real estate deal that may be several years down the line or, more likely, gain positive referrals to other buyers and sellers.

Today, many organizations have embraced an alternative approach. Relationship marketing views customers as equal partners in buyer–seller transactions. By motivating customers to enter a long-term relationship in which they repeat purchases or buy multiple brands from the firm, marketers obtain a clearer understanding of customer needs over time. This process leads to improved goods or customer service, which pays off through increased sales and lower marketing costs. In addition, marketers have discovered it is less expensive to retain satisfied customers than it is to attract new ones or repair damaged relationships.

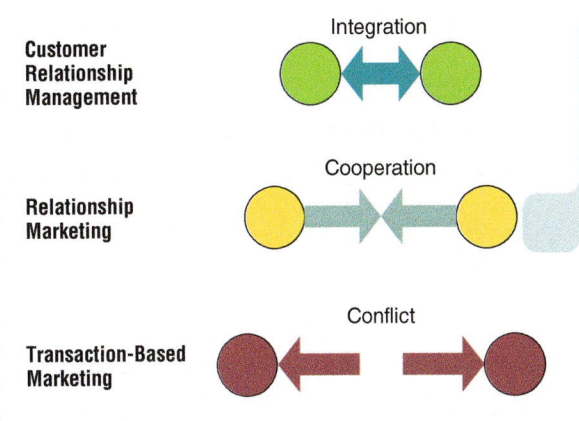

FIGURE 11.1
Forms of Buyer–Seller Interactions from Conflict to Integration

As Figure 11.1 illustrates, relationship marketing emphasizes cooperation rather than conflict between all of the parties involved. This ongoing collaborative exchange creates value for both parties and builds customer loyalty. Customer relationship management goes a step further and integrates the customer's needs into all aspects of the firm's operations and its relationships with suppliers, distributors, and strategic partners. It combines people, processes, and technology with the long-term goal of maximizing customer value through mutually satisfying interactions and transactions.

Marketers now understand they must do more than simply create products and then sell them. With so many goods and services to choose from, customers look for added value from their marketing relationships. With more than 100 stores nationwide, Unleashed, Petco's line of smaller neighborhood retail stores, not only charges lower prices than grocery stores for pet products but also offers a huge selection—everything from premium and national brands of food, toys and bedding, leashes, and other supplies to comprehensive services such as dog training, grooming, day and overnight boarding, and veterinary care and hospitalization. You can even buy—or better, adopt—your pet there. These offerings help build customer loyalty in the pet ownership market, where the number of consumers and the level of spending per pet continue to rise.[2]

In general, the differences between the narrow focus of transaction marketing and the much broader view of relationship marketing can be summarized as follows.

Unleashed, Petco's smaller neighborhood stores, offers the same goods and services as its larger locations but adds a local flavor.

Relationship marketing:

- focuses on the long term rather than the short term
- emphasizes retaining customers over making a sale
- ranks customer service as a high priority
- encourages frequent customer contact
- fosters customer commitment with the firm
- bases customer interactions on cooperation and trust
- commits all employees to provide high-quality products

As a result, the buyer–seller bonds developed in a relationship marketing partnership last longer and cover a much wider scope than those developed in transaction marketing.

> **ASSESSMENT CHECK**
>
> 1.1 What are the major differences between transaction-based marketing and relationship marketing?

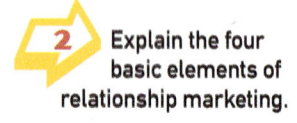

ELEMENTS OF RELATIONSHIP MARKETING

2 Explain the four basic elements of relationship marketing.

To build long-term customer relationships, marketers need to place customers at the center of their efforts. When a company integrates customer service and quality with marketing, the result is a relationship marketing orientation.

But how do firms achieve these long-term relationships? They build them with four basic elements.

1. They gather information about their customers.
2. They analyze the data collected and use it to modify their marketing mix to deliver differentiated messages and customized marketing programs to individual consumers.
3. Through relationship marketing, they monitor their interactions with customers. They can then assess the customer's level of satisfaction or dissatisfaction with their service. Marketers can also calculate the cost of attracting one new customer and figure out how much profit that customer will generate during the relationship. Information is fed back, and they then can seek ways to add value to the buyer–seller transaction so the relationship will continue.
4. With customer relationship management (CRM) software, they use intimate knowledge of customers and customer preferences to orient every part of the organization toward building a unique company differentiation based on strong, unbreakable bonds with customers.

See the "Marketing Success" feature to learn how one company, Motel 6, recently celebrated its 50-year relationship with customers.

INTERNAL MARKETING

external customers
People or organizations that buy or use a firm's goods or services.

internal customers
Employees or departments within an organization that depend on the work of another employee or department.

The concepts of customer satisfaction and relationship marketing usually are discussed in terms of **external customers**—people or organizations that buy or use a firm's goods or services. But marketing in organizations concerned with customer satisfaction and long-term relationships must also address **internal customers**—employees or departments within the organization whose success depends on the work of other employees or departments. A person processing an order for a new piece of equipment is the internal customer of the salesperson who completed the sale, just as the person who bought the product is the salesperson's external customer. Although the order processor might never directly encounter an external customer, his or her performance can have a direct impact on the overall value the firm is able to deliver.

MARKETING SUCCESS
Motel 6 Still Going Strong After 50

Background. Motel 6, founded in 1962 in Santa Barbara, California, started simply by offering free coffee and clean, comfortable rooms for $6 a night. With more than 1,100 company-owned and franchised locations offering cable, wi-fi, and swimming pools, the company recently celebrated its 50th anniversary.

The Challenge. The chain wanted to attract a new generation of customers and remind older travelers about what they had always valued in the brand, which has served millions of travelers over the years.

The Strategy. Motel 6 created a new marketing campaign, including radio and TV commercials, digital ads, and outreach efforts on Facebook and YouTube. The television commercial, narrated by longtime announcer Tom Bodett ("We'll leave the light on for you"), used special effects to illustrate the passage of time since 1962 via changing styles as a family drives up to a Motel 6. Much has changed, says Bodett, but, "50 years and the light's still on."

The Outcome. Motel 6 still offers the lowest price and highest occupancy of any national hotel chain. Its campaign effectively captured the idea that its quality has stood the test of time, giving budget-minded travelers a good reason to celebrate.

Sources: Corporate website, www.motel6.com, accessed March 13, 2014; "Motel 6 Celebrates 50-Year Heritage," *PR Newswire*, accessed March 13, 2014, www.prnewswire.com; Gary A. Warner, "Motel 6 and Sambo's in Santa Barbara," *OC Register*, accessed March 13, 2014, www.ocregister.com; Stuart Elliott, "Brands Cheer Their Virtues with Anniversary Candles," *The New York Times*, accessed March 13, 2014, www.nytimes.com.

Internal marketing depends on managerial actions that enable all members of an organization to understand, accept, and fulfill their respective roles in implementing a marketing strategy. Good internal customer satisfaction helps organizations attract, select, and retain outstanding employees who appreciate and value their role in the delivery of superior service to external customers. Farmers Insurance has an award-winning training program called the University of Farmers. Located in Agoura Hills, California, the program is available to Farmers' insurance agents, claims personnel, and management in four areas: (1) sales, (2) marketing, (3) operations, and (4) management.

As touted in its comedic TV commercials, what makes Farmers stand out is its training for insurance agents in "non-traditional" courses involving things such as a car rotisserie and an all-weather model home. Farmers' learning programs have won the company a place in *Training* magazine's Top 10 Hall of Fame.[3]

Employee knowledge and involvement are important goals of internal marketing. Companies that excel at satisfying customers typically place a priority on keeping employees informed about corporate goals, strategies, and customer needs. Employees must also have the necessary tools to address customer requests and problems in a timely manner. Companywide computer networks aid the flow of communications between departments and functions. Several companies also include key suppliers in their networks to speed and ease communication of all aspects of business, from product design to inventory control.

Employee satisfaction is another critical objective of internal marketing. Employees seldom, if ever, satisfy customers when they themselves are unhappy. Dissatisfied employees are likely to spread negative word-of-mouth messages to relatives, friends, and acquaintances, and these reports can affect purchasing behavior. Satisfied employees buy their employer's products, tell friends and families how good the customer service is, and ultimately send a powerful message to customers. One recommended strategy for offering consistently good service is to attract

internal marketing Managerial actions that help all members of the organization understand, accept, and fulfill their respective roles in implementing a marketing strategy.

employee satisfaction Employee's level of satisfaction in his or her company and the extent to which that loyalty—or lack thereof—is communicated to external customers.

Upscale hotel chain Four Seasons pampers its customers and relates its high-service standards directly to maintaining satisfied employees.

ASSESSMENT CHECK

2.1 What are the four basic elements of relationship marketing?

2.2 Why is internal marketing important to a firm?

good employees, hire good employees, and retain good employees. Upscale hotel chain Four Seasons pampers its customers and generates a loyal following. But the company relates its high service standards directly to its hiring policies and to maintaining satisfied employees. Four Seasons was recently named one of *Fortune* magazine's 100 Best Companies to Work For, one of only 13 companies that have been on the list every year since it began.[4]

LEVELS OF RELATIONSHIP MARKETING

> 3 Identify the three levels of relationship marketing.

Like all other interpersonal relationships, buyer–seller relationships function at various levels. As an individual or firm progresses from the lowest level to the highest level of relationship marketing as shown in Table 11.1, the strength of commitment between the parties grows. The likelihood of a continuing, long-term relationship grows as well. Whenever possible, marketers want to move their customers to higher levels, converting them from level one purchasers, who focus mainly on price, to level three customers, who receive specialized services and value-added benefits that may not be available from another firm.

TABLE 11.1 Three Levels of Relationship Marketing

Characteristic	Level One	Level Two	Level Three
Primary bond	Financial	Social	Structural
Degree of customization	Low	Medium	Medium to High
Potential for sustained competitive advantage	Low	Moderate	High

Source: Adapted from Leonard L. Berry, "Relationship Marketing of Services—Growing Internet, Emerging Perspectives," *Journal of the Academy of Marketing Science*, Fall 1995, p. 240.

LEVEL ONE: FOCUS ON PRICE

Interactions at the first level of relationship marketing are the most superficial and the least likely to lead to a long-term relationship. In the most prevalent examples of this first level, relationship marketing efforts rely on pricing and other financial incentives to motivate customers to enter into buying relationships with a seller. Fast-food chains, for instance, regularly use value- and dollar-menu promotions, offering more food for less, to attract fickle customers. In a challenging economy, lower prices are especially attractive. Service providers offer price savings, too. T-Mobile's unlimited talk, text, and Web plans offer new and existing customers low flat rates for unlimited calls anytime, anywhere in the United States.[5]

Although these programs can be attractive to users, they may not create long-term buyer relationships. Because the programs are not customized to the needs of individual buyers, they are easily duplicated by competitors. The lesson? It takes more than a low price or other financial incentives to create a long-term relationship between buyers and sellers.

LEVEL TWO: SOCIAL INTERACTIONS

As buyers and sellers reach the second level of relationship marketing, their interactions develop on a social level—one that features deeper and less superficial links than the financially motivated first level. Sellers have begun to learn that social relationships with buyers can be very effective marketing tools. Customer service and communication are key factors at this stage.

Social interaction can take many forms. The owner of a local clothing store or dry cleaner might chat with customers about local events. A local restaurant may host a wine-tasting event. The service department of an auto dealership might call a customer after a repair to see whether or not the customer is satisfied or has any questions. An accounting firm may send holiday cards to all its customers. Even television watching, once passive, is getting more social. Twitter recently spent $90 million to purchase Bluefin Labs, a social analytics company that collects data on viewers who post comments on Twitter, Facebook, and other social media sites while watching their favorite TV shows. Bluefin then analyzes those comments to learn what TV watchers are saying

> **Briefly Speaking**
>
> "The achievements of an organization are the results of the combined effort of each individual."
>
> —Vince Lombardi
> (1913–1970)
> *National Football League coach*

As buyers and sellers reach the second level of relationship marketing, their interactions develop on a social level.

Tim Boyle/Bloomberg/Getty Images

about the shows and commercials and profiles viewers based on their previous social media comments.[6] Marketers continue to learn the potential for more precise targeting through the use of social media sites.

LEVEL THREE: INTERDEPENDENT PARTNERSHIP

At the third level of relationship marketing, relationships are transformed into structural changes that ensure buyer and seller are true business partners. As buyer and seller work more closely together, they develop a dependence on one another that continues to grow over time. Angie's List is a member-based website that connects quality local service providers and contractors with consumers in the United States and Canada. From the service side of the business, the company seeks suppliers willing to contract with Angie's List to participate in the company's Big Deal program—a "daily deal" initiative similar to Groupon. Members sign up to receive exclusive deals via email offers and discounts.

In the process of signing up local contractors and structuring a deal with them, Angie's List had a difficult time getting them to finalize applications and contracts, which caused significant drop-off when it came to adding new discounts and deals for website members. Angie's List had relied on an internal set of tools to generate contract proposals, but the company found it was losing potential suppliers because the proposals were not completed and the internal tracking of this process was not effective. As a result, Angie's List turned to TinderBox, an outside enterprise company, which created a customized proposal program to track each stage of the process and alert sales representatives when the process wasn't proceeding in a timely fashion. Using the outside business partner, Angie's List was able to close more than 85 percent of its supplier proposals.[7]

> **ASSESSMENT CHECK**
>
> 3.1 Identify the three levels of the marketing relationship.
>
> 3.2 Which level is the most complicated? Why?

ENHANCING CUSTOMER SATISFACTION

4 Explain how firms can enhance customer satisfaction.

Marketers monitor customer satisfaction through various methods of marketing research. As part of an ongoing relationship with customers, marketers must continually measure and improve how well they meet customer needs. As Figure 11.2 shows, three major steps are involved in this process: understanding customer needs, obtaining customer feedback, and instituting an ongoing program to ensure customer satisfaction.

UNDERSTANDING CUSTOMER NEEDS

Knowledge of what customers need, want, and expect is a central concern of companies focused on building long-term relationships. This information is also a vital first step in setting up a system to measure **customer satisfaction**. Marketers must carefully monitor the characteristics of their product that really matter to customers. They also must remain constantly alert to new elements that might affect satisfaction.

customer satisfaction Extent to which customers are satisfied with their purchases.

Satisfaction can be measured in terms of the gaps between what customers expect and what they perceive they have received. Such gaps can produce favorable or unfavorable impressions. Goods or services may be better or worse than expected. If they are better, marketers can use the opportunity to create loyal customers. If goods or services are worse than expected, a company may start to lose customers. The American Customer Satisfaction Index (ACSI) is a nationwide tool to provide information about customer satisfaction with product quality. Conducting more than 70,000 telephone interviews a year, it tracks customer responses to more than 5,000 brands produced by more than 230 companies. Some of the firms ACSI rates include Hershey, General Mills, Mercedes-Benz, Nordstrom, and Lowe's. Each rating is based on 250 customer interviews.[8] Marketers at the companies profiled can use such rankings to measure how well they satisfy customer needs.

To avoid unfavorable service gaps, marketers need to keep in touch with the needs of current and potential customers. They must look beyond traditional performance measures and explore the factors that determine purchasing behavior to formulate customer-based missions, goals, and performance standards.

FIGURE 11.2 Three Steps to Measure Customer Satisfaction

(Pyramid: Ongoing Measurement / Customer Feedback / Understanding Customer Needs)

OBTAINING CUSTOMER FEEDBACK AND ENSURING SATISFACTION

The second step in measuring customer satisfaction is to compile feedback from customers regarding present performance. Increasingly, marketers try to improve customers' access to their companies by including toll-free phone numbers or website addresses in their advertising. Most firms rely on reactive methods of collecting feedback. Rather than solicit complaints, they might, for example, monitor social media sites such as Twitter, online discussion groups, and popular blogs to track customer comments and attitudes about the value received. Marketers at telecommunications giant Comcast review postings on blogs, message boards, and social networking sites. Dell learned the hard way that ignoring negative blog and other social media posts annoyed customers and failed to solve underlying problems. It now monitors its online mentions 24/7 in 14 languages through its @DellCares feed on Twitter. The turnaround Dell made to achieve customer service excellence is now legendary.[9] Even the late Steve Jobs, Apple's co-founder, occasionally answered customer emails, creating waves of excitement among Apple users around the world. His successor, Tim Cook, also answers customer emails.[10] Some companies hire mystery shoppers who visit or call businesses posing as customers to evaluate the service they receive. Their unbiased appraisals usually are conducted semiannually or quarterly to monitor employees, diagnose problem areas in customer service, and measure the impact of employee training.

Because unhappy customers typically talk about their buying experiences more than happy customers do, the cost of dissatisfaction can be high. One instance of poor complaint handling at an upscale fitness club, for instance, could cost the gym thousands of dollars in lost membership fees. So it makes sense to try to resolve problems quickly. In addition to training employees to resolve complaints, firms can benefit from providing several different ways for customers to make their dissatisfaction known, including online questionnaires, telephone help lines, and face-to-face exit surveys as people leave the premises. Any method that makes it easier for customers to complain actually benefits a firm. Customer complaints offer firms the opportunity to overcome problems and prove their commitment to service. People often have greater loyalty to a company after a conflict has been resolved than if they had never complained at all.

Many organizations also use proactive methods to assess customer satisfaction, including visiting, calling, or mailing surveys to customers to gauge their level of satisfaction with the products or services. Many retailers, such as Burger King, Dunkin' Donuts, and Macy's, use their receipts to initiate a customer survey. Customers are directed to a website to complete a survey, and respondents receive a code that entitles them to a discount on a future purchase. The Denny's restaurant chain maintains a special website, www.DennysListens.com, where customers can leave feedback about their recent dining experience. Customers answer questions about the service, including how long they waited to be greeted, seated, and served. Denny's management uses the feedback to improve service standards.[11]

ASSESSMENT CHECK

4.1 How is customer **satisfaction measured?**

4.2 Identify the ways **marketers may obtain customer feedback.**

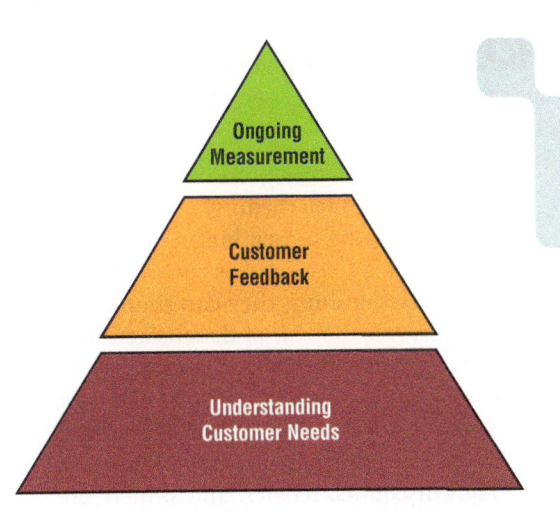

> **Briefly Speaking**
>
> "If you work just for money, you'll never make it, but if you love what you're doing and you always put the customer first, success will be yours."
>
> —Ray Kroc
> *Founder of McDonald's*

BUILDING BUYER–SELLER RELATIONSHIPS

5 Describe how companies build buyer–seller relationships.

Marketers of consumer goods and services have discovered they must do more than simply create products and then sell them. With a dizzying array of products to choose from, many customers seek ways to simplify both their business and personal lives, and relationships provide a way to do this.

One reason consumers form continuing relationships is their desire to reduce choices. Through relationships, they can simplify information gathering and the entire buying process as well as decrease the risk of dissatisfaction. They find comfort in brands that have become familiar through their ongoing relationships with companies. Such relationships may lead to more efficient decision making by customers and higher levels of customer satisfaction. A key benefit to consumers in long-term buyer–seller relationships is the perceived positive value they receive. Relationships add value because of increased opportunities for frequent customers to save money through discounts, rebates, and similar offers; via special recognition from the relationship programs; and through convenience in shopping.

Marketers should also understand why consumers end relationships. Technology and the Internet have made consumers better informed by giving them unprecedented abilities to compare prices, merchandise, and customer service. If they perceive a competitor's product or customer service is better, customers may switch loyalties. Many consumers dislike feeling locked into a relationship with one company, and that is reason enough for them to try a competing item the next time they buy. Some customers simply become bored with their current providers and decide to sample the competition.

HOW MARKETERS KEEP CUSTOMERS

One of the major forces driving the push from transaction-based marketing to relationship marketing is the realization that retaining customers is an important component of maintaining a successful business. A recent World Retail Banking Report asked more than 18,000 customers in 35 countries about their experiences with their banks. The survey revealed that 10 percent of retail banking customers are likely to change banks sometime in the next six months, and an additional 41 percent were unsure about staying in the long run. This **customer churn**, or turnover, is expensive. But the survey indicated that banks have the opportunity to increase customer loyalty by improving those services that customers consider most important: quality of service; lower fees; relationship building; and mobile banking.[12]

customer churn Turnover in a company's customer base.

In the telecom industry, wireless services estimate the gross cost per new subscriber ranges from $275 to $425. Considering that many customers sign two-year contracts—and that this cost that can take well over a year for a company such as Verizon or AT&T to recover—some observers advise wireless carriers to alert customers *before* their contracts are due to run out and to even offer them new plans better suited to their actual mobile-phone habits. The two-year contract for wireless customers may be in jeopardy, thanks to T-Mobile's recent strategy of no contracts for mobile customers. This move may shake up the wireless industry, as consumers look to get the best service deal for their wireless devices.[13]

Also, customers usually enable a firm to generate more profits with each additional year of the relationship. Unlike most customer reward programs, which award points that the customer might or might not use, Amazon Prime charges its members $99 a year for free shipping on eligible items, free streaming of more than 150,000 movies and TV shows, and free e-book borrowing from a library of more than 475,000 titles. Amazon shoppers in the United States, France, Germany, Great Britain, and Japan can sign up for the program. Although Amazon Prime now has a free-shipping minimum of $35, one analyst found that Prime members spend 40 percent more than they did before they were members. Amazon Prime now has more than 40 million members worldwide, and the program brings in more than $1.7 billion in revenues on an annual basis. And as it does with all its other customers, Amazon regularly emails its Prime members purchase suggestions similar or related to their previous purchases.[14]

frequency marketing Frequent-buyer or -user marketing programs that reward customers with cash, rebates, merchandise, or other premiums.

Programs such as Amazon Prime are an example of **frequency marketing**. These programs reward top customers with cash, rebates, merchandise, or other premiums. Buyers who purchase an item more often earn higher rewards. Frequency marketing focuses on a company's best customers with the goal of increasing their motivation to buy even more of the same or other products from the seller.

Many types of companies use frequency programs: fast-food restaurants, retail stores, telecommunications companies, and travel firms. Popular programs include airline frequent-flyer programs, such as United's Mileage Plus, and retail programs, such as Sephora's Beauty Insider.

About 80 percent of credit card purchases (by value) now include some sort of reward, such as cash back, frequent-flyer miles, price rebates, and other offerings. Eighty million U.S. consumers use such cards, although credit counselors caution that their rewards aren't strictly free. Most companies charge higher interest payments and fees to finance the give-backs, making some cards more costly to consumers than the "rewards" they offer.[15]

In addition to frequency programs or other incentives, companies use **affinity marketing** to retain customers. Each of us holds certain things dear. Some may feel strongly about Eastern Michigan University; others admire the Seattle Seahawks or the Tampa Bay Rays. These examples, along with an almost unending variety of others, are subjects of affinity programs. An affinity program is a marketing effort sponsored by an organization that solicits involvement by individuals who share common interests and activities. With affinity programs, organizations create extra value for members and encourage stronger relationships. And sometimes those relationships are geared toward eternity: The University of Florida is one of a handful of colleges that allow alumni to have their ashes buried on campus grounds after paying for the upkeep. Others include Notre Dame, Duke, and Iowa State.[16]

Avid sports fans are another target for affinity programs. The U.S. Olympic Committee chose the clothing giant Ralph Lauren to design the uniforms for the U.S. Olympic and Paralympic closing ceremonies at the Sochi, Russia, winter games, as well as the clothes the athletes wore in the Olympic village. Already a world-famous brand, Ralph Lauren doesn't really need more publicity for its label—but the goodwill resulting from this association with the Olympic Games can be priceless. The apparel was sold online and at selected department stores.[17]

Not all affinity programs involve credit cards. WNET, the New York public television station, thanks members who contribute more than $60 a year with a card that entitles them to discounts at participating restaurants, museums, theaters, hotels, and car rental companies.[18]

Amazon Prime, an example of frequency marketing, offers members free shipping on eligible items for an annual fee.

affinity marketing Marketing effort sponsored by an organization that solicits responses from individuals who share common interests and activities.

DATABASE MARKETING

The use of information technology to analyze data about customers and their transactions is referred to as **database marketing**. The results form the basis of new advertising or promotions targeted to carefully identified groups of customers. Database marketing is a particularly effective tool for building relationships because it allows sellers to sort through huge quantities of data from multiple sources on the buying habits or preferences of thousands or even millions of customers. Companies can then track buying patterns, develop customer relationship profiles, customize their offerings and sales promotions, and even personalize customer service to suit the needs of targeted groups of customers. Properly used, databases can help companies in several ways, including:

- identifying their most profitable customers
- calculating the lifetime value of each customer's business
- creating a meaningful dialogue that builds relationships and encourages genuine brand loyalty

database marketing Use of software to analyze marketing information, identifying and targeting messages toward specific groups of potential customers.

- improving customer retention and referral rates
- reducing marketing and promotion costs
- boosting sales volume per customer or targeted customer group
- expanding loyalty programs[19]

Where do organizations find all the data that fill these vast marketing databases? Everywhere! Credit card applications, software registration, and product warranties all provide vital statistics of individual consumers. Point-of-sale register scanners, customer opinion surveys, and sweepstakes entry forms may offer not just details of name and address but information about preferred brands and shopping habits. Websites offer free access in return for personal data, allowing companies to amass increasingly rich marketing information.

Google Personalized Search is a platform that can track users' past online history and use it to improve and tailor the results of future searches. One of the features of Google+ is Hangouts. Similar in some ways to Twitter or Facebook, Hangouts lets users gather, either publicly or privately, with other users in real time. The goal of these features is to make Google search experiences better based on the user's preferences, without the customer having to enter any additional information. Some see personalized search results as a breakthrough that allows the company to target its ads to those who will be most interested in them. Others have privacy concerns, however, and some simply prefer the open-ended nature of searches without personalization.[20]

The Nielsen Company carefully tracks Super Bowl viewership each year to help the network that airs the game and other football broadcasters determine ad rates for the following year, among other results. A recent Super Bowl audience numbered 111.5 million. The Super Bowl is the most-watched TV program in U.S. history.[21]

Interactive television, including smart TVs, delivers even more valuable data—information on real consumer behavior and attitudes toward brands. Linked to digital devices, sophisticated set-top boxes already collect vast amounts of data on television viewer behavior, organized in incredible detail. As Internet-connected TVs make their way into more homes, marketers receive firsthand knowledge of the kind of programming and products their targeted customers want. According to researchers, almost 40 percent of U.S. consumers have their televisions connected in some way to the Internet—by smart TVs, set-top boxes such as Roku, or Apple TV technology.[22]

Mobile apps have become a multi-billion-dollar economy in recent years. Analysts estimate that companies will spend more than $18 billion annually on mobile advertising in the near future, taking advantage of access to users' personal data, credit card information, and current location.[23]

CUSTOMERS AS ADVOCATES

Recent relationship marketing efforts focus on turning customers from passive partners into active proponents of a product. **Grassroots marketing** involves connecting directly with existing and potential customers through non-mainstream channels. The grassroots approach relies on marketing strategies that are unconventional, nontraditional, and extremely flexible. Grassroots marketing sometimes is characterized by a relatively small budget and lots of legwork, but its hallmark is the ability to develop long-lasting, individual relationships with loyal customers.

With **viral marketing**, firms let satisfied customers spread the word about products to other consumers. The clothing company The Gap originally launched its Product Red brand almost a decade ago with its iconic T-shirts inscribed desi(RED), ado(RED), and inspi(RED). Since then, the brand has gone viral, with social media campaigns and partnerships with brands such as Coca-Cola, Apple, and Bank of America. (RED) has expanded to include hundreds of products that can be purchased in more than 70 countries. A portion of the profits from every purchase goes to the Global Fund to help fight HIV/AIDS in Africa. The fund has passed $275 million and help has reached more than 55 million people. (RED) has a total of almost 4 million followers on all platforms, including Facebook, Pinterest, and Twitter.[24] See the "Solving an Ethical Controversy" feature to find out what happened when another marketer attempted to do something for a good cause.

interactive television Television service package that includes a return path for viewers to interact with programs or commercials by clicking their remote controls.

grassroots marketing Efforts that connect directly with existing and potential customers through non-mainstream channels.

viral marketing Efforts that allow satisfied customers to spread the word about products to other consumers.

SOLVING AN ETHICAL CONTROVERSY
Helping the Homeless?

At a recent South by Southwest (SXSW) conference in Austin, Texas, BBH Labs—part of an international marketing agency—gave mobile wi-fi devices to 13 volunteers from a nearby homeless shelter. The volunteers were paid $50 a day plus whatever donations they received from conference attendees who used their wi-fi devices to get online. Reactions were swift, including approval of the opportunity for the homeless to earn money and outrage that they were exploited.

Was it ethical for marketers at SXSW to recruit homeless people as mobile hot spots?

PRO

1. The volunteers wore no brand names, and BBH wasn't promoting anything.
2. The volunteers benefited by using their own initiative to earn money they would not otherwise have had.

CON

1. At the end of the four-day event, the volunteers were thrown back on their own luck with no long-term commitment of help.
2. Turning people into walking wi-fi towers robs them of their dignity and humanity without addressing the real causes of homelessness.

Summary

BBH saw the effort as a successful awareness-raising effort that gave some homeless people a temporary voice in mainstream society. One volunteer said, "I love talking to people and it's a job. An honest day of work and pay."

Sources: Company website, "Homeless Hotspots: A Charitable Experiment at SXSWi," *BBH Labs*, http://bbh-labs.com, accessed March 13, 2014; Jim LoBianco, "Homeless Hotspots: Beyond the Rhetoric," *Streetwise*, accessed March 13, 2014, http://streetwise.org; Daniel Terdiman, "Homeless Hot Spots at SXSW: A Manufactured Controversy," *CNET News*, accessed March 13, 2014, http://news.cnet.com; Jenna Wortham, "Use of Homeless as Internet Hot Spots Backfires on Marketer," *The New York Times*, accessed March 13, 2014, www.nytimes.com; Molly Hennessy-Fiske, "At SXSW, the 'Homeless Hotspot' Experiment Spurs Slams, Sarcasm," *Los Angeles Times*, accessed March 13, 2014, http://articles.latimes.com.

Buzz marketing gathers volunteers to try products and then relies on them to talk about their experiences with friends and colleagues. *Influencers*, or early adopters of products, are ideal carriers of buzz marketing messages, because their credibility makes their choices valuable among their peers. They are often recruited online through chat rooms, blogs, and instant messaging. Word-of-mouth—the idea behind buzz marketing—isn't new, but by accelerating communication, technology has made many more applications possible. Procter & Gamble's Tremor division relies on the buzz created by an online community called Vocalpoint, which numbers more than half a million mothers.[25] Techniques in this area are still evolving, and the Word of Mouth Marketing Association has developed rules and standards for buzz marketing and other types of social media it hopes will prevent fraud and preserve the value of buzz marketing.[26]

buzz marketing
Marketing that gathers volunteers to try products and then relies on them to talk about their experiences with their friends and colleagues.

ASSESSMENT CHECK

5.1 Describe two ways marketers keep customers.

5.2 List three efforts that turn customers into advocates for products.

CUSTOMER RELATIONSHIP MANAGEMENT

6 Explain customer relationship management (CRM) and the role of technology in building customer relationships.

customer relationship management (CRM) Combination of strategies and tools that drives relationship programs, reorienting the entire organization to a concentrated focus on satisfying customers.

Emerging from—and closely linked to—relationship marketing, **customer relationship management (CRM)** is the combination of strategies and technologies that empowers relationship programs, reorienting the entire organization to a concentrated focus on satisfying customers. CRM leverages technology as a means to manage customer relationships and to integrate all stakeholders into a company's product design and development, manufacturing, marketing, sales, and customer service processes.

CRM represents a shift in thinking for everyone involved with a firm—from the CEO down and encompassing all other key stakeholders, including suppliers, dealers, and other partners. All recognize that solid customer relations are fostered by similarly strong relationships with other major stakeholders. Because CRM goes well beyond traditional sales, marketing, or customer service functions, it requires a top-down commitment and must permeate every aspect of a firm's business. Technology makes that possible by allowing firms—regardless of size and no matter how far-flung their operations—to manage activities across functions, from location to location, and among their internal and external partners.

BENEFITS OF CRM

CRM software systems are capable of making sense of the vast amounts of customer data that technology allows firms to collect. Another key benefit of CRM systems is that they simplify complex business processes while keeping the best interests of customers at heart.

Selecting the right CRM software system is critical to the success of a firm's entire CRM program. CRM can be used at two different levels: on demand, accessed via the Internet as a Web-based service; and on premises, installed on a company's computer system on site. A firm may choose to buy a system from a company such as SAP or Oracle or rent hosted CRM applications through websites such as Salesforce.com or Salesnet.com. Purchasing a customized system can cost millions of dollars and take months to implement. Hosted solutions—rented through a website—are cheaper and quicker to get up and running. But purchasing a system allows a firm to expand and customize, whereas hosted systems are more limited. Experienced marketers also warn that it is easy to get mired in a system too complicated for staff to use.

Software solutions are just one component of a successful CRM initiative. The most effective companies approach customer relationship management as a complete business strategy in which people, processes, and technology are organized around delivering superior value to customers.

Successful CRM systems share the following qualities:

- They create partnerships with customers in ways that align with the company's mission and goals.
- They reduce costs by empowering customers to find the information they need to manage their own orders.
- They improve customer service by centralizing data and help sales representatives guide customers to information.
- They reduce response time and thus increase customer satisfaction.
- They improve customer retention and loyalty, leading to more repeat business and new business from word-of-mouth.
- They provide access to vital customer information anytime or anywhere.
- Their results are measurable.[27]

PROBLEMS WITH CRM

CRM is not a magic wand. The strategy needs to be thought out in advance, and everyone in the firm must be committed to it and understand how to use it. If no one can put the system to work, it is an expensive mistake.

Experts explain that failures with CRM often result from failure to organize—or reorganize—the company's people and business processes to take advantage of the benefits the CRM system offers. For instance, it might be important to empower salespeople to negotiate price with their customers to close more sales with CRM, but if a company does not adapt its centralized pricing system, its CRM efforts will be hampered. Second, if sales and service employees do not have input in the CRM process during its design phase, they might be less willing to use its tools—no matter how much training is offered. A third factor is some CRM "failures" are actually at least partially successful, but companies or their executives have set their expectations too high. Having a realistic idea of what CRM can accomplish is as important to success as properly implementing the program. Finally, truly understanding customers, their needs, and the ways they differ from customers of the past is a critical element in any successful CRM project.[28]

RETRIEVING LOST CUSTOMERS

Repeat customers are important, and the "Career Readiness" feature presents some strategies for building the kind of loyalty that keeps buyers coming back. However, customers defect from a firm's goods or services for many reasons. They may be bored, they move away, they don't need the product anymore, or they discover they prefer a competitor's product. Figure 11.3 illustrates differing levels of customer retention in the auto industry. An increasingly important part of an effective CRM strategy is **customer win-back**, the process of rejuvenating lost relationships with customers.

In many cases, a lost relationship can be found again with the right approach. Saddleback Leather Company, based in San Antonio, Texas, makes handmade leather bags that come with a 100-year warranty. Recently it came to the CEO's attention that other companies were making inexpensive "knock-off" versions of Saddleback products. Rather than go after the counterfeiters, the company decided to create a video to show customers how the other companies were making imitations while demonstrating the true quality and value of the Saddleback bags. The video on the company's website has been viewed more than 160,000 times, with consumers expressing keen interest in purchasing Saddleback bags. The CEO acknowledges that competitors will continue to make imitations, but customers who value the quality and detail that goes into Saddleback products will increase the company's overall business.[29]

customer win-back Process of rejuvenating lost relationships with customers.

FIGURE 11.3
Customer Retention in the Auto Industry

Source: J.D. Power and Associates, *2012 Customer Retention Study*, accessed March 13, 2014, www.jdpower.com.

Note: Industry average for customer retention is 49 percent.

(Bar chart showing % of Customer Retention by brand, in order: Hyundai, Ford, Honda, BMW, Kia, Toyota, Chevrolet, Mercedes-Benz, Lexus, Cadillac)

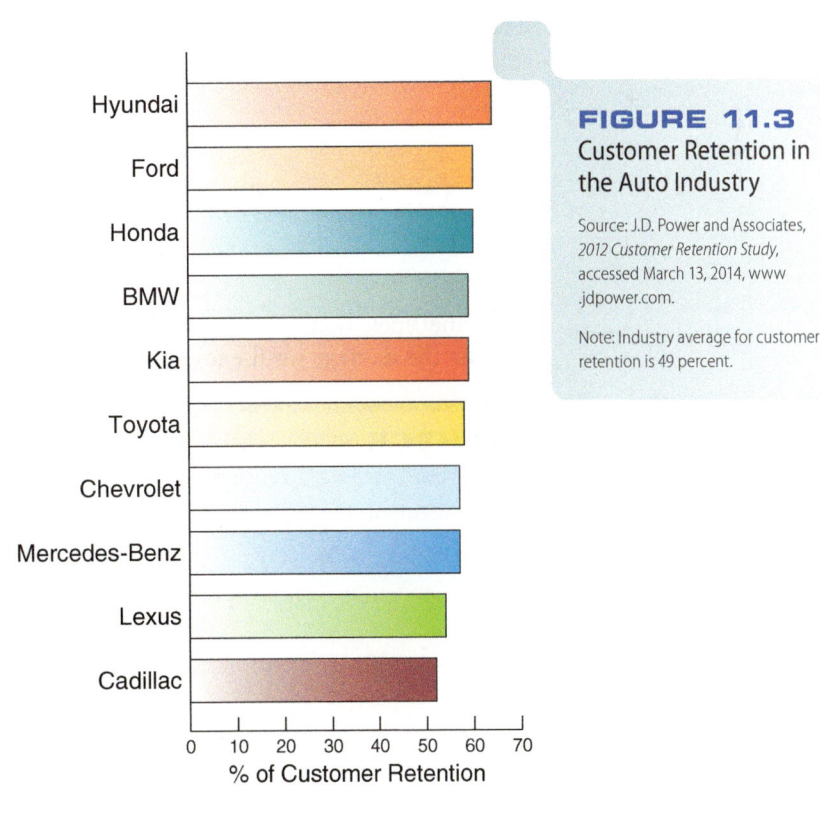

CAREER READINESS
Ways to Build Customer Loyalty

Almost 70 percent of new business comes from a firm's existing customers, and acquiring new customers can cost five to ten times as much as maintaining current ones. Given that, companies are focusing on building customer loyalty as never before. How can you achieve this valuable goal?

1. Know who your customers really are and what they really want.
2. Make every customer contact a positive one, and let customers know what you are doing for them.
3. Hire only people who share your customer-responsive orientation, and motivate them to make customer service their top priority every day.
4. Get to know your best customers so you can offer personalized service.
5. Avoid training customers to wait for sales, since bargain hunters are seldom loyal.
6. Make sure your customer loyalty program is easy and rewarding to use. Upgrade it to the digital age so it can gather customer data for you.
7. Make sure customer phone calls and emails are answered right away.
8. Resolve customer problems immediately. Apologize and make it right without trying to close a sale, and learn from customer service mistakes so they don't happen again.
9. Let unprofitable customers go; it's too expensive to retain them.

Sources: Micah Solomon, "Building Customer Loyalty the Hard (and Only) Way," *Forbes*, accessed March 12, 2014, www.forbes.com; Christine Crandell, "Stop Kicking the Can on Customer Loyalty," *Forbes*, accessed March 12, 2014, www.forbes.com; "Ten Tips to Build Customer Loyalty," *All Business*, accessed March 12, 2014, www.allbusiness.com; Joanna Lord, "6 Ways to Build Customer Loyalty," *Entrepreneur*, accessed March 12, 2014, www.entrepreneur.com; Geoffrey James, "8 Ways to Build Customer Loyalty," *Inc.*, accessed March 12, 2014, www.inc.com.

Sometimes, however, the missteps are so great that it is almost impossible for a company to repair the damage until enough time has passed for attention to simply turn elsewhere. This was the case for BP, the energy company whose reputation suffered a severe blow following the Deepwater Horizon oil rig disaster in the Gulf of Mexico. Many observers felt the company's public response compounded the damage, which included threats to plant and animal life in the Gulf and the widespread loss of residents' livelihoods. More than five years after the event, the Gulf Coast continues to recover, and tourism and other businesses are coming back. For its part in the oil spill disaster, BP has already paid out more than $28 billion in damages with some legal claims still pending.[30]

ASSESSMENT CHECK

6.1 Define customer relationship management.

6.2 What are the two major types of CRM systems?

6.3 Describe two steps a firm can take to rejuvenate a lost relationship.

To highlight the quality of its products and to attract former and new customers, Saddleback Leather Company created a video that shows how counterfeit leather bags are made. Built to last, Saddleback bags come with a 100-year warranty.

BUYER–SELLER RELATIONSHIPS IN BUSINESS-TO-BUSINESS MARKETS

Customer relationship management and relationship marketing are not limited to consumer goods and services. Building strong buyer–seller relationships is a critical component of business-to-business (B2B) marketing as well.

As discussed in Chapter 7, business-to-business marketing includes an organization's purchase of goods and services to support company operations or the production of other products. Buyer–seller relationships between companies involve working together to provide advantages that benefit both parties. These advantages might include lower prices for supplies, quicker delivery of inventory, improved quality and reliability, customized product features, and more favorable financing terms.

A **partnership** is an affiliation of two or more companies that help each other achieve common goals. Partnerships cover a wide spectrum of relationships, from informal cooperative purchasing arrangements to formal production and marketing agreements. In business-to-business markets, partnerships form the basis of relationship marketing.

Various common goals motivate firms to form partnerships. Companies may want to protect or improve their positions in existing markets, gain access to new domestic or international markets, or quickly enter new markets. Expansion of a product line—to fill in gaps, broaden the product line, or differentiate the product—is another key reason for joining forces. Other motives include sharing resources, reducing costs, warding off threats of future competition, raising or creating barriers to entry, and learning new skills.

> Describe the buyer–seller relationship in business-to-business marketing and the four types of business partnerships.

partnership Affiliation of two or more companies that help each other achieve common goals.

Briefly Speaking

"The more you engage with customers, the clearer things become, and the easier it is to determine what you should be doing."

—**John Russell**
President, Harley Davidson

CHOOSING BUSINESS PARTNERS

How does an organization decide which companies to select as partners? The first priority is to locate firms that can add value to the relationship—whether through financial resources, contacts, extra manufacturing capacity, technical know-how, or distribution capabilities. The greater the value added, the greater the desirability of the partnership. In many cases, the attributes of each partner complement those of the other; each firm brings something to the relationship the other party needs but cannot provide on its own. Other partnerships join firms with similar skills and resources to reduce costs. Organizations must share similar values and goals for a partnership to succeed in the long run.

TYPES OF PARTNERSHIPS

Companies form four key types of partnerships in business-to-business markets: buyer, seller, internal, and lateral partnerships. This section briefly examines each category.

In a **buyer partnership**, a firm purchases goods and services from one or more providers. American Express, for example, has partnered with Walmart to issue a prepaid card called Bluebird aimed at millions of customers eager to avoid fees charged by banks. The card is available online and at Walmart stores.[31] When a company assumes the buyer position in a relationship, it has a unique set of needs and requirements vendors must meet to make the relationship successful. Although buyers want sellers to provide fair prices, quick delivery, and high quality levels, a lasting relationship often requires more effort. To induce a buyer to form a long-term partnership, a supplier must also be responsive to the purchaser's unique needs.

Seller partnerships set up long-term exchanges of goods and services in return for cash or other considerations. Sellers, too, have specific needs as partners in ongoing relationships. Most prefer to develop long-term relationships with their partners. Sellers also want prompt payment.

The importance of **internal partnerships** is widely recognized in business today. The classic definition of the word *customer* as the buyer of a good or service is now more carefully defined in terms of external customers. However, customers within an organization also have their own needs. Internal partnerships are the foundation of an organization and its ability to meet its commitments to external entities. If the purchasing department selects a parts vendor that fails to ship on the dates required by manufacturing, production will halt and products will not be delivered to customers as promised. As a result, external customers will likely seek other, more reliable suppliers. Without building and maintaining internal partnerships, an organization will have difficulty meeting the needs of its external partnerships.

Lateral partnerships include strategic alliances with other companies or with not-for-profit organizations and research alliances between for-profit firms and colleges and universities. The relationship focuses on external entities—such as customers of the partner firm—and involves no direct buyer–seller interactions. Strategic alliances are discussed later in this chapter.

COBRANDING AND COMARKETING

Two other types of business marketing relationships include cobranding and comarketing. **Cobranding** joins two strong brand names, perhaps owned by two different entities, to sell a product. More than three decades ago, Nike signed then-rookie NBA player Michael Jordan to market a line of basketball shoes. Over the years, the relationship has been quite successful, including six championship rings for Jordan and more than half of the shoe market in the United States for Nike. The Jordan Brand, a division of Nike, helps Jordan earn $90 million annually in retirement, and the company recently released its 30th athletic shoe.[32]

In a **comarketing** effort, two or more organizations join to sell their products in an allied marketing campaign. ConAgra and Kraft Foods teamed up in a marketing campaign to tout Hunt's Diced Tomatoes and Kraft's 100% Grated Parmesan as part of a quick and easy weeknight

---

buyer partnership Relationship in which a firm purchases goods and services from one or more providers.

seller partnerships Relationship involving long-term exchanges of goods or services in return for cash or other valuable consideration.

internal partnerships Relationship involving customers within an organization.

lateral partnerships Strategic relationship that extends to external entities but involves no direct buyer–seller interactions.

cobranding Cooperative arrangement in which two or more businesses team up to closely link their names on a single product.

comarketing Cooperative arrangement in which two or more businesses jointly market each other's products.

RECIPES

Hunt's Tomato & Kraft Parmesan Cheese Recipes

ConAgra and Kraft Foods launched a comarketing effort for two of their products in an effort to help busy moms and dads with quick weeknight dinner decisions.

> **ASSESSMENT CHECK**
>
> 7.1 What are the four key types of business marketing partnerships?
>
> 7.2 Distinguish between cobranding and comarketing.

dinner decision for busy moms and dads. The two brands started the comarketing effort by developing a dinner recipe collection that uses both brands. Additional marketing efforts include promotions on both brands' social media sites as well as a sweepstakes, coupons, and in-store displays with recipes.[33]

IMPROVING BUYER–SELLER RELATIONSHIPS IN BUSINESS-TO-BUSINESS MARKETS

Organizations that know how to find and nurture partner relationships, whether through informal deals or contracted partnerships, can enhance revenues and increase profits. Partnering often leads to lower prices, better products, and improved distribution—resulting in higher levels of customer satisfaction. Partners who know each other's needs and expectations are more likely to satisfy them and forge stronger long-term bonds. Often, partnerships can be cemented through personal relationships, no matter where firms are located.

In the past, business relationships were conducted primarily in person, over the phone, or by mail. Today, businesses use the latest electronic, computer, and communications technology to link up. Email, the Internet, and other telecommunications services allow businesses to communicate any time and any place. Chapter 5 discussed the business role of the Internet in detail. The following sections explore other ways buyers and sellers cooperate in business-to-business markets.

Describe the six key elements of business-to-business marketing. **8**

NATIONAL ACCOUNT SELLING

Some relationships are more important than others due to the large investments at stake. Large manufacturers such as Procter & Gamble and Clorox pay special attention to the needs of major retailers, such as Walmart and Kohl's. Manufacturers use a technique called **national account selling** to serve their largest, most profitable customers. The large collection of supplier offices in northwest Arkansas, near Walmart's home office, suggests how national account selling might be implemented. These offices are usually called *teams* or *support teams*.

The advantages of national account selling are many. By assembling a team of individuals to serve just one account, the seller demonstrates the depth of its commitment to the customer.

national account selling Promotional effort in which a dedicated sales team is assigned to a firm's major customers to provide sales and service.

The buyer–seller relationship is strengthened as both collaborate to find mutually beneficial solutions. Finally, cooperative buyer–seller efforts can bring about dramatic improvements in both efficiency and effectiveness for both partners. These improvements find their way to the bottom line in the form of decreased costs and increased profits.

BUSINESS-TO-BUSINESS DATABASES

As noted earlier, databases are indispensable tools in relationship marketing. They are also essential in building business-to-business relationships. Using information generated from sales reports, scanners, and many other sources, sellers can create databases that help guide their own efforts and those of buyers who resell products to final users.

ELECTRONIC DATA INTERCHANGE AND WEB SERVICES

electronic data interchanges (EDIs) Computer-to-computer exchanges of invoices, orders, and other business documents.

quick-response merchandising Just-in-time strategy that reduces the time a retailer must hold merchandise in inventory, resulting in substantial cost savings.

web services Platform-independent information exchange systems that use the Internet to allow interaction between firms.

Technology has transformed the ways companies control their inventories and replenish stock. Gone are the days when a retailer would notice stocks were running low, call the vendor, check prices, and reorder. Today's **electronic data interchanges (EDIs)** automate the entire process. EDI involves computer-to-computer exchanges of invoices, orders, and other business documents. It allows firms to reduce costs and improve efficiency and competitiveness. Retailers such as Dillard's and Lowe's require vendors to use EDI as a core **quick-response merchandising** tool. Quick-response merchandising is a just-in-time strategy that reduces the time merchandise is held in inventory, resulting in substantial cost savings. An added advantage of EDI is it opens new channels for gathering marketing information helpful in developing long-term business-to-business relationships.

Web services provide a way for companies to communicate even if they are not running the same or compatible software, hardware, databases, or network platforms. Companies in a customer–supplier relationship, or a partnership such as an airline and car rental firm, may have difficulty getting their computer systems to work together or exchange data easily. Web services are platform-independent information exchange systems that use the Internet to allow interaction between the firms. They usually are simple, self-contained applications that handle functions from the simple to the complex.

VENDOR-MANAGED INVENTORY

vendor-managed inventory (VMI) Inventory management system in which the seller—in an existing agreement with a buyer—determines how much of a product is needed.

collaborative planning, forecasting, and replenishment (CPFR) Planning and forecasting approach based on collaboration between buyers and sellers.

supply chain Sequence of suppliers that contribute to the creation and delivery of a product.

The proliferation of electronic communication technologies and the constant pressure on suppliers to improve response time have led to another way for buyers and sellers to do business. **Vendor-managed inventory (VMI)** has replaced buyer-managed inventory in many instances. It is an inventory management system in which the seller, based on an existing agreement with the buyer, determines how much of a product a buyer needs and automatically ships new supplies to that buyer.

Some firms have modified VMI to an approach called **collaborative planning, forecasting, and replenishment (CPFR)**, a planning and forecasting technique involving collaborative efforts by both purchasers and vendors. Rite Aid Corporation is a nationwide drugstore chain with almost 4,600 stores in 31 states. Rite Aid's CPFR program involves about 50 suppliers, including Kimberly-Clark Corporation, which manufactures brands such as Kleenex facial tissues, Huggies diapers, and Scott toilet tissue. Rite Aid and Kimberley-Clark teamed up to collaborate on a shared demand forecast that keeps inventory running smoothly.[34]

MANAGING THE SUPPLY CHAIN

Good relationships between businesses require careful management of the **supply chain**—sometimes called the *value chain*—the entire sequence of suppliers that contribute to the creation and delivery of a product. This process affects both upstream relationships between the company and its suppliers and downstream relationships with the product's end users. The supply chain is discussed in greater detail in Chapter 14.

Effective supply chain management can provide an important competitive advantage that results in:

- increased innovation
- decreased costs
- improved conflict resolution within the chain
- improved communication and involvement among members of the chain

By coordinating operations with the other companies in the chain, boosting quality, and improving its operating systems, a firm can improve speed and efficiency. Because companies spend considerable resources on goods and services from outside suppliers, cooperative relationships can pay off in many ways.

BUSINESS-TO-BUSINESS ALLIANCES

Strategic alliances—the ultimate expression of relationship marketing—are partnerships formed to create a competitive advantage. These more formal long-term arrangements improve each partner's supply chain relationships and enhance operating flexibility in today's complex and rapidly changing marketplace. The size and location of strategic partners are not important. Strategic alliances include businesses of all sizes, of all kinds, and in many locations; it is what each partner can offer the other that is important. When it launched its Nexus One smartphone, for instance, Google needed business partners that could manufacture mobile devices for its Android operating system and provide customers with wireless telecom service.

Companies can structure strategic alliances in two ways. Alliance partners can establish a new business unit in which each takes an ownership position. In such a joint venture, one partner might own 40 percent, while the other owns 60 percent. Alternatively, the partners may decide to form a less formal cooperative relationship that does not involve ownership—for example, a joint new-product design team. The cooperative alliance can operate more flexibly and change more easily as market forces or other conditions dictate. In either arrangement, the partners agree

strategic alliances Partnership in which two or more companies combine resources and capital to create competitive advantages in a new market.

Good relationships between businesses require careful management of the supply chain—the entire sequence of suppliers that contribute to the creation and delivery of a product.

in advance on the skills and resources each will bring into the alliance to achieve their mutual objectives and gain a competitive advantage. Resources typically include patents; product lines; brand equity; product and market knowledge; company and brand image; and reputation for product quality, innovation, or customer service. Relationships with customers and suppliers are also desirable resources as are a convenient manufacturing facility, economies of scale and scope, information technology, and a large sales force. Alliance partners can contribute marketing skills, such as innovation and product development; manufacturing skills, including low-cost or flexible manufacturing; and planning, research, and development expertise.

Companies form many types of strategic alliances. Some create horizontal alliances between firms at the same level in the supply chain; others define vertical links between firms at adjacent stages. The firms may also serve the same or different industries. Under a professional partnership with the U.S. Golf Association, Fox Sports will broadcast exclusive coverage of the U.S. Open through 2026.[35] Alliances can also involve cooperation among rivals who are market leaders or between a market leader and a follower.

ASSESSMENT CHECK

8.1 Name four technologies businesses can use to improve buyer–seller relationships in B2B markets.

8.2 What are the benefits of effective supply chain management?

EVALUATING CUSTOMER RELATIONSHIP PROGRAMS

9 Describe the six techniques used to evaluate relationship marketing programs.

lifetime value of a customer Revenues and intangible benefits, such as referrals and customer feedback, a customer brings to the seller over an average lifetime of their relationship, less the amount the company must spend to acquire, market to, and service the customer.

One of the most important measures of relationship marketing programs, whether in consumer or business-to-business markets, is the **lifetime value of a customer**. This concept can be defined as the revenues and intangible benefits, such as referrals and customer feedback, a customer brings to the seller over an average lifetime of their relationship, less the amount the company must spend to acquire, market to, and serve the customer. Long-term customers are usually more valuable assets than new ones because they buy more, cost less to serve, refer other customers, and provide valuable feedback. The "average lifetime" of a customer relationship depends on industry and product characteristics. Customer lifetime for a consumer product such as microwave pizza may be very short, while that for an automobile or computer will last longer.

For a simple example of a lifetime value calculation, assume a Chinese takeout restaurant's typical customer buys dinner twice a month at an average cost of $25 per order over a lifetime of five years. That business results in revenues of $600 per year and $3,000 for five years. The restaurant can calculate and subtract its average costs for food, labor, and overhead to arrive at the per-customer profit. This figure serves as a baseline against which to measure strategies to increase the restaurant's sales volume, customer retention, or customer referral rate.

Another approach is to calculate the payback from a customer relationship, or the length of time it takes to breakeven on customer acquisition costs. Assume an Internet service provider spends $75 per new customer on direct mail and enrollment incentives. Based on average revenues per subscriber, the company takes about three months to recover that $75. If an average customer stays with the service 32 months and generates $800 in revenues, the rate of return is nearly 11 times the original investment. Once the customer stays past the payback period, the provider should make a profit on that business.

In addition to lifetime value analysis and payback, companies use many other techniques to evaluate relationship programs, including:

- reviewing customer comments and feedback on social media sites such as Facebook and Twitter
- tracking rebate requests, coupon redemption, credit card purchases, and product registrations

- monitoring returned merchandise and analyzing why customers leave
- reviewing reply cards, comment forms, and surveys
- monitoring click-through behavior on websites to identify why customers stay and why they leave

These tools give the organization information about customer priorities so managers can make changes to their systems if necessary and set appropriate, measurable goals for relationship programs.

In developing the kind of loyalty that makes lifetime customers valuable, attracting the right buyers is just as important as treating them well. For example, USAA Insurance targets a special niche of customers: active duty military personnel who typically are loyal, reliable, and honest customers. As a result, less than 2 percent of USAA policyholders defect each year.[36]

A hotel chain may set a goal of improving the rate of repeat visits from 44 to 52 percent. If a customer survey reveals late flight arrivals as the number-one complaint of an airline's passengers, the airline may set an objective of increasing the number of on-time arrivals from 87 to 93 percent.

Companies large and small can implement technology to help measure the value of customers and the return on investment from expenditures in developing customer relationships. They can choose from a growing number of software products, many tailored to specific industries or flexible enough to suit companies of varying sizes.

For a simple example of lifetime value, imagine the profit from a Chinese takeout restaurant's average customer.

ASSESSMENT CHECK

9.1 Define lifetime value of a customer.

9.2 Why are customer complaints valuable in evaluating customer relationship programs?

SALES FORECASTING

A basic building block of any marketing plan is a **sales forecast**, an estimate of a firm's revenue for a specified future period. Sales forecasts play major roles in new-product decisions, production scheduling, financial planning, inventory planning and procurement, distribution, and human resources planning. An inaccurate forecast may lead to incorrect decisions in each of these areas. Numerous software programs offer companies sales forecasting applications to help automate the forecasting process.

Planners rely on short-run, intermediate, and long-run sales forecasts. A short-run forecast usually covers a period of up to one year, an intermediate forecast covers one to five years, and a long-run forecast extends beyond five years. Although sales forecasters use an array of techniques to predict the future—ranging from computer simulations to studying trends identified by futurists—their methods fall into two broad categories: qualitative and quantitative forecasting.

Identify the two major types of sales forecasting methods. 10

sales forecast Estimate of a firm's revenue for a specified future period.

qualitative forecasting Use of subjective techniques to forecast sales, such as the jury of executive opinion, Delphi technique, sales force composite, and surveys of buyer intention.

quantitative forecasting Use of statistical forecasting techniques such as trend analysis and exponential smoothing.

jury of executive opinion Qualitative sales forecasting method that assesses the sales expectations of various executives.

delphi technique Qualitative sales forecasting method that gathers and redistributes several rounds of anonymous forecasts until the participants reach a consensus.

sales force composite Qualitative sales forecasting method based on the combined sales estimates of the firm's salespeople.

survey of buyer intentions Qualitative sales forecasting method that samples opinions among groups of current and potential customers concerning their purchasing plans.

Qualitative forecasting techniques rely on subjective data that reports opinions rather than exact historical data. **Quantitative forecasting** methods, by contrast, use statistical computations, such as trend extensions based on past data, computer simulations, and econometric models. As Table 11.2 shows, each method has benefits and limitations. Consequently, most organizations use a combination of both techniques.

QUALITATIVE FORECASTING TECHNIQUES

Planners apply qualitative forecasting methods when they want judgmental or subjective indicators. Qualitative forecasting techniques include the jury of executive opinion, Delphi technique, sales force composite, and survey of buyer intentions.

Jury of Executive Opinion

The technique called the **jury of executive opinion** combines and averages the outlooks of top executives from such areas as marketing, finance, and production. Top managers bring the following capabilities to the process: experience and knowledge about situations that influence sales, open-minded attitudes toward the future, and awareness of the bases for their judgments. This quick and inexpensive method generates good forecasts for sales and new-product development. It works best for short-run forecasting.

Delphi Technique

Like the jury of executive opinion, the **Delphi technique** solicits opinions from several people, but it also gathers input from experts outside the firm, such as academic researchers, rather than relying completely on company executives. It is most appropriately used to predict long-run issues, such as technological breakthroughs, that could affect future sales and the market potential for new products.

The Delphi technique works as follows: A firm selects a panel of experts and sends each a questionnaire relating to a future event. After combining and averaging the answers, the firm develops another questionnaire based on these results and sends it back to the same people. The process continues until it identifies a consensus. Although firms have successfully used Delphi to predict future technological breakthroughs, the method is both expensive and time-consuming.

Sales Force Composite

The **sales force composite** technique develops forecasts based on the belief that organization members closest to the marketplace—those with specialized product, customer, and competitive knowledge—offer the best insights concerning short-term future sales. It typically works from the bottom up. Management consolidates salespeople's estimates first at the district level, then at the regional level, and finally nationwide to obtain an aggregate forecast of sales that reflects all three levels.

The sales force composite approach has some weaknesses, however. Because salespeople recognize the role of their sales forecasts in determining sales quotas for their territories, they are likely to make conservative estimates. Moreover, their narrow perspectives from within their limited geographic territories may prevent them from considering the impact on sales of trends developing in other territories, forthcoming technological innovations, or the major changes in marketing strategies. Consequently, the sales force composite gives the best forecasts in combination with other techniques.

Survey of Buyer Intentions

A **survey of buyer intentions** gathers input through mail-in questionnaires, online feedback, telephone polls, and personal interviews to determine the purchasing intentions of a representative group of current and potential customers. This method suits firms that serve limited numbers of customers but often proves impractical for those with millions of customers. Also, buyer surveys gather useful information only when customers willingly reveal their buying intentions. Moreover, customer intentions do not necessarily translate into actual purchases. These surveys may help a firm predict short-run or intermediate sales, but they employ time-consuming and expensive methods.

TABLE 11.2 Benefits and Limitations of Various Forecasting Techniques

Techniques	Benefits	Limitations
Qualitative Methods		
Jury of executive opinion	Opinions come from executives in many different departments; quick; inexpensive	Managers may lack background knowledge and experience to make meaningful predictions
Delphi technique	Group of experts may predict long-term events such as technological breakthroughs	Time-consuming; expensive
Sales force composite	Salespeople have expert customer, product, and competitor knowledge; quick; inexpensive	Inaccurate forecasts may result from low estimates of salespeople concerned about their influence on quotas
Survey of buyerintentions	Useful in predicting short-term and intermediate sales for firms that serve selected customers	Intentions to buy may not result in actual purchases; time-consuming; expensive
Quantitative Methods		
Test market	Provides realistic information on actual purchases rather than on intent to buy	Alerts competition to new-product plans; time-consuming; expensive
Trend analysis	Quick; inexpensive; effective with stable customer demand and environment	Assumes the future will continue the past; ignores environmental changes
Exponential smoothing	Same benefits as trend analysis, but emphasizes more recent data	Same limitations as trend analysis, but not as severe due to emphasis on recent data

QUANTITATIVE FORECASTING TECHNIQUES

Quantitative techniques attempt to eliminate the subjectivity of the qualitative methods. They include methods such as test markets, trend analysis, and exponential smoothing.

Test Markets

One quantitative technique, the test market, frequently helps planners assess consumer responses to new-product offerings. The procedure typically begins by establishing one or more test markets to gauge consumer responses to a new product under actual marketplace conditions. These tests also permit experimenters to evaluate the effects of different prices, alternative promotional strategies, and other marketing mix variations by comparing results among different test markets. The primary advantage of test markets is the realism they provide for the marketer. On the other hand, these expensive and time-consuming experiments may also communicate marketing plans to competitors.

Trend Analysis

Trend analysis develops forecasts for future sales by analyzing the historical relationship between sales and time. It implicitly assumes the collective causes of past sales will continue to exert similar influences in the future. When historical data is available, planners can quickly and inexpensively complete trend analysis. Software programs can calculate the average annual increment of change for the available sales data. This average increment of change is then projected into the future to come up with the sales forecast. So if the sales of a firm have been growing $5.3 million on average per year, this amount of sales could be added to last year's sales total to arrive at next year's forecast.

Of course, trend analysis cannot be used if historical data is not available, as in new-product forecasting. Also, trend analysis makes the dangerous assumption that future events will continue in the same manner as the past. Any variations in the determinants of future sales will

> **Briefly Speaking**
>
> "Big companies often make the mistake of thinking forecasting is just looking at the sales history and taking an average over time. Instead, they need to look at many additional factors."
>
> —Glen Margolis
> *Founder and CEO, Steelwedge Software*

trend analysis
Quantitative sales forecasting method that estimates future sales through statistical analyses of historical sales patterns.

exponential smoothing Quantitative forecasting technique that assigns weights to historical sales data, giving the greatest weight to the most recent data.

cause deviations from the forecast. In other words, this method gives reliable forecasts during periods of steady growth and stable demand. If conditions change, predictions based on trend analysis may become worthless. For this reason, forecasters have applied more sophisticated techniques and complex, new forecasting models to anticipate the effects of various possible changes in the future.

Exponential Smoothing

A more sophisticated method of trend analysis, the **exponential smoothing** technique, weighs each year's sales data, giving greater weight to results from the most recent years. Otherwise, the statistical approach used in trend analysis is applied here. For example, last year's sales might receive a 1.5 weight, while sales data from two years ago could get a 1.4 weighting. Exponential smoothing is the most commonly used quantitative forecasting technique.

ASSESSMENT CHECK

10.1 Describe the jury of executive opinion.
10.2 What is the Delphi technique?
10.3 How does the exponential smoothing technique forecast sales?

Strategic Implications of Marketing in the 21st Century

A focus on relationship marketing helps companies create better ways to communicate with customers and develop long-term relationships. This focus challenges managers to develop strategies that closely integrate customer service, quality, and marketing functions. By leveraging technology—both through database marketing and through customer relationship management applications—companies can compare costs of acquiring and maintaining customer relationships with profits received from these customers. This information allows managers to evaluate the potential returns from investing in relationship marketing programs.

Relationships include doing business with consumers as well as partners, such as vendors, suppliers, and other companies. Partners can structure relationships in many ways to improve performance, and these choices vary for consumer and business markets. In all marketing relationships, it is important to build shared trust. For long-term customer satisfaction and success, marketers must make promises they can keep. Marketers must also have a solid marketing plan in place, and a key component of any marketing plan is an accurate sales forecast.

Get online now for additional learning tools to help you master your marketing knowledge—visit **WWW.CENGAGEBRAIN.COM** today!

REVIEW OF CHAPTER OBJECTIVES

1 Contrast transaction-based marketing with relationship marketing.

Transaction-based marketing refers to buyer–seller exchanges characterized by limited communications and little or no ongoing relationship between the parties. Relationship marketing is the development and maintenance of long-term, cost-effective relationships with individual customers, suppliers, employees, and other partners for mutual benefit.

2 Explain the four basic elements of relationship marketing, as well as the importance of internal marketing.

The four basic elements of relationship marketing are database technology, database marketing, monitoring relationships, and customer relationship management (CRM). Database technology helps identify current and potential customers. Database marketing analyzes the information provided by the database. Through relationship marketing, a firm monitors each relationship. With CRM, the firm orients every part of the organization toward building a unique company with an unbreakable bond with customers. Internal marketing involves activities within the company designed to help all employees understand, accept, and fulfill their roles in the marketing strategy.

3 Identify the three levels of relationship marketing.

The three levels of relationship marketing are (1) focus on price, (2) social interaction, and (3) interdependent partnership. At the first level, marketers use financial incentives to attract customers. At the second level, marketers engage in social interaction with buyers. At the third level, buyers and sellers become true business partners.

4 Explain how firms can enhance customer satisfaction.

Marketers monitor customer satisfaction through various methods of marketing research. They look to understand what customers want—including what they expect—from goods or services. They also obtain customer feedback through means such as toll-free phone numbers, websites, and social media. Then they use this information to improve.

5 Describe how companies build buyer–seller relationships.

Marketers of consumer goods and services have discovered they must do more than simply create products and then sell them. One reason consumers form continuing relationships is their desire to reduce choices. Through relationships, they can simplify information gathering and the entire buying process as well as decrease the risk of dissatisfaction. One of the major forces driving the push from transaction-based marketing to relationship marketing is the realization that retaining customers is an important component of any successful business. Database marketing is a particularly effective tool for building relationships because it allows sellers to sort through huge quantities of data from multiple sources on the buying habits or preferences of many customers.

6 Explain customer relationship management (CRM) and the role of technology in building customer relationships.

Customer relationship management is the combination of strategies and technologies that empowers relationship programs, reorienting the entire organization to a concentrated focus on satisfying customers. Made possible by technological advances, it leverages technology as a means to manage customer relationships and to integrate all stakeholders into a company's product design and development, manufacturing, marketing, sales, and customer service processes. CRM allows firms to manage vast amounts of data from multiple sources to improve overall customer satisfaction. The most effective companies approach CRM as a complete business strategy in which people, processes, and technology are organized around delivering superior value to customers. A recent outgrowth of CRM is virtual relationships, in which buyers and sellers rarely, if ever, meet face to face.

7 Describe the buyer–seller relationship in business-to-business marketing and the four types of business partnerships.

By developing buyer–seller relationships, companies work together for their mutual benefit. Advantages may include lower prices for supplies, faster delivery of inventory, improved quality or reliability, customized product features, or more favorable financing terms. The four types of business partnerships are buyer, seller, internal, and lateral. Regardless of the type of partnership, partners usually share similar values and goals that help the alliance endure over time. Two other types of business marketing relationships are cobranding and comarketing.

8 Describe the six key elements of business-to-business marketing.

National account selling helps firms form a strong commitment with key buyers, resulting in improvements in efficiency and effectiveness for both parties. The use of electronic data interchanges allows firms to reduce costs and improve efficiency and competitiveness. Web services are software applications that allow firms with different technology platforms to communicate and exchange information over the Internet. Vendor-managed inventory (VMI) is a system in which sellers can automatically restock to previously requested levels. The collaborative planning, forecasting, and replenishment (CPFR) approach bases plans and forecasts on collaborative seller–vendor efforts. Managing the supply chain provides increased innovation, decreased costs, conflict resolution, and improved communications. Strategic alliances can help both partners gain a competitive advantage in the marketplace.

9 Describe the six techniques used to evaluate relationship marketing programs.

The effectiveness of relationship marketing programs can be measured using several methods. In the lifetime value of a customer, the revenues and intangible benefits a customer brings to the seller over an average lifetime—less the amount the company must spend to acquire, market to, and service the customer—are calculated. With this method, a company can determine its costs to serve each customer and develop ways to increase profitability.

The payback method calculates how long it takes to breakeven on customer acquisition costs. Other measurements include reviewing customer comments on social media sites; tracking rebates, coupons, and credit card purchases; monitoring complaints and returns; and reviewing reply cards, comment forms, and surveys. These tools give the organization information about customer priorities so managers can make changes to their systems and set measurable goals.

10 Identify the two major types of sales forecasting methods.

The two categories of forecasting methods are qualitative and quantitative. Qualitative methods are more subjective because they are based on opinions rather than exact historical data. They include the jury of executive opinion, the Delphi technique, the sales force composite, and the survey of buyer intentions. Quantitative methods include more factual and numerical measures, such as test markets, trend analysis, and exponential smoothing.

ASSESSMENT CHECK: ANSWERS

1.1 What are the major differences between transaction-based marketing and relationship marketing? Transaction-based marketing refers to buyer–seller exchanges involving limited communications and little or no ongoing relationship between the parties. Relationship marketing is the development and maintenance of long-term, cost-effective relationships with individual customers, suppliers, employees, and other partners for mutual benefit.

2.1 What are the four basic elements of relationship marketing? The four basic elements are database technology, database marketing, monitoring relationships, and customer relationship management (CRM).

2.2 Why is internal marketing important to a firm? Internal marketing enables all members of the organization to understand, accept, and fulfill their respective roles in implementing a marketing strategy.

3.1 Identify the three levels of the marketing relationship. The three levels of the relationship marketing are (1) focus on price, (2) social interaction, and (3) interdependent partnership.

3.2 Which level is the most complicated? Why? The third level is the most complex because the strength of commitment between the parties grows.

4.1 How is customer satisfaction measured? Marketers monitor customer satisfaction through various marketing research methods.

4.2 Identify the ways marketers may obtain customer feedback. Marketers can include a toll-free phone number or website address in their advertising; monitor social media and blogs; and hire mystery shoppers to personally check on products.

5.1 Describe two ways marketers keep customers. Marketers keep customers through frequency marketing—frequent-buyer or -user marketing programs that reward customers with rebates, merchandise, or other premiums. A second way is through affinity marketing—a marketing effort sponsored by an organization that solicits responses from individuals who share common interests and activities.

5.2 List three efforts that turn customers into advocates for products. Relationship marketing efforts that turn customers from passive partners into advocates include grassroots marketing, viral marketing, and buzz marketing.

6.1 Define customer relationship management. Customer relationship management is the combination of strategies and technologies that empowers relationship programs, reorienting the entire organization to a concentrated focus on satisfying customers.

6.2 What are the two major types of CRM systems? The two major types of CRM systems are ones that are purchased and ones that are rented and hosted by another company.

6.3 Describe two steps a firm can take to rejuvenate a lost relationship. Marketers can rejuvenate a lost relationship by changing the product mix, if necessary, or changing some of their processes.

7.1 What are the four key types of business marketing partnerships? The four key types of business partnerships are buyer, seller, internal, and lateral.

7.2 Distinguish between cobranding and comarketing. Cobranding joins two strong brand names—perhaps owned by two different companies—to sell a product. In a comarketing effort, two or more organizations join to sell their products in an allied marketing campaign.

8.1 Name four technologies businesses can use to improve buyer–seller relationships in B2B markets. The use of electronic data interchanges (EDIs) allows firms to reduce costs and improve efficiency and competitiveness. Web services provide a way for companies to communicate even if they are not running the same or compatible software, hardware, databases, or network platforms. In a vendor-managed inventory (VMI) system, sellers can automatically restock to previously requested levels. The collaborative planning, forecasting, and replenishment (CPFR) approach bases plans and forecasts on collaborative seller–vendor efforts.

8.2 What are the benefits of effective supply chain management? Managing the supply chain increases innovation, decreases costs, resolves conflicts, and improves communications.

9.1 Define lifetime value of a customer. In the lifetime value of a customer, the revenues and intangible benefits a customer brings to the seller over an average lifetime—less the amount the company must spend to acquire, market to, and service the customer—are calculated.

9.2 Why are customer complaints valuable in evaluating customer relationship programs? Customer complaints give the organization information about customer priorities so managers can make changes to their systems, if necessary, and set appropriate, measurable goals for relationship programs.

10.1 Describe the jury of executive opinion. The jury of executive opinion combines and averages the outlooks of top executives from areas like marketing, finance, production, and purchasing.

10.2 What is the Delphi technique? The Delphi technique solicits opinions from several people but also includes input from experts outside the firm.

10.3 How does the exponential smoothing technique forecast sales? Exponential smoothing weighs each year's sales data, giving greater weight to results from the most recent years.

MARKETING TERMS YOU NEED TO KNOW

transaction-based marketing 340
relationship marketing 340
external customers 342
internal customers 342
internal marketing 343
employee satisfaction 343
customer satisfaction 346
customer churn 348
frequency marketing 348
affinity marketing 349
database marketing 349
interactive television 350
grassroots marketing 350

viral marketing 350
buzz marketing 351
customer relationship management (CRM) 352
customer win-back 353
partnership 355
buyer partnership 356
seller partnership 356
internal partnership 356
lateral partnership 356
cobranding 356
comarketing 356
national account selling 357

electronic data interchange (EDI) 358
quick-response merchandising 358
web services 358
vendor-managed inventory (VMI) 358
collaborative planning, forecasting, and replenishment (CPFR) 358
supply chain 358
strategic alliance 359
lifetime value of a customer 360
sales forecast 361

qualitative forecasting 362
quantitative forecasting 362
jury of executive opinion 362
delphi technique 362
sales force composite 362
survey of buyer intentions 362
trend analysis 363
exponential smoothing 364

ASSURANCE OF LEARNING REVIEW

1. Describe the benefits of relationship marketing. How does database technology help firms build relationships with customers?
2. What types of factors might the firm monitor in its relationships?
3. What is an affinity marketing program?
4. Distinguish between grassroots marketing, viral marketing, and buzz marketing.
5. Describe at least four qualities of a successful CRM system.
6. Describe each of the four types of business partnerships.
7. Why is it important for a firm to manage the relationships along its supply chain?
8. What is the most important factor in a strategic alliance?
9. Explain how a firm goes about evaluating the lifetime value of a customer.
10. Contrast qualitative and quantitative sales forecasting methods.

PROJECTS AND TEAMWORK EXERCISES

1. With a teammate, choose one of the following companies. Create a plan to attract customers at the first level of the relationship marketing continuum—price—and move them to the next levels with social interactions. Present your plan to the class.
    a. dog-grooming service
    b. fitness club
    c. surfboard or snowmobile manufacturer
    d. sandwich shop
2. With a teammate, select a business you are familiar with and design a frequency marketing program for that firm. Now design a grassroots, viral marketing, or buzz marketing campaign for the company you selected. Present your campaign to the class.
3. A hotel chain's database has information on guests that includes demographics, number of visits, and room preferences. Describe how the chain can use this information to develop several relationship marketing programs. How can it use a more general database to identify potential customers and personalize its communications with them?
4. Select a local business enterprise. Find out as much as you can about its customer base, marketing strategies, and internal functions. Consider whether a customer relationship management focus would sharpen the enterprise's competitive edge. Argue your position in class.
5. Choose a company that makes great stuff—something you really like, whether it is tennis racquets, electronics, ice cream, or the jeans. Now come up with a partner for your firm that you think would make a terrific strategic alliance. Write a plan for your alliance, explaining why you made the choice, what you want the two firms to accomplish, and why you think the alliance will be successful.

CRITICAL-THINKING EXERCISES

1. Suppose you were asked to be a marketing consultant for a restaurant specializing in a regional cuisine such as Tex-Mex, Cuban, or New England fare. The owner is concerned about employee satisfaction. When you visit the restaurant, what clues would you look for to determine employee satisfaction? What questions might you ask employees?
2. What types of social interaction might be appropriate—and effective—for a local hair salon to engage in with its customers?
3. What steps might a clothing store take to win back its lost customers?
4. Explain why a large firm like General Mills might use national account selling to strengthen its relationship with a major supermarket chain.
5. Why is it important for a company to calculate the lifetime value of a customer?

ETHICS EXERCISE

Suppose you work for a firm that sells home appliances, such as refrigerators, microwaves, and washers and dryers. Your company has been slowly losing customers, but no one seems to know why. Employee morale is sliding as well. You believe the company is run by honest, dedicated owners who want to please their customers. One day, you overhear an employee quietly advising a potential customer to shop at another store. You realize your firm's biggest problem may be a lack of employee satisfaction—which is leading to external customer loss.

1. Would you approach the employee to discuss the problem?
2. Would you ask the employee why he or she is turning customers away?
3. What steps do you think your employer could take to turn the situation around?

INTERNET EXERCISES

1. **Cobranding.** Use a search engine such as Google or Bing to find three examples of cobranding similar to the Delta SkyMiles credit card from American Express.

   http://www.delta.com/skymiles/about_skymiles/benefits_at_glance/dl_amex_credit_card/index.jsp

2. **CRM software.** Act! is a type of customer relationship management software. Visit the website shown here and prepare a brief report about Act! software and how it can improve marketing relationships.

   www.act.com

3. **Rewards programs.** Virtually all hotels and airlines have customer loyalty rewards programs. Go to the websites listed here to learn more about the rewards programs offered by United Airlines and Hilton hotels. Prepare a brief report comparing the two programs.

   http://www.united.com/web/en-us/content/mileageplus/default.aspx

   http://hhonors3.hilton.com/en/index.html

Note: Internet Web addresses change frequently. If you don't find the exact site listed, you may need to access the organization's home page and search from there or use a search engine such as Google or Bing.

CASE 11.1
Teaching Customer Service at the Disney Institute

Visitors to Disney's fabled theme parks are delighted by immaculate facilities, unfailingly cheerful and friendly service, personalized attention, and knowledgeable and helpful staff The company's top-notch customer service is widely admired, and some years ago other firms asked Disney to share its customer-service secrets. So Disney created its own consulting company, called the Disney Institute. The Disney Institute keeps a low profile (not everyone can make the imaginative leap from mouse ears to skilled advice on best business practices), but nevertheless it has helped clients ranging from a single hair salon in Michigan and a youth counseling center in Boston to hospital chains, car dealerships, Häagen-Dazs International, United Airlines, and the NBA. Caught between a sluggish economy and multiple social media sites where consumers can express dissatisfaction, many companies are urgently seeking ways to please their customers.

Sometimes the stakes for the Disney Institute's clients are especially high. Hospitals, for instance, must earn high scores on patient satisfaction surveys to qualify for Medicare reimbursements. One Florida hospital went from the bottom 10 percent in the country on patient satisfaction to the top 10 percent after consulting with the institute's experts.

The core of the institute's customized program focuses on five principles: leadership, training, customer experience, brand loyalty, and creativity. Some of the customer service lessons Disney's clients can hope to learn are the importance of surprising customers in small ways, creating and delivering on a brand promise (Disney's is "Entertainment with heart"), and learning to say yes to customers whenever possible. Perhaps the lesson Disney itself best exemplifies is the need for employees to become the face of the brand, interacting with customers as much as possible, offering help instead of waiting to be asked, and becoming thoroughly knowledgeable about the product. The corollary lesson? Companies should keep employees happy to ensure they can focus on the positive in their customer interactions, instead of falling back on rote behavior and just taking the customer's money.

QUESTIONS FOR CRITICAL THINKING

1. The Disney Institute says clients can't "take Disney and just plug it in." In what ways can companies best adapt Disney's advice to their own customer service situations?

2. Do you agree that keeping employees happy is important for sustaining a customer satisfaction orientation? Why or why not?

Sources: Company website, "Our Story," http://disneyinstitute.com, accessed March 14, 2014; John Lombardo, "Disney Institute, NBA Align," *Sports Business Daily*, accessed March 14, 2014, www.sportsbusinessdaily.com; Anthony Schoettle, "Pacers Hire Disney to Upgrade Service," *Indianapolis Business Journal*, accessed March 14, 2014, www.ibj.com; "Case Study: Häagen-Dazs," *Disney Institute*, accessed March 14, 2014, http://disneyinstitute.com; Brooks Barnes, "In Customer Service Consulting, Disney's Small World Is Growing," *The New York Times*, accessed March 14, 2014, www.nytimes.com; Carmine Gallo, "Customer Service the Disney Way," *Forbes*, accessed March 14, 2014, www.forbes.com.

VIDEO CASE 11.2
Pepe's Pizzeria Serves Success One Customer at a Time

People love Pepe's pizza so much they'll line up around the block waiting for a chance to sink their teeth into fresh dough, homemade sauce, and toppings—all roasted in a coal oven while they sip a root beer or iced tea Regular customers may even choose a table at Pepe's Pizzeria near the open kitchen, where they can watch their crust being spun and tossed, then slipped into the oven. The open kitchen isn't just a nod to the latest trend in restaurant design; it's an acknowledgement of the importance of Pepe's nearly 90-year relationship with its customers. "I treat the customers as if they are part of my family," says Jennifer Kelly, granddaughter of founder Frank Pepe. From 1925, when Pepe began selling pizzas off a pushcart, until today, when hundreds of hungry diners pass through the doors of Pepe's New England restaurants every day, customers have been considered family and friends. Pepe's Pizzeria has built its brand equity not only on the high quality of its food but on its social interaction with customers. "They relate to their customers," says Pepe's CEO Ken Berry. Kelly is a co-owner of Pepe's, along with several siblings and cousins. She is also a server at the New Haven, Connecticut, flagship restaurant. This means that Kelly sees her customers every single day and gets to know them well. She understands how they feel. "When I go out to dinner, I like to be treated with respect," Kelly explains. "I treat them the same way." She listens to them and cares about getting their orders exactly right. If a group of diners has waited in line for a long time, she's empathetic about that too. "They're hungry," Kelly says. "I try to get them their drinks and salads right away."

Kelly also notes that hiring the right staff is critical to the restaurant's success. The wait staff does make transactions; but the relationships they create in just an hour or two ensure that diners will return. "We hire people who know what to do," Kelly says. "We aren't going to hire someone who doesn't have our values."

Even as the price of everything rises, Pepe's pizza prices stay relatively the same. But it's not a focus on price for the purpose of cutting costs or skimping on ingredients—it's one of Pepe's original values, treating his customers as if they were friends and family. "Frank's business survived the Great Depression because he didn't increase prices. He gave to people," Kelly explains. "He was a contributor to the war-time veterans . . . my grandfather never charged them. This is the type of man my grandfather was. This is the type of heritage that we follow." As for prices in today's economy, Kelly asks, "Why would we increase prices right now? People are struggling." She comments that a family of four can eat at the restaurant for around $20 and be satisfied—which means they are very likely to return.

Pepe's doesn't need to do a lot more in the way of marketing to enhance its relationships, but there are thousands of pizza joints littered across the nation, translating to competition. Valuing its roots—but not wanting to be stuck in the last century—the company does engage in social marketing for broader relationship building. On Pepe's Facebook page, which has more than 14,000 "likes," customers post comments such as, "I have driven 50 miles—each way—for one of these pizzas." The company advertises new menu items there, including beverages. Fans can also enter the current "Where in the World Is Pepe's?" contest for a chance to win a $300 Pepe's gift card and an iPad. Or they can log on to their Twitter accounts to enter #MyPepes contest by tweeting a picture of their pizza from the restaurant.

Still, Pepe's will always maintain its old-world family feel. Berry describes how Pepe sometimes spent 24 hours at a time in his pizzeria, fashioning new recipes, making dough, cleaning the kitchen. People tossed pebbles at the windows late at night or early in the morning to catch his attention and ask him to make them a pizza—which he did. In this regard, the transition of Pepe's from 1925 to today's world is seamless. "It goes back to the people from our community and our neighborhood," says Kelly. "Those are the people who made us famous. Those are the people who made us who we are today."

QUESTIONS FOR CRITICAL THINKING

1. How does Pepe's Pizzeria use price and social interactions to build relationships with its customers?
2. How does Pepe's Pizzeria ensure customer satisfaction?

Sources: Company website, www.pepespizzeria.com, accessed March 14, 2014; company Facebook page, www.facebook.com/FrankPepes, accessed March 14, 2014; Jacky Smith, "Free Pizza at Pepe's in Danbury Tuesday Night," *News Times*, accessed March 14, 2014, http://blog.ctnews.com.

NOTES

1. Corporate website, "About Publix," www.publix.com, accessed October 7, 2014; Jennifer Thomas, "Publix Among Fortune's 100 Best Companies to Work For in 2014," *Charlotte Business Journal*, accessed March 12, 2014, www.bizjournals.com; Brian Solomon, "The Wal-Mart Slayer: How Publix's People-First Culture Is Winning the Grocer War," *Forbes*, accessed March 12, 2014, www.forbes.com; David Bracken and Andrew Kenney, "Publix Enters Crowded Triangle Grocery Market with Cary Store," *The News & Observer*, accessed March 12, 2014, www.newsobserver.com; "Supermarket Sweep: Publix's Maria Brous on Media and Community Relations," *Public Relations Tactics*, accessed March 12, 2014, www.prsa.org; Megan Ribbens, "Publix Takes Top Spot on Temkin Customer Service List," *Orlando Business Journal*, accessed March 12, 2014, www.bizjournals.com.
2. Company website, "About Us," http://unleashedbypetco.com, accessed March 12, 2014; Clarice Brough, "Pet Businesses Will Prosper: Industry Trends for 2014 and Beyond," *Multibriefs*, accessed March 12, 2014, www.multibriefs.com.
3. "Training Magazine Announces 2014 Top 125 Winners and Hall of Fame Inductees," *Training* magazine, accessed March 12, 2014, www.trainingmag.com; "Farmers Insurance Finishes in the Top 5 of the Training Magazine Top 125 Awards, Will Join Hall of Fame," *PRNewswire*, accessed March 12, 2014, www.prnewswire.com; company district website, "University of Farmers," www.farmersagent.com, accessed March 12, 2014.
4. "Four Seasons Hotels and Resorts Named to *Fortune* List of the '100 Best Companies to Work For'" (press release), accessed March 12, 2014, http://press.fourseasons.com.
5. Company website, http://t-mobile.com, accessed March 12, 2014.
6. Mike Isaac, "Why Twitter Dropped Close to $90 Million on Bluefin Labs," *All Things Digital*, accessed March 12, 2014, http://allthingsd.com.
7. "The 2013 CRM Elite: Angie's List: Unifying Member Promotions Using TinderBox," *CRM Magazine*, accessed March 12, 2014, www.destinationcrm.com.
8. Organization website, www.theacsi.org, accessed October 7, 2014.
9. Melinda F. Emerson, "Learning Social Media Tricks from the Big Boys," *The New York Times*, accessed March 12, 2014, http://boss.blogs.nytimes.com.
10. Saiyai Sakawee, "When It Comes to Customer Service in Thailand, Apple's Tim Cook Wins," *Tech in Asia*, accessed March 12, 2014, www.techinasia.com.
11. Company website, "Guest Satisfaction Survey," http://www.dennyslistens.com, accessed March 12, 2014.
12. Company website, "World Retail Banking Report 2013," www.capgemini.com, accessed March 12, 2014.
13. Michael B. Farrell and Hiawatha Bray, "Cellphone Giants Cling to 2-Year Contracts," *The Boston Globe*, accessed March 13, 2014, www.bostonglobe.com.
14. Jason Del Rey, "Amazon Prime May Have 50 Million Members, Analyst Says," *Recode*, accessed October 7, 2014, http://recode.net; company website, Amazon Prime, www.amazon.com, accessed October 7, 2014; David Streitfeld, "Complaints as Amazon Raises Cost of Prime," *The New York Times*, March 13, 2014, www.nytimes.com; Trefis, "Re-Evaluating Amazon Prime's Strength," *Forbes*, accessed March 13, 2014, www.forbes.com; Kelli B. Grant, "Amazon Prime Membership Could Be a Budget Buster," *CNBC*, accessed March 13, 2014, www.cnbc.com; Paul Greenberg, "Why Customer-Based Amazon Is Our Most-Important Business Force," *ZDNet*, accessed March 13, 2014, www.zdnet.com.
15. Daniel P. Ray and Yasmin Ghahremani, "Credit Card Statistics, Industry Facts, Debt Statistics," *CreditCards.com*, accessed March 13, 2014, www.creditcards.com.
16. April Lentini, "College Campuses with Cemeteries," *Half Past Nine*, accessed March 13, 2014, http://halfpastnine.com.
17. David Wharton, "Ralph Lauren Unveils Opening Ceremony Outfits for 2014 Sochi Olympics," *Los Angeles Times*, accessed March 13, 2014, www.latimes.com.
18. Organization website, "Membership & Benefits," www.thirteen.org, accessed March 13, 2014.
19. Arthur Middleton Hughes, "The 24 Essential Database Marketing Techniques," *Database Marketing Institute*, accessed March 13, 2014, www.dbmarketing.com.
20. Greg Sterling, "Google Brings More 'Now' to Search with New Quick Answers," *Search Engine Land*, accessed March 13, 2014, http://searchengineland.com; Jon Fingas, "Google+ Hangouts App Hands-On," *Engadget*, accessed March 13, 2014, www.engadget.com; Larry Magid, "How (and Why) to Turn Off Google's Personalized Search," *Forbes*, accessed March 13, 2014, www.forbes.com.
21. "Super Bowl 2014 Ratings Set New Record," *CBS News*, accessed March 13, 2014, www.cbsnews.com.
22. David Salway, "Internet Connected TV's in the US Reaches 40%," *About Technology*, accessed October 7, 2014, http://broadband.about.com.
23. Parmy Olson, "Mobile Advertisers Aim to Be More Useful, Less Annoying and Creepy," *Forbes*, accessed March 13, 2014, www.forbes.com.
24. Organization website, www.red.org, accessed October 7, 2014; organization website, www.theglobalfund.org, accessed March 13, 2014; Zoe Fox, "How (RED) United the Social Web in the Fight against AIDS," *Mashable*, accessed March 13, 2014, http://mashable.com.
25. Company website, www.tremor.com, accessed March 13, 2014.
26. Organization website, "About WOMMA," Word of Mouth Marketing Association, www.womma.org, accessed March 13, 2014.
27. "The Benefits of CRM Systems," *Benefits of CRM*, accessed March 14, 2014, www.benefitsofcrm.com; "7 Key Benefits to Your Business with CRM," *Success with CRM*, accessed March 14, 2014, www.successwithcrm.com.
28. "Top 10 Factors Attributed to CRM Implementation Failures," *CRM Blog Guy*, accessed March 14, 2014, www.crmblogguy.com.
29. Erika Napoletano, "How to Gracefully Deal with Haters," *OPEN Forum*, accessed March 14, 2014, https://www.openforum.com; company website, "How to Knock Off a Bag," www.saddlebackleather.com, accessed March 14, 2014.
30. Laurel Brubaker Calkins, "BP Still Trying to Undo Some Oil Spill Claims Payments to Nonprofits," *Insurance Journal*, accessed October 7, 2014, www.insurancejournal.com; Campbell Robertson and John Schwartz, "How a Gulf Settlement That BP Once Hailed Became Its Target," *The New York Times*, accessed October 7, 2014, www.nytimes.com.
31. Robin Sidel and Andrew R. Johnson, "Prepaid Enters Mainstream," *The Wall Street Journal*, accessed March 14, 2014, http://online.wsj.com; company website, "Say Hello to Bluebird," www.walmart.com, accessed March 14, 2014.
32. Kurt Badenhausen, "How Michael Jordan Made $90 Million in 2013," *Forbes*, accessed October 7, 2014, www.forbes.com; Kavitha A. Davidson, "Michael Jordan, Fueled by Nike's Jordan Brand Sales, Enters Billionaires Club," *Bloomberg News*, accessed October 7, 2014, www.bloombergnews.com.
33. Karlene Lukovitz, "ConAgra, Kraft Expand Marketing Partnerships," *Marketing Daily*, accessed March 14, 2014, www.mediapost.com.
34. Company website, "The Right Stuff: Rite Aid and Kimberly-Clark Succeed at Collaboration with the Support of JDA Marketplace Replenish," *Real Results*, www.jda.com, accessed March 14, 2014.
35. Organization website, "Fox Sports Inks Deal to Televise U.S. Open" (press release), www.pgatour.com, accessed March 14, 2014.
36. Bryan Yurcan, "USAA, ING Direct, PNC Leaders in Customer Retention, Report Says," *Bank Tech*, accessed March 14, 2014, www.banktech.com; Arthur Middleton Hughes, "The Loyalty Effect: A New Look at Lifetime Value," *Database Marketing Institute*, accessed March 14, 2014, www.dbmarketing.com.

Scripps Networks Interactive & Food Network

PART 3
Target Market Selection

Scooping Up Consumer Insight

"Food is such a huge topic in people's lives," comments Susie Fogelson, senior vice president, marketing, creative services, and public relations for Food Network and the Cooking Channel. "Social media gives us an opportunity to be relevant in people's lives almost every minute of every day, as long as we can make the content valuable, compelling, unique, and authentic." That's a large order to fill, but marketers for Scripps Networks Interactive and its branded networks, including Food Network, recognize that social media is not only a way to reach consumers but also for consumers to reach them.

The social media conversation begins naturally and becomes marketing research as marketers tease out data that help them identify consumer trends, preferences, lifestyle choices and habits, and the like. "We're always looking for better ways to get more interesting information," says Gabe Gordon, vice president of research for the food category at Scripps. While the networks themselves may look specifically for food trends, Gordon's team researches a broader scope—what he calls "emotional" trends. If the defined problem is loss of market share for a certain type of cooking show, then researchers will attempt to find out why. If Scripps wants to develop a new show to compete head-on with a show from a rival network such as Bravo or TLC, researchers may initiate a social media conversation to learn what viewers especially like about the other network's show. Once they gather enough information on viewers' preferences, they can do targeted messaging that encourages viewers to visit Food Network to watch shows, such as "Food Network Star" or "Chopped."

Social media allows marketers to collect a lot of primary data through conversations directly with consumers. "We want our social media conversations to be as non-invasive as possible," says Gordon. Computer technology allows these exchanges to take place as naturally as possible—Scripps might give participants a smartphone or tablet to carry, so they can chat or comment at any given moment during the day. Scripps still conducts traditional surveys (usually online) and focus groups, because they do contain value. "But there are always drawbacks to any sort of research process," acknowledges Gordon. "One of the biggest is having people in an artificial environment."

Social media gives marketers a peek into nearly every aspect of consumers' lives that they're willing to share, including the most mundane details. "Consumers are out there in the social spaces telling us what they're eating for breakfast, what they're doing over the weekend," says Jonah Spegman, director of digital media and database marketing for Scripps. "They're leaving all sorts of data elements out there for us on the marketing side." But just knowing that one consumer ate cereal for breakfast while another went running instead isn't enough. Marketers must be able to identify groups of people and interpret the gathered data so it becomes valuable information. "We pick up on those data elements and start building out segments about people who are interested and have certain passions around what our brands can offer," explains Spegman. For example, after airing the Food Network documentary "Hunger Hits Home," marketers used targeted Facebook ads to pinpoint people who were interested in charity work. "Social media allowed us to use mechanisms to identify who those people are and then reach out to them with a message that spoke to what the documentary had to offer," recalls Spegman.

Food Network marketers already know that the overwhelming majority of their audience is women; but more and more men are tuning in, says Kate Gold, director of social media. In social media interactions, she notes a similar trend—but younger consumers tend to communicate via Twitter while Facebook is more across the board in terms of age groups. Food Network targets female viewers with decision-making and buying power—preferably with the ability and desire to spend money on restaurants, fine food and beverages, and higher-end cooking supplies. Although Engel's law states that the greater a person's household income is, the lower the percentage spent on food items will be, in this case, food expenditures blend with luxury and entertainment.

Social media reaches directly to Food Network's segmented audience—consumers who care about food, cooking, and dining. Fogelson thinks about the ways that Food Network can interact with consumers long after they've turned off the TV. Shoppers could access Food Network from their smartphones while in the grocery store and learn which ingredients to buy for a quick dinner. While standing at the fish or produce counter, they could find out which fish or vegetables are in season. "The possibilities are infinite if we can talk to consumers all day, what we can do for them," says Fogelson. "Consumer insights are the most important thing when you think about how to program social media."

This kind of activity underscores the idea of conversation—building relationships with viewers and consumers in general. For example, Food Network celebrity chefs such as Bobby Flay and Giada De Laurentiis tweet and answer questions from consumers on Facebook several times a day. "It's a great opportunity for the network to cultivate those relationships," remarks Gold. "It's broken down that barrier—seeing someone on TV and then being able to interact with them in social media. These are real people, and viewers get real insights into the talents' everyday life."

QUESTIONS FOR CRITICAL THINKING

1. Using the VALS framework, how would you segment the average viewer of Food Network programming?
2. Using social media, what steps might Food Network take to expand its viewership to include more teens? What about viewers from different ethnic groups?
3. What types of secondary data could be helpful to Food Network marketing researchers? How could they put this data to use?
4. Through social media, how do Food Network viewers become advocates for the network?

Part 4
Product Decisions

12 **Product and Service Strategies**

13 **Developing and Managing Brand and Product Categories**

Chapter 12

Product and Service Strategies

APPLE'S "A" FOR INNOVATION

1. Define the term *product*.
2. Distinguish between goods and services and how they relate to the goods–services continuum.
3. Outline the importance of the service sector in today's marketplace.
4. Describe the three classifications of consumer goods and services.
5. Identify the six types of business goods and services.
6. Discuss how marketers use quality as a product strategy.
7. Explain why firms develop lines of related products.
8. Describe the way marketers typically measure product mixes and make product mix decisions.
9. Explain the four stages of the product lifecycle.
10. Describe the four strategies for extending a product's lifecycle and why certain products may be eliminated.

Apple has become one of the most successful and innovative companies in the world. It is no accident that the maker of the Mac, the iPhone, the iPod, and the iPad draws millions of people to its more than 428 stores every day, or that it generates more than $171 billion in sales each year. *Forbes* recently named Apple the most powerful brand in the world. What is the strategy behind the company's success? It relies on both superior products and exceptional customer service.

Apple leads the industry in the design of sleek and highly functional products that are dependable and intuitively easy to use. Nearly all its products have revolutionized or created and then dominated a market. Because of the quality, features, and high-tech appeal of Apple products, more than half of all U.S. homes own at least one. In fact, the average number owned is 1.6 devices per household, with more than three of five consumers in the 18–49 age groups owning at least one Apple product. Though the most typical customers are young, college-educated males, the popularity of Apple devices cuts across all age groups, geographic areas, and even political parties, with Democrats and Republicans owning them in about equal numbers. The vice president of one marketing research firm says, "It's a fantastic business model—the more [Apple] products you own, the more likely you are to buy more."

Apple also introduces new devices and new versions of existing products at a dizzying rate. Innovation truly drives the firm, and it is not afraid to let new products take sales away from older ones. CEO Tim Cook says the company would rather let the iPad cannibalize sales of the Mac than lose those sales to a competing company.

Another big factor in Apple's continued success is the care with which it treats customers in its stores. Steve Jobs, the company's late founder, helped select "Enriching Lives" as Apple's retail vision, rather than focusing on selling per se. Staff in the stores don't earn commissions and are trained to create memorable customer experiences, even for visitors who don't buy anything. Apple focuses on building relationships, offering help and training, troubleshooting, and solving problems in an effort to touch customers at an emotional level and motivate them to become loyal to the Apple brand. That's why customers recommend it to others.

With all this to offer, Apple can feel confident that its merchandise and customer service can command a premium price.[1]

EVOLUTION OF A BRAND

From the Macintosh computer to the iPhone, iPod, and iPad, the Apple brand is an indisputable success story. But success didn't come without a plan and a vision. Steve Jobs's vision for Apple centered around products that were well-made, functional, and easy to use—products that would become part of the fabric of life for consumers worldwide.

- More than a million apps are available in the App Store for iPhone, iPad, or iPod across 169 countries. How does the development of new applications help extend the lifecycle of these products?
- After Apple partnered with China Mobile, the world's largest mobile carrier, to sell iPhones, Chinese consumers were said to prefer screens larger than the iPhone's. How might the availability of iPhones in China lead to other product innovations?
- Apple recently paid $3 billion to acquire Beats Electronics, which offers a music-streaming service as well as high-end headphones. How might this acquisition change Apple's business strategy going forward?

Chapter Overview

marketing mix Blending of the four strategy elements—product, distribution, promotion, and price—to fit the needs and preferences of a specific target market.

We've discussed how marketers conduct research to determine unfilled needs in their markets, how customers behave during the purchasing process, and how firms expand their horizons overseas. Now our attention shifts to a company's **marketing mix**, the blend of four elements of a marketing strategy—product, distribution, promotion, and price—to satisfy the target market. This chapter focuses on how companies like Apple select and develop the goods and services they offer, starting with planning which products to offer. The other variables of the marketing mix—distribution channels, promotional plans, and pricing decisions—must accommodate the product strategy selected.

Marketers develop strategies to promote both tangible goods and intangible services. Any such strategy begins with investigation, analysis, and selection of a particular target market, and it continues with the creation of a marketing mix designed to satisfy that segment. Tangible goods and intangible services both intend to satisfy consumer wants and needs, but the marketing efforts supporting them may be vastly different. Many firms sell both types of products, offering innovative goods and ongoing service to attract and retain customers for the long term. Doing so can be profitable, as you'll see in this chapter.

This chapter examines the similarities and differences in marketing goods and services. It then presents basic concepts—product classifications, development of product lines, and the product lifecycle—marketers apply in developing successful products. Finally, the chapter discusses product deletion and product mix decisions.

> **Briefly Speaking**
>
> "What's a brand? A singular idea or concept that you own inside the mind of the prospect."
>
> —Al Ries
> American marketer and author,
> *Positioning: The Battle for Your Mind*

WHAT IS A PRODUCT?

1 Define the term *product*.

At first, you might think of a product as an object you hold in your hand, such as a baseball or a toothbrush. You might also think of the car you drive as a product. But this doesn't take into account the idea of a service as a product. Nor does it consider the idea of what the product is used for. So a television is more than a box with a screen and a remote control. It's really a means of providing entertainment—your favorite movies, news programs, or reality shows. Marketers acknowledge this broader conception of product; they realize that people buy *want satisfaction* rather than objects.

You might feel a need for a television to satisfy a want for entertainment. You might not know a lot about how the device itself works, but you understand the results. If you are entertained by watching TV, then your wants are satisfied. If, however, the television is working just fine, but you don't like the programming offered, you may need to satisfy your desire for entertainment by changing your service package to include premium channels. The service—and its offerings—is a product.

ASSESSMENT CHECK

1.1. Define product.
1.2. Why is the understanding of want satisfaction so important to marketers?

Chapter 12 Product and Service Strategies

Marketers think in terms of a product as a compilation of package design and labeling, brand name, price, availability, warranty, reputation, image, and customer service activities that add value for the customer. Consequently, a **product** is a bundle of physical, service, and symbolic attributes designed to satisfy a customer's wants and needs.

> **product** Bundle of physical, service, and symbolic attributes designed to satisfy a customer's wants and needs.

WHAT ARE GOODS AND SERVICES?

Services are intangible products. A general definition identifies **services** as intangible tasks that satisfy the needs of consumer and business users. But you can't hold a service in your hand the way you can **goods**—tangible products customers can see, hear, smell, taste, or touch. Most service providers cannot transport or store their products; customers simultaneously buy and consume these products, such as haircuts, car repairs, and visits to the dentist. One way to distinguish services from goods is the **goods–services continuum**, as shown in Figure 12.1.

This spectrum helps marketers visualize the differences and similarities between goods and services. A car is a *pure good*, but the dealer also offers repair and maintenance services or includes the services in the price of a lease. The car falls at the pure good extreme of the continuum, because the repair or maintenance services are an adjunct to the purchase. A dinner at an exclusive restaurant is a mix of goods and services. It combines the physical goods of gourmet food with the intangible services of an attentive wait staff, elegant surroundings, and perhaps a visit to your table by the chef or restaurant owner to make sure your meal is perfect. At the other extreme, a dentist provides *pure service*—cleaning teeth, filling cavities, taking X-rays. The dentist's office may also sell items like night guards, but it is the service that is primary in patients' minds.

Services can be distinguished from goods in several ways:

1. *Services are intangible.* Services do not have physical features buyers can see, hear, smell, taste, or touch prior to purchase. Service firms essentially ask their customers to buy a promise—the haircut will be stylish, the insurance will cover injuries, the lawn will be mowed, and so on.
2. *Services are inseparable from the service providers.* Consumer perceptions of a service provider become their perceptions of the service itself. The name of a doctor, lawyer, or hair stylist is synonymous with the service they provide. A bad haircut can deter customers, while a good one will attract more to the salon. A house-cleaning service like Merry Maids depends on its workers to leave each house spotless, because its reputation is built on this service.
3. *Services are perishable.* Providers cannot maintain inventories of their services. A day spa can't stockpile facials or pedicures. A travel agent can't keep quantities of vacations on a shelf. For this reason some service providers, such as airlines and hotels, may raise their prices during times of peak demand—during spring break from school, for example—and reduce them when demand declines.
4. *Companies cannot easily standardize services.* However, many firms are trying to change this. Most fast-food chains promise you'll get your meal within a certain number of minutes, and it will taste the way you expect it to. A hotel chain may have the same amenities at each location—a pool, fitness room, free breakfast, and cable movies.

> **2** Distinguish between goods and services and how they relate to the goods–services continuum.
>
> **services** Intangible tasks that satisfy the needs of consumer and business users.
>
> **goods** Tangible products customers can see, hear, smell, taste, or touch.
>
> **goods–services continuum** Spectrum along which goods and services fall according to their attributes, from pure good to pure service.

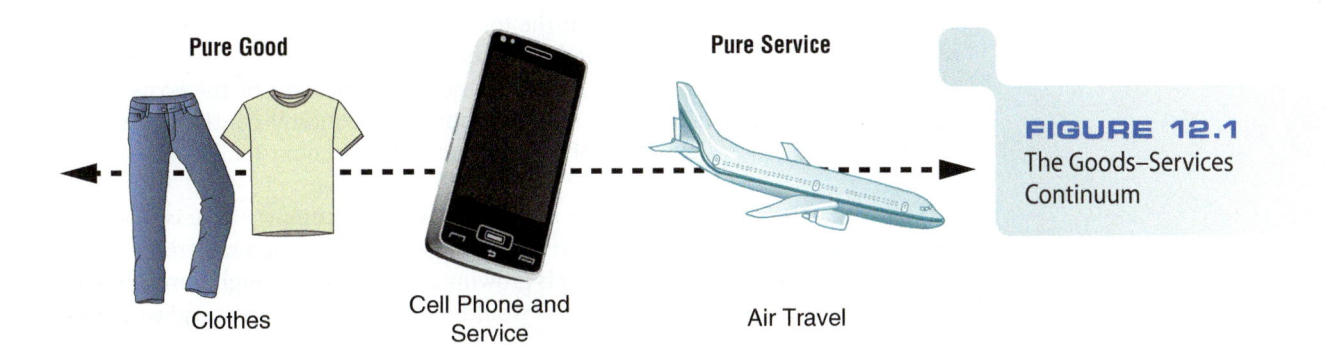

Pure Good ← Clothes — Cell Phone and Service — Air Travel → Pure Service

FIGURE 12.1 The Goods–Services Continuum

It is not easy for companies to standardize services, but they do try. For example, a hotel chain might have the same amenities at each location, including a beautiful indoor pool.

5. *Buyers often play important roles in the creation and distribution of services.* Service transactions frequently require interaction between buyer and seller at the production and distribution stages. When a traveler arrives at the airport to pick up a rental car, he or she may have a choice of vehicle and additional amenities such as a GPS unit or car seat for a child. If the car is ready to go immediately, the customer will likely be satisfied. If the desired car is not available, not clean, or doesn't have a full tank of gas, the customer may not book with this company again.

6. *Service standards show wide variations.* New York City's posh Le Cirque and your local Pizza Hut are both restaurants. Depending on your expectations, both can be considered good restaurants. However, the service standards at each vary greatly. At Le Cirque, you'll experience finely prepared cuisine served by a highly trained wait staff. At Pizza Hut, you may serve yourself fresh pizza from the buffet. If you receive your dinner from attentive wait staff at Le Cirque, you will be satisfied by the service standards. If the pizza at Pizza Hut is hot and fresh, and the buffet is replenished frequently, you will be satisfied by those standards as well.

Keep in mind that a product often blurs the distinction between services and goods. U-Haul is a service that rents trucks and moving vans, which are goods. LensCrafters provides eye examinations—services from optometrists—while also selling eyeglasses and contact lenses, which are goods.

ASSESSMENT CHECK

2.1 Describe the goods–services continuum.

2.2 List the six characteristics distinguishing services from goods.

IMPORTANCE OF THE SERVICE SECTOR

3 Outline the importance of the service sector in today's marketplace.

You would live a very different life without service firms to fill many needs. You could not place a phone call, log on to the Internet, flip a switch for electricity, or even take a college course if organizations did not provide such services. During an average day, you probably use many services without much thought, but these products play an integral role in your life.

The service sector makes a crucial contribution to the U.S. economy in terms of products and jobs. Yet, only two of *Fortune*'s top ten most-admired companies are pure service firms—Google and FedEx. The other eight firms in the top ten, all listed in Figure 12.2, provide highly regarded services in conjunction with the goods they sell.[2]

The U.S. service sector now makes up nearly 80 percent of the economy, as the shift from a goods-producing economy to a service-producing economy continues. According to the U.S. Department of Labor, service industries are expected to account for 14 million new jobs by the year 2022.[3]

Services also play a crucial role in the international competitiveness of U.S. firms. While the United States runs a continuing trade deficit in goods, it has maintained a trade surplus in services every year since 1992, and the surplus is growing.[4] However, although some economists believe more precise measurements of service exports would reveal an even larger surplus, others worry about the effect of offshoring service jobs.

While some firms have found success with offshoring certain of their work functions, such as call centers and IT, others have returned those functions to the United States after determining they would save money and improve quality by doing so.[5] Termed *backshoring*, this trend is growing and actually becoming a marketing tool for firms. "Foreign call centers feed into the perception that companies aren't interested in their customers," notes one marketing researcher.

Some companies bringing their call centers back to the United States are taking another approach using home-based hourly workers, often managed by a private firm.[6] This emerging trend, known as **homeshoring**, enables firms to save on office space, furnishings, and supplies. In addition, most also save on health care and other benefits. Carnival Cruise Lines, JetBlue, and Sears practice homeshoring. Miramar, Florida–based Arise Virtual Solutions supplies home-based employees to other companies, much the way an employment agency does.[7] Firms that practice homeshoring are experiencing another benefit: a reduction in the use of energy and other natural resources, which decreases these firms' impact on the environment. Because employees are not commuting to work every day, and because an office does not have to be heated, cooled, and supplied with electricity and water every day, firms not only experience reduced costs but also a drop in emissions. These companies can highlight their green practices in marketing messages to customers.

Observers cite several reasons for the growing importance of services, including consumer desire for speed and convenience and technological advances that allow firms to fulfill this demand. Services involving wireless communications, data backup and storage, and even meal preparation for busy families are on the rise. Grocery chain Trader Joe's is benefiting from this need for quick meals by offering partially cooked, fully cooked, and flash-frozen entrées that can be picked up and prepared in less time than meals made from scratch. Many traditional supermarkets offer prepared entrées and side dishes shoppers can buy at the store and heat quickly in the microwave at home. Consumers are also looking to advisors to help plan for a financially secure future and insurance to protect their homes and families.

Most service firms emphasize marketing as a significant activity for two reasons. First, the growth potential of service transactions represents a vast marketing opportunity. Second, the environment for services is changing. For instance, increased competition is forcing traditional service industries to differentiate themselves from their competitors. Providing superior service is one way to develop long-term customer relationships and compete more effectively. As we discussed earlier, relationship marketing is just one of the ways service firms can develop and solidify their customer relationships.

FIGURE 12.2
World's Most Admired Companies

Source: "World's Most Admired Companies 2014," *Fortune*, accessed October 9, 2014, http://fortune.com.

1. Apple
2. Amazon.com
3. Google
4. Berkshire Hathaway
5. Starbucks
6. The Coca-Cola Company
7. The Walt Disney Company
8. FedEx
9. Southwest Airlines
10. GE

homeshoring Hiring workers to do jobs from their homes.

Homeshoring, or using home-based hourly workers, allows companies to save on office space, furnishings, and supplies.

ASSESSMENT CHECK

3.1 Identify two reasons services are important to the U.S. economy and business environment.

3.2 Why do service firms emphasize marketing?

CLASSIFYING GOODS AND SERVICES FOR CONSUMER AND BUSINESS MARKETS

4 Describe the three classifications of consumer goods and services.

A firm's choices for marketing a good or service depend largely on the offering itself and on the nature of the target market. Product strategies differ for consumer and business markets. **Business-to-consumer (B2C) products** are those destined for use by ultimate consumers, while **business-to-business (B2B) products** (also called *industrial* or *organizational products*) contribute directly or indirectly to the output of other products for resale. Marketers further subdivide these two major categories into more specific categories, as discussed in this section.

Some products fall into both categories. A case in point is prescription drugs. Traditionally, pharmaceutical companies marketed prescription drugs to doctors, who then made the purchase decision for their patients by writing the prescription. These medications would be classified as a business product. However, many drug companies now advertise their products in consumer-oriented media, including magazines, television, and the Internet. The ads suggest that consumers inquire about a certain drug when they go to their doctors. This direct-to-consumer advertising topped $3.8 billion in a recent year.[8]

business-to-consumer (B2C) products Product destined for use by ultimate consumers.

business-to-business (B2B) products Product that contributes directly or indirectly to the output of other products for resale; also called industrial or organizational product.

unsought products Products marketed to consumers who may not yet recognize a need for them.

convenience products Goods and services consumers want to purchase frequently, immediately, and with minimal effort.

TYPES OF CONSUMER PRODUCTS

The most widely used product classification system focuses on the buyer's perception of a need for the product and his or her buying behavior. However, **unsought products** are marketed to consumers who may not yet recognize any need for them. Examples of unsought products are long-term-care insurance and funeral services.

Relatively few products fall into the unsought category. Most consumers recognize their own needs for various types of consumer purchases and actively seek them, so the customer buying-behavior variations are key in distinguishing the various categories. The most common classification scheme for sought products divides consumer goods and services into three groups based on customers' buying behavior: convenience, shopping, and specialty. Figure 12.3 illustrates samples of these categories, together with the unsought classification.

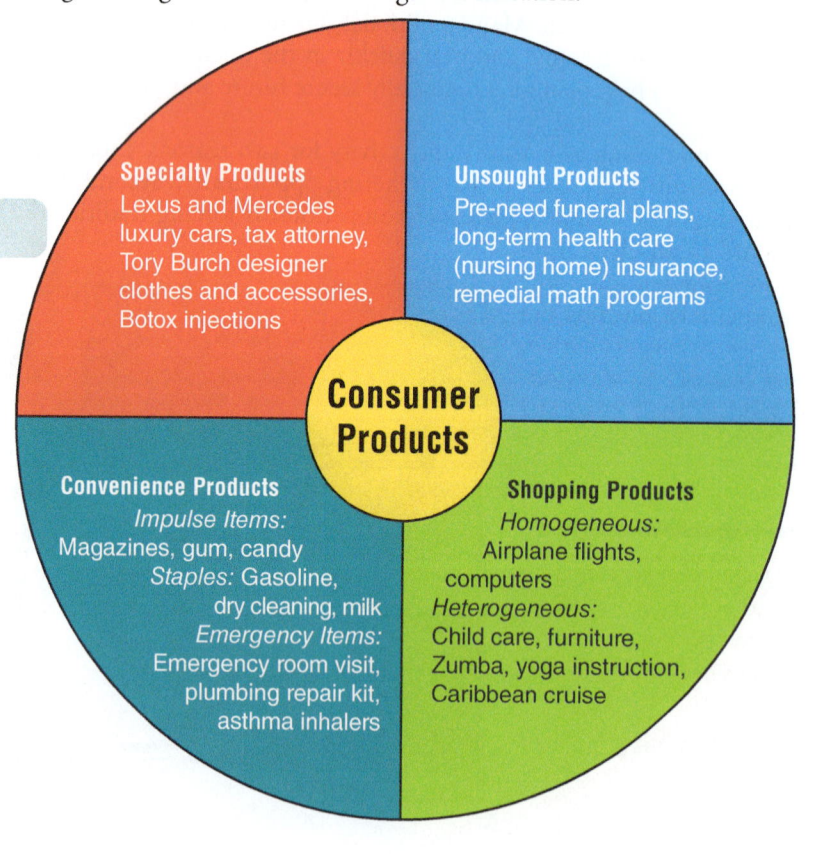

FIGURE 12.3 Classification of Consumer Products

Specialty Products
Lexus and Mercedes luxury cars, tax attorney, Tory Burch designer clothes and accessories, Botox injections

Unsought Products
Pre-need funeral plans, long-term health care (nursing home) insurance, remedial math programs

Convenience Products
Impulse Items: Magazines, gum, candy
Staples: Gasoline, dry cleaning, milk
Emergency Items: Emergency room visit, plumbing repair kit, asthma inhalers

Shopping Products
Homogeneous: Airplane flights, computers
Heterogeneous: Child care, furniture, Zumba, yoga instruction, Caribbean cruise

Convenience Products

Convenience products refer to goods and services consumers want to purchase frequently, immediately, and with minimal effort. Milk, bread, and toothpaste are convenience products. Convenience services include 24-hour quick-stop stores, walk-in hair or nail salons, copy shops, and dry cleaners.

Marketers further subdivide the convenience category into impulse items, staples, or emergency items. **Impulse goods and services** are purchased on the spur of the moment—for example, visiting a car wash or a picking up a pack of gum at the supermarket register. Some marketers have even come up with ways to attract impulse shopping on the Internet. For example, ArtTownGifts.com offers a last-minute and emergency gifts service that allows shoppers to choose and ship gifts quickly, even for same-day delivery. They can select balloon bouquets, flowers, fruit or wine baskets, and more. Emergency gifts don't come cheap—they range in price from about $45 to $300—but they fulfill an immediate need for goods and services.[9]

Staples are convenience goods and services consumers constantly replenish to maintain a ready inventory: gasoline, shampoo, and dry cleaning are good examples. Marketers spend many hours and dollars creating messages for consumers about these products, partly because there are so many competitors.

Emergency goods and services are bought in response to unexpected and urgent needs. A snow blower purchased during a snowstorm and a visit to a hospital emergency room to treat a broken ankle are examples. Depending on your viewpoint, the products offered by ArtTownGifts.com's emergency service also could fall into this category.

Because consumers devote little effort to convenience-product purchase decisions, marketers must strive to make these exchanges as simple as possible. Store location can boost a convenience product's visibility. Marketers compete vigorously for prime locations, which can make all the difference between a consumer choosing one gas station, vending machine, or dry cleaner over another.

Location *within* a store also can make the difference between success and failure of a product, which is why manufacturers fight so hard for the right spot on supermarket shelves. Typically, the largest grocery suppliers, such as Kellogg and General Mills, get the most visible spots. But visibility to consumers sometimes comes at a price, often via a practice called *slotting allowances*, or *slotting fees*— money paid by producers to retailers to guarantee a priority display of their merchandise. According to retailers, the purpose of slotting allowances is to cover their losses if products don't sell. When the Federal Trade Commission (FTC) investigated the practice of slotting allowances, it found these fees vary greatly across product categories. In addition, a new trend regarding slotting allowances is emerging: Growth in the private-label goods category has been so great over the past few years that retailers are willing to forfeit allowances they might receive so they can get into the manufacturing end themselves. This is particularly true of private-label organic and ethnic foods.

Shopping Products

In contrast to the purchase of convenience items, consumers buy **shopping products** only after comparing competing offerings on such characteristics as price, quality, style, and color. Shopping products typically cost more than convenience purchases. This category includes tangible items— such as clothing, furniture, electronics, and appliances—as well as services like child care, auto repairs, insurance, and hotel stays. The purchaser of a shopping product lacks complete information prior to the buying trip and gathers information during the buying process.

Several important features distinguish shopping products: physical attributes; service attributes, such as warranties and after-sale service terms; prices; styling; and places of purchase. A store's name and reputation have considerable influence on people's buying behavior. The personal selling efforts of salespeople also provide important promotional support.

---

impulse goods and services Products purchased on the spur of the moment.

staples Convenience goods and services consumers constantly replenish to maintain a ready inventory.

emergency goods and services Products bought in response to unexpected and urgent needs.

shopping products Products consumers purchase after comparing competing offerings.

Emergency goods and services, such as this battery-powered lantern, are purchased in response to urgent needs.

Buyers and marketers treat some shopping products, such as microwave ovens and washing machines, as relatively homogeneous products. To the consumer, one brand seems largely the same as another. Marketers may try to differentiate homogeneous products from competing products in several ways. They may emphasize price and value, or they may attempt to educate buyers about less-obvious features that contribute to a product's quality, appeal, and uniqueness.

Other shopping products seem heterogeneous because of basic differences among them. Examples include furniture, physical-fitness training, vacations, and clothing. Differences in features often separate competing heterogeneous shopping products in the minds of consumers. Perceptions of style, color, and fit can all affect consumer choices.

Specialty Products

specialty products
Products with unique characteristics that cause buyers to prize those particular brands.

Specialty products offer unique characteristics that cause buyers to prize those particular brands. They typically carry high prices, and many represent well-known brands. Examples of specialty goods include Hermès scarves, Kate Spade handbags, Ritz-Carlton resorts, Tiffany jewelry, and Ducati motorcycles. Specialty services include professional services such as financial advice, legal counsel, and cosmetic surgery.

Purchasers of specialty goods and services know exactly what they want—and they are willing to pay accordingly. See the "Marketing Success" feature to find out how one consumer who knew what car she wanted was able to drive it free for 24 hours. These buyers begin shopping with complete information, and they refuse to accept substitutes. Because consumers are willing to exert considerable effort to obtain specialty products, producers can promote them through relatively few retail locations. In fact, some firms intentionally limit the range of retailers carrying their products to add to their cachet. Both highly personalized service by sales associates and image advertising help marketers promote specialty items. Because these products are available in so few retail outlets, advertisements frequently list their locations or give toll-free telephone numbers that provide customers with this information.

MARKETING SUCCESS
Audi Goes Social to Promote Brand

Background. A woman in Washington, DC, was so sold on Audi's marketing campaign for its R8 model that she started a Twitter campaign using the hashtag #WantAnR8. Audi took note of the woman's high Klout scores and sent a brand-new R8 to her home, lending her the car to drive for 24 hours.

The Challenge. "These kinds of opportunities are out there for marketers," said Audi's CMO. What Audi needed to do was figure out how to make the most of it.

The Strategy. Audi asked Twitter users whether they would like an R8 as well, and 75,000 people around the country said yes, so the company created a contest enabling four more people to drive an R8 for the day. The automaker used the promotion for two consecutive years, looking for creativity in the eight winning submissions, which can now include photos and videos, and adding a second prize option—a trip for two to an R8 One-Day Program at Infineon Raceway. Audi also put together a 30-second television spot (available on YouTube) to publicize the promotion.

The Outcome. "Why not merge the social and real world and make dreams come true?" asks Audi's CMO. Audi's inventive promotion may achieve even more. The company has more than 9 million "likes" on its Facebook page.

Sources: Annie White, "Who Wants to Drive an Audi R8?" *JeanKnowsCars.com*, accessed March 13, 2014, www.jeanknowscars.com; company website, "Audi @ WantAnR8 Contest Returns, Putting Fans in the Director's Chair for a Chance to Win a Day with the 2014 Audi R8," press release, www.audiusa.com, accessed March 13, 2014; "#WantAnR8 Contest Returns, Putting Fans in the Director's Chair for a Chance to Win a Day with the Audi 2014 R8," *Audizine.com*, accessed March 13, 2014, www.audizine.com; "Audi Giving Tweeting Fans R8 for a Day…Will You Be Next?" *Auto Blog*, accessed March 13, 2014, www.autoblog.com.

In recent years, makers of some specialty products, such as Coach handbags and Salvatore Ferragamo shoes, have broadened their market by selling some of their goods through company-owned discount outlets. The stores attract consumers who want to own specialty items but who cannot or do not wish to pay their regular prices. The goods offered are usually last season's styles. Tiffany has taken a different approach—broadening its base within its own store. Shoppers who visit the store on Fifth Avenue in New York City can take the elevator to the second floor, where they may purchase a variety of items in sterling silver at prices significantly lower than those for gold and gemstone jewelry. A number of these items are also available in Tiffany's mail-order catalog.

CLASSIFYING CONSUMER SERVICES

Like tangible goods, services are also classified based on the convenience, shopping, and specialty products categories. Companies also may examine several additional factors unique to classifying services. Service firms may serve consumer markets, business markets, or both. A firm offering architectural services may design either residential or commercial buildings or both. A cleaning service may clean houses, offices, or both. In addition, services can be classified as equipment based or people based. A car wash is an equipment-based service, whereas a law office is people based. Marketers may ask themselves any of these five questions to help classify certain services:

1. What is the nature of the service?
2. What type of relationship does the service organization have with its customers?
3. How much flexibility is there for customization and judgment on the part of the service provider?
4. Do demand and supply for the service fluctuate?
5. How is the service delivered?[10]

A person attempting to classify the activities of a boarding kennel would answer these questions in one way; a person evaluating a lawn-care service would come up with different answers. For example, customers would bring their pets to the kennel to receive service, while the lawn-care staff would travel to customers' homes to provide service. Workers at the kennel are likely to have closer interpersonal relationships with pet owners—and their pets—than lawn-care workers, who might not meet their customers at all. Someone assessing demand for the services of a ski resort or a food concession at the beach is likely to find fluctuations by season. And a dentist has flexibility in making decisions about a patient's care, whereas a delivery service must arrive with a package at the correct destination, on time.

Shoppers who visit the Tiffany & Company store in New York will notice a large variety of items at lower prices than those for gold and diamond jewelry.

TABLE 12.1 Marketing Impact of the Consumer Products Classification System

	Convenience Product	Shopping Product	Specialty Product
Consumer Factors			
Planning time involved in purchase	Very little	Considerable	Extensive
Purchase frequency	Frequent	Less frequent	Infrequent
Importance of convenient location	Critical	Important	Unimportant
Comparison of price and quality	Very little	Considerable	Very little
Marketing Mix Factors			
Price	Low	Relatively high	High
Importance of seller's image	Unimportant	Very important	Important
Distribution channel length	Long	Relatively short	Short
Number of sales outlets	Many	Few	Very few
Promotion	Advertising and promotion by producer	Personal selling and advertising by producer and retailer	Personal selling and advertising by producer and retailer

APPLYING THE CONSUMER PRODUCTS CLASSIFICATION SYSTEM

The three-way classification system of convenience, shopping, and specialty goods and services helps guide marketers in developing a successful marketing strategy. Buyer behavior patterns differ for the three types of purchases. For example, classifying a new food item as a convenience product leads to insights about marketing needs in branding, promotion, pricing, and distribution decisions. Table 12.1 summarizes the impact of this classification system on the development of an effective marketing mix.

The classification system also poses a few problems. The major obstacle to implementing this system results from the suggestion that all goods and services must fit within one of the three categories. Some fit neatly into one category, but others share characteristics of more than one. How would you classify the purchase of a new automobile? Before classifying the expensive good, which is handled by only a few dealers in the area as a specialty product, consider other characteristics. New-car buyers often shop extensively among competing models and dealers before deciding on the best deal, and they have a wide range of models, features, and prices to consider. At one end of the spectrum is a basic car like a Nissan Versa or a Chevy Spark that could be purchased for under $13,000. At the other end is what people are calling European supercars, such as the Lamborghini Veneno roadster, starting at $4.5 million, or the hybrid gas–electric Porsche 918 Spyder, priced at $845,000. These cars are fast, powerful, and hard to find—which boosts their value.[11]

Think of the categorization process in terms of a continuum representing degrees of effort expended by consumers. At one end of the continuum, consumers casually pick up convenience items; at the other end, they search extensively for specialty products. Shopping products fall between these extremes. In addition, car dealers may offer services both during and after the sale that play a big role in the purchase decision. On this continuum, the new-car purchase might appear between the categories of shopping and specialty products but closer to specialty products.

A second problem with the classification system emerges because consumers differ in their buying patterns. One person may walk into a hair salon and request a haircut without an appointment, while another may check references and compare prices before selecting a stylist. The first consumer's impulse purchase of a haircut does not make hair styling services a convenience item, however. Marketers classify goods and services by considering the purchase patterns of the majority of buyers.

ASSESSMENT CHECK

4.1 What are the three major classifications of consumer products?

4.2 Identify five factors marketers should consider in classifying consumer services.

TYPES OF BUSINESS PRODUCTS

Business buyers are professional customers. Their job duties require rational, cost-effective purchase decisions. For instance, General Mills applies much of the same purchase decision process to buying flour that Kellogg's does.

The classification system for business products emphasizes product uses rather than customer buying behavior. B2B products generally fall into one of six categories for product uses: installations, accessory equipment, component parts and materials, raw materials, supplies, and business services. Figure 12.4 illustrates the six types of business products.

> Identify the six types of business goods and services.

Installations

The specialty products of the business market are called **installations**. This classification includes major capital investments for new factories and heavy machinery and for telecommunications systems. Purchases of Boeing's 787 Dreamliner airplanes by Qantas and Kenya Airways are considered installations for those airlines.

Because installations last for long periods of time and their purchases involve large sums of money, they represent major decisions for organizations. Negotiations often extend over several months and involve numerous decision makers. Vendors often provide technical expertise along with tangible goods. Representatives who sell custom-made equipment work closely with buying firms' engineers and production personnel to design the most satisfactory products possible.

Price typically does not dominate purchase decisions for installations, although a recent order for 234 Airbus jets by the Indonesia-based carrier Lion Air totaled a record $24 billion.[12] A purchasing firm buys such a product for its efficiency and performance over its useful life. The firm also wants to minimize breakdowns. Downtime is expensive because the firm must pay employees while they wait for repairs on a machine. In addition, customers may be lost during downtime; in this case, travelers might choose to fly with another airline. Installations are major investments often designed specifically for the purchasers. Training of the buyer's workforce to operate the equipment correctly, along with significant after-sale service, is usually also involved. As a result, marketers of these systems typically focus their promotional efforts on employing highly trained sales representatives, often

installations Major capital investments in the B2B market.

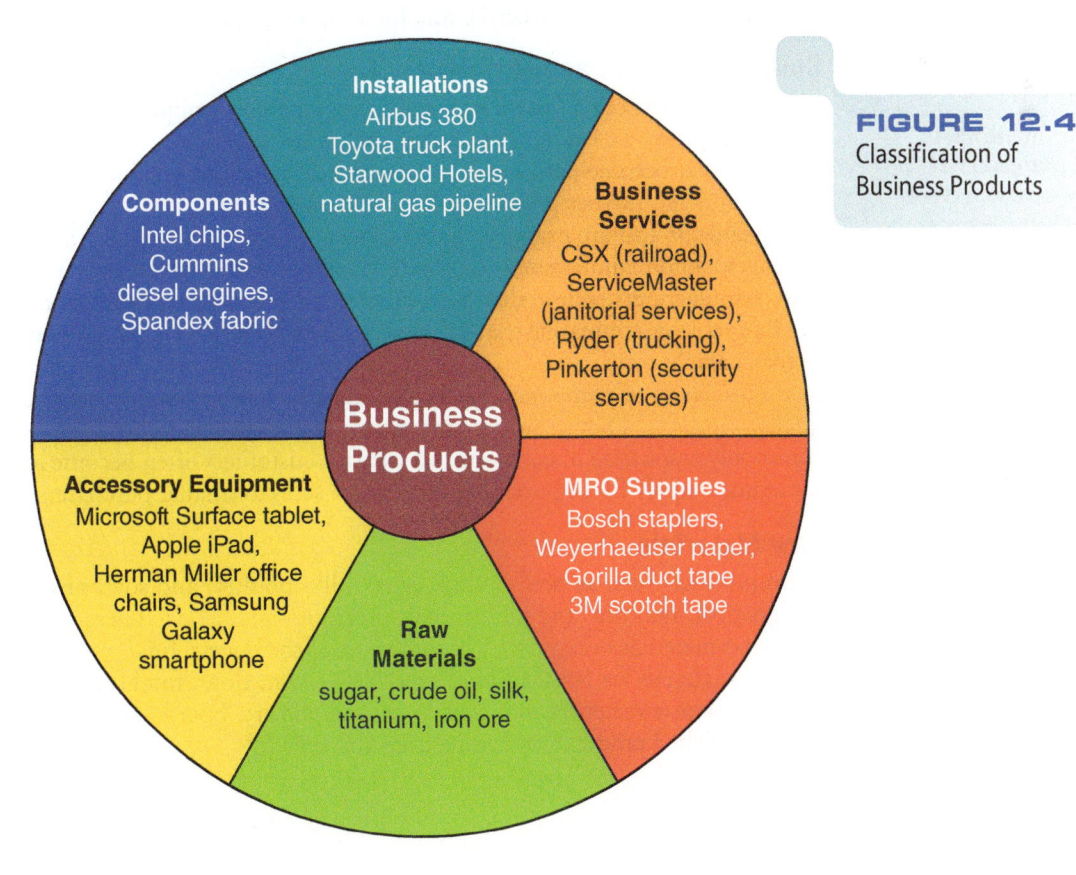

FIGURE 12.4
Classification of Business Products

- **Installations**: Airbus 380, Toyota truck plant, Starwood Hotels, natural gas pipeline
- **Business Services**: CSX (railroad), ServiceMaster (janitorial services), Ryder (trucking), Pinkerton (security services)
- **MRO Supplies**: Bosch staplers, Weyerhaeuser paper, Gorilla duct tape, 3M scotch tape
- **Raw Materials**: sugar, crude oil, silk, titanium, iron ore
- **Accessory Equipment**: Microsoft Surface tablet, Apple iPad, Herman Miller office chairs, Samsung Galaxy smartphone
- **Components**: Intel chips, Cummins diesel engines, Spandex fabric

Indonesia-based Lion Air recently bought an installation—a major capital investment—by purchasing the first Airbus jets for its fleet.

with technical backgrounds. Advertising, if the firm uses it at all, emphasizes company reputation and directs potential buyers to contact local sales representatives.

Most installations are marketed directly from manufacturers to users. Even a one-time sale may require continuing contacts for regular product servicing. Some manufacturers prefer to lease extremely expensive installations to customers rather than sell the items outright, and they assign personnel directly to the lessees' sites to operate or maintain the equipment.

Accessory Equipment

accessory equipment Capital items, such as desktop computers and printers, that typically cost less and last for shorter periods than installations.

Only a few decision makers may participate in a purchase of **accessory equipment**—capital items that typically cost less and last for shorter periods than installations. Although quality and service exert important influences on purchases of accessory equipment, price may significantly affect these decisions. Accessory equipment includes products such as power tools, computers, smartphones, and office furniture. Although these products are considered capital investments and buyers depreciate their costs over several years, their useful lives are generally much shorter than those of installations.

industrial distributor Channel intermediary that takes title to goods it handles and then distributes these goods to retailers, other distributors, or business or B2B customers; also called a *wholesaler*.

Marketing these products requires continuous representation and dealing with the widespread geographic dispersion of purchasers. To cope with these market characteristics, a wholesaler—often called an **industrial distributor**—might be used to contact potential customers in its own geographic area. Customers usually do not require technical assistance, and a manufacturer of accessory equipment can often distribute its products effectively through wholesalers. Advertising is an important component in the marketing mix for accessory equipment.

Component Parts and Materials

component parts and materials Finished business products of one producer that become part of the final products of another producer.

Whereas business buyers use installations and accessory equipment in the process of producing their own final products, **component parts and materials** represent finished business products of one producer that become part of the final products of another producer. Some materials—for example, flour—undergo further processing before becoming part of finished products. Textiles, paper pulp, and chemicals also are examples of component parts and materials. Bose supplies its luxury sound systems to auto manufacturers like Audi, Cadillac, Infiniti, Maserati, and Porsche. Marketers for the auto manufacturers believe that Bose systems are a good match between premium sound and their top-line vehicles, comparing the high performance of the Bose sound systems to the high performance of their cars.[13]

Purchasers of component parts and materials need regular, continuous supplies of uniform-quality products. They generally contract to purchase these items for set periods of time. Marketers commonly emphasize direct sales, and satisfied customers often become regular buyers. Wholesalers sometimes supply fill-in purchases and handle sales to smaller purchasers.

Raw Materials

raw materials Natural resources, such as farm products, coal, copper, or lumber that become part of a final product.

Farm products such as beef, cotton, eggs, milk, poultry, and soybeans, and natural resources like coal, copper, iron ore, and lumber, constitute **raw materials**. These products resemble component parts and materials because they become part of the buyers' final products. Cargill supplies many of the raw materials for finished food products—corn, flour, food starch, oils and shortenings, cocoa and chocolate, sweeteners, and beef, pork, and poultry. Food manufacturers then turn these materials into finished products, including cake and bread.[14]

See the "Solving an Ethical Controversy" feature to find out what happened when one cereal company discovered that consumers don't distinguish between "natural" and "organic" ingredients.

Most raw materials carry grades determined according to set criteria, assuring purchasers of the receipt of standardized products of uniform quality. As with component parts and materials, vendors commonly market raw materials directly to buying organizations. Wholesalers are increasingly involved in purchasing raw materials from foreign suppliers.

Price is seldom a deciding factor in a raw materials purchase because the costs are often set at central markets; this ensures virtually identical transactions among competing sellers. Purchasers buy raw materials from the firms they consider best able to deliver the required quantities and qualities.

Supplies

If installations represent the specialty products of the business market, operating supplies represent its convenience products. **Supplies** constitute the regular expenses a firm incurs in its daily operations. These expenses do not become part of the buyer's final products.

supplies Regular expenses a firm incurs in its daily operations.

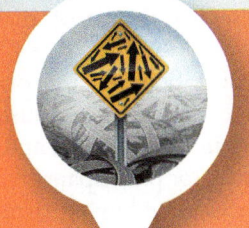

SOLVING AN ETHICAL CONTROVERSY
Natural vs. Organic: Who Is Responsible for Knowing the Difference?

Buyers of Kashi brand cereal were recently shocked to realize that the product, billed as "natural" by its maker, Kellogg Co., contained nonorganic soybeans, genetically modified as protection against a popular weed killer. An organic grocer in Rhode Island took the cereal off the shelves, and the news quickly went viral, resulting in an online uproar to which Kashi responded with a Facebook video. Kashi said it did not violate consumers' trust by labeling its product "natural," which it defines as minimally processed without artificial ingredients. The use of the term "organic," on the other hand, is federally regulated and excludes products with genetically engineered ingredients. Kashi did not call its cereal organic.

Are companies responsible for noting the difference between natural and organic in their products?

PRO
1. Consumers want wholesome products, and companies that want their business should be up-front about what is in their products.
2. Companies are taking advantage of consumers' confusion about the difference between "natural" and "organic."

CON
1. Consumers should educate themselves about what "organic" means under the law.
2. The Food and Drug Administration does not regulate the word "natural," so companies can define it as they wish.

Summary

Kashi is working with the Non-GMO Project, a not-for-profit organization that promotes non-genetically modified foods, to certify its all-natural products. Meanwhile, "natural" can mean whatever anyone wants it to.

Sources: Organization website, www.nongmoproject.org, accessed March 13, 2014; Candice Choi, "Has Kashi Lost Its Cool?" *Associated Press*, accessed March 13, 2014, www.mercurynews.com ; Tara Dodrill, "Is Your All-Natural Cereal Made from GMO Corn?" *Off The Grid News*, accessed March 13, 2014, www.offthegridnews.com ; Lance Johnson, "Are GMO Foods Safe?" *Natural News*, accessed March 13, 2014, www.naturalnews.com ; Lindsey Blomberg, "GMOs and Pesticides Found in Kashi Cereal," *EMagazine.com*, accessed March 13, 2014, www.emagazine.com.

MRO items Business supplies that include maintenance items, repair items, and operating supplies.

Supplies are also called **MRO items** because they fall into three categories: (1) maintenance items such as brooms, filters, and light bulbs; (2) repair items such as nuts and bolts used in repairing equipment; and (3) operating supplies such as printer paper and cartridges, mouse batteries, and pens. Office Max sells all kinds of supplies to small, medium, and large businesses. Companies can purchase everything from paper and labels to filing cabinets, lighting, office furniture, computers, and copiers. The firm also offers printing and binding services, downloadable forms, and more.[15]

A purchasing manager regularly buys operating supplies as a routine job duty. Wholesalers often facilitate sales of supplies because of the low unit prices, the small order size, and the large number of potential buyers. Because supplies are relatively standardized, heavy price competition frequently keeps costs under control. However, a business buyer spends little time making decisions about these products. Exchanges of products involve simple telephone orders, Web or EDI orders, or regular purchases from a sales representative of a local wholesaler.

Business Services

business services Intangible products firms buy to facilitate their production and operating processes.

The **business services** category includes the intangible products firms buy to facilitate their production and operating processes. Examples of business services are financial services, leasing and rental services that supply equipment and vehicles, insurance, security, legal advice, and consulting. As mentioned earlier, many service providers sell the same services to both consumers and organizational buyers—telephone, gas, and electricity, for example—although service firms may maintain separate marketing groups for the two customer segments.

Organizations also purchase many adjunct services that assist their operations but are not essentially a part of the final product. Cisco Systems offers its TelePresence meeting service to businesses seeking to link people in a single interactive conference. The service combines voice, data, and video on the same network, providing an interactive and collaborative experience for participants.[16]

Price may strongly influence purchase decisions for business services. The buying firm must decide whether to purchase a service or provide that service internally. This decision may depend on how frequently the firm needs the service and the specialized knowledge required to provide it. In the case of TelePresence, firms may decide the cost of the service is offset by savings in travel expenses for meeting participants. In addition, the service offers convenience.

Purchase decision processes vary considerably for different types of business services. A firm may purchase window-cleaning services through a routine and straightforward process similar to buying operating supplies. By contrast, a purchase decision for highly specialized environmental engineering advice requires complex analysis and perhaps lengthy negotiations similar to purchases of installations. This variability of the marketing mix for business services and other business products is outlined in Table 12.2.

TABLE 12.2 Marketing Impact of the Business Products Classification System

Factor	Installations	Accessory Equipment	Component Parts and Materials	Raw Materials	Supplies	Business Services
Organizational						
Planning time	Extensive	Less extensive	Less extensive	Varies	Very little	Varies
Purchase frequency	Infrequent	More frequent	Frequent	Infrequent	Frequent	Varies
Comparison of price and quality	Quality very important	Quality and price important	Quality important	Quality important	Price important	Varies
Marketing Mix						
Price	High	Relatively high	Low to high	Low to high	Low	Varies
Distribution channel length	Very short	Relatively short	Short	Short	Long	Varies
Promotion method	Personal selling by producer	Advertising	Personal selling	Personal selling	Advertising by producer	Varies

Cisco Systems offers its TelePresence meeting service to businesses to link people from around the world in a single interactive conference.

The purchase of the right business services can make a difference in a firm's competitiveness. The Regus Group provides businesses with facilities for meetings and conferences in 750 cities across 100 countries. The firm's more than 2,000 business centers are fully furnished and equipped with every electronic medium and amenity a business could possibly need and are staffed by trained support personnel. Regus serves large and small companies, including those relying on mobile and home-based workers. The firm's services allow businesses to customize their office and meeting needs while saving money during periods when office space is not necessary.[17]

ASSESSMENT CHECK

5.1 What are the six main classifications of business products?

5.2 What are the three categories of supplies?

QUALITY AS A PRODUCT STRATEGY

No matter how a product is classified, nothing is more frustrating to a customer than having a new item break after just a few uses or having it not live up to expectations. The cell phone that hisses static at you unless you stand still or the seam that rips out of your new jacket aren't life-altering experiences, but they do leave an impression of poor quality that likely may lead you to make different purchases in the future. Then there's the issue of service quality—the department store that seems to have no salespeople, or the computer help line that leaves you on hold for 20 minutes.

Quality is a key component to a firm's success in a competitive marketplace. The efforts to create and market high-quality goods and services have been referred to as **total quality management (TQM)**. TQM expects all of a firm's employees to continually improve products and work processes with the goal of achieving customer satisfaction and world-class performance. This means engineers design products that work, marketers develop products people want, and salespeople deliver on their promises. Managers are responsible for communicating the goals of total quality management to all staff members and for encouraging workers to improve themselves and take pride in their work. Of course, achieving maximum quality is easier said than done, and the process is never complete. Many companies solicit reviews or feedback from customers to improve their goods and services.

Discuss how marketers use quality as a product strategy.

total quality management (TQM) Continuous effort to improve products and work processes with the goal of achieving customer satisfaction and world-class performance.

WORLDWIDE QUALITY PROGRAMS

Although the movement began in the United States in the 1920s as an attempt to increase product quality by improving the manufacturing process, the quality revolution did not pick up speed in U.S. corporations until the 1980s. The campaign to improve quality found the leaders at large manufacturing firms—such as Ford, Xerox, and Motorola—had lost market share to Japanese competitors. Smaller companies that supplied parts to large firms then began to recognize quality as a requirement for success. Today, commitment to quality has spread to service industries, not-for-profit organizations, government agencies, and educational institutions.

Congress established the Malcolm Baldrige National Quality Award to recognize excellence in quality management. Named after the late secretary of commerce Malcolm Baldrige, the award is the highest national recognition for quality a U.S. company can receive. The award works toward promoting quality awareness, recognizing quality achievements of U.S. companies, and publicizing successful quality strategies.

The quality movement is also strong in European countries. The European Union's **ISO 9001:2008** standards define international, generic criteria for quality management and quality assurance. Originally developed by the International Organization for Standardization in Switzerland to ensure consistent quality among products manufactured and sold throughout the European Union (EU), the standards now include criteria for systems of management as well. Although most other ISO standards are specific to particular products or processes, ISO 9001 applies to any organization, regardless of the goods or services it produces. Many European companies require suppliers to achieve ISO certification, a rigorous process that takes several months to complete, as a condition of doing business with them. The U.S. member body of ISO is the National Institute of Standards and Technology (NIST).[18]

ISO 9001:2008 Standards developed by the International Organization for Standardization based in Switzerland to ensure consistent quality management and quality assurance for goods and services throughout the European Union.

BENCHMARKING

Firms often rely on an important tool called benchmarking to set performance standards. The purpose of **benchmarking** is to achieve superior performance that results in a competitive advantage in the marketplace. A typical benchmarking process involves three main activities: identifying manufacturing or business processes that need improvement, comparing internal processes to those of industry leaders, and implementing changes for quality improvement. The practice of benchmarking has been around for a long time. Henry Ford is known to have developed his own version of the assembly line—an improvement to gain competitive advantage—by observing the way meat-packing plants processed their meat products.[19]

Benchmarking requires two types of analyses: internal and external. Before a company can compare itself with another, it must first analyze its own activities to determine strengths and weaknesses. This assessment establishes a baseline for comparison. External analysis involves gathering information about the benchmark partner to find out why the partner is perceived as the industry's best. A comparison of the results of the analysis provides an objective basis for making improvements. From time to time, firms of all sizes—particularly large firms—benchmark their operations and practices against their competitors and other players in their industry. Often, organizations follow a formal, complex program, but benchmarking can also take a simpler, more informal approach as well.

benchmarking Method of measuring quality by comparing performance against industry leaders.

> **Briefly Speaking**
>
> "Your premium brand had better be delivering something special, or it's not going to get the business."
>
> —Warren Buffett
> *American business magnate, investor, and philanthropist*

QUALITY OF SERVICES

Everyone has a story about bad and good service—the waiter who lost a dinner order, a car mechanic who offered a ride to and from the repair shop. As a consumer, your perception of the quality of the service you have purchased is usually determined during the **service encounter**—the point at which the customer and service provider interact. Employees such as bank tellers, cashiers, and customer service representatives have a powerful impact on their customers' decision to return or not. You might pass the word to your friends about the friendly staff at your local breakfast eatery, the slow cashiers at a local supermarket, or the huge scoops of ice cream

service encounter Point at which the customer and service provider interact.

you got at the nearby ice cream stand. Those words form powerful marketing messages about the services you received.

Service quality refers to the expected and perceived quality of a service offering, and it has a huge effect on the competitiveness of a company. Online retailer Zappos.com (now part of Amazon) built its business on delivering exceptional customer service by, among other things, providing free shipping, maintaining a 365-day return policy, and paying rigorous attention to hiring only those whose passion for customer service matched the company's high standards. The decision to focus on customer service rather than on marketing enabled Zappos to grow to a billion-dollar company. In fact, consumers regularly name Zappos number one in customer service.[20]

Poor service can cut into a firm's competitiveness. When server problems hit an Amazon data center recently, its cloud computing platform shut down. The outage also brought down several websites that rent cloud space from Amazon: Instagram, Vine, and others. In all, the sites were out of commission, or at least partly disabled, for about an hour. Although Amazon issued an apology and explanation, this latest outage and other past events underscored the unreliability of cloud computing.[21] Deserved or not, consumers often perceive such technology glitches as customer-service problems and, dissatisfied, they may begin to seek alternatives.

Service quality is determined by five variables:

1. *Tangibles*, or physical evidence. A tidy office and clean uniforms are examples.

2. *Reliability*, or consistency of performance and dependability. "The right technology. Right away," asserts software-solutions provider CDW.

3. *Responsiveness*, or the readiness to serve. "Citi never sleeps," say the ads for the banking giant.

4. *Assurances*, or the confidence communicated by the service provider. "Let your worries go," reassures Northwestern Mutual, an investment and insurance firm.

5. *Empathy*, which shows the service provider understands customers' needs and is ready to fulfill them. "Lift your spirits," says Canyon Ranch Resorts, a popular health spa.

A gap that exists between the level of service customers expect and the level they think they received can be favorable or unfavorable. If you get a larger steak than you expected, or your plane arrives ahead of schedule, the gap is favorable, and you are likely to try that service again. If your steak is tiny, overcooked, and cold, or your plane is two hours late, the gap is unfavorable,

Customers expect the items they purchase online to arrive in a timely manner.

service quality Expected and perceived quality of a service offering.

> **Briefly Speaking**
>
> "A brand is a living entity—and it is enriched or undermined cumulatively over time, the product of a thousand small gestures."
>
> —**Michael Eisner**
> *American businessman and former CEO, Walt Disney Company*

CAREER READINESS
Email: Think Before You Send

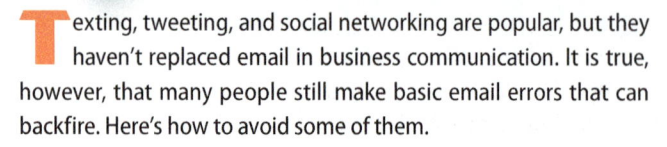

Texting, tweeting, and social networking are popular, but they haven't replaced email in business communication. It is true, however, that many people still make basic email errors that can backfire. Here's how to avoid some of them.

1. Be concise and use good grammar. Avoid abbreviations and jargon, and watch your tone. Sarcasm and humor are easily misunderstood.
2. Proofread everything.
3. Never send an email that you would be embarrassed to see on the front page of a newspaper. If you're angry, wait an hour before writing anything, and then think twice before sending it. You never know who is storing your message.
4. Make one point per email; many readers don't notice the second or third. If you must make more than one point, use a bulleted list.
5. Give your message a clear subject line so your recipient can prioritize incoming messages.
6. Be cautious about forwarding other people's emails, about blind copying others on your emails, and about hitting the infamous "Reply all" button.
7. Never forward chain emails.
8. Answer incoming email promptly and completely.
9. Finally, remember the human touch. A phone call or quick visit to someone's office can be more effective than a long, complicated email.

Sources: "101 Email Etiquette Tips," *I Studio*, accessed March 13, 2014, www.101emailetiquettetips.com; "12 Tips for Better E-Mail Etiquette," *Office.com*, accessed March 13, 2014, http://office.microsoft.com; Virginia Tech Division of Student Affairs, "E-Mail Guidelines and Etiquette," accessed March 13, 2014, www.career.vt.edu; "37 Tips for Writing Emails That Get Opened, Read, and Clicked," *Copyblogger.com*, accessed March 13, 2014, www.copyblogger.com.

ASSESSMENT CHECK

6.1 What is TQM?
6.2 What are the five variables of service quality?

and you may seek out another restaurant or decide to drive the next time. Emails are another way in which customers judge a company's service. See the "Career Readiness" feature for some tips about sending effective emails, both within and outside the company.

DEVELOPMENT OF PRODUCT LINES

> **7** Explain why firms develop lines of related products.

Few firms today market only one product. A typical firm offers its customers a **product line**—that is, a series of related products. The motivations for marketing complete product lines rather than concentrating on a single product include the desire to grow, enhancing the company's position in the market, optimal use of company resources, and exploiting the product lifecycle. The following subsections examine each of the first three reasons. The final reason, exploiting the stages of the product lifecycle, is discussed in the section that focuses on strategic implications of the product lifecycle concept.

product line Series of related products offered by one company.

DESIRE TO GROW

A company limits its growth potential when it concentrates on a single product, even though the company may have started that way, as retailer L.L.Bean did with its single style of boots called

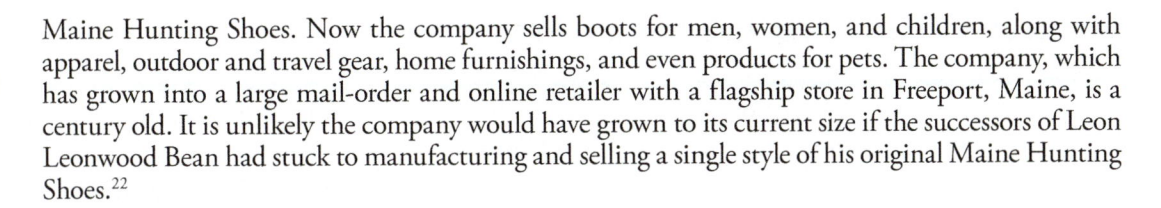

Maine Hunting Shoes. Now the company sells boots for men, women, and children, along with apparel, outdoor and travel gear, home furnishings, and even products for pets. The company, which has grown into a large mail-order and online retailer with a flagship store in Freeport, Maine, is a century old. It is unlikely the company would have grown to its current size if the successors of Leon Leonwood Bean had stuck to manufacturing and selling a single style of his original Maine Hunting Shoes.[22]

ENHANCING THE COMPANY'S MARKET POSITION

A company with a line of products often makes itself more important to both consumers and marketing intermediaries than a firm with only one product. A shopper who purchases a tent often buys related camping items. For instance, L.L.Bean now offers a wide range of products with which consumers can completely outfit themselves for outdoor activities or travel. They can purchase hiking boots, sleeping bags and tents, fishing gear, duffel bags, kayaks and canoes, bicycles, snowshoes and skis, as well as clothing for their adventures. In addition, the firm offers Outdoor Discovery Schools programs that teach customers the basics of kayaking, fly fishing, and other sports directly related to the products they purchase from the retailer. L.L.Bean also offers many of its products sized to fit children—from fleece vests to school backpacks.[23] If children grow up wearing L.L.Bean clothes and skiing on L.L.Bean skis, they are more likely to continue as customers when they become adults.

Servicing the variety of products a company sells can also enhance its position in the market. Bean's Outdoor Discovery Schools programs are a form of service, as are its policy to accept returns—no matter what. Schoolchildren who purchase the firm's backpacks can return them anytime for a new one—even if the child has simply outgrown the pack. Policies like this make consumers feel comfortable about purchasing many different products from L.L.Bean.

ASSESSMENT CHECK

7.1 List the four reasons for developing a product line.

7.2 Give an example of a product line with which you are familiar.

THE PRODUCT MIX

A company's **product mix** is its assortment of product lines and individual product offerings. The right blend of product lines and individual products allows a firm to maximize sales opportunities within the limitations of its resources. Marketers typically measure product mixes according to width, length, and depth.

> Describe the way marketers typically measure product mixes and make product mix decisions.
>
> **8**

product mix
Assortment of product lines and individual product offerings a company sells.

PRODUCT MIX WIDTH

The *width* of a product mix refers to the number of product lines the firm offers. Johnson & Johnson offers a broad line of retail consumer products in the U.S. market as well as business-to-business products to the medical community. Consumers can purchase prescription and over-the-counter medications, nutritional products, dental care products, and first-aid products, among others. Health-care professionals can prescribe prescription drugs and obtain medical and diagnostic devices, wound treatments. LifeScan, one of the firm's subsidiaries, offers an entire suite of products designed to help diabetes patients manage their condition. DePuy, another subsidiary, manufactures orthopedic implants and joint replacement products. At the drugstore, consumers can pick up some of J&J's classic products, such as Motrin and Visine.[24]

TABLE 12.3 Johnson & Johnson's Mix of Health Care Products

Over-the-Counter Medicines	Nutritionals	Skin and Hair Care	Oral Care	Medical Devices and Diagnostics
Motrin pain reliever	Lactaid digestive aid	Aveeno lotions	Listerine oral rinse	Ethicon surgical instruments and systems
Tylenol pain reliever	Splenda artificial sweetener	Clean & Clear facial cleansers and toners	REACH dental floss	LifeScan diabetes management products
Benadryl antihistamine	Viactiv calcium supplement	Johnson's baby shampoo	Rembrandt whitening toothpaste	Orthopedic joint replacement products
Mylanta antacid	Benecol	Neutrogena soaps and shampoos	Listerine whitening strips	Veridex diagnostic tests

Source: Company website, www.jnj.com, accessed March 13, 2014.

> **Briefly Speaking**
>
> "Success means never letting the competition define you. Instead, you have to define yourself based on a point of view you care deeply about."
>
> —**Tom Chappell**
> *American businessman and co-founder, Tom's of Maine*

PRODUCT MIX LENGTH

The *length* of a product mix refers to the number of different products a firm sells. Table 12.3 identifies some of the categories and a few of the hundreds of health care products offered by Johnson & Johnson. Some of J&J's most recognizable brands are Band-Aid, Tylenol, and Listerine.

PRODUCT MIX DEPTH

Depth refers to variations in each product the firm markets in its mix. Johnson & Johnson's Band-Aid brand bandages come in a variety of shapes and sizes, including Finger-Care Tough Strips, Comfort-Flex and Activ-Flex for elbows and knees, and Advance Healing Blister bandages.

PRODUCT MIX DECISIONS

Establishing and managing the product mix have become increasingly important marketing tasks. Adding depth, length, and width to the product mix requires careful thinking and planning; otherwise, a firm can end up with too many products, including some that don't sell well. To evaluate a firm's product mix, marketers look at the effectiveness of its depth, length, and width. Has the firm ignored a viable consumer segment? It may improve performance by increasing product-line depth to offer a product variation that will attract the new segment. Can the firm achieve economies in its sales and distribution efforts by adding complementary product lines to the mix? If so, a wider product mix may seem appropriate. Does the firm gain equal contributions from all items in its portfolio? If not, it may decide to lengthen or shorten the product mix to increase revenues. Italian shoe manufacturer Geox is known for its patented breathable fabric that keeps feet cool and comfortable. With annual sales near $1 billion, Geox is expanding both ways—in width and length. The firm offers trendy shoe styles including strappy sandals and retro-inspired high-top sneakers. In addition, Geox features apparel and shoe lines for men and children, made of similar breathable fabrics that help keep consumers cool and dry.[25]

Another way to add to the mix is to purchase a product line from another company or acquire an entire company through merger or acquisition. Entrepreneurial startup Nest Labs in Palo Alto, California, redesigned the traditional home thermostat to function as the hub of an energy-conserving home. Google had also entered the home-energy conservation space with its PowerMeter tool, but exited the market when PowerMeter didn't take off. Google recently acquired Nest Labs for $3.2 billion—effectively re-entering the smart home hardware and software space.[26]

A firm should assess its current product mix for another important reason: to determine the feasibility of a **line extension**. A line extension adds individual offerings that appeal to different market

line extension
Development of individual offerings that appeal to different market segments while remaining closely related to the existing product line.

segments while remaining closely related to the existing product line. Adidas currently markets a broad assortment of athletic goods for men, women, and children, from shoes for virtually any sport to apparel and accessories. In keeping with its focus on athleticism, Adidas recently introduced the Smart Run watch, a fitness device that—besides telling time—measures the wearer's steps; uses GPS to track routes, speed, and distance; monitors heart rate; and offers coaching tips. The watch even includes an earpiece and a built-in MP3 player.[27]

The marketing environment also plays a role in a marketer's evaluation of a firm's product mix and the decision to extend a product line. In the case of Adidas, several factors may have been in play: a rise in GPS technologies; a variety of sectors—from tech firms to automakers—introducing activity-tracking devices; continued interest in getting and staying healthy; and the recent surge in wearable technology.

Careful evaluation of a firm's current product mix can also help marketers make decisions about brand management and new-product introductions.

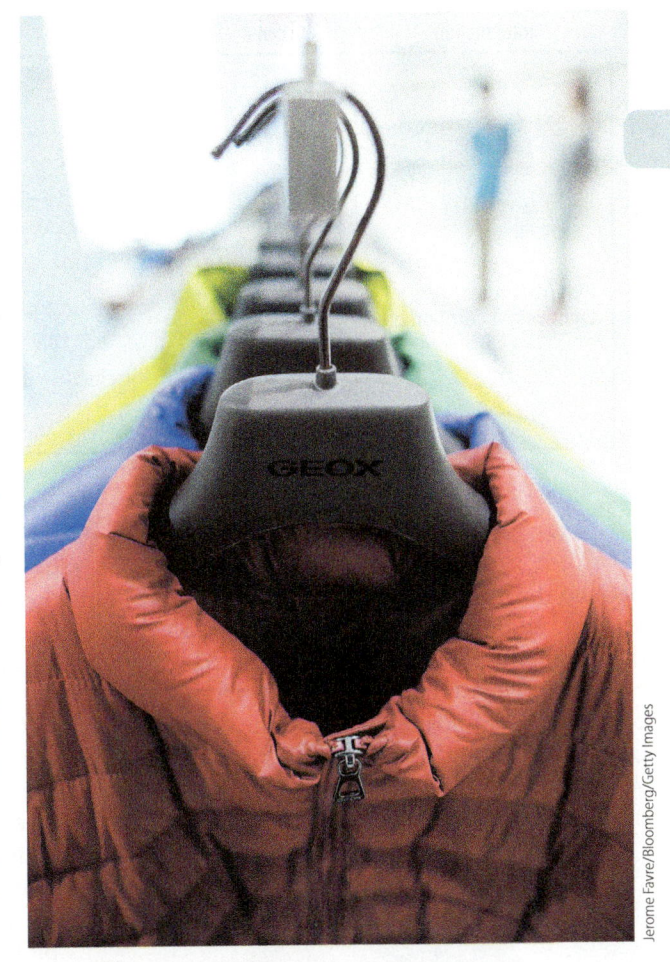

After successfully marketing to women, Geox expanded its product mix to include shoes and apparel for men and children.

ASSESSMENT CHECK

8.1. Define product mix.
8.2. How do marketers typically measure product mixes?

Chapter 13 examines the importance of branding, brand management, and the development and introduction of new products.

THE PRODUCT LIFECYCLE

Products, like people, pass through stages as they age. Successful products progress through four basic stages: introduction, growth, maturity, and decline. This progression, known as the **product lifecycle**, is shown in Figure 12.5.

The product lifecycle concept applies to products or product categories within an industry, not to individual brands. For instance, camera cell phones are moving rapidly from the introductory stage to the growth stage. Digital cameras are still in the growth stage but moving toward maturity. Film cameras have declined so much that it is difficult for consumers to purchase film for them. There is no set schedule or time frame for a particular stage of the lifecycle. CDs have been around for more than a quarter of a century but sales have been declining, in part due to the increase in digital music downloads.

Explain the four stages of the product lifecycle.

product lifecycle Progression of a product through introduction, growth, maturity, and decline stages.

INTRODUCTORY STAGE

During the **introductory stage** of the product lifecycle, a firm works to stimulate demand for the new-market entry. Merchandise in this stage might bring new technology to a product category.

introductory stage First stage of the product lifecycle, in which a firm works to stimulate sales of a new-market entry.

FIGURE 12.5
Stages in the Product Lifecycle

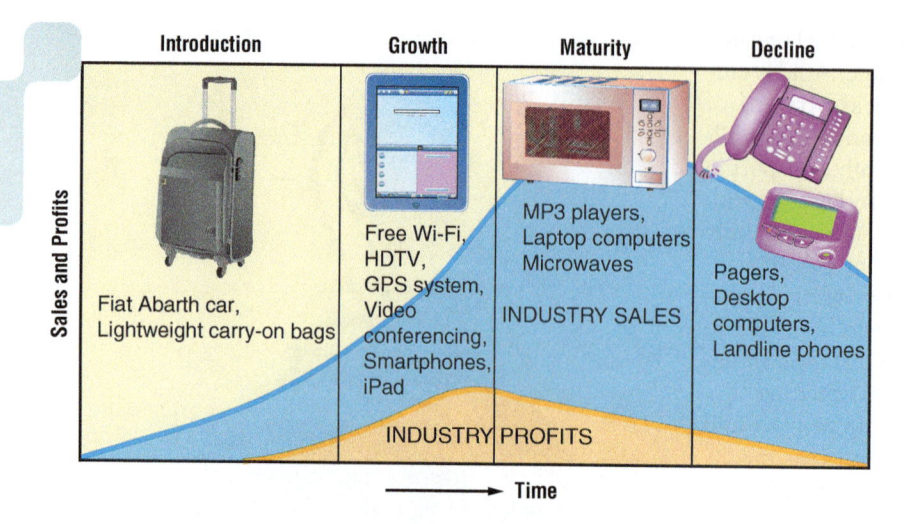

Introduction	Growth	Maturity	Decline
Fiat Abarth car, Lightweight carry-on bags	Free Wi-Fi, HDTV, GPS system, Video conferencing, Smartphones, iPad	MP3 players, Laptop computers, Microwaves	Pagers, Desktop computers, Landline phones

INDUSTRY SALES
INDUSTRY PROFITS
Sales and Profits → Time

Because the product is unknown to the public, promotional campaigns stress information about its features. Additional promotions try to induce distribution channel members to carry the product. In this phase, the public becomes acquainted with the item's merits and begins to accept it.

A product in the introductory stage is Google Glass, a lightweight, wearable Android-powered computer built into an eyeglass frame. Worn like a pair of eyeglasses, Google Glass features a small computer display that can be seen without obstructing the user's vision. Google Glass responds to voice commands and gestures, and taps on the frame. Bluetooth and Wi-Fi are built in, and a wealth of third-party developers are creating apps to make Google Glass even more versatile.[28]

Technical problems and financial losses are common during the introductory stage as companies fine-tune product design and spend money on advertising. Many users remember early problems with the Internet—jammed portals, order fulfilling glitches, dot-coms that went bust. But DVD players and camera phones experienced few of these setbacks. Users of GPS devices also reported some glitches but conceded that some problems stem from learning how to operate the devices correctly.

growth stage Second stage of the product lifecycle that begins when a firm starts to realize substantial profits from its investment in a product.

Google Glass, an Android-powered computer in an eyeglass frame, is in the introductory stage of the product lifecycle.

GROWTH STAGE

Sales volume rises rapidly during the growth stage as new customers make initial purchases and early buyers repurchase the product, such as camera phones and GPS devices. The **growth stage** usually begins when a firm starts to realize substantial profits from its investment. Word-of-mouth reports, mass advertising, and lowered prices all encourage hesitant buyers to make trial purchases of new products. In the case of big-screen TVs, low prices generally were not a factor. "Big screen" now refers to a TV that is about 60 inches. As sales volume rises, competitors enter the marketplace, creating new challenges for marketers. As LED models gradually replace plasma technology, companies with competing technologies vie for dominance; the TVs themselves grow larger, and prices continue to range widely. Shoppers can purchase a 60-inch Sharp LED HDTV for about $1,000, a 47-inch Sony LED HDTV with 3D for just under $1,100, or opt for the less-expensive 32-inch Sharp LED model at less than $300.[29]

MATURITY STAGE

Sales of a product category continue to grow during the early part of the **maturity stage**, but they eventually reach a plateau as the backlog of potential customers dwindles. By this time, many competitors have entered the market, and the firm's profits begin to decline as competition intensifies.

At this stage in the product lifecycle, differences between competing products diminish as competitors discover the product and promotional characteristics most desired by customers. Available supplies exceed industry demand for the first time. Companies can increase their sales and market shares only at the expense of competitors, so the competitive environment becomes increasingly important. In the maturity stage, heavy promotional outlays emphasize any differences still separating competing products, and brand competition intensifies. Some firms try to differentiate their products by focusing on attributes like quality, reliability, and service. Others focus on redesign or other ways of extending the product lifecycle.

Baltimore-based Marlin Steel manufactured one product for a single industry: wire baskets for bagel stores to display their wares. But competition from China was undercutting Marlin Steel on price: $6 for a Chinese-made basket, compared to Marlin's $12. "We were going to go extinct," says Marlin Steel CEO Drew Greenblatt—and then his company discovered demand for wire baskets in an altogether different industry: aerospace.

An inquiry from Boeing for precision made baskets to hold airplane parts helped change the way Marlin Steel did business. By expanding its target market to manufacturing, the company was able to fine-tune its operations and produce baskets to customers' precise specifications. In a decade, Marlin Steel grew from a small concern with a handful of customers to a multimillion-dollar firm with a broad array of manufacturing customers. (The bagel stores now account for less than half of 1 percent of its business.)[30]

DECLINE STAGE

In the **decline stage** of a product's life, innovations or shifts in consumer preferences bring about an absolute decline in industry sales. Dial telephones became touch-tone phones, which evolved into portable phones, which are now being replaced with conventional cell phones, which in turn are being replaced with camera phones. Thirty-five-millimeter home-movie film was replaced with videotape, which is now being replaced with DVD technology.

maturity stage Third stage of the product lifecycle, in which industry sales level out.

> **Briefly Speaking**
>
> "In business, you get what you want by giving other people what they want."
>
> —Alice Foote MacDougall
> *1920s American restaurateur*

decline stage Final stage of the product lifecycle, in which a decline in total industry sales occurs.

At the maturity stage in the product lifecycle, Marlin Steel was able to grow its business by expanding its target market to manufacturing and supply wire baskets to a broad range of customers.

Some manufacturers refuse to give up in the decline stage. Young consumers, accustomed to CDs and digital downloads, are beginning to turn their attention to vinyl records. They have discovered their parents' and grandparents' collections of LPs and have hauled old record turntables out of the attic. If curiosity led them to the discovery, the sound and graphics of a record seem to be holding their interest. Marketers in the music industry have taken notice, and some bands have begun to issue limited numbers of records along with CDs and MP3 formats. They don't expect vinyl to become the primary medium for music but are happy to resurrect a classic product for a new generation of listeners.[31] The next section of this chapter discusses more specific strategies for extending the lifecycle of a product.

It is important to remember that the traditional product lifecycle differs from fad cycles. Fashions and fads profoundly influence marketing strategies. Fashions are currently popular products that tend to follow recurring lifecycles. For example, bell-bottom pants popular in the 1960s and 1970s have returned as flares or boot-cut pants. In contrast, fads are products with abbreviated lifecycles. Most fads experience short-lived popularity and then quickly fade, although some maintain residual markets among certain segments. Webkinz (the stuffed animals that have their own online Webkinz World) are an example of a fad.

> **ASSESSMENT CHECK**
>
> 9.1 Identify the four stages of the product lifecycle.
>
> 9.2 During which stage or stages are products likely to attract the most new customers?

EXTENDING THE PRODUCT LIFECYCLE

10 Describe the four strategies for extending a product's lifecycle and why certain products may be eliminated.

Marketers usually try to extend each stage of the lifecycles for their products as long as possible. Product lifecycles can stretch indefinitely as a result of decisions designed to increase the frequency of use by current customers; increase the number of users for the product; find new uses; or change package sizes, labels, or product quality.

INCREASING FREQUENCY OF USE

During the maturity stage, the sales curve for a product category reaches a maximum point if the competitors exhaust the supply of potential customers who previously had not made purchases. If current customers buy more frequently than they formerly did, total sales will rise even though no new buyers enter the market.

For instance, consumers buy some products during certain seasons of the year. Marketers can boost purchase frequency by persuading these people to try the product year-round. For decades, most people used sunscreen only during warm and sunny seasons of the year. With greater warnings about the risks of sun damage and skin cancer, companies now advertise the benefits of using sunscreen year-round. In another change, Hershey now offers its famous Hershey's Kisses with personalized messages like "Congratulations," "It's a Boy," and "Happy Birthday" to celebrate personal events.

INCREASING THE NUMBER OF USERS

A second strategy for extending the product lifecycle seeks to increase the overall market size by attracting new customers who previously have not used the product. Marketers may find their products in different stages of the lifecycle in different countries. This difference can help firms extend product growth. Items that have reached the maturity stage in the United States may still be in the introductory stage somewhere else.

After years of operating exclusively in the United States and Canada, retail chain J.Crew recently opened three stores in London, with two stores scheduled for Hong Kong. Previously J.Crew's management believed expanding overseas would distract the company from its North American operations. Now the company sees stores in Europe and Asia as a way to grow sales.[32]

FINDING NEW USES

Finding new uses for a product is an excellent strategy for extending a product's lifecycle. New applications for mature products include oatmeal as a cholesterol reducer, antacids as a calcium supplement, and aspirin for promoting heart health.

Marketers sometimes conduct contests or surveys to identify new uses for their products. They may post the results or their own new ideas on their websites. Arm & Hammer's website lists dozens of alternative uses throughout the house for its baking soda. Consumers can use baking soda to clean crayon off walls, to fuel an "erupting volcano" science experiment, or as an agent to balance the pH in swimming pool water. The firm has even developed products for using baking soda in household tasks, such as a plastic shaker container and an air filter that adheres to the inside of the refrigerator.[33]

Changes in packaging can lengthen a product's lifecycle. Consider the new market for single-portion coffee pods used in single-cup brewing machines.

CHANGING PACKAGE SIZES, LABELS, OR PRODUCT QUALITY

Many firms try to extend their product lifecycles by introducing physical changes in their offerings. Alternatively, new packaging and labels with updated images and slogans can help revitalize a product. General Mills found a way to remodel the packaging for its iconic Cheerios brand and create a more sustainable design. Previously, Cheerios sold at club stores like Costco and BJ's Wholesale came in an oversized box with two bags of cereal inside; for many homes, the box was cumbersome and didn't fit on a pantry shelf. In addition, the bags contained a considerable amount of head space because the cereal would settle during transit. However, a new technology developed at General Mills permits the Cheerios to settle while still on the production line, allowing more dense packing. For club shoppers, the new package actually consists of two smaller, detachable boxes—easier to store and serve. The new design also saves paperboard and allows more boxes to fit on a truck.[34]

Changes in packaging can lengthen a product's lifecycle. Food marketers have brought out small packages designed to appeal to one-person households and extra-large containers for customers who want to buy in bulk. Other firms offer their products in convenient packages for use away from home or at the office. The popularity of the Keurig single-cup brewing machine has skyrocketed, leading numerous coffee sellers to introduce "K-cup" portions of their brands. Starbucks was one such company that had inked a deal with Green Mountain Coffee Roasters—owners of the Keurig machine—to sell single-serve packs of Starbucks and Tazo coffees and teas. Starbucks later introduced its own single-serve brewing machine, the Verismo, which prepares espresso drinks, lattes, and chai tea as well as brewed coffee.[35]

PRODUCT DELETION DECISIONS

To avoid wasting resources promoting unpromising products, marketers must sometimes prune product lines and eliminate marginal products. Marketers typically face this decision during the late maturity and early decline stages of the product lifecycle. Periodic reviews of weak products should justify either eliminating or retaining them. After battling it out with Sony in the DVD player arena, Toshiba finally conceded defeat and announced it would stop making its HD DVD player. That left Sony the winner in the marketplace with its Blu-ray format.

A firm may continue to carry an unprofitable item to provide a complete line for its customers. Some grocery stores may lose money on bulky, low-unit-value items like salt, but they continue to carry these items to meet shopper demand.

Shortages of raw materials sometimes prompt companies to discontinue production and marketing of previously profitable items. A firm may even drop a profitable product that fails to fit into its existing line or doesn't fit the direction in which the firm wants to grow. Some of these so-called orphan brands return to the market when other firms purchase and relaunch them. In the largest relaunch in hotel history, InterContinental Hotels Group (IHG) reinvigorated its Holiday Inn brand with a three-year, $1 billion makeover of the hotel chain. Approximately 1,250 Holiday Inns received a redesigned logo; upgraded lobbies and guest bathrooms; and new signage, landscaping, lighting, and bedding. Next, IHG turned its attention to Holiday Inn Express, reviving that brand with a $20 million advertising campaign and physical enhancements at 2,200 locations.[36]

ASSESSMENT CHECK

10.1 Describe the four strategies for extending a product's lifecycle.

10.2 Under what circumstances do firms decide to delete a product from their line?

Strategic Implications of Marketing in the 21st Century

Marketers who want their businesses to succeed continue to develop new goods and services to attract and satisfy customers. They engage in continuous improvement activities, focusing on quality and customer service, and they continually evaluate their company's mix of products.

Marketers everywhere are constantly developing new and better products that fit their firm's overall strategy. Technological innovations are one area in which new products quickly replace old ones. Marketers are sometimes faced with the dilemma of lagging sales for formerly popular products. They must come up with ways to extend the lives of certain products to extend their firms' profitability and sometimes must recognize and delete those that no longer meet expectations.

Get online now for additional learning tools to help you master your marketing knowledge—visit **WWW.CENGAGEBRAIN.COM** today!

REVIEW OF CHAPTER OBJECTIVES

1 Define the term *product*.

Marketers define a product as the bundle of physical, service, and symbolic attributes designed to satisfy customers' wants and needs.

2 Distinguish between goods and services and how they relate to the goods–service continuum.

Goods are tangible products customers can see, hear, smell, taste, or touch. Services are intangible tasks that satisfy the needs of customers. Goods represent one end of a continuum, and services represent the other.

3 Outline the importance of the service sector in today's marketplace.

The service sector makes a crucial contribution to the U.S. economy in terms of products and jobs. The U.S. service sector now makes up more than three-fourths of the economy. Services have grown because of consumers' desire for speed, convenience, and technological advances.

4 Describe the three classifications of consumer goods and services.

Consumer products—goods and services—are classified as convenience products (frequently purchased items), shopping products (products purchased after comparison), and specialty products (those offering unique characteristics that consumers prize).

5 Identify the six types of business goods and services.

Business products are classified as installations (major capital investments), accessory equipment (capital items that cost less and last for shorter periods than installations), component parts and materials (finished business products of one producer that become part of the final products of another producer), raw materials (natural resources such as lumber, beef, or cotton), supplies (regular expenses a firm incurs in daily operations), and business services (the intangible products firms buy to facilitate their production and operating processes).

6 Discuss how marketers use quality as a product strategy.

Many companies use total quality management (TQM) in an effort to encourage all employees to participate in producing the best goods and services possible. Companies may also participate in ISO 9001:2008 certification or benchmarking to evaluate and improve quality. Consumers often evaluate service quality on the basis of tangibles, reliability, responsiveness, assurance, and empathy, so marketers of service firms strive to excel in all of these areas.

7 Explain why firms develop lines of related products.

Companies usually produce several related products rather than individual ones to achieve the objectives of growth, optimal use of company resources, and increased company importance in the market, and to make optimal use of the product lifecycle.

8 Describe the way marketers typically measure product mixes and make product mix decisions.

Marketers must decide the right width, length, and depth of product lines. Width is the number of product lines. Length is the number of products a company sells. Depth refers to the number of variations of a product available in a product line. Marketers evaluate the effectiveness of all three elements of the product mix. They may purchase product lines from other companies or extend the product line, if necessary. Firms may also acquire entire companies and their product lines through mergers and acquisitions.

9 Explain the four stages of the product lifecycle.

The product lifecycle outlines the stages a product goes through, including introduction, growth, maturity, and decline. During the introductory stage, marketers work to stimulate demand for the new product. New customers make initial purchases and repurchases of the product in the growth stage. Sales continue to grow during the maturity stage but eventually level off. In the decline stage, sales are reduced due to innovations or a shift in consumer preferences.

10 Describe the four strategies for extending a product's lifecycle and why certain products may be eliminated.

Marketers can extend the product lifecycle by increasing frequency of use or number of users; finding new uses for the product; or changing package size, label, or quality. If none of these is successful, or if the product no longer fits a firm's line, the firm may decide to eliminate it from its line.

ASSESSMENT CHECK: ANSWERS

1.1 Define the term *product*. A product is a bundle of physical, service, and symbolic attributes designed to satisfy a customer's wants and needs.

1.2 Why is the understanding of want satisfaction so important to marketers? The understanding of want satisfaction is important to marketers because it helps them understand why people purchase certain goods and services.

2.1 Describe the goods–services continuum. The goods–services continuum is a spectrum that helps marketers visualize the differences and similarities between goods and services.

2.2 List the six characteristics distinguishing services from goods. The six characteristics distinguishing services from goods are the following: (1) services are intangible, (2) services are inseparable from the service providers, (3) services are perishable, (4) companies cannot easily standardize services, (5) buyers often play important roles in the creation and distribution of services, and (6) service standards show wide variations.

3.1 Identify two reasons services are important to the U.S. economy and business environment. The service sector makes an important contribution to the economy in terms of products and jobs. Services also play a vital role in the international competitiveness of U.S. firms.

3.2 Why do service firms emphasize marketing? The growth of potential service transactions represents a vast marketing opportunity, and the environment for services is changing—so marketers need to find new ways to reach customers.

4.1 What are the three major classifications of consumer products? The three major classifications are convenience products, shopping products, and specialty products.

4.2 Identify five factors marketers should consider in classifying consumer services. Five factors are the following: (1) the nature of the service, (2) the relationship between the service organization and its customers, (3) flexibility for customization, (4) fluctuation of supply and demand, and (5) the way the service is delivered.

5.1 What are the six main classifications of business products? The six main classifications of business products are the following: (1) installations, (2) accessory equipment, (3) component parts and materials, (4) raw materials, (5) supplies, and (6) business services.

5.2 What are the three categories of supplies? The three categories of supplies are maintenance items, repair items, and operating supplies.

6.1 What is TQM? TQM stands for total quality management, a process that expects all of a firm's employees to continually improve its products and work processes.

6.2 What are the five variables of service quality? The five variables of service quality are tangibles, reliability, responsiveness, assurances, and empathy.

7.1 List the four reasons for developing a product line. The four reasons firms want to develop product lines are the following: (1) a desire to grow, (2) enhancing the company's position in the market, (3) optimal use of company resources, and (4) exploiting the stages of the product lifecycle.

7.2 Give an example of a product line with which you are familiar. Product lines could include salad dressings, hybrid automobiles, sporting equipment, hotel chains, and so on.

8.1 Define product mix. The product mix is a company's assortment of product lines and individual product offerings.

8.2 How do marketers typically measure product mixes? The product mix is measured by width, length, and depth.

9.1 Identify the four stages of the product lifecycle. The four stages of the product lifecycle are introduction, growth, maturity, and decline.

9.2 During which stage or stages are products likely to attract the most new customers? Products usually attract the most new customers during the introductory and growth stages.

10.1 Describe the four strategies for extending a product's lifecycle. The four strategies are increasing frequency of use, increasing the number of users, finding new users, and changing packaging or quality.

10.2 Under what circumstances do firms decide to delete a product from their line? Firms may decide to delete a product if none of their strategies work, if raw materials become unavailable, or if the product no longer fits the existing or future product line.

Chapter 12 Product and Service Strategies

MARKETING TERMS YOU NEED TO KNOW

marketing mix 376
product 377
services 377
goods 377
goods–services continuum 377
homeshoring 379
business-to-consumer (B2C) product 380
business-to-business (B2B) products 380
unsought products 380
convenience products 380
impulse goods and services 381
staples 381
emergency goods and services 381
shopping products 381
specialty products 382
installations 385
accessory equipment 386
industrial distributor 386
component parts and materials 386
raw materials 386
supplies 387
MRO items 388
business services 388
total quality management (TQM) 389
ISO 9001:2008 390
benchmarking 390
service encounter 390
service quality 391
product line 392
product mix 393
line extension 394
product lifecycle 395
introductory stage 395
growth stage 396
maturity stage 397
decline stage 397

ASSURANCE OF LEARNING REVIEW

1. Choose one of the following products and explain how it blurs the distinction between goods and services.
   a. knee replacement surgery
   b. dinner at a popular restaurant
   c. purchase and installation of new roof
   d. live concert
   e. custom-made suit
2. What are the differences between consumer products and B2B products? Describe a product that could be used as both.
3. What are unsought products? Give an example of an unsought product, and explain how it might be marketed.
4. What important features distinguish shopping products from one another?
5. How do marketing for installations and accessory equipment differ?
6. How do firms use benchmarking?
7. Briefly describe how L.L.Bean achieved each of the objectives for developing a product line. Why do you think the firm has been successful?
8. What is a line extension? Describe how *one* of the following might create a line extension:
   a. Angel Soft toilet tissue
   b. Kellogg's Frosted Flakes
   c. Dunkin' Donuts ground coffee
   d. Gain laundry detergent
9. What steps do marketers take to make the introductory stage of the product lifecycle successful enough to reach the growth stage? What are some of the challenges they face?
10. Arm & Hammer extended the lifecycle of its baking soda by coming up with new uses for the product. Think of a product whose lifecycle you believe could be extended by finding new uses. Describe the product and your ideas for new uses.

PROJECTS AND TEAMWORK EXERCISES

1. On your own or with a classmate, choose one of the following goods (or choose one of your own). Visit the company's website to learn as much as you can about your product and the way it is marketed. Then create a marketing strategy for developing the services to support your product and make it stand out from others.
   a. True Religion jeans
   b. HTC Desire smartphone
   c. Sephora makeup
   d. Brother printer
   e. MINI Cooper car
2. On your own or with a classmate, create an advertisement for an unsought product, such as a remedial reading or math course, cremation services, a first-aid kit, or the like. How can your ad turn an unsought product into one actually desired by consumers?
3. Consider a customer service experience you have had in the last month or so. Was it positive or negative? Describe your experience to the class and then discuss how the firm might improve the quality of its customer service—even if it is already positive.

4. With a classmate, choose one of the following firms or another that interests you. Visit the firm's website and review its product mix. Then create a chart like the one for Johnson & Johnson in Table 12.3 (on page 396), identifying the company's major product lines, along with a few specific examples.
   a. Under Armour athletic clothing
   b. Condé Nast magazines
   c. Wyndham Hotels
   d. LG Appliances
   e. Volkswagen

5. With the same classmate, create a plan for further extending one of the firm's product lines. Describe the strategy you would recommend for extending the line as well as new products that might be included.

CRITICAL-THINKING EXERCISES

1. Draw a line representing the goods–services continuum. Then place each of the following along the continuum. Briefly explain your decision.
   a. Skype
   b. Teleflora.com
   c. Pottery Barn
   d. Hyundai dealership
   e. Redbox

2. Make a list of all the convenience products you buy in a week. Does the list change from week to week based on need or your budget? What would it take to make you switch from one product to another?

3. Imagine your favorite restaurant. List as many installations, raw materials, and supplies as you can that you think the restaurant owner or manager must be responsible for purchasing.

4. Why is it important for even a small firm to develop a line of products?

5. Choose one of the following goods and services and describe your strategy for taking it to the next stage in its product lifecycle. For products in the maturity or decline stage, describe a strategy for extending their lifecycle.
   a. iPad (growth)
   b. MP3 player (maturity)
   c. Text messaging (growth)
   d. Landline phone (decline)
   e. Duct tape (maturity)

6. Describe a fad that has come and gone during your lifetime, such as Beanie Babies or Pokemon. Did you take part in the fad? Why or why not? How long did it last? Why do you think it faded?

ETHICS EXERCISE

The airline industry has suffered recent setbacks, such as the high cost of fuel, which have forced the major carriers to cut back on many of their services. Many airlines, like Delta and United, charge passengers a fee for checked baggage. Spirit Air announced it would charge for both checked and carry-on bags.[37] Most airlines charge for in-flight snacks or don't serve any at all. Airlines have reduced the number of flights they operate to certain destinations, packing planes full to overflowing, and recent restrictions on the use of frequent-flyer miles make it difficult to cash them in. Then there are the record-setting delays and lost-luggage claims. All of these factors add up to less-than-enjoyable flying experiences for most travelers, many of whom are opting to find other modes of transportation or just staying home. Suppose you are a marketer for one of the major airlines. Your company is facing difficulty providing acceptable service to the passengers on its flights, but you need to find a way to emphasize the positive features of your airline's service.

1. Using the five variables of service quality as your guideline, what steps would you take—within your realm of control—to close the gap between the level of service passengers expect and the level they have been receiving?

2. How might you attract business customers? Would you give them a level of service that is different from families and other consumers who are flying for pleasure?

INTERNET EXERCISES

1. **Product classification.** Visit the website of a company like Reckitt Benckiser, Colgate, or Unilever. Choose at least five different products and classify each as a convenience or shopping product. Explain your reasoning.

   www.rb.com

   www.colgate.com

   www.unilever.com

2. **ISO certification.** The International Organization for Standardization (ISO) is responsible for the development and implementation of product standards. Go to the ISO's website and answer the following questions:

   a. Who belongs to ISO and how is it administered?

   b. How are ISO standards developed?

   c. What are some of the advantages of ISO certification?

   www.iso.org

3. **Product lifecycle.** Arm & Hammer baking soda was first sold more than 100 years ago. Visit the Arm & Hammer website. Review the history of the product and then prepare a brief report outlining how the makers of Arm & Hammer baking soda have been able to extend the product's lifecycle.

   www.armandhammer.com

4. *Note:* Internet Web addresses change frequently. If you don't find the exact site listed, you may need to access the organization's home page and search from there or use a search engine such as Google or Bing.

CASE 12.1
Nike Back in the Limelight

Nike has long been known for innovation. Its instantly recognizable "swoosh" and blunt advertising tag lines such as "There is no finish line" once combined with a lineup of noted athlete–spokespersons to ensure its popularity with amateurs in every sport. Its cutting-edge marketing strategies were widely imitated, and with many of its original fans entering middle age, Nike now finds itself ranked fifth in popularity among coveted buyers between 18 and 24.

The $28 billion company is not about to settle for fifth place, however. Its drive to innovate is stronger, and it has geared up to unleash an array of patented athletic gear that marries the newest technology and enhanced product performance. With dozens of physiologists and specialists in biomechanics among its employees, the firm has been adding to its array of high-tech patents, filing almost 300 patents in one recent year, including ones for footwear, for digital technologies to measure physical exertion, and for improved manufacturing processes. Prototypes are currently being developed for biofeedback products including shoes that change color based on the wearer's activity level, sensor-dotted workout clothing, and golfing glasses that describe the flight of a ball. Nike was recently named Inc. magazine's Most Innovative Company.

One product already on the market is shoes made with Nike's Flyknit technology, a means of knitting footwear that eliminates manufacturing waste and ensures a compression fit, for a shoe so flexible it feels like going barefoot. Free Hyperfeel is another new running shoe designed to feel like no shoe at all, while Dri-Fit Knit and Aeroloft clothing use new moisture-wicking and ventilation technologies to keep wearers dry and comfortable. The FuelBand, a bracelet device that measures the wearer's rate of physical activity, has also become popular, and many more shoes and other products are in the works, including golf clubs with bigger sweet spots and customizable golf balls.

Nike's CEO calls innovation the core of the company's character, the big differentiator between Nike and its competitors. He envisions even more ways to give athletes useful feedback on their bodies, whether their goal is to be more competitive, more fit, or just more inspired by their workouts. For instance, new Nike technologies could use your movements or speed to change the tempo of the music you're listening to, or to change the color of something you're wearing.

QUESTIONS FOR CRITICAL THINKING

1. In your opinion, does a spirit of innovation create a competitive advantage for a company? How can Nike use its innovative spirit to its advantage in the marketplace?

2. What other product extensions might Nike consider for its Flyknit technology?

Sources: Company website, **www.nike.com**, accessed October 9, 2014; Matthew Kish and Mason Walker, "A Peek Inside Nike's Patent Vault," *Portland Business Journal*, accessed October 9, 2014, **www.bizjournals.com**; Joel Makower, "Hannah Jones and Nike's Innovation Juggernaut," *GreenBiz.com*, accessed March 14, 2014, **www.greenbiz.com**; Stuart Elliott, "Losing a Step, Nike Seeks to Regain Its Edge," *The New York Times*, accessed March 14, 2014, **www.nytimes.com**; Austin Carr, "Nike CEO Mark Parker on His Company's Digital Future," *Fast Company*, accessed March 14, 2014, **www.fastcompany.com** ; Austin Carr, "Nike: The No. 1 Most Innovative Company of 2013," *Fast Company*, accessed March 14, 2014, **www.fastcompany.com**.

VIDEO CASE 12.2
BoltBus Gives Bus Travel a Jump Start

You see them rocketing down the interstate: black-and-orange buses slashed by a gray lightning bolt. This is not old-style bus travel where you bought your ticket at a seedy terminal counter and then squeezed into a sweltering or freezing seat and wished your journey would end before it began. This is BoltBus, a division of Greyhound Lines and part of a new generation of bus companies that offer a surprising combination of cheap rates and upscale amenities.

BoltBus is a bundle of goods and services designed to meet the needs of travelers along the Northeastern corridor and recently in the Pacific Northwest. "BoltBus is a bus company that meets the needs of the urban, educated, and adventurous type of customer," says Nicole Recker, senior marketing manager for the company. "We target college students, young professionals, and young families." The goods are the updated buses themselves—comfortable seating with extra legroom, along with power outlets and free Wi-Fi. The services include online ticket purchasing, confirmed reservations, express routes, and real-time status updates on Twitter. "It's more like an airline than it is like a traditional bus," observes David Hall, the company's general manager. "It's a reservation service, so when you buy a ticket you have a reservation on that bus."

Bus travel has been around for a long time. In fact, for a number of years, ridership experienced a steady decline. Customers were fed up with high prices (compared with train or air travel), inconvenient schedules, uncomfortable seating, and poor safety records. But in recent years the industry has changed dramatically. During the late 1990s, a different business model emerged: Companies began selling tickets on the Internet instead of at ticket counters in terminals. Hall and his team observed that there might be an opportunity to jump start bus travel from a declining phase in the product lifecycle. Roughly 15 competitors already shared the Northeast market, many of whom had introduced online ticket sales. So BoltBus had to find ways to distinguish its brand from rivals. The average ticket price for a BoltBus trip is $20, which is a bargain in the Northeast. The combination of low prices and higher-end amenities has been a hit with travelers. In fact, BoltBus seats sell out so quickly that regular passengers know to book well in advance or they'll be riding another bus line. Travelers clearly appreciate the easily accessible power outlets and free Wi-Fi, in addition to the express-type service, which means the buses don't make many stops. Hall likes to compare BoltBus to Southwest Airlines. "We wanted a brand that was affordable . . . a fun, easy-to-use brand. We don't have a lot of rules and regulations."

BoltBus was launched in 2008 from its primary hub of New York City, running buses from there to Washington, DC, Philadelphia, and Boston. Other cities—including Baltimore and Newark—were added later. BoltBus hit the Pacific Northwest in 2012 and Southern California in 2013. Today, the company employs about 200 workers and operates 92 buses that carry more than 2 million passengers a year. "We try to stay lean and keep our costs down, which keeps ticket prices down," says Hall.

The marketing budget for BoltBus is lean, too. The company relies heavily on word-of-mouth and social media. "We pride ourselves on offering customers the best possible rate they can get, which means we operate on a fixed budget when it comes to marketing," explains Nicole Recker, the company's senior marketing manager. "We don't take part in traditional marketing initiatives. We focus on local grassroots efforts." Because many of the bus line's passengers are young and tech-savvy, Recker says that Twitter has given the company its biggest marketing boost. "The customers enjoy that real-time feedback. They can engage with us as a business." Passengers might tweet about a delay while en route, receiving immediate responses and real-time updates from BoltBus about the status of the situation. BoltBus may tweet to passengers about weather or road conditions that could affect the schedule. "This has proved to be extremely beneficial," says Recker. The company has found customer interactions via Twitter to be so effective that it has hired staff to monitor its Twitter account. Bus travel has taken to the highways again, and BoltBus is driving in the express lane.

QUESTIONS FOR CRITICAL THINKING

1. Where does BoltBus fall on the goods–services continuum? With this in mind, what strategies might BoltBus use to gain a competitive advantage over rival bus companies?
2. What steps could BoltBus marketers take to extend its product lifecycle?

Sources: Company website, www.boltbus.com, accessed March 14, 2014; Christine Whittemore, "Travel Marketing: What the Revitalized Bus Travel Industry Can Teach You about Reinventing Your Travel Brand," *5 to 9 Branding*, accessed March 14, 2014, http://5to9branding.com; Jennifer Sokolowsky, "BoltBus to Offer $1 Fares Between Seattle, Portland," *Puget Sound Business Journal*, accessed March 14, 2014, www.bizjournals.com ; "BoltBus," *Portland a Foot*, accessed March 14, 2014, http://portlandafoot.org.

NOTES

1. Company website, "At a Glance," www.infoapplestore.com, accessed October 10, 2014; Hannah Karp and Alistair Barr, "Apple Buys Beats for $3 Billion, Tapping Tastemakers to Regain Music Mojo," *The Wall Street Journal*, accessed October 10, 2014, http://online.wsj.com; Farquar McIntosh, "Apple Share Price: CEO Cook Promises 'Great Things' to Chinese Customers," *Invezz*, accessed March 13, 2014, http://invezz.com; Kofi Bofah, "2014 Outlook: No Apple iPhone Killer," *Seeking Alpha*, accessed March 13, 2014, http://seekingalpha.com; Thomas Claburn, "Apple App Store Annual Sales Exceed $10 Billion," *Information Week*, accessed March 13, 2014, http://www.informationweek.com; company website, "App Store Sales Top $10 Billion in 2013," press release, https://www.apple.com, accessed March 13, 2014; Cory Gunther, "Apple Retail Stores Serve 1 Million Customers, Daily, 407 Locations Worldwide," *Slashgear*, accessed March 13, 2014, www.slashgear.com; Jordan Golson, "51% of US Households Own an Apple Product," *Mac Rumors*, accessed March 13, 2014, www.macrumors.com.
2. "World's Most Admired Companies 2014," *CNNMoney.com*, accessed March 13, 2014, http://money.cnn.com.
3. U.S. Bureau of Labor Statistics, "Table 2.1 Employment by Major Industry Sector," accessed March 13, 2014, www.bls.gov.
4. U.S. Department of Commerce, "U.S. International Trade in Goods and Services: January 2014," press release, March 13, 2014, www.commerce.gov.
5. Erik Savitz, "Why Some U.S. Companies Are Giving up on Outsourcing," *Forbes*, accessed March 13, 2014, www.forbes.com.
6. "Backshoring: Why Is It Becoming a Growing Trend?" *Outsource*, accessed March 13, 2014, www.outsourcemagazine.com.
7. Tacoma Perry, "Homeshoring Gives Stay-at-Home Parents Job Opportunities," *FOX 5*, accessed March 13, 2014, www.myfoxatlanta.com.
8. "The Top 20 DTC Ad Spenders in 2013 Virtually Ignored Digital," *Pharma Marketing Blog*, accessed October 9, 2014, http://pharmamktingblogspot.com.
9. Company website, accessed March 13, 2014, www.arttowngifts.com.
10. This concept was introduced in Christopher H. Lovelock, "Classifying Services to Gain Strategic Marketing Insights," *Journal of Marketing*, Summer 1983, p. 9.
11. James R. Healey, "10 Cheapest Cars: Why (Almost) Nobody Buys Them," *USA Today*, accessed March 13, 2014, www.usatoday.com; Jim Henry, "10 Most Expensive Cars of 2014: Keeping Up with the 1 Percent," *Forbes*, accessed March 13, 2014, www.forbes.com.
12. "Airbus Lands $24B Order from Indonesia's Lion Air," *USA Today*, accessed March 13, 2014, www.usatoday.com.
13. Company website, www.bose.com, accessed March 14, 2014.
14. Company website, www.cargill.com, accessed March 14, 2014.
15. Company website, www.officemax.com, accessed March 14, 2014.
16. Company website, www.cisco.com, accessed March 14, 2014.
17. Company website, www.regus.com, accessed October 9, 2014.
18. Organization website, "ISO 9001:2008," www.iso.org, accessed March 14, 2014; organization website, www.nist.gov, March 14, 2014.
19. Public Broadcasting System, "Who Made America: Henry Ford," www.pbs.org, accessed March 14, 2014.
20. Barry Glassman, What Zappos Taught Us about Creating the Ultimate Client Experience," *Forbes*, accessed March 14, 2014, www.forbes.com.
21. Zack Whittaker, "Amazon Web Services Suffers Outage, Takes Down Vine, Instagram, Others with It," *ZDNet*, accessed March 14, 2014, www.zdnet.com.
22. Company website, www.llbean.com, accessed March 14, 2014.
23. Ibid.
24. Company website, www.jnj.com, accessed March 14, 2014; company website, www.lifescan.com, accessed March 14, 2014; company website, www.depuy.com, accessed March 14, 2014.
25. Company website, www.geox.com, accessed March 14, 2014; "Geox Sees EMEA, Americas Stabilizing in 2014, Growing in 2015," *Reuters*, accessed March 14, 2014, www.reuters.com.
26. Katie Fehrenbacher, "The Winners and Losers in Google's Acquisition of Nest," *Gigaom.com*, accessed March 14, 2014, http://gigaom.com; "5 Reasons Google PowerMeter Didn't Take Off," *Gigaom.com*, accessed March 13, 2014, http://gigaom.com.
27. Robert Klara, "The Best Brand Extensions of 2013," *Adweek*, accessed March 14, 2014, www.adweek.com; Damon Poeter, "Adidas Lifts Curtain on $399 Smart Run Fitness Watch," *PC Magazine*, accessed March 14, 2014, www.pcmag.com.
28. Stuart Houghton, "Google Glass: Release Date, News and Features," *Tech Radar*, accessed March 13, 2014, www.techradar.com.
29. Company website, www.bestbuy.com, accessed March 13, 2014.
30. Charles Fishman, "The Road to Resilience: How Unscientific Innovation Saved Marlin Steel," *Fast Company*, accessed March 14, 2014, www.fastcompany.com
31. Jeanine Poggi, "Despite Rise of Digital Music, Vinyl Makes a Comeback," *Advertising Age*, accessed March 14, 2014, http://adage.com.
32. Emma Rosenblum, "The J.Crew Invasion," *Bloomberg Businessweek*, accessed March 14, 2014, www.businessweek.com
33. Company website, www.armandhammer.com, accessed March 14, 2014.
34. Company website, "More Cereal, Less Packaging," press release, accessed March 14, 2014, www.generalmills.com.
35. Company website, "Starbucks Invites Customers to Share the Spirit of the Season This Black Friday," press release, http://news.starbucks.com, accessed March 14, 2014.
36. Nancy Trejos, "Holiday Inn Express Revives Stay Smart Ad Campaign," *USA Today*, accessed March 13, 2014, www.usatoday.com.
37. Company website, "Our Optional Services," www.spirit.com, accessed March 14, 2014.

Chapter 13

Developing and Managing Brand and Product Categories

1. Discuss how to define a brand.
2. Identify the five different types of brands.
3. Explain the strategic value of brand equity.
4. Explain the benefits of category and brand management.
5. Discuss how companies develop a strong identity for their product or brand.
6. Describe the four new-product development strategies.
7. Describe the five steps in the consumer adoption process.
8. Explain the six steps in the new-product development process.
9. Explain the relationship between product safety and product liability.

UNDER ARMOUR BRAND SOARS

It might seem unlikely that a college athlete's efforts to overcome being "short and slow" could grow into a billion-dollar sports apparel company, but that's the story behind Under Armour, based in Baltimore. Founder Kevin Plank was a college football player who believed the sweat-collecting properties of cotton gear slowed him down on the field. Soon he was spending most of his spare time and meager savings on testing fabrics from tailors' shops to find a material that would carry moisture away from the body.

If he had been working in the apparel industry, Plank says, "I would have been too scared to do anything." But by being dogged and depending on his former teammates and their friends to test his sample shirts, Plank not only refined his product ideas, he also managed to start a successful word-of-mouth campaign that soon had him scrambling to fill orders from college teams.

Now the company has more than $2.3 billion in revenues and is expanding internationally, opening offices and expanding its retail distribution around the world. Under Armour still makes its iconic moisture-wicking shirts, but it has added other athletic gear, including mouth guards, sports bras, basketball shoes, running shoes, and football cleats. It is the official uniform sponsor of a number of overseas teams, including the Tottenham Hotspur Football Club in England, the Welsh Rugby Union, and soccer teams in Israel, Japan, and Mexico. The company has also turned its marketing focus to Latin America, launching an office in Brazil in the run-up to soccer's World Cup and the Summer Olympics to be held there. Under Armour sponsors some U.S. Olympic teams and has positioned itself as the go-to supplier for young athletes who can grow up with the company.

The company's plans include even more growth and expansion. Its first-ever football cleat sold out online in two hours before moving into stores, and next up is the Apollo SpeedForm running shoe, manufactured in a clothing factory to ensure a better fit. Plank sees many opportunities for the brand, and Under Armour is poised to take them.[1]

EVOLUTION OF A BRAND

Under Armour has expanded its business to Europe, Latin America, and China, launching TV and social media campaigns in several countries and believing the future success of its brand depends on developing business outside of North America. The company recently opened a retail theater specialty store in Shanghai, China, complete with a video experience for shoppers that will tell the company's story. Under Armour's strategy is to introduce totally new customers to its brand first and then get them to buy its products.

- In the United States, Under Armour is associated with baseball and football. How will the company need to adapt its approach to reach global consumers whose most important sport is soccer?
- How do you think Under Armour's marketing to a youthful audience will serve the company in the future?
- Under Armour signed a ten-year apparel contract with the University of Notre Dame to supply uniforms, footwear, and apparel for all 26 Fighting Irish varsity teams. What effect will this deal have on the company's marketing strategy? On its competitors?
- To expand its brand appeal to women, Under Armour recently promoted its athletic apparel with a commercial starring Misty Copeland, a soloist in the American Ballet Theatre and the first "nonathlete" featured in the company's marketing efforts. How do you think this marketing approach will increase the company's brand among consumers?

Chapter Overview

Brands play a huge role in our lives. We try certain brands for all kinds of reasons: on recommendations from friends, because we want to associate ourselves with the images certain brands convey, or because we remember colorful advertisements. We develop loyalty to certain brands and product lines for varying reasons as well—quality of a product, price, and habit are a few examples. This chapter examines the way companies make decisions about developing and managing the products and product lines they hope will become consumer necessities. Developing and marketing a product and product line and building a desired brand image are costly propositions. To protect its investment, a specialized marketer called a *category manager* must carefully nurture both existing and new products. The category manager is responsible for an entire product line.

This chapter focuses on two critical elements of product planning and strategy. First, it looks at how firms build and maintain identity and competitive advantage for their products through branding. Second, it focuses on the new-product planning and development process. A category manager's responsibility for new-product planning and meeting the profit requirements take careful preparation. The needs and desires of consumers change constantly, and successful marketers manage to keep up with—or stay just ahead of—those changes.

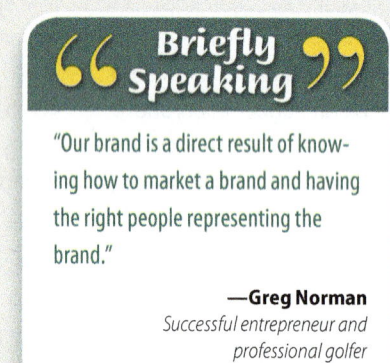

> **Briefly Speaking**
>
> "Our brand is a direct result of knowing how to market a brand and having the right people representing the brand."
>
> —**Greg Norman**
> *Successful entrepreneur and professional golfer*

MANAGING BRANDS FOR COMPETITIVE ADVANTAGE

1 Discuss how to define a brand.

Think of the last time you went shopping for groceries. As you moved through the store, chances are your recognition of various brand names influenced many of your purchasing decisions. Perhaps you chose Colgate toothpaste over competitive offerings or loaded Heinz ketchup into your cart instead of the store brand. Walking through the snack food aisle, you might have reached for Orville Redenbacher popcorn or Lay's potato chips without much thought.

Marketers recognize the powerful influence products and product lines have on customer behavior, and they work to create strong identities for their products and protect them. Branding is the process of creating that identity. A **brand** is a name, term, sign, symbol, design, or some combination that identifies the products of one firm while differentiating these products from competitors' offerings. The tradition of excellence created by the Gucci Group is carried through in all the brands in its lineup—Gucci, Saint Laurent, Stella McCartney, and Balenciaga, to name a few.

As you read this chapter, consider how many brands you are aware of, both those you are loyal to and those you have never tried or have sampled and abandoned. Table 13.1 shows some selected brands, brand names, and brand marks. Satisfied buyers respond to branding by making repeat purchases of the same product because they identify the item with the name of its producer. One buyer might derive satisfaction from an ice cream bar with the brand name Dove; another might derive the same satisfaction from one with the name Ben & Jerry's.

brand Name, term, sign, symbol, design, or some combination that identifies the products of one firm while differentiating them from those of the competition.

TABLE 13.1 Selected Brands, Brand Names, and Brand Marks

Brand type	Dr Pepper or Mountain Dew
Private brand	Craftsman tools (Sears) or Trader José's Chunky Salsa (Trader Joe's)
Family brand	RAID insect sprays or Progresso soups
Individual brand	Purex or Clorox
Brand name	Kleenex or Cheetos
Brand mark	Colonel Sanders for KFC or the Geico Insurance gecko

BRAND LOYALTY

Brands achieve widely varying consumer familiarity and acceptance. A snowboarder might insist on a Burton snowboard, but the same consumer might show little loyalty to particular brands in another product category such as bath soap. Marketers measure brand loyalty in three stages: brand recognition, brand preference, and brand insistence.

Brand recognition is a company's first objective for newly introduced products. Marketers begin the promotion of new items by trying to make them familiar to the public. Advertising offers one effective way for increasing consumer awareness of a brand. Coca-Cola is a familiar brand worldwide, and it drew on customers' recognition of its familiar bottle shape when it introduced the PlantBottle, made from 30 percent plant fiber. In collaboration with Ford, the company recently announced its PlantBottle technology will be used in the fabric interior of the Ford Fusion Energi. Other tactics for creating brand recognition include offering free samples or discount coupons for purchases. Once consumers have used a product, seen it advertised, or noticed it in stores, it moves from the unknown to the known category, increasing the probability that some of those consumers will purchase it. Sometimes customers can misinterpret a marketing message, however, as happened to Nutella. See the "Solving an Ethical Controversy" feature to find out the result.

At the second level of brand loyalty, **brand preference**, buyers rely on previous experiences with the product when choosing it, if available, over competitors' products. You may prefer Tory Burch shoes or Juicy Couture clothes to other brands and buy their new lines as soon as they are offered. If so, those products have established brand preference.

brand recognition
Consumer awareness and identification of a brand.

brand preference
Consumer choice of a product on the basis of a previous experience.

Familiar brand Coca-Cola drew on customers' recognition of its popular bottle shape when it introduced the PlantBottle, made partially from vegetable fiber. Coke's PlantBottle technology will also be used for the fabric interior of the Ford Fusion Energi hybrid car.

Source: www.psfk.com

SOLVING AN ETHICAL CONTROVERSY
Who Is Responsible for the Truth of Advertising Claims?

Some customers were shocked to find that Nutella, the chocolate-hazelnut spread from Europe that's increasingly popular in the United States, was not an especially nutritious food, despite commercials showing a mother and children eating it in their kitchen. These customers believe the scene suggested Nutella might be part of a healthy breakfast for kids. A class-action suit against Ferrero USA Inc., which markets the spread in the United States, was settled in favor of consumers, who will be entitled to a token cash payment that could cost the company more than $3 million if all the money is claimed.

Should consumers be responsible for correctly interpreting advertising claims?

PRO
1. Anyone reading the product label would know it contains 21 grams of sugar and 11 grams of fat per serving.
2. When has chocolate ever been a healthy breakfast food?

CON
1. Ferrero's marketing deliberately put the product in a wholesome setting, suggesting it has nutritional value.
2. The ads market Nutella as particularly suitable for kids' breakfasts, despite its high calorie content.

Summary
Some consumers ridiculed the lawsuit, but Ferrero is also changing the product's labeling, withdrawing the commercials, producing new ones that the suit's plaintiffs will approve before filming, and altering its website. Nutella's caloric, fat, sodium, and sugar content now appear on the front of the jar.

Sources: Company website, "Frequently Asked Questions," www.nutellausa.com, accessed March 21, 2014; Ishmael N. Daro, "This Video Will Make You Think Twice About Eating Nutella," *O Canada*, accessed February 11, 2014, http://o.canada.com; "Nutella Health Claims Net $3.05 Million Settlement in Class-Action Lawsuit," *CBS News*, accessed March 21, 2014, www.cbs.news.com; Caroline Scott-Thomas, "Ferrero Backs Away from Nutella Health Claims in $3M Class Action Settlement," *Food Navigator USA*, accessed March 21, 2014, www.foodnavigator-usa.com; Laurent Belsie, "Nutella Settles Lawsuit. You Can Get $20," *The Christian Science Monitor*, accessed March 21, 2014, www.csmonitor.com.

ASSESSMENT CHECK
1.1 What is a brand?
1.2 Differentiate among brand recognition, brand preference, and brand insistence.

Brand insistence, the ultimate stage in brand loyalty, leads consumers to refuse alternatives and to search extensively for the desired merchandise. A product at this stage has achieved a monopoly position with its consumers. Although many firms try to establish brand insistence with all consumers, few achieve this ambitious goal. Companies that offer specialty or luxury goods and services, such as Rolex watches or Lexus automobiles, are more likely to achieve this status than those offering mass-marketed goods and services.

TYPES OF BRANDS

> **2** Identify the five different types of brands.

Brands are classified in many ways: private, manufacturer's or national, family, and individual brands. In making branding decisions, firms weigh the benefits and drawbacks of each type of brand. Some firms, however, sell their goods without any efforts at branding. These items are called **generic products**. They are characterized by plain labels, little or no advertising, and no brand names. Common categories of generic products include food and household staples. These no-name products were first sold in Europe at prices as much as 30 percent below those of branded products. This product strategy was introduced in the United States three decades ago. The market shares for generic products increase during economic downturns but subside when the economy improves. However, many consumers request generic substitutions for brand-name prescriptions at the pharmacy whenever they are available.

Manufacturers' Brands versus Private Brands

Manufacturers' brands, also called *national brands*, define the image most people form when they think of a brand. A **manufacturer's brand** refers to a brand name owned by a manufacturer or other producer. Well-known manufacturers' brands include Hewlett-Packard, Sony, Pepsi-Cola, Dell, and French's. In contrast, many large wholesalers and retailers place their own brands on the merchandise they market. The brands offered by wholesalers and retailers usually are called **private brands** (or *private labels*). Although some manufacturers refuse to produce private-label goods, most regard such production as a way to reach additional market segments. Supervalu offers many private-label products in its retail grocery stores, including Culinary Circle and Essential Everyday food products, Wild Harvest organic products, and Baby Basic products.

The growth of private brands has paralleled that of chain stores in the United States. Manufacturers not only sell their well-known brands to stores but also put the store's own label on similar products. Leading manufacturers such as Westinghouse, Armstrong Rubber, and Heinz generate ever-increasing percentages of their total incomes by producing goods for sale under retailers' private labels. A recent survey found that private-label purchases make up more than 50 percent of in-store buying. Some 78 percent of shoppers buy many private-label brands because they are less expensive. More than half of consumers surveyed said it would take a permanent price reduction of brand-name products—to the same price as the store brand—to persuade them to return to purchasing brand-name products.[2]

Consistent with its corporate goal to buy and sell green products, office supply retailer Office Depot launched Office Depot Green, a private-label line of environmentally sound products. The line includes recycled paper and paper products, ink and toner cartridges, compact fluorescent light bulbs, and other items that create minimal impact on the environment.[3]

Captive Brands

The nation's major discounters—such as Walmart, Target, and Kohl's—have come up with a spinoff of the private-label idea. So-called **captive brands** are national brands sold exclusively by a retail chain. Captive brands typically provide better profit margins than private labels. Target's captive brands include linens by designer Rachel Ashwell, snowboarder Shaun White's gear for boys, Liz Lange maternity wear, and cookware by chef Giada De Laurentiis.[4]

Family and Individual Brands

A **family brand** is a single brand name that identifies several related products. For example, All-Clad Metalcrafters markets a complete line of cookware under the All-Clad name, and Johnson & Johnson offers a line of baby powder, lotions, plastic pants, and baby shampoo under its name. All Pepperidge Farm products, including bread, rolls, and cookies, carry the Pepperidge Farm brand. Frito-Lay markets both chips and salsa under its Tostitos family brand.

Alternatively, a manufacturer may choose to market a product as an **individual brand**, which uniquely identifies the item itself, rather than promoting it under the name of the company or under an umbrella name covering similar items. Unilever, for example, markets Ben & Jerry's, Bertolli, Lipton, and Promise food products; TRESemmé and St. Ives beauty products; and Lever 2000 and Dove soaps. PepsiCo's Quaker Oats unit markets Aunt Jemima breakfast products, Life and Cap'n Crunch cereals, and Rice-a-Roni side dishes along with Quaker oatmeal. Its Frito-Lay division makes Lays, Ruffles, and Doritos chips and Smartfood popcorn. Pepsi-Cola brands include Mountain Dew, Sierra Mist, SoBe juices and teas, and Aquafina water. Individual brands cost more than family brands to market because the firm must develop a new promotional campaign to introduce each new product. Distinctive brands are extremely effective aids in implementing market segmentation strategies, however.

---

brand insistence Consumer refusal of alternatives and extensive search for desired merchandise.

generic products Products characterized by plain labels, no advertising, and the absence of brand names.

manufacturer's brand Brand name owned by a manufacturer or other producer.

private brands Brand offered by a wholesaler or retailer.

captive brands National brand sold exclusively by a retail chain.

family brand Single brand name that identifies several related products.

individual brand Single brand that uniquely identifies a product.

A family brand is a single brand name that identifies several related products. Johnson & Johnson markets a complete line of baby products under its name.

On the other hand, a promotional outlay for a family brand can benefit all items in the line. Family brands also help marketers introduce new products to both customers and retailers. Because supermarkets stock thousands of items, they hesitate to add new products unless they are confident they will be in demand.

Family brands should identify products of similar quality, or the firm risks harming its overall product image. If Rolls-Royce marketers were to place the Rolls name on a low-end car or a line of discounted clothing, they would severely tarnish the image of the luxury car line. Conversely, Lexus, Infiniti, and Porsche put their names on luxury sport-utility vehicles to capitalize on their reputations and to enhance the acceptance of the new models in a competitive market.

Individual brand names should, however, distinguish dissimilar products. Kimberly-Clark markets two different types of diapers for infants under its Huggies and Pull-Ups names. Procter & Gamble offers shaving products under its Gillette name; laundry detergent under Cheer, Tide, and other brands; and dishwasher detergent under Cascade.

ASSESSMENT CHECK

2.1 Identify the five different types of brands.
2.2 How are generic products different from branded products?

BRAND EQUITY

3 Explain the strategic value of brand equity.

As individuals, we often like to say our strongest asset is our reputation. The same is true of organizations. A brand can go a long way toward making or breaking a company's reputation. A strong brand identity backed by superior quality offers important strategic advantages for a firm. First, it increases the likelihood that consumers will recognize the firm's product or product line when they make purchase decisions. Second, a strong brand identity can contribute to buyers' perceptions of product quality. Branding can also reinforce customer loyalty and repeat purchases. A consumer who tries a brand and likes it will probably look for that brand on future store visits. All of these benefits contribute to a valuable form of competitive advantage called *brand equity*.

brand equity Added value that a respected, well-known brand name gives to a product in the marketplace.

Brand equity refers to the added value a certain brand name gives to a product in the marketplace. Brands with high equity confer financial advantages on a firm because they often command comparatively large market shares and consumers may pay little attention to differences in prices. Studies have also linked brand equity to high profits and stock returns. Service companies are also aware of the value of brand equity.

In global operations, high brand equity often facilitates expansion into new markets. Currently, Apple, Google, and Coca-Cola are the most valuable—and most recognized—brands in the world.[5] Similarly, Disney's brand equity allows it to market its goods and services in Europe and Japan—and now, China. What makes a global brand powerful? According to Interbrand, which measures brand equity in dollar values, a strong brand has the power to increase a company's sales and earnings. A global brand generally is defined as one that sells at least 30 percent outside its home country.

Global advertising agency Young & Rubicam developed another brand equity system called the BrandAsset Valuator. Y&R's database of consumers' brand perceptions contains more than 800,000 consumer interviews and information on 44,000 brands across 50 countries. According to Y&R, a firm builds brand equity sequentially on four dimensions of brand personality. These four dimensions are differentiation, relevance, esteem, and knowledge:

> **Briefly Speaking**
>
> "Any ... fool can put on a deal, but it takes genius, faith and perseverance to create a brand."
>
> —David Ogilvy
> American advertising pioneer

- *Differentiation* refers to a brand's ability to stand apart from competitors. Brands such as Porsche and Victoria's Secret stand out in consumers' minds as symbols of unique product characteristics.

- *Relevance* refers to the real and perceived appropriateness of a brand to a big consumer segment. A large number of consumers must feel a need for the benefits offered by the brand. Brands with high relevance include Apple and Hallmark.

- *Esteem* is a combination of perceived quality and consumer perceptions about a brand's growing or declining popularity. A rise in perceived quality or in public opinion about a brand enhances a brand's esteem. But negative impressions reduce esteem. Brands with high esteem include Coca-Cola and Honda.

- *Knowledge* refers to the extent of customers' awareness of the brand and understanding of what a good or service stands for. Knowledge implies that customers feel an intimate relationship with a specific brand. Examples include Kraft Macaroni & Cheese and North Face.[6]

Most customers have knowledge, awareness, and understanding of the North Face brand.

ASSESSMENT CHECK

3.1 What is brand equity?
3.2 What are the four dimensions of brand personality?

THE ROLE OF CATEGORY AND BRAND MANAGEMENT

Because of the tangible and intangible value associated with strong brand equity, marketing organizations invest considerable resources and effort in developing and maintaining these dimensions of brand personality. Traditionally, companies assigned the task of managing a brand's marketing strategies to a **brand manager**. Today, because they sell about 80 percent of their products to national retail chains, major consumer goods companies have adopted a strategy called **category management**. In this strategy, a manufacturer's *category manager* maximizes sales for the retailer by overseeing an entire product line, often tracking sales history with data from the retail checkout point and aggregating it with sales data for the entire category (obtained from third-party vendors) and qualitative data, such as customer surveys.[7]

Unlike traditional product managers, category managers have profit responsibility for their product group and help the retailer's category buyer maximize sales for the whole category, not just the particular manufacturer's product. These managers are assisted by associates usually called *analysts*. Part of the shift to category management was initiated by large retailers, who realized they could benefit from the marketing muscle of large grocery and household goods producers such as SC Johnson and Procter & Gamble. As a result, producers began to focus their attention on in-store merchandising instead of mass-market advertising. Some manufacturers that are too small to dedicate a category manager to each retail chain assign a category manager to each major channel, such as convenience stores, drugstores, grocery stores, and so on.[8]

Some of the steps companies follow in the category management process include defining the category based on the target market's needs, scoping out a consumer's decision process when shopping the category, identifying consumer groups and the store clusters with the

Explain the benefits of category and brand management. 4

brand manager Marketer responsible for a single brand.

category management Product management system in which a category manager—with profit and loss responsibility—oversees a product line.

ASSESSMENT CHECK

4.1 Define brand manager.

4.2 How does category management help retailers?

greatest sales potential, creating a marketing strategy and performance goal for each cluster and using a scorecard to measure progress, defining and executing the tactics, and tracking progress.[9] Hershey's vending division offers category management services to its institutional customers, providing reduced inventory costs, improved warehouse efficiency, and increased sales.[10]

PRODUCT IDENTIFICATION

> **5** Discuss how companies develop a strong identity for their product or brand.

Organizations identify their products in the marketplace with brand names, symbols, and distinctive packaging. Almost every product distinguishable from another gives buyers some means of identifying it. Sunkist Growers, for instance, stamps its oranges with the name Sunkist. Iams stamps a paw print on all of its pet food packages. For well over a century, Prudential Financial has used the Rock of Gibraltar as its symbol.

Choosing how to identify a firm's output represents a major strategic decision for marketers. Produce growers have another option besides gummed paper stickers for identifying fruits and vegetables: dissolvable fruit stickers. Amron Vanishing Fruitwash Labels include the PLU (price look-up) code and eliminate sticky labels. Washing the fruit dissolves the label, which turns into an organic produce wash that eliminates wax, pesticides, dirt, and bacteria.[11]

BRAND NAMES AND BRAND MARKS

brand name Part of a brand, consisting of letters, numbers, or words, that can be spoken and that identifies and distinguishes a firm's offerings from those of its competitors.

brand mark Symbol or pictorial design that distinguishes a product.

A name plays a central role in establishing brand and product identity. The American Marketing Association defines a **brand name** as the part of a brand that can be spoken. It can consist of letters, numbers, or words and forms a name that identifies and distinguishes the firm's offerings from those of its competitors. Firms can also identify their brands by brand marks. A **brand mark** is a symbol or pictorial design that distinguishes a product, such as the Jolly Green Giant for Green Giant Vegetables.

Effective brand names are easy to pronounce, recognize, and remember. Short names, such as Nike, Ford, and Bounty, meet these requirements. Marketers try to overcome problems with easily mispronounced brand names by teaching consumers the correct pronunciations. For example, early advertisements for the Korean carmaker Hyundai explained that the name rhymes with *Sunday*. Sensitivity to clear communication doesn't end with the choice of brand name; marketers should also be aware of how well they get their point across in interpersonal communications.

A brand name should give buyers the correct connotation of the product's image. The name of Apple's iPad Mini suggests its small size.

©iStockphoto.com/franckreporter

A brand name should also give buyers the correct connotation of the product's image. Nissan's Xterra connotes youth and extreme sports to promote the off-road SUV. ConAgra's Healthy Choice food line presents an alternative to fast foods that may be high in sodium or fat, and the iPad Mini uses a name that aptly suggests its small size. A brand name must also qualify for legal protection. The Lanham Act of 1946 states that registered trademarks must not contain words or phrases in general use, such as *automobile* or *suntan lotion*. These generic words actually describe particular types of products, and no company can claim exclusive rights to them.

Marketers feel increasingly hard-pressed to coin effective brand names, as multitudes of competitors rush to stake out names for their own products. Some companies register names before they have products to fit them to prevent competitors from using them. Some marketers use humor to connect with potential customers. Harley Davidson's Fat Boy series of motorcycles have become very successful because buyers liked the name.[12]

When a class of products becomes generally known by the original brand name of a specific offering, the brand name may become a descriptive generic name. If this occurs, the original owner loses exclusive claim to the brand name. The generic names nylon, aspirin, escalator, kerosene, and zipper started as brand names. Other generic names that were once brand names include cola, yo-yo, linoleum, and shredded wheat.

Marketers must distinguish between brand names that have become legally generic terms and those that seem generic only in many consumers' eyes. Consumers often adopt legal brand names as descriptive names. Many people use the term Kleenex to refer to any brand of facial tissues. English and Australian consumers use the brand name Hoover as a verb for vacuuming. One popular way to look something up on the Internet is to "Google it." Xerox is such a well-known brand name that people frequently—though incorrectly—use it as a verb to mean photocopying. To protect its valuable trademark, Xerox Corporation has created advertisements explaining that Xerox is a brand name and registered trademark and should not be used as a verb.

> **Briefly Speaking**
>
> "Products are made in the factory, but brands are created in the mind."
>
> —**Walter Landor**
> *Founder of the industrial design firm Walter Landor & Associates*

TRADEMARKS

Businesses invest considerable resources in developing and promoting brands and brand identities. The high value of brand equity encourages firms to take steps in protecting the expenditures they invest in their brands.

A **trademark** is a brand for which the owner claims exclusive legal protection. A trademark should not be confused with a trade name, which identifies a company. The Coca-Cola Company is a trade name, but Coke is a trademark of the company's product. Some trade names duplicate companies' brand names.

trademark Brand for which the owner claims exclusive legal protection.

Protecting Trademarks

Trademark protection confers the exclusive legal right to use a brand name, brand mark, and any slogan or product name abbreviation. It designates the origin or source of a good or service. Frequently, trademark protection is applied to words or phrases, such as *Bud* for Budweiser or *the Met* for the Metropolitan Opera in New York City. Robert Burck, better known as the Naked Cowboy—a New York street performer who plays guitar in Times Square wearing nothing but white cowboy boots, cowboy hat, and underpants—registered his likeness and the words "Naked Cowboy" as a trademark. Burck sued Mars, the makers of M&Ms, for trademark infringement after they erected a video billboard showing a blue M&M playing the guitar and clad only in white boots, hat, and underpants. The case was settled out of court, with Burck's lawyers arguing that Mars had infringed on his trademark rights. More recently, Burck sued CBS, whose soap opera *The Bold and the Beautiful* featured a character wearing only briefs and playing a guitar. CBS later uploaded the episode onto YouTube and labeled it "The Bold and the Beautiful—Naked Cowboy." Burck accused the network of harming his reputation, but he lost that lawsuit when the judge ruled that "even an unsophisticated viewer" would not mistake Burck for the character in the soap opera.[13]

Firms can also receive trademark protection for packaging elements and product features, such as shape, design, and typeface. U.S. law has fortified trademark protection in recent years. The Federal Trademark Dilution Act of 1995 gives a trademark holder the right to sue for trademark infringement even if other products using its brand are not particularly similar or easily confused in the minds of consumers. The infringing company does not even have to know it is diluting another's trademark. The act also gives a trademark holder the right to sue if another party imitates its trademark.

The Internet is the next battlefield for trademark infringement cases. Some companies are attempting to protect their trademarks by filing infringement cases against companies using similar names. Pinterest, a social-networking site, recently filed a lawsuit against Pintrips, a personal travel planning site, for trademark infringement based on its similar sounding name and graphic brand. Pinterest encourages visitors to its site to pin images and create collections that users can share with each other. The current graphic used by Pintrips is called a PIN button and allows visitors to track prices for flights they might be interested in taking and marking possible travel destinations with a blue pin. In its lawsuit Pinterest alleges that the Pintrips name sounds too much like Pinterest, causing confusion among consumers and implying a connection between the two brands. Pintrips filed a motion to dismiss the trademark case in federal court, saying "pin" is a generic term; however, the motion to dismiss the case was denied.[14]

Trade Dress

trade dress Visual components that contribute to the overall look of a brand.

Visual cues used in branding create an overall look sometimes referred to as **trade dress**. These visual components may be related to color selections, sizes, package and label shapes, and similar factors. For example, the McDonald's golden arches, Merrill Lynch's bull, and the yellow of Shell's seashell are all part of these products' trade dress. Owens Corning has registered the color pink to distinguish its fiberglass insulation from that of its competition. A combination of visual cues can also constitute trade dress. Consider a Mexican food product that uses the colors of the Mexican flag: green, white, and red.

Trade dress disputes have led to numerous courtroom battles but no apparent consensus from the Supreme Court. Apple sued Samsung, charging that the Korean electronics giant had infringed on Apple's trade dress, trademark, and design patents in manufacturing its Android smartphone. In an unusual twist, Samsung happens to be one of Apple's major parts suppliers. The courts awarded Apple more than $1 billion in damages, finding that Samsung had infringed on some of Apple's patents.[15]

DEVELOPING GLOBAL BRAND NAMES AND TRADEMARKS

Cultural and language variations make brand-name selection a difficult undertaking for international marketers; an excellent brand name or symbol in one country may prove disastrous in another. An advertising campaign for E-Z washing machines failed in the United Kingdom, because the British pronounce *z* as "zed." A firm marketing a product in multiple countries must also decide whether to use a single brand name for universal promotions or tailor names to individual countries. Most languages contain *o* and *k* sounds, so *okay* has become an international word. Most languages also have a short *a,* so Coca-Cola, Kodak, and Texaco are effective brands abroad.

In a recent dispute, two global companies squared off, with distiller Maker's Mark winning a judgment against Jose Cuervo International. As part of the manufacturing process of its Maker's Mark bourbon, the company seals the bottles by hand-dipping the tops in red wax, creating a free-form red seal. Makers of Jose Cuervo tequila had recently begun affixing a red wax seal on its bottles. The court agreed that the red wax seal was part of the Maker's Mark trademark and barred Jose Cuervo International from its further use.[16]

PACKAGING

A firm's product strategy must also address questions about packaging. Like its brand name, a product's package can powerfully influence buyers' purchase decisions.

Marketers apply increasingly scientific methods to their packaging decisions. Rather than experimenting with physical models or drawings, more and more package designers work on special computer graphics programs that create three-dimensional images of packages in thousands of colors, shapes, and typefaces. Another software program helps marketers design effective packaging by simulating the displays shoppers see when they walk down supermarket aisles.

Companies conduct marketing research to evaluate current packages and to test alternative package designs. When Nestlé USA Prepared Foods wanted to update the packaging of its Lean Cuisine line of frozen entrees and dinners, the company conducted extensive marketing research. Lean Cuisine was first introduced more than 30 years ago as a line of healthful meals, but as the company's design manager put it, the brand is about bringing out the best by helping people to eat healthier every day. The company believed the old package design didn't reflect this attitude. Nestlé USA worked with a

Chapter 13 Developing and Managing Brand and Product Categories

design firm to develop packaging that would reflect Lean Cuisine's "vibrant and optimistic personality." The company recently debuted Lean Cuisine Honestly Good, a frozen meal of quality ingredients that contain no preservatives. The product features new packaging with a 100 percent recyclable outer sleeve and translucent tray, which allows consumers to see the meal they're about to eat.[17] Changes to packaging can take a long time. Heinz spent years testing pouch-style packaging for its ketchup. See the "Marketing Success" feature for the story.

A package serves three major objectives: (1) protection against damage, spoilage, and pilferage; (2) assistance in marketing the product; and (3) cost effectiveness. Let's briefly consider each of these objectives.

Protection against Damage, Spoilage, and Pilferage

The original objective of packaging was to offer physical protection for the merchandise. Products typically pass through several stages of handling between manufacturing and customer purchases, and a package must protect its contents from damage. Furthermore, packages

The globe is part of AT&T's trade dress, which gives visual cues about the company's brand.

MARKETING SUCCESS
Packaging Gives Heinz a Boost

Background. Flexible food pouches have been slower to catch on in the United States than in Europe, even though they are cheaper to manufacture than plastic bottles, have a modern look, and are easy to use. They also keep food exceptionally fresh.

The Challenge. While H.J. Heinz Co. hadn't redesigned its ketchup bottle since 1983, the company recognized that consumers today want smaller sizes, lower prices, and convenience but are unwilling to give up quality. Heinz wanted its iconic product to remain competitive even in discount groceries, where value is especially important.

The Strategy. Heinz introduced a flexible, 10-ounce ketchup pouch with pouring spout for half the price of the traditional 20-ounce bottle. There is also a food-service version of the pouch, whose unique "Dip and Squeeze" design holds three times as much ketchup as the original restaurant packets, so fewer are needed per order.

The Outcome. Heinz hopes the pouches' design and convenience appeals to younger consumers, both in grocery stores and in food-service outlets. The company says it didn't change the ketchup's formula but how the product is delivered. The food-service pouch has already sold more than 1 billion units, including to Wendy's and Chick-fil-A.

Sources: Company website "Innovation in Packaging," www.heinz.com, accessed March 21, 2014; Pat Reynolds, "Dip & Squeeze Boasts Dual Functionality," *Packaging World*, accessed March 21, 2014, www.packworld.com; Elaine Watson, "Quote/Unquote: Heinz on Rocking the Boat…" *Food Navigator*, accessed March 21, 2014, www.foodnavigator-usa.com; Emily Bryson York, "More Foods Going to Pouch Packaging," *Chicago Tribune*, accessed March 21, 2014, http://articles.chicagotribune.com; Sarah Nassauer, "Old Ketchup Packet Heads for Trash," *The Wall Street Journal*, accessed March 21, 2014, http://onlinewsj.com.

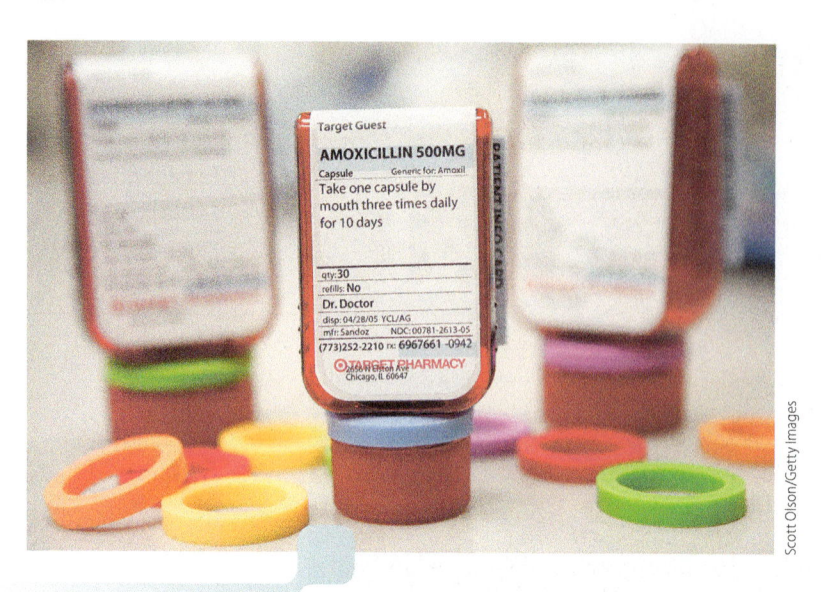

Target's ClearRx prescription bottles offer easy-to-read labels in a shape designed to fit in the palm of the hand; an information card about the prescription tucked into a sleeve on the back of the bottle; and color-coded rings on the bottle's neck to help family members identify their medications at a glance.

of perishable products must protect the contents against spoilage in transit and in storage until purchased by the consumer. Fears of product tampering have forced many firms to improve package designs. Over-the-counter medicines are sold in tamper-resistant packages covered with warnings informing consumers not to purchase merchandise without protective seals intact. Many grocery items and light-sensitive products are packaged in tamper-resistant containers as well. Products in glass jars, such as spaghetti sauce and jams, often come with vacuum-depressed buttons in the lids that pop up the first time the lids are opened.

Even prescription medicine packaging can be revolutionized for the consumer's benefit, as Target found. Its ClearRx prescription dispensing system offers bottles with easy-to-read labels, in a shape designed to fit in the palm of the hand and to stand upright on either end of the container. An information card tucked into a sleeve on the back of the bottle provides a brief summary of the medication's uses and side effects. For households where several people are taking medication, color-coded rings on the neck of the bottle help family members identify their medication at a glance.[18]

Many packages offer important safeguards against pilferage for retailers. Shoplifting and employee theft cost retailers several billion dollars each year. To limit this activity, many packages feature oversized cardboard backings too large to fit into a shoplifter's pocket or purse. Efficient packaging that protects against damage, spoilage, and theft is especially important for international marketers, which must contend with varying climatic conditions and the added time and stress involved in overseas shipping.

Assistance in Marketing the Product

The proliferation of new products, changes in consumer lifestyles and buying habits, and marketers' emphasis on targeting smaller market segments have increased the importance of packaging as a promotional tool. Many firms address consumer concerns about protecting the environment by designing packages made of biodegradable and recyclable materials. To demonstrate serious concern regarding environmental protection, Procter & Gamble, McDonald's, and other firms have created ads that describe their efforts in developing environmentally sound packaging.

In a grocery store where thousands of different items compete for notice, a product must capture the shopper's attention. Marketers combine colors, sizes, shapes, graphics, and typefaces to establish distinctive trade dress that sets their products apart from the competition. Packaging can help establish a common identity for a group of items sold under the same brand name. Like the brand name, a package should evoke the product's image and communicate its value.

Some packages enhance convenience. Pump dispensers, for example, facilitate the use of products ranging from mustard to insect repellent. Squeezable bottles of honey and ketchup make those products easier to use and store. Packaging provides key benefits for convenience foods such as meals and soups packaged in microwavable containers, juice drinks in aseptic packages, and frozen entrées and vegetables packaged in single-serving portions.

Cost-Effective Packaging

Although packaging must perform a number of functions for the producer, marketers, and consumers, it must do so at a reasonable cost. Sometimes changes in the packaging can make packages both cheaper and better for the environment. A redesign of the standard gallon milk jug has cut shipping costs and lessened its environmental impact. Kimberly-Clark is best known to consumers for its Kleenex, Scott, and Huggies brands, but its Kimberly-Clark Health Care and Kimberly-Clark Professional divisions make products for the medical field. Working together, the two divisions introduced new packaging for disposable medical gloves. Someone trying to take one glove out of a package often pulls out several, which have to be discarded. The SmartPULL packaging has a dual-opening tab for its paper cartons that greatly reduces wasted gloves.[19]

Labeling

Labels were once a separate element applied to a package; today, they are an integral part of a typical package. Labels perform both promotional and informational functions. A **label** carries an item's brand name or symbol, the name and address of the manufacturer or distributor, information about the product's composition and size, and recommended uses. The right label can play an important role in attracting consumer attention and encouraging purchases.

Consumer confusion and dissatisfaction over descriptions such as *giant economy size*, *king size*, and *family size* led to the passage of the Fair Packaging and Labeling Act in 1966. The act requires that a label offer adequate information concerning the package contents and that a package design facilitate value comparisons among competing products.

The Nutrition Labeling and Education Act of 1990 imposes a uniform format in which food manufacturers must disclose nutritional information about their products. In addition, the Food and Drug Administration (FDA) has mandated design standards for nutritional labels that provide clear guidelines to consumers about food products. The FDA has also tightened definitions for loosely used terms such as *light*, *fat free*, *lean*, and *extra lean*, and it mandates that labels list the amounts of fat, sodium, dietary fiber, calcium, vitamins, and other components in typical servings. The latest ruling requires food manufacturers to include on nutritional labels the total amount of trans fats—hydrogenated oils that improve texture and freshness but contribute to high levels of cholesterol—in each product.

The Food Allergen Labeling and Consumer Protection Act of 2004 requires that food labeling disclose all major food allergens in terms the average consumer can understand. According to the FDA, eight allergens account for most documented allergic reactions to food, and all must be identified. They are milk, eggs, peanuts, tree nuts (such as almonds, cashews, and walnuts), fish (like bass, cod, and flounder), shellfish (such as crab, lobster, and shrimp), soy, and wheat.[20]

Labeling requirements differ elsewhere in the world. In Canada, for example, labels must provide information in both English and French. The type and amount of information required on labels also vary among nations. International marketers must carefully design labels to conform to the regulations of each country in which they market their merchandise.

The **universal product code (UPC)** designation is another important aspect of a label or package. Introduced in 1974 as a method for cutting expenses in the supermarket industry, UPCs are numerical barcodes printed on packages. Optical scanner systems read these codes, and computer systems recognize items and print their prices on cash register receipts. Although UPC scanners are costly, they permit both considerable labor savings over manual pricing and improved inventory control. The universal product code is also a major asset for marketing research. However, many consumers feel frustrated when only a UPC is placed on a package without an additional price tag, because they do not always know how much an item costs if the price labels are missing from the shelf.

Radio-frequency identification (RFID) tags—electronic chips that carry encoded product identification—may replace some of the functions of UPC codes, such as price identification and inventory tracking. But consumer privacy concerns about the amount of information RFID tracking can accumulate may limit their use to aggregate packaging, such as pallets, rather than units sized for individual sale. When the FDA decided to require drug makers and marketers to place a scannable code on all drugs sold to U.S. hospitals at the level of patient unit doses, it chose UPC codes.

BRAND EXTENSIONS

Some brands become so popular that marketers may decide to use them on unrelated products in pursuit of instant recognition for the new offerings. The strategy of attaching a popular brand name to a new product in an unrelated product category is known as **brand extension**. This practice should not be confused with **line extensions**, which refers to new sizes, styles, or related products. A brand extension, in contrast, carries over from one product nothing but the brand name. In establishing brand extensions, marketers hope to gain access to new customers and markets by building on the

---

label Branding component that carries an item's brand name or symbol, the name and address of the manufacturer or distributor, information about the product, and recommended uses.

universal product code (UPC) Numerical barcode system used to record product and price information.

brand extension Strategy of attaching a popular brand name to a new product in an unrelated product category.

line extensions Development of individual offerings that appeal to different market segments while remaining closely related to the existing product line.

equity already established in their existing brands. This is the strategy behind Tommy Bahama's brand extension from fashion to furniture and restaurants.[21]

Targeting girls from preschool through the tween years, American Girl "celebrates girls and all they can be." Founded more than 25 years ago, American Girl introduced a set of historical characters—fictional nine-year-old heroines whose stories are set in America's past—and featured them in high-quality books, as 18-inch dolls, and in clothes, toys, and more. American Girl further extended its brand with the My American Girl line, dolls whose appearance can be customized with different hair and eye color and skin tone, plus other features such as braces, glasses, and earrings.

But the American Girl brand extends far beyond the dolls themselves. Girls can play on Innerstar University, American Girl's secure online site offering games, activities, and networking. The company publishes *American Girl* magazine, which encourages girls' creativity and affirms their self-esteem. American Girl retail stores in selected U.S. cities offer shopping, dining, and special events such as crafts workshops and cooking classes, and even salons where girls can have their dolls' hair cut and styled.[22]

BRAND LICENSING

brand licensing
Practice that expands a firm's exposure in the marketplace.

A growing number of firms authorize other companies to use their brand names. Even colleges license their logos and trademarks. Known as **brand licensing**, this practice expands a firm's exposure in the marketplace, much as a brand extension does. The brand name's owner also receives an extra source of income in the form of royalties from licensees, typically 10 percent of wholesale revenues.[23]

Brand experts note several potential problems with licensing, however. Brand names do not transfer well to all products. The PetSmart PetsHotel was a winner, as was *American Idol* camp, but recent losers were Precious Moments coffins, Dr Pepper Marinade, and Zippo Fragrances. Also, if a licensee produces a poor-quality product or an item ethically incompatible with the original brand, the arrangement could damage the reputation of the brand.[24]

American Girl has extended its brand with the Innerstar University website, where girls can play games, watch videos, and download apps related to the company's products.

Chapter 13 Developing and Managing Brand and Product Categories   423

Harley Davidson has been selling motorcycles for more than 100 years, basing its marketing campaigns on the association of its bikes with masculinity and the open road. Although some fans have gone so far as to get tattooed with the Harley Davidson name and logo, most are content with buying branded T-shirts, ornaments, and socks. Thinking that introducing more branded products would bring more sales, the company launched Harley Davidson aftershave, perfume, and even wine coolers. But those brand extensions were too much for even the most devoted fans.[25]

> **ASSESSMENT CHECK**
>
> 5.1 Distinguish between a brand name and a trademark.
> 5.2 What are the three purposes of packaging?
> 5.3 Describe brand extension and brand licensing.

NEW-PRODUCT PLANNING

As its offerings enter the maturity and decline stages of the product lifecycle, a firm must add new items to continue to prosper. Regular additions of new products to the firm's line help protect it from product obsolescence.

New products are the lifeblood of any business, and survival depends on a steady flow of new entries. Some new products may implement major technological breakthroughs. Other new products simply extend existing product lines. In other words, a new product is one that either the company or the customer has not handled before.

PRODUCT DEVELOPMENT STRATEGIES

A firm's strategy for new-product development varies according to its existing product mix and the match between current offerings and the firm's overall marketing objectives. The current market positions of products also affect product development strategy. Figure 13.1 identifies four alternative development strategies: market penetration, market development, product development, and product diversification.

A **market penetration strategy** seeks to increase sales of existing products in existing markets. Firms can attempt to extend their penetration of markets in several ways. They may modify products, improve product quality, or promote new and different ways to use products. Packaged-goods marketers often pursue this strategy to boost market share for mature products in mature markets. Product positioning often plays a major role in such a strategy.

Product positioning refers to consumers' perceptions of a product's attributes, uses, quality, advantages, and disadvantages relative to competing brands. Marketers often conduct studies to analyze consumer preferences and to construct product-positioning maps that plot their products' positions in relation to those of competitors' offerings.

Hyundai Motors has repositioned its Hyundai brand in the United States. Although the Hyundai entered the U.S. market as an inexpensive alternative to other cars, the company has ratcheted up the look and feel of its sedans to emphasize quality and safety as well as eco-friendliness. To attract buyers, Hyundai was one of the first brands to offer a ten-year, 100,000-mile warranty. The company frequently ranks first in customer loyalty.[26]

A **market development strategy** concentrates on finding new markets for existing products. Market segmentation, discussed in Chapter 9, provides useful support for such an effort. New Jersey–based supermarket chain Asian Food Markets once targeted chiefly Asian shoppers from China, Taiwan, Korea, and

> **6** Describe the four new-product development strategies.
>
> **market penetration strategy** Strategy that seeks to increase sales of existing products in existing markets.
>
> **product positioning** Consumers' perceptions of a product's attributes, uses, quality, advantages, and disadvantages relative to competing brands.
>
> **market development strategy** Strategy that concentrates on finding new markets for existing products.

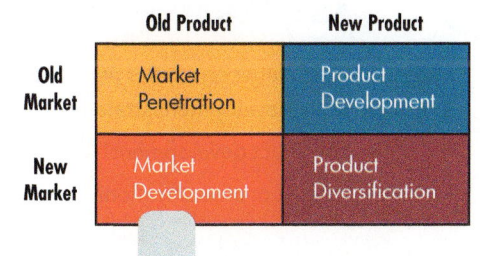

	Old Product	New Product
Old Market	Market Penetration	Product Development
New Market	Market Development	Product Diversification

FIGURE 13.1 Alternative Product Development Strategies

In addition to the original Calvin Klein scent for men, customers can choose flanker brands such as Euphoria and Obsession, both in men's and women's fragrances. Flanker brands are common in the fragrance industry.

product development Introduction of new products into identifiable or established markets.

product diversification strategy Developing entirely new products for new markets.

cannibalization Loss of sales of an existing product due to competition from a new product in the same line.

Japan to the Philippines, Southeast Asia, and India. Today, however, the family-owned enterprise has expanded its reach beyond Asian customers by offering a wide selection of fresh produce, meat and poultry, and fresh baked goods as well as Chinese-inspired dishes for takeout.[27]

The strategy of **product development** refers to the introduction of new products into identifiable or established markets. With its origins in the film industry, 4K technology, also called ultra high definition or UHD, is the latest product development in TVs, promising brighter and crisper images than those shown on 3D TVs. The introduction of 4K has spurred development of new technologies for streaming content, cable boxes, and Blu-ray converters compatible with 4K TVs.[28]

Firms may also choose to introduce new products into markets in which they have already established positions to try to increase overall market share. These new offerings are called *flanker brands*. The fragrance industry uses this strategy extensively when it develops scents related to their most popular products. The flanker scents are related in both their smell and their names. Calvin Klein has built a family of flanker brands around its original Calvin fragrance for men. The flanker brands include Eternity, Obsession, CK One, and Euphoria, all in men's and women's scents; and Beauty for women and CK Free for men. Recently, the company introduced new versions of CK One and Euphoria: CK One Red and Endless Euphoria.[29]

Finally, a **product diversification strategy** focuses on developing entirely new products for new markets. Some firms look for new target markets that complement their existing markets; others look in completely new directions. PepsiCo began diversifying its product lines beyond items that are "fun for you" to items that are "good for you"—including juices, nuts, and oatmeal—several years ago. However, the company recently announced that, while it will continue to promote "good for you" items, it will also spend an additional $5 billion on advertising and marketing Pepsi's traditionally more profitable soft drinks and snacks in other countries, with a renewed emphasis on new-product development.[30]

In selecting a new-product strategy, marketers should keep in mind an additional potential problem: **cannibalization**. Any firm wants to avoid investing resources in a new-product introduction that will adversely affect sales of existing products. A product that takes sales from another offering in the same product line is said to cannibalize that line. A company can accept some loss of sales from existing products if the new offering will generate sufficient additional sales to warrant the investment in its development and market introduction.

ASSESSMENT CHECK

6.1 Distinguish between market penetration and market development strategies.
6.2 What is product development?
6.3 What is product diversification?

7 Describe the five steps in the consumer adoption process.

THE CONSUMER ADOPTION PROCESS

In the **adoption process**, consumers go through a series of stages from first learning about the new product to trying it and deciding whether to purchase it regularly or reject it. These stages in the consumer adoption process can be classified as follows:

Burt's Bees launched an all-out marketing campaign via various channels to introduce its new product line called güd, which is targeted to younger consumers who are attracted by a product's fragrance.

1. *Awareness.* Individuals first learn of the new product, but they lack full information about it.
2. *Interest.* Potential buyers begin to seek information about it.
3. *Evaluation.* They consider the likely benefits of the product.
4. *Trial.* They make trial purchases to determine its usefulness.
5. *Adoption/Rejection.* If the trial purchase produces satisfactory results, they decide to use the product regularly.

adoption process Stages consumers go through in learning about a new product, trying it, and deciding whether to purchase it again.

Marketers must understand the adoption process to move potential consumers to the adoption stage. Once marketers recognize a large number of consumers at the interest stage, they can take steps to stimulate sales by moving these buyers through the evaluation and trial stages. Burt's Bees, which offers natural skin-care, beauty, and personal-care products, introduced güd (pronounced "good"), a new line of products geared to younger buyers who are attracted by a product's scent. Before launching the line, güd's marketing team worked with a fragrance consultant to develop scents not typically available in natural personal care products. The company created 15 fragrances, tested 10 with consumers, and launched 4 to the marketplace. The products have names such as Mango Moonbreeze, Orange Petalooza, Pearanormal Activity, and Red Ruby Groovy. The company recently named singer Carly Rae Jepsen as a product ambassador to its teenage audience.[31]

ADOPTER CATEGORIES

First buyers of new products, the **consumer innovators**, are people who purchase new products almost as soon as these products reach the market. Later adopters wait for additional information and rely on the experiences of initial buyers before making trial purchases. Consumer innovators welcome innovations in each product area. Some computer users, for instance, rush to install new software immediately after each update becomes available.

A number of studies about the adoption of new products have identified five categories of purchasers based on relative times of adoption. These categories, shown in Figure 13.2, are consumer innovators, early adopters, early majority, late majority, and laggards.

consumer innovators Someone who purchases a new product almost as soon as the product reaches the market.

FIGURE 13.2
Categories of Adopters Based on Relative Times of Adoption

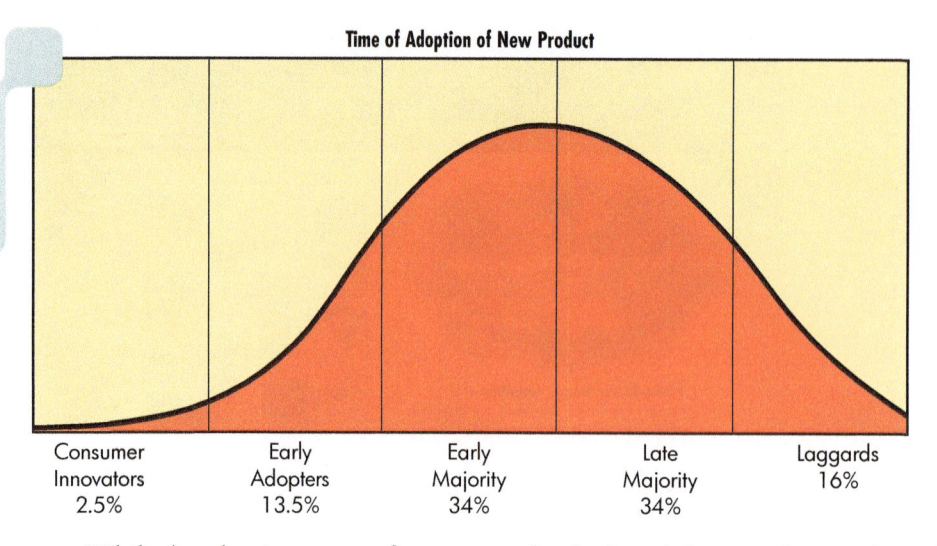

Time of Adoption of New Product

| Consumer Innovators 2.5% | Early Adopters 13.5% | Early Majority 34% | Late Majority 34% | Laggards 16% |

diffusion process
Process by which new goods or services are accepted in the marketplace.

While the adoption process focuses on individuals and the steps they go through in making the ultimate decision of whether to become repeat purchasers of the new product or reject it as failing to satisfy their needs, the **diffusion process** focuses on all members of a community. The focus here is on the speed at which an innovative product is accepted or rejected by all group members.

Figure 13.2 shows the diffusion process as following a normal distribution from a small group of early purchasers (*innovators*) to the final group of consumers (*laggards*) to make trial purchases of the new product. A few people adopt at first, and then the number of adopters increases rapidly as the value of the product becomes apparent. The adoption rate finally diminishes as the number of potential consumers who have not adopted, or purchased, the product diminishes. Typically, innovators make up the first 2.5 percent of buyers who adopt the new product; laggards are the last 16 percent to do so. Figure 13.2 excludes those who never adopt the product.

IDENTIFYING EARLY ADOPTERS

It's no surprise that identifying consumers or organizations most likely to try a new product can be vital to a product's success. By reaching these buyers early in the product's development or introduction, marketers can treat these adopters as a test market, evaluating the product and discovering suggestions for modifications. Because early purchasers often act as opinion leaders from whom others seek advice, their attitudes toward new products quickly spread to others. Acceptance or rejection of the innovation by these purchasers can help forecast its expected success. New car models are multiplying, for instance, and many are sporting a dizzying variety of options such as ports to accommodate—and integrate—the driver's smartphone and other mobile devices. Improved stability controls, collision warnings, and smart engines that save fuel are also available.

A large number of studies have established the general characteristics of first adopters. These pioneers tend to be younger, are better educated, and enjoy higher incomes than other consumers. They are more mobile than later adopters and change both their jobs and addresses more often. They also rely more heavily than later adopters on impersonal information sources; more hesitant buyers depend primarily on company-generated promotional information and word-of-mouth communications.

Rate of Adoption Determinants

Frisbees progressed from the product introduction stage to the market maturity stage in a period of six months. By contrast, the U.S. Department of Agriculture tried for 13 years to persuade corn farmers to use hybrid seed corn, an innovation capable of doubling crop yields. Five characteristics of a product innovation influence its adoption rate:

1. *Relative advantage.* An innovation that appears far superior to previous ideas offers a greater relative advantage—reflected in terms of lower price, physical improvements, or ease of use—and increases the product's adoption rate.

2. *Compatibility.* An innovation consistent with the values and experiences of potential adopters attracts new buyers at a relatively rapid rate. Consumers comfortable with the miniaturization of communications technology are attracted to smartphones, for instance, and the size of their display screens.

3. *Complexity.* The relative difficulty of understanding the innovation influences the speed of acceptance. In most cases, consumers move slowly in adopting new products they find difficult to understand or use. Farmers' cautious acceptance of hybrid seed corn illustrates how long an adoption can take.

4. *Possibility of trial use.* An initial free or discounted trial of a good or service means adopters can reduce their risk of financial loss when they try the product. A coupon for a free item or a free night's stay at a hotel can accelerate the rate of adoption.

5. *Observability.* If potential buyers can observe an innovation's superiority in a tangible form, the adoption rate increases. In-store demonstrations or even advertisements that focus on the superiority of a product can encourage buyers to adopt a product.

Marketers who want to accelerate the rate of adoption can manipulate these five characteristics at least to some extent. An informative promotional message about a new allergy drug could help consumers overcome their hesitation in adopting this product. Effective product design can emphasize an item's advantages over the competition. Everyone likes to receive something for free, so giving away small samples of a new product lets consumers try it at little or no risk. Marketers must also make positive attempts to ensure the innovation's compatibility with adopters' value systems.

ORGANIZING FOR NEW-PRODUCT DEVELOPMENT

A firm needs to be organized in such a way that its personnel can stimulate and coordinate new-product development. Some companies contract with independent design firms to develop new products. Many assign product-innovation functions to one or more of the following entities: new-product committees, new-product departments, product managers, and venture teams.

New-Product Committees
The most common organizational arrangement for activities in developing a new product is to center these functions in a new-product committee. This group typically brings together experts in areas such as marketing, finance, manufacturing, engineering, and research. Committee members spend less time conceiving and developing their own new-product ideas than reviewing and approving new-product plans that arise elsewhere in the organization. The committee might review ideas from the engineering and design staff or perhaps from marketers and salespeople who are in constant contact with customers.

Because members of a new-product committee hold important jobs in the firm's functional areas, their support for any new-product plan likely foreshadows approval for further development. However, new-product committees in large companies tend to reach decisions slowly and maintain conservative views. Sometimes members compromise so they can return to their regular work responsibilities.

New-Product Departments
Many companies establish separate, formally organized departments to generate and refine new-product ideas. The departmental structure overcomes the limitations of the new-product committee system and encourages innovation as a permanent full-time activity. The new-product department is responsible for all phases of a development project within the firm, including screening decisions, developing product specifications, and coordinating product testing. The head of the department wields substantial authority and typically reports to the chief executive officer, chief operating officer, or a top marketing executive.

Product Managers
A **product manager** is another term for a brand manager, a function mentioned earlier in the chapter. This marketer supports the marketing strategies of an individual product or product line.

product manager
Marketer responsible for an individual product or product line; also called a brand manager.

Product managers set prices, develop advertising and sales promotion programs, and work with sales representatives in the field. In a company that sells multiple products, product managers fulfill key functions in the marketing department. They provide individual attention for each product and support and coordinate efforts of the firm's sales force, marketing researchers, and advertising department. Product managers often lead new-product development programs, including creation of new-product ideas and recommendations for improving existing products.

However, most consumer-goods companies, such as Procter & Gamble and General Mills, have either modified the product manager structure or done away with it all together in favor of a category management structure. Category managers have profit and loss responsibility, which is not characteristic of the product management system. This change has largely come about because of customer preference, but it can also benefit a manufacturer by avoiding duplication of some jobs and competition among the company's own brands and its managers.

Venture Teams

venture team Group of personnel from different areas of an organization who work together in developing new products.

A **venture team** gathers a group of specialists from different areas of an organization to work together in developing new products. The venture team must meet criteria for return on investment, uniqueness of product, serving a well-defined need, compatibility of the product with existing technology, and strength of patent protection. Although the organization sets up the venture team as a temporary entity, its flexible life span may extend over a number of years. When purchases confirm the commercial potential of a new product, an existing division may take responsibility for that product, or it may serve as the nucleus of a new business unit or of an entirely new company.

Some marketing organizations differentiate between venture teams and task forces. A new-product task force assembles an interdisciplinary group working on temporary assignment through their functional departments. Its basic activities center around coordinating and integrating the

CAREER READINESS
How to Be a Team Player

Work groups and teams are more popular than ever. How can you turn your team assignment into a success for you and for your teammates?

1. Be reliable. That means be on time and come prepared to meetings, complete your assigned tasks, communicate clearly, and contribute actively to discussions.

2. Help others in the group. Volunteer your assistance; perhaps you can help a team member catch up on his or her assignment or lend an extra effort to achieving a group goal.

3. Be respectful of others. Listen to others' opinions with an open mind, accommodate their differences, and avoid criticizing.

4. Play an active social role and build solid work relationships. Go to lunch with team members or join company extracurricular activities. You'll get to know team members in a different setting and might even make new connections across the organization that can help you and the team.

5. Set the example and promote a positive team atmosphere. Some conflict is unavoidable, but don't be the source or the cause of it. Keep a positive attitude and avoid complainers and troublemakers.

6. Be the person who gets things done. Your efforts won't go unnoticed.

Sources: Jon Gordon, "9 Ways to Be a Great Team Member," (blog), accessed March 21, 2014, www.jongordon.com; Tatyana Sussex, "6 Tips to Become a Highly Valued Member of Your Team," *Liquid Planner*, accessed March 21, 2014, www.liquidplanner.com; "How to Be a Successful Team Player at Work," *eHow*, accessed March 21, 2014, www.ehow.com; "How to Be a Team Player," *Doostang News*, accessed March 21, 2014, http://blog.doostang.com; Marty Brounstein, "Ten Qualities of an Effective Team Player," *Managing Teams for Dummies*, accessed March 21, 2014, www.dummies.com.

work of the firm's functional departments for a specific project. Check out the "Career Readiness" feature for some tips about working successfully in a group or team.

Unlike a new-product committee, a venture team does not disband after every meeting. Team members accept project assignments as major responsibilities, and the team exercises the authority it needs to both plan and implement a course of action. To stimulate product innovation, the venture team typically communicates directly with top management but functions as an entity separate from the basic organization.

ASSESSMENT CHECK

7.1 Who are consumer innovators?

7.2 What characteristics of a product innovation can influence its adoption rate?

THE NEW-PRODUCT DEVELOPMENT PROCESS

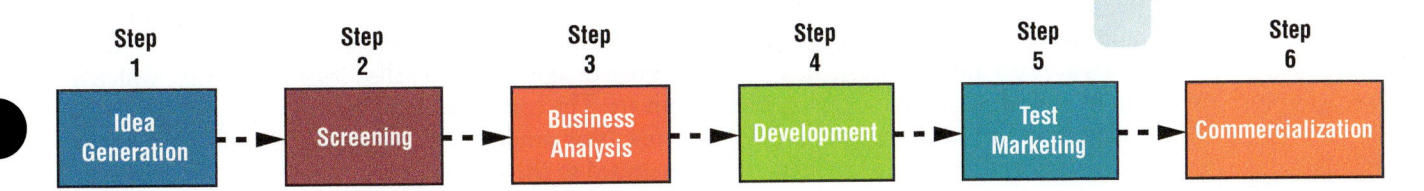

Once a firm is organized for new-product development, it can establish procedures for moving new-product ideas to the marketplace. Developing a new product is often time-consuming, risky, and expensive. Usually, firms must generate dozens of new-product ideas to produce even one successful product. In fact, the failure rate of new products averages 80 percent. Products fail for a number of reasons, including inadequate market assessments, lack of market orientation, poor screening and project evaluation, product defects, and inadequate launch efforts. And these blunders cost a bundle: Firms invest nearly half of the total resources devoted to product innovation on products that become commercial failures.

A new product is more likely to become successful if the firm follows the six-step development process shown in Figure 13.3: (1) idea generation, (2) screening, (3) business analysis, (4) development, (5) test marketing, and (6) commercialization. Of course, each step requires decisions about whether to proceed further or abandon the project. And each step involves a greater financial investment.

Traditionally, most companies developed new products through phased development, which follows the six steps in an orderly sequence. Responsibility for each phase passes first from product planners to designers and engineers, then to manufacturers, and finally to marketers. The phased development method can work well for firms that dominate mature markets and can develop variations on existing products. But with rapid changes in technology and markets, companies often feel pressured to speed up the development process.

Many firms respond by implementing accelerated product development programs. These programs generally consist of teams with design, manufacturing, marketing, and sales personnel who carry out development projects from idea generation to commercialization. This method can reduce the time needed to develop products, because team members work on the six steps concurrently rather than in sequence.

Whether a firm pursues phased development or parallel product development, all phases can benefit from planning tools and scheduling methods, such as the program evaluation and review technique (PERT) and the critical path method (CPM). These techniques, originally developed by the U.S. Navy in connection with construction of the Polaris missile and submarine, map out the sequence of each step in a process and show the time allotments for each activity. Detailed PERT and CPM flowcharts help marketers coordinate all activities in the development and introduction of new products.

Explain the six steps in the new-product development process.

FIGURE 13.3
Steps in the New-Product Development Process

Step 1	Step 2	Step 3	Step 4	Step 5	Step 6
Idea Generation	Screening	Business Analysis	Development	Test Marketing	Commercialization

New-product development begins with ideas from many sources: suggestions from customers, the sales force, research and development specialists, competing products, suppliers, retailers, and independent inventors. Bose Corporation has built its brand by staying at the forefront of technology. Spending an estimated $100 million a year on research, the company leads the market for products using advanced technology: sound systems for businesses, cars, and consumer use, including noise-cancelling headphones, wireless speakers, TV sound systems, and Wave music systems.[32]

With the goal of winning 1 billion new customers over the next decade, the cosmetics and beauty company L'Oréal opened a global research center in Paris for the sole purpose of developing new hair-coloring, hair-care, and hair-styling products.[33] Similarly, ongoing research by scientists at lawn-care industry leader Scotts Miracle-Gro helps the company fine-tune its understanding of consumer needs as it develops products and incorporates environmentally responsible behavior throughout its operations.[34]

SCREENING

Screening separates ideas with commercial potential from those that cannot meet company objectives. Some organizations maintain checklists of development standards in determining whether a project should be abandoned or considered further. These checklists typically include factors such as product uniqueness, availability of raw materials, and the proposed product's compatibility with current product offerings, facilities, and, capabilities. The screening stage may also allow for open discussions of new-product ideas among different parts of the organization.

BUSINESS ANALYSIS

A product idea that survives the initial screening must then pass thorough business analysis. This stage consists of assessing the new product's potential market, growth rate, and likely competitive strengths. Marketers must evaluate the compatibility of the proposed product with organizational resources.

concept testing Method for subjecting a product idea to additional study before actual development by involving consumers through focus groups, surveys, in-store polling, and similar strategies.

Concept testing subjects the product idea to additional study prior to its actual development. This important aspect of a new product's business analysis represents a marketing research project that attempts to measure consumer attitudes and perceptions about the new-product idea. Focus groups and in-store polling can contribute effectively to concept testing. The Eclipse 500 Jet, a six-passenger airplane that weighs under 10,000 pounds, can fly faster and higher than other aircraft in its class. Before manufacturing the plane, Eclipse Aviation spent years testing its concept. During its research phase, the company sought input from small- and large-plane pilots as well as experts from both inside and outside the aviation industry.[35] The screening and business analysis stages generate extremely important information for new-product development because they (1) define the proposed product's target market and customers' needs and wants and (2) determine the product's financial and technical requirements. Firms willing to invest money and time during these stages tend to be more successful at generating viable ideas and creating successful products.

DEVELOPMENT

Financial outlays increase substantially as a firm converts an idea into a visible product. The conversion process is the joint responsibility of the firm's development engineers, who turn the original concept into a product, and its marketers, who provide feedback on consumer reactions to the product design, package, color, and other physical features. Many firms implement computer-aided design and manufacturing (CAD/CAM) systems to streamline the development stage, and prototypes may go through numerous changes before the original mock-up becomes a final product. Southern California–based sports eyewear and apparel marketer Oakley uses a design approach called *sculptural physics,* which it views as the discipline of wrapping science with art. The company's ideas are born using CAD/CAM engineering and are given form as 3D prototypes. New products are evaluated and field-tested by the world's top athletes. Once finalized, they are released to the general public.

Chapter 13 Developing and Managing Brand and Product Categories

TEST MARKETING

As discussed in Chapter 10, many firms test market their new-product offerings to gauge consumer reaction. After a company develops a prototype, it may decide to test market it to measure consumer reactions under normal competitive conditions. Test marketing's purpose is to verify that the product will perform well in a real-life environment. If the product does well, the company can proceed to commercialization. If it flops, the company can fine-tune certain features and reintroduce it or pull the plug on the project altogether. Industries that rely heavily on test marketing are snack foods, automobiles, and movies. Of course, even if a product tests well and reaches the commercialization stage, it may still take a while to catch on with the general public.

> **Briefly Speaking**
>
> "Innovation is not about saying yes to everything. It's about saying NO to all but the most crucial features."
>
> —Steve Jobs
> *Co-founder, Apple*

COMMERCIALIZATION

When a new-product idea reaches the commercialization stage, it is ready for full-scale marketing. Commercialization of a major new product can expose the firm to substantial expenses. It must establish marketing strategies; fund outlays for production facilities; and acquaint the sales force, marketing intermediaries, and potential customers with the new product.

> **ASSESSMENT CHECK**
>
> 8.1 Where do ideas for new products come from?
> 8.2 What is concept testing?
> 8.3 What happens in the commercialization stage?

PRODUCT SAFETY AND LIABILITY

A product can fulfill its mission of satisfying consumer needs only if it ensures safe operation. Manufacturers must design their products to protect users from harm. Products that lead to injuries, either directly or indirectly, can have disastrous consequences for their makers. **Product liability** refers to the responsibility of manufacturers and marketers for injuries and damages caused by their products. Chapter 3 discussed some of the major consumer protection laws that affect product safety. These laws include the Flammable Fabrics Act of 1953, the Fair Packaging and Labeling Act of 1966, the Poison Prevention Packaging Act of 1970, and the Consumer Product Safety Act of 1972.

Federal and state legislation play a major role in regulating product safety. The Poison Prevention Packaging Act requires drug manufacturers to place their products in packaging that is child resistant yet accessible to all adults, even ones who have difficulty opening containers. The Consumer Product Safety Act created a powerful regulatory agency—the Consumer Product Safety Commission (CPSC). This agency has assumed jurisdiction over every consumer product category except food, automobiles, and a few other products already regulated by other agencies. The CPSC has the authority to ban products without court hearings, order recalls or redesigns of products, and inspect production facilities. It can charge managers of negligent companies with criminal offenses. The CPSC is especially watchful of products aimed at infants and young children.

The federal Food and Drug Administration must approve food, medications, and health-related devices such as wheelchairs. The Food Allergen Labeling and Consumer Protection Act mentioned earlier increased the requirements for food labeling. The FDA can also take products off the market if concerns arise about the safety of these products.

The number of product liability lawsuits filed against manufacturers skyrocketed in recent years. Marketers' exposure to potential liability and litigation is also on the rise in many overseas markets. Many of these claims reach settlements out of court. DePuy Orthopaedics, a division of Johnson & Johnson, agreed to pay $4 billion to settle consumer lawsuits related to its hip implant devices, which had to be replaced.[36]

The threat of lawsuit has led most companies to step up efforts to ensure product safety. Safety warnings appear prominently on the labels of potentially hazardous products such as cleaning fluids and drain cleaners to inform users of the dangers of these products, particularly to children. Changes

9 Explain the relationship between product safety and product liability.

product liability Responsibility of manufacturers and marketers for injuries and damages caused by their products.

Volvo built a reputation for engineering safety features into its autos. Geely Holding Group, a private Chinese firm that bought the Sweden-based automaker, recently opened the China Sweden Research Centre for Traffic Safety in Beijing in collaboration with several other partners, including Chalmers University of Technology.

Chalmers partners Sino-Swedish research centre on traffic safety

in product design have reduced the hazards posed by products such as lawn mowers, hedge trimmers, and toys. Product liability insurance has become an essential element for any new or existing product strategy. Premiums for this insurance have risen alarmingly, however, and insurers have almost entirely abandoned some kinds of coverage.

Regulatory activities and the increased number of liability claims have prompted companies to sponsor voluntary improvements in safety standards. Many companies, including Walmart and Mattel, have worked with the Consumer Product Safety Commission to improve their safety protocols. Walmart uses its Retailer Reporting Model to provide CPSC with detailed weekly reports about customer product safety complaints and concerns. Safety planning is now a vital element of product strategy, and many companies now publicize the safety planning and testing that go into the development of their products. Volvo, for example, is well known for the safety features it designs into its automobiles, and consumers recognize that fact when they decide to purchase a Volvo.

ASSESSMENT CHECK

9.1 What is the role of the Consumer Product Safety Commission?

9.2 What safety issues come under the jurisdiction of the Food and Drug Administration?

Strategic Implications of Marketing in the 21st Century

Marketers who want to see their products reach the marketplace successfully have a number of options for developing them, branding them, and developing a strong brand identity among consumers and business customers. The key is to integrate all of the options so they are compatible with a firm's overall business and marketing strategy and, ultimately, the firm's mission. As marketers consider ideas for new products, they need to be careful not to send their companies in so many different directions as to dilute the identities of their brands, making it nearly impossible to keep track of what their companies do well. Category management can help companies develop a consistent product mix with strong branding, while at the same time meeting the needs of customers. Looking for ways to extend a brand without diluting it or compromising brand equity is also an important marketing strategy. Finally, marketers must continue to work to produce high-quality products that are safe for all users.

Get online now for additional learning tools to help you master your marketing knowledge—visit **WWW.CENGAGEBRAIN.COM** today!

REVIEW OF CHAPTER OBJECTIVES

1 Discuss how to define a brand.

Marketers recognize the powerful influence products and product lines have on customer behavior, and they work to create strong identities for their products and protect them. Branding is the process of creating that identity. A brand is a name, term, sign, symbol, design, or some combination that identifies the products of one firm while differentiating these products from competitors' offerings.

2 Identify the five different types of brands.

A generic product is an item characterized by a plain label—no advertising, no brand name. A manufacturer's brand is a brand name owned by a manufacturer or other producer. Private brands are brand names placed on products marketed by a wholesaler or retailer. Captive brands are national brands sold exclusively by a retail chain. A family brand is a brand name that identifies several related products. An individual brand is a unique brand name that identifies a specific offering within a firm's product line to avoid grouping it under a family brand.

3 Explain the strategic value of brand equity.

Brand equity provides a competitive advantage for a firm, because consumers are more likely to buy a product that carries a respected, well-known brand name. Brand equity also eases the path for global expansion.

4 Explain the benefits of category and brand management.

Category management is beneficial to a business because it gives direct responsibility for creating profitable product lines to category managers and their product group. Consumers respond to branding by making repeat purchases of favored goods and services. Therefore, good management of brands and categories of brands or product lines can result in a direct response from consumers, increasing profits and revenues for companies and creating consumer satisfaction. Brand and category managers can also enhance relationships with business customers such as retailers.

5 Discuss how companies develop a strong identity for their product or brand.

Effective brands communicate to a buyer an idea of the product's image. Trademarks, brand names, slogans, and brand icons create associations that satisfy the customer's expectation of the benefits that using or having those products will yield.

6 Describe the four new-product development strategies.

The success of a new product can result from four product development strategies: market penetration, in which a company seeks to increase sales of an existing product in an existing market; (1) market development, which concentrates on finding new markets for existing products; (2) product development, the introduction of new products into identifiable or established markets; and (3) product diversification, which focuses on developing entirely new products for new markets.

7 Describe the five steps in the consumer adoption process.

In the adoption process, consumers go through a series of stages, from learning about the new product to trying it and deciding whether to purchase it again. The stages are called awareness, interest, evaluation, trial, and adoption/rejection.

8 Explain the six steps in the new-product development process.

The stages in the six-step new-product development process are (1) idea generation, (2) screening, (3) business analysis, (4) development, (5) test marketing, and (6) commercialization. These steps can be performed sequentially or, in some cases, concurrently.

9 Explain the relationship between product safety and product liability.

Product safety refers to a manufacturer's goal of creating products that can be used safely and will protect consumers from harm. Product liability is the responsibility of marketers and manufacturers for injuries and damages caused by their products. Major consumer protection laws are in place to protect consumers from faulty products.

ASSESSMENT CHECK: ANSWERS

1.1 What is a brand? A brand is a name, term, sign, symbol, design, or some combination that identifies the products of one firm while differentiating these products from competitors' offerings.

1.2 Differentiate among brand recognition, brand preference, and brand insistence. Brand recognition is a company's first objective for newly introduced products and aims to make these items familiar to the public. Brand preference is buyers' reliance on previous experiences with the product when choosing it over competitors' products. Brand insistence leads consumers to refuse alternatives and to search extensively for the desired merchandise.

2.1 Identify the five different types of brands. The different types of brands are manufacturer's (or national) brands, private brands, captive brands, family brands, and individual brands.

2.2 How are generic products different from branded products? Generic products are characterized by plain labels, little or no advertising, and no brand names.

3.1 What is brand equity? Brand equity refers to the added value a certain brand name gives to a product in the marketplace.

3.2 What are the four dimensions of brand personality? The four dimensions of brand personality are differentiation, relevance, esteem, and knowledge.

4.1 Define brand manager. A brand manager is the person at a company with the task of managing a brand's marketing strategies.

4.2 How does category management help retailers? Category management helps retailers by providing a person—a category manager—who oversees an entire product line and maximizes sales for that retailer. Category management teams the consumer goods producer's marketing expertise with the retailer's in-store merchandising efforts to track and identify new opportunities for growth.

5.1 Distinguish between a brand name and a trademark. A brand name is the part of the brand consisting of letters, numbers, or words that can be spoken and that forms a name distinguishing a firm's offerings from those of its competitors. A trademark is a brand for which the owner claims exclusive legal protection.

5.2 What are the three purposes of packaging? A package serves three major objectives: (1) protection against damage, spoilage, and pilferage; (2) assistance in marketing the product; and (3) cost effectiveness.

5.3 Describe brand extension and brand licensing. Brand extension is the strategy of attaching a popular brand name to a new product in an unrelated product category. Brand licensing is the strategy of authorizing other companies to use a brand name.

6.1 Distinguish between market penetration and market development strategies. In a market penetration strategy, a company seeks to increase sales of an existing product in an existing market. In a market development strategy, the company concentrates on finding new markets for existing products.

6.2 What is product development? Product development is the introduction of new products into identifiable or established markets.

6.3 What is product diversification? A product diversification strategy focuses on developing entirely new products for new markets.

7.1 Who are consumer innovators? Consumer innovators are the first buyers of new products—people who purchase new products almost as soon as these products reach the market.

7.2 What characteristics of a product innovation can influence its adoption rate? Five characteristics of a product innovation influence its adoption rate: relative advantage, compatibility, complexity, possibility of trial use, and observability.

8.1 Where do ideas for new products come from? New-product development begins with ideas from many sources: suggestions from customers; the sales force, or research and development specialists; suppliers, retailers, and independent inventors; and assessments of competing products.

8.2 What is concept testing? Concept testing subjects a product idea to additional study prior to its actual development.

8.3 What happens in the commercialization stage? When a new-product idea reaches the commercialization stage, it is ready for full-scale marketing.

9.1 What is the role of the Consumer Product Safety Commission? The Consumer Product Safety Commission is a powerful regulatory agency with jurisdiction over every consumer product category except food, automobiles, and a few other products already regulated by other agencies.

9.2 What safety issues come under the jurisdiction of the Food and Drug Administration? The Food and Drug Administration must approve food, medications, and health-related devices such as wheelchairs.

Chapter 13 Developing and Managing Brand and Product Categories

MARKETING TERMS YOU NEED TO KNOW

brand 410
brand recognition 411
brand preference 411
brand insistence 413
generic products 413
manufacturer's brand 413
private brands 413
captive brands 413
family brand 413
individual brand 413
brand equity 414
brand manager 415
category management 415
brand name 416
brand mark 416
trademark 417
trade dress 418
label 421
universal product code (UPC) 421
brand extension 421
line extensions 421
brand licensing 422
market penetration strategy 423
product positioning 423
market development strategy 423
product development 424
product diversification strategy 424
cannibalization 424
adoption process 425
consumer innovators 425
diffusion process 426
product manager 427
venture team 428
concept testing 430
product liability 431

ASSURANCE OF LEARNING REVIEW

1. What are the three stages marketers use to measure brand loyalty?
2. Identify and briefly describe the different types of brands.
3. Why is brand equity so important to companies?
4. What are the characteristics of an effective brand name?
5. What role does packaging play in helping create brand loyalty and brand equity?
6. What is category management, and what role does it play in the success of a product line?
7. Describe the different product development strategies.
8. What are the five stages of the consumer adoption process?
9. Describe the ways companies can organize to develop new products.
10. List the six steps in the new-product development process.

PROJECTS AND TEAMWORK EXERCISES

1. Locate an advertisement for a product that illustrates an especially effective brand name, brand mark, packaging, and overall trade dress. Explain to the class why you think this product has a strong brand identity.
2. With a classmate, search a grocery store for a product you think could benefit from updated or new package design. Then sketch out a new package design for the product, identifying and explaining your changes as well as your reasons for the changes. Bring the old package and your new package design to class to share with your classmates.
3. What category of consumer adopter best describes you? Do you follow the same adoption pattern for all products? Or are you an early adopter for some and a laggard for others? Create a graph or chart showing your own consumer adoption patterns for different products.
4. Which product labels do you read? Over the next several days, keep a brief record of the labels you check while shopping. Do you read nutritional information when buying food products? Do you check care labels on clothes before you buy them? Do you read the directions or warnings on a product you haven't used before? Make notes about what influenced your decision to read or not read the product labels. Did you think they provided enough information, too little, or too much?
5. Some brands achieve customer loyalty by retaining an air of exclusivity and privilege, even though that often comes with high price tags. Louis Vuitton, the maker of luxury leather goods, is one such firm. What kind of brand loyalty is this, and how does Vuitton achieve it?

CRITICAL-THINKING EXERCISES

1. In this chapter, you learned that American Girl has expanded its products beyond the original American Girl dolls, intended for nine-year-old girls. Why has this strategy worked for the company? Identify another well-known product that appeals to a specific age group. Do you think a similar strategy would be successful? Why or why not?
2. General Mills and several other major food makers have begun producing organic foods. But they have deliberately kept

their brand names off the packaging of these new products, thinking that the kind of customer who goes out of his or her way to buy organic products is unlikely to trust multinational brands. Other companies, however, such as Heinz, PepsiCo, and Tyson Foods, are betting that their brand names will prove to be persuasive in the $35 billion organic foods market. Which strategy do you think is more likely to be successful? Why?

3. The former mayor of New York City called for a ban on super-sized sugary drinks at delis, fast-food restaurants, and sports areas in the city, saying that obesity is a national epidemic and New York should take the lead in doing something about the problem. While some consumer groups backed the proposed ban, other industry groups and companies objected. Do you think such a ban would help in the fight against obesity? If you were a marketing manager for a fast-food restaurant chain, how would you handle the situation if such a ban gets approved?

4. Brand names contribute enormously to consumers' perception of a brand. One writer has argued that alphanumeric brand names, such as the Toyota RAV4, Jaguar's XF-type sedan, the Xbox game console, and the GTI from Volkswagen, can translate more easily overseas than "real" names such as Golf, Jetta, and Escalade. What other advantages and disadvantages can you think of for each type of brand name? Do you think one type is preferable to the other? Why?

ETHICS EXERCISE

As mentioned in the chapter, some analysts predict barcodes may be replaced by a wireless technology called *radio-frequency identification (RFID)*. RFID is a system of installing tags containing tiny computer chips on, say, supermarket items. These chips automatically radio the location of the item to a computer network where inventory data is stored, letting store managers know not only where the item is at all times but also when and where it was made and its color and size. Proponents believe RFID cuts costs and simplifies inventory tracking and reordering. It may also allow marketers to respond quickly to shifts in demand, avoid under- and overstocking, and reduce spoilage by automatically removing outdated perishables from the shelves. Privacy advocates, however, think the chips provide too much product-preference information that might be identified with individual consumers. In the meantime, Walmart requires its major suppliers to use the new technology on products stocked by the giant retailer.

1. Do you think RFID poses a threat to consumer privacy? Why or why not?
2. Do you think the technology's possible benefits to marketers outweigh the potential privacy concerns? Are there also potential benefits to consumers? If so, what are they?
3. How can marketers reassure consumers about privacy concerns if RFID comes into widespread use?

INTERNET EXERCISES

1. **Ferrari brand.** Visit the Ferrari website. Review the material and prepare a report outlining how Ferrari—a company that produces products that only a handful of consumers can afford—has been able to build such a strong, recognizable brand.

   www.ferrari.com

2. **Trademark disputes.** Search an Internet news site, such as Google News, and the U.S. Patent and Trademark Office for recent trademark dispute cases. Select two of these cases and prepare a summary of each. Does the number of trademark dispute cases appear to be growing? If so, what is one possible explanation for this increase?

   http://news.google.com
   www.uspto.gov

3. **Brand equity.** Several sources compile lists each year of the world's most valuable brands. Two are *Bloomberg Businessweek* magazine and a consulting firm called Brand Finance. Visit both websites and review the most recent lists of the world's most valuable brands. How many firms are represented on both lists? Where are these firms located? What criteria do *Businessweek* and Brand Finance use in determining brand equity? Which brands have improved their values the most over the past couple of years?

   www.businessweek.com
   www.brandfinance.com

Note: Internet Web addresses change frequently. If you don't find the exact site listed, you may need to access the organization's home page and search from there or use a search engine such as Google or Bing.

CASE 13.1
Chobani Greek Yogurt Focuses on Tradition

When a Turkish immigrant converted an old food plant in upstate New York to create a kind of yogurt unlike anything many U.S. consumers had ever tasted, little did he dream his company would receive an Entrepreneurial Success of the Year award a few years later. Chobani, the company Hamdi Ulukaya founded with five employees almost a decade ago, has become the number-one producer of Greek yogurt in the United States and is driving a dramatically rising trend.

Greek yogurt, with its thicker, creamier texture and slightly tart taste, now accounts for 52 percent of U.S. yogurt sales, and some observers believe there is no end in sight. Chobani and other brands of Greek yogurt have more protein and less sugar than products made by most U.S. firms, and consumers—especially women and upper-income shoppers—are snapping it up as quickly as producers can manufacture it.

Chobani and Fage, one of its competitors, both have ambitious expansion plans, including enlarging their plants, which lie about an hour apart in New York State, where they have given a strong boost to the local economy. The state now has six yogurt plants and recently surpassed California as the top yogurt-producing state. Chobani also spent more than $250 million to open the largest plant of its kind in Twin Falls, Idaho, in part to ease distribution of its products to western states. Meanwhile, mainstream yogurt makers such as Dannon have introduced Greek-style yogurt products, too.

Chobani has 3,000 employees and ships 2.2 million cases of yogurt across the United States every week, racking up annual sales of over $1 billion. With "How Matters" as its corporate motto, the firm still pays individual attention to each batch. "We aimed at people who never liked yogurt," Ulukaya says, explaining that these consumers had never tasted Greek yogurt before, so they couldn't be blamed for not realizing how tasty it could be. Chobani's founder recently won the Ernst & Young World Entrepreneur Award for his business efforts.

QUESTIONS FOR CRITICAL THINKING

1. What factors account for the rising popularity of Greek yogurt?
2. Do you think the sales trend will continue upward? Why or why not?

Sources: Company website, www.chobani.com, accessed October 16, 2014; Elaine Watson, "Chobani Simply 100 Greek Yogurt Snags 1.3% Share of U.S. Yogurt Market Just Six Weeks after Launch," *Food Navigator*, accessed October 16, 2014, www.foodnavigator-usa.com; Megan Durisin, "Chobani CEO: Our Success Has Nothing to Do with Yogurt," *Business Insider*, accessed March 21, 2014, www.businessinsider.com; Bryan Gruley, "At Chobani, the Turkish King of Greek Yogurt," *Bloomberg Businessweek*, accessed March 21, 2014, www.businessweek.com; Brian Smith, "Chobani to Increase Twin Falls Production, Add New Product," *Twin Falls Times-News*, accessed March 21, 2014, http://magicvalley.com; Oliver Pursche, "What Investors Can Learn from Chobani's Hamdi Ulukaya's Success," *Forbes*, accessed March 21, 2014, www.forbes.com; J.D. Harrison, "Greek Yogurt Maker Chobani Takes Home 2012 SBA Entrepreneurship Award," *The Washington Post*, accessed March 21, 2014, www.washingtonpost.com; William Neuman, "Greek Yogurt a Boon for New York State," *The New York Times*, accessed March 21, 2014, www.nytimes.com.

VIDEO CASE 13.2
At Zappos, Passion Is Paramount

From its humble beginnings as the first online shoe store, Zappos has grown to nearly gargantuan proportions. Now owned by Amazon, the online retailer carries most of the top footwear and apparel brands, along with handbags and luggage, and last but not least, home furnishings and beauty products. In other words, if Zappos were a brick-and-mortar store, you could live there.

"When Zappos first started out, it was all about the best selection of products," recalls Steve Hill, vice president of merchandising. In many respects that's still true—but as the company has expanded, it has adjusted the way it manages brands as well as entire categories of goods. A decade ago, Fred Mossler (former vice president of merchandising, recently promoted to the position of "No Title") went to the annual World Shoe Accessories show in Las Vegas in hopes of luring a few brands to the site. (According to the company, Mossler's "No Title" enables him to oversee a variety of departments within the organization.) He talked with more than 100 vendors there, but only 3 agreed to offer their products on Zappos. Today, the company carries 1,165 brands and counting. "We carry the top brands," says Hill.

The merchandising team, which includes lead buyers, buyers, assistant buyers, and merchandising assistants, scours the earth for the best brands in any product category—then meets with vendors and decides which will sell best at Zappos. The company's buyers concentrate entirely on a single category of products. "Our buyers are aligned around lifestyles—so our hiking buyer will buy only hiking products and our running buyer will buy only running products." But specialization doesn't stop there. "Our buyers buy stuff that they're passionate about," explains Hill. "For example, our running buyers are running marathons and half-marathons and 5Ks." This makes them virtual experts in the category of goods they buy for Zappos to sell online to consumers.

Zappos prefers to hire its buyers based on their passion for a specific activity or product category. "If we can hire them for their passion for the category, we can teach them all the skills of buying," says Hill. In fact, the buyers themselves have created categories at Zappos, based on their own interests. That's how Zappos began selling outdoor apparel and footwear, as well as designer fashions. The other avenue that Zappos takes for developing categories is through customer feedback—if enough customers request a new category or specific brand, Zappos will work hard to bring it to them.

Although Zappos remains focused on manufacturers' brands with names such as Nike, Billabong, Guess, Lacoste, Steve Madden, and Mountain Hardwear, the retailer also has a few couture offerings, such as the family brands 10 Crosby by Derek Lam and Adidas by Stella McCartney. Recently, the company has been testing the waters with its own private footwear and apparel label called The Cool People. It's not a huge chunk of business—instead filling niches not covered by Zappos' branded partners. One of the most successful private-label products for Zappos is a wide-calf boot for women—so much so that branded manufacturers have begun to create their own wide-calf boots.

While Zappos is the self-proclaimed merchant of happiness, managing the growing collection of brands is serious business. This doesn't mean Zappos employees don't have fun or enjoy what they are doing—it's quite the opposite. It's just that Zappos inspires its buyers with a sense of entrepreneurship within a large company. "We want buyers to feel like they're buying for their own boutique or storefront," explains Hill. "We call it the shopkeeper's mentality. We want them to feel if they don't buy the right stuff, they won't be able to keep the lights on. We are part of a much bigger company now, but we want everyone to feel like they're running their own business and in control of what they're doing."

Hill acknowledges that, despite the huge success of online retailing over the last decade, it still represents only about 8 to 9 percent of overall retailing in the United States. However, he and other marketing experts predict that number will grow to 30 percent in the next ten years. This means that Zappos is poised to make huge gains if it continues to offer an expanding array of brands backed by superior customer service. Hill believes that his company's mix of goods and services will keep shoppers coming back. "Once they find us," he says, "they'll stick with us and be loyal to us."

QUESTIONS FOR CRITICAL THINKING

1. Describe how Zappos builds brand equity along the four dimensions of brand personality.
2. What steps might Zappos take to build its private brands without endangering its relationship with the producers of manufacturing brands?

Sources: Company website, www.zappos.com, accessed March 21, 2014; Tricia Duryee, "Zappos Founder Focuses on Brand Loyalty for His Next Gig," *All Things Digital*, accessed March 21, 2014, http://allthingsd.com; "Show or Tell?" *Brand Story Online*, accessed March 21, 2014, www.brandstoryonline.com.

NOTES

1. Company website, www.ua.com, accessed October 16, 2014; Andrew Adam Newman, "Under Armour Heads Off the Sidelines for a Campaign Aimed at Women," *The New York Times*, accessed October 16, 2014, www.nytimes.com; Lydia DePillis, "Five Smart Things Under Armour Did to Take On the Sports Retail Giants," *The Washington Post*, accessed March 21, 2014, www.washingtonpost.com; Sarah Meehan, "This $100 Premium Running Shoe Could Be Under Armour's Breakout Footwear Product," *Baltimore Business Journal*, accessed March 21, 2014, www.bizjournals.com; Eben Novy-Williams, "Notre Dame Says Under Armour Deal Is Biggest in College History," *Bloomberg News*, accessed March 21, 2014, www.bloomberg.com; Monte Burke, "Under Armour's Aggressive Plan to Expand Overseas," *Forbes*, accessed March 21, 2014, www.forbes.com; Richard Woodard, "In the Money: Under Armour Gears Up for the Future," *Just Style*, accessed March 21, 2014, www.just-style.com; Trey Palmisano, "From Rags to Microfiber: Inside the Rapid Rise of Under Armour," *Sports Illustrated*, accessed March 21, 2014, http://sportsillustrated.cnn.com; "Under Armour's Kevin Plank: Creating the 'Biggest, Baddest Brand on the Planet,'" *Knowledge@Wharton*, accessed March 21, 2014, http://knowledge.wharton.upenn.edu.
2. "Study: Nearly All Shoppers Buy Private Label Groceries," *Store Brands Decisions*, accessed March 21, 2014, www.storebrandsdecisions.com.
3. Company website, "Here's Your Guide to Buying Green," www.officedepot.com, accessed March 21, 2014.
4. Company website, "Brand Shop," www.target.com, accessed March 21, 2014.
5. Lara O'Reilly, "The 20 Most Valuable Brands in the World," *Business Insider*, accessed October 16, 2014, www.businessinsider.com.
6. Company website, "About Y&R," www.yr.com, accessed March 22, 2014; company website, http://bavconsulting.com, accessed March 22, 2014.
7. Organization website, "What Is Category Management?" www.cpgcatnet.org, accessed March 22, 2014.
8. Ibid.
9. Company website, www.igd.com, accessed March 23, 2014.
10. Company website, "Hershey's Convenience," www.hersheys.com, accessed March 23, 2014.
11. Company website, www.amronexperimental.com, accessed March 22, 2014; Audrey Quinn, "Dissolving Fruit Stickers," *Smart Planet*, accessed March 22, 2014, www.smartplanet.com.
12. Steve McKee, "Funny Ads Make Brands Stronger. No Joke," *Bloomberg Businessweek*, accessed March 23, 2014, www.businessweek.com; company website, www.harley-davidson.com, accessed March 23, 2014.

13. Matthew Swyers, "Can a Shoe Color Really Be Trademarked?" *Inc.*, accessed March 22, 2014, www.inc.com; Judith Welikala, "Naked Cowboy to Sue Naked Indian over Times Square Turf," *Time*, accessed March 22, 2014, http://newsfeed.time.com.
14. Beth Winegarner, "Pintrips Can't Escape Pinterest Trademark Suit," *Law360*, accessed March 31, 2014, www.law360.com; Ingrid Lunden, "Pintrips Files a Motion to Dismiss Pinterest's Trademark Suit, Says 'Pin' Is Too Generic," *TechCrunch*, accessed March 23, 2014, http://techcrunch.com; Ingrid Lunden, "Pinterest or Pintrips? Pinterest Files a Trademark Infringement Suit against Travel Planning Startup," *TechCrunch*, accessed March 23, 2014, http://techcrunch.com.
15. Sarah Burstein, "Design Patents, Trade Dress & Apple III," *Patently O*, accessed March 23, 2014, http://patentlyo.com; Nick Wingfield, "Jury Awards $1 Billion to Apple in Samsung Patent Case," *The New York Times*, accessed March 23, 2014, www.nytimes.com.
16. Brett Barrouquere, "Maker's Mark Bourbon Wins Right to Dripping Wax Seal," *USA Today*, accessed March 23, 2014, http://usatoday30.usatoday.com.
17. Kari Embree, "Lean Cuisine Rolls Out All Natural Ingredients in New Frozen Line," *Packaging Digest*, accessed March 23, 2014, www.packagingdigest.com.
18. Company website, "Make No Mistake with ClearRx," www.target.com, accessed March 23, 2014.
19. Jim Butschli, "Kimberly-Clark Uses Packaging to Reduce Product Waste," *Packaging World*, accessed March 23, 2014, www.packworld.com.
20. "Food Allergies: Understanding Food Labels," *Mayo Clinic* website, accessed March 23, 2014, www.mayoclinic.com.
21. Company website, www.tommybahama.com, accessed March 23, 2014.
22. Company website, "About Us," www.americangirl.com, accessed March 23, 2014.
23. "How Brand Licensing Works," *Perpetual Licensing*, accessed March 23, 2014, www.perpetuallicensing.com.
24. Robert Klara, "The Best (and Worst) Brand Extensions," *AdWeek*, accessed March 23, 2014, www.adweek.com.
25. Steve Reeves, "Top 5 Worst Brand Extensions," *The Value Engineers*, accessed March 23, 2014, www.thevalueengineers.com.
26. Company website, "Hyundai Takes Top Honors in Brand Keys 2013 Loyalty Engagement Index" (press release), www.hyundainews.com, accessed March 23, 2014.
27. Company website, www.asianfoodmarkets.com, accessed March 23, 2014.
28. Lee Neikirk, "Samsung's Curved 4K TV Is Fit to Rule," *USA Today*, accessed March 23, 2014, www.usatoday.com; Ty Pendlebury, "What Is 4K UHD? Next-Generation Resolution Explained," *CNET*, accessed March 23, 2014, http://reviews.cnet.com.
29. "Calvin Klein to Launch CK One and Euphoria Flankers Next Year," *Base Notes*, accessed March 23, 2014, www.basenotes.net.
30. Amy Kazmin, "India Pressures Pepsi to Reduce Sugar in Drinks and Snacks," *Financial Times*, accessed October 16, 2014, www.ft.com.
31. Company website, www.gudhappens.com, accessed March 23, 2014; "Güd Scents," *The Diamond Report*, accessed March 23, 2014, https://www.thecloroxcompany.com.
32. Company website, www.bose.com, accessed March 23, 2014.
33. Company website, "A New Global Hair Research Center," www.lorealusa.com, accessed March 23, 2014.
34. Company website, www.thescottsmiraclegrocompany.com, accessed March 23, 2014.
35. Company website, www.eclipse.aero, accessed March 23, 2014.
36. Jef Feeley and David Voreacos, "J&J Said to Reach $4 Billion Deal to Settle Hip Lawsuits," *Bloomberg News*, accessed March 23, 2014, www.bloomberg.com.

Scripps Networks Interactive & Food Network

PART 4
Product Decisions

The Line between Content and Commerce

When you're watching a cooking show, how do you define the product? Is it the show itself, the celebrity chef, the recipes demonstrated, or the sizzling pots and pans? In this case, the product is a little bit of everything—talent, entertainment, and food. It's a combination of goods and services bundled together in a single brand: Food Network. And while the selling of the brand is important, part of its value lies in its mission to entertain and inspire. "There's a line between where a brand is inspiring and when it becomes overtly commercial," points out Sergei Kuharsky, senior vice president and general manager of licensing and merchandising at Scripps Networks Interactive, which produces and markets Food Network. "Everyone walks that line."

Food Network's product mix serves up an array of popular shows that appeal to food-loving viewers. Cooking shows such as Barefoot Contessa and Giada at Home demonstrate how to whip up delicious meals in various styles. Competition shows, such as Food Network Star, Great Food Truck Race, and Chopped, entertain viewers as they watch contestants cook off for bragging rights, cash, or a television contract. Celebrity shows such as Diners, Drive-ins, and Dives and Restaurant: Impossible showcase famous chefs in various scenarios as they visit favorite eateries or try to help restaurant owners save their businesses. Each of these individual shows fits into the product line and overall product mix in a certain way—but all are designed to entertain and inspire.

Inspiration about food and cooking is integral to the Food Network brand—the challenge for marketers is to take this to the next level, from the TV screen to wherever consumers are in their daily lives. Social media has emerged as a major tool for Food Network marketers to converse with viewers on a regular basis. "Social media does so much for our brand," says Kate Gold, director of social media for the company. "It's really about being able to have a dialogue with our audience. It's being able to listen to them. It's the one platform where all day, every day, we're getting feedback." Several years ago, Scripps reorganized its social media marketing to reflect consumer categories: food, home, and travel. The shows offered by Food Network and the Cooking Channel fall into the first category. This reorganization helped marketers understand more clearly how consumers behaved with social media and what those consumers wanted from the Food Network brand.

"We saw what was in the competitive market, and people not only wanted recipes, they wanted the tools to accompany them," observes Leora Schachter, vice president of digital strategy and planning for Scripps. So the company developed various apps to meet this need—and solidify the Food Network brand in consumers' minds. For example, the "Cupcakes" app stems from the popular shows Cupcake Wars and Cupcake Champions. The app provides additional content that consumers can use and enjoy—videos, recipes, and cooking or shopping tips. "In the Kitchen" is another popular Food Network app among consumers—listed as one of the top-five paid apps in the lifestyle category at Apple.

On a broader scale, Food Network's core social media platforms are Facebook, Twitter, and Pinterest. But the network is also active on Google+, Instagram, Foursquare, and Tumblr. Marketers use Foursquare to support location-based shows; for example, many viewers request a list of all the restaurants visited by host Guy Fieri in Diners, Drive-ins, and Dives. "We're very careful about the new platforms that we expand into, based on audiences that are there, the actions that people are taking, and how our brand could fit in," explains Gold. For example, Facebook is the ideal platform for Food Network to hold chats with celebrity chefs, while Twitter can give quick updates behind the scenes from a TV show.

Customer feedback is one of the most important factors in category and brand management. By its very nature, social media provides plenty of feedback to Food Network about its shows, celebrities, recipes, choice of restaurants to feature—the list is endless. Marketers also receive feedback on their choices about social media, including Facebook posts and tweets. Apps are no exception. "When you're in an app store, you get direct feedback from your audience, which is unlike any other channel we have at Food Network," says Schachter. People rate and review an app immediately after using it, which means that Food Network can update and improve the app on a regular basis. "It's expensive," notes Schachter, "but worthwhile."

QUESTIONS FOR CRITICAL THINKING

1. How would you describe Food Network's product mix in terms of width, length, and depth?

2. Where would you place Food Network in the product lifecycle? What steps could marketers take to extend its lifecycle?

3. What sets Food Network brand apart from the brands of other networks? How has social media helped Food Network enhance its brand equity?

4. How might Food Network marketers use social media to speed the adoption rate of a new television show?

Part 5
Distribution Decisions

14 Marketing Channels and Supply Chain Management

15 Retailers, Wholesalers, and Direct Marketers

Chapter 14

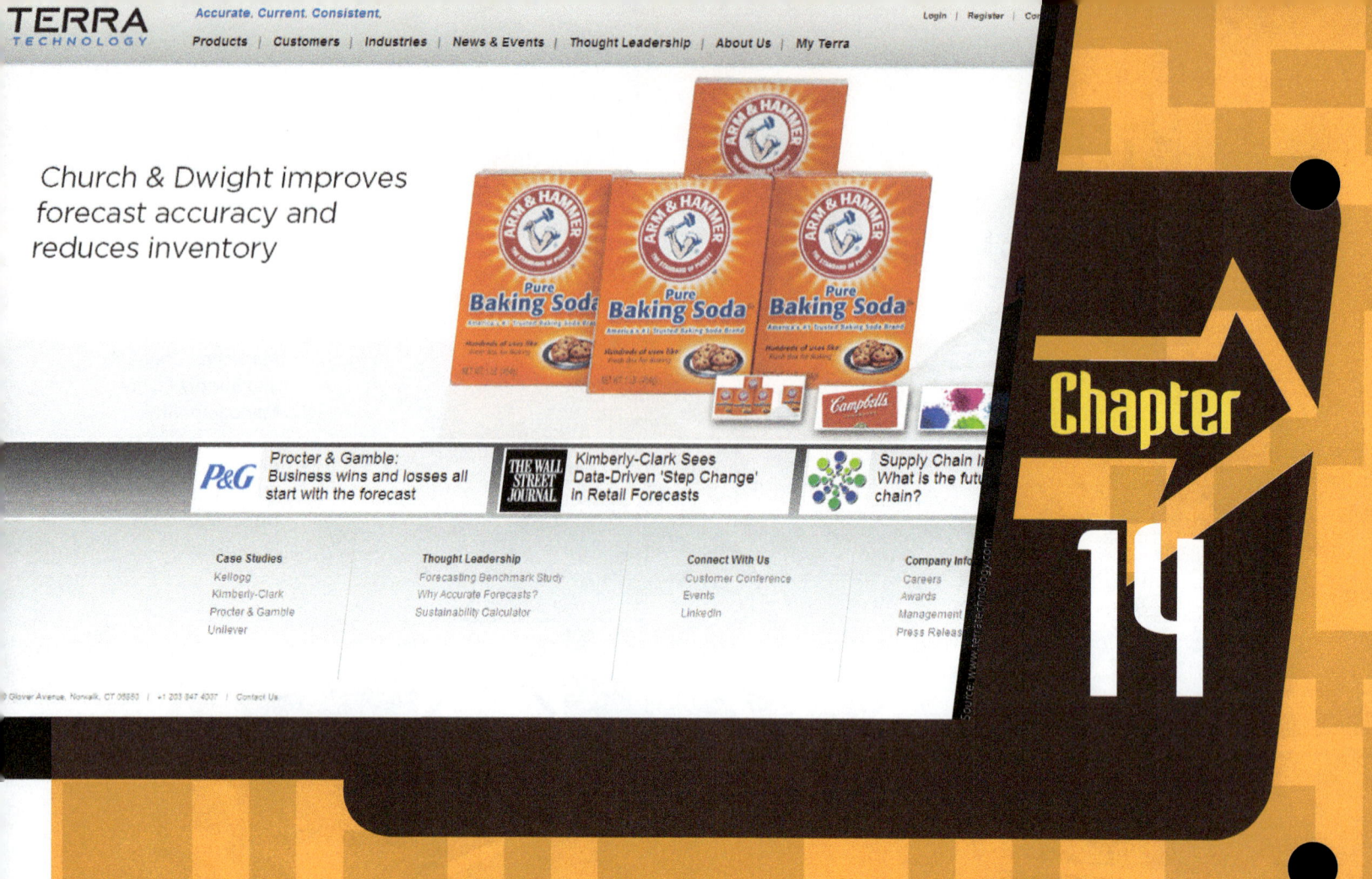

Marketing Channels and Supply Chain Management

TERRA TECHNOLOGY HELPS MANAGE GLOBAL SUPPLY CHAIN

1. Describe the four types of marketing channels and the roles they play in marketing strategy.
2. Outline the three major channel strategy decisions.
3. Describe the concepts of channel management, conflict, and cooperation.
4. Describe the three different vertical marketing systems.
5. Explain the roles of logistics and supply chain management in an overall distribution strategy.
6. Identify the six major components of a physical distribution system.
7. Compare the five major modes of transportation.
8. Discuss the role of transportation intermediaries, combined transportation modes, and warehousing in improving physical distribution.

If, as Robert Byrne tells it, $8 trillion worth of goods held in inventory worldwide accounts for 11 percent of the world's environmental footprint and 40 percent of our annual water consumption, then you can appreciate his view that more efficient supply chains are good for business and good for the earth as well.

As CEO and co-founder of Terra Technology, a supply chain solutions provider, Byrne has helped develop sophisticated software systems that show companies how to do a better job of forecasting demand for their products thus better managing their inventories and supply chains. Terra's software has won numerous industry awards for the firm, based on its enviable track record for cutting costs and improving supply chain management. Among its clients are global companies including Shell Oil,

Procter & Gamble, Unilever, Kimberly-Clark, Kraft Foods, General Mills, Campbell Soup, and Kellogg. In fact, its clients operate in more than 160 countries and represent a wide range of industries, including chemicals, high tech, consumer products, petroleum, and food and beverage manufacturing.

Managers in the United States, Europe, and India are looking to Terra for ways to streamline inventory, improve customer service, cut costs, and reduce their environmental impact while efficiently matching their product output to a growing global population. Saving money by transporting and warehousing less inventory is another top goal, and that's where improved forecasting comes in. Terra's employees have helped Procter & Gamble save $100 million and reduce forecasting errors by 40 percent. Campbell Soup saw a 50 percent improvement in forecasting. Successes like these have earned Terra a spot in the top five supply chain planning companies for several years in a row and placed it among *SupplyChainBrain's* 100 great supply chain partners.

Terra, which is privately owned, is so confident about the value of its forecasting capabilities that it gives its corporate clients a money-back guarantee that they will see a 40 percent improvement in demand projections when they use its services. One of the company's newest products is a sustainability calculator that shows customers how better forecasting leads to reduced inventory and then spells out the measurable environmental benefits. Byrne says Terra is "really a math company," and it seems he's right.[1]

EVOLUTION OF A BRAND

Regardless of its size or the market in which it operates, no business can survive for long without an efficient supply chain system. As competition becomes increasingly global, organizations look for every opportunity to enhance their profitability. Using Terra Technology's proprietary forecasting software, some of the world's most successful organizations can realize greater profitability in more efficient management of their inventory.

- Why has inventory management become such an important activity, particularly for consumer packaged-goods companies?
- Might the capabilities of a company like Terra Technology be more important to some marketing channels than others? Which channels? Why?
- In your opinion, is there a limit to supply chain efficiency?

Chapter Overview

distribution Movement of goods and services from producers to customers.

marketing (distribution) channel System of marketing institutions that enhances the physical flow of goods and services, along with ownership title, from producer to consumer or business user.

logistics Process of coordinating the flow of information, goods, and services among members of the distribution channel.

supply chain management Complete sequence of suppliers and activities that contribute to the creation and delivery of merchandise.

Distribution—moving goods and services from producers to customers—is the second marketing mix variable and an important marketing concern. Firms depend on distribution systems to be able to move their goods from one destination to another. A distribution strategy has two critical components: (1) marketing channels and (2) logistics and supply chain management.

A **marketing channel**—also called a **channel distribution**—is an organized system of marketing institutions and their interrelationships that enhances the physical flow and ownership of goods and services from producer to consumer or business user. The choice of marketing channels should support the firm's overall marketing strategy. In contrast, **logistics** refers to the process of coordinating the flow of information, goods, and services among members of the marketing channel. **Supply chain management** is the control of activities of purchasing, processing, and delivery through which raw materials are transformed into products and made available to final consumers. Efficient logistical systems support customer service—enhancing customer relationships—an important goal of any marketing strategy.

A key aspect of logistics is physical distribution, which covers a broad range of activities aimed at efficient movement of finished goods from the end of the production line to the consumer. Although some marketers use the terms *transportation and physical distribution* interchangeably, these terms do not carry the same meaning. **Physical distribution** extends beyond transportation to include such important decision areas as customer service, inventory control, materials handling, protective packaging, order processing, and warehousing.

Well-planned marketing channels and effective logistics and supply chain management provide ultimate users with convenient ways for obtaining the goods and services they desire. This chapter discusses the activities, decisions, and marketing intermediaries involved in managing marketing channels and logistics. Chapter 15 looks at other players in the marketing channel: retailers, direct marketers, and wholesalers.

THE ROLE OF MARKETING CHANNELS IN MARKETING STRATEGY

1 Describe the four types of marketing channels and the roles they play in marketing strategy.

A firm's distribution channels play a key role in its overall marketing strategy because these channels provide the means by which the firm makes the goods and services available to ultimate users. Channels perform four important functions. First, they facilitate the exchange process by reducing the number of marketplace contacts necessary to make a sale. Suppose you've had a Nintendo Wii handheld game player in the past and been satisfied with it, so when you see an ad for the Nintendo Wii U you are interested. You visit the Nintendo website where you learn more about the Wii U and its unique features. You are particularly drawn to the games *LEGO Marvel Super Heroes* and *Super Smash Bros*. You want to see the game console in person, so you locate a dealer near enough for you to visit. The dealer forms part of the channel that brings you—a potential buyer—and

Nintendo—the seller—together to complete the exchange process. Keep in mind that all channel members benefit when they work together; when they begin to disagree or—worse yet—compete directly with each other, everyone loses.

Distributors adjust for discrepancies in the market's assortment of goods and services via a process known as *sorting*, the second channel function. A single producer tends to maximize the quantity it makes of a limited line of goods, while a single buyer needs a limited quantity of a wide selection of merchandise. Sorting alleviates such discrepancies by channeling products to suit both the buyer's and the producer's needs.

The third function of marketing channels involves standardizing exchange transactions by setting expectations for products, and it involves the transfer process itself. Channel members tend to standardize payment terms, delivery schedules, prices, and purchase lots, among other conditions. Standardization helps make transactions efficient and fair.

The final marketing channel function is to facilitate searches by both buyers and sellers. Buyers search for specific goods and services to fill their needs, while sellers attempt to learn what buyers want. Channels bring buyers and sellers together to complete the exchange process. Hundreds of distribution channels exist today, and no single channel best serves the needs of every company. Instead of searching for the best channel for all products, a marketing manager must analyze alternative channels in light of consumer needs to determine the most appropriate channel or channels for the firm's goods and services.

Marketers must remain flexible because channels may change over time. Today's ideal channel may prove inappropriate in a few years, or the way a company uses that channel may have to change. Like many other companies, Procter & Gamble has used digital advertising for many years, taking advantage of digital's ability to home in on customers' needs. Finding the right combination of tactics—apps, tablets, mobile, social, and many others—is never easy. The world's largest advertiser, the company recently announced it would shift its marketing focus even further to digital. P&G's vice president of global e-business says the evolving nature of digital media prompted a change from static marketing campaigns to real-time brand building.[2]

The following sections examine the diverse types of channels available to marketers and the decisions marketers must make to develop an effective distribution strategy that supports their firm's marketing objectives.

A local dealer for Nintendo's Wii U forms part of the marketing channel that brings potential buyers (consumers) and sellers (Nintendo) together.

Briefly Speaking

"Confidence delivered"
—**YRC Freight motto**

physical distribution Broad range of activities aimed at efficient movement of finished goods from the end of the production line to the consumer.

marketing intermediary (middleman) Wholesaler or retailer that operates between producers and consumers or business users.

wholesaler Channel intermediary that takes title to the goods it handles and then distributes these goods to retailers, other distributors, or business or B2B customers.

TYPES OF MARKETING CHANNELS

The first step in selecting a marketing channel is determining which type of channel will best meet both the seller's objectives and the distribution needs of customers. Figure 14.1 depicts the major channels available to marketers of consumer and business goods and services.

Most channel options involve at least one marketing intermediary. A **marketing intermediary** (or **middleman**) is an organization that operates between producers and consumers or business users. Retailers and wholesalers are both marketing intermediaries. A retail store owned and operated by someone other than the manufacturer of the products it sells is one type of marketing intermediary. A **wholesaler** is an intermediary that takes title to the goods it handles and then distributes these goods to retailers, other distributors, or end consumers. Wholesalers are able to

FIGURE 14.1
Alternative Marketing Channels

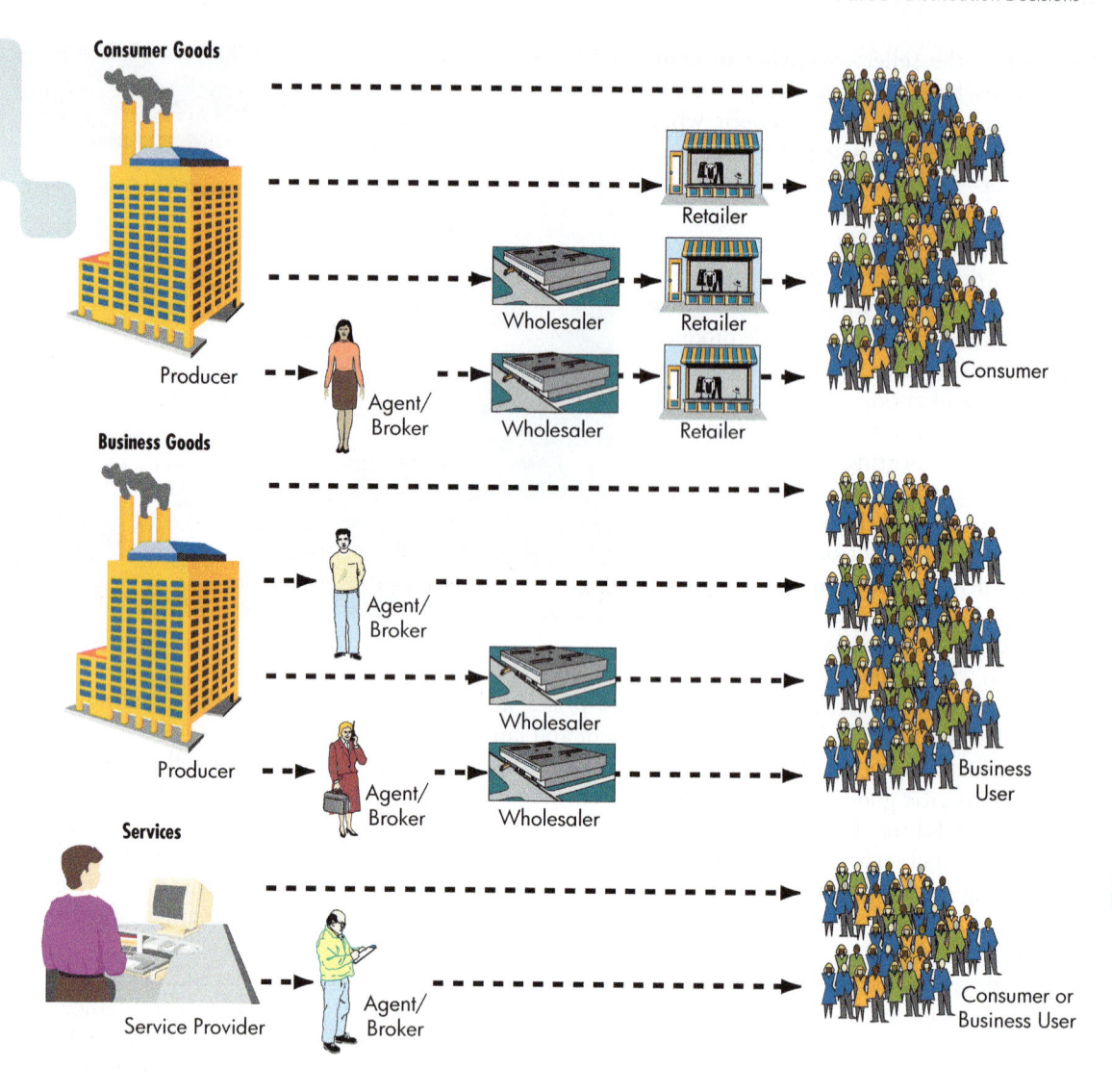

Consumer Goods

Producer → Consumer
Producer → Retailer → Consumer
Producer → Wholesaler → Retailer → Consumer
Producer → Agent/Broker → Wholesaler → Retailer → Consumer

Business Goods

Producer → Business User
Producer → Agent/Broker → Business User
Producer → Wholesaler → Business User
Producer → Agent/Broker → Wholesaler → Business User

Services

Service Provider → Consumer or Business User
Service Provider → Agent/Broker → Consumer or Business User

---

stockpile nonperishable goods, but perishables are another story. The specialty coffee market in the United States, once only 1 percent of the total mark, has increased to more than 35 percent in recent years. At the same time, a worldwide increase in demand threatens to make the finite coffee supply less accessible in the future for both wholesalers and independent specialty retailers.[3]

Marketers must remain flexible, because channels change over time. Procter & Gamble, which once emphasized TV and print ads to sell its products, now relies more on digital media.

A short marketing channel involves few intermediaries. By contrast, a long marketing channel involves several intermediaries working in succession to move goods from producers to consumers. Business products usually move through short channels due to geographic concentrations and comparatively fewer business purchasers. Service firms market primarily through short channels, because they sell intangible products and need to maintain personal relationships within their channels. Haircuts, manicures, and dental cleanings all operate through short channels. Not-for-profit organizations also tend to work with short, simple, and direct channels. Any marketing intermediaries in such channels usually act as agents, such as independent ticket agencies or fund-raising specialists.

DIRECT SELLING

The simplest and shortest marketing channel is a direct channel. A **direct channel** carries goods directly from a producer to the business purchaser or ultimate user. This channel forms part of **direct selling**, a marketing strategy in which a producer establishes direct sales contact with its product's final users. Direct selling is an important option for goods requiring extensive demonstrations in persuading customers to buy. The "Career Readiness" feature contains suggestions for closing a successful sale.

Direct selling plays a significant role in business-to-business marketing. Most major installations, accessory equipment, and even component parts and raw materials are sold through direct contacts between producing firms and final buyers. Many people in business enjoy successful sales careers. According to the *Occupational Outlook Handbook*, published by the U.S. Department of Labor, more than 1.9 million people are employed as sales representatives in manufacturing and wholesaling industries.[4]

Direct selling is also important in consumer-goods markets. Direct sellers, such as Avon, Pampered Chef, and Tastefully Simple, sidestep competition in store aisles by developing networks

direct channel Marketing channel that moves goods directly from a producer to the business purchaser or ultimate user.

direct selling Strategy designed to establish direct sales contact between producer and final user.

CAREER READINESS
How to Successfully Close a Sale

Closing a sale is often a challenge, but several steps can improve your success rate. Here are some basic strategies, and a few you might not have thought of.

1. There's no substitute for preparation. Research your customer so you know what their needs are and what they've purchased before.

2. Know the value of your product. It's not the same thing as the price.

3. During the sales call, listen more than you speak. Some experienced salespeople say you should be talking only 20 percent of the time and listening the rest.

4. Use your speaking time to ask about the challenges your customer faces, who all the decision makers are that you need to influence, and how you can help solve their problems.

5. Assume that your customer wants to buy, and gear your presentation to that assumption. Using statements that reflect a customer's perceived interest ("I think you'll like how this works" or "You'll be happy with how this meets your needs") helps you build confidence.

6. Also assume that your customer's objections are legitimate and address them as such. Your response to objections tells the prospect a lot about how you will treat him or her as a customer.

7. Remain seated. Standing up, even if the prospect has done so, signals a change in the situation and can end negotiations before you're ready.

8. Always carry a pen. More than one sale has been lost for want of a pen to sign it with.

9. Don't forget to say thank you.

Sources: Rochelle Togo-Figa, "7 Key Steps to Closing Every Sale," *Salesopedia.com*, accessed March 25, 2014, http://salesopedia.com; Tim Conner, "12 Things Every Sales Super Star Knows," *Experience.com*, accessed March 25, 2014, www.experience.com; Barry Farber, "8 Steps to a Successful Sales Call," *Entrepreneur*, accessed March 25, 2014, www.entrepreneur.com; Steve W. Martin, "How to Close a Sales Call," *HBR Blog Network*, accessed March 25, 2014, http://blogs.hbr.org.

> **Briefly Speaking**
>
> "You can do away with middlemen, but you can't do away with the functions they perform."
>
> —American business saying

of independent representatives who sell their products directly to consumers. Many of these companies practice a direct selling strategy called the *party plan*, originally popularized by Tupperware. San Francisco–based jewelry boutique company Stella & Dot is one such business. Launched by entrepreneur Jessica Herrin, Stella & Dot jewelry is sold at home-based parties, or "trunk shows," by independent sales representatives in North America, Germany, and the UK. The jewelry, which appeals to women of all ages, is accessible and affordable—and is often worn by TV celebrities. Stella & Dot recently paid its sales representatives more than $150 million in commissions.[5]

The Internet provides another direct selling channel for both B2B and B2C purchases. Consumers who want to sport designer handbags, but don't want to pay full price for them, can rent them from Bag Borrow or Steal, an e-commerce business. For those who like to change purses often but can't or won't pay the hundreds or thousands of dollars for Chanel's, Prada's, or Gucci's latest, Bag Borrow or Steal may be a real bargain. In addition to designer handbags, shoppers can find sunglasses and jewelry to complete their look.[6]

Direct mail can also be an important part of direct selling—or it can encourage a potential customer to contact an intermediary such as a retailer. Either way, it is a vital communication piece for many marketers.

CHANNELS USING MARKETING INTERMEDIARIES

Although direct channels allow simple and straightforward marketing, they are not practical in every case. Some products serve markets in different areas of the country or world, or have large numbers of potential end users. Other categories of goods rely heavily on repeat purchases. The producers of these goods may find more efficient, less expensive, and less time-consuming alternatives to direct channels by using marketing intermediaries. This section considers five channels that involve marketing intermediaries.

Producer to Wholesaler to Retailer to Consumer

The traditional channel for consumer goods proceeds from producer to wholesaler to retailer to user. This method carries goods between thousands of small producers with limited lines and local retailers. A firm with limited financial resources will rely on the services of a wholesaler that serves as an immediate source of funds and then markets to hundreds of retailers. On the other hand, a small retailer can draw on a wholesaler's specialized distribution skills. In addition, many manufacturers hire their own field representatives to service retail accounts with marketing information. Wholesalers may then handle the actual sales transactions.

Producer to Wholesaler to Business User

Similar characteristics in the organizational market often attract marketing intermediaries to operate between producers and business purchasers. The term *industrial distributor* commonly refers to intermediaries in the business market that take title to the goods.

Producer to Agent to Wholesaler to Retailer to Consumer

In markets served by many small companies, a unique intermediary—the agent—performs the basic function of bringing buyer and seller together. An agent may or may not take possession of the goods but never takes title. The agent merely represents a producer by seeking a market for its products or a wholesaler, which does take title to the goods by locating a supply source.

Producer to Agent to Wholesaler to Business User

Like agents, brokers are independent intermediaries who may or may not take possession of goods but never take title to these goods. Agents and brokers also serve the business market when small producers attempt to market their offerings through large wholesalers. Such an intermediary, often called a **manufacturer's representative**, provides an independent sales force to contact wholesale buyers. A kitchen equipment manufacturer may have its own manufacturer's representatives to market its goods, for example.

manufacturer's representative Agents wholesaling intermediary that represents manufacturers of related but noncompeting products and receives a commission on each sale.

Chapter 14 Marketing Channels and Supply Chain Management

Producer to Agent to Business User

For products sold in small units, only merchant wholesalers can economically cover the markets. A merchant wholesaler is an independently owned wholesaler that takes title to the goods. By maintaining regional inventories, this wholesaler achieves transportation economies, stockpiling goods and making small shipments over short distances. For a product with large unit sales, however, and for which transportation accounts for a small percentage of the total cost, the producer-agent-business user channel is usually employed. The agent in effect becomes the producer's sales force, but bulk shipments of the product reduce the intermediary's inventory management function.

DUAL DISTRIBUTION

Dual distribution refers to the movement of products through more than one channel to reach the firm's target market. Nordstrom, for instance, has a three-pronged distribution system, selling through stores, catalogs, and the Internet. Marketers usually adopt a dual distribution strategy either to maximize their firm's coverage in the marketplace or to increase the cost-effectiveness of the firm's marketing effort. Nintendo and Netflix partner to offer entertainment through more than one channel. Previously Netflix customers ordered their favorite movies online and had the DVDs delivered to their mailboxes. Now, under their $7.99 monthly subscription, Netflix subscribers can stream movies and TV programs and view them on their Wii consoles at no extra cost.[7]

REVERSE CHANNELS

While the traditional concept of marketing channels involves the movement of goods and services from producer to consumer or business user, marketers should not ignore **reverse channels**—channels designed to return goods to their producers. Reverse channels have gained increased importance with rising prices for raw materials, increasing availability of recycling facilities, and passage of additional antipollution and conservation laws. Purchase a new set of tires, and you'll find a recycling charge for disposing of the old tires. The intent is to halt the growing litter problem of illegal tire dumps. Automotive and marine batteries contain potentially toxic materials, including 25 pounds of lead, plastic, and sulfuric acid. Yet 99 percent of the elements in a spent battery can be reclaimed, recycled, and reused in new batteries. Forty-five states have laws requiring the proper recycling of auto batteries. To help in this effort, AutoZone stores accept old car batteries without charge—and even offers a $5 merchandise card in exchange.[8]

Some reverse channels move through the facilities of traditional marketing intermediaries. In states that require bottle deposits, retailers and local bottlers perform these functions in the soft-drink industry. For other products, manufacturers establish redemption centers, develop systems for rechanneling products for recycling, and create specialized organizations to handle disposal and recycling. Nike's Reuse-A-Shoe program has

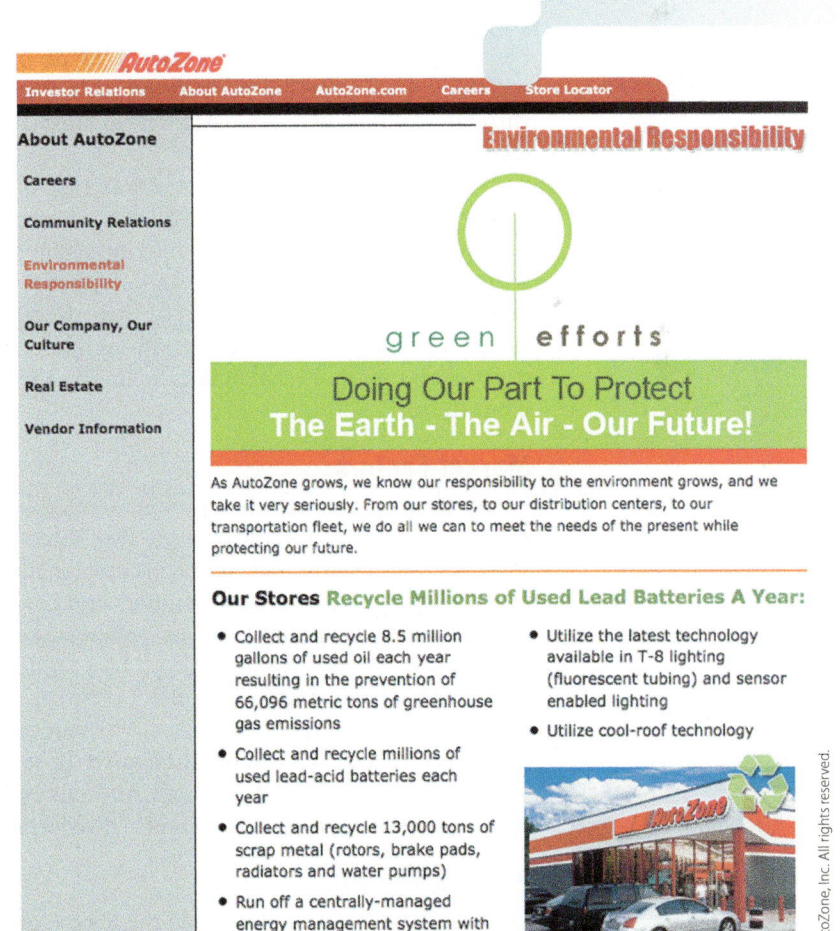

dual distribution Network that moves products to a firm's target market through more than one marketing channel.

reverse channels Channel designed to return goods to their producers.

AutoZone stores promote eco-friendly practices by helping customers recycle their old car batteries and providing other helpful information on their website.

ASSESSMENT CHECK

1.1 Distinguish between a marketing channel and logistics.
1.2 What are the different types of marketing channels?
1.3 What four functions do marketing channels perform?

been collecting people's cast-off athletic shoes since 1990 and recycling them to create a high-quality sports surface for tennis courts, turf fields, and more. This recycling effort is likely to help build customer loyalty and enhance the brand's reputation.[9]

Reverse channels also handle product recalls and repairs. An appliance manufacturer might send recall notices to the buyers of a washing machine. An auto manufacturer might send notices to car owners advising them of a potential problem and offering to repair the problem at no cost through local dealerships.

CHANNEL STRATEGY DECISIONS

2 Outline the three major channel strategy decisions.

Marketers face several strategic decisions in choosing channels and marketing intermediaries for their products. Selecting a specific channel is the most basic of these decisions. Marketers must also resolve questions about the level of distribution intensity, assess the desirability of vertical marketing systems, and evaluate the performance of current intermediaries.

SELECTION OF A MARKETING CHANNEL

Consider the following questions: What characteristics of a franchised dealer network make it the best channel option for a company? Why do operating supplies often go through both agents and merchant wholesalers before reaching their actual users? Why would a firm market a single product through multiple channels? Marketers must answer many such questions in choosing marketing channels.

A variety of factors affect the selection of a marketing channel. Some channel decisions are dictated by the marketplace in which the company operates. In other cases, the product itself may be a key variable in picking a marketing channel. Finally, the marketing organization could base its selection of channels on its size and competitive factors. Individual firms in a single industry may choose different channels as part of their overall strategy to gain a competitive edge. Book publishers, for instance, could sell books through bookstores, directly to consumers on their own websites, or through nontraditional outlets including specialty retailers such as craft stores or home-improvement stores.

Market Factors

Channel structure reflects a product's intended markets for either consumers or business users. Business purchasers usually prefer to deal directly with manufacturers (except for routine supplies or small accessory items), but most consumers make their purchases from retailers. Marketers often sell products that serve both business users and consumers through more than one channel. Sometimes marketers must adapt to customers' preferences for ethical supply chain behavior. See the "Solving an Ethical Controversy" feature to learn how consumers brought about change in the cocoa industry.

Other market factors also affect channel choice, including the market's needs, its geographic location, and its average order size. To serve a concentrated market with a small number of buyers, a direct channel offers a feasible alternative. In serving a geographically dispersed potential trade area in which customers purchase small amounts in individual transactions—the conditions that characterize the consumer goods market—distribution through marketing intermediaries makes sense.

Product Factors

Product characteristics also guide the choice of an optimal marketing channel strategy. Perishable goods, such as fresh fruit and vegetables, milk, and fruit juice, move through short channels. Trendy or seasonal fashions, such as swimsuits and skiwear, are also examples.

SOLVING AN ETHICAL CONTROVERSY
Hershey's Takes Responsibility for Its Supply Chain

When consumers learned of abusive conditions under which thousands of children were forced to work in Africa's cocoa industry, most major chocolate manufacturers bowed to public pressure. They promised to end human trafficking and child labor in West Africa, which produces more than 70 percent of the world's cocoa, and to buy sustainably produced ingredients. Hershey's, however, lagged behind other chocolate producers in committing to ensure its products were made without child labor. Several human rights organizations banded together on Hershey's Facebook page asking the company to stop using suppliers who abused their young workers.

Should companies be responsible for the actions of their suppliers?

PRO
1. Consumers want to know the products they're buying are not associated with abusive labor practices.
2. Multinational companies with small, unregulated suppliers that depend on their business have an opportunity to do good by insisting on fair labor practices.

CON
1. Companies should not try to control what their suppliers in other cultures do or impose their own (or their customers') value systems on them.
2. Companies are responsible to their shareholders for finding the lowest-cost and most efficient production methods.

Summary
As a result of several groups banding together to alert consumers about some of its suppliers' practices, Hershey's recently pledged $10 million over five years to educate West African farmers who supply cocoa for Hershey's products on improving their trade and combating child labor abuses.

Sources: Katrina Rabeler, "What 11-Year-Olds Get—and Adults Forget—about Child Labor in Chocolate," *Yes Magazine*, accessed March 25, 2014, www.yesmagazine.com; Jeff Mordock, "Court Dismisses Child Labor Claims against Hershey," *Pittsburgh Post-Gazette*, accessed March 25, 2014, www.post-gazette.com; City University of New York, "Hershey's & Child Labor: The Facts," blog entry, accessed March 25, 2014, http://blsciblogs.baruch.cuny.edu; Phil Milford and Dawn McCarty, "Hershey Should Supply Child-Labor Records, Academics Say," *Bloomberg News*, accessed March 25, 2014, www.bloomberg.com; Eleanor Bloxham, "Chocolate and Child Labor: A Hurdle for Hershey," *Fortune*, accessed March 25, 2014, http://management.fortune.cnn.com.

Vending machines represent another short channel. Typically, you can buy Skittles, SunChips, or a bottle of Dasani water from a vending machine. But how about cupcakes? Beverly Hills–based Sprinkles Cupcakes is installing "cupcake ATMs" across the United States that dispense cupcakes 24 hours a day.[10]

Complex products, such as custom-made installations and computer equipment, are often sold directly to ultimate buyers. In general, relatively standardized items that are also nonperishable pass through comparatively long channels. Products with low unit costs—such as cans of dog food, bars of soap, and packages of gum—typically travel through long channels. Perishable items—fresh flowers, meat, and produce—require much shorter channels.

Organizational and Competitive Factors

Companies with strong financial, management, and marketing resources feel less need for help from intermediaries. A large, financially strong manufacturer can hire its own sales force, warehouse its own goods, and extend credit to retailers or consumers. A small firm with fewer resources may do better with the aid of intermediaries. Christine and Robert Hackett founded Petropics, a small, Hawaii-based pet-food company that makes gourmet, unprocessed and unrefined dog and cat foods in Hawaiian-themed flavors, such as Lanai Luau for cats and Maui Luau for dogs. Petropics sells its products through local retailers and on the Web with big e-tail partners like Amazon, PawsChoice, and the Pet Center.[11]

A firm with a broad product line can usually market its products directly to retailers or business users, because its own sales force can offer a variety of products. High sales volume spreads selling costs over a large number of items, generating adequate returns from direct sales. Single-product firms often view direct selling as unaffordable.

The manufacturer's desire for control over marketing its products also influences channel selection. Some manufacturers sell their products only at their own stores. Manufacturers of specialty or luxury goods, such as Hermès scarves and Rolex watches, limit the number of retailers that can carry their products.

Businesses that explore new marketing channels must be careful to avoid upsetting their channel intermediaries. Conflicts frequently arose as companies began to establish an Internet presence in addition to traditional outlets. Today firms look for new ways to handle both without damaging relationships. In a social media campaign, the athletic apparel and equipment manufacturer Under Armour recently unveiled a revamped website to showcase its new products, such as shoes, athletic bags, and hats. The site also has live chat and customer review apps. However, retail sales—most notably through Dick's Sporting Goods and The Sports Authority—still account for 26 percent of Under Armour sales. The new website also features a much more conspicuous brick-and-mortar store locator. Under Armour's vice president of global e-commerce says the new store finder ensures consumers can locate the brick-and-mortar stores near them to touch, feel, and try on Under Armour gear, but online the company focuses on telling the innovation and leadership product stories that create strong desire for its products.[12]

Table 14.1 summarizes the factors that affect the selection of a marketing channel and examines the effect of each factor on the channel's overall length.

Vending machines are considered a short marketing channel. This cupcake ATM from Sprinkles Cupcakes recently was installed in New York City.

TABLE 14.1 Factors Influencing Marketing Channel Strategies

	Characteristics of Short Channels	**Characteristics of Long Channels**
Market Factors	Business users	Consumers
	Geographically concentrated	Geographically dispersed
	Extensive technical knowledge and regular servicing required	Little technical knowledge and regular servicing not required
	Large orders	Small orders
Product Factors	Perishable	Durable
	Complex	Standardized
	Expensive	Inexpensive
Organizational Factors	Manufacturer has adequate resources to perform channel functions	Manufacturer lacks adequate resources to perform channel functions
	Broad product line	Limited product line
	Channel control important	Channel control not important
Competitive Factors	Manufacturer feels satisfied with marketing intermediaries' performance in promoting products	Manufacturer feels dissatisfied with marketing intermediaries' performance in promoting products

DETERMINING DISTRIBUTION INTENSITY

Another key channel strategy decision is the intensity of distribution. *Distribution intensity* refers to the number of intermediaries through which a manufacturer distributes its goods in a particular market. Optimal distribution intensity should ensure adequate market coverage for a product. Adequate market coverage varies depending on the goals of the individual firm, the type of product, and the consumer segments in its target market. In general, distribution intensity varies along a continuum with three general categories: intensive distribution, selective distribution, and exclusive distribution.

Intensive Distribution

An **intensive distribution** strategy seeks to distribute a product through all available channels in a trade area. Because Dove practices intensive distribution for many of its products, you can pick up one of its chocolate bars or ice cream products just about anywhere—the supermarket, the convenience store, and even the drugstore. Usually, an intensive distribution strategy suits items with wide appeal across broad groups of consumers.

Selective Distribution

In another market coverage strategy, **selective distribution**, a firm chooses only a limited number of retailers in a market area to handle its line. Italian design firm Gucci sells its merchandise only through a limited number of select boutiques worldwide. By limiting the number of retailers, marketers can reduce total marketing costs while establishing strong working relationships within the channel. Moreover, selected retailers often agree to comply with the company's strict rules for advertising, pricing, and displaying its products. *Cooperative advertising*—in which the manufacturer pays a percentage of the retailer's advertising expenditures and the retailer prominently displays the firm's products—can be used for mutual benefit, and marginal retailers can be avoided. Where service is important, the manufacturer usually provides training and assistance to the dealers it chooses.

Exclusive Distribution

When a producer grants exclusive rights to a wholesaler or retailer to sell its products in a specific geographic region, it practices **exclusive distribution**. The automobile industry provides a good example of exclusive distribution. A city with a population of 100,000 probably has a single Jaguar dealer. Exclusive distribution agreements also govern marketing for some major appliance and apparel brands.

Marketers may sacrifice some market coverage by implementing a policy of exclusive distribution. However, they often develop and maintain an image of quality and prestige for the product. If it is harder to find a Free People silk dress, the item seems more valuable. In addition, exclusive distribution limits marketing costs because the firm deals with a smaller number of accounts. In exclusive distribution, producers and retailers cooperate closely in decisions concerning advertising and promotion, inventory carried by the retailers, and prices.

Legal Problems of Exclusive Distribution

Exclusive distribution presents potential legal problems in three main areas: exclusive dealing agreements, closed sales territories, and tying agreements. Although none of these practices is illegal per se, all may break the law if they reduce competition or tend to create monopolies.

As part of an exclusive distribution strategy, marketers may try to enforce an exclusive dealing agreement, which prohibits a marketing

---

intensive distribution Distribution of a product through all available channels.

selective distribution Distribution of a product through a limited number of channels.

Dove uses intensive distribution for many of its products, which means you can pick up a Dove ice cream bar just about anywhere—the supermarket, the convenience store, or even the drugstore.

exclusive distribution Distribution of a product through a single wholesaler or retailer in a specific geographic region.

closed sales territories Exclusive geographic selling region of a distributor.

intermediary (a wholesaler or, more typically, a retailer) from handling competing products. Producers of high-priced shopping goods, specialty goods, and accessory equipment often require such agreements to ensure total concentration on their own product lines. Such contracts violate the Clayton Act only if the producer's or dealer's sales volumes represent a substantial percentage of total sales in the market area. While exclusive distribution is legal for companies first entering a market, such agreements violate the Clayton Act if used by firms with a sizable market share seeking to bar competitors from the market.

Producers may also try to set up **closed sales territories** to restrict their distributors to certain geographic regions, reasoning that the distributors gain protection from rival dealers in their exclusive territories. Some beverage distributors have closed territories, as do distributors of plumbing fixtures. The downside of this practice is that the distributors sacrifice opportunities to open new facilities or market the manufacturers' products outside their assigned territories. The legality of a system of closed sales territories depends on whether the restriction decreases competition. If so, it violates the Federal Trade Commission Act and provisions of the Sherman and Clayton Acts.

The legality of closed sales territories also depends on whether the system imposes horizontal or vertical restrictions. Horizontal territorial restrictions result from agreements between retailers or wholesalers to avoid competition among sellers of products from the same producer. Such agreements consistently have been declared illegal. However, the U.S. Supreme Court has ruled that vertical territorial restrictions—those between producers and wholesalers or retailers—may meet legal criteria. The ruling gives no clear-cut answer, but such agreements likely satisfy the law in cases in which manufacturers occupy relatively small parts of their markets. In such instances, the restrictions may actually increase competition among competing brands; the wholesaler or retailer faces no competition from other dealers carrying the manufacturer's brand, so it can concentrate on competing effectively with other brands.

tying agreements Arrangement that requires a marketing intermediary to carry items other than those they want to sell.

The third legal question of exclusive distribution involves **tying agreements**, which allow channel members to become exclusive dealers only if they also carry products other than those they want to sell. In the apparel industry, for example, an agreement might require a dealer to carry a comparatively unpopular line of clothing in exchange for the desirable, fast-moving items. Tying agreements violate the Sherman Act and the Clayton Act when they reduce competition or create monopolies that keep competitors out of major markets.

WHO SHOULD PERFORM CHANNEL FUNCTIONS?

A fundamental marketing principle governs channel decisions. A member of the channel must perform certain central marketing functions. Responsibilities of the different members may vary, however. Although independent wholesalers perform many functions for manufacturers, retailers, and other wholesaler clients, other channel members could fulfill these roles instead. A manufacturer might bypass its wholesalers by establishing regional warehouses, maintaining field sales forces, serving as sources of information for retail customers, or arranging details of financing. For years, auto manufacturers have operated credit units that offer new-car financing; some have even established their own banks.

An independent intermediary earns a profit in exchange for providing services to manufacturers and retailers. This profit margin is low, ranging from 1 percent for food wholesalers to 5 percent for durable goods wholesalers. Manufacturers and retailers could retain these costs, or they could market directly and reduce retail prices—but only if they could perform the channel functions and match the efficiency of the independent intermediaries.

To grow profitably in a competitive environment, an intermediary must provide better service at lower costs than manufacturers or retailers can provide for themselves. In this case, consolidation of channel functions can represent a strategic opportunity for a company.

ASSESSMENT CHECK

2.1 Identify four major factors in selecting a marketing channel.

2.2 Describe the three general categories of distribution intensity.

CHANNEL MANAGEMENT AND LEADERSHIP

Distribution strategy does not end with the choice of a channel. Manufacturers must also focus on channel management by developing and maintaining relationships with the intermediaries in their marketing channels. Positive channel relationships encourage channel members to remember their partners' goods and market them. Manufacturers also must carefully manage the incentives they offer to induce channel members to promote their products. This effort includes weighing decisions about pricing, promotion, and other support efforts the manufacturer performs.

Increasingly, marketers are managing channels in partnership with other channel members. Effective cooperation allows all channel members to achieve goals they could not achieve on their own. Keys to successful management of channel relationships include the development of high levels of coordination, commitment, and trust between channel members.

Not all channel members wield equal power in the distribution chain, however. The dominant member of a marketing channel is called the **channel captain**. This firm's power to control a channel may result from its control over some type of reward or punishment to other channel members such as granting an exclusive sales territory or taking away a dealership. Power might also result from contractual arrangements, specialized expert knowledge, or agreement among channel members about their mutual best interests.

In the grocery industry, food producers once were considered channel captains. Today, retail giants like Kroger, SuperValu, and Safeway face competition from all quarters: discounters like ALDI and Save-A-Lot, club stores like Costco and Sam's Club, and even dollar stores. Just as they do when shopping for clothes or other items, grocery shoppers use their smartphones or tablets to look for bargains either before or during their trips to the store. To survive in the competitive grocery industry, supermarket owners are diversifying their retail formats from traditional stores to include natural and organic foods and upscale specialty merchandise to satisfy a wider variety of customers to compete with such chains as Whole Foods Market and Trader Joe's.[13] Pressure on traditional chains also comes from supercenters like Walmart and Target and their continued expansion into the grocery market.

> Describe the concepts of channel management, conflict, and cooperation.

channel captain Dominant and controlling member of a marketing channel.

CHANNEL CONFLICT

Marketing channels work smoothly only when members cooperate in well-organized efforts to achieve maximum operating efficiencies. Yet channel members often perform as separate, independent, and even competing forces. Two types of conflict—horizontal and vertical—may hinder the normal functioning of a marketing channel.

Horizontal Conflict

Horizontal conflict sometimes results from disagreements among channel members at the same level, such as two or more wholesalers or retailers, or among marketing intermediaries of the same type, such as two competing discount stores or several retail florists. More often, horizontal conflict causes problems between different types of marketing intermediaries that handle similar products. For example, Hulu, Netflix, Streampix, and Amazon all offer streaming video service, allowing subscribers to view movies and TV shows on their televisions, computers, or mobile devices. The networking equipment maker Cisco predicts soon there will be 10 billion mobile devices, including sensors, tablets, and smartphones—more devices, in fact, than the world's projected population. The company also estimates that more than two-thirds of Internet traffic will be streamed video. Although carriers are trying to slow down the rush of video use on mobile devices by charging higher prices for heavy data consumption, more people are buying and using smartphones that can carry videos, especially with smartphones costing only about $100 in some regions.[14]

> **Briefly Speaking**
>
> "We expanded the brand to include a whole line of apparel and accessories, but we quickly learned it was not good to have one channel of distribution."
>
> —**Kathy Ireland**
> *Founder and CEO, Kathy Ireland Worldwide*

Vertical Conflict

Vertical relationships may result in frequent and severe conflict. Channel members at different levels find many reasons for disputes. For example, retailers may develop private brands to compete with producers' brands or producers may establish their own retail stores or create mail-order operations that compete with retailers. Producers also may annoy wholesalers and retailers when they attempt to bypass these intermediaries and sell directly to consumers. When booking plane flights and other travel arrangements online first became feasible, many travelers stopped using the services of travel agents and made their own arrangements. However, they found it could sometimes take several hours to search airline websites to find the best combination of price and travel dates. As the economy continues to recover, consumers have become more selective about exactly what kind of vacation they want, how to find the very best deals, and when to work with an industry expert who can guide them through the travel planning process. Thus, travel agencies are experiencing a revival. Their job is also changing as they develop long-term, more advisory relationships with their clients.[15]

The vertical conflict that arose when consumers made their own travel arrangements online has been resolved as they rely more on travel advisors to help them plan the right vacation.

The Gray Market

Another type of channel conflict results from activities in the so-called gray market. As U.S. manufacturers license their technology and brands abroad, they sometimes find themselves in competition in the U.S. market against versions of their own brands produced by overseas affiliates. These **gray goods**, goods produced for overseas markets often at reduced prices, enter U.S. channels through the actions of unauthorized foreign distributors—typically individuals who buy the goods in the United States for resale in their home markets. While licensing agreements usually prohibit foreign licensees from selling in the United States, no such rules inhibit their distributors. Other countries have gray markets as well. For example, before Amazon became licensed to sell its Kindle products in China, the e-readers were readily available on China's gray market.

gray goods Products manufactured abroad under license from a U.S. firm and then sold in the U.S. market in competition with that firm's own domestic output.

Similarly, when Apple made the iPhone available in China on the same day as it launched worldwide, the company's decision put a major crimp in Hong Kong's gray market. Historically, customers from mainland China had flocked to Hong Kong and willingly paid a premium for the iPhone—often more than $1,000 for a phone that typically retails at $700.[16]

ACHIEVING CHANNEL COOPERATION

The basic antidote to channel conflict is effective cooperation among channel members. Cooperation is best achieved when all channel members regard themselves as equal components of the same organization. The channel captain is primarily responsible for providing the leadership necessary to achieve this kind of cooperation.

IMAX, Sony, and Discovery Communications formed a joint venture to create 3net, a 3D television channel. Distributed by Discovery, the new channel offers a broad programming mix that includes sports, entertainment, nature shows, and more.[17]

ASSESSMENT CHECK

3.1 What is a channel captain? What is its role in channel cooperation?

3.2 Identify and describe the three types of channel conflict.

VERTICAL MARKETING SYSTEMS

Efforts to reduce channel conflict and improve the effectiveness of distribution have led to the development of vertical marketing systems. A **vertical marketing system (VMS)** is a planned channel system designed to improve distribution efficiency and cost effectiveness by integrating various functions throughout the distribution chain.

A vertical marketing system can achieve this goal through either forward or backward integration. In **forward integration**, a firm attempts to control downstream distribution. For example, a manufacturer might set up a retail chain to sell its products. **Backward integration** occurs when a manufacturer attempts to gain greater control over inputs in its production process. A manufacturer might acquire the supplier of a raw material the manufacturer uses in the production of its products. Backward integration also can extend the control of retailers and wholesalers over producers that supply them.

A VMS offers several benefits. First, it improves chances for controlling and coordinating the steps in the distribution or production process. It may lead to the development of economies of scale that ultimately saves money. A VMS may also let a manufacturer expand into profitable new businesses. However, a VMS also involves some costs. A manufacturer assumes increased risk when it takes control of an entire distribution chain. Manufacturers also may discover they lose some flexibility in responding to market changes.

Marketers have developed three categories of VMSs: corporate systems, administered systems, and contractual systems. These categories are outlined in the following sections.

CORPORATE AND ADMINISTERED SYSTEMS

When a single owner runs an organization at each stage of the marketing channel, it operates a **corporate marketing system**. Phillips, the international auction house based in New York City, runs a corporate marketing system. An **administered marketing system** achieves channel coordination when a dominant channel member exercises its power. Even though Goodyear sells its tires through independently owned and operated dealerships, it controls the stock these dealerships carry. Another example of channel captains leading administered channels is McKesson, a health care technology company and pharmaceutical distributor.

CONTRACTUAL SYSTEMS

Instead of common ownership of intermediaries within a corporate VMS or the exercising of power within an administered system, a **contractual marketing system** coordinates distribution through formal agreements among channel members. In practice, three types of agreements set up these systems: wholesaler-sponsored voluntary chains, retail cooperatives, and franchises.

Wholesaler-Sponsored Voluntary Chain

Sometimes an independent wholesaler tries to preserve a market by strengthening its retail customers through a wholesaler-sponsored voluntary chain. The wholesaler adopts a formal agreement with its retailers to use a common name and standardized facilities and to purchase the wholesaler's goods. The wholesaler may even develop a line of private brands to be stocked by the retailers. This practice often helps smaller retailers compete with rival chains—and strengthens the wholesaler's position as well.

IGA (Independent Grocers Alliance) Food Stores is a good example of a voluntary chain. Because a single advertisement promotes all the retailers in the trading area, a common store name and similar inventories allow the retailers to save on advertising costs.

Retail Cooperative

In a second type of contractual VMS, a group of retailers establishes a shared wholesaling operation to help them compete with chains. This is known as a **retail cooperative**. The retailers purchase ownership shares in the wholesaling operation and agree to buy a minimum percentage of their

---

Describe the three different vertical marketing systems.

vertical marketing system (VMS) Planned channel system designed to improve distribution efficiency and cost-effectiveness by integrating various functions throughout the distribution chain.

forward integration Process through which a firm attempts to control downstream distribution.

backward integration Process through which a manufacturer attempts to gain greater control over inputs in its production process, such as raw materials.

corporate marketing system VMS in which a single owner operates the entire marketing channel.

administered marketing system VMS that achieves channel coordination when a dominant channel member exercises its power.

contractual marketing system VMS that coordinates channel activities through formal agreements among participants.

retail cooperative Group of retailers that establish a shared wholesaling operation to help them compete with chains.

inventories from this operation. The members typically adopt a common store name and develop common private brands. Ace Hardware is an example of a retail cooperative.

Franchise

franchise Contractual arrangement in which a wholesaler or retailer agrees to meet the operating requirements of a manufacturer or other franchiser.

A third type of contractual vertical marketing system is the **franchise**, in which a wholesaler or dealer (the franchisee) agrees to meet the operating requirements of a manufacturer or other franchiser. Franchising is a huge and growing industry—an estimated 3,000 U.S. companies distribute goods and services through systems of franchised dealers, and numerous firms also offer franchises in international markets. Nationwide, more than 900,000 retail outlets represent franchises, generating over $2.1 trillion to the U.S. economy.[18] Table 14.2 shows the 20 fastest-growing franchises in the United States, with Subway, 7-Eleven, and Mac Tools topping the list.

Franchise owners pay anywhere from several thousand to more than a million dollars to purchase and set up a franchise. Typically, they also pay a royalty on sales to the franchising company. In exchange for these initial and ongoing fees, franchise owners receive the right to use the company's brand name as well as services like training, marketing, advertising, and volume discounts. Major franchise chains justify the steep price of entry because it allows new businesses to sell winning brands. If the brand enters a slump or the corporation behind the franchise makes poor strategic decisions, franchisees are often hurt.

ASSESSMENT CHECK

4.1 What are vertical marketing systems? Identify the major types.

4.2 Identify the three types of contractual marketing systems.

TABLE 14.2 The Top 20 Fastest-Growing Franchises

Rank	Company and Product(s)
1	Subway: submarine sandwiches and salads
2	7-Eleven: convenience stores
3	Mac Tools: automotive tools and equipment
4	Jan-Pro Franchising International: commercial cleaning
5	Dunkin' Donuts: coffee, doughnuts, baked goods
6	Cruise Planners-American Express Travel: cruise and tour travel agency
7	Vanguard Cleaning Systems: commercial cleaning
8	Jimmy John's Gourmet Sandwich Shops: gourmet sandwiches
9	Great Clips: hair salon
10	Pizza Hut: pizza, pasta, wings
11	Taco Bell: quick-service Mexican restaurant
12	Bricks 4 Kidz: Lego engineering classes, camps, parties
13	Liberty Tax Service: income tax preparation
14	Chester's: quick-service chicken restaurants
15	Anytime Fitness: fitness centers
16	RE/MAX LLC: real estate
16	Sport Clips: men's sports-themed hair salon
18	Coverall Health-Based Cleaning System: commercial cleaning
19	McDonald's: burgers, chicken, salads, beverages
20	Kona Ice: shaved ice cones served from trucks

Source: "2014 Fastest-Growing Franchise Rankings," *Entrepreneur*, accessed March 25, 2014, www.entrepreneur.com.

LOGISTICS AND SUPPLY CHAIN MANAGEMENT

Pier 1 Imports buys its eclectic mix of items from vendors in more than 50 countries, most representing small companies. If high-demand items or seasonal products arrive late to its six North American distribution centers or are shipped in insufficient quantities, the company may miss opportunities to deliver popular shopping choices to its more than 1,000 retail stores and could lose ground to such competitors as Pottery Barn and Crate & Barrel. The situation facing Pier 1 illustrates the importance of logistics. Careful coordination of Pier 1's supplier network, shipping processes, and inventory control is the key to its continuing success. In addition, the store's buyers develop relationships with suppliers in all participating countries.[19]

Effective logistics requires proper supply chain management, control of the activities of purchasing, processing, and delivery through which raw materials are transformed into products and made available to final consumers. The **supply chain**, also known as the *value chain*, is the complete sequence of suppliers and activities that contribute to the creation and delivery of goods and services. The supply chain begins with the raw material inputs for the manufacturing process of a product and then proceeds to the actual production activities. The final link in the supply chain is the movement of finished products through the marketing channel to customers. Each link of the chain benefits the consumers as raw materials move through manufacturing to distribution. The chain encompasses all activities that enhance the value of the finished goods, including design, quality manufacturing, customer service, and delivery. Customer satisfaction results directly from the perceived value of a purchase to its buyer. Read the "Marketing Success" feature to see how one restaurant chain manages its seafood supply chain.

To manage the supply chain, businesses must look for ways to maximize customer value in each activity they perform. Supply chain management takes place in two directions: upstream and downstream, as illustrated in Figure 14.2. **Upstream management** involves managing raw materials, inbound logistics, and warehouse and storage facilities. **Downstream management** involves managing finished product storage, outbound logistics, marketing and sales, and customer service.

> **5** Explain the roles of logistics and supply chain management in an overall distribution strategy.
>
> **supply chain** Control of the activities of purchasing, processing, and delivery through which raw materials are transformed into products and made available to final consumers.
>
> **upstream management** Controlling part of the supply chain that involves raw materials, inbound logistics, and warehouse and storage facilities.
>
> **downstream management** Controlling part of the supply chain that involves finished product storage, outbound logistics, marketing and sales, and customer service.

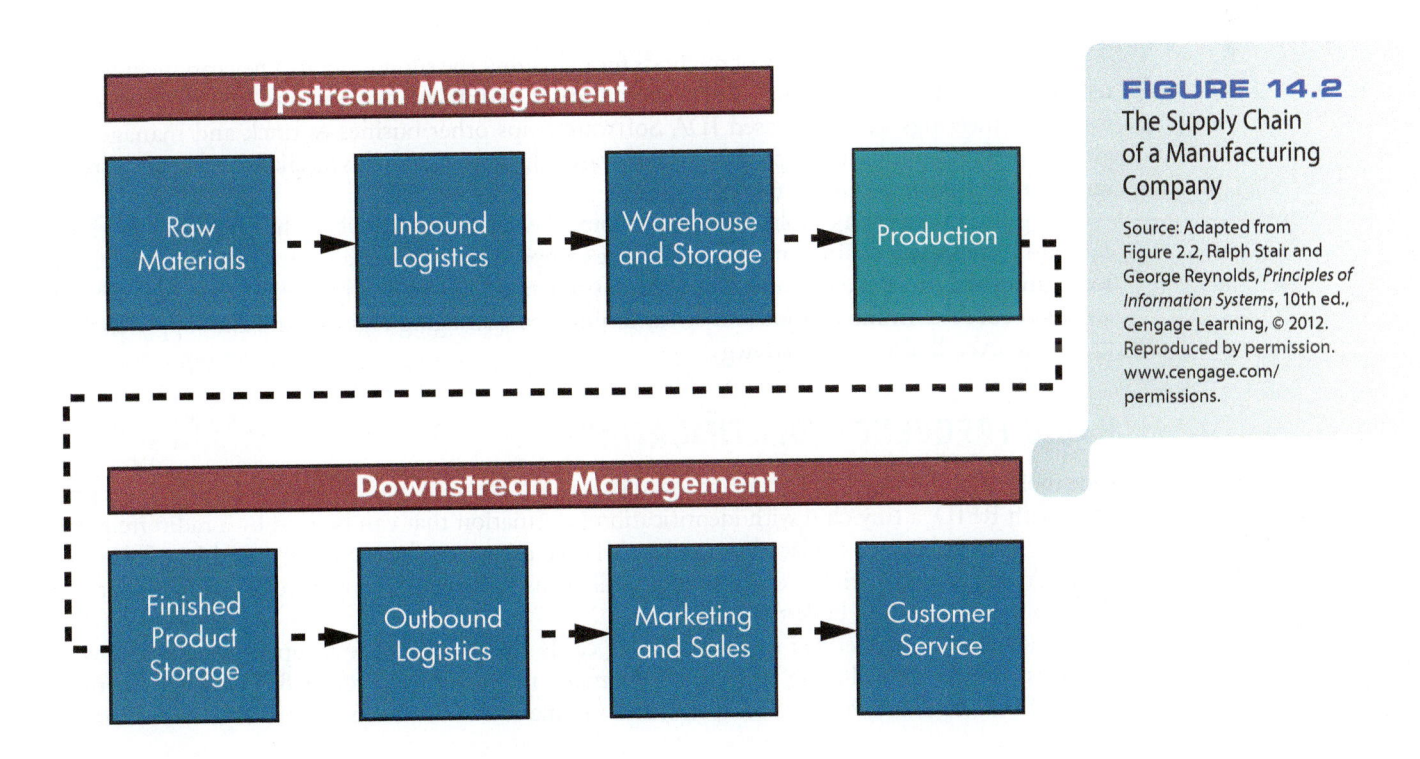

FIGURE 14.2
The Supply Chain of a Manufacturing Company

Upstream Management
Raw Materials → Inbound Logistics → Warehouse and Storage → Production

Downstream Management
Finished Product Storage → Outbound Logistics → Marketing and Sales → Customer Service

Source: Adapted from Figure 2.2, Ralph Stair and George Reynolds, *Principles of Information Systems*, 10th ed., Cengage Learning, © 2012. Reproduced by permission. www.cengage.com/permissions.

MARKETING SUCCESS
Red Lobster "Seas" Food Differently

Background. Red Lobster has been a popular seafood destination since 1968, serving reasonably priced fish and lobster dishes in more than 700 family-friendly locations in the United States and Canada.

The Challenge. Families are eating out more cheaply or less often, and Red Lobster wants to maintain its position as a desirable dining option, serving fresh and wholesome seafood at reasonable prices. Yet the world's supply of some ocean species is dwindling, and concerns about sustainability as well as food safety are more urgent than ever before.

The Strategy. Red Lobster has responded to the reduction of some ocean populations with menu changes that respect scarcity and with initiatives that it hopes will improve sustainability. The company sources fish from only certified, sustainable farms, and it requires suppliers to adhere to Best Aquaculture Practices set by the Global Aquaculture Alliance.

The Outcome. Red Lobster unveiled a new "Sea Food Differently" marketing campaign focusing on individuals in its supply chain and operations areas. Since the campaign, Red Lobster reported increased annual sales in its stores. The chain's parent company, Darden Restaurants, recently sold Red Lobster to private equity firm Golden Gate Capital for more than $2 billion in cash.

Sources: Michael J. De La Merced, "With Sale of Red Lobster Complete, Chief of Darden Restaurants to Step Down," *The New York Times*, accessed October 17, 2014, http://dealbook.nytimes.com; Reuters, "Darden Sells Red Lobster to Golden Gate Capital for $2.1B," *CNBC*, accessed June 3, 2014, www.cnbc.com; L. Z. Granderson, "It Hurts to Lose Red Lobster, But Money Is Tight," *CNN Opinion*, accessed March 25, 2014, www.cnn.com; Sunando Basu, "Red Lobster: Not Immediately Closing, Darden Inc. Claims," *Liberty Voice*, accessed March 25, 2014, http://guardianlv.com; Erica McClain, "Southgate: Red Lobster Denies Rumors of Closure," *News-Herald*, accessed March 25, 2014, www.thenewsherald.com; Bret Thorn, "Darden Details Seafood Sustainability Efforts," *Nation's Restaurant News*, accessed March 25, 2014, http://nrn.com; Stuart Elliott, "Red Lobster Campaign to Showcase Some of Its Own Workers," *The New York Times*, accessed March 25, 2014, www.nytimes.com.

Companies choose a variety of methods for managing the supply chain. They can include high-tech systems like radio frequency identification (discussed in the next section) and regular person-to-person meetings. Arizona-based JDA Software helps other businesses track and manage their global supply chains. Using its proprietary software solutions, JDA helps its clients enhance customer service and improve inventory management.[20]

Logistics plays a major role in giving customers what they need when they need it, and thus is central in the supply chain. Another important component of this chain, *value-added service*, adds some improved or supplemental service that customers do not normally receive or expect. The following sections examine methods for streamlining and managing logistics and the supply chain as part of an overall distribution strategy.

RADIO FREQUENCY IDENTIFICATION

radio frequency identification (RFID) Technology that uses a tiny chip with identification information that can be read by a scanner using radio waves from a distance.

One tool marketers use to help manage logistics is **radio frequency identification (RFID)** technology. With RFID, a tiny chip with identification information that can be read by a radio frequency scanner from a distance is placed on an item. These chips are already widely used in tollway pass transmitters, allowing drivers to zip through tollbooths without stopping or rolling down their windows to toss change into baskets.

They are also embedded in employee ID cards that workers use to open office doors without keys. Businesses including retail giant Walmart, manufacturer Procter & Gamble, credit-card firms MasterCard and American Express, and German retailer Metro AG are eagerly putting this technology to wider use; they say it will speed deliveries, make consumer barcodes obsolete, and provide marketers with valuable information about consumer preferences. Walmart requires its biggest suppliers to attach RFID tags to pallets and cases of products like Coca-Cola and Dove soap, saying the technology vastly improves its ability to track inventory and keep the right amount of products in stock.

RFID technology also may make lost luggage a thing of the past. Aircraft manufacturer Airbus has unveiled Bag2Go, luggage that contains an embedded RFID chip. The chip enables the bag's owner to track the luggage using a smartphone—even notifying the owner if the bag is opened.[21]

Careful coordination of Pier 1's supplier network, shipping process, and inventory control is the key to the company's continuing success.

ENTERPRISE RESOURCE PLANNING

Software is an important aspect of logistics management and the supply chain. An **enterprise resource planning (ERP) system** is an integrated software system that consolidates data from among the firm's units. Roughly two-thirds of ERP system users are manufacturers concerned with production issues such as sequencing and scheduling. German software giant SAP offers systems that allow businesses to manage their customer relations. Recently, ERP suppliers have begun offering cloud-based technology, with its emphasis on subscription-based solutions.[22]

As valuable as it is, ERP and its related software aren't always perfect. ERP failures were blamed for Hershey's inability to fulfill all of its candy orders during one Halloween period when a decrease in sales was blamed on a combination of shipping delays, inability to fill orders, and partial shipments while candy accumulated in warehouses. The nation's major retailers were forced to shift their purchases to other candy vendors.

enterprise resource planning (ERP) system Software system that consolidates data from among a firm's various business units.

third-party (contract) logistics firms Company that specializes in handling logistics activities for other firms.

LOGISTICAL COST CONTROL

In addition to enhancing products by providing value-added services to customers, many firms focus on logistics for another important reason: to cut costs. Distribution functions currently represent almost half of a typical firm's total marketing costs. To reduce logistical costs, businesses are reexamining each link in their supply chains to identify activities that do not add value for customers. By eliminating, reducing, or redesigning these activities, they can often cut costs and boost efficiency. As just described, new technologies like RFID can save businesses millions—or even billions—of dollars.

Because of increased security requirements in recent years, businesses involved in importing and exporting have faced a major rise in logistical costs. The U.S. Transportation Security Administration (TSA) is charged with screening cargo on passenger planes, which increases the cost of transporting goods even more.[23]

Third-Party Logistics

Some companies try to cut costs and offer value-added services by outsourcing some or all of their logistics functions to specialist firms. **Third-party (contract) logistics firms** (3PL firms) specialize in handling logistical activities for their clients. Third-party logistics is a huge industry, estimated at more than $171 billion in the United States alone. More than 90 percent of domestic Fortune 500 companies report using third-party logistics providers.[24]

> **Briefly Speaking**
>
> "Be prepared for all possible instances of demand, whenever and wherever they may occur."
>
> —Michael Dell
> *Founder, Dell Inc.*

> **ASSESSMENT CHECK**
>
> 5.1 What is upstream management? What is downstream management?
>
> 5.2 Identify three methods for managing logistics.

Through outsourcing alliances, producers and logistical service suppliers cooperate in developing innovative, customized systems that speed goods through carefully constructed manufacturing and distribution pipelines. Although many companies have long outsourced transportation and warehousing functions, today's alliance partners use similar methods to combine their operations.

PHYSICAL DISTRIBUTION

> **6** Identify the six major components of a physical distribution system.

A firm's physical distribution system is an organized group of components linked according to a plan for achieving specific distribution objectives. It contains the following elements:

1. *Customer service*—level of customer service the distribution activities support
2. *Transportation*—how the firm ships its products
3. *Inventory control*—quantity of inventory the firm maintains at each location
4. *Protective packaging and materials handling*—how the firm packages and efficiently handles goods in the factory, warehouse, and transport terminals
5. *Order processing*—how the firm handles orders
6. *Warehousing*—the distribution system's location of stock and the number of warehouses the firm maintains

All these components function in interrelated ways. Decisions made in one area affect efficiency in others. The physical distribution manager must balance each component so the system avoids stressing any single aspect to the detriment of overall functioning. A firm might decide to reduce transportation costs by shipping its products by less costly—but slower—water transportation. Slow deliveries would likely force the firm to maintain higher inventory levels, raising those costs. This mismatch between system elements often leads to increased production costs, so balancing the components is crucial.

The general shift from a manufacturing economy to a service economy in the United States has affected physical distribution in two key ways. First, customers require more flexible—yet reliable—transportation service. Second, the number of smaller shipments is growing much faster than the number of large shipments. Although traditional high-volume shipments will continue to grow, they will represent a lower percentage of the transportation industry's revenues and volume.

THE PROBLEM OF SUBOPTIMIZATION

Logistics managers seek to establish a specified level of customer service while minimizing the costs of physically moving and storing goods. Marketers must first decide on their priorities for customer service and then determine how to fulfill those goals by moving goods at the least cost. Meshing together all the physical distribution elements is a huge challenge that firms don't always meet.

suboptimization
Condition that results when individual operations achieve their objectives but interfere with progress toward broader organizational goals.

Suboptimization results when the managers of individual physical distribution functions attempt to minimize costs, but the impact of one task leads to less than optimal results on the others. Imagine a hockey team composed of star players. Unfortunately, despite the individual talents of the players, the team fails to win a game. This is an example of suboptimization. The same thing can happen at a company when each logistics activity is judged by its own accomplishments instead of the way it contributes to the overall goals of the firm. Suboptimization often happens when a firm introduces a new product that may not fit easily into its current physical distribution system.

Effective management of the physical distribution function requires some cost trade-offs. By accepting relatively high costs in some functional areas to cut costs in others, managers can minimize their firm's total physical distribution costs. Of course, any reduction in logistical costs should support progress toward the goal of maintaining customer service standards.

CUSTOMER SERVICE STANDARDS

Customer service standards state the goals and define acceptable performance for the quality of service a firm expects to deliver to its customers. Internet retailers like RoadRunnerSports.com thrive because of their ability to ship within hours of receiving an order. Zappos.com has a 365-day return policy, which means a customer can return a purchase up to a year later for a full refund, as long as the merchandise has not been worn, is in the state it was received, and is in the original packaging.[25] A pizza restaurant might set a standard to deliver customers' pizzas hot and fresh within 30 minutes. An auto repair shop may set a standard to complete all oil changes in a half hour. All are examples of customer service standards.

Designers of a physical distribution system begin by establishing acceptable levels of customer service. These designers then assemble physical distribution components in a way that will achieve this standard at the lowest possible total cost. This overall cost breaks down into five components: (1) transportation, (2) warehousing, (3) inventory control, (4) customer service/order processing, and (5) administrative costs.

TRANSPORTATION

The transportation industry was largely deregulated a number of years ago. Deregulation has been particularly important for motor carriers, railroads, and air carriers. Today, an estimated 15.5 million trucks are transporting goods throughout the United States; 2 million of these are tractor trailers. It is estimated that nearly 3.5 million truck drivers operate in the country.[26] Railroads are enjoying a new boom: Once hauling mostly commodities like corn and grain, they now transport cross country the huge loads of goods coming from China through West Coast ports. Railroads can move a greater amount of freight for less fuel than trucks. In the United States, more than 1.3 million rail cars carry freight on over 138,000 miles of track, with the industry generating more than $73 billion in annual revenues.[27]

Typically adding about 10 percent to the cost of a product, transportation and delivery expenses are the largest category of logistics-related costs for most firms. Also, for many items—particularly perishable ones such as fresh fish or produce—transportation makes a central contribution to satisfactory customer service.

Many logistics managers have found that the key to controlling shipping costs is careful management of relationships with shipping firms. Freight carriers use two basic rates: class and commodity rates. A class rate is a standard rate for a specific commodity moving between any pair of destinations. A carrier may charge a lower commodity rate, sometimes called a *special rate*, to a favored shipper as a reward for either regular business or a large shipment. Railroads and inland water carriers frequently reward customers in this way. In addition, the railroad and motor carrier industries sometimes supplement this rate structure with negotiated, or contract, rates. In other words, the two parties finalize the terms of rates, services, and other variables in a contract.

Classes of Carriers

Freight carriers are classified as common, contract, and private carriers. **Common carriers**, often considered the backbone of the transportation industry, provide transportation services as for-hire carriers to the general public. The government still regulates their rates and services, and they cannot conduct their operations without permission from the appropriate regulatory authority. Common carriers move freight via all modes of transport. FedEx is a major common carrier serving businesses and consumers. One way the firm remains competitive is by developing new methods for enhancing customer service. FedEx has a service called InSight, a free online service that essentially reverses the package-tracking process. Instead of following a package from shipment to delivery, customers can go online to find out what will be delivered to them that day.

The logistics systems of common carriers like FedEx and UPS came under fire during a recent Christmas season when thousands of deliveries failed to arrive in time for the holidays—and, in some cases, didn't arrive at all. The carriers blamed the problems on a confluence of factors, including bad weather that crippled the transportation system and an unexpected spike in delivery volume that swamped their systems. Despite the unpredictability of winter weather, consumers nationwide were unhappy with the companies' performance.[28]

common carriers Businesses that provide transportation services as for-hire carriers to the general public.

FedEx serves businesses and consumers as a common carrier and offers customers a free online service called InSight to track deliveries.

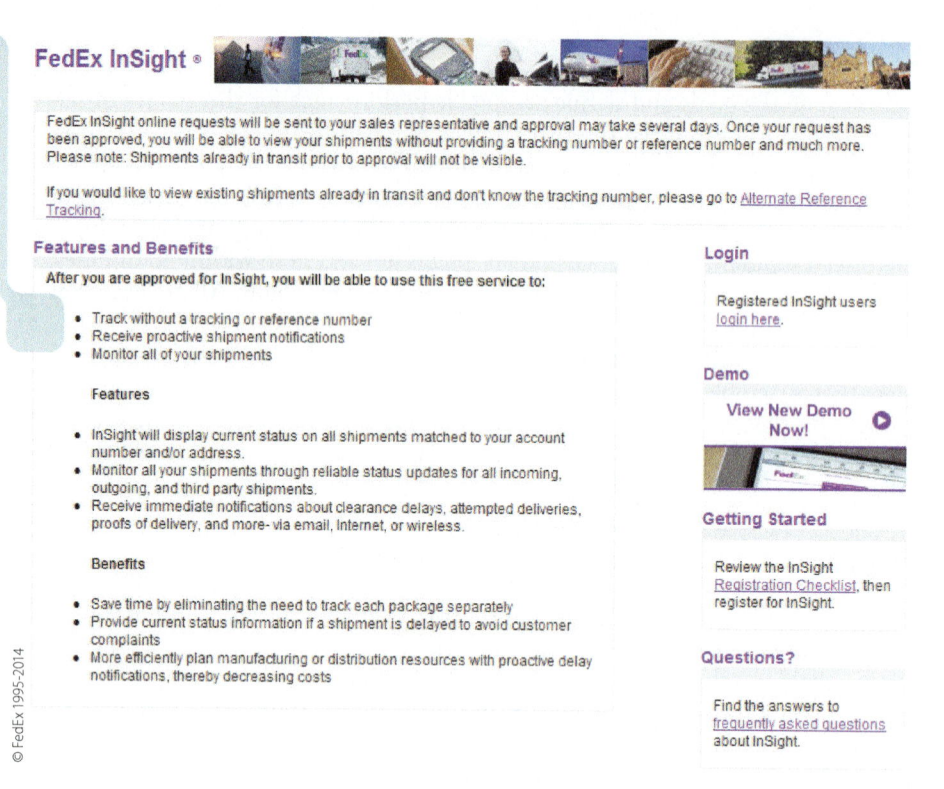

contract carriers For-hire transporters that do not offer their services to the general public.

private carriers Transporters that provide service solely for internally generated freight.

ASSESSMENT CHECK

6.1 What are the six major elements of physical distribution?

6.2 What is suboptimization?

Contract carriers are for-hire transporters that do not offer their services to the general public. Instead they establish contracts with individual customers and operate exclusively for particular industries, such as the motor freight industry. These carriers operate under much looser regulations than common carriers.

Private carriers do not offer services for hire. These carriers provide transportation services solely for internally generated freight. As a result, they observe no rate or service regulations. The Interstate Commerce Commission (ICC), a federal regulatory agency, permits private carriers to operate as common or contract carriers as well. Many private carriers have taken advantage of this rule by operating their trucks fully loaded at all times.

MAJOR TRANSPORTATION MODES

7 Compare the five major modes of transportation.

Logistics managers choose among five major transportation alternatives: railroads, motor carriers, water carriers, pipelines, and air freight. Each mode has its own unique characteristics. Logistics managers select the best options by matching these features to their specific transportation needs.

Railroads

intermodal operations Combination of transport modes, such as rail and highway carriers (piggyback), air and highway carriers (birdyback), and water and air carriers (fishyback), to improve customer service and achieve cost advantages.

Railroads continue to control the largest share of the freight business as measured by ton-miles. The term *ton-mile* indicates shipping activity required to move one ton of freight one mile. Rail shipments quickly rack up ton-miles because this mode provides the most efficient way for moving bulky commodities over long distances. Rail carriers generally transport huge quantities of coal, chemicals, grain, nonmetallic minerals, lumber and wood products, and automobiles. The railroads have improved their service standards through a number of innovative concepts, such as unit trains, run-through trains, **intermodal operations**, and double-stack container trains. Unit trains carry much of the coal, grain, and other high-volume commodities shipped. They run back and forth between single loading points (such as a mine) and single destinations (like a power plant) to deliver a commodity. Run-through trains bypass intermediate terminals to speed up schedules. They work like unit trains, but a run-through train may carry a variety of commodities.

In piggyback operations, one of the intermodal operations, highway trailers and containers ride on railroad flatcars, combining the long-haul capacity of the train with the door-to-door flexibility of the truck. A double-stack container train pulls special rail cars equipped with bathtub-shaped wells so they can carry two containers stacked on top of one another. By nearly doubling train capacity and slashing costs, this system offers enormous advantages to rail customers.

As mentioned earlier, the railroad industry is enjoying a resurgence—this also means it must build a better infrastructure to handle the increase in demand. Recently, the Association of American Railroads announced it would invest more than $25 billion on improvements to the U.S. freight rail system.[29]

Motor Carriers

The trucking industry is also an important factor in the freight industry—the American Trucking Association reports that trucks haul more than 9.2 billion tons of freight each year, making deliveries to areas railroads simply can't reach.[30]

Trucking offers some important advantages over the other transportation modes, including relatively fast and consistent service for both large and small shipments. Motor carriers concentrate on shipping manufactured products, while railroads typically haul bulk shipments of raw materials. Motor carriers therefore receive greater revenue per ton shipped, because the cost for shipping raw materials is higher than shipping manufactured products.

Technology has also improved the efficiency of trucking. Many trucking firms now track their fleets via satellite communications systems. In-truck computer systems allow drivers and dispatchers to make last-minute changes in scheduling and delivery. The Internet is also adding new features to motor carrier services.

Even so, the trucking industry must adjust to changes in the marketing environment. Trucking firms report a shortage of long-haul drivers, causing delays in some deliveries and higher costs, along with the rising cost of fuel, to customers. Some firms offer drivers regional runs and dedicated routes for more predictable work hours, as well as better pay. They also recruit husband-and-wife teams for the long-haul routes. Currently, long-haul trucks in the United States use an estimated 37 billion gallons of diesel fuel annually. With government tax incentives for more fuel-efficient trucks, the trucking industry is slowly moving away from petroleum toward cleaner-burning, less-costly natural gas.[31]

Water Carriers

Two basic types of transport methods move products over water: inland or barge lines and oceangoing, deepwater ships. Barge lines efficiently transport bulky, low-unit-value commodities such as grain, gravel, lumber, sand, and steel. A typical lower Mississippi River barge line may stretch more than a quarter mile across.

Large ships also operate on the Great Lakes, transporting materials like iron ore from Minnesota and harvested grain for market. These lake carrier ships range in size from roughly 400 feet to more than 1,000 feet in length.

Oceangoing supertankers from global companies like the Maersk Line are the size of three football fields and almost double the capacity of other vessels. At full capacity, the ships can cut one-fifth of the cost of shipping a container across the Pacific Ocean. Shippers that transport goods via water carriers incur low costs compared with the rates for other transportation modes. Standardized modular shipping containers maximize savings by limiting loading, unloading, and other handling.

Ships often carry large refrigerated containers called "reefers" for transporting everything from fresh produce to medical supplies. These containers, along with their nonrefrigerated counterparts, improve shipping efficiency because they can easily be removed from a ship and attached to trucks or trains. Although shipping by water traditionally has been less expensive than other modes of transportation, as explained earlier, costs for this mode have increased dramatically because of tightened security measures. Freight rates are based on the size of the vessel, the cost of fuel, and security requirements. Container shipping experienced a downturn during the recent recession. As global economies improve, however, experts are optimistic that the industry will recover.[32]

DHL XML Services offers fully integrated Web service that provides clients with DHL's availability, shipping times, rates, shipment, and courier booking, as well as shipment tracking capability from more than 140 countries. It also features in-house label printing and tracking.

> **Briefly Speaking**
>
> "The American people have done much for the locomotive, and the locomotive has done much for them."
>
> —**James A. Garfield**
> 20th president of the United States

DHL's XML Services and EDI Solutions offer customizable, fully integrated Web service for both large and small businesses.

The company's totally customizable EDI Solutions provides for large-volume shipping and multi-site logistical operations.[33]

The expansion of the Panama Canal should be completed within the next several years. Once it is widened and deepened, the Panama Canal will allow larger ships to pass through the all-water route from Asia to the U.S. Atlantic coast. The expansion doubles the amount of freight that can go through the canal and will have a significant impact on distribution. Ports in New York, New Jersey, Maryland, and Florida are racing to prepare for the arrival of the larger ships by investing in new infrastructure to allow the big ships to dock and unload their cargo.[34]

Pipelines

Although the pipeline industry ranks third after railroads and motor carriers in ton-miles transported, many people scarcely recognize its existence. More than 2.5 million miles of pipelines crisscross the United States in an extremely efficient network for transporting energy products—enough to circle the planet 100 times. The pipelines are operated by about 3,000 large and small firms.[35] Oil pipelines carry two types of commodities: crude (unprocessed) oil and refined products, such as gasoline, jet fuel, and kerosene. The planned Keystone XL Pipeline will move crude oil from Alberta, Canada, to the Gulf Coast.

Although pipelines offer low maintenance and dependable methods of transportation, a number of characteristics limit their applications. They have fewer locations than water carriers, and they can accommodate shipments of only a small number of products. Finally, pipelines represent a relatively slow method of transportation; liquids travel through this method at an average speed of only three to four miles per hour.

Air Freight

Companies involved in air freight are adapting their services as the economy starts to rebound. UPS recently revamped its services, now offering an expanded international express service called UPS Express Freight. The service provides guaranteed time-definite, overnight to three-day, door-to-door delivery, including customs clearance, to large global metropolitan areas. UPS is also offering two less-expensive, nonguaranteed services: UPS Air Freight Direct and UPS Air Freight Consolidated. Both are available worldwide and provide package pickup, delivery, and customs clearance.[36]

Comparing the Five Modes of Transport

Table 14.3 compares the five transportation modes on several operating characteristics. Although all shippers judge reliability, speed, and cost in choosing the most appropriate transportation methods, they assign varying importance to specific criteria when shipping different goods. For example, while motor carriers rank highest in availability in different locations, shippers of petroleum products frequently choose the lowest-ranked alternative, pipelines, for their low cost. Examples of types of goods most often handled by the different modes of transport include:

- *Railroads*—lumber, iron, steel, coal, automobiles, grain, and chemicals
- *Motor carriers*—clothing, furniture, fixtures, lumber, plastic, food, leather, and machinery
- *Water carriers*—fuel, oil, coal, chemicals, minerals, and petroleum products; automobiles and electronics from foreign manufacturers; and low-value products such as clothing and toys from foreign manufacturers

TABLE 14.3 Comparison of Transport Modes

Mode	Speed	Dependability in Meeting Schedules	Frequency of Shipments	Availability in Different Locations	Flexibility in Handling	Cost
Rail	Average	Average	Low	Low	High	Average
Water	Very slow	Average	Very low	Limited	Very high	Very low
Truck	Fast	High	High	Very extensive	Average	High
Pipeline	Slow	High	High	Very limited	Very low	Low
Air	Very fast	High	Average	Average	Low	Very high

ASSESSMENT CHECK

7.1 Identify the five major modes of transport.

7.2 Which mode of transport is currently experiencing a resurgence, and why?

- *Pipelines*—oil, diesel fuel, jet fuel, kerosene, and natural gas
- *Air freight*—flowers, medical testing kits, and gourmet food products sent directly to consumers

FREIGHT FORWARDERS AND SUPPLEMENTAL CARRIERS

Freight forwarders act as transportation intermediaries, consolidating shipments to gain lower rates for their customers. The transport rates on less-than-truckload (LTL) and less-than-carload (LCL) shipments often double the per-unit rates on truckload (TL) and carload (CL) shipments. Freight forwarders charge less than the highest rates but more than the lowest rates. They profit by consolidating shipments from multiple customers until they can ship at TL and CL rates. The customers gain two advantages from these services: lower costs on small shipments and faster delivery service than they could achieve with their own LTL and LCL shipments.

In addition to the transportation options reviewed so far, a logistics manager can ship products via a number of auxiliary, or supplemental, carriers that specialize in small shipments. These carriers include UPS, FedEx, and the U.S. Postal Service.

> **8** Discuss the role of transportation intermediaries, combined transportation modes, and warehousing in improving physical distribution.

INTERMODAL COORDINATION

Transportation companies emphasize specific modes and serve certain kinds of customers, but they sometimes combine their services to give shippers the service and cost advantages of each. *Piggyback* service, mentioned in the section on rail transport, is the most widely used form of intermodal coordination. *Birdyback* service, another form of intermodal coordination, sends motor carriers to pick up a shipment locally and deliver that shipment to local destinations; an air carrier takes it between airports near those locations. *Fishyback* service sets up a similar intermodal coordination system between motor carriers and water carriers.

Intermodal transportation generally gives shippers faster service and lower rates than either mode could match individually because each method carries freight in its most efficient way. Intermodal arrangements require close coordination between transportation providers.

Recognizing this need, multimodal transportation companies have formed to offer combined activities within single operations. Piggyback service generally joins two separate companies: a railroad and a trucking company. A multimodal firm provides intermodal service through its own internal transportation resources. Shippers benefit because the single service assumes responsibility from origin to destination. This unification prevents disputes over which carrier delayed or damaged a shipment.

Neovia Logistics Services, a global provider of logistics solutions to more than 190 countries, recently finalized plans to open a 405,000-square-foot warehouse in a 6,400-acre intermodal center near Chicago. A company executive says the new warehouse will minimize over-the-road transit and reduce transportation costs and transit time.[37]

WAREHOUSING

Products flow through two types of warehouses: storage and distribution warehouses. A *storage warehouse* holds goods for moderate to long periods in an attempt to balance supply and demand for producers and purchasers. Controlled-atmosphere—also called *cold storage*—warehouses in Yakima and Wenatchee, Washington, serve nearby apple orchards. By contrast, a *distribution warehouse* assembles and redistributes goods, keeping them moving as much as possible. Many distribution warehouses or centers physically store goods for less than 24 hours before shipping them to customers.

A storage warehouse holds goods for a moderate to long period of time while a distribution warehouse assembles and redistributes goods quickly.

Logistics managers have attempted to save on transportation costs by developing central distribution centers. A manufacturer might send a single, large, consolidated shipment to a break-bulk center—a central distribution center that breaks down large shipments into several smaller ones and delivers them to individual customers in the area. Many Internet retailers use break-bulk distribution centers.

Automated Warehouse Technology

Logistics managers can cut distribution costs and improve customer service dramatically by automating their warehouse systems. Although automation technology represents an expensive investment, it can provide major labor savings for high-volume distributors like grocery chains. A computerized system might store orders, choose the correct number of cases, and move those cases in the desired sequence to loading docks. This kind of warehouse system reduces labor costs, worker injuries, pilferage, fires, and breakage.

Warehouse Locations

Every company must make a major logistics decision when it determines the number and locations of its storage facilities. Two categories of costs influence this choice: (1) warehousing and materials handling costs and (2) delivery costs from warehouses to customers. Large facilities offer economies of scale in facilities and materials handling systems; per-unit costs for these systems decrease as volume increases. Delivery costs, on the other hand, rise as the distance from warehouse to customer increases.

Warehouse location also affects customer service. Businesses must place their storage and distribution facilities in locations from which they can meet customer demands for product availability and delivery times. They must also consider population and employment trends. The rapid growth of metropolitan areas in the southern and western United States has caused some firms to open more distribution centers in these areas. From its distribution center in Four Oaks, North Carolina, medical technology firm Becton, Dickinson and Company ships 40 percent of its products to northern and southern destinations as well as to Europe. The facility's workers use state-of-the-art technology to track shipments. Forklifts carrying large boxes from high shelves take advantage of gravity; the motion recharges their batteries. Skylights supply most of the building's light. Solar panels provide about one-fifth of the electricity supply, and the remainder of the roof is a "cool roof" that reflects sunlight. The facility became the company's first warehouse to earn gold certification from the LEED program.[38]

INVENTORY CONTROL SYSTEMS

Inventory control captures a large share of a logistics manager's attention, because companies need to maintain enough inventory to meet customer demand without incurring costs for carrying excess inventory. Some firms attempt to keep inventory levels under control by implementing just-in-time (JIT) production. Others, as discussed earlier in this chapter, are beginning to use RFID technology.

Retailers often shift the responsibility—and costs—for inventory from themselves back to individual manufacturers. Vendor-managed inventory (VMI) systems like this are based on the assumption that suppliers are in the best position to spot understocks or surpluses, cutting costs along the supply chain that can be translated into lower prices at the checkout. Datalliance provides VMI platform services in consumer and industrial applications. In the retail sector, the company helps manufacturers that want to replenish supplies by sending them directly to retail stores rather than to distribution centers. Among its clients are Honeywell, Johnson & Johnson, and Sunny D.[39]

ORDER PROCESSING

Like inventory control, order processing directly affects the firm's ability to meet its customer-service standards. A company may need to compensate for inefficiencies in its order-processing system by shipping products via costly transportation modes or by maintaining large inventories at many expensive field warehouses.

Order processing typically consists of four major activities: (1) conducting a credit check; (2) keeping a record of the sale, which involves tasks like crediting a sales representative's commission account; (3) making appropriate accounting entries; and (4) locating orders, shipping them, and adjusting inventory records. A stockout occurs when an order for an item is not available for shipment. A firm's order-processing system must advise customers of a stockout and offer a choice of alternative actions.

As in other areas of physical distribution, technological innovations improve efficiency in order processing. Many firms are streamlining their order-processing procedures by using email and the Internet. The outdoor-gear retailer REI, for example, pushes customers toward Web ordering—its least costly fulfillment channel—in its catalogs, store receipts, signs, mailers, and membership letters.

PROTECTIVE PACKAGING AND MATERIALS HANDLING

Logistics managers arrange and control activities for moving products within plants, warehouses, and transportation terminals. These activities compose the **materials handling system**. Two important concepts influence many materials handling choices: unitizing and containerization.

Unitizing combines as many packages as possible into each load that moves within or outside a facility. Logistics managers prefer to handle materials on pallets (platforms, generally made of wood, on which goods are transported). Unitizing systems often lash materials in place with steel bands or shrink packaging. A shrink package surrounds a batch of materials with a sheet of plastic that shrinks after heating, securely holding individual pieces together. Unitizing promotes efficient materials handling because each package requires minimal labor to move. Securing the materials together also minimizes damage and pilferage. Ridley Inc. manufactures animal feeds for breeders and growers across North America. At its Beloit, Kansas, plant, Ridley uses an efficient process in distributing its products as *unitized pallets*—that is, a pallet holding merchandise ready for storage and shipping to customers. To create these pallets, the company invested in a palletizing line that can handle 24 bags of feed per minute. The machine sprays a food-grade, water-soluble material called Lock n'Pop onto each bag, preventing spillage. The bags then enter a robotic palletizer. Instead of stretch wrap, the palletizer can be programmed with two types of adhesive spray for stacking the pallets.[40]

Logistics managers extend the same concept through **containerization**—combining several unitized loads. A container of oil rig parts, for example, can be loaded in Topeka and trucked to Kansas City, where rail facilities place the shipment on a high-speed run-through train to New York City. There, the parts are loaded onto a ship headed to Saudi Arabia.

materials handling system Set of activities that move production inputs and other goods within factories, warehouses, and transportation terminals.

containerization Process of combining several unitized loads into a single, well-protected load for shipment.

ASSESSMENT CHECK

8.1 What are the benefits of intermodal transportation?

8.2 Identify the two types of warehouses, and explain their function.

In addition to the benefits outlined for unitizing, containerization also markedly reduces the time required to load and unload ships. Containers limit in-transit damage to freight because individual packages pass through fewer handling systems en route to purchasers.

STRATEGIC IMPLICATIONS OF MARKETING IN THE 21ST CENTURY

Several factors, including the e-business environment, security issues, and the cost of fuel, are driving changes in channel development, logistics, and supply chain management. As the Internet continues to revolutionize the ways manufacturers deliver goods to ultimate consumers, marketers must find ways to promote cooperation between existing dealer, retailer, and distributor networks while harnessing the power of the Web as a channel. This system demands not only delivery of goods and services faster and more efficiently than ever before, it also provides superior service to Web-based customers.

In addition, increased product proliferation—grocery stores typically stock almost 50,000 different items—demands logistics systems that can manage multiple brands delivered through multiple channels worldwide. Those channels must be finely tuned to identify and rapidly rectify problems like retail shortfalls or costly overstocks. The trend toward leaner retailing, in which the burden of merchandise tracking and inventory control is switching from retailers to manufacturers, means that to be effective, logistics and supply chain systems must result in cost savings.

Get online now for additional learning tools to help you master your marketing knowledge—visit **WWW.CENGAGEBRAIN.COM** today!

REVIEW OF CHAPTER OBJECTIVES

1 Describe the four types of marketing channels and the roles they play in marketing strategy.

Marketing (distribution) channels are the systems of marketing institutions that enhance the physical flow of goods and services, along with ownership title, from producer to consumer or business user. In other words, they help bridge the gap between producer or manufacturer and business customer or consumer. Types of channels include direct selling, selling through intermediaries, dual distribution, and reverse channels. Channels perform four functions: facilitating the exchange process, sorting, standardizing exchange processes, and facilitating searches by buyers and sellers.

2 Outline the three major channel strategy decisions.

Decisions include selecting a marketing channel and determining distribution intensity. Selection of a marketing channel may be based on market factors, product factors, organizational factors, or competitive factors. Distribution may be intensive, selective, or exclusive.

3 Describe the concepts of channel management, conflict, and cooperation.

Manufacturers must practice channel management by developing and maintaining relationships with the intermediaries in their marketing channels. The channel captain is the dominant member of the channel. Horizontal and vertical conflict can arise when disagreement exists among channel members. Cooperation is best achieved when all channel members regard themselves as equal components of the same organization.

4 Describe the three different vertical marketing systems.

A vertical marketing system (VMS) is a planned channel system designed to improve distribution efficiency and cost-effectiveness by integrating various functions throughout the distribution chain. This coordination can be achieved by forward integration or backward integration. Options include a corporate marketing system, operated by a single owner; an administered marketing system, run by a dominant channel member; and contractual marketing systems, based on formal agreements among channel members.

5 Explain the roles of logistics and supply chain management in an overall distribution strategy.

Effective logistics requires proper supply chain management. The supply chain begins with raw materials, proceeds through actual production, and then continues with the movement of finished products through the marketing channel to customers. Supply chain management takes place in two directions: upstream and downstream. Tools that marketers use to streamline and manage logistics include radio frequency identification (RFID), enterprise resource planning (ERP), and logistical cost control.

6 Identify the six major components of a physical distribution system.

Physical distribution involves a broad range of activities concerned with efficient movement of finished goods from the end of the production line to the consumer. As a system, physical distribution consists of six elements: (1) customer service, (2) transportation, (3) inventory control, (4) materials handling and protective packaging, (5) order processing, and (6) warehousing. These elements are interrelated and must be balanced to create a smoothly functioning distribution system and to avoid suboptimization.

7 Compare the five major modes of transportation.

The five major modes of transport are railroads, motor carriers, water freight, pipelines, and air freight. Railroads rank high on flexibility in handling products; average on speed, dependability in meeting schedules, and cost; and lower on frequency of shipments. Motor carriers are relatively high in cost but rank high on speed, dependability, shipment frequency, and availability in different locations. Water carriers balance their slow speed, low shipment frequency, and limited availability with lower costs. The special nature of pipelines makes them rank relatively low on availability, flexibility, and speed, but they are also lower in cost. Air transportation is high in cost but offers very fast and dependable delivery schedules.

8 Discuss the role of transportation intermediaries, combined transportation modes, and warehousing in improving physical distribution.

Transportation intermediaries facilitate movement of goods in a variety of ways, including piggyback, birdyback, and fishyback services—all forms of intermodal coordination. Methods like unitization and containerization facilitate intermodal transfers.

ASSESSMENT CHECK: ANSWERS

1.1 Distinguish between a marketing channel and logistics. A marketing channel is an organized system of marketing institutions and their interrelationships, designed to enhance the flow and ownership of goods and services from producer to user. Logistics is the actual process of coordinating the flow of information, goods, and services among members of the marketing channel.

1.2 What are the different types of marketing channels? The different types of marketing channels are direct selling, selling through intermediaries, dual distribution, and reverse channels.

1.3 What four functions do marketing channels perform? The four functions of marketing channels are (1) facilitating the exchange process by reducing the number of marketplace contacts necessary for a sale, (2) sorting, (3) standardizing exchange transactions, and (4) facilitating searches by buyers and sellers.

2.1 Identify four major factors in selecting a marketing channel. The four major factors in selecting a marketing channel are market, product, organizational, and competitive.

2.2 Describe the three general categories of distribution intensity. Intensive distribution seeks to distribute a product through all available channels in a trade area. Selective distribution chooses a limited number of retailers in a market area. Exclusive distribution grants exclusive rights to a wholesaler or retailer to sell a manufacturer's products.

3.1 What is a channel captain? What is its role in channel cooperation? A channel captain is the dominant member of the marketing channel. Its role in channel cooperation is to provide the necessary leadership.

3.2 Identify and describe the three types of channel conflict. Horizontal conflict results from disagreements among channel members at the same level. Vertical conflict occurs when channel members at different levels disagree. The gray market causes conflict because it involves competition in the U.S. market of brands produced by overseas affiliates.

4.1 What are vertical marketing systems? Identify the major types. Vertical marketing systems are planned channel systems designed to improve the effectiveness of distribution, including efficiency and cost. The three major types are corporate, administered, and contractual.

4.2 Identify the three types of contractual marketing systems. The three types of contractual systems are wholesale-sponsored voluntary chains, retail cooperatives, and franchises.

5.1 What is upstream management? What is downstream management? Upstream management involves managing raw materials, inbound logistics, and warehouse and storage facilities. Downstream management involves managing finished product storage, outbound logistics, marketing and sales, and customer service.

5.2 Identify three methods for managing logistics. Methods for managing logistics include RFID technology, enterprise resource planning (ERP) systems, and logistical cost control.

6.1 What are the six major elements of physical distribution? The major elements of physical distribution are customer service, transportation, inventory control, materials handling and protective packaging, order processing, and warehousing.

6.2 What is suboptimization? Suboptimization occurs when managers of individual functions try to reduce costs but create less than optimal results.

7.1 Identify the five major modes of transport. The five major modes of transport are railroads, motor carriers, water carriers, pipelines, and air freight.

7.2 Which mode of transport is currently experiencing a resurgence, and why? Railroad transport is currently experiencing a resurgence because of the cost of fuel and its efficiency in transporting large amounts of freight while using less fuel.

8.1 What are the benefits of intermodal transportation? Intermodal transportation usually provides shippers faster service and lower rates than a single mode could offer.

8.2 Identify the two types of warehouses, and explain their function. The two types of warehouses are storage and distribution. Storage warehouses hold goods for moderate to long periods of time to balance supply and demand. Distribution warehouses assemble and redistribute goods as quickly as possible.

MARKETING TERMS YOU NEED TO KNOW

distribution 444
marketing (distribution) channel 444
logistics 444
supply chain management 444
physical distribution 445
marketing intermediary (middleman) 445
wholesaler 445
direct channel 447
direct selling 447
manufacturer's representative 448

dual distribution 449
reverse channels 449
intensive distribution 453
selective distribution 453
exclusive distribution 454
closed sales territories 454
tying agreements 454
channel captain 455
gray goods 456
vertical marketing system (VMS) 457
forward integration 457
backward integration 457

corporate marketing system 457
administered marketing system 457
contractual marketing system 457
retail cooperative 457
franchise 458
supply chain 459
upstream management 459
downstream management 459
radio frequency identification (RFID) 460

enterprise resource planning (ERP) system 461
third-party (contract) logistics firms 461
suboptimization 462
common carriers 463
contract carriers 464
private carriers 464
intermodal operations 464
materials handling system 469
containerization 469

ASSURANCE OF LEARNING REVIEW

1. What is a marketing intermediary? What is the intermediary's role?
2. Explain why the following firms might choose a dual distribution strategy:
    a. Netflix
    b. Home Shopping Network
    c. The Gap
3. Describe the three levels of distribution intensity. Give an example of a product in each level.
4. Compare and contrast the two types of channel conflict. Why is channel conflict damaging to all parties?
5. What are the benefits of owning a franchise? What are the drawbacks?
6. Why do firms choose to streamline their supply chains? Describe two or three ways a firm might go about streamlining its supply chain.
7. What are the five components associated with the cost of achieving customer service standards in a physical distribution system?
8. Which mode of transport would probably be most appropriate for the following goods?
    a. diesel fuel
    b. chain-link fencing
    c. locally grown peaches
    d. automobiles made in South Korea
    e. T-shirts manufactured in Guatemala
    f. grain grown in North Dakota
9. Which two categories of costs influence the choice of how many storage facilities a firm might have and where they are located?
10. Describe the two concepts that influence materials handling choices. Give an example of a product that would be appropriate for each.

PROJECTS AND TEAMWORK EXERCISES

1. The traditional channel for consumer goods runs from producer to wholesaler to retailer to user. With a classmate, select a product from the following list (or choose one of your own) and create a chart that traces its distribution system. You may go online to the firm's website for additional information.
    a. kayak from the Orvis catalog or website
    b. tickets to an NBA game
    c. HD TV from Sam's Club
2. On your own or with a classmate, identify, draw, and explain a reverse channel with which you are familiar. What purpose does this reverse channel serve for businesses? For the community? For consumers?
3. With a classmate, choose a product you think would sell best through a direct channel. Then create a brief sales presentation for your product and present it to the class. Ask for feedback.
4. With a classmate, choose a franchise that interests you. Visit the website of the company to learn more about how its goods and services are distributed. Create a chart outlining the firm's physical distribution system.
5. It takes a lot to move an elaborate stage show like Cirque du Soleil, Big Apple Circus, or a rock band from one location to another while it is on tour. With a classmate, choose a touring performance that interests you—a music group, a circus, a theater performance, or the like—and imagine you are in charge of logistics. Create a chart showing what modes of transportation you would select to move the performance, how you would warehouse certain items during downtime, and what methods you would use to control costs.

CRITICAL-THINKING EXERCISES

1. Imagine a vending machine that would charge more for hot drinks—coffee, tea, and cocoa—during cold weather. What is your opinion of a temperature-sensitive vending machine? Consumers who live in colder climates might pay more over a longer time period each year than consumers who live in warmer climates. Would your opinion change if alternatives were nearby, such as a convenience store or a vending machine that is not temperature-sensitive? Do you think such a machine would be successful? Why or why not?
2. Auto dealerships typically have exclusive distribution rights in their local markets. How might this affect the purchase choices consumers make? What problems might a dealership encounter with this type of distribution?

3. Choose one of the following firms and identify which marketing channel or channels you think would be best for its goods or services. Then explain the **market factors**, **product factors**, and **organizational and competitive factors** contributing to your selection.
    a. Williams-Sonoma
    b. Quiznos Restaurants
    c. *National Geographic Traveler* magazine
    d. LPGA
    e. Kohl's
4. In their most basic form, RFID tags track the progress of products from warehouse to retail shelf to checkout counter. They have great potential to provide marketers with more information about consumers' purchase patterns. In what ways might RFID technology be used to serve customers better? What problems might arise?
5. After a trip to Turkey where you were inspired by the craftsmanship of artisans who make jewelry and decorative artifacts, you decide to establish an import business focusing on their work. How would you determine distribution intensity for your business? What mode or modes of transportation would you use to get the goods to the United States? How and where would you warehouse the goods? Explain your answers.

ETHICS EXERCISE

As more and more firms do business globally, transporting goods from one part of the world to another, there has been a surge in piracy—criminals making off with cargo shipments of all kinds and selling them on the black market. A tractor trailer loaded with electronics might be stolen from a truck stop; a warehouse with pallets of clothing, food, video games, or other goods is susceptible to theft. Large, sophisticated cargo theft gangs have been identified by police in California, Florida, New Jersey, New York, and Texas. However, members of the supply chain can work together to close the net around would-be thieves, developing stronger relationships with each other and law enforcement.[41]

1. What steps might manufacturers take to achieve the kind of channel cooperation that could reduce or prevent cargo theft?
2. How might transportation firms use security measures to build trust with customers and strengthen their position in the marketplace?

INTERNET EXERCISES

1. **Channel conflicts.** Garmin produces a wide range of GPS devices for a variety of applications. Garmin uses several channels to sell its products, including its own Web store. Visit the Garmin USA website. How does Garmin avoid channel conflict? Explain your answer.
    www.garmin.com/us
2. **RFID developments.** Go to the website of the *RFID Journal*. Review the material and prepare a report outlining some of the more significant developments in RFID technology.
    www.rfidjournal.com
3. **Barge transportation statistics.** Visit the website of the American Waterways Operators. Select "Media," then "Industry Facts," and answer the following questions:
    a. How many barges are in operation in the United States?
    b. What commodities are typically shipped by barge in the United States?
    c. Compared to railroads and trucks, why are barges a more economical way to ship certain types of commodities?
    www.americanwaterways.com

Note: Internet Web addresses change frequently. If you don't find the exact site listed, you may need to access the organization's home page and search from there or use a search engine such as Google or Bing.

CASE 14.1
Superstorm Sandy Disrupts Global Supply Chain

Superstorm Sandy surged through New York and New Jersey several years ago, bringing winds of more than 80 miles an hour and a 14-foot flood surge. Airports closed, subways flooded, power and communications were disrupted. In addition to more than 100 deaths, thousands of homes and businesses were damaged or destroyed by flood, fire, and wind. In the aftermath, bridges and roads were closed, gasoline had to be rationed, and crews from as far away as Canada arrived to repair power lines, an effort that took weeks. The storm is estimated to have cost more than $60 billion in property damage and lost business.

While many soon returned to normal routines, the storm's full effects across 15 states were deep and long lasting. A major reason was the disruption of the area's supply chains. New York's and New Jersey's international shipping harbors and three major airports were closed for two to three days, and road traffic was nearly halted for up to several days. Some cargoes were quickly diverted, but shipping volume in the area is so heavy—second only to that of Long Beach/Los Angeles—that disruptions were widespread. Incoming and outgoing shipments were delayed, with ripple effects that went worldwide. Some businesses were hurt by these delays as the critical holiday season approached; some never reopened.

Perhaps most frustrating to many consumers was the unexpected shortage of gasoline left in Sandy's wake, resulting from power outages at gas stations and the shutdown of the area's two main refineries due to flooding. Once the stations that could power their pumps ran out of fuel, no new supplies could reach them for days.

Government officials and business managers alike agree that better preparation can prevent some of these losses and difficulties should another superstorm hit the area. One consultant suggests that businesses learn the risks their suppliers face, plan their production schedules and deliveries in light of those risks, and seek multiple suppliers—ones that are not too far away.

QUESTIONS FOR CRITICAL THINKING

1. Consumers are often advised to stock up on necessities in advance of a major storm. Would this kind of strategy work for businesses? Why or why not?

2. One writer suggests that disaster preparedness includes understanding the risks faced by your supplier's suppliers. Do you agree? Why or why not?

Sources: Sabina Zawadzki and Anna Louie Sussman, "Analysis: Six Months after Sandy, New York Fuel Supply Chain Still Vulnerable," *Reuters*, accessed March 17, 2014, www.reuters.com; Denise Deveau, "Hurricane Sandy a Harsh Reminder of Supply Chain Vulnerability," *National Post*, accessed March 17, 2014, http://business.financialpost.com; "Hurricane Sandy: A Reminder to Plan for Supply Chain Disruption," *HICX Solutions*, accessed March 17, 2014, www.hicxsolutions.com; Chris Merritt, "Impact of Hurricane Sandy on Retail Supply Chains," *Chain Store Age*, accessed March 17, 2014, http://chainstoreage.com; "As the Clear-Up Begins, A Look at Hurricane Sandy's Likely Economic Toll," *HIS Global Insight*, accessed March 17, 2014, www.ihs.com.

VIDEO CASE 14.2
Geoffrey B. Small Keeps Marketing Channels Tight

Designer Geoffrey B. Small doesn't want you to buy his clothes. In fact, he might be disappointed if you were able to find them in a store at all. Small is an American designer who cut his teeth in the clothing industry by selling jeans at The Gap in Boston. Today, Small's overall marketing channel strategy is the opposite of The Gap's: the fewer pieces he sells, the more successful he becomes.

Small is blunt about the importance of exclusive distribution to the image of his goods and his relationships with retail partners as well as consumers. "We have one of the tightest distributions in the world-designer industry," says Small. "It's very difficult to find our collection. So it's very exclusive, and that's by choice, that's important for our customer. We're not for everybody, and we're not interested in being available to everybody." Small explains that the benefits of exclusive distribution outweigh the drawbacks. While it's true that his firm doesn't sell as many clothes as other clothing manufacturers (sometimes Small only makes four pieces of one design), he believes that reverse psychology works. "People want what they can't have," he observes. "Exclusivity is a fundamental part of our field," he comments. "If you're too available, nobody makes money." Small makes his profit by selling less—not more.

The flip side to the exclusivity coin is the mandate that a product represent the very best quality of its type in the world. Small is confident that his clothes meet the highest standards for fabric, tailoring, and workmanship. To achieve this goal, he headquarters his business in Italy right near his suppliers. "If you're trying to make the very best clothes in the world today in terms of materials, components, and accessories in collaborative work-partnerships, there's only one place in the world—and that's Italy." The designer deliberately keeps his supply chain very short. "We're in a region in Italy where we're very close to the best suppliers in the world, and we work with them," Small says.

Small partners with two fabric makers: one is the oldest woolen maker in the world and the other is a multigenerational family company. Small is working with the second firm to develop what he hopes will be the world's best organic fiber, with the ultimate goal of making the world's best sustainable fabrics to be used in luxury fashion design. He is proud of the way these textile manufacturers complement the expertise his team brings to the design table. They bring "a level of artisanal excellence that is unique in the world," says Small. He also notes that the components of his garments reflect the highest concentration of handwork available that he's aware of.

Small also maintains a close relationship with his other channel partners, the retailers who carry his finished garments. Despite the extremely limited production runs of his clothing, Small's designs can be found in 10 countries. In addition to producing a handful of items to be sold across retailers (sometimes one jacket or pair of pants per country), Small works with his retail partners to come up with designs exclusively for the customers of a particular store. Because so few items are produced in any given year, Small says that visiting every store is difficult—but he does it. "The store is where the action is," he explains. He likes to meet with retail staff who, he believes, are the most connected to customers—yet are often underappreciated. Small believes that the retail staff holds key information about consumer needs and preferences. Small also likes to speak directly with customers on his retail visits, engaging in one-on-one communication with the people who buy his clothes.

You won't see a Geoffrey B. Small line at Target or even at Gap any time soon. Small doesn't want to sell you his clothes unless you share his outlook on fashion, appreciate his designs and fabrics, will happily pay top dollar for them, and know the right retailers. Although he wants to grow his business, he insists on doing it his own way: with the marketing channels as precise and tight as one of his hand-sewn stitches.

QUESTIONS FOR CRITICAL THINKING

1. Over the next 10 years, do you think Small's insistence on exclusivity will continue to benefit his business or begin to be detrimental? Why?
2. In your opinion, why does Small have such successful partnerships throughout his marketing channels?

Sources: "The Amazing Geoffrey B. Small Story," company website, www.geoffreybsmall.net/gbstory.htm, accessed March 20, 2014; Geoffrey B. Small, "The Environment of Young Designers," *Not Just a Label*, accessed March 20, 2014, www.notjustalabel.com; Claire Ruhlin, "Recycle, Reconstruct, Redesign," *Community*, accessed March 20, 2014, http://communityathens.blogspot.com; "Independent Luxury, Timeless Style: Geoffrey B. Small on What's the Fashion?" *Irenebrination*, accessed March 20, 2014, http://irenebrinationItypepad.com.

NOTES

1. Company website, "Terra Technology's Award Winning Supply Chain Solutions Help Company Expand Footprint into New Markets," company press release, www.terratechnology.com, accessed March 25, 2014; "Procter & Gamble Implement Demand Sensing," *Supply Chain Movement*, accessed March 25, 2014, www.supplychainmovement.com; "Unilever Uses Terra Technology for Optimization in Europe," *Retaining Today*, accessed March 25, 2014, http://retailingtoday.com; Bruce Rogers, "Robert Byrne's Terra Technology's Mission to Make Business More Efficient," *Forbes*, accessed March 25, 2014, www.forbes.com.
2. Company website, www.pg.com, accessed March 25, 2014; Paula Bernstein, "The Right Fit: Social, Mobile, Display, Search, Video …How Marketers Are Choosing Their Digital Options," *Adweek*, accessed March 25, 2014, www.adweek.com.
3. Specialty Coffee Association of America, "Specialty Coffee Facts & Figures," www.scaa.org, accessed March 25, 2014.
4. "Sales Representatives, Wholesale and Manufacturing," *Occupational Outlook Handbook, 2014–2015*, Bureau of Labor Statistics, accessed October 17, 2014, www.bls.gov.
5. Vikram Alexei Kansara, "Jessica Herrin of Stella & Dot on Remaking Direct Sales for the Digital Age," *Business of Fashion*, accessed October 17, 2014, www.businessoffashion.com.
6. Company website, www.bagborroworsteal.com, accessed March 24, 2014.
7. Thomas Whitehead, "Netflix Wii U App Update Goes Live," *Nintendo Life*, accessed March 25, 2014, www.nintendolife.com.
8. Company website, www.autozone.com, accessed March 24, 2014; Battery Council International, "State Recycling Laws," http://batterycouncil.org, accessed March 24, 2014.
9. Company website, "Reuse-A-Shoe," www.nike.com, accessed March 14, 2014.
10. Josh Davis, "'Cupcake ATM' Opens in Dallas," *WFAA*, accessed March 17, 2014, www.wfaa.com; "Sprinkles Cupcakes Poised for Growth as It Announces Partnership with KarpReilly," press release, *PRNewswire*, accessed March 17, 2014, www.prnewswire.com.
11. Company website, www.petropics.com, accessed March 24, 2014.
12. Mark Brohan, "A Conflicted Group: Top 500 Manufacturers Need to Address Channel Conflict and Speed Up Online Productivity," *Internet Retailer*, accessed March 25, 2014, www.internetretailer.com.
13. "Supermarket Chains Expand Natural & Organic Private Label," *Organic and Wellness News*, accessed March 25, 2014, http://organicwellnessnews.com.
14. Company website, "Cisco Visual Networking Index: Global Mobile Data Traffic Forecast Update, 2013–2018," www.cisco.com, accessed March 25, 2014.
15. Nancy Trejos, "Travel Agents Still Play Vital Role for Business Travelers," *USA Today*, accessed March 25, 2014, www.usatoday.com.
16. Lorraine Luk, "iPhone's China Launch Pinches Gray Market," *The Wall Street Journal*, accessed March 25, 2014, http://blogs.wsj.com.
17. "3net Marks Second Anniversary with Dramatic Growth in Consumer Base and New Original 3D Series Premieres," press release, *The Futon Critic*, accessed March 25, 2014, www.thefutoncritic.com.
18. "Quick Franchise Facts, Franchising Industry Statistics," *A–Z Franchises*, accessed March 25, 2014, www.azfranchises.com.
19. Company website, "2014 Annual Report," www.pier1.com, accessed October 17, 2014.
20. Company website, www.jda.com, accessed March 25, 2014.

21. Adario Strange, "Airbus Unveils iPhone-enabled RFID Luggage Tracking System," *DVICE*, accessed March 25, 2014, www.dvice.com.
22. Colin Barker, "How the Cloud Is Going to Reinvent ERP—and How Long It Will Take," *ZDNet*, accessed March 26, 2014, www.zdnet.com.
23. Organization website, "Frequently Asked Questions," http://www.tsa.gov, accessed March 26, 2014.
24. "Statistics and Facts about the U.S. Logistics Industry," *Statista*, accessed October 19, 2014, www.statista.com.
25. Company website, www.zappos.com, accessed March 26, 2014.
26. "Trucking Statistics," *Truck Info*, accessed October 19, 2014, www.truckinfo.net.
27. Organization website, "Class I Railroad Statistics," www.aar.org, accessed October 19, 2014.
28. Tony Dokoupil, "UPS, FedEx Draw Fire after Christmas Delivery Problems," *U.S. News*, accessed March 26, 2014, http://usnews.nbcnews.com.
29. Association of American Railroads, "Railroad Infrastructure Investment," www.aar.org, accessed October 19, 2014.
30. Organization website, "Reports, Trends & Statistics," www.truckline.com, accessed March 26, 2014.
31. Diane Cardwell and Clifford Krauss, "Trucking Industry Is Set to Expand Its Use of Natural Gas," *The New York Times*, accessed March 26, 2014, www.nytimes.com.
32. Holly Ellyatt, "Shipping Industry Not Out of Danger Yet: Analyst," *CNBC*, accessed March 25, 2014, www.cnbc.com.
33. Company website, www.dhl.com, accessed March 26, 2014.
34. "Cost Dispute Halts Work on Project to Expand Panama Canal," *The New York Times*, accessed March 26, 2014, www.nytimes.com.
35. U.S. Department of Transportation, Office of Pipeline Safety, "Pipeline Basics," PHMSA Stakeholder Communications, http://primis.phmsa.dot.gov, accessed March 26, 2014.
36. Company website, www.ups-scs.com, accessed March 26, 2014.
37. Todd J. Behme, "Shipping Firm to Lease Big New Warehouse in Joliet Development," *Crain's Chicago Business*, accessed March 26, 2014, www.chicagobusiness.com.
38. Company website, "BD Opens Major Distribution Center in Four Oaks, North Carolina," press release, www.bd.com, accessed March 27, 2014.
39. Company website, www.datalliance.com, accessed March 27, 2014.
40. Company website, www.ridleyinc.com, accessed March 27, 2014; company website, "Bags Shipped Trouble-Free without Stretch Wrap," case study, www.itwpackaginsolutions.com, accessed March 27, 2014.
41. Roxana Hegeman, "Thieves Pose as Truckers to Steal Huge Cargo Loads," *Chicago Sun Times*, accessed March 27, 2014, www.suntimes.com.

Chapter 15

Retailers, Wholesalers, and Direct Marketers

1. Explain the wheel of retailing.
2. Describe the five key strategies for selecting target markets.
3. Describe how the four elements of the marketing mix apply to retailing strategy.
4. Explain the concepts of retail convergence and scrambled merchandising.
5. Describe the three functions performed by wholesaling intermediaries.
6. Describe the two major types of independent wholesaling intermediaries and the appropriate situations for using each.
7. Describe the six basic types of direct marketing and nonstore retailing.
8. Explain how the Internet has altered the retailing, wholesaling, and direct marketing environments.

MACY'S MULTI-LEVEL PLAN YIELDS BIG REWARDS

Macy's, the retail giant with more than 840 stores, competes in a tough market. Its rivals include not only upscale chains such as Saks but also off-price retailers such as T.J. Maxx and Marshalls—and of course shopping websites. Yet profits are up for Macy's, in stores, online, and through mobile apps. What drives the chain's success?

Macy's uses several strategic tools to keep its edge by focusing on its customers. Its database holds information about 500 million sales transactions with some 33 million households, which helps it identify and cater to its most loyal shoppers. These individuals, Macy's learned, are not always the biggest spenders. The company's group vice president of marketing reveals that dollars spent don't always relate to customer retention, so Macy's cultivates loyal spenders with personalized outreach such as free manicures or lunches, or coupons for specific items these shoppers want.

The $2.7 billion company is also forging ahead with inventory improvements that let sales associates locate merchandise on iPod Touch devices and ship it to customers immediately, not only from a warehouse but also from another Macy's store that has the item in stock. Shipping items from stores that could be overstocked helps the company move more merchandise at full price instead of marking it down to sell it in the original store. Some 10 percent of online purchases are also filled this way.

Macy's also maintains a mobile website and mobile apps, where its Fashion Star campaign lets valued younger customers buy trendy featured items in real time. Efforts such as these ensure that the chain's future market will be as profitable as its current core consumer target, the now-aging baby boomers.

Finally, Macy's keeps close tabs on its local markets so it can tailor buying strategies to individual stores. Unlike other chains that strive for uniformity, Macy's monitors 69 different cities around the United States and customizes its offerings by size, color, and style as local customers prefer. This strategy, unique among the big retailers, has been so successful that not only are sales and profitability up, but government officials regularly call the company for its insights into how consumers are faring. You can't get more customer-oriented than that.[1]

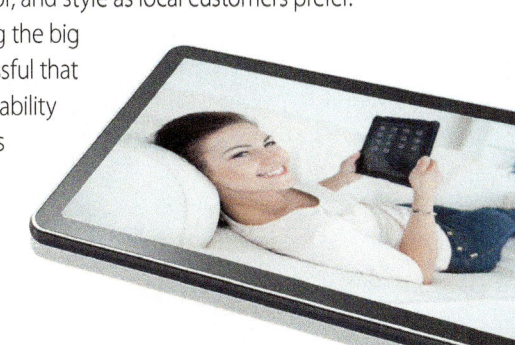

EVOLUTION OF A BRAND

Despite operating in a challenging mid-level retail market, Macy's has implemented a marketing strategy that makes the retailer a recognized brand across many channels. Introducing its mobile app in the lead-up to a recent holiday season, even the retailer was surprised at the strong interest from shoppers—the app was downloaded more than 2 million times before the busy season started.

- Macy's Star Rewards program recently was named one of the top ten loyalty programs in the retail sector, along with Starbucks, Walgreens, and others. How can the company use the loyalty program to attract a new generation of younger, mobile shoppers?
- As consolidation has occurred in the mid-level department store market, more specialized retailers have come online vying for Macy's customers. How can the company compete with these online businesses?
- Macy's shoppers are characterized as loyal followers of the brand, although they may not spend the most money on their purchases. How does offering serious discounts via coupons and other special offers contribute to the company's bottom line?

Chapter Overview

In exploring how today's retailing sector operates, this chapter introduces many examples that explain the combination of activities involved in selling goods to ultimate consumers. Then the chapter discusses the role of wholesalers and other intermediaries who deliver goods from the manufacturers into the hands of retailers or other intermediaries. Finally, the chapter looks at nonstore retailing. Direct marketing, a channel consisting of direct communication to consumers or business users, is a major form of nonstore retailing. It includes not just direct mail and telemarketing but also direct-response advertising, infomercials, and Internet marketing. The chapter concludes by looking at a less pervasive but growing aspect of nonstore retailing—automatic merchandising.

RETAILING

1 Explain the wheel of retailing.

retailing Activities involved in selling merchandise to ultimate consumers.

Retailers are the marketing intermediaries in direct contact with ultimate consumers. **Retailing** describes the activities involved in selling merchandise to these consumers. Retail outlets are contact points between channel members and ultimate consumers. In a very real sense, retailers represent the distribution channel to most consumers, because a typical shopper has little contact with manufacturers and virtually no contact with wholesaling intermediaries. Retailers determine locations, store hours, number of sales personnel, store layouts, merchandise selections, and return policies—factors that often influence consumers' images of the offerings more strongly than consumers' images of the products themselves. Both large and small retailers perform the major channel activities: creating time, place, and ownership utilities.

Retailers act as both customers and marketers in their channels. They sell products to ultimate consumers, and at the same time, they buy from wholesalers and manufacturers. Because of their critical location in the marketing channel, retailers often perform a vital feedback role. They obtain information from customers and transmit that information to manufacturers and other channel members.

Retail outlets such as Nordstrom are contact points between channel members and ultimate consumers.

David L. Moore – CA/Alamy

EVOLUTION OF RETAILING

The development of retailing illustrates the marketing concept in operation. Early retailing in North America can be traced to the establishment of trading posts, such as the Hudson's Bay Company, and to pack peddlers who carried their wares to outlying settlements. The first type of retail institution, the general store, stocked a wide range of merchandise that met the needs of an isolated community or rural area. Supermarkets appeared in the early 1930s in response to consumers' desire for lower prices. In the 1950s and 1960s, discount stores delivered lower prices in exchange for reduced services. The emergence of convenience food stores in the 1960s satisfied consumer demand for fast service, convenient locations, and expanded hours of operation. The development of off-price retailers in the 1980s and 1990s reflected consumer demand for brand-name merchandise at prices considerably lower than those of traditional retailers. In recent years, online retailing has increased in influence and importance.

A key concept known as the **wheel of retailing** attempts to explain the patterns of change in retailing. According to the wheel of retailing, a new type of retailer gains a competitive foothold by offering customers lower prices than current outlets charge and maintains profits by reducing or eliminating services. Once established, however, the innovator begins to add more services, and its prices gradually rise. It then becomes vulnerable to new low-price retailers that enter with minimum services—and so the wheel turns. The retail graveyard is littered with the likes of Gottschalks, Sharper Image, Linens N Things, KB Toys, Circuit City, Harold's, and Levitz Furniture.

Many major developments in the history of retailing appear to fit the wheel's pattern. Early department stores, chain stores, supermarkets, discount stores, hypermarkets, and catalog retailers all emphasized limited service and low prices. Most of these retailers gradually increased their prices as they added services.

Some exceptions disrupt this pattern, however. Suburban shopping centers, convenience food stores, and vending machines never built their appeals around low prices. Still, the wheel pattern has been a good indicator enough times in the past to make it an accurate indicator of future retailing developments.

The wheel of retailing suggests that retailing is always changing. CVS, the top pharmacy chain in the United States, recently announced that its 7,700 stores will no longer sell cigarettes and other tobacco products. With more than 26,000 pharmacists and nurse practitioners working in the company's pharmacies and in-store health care clinics, the chain's CEO says there is no place for cigarettes in an environment where health care is being delivered. While the decision was praised by leading consumer and health care organizations, CVS's strategy will cost the company almost $2 billion in annual sales.[2]

wheel of retailing Hypothesis that each new type of retailer gains a competitive foothold by offering lower prices than current suppliers charge, the result of reducing or eliminating services.

> **Briefly Speaking**
>
> "No sale is really complete until the product is worn out, and the customer is satisfied."
>
> —**Leon Leonwood Bean**
> Founder, L.L.Bean

ASSESSMENT CHECK

1.1 What is retailing?

1.2 Explain the wheel-of-retailing concept.

RETAILING STRATEGY

Like manufacturers and wholesalers, a retailer develops a marketing strategy based on the firm's goals and strategic plans. The organization monitors environmental influences and assesses its own strengths and weaknesses in identifying marketing opportunities and constraints. A retailer bases its key decisions on two fundamental steps in the marketing strategy process:

1. selecting a target market
2. developing a retailing mix to satisfy the chosen market

The retailing mix specifies merchandise strategy, customer service standards, pricing guidelines, target market analysis, promotion goals, location/distribution decisions, and store atmosphere choices. The combination of these elements projects a desired retail image. Retail image

FIGURE 15.1 Components of Retail Strategy

communicates the store's identity to consumers. Kohl's, for instance, counts on its trendy, contemporary image to attract consumers. As Figure 15.1 points out, components of retailing strategy must work together to create a consistent image that appeals to the store's target market.

Operating more than 175 stores in 10 states and with plans for expansion, Phoenix-based Sprouts Farmers Market portrays itself as a neighborhood grocery store that specializes in healthy living at affordable prices. Its stores are half the size of typical grocery stores but contain all the departments found in other supermarkets. The company, which recently went public, focuses its business on four strategies: health, selection, value, and customer services.[3] Whole Foods, in contrast, is an upscale retailer that has succeeded despite the sluggish economy by focusing its expansion on college towns. To learn more, see the story in the "Marketing Success" feature.

Marketing Success
College Towns Help Whole Foods Expand

Background. Although consumers are increasingly interested in Whole Foods' natural and organic products, grocery industry earnings remain flat as the economy tries to regain its footing.

The Challenge. Whole Foods sought a way to grow, while maintaining its signature focus on healthy products and environmentally friendly practices rather than on price cutting.

The Strategy. The company takes a two-pronged approach to growth. First, it's opening stores in and around college towns to tap a young, educated, environmentally aware, and affluent market segment. These locations also offer good real estate value, so even smaller stores can perform well. Second, it has fine-tuned its social media strategy to include not only its own website and blog but also Twitter, Facebook, Google+, Instagram, Pinterest, YouTube, and LinkedIn. The company maintains Facebook and Twitter accounts not just for each of its more than 400 stores but also for its specialty departments such as wine and cheese, allowing finely targeted marketing appeals. It recently established a team dedicated to monitoring all of its social channels for customer questions, concerns, and praise to ensure that customer service remains a top priority for its more than 80,000 employees.

The Outcome. Whole Foods' stock continues to hold steady as it opens new stores both in the United States and abroad. Analysts say it is a strong force in the upscale segment of the grocery market, a sector that is getting increasingly crowded with other grocery retailers.

Sources: Company website, http://wholefoodsmarket.com, accessed October 21, 2014; Robert Channick and Jessica Wohl, "Whole's New Ballgame," *The Chicago Tribune*, October 21, 2014, www.chicagotribune.com; "Social Media Superstars 2014," *CNNMoney*, accessed March 27, 2014, http://money.cnn.com; Asit Sharma, "Three Potential Strategy Tweaks for Whole Foods Market in 2014," *Motley Fool*, accessed March 27, 2014, www.fool.com; Jacqui MacKenzie, "Why I Follow Whole Foods," *Social Media Today*, accessed March 27, 2014, http://socialmediatoday.com; "How Whole Foods Marketing Uses Social Media to Be a Difference Maker," *Digital Spark Marketing*, accessed March 27, 2014, www.digitalsparkmarketing.com; Rebecca Coleman, "Social Media Marketing Case Study: Whole Foods," *Rebecca Coleman.com*, accessed March 27, 2014, www.rebeccacoleman.ca.

SELECTING A TARGET MARKET

A retailer starts to define its strategy by selecting a target market. Factors that influence the retailer's selection are the size and profit potential of the market and the level of competition for its business.

Retailers pore over demographic, geographic, and psychographic profiles to segment markets. In the end, most retailers identify their target markets in terms of certain demographics.

The importance of identifying and targeting the right market is dramatically illustrated by the erosion of department store retailing. While mall anchor stores struggle to attract customers, stand-alone store Target makes a memorable splash with edgy advertising that incorporates its signature red doughnut-shaped logo in imaginative ways. And although Target can be categorized as a discount retailer, it has differentiated itself from competitors such as Walmart and Kmart by offering trendy, quality merchandise at low prices.[4]

Deep-discount chains, such as Dollar General, Dollar Tree, and 99¢ Only, with their less-glamorous locations and low-price merchandise displayed in narrow aisles, target lower-income bargain hunters. Attracted by cents-off basics such as shampoo, cereal, and laundry detergent, customers typically pick up higher-margin goods—toys or chocolates—on their way to the checkout.

By creating stores with wide aisles and clean presentation and offering friendly service and high-end product lines, such as Laura Ashley paints, home improvement chain Lowe's competes with its archrival, Home Depot. Lowe's ambiance helps make the store more appealing to female shoppers, who initiate 80 percent of home improvement purchases.[5]

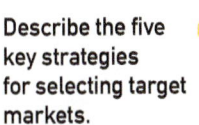

> **Describe the five key strategies for selecting target markets.** [2]

ASSESSMENT CHECK

2.1 How does a retailer develop a marketing strategy?

2.2 How do retailers select target markets?

After identifying a target market, a retailer must then develop marketing strategies to attract these chosen customers to its stores or website. The following sections discuss tactics for implementing different strategies.

MERCHANDISING STRATEGY

A retailer's merchandising strategy guides decisions regarding the items it will offer. A retailer must decide on general merchandise categories, product lines, specific items within lines, and the depth and width of its assortments. Shoe retailer DSW specializes in high-fashion, high-quality footwear.[6] Furnishings retailer West Elm focuses on modern design and contemporary home accessories.[7]

To develop a successful merchandise mix, a retailer must weigh several priorities. First, it must consider the preferences and needs of its previously defined target market, keeping in mind that the competitive environment influences these choices. The retailer must also consider the overall profitability of each product line and product category.

> **Describe how the four elements of the marketing mix apply to retailing strategy.** [3]

Category Management

As mentioned in Chapter 13, a popular merchandising strategy is *category management*, in which a category manager oversees an entire product line and is responsible for the profitability of the product group. Both vendors and retailers use this strategy. Category management seeks to improve the retailer's product category performance through more coordinated buying, merchandising, and pricing. Rather than focusing on the performance of individual brands, such as Suave shampoo or Puffs tissue, category management evaluates performance according to each product category. Laundry detergent, skin-care products, and paper goods, for example, are each viewed as individual profit centers, and different category managers supervise each group. Those that underperform are at risk of being dropped from inventory, regardless of the strength of individual brands. To improve their profitability, for example, some department stores have narrowed their traditionally broad product categories to eliminate high-overhead, low-profit lines such as toys, appliances, and furniture.

The Battle for Shelf Space

As discussed in Chapter 14, large-scale retailers are increasingly taking on the role of channel captain within many distribution networks. Some have assumed traditional wholesaling functions, while others dictate product design and specifications to manufacturers. The result is a shift in power from the manufacturers of top-selling brands to the retailer who makes them available to customers.

Adding to the pressure is the increase in the number of new products and variations on existing products. To identify the varying items within a product line, retailers refer to a specific product offering as a **stock-keeping unit (SKU)**. Within the skin-care category, for example, each facial cream, body moisturizer, and sunscreen in various sizes and formulations is a separate SKU. The proliferation of new SKUs has resulted in a fierce battle for product space on store shelves.

Increasingly, major retailers make demands in return for providing shelf space. They may, for example, seek pricing and promotional concessions from manufacturers as conditions for selling their products. Retailers such as Walmart also require manufacturers to participate in their electronic data interchange (EDI) and quick-response systems. Manufacturers unable to comply may find themselves unable to penetrate this marketplace.

Slotting allowances are just one of the many nonrefundable fees grocery retailers receive from manufacturers to secure shelf space for new products. Manufacturers may pay a national retailer thousands of dollars to get their new product displayed on store shelves.[8] Other fees include failure fees that are imposed if a new product does not meet sales projections; annual renewal fees, a "pay to stay" inducement for retailers to continue carrying brands; trade allowances; discounts on high-volume purchases; and survey fees for research done by the retailers.

Lowe's has designed its stores and overall ambience to appeal to female shoppers, who initiate the major of home improvement purchases.

stock-keeping unit (SKU) Offering within a product line, such as a specific size of liquid detergent.

CUSTOMER SERVICE STRATEGY

Some stores build their retailing strategy around heightened customer services for shoppers. Gift wrapping, alterations, return privileges, bridal registries, consultants, interior design services, delivery and installation, and online shopping via store websites are all examples of services that add value to the shopping experience. A retailer's customer service strategy must specify which services the firm will offer and whether it will charge customers for these services. Those decisions depend on several conditions: store size, type, and location; merchandise assortment; services offered by competitors; customer expectations; and financial resources.

The basic objective of all customer services focuses on attracting and retaining target customers, thus increasing sales and profits. Some services—such as convenient restrooms, lounges, and complimentary coffee—enhance shoppers' comfort. Other services are intended to attract customers by making shopping easier and faster than it would be without the services. Some retailers, for example, offer child-care services for customers. Consumers can also get "virtual assistance" from companies such as Virtuosity, whose Maestro Virtual Assistant can answer, screen, and route calls much like a living, breathing administrative assistant.[9]

A customer service strategy can also support efforts in building demand for a line of merchandise. For more than 90 years, Ace Hardware stores have been a familiar sight, with more than 4,700 stores in cities and towns across the United States and around the world. Each store is independently owned; together, they form the largest cooperative in the hardware industry. The stores sell Ace's own private-label tools—over 11,000 kinds. The company refers to store personnel as the "Helpful Hardware Folks," in line with its familiar slogan, "The helpful place."

Ace Hardware reassures customers with its familiar slogan, "The helpful place."

PRICING STRATEGY

Prices reflect a retailer's marketing objectives and policies. They also play a major role in consumer perceptions of a retailer. Consumers realize, for example, that when they enter an Hermès boutique, they will find expensive merchandise such as leather handbags priced at $3,800 and up, along with men's belts at $720 and up. In contrast, customers of Tuesday Morning or Big Lots expect totally different merchandise and prices.

Markups and Markdowns

The amount a retailer adds to a product's cost to set the final selling price is the **markup**. The amount of the markup typically results from two marketing decisions:

1. *Services performed by the retailer.* Other things being equal, stores that offer more services charge larger markups to cover their costs.
2. *Inventory turnover* rate. Other things being equal, stores with a higher turnover rate can cover their costs and earn a profit while charging a smaller markup.

A retailer's markup exerts an important influence on its image among present and potential customers. In addition, the markup affects the retailer's ability to attract shoppers. An excessive markup may drive away customers; an inadequate markup may not generate sufficient revenue to cover costs and return a profit. Retailers typically state markups as percentages of either the selling prices or the costs of the products.

Marketers determine markups based partly on their judgments of the price that consumers will pay for a given product. When buyers refuse to pay a product's stated price, however, or when improvements in other items or fashion changes reduce the appeal of current merchandise, a retailer must take a markdown. The **markdown** is the amount by which a retailer reduces the original selling price—the discount typically advertised for a sale item. Markdowns are sometimes used to evaluate merchandisers. For example, a department store might base its evaluations of merchandise buyers partly on the average markdown percentages for the product lines for which they are responsible.

The formulas for calculating markups and markdowns are provided in the "Financial Analysis in Marketing" appendix at the end of this textbook.

markup Amount a retailer adds to the cost of a product to determine its selling price.

markdown Amount by which a retailer reduces the original selling price of a product.

LOCATION/DISTRIBUTION STRATEGY

Retail experts often cite location as a potential determining factor in the success or failure of a retail business. A retailer may locate at an isolated site, in a central business district, or in a planned shopping center. The location decision depends on many factors, including the type of merchandise, the retailer's financial resources, characteristics of the target market, and site availability.

In recent years, many localities have become saturated with stores. As a result, some retailers have reevaluated their location strategies. A chain may close individual stores that do not meet sales and profit goals. Other retailers have experimented with nontraditional location strategies. For instance, Starbucks is now found in some Macy's and Target stores as well as Barnes & Noble bookstores.

Locations in Planned Shopping Centers

Over the past several decades, retail trade has shifted away from traditional downtown retailing districts and toward suburban shopping centers. A **planned shopping center** is a group of retail stores designed, coordinated, and marketed to shoppers in a geographic trade area. Together, the stores provide shoppers with a single convenient location as well as free parking. They facilitate shopping by maintaining uniform hours of operation, including evening and weekend hours.

There are five main types of planned shopping centers. The smallest, the *neighborhood shopping center,* is likely to consist of a group of smaller stores, such as a drugstore, a dry cleaner, a card and gift shop, and perhaps a hair or nail salon. This kind of center provides convenient shopping for 5,000 to 50,000 shoppers who live within a few minutes' commute. It contains 5 to 20 stores, and the product mix usually is confined to convenience items and some limited shopping goods.

A *community shopping center* serves 20,000 to 100,000 people in a trade area extending a few miles from its location. It contains anywhere from 15 to 40 retail stores, with a branch of a local department store or some other large specialty discount store as the primary tenant. In addition to the stores found in a neighborhood center, a community center probably encompasses more stores featuring shopping goods, some professional offices, a branch bank, and perhaps a movie theater or supermarket.

Community shopping centers typically offer ample parking, and tenants often share some promotion costs. With the advent of stand-alone, big-box retailers, some community shopping centers have declined in popularity. Some department stores are also moving away from the strategy of locating in shopping centers and opting for freestanding stores.

A *regional shopping center* is a large facility with at least 400,000 square feet of shopping space. Its marketing appeal usually emphasizes major department stores with the power to draw customers, supplemented by as many as 200 smaller stores. A successful regional center needs a location within 30 minutes' driving time of at least 250,000 people. A regional center such as Indianapolis's Fashion Mall at Keystone or a super-regional center such as the Streets at Southpoint in Durham, North Carolina, provides a wide assortment of convenience, shopping, and specialty goods, plus many personal service facilities. Some shopping centers are going green, working to reduce their environmental impact with mandatory recycling programs, maximizing the use of natural light, and installing heat-reflecting roofing that reduces the need for air-conditioning.[10]

A *power center,* usually located near a regional or super-regional mall, brings together several huge specialty stores, such as Sports Authority, Home Depot, and Bed Bath & Beyond, as stand-alone stores in a single trading area. Rising in popularity during the 1990s, power centers offered value because they underpriced department stores while providing a huge selection of specialty merchandise. Heated competition from cost-cutter Walmart and inroads from more upscale discounters, such as Target and Kohl's, are currently hurting the drawing power of these centers.

A fifth type of planned center, the *lifestyle center,* is a retailing format offering a combination of shopping, movie theaters, stages for concerts and live entertainment, decorative fountains and park benches in greenways, and restaurants and bistros in an attractive outdoor environment. Some also include office parks, townhouses, and condominiums. At around 300,000 to 1 million square feet, the centers are large, but they seek to offer the intimacy and easy access of neighborhood village retailing with a fashionable cachet. Convenience and pleasant ambiance are also part of the appeal. Here, shoppers find a mix of just the right upscale tenants—Williams-Sonoma, Banana

planned shopping center Group of retail stores planned, coordinated, and marketed as a unit.

Chapter 15 Retailers, Wholesalers, and Direct Marketers

Republic, Ann Taylor, Pottery Barn, and Restoration Hardware, for instance. Customers can find these lifestyle centers in places such as Santana Row in San Jose, California; Kierland Commons in Scottsdale, Arizona; The Glen Town Center in Glenview, Illinois; and St. John's Town Center in Jacksonville, Florida.[11]

To fill the empty spaces in malls and attract shoppers, malls increasingly add businesses that offer entertainment and experiences. Today, many shopping centers include restaurants, movie-theater complexes, indoor playgrounds, art galleries, arcade games, bowling alleys, and more. The upscale NorthPark Center in Dallas exhibits works by artists such as Andy Warhol and Roy Lichtenstein and acts as a venue for the Dallas International Film Festival.[12]

PROMOTIONAL STRATEGY

To establish store images that entice more shoppers, retailers use various promotional techniques. Through its promotional strategy, a retailer seeks to communicate to consumers information about its stores—locations, merchandise selections, hours of operation, and prices. If merchandise selection changes frequently to follow fashion trends, advertising is typically used to promote current styles effectively. In addition, promotions help retailers attract shoppers and build customer loyalty.

Innovative promotions can have interesting results. Chipotle Mexican Grill recently produced a four-episode satirical Web series on the content-streaming platform Hulu to raise consumers' awareness about genetically modified farming practices. The socially conscious fast-casual restaurant chain is barely mentioned in the episodes, but the series contains trivia tie-ins, video games, and links to the company's foundation that supports sustainable farming. The company hopes the Web series will translate into consumers' buying meals at its Chipotle stores, whose slogan is "Food with Integrity."[13]

National retail chains often purchase advertising space in newspapers, on radio, and on television. Other retailers promote their goods over the Internet or use wireless technology to send marketing messages to customers' cell phones. Consumers are increasingly using their smartphones and tablet devices to surf the Web. Flurry, a California–based analytics firm recently acquired by Yahoo, provides clients with details on how mobile phone and tablet users engage with apps. They launched Ad Analytics, which measures data on how smartphone and tablet users interact with advertisements *within* apps. More than 540,000 apps use Flurry's product, and the company tracks activity from more than 1.2 billion smartphones and tablets.[14]

Retailers also try to combine advertising with in-store merchandising techniques that influence buyer behavior at the point of purchase. As part of Whole Foods Market's goal of "satisfying and delighting our customers," stores reach out to engage their communities by offering in-store education on food, free samples, and lively social media content.[15]

> **Briefly Speaking**
>
> "Save people money so that they can live better—that's Walmart's real mission. And we can do that and get good returns."
>
> **—Rob Walton**
> *Chairman, Walmart*

Lifestyle centers, such as Navy Pier in Chicago, offer a combination of shopping, movie theaters, restaurants, carnival rides, and other forms of entertainment.

From anywhere in the world, a shopper can launch the IMAN Cosmetics beauty app to find just the right makeup for her skin tone.

A friendly, well-trained, and knowledgeable salesperson plays a vital role in conveying the store's image to consumers and in persuading shoppers to buy. To serve as a source of information, a salesperson must possess extensive knowledge regarding credit policies, discounts, special sales, delivery terms, layaways, and returns. To increase store sales, the salesperson must persuade customers that the store sells what those customers need. To this end, salespeople should receive training in selling up and suggestive selling.

By *selling up*, salespeople try to convince customers to buy higher-priced items than originally intended. For example, an automobile salesperson might persuade a customer to buy a more expensive model than the car the buyer had initially considered. Of course, the practice of selling up must always respect the constraints of a customer's real needs. If a salesperson sells customers something they really do not need, the potential for repeat sales dramatically diminishes.

Another technique, *suggestive selling*, seeks to broaden a customer's original purchase by adding related items, special promotional products, or holiday or seasonal merchandise. Here, too, the salesperson tries to help a customer recognize true needs rather than unwanted merchandise. Beauty advisors in upscale department stores are masters of suggestive selling. Smartphones can become beauty advisors, too. Recently, IMAN Cosmetics, which specializes in cosmetics for women of color, introduced a beauty app that helps women find the correct color of makeup to match their skin tone. Using the app, a woman can take a picture of herself and the app reads her skin tone and finds the right IMAN product match for her coloring.[16]

Just as knowledgeable and helpful sales personnel can both boost sales and set retailers apart from competitors, poor service influences customers' attitudes toward a retailer. Increasing customer complaints about unfriendly, inattentive, and uninformed salespeople have prompted many retailers to intensify their attention to training and motivating salespeople. Older training methods are giving way to online learning in many firms.

STORE ATMOSPHERICS

While store location, merchandise selection, customer service, pricing, and promotional activities all contribute to a store's consumer awareness, stores also project their personalities through **atmospherics**—physical characteristics and amenities that attract customers and satisfy their shopping needs. Atmospherics include both a store's exterior and interior décor.

A store's exterior appearance, including architectural design, window displays, signs, and entryways, helps identify the retailer and attract its target market shoppers. The Saks Fifth Avenue script logo on a storefront and McDonald's golden arches are exterior elements that readily identify these retailers. Other retailers design eye-catching exterior elements aimed at getting customers' attention. Colorful, lifelike recreations of jungle animals flank the theatrically lit entrances of the popular Rainforest Cafés, and the tropical motif carries over to the interiors, decorated with wall-sized

atmospherics Combination of physical characteristics and amenities that contribute to a store's image.

SOLVING AN ETHICAL CONTROVERSY
Who Should Control the Spread of Fake Stores and Counterfeit Products?

New York City police who stopped an unlicensed street vendor hawking an iPhone for $150 were surprised at the defense he offered: The phone was just a fake. It came from a nearby store, where officers confiscated thousands of others. A U.S. blogger made worldwide headlines after posting pictures of a fully staffed, authentic-looking Apple store in China that also proved a fake, as did all the products inside. The store was so authentic that the Chinese staff members really believed they were working for Apple. The global proliferation of counterfeit electronics continues unabated, especially in Asia, with counterfeit products cobbled together from fake or stolen parts.

Should governments step in to stop the flood of fakes?

PRO
1. All governments should respect intellectual property rights so multinational companies can safely bring jobs and investment dollars to their countries.
2. Governments should protect their citizens from fake products that perform poorly, if at all.

CON
1. In some cultures, such as China's, innovation is difficult, intellectual property is not protected, and functioning fakes are accepted.
2. Governments should not restrict what companies manufacture, and consumers should look out for themselves.

Summary
Wide-scale government action abroad seems unlikely, especially in Asia, where customers often prefer sophisticated fakes—such as replaceable-battery iPhones—because the products are less expensive than the real thing.

Sources: Christopher Magoon and Katie Martin, "China's Copycat Phenomenon: Fake Apple Stores Still Booming in Southern China," *Tea Leaf Nation*, accessed March 27, 2014, www.tealeafnation.com; Ben Reid, "Chinese Gold iPhone 5s and iPhone 5c Knockoffs Now Available, Runs Android," *Redmond Pie*, accessed March 27, 2014, www.redmondpie.com; Abe Sauer, "How Western Brands Get Shanghaied on China's Shanzhai Express," *Brand Channel*, accessed March 27, 2014, www.brandchannel.com; Panos Mourdoukoutas, "Why China Imitates Western Brands," *Forbes*, accessed March 27, 2014, www.forbes.com; Rick Marshall, "A Video Tour of China's Fake Apple Stores," *Digital Trends*, accessed March 27, 2014, www.digitaltrends.com; Nick Bilton, "Fake Apple Stores Get Fake News Video," *The New York Times*, accessed March 27, 2014, http://bits.blogs.nytimes.com; "Are You Listening, Steve Jobs?" *WordPress.com*, accessed March 27, 2014, http://birdabroad.wordpress.com; Michael Wilson, "An iPhone That's Cheaper, But Fake," *The New York Times*, accessed March 27, 2014, www.nytimes.com; Louis Bedigian, "Apple's Worst Nightmare Comes from an Unlikely Source," *Forbes*, accessed March 27, 2014, www.forbes.com.

---

aquariums. Sometimes the design can be too good to be true; as fake electronics continue to flood global markets, counterfeiters have even managed to open fake Apple stores in China. See the "Solving an Ethical Controversy" feature to read more.

The interior décor of a store should also complement the retailer's image, respond to customers' interests, and, most importantly, induce shoppers to buy. Interior atmospheric elements include store layout, merchandise presentation, lighting, color, sounds, scents, and cleanliness. By strategically positioning the sections where aroma or fragrance is key—the flower shop, the bakery, and the deli, where table-ready roasted chicken or pizza is sold—supermarkets can boost impulse sales. Some hotels even use hidden devices to waft a fragrance throughout their lobbies.[17]

When designing the interior and exterior of a store, marketers must remember that many people shop for reasons other than just purchasing needed products. Other common reasons for shopping include escaping the routine of daily life, avoiding weather extremes,

The Samsung Experience Shop within Best Buy stores sells selected merchandise in an intimate setting, providing a welcoming environment that attracts shoppers with a "store within a store" retail strategy.

ASSESSMENT CHECK

3.1 What is an SKU?

3.2 What are the two components of a markup?

3.3 What are store atmospherics?

fulfilling fantasies, and socializing with family and friends. Retailers expand beyond interior design to create welcoming and entertaining environments that draw shoppers. Some retailers offer a "store within a store" to sell selected merchandise in a more intimate setting—for example, the Samsung Experience Shop within Best Buy stores and British clothing retailer TOPSHOP within Nordstrom stores.[18]

TYPES OF RETAILERS

Because new types of retailers continue to evolve in response to changes in consumer demand, a universal classification system for retailers has yet to be devised. Certain differences do, however, define several categories of retailers: (1) forms of ownership, (2) shopping effort expended by customers, (3) services provided to customers, (4) product lines, and (5) location of retail transactions.

As Figure 15.2 points out, most retailing operations fit in several different categories. A 7-Eleven outlet may be classified as a convenience store (category 2) with self-service (category 3) and a relatively broad product line (category 4). It is both a store-type retailer (category 5) and a member of a chain (category 1).

CLASSIFICATION OF RETAILERS BY FORM OF OWNERSHIP

Perhaps the easiest method for categorizing retailers is by ownership structure, distinguishing between chain stores and independent retailers. In addition, independent retailers may join wholesaler-sponsored voluntary chains, band together to form retail cooperatives, or enter into franchise agreements with manufacturers, wholesalers, or service provider organizations. Each type of ownership has its own unique advantages and strategies.

Chain Stores

Chain stores are groups of retail outlets that operate under central ownership and management and handle the same product lines. Chains have an advantage over independent retailers in economies of scale. Volume purchases allow chains to pay lower prices than their independent rivals must pay.

Because a chain may have hundreds of retail stores, it can afford extensive advertising, sales training, and computerized systems for merchandise ordering, inventory management, forecasting, and accounting. Also, the large sales volume and wide geographic reach of a chain may enable it to advertise in various media.

Independent Retailers

As the second-largest industry in the United States by number of establishments as well as number of employees, the independent retailing structure supports a large number of small stores, many medium-size stores, and a small number of large stores. It generated about $4.7 trillion in retail sales in a recent year. Of the total U.S. gross domestic product, an estimated two-thirds is retail consumption.[19]

Independent retailers compete with chains in a number of ways. The traditional advantage of independent stores is friendly, personalized service. Cooperatives offer another strategy for independents. For instance, cooperatives such as Valu-Rite Pharmacies help independents compete by providing volume buying power as well as advertising and marketing programs.

FIGURE 15.2
Bases for Categorizing Retailers

CLASSIFICATION BY SHOPPING EFFORT

Another classification system is based on the reasons consumers shop at particular retail outlets. This approach categorizes stores as convenience, shopping, or specialty retailers.

Convenience retailers focus their marketing appeals on accessible locations, extended store hours, rapid checkout service, and adequate parking facilities. Local food stores, gasoline stations, and dry cleaners fit this category. Pennsylvania-based Wawa convenience stores offer customers various items, including gasoline and private-label breakfast treats, deli sandwiches, ready-to-eat salads, and seasonal fresh fruit. In addition to its stores in the Mid-Atlantic states, Wawa has opened locations in central Florida.

Shopping stores typically include furniture stores such as Ethan Allen, appliance retailers, clothing outlets, and sporting goods stores. Consumers usually compare prices, assortments, and quality levels at competing outlets before making purchase decisions. Consequently, managers of shopping stores attempt to differentiate their outlets through advertising, in-store displays, well-trained and knowledgeable salespeople, and appropriate merchandise assortments.

Specialty retailers combine carefully defined product lines, services, and reputations in attempts to persuade consumers to expend considerable effort to shop at their stores. Examples include Neiman Marcus, Nordstrom, and Dillard's.

convenience retailers Store that appeals to customers by having an accessible location, long hours, rapid checkout, and adequate parking.

specialty retailers Store that combines carefully defined product lines, services, and reputation to persuade shoppers to spend considerable shopping effort there.

CLASSIFICATION BY SERVICES PROVIDED

Another category differentiates retailers by the services they provide to customers. This classification system consists of three retail types: self-service, self-selection, or full-service retailers.

The AM PM mini-mart is classified as a self-service store, while Albertsons and Kroger grocery stores are examples of self-selection stores. Both categories sell convenience products people can purchase frequently with little assistance. In the clothing industry, the catalog retailer Lands' End is a self-selection store. Full-service retailers such as Macy's focus on fashion-oriented merchandise, backed by a complete array of customer services.

CLASSIFICATION BY PRODUCT LINES

Product lines also define a set of retail categories and the marketing strategies appropriate for firms within those categories. Grouping retailers by product lines produces three major categories: specialty stores, limited-line retailers, and general-merchandise retailers.

Specialty Stores

A *specialty store* typically handles only part of a single product line. However, it stocks this portion in considerable depth or variety. Specialty stores include a wide range of retail outlets, including fish markets, grocery stores, men's and women's shoe stores, and bakeries. Although some specialty stores are chain outlets, most are independent, small-scale operations. They represent perhaps the greatest concentration of independent retailers who develop expertise in one product area and provide narrow lines of products for their local markets.

Specialty stores should not be confused with specialty products. Specialty stores typically carry convenience and shopping goods. The label *specialty* reflects the practice of handling a specific, narrow line of merchandise. For example, Lady Foot Locker is a specialty store that offers a wide selection of name-brand athletic footwear, apparel, and accessories made specifically for women. Gloria Jean's Coffees sells whole-bean coffees, beverages, and gifts.[20]

Limited-Line Retailers

Customers find a large assortment of products within one product line or a few related lines in a **limited-line store**. This type of retail operation typically develops in areas with a large enough population to sufficiently support it. Examples of limited-line stores are IKEA (home furnishings and housewares) and Rubensteins of New Orleans (men's clothing). These retailers cater to the needs of people who want to select from complete lines in purchasing particular products.

A unique type of limited-line retailer is known as a **category killer**. These stores offer huge selections and low prices in single product lines. Stores within this category, such as Bed Bath & Beyond, Home Depot, and Best Buy are among the most successful retailers in the nation. Category killers at first took business away from general merchandise discounters, which were not able to compete in selection or price. Recently, however, expanded merchandise and aggressive cost cutting by warehouse clubs and Walmart have turned the tables. Competition from online companies such as Amazon, which can offer unlimited selection and speedy delivery, has also taken customers away. While they still remain a powerful force in retailing, especially for local businesses, category killers are not invulnerable.

General Merchandise Retailers

General merchandise retailers, carrying a wide variety of product lines stocked in some depth, distinguish themselves from limited-line and specialty retailers by the large number of product lines they carry. Target stores are examples of general merchandise retailers. The general store described earlier in this chapter was an early form of a general merchandise retailer. This category includes variety stores, department stores, and mass merchandisers, such as discount houses, off-price retailers, and hypermarkets.

Variety Stores

A retail outlet that offers an extensive range and assortment of low-price merchandise is called a *variety store*. Less popular today than they once were, many of these stores have evolved into or given way to other types of retailers such as discount stores. In recent years, many pharmacies have become drugstore–variety store combinations. Walgreens, for example, has more than 8,300 drugstores nationwide and filled more than 821 million prescriptions during a recent year.[21] The nation's variety stores now account for less than 1 percent of all retail sales. However, variety stores remain popular in other parts of the world.

Department Stores

In essence, a **department store** is a series of limited-line and specialty stores under one roof. By definition, this large retailer handles a variety of merchandise, including men's, women's, and children's clothing and accessories; household linens and dry goods; home furnishings; and furniture. It is a one-stop shopping destination for almost all personal and household products.

> "I wanted to create a new way of looking at retail."
>
> —Tory Burch
> *American entrepreneur, fashion designer, and CEO, Tory Burch*

limited-line store Retailer that offers a large assortment within a single product line or within a few related product lines.

category killer Store offering huge selections and low prices in single product lines.

general merchandise retailers Store that carries a wide variety of product lines.

department store Large store that handles a variety of merchandise, including clothing, household goods, appliances, and furniture.

Department stores such as Bloomingdale's built their reputations by offering wide varieties of services, including charge accounts, delivery, gift wrapping, and liberal return privileges. As a result, they incur relatively high operating costs, averaging about 45 to 60 percent of sales.

Department stores have faced intense competition over the past several years. Relatively high operating costs have left them vulnerable to retailing innovations, such as discount stores, Internet retailers, and hypermarkets. In addition, department stores' original locations in downtown business districts have suffered from problems associated with limited parking, traffic congestion, and population migration to the suburbs.

Department stores have fought back in various ways. Many have closed certain sections, such as electronics, in which high costs kept them from competing with discount houses and category killers. They have added bargain outlets, expanded parking facilities, and opened major branches in regional shopping centers. Marketers have attempted to revitalize downtown retailing in many cities by modernizing their stores, expanding store hours, making special efforts to attract the tourist and convention trade, and serving the needs of urban residents. Over the years, U.S. department stores have also undergone massive consolidation, with only a handful of companies owning many department-store chains that were once freestanding.[22]

Considered a category killer, Bed Bath & Beyond offers large selections and low prices.

Mass Merchandisers

Mass merchandising has made major inroads into department store sales by emphasizing lower prices for well-known brand-name products, high product turnover, and limited services. A **mass merchandiser** often stocks a wider line of items than a department store but usually without the same depth of assortment within each line. Discount houses, off-price retailers, hypermarkets, and catalog retailers are all examples of mass merchandisers. Examples include Sears and West Coast–based Fred Meyer stores.

Discount Houses A **discount house** charges low prices and offers fewer services. Early discount stores sold mostly appliances. Today, they offer soft goods, drugs, food, gasoline, and furniture.

By eliminating many of the "free" services provided by traditional retailers, these operations can keep their markups 10 to 25 percent below those of their competitors. Some of the early discounters have since added services, stocked well-known name brands, and boosted their prices. In fact, many now resemble department stores.

A discount format gaining strength is the *warehouse club.* Costco, BJ's, and Sam's Club are the largest warehouse clubs in the United States. These no-frills, cash-and-carry outlets offer consumers access to name-brand products at deeply discounted prices. Selection at warehouse clubs includes gourmet popcorn, printers, peanut butter, luggage, and sunglasses sold in vast, warehouse-like settings. Attracting business away from almost every retailing segment, warehouse clubs offer fresh food and gasoline. Customers must be members to shop at warehouse clubs.

Off-Price Retailers Another version of a discount house is an *off-price retailer.* This kind of store stocks only designer labels or well-known brand-name clothing at prices equal to or below regular wholesale prices and then passes the cost savings along to buyers. While many off-price retailers are located in outlets in downtown areas or in freestanding buildings, a growing number are concentrating in *outlet malls*—shopping centers that house only off-price retailers.

mass merchandiser Store that stocks a wider line of goods than a department store, usually without the same depth of assortment within each line.

discount house Store that charges low prices but may not offer some services.

> **Briefly Speaking**
>
> "If you don't sell, it's not the product that's wrong, it's you."
>
> —Estée Lauder
> *American businesswoman and founder of Estée Lauder Cosmetics*

Off-price retailers such as Marshalls keep their prices below those of traditional retailers by offering fewer services.

hypermarkets Giant one-stop shopping facility offering wide selections of grocery items and general merchandise at discount prices, typically filling up 200,000 or more square feet of selling space.

supercenters Large store, usually smaller than a hypermarket, that combines groceries with discount store merchandise.

4 Explain the concepts of retail convergence and scrambled merchandising.

retail convergence Situation in which similar merchandise is available from multiple retail outlets, resulting in the blurring of distinctions between types of retailers and merchandise offered.

Inventory at off-price stores changes frequently as buyers take advantage of special price offers from manufacturers selling excess merchandise. Off-price retailers, such as Burlington, Marshalls, Ross, Stein Mart, and T.J. Maxx, also keep their prices below those of traditional retailers by offering fewer services. Off-price retailing has been well received by today's shoppers. France-based retailer Vente-privée.com sells high-fashion overstock merchandise through invitation-only clearance sales conducted solely on the Web.[23]

Hypermarkets and Supercenters Another innovation in discount retailing is the creation of **hypermarkets**—giant, one-stop shopping facilities that offer wide selections of grocery and general merchandise products at discount prices. Store size determines the major difference between hypermarkets and supercenters. Hypermarkets typically fill up 200,000 or more square feet of selling space, usually larger than most **supercenters**. Michigan-based Meijer, with more than 190 stores in five states, offers a vast array of items in dozens of departments, including housewares, groceries, apparel, drugs, hardware, electronics, and photo finishing.[24]

CLASSIFICATION OF RETAIL TRANSACTIONS BY LOCATION

Although most retail transactions occur in stores, nonstore retailing serves as an important marketing channel for many products. In addition, both consumer and business-to-business marketers rely on nonstore retailing to generate orders or requests for more information that may result in future orders.

Direct marketing is a broad concept that includes direct mail, direct selling, direct-response retailing, telemarketing, Internet retailing, and automatic merchandising. The last sections of this chapter consider each type of nonstore retailing.

RETAIL CONVERGENCE AND SCRAMBLED MERCHANDISING

Many traditional differences no longer distinguish familiar types of retailers, rendering any set of classifications less useful. **Retail convergence**, whereby similar merchandise is available from multiple retail outlets distinguished by price more than any other factor, blurs distinctions between types of retailers and the merchandise mix they offer. A few years ago, a customer looking for a fashionable coffeemaker might have headed straight for Williams-Sonoma or Starbucks. Today, one is just as likely to pick that product up at Target or Sam's Club, where that customer can also check out new spring fashions and stock up on paper goods. The Gap is no longer pitted only against American Eagle Outfitters or L.L.Bean but against designer-label brands at department stores and Kohl's, too. Grocery stores compete with Walmart Supercenter, Sam's Club, and Costco. Walmart has beefed up its already-robust product mix to include VUDU broadband streaming services for the consumer electronics products it sells alongside apparel, housewares, fine jewelry, and more.[25] All these examples highlight how important it is to know your competition. See the "Career Readiness" feature for some tips on how to stay ahead of your competitors.

Scrambled merchandising—in which a retailer combines dissimilar product lines in an attempt to boost sales volume—has also muddied the waters. Drugstores not only fill prescriptions

CAREER READINESS
Tips on Knowing Your Competition

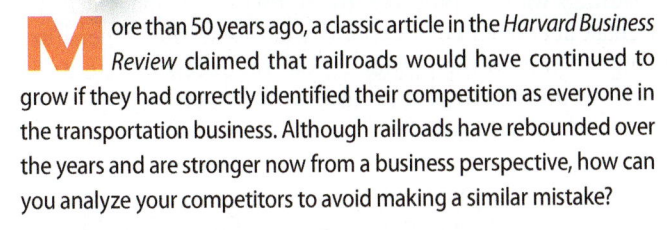

More than 50 years ago, a classic article in the *Harvard Business Review* claimed that railroads would have continued to grow if they had correctly identified their competition as everyone in the transportation business. Although railroads have rebounded over the years and are stronger now from a business perspective, how can you analyze your competitors to avoid making a similar mistake?

1. Define "competition" to include anything and everything that might take your customers away. Anticipate market entries from existing and new directions. Movie theaters compete with all forms of live and recorded entertainment, for instance, not just other theater chains.

2. Become your competitors' customer. Buy and try the product, visit the store and the website, talk to other customers in person or online. What are your competitors doing well? Where are they weak?

3. Go to trade shows and conferences, and let competitors' reps tell you all about their new products, goals, and selling strategies.

4. Investigate competitors' company websites, Facebook and Twitter pages, and blogs. Sign up for their marketing messages, including newsletters and mobile ads. How effectively are they reaching their customers—and yours?

5. On a search engine, type in "Link:" followed by the full URL of your competitors' website, to see which sites are sending Web traffic to your rivals. Will they do the same for you?

Sources: Ben Harper, "How to Analyze Your Competitors Using Social Data," *Social Media Explorer*, accessed March 27, 2014, www.socialmediaexplorer.com; "Analyze the Competition to Keep Your Edge," *All Business*, accessed March 27, 2014, www.allbusiness.com; Rhonda Abrams, "7 Tips for Analyzing the Business Competition," *USA Today*, accessed March 27, 2014, http://usatoday30.usatoday.com.

ASSESSMENT CHECK

4.1 How do we classify retailers by form of ownership?

4.2 Categorize retailers by shopping effort and by services provided.

4.3 List several ways to classify retailers by product line.

but sell cameras, cards, housewares, magazines, and even small appliances. In addition, Walgreens, CVS, Target, and other stores have discovered another consumer need: in-store health clinics that diagnose and treat minor illnesses and injuries quickly and affordably.[26]

scrambled merchandising Retailing practice of combining dissimilar product lines to boost sales volume.

WHOLESALING INTERMEDIARIES

Recall from Chapter 14 that several distribution channels involve marketing intermediaries called **wholesalers**. These firms take title to the goods they handle and sell those products primarily to retailers or to other wholesalers or business users. They sell to ultimate consumers only in insignificant quantities, if at all. **Wholesaling intermediaries**, a broader category, include not only wholesalers but also agents and brokers who perform important wholesaling activities without taking title to the goods.

wholesalers Channel intermediary that takes title to goods it handles and then distributes those goods to retailers, other distributors, or B2B customers.

wholesaling intermediaries Comprehensive term that describes wholesalers as well as agents and brokers.

FUNCTIONS OF WHOLESALING INTERMEDIARIES

> **5** Describe the three functions performed by wholesaling intermediaries.

As specialists in certain marketing functions—as opposed to production or manufacturing functions—wholesaling intermediaries can perform these functions more efficiently than producers or consumers. The importance of these activities results from the utility they create, the services they provide, and the cost reductions they allow.

Creating Utility

Wholesaling intermediaries create three types of utility for consumers: They enhance time utility by making products available for sale when consumers want to purchase them; they create place utility by helping deliver goods and services for purchase at convenient locations; and they create ownership (or possession) utility when a smooth exchange of title to the products from producers or intermediaries to final purchasers is complete. Possession utility can also result from transactions in which actual title does not pass to purchasers, as in rental car services.

Providing Services

Table 15.1 lists a number of services provided by wholesaling intermediaries. The list clearly indicates the marketing utilities—time, place, and possession utility—that wholesaling intermediaries

TABLE 15.1 Wholesaling Services for Customers and Producer-Suppliers

Service	Customers	Producer-Suppliers
Buying	Yes	No
Anticipates customer demands and applies knowledge of alternative sources of supply; acts as purchasing agent for customers.		
Selling	No	Yes
Provides a sales force to call on customers, creating a low-cost method for servicing smaller retailers and business users.		
Storing	Yes	Yes
Maintains warehouse facilities at lower costs than most individual producers or retailers could achieve. Reduces risk and cost of maintaining inventory for producers.		
Transporting	Yes	Yes
Customers receive prompt delivery in response to their demands, reducing their inventory investments. Wholesalers also break bulk by purchasing in economical carload or truckload lots, then reselling in smaller quantities, thereby reducing overall transportation costs.		
Providing Marketing Information	Yes	Yes
Offers important marketing research input for producers through regular contacts with retail and business buyers. Provides customers with information about new products, technical information about product lines, reports on competitors' activities and industry trends, and advisory information concerning pricing changes, legal changes, and so forth.		
Financing	Yes	Yes
Grants credit that might be unavailable for purchases directly from manufacturers. Provides financing assistance to producers by purchasing products in advance of sale by promptly paying bills.		
Risk Taking	Yes	Yes
Evaluates credit risks of numerous, distant retail customers and small-business users. Extends credit to customers that qualify. By transporting and stocking products in inventory, the wholesaler assumes risk of spoilage, theft, or obsolescence.		

Beneficiaries of Service

create or enhance. These services also reflect the basic marketing functions of buying, selling, storing, transporting, providing marketing information, financing, and risk taking.

Of course, wholesaling intermediary services can vary, and not all of them perform every service listed in the table. Producer-suppliers rely on wholesaling intermediaries for distribution and selection of firms that offer the desired combinations of services. In general, however, the critical marketing functions listed in the table form the basis for any evaluation of a marketing intermediary's efficiency. The risk-taking function affects each service of the intermediary.

California-based Ingram Micro is a leading technology distributor with business clients in about 170 countries and vendors all over the world. Ranking number 69 in the Fortune 500, it offers a wide range of information technology services for order management and fulfillment, contract manufacturing and warehousing, transportation management, and credit and collection management, as well as distributing and marketing information technology products to businesses worldwide.[27]

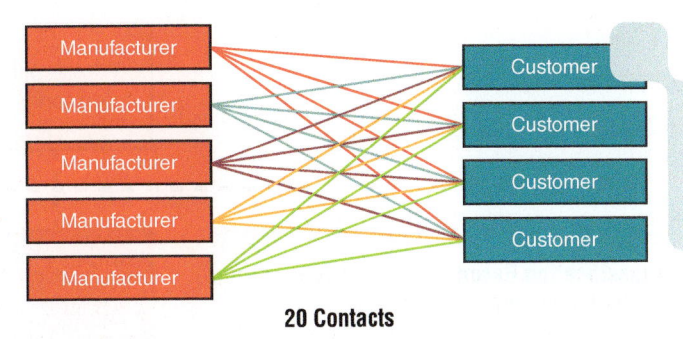

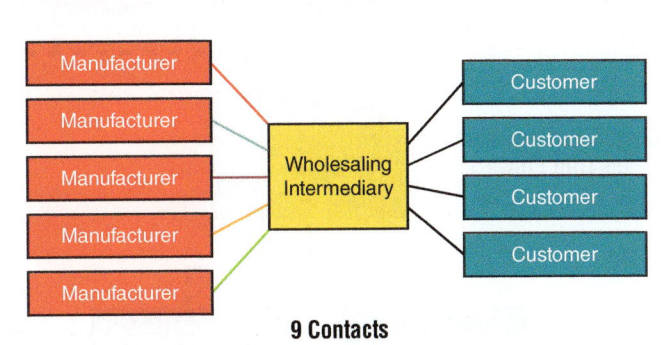

FIGURE 15.3
Transaction Economies through Wholesaling Intermediaries

Lowering Costs by Limiting Contacts

When an intermediary represents numerous producers, it often cuts the costs of buying and selling. The transaction economies are illustrated in Figure 15.3, which shows five manufacturers marketing their outputs to four different retail outlets. Without an intermediary, these exchanges would require 20 transactions. Adding a wholesaling intermediary reduces the number of transactions to nine.

United Stationers is a wholesale distributor of business products ranging from paper clips to technology equipment and office furniture. It serves discount chains, independent stores, and Internet resellers. Although big-box retailers buy in bulk directly from manufacturers, they can order low-volume specialty goods faster and more efficiently from United Stationers. By ordering online, mom-and-pop stores have access to about 100,000 items from more than 1,000 manufacturers, delivered either to the store or directly to customers overnight. A one-stop warehousing, logistics, and distribution network, United Stationers has a product mix that even includes industrial products and janitorial and break-room supplies.[28]

ASSESSMENT CHECK

5.1 What is a wholesaler? How does it differ from a wholesaling intermediary?

5.2 How do wholesaling intermediaries help sellers lower costs?

TYPES OF WHOLESALING INTERMEDIARIES

Various types of wholesaling intermediaries operate in different distribution channels. Some provide wide ranges of services or handle broad lines of goods, while others specialize in individual services, goods, or industries. Figure 15.4 classifies wholesaling intermediaries by two characteristics: ownership and title flows—whether title passes from manufacturer or wholesaling intermediary. The three basic ownership structures are (1) manufacturer-owned facilities, (2) independent wholesaling intermediaries, and (3) retailer-owned cooperatives and buying offices.

Describe the two major types of independent wholesaling intermediaries and the appropriate situations for using each. **6**

FIGURE 15.4 Major Types of Wholesaling Intermediaries

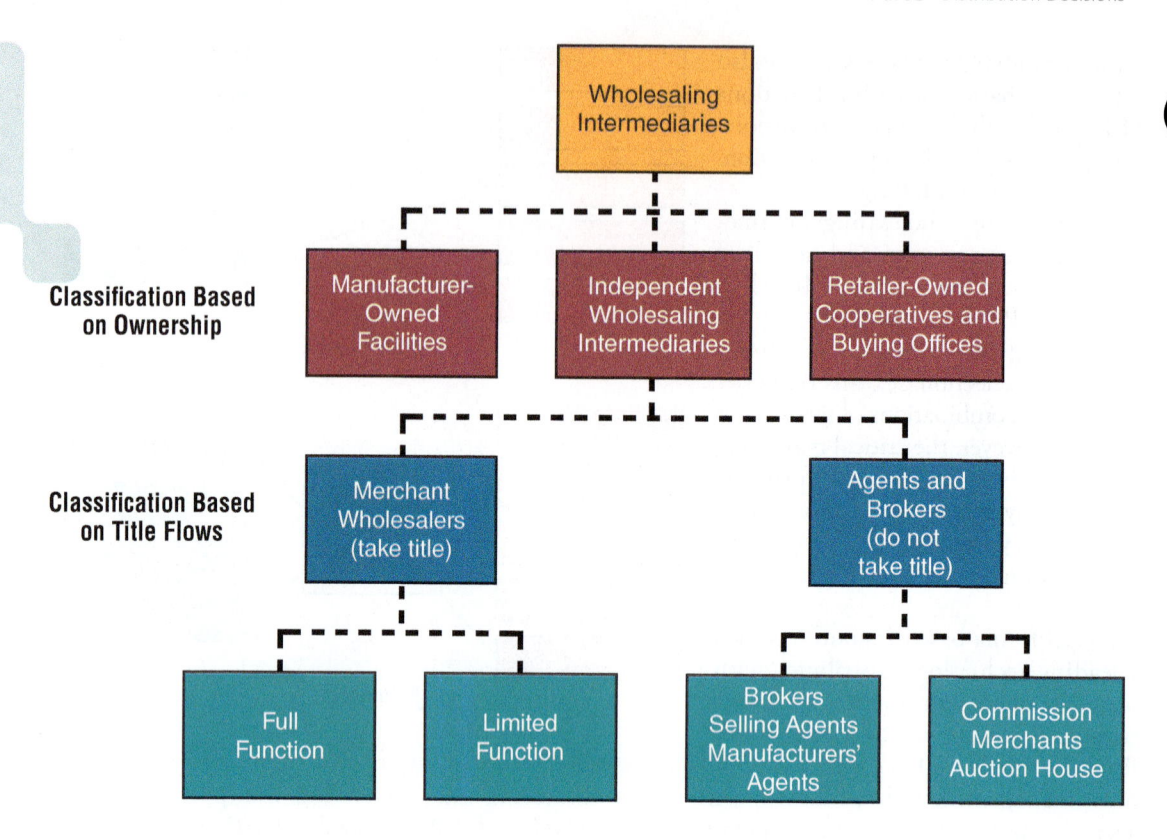

```
                              Wholesaling
                              Intermediaries
                                   |
          ┌────────────────────────┼────────────────────────┐
Classification Based      Manufacturer-        Independent           Retailer-Owned
on Ownership              Owned                Wholesaling           Cooperatives and
                          Facilities           Intermediaries        Buying Offices
                                                   |
                                    ┌──────────────┴──────────────┐
Classification Based            Merchant                      Agents and
on Title Flows                  Wholesalers                   Brokers
                                (take title)                  (do not take title)
                                    |                              |
                            ┌───────┴───────┐              ┌───────┴───────┐
                          Full           Limited         Brokers         Commission
                          Function       Function        Selling Agents  Merchants
                                                         Manufacturers'  Auction House
                                                         Agents
```

The two types of independent wholesaling intermediaries are merchant wholesalers, which take title of the goods, and agents and brokers, which do not.

Several reasons lead manufacturers to distribute their goods directly through company-owned facilities. Some perishable goods need rigid control of distribution to avoid spoilage; other goods require complex installation or servicing. Some goods need aggressive promotion. Goods with high unit values allow profitable sales by manufacturers directly to ultimate purchasers. Manufacturer-owned facilities include sales branches, sales offices, trade fairs, and merchandise marts.

A *sales branch* carries inventory and processes orders for customers from available stock. Branches provide a storage function like independent wholesalers and serve as offices for sales representatives in their territories. They are prevalent in marketing channels for chemicals, commercial machinery and equipment, and petroleum products.

A *sales office*, in contrast, does not carry inventory, but it does serve as a regional office for a manufacturer's sales personnel. Locations close to the firm's customers help limit selling costs and support effective customer service. For example, numerous sales offices in the Detroit area serve the domestic automobile industry.

A *trade fair* (or trade exhibition) is a periodic show at which manufacturers in a particular industry display their wares for visiting retail and wholesale buyers. The annual International Consumer Electronics Show (CES), which is the world's largest consumer technology trade show and the largest trade show of any kind in America, takes place in January in Las Vegas. In a recent year, CES attracted more than 150,000 industry professionals from more than 140 countries and featured more than 3,500 exhibitors.[29]

A *merchandise mart* provides space for permanent showrooms and exhibits, which manufacturers rent to market their goods. One of the world's largest merchandise marts is Chicago's Merchandise Mart, a 4.2-million-square-foot complex with its own ZIP code that hosts more than 30 seasonal buying markets each year.

Independent Wholesaling Intermediaries

Many wholesaling intermediaries are independently owned. These firms fall into two major categories: (1) merchant wholesalers and (2) agents and brokers.

Held annually in Las Vegas, the International Consumer Electronics Show is the world's largest consumer technology trade show.

Merchant Wholesalers

A **merchant wholesaler** takes title to the goods it handles. Merchant wholesalers account for roughly 60 percent of all sales at the wholesale level. Further classifications divide these wholesalers into full-function or limited-function wholesalers, as indicated in Figure 15.4.

A full-function merchant wholesaler provides a complete array of services for retailers and business purchasers. Such a wholesaler stores merchandise in a convenient location, allowing customers to make purchases on short notice and minimizing inventory requirements. The firm typically maintains a sales force that calls on retailers, arranges deliveries, and extends credit to qualified buyers. Full-function wholesalers are common in the drug, grocery, and hardware industries. In the business-goods market, full-function merchant wholesalers—often called *industrial distributors*—sell machinery, inexpensive accessory equipment, and supplies.

A **rack jobber** is a full-function merchant wholesaler that markets specialized lines of merchandise to retailers. A rack jobber supplies the racks, stocks the merchandise, prices the goods, and makes regular visits to refill shelves. Sometimes rack jobbers are the exclusive supplier of a retailer—as in the case of Anderson Merchandisers, a rack jobber in the entertainment sector, which grew by being the supplier to Walmart stores' consumer electronics departments.[30]

Limited-function merchant wholesalers fit into four categories: cash-and-carry wholesalers, truck wholesalers, drop shippers, and mail-order wholesalers. Limited-function wholesalers serve the food, coal, lumber, cosmetics, jewelry, sporting goods, and general merchandise industries.

A *cash-and-carry* wholesaler performs most wholesaling functions, except for financing and delivery. Although feasible for small stores, this kind of wholesaling generally is unworkable for large-scale grocery stores. Today, cash-and-carry operations typically function as departments within regular full-service wholesale operations. Cash-and-carry wholesalers are commonplace outside the United States, such as in the United Kingdom.

A **truck wholesaler (or truck jobber)** markets perishable food items such as bread, potato chips, candy, and dairy products. Truck wholesalers make regular deliveries to retailers, perform sales and collection functions, and promote product lines. Regional wholesale distributor S. Abraham & Sons delivers brand-name groceries, health and beauty aids, and other merchandise to convenience, drug, and grocery stores in the Midwest.[31]

merchant wholesaler Independently owned wholesaling intermediary that takes title to the goods it handles; also known as an industrial distributor in the business goods market.

rack jobber Full-function merchant wholesaler that markets specialized lines of merchandise to retail stores.

truck wholesaler (or truck jobber) Limited-function merchant wholesaler that markets perishable food items.

TABLE 15.2 Comparison of the Types of Merchant Wholesalers and Their Services

		Limited-Function Wholesaler			
Service	Full-Function	Cash-and-Carry	Truck	Drop Shipper	Mail-Order
Anticipates customer needs	Yes	Yes	Yes	No	Yes
Carries inventory	Yes	Yes	Yes	No	Yes
Delivers	Yes	No	Yes	No	No
Provides marketing information	Yes	Rarely	Yes	Yes	No
Provides credit	Yes	No	No	Yes	Sometimes
Assumes ownership risk by taking title	Yes	Yes	Yes	Yes	Yes

drop shipper Limited-function merchant wholesaler that accepts orders from customers and forwards those orders to producers, which then ship directly to the buyers.

mail-order wholesaler Limited-function merchant wholesaler that distributes catalogs instead of sending sales personnel to contact customers.

A **drop shipper**, such as ONEinc, based in Tampa, Florida, accepts orders from customers and forwards these orders to producers, which then ship the desired products directly to customers. Although drop shippers take title to goods, they never physically handle or even see the merchandise. These intermediaries often operate in industries selling bulky goods, such as coal and lumber, which customers buy in large lots.

A **mail-order wholesaler** is a limited-function merchant wholesaler that distributes physical or online catalogs as opposed to sending sales representatives to contact retail, business, and institutional customers. Customers then make purchases by mail, by phone, or online. Such a wholesaler often serves relatively small customers in outlying areas. Mail-order operations mainly exist in the hardware, cosmetics, jewelry, sporting goods, and specialty food lines as well as in general merchandise. Some popular mail-order products are pharmaceuticals, roasted bean coffee, Christmas trees and wreaths, and popcorn.

Table 15.2 compares the various types of merchant wholesalers and the services they provide. Full-function merchant wholesalers and truck wholesalers rank as relatively high-cost intermediaries because of the number of services they perform, while cash-and-carry wholesalers, drop shippers, and mail-order wholesalers provide fewer services and set lower prices because they incur lower operating costs.

Agents and Brokers

A second group of independent wholesaling intermediaries, agents and brokers, may or may not take possession of the goods they handle, but they never take title. They normally perform fewer services than merchant wholesalers, working mainly to bring together buyers and sellers. Agents and brokers fall into five categories: commission merchants, auction houses, brokers, selling agents, and manufacturers' representatives (reps).

commission merchants Agent wholesaling intermediary that takes possession of goods shipped to a central market for sale, acts as the producer's agent, and collects an agreed-upon fee at the time of the sale.

brokers Agent wholesaling intermediary that does not take title to or possession of goods in the course of its primary function, which is to bring together buyers and sellers.

Commission merchants, which predominate in the markets for agricultural products, take possession when producers ship goods such as grain, produce, and livestock to central markets for sale. Commission merchants act as producers' agents and receive agreed-upon fees when they make sales. Because customers inspect the products and prices fluctuate, commission merchants receive considerable latitude in marketing decisions. The owners of the goods may specify minimum prices, but the commission merchants sell these goods at the best possible prices. The commission merchants then deduct their fees from the sales' proceeds.

An *auction house* gathers buyers and sellers in one location and allows potential buyers to inspect merchandise before submitting competing purchase offers. Auction house commissions typically reflect specified percentages of the sales prices of the auctioned items. Auctions are common in the distribution of tobacco, used cars, artwork, livestock, furs, and fruit. The Internet has led to a new type of auction house that connects customers and sellers in the online world. A well-known example is eBay, which auctions a wide variety of products in all price ranges.

Brokers work mainly to bring together buyers and sellers. A broker represents either the buyer or the seller—but not both—in a given transaction, and the broker receives a fee from the client when the transaction is completed. Intermediaries that specialize in arranging buying and selling transactions between domestic producers and foreign buyers are called *export brokers*. Brokers operate in industries characterized by large numbers of small suppliers and purchasers, such as real estate, frozen foods, and used machinery. Because they provide one-time services for sellers or buyers, they cannot serve as effective channels for manufacturers seeking regular, continuing service. A firm that seeks to develop a more permanent channel might choose instead to use a selling agent or manufacturer's agent.

A **selling agent** typically exerts full authority over pricing decisions and promotional outlays, and it often provides financial assistance for the manufacturer. Selling agents act as independent marketing departments, because they can assume responsibility for the total marketing programs of client firms' product lines. Selling agents mainly operate in the coal, lumber, and textiles industries. For a small, weakly financed, production-oriented firm, such an intermediary might prove the ideal marketing channel.

While a manufacturer may deal with only one selling agent, a firm that uses **manufacturers' representatives** often delegates marketing tasks to many of these agents. Such an independent salesperson may work for a number of firms that produce related, noncompeting products. Manufacturers' reps are paid on a commission basis, such as 7 percent of sales. Unlike selling agents, who may contract for exclusive rights to market a product, manufacturers' agents operate in specific territories. They may develop new sales territories or represent relatively small firms and those firms with unrelated lines.

Spirit Group, an Orlando-based manufacturers representative agency, focuses its business on commercial and residential plumbing supplies. The company represents 19 manufacturers, and its territory covers most of Florida. Spirit Group places its emphasis on superior customer service and strong relationships with key partners, including supply houses and wholesale distributors. Spirit Group was recently named Manufacturers' Representative of the Year by *Supply House Times*.[32]

The importance of selling agents in many markets has declined because manufacturers want better control of their marketing programs than these intermediaries allow. In contrast, the volume of sales by manufacturers' agents has more than doubled, to about 37 percent of all sales by agents and brokers. Table 15.3 compares the major types of agents and brokers on the basis of the services they perform.

Auction house eBay offers a wide variety of products in all price ranges.

selling agent Agent wholesaling intermediary for the entire marketing program of a firm's product line.

manufacturers' representatives Agent wholesaling intermediary who represents manufacturers of related but noncompeting products and receives a commission on each sale.

ASSESSMENT CHECK

6.1 What is the difference between a merchant wholesaler and a rack jobber?

6.2 Differentiate between agents and brokers.

TABLE 15.3 Services Provided by Agents and Brokers

Service	Commission Merchant	Auction House	Broker	Selling Agent	Manufacturers' Rep
Anticipates customer needs	Yes	Sometimes	Sometimes	Yes	Yes
Carries inventory	Yes	Yes	No	No	No
Delivers	Yes	No	No	No	Sometimes
Provides marketing information	Yes	Yes	Yes	Yes	Yes
Provides credit	Sometimes	No	No	Sometimes	No
Assumes ownership risk by taking title	No	No	No	No	No

RETAILER-OWNED COOPERATIVES AND BUYING OFFICES

Retailers may assume numerous wholesaling functions in an attempt to reduce costs or provide special services. Independent retailers sometimes band together to form buying groups that can achieve cost savings through quantity purchases. Other groups of retailers establish retailer-owned wholesale facilities by forming cooperative chains. Large chain retailers often establish centralized buying offices to negotiate large-scale purchases directly with manufacturers.

DIRECT MARKETING AND OTHER NONSTORE RETAILING

> **7** Describe the six basic types of direct marketing and nonstore retailing.
>
> **direct marketing**
> Direct communications, other than personal sales contacts, between buyer and seller, designed to generate sales, information requests, or store or website visits.

Although most retail transactions occur in stores, nonstore retailing is an important marketing channel for many products. Both consumer and business-to-business marketers rely on nonstore retailing to generate leads or requests for more information that may result in future orders.

Direct marketing is a broad concept that includes direct mail, direct selling, direct-response retailing, telemarketing, Internet retailing, and automatic merchandising. Direct and interactive marketing expenditures amount to hundreds of billions of dollars in yearly purchases. The last sections of this chapter consider each type of nonstore retailing.

DIRECT MAIL

Direct mail is a major component of direct marketing. It comes in many forms: sales letters, postcards, brochures, booklets, catalogs, house organs (periodicals published by organizations to cover internal issues), and DVDs. Both not-for-profit and profit-seeking organizations make extensive use of this distribution channel.

Direct mail offers several advantages, such as the ability to select a narrow target market, achieve intensive coverage, send messages quickly, choose from various formats, provide complete information, and personalize each mailing piece. Response rates are measurable and higher than other types of advertising. In addition, direct mailings stand alone and do not compete for attention with magazine articles and television programs. On the other hand, the per-reader cost of direct mail is high, effectiveness depends on the quality of the mailing list, and some consumers object to direct mail, considering it "junk mail."

Direct-mail marketing relies heavily on database technology in managing lists of names and in segmenting these lists according to the objectives of the campaign. Recipients get targeted materials, often personalized with their names within the ad's content.

Catalogs are still a popular form of direct mail, with more than 20,000 consumer specialty mail-order catalog companies—and thousands more for business-to-business sales—whose catalogs find their way to almost every mailbox in the United States. In a typical year, almost 12 billion mail-order catalogs are mailed; more than half of all American consumers buy from catalogs.[33] Catalog marketing continues to grow at a faster rate than brick-and-mortar retailers. Catalogs can be a company's only or primary sales method. Pajamagram, Fetch Dog, Popcorn Factory, and Improvements are well-known examples. Brick-and-mortar retailers such as Crate & Barrel, Chico's, Williams-Sonoma, and Orvis also distribute catalogs through the mail.

Environmental concerns and new technologies are changing catalog marketing. More than 2 million American consumers have used TrustedID Mail Preference Service to have their names removed from catalog mailing lists. Most cite a desire to save natural resources for their decision to stop receiving a blizzard of paper catalogs by mail.[34] By moving a catalog online, a merchant can update content easily and quickly, providing consumers with the latest information and prices. Online technology also allows marketers to use video and other techniques to display their merchandise. For example, Nordstrom's online shoe store catalog allows browsers to zoom in and out and view a shoe from different angles and in different colors.

DIRECT SELLING

Through direct selling, manufacturers completely bypass retailers and wholesalers. Instead, they set up their own channels to sell their products directly to consumers. Amway, Avon, Pampered Chef, and Tupperware are all direct sellers. This channel was discussed in detail in Chapter 14.

DIRECT-RESPONSE RETAILING

Customers of a direct-response retailer can order merchandise by mail or telephone, by visiting a mail-order desk in a retail store, or by computer. The retailer then ships the merchandise to the customer's home or to a local retail store for pickup.

Many direct-response retailers rely on direct mail, such as catalogs, to create telephone and mail-order sales and to promote in-store purchases of products featured in the catalogs. Some firms, such as Lillian Vernon, make almost all their sales through catalog orders. Mail-order sales have grown at about twice the rate of retail store sales in recent years.

Direct-response retailers are increasingly reaching buyers through the Internet and through unique catalogs that serve special market niches. Many catalogs sell specialty products, such as kitchenware for the professional cook, art supplies, or supplies for the home renovator.

Direct-response retailing also includes home shopping, which runs promotions on cable television networks to sell merchandise through telephone orders. One form of home shopping, the *infomercial*, has existed for years. Infomercials can be short—one to two minutes—or run up to 30 minutes. Both have demonstrated success at generating revenues. Collette Liantonio is known as the "Queen of Infomercials," having produced more than 2,000 of them over 35 years. Among them are pitches for the George Foreman Grill, the Perfect Pasta Pot, and Pajama Jeans.[35]

> **Briefly Speaking**
>
> "People shop and learn in a whole new way compared to just a few years ago, so marketers need to adapt or risk extinction."
>
> —**Brian Halligan**
> CEO and co-founder, Hubspot

ASSESSMENT CHECK

7.1 What is direct marketing?
7.2 What is direct mail?

TELEMARKETING

Telemarketing refers to direct marketing conducted entirely by telephone. It is the most frequently used form of direct marketing. It provides marketers with a high return on their expenditures, an immediate response, and the opportunity for personalized two-way conversations. Telemarketing is discussed in further detail in Chapter 17.

INTERNET RETAILING

As discussed in detail in Chapter 5, Internet-based retailers sell directly to customers via sites on the Internet. They usually maintain little or no inventory, ordering directly from vendors to fill customer orders received via their websites. Pinrose, a recent start-up business, sells fragrances online and tries to personalize the retail experience of finding the right scent. Using a profiling quiz, Pinrose matches your preferences for colors, sounds, and textures with your olfactory likes and dislikes. Once scent matches are determined, Pinrose suggests three of its fragrances and sends you samples to try with explanations that describe the personality type the scents appeal to. The founders keep their costs low by selling via the Internet, eliminating intermediaries.[36]

In the past decade, conventional retailers have recognized the increasing power of the Internet by adding e-commerce sites to complement their brick-and-mortar stores. The Gap, Home Depot, and Macy's, for example, succeeded in extending their success to the Web. Staples offers thousands of office-supply products on its website, which also offers email alerts, favorite-item lists, and a customer loyalty program.

> **8** Explain how the Internet has altered the retailing, wholesaling, and direct marketing environments.

AUTOMATIC MERCHANDISING

The world's first vending machines dispensed holy water for five drachma coins in Egyptian temples around 215 B.C. This retailing method has grown rapidly ever since; today, nearly 26,000 vending machine operators sell about $7 billion in convenience goods annually in the United States alone.[37]

Although U.S. vending machines primarily sell items such as snacks, soft drinks, or lottery tickets, Japanese consumers use automatic merchandising for everything, including fresh sushi and new underwear. Recently, U.S. marketers have begun to realize the potential of this underused marketing tool. Several vending-machine companies, such as the California-based Fresh Healthy Vending and HUMAN Healthy Vending, with offices on both coasts, work with schools to replace traditional vending-machine offerings with fresh, healthy snacks.[38] The three major soft-drink companies recently agreed to remove sweetened drinks, such as soda and iced tea, from vending machines in elementary and high schools nationwide. The calorie-laden drinks will be replaced by bottled water, low-fat milk, and 100 percent fruit juice or sports drinks. The ability to accept credit cards has enabled vending machines to sell high-end items, such as iPads, headphones, and Sony PlayStation games. Technological advances such as touchscreens, animation, and digital imagery make the buying experience fun—and even allow customers to read the back of the package before they buy.[39]

> **ASSESSMENT CHECK**
>
> 8.1 Describe Internet-based retailers.
>
> 8.2 Explain how the Internet has enhanced retailers' functions.

Strategic Implications of Marketing in the 21st Century

As the Internet revolution steadily becomes a way of life—both for consumers and for the businesses marketing goods and services to them—technology will continue to transform the ways in which retailers, wholesalers, and direct marketers connect with customers.

In the retail sector, the unstoppable march toward lower prices has forced retailers from Neiman Marcus to dollar stores to reevaluate everything, including their logistics and supply networks and their profit margins. Many have used the power of the Internet to strengthen such factors as store image, the merchandising mix, customer service, and the development of long-term relationships with customers.

Although manufacturers first anticipated that Internet technology would enable them to bypass intermediaries such as wholesalers and agents, bringing them closer to the customer, the reality is quite different. Successful wholesalers have established themselves as essential links in the supply, distribution, and customer service network. By leveraging technology, they have carved out new roles, providing expert services such as warehousing and fulfillment to multiple retail clients.

The Internet has empowered direct marketers by facilitating more sophisticated database segmentation. Traditional catalog and direct-mail marketers have integrated Internet sites, Web advertising, and emailing programs into a cohesive targeting, distribution, and repeat-buying strategy.

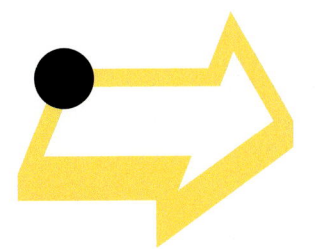

Get online now for additional learning tools to help you master your marketing knowledge—visit **WWW.CENGAGEBRAIN.COM** today!

REVIEW OF CHAPTER OBJECTIVES

1 Explain the wheel of retailing.

The wheel of retailing is the hypothesis that each new type of retailer gains a competitive foothold by offering lower prices than current suppliers and maintains profits by reducing or eliminating services. Once established, the innovator begins to add more services. Its prices gradually rise, making it vulnerable to new low-price retailers. This turns the wheel again.

2 Describe the five key strategies for selecting target markets.

A retailer starts to define its strategy by selecting a target market. The target market dictates, among other things, the product mix, pricing strategy, and location strategy. Retailers deal with consumer behavior at the most complicated level, and a clear understanding of the target market is critical. Strategies for selecting target markets include merchandising, customer services, pricing, location/distribution, and promotional strategies.

3 Describe how the four elements of the marketing mix apply to retailing strategy.

A retailer must first identify a target market and then develop a product strategy. Next, it must establish a customer service strategy. Retail pricing strategy involves decisions on markups and markdowns. Location is often the determining factor in a retailer's success or failure. A retailer's promotional strategy and store atmosphere play important roles in establishing a store's image.

4 Explain the concepts of retail convergence and scrambled merchandising.

Retail convergence is the coming together of shoppers, goods, and prices, resulting in the blurring of distinctions among types of retailers and the merchandise mix they offer. Similar selections are available from multiple sources and are differentiated mainly by price. Scrambled merchandising refers to retailers' practice of carrying dissimilar product lines in an attempt to generate additional sales volume. Retail convergence and scrambled merchandising have made it increasingly difficult to classify retailers.

5 Describe the three functions performed by wholesaling intermediaries.

The functions of wholesaling intermediaries include creating utility, providing services, and lowering costs by limiting contacts.

6 Describe the two major types of independent wholesaling intermediaries and the appropriate situations for using each.

Independent wholesaling intermediaries can be divided into two categories: (1) merchant wholesalers and (2) agents and brokers. The two major types of merchant wholesalers are full-function merchant wholesalers, such as rack jobbers; and limited-function merchant wholesalers, including cash-and-carry wholesalers, truck wholesalers, drop shippers, and mail-order wholesalers. Full-function wholesalers are common in the pharmaceutical, grocery, and hardware industries.

The food, coal, lumber, cosmetics, jewelry, sporting goods, and general-merchandise industries sometimes use limited-function wholesalers. Agents and brokers do not take title to the products they sell; this category includes commission merchants, auction houses, brokers, selling agents, and manufacturers' reps. Companies seeking to develop new sales territories, firms with unrelated lines, and smaller firms use manufacturers' reps. Commission merchants are common in the marketing of agricultural products. Auction houses are used to sell tobacco, used cars, livestock, furs, and fruit. Brokers are prevalent in the real estate, frozen foods, and used machinery industries.

7 Describe the six basic types of direct marketing and nonstore retailing.

Direct marketing is a distribution channel consisting of direct communication to a consumer or business recipient. It generates orders and sales leads that may result in future orders. Because direct marketing responds to fragmented media markets and audiences, growth of customized products, and shrinking network broadcast audiences, marketers consider it an important part of their planning efforts. Although most U.S. retail sales take place in stores, nonstore retailing activities such as direct mail, direct selling, direct-response retailing, telemarketing, Internet retailing, and automatic merchandising are important in marketing many types of goods and services.

8 Explain how the Internet has altered the retailing, wholesaling, and direct marketing environments.

The Internet has affected every aspect of marketing, including how supply networks operate and how relationships are formed with customers. The Internet has allowed retailers to enhance their merchandising mix and their customer service by, among other things, giving them access to much broader selections of goods. Successful wholesalers have carved out a niche as a source of expertise offering faster, more efficient, Web-enabled distribution and fulfillment. Direct marketers have merged their traditional catalog or direct-mail programs with an Internet interface that allows for faster, more efficient, and more frequent contact with customers and prospects.

ASSESSMENT CHECK: ANSWERS

1.1 What is retailing? Retailing refers to the activities involved in selling merchandise to ultimate consumers.

1.2 Explain the wheel-of-retailing concept. The wheel of retailing is the hypothesis that each new type of retailer gains a competitive foothold by offering lower prices than current suppliers and maintains profits by reducing or eliminating services.

2.1 How does a retailer develop a marketing strategy? A retailer develops a marketing strategy that is based on its goals and strategic plans.

2.2 How do retailers select target markets? Strategies for selecting target markets include merchandising, customer services, pricing, location/distribution, and promotional strategies.

3.1 What is an SKU? An SKU, or stock-keeping unit, is a specific product offering within a product line.

3.2 What are the two components of a markup? A markup consists of the product's cost and an amount added by the retailer to determine its selling price.

3.3 What are store atmospherics? Store atmospherics are the physical characteristics and amenities that attract customers and satisfy their shopping needs.

4.1 How do we classify retailers by form of ownership? There are two types of retailers by form of ownership: chain stores and independent retailers.

4.2 Categorize retailers by shopping effort and by services provided. Convenience retailers and specialty retailers are classified by shopping effort; self-service, self-selection, and full-service describe retailers in terms of services provided.

4.3 List several ways to classify retailers by product line. Retailers classified by product line include specialty stores, limited-line retailers, and general merchandise retailers. General merchandise retailers include variety stores, department stores, and mass merchandisers.

5.1 What is a wholesaler? How does it differ from a wholesaling intermediary? A wholesaler is a channel intermediary that takes title to goods it handles and then distributes these goods to retailers, other distributors, or B2B customers. A wholesaling intermediary can be a wholesaler, an agent, or a broker and can perform wholesaling activities without taking title to the goods.

5.2 How do wholesaling intermediaries help sellers lower costs? Wholesaling intermediaries reduce the number of transactions between manufacturers and retail outlets, thus lowering distribution costs.

6.1 What is the difference between a merchant wholesaler and a rack jobber? A merchant wholesaler takes title to the goods it handles. A rack jobber is a full-function merchant wholesaler that markets specialized lines of merchandise to retailers.

6.2 Differentiate between agents and brokers. Agents and brokers may or may not take possession of the goods they handle, but they never take title. Brokers work mainly to bring together buyers and sellers. A selling agent typically exerts full authority over pricing decisions and promotional outlays and often provides financial assistance for the manufacturer.

7.1 What is direct marketing? Direct marketing is a distribution channel consisting of direct communication to a consumer or business recipient. It generates orders and sales leads that may result in future orders.

7.2 What is direct mail? Direct mail is a form of direct marketing that includes sales letters, postcards, brochures, booklets, catalogs, house organs, and DVDs.

8.1 Describe Internet-based retailers. Internet-based retailers sell directly to customers via virtual storefronts on the Web. They usually maintain little or no inventory, ordering directly from vendors to fill customers' orders.

8.2 Explain how the Internet has enhanced retailers' functions. The Internet has allowed retailers to enhance their merchandising mix and their customer service by, among other things, giving them access to much broader selections of goods. Direct marketers have merged their traditional catalog or direct-mail programs with an Internet interface that allows for faster, more efficient, and more frequent contact with customers and prospects.

MARKETING TERMS YOU NEED TO KNOW

retailing 480	limited-line store 492	retail convergence 494	mail-order wholesaler 500
wheel of retailing 481	category killer 492	scrambled merchandising 495	commission merchants 500
stock-keeping unit (SKU) 484	general merchandise retailers 492	wholesalers 495	broker 500
markup 485	department store 492	wholesaling intermediaries 495	selling agent 501
markdown 485	mass merchandiser 493	merchant wholesaler 499	manufacturers' representative 501
planned shopping center 486	discount house 493	rack jobber 499	direct marketing 502
atmospherics 488	hypermarkets 494	truck wholesaler (truck jobber) 499	
convenience retailer 491	supercenters 494	drop shipper 500	
specialty retailer 491			

ASSURANCE OF LEARNING REVIEW

1. Find some examples of retailers that demonstrate the concept of the wheel of retailing. Explain the stages they have gone through and which stage they are in currently.
2. How do retailers identify target markets? Explain the major strategies by which retailers reach their target markets.
3. Explain the importance of a retailer's location to its strategy.
4. What is retail convergence?
5. Define scrambled merchandising. Why has this practice become so common in retailing?
6. What is a wholesaling intermediary? Describe the activities it performs.
7. Distinguish among the different types of manufacturer-owned wholesaling intermediaries. What conditions might suit each one?
8. Differentiate between direct selling and direct-response retailing. Cite examples of both.
9. In what ways has the Internet changed direct-response retailing?
10. Define automatic merchandising, and explain its role in U.S. retailing today and in the future.

PROJECTS AND TEAMWORK EXERCISES

1. Research and then classify each of the following retailers:
   a. Home Depot
   b. H&M
   c. h.h. gregg
   d. Dillard's
   e. Gymboree
2. Visit a local Walmart store and observe product placement, shelf placement, inventory levels on shelves, traffic patterns, customer service, and checkout efficiency. Discuss what makes Walmart the world's most successful retailer.
3. Target has become known for trendy clothes and stylish housewares, all readily available in spacious stores at reasonable prices. Visit a local Target store or the company's website and compare its product selection to that of your local hardware store or a department store. Make a list of each store's advantages and disadvantages, including convenience, location, selection, service, and general prices. Do any of their product lines overlap? How are they different from each other?
4. Match each industry with the most appropriate type of wholesaling intermediary.

   ___ hardware   a. drop shipper
   ___ perishable foods   b. truck wholesaler
   ___ lumber   c. auction house
   ___ wheat   d. full-function merchant wholesaler
   ___ used cars   e. commission merchant

5. In teams, develop a retailing strategy for an Internet retailer. Identify a target market and then suggest a mix of merchandise, promotion, service, and pricing strategies that would help a retailer reach that market via the Internet. What issues must Internet retailers address that do not affect traditional store retailers?
6. With a classmate, visit two or three retail stores that compete with each other in your area and compare their customer service strategies. (You might want to visit each store more than once to avoid making a snap judgment.) Select at least five criteria and use them to assess each store. How do you think each store sees its customer service strategy as fitting into its

overall retailing strategy? Present your findings in detail to the class.

7. Visit a department store and compare at least two departments' pricing strategies based on the number of markdowns you find and the size of the discount. What, if anything, can you conclude about the success of each department's retailing strategy?

8. Think of a large purchase you make on a nonroutine basis, such as a new winter coat or expensive clothing for a special occasion. Where will you shop for such items? Will you travel out of your way? Will you go to the nearest shopping center? Will you look on the Internet? Once you have made your decision, describe any strategies used by the retailer that led you to this decision. What might make you change your mind about where to shop for this item?

9. Outlet malls are a growing segment of the retail market. Visit a local outlet mall or research one on the Internet. What types of stores are located there? How do the product selection and price compare with typical stores?

10. Torrid is a national chain of about 170 stores that feature clothing for plus-size women. Recommend an appropriate retailing strategy for this type of retailer.

CRITICAL-THINKING EXERCISES

1. The retail chain Anthropologie sells a unique mix of women's clothing and home furnishings. Since its founding in 1992, Anthropologie has opened stores across the United States, Canada, and Great Britain. The retailer aims to create a shopping "experience" where its customers—independent-minded, college-educated female professionals between ages 30 and 45—can find their own look. No two Anthropologie stores are exactly alike, and the chain does not use advertising. Visit the website at www.anthropologie.com. How does it differentiate itself from its competitors?

2. Several major retailers have begun to test the extreme markdown strategy that lies behind popular dollar stores such as Dollar General and Dollar Tree Stores. Kroger, Walmart, and others have opened sections in selected stores that feature items from snacks to beauty supplies, all priced at $1. Is this experiment simply a test of pricing strategy? What else might motivate these retailers to offer such deep discounts?

3. Industry watchers blame the introduction of iTunes and other online music streaming sites for the overall decline of the retail music store. Most, however, feel that music stores will somehow remain viable. What are some changes these retailers could make in their merchandising, customer service, pricing, location, and other strategies to try to reinvent their business?

4. McDonald's has traditionally relied on a cookie-cutter approach to its restaurant design. One store looked essentially like every other—until recently. The chain has decided to loosen its corporate design mandate to fit within special markets and to update its image with customers. Research McDonald's makeover efforts. What types of changes has the company made and where? How have changes in atmospherics helped the chain with customers? Have the changes you researched modified your perception of McDonald's at all? If so, how?

ETHICS EXERCISE

As the largest company in the world, with more than two million employees worldwide and more than $473 billion in sales in a recent year, Walmart has become big and powerful enough to influence the U.S. economy. Some observers believe Walmart is also responsible for the low U.S. inflation rates of recent years.

1. Some economists fear what might happen to the U.S. economy if Walmart has a bad year. (So far, it has had more than four decades of growth.) Should a single retailer have that much influence on the economy? Why or why not?

2. Walmart is selective about what it sells—refusing, for instance, to carry music or computer games with mature ratings, magazines with content it considers too adult, or, in some of its stores, handguns. Because of its sheer size, these decisions can influence American culture. Do you think this is a positive or negative effect of the growth of this retailer? Why?

INTERNET EXERCISES

1. **Shopping center trends.** Read the article at the URL listed below. Review the material and prepare a brief report on some of the major trends in shopping center development.
   http://www.washingtonpost.com/business/capitalbusiness/five-retail-trends-to-watch-in-2014/2014/02/21/fca8180e-99ab-11e3-b931-0204122c514b_story.html

2. **Online retailing strategy.** Visit Kohl's website. Using the material in this chapter on retailing strategy, answer the following questions:
   a. How does the design and layout of Kohl's online store appeal to the retailer's target market?
   b. In your opinion, what is the main strategic objective of Kohl's online store? Is it to generate revenue independent of its brick-and-mortar stores? Or is the online store's main purpose to support so-called Web-to-store shoppers (shoppers who use the Web mainly to obtain product information and prices but make actual purchases at brick-and-mortar stores)?
   www.kohls.com

3. **Wholesale-distribution industry.** Visit the website of the National Association of Wholesaler-Distributors. Click on "About NAW" and scroll down and click on "About the Industry." Review the data and prepare a brief report describing the state of the U.S. wholesale distribution industry.
   www.naw.org/about/industry.php

Note: Internet Web addresses change frequently. If you don't find the exact site listed, you may need to access the organization's home page and search from there or use a search engine such as Google or Bing.

CASE 15.1
Costco Plays Catch-Up in Online Sales

Costco, the $108 billion warehouse-style chain, is the third-largest retailer in the United States. With low prices, low employee turnover, and steady growth, the company would seem to be an all-around success. It even boasts above-average survey scores on the quality of the shopping experience and customer service in its more than 663 stores worldwide.

But Costco is playing catch-up online, a sector that's growing faster than in-store retailing and where nimble competitors such as Walmart hope to gain most of their future expansion. A rarity in store retailing because it has been profitable since day one, Costco has big plans for boosting its e-commerce business, but it has also missed some opportunities.

Costco.com takes in more than $3 billion a year with a broad assortment of products that are not always found in the stores. These range from electronics and lawn furniture to caskets and pricey diamond jewelry. The convenience of free shipping and assembly are usually included. Most of Costco's online customers are a bit more affluent than customers of other warehouse stores, and their average purchases tend to be bigger, too.

But despite being a brick-and-mortar presence in eight countries abroad, Costco currently limits its online operations to the United States, Mexico, and Canada. Some critics have found weaknesses in the company's online marketing efforts. Customers are not always aware of the product variety online, nor do they realize that the special offers outlined in the company's emails, which go to more than 12 million registered customers, promote products unique to the website. Another issue is that products on the website don't turn up in shoppers' search engine results because of the way the website's pages are named, a condition Costco hopes to improve via the technical process of search engine optimization. The website could also be more user-friendly, say critics, with less visual clutter and fewer poorly labeled photographs. One search engine consultant said the company's online division is "undoubtedly leaving some sales on the table."

QUESTIONS FOR CRITICAL THINKING

1. How can Costco.com better inform its online customers of the product variety available and the real value of its special offers?

2. What priority do you think Costco should put on expanding its online business abroad? Is this more or less important than improving sales from the existing e-commerce operations in North America? Explain your reasoning.

Sources: Company profile, http://phx.corporate.ir.net, accessed October 20, 2014; Trefis, "Costco Beats Estimates on Strong Online & Membership Growth," *Forbes*, October 9, 2014, www.forbes.com; Elliot Zwiebach, "Costco Takes Wait-and-See Approach to E-Commerce," *Supermarket News*, accessed March 26, 2014, http://supermarketnews.com; Melissa Allison, "Costco Makes Plans for Boosting Its Online Sales," *The Seattle Times*, accessed March 26, 2014, http://seattletimes.nwsource.com.

VIDEO CASE 15.2
GaGa SherBetter: Coming to a Market Near You?

Everyone likes ice cream—or sherbet. But suppose you could have the best of both, in one cup or cone? And what if you could buy your favorite treat at your local market? Jim King, founder and CEO of GaGa, is doing his best to see that your frozen dessert wishes come true. Nearly 10 years ago, King—a former TV news anchor—began experimenting with his grandmother GaGa's recipe for lemon sherbet. He made a few batches and peddled them to retailers in his home state of Rhode Island before stopping in at Munroe Dairy, a home-delivery dairy farm. The owner ordered 500 pints on the spot—and GaGa was in business. Suddenly, King and his wife Michelle had to figure out how to make and store a large batch of the "SherBetter"—Jim's name for the product, which he described as "sherbet but better." Eventually, he purchased a batch freezer for $2,800 at an IRS auction.

Once the Munroe Dairy order was filled, the Kings had to decide where and how to sell their product—directly to consumers, via wholesalers, or to retailers. Early on, they tried selling through an ice cream company. "We sold zero," recalls Michelle. Consumers would have to pay about $100 for a six-pint order instead of $4.99 for a pint at the grocery market, because the cost of shipping was astronomical—the SherBetter had to be shipped overnight in a heavy box with dry ice. The television shopping networks HSN and QVC also invited the Kings to sell their product on television; as a former news anchor, Jim would be a natural on camera. But the Kings declined—again because of the high cost of shipping directly to consumers.

Jim also researched the possibility of becoming a retailer himself—opening his scoop shop. But he quickly realized that the business model just wouldn't work for his company. Successful scoop shops must be located near a beach, lake, or other recreational area, and have no other direct competitors nearby. Furthermore, in New England, ice cream shops are mostly seasonal. Jim also determined that the projected expense of purchasing and maintaining a building and property was too high for GaGa. In addition, ice cream shops generally offer a wide variety of products, including ice cream, sherbet, frozen yogurt, diabetic-friendly and dairy-free frozen desserts, smoothies, shakes, and more. GaGa just had SherBetter—albeit in a growing array of flavors.

So the Kings decided that retailers would be the best outlet for their product. "Basically, we're a marketing agency," Jim comments. Jim works with a broker who arranges for Jim and Michelle to meet with retailers and demonstrate GaGa SherBetter at their stores, giving out free samples and promoting the product. If the retailers and their customers like the product, it is added to the grocery shelves. The smaller or specialty markets such as Whole Foods generally stock GaGa, because the Kings can't afford the huge slotting allowances charged by larger supermarkets. Jim explains that a slotting fee in the frozen section of a large supermarket chain could run as much as $35,000 to $40,000 just to place one product on the shelf at 600 to 800 stores. Jim notes that Whole Foods, which doesn't require a slotting allowance, may initially ask for free products to see if they will sell. "That's affordable," acknowledges Jim. "We can make that back pretty quickly." Not only is the cost of putting a product on the shelves of a large supermarket chain prohibitive, those customers aren't necessarily the consumers who would buy GaGa anyway. "Because we are a super-premium product and perceived as expensive, we don't sell well" in those stores, Michelle points out. "People who go into a market like that are looking for a deal." So they've decided to target the specialty markets, because that's where their true customers shop.

Looking to the future, Jim believes that ultimately GaGa could become an umbrella brand for a wider range of products, by building out the current line of SherBetter products and eventually adding new categories. He also wants to make a second stab at the wholesale food service channel, since the first attempt didn't work out. He tried to make a push into food wholesaler Sysco but was unsuccessful—largely because the price of GaGa was double that of Sysco's price for super-premium ice cream. "Restaurants are more concerned about price," says Jim. He's now searching for a wholesale outlet connected with a nationwide restaurant chain that would agree to put GaGa dessert on the menu.

For now, Jim remains focused on the job at hand—getting GaGa into the stores. "We've got this great name," he remarks. "We've got this great product."

QUESTIONS FOR CRITICAL THINKING

1. Experience has taught the Kings that smaller, specialty markets are the strongest retail outlets for their GaGa SherBetter. Under what conditions might they begin to make a successful move into the larger supermarket chains?

2. How might the right wholesaler ultimately create marketing utility for GaGa?

Sources: Company website, www.gonegaga.net, accessed March 26, 2014; "GaGa's Rainbow SherBetter," *On Second Scoop*, accessed March 26, 2014, www.onsecondscoop.com; Judi Atkins Bridges, "Summer Market Blackberries," *AL.com*, accessed March 26, 2014, http://blog.al.com; Curt Nickisch, "GaGa's for Lady Gaga? Coincidental Celebrity Lifts Local Brands," *NPR* (Boston), accessed March 26, 2014, www.wbur.org.

NOTES

1. "Macy's, Inc. At-A-Glance," 2014 *Corporate Fact Book*, www.macys.com, accessed October 20, 2014; Natalie Zmuda, "Macy's Uses Media Muscle to Push App, Other Services," *Advertising Age*, accessed March 26, 2014, http://adage.com; "Top Ten Retail Loyalty Programs," *Big Door*, accessed March 26, 2014, http://bigdoor.com; Lee Brodie, "Cramer: Macy's Hyper-Local Strategy to Drive Sales," *CNBC*, accessed March 26, 2014, www.cnbc.com; Allison Berry, "Macy's Sets Its Sights on Millennial Customers with Three New Brand Launches," *Time*, accessed March 26, 2014, http://style.time.com; Rimma Kats, "Macy's Exec: Mobile Amplifies Multichannel, Multiscreen Marketing," *Mobile Commerce Daily*, accessed March 26, 2014, www.mobilecommercedaily.com; James Tenser, "Omni-Channel at Macy's: It's About Inventory Too," *Retail Wire*, accessed March 26, 2014, www.retailwire.com; Jennifer Marlo, "The Strategy That Made Macy's a Success," *iMedia Connection*, accessed March 26, 2014, www.imediaconnection.com; Adrianne Pasquarelli, "Macy's Shows It Can Make Big Bucks Online," *Crain's*, accessed March 26, 2016, www.crainsnewyork.com.
2. Rachel Abrams, "CVS Stores Stop Selling All Tobacco Products," *The New York Times*, accessed October 20, 2014, www.nytimes.com.
3. Company website, www.sprouts.com, accessed October 20, 2014; Brendan Byrnes, "Meet Sprouts Farmers Market, Inc. CFO Amin Maredia," *The Motley Fool*, February 26, 2014, www.fool.com.
4. Ashley Lutz and Kim Bhasin, "51 Companies That Are Changing the Way We Shop," *Business Insider*, accessed March 26, 2014, www.businessinsider.com.
5. Angela Bender, "Women Turning Out to Be Home Improvement Gems," *Beacon News*, accessed March 28, 2014, http://beaconnews.suntimes.com.
6. Company website, www.dswinc.com, accessed March 28, 2014.
7. Anna Prior, "West Elm, Pottery Barn Boost Williams-Sonoma's Sales," *The Wall Street Journal*, March 22, 2014, http://online.wsj.com; company website, "Who We Are," accessed March 22, 2014, www.westelm.com.
8. "Business Idea Center: Specialty Foods," *Entrepreneur*, accessed March 28, 2014, www.entrepreneur.com.
9. Company website, www.maestrovirtualassistant.com, accessed March 28, 2014.
10. Organization website, "U.S. Shopping-Center Classifications and Characteristics," www.icsc.org, accessed March 28, 2014; company website, www.streetsatsouthpoint.com, accessed March 28, 2014.
11. Judy Keen, "As Enclosed Malls Decline, 'Lifestyle Centers' Proliferate," *MinnPost*, accessed March 21, 2014, www.minnpost.com.
12. Company website www.northparkcenter.com, accessed March 21, 2014.
13. "Chipotle Releases 'Farmed and Dangerous' Web Series on Hulu," *United Press International*, March 27, 2014, www.upi.com; Noam Cohen, "Chipotle Blurs Lines with a Satirical Series About Industrial Farming," *The New York Times*, accessed March 27, 2014, www.nytimes.com.
14. Company website, www.flurry.com, accessed October 20, 2014; Ingrid Lunden, "Yahoo Buys Mobile Analytics Firm Flurry for North of $200M," *Tech Crunch*, accessed October 20, 2014, http://techcrunch.com.
15. Company website, "We Satisfy, Delight and Nourish Our Customers," www.wholefoodsmarket.com, accessed March 21, 2014.
16. Company website, "Introducing the IMAN Cosmetics Beauty App for iOS," www.imancosmetics.com, accessed March 21, 2014.
17. Gus Lubin, "15 Ways Supermarkets Trick You into Spending More Money," *Business Insider*, accessed March 22, 2014, www.businessinsider.com; "The Secret Weapon Luxe Hotels Use to Lure Guests In," *Forbes*, accessed March 22, 2014, www.forbes.com.
18. Brad Tuttle, "Can the Boutique 'Store-Within-a-Store' Concept Save Big Box Retailers from Extinction?" *Time*, accessed March 21, 2014, http://business.time.com; "Nordstrom to Expand Topshop and Topman Partnership to 28 Additional Stores This Fall," *PRNewswire*, accessed March 21, 2014, www.prnewswire.com.
19. Barbara Farfan, "2014 US Retail Industry Overview—Info, Facts, Research, Data, and Trivia," *About.com*, accessed March 26, 2014, http://retailindustry.about.com.
20. Company website, www.gloriajeans.com, accessed March 26, 2014.
21. Company website, http://news.walgreens.com, accessed October 20, 2014.
22. Allison Collins, "Boutique Appeal: Against the Backdrop of Department Store Consolidation, Retailers and Investors Seek Specialty Shops," *Mergers & Acquisitions*, accessed March 26, 2014, www.themiddlemarket.com.
23. Company website, http://sale.vente-privee.com, accessed March 26, 2014.
24. Company website, www.meijer.com, accessed October 20, 2014.
25. Company website, "VUDU Brand Shop," www.walmart.com, accessed March 26, 2014.
26. "Retail Clinics Play Growing Role in Health Care Marketplace," *RAND Health*, accessed March 26, 2014, www.rand.org.
27. Company website, "About Us," http://corp.ingrammicro.com, accessed October 20, 2014.
28. Company website, www.unitedstationers.com, accessed March 26, 2014.
29. Organization website, "About Us," www.cesweb.org, accessed March 26, 2014.
30. Company website, www.amerch.com, accessed March 26, 2014.
31. Company website, www.sasinc.com, accessed March 26, 2014.
32. Mike Miazga, "2013 Manufacturers' Rep of the Year: Spirit Group," *Supply House Times*, accessed March 26, 2014, www.supplyht.com.
33. Elizabeth Holmes, "Why Online Retailers Like Bonobos, Boden, Athleta Mail So Many Catalogs," *The Wall Street Journal*, accessed October 20, 2014, http://online.wsj.com.
34. Alina Tugend, "Working to Block Those Advertising Annoyances," *The New York Times*, March 22, 2014, www.nytimes.com.
35. Tammy La Gorce, "Collette Liantonio: The Infomercial Queen," *New Jersey Monthly*, accessed March 26, 2014, http://njmonthly.com.
36. Company website, www.pinrose.com, accessed March 27, 2014; Ashlee Vance, "Pinrose Tries Selling Perfume by Algorithm, No Charlize Therons Required," *Bloomberg Businessweek*, accessed March 27, 2014, www.businessweek.com.
37. "Vending Machine Operators in the U.S.: Market Research Report," *IBIS World*, accessed March 26, 2014, www.ibisworld.com.
38. Kate Taylor, "High-Tech Vending Machines That Serve Healthy Snacks See Rapid Growth," *Entrepreneur*, accessed March 26, 2014, www.entrepreneur.com.
39. Olga Kharif, "Vending Machines Get Smart to Accommodate the Cashless," *Bloomberg Businessweek*, accessed March 26, 2014, www.businessweek.com; company website, "Our Clients," www.zoomsystems.com, accessed March 26, 2014.

Scripps Networks Interactive & Food Network

**PART 5
Distribution Decisions**

Pushing Content into New Channels

"We're a content-first company," notes Sergei Kuharsky, senior vice president and general manager of licensing and merchandising for Scripps Networks Interactive. How do you build a distribution (or marketing) channel system for content featuring a product that customers can't actually see, smell, hear, touch, or taste? Food Network, one of the branded networks owned by Scripps Networks Interactive, creates and produces the content (concept, script, and other programming details) for an array of television shows focused on food and cooking. Television is the first distribution channel that comes to mind—but the company's website and magazine are also two important channels for getting the content out to consumers. Then there are all the social and digital options: Facebook, Twitter, Pinterest, and more. Finally, there is the retailer who agrees to stock its shelves with Food Network's branded kitchen supplies.

Scripps and Food Network marketers partner to handle the logistics of delivering Food Network's products—ranging from programming to frying pans. By coordinating the flow of marketing information, goods, programming content, and services to members of the overall marketing channel, marketers extend Food Network's reach. Food Network's huge cache of original recipes is a good example. Viewers love to try recipes they see on Food Network's various cooking shows, whether it's Bobby Flay's *Barbecue Addiction* or Melissa D'Arabian's *Ten Dollar Dinners*. Marketers had to determine the best way to get those recipes into the kitchens of viewers by facilitating searches. So they posted the recipes on the Food Network website, making it easy for consumers to locate and use. Then they pushed the recipes out farther by creating digital and print cookbooks (often in partnership with Food Network stars such as Rachael Ray or Giada De Laurentiis). The cookbooks have been extremely popular; during one recent year, ten Food Network cookbooks hit the *New York Times* best seller list.

When Food Network decided to create a line of kitchen and cooking supplies—cookware, dinnerware, table linens, and more—marketers considered the options and settled on an exclusive distribution partnership with Kohl's. Kuharsky notes that while being everywhere can be a very good thing because it eliminates barriers to consumers, it also poses challenges. "With it, you lose control, and then you risk quality," he explains. So Food Network remains selective in its choice of distribution channels. Today, Kohl's sells more than 1,100 Food Network items at its retail stores and online. And since food is, after all, about the senses, Food Network has partnered with about 2,200 sports arenas across the country to offer everything from sizzling burgers to crispy fries at exclusive concessions. Sports fans can belly up to the Food Network stand and enjoy their favorite arena snacks while cheering their teams. Kuharsky summarizes the company's overall distribution strategy this way: "You look at all the different consumer touch points and what the challenges are. You want the ones that give you the best opportunity to present the brand and deepen your relationship."

Managing all of the interactive digital channels for delivering content as well as marketing messages is a vital job for Scripps and Food Network marketers. "I think our strongest channel right now is probably the Food Network website, for its reach," observes Tanya Edwards, digital programming director. One reason for this is that people engage online while they are watching the television shows, giving Food Network a prime opportunity to hold onto viewers' attention after a show is over. For example, at the end of Restaurant: Impossible, viewers see a prompt to the Food Network website, where they learn more about the featured restaurant. They might catch an interview with the owners or updates on the restaurant's success.

Edwards notes that Food Network has enjoyed great success with its apps, especially those that focus on recipes and cooking tips, such as "In the Kitchen." The app delivers content right to consumers wherever they are, whether it's the grocery store, farmers' market, or kitchen. This also helps build brand loyalty. "People trust our brand as someone who will help them get dinner, create a great dessert, or bake cupcakes to take to a party," Edwards says.

Because social media is by definition interactive, it creates some unique challenges as part of the overall marketing channel system. For example, it's unclear how to monetize a social media presence. But social media is still one of the best ways to capture valuable data as people talk about the brand. In the end, says Kuharsky, it's all about "looking for all those fun touch points that food goes where we go, and trying to be people's best friend in food."

QUESTIONS FOR CRITICAL THINKING

1. Food Network adopts a dual distribution strategy. In your opinion, what are the benefits of this?
2. Scripps and Food Network appear to have achieved channel cooperation. However, describe a scenario in which channel conflict might arise.
3. How does social media marketing support Food Network's distribution strategy?
4. Do you think Kohl's is the best choice of retail outlet for Food Network's products? Why or why not?

Part 6
Promotional Decisions

16 Integrated Marketing Communications, Advertising, and Public Relations

17 Personal Selling and Sales Promotion

Chapter 16

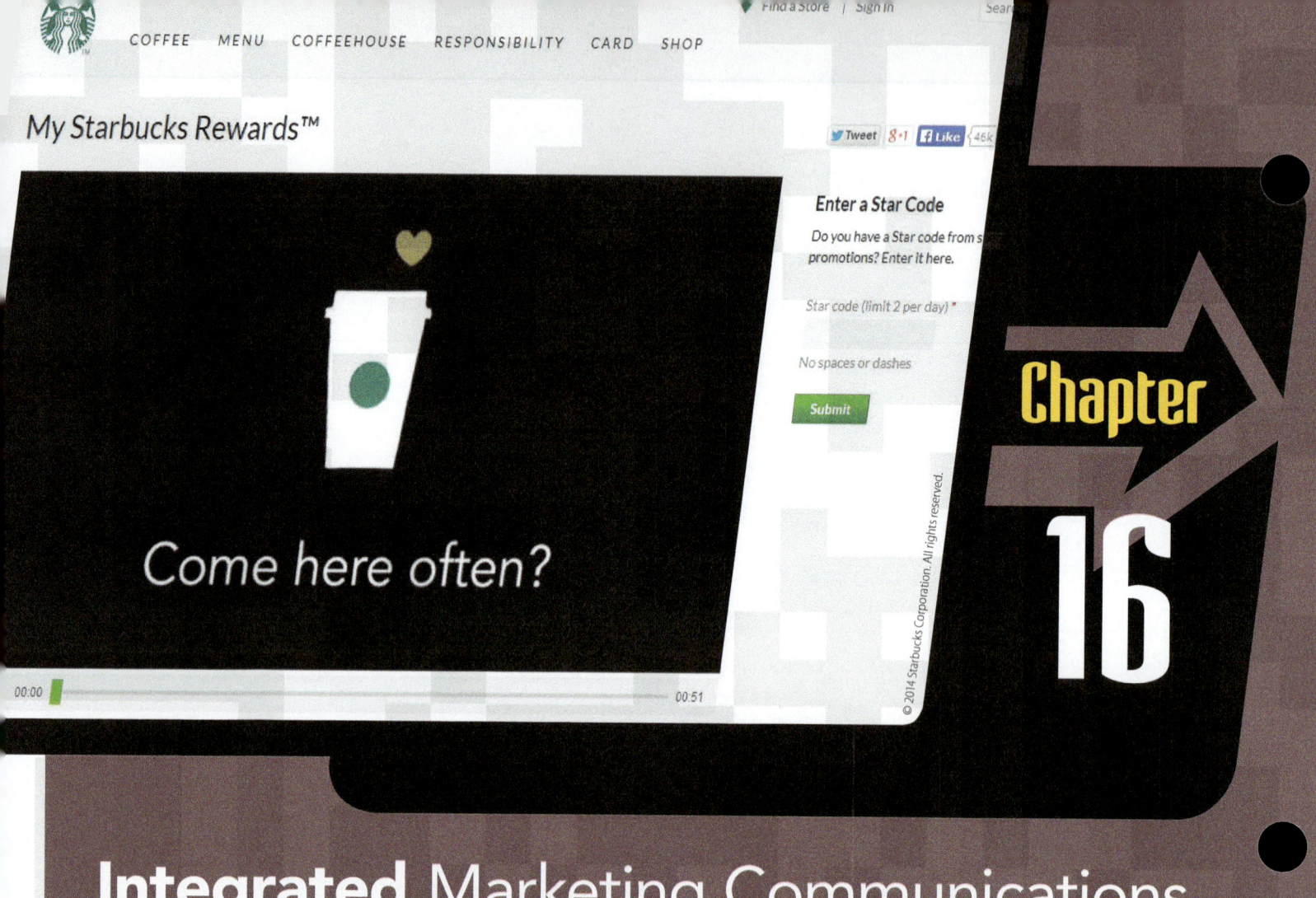

Integrated Marketing Communications, Advertising, and Public Relations

1. Describe integrated marketing communications and how it relates to the development of an optimal promotional mix.
2. Describe the communication process and how it relates to the AIDA concept.
3. Identify the seven components of the promotional mix.
4. Name the three basic advertising objectives and the two basic categories of advertising.
5. Identify the four major advertising strategies.
6. Describe the various types of advertising appeals and their uses.
7. Compare the seven different advertising media.
8. Explain the roles of public relations, publicity, and cross-promotion in an organization's promotional strategy.
9. Discuss the five factors that influence the effectiveness of a promotional mix and how marketers measure promotional effectiveness.

STARBUCKS SERVES UP SUCCESSFUL MARKETING "BREW"

Starbucks doesn't only serve great coffee drinks in the comfortable cafés it calls the "third place" between home and office. It also engages customers with an integrated marketing message that builds loyalty and keeps them coming back. In fact, an advertising research firm recently rated the company number one in a study of "most socially engaged companies."

Starbucks' marketing approach is multilayered, reaches across various platforms, and continues to evolve. The company knows its customers appreciate marketing messages that recognize how they want to be perceived by others in their everyday lives as well as in their social networks. Its media efforts thus consistently appeal to, and let customers express, their "idealized self." For instance, Starbucks' Web page invites visitors to post their unique product preferences and share their own personal Starbucks experiences.

Starbucks supports one-to-one marketing communications with its mobile marketing strategy. This strategy offers purchase and special-occasion incentives through a loyalty program as well as a store finder and nutrition information. It also allows users to to check their My Starbucks Rewards balances and reload payment cards, and to pay for purchases with their smartphones. The loyalty program quickly grew to more than 10 million members, with 5 million weekly transactions, on average, representing a staggering $1 billion in revenues in a recent year. Starbucks invites customers to sign up for informative emails and receive text messages about its products. The company hopes recipients will share this information with friends.

Starbucks' media strategy is also visible in its cafés. The Starbucks Digital Network provides unique news and entertainment content delivered on its free in-store wi-fi service. Free access to subscription content from *The Wall Street Journal* and *The New York Times* is available, along with *USA Today*, *The Economist*, and *ESPN Insider*. When it's time for customers to collect rewards benefits, Starbucks quickly loads rewards on members' loyalty cards and mobile devices.[1]

EVOLUTION OF A BRAND

From the opening of its first store in Seattle's Pike Place Market in 1971, Starbucks has known success—in large part because of its uncanny ability to identify and understand its audience and develop products with that audience in mind. Since then, in what has grown to be a $100 billion-plus market, Starbucks marketers have promoted their iconic brand using every medium available to them, building lasting relationships with their customers.

Starbucks understands that mobile marketing strategies can help extend its brand exponentially. Its payment app for iPhone users allows customers to shake their phones for the payment barcode to be displayed. The company also launched a digital tipping option where customers can tip Starbucks baristas through their phones. This innovative approach to mobile payments drove more than $1 billion in revenue in a recent year.

- How does Starbucks use social media and other mobile strategies to keep its marketing approach fresh and relevant?
- Rewards programs have become a popular means of building customer loyalty. Yet, according to some industry experts, many such programs are failing. What steps can Starbucks take to ensure that its loyalty program remains successful?

Chapter Overview

Two of the four components of the marketing mix—product and distribution strategies—were discussed in previous chapters. The two chapters in Part 6 analyze the third marketing mix variable—promotion. **Promotion** is the function of informing, persuading, and influencing the consumer's purchase decision.

This chapter introduces the concept of integrated marketing communications. It describes the elements of a promotional mix and discusses the factors that influence its effectiveness. Chapter 17 completes this part of the book by focusing on two other elements of the promotional mix: personal selling and sales promotion.

Throughout *Contemporary Marketing*, special emphasis has been given to showing how technology is changing the way marketers approach *communication,* the transmission of a message from a sender to a receiver. Consumers receive **marketing communications**—messages that deal with buyer–seller relationships—from a variety of media, including television, radio, magazines, direct mail, the Internet, and smartphones. Marketers can broadcast an ad on the Web to mass markets or design a customized appeal targeted to a small market segment. Each message the customer receives from any source represents the brand, company, or organization. A company must coordinate the messages for maximum total impact and to reduce the likelihood that the consumer will completely tune them out.

To prevent this loss of attention, marketers turn to **integrated marketing communications (IMC)**, which coordinates all promotional activities—media advertising, direct mail, personal selling, sales promotion, public relations, and sponsorships—to produce a unified, customer-focused promotional message, as shown in Figure 16.1. IMC is a broader concept than marketing communications and promotional strategy. It uses database technology to refine the marketer's understanding of the target audience, segment this audience, and select the best type of media for each segment.

IMC involves not only the marketer but all other organizational units that interact with the consumer. Marketing managers set the goals and objectives of the firm's promotional strategy in accordance with overall organizational objectives and marketing goals. Based on these objectives, elements of the promotional strategy are formulated into an integrated communications plan, which becomes a central part of the firm's total marketing strategy. The feedback mechanism, including marketing research and field reports, identifies any deviations from the plan and suggests improvements.

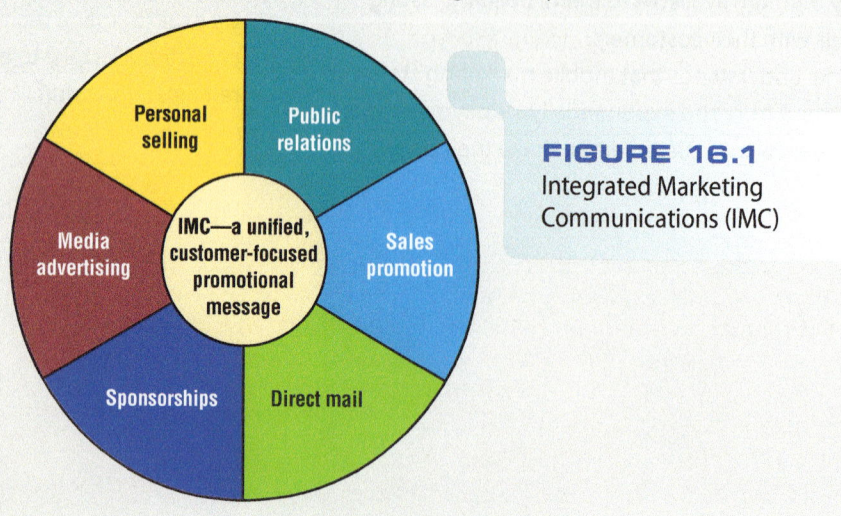

promotion Communication link between buyers and sellers; the function of informing, persuading, and influencing a consumer's purchase decision.

marketing communications Messages that deal with buyer–seller relationships.

integrated marketing communications (IMC) Coordination of all promotional activities to produce a unified, customer-focused promotional message.

FIGURE 16.1 Integrated Marketing Communications (IMC)

INTEGRATED MARKETING COMMUNICATIONS

Stop and think for a moment about all the marketing messages you receive in a day. Click on the TV for the news, and you see commercials. Listen to the car radio on the way to work or school, and you can sing along with the jingles. You get catalogs and coupons in the mail. Online you see banner and pop-up ads and marketing-related emails. Marketers know you receive many types of communication. They compete for your attention, so they look for ways to reach you in a coordinated manner through integrated marketing communications.

Successful marketers use the marketing concept and relationship marketing to develop customer-oriented marketing programs. The customer is at the heart of integrated marketing communications. An IMC strategy begins not with the organization's goods and services but with consumer wants or needs, and then works in reverse to the product, brand, or organization. It sends receiver-focused (rather than product-focused) messages.

Instead of separating the parts of the promotional mix and viewing them as isolated components, IMC looks at these elements from the consumer's viewpoint—as information about the brand, company, or organization. Although messages come from different sources—sales presentations, word of mouth, TV, radio, newspapers, billboards, direct mail, coupons, public relations, social media—consumers may perceive all of them as "advertising" or a "sales pitch." IMC broadens promotion to include all the ways a customer has contact with an organization, adding to traditional media and direct mail with such sources as package design, store displays, sales literature, and online and interactive media. Unless the organization takes an integrated approach to present a unified, consistent message, it may send conflicting information that confuses consumers.

Today's business environment is characterized by many diverse markets and media creating both opportunities and challenges. The success of any IMC program depends on identifying the members of an audience and understanding what they want. Without accurate, current information about existing and potential customers and their purchase histories, needs, and wants, marketers may send the wrong message. But they cannot succeed simply by improving the quality of the messages or by sending more of them. IMC must not only deliver messages to intended audiences but also gather responses from them. Databases and interactive marketing are important IMC tools that help marketers collect information from customers and then segment markets according to demographics and preferences. Marketers can then design specialized communications programs to meet the needs of each segment.

Young male consumers can be hard to pin down. That's why the U.S. Navy became a sponsor of the Winter X Games, a favorite of extreme sports fans—usually males 13 to 17 years of age. By signing on for the highest level of sponsorship rights, the Navy enjoys a variety of perks, including on-site signage and activation and integrated media exposure across ESPN's TV, digital, print, and radio platforms.[2]

The increase in media options provides more ways to give consumers product information; however, it can also create information overload. Marketers have to spread available dollars across fragmented media markets and a wider range of promotional activities to achieve their communication goals. Mass media like TV ads, while still useful, are no longer the mainstay of marketing campaigns. In 1960, a marketer could reach about 90 percent of U.S. consumers by advertising on the three major TV networks—CBS, NBC, and ABC. Today, even though overall TV viewing is at an all-time high, consumers spend considerably fewer viewing hours watching these stations. Instead, they turn to such cable channels as ESPN, FOX, CNN, TNT, the History Channel, Disney, and the Food Network. To reach targeted groups of consumers, organizations must turn to niche marketing—advertising in special-interest magazines, buying time on cable TV channels, reaching out through telecommunications media like smartphones and the Internet, and sponsoring events and activities. Without an IMC program, marketers often encounter problems within their own organizations, because separate departments have authority and responsibility for planning and implementing specific promotional mix elements.

> **1** Describe integrated marketing communications and how it relates to the development of an optimal promotional mix.

The U.S. Navy sponsors the Winter X Games to reach potential recruits.

The coordination of an IMC program often produces a competitive advantage based on synergy and interdependence among the various elements of the promotional mix. With an IMC strategy, marketers can create a unified personality for the product or brand by choosing the right elements from the promotional mix to send the message. At the same time, they can develop more narrowly focused plans to reach specific market segments and choose the best form of communication to send a particular message to a specific target audience. IMC provides a more effective way to reach and serve target markets than less-coordinated strategies. See how global retailer H&M accomplished this strategy by reading the "Marketing Success" feature.

IMPORTANCE OF TEAMWORK

IMC requires a big-picture view of promotional planning, a total strategy that includes all marketing activities, not just promotion. Successful implementation of IMC requires

MARKETING SUCCESS
H&M Integrates Its Beckham Campaign

Background. H&M, the Swedish fashion retailer with 3,300 stores in 55 countries, collaborated with international soccer star and veteran brand spokesman David Beckham on a new line of men's bodywear.

The Challenge. The company wanted to ensure the success of the Beckham line in North America and integrated all of its related marketing communications.

The Strategy. H&M took the bold step of airing an ad during the Super Bowl, a hip, black-and-white 30-second spot featuring Beckham modeling the new collection. It also took out national and local print ads and out-of-home advertising, including a giant billboard in midtown Manhattan with a body-length image of Beckham wearing trunks. The image was hand-painted over a two-week period leading up to the Super Bowl, and the process was captured in a time-lapse video uploaded to YouTube. H&M also bought numerous search ads, uploaded the Super Bowl ad to its home page, inserted poster-sized images from the ad in free New York City newspapers, and gave away booklet ads and Beckham shopping bags in its stores. Beckham appeared as a fashion mannequin on the company's website, and the campaign was featured on the company's Facebook and Twitter pages.

The Outcome. By using a variety of marketing media, H&M's Beckham campaign has generated an increasing volume of online buzz and created more opportunities to engage with consumers. Riding on the success of that campaign, two years later H&M showcased Beckham in another Super Bowl commercial that generated similar buzz when he stripped down to a pair of briefs from his bodywear line. The only retailer to secure ad space during the big game, H&M shot two versions of the ad and invited fans to vote on the version they wanted to see during the big game: "Covered" or "Uncovered."

Sources: Company website, www.hm.com, accessed October 23, 2014; Katrina Mitzeliotis, "David Beckham Naked in H&M's Super Bowl Commercial: WATCH," *Hollywood Life*, April 2, 2014, http://hollywoodlife.com; Laura Heller, "David Beckham and H&M's Super Bowl Ad Could Change Advertising Forever," *Forbes*, April 2, 2014, www.forbes.com; Jason Belzer, "H&M Lets Fans Undress David Beckham in Latest Super Bowl Commercial," *Forbes*, April 4, 2014, www.forbes.com.

that everyone involved in each aspect of promotion function as a team. This saves time and money, avoids duplication of effort, and increases effectiveness. In other words, the result is greater than the sum of its parts.

Teamwork involves both in-house resources and outside vendors. For example, a firm gains nothing from a terrific advertising campaign if customers encounter unhelpful salespeople. The company must train its representatives to send a single positive message to consumers and to solicit information for the firm's customer database.

IMC also challenges the traditional role of the outside advertising agency. A single agency may no longer fulfill all of a client's communications requirements. To best serve client needs, agencies must often partner with other firms to get the job done.

Networking, another form of teamwork, is an important skill for building a career. The "Career Readiness" feature provides networking tips.

ROLE OF DATABASES IN EFFECTIVE IMC PROGRAMS

The Internet empowers marketers to gather more information faster and to organize it more easily than ever before. By sharing this detailed knowledge appropriately among all relevant parties, a company can lay the foundation for a successful IMC program.

The move from mass marketing to a customer-specific marketing strategy—a characteristic of online marketing—requires not only a means of identifying and communicating with the firm's target market but also information regarding important characteristics of each prospective customer. As discussed in Chapter 11, organizations can compile different kinds of data into complete databases with customer information, including names, addresses, demographics, lifestyle

CAREER READINESS
Tips for Career Networking

You may already have a wide network of friends, but what about your professional network? Here are ideas for building and maintaining a network for your career and future job searches.

1. Keep in mind that most job openings are filled by word of mouth, not by advertising, and that people like to deal with those they know or who are recommended to them.

2. Start with friends, family, neighbors, current and former colleagues, teachers, former bosses, and anyone you would use as a reference. Ask them for other recommendations to add to your network.

3. Remember that successful networking is a two-way street: Don't focus exclusively on what's in it for you. Be prepared to give as much as you get; that's what motivates people to help you.

4. Use social media to keep your network fresh and active.

5. For best results, organize your job search with a spreadsheet or other system that works best for you. At some point, your search is likely to uncover several opportunities, and you don't want anything to fall through the cracks.

6. Follow up, thank people for helping you, let them know the result, and stay in touch.

Sources: Alison Doyle, "Job Search and Career Networking Tips," *About.com*, accessed April 2, 2014, http://jobsearch.about.com; Lindsay Olson, "6 Networking Tips for Your Job Search," *U.S. News & World Report*, accessed April 2, 2014, http://money.usnews.com; Lou Adler, "Networking Rules for Job-seekers: the Good, the Bad, and the Almost Perfect," *LinkedIn*, accessed April 2, 2014, www.linkedin.com.

ASSESSMENT CHECK

1.1 Define promotion.
1.2 What is the difference between marketing communications and integrated marketing communications (IMC)?

considerations, brand preferences, and buying behavior. This information provides critical guidance in designing an effective IMC strategy that achieves organizational goals and finds new opportunities for increased sales and profits. This increased ability to acquire data poses a new challenge: how to sift through it efficiently so it becomes useful information. Technology allows researchers to do exactly that—work with millions of sets of data to make very specific analyses.

THE COMMUNICATION PROCESS

> **2** Describe the communication process and how it relates to the AIDA concept.

When you have a conversation with someone, do you wonder whether the person understood your message? Do you worry that you might not have heard the person correctly? Marketers have the same concerns: When they send a message to an intended audience or market, they want to make sure it gets through clearly and persuasively. That is why the communication process is so important to marketing. The top portion of Table 16.1 shows a general model of the communication process and its application to promotional strategy.

The **sender** acts as the source in the communication system as he or she seeks to convey a **message** (a communication of information, advice, or a request) to a receiver. An effective message accomplishes three tasks:

1. It gains the receiver's attention.
2. It achieves understanding by both receiver and sender.
3. It stimulates the receiver's needs and suggests an appropriate method of satisfying them.

> **Briefly Speaking**
>
> "Every advertisement should be thought of as a contribution to the complex symbol which is the brand image."
>
> —David Ogilvy
> *American advertising pioneer*

Table 16.1 also offers examples of promotional messages. Although the types of promotion may vary from a highly personalized sales presentation to such nonpersonal promotions as TV advertising and coupons, each goes through every stage in the communications process.

The three tasks just listed are related to the **AIDA concept** (**a**ttention, **i**nterest, **d**esire, **a**ction), the steps consumers take in reaching a purchase decision. First, the promotional message must gain

TABLE 16.1 Relating Promotion to the Communication Process

Type of Promotion	Message Sender	Encoding by Sender	Channel	Decoding by Receiver	Response	Feedback
Personal selling	SAP system	Sales presentation on new applications of system	SAP sales representative	Office manager and employees discuss sales presentation and those of competing suppliers.	Customer places order for SAP system.	Customer asks about a second system for a subsidiary company.
Dollar-off coupon (sales promotion)	SC Johnson	Coupon for Pledge Duster Plus	Coupon insert in Sunday newspaper	Newspaper reader sees coupon for Pledge Duster Plus.	Shopper buys product using the coupon.	SC Johnson researchers see increase in market share.
Television advertising	Capital One	Advertisement featuring "What's in Your Wallet" slogan	Network television ads during program with high percentages of adult viewers	Adults see an ad and decide to try out the card.	Customer applies for Capital One card.	Customer makes purchases with Capital One card.

the potential consumer's attention. It then seeks to arouse interest in the good or service. Next, it stimulates desire by convincing the would-be buyer of the product's ability to satisfy his or her needs. Finally, the sales presentation, advertisement, or sales promotion technique attempts to produce action in the form of a purchase now or in the future.

The message begins with *encoding*—that is, translating it into understandable terms and transmitting it through a communications channel. *Decoding* is the receiver's interpretation of the message. The receiver's response, known as *feedback*, completes the system. Throughout the process, *noise* (in such forms as ineffective promotional appeals, inappropriate advertising media, or poor radio or television reception) can interfere with the transmission of the message and reduce its effectiveness.

The marketer is the message sender in Table 16.1. He or she encodes the message in the form of sales presentations, advertising, displays, or publicity releases. The *channel* for delivering the message may be a salesperson, a PR outlet, a website, or an advertising medium. Decoding is often the toughest step in marketing communications because consumers do not always interpret messages the same way as senders do. Because receivers usually decode messages according to their own frame of reference or experience, a sender must carefully encode a message to match the target's frame of reference. Consumers are exposed daily to thousands of messages through many media channels. This exposure can create confusion as noise in the channel increases. Because the typical person will choose to process only a few messages, ignored messages are wasted communications expenditures.

The AIDA concept is also vital to online marketers. It is not enough to say a website has effective content or high response rates. Marketers must know just how many "eyeballs" are looking at the site, how often they return, and what they are reading. Most important, they must find out what consumers do besides just look. The bottom line: If no one responds to a website, it might as well not exist. Experts suggest attracting users' attention by including people in advertisements and other communications in addition to new content and formats.

For the recent FIFA World Cup in Brazil, eight advertisers paid more than $600 million to the Brazilian TV network Globo for a major media presence during the month-long soccer competition that was watched around the world. Brands that signed up for the sporting event, including The Coca-Cola Company, AmBev (makers of Budweiser and other beverages), Johnson & Johnson, Hyundai, and Nestlé, paid the equivalent of almost 20 thirty-second Super Bowl spots to advertise their brands to a global audience.[3]

Feedback lets marketers evaluate the effectiveness of the message and tailor their responses accordingly. It may take the form of attitude change, a purchase, or a nonpurchase. In some instances, marketers use promotion to create favorable attitudes toward their goods or services in the hope of future purchases. Other promotional communications aim to stimulate consumer purchases directly. Marketers using infomercials that urge the viewer to call a toll-free number to place orders for their products can easily measure success by counting the number of calls they receive that result in orders.

Even a nonpurchase is feedback. Failure to purchase may result from ineffective communication: Do receivers believe the message? Do they even remember it? And do they associate it with the correct firm? Receivers may remember it correctly, but the message may have failed to persuade them to buy. Marketers must be keenly aware of why messages fail.

Noise represents interference at some stage in the communication process. It may result from disruptions such as transmissions of competing promotional messages over the same communications channel, misinterpretation of a sales presentation or advertising message, receipt of the promotional message by the wrong person, or random events like people conversing or leaving the room during a television commercial. Noise can also result from distractions within an advertising message itself. Buzzwords and jargon can create confusion for consumers who are just trying to find out more about a product.

Noise can be especially problematic in international communications. One problem is that there may be too many competing messages. Or technology may be poor, and language translations, inaccurate. Nonverbal cues like body language and tone of voice are important to the

sender Source of the message communicated to the receiver.

message Communication of information, advice, or a request by the sender to the receiver.

AIDA concept Steps through which an individual reaches a purchase decision: attention, interest, desire, and action.

> **ASSESSMENT CHECK**
>
> 2.1 Identify the four steps of the AIDA concept.
> 2.2 What is noise as it relates to the communication process?

communication process, and cultural differences may lead to noise and misunderstandings. For example, in the United States, the round "O" sign made with the thumb and index finger means "okay." In Mediterranean countries, the same gesture means "zero" or "the worst." A Tunisian interprets this sign as "I'll kill you," and to the Japanese, it means "money." It's easy to see how misunderstandings could arise from a single gesture.

ELEMENTS OF THE PROMOTIONAL MIX

3 Identify the seven components of the promotional mix.

promotional mix Subset of the marketing mix in which marketers attempt to achieve the optimal blending of the elements of personal and nonpersonal selling to achieve promotional objectives.

Like the marketing mix, the promotional mix requires a carefully designed blend of variables to satisfy the needs of a company's customers and achieve organizational objectives. The **promotional mix** works like a subset of the marketing mix with its product, distribution, promotion, and pricing elements. With the promotional mix, the marketers attempt to create an optimal blend of various elements to achieve promotional objectives. The components of the promotional mix are personal selling and nonpersonal selling, including advertising, sales promotion, direct marketing, public relations, and guerrilla marketing.

Personal selling, advertising, and sales promotion usually account for the bulk of a firm's promotional expenditures. However, direct marketing, guerrilla marketing, sponsorships, and public relations also contribute to integrated marketing communications. These activities will be discussed later in the chapter.

PERSONAL SELLING

personal selling Interpersonal influence process involving a seller's promotional presentation conducted on a person-to-person basis with the buyer.

Personal selling, the oldest form of promotion, dates back to the beginning of trading and commerce. Traders vastly expanded markets and product varieties as they led horses and camels along the Silk Road from China to Europe from 300 BCE to 1600 CE, conducting personal selling at both ends. Personal selling may be defined as a seller's promotional presentation conducted person-to-person with the buyer. It may take place face-to-face, over the telephone, through videoconferencing, or by computer links between buyer and seller.

Today, more than 18 million people in the United States have careers in sales and related occupations. They may sell real estate, insurance, and financial investments or tractors, automobiles, and vacuum cleaners; they may work in retail or wholesaling; they may be regional managers or in the field. In other words, the range of selling jobs, as well as the products they represent, is huge.[4]

NONPERSONAL SELLING

nonpersonal selling Promotion that includes advertising, product placement, sales promotion, direct marketing, public relations, and guerrilla marketing—all conducted without being face-to-face with the buyer.

Nonpersonal selling includes advertising, product placement, sales promotion, direct marketing, public relations, and guerrilla marketing. Advertising and sales promotion are usually regarded as the most important forms of nonpersonal selling. About one-third of marketing dollars spent on nonpersonal selling activities are allocated for media advertising; the other two-thirds fund trade and consumer sales promotions.

ADVERTISING

advertising Paid, nonpersonal communication through various media about a business firm, not-for-profit organization, product, or idea by a sponsor identified in a message intended to inform or persuade members of a particular audience.

Advertising is any paid, nonpersonal communication through various media about a business firm, not-for-profit organization, product, or idea by a sponsor identified in a message intended to inform, persuade, or remind members of a particular audience. It is a major promotional mix component for thousands of organizations—total ad spending in the United States rose to more than $180 billion in a recent year, and online ad spending was estimated at more than $50 billion.[5] Mass consumption and geographically dispersed markets make advertising particularly appropriate for marketing goods and services aimed at large audiences likely to respond to the same promotional messages.

Advertising involves the mass media, such as newspapers, television, radio, magazines, movie screens, and billboards, as well as electronic and computerized forms of promotion like Internet commercials, streaming videos, and TV monitors at supermarkets. Marketers are increasingly using the Internet to reach millions of people—one at a time.

PRODUCT PLACEMENT

Product placement is a form of nonpersonal selling in which the marketer pays a fee to display a product prominently in a film or TV show. The practice gained attention more than two decades ago in the movie *E.T.: The Extra-Terrestrial* when Elliott, the boy who befriends E.T., lays out a trail of Reese's Pieces candy to draw the alien from his hiding place. Product sales for Reese's Pieces went through the roof. Interestingly, this was not the moviemaker's first choice of candy: Mars turned down the opportunity to have its M&Ms appear in the film. Today, hundreds of products appear in movies and on television shows, and the fees charged for these placements have soared. Recently, product placement even became the reason for making a movie—as in the case of *The LEGO Movie*.[6]

Product placement figures prominently in the recent box-office hit, *The LEGO Movie.*

product placement Form of promotion in which a marketer pays a motion picture or television program owner a fee to display a product prominently in the film or show.

SALES PROMOTION

Sales promotion consists of marketing activities other than personal selling, advertising, guerrilla marketing, and public relations that stimulate consumer purchasing and dealer effectiveness. This broad category includes displays, trade shows, coupons, contests, samples, premiums, product demonstrations, and various one-time selling efforts. Sales promotion provides a short-term incentive, usually in combination with other forms of promotion, to emphasize, assist, supplement, or otherwise support the objectives of the promotional program. Restaurants, including those serving fast food, often place certain items on the menu at a lower price "for a limited time only." Advertisements may contain coupons for free or discounted items for a specified period of time. Or companies may conduct sweepstakes for prizes, such as new cars or vacations, which may even be completely unrelated to the products the companies are selling.

Sales promotion geared to marketing intermediaries is called **trade promotion**. Companies spend about as much on trade promotion as on advertising and consumer-oriented sales promotion combined. Trade-promotion strategies include offering free merchandise, buyback allowances, and merchandise allowances, along with sales contests to encourage wholesalers and retailers to sell more of certain items or product lines.

sales promotion Marketing activities other than personal selling, advertising, guerrilla marketing, and public relations that stimulate consumer purchasing and dealer effectiveness.

trade promotion Sales promotion that appeals to marketing intermediaries rather than to consumers.

DIRECT MARKETING

Another element in a firm's integrated promotional mix is **direct marketing**, the use of direct communication to a consumer or business recipient designed to generate a response in the form of an order, a request for further information (lead generation), or a visit to a place of business to purchase specific goods or services (traffic generation). While many people equate direct marketing with direct mail, this important promotional category also includes telemarketing, direct-response advertising and infomercials on television, direct-response print advertising, and electronic media.

direct marketing Direct communications, other than personal sales contacts, between buyer and seller, designed to generate sales, information requests, or store or website visits.

PUBLIC RELATIONS

Public relations refers to a firm's communications and relationships with its various publics. These publics include customers, suppliers, stockholders, employees, the government, and the general public. Public relations programs can conduct either formal or informal contacts. The critical point is

public relations Firm's communications and relationships with its various publics.

that every organization, whether or not it has a formally organized program, must be concerned about its public relations.

Publicity is the marketing-oriented aspect of public relations. It can be defined as nonpersonal stimulation of demand for a good, service, person, cause, or organization through unpaid placement of significant news about it in a published medium, on social media sites, or through a favorable presentation of it on the radio or television. Compared with personal selling, advertising, and sales promotion, expenditures for public relations are usually low in most firms. Because companies do not pay for publicity, they have less control over whether the press or electronic media publish good or bad news. This often means consumers find this type of news source more believable than company-disseminated information. Of course, bad publicity can damage a company's reputation and diminish brand equity. Organizations that enjoy good publicity generally try to make the most of it. Those who have suffered from bad publicity try to turn the situation around.

GUERRILLA MARKETING

guerrilla marketing
Unconventional, innovative, and low-cost marketing techniques designed to get consumers' attention in unusual ways.

Guerrilla marketing—using unconventional, innovative, and low-cost techniques to attract consumers' attention—is a relatively new approach typically used when an organization doesn't have the funds for a full marketing program. Firms that can't afford the huge costs of print and broadcasting often look for an innovative, low-cost way to reach their market. Some large companies, such as PepsiCo and Toyota, engage in guerrilla marketing as well.

As mentioned in Chapter 11, *buzz marketing* can be part of guerrilla marketing. This type of marketing works well to reach college students and other young adults. Marketing firms may hire students to mingle among their own classmates and friends, creating buzz about a product. Often called *campus ambassadors,* they may wear logo-bearing T-shirts or caps, leave Post-it notes with marketing messages around campus, and chat about the good or service with friends during class breaks or over meals.

Viral marketing, also mentioned in Chapter 11, is another form of guerrilla marketing that has rapidly caught on with large and small firms. In Dove's "Real Beauty Sketches" ad video, an FBI-trained artist sits behind a screen and sketches faces of women, first based on their self-description, then on the description by a stranger. The strangers' descriptions often were uncannily close to the subject's appearance—underscoring the marketer's point that most women are their own worst beauty critic. The video's message struck an emotional chord with consumers, with more than 163 million views across more than 110 countries.[7]

The results of guerrilla marketing can be funny and outrageous—even offensive to some people, but they almost always get consumers' attention. Some guerrilla marketers stencil their company and product names anywhere graffiti might appear. Street artists are hired to plaster company and product logos on blank walls or billboards.

Viral marketing has caught on rapidly with companies of all sizes. Dove's "Real Beauty Sketches" ad video struck an emotional chord with consumers, with more than 163 million views across the globe.

ADVANTAGES AND DISADVANTAGES OF TYPES OF PROMOTION

Each type of promotion has both advantages and shortcomings. Although personal selling entails a relatively high per-contact cost, it involves less wasted effort than nonpersonal forms of promotion like advertising. Personal selling often provides more flexibility than the other forms because the salesperson can tailor the sales message to meet the unique needs—or objections—of each potential customer.

The major advantages of advertising stem from its ability to create instant awareness of a good, service, or idea; build brand equity; and deliver the marketer's message to mass audiences for a relatively low cost per contact. Major disadvantages include the difficulty of measuring advertising effectiveness and high media costs. Sales promotions, by contrast, can be more accurately monitored and measured than advertising, produce immediate consumer responses, and provide short-term sales increases. Direct marketing gives potential customers an action-oriented choice, permits segmentation and customization of communications, and produces measurable results. Public relations efforts like publicity frequently offer greater credibility than other promotional techniques. For marketers with limited funds, guerrilla marketing can be innovative and effective at a low cost, as long as the tactics are not too outrageous, but it is more difficult to reach people. Marketers must determine the appropriate blend of these promotional mix elements to effectively market their goods and services.

SPONSORSHIPS

Commercial sponsorship of an event or activity involves personal selling, advertising, sales promotion, and public relations in achieving specific promotional goals. Sponsorships have become a multi-billion-dollar business.

Sponsorship consists of an organization providing money or in-kind resources in exchange for a direct association with an event or activity. The sponsor purchases access to the activity's audience and the image associated with the activity. Sponsorships typically involve advertising, direct mail and sales promotion, publicity in the form of media coverage of the event, and personal selling at the event itself. They also involve relationship marketing, bringing together the event, its participants, sponsoring firms, and channel members and major customers. Marketers underwrite varying levels of sponsorships depending on types of events and the amount their company wants to spend.

Commercial sponsorship is not a new concept. It dates back to ancient Rome, where aristocrats sponsored gladiator competitions and chariot races featuring teams supported financially by competing businesses. During the 1880s, some local baseball teams in the United States were sponsored by streetcar companies.

Today's sponsorships are most prevalent in sports—LPGA events, NASCAR, the World Cup, the Super Bowl, NCAA basketball, and more. Companies may also sponsor reading and child-care programs, concerts, art exhibits, and humanitarian programs.

The escalating costs of traditional advertising make commercial sponsorships a cost-effective alternative. Except for really large events, which often have multiple sponsors, most sponsorships are less costly than an advertising campaign that employs television, print, and other media. In addition, sponsors often gain the benefit of media coverage anyway, because associated events are covered as news. In the case of naming rights of venues like sports arenas or subway stations, the name serves as a perpetual advertisement. The city of Boston recently announced it would grant naming rights to sponsoring companies on station stops along its public transit system. The asking price for a five-year deal begins at $1 million per year per station.[8]

While marketers have considerable control over the quantity and quality of market coverage when they advertise, sponsors have little control of sponsored events beyond matching the audiences to profiles of their own target markets. Instead, event organizers control the coverage, which typically focuses on the event, not the sponsor. By contrast, a traditional advertisement allows a marketer to create an individual message containing an introduction, a theme, and a conclusion.

sponsorship
Relationship in which an organization provides funds or in-kind resources to an event or activity in exchange for a direct association with that event or activity.

ASSESSMENT CHECK

3.1 Differentiate between personal and nonpersonal selling.

3.2 What are the six major categories of nonpersonal selling?

3.3 How is sponsorship different from advertising?

ADVERTISING

4 Name the three basic advertising objectives and the two basic categories of advertising.

Advertising in the 21st century is closely linked to integrated marketing communications (IMC) in many respects. While IMC involves a message dealing with buyer–seller relationships, advertising seeks to inform or persuade members of a particular audience. Marketers use advertising to reach target markets with messages designed to appeal to business firms, not-for-profit organizations, or ultimate consumers.

The United States is home to many of the world's leading advertisers. Procter & Gamble, AT&T, and Comcast top a recent list, with P&G spending close to $2.4 billion in advertising during a recent period.[9] Advertising varies among industries as well as companies. Automotive, retail, local services, and telecom services make up the top four categories.[10]

product advertising Nonpersonal selling of a particular good or service.

institutional advertising Promotion of a concept, an idea, a philosophy, or the goodwill of an industry, company, organization, person, geographic location, or government agency.

TYPES OF ADVERTISING

Advertisements fall into two broad categories: product and institutional. **Product advertising** is nonpersonal selling of a particular good or service. This is the type of advertising the average person usually thinks of when talking about most promotional activities.

Institutional advertising, in contrast, promotes a concept, an idea, a philosophy, or the goodwill of an industry, company, organization, person, geographic location, or government agency. This term has a broader meaning than *corporate advertising* that is typically limited to advertising sponsored by a specific profit-seeking firm. Institutional advertising is sometimes related to the public relations function.

informative advertising Promotion that seeks to develop initial demand for a good, service, organization, person, place, idea, or cause.

persuasive advertising Promotion that attempts to increase demand for an existing good, service, organization, person, place, idea, or cause.

reminder advertising Advertising that reinforces previous promotional activity by keeping the name of a good, service, organization, person, place, idea, or cause before the public.

OBJECTIVES OF ADVERTISING

Marketers use advertising messages to accomplish the following objectives: to inform, to persuade, and to remind. These objectives may be used individually or, more typically, in conjunction with each other. For example, an ad for a not-for-profit agency may inform the public of the existence of the organization and at the same time persuade the audience to make a donation, join the organization, or attend a function.

Informative advertising develops initial demand for a good, service, organization, person, place, idea, or cause. The success of a new market entry often depends simply on announcing its availability or explaining its benefits, as in the case of Activia, the yogurt whose global ad campaign features pop singer Shakira.

Persuasive advertising works to increase demand for an existing good, service, organization, person, place, idea, or cause. Persuasive advertising is typically used during the growth stage and the early part of the maturity stage of the product lifecycle.

Reminder advertising strives to reinforce previous promotional activity by keeping the name of a good, service, organization, person, place, idea, or cause before the public. It is common in the latter part of the maturity stage and throughout the decline stage of the product lifecycle. In the competitive beer market, the Dos Equis brand languished until an ad campaign introduced The Most Interesting Man in the World—a Dos Equis drinker whose personal résumé is as entertaining as it is astonishing. With his signature signoff, "Stay thirsty, my friends," the campaign caused Dos Equis sales to soar.[11]

The Most Interesting Man in the World campaign—with the signature signoff, "Stay thirsty, my friends"—revitalized sales of the Dos Equis brand.

Traditionally, marketers stated their advertising objectives as direct sales goals. A more current and realistic standard, however, views advertising as a way to achieve communications objectives—including informing, persuading, and reminding potential customers of the product. Advertising attempts to condition consumers to adopt favorable viewpoints toward a promotional message. The goal of an ad is to improve the likelihood that a customer will buy a particular good or service. In this sense, advertising illustrates the close relationship between marketing communications and promotional strategy.

To get the best value for a firm's advertising investment, marketers must first determine a firm's advertising objectives. Effective advertising can enhance consumer perceptions of quality in a product, leading to increased customer loyalty, repeat purchases, and protection against price wars. In addition, perceptions of superiority pay off in the firm's ability to raise prices without losing market share.

> **ASSESSMENT CHECK**
>
> 4.1 What are the goals of institutional advertising?
>
> 4.2 At what stage in the product lifecycle are informative ads used?

ADVERTISING STRATEGIES

If the primary function of marketing is to bring buyers and sellers together, then advertising is the means to an end. Effective advertising strategies accomplish at least one of three tasks: informing, persuading, or reminding consumers. The secret to choosing the best strategy is developing a message that best positions a firm's product in the audience's mind. Among the advertising strategies available for use by 21st century marketers are comparative advertising and celebrity advertising, as well as decisions about global and interactive ads. Channel-oriented decisions, such as retail and cooperative advertising, can also be devised.

Marketers often combine several of these advertising strategies to ensure the advertisement accomplishes set objectives. As markets become more segmented, the need for personalized advertising increases.

Identify the four major advertising strategies.

COMPARATIVE ADVERTISING

Firms whose products are not the leaders in their markets often favor **comparative advertising**, an approach that emphasizes advertising messages with direct or indirect comparisons to dominant brands in the industry. By contrast, advertising by market leaders seldom acknowledges that competing products even exist, and when they do, they do not point out any benefits of the competing brands.

Wireless telecommunications carriers have been battling it out in media advertising, promoting their calling plans and inviting comparison to competitors. Some offer free text messaging, no roaming charges, or extended hours at reduced rates.

Comparative advertising was once frowned upon, but the Federal Trade Commission now encourages it, believing such ads keep marketers competitive and consumers better informed about their choices. Scotts and Pennington have long waged a battle on the airwaves, comparing their respective brands of grass seed—each claiming its brand is superior.[12]

Generally speaking, when competition through advertising exists, prices tend to go down because people can shop around. This benefit has proved increasingly true for online consumers, who now use shopping bots to help find the best prices on goods and services.

comparative advertising Advertising strategy that emphasizes messages with direct or indirect promotional comparisons between competing brands.

> **Briefly Speaking**
>
> "Advertising says to people, 'Here's what we've got. Here's what it will do for you. Here's how to get it.'"
>
> —Leo Burnett
> *Twentieth-century American advertising executive*

CELEBRITY TESTIMONIALS

A popular technique for increasing advertising readership and improving effectiveness involves the use of celebrity spokespeople. This type of advertising is also popular in foreign countries. Both the number of celebrity ads and the dollars spent on them have risen in recent years. Professional athletes

The evidence against vacuum cleaners with bags keeps piling up.

Because bags clog, bag cleaners lose suction... ...leaving this behind in your home.

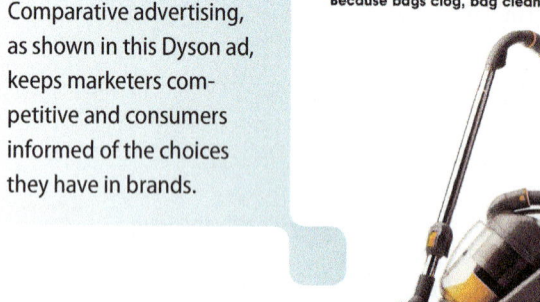

The Dyson has no bag, so it's the only cleaner to maintain 100% suction, 100% of the time.

dyson

Source: www.dyson.com

Comparative advertising, as shown in this Dyson ad, keeps marketers competitive and consumers informed of the choices they have in brands.

like NBA star LeBron James are among the highest-paid product endorsers. In a recent year, James reportedly earned $42 million from endorsement deals with such firms as The Coca-Cola Company, McDonald's, Nike, Samsung, and State Farm. With the exception of Nike, none of these has anything to do with basketball.[13]

One advantage of associations with big-name personalities is improved product recognition in a promotional environment filled with hundreds of competing 15- and 30-second commercials. Advertisers use the term *clutter* to describe this situation. As e-marketing continues to soar, one inevitable result has been the increase in advertising clutter as companies rush to market their goods and services online.

A celebrity testimonial generally succeeds when the celebrity is a credible source of information for the product. The most effective testimonial ads link the celebrity and the advertised good or service. Studies of consumer behavior show that celebrities improve the product's believability, product recall, and brand recognition.

However, celebrity endorsements can also go awry. A personality who endorses too many products may create marketplace confusion. Customers may remember the celebrity but not the product or brand; worse, they might connect the celebrity to a competing brand. Another problem arises if a celebrity isn't credible. A recent series of Subway commercials features current and former Olympians touting the healthy sandwiches: gymnast Nastia Liukin, speed skater Apolo Ohno, and snowboarder Torah Bright. But Subway added a jarring note when it included light heavyweight boxer Michael Lee in one of the commercials. As a relative unknown, media critics observed, Lee lacks the stature of the Olympic medal winners—and, therefore, the credibility.[14]

Some advertisers try to avoid problems with celebrity endorsers by using cartoon characters as endorsers. The GEICO gecko, the humorous reptile with a British accent, has appeared in GEICO ads for years.[15] Some advertisers may actually prefer cartoon characters because the characters never say anything negative about the product, they do exactly what the marketers want them to do, and they cannot get involved in scandals.

RETAIL ADVERTISING

retail advertising Advertising by stores that sell goods or services directly to the consuming public.

cooperative advertising Strategy in which a retailer shares advertising costs with a manufacturer or wholesaler.

Most consumers are confronted daily with **retail advertising**, which includes all advertising by retail stores that sell goods or services directly to the consuming public. While this activity accounts for a sizable portion of total annual advertising expenditures, retail advertising varies widely in its effectiveness. One study showed that consumers often respond with suspicion to retail price advertisements.

A retailer often shares advertising costs with a manufacturer or wholesaler in a technique called **cooperative advertising**. For example, an apparel marketer may pay a percentage of the cost of a retail store's newspaper advertisement featuring its product lines. Cooperative advertising campaigns originated to take advantage of the media's practice of offering lower rates to local advertisers than to national ones. Later, cooperative advertising became part of programs to improve dealer relations. The retailer likes the chance to secure advertising that it might not be able to afford otherwise. Cooperative advertising can strengthen vertical links in the marketing channel, as when a manufacturer and retailer coordinate their resources. It can also involve firms at the same level of the supply chain. In a horizontal arrangement, a group of retailers—for example, all the Ford dealers in a state—might pool their resources.

INTERACTIVE ADVERTISING

Because marketers realize that two-way communications are more effective in achieving promotional objectives, they are interested in interactive media. **Interactive advertising** involves two-way promotional messages transmitted through communication channels that induce message recipients to participate actively in the promotional effort. Achieving this involvement is the difficult task facing contemporary marketers. Although interactive advertising has become synonymous with the Internet, it also includes other formats like kiosks in shopping malls and text messages on cell phones. Multimedia technology, the Internet, and commercial online services are changing the nature of advertising from a one-way, passive communication technique to more effective, two-way marketing communications. Interactive advertising creates dialogue between marketers and individual shoppers, providing more materials at the user's request. The advertiser's challenge is to gain and hold consumer interest in an environment where these individuals control what they want to see.

Successful interactive advertising adds value by offering the viewer more than just product-related information. A website can do more than display an ad to promote a brand; it can create a company store, provide customer service, and offer additional content. Many marketers believe such ads can be so finely targeted that they cut through increasing advertising clutter and reach only consumers ready to hear their messages.

CREATING AN ADVERTISEMENT

With millions of dollars at stake, marketers must create effective, memorable ads that increase sales and enhance their organization's image. Research helps them by pinpointing the three goals an ad needs to accomplish: educating consumers about product features, enhancing brand loyalty, or improving consumer perception of the brand. These objectives should guide the design of the ad. Marketers can also discover what appeals to consumers and can test ads with potential buyers before committing funds for a campaign.

Marketers sometimes face specific challenges as they develop advertising objectives for services. They must find a creative way to fill out the intangible images of most services and successfully convey the benefits consumers receive. With the words "Like a good neighbor, State Farm is there," State Farm demonstrates how advertising can make the intangible nature of its services—insurance—tangible to consumers.

TRANSLATING ADVERTISING OBJECTIVES INTO ADVERTISING PLANS

Once a company defines its objectives for an advertising campaign, it can develop its advertising plan. Marketing research helps managers make strategic decisions that guide choices in technical areas such as budgeting, copywriting, scheduling, and media selection. Posttests, discussed in greater detail later in the chapter, measure the effectiveness of advertising and form the basis for feedback concerning possible adjustments. The elements of advertising planning are shown in Figure 16.2. Experienced marketers know the importance of following even the most basic steps in the process, such as market analysis.

As Chapter 9 explained, positioning involves developing a marketing strategy that aims to achieve a desired position in a prospective buyer's mind. Effective advertising communicates the desired position by emphasizing certain product characteristics such

interactive advertising Two-way promotional messages transmitted through communication channels that induce message recipients to participate actively in the promotional effort.

FIGURE 16.2
Elements of the Advertising Planning Process

Consideration of constraints and uncontrollable factors

Research Inputs
Consumer research
Product research
Market analysis
Competitive analysis

Strategic Decisions
Setting objectives
Identifying and selecting target markets
Selecting message and media strategy
Coordinating with other marketing mix elements

Tactical Execution
Establish advertising budget
Establish controls
Write and produce ads and commercials
Select and schedule media choices
Pretest advertising alternatives

Feedback

Measuring Advertising Effectiveness
Use posttests to determine the effectiveness of advertising

Advertising Evaluation
Evaluate results of advertising
Make necessary adjustments

advertising campaign Series of different but related ads that use a single theme and appear in different media within a specified time period.

as performance attributes, price, quality, competitors' shortcomings, applications, user needs, and product classes.

ADVERTISING MESSAGES

Message creation starts with the benefits a product offers and moves to the creative concept phase in which marketers strive to bring an appropriate message to consumers using both visual and verbal components. Marketers work to create an ad with meaningful, believable, and distinctive appeals—one that stands out from the clutter and is more likely to escape being skipped over by consumers.

Ads usually are created not individually, but as part of specific campaigns. An **advertising campaign** is a series of different but related ads that use a single theme and appear in different media within a specified time period. In developing a creative strategy, advertisers must decide how to communicate their marketing story. They must balance message characteristics—the tone of the appeal, the information provided, and the conclusion to which it leads the consumer—with the side of the story the ad tells, and its emphasis on verbal or visual primary elements.

ASSESSMENT CHECK

5.1 What is comparative advertising?
5.2 What makes for a successful celebrity testimonial?
5.3 What is an advertising campaign?
5.4 What are an advertisement's three main goals?

ADVERTISING APPEALS

6 Describe the various types of advertising appeals and their uses.

Humorous ads seek to create a positive mood related to a firm's goods or services. These hamster characters provide humor in a series of Kia TV commercials.

Should the tone of the advertisement focus on a practical appeal such as price or gas mileage, or should it evoke an emotional response by appealing to, say, fear, humor, or sex? This is another critical decision in the creation of memorable ads that possess the strengths needed to accomplish promotional objectives.

FEAR APPEALS

In recent years, marketers have relied increasingly on fear appeals. Ads for insurance, autos, and even batteries imply that the wrong buying decision could lead to property loss, injury, or other bad outcomes. Recent Allstate commercials feature "Mayhem," a wild-eyed character who describes the adverse consequences of being uninsured.[16]

Pharmaceutical companies spend several billion dollars a year on advertising, much of it directed toward consumer fears of health conditions. Drug ads have flourished in print, online, and broadcast media since the Food and Drug Administration lifted a ban on such advertising on TV. Fear appeals can backfire when viewers practice selective perception and tune out statements they perceive as too strong or not credible. Some consumer researchers believe viewer or reader backlash will eventually occur due to the amount of prescription drug advertising based on fear appeals.

HUMOR IN ADVERTISING MESSAGES

A humorous ad seeks to create a positive mood related to a firm's goods or services, but advertising professionals differ in their opinions of the ads' effectiveness. Some believe humor distracts attention from brand and product features; consumers remember the humor but not the product. Humorous ads, because they are so memorable, may lose their effectiveness sooner than ads with other kinds of appeals. In addition, humor can be tricky because what one group of consumers finds funny may not be funny at all to another group. Men and women sometimes have a different sense of humor, as do people of different ages. This distinction may become even greater across cultures.

ADS BASED ON SEX

Ads with sex-based appeals immediately attract attention. Advertisements for Victoria's Secret lingerie and clothing are designed this way. While many people accept these and other ads, they do not appeal to everyone. Marketers using sex-based appeals know they walk a fine line between what is acceptable to the consumers they want to reach and what is not.

DEVELOPING AND PREPARING ADS

The final step in the advertising process—the development and preparation of an advertisement—should flow logically from the promotional theme selected. This process should create an ad that becomes a complementary part of the marketing mix with a carefully determined role in the total marketing strategy. Preparation of an advertisement should emphasize features such as its creativity, its continuity with past advertisements, and possibly its association with other company products.

What immediate tasks should an advertisement accomplish? Regardless of the chosen target, an ad should (1) gain attention and interest, (2) inform or persuade, and (3) eventually lead to a purchase or other desired action. It should gain attention in a productive way; that is, it should instill some recall of the good or service. Otherwise, it will not drive a purchase.

Gaining attention and generating interest—cutting through the clutter—can be formidable tasks. Stimulating buying action is often difficult because an advertisement cannot actually close a sale. Nevertheless, if an ad gains attention and informs or persuades, it probably represents a worthwhile investment of marketing resources. Too many advertisers fail to tell consumers how to buy the product. Creative design should eliminate this shortcoming.

Figure 16.3 shows the four major elements of a print advertisement: headline, illustration, body copy, and signature. *Headlines* and *illustrations* (photographs, drawings, or other artwork) should work together to generate interest and attention. *Body copy* informs, persuades, and stimulates buying action. The *signature*—which may include the company name, address, phone number, Web address, slogan, trademark, or simply a product photo—names the sponsoring

FIGURE 16.3
Elements of a Typical Ad

organization. An ad may also have one or more subheadings that either link the main headline to the body copy or subdivide sections of the body copy.

Once advertisers conceive an idea for an ad that gains attention, informs and persuades, and stimulates purchases, their next step involves refining the thought sketch into a rough layout. Continued refinements of the rough layout eventually produce the final version of the advertisement design ready to be executed, printed, or recorded.

The creation of each advertisement in a campaign requires an evolutionary process that begins with an idea and ultimately results in a finished ad ready for distribution through print or electronic media. The idea itself must first be converted into a thought sketch—a tangible summary of the intended message. Advances in technology allow advertisers to create novel, eye-catching advertisements. Innovative software packages allow artists to merge multiple images to create a single image with a natural, seamless appearance.

CREATING INTERACTIVE ADS

Internet users want engaging, lively content that takes advantage of the medium's capabilities and goes beyond what they find elsewhere. The Internet's major advantages enable advertisers to provide that, offering speed, information, two-way communications, self-directed entertainment, and personal choice. Internet ads are also vibrant in their visual appeal, and some believe they will not experience the swings in spending that traditional ad media do.

Internet ads have grown from information-based home pages to innovative, interactive channels for transmitting messages to online audiences, including banners, pop-ups, keyword ads, advertorials, and interstitials. *Advergames* are either online games created by marketers to promote their products to targeted audiences in an interactive way or ads or product placements inserted into online video games. Recently, Coke Zero partnered with Sony to create an advergame for PlayStation known as "PlayStation All-Stars Island." Players compete in four mini-games on PlayStation.[17]

Banner advertisements on a Web page that link to an advertiser's site are the most common type of advertising on the Internet. They can be free of charge or cost thousands of dollars per month, depending on the amount of hits the site receives. Online advertisers often describe their Internet ads in terms of "richness," referring to the degree to which such technologies as streaming video, 3D animation, and interactive capabilities are implemented in the banners.

Keyword ads are an outcropping of banner ads. Used in search engines, keyword ads appear on the results page of a search and are specific to the searched term. Advertisers pay search engines to target their ads and display the banners only when users search for relevant keywords, allowing marketers to target specific audiences. For example, if a user searched for the term "digital camera," keyword ads might appear for electronic boutiques or camera shops that sell digital cameras and film.

Then there are *pop-ups*—little advertising windows appearing in front of the top window of a user's screen—and *pop-unders* that appear under the top window. Many users complain that interstitials, like pop-ups, are intrusive and unwanted. Interstitials are more likely to contain large graphics and streaming

> Banner ads on a Web page that link to an advertiser's site are the most common type of advertising on the Internet.

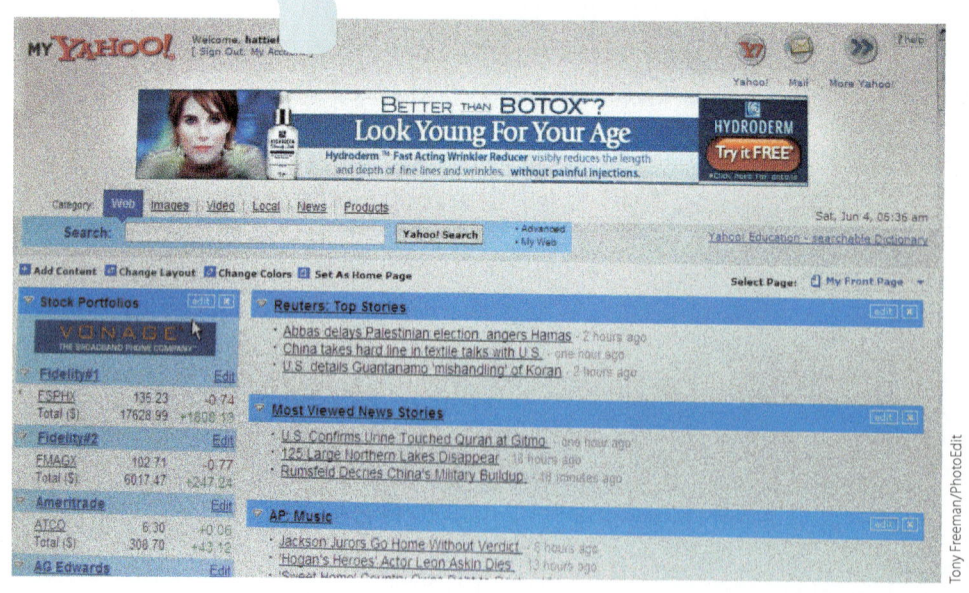

presentations than banner ads and are more difficult to ignore than typical banner ads. But despite complaints, some studies show that users are more likely to click interstitials than banners.

Perhaps the most intrusive form of online advertising is *adware*, which allows ads to be shown on users' screens via software downloaded to their computers without their consent or through trickery. Such software can be difficult to remove, and some industry experts believe marketers should avoid dealing with Internet marketing firms that promote the use of adware.

Revenues for *social media advertising* on sites like Facebook and LinkedIn continue to skyrocket. In a recent year, revenues totaled more than $4 billion, and industry observers predict continued double-digit growth.[18] However, the very nature of the advertising makes it difficult to evaluate and measure its effectiveness. If a virtual bottle of Coca-Cola appears on Facebook or LinkedIn, how likely is it that consumers will actually purchase Coke the next time they want something to drink?

ASSESSMENT CHECK

6.1 What are some common emotional appeals used in advertising?

6.2 What are the main types of interactive ads?

MEDIA SELECTION AND SCHEDULING

One of the most important decisions in developing an advertising strategy is the selection of appropriate media to carry a firm's message to its audience. The media selected must be capable of accomplishing the communications objectives of informing, persuading, and reminding potential customers of the good, service, person, or idea advertised.

Research identifies the ad's target market to determine the market's size and characteristics. Advertisers then match the target characteristics with the media best able to reach that particular audience. The objective of media selection is to achieve adequate media coverage without advertising beyond the identifiable limits of the potential market. Finally, cost comparisons between alternatives should determine the best possible media purchase.

Compare the seven different advertising media.

TELEVISION

Television—network and cable combined—still accounts for nearly 40 cents of every advertising dollar spent in the world.[19] Television advertising is attractive because it allows marketers to reach local and national markets. Whereas most newspaper advertising revenues come from local advertisers, the greatest share of television advertising revenues comes from organizations that advertise nationally. Virtual ads are banner-type logos and brief advertising messages superimposed onto television coverage of sporting events so they seem to be a part of the arena's signage but cannot be seen by anyone attending the game Streaming headlines are paid for by corporate sponsors whose names and logos appear within the news stream.

Other trends in TV advertising include the abbreviated spot—a 15- or 30-second ad that costs less to make and buy and is over before most viewers can zap it with their remote control—and single-advertiser shows. These advertisements work well when viewers are watching live, but as more consumers record programs with DVRs, many fast-forward past even the briefest commercials. In fact, Dish Network installs "ad erasers" in its DVRs, enabling viewers to skip over commercial content altogether.[20]

Websites that aggregate TV programming have become top video destinations on the Internet, where viewers can watch complete, high-resolution episodes of current TV programs on their computer, smartphone, or other wireless device. The sites are free and require no additional wires or boxes for access. Instead, viewers see brief ads in order to watch their favorite programming.

Dish Network began installing "ad erasers" in its DVRs to permit viewers to skip TV commercials.

Under Hulu's Hulu Plus feature, viewers can pay a monthly fee to watch a complete season of TV shows. Other aggregators offer movies, music videos, and more.

In the past decade, cable television's share of ad spending and revenues has grown tremendously. Satellite television has contributed to increased cable penetration; almost three-fourths of all Americans now have cable installed in their homes. In response to declining ratings and soaring costs, network television companies like NBC, CBS, and ABC are refocusing their advertising strategies with a heavy emphasis on moving onto the Internet and social media sites to capture younger audiences.

Because cable audiences have grown, programming has improved, and ratings have increased, advertisers have earmarked more of their advertising budgets for this medium. Cable advertising offers marketers access to more narrowly defined target audiences than other broadcast media can provide—a characteristic referred to as *narrowcasting*. The great variety of special-interest channels devoted to subjects like cooking, golf, history, home and garden, health, fitness, and shopping attract specialized audiences and permit niche marketing.

Television advertising offers the advantages of mass coverage, powerful impact on viewers, repetition of messages, flexibility, and prestige. Its disadvantages include loss of control of the promotional message to the telecaster, which can influence its impact and result in high costs and some viewer distrust. Compared with other media, television can suffer from lack of selectivity because specific TV programs may not reach consumers in a precisely defined target market without a significant degree of wasted coverage. However, the growing specialization of cable TV channels can help resolve the problem. Finally, some types of products are banned from television advertising. Tobacco goods, such as cigarettes, fall into this category.

With the high cost of television advertising, some companies seek cheaper alternatives—such as print ads, online blogs, and Facebook—for launch campaigns. When Orabrush, maker of a tongue cleaner, decided to branch out with a breath-cleaning device for dogs, it turned to the Internet to build demand. Advertising on YouTube quickly went viral, with more than 4 million views.[21]

Television commercials can promote more than a firm's products; they can highlight the organization's efforts to address a crisis, repair a corporate reputation, and attempt to solidify customer loyalty. BP used TV commercials for all these reasons in the aftermath of a massive oil spill in the Gulf of Mexico.

RADIO

Radio advertising has always been a popular media choice for delivering up-to-the-minute newscasts and targeting advertising messages to local audiences. But in recent years, radio also has become one of the fastest-growing media alternatives. As more and more people find they have less and less time, radio provides immediate information and entertainment at work, at play, and in the car.

Marketers frequently use radio advertising to reach local audiences. Recently it has played an increasingly important role as a national—and even global—listening favorite. Thousands of online listeners use the Internet to tune in to radio stations from almost every city—an easy-listening station in London, a top-40 Hong Kong broadcaster, or a chat show from Toronto. Other listeners equip their vehicles with satellite radio to maintain contact with hometown or destination stations during long trips.

Satellite radio offers higher-quality digital signals than regular radio stations, with many more channels mostly free of Federal Communications Commission oversight as well as commercials. XM Radio, the first such service to be licensed, began airing commercials on a few of its nearly 200 music, sports, and talk channels. Both XM and its competitor, Sirius, charged an annual subscription fee. When the two merged, they initially agreed to offer à la carte pricing, under which subscribers could select the programming they preferred. Now the satellite radio service offers several different monthly subscription packages.

Advertisers like radio for its ability to reach people while they drive because they are a captive audience. Other benefits include low cost, flexibility, and mobility. Stations can adapt to local preferences by changing format, such as going from country and western to an all-news or all-sports station. The variety of stations allows advertisers to easily target audiences and tailor their messages to those listeners.

Disadvantages to radio advertising include highly segmented audiences (reaching most people in a market may require ads placed on multiple stations), the temporary nature of messages (unlike print, radio and TV ads are instantaneous and must be rebroadcast to reach consumers a second time), and a minimum of research information compared with television.

While most radio listening is often done in cars or with headset-equipped portables, technology has given birth to Internet radio. Webcast radio allows customers to widen their listening times and choices through computers and mobile devices. With an estimated monthly audience of more than 160 million people, online radio listenership continues to grow.[22]

NEWSPAPERS

Newspaper advertising continues to dominate local markets and is estimated to account for slightly less than $18 billion of annual advertising expenditures.[23] In addition to retail advertisements, classified advertising is an important part of newspaper revenues. Although some predict the decline of newspaper audiences, when online readers are included in circulation figures, newspapers are as popular as ever. Most newspapers have their own websites, which attract growing numbers of visitors—164 million unique visits in a recent month and 80 percent of the total U.S. adult population accessing any digital content in that same time period.[24] Although newspaper advertising as a whole has decreased, activity on newspaper websites creates new opportunities for marketers.

The primary advantage of newspaper advertising is the flexibility it offers, because the ads can vary from one locality to the next. Newspapers also allow a larger audience for ads. Unlike television or radio advertising messages, newspaper readers can keep the printed advertising message and refer back to it. Newspaper advertising does have some disadvantages. One of these is relatively poor reproduction quality, although that is changing as technology improves. The high quality of ads in *USA Today* is an example of the strides in newspaper ad quality made possible by new technologies. Newspapers also struggle to "get through the noise" of other advertisers. To retain big advertisers like trendy designers and national retailers, some newspapers like *The New York Times* have launched their own annual or semiannual fashion magazines, taking advantage of their finely tuned distribution capabilities.

MAGAZINES

Advertisers divide magazines into two broad categories: consumer magazines and business magazines. These categories are also subdivided into monthly and weekly publications. The top magazine by circulation is *AARP The Magazine*.[25] The primary advantages of magazine advertising include the ability to reach precise target markets, quality reproduction, long life, and the prestige associated with some magazines (such as *National Geographic*). The primary disadvantage is that magazines lack the flexibility of newspaper, radio, and TV.

Media buyers study circulation numbers and demographic information for various publications before choosing optimal placement opportunities and negotiating rates. The same advertising categories have claimed the title for big spenders for several years running. Automotive, retail, and movies and media advertising have held their first, second, and third places, respectively, each year and continue to show strong growth. Advertisers can reach their target markets by advertising in the appropriate magazines.

DIRECT MAIL

As discussed in Chapter 15, direct-mail advertising includes sales letters, postcards, leaflets, folders, booklets, catalogs, and house organs—periodicals published by organizations to cover internal issues. Its advantages come from direct mail's ability to segment large numbers of prospective customers into narrow market niches, speed, flexibility, detailed information, and personalization. Disadvantages of direct mail include high production costs, reliance on the quality of mailing lists, and some consumers' resistance to it.

The advantages of direct mail explain its widespread use. Data are available on previous purchase patterns and preferred payment methods as well as household characteristics, such as number of children or seniors. Direct mail accounted for more than $50 billion of advertising spending in a recent year.[26] The downside to direct mail is clutter, otherwise known as *junk mail*. So much advertising material is stuffed into people's mailboxes every day that the task of grabbing consumers' attention and evoking some interest can be daunting to direct-mail advertisers.

OUTDOOR ADVERTISING

Outdoor advertising, sometimes called *out-of-home advertising,* is one of the oldest and simplest media businesses. Advertisers in the United States spent about $6.9 billion on outdoor advertising in a recent year.[27] Traditional outdoor advertising takes the form of billboards, painted displays such as those that appear on the walls of buildings, and electronic displays. Transit advertising includes ads placed inside and outside buses, subway trains, commuter trains, and stations. Some firms place ads on the roofs of taxicabs, on bus shelters and benches, on entertainment and sporting event turnstiles, in public restrooms, and even on parking meters. A section of highway might be cleaned up by a local real estate company or restaurant, with a nearby sign indicating the firm's contribution. All of these are forms of outdoor advertising.

Outdoor advertising quickly communicates simple ideas. It also offers repeated exposure to a message and strong promotion for locally available products. Outdoor advertising is particularly effective along metropolitan streets and in other high-traffic areas. But like every other type of ad, outdoor advertising produces clutter. It also suffers from the brevity of exposure to its messages by passing motorists. Driver concerns about rush-hour safety and limited time also combine to limit the length of exposure to outdoor messages. As a result, most of these ads use striking, simple illustrations, short selling points, and humor to attract people interested in products, such as beverages, vacations, local entertainment, and lodging.

Another problem relates to public concerns over aesthetics. Legislation regulates the placement of outdoor advertising near interstate highways. Also, local ordinances in many cities regulate the size and placement of outdoor messages. Hawaii prohibits them altogether.

New technologies are helping revive outdoor advertising, livening up the billboards themselves with animation, large sculptures, and laser images. Of the 400,000 billboards in the United States, more than 5,200 are digitized, and their numbers are growing. While safety advocates express concern that such billboards constitute a driving hazard, studies are under way to confirm that the high-tech signage poses no risk.[28]

INTERACTIVE MEDIA

Interactive media—especially on the Internet and social media sites—are being used more and more by advertisers. Keyword ads dominate online advertising. In a recent year, Google's ad revenues totaled nearly $58 billion, and many firms are increasing their interactive advertising budgets.[29]

As video and broadcast capabilities expand, advertising comes to cell phones in interesting ways. In a recent year mobile advertising revenues in the United States hit an estimated $18 billion and are expected to continue their explosive growth.[30] Through an emerging technology known as *augmented reality*, virtual imaging can be incorporated into real-time video on a mobile phone, creating an exciting new experience for cell phone users.[31]

MEDIA SCHEDULING

Once advertisers have selected the media that best match their advertising objectives and promotional budget, they shift their attention to **media scheduling**—setting the timing and sequence for a series of advertisements. A variety of factors influence this decision—sales patterns, repurchase cycles, and competitors' activities are the most important variables.

Seasonal sales patterns are common in many industries. An airline might reduce advertising during peak travel periods and boost its media schedule during low travel months. A harsh winter in the Midwest saw increased advertising to local consumers for warm weather vacations in Florida and the Caribbean. Repurchase cycles also may play a role in media scheduling—products with shorter repurchase cycles will more likely require consistent media schedules throughout the year. Competitors' activities are still other influences on media scheduling. A small firm may avoid advertising during periods of heavy advertising by its rivals.

Recently marketers have questioned the effectiveness of reach and frequency to measure ad success online. The theory behind frequency is that the average advertising viewer needs a minimum of three exposures to a message to understand it and connect it to a specific brand. For Internet users, the connection time is much quicker—hence, the greater importance of building customer relationships through advertisements.

A media schedule is typically created as follows. Suppose an auto manufacturer wants to advertise a new model designed primarily to appeal to professional consumers in their 40s. The model would be introduced in November with a direct-mail piece offering test drives. Outdoor, newspaper, and magazine advertising would support the direct-mail campaign but also follow through the winter and into the spring and summer. Early television commercials might air during a holiday television special in mid-December, and then one or more expensively produced, highly creative spots would be first aired during the Super Bowl in late January. Another television commercial—along with new print ads—might be scheduled for fall clearance sales as the manufacturer gets ready to introduce next year's models. This example illustrates how marketers might plan their advertising year for just one product.

Technology is helping to revive outdoor advertising with digital billboards that use animation and laser images.

media scheduling Setting the timing and sequence for a series of advertisements.

ASSESSMENT CHECK

7.1 What types of products are banned from advertising on television?

7.2 What are some advantages radio offers to advertisers? What about newspapers?

7.3 Define media scheduling, and identify the most important factors influencing the scheduling decision.

PUBLIC RELATIONS

> **8** Explain the roles of public relations, publicity, and cross-promotion in an organization's promotional strategy.

Earlier we defined public relations as the firm's communications and relationships with its various publics, including customers, employees, stockholders, suppliers, government agencies, and the society in which it operates. Organizational public relations efforts date back to 1889, when George Westinghouse hired two people to publicize the advantages of alternating current electricity and refute arguments originally championed by Thomas Edison for direct-current systems.

Today, public relations is concerned with the prestige and image of all parts of the organization. It plays a larger role than ever within the promotional mix, and it may emphasize more marketing-oriented information. In addition to its traditional activities, such as surveying public attitudes and creating a good corporate image, PR also supports advertising in promoting the organization's goods and services.

In the United States, more than 229,000 people work in the public relations field for both profit-centered and not-for-profit organizations, with about 62,000 working as public relations managers.[32] Public relations has grown in importance as a result of increased public pressure on industries regarding corporate ethical conduct and environmental and international issues. Many top executives have become more involved in public relations as the public expects top managers to take greater responsibility for company actions.

The PR department is the link between the firm and the media. It provides press releases and holds news conferences to announce new products, the formation of strategic alliances, management changes, financial results, or similar developments. The PR department may also issue publications and documents such as newsletters, brochures, and reports.

PUBLICITY

> **Briefly Speaking**
>
> "Without publicity a terrible thing happens: nothing."
>
> —P. T. Barnum
> *Nineteenth-century American showman and businessman*

The aspect of public relations most directly related to promoting a firm's products is *publicity*, the nonpersonal stimulation of demand for a good, service, place, idea, person, or organization by unpaid placement of significant news regarding the product in a print, social, or broadcast medium. Firms generate publicity by creating special events, holding press conferences, and preparing news releases and media kits. Many businesses, like Starbucks and Sam's Club, built their brands with virtually no advertising.

While publicity generates minimal costs compared with other forms of promotion, it does not deliver its message entirely for free. Publicity-related expenses include the costs of employing staff assigned to create and submit publicity releases, printing and mailing costs, and related expenses. Firms often pursue publicity to promote their images or viewpoints. Other publicity efforts involve organizational activities such as plant expansions, mergers and acquisitions, management changes, and research breakthroughs. A significant amount of publicity provides information about goods and services, particularly new products.

Because many consumers consider news stories to be more credible than advertisements as sources of information, publicity releases are often sent to media editors for possible inclusion in news stories. The media audiences perceive the news as coming from the communications media, not the sponsors. The information in a publicity release about a new good or service can provide valuable assistance for a television, newspaper, or magazine writer, leading to eventual broadcast or publication.

CROSS-PROMOTION

> **cross-promotion** Promotional technique in which marketing partners share the cost of a promotional campaign that meets their mutual needs.

In recent years marketers have begun to combine their promotional efforts for related products using a technique called **cross-promotion**, in which marketing partners share the cost of a promotional campaign that meets their mutual needs. Relationship marketing strategies like comarketing and cobranding, discussed in Chapter 11, are forms of cross-promotion. Marketers realize these joint efforts between established brands provide greater benefits in return for both organizations; investments of time and money on such promotions will become increasingly important to many partners' growth prospects.

ETHICS AND PROMOTIONAL STRATEGIES

Chapter 3 introduced the topic of marketing ethics and noted that promotion is the element in the marketing mix that raises the most ethical questions. People actively debate the question of whether marketing communications contribute to better lives. The final section of this chapter takes a closer look at ethical concerns in advertising and public relations.

Even though ads targeting children are technically legal, these types of promotions raise ethical issues. In the case of advertising aimed at children, when it comes to influencing parents' purchase decisions, nothing beats influencing kids. By promoting goods and services directly to children, firms can sell not only to them but to the rest of the household, too. However, as the feature "Solving an Ethical Controversy" points out, many people question the ethics of promoting directly to children.

Another issue is the insertion of product messages in media programs without full disclosure of the marketing relationship to audiences. To woo younger consumers, especially teens and those in their 20s, advertisers attempt to make these messages appear as different from advertisements as possible; they design ads that seem more like entertainment.

In online ads, it is often difficult to separate advertising from editorial content, because many sites resemble magazine and newspaper ads or television infomercials. Another ethical issue

SOLVING AN ETHICAL CONTROVERSY
Fast-Food Advertising Directed to Children

The U.S. Centers for Disease Control and Prevention reports that one child in six is overweight or obese, triple the number 30 years ago. Many blame the increased role of fast food and the heavy influence of colorful advertising aimed at children. The American Academy of Pediatrics' 65,000 member doctors recently called for a ban of fast-food advertising during children's TV programs.

Should fast-food advertising to children be banned?

PRO

1. Research shows digital media has changed the advertising landscape, making it even more difficult for children to discern advertising from entertainment and make critical judgments about what they see.
2. The incidence of child obesity is of national concern. One study reported that banning fast-food ads could decrease obesity, which may result in serious health problems in adulthood, by 17 percent.

CON

1. Parents buy fast food for their children; banning ads on kids' programs won't affect their purchases.
2. Advertising pays for most network TV programming.

Summary

Disney announced new nutritional standards for all products advertised on its TV channels, websites, and radio stations, banning candy, sugared cereal, and fast food. Foods sold in Disney theme parks will contain 25 percent less sodium. McDonald's rejected shareholder calls for menu changes aimed at curbing childhood obesity but announced that new kids' advertising will feature messages about physical activity and nutrition.

Sources: James Steyer, "Super Bowl Ad Blitz: Are Kids Vulnerable?" CNN, accessed April 2, 2014, www.cnn.com; Katy Bachman, "Big Food Cuts the Fat in Advertising to Kids," Adweek, accessed April 2, 2014, www.adage.com; "Advertising to Children," The Economist, accessed April 2, 2014, www.economist.com; Romeo Vitelli, "Television, Commercials, and Your Child," Psychology Today, accessed April 2, 2014, www.psychologytoday.com; Perry Klass, "How Advertising Targets Our Children," The New York Times, accessed April 2, 2014, http://well.blogs.nytimes.com.

surrounding online advertising is the use of *cookies*, small text files automatically downloaded to a user's computer or mobile device whenever a site is visited. Each time the user returns to that site, the site's server accesses the cookie and gathers information: What site was visited last? How long did the user stay? What was the next site visited? Marketers claim this device helps them determine consumer preferences and argue that cookies are stored in the user's PC, not the company's website. The problem is that cookies can and do collect personal information without the user's knowledge.

Puffery and Deception

Puffery refers to exaggerated claims of a product's superiority or the use of subjective or vague statements that may not be literally true. A company might advertise the "most advanced system" or claim that its product is "most effective" in accomplishing its purpose.

Exaggeration in ads is not new. Consumers seem to accept advertisers' tendencies to stretch the truth in their efforts to distinguish their products and get consumers to buy them. This inclination may provide one reason that advertising does not encourage purchase behavior as successfully as sales promotions do. A tendency toward puffery does raise ethical questions, though: Where is the line between claims that attract attention and those that provide implied guarantees? To what degree do advertisers deliberately make misleading statements?

The Uniform Commercial Code standardizes sales and business practices throughout the United States. It makes a distinction between puffery and any specific or quantifiable statement about product quality or performance that constitutes an "express warranty," which obligates the company to stand behind its claim. Boasts of product superiority and vague claims are puffery, not warranties. They are considered so self-praising or exaggerated that the average consumer would not rely on them to make a buying decision. A quantifiable statement, on the other hand, implies a certain level of performance.

> **ASSESSMENT CHECK**
>
> 8.1 What is the role of the PR department in an organization?
>
> 8.2 What is publicity?
>
> 8.3 What are the advantages of cross-promotion?

PROMOTIONAL MIX EFFECTIVENESS

> **9** Discuss the five factors that influence the effectiveness of a promotional mix and how marketers measure promotional effectiveness.

Because quantitative measures are not available to determine the effectiveness of each component of a promotional mix in a given market segment, developing an effective promotional mix is one of a marketer's most difficult tasks. Several factors influence the effectiveness of a promotional mix.

NATURE OF THE MARKET

The marketer's target audience has a major impact on the choice of a promotion method. When a market includes a limited number of buyers, personal selling may prove a highly effective technique. However, markets characterized by large numbers of potential customers scattered over sizable geographic areas may make the cost of contact by salespeople prohibitive. In such instances, extensive use of advertising often makes sense. The type of customer also affects the promotional mix. Personal selling works better in high-priced, high-involvement purchases—for instance, a target market made up of business purchasers or wholesale buyers—than in a target market consisting of ultimate consumers. Similarly, pharmaceutical firms use large sales forces to sell prescription drugs directly to physicians and hospitals, but they also advertise to promote over-the-counter and prescription drugs for the consumer market. The drug firm must switch its promotional strategy from personal selling to consumer advertising based on the market it is targeting.

NATURE OF THE PRODUCT

The product itself is an important factor in determining promotional mix effectiveness. Highly standardized products with minimal servicing requirements usually depend less on personal selling than custom products with technically complex features or requirements for frequent maintenance.

Marketers of consumer products are more likely to rely heavily on advertising than business products. For example, soft drinks lend themselves more readily to advertising than large pieces of business machinery.

Promotional mixes vary within each product category. In the B2B market, for example, installations typically rely more heavily on personal selling than marketing of operating supplies. In contrast, the promotional mix for a convenience product is likely to involve more emphasis on manufacturer advertising and less on personal selling.

STAGE IN THE PRODUCT LIFECYCLE

The promotional mix also must be tailored to the product lifecycle as shown in Figure 16.4. In the introductory stage, both nonpersonal and personal selling are used to acquaint marketing intermediaries and final consumers with the merits of the new product. Heavy emphasis on personal selling helps inform the marketplace of the merits of the new good or service.

Salespeople contact marketing intermediaries to secure interest in and commitment to handling the newly introduced item. Trade shows are frequently used to inform and educate prospective dealers and ultimate consumers about its merits over current competitive offerings. Advertising and sales promotion are also used during this stage to create awareness, answer questions, and stimulate initial purchases.

As the product moves into the growth and maturity stages, advertising gains relative importance in persuading consumers to make purchases. Marketers continue to direct personal selling efforts at marketing intermediaries in an attempt to expand distribution. As more competitors enter the marketplace, advertising begins to stress product differences to persuade consumers to purchase the firm's brand. In the maturity and early decline stages, firms frequently reduce advertising and sales promotion expenditures as market saturation is reached and newer items with their own competitive strengths begin to enter the market.

PRICE

The price of an item is the fourth factor that affects the choice of a promotional mix. Advertising dominates the promotional mixes for low-unit-value products due to the high per-contact costs in personal selling. Advertising permits a low promotional expenditure per sales unit because it reaches mass audiences. For low-value consumer goods, such as chewing gum, soft drinks, and snack foods, advertising is the most feasible means of promotion. On the other hand, consumers of high-priced items like luxury cars expect lots of well-presented information from qualified salespeople. High-tech direct marketing promotions, such as video presentations on a tablet or smartphone, brochures, and personal selling by informed, professional salespeople, appeal to these potential customers.

FUNDS AVAILABLE FOR PROMOTION

Budget size can present a stumbling block to implementing promotional strategy. For example, the average cost of a single 30-second slot during a recent Super Bowl telecast was $4 million.[33] While millions of viewers may see the commercial, making the cost per contact relatively low, such an expenditure exceeds the entire promotional budgets of thousands of firms, a dilemma that at least partially explains how guerrilla marketing got its start. And if a company wants to hire a celebrity to promote its goods and services, the fee can run into millions of dollars a year.

Traditional methods used for creating a promotional budget include the percentage-of-sales and fixed-sum-per-unit methods, along with techniques for meeting the competition and achieving task objectives.

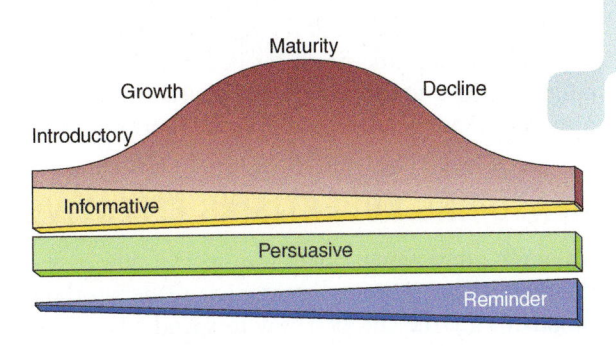

FIGURE 16.4
Advertising Objectives in Relation to Stage in the Product Lifecycle

The *percentage-of-sales method* is perhaps the most common way of establishing promotional budgets. The percentage can be based on sales either from some past period (such as the previous year) or forecasted for a future period (the current year). While this plan is appealingly simple, it does not effectively support the achievement of basic promotional objectives. Arbitrary percentage allocations can't provide needed flexibility. In addition, sales should depend on promotional allocation rather than vice versa.

The *fixed-sum-per-unit method* allocates a predetermined amount to each sales or production unit. This amount can also reflect either historical or forecasted figures. Producers of high-value consumer durable goods, such as automobiles, often use this budgeting method.

The *meeting competition method* simply matches competitors' outlays, either in absolute amounts or relative to the firm's market shares. But this method doesn't help marketers gain a competitive edge. A budget appropriate for one company may not be appropriate for another.

The *task-objective method* develops a promotional budget based on a sound evaluation of the firm's promotional objectives. The method has two steps:

1. Define realistic and quantifiable communication goals for the promotional mix (for example, "Achieve a 25 percent increase in brand awareness"). Such objectives become an integral part of the promotional plan.

2. Determine the amount and type of promotional activity required for each objective. Combined, these units become the firm's promotional budget.

A crucial assumption underlies the task-objective approach: Marketers can measure the productivity of each promotional dollar. That assumption explains why the objectives must be carefully chosen, quantified, and accomplished through promotional efforts. Generally, budgeters should avoid such general marketing objectives as "Achieve a 5 percent increase in sales." A sale is a culmination of the effects of all elements of the marketing mix. A more appropriate promotional objective might be "Achieve an 8 percent response rate from a targeted direct-mail advertisement."

EVALUATING PROMOTIONAL EFFECTIVENESS

Evaluating the effectiveness of a promotion today is a far different exercise in marketing research than it was even a decade ago. Social media and the Internet have helped marketing research to evolve. Now marketers can find information about each customer's purchase behavior, lifestyle, preferences, opinions, and buying habits in a matter of seconds.

Most marketers would prefer to use a *direct sales results test* to measure the effectiveness of promotion. Such an approach would reveal the specific impact on sales revenues for each dollar of promotional spending. This type of technique has always eluded marketers because of their inability to control other variables operating in the marketplace. A firm may receive $20 million in additional sales orders following a new $1.5 million advertising campaign, but the market success actually may have resulted from the products receiving more intensive distribution, as more stores decide to carry them, or price increases for competing products rather.

Marketers often encounter difficulty isolating the effects of promotion from those of other market elements and outside environmental variables. *Indirect evaluation* helps researchers concentrate on quantifiable indicators of effectiveness, such as recall and readership. The basic problem with indirect measurement is the difficulty in relating these variables to sales.

Marketers need to ask the right questions and understand what they are measuring. Promotion to build sales volume produces measurable results in the form of short-term returns, but brand-building efforts to generate or enhance consumers' perceptions of value in a product, brand, or organization cannot be measured over the short term.

MEASURING ADVERTISING EFFECTIVENESS

Although promotional prices vary widely, advertisers typically pay a fee based on the cost to deliver the message to viewers, listeners, or readers—the so-called *cost per thousand impressions (CPM)*. Billboards are the cheapest way to spend advertising dollars, with television and some newspapers the most expensive. While price is an important factor in media selection, it is by no means the only one—or all ads would appear on billboards.

Because promotion represents such a major expenditure for many firms, they need to determine whether their campaigns accomplish appropriate promotional objectives. Companies want their advertising agencies and in-house marketers to demonstrate how promotional programs contribute to increased sales and profits. Marketers are well aware of the number of advertising messages and sales promotions consumers encounter daily, and they know these people practice selective perception and simply screen out many messages.

By measuring promotional effectiveness, organizations can evaluate different strategies, prevent mistakes before spending money on specific programs, and improve their promotional programs. As the earlier discussion of promotional planning explained, any evaluation program starts with objectives and goals; otherwise, marketers have no yardstick against which to measure effectiveness. Determining whether an advertising message has achieved its intended objective is one of the most difficult undertakings in marketing. Sales promotions and direct marketing are somewhat easier to evaluate, because they evoke measurable consumer responses. Like advertising, public relations is also difficult to assess on purely objective terms.

MEDIA AND MESSAGE RESEARCH

Measures to evaluate the effectiveness of advertising, although difficult and costly, are essential parts of any marketing plan. Without an assessment strategy, marketers will not know whether their advertising achieves the objectives of the marketing plan or whether the dollars in the advertising budget are well spent. To answer these questions, marketers can conduct two types of research. **Media research** assesses how well a particular medium delivers the advertiser's message, where and when to place the advertisement, and the size of the audience. Buyers of broadcast time base their purchases on estimated Nielsen rating points, and the networks have to make good if ratings do not reach promised levels. Buyers of print advertising space pay fees based on circulation. Circulation figures are independently certified by specialized research firms.

The other major category, **message research**, tests consumer reactions to an advertisement's creative message. Pretesting and posttesting, the two methods for performing message research, are discussed in the following sections.

As the role of marketing expands in many organizations, marketers are employing increasingly sophisticated techniques to measure marketing effectiveness not only throughout the company but through the entire marketing channel. As more firms conduct multichannel promotional efforts, keeping track of the data continues to be a challenge.

Pretesting

To assess an advertisement's likely effectiveness before it actually appears in the chosen medium, marketers often conduct **pretesting**. The obvious advantage of this technique is the opportunity to evaluate ads when they are being developed. Marketers can conduct a number of different pretests, beginning during the concept phase in the campaign's earliest stages, when they have only rough copy of the ad, and continuing until the ad layout and design are almost completed.

Pretesting uses several evaluation methods. For example, focus groups can discuss their reactions to mock-ups of ads. To screen potential radio and television advertisements, marketers often recruit consumers to sit in a studio and indicate their preferences by pressing two buttons, one for a positive reaction to the commercial and the other for a negative reaction. Sometimes proposed ad copy is printed on a postcard that also offers a free product; the number of cards returned represents an indication of the copy's effectiveness. In a *blind product test*, people are asked to select unidentified products on the basis of available advertising copy.

Mechanical and electronic devices offer yet another method of assessing how people read advertising copy. One mechanical test uses a hidden camera to photograph eye movements of readers. The results help advertisers determine headline placement and copy length. Another mechanical approach measures the galvanic skin response—changes in the electrical resistance of the skin produced by emotional reactions.

media research Advertising research that assesses how well a particular medium delivers an advertiser's message, where and when to place the advertisement, and the size of the audience.

message research Advertising research that tests consumer reactions to an advertisement's creative message.

pretesting Research that evaluates an ad during its development stage.

Posttesting

posttesting Research that assesses advertising effectiveness after it has appeared in a print or broadcast medium.

Posttesting assesses advertising copy after it has appeared in the appropriate medium. Pretesting generally is a more desirable measurement method than posttesting because it can save the cost of placing ineffective ads. However, posttesting can help in planning future advertisements and adjusting current advertising programs.

In one of the most popular posttests, the *Starch Readership Report* interviews people who have read selected magazines to determine whether they observed various ads in them. A copy of the magazine is used as an interviewing aid, and each interviewer starts at a different point in the magazine. For larger ads, respondents are also asked about specifics, such as headlines and copy. All such *readership tests,* also called recognition tests, assume that future sales are related to advertising readership.

Unaided recall tests are another method of posttesting the effectiveness of advertisements. Respondents do not see copies of the magazine after their initial reading but are asked to recall the ads from memory. Podcasts are a popular medium for advertisers because posttests reveal that unaided recall among respondents is high. *Inquiry tests* are another popular form of posttest. Advertisements sometimes offer gifts—generally product samples—to people who respond to them. The number of inquiries relative to the advertisement's cost forms a measure of its effectiveness.

split runs Methods of testing alternate ads by dividing a cable TV audience or a publication's subscribers in two, using two different ads, and then evaluating the relative effectiveness of each.

Split runs allow advertisers to test two or more ads at the same time. Although advertisers traditionally place different versions in newspapers and magazines, split runs on cable television systems frequently test the effectiveness of TV ads. With this method, advertisers divide the cable TV audience or a publication's subscribers in two; half view advertisement A and the other half view advertisement B. The relative effectiveness of the alternatives is then determined through inquiries or recall and recognition tests.

MEASURING PUBLIC RELATIONS EFFECTIVENESS

Organizations must measure PR results based on their objectives both for the PR program as a whole and for specific activities. In the next step, marketers must decide what they want to measure. This choice includes determining whether the message was heard by the target audience and whether it had the desired influence on public opinion.

The simplest and least costly level of assessment measures outputs of the PR program: whether the target audience received, paid attention to, understood, and retained the messages directed to them. To make this judgment, the staff could count the number of media placements and gauge the extent of media coverage. They could count attendees at any press conference, evaluate the quality of brochures and other materials, and pursue similar activities. Formal techniques include tracking publicity placements, analyzing how favorably their contents portrayed the company, and conducting public-opinion polls.

To analyze PR effectiveness more deeply, firms conduct focus groups, interviews with opinion leaders, and more detailed and extensive opinion polls. The highest level of effectiveness measurement looks at outcomes: Did the program change people's opinions, attitudes, and behavior? PR professionals measure outcomes through before-and-after polls and more advanced techniques, such as psychographic analysis (discussed in Chapter 9).

EVALUATING INTERACTIVE MEDIA

Marketers have used various methods to measure the effectiveness of Web communication: *hits* (user requests for information), *impressions* (the number of times a viewer sees an ad), and *click-throughs* (when the user clicks the ad to get more information). *View-through* rates measure responses over time. However, all of these measures can be misleading: It takes more than "eyeballs" to measure the effectiveness of online media. What matters is not how many times a website is visited but how well the communication elicits the desired behavior.

Traditional numbers that work for other media forms are not necessarily relevant indicators of effectiveness for a website. For one thing, the Web combines both advertising and direct marketing. Web pages effectively integrate advertising and other content, such as demonstrations, coupons, product information, and interactive features, which may often prove to be the page's main—and most effective—feature. For another consideration, consumers generally choose the advertisements they want to see on the Internet, whereas traditional broadcast or print media automatically expose consumers to ads.

Two major techniques for setting Internet advertising rates are cost per impression and cost per response. *Cost per impression* is a measurement technique that relates the cost of an ad to every thousand people who view it. In other words, anyone who sees the page containing the banner or other form of ad creates one impression. This measure assumes the site's primary purpose is to display the advertising message. *Cost per response* (or *click-throughs*) is a direct marketing technique that relates the cost of an ad to the number of people who click it. However, not everyone who clicks on an ad makes a purchase. So marketers may use a third technique: Measuring the *conversion rate*—the percentage of website visitors who actually make a purchase. All three rating techniques have merit. Site publishers point out that click-through rates are influenced by the creativity of the ad's message. Advertisers, on the other hand, point out that the Web ad has value to those who click it for additional information.

Internet marketers price ad banners based on CPM. Websites that sell advertising typically guarantee a certain number of impressions—the number of times an ad banner is downloaded and presumably seen by visitors. Marketers then set a rate based on that guarantee times the CPM rate.

Marketers can measure performance by incorporating some form of direct response into their promotions. This technique also helps them compare different promotions for effectiveness and rely on facts rather than opinions.

ASSESSMENT CHECK

9.1 What five factors affect the choice of a promotional mix?

9.2 Why is the choice of a mix a difficult task for marketers?

9.3 What is the most common way of establishing a promotional budget?

9.4 What is the direct sales results test? Why is it difficult to administer?

Strategic Implications of Marketing in the 21st Century

With the incredible proliferation of promotional messages in the media, today's marketers—consumers themselves—must find new ways to reach customers without overloading them with unnecessary or unwanted communications. Integrating marketing communications into an overall consumer-focused strategy has become more and more critical in a busy global marketplace.

It is difficult to overstate the impact of the Internet and social media on the promotional mix of 21st century marketers. As greater portions of corporate ad budgets continue to migrate to the Web, marketers must be increasingly aware of the benefits and pitfalls of Internet advertising. They should not forget the benefits of other types of advertising as well.

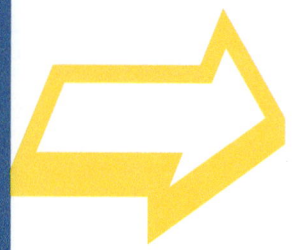

REVIEW OF CHAPTER OBJECTIVES

1 Define integrated marketing communications and explain how it relates to the development of an optimal promotional mix.

Integrated marketing communications (IMC) refers to the coordination of all promotional activities to produce a unified, customer-focused promotional message. Developing an optimal promotional mix involves selecting the personal and nonpersonal selling strategies that will work best to deliver the overall marketing message as defined by IMC.

2 Describe the communication process and how it relates to the AIDA concept.

In the communication process, a message is encoded and transmitted through a communications channel; then it is decoded, or interpreted by the receiver; finally, the receiver provides feedback, which completes the system. The AIDA concept (attention, interest, desire, action) explains the steps through which a person reaches a purchase decision after being exposed to a promotional message. The marketer sends the promotional message, and the consumer receives and responds to it via the communication process.

3 Identify the seven components of the promotional mix.

The components of the promotional mix include personal selling and nonpersonal selling (advertising, product placement, sales promotion, direct marketing, public relations, and guerilla marketing). Guerrilla marketing is frequently used by marketers with limited funds and firms attempting to attract attention for new-product offerings with innovative promotional approaches. Sponsorship occurs when an organization pays money or in-kind resources to an event or activity in exchange for a direct association with it.

4 Name the three basic advertising objectives and the two basic categories of advertising.

The three basic objectives of advertising are to inform, persuade, and remind. The two major categories of advertising are product advertising and institutional advertising. Product advertising involves the nonpersonal selling of a good or service. Institutional advertising is the nonpersonal promotion of a concept, idea, or philosophy of a company or organization.

5 Identify the four major advertising strategies.

The major strategies are comparative advertising, which makes extensive use of messages with direct comparisons between competing brands; celebrity, which uses famous spokespeople to boost an advertising message; retail, which includes all advertising by retail stores selling products directly to consumers; and interactive, which encourages two-way communication via the Internet, social media sites, or kiosks.

An advertisement evolves from pinpointing goals, such as educating consumers, enhancing brand loyalty, or improving a product's image. From those goals, marketers move to the next stages: creating a plan, developing a message, developing and preparing the ad, and selecting the appropriate medium (or media).

6 Describe the various types of advertising appeals and their uses.

Advertisements often appeal to consumers' emotions. These appeals such as fear, humor, or sex, can be effective. Marketers need to recognize that fear appeals can backfire; people's sense of humor can differ according to sex, age, and other factors; and use of sexual imagery must not overstep the bounds of taste.

Chapter 16 Integrated Marketing Communications, Advertising, and Public Relations   547

7 Compare the seven different advertising media.

The major media include broadcast (TV and radio), newspapers and magazines, direct mail, outdoor, and interactive. Each medium has benefits and drawbacks. Newspapers are flexible and dominate local markets. Magazines can target niche markets. Interactive media fosters two-way communication. Outdoor advertising in a high-traffic location reaches many people every day; television and radio reach even more. Direct mail allows effective segmentation. Once advertisers select the media that best matches their advertising objectives and promotional budgets, their attention shifts to setting the time and sequence for a series of ads.

8 Explain the roles of public relations, publicity, and cross-promotion in an organization's promotional strategy.

Public relations consists of the firm's communications and relationships with its various publics, including customers, employees, stockholders, suppliers, government, and the society in which it operates. Publicity is the dissemination of newsworthy information about a product or organization. This information activity is frequently used in new-product introductions. Cross-promotion, illustrated by tie-ins between popular movies and fast-food restaurants, permits marketing partners to share the cost of a promotional campaign that meets their mutual needs. Marketers should be careful to construct ethically sound promotional campaigns, avoiding such practices as puffery and deceit. In addition, negative publicity may occur as a result of some action a firm takes—or fails to take—such as a product recall.

9 Discuss the five factors that influence the effectiveness of a promotional mix and how marketers measure effectiveness.

Marketers face the challenge of determining the best mix of components for an overall promotional strategy. Several factors influence the effectiveness of the promotional mix: (1) the nature of the market, (2) the nature of the product, (3) the stage in the product lifecycle, (4) price, and (5) the funds available for promotion.

Marketers may choose among several methods for determining promotional budgets, including percentage-of-sales, fixed-sum-per-unit, meeting competition, or task-objective, which is considered the most flexible and most effective. Today, marketers use either direct sales results tests or indirect evaluation to measure effectiveness. Both methods have their benefits and drawbacks because of the difficulty of controlling variables.

The effectiveness of advertising can be measured by pretesting and posttesting. Pretesting assesses an ad's effectiveness before it is actually used. Posttesting assesses an ad's effectiveness after it has been used. Commonly used posttests include readership tests, unaided recall tests, inquiry tests, and split runs.

ASSESSMENT CHECK: ANSWERS

1.1 **Define promotion.** Promotion is the function of informing, persuading, and influencing the consumer's purchase decision.

1.2 **What is the difference between marketing communications and integrated marketing communications (IMC)?** Marketing communications are messages that deal with buyer–seller relationships from a variety of media. IMC coordinates all promotional activities to produce a unified, customer-focused promotional message.

2.1 **Identify the four steps of the AIDA concept.** The four steps of the AIDA concept are attention, interest, desire, and action.

2.2 **What is noise as it relates to the communication process?** Noise represents interference at some stage in the communication process.

3.1 **Differentiate between personal and nonpersonal selling.** Personal selling is promotion conducted person-to-person between a seller and a buyer. It may take place face-to-face, over the telephone, through videoconferencing, or by computer links between buyer and seller. Nonpersonal selling is promotion conducted without being face-to-face with the buyer.

3.2 **What are the six major categories of nonpersonal selling?** The six categories of nonpersonal selling are advertising, product placement, sales promotion, direct marketing, public relations, and guerrilla marketing.

3.3 **How is sponsorship different from advertising?** Although sponsorship generates brand awareness, the sponsor has little control over the message or even the coverage, unlike advertising.

4.1 **What are the goals of institutional advertising?** Institutional advertising promotes a concept, an idea, a philosophy, or the goodwill of an industry, company, organization, person, geographic location, or government agency.

4.2 **At what stage in the product lifecycle are informative ads used?** Informative ads are common in the introductory stage of the product lifecycle.

5.1 What is comparative advertising? Comparative advertising makes extensive use of messages with direct comparisons between competing brands.

5.2 What makes a successful celebrity testimonial? Successful celebrity ads feature figures who are credible sources of information for the item being promoted.

5.3 What is an advertising campaign? An advertising campaign is a series of different but related ads that use a single theme and appear in different media within a specified time period.

5.4 What are an advertisement's three main goals? Advertising's three main goals are to educate consumers about product features, enhance brand loyalty, and improve consumer perception of the brand.

6.1 What are some common emotional appeals used in advertising? Advertisers often focus on making emotional appeals to fear, humor, or sex.

6.2 What are the main types of interactive ads? Interactive ads include Internet banners, pop-ups, keyword ads, advertorials, advergames, and interstitials.

7.1 What types of products are banned from advertising on television? Tobacco goods like cigarettes are banned from television advertising.

7.2 What are some advantages radio offers to advertisers? What about newspapers? Radio ads allow marketers to target a captive audience and offer low cost, flexibility, and mobility. Newspaper ads are flexible and provide nearly complete coverage of the market. Readers can also refer back to newspaper ads.

7.3 Define media scheduling, and identify the most important factors influencing the scheduling decision. Media scheduling sets the timing and sequence for a series of advertisements. Sales patterns, repurchase cycles, and competitors' activities are the most important variables in the scheduling decision.

8.1 What is the role of the PR department in an organization? The PR department is the link between the firm and the media. It provides press releases and holds news conferences to announce new products, the formation of strategic alliances, management changes, or similar developments. The PR department may also issue its own publications, including newsletters, brochures, and reports.

8.2 What is publicity? Publicity is nonpersonal stimulation of demand for a good, service, place, idea, person, or organization by unpaid placement of significant news regarding the subject in a print or broadcast medium.

8.3 What are the advantages of cross-promotion? Cross-promotion divides the cost of a promotional campaign that meets the mutual needs of marketing partners and provides greater benefits for both in return.

9.1 What five factors affect the choice of a promotional mix? The five factors are (1) nature of the market, (2) nature of the product, (3) stage in the product lifecycle, (4) price, and (5) funds available for promotion.

9.2 Why is the choice of a mix a difficult task for marketers? Developing an effective promotional mix is difficult, because marketers lack quantitative measures to determine the effectiveness of each component of a promotional mix in a given market segment.

9.3 What is the most common way of establishing a promotional budget? The most common method of establishing a promotional budget is the percentage-of-sales method.

9.4 What is the direct sales results test? Why is it difficult to administer? The direct sales results test reveals the specific impact on sales revenues for each dollar of promotional spending. Administering this test is difficult because marketers cannot control other variables operating in the marketplace.

MARKETING TERMS YOU NEED TO KNOW

promotion 516
marketing communications 516
integrated marketing communications (IMC) 516
sender 521
message 521
AIDA concept 521
promotional mix 522

personal selling 522
nonpersonal selling 522
advertising 522
product placement 523
sales promotion 523
trade promotion 523
direct marketing 523
public relations 523
guerrilla marketing 524

sponsorship 525
product advertising 526
institutional advertising 526
informative advertising 526
persuasive advertising 526
reminder advertising 526
comparative advertising 527
retail advertising 528
cooperative advertising 528

interactive advertising 529
advertising campaign 530
media scheduling 537
cross-promotion 538
media research 543
message research 543
pretesting 543
posttesting 544
split runs 544

ASSURANCE OF LEARNING REVIEW

1. What is the role of integrated marketing communications (IMC) in a firm's overall marketing strategy? When executed well, what are its benefits?
2. Differentiate between advertising and product placement. Which do you think is more effective, and why?
3. Why is sponsorship such an important part of a firm's IMC?
4. For each of the following goods and services, indicate which direct marketing channel or channels you think would be best:
   a. Kansas City Royals tickets
   b. athletic apparel
   c. custom-made earrings
   d. lawn-care service
   e. museum membership
5. How does the nature of the market for a firm's goods or services affect the choice of a promotion method?
6. What are the three primary objectives of advertising? Give an example of when each one might be used.
7. Identify the different types of emotional appeals in advertising. What are the benefits and pitfalls of each?
8. Compare and contrast interactive ads and traditional ads.
9. Identify and describe the different advertising media. Which are on the rise? Which are facing possible decline?
10. Describe how marketers assess promotional effectiveness.

PROJECTS AND TEAMWORK EXERCISES

1. On your own or with a classmate, select a print advertisement that catches your attention and analyze it according to the AIDA concept (attention, interest, desire, action). Identify features of the ad that catch your attention, pique your interest, make you desire the product, and spur you toward a purchase. Present your findings to the class.
2. Watch a television show and see how many products you can find placed within the show. Present your findings to the class.
3. With a classmate, choose a good or service you think could benefit from guerrilla marketing. Imagine you have a limited promotional budget, and come up with a plan for a guerrilla approach. Outline several ideas, and explain how you plan to carry them out. Present your plan to the class.
4. Cut out a print ad and place it on a poster board. With a marker, identify all the elements of the ad. Then identify what you believe is the ad's objective. Next, identify the strategy used. If the ad has an interactive component, note that as well.

CRITICAL-THINKING EXERCISES

1. What are some benefits and drawbacks of using celebrity testimonials in advertising? Identify an ad that uses a celebrity's endorsement effectively, and explain why.
2. Identify a corporate sponsorship for a cause or event in your area, or find a local company that sponsors a local charity or other organization. What does the sponsor gain from its actions? Be specific. What does the sponsored organization receive? Is this sponsorship good for your community? Explain.
3. Select two different advertisers' TV or print ads for the same product category (cars or soft drinks, for instance) and decide what emotion each appeals to. Which ad is more effective, and why?
4. Think back to publicity you have heard recently about a company or its products. If it was good publicity, how was it generated, and what media were used? If it was bad publicity, where did you learn about it, and how did the firm try to control or neutralize it?

ETHICS EXERCISE

Pop-up ads, those unsolicited messages that sometimes pop onto your computer screen and block the site or information you're looking for until you close or respond to them, are inexpensive to produce and cost nearly nothing to send. They are so annoying to some computer users that dozens of special programs have been written to block them from appearing on the screen during Internet use.

1. Do you think that, because they are unsolicited, pop-up ads are also disruptive? Are they an invasion of privacy? Explain your reasoning.
2. Do you consider the use of pop-up ads to be unethical? Why or why not?

INTERNET EXERCISES

1. **Super Bowl advertising.** Visit the websites listed here. How many different organizations ran ads during the most recent Super Bowl? Which organizations have run the most ads in Super Bowls? During the most recent Super Bowl, which ads were the highest rated? The lowest rated? How much has the cost of a 30-second Super Bowl ad changed since the first game was played?

   www.superbowl-commericials.org

   http://viralvideochart.unrulymedia.com/chart_keyword/Super_Bowl_2014?interval=week

2. **Not-for-profit advertising.** Review the material in the chapter on creating an advertisement and then go to the website listed here. It outlines the basic steps involved in creating an advertisement for a not-for-profit organization. Review the material and prepare a brief report comparing and contrasting the process of creating an advertisement for a for-profit and a not-for-profit organization.

   http://marketing.about.com/cs/nonprofitmrktg/a/8stepnonprofit.htm

3. **Public relations.** Visit the websites of at least three large, multinational corporations. Examples include Siemens, DuPont, and ExxonMobil. Review the material on the websites and prepare a brief report outlining how each firm includes public relations as part of its promotional strategy.

   www.siemens.com

   www.dupont.com

   www.exxonmobil.com

Note: Internet Web addresses change frequently. If you don't find the exact site listed, you may need to access the organization's home page and search from there or use a search engine such as Google or Bing.

CASE 16.1
The Richards Group: A Unique Advertising Group

The popular image of an advertising agency is of a vibrantly creative place without much corporate structure, where copywriters, artists, and executives enjoy free rein, an anything-goes culture, and freedom to come and go at will. That picture usually doesn't include a list of rules employees must follow, such as punching a time clock, logging work time in precise 15-minute intervals, paying a fine for tardiness, getting closed out of meetings if late, and going home at precisely 6 P.M. But those are some of the strictly enforced practices at The Richards Group, a successful independent Dallas agency in business for more than three decades and recently named one of Advertising Age's Best Places to Work.

If the rules sound repressive, Stan Richards, the company's 80+ year-old founder, admits they aren't for everybody. One of his former writers says, "The genius of the place is completely counterintuitive." But that genius has produced a steady stream of memorable campaigns for clients such as Chick-fil-A, Motel 6, and Corona beer, and it has kept more than 30 creative group heads on board with Richards for an average tenure of 17 years.

Life at the agency isn't all about the rules, either. Richards learned early in his advertising design education at New York's Pratt Institute that creativity comes from any source, but that expressing it requires meticulous hard work and limited shortcuts. Since founding the agency, Richards has relaxed a few rules, such as the dress code, and he no longer personally approves every piece of work. But he still encourages face time with colleagues and clients instead of emails. And there are perks—though fancy titles are not among them. In fact, there are no titles. Instead, every employee is expected to be "a leader in every situation." Those who have the longest tenure get the best parking spots and the desks nearest the windows, but any of Richards' 670 employees can take the company's private plane to client meetings. And after 20 years with the company, they can use the plane to take their families on a free trip anywhere in the world, even as far away as the Galapagos Islands.

QUESTIONS FOR CRITICAL THINKING

1. Stan Richards believes that "the way you treat your people is exactly how they treat clients." Do you agree or disagree? Explain your reasoning.

2. Evaluate Richards' belief that creativity requires hard work. Do you think this is true? Does it apply only to marketing and advertising? Why or why not?

Sources: Company website, www.richards.com, accessed June 3, 2014; Burt Helm, "Stan Richards's Unique Management Style," *Inc.*, accessed June 3, 2014, www.inc.com; "Richards Group Is No. 37 on *Ad Age's* Best Places to Work List," *Advertising Age*, accessed June 3, 2014, http://adage.com; "Pete Lerman, Minority Business Leader Awards," *Dallas Business Journal*, accessed June 3, 2014, www.bizjournals.com.

VIDEO CASE 16.2
Pepe's Pizzeria Delivers Every Day

If you're a pizza lover, you'd say that a sizzling hot, fresh pizza sells itself. If you happen to live in southern New England—and be a pizza lover—you'd probably say that everyone knows about Pepe's Pizzeria But Ken Berry, CEO of Pepe's, understands the importance of spreading the word about his company's pizza, even though it's practically got a cult following. Founded by Frank Pepe in New Haven, Connecticut, pizzeria employees still hand-toss every single pizza. "Our pizza really has a heritage," observes Berry. "It goes back 87 years, virtually unchanged during those 87 years." He notes that the company has added refrigerators and air-conditioning, but that's about all. When diners visit the restaurant, they enjoy the sights, sounds, smells, and flavors of this heritage. "It's a way for people to step back in time," Berry says. The pizza dough is still made fresh daily, and the ingredients come from many of the same sources they did decades ago.

Pepe's has built a loyal following through the years. "People have adopted Pepe's as their own through generations," notes Berry. This word-of-mouth advertising is impossible to buy or replicate, and it helps strengthen the brand. It also represents a challenge, in that these loyal customers arrive at the restaurant with high expectations. If they bring friends or family, they expect those guests to be served a top-notch meal, much as if they were entertaining in their own home. "If you don't deliver on your promise, they'll let you know right away," warns Berry.

When Pepe's co-owners decided to expand from its initial location several years ago, their strategy included replicating every aspect of the Pepe's dining experience—right down to the furniture and uniforms of the wait staff. They wanted customers to walk into the new location in Fairfield, Connecticut, and feel right at home. They didn't anticipate a backlash—a small core of regular New Haven customers who objected to the expansion of their beloved Pepe's. These customers staged a protest outside the new restaurant as it opened to the public. But publicity surrounding the opening of a new Pepe's swelled beyond the protestors—and 200 people showed up to wait in line for their own piece of Pepe's pie. If anything, the buzz surrounding the protest likely attracted more customers to the new location.

Pepe's approach to advertising is pretty straightforward. The pizza sells itself—one bite, and pizza lovers are hooked. So the main objective is to make consumers aware of the restaurant, which now has several locations in the tri-state area surrounding New York City. As the Fairfield restaurant neared its opening date, Pepe's alerted current customers with a simple message printed on top of each pizza box (coincidentally, many of Pepe's regular New Haven diners actually lived in Fairfield). The company also published press releases and advertised the grand opening of the new restaurant. Billboards along the interstate highway proved to be effective with travelers, as did some direct-mail efforts. Pepe's recently ventured into social media with a Facebook page and Twitter account, which Berry refers to as "the new word of mouth." Pepe's posts photos, blurbs about menu items, and relives a few proud moments on Facebook. Customers comment about their favorite pizza flavors (such as spinach and gorgonzola), and share experiences (like driving 50 miles each way for a Pepe's pizza). Berry notes that Pepe's presence in social media keeps the relationships with customers going.

Educating consumers about Pepe's is the second advertising objective. With such a tasty product, what better way to attract new customers than to let them discover that the proof really is in the pie? Now when Pepe's launches a new restaurant, they give away free pizza for about a week before the grand opening. That's right: free pizza, for a week. Ken Berry explains that this promotion serves three purposes: It trains the new employees, tests the new ovens, and introduces Pepe's pizza to new customers. The giveaway generates plenty of good buzz about Pepe's pizzas and makes an important statement to the public: Pepe's is so confident about the quality of its food that they're willing to give it away for a week—certain that consumers will become regular customers.

Pepe's also enjoys positive public relations surrounding its charitable giving. The company website has a tab allowing customers to request donations for their particular charities, and the restaurant conducts regular "Good Neighbors Nights," from which it donates 15 percent of its proceeds to a designated not-for-profit group. All of these efforts roll together into cohesive marketing communications with one major goal. "Our challenge is to build our brand and protect it," says Berry, "and to make sure we deliver every day."

QUESTIONS FOR CRITICAL THINKING

1. Describe how the Pepe's pizza giveaway promotion relates to each step in the AIDA concept.
2. How might Pepe's use guerilla marketing to promote its brand among college students?

Sources: Company website, www.pepespizzeria.com, accessed April 2, 2014; company Facebook page, www.facebook.com/pepesnewhaven, accessed April 2, 2014; company Twitter page, https://twitter.com/pepespizzeria, accessed April 2, 2014.

NOTES

1. Company website, www.starbucks.com, accessed October 23, 2014; Soo Jin Oh, "From Coffee to Mobile King: How Starbucks Serves Up Its Mobile Strategy," *Marketing Land*, accessed October 23, 2014, http://marketingland.com; Joseph Ruiz, "Starbucks Brand; Starbucks Brand Identity, Personality & Experience," *Social Media Today*, accessed April 2, 2014, www.socialmediatoday.com; Adam Chandler, "NBC Smuggled an Entire Starbucks into Sochi," *The Wire*, accessed April 2, 2014, www.thewire.com; Bryan Gruley and Leslie Patton, "To Stop the Coffee Apocalypse, Starbucks Buys a Farm," *Bloomberg Businessweek*, accessed April 2, 2014, www.businessweek.com; "Starbucks Hits $1B in Mobile Payment Revenues in 2013, Analysis Says," *Computerworld*, accessed April 2, 2014, www.computerworld.com; Maggie McGrath, "New Store Openings Push Starbucks Revenue Up 13%," *Forbes*, accessed April 2, 2014, www.forbes.com.
2. Ana Livia Coelho, "ESPN's X Games Announces Sponsors for X Games Aspen 2014," press release, *ESPN Media Zone*, accessed April 2, 2014, http://espnmediazone.com.
3. Laurel Wentz, "Super What? World Cup Sponsors Spending $600M on Brazil Network," *Advertising Age*, accessed October 23, 2014, http://adage.com.
4. Gerhard Gschwandtner, "How Many Salespeople Will Be Left by 2020?" *Selling Power*, accessed October 23, 2014, www.sellingpower.com; Paul Davidson, "Bosses Lament: Sales Jobs Hard to Fill," *USA Today*, accessed March 19, 2014, www.usatoday.com.
5. Total US Ad Spending to See Largest Increase Since 2004," *eMarketer*, accessed October 23, 2014, www.emarketer.com.
6. Brad Slager, "'Lego Movie's' Success Portends New Product Placement Possibilities," *Breitbart.com*, accessed March 22, 2014, www.breitbart.com.
7. "Case Study: Real Beauty Shines Through: Dove Wins Titanium Grand Prix, 163 Million Views on YouTube," *Think* newsletter, accessed October 23, 2014, www.thinkwithgoogle.com; "How Dove's 'Real Beauty Sketches' Becomes the Most Viral Video Ad of All Time," *Business Insider*, accessed March 19, 2014, www.businessinsider.com.
8. Steve Annear, "For $1 Million, Your Company Can Name an MBTA Station," *Boston Magazine*, accessed March 19, 2014, www.bostonmagazine.com.
9. "Kantar Media Reports U.S. Advertising Expenditures Declined in Q3 2013, Due to Comparison against High Olympics, Election Year Spend in 2012," press release, *Kantar Media*, accessed March 22, 2014, http://kantarmedia.us.
10. "Kantar Media Reports U.S. Advertising Expenditures Declined in Q3 2013, Due to Comparison against High Olympics, Election Year Spend in 2012," press release, *Kantar Media*, accessed March 22, 2014, http://kantarmedia.us.
11. Graham Flanagan, "The Truth About 'The Most Interesting Man in the World,'" *Business Insider*, accessed March 27, 2014, www.businessinsider.com; Michael Lowenstein, "The Most Interesting Beer (Consumer) in the World: How Dos Equis Built Its Powerhouse Brand," *Customer Think*, accessed March 27, 2014, http://customerthink.com; E. J. Schultz, "How This Man Made Dos Equis a Most Interesting Marketing Story," *Advertising Age*, accessed March 27, 2014, www.adage.com.
12. Gillian Mohney, "Turf-Grass War Heats Up Airwaves," *ABC News*, accessed March 19, 2014, http://abcnews.go.com.
13. Ben Leibowitz, "LeBron James, Kobe Bryant Top Forbes' List of 2013 NBA Endorsement Deal Earners," *Bleacher Report*, accessed March 27, 2014, http://bleacherreport.com; Sean Highkin, "Magic Johnson Thinks LeBron Doesn't Have Enough Endorsements," *USA Today*, accessed March 27, 2014, www.usatoday.com.
14. Ira Boudway, "Does a $5 Footlong Make You Think of the Olympics?" *Bloomberg Businessweek*, accessed April 3, 2014, www.businessweek.com.
15. Company website, www.geico.com, accessed March 19, 2014.
16. Aaron Perlut, "Allstate Bringing Mayhem to Twitter," *Forbes*, accessed March 19, 2014, www.forbes.com.
17. Roger Riddell, "Coke Partners with Sony for PlayStation All-Stars Mobile Advergame," *Food Dive*, accessed March 19, 2014, www.fooddive.com.
18. Justin Freid, "Social Advertising Revenues Forecast to Grow 31% in 2014," *Search Engine Watch*, accessed March 25, 2014, http://searchenginewatch.com.
19. "US Total Media Ad Spend Inches Up, Pushed by Digital," *eMarketer*, accessed March 23, 2014, www.emarketer.com.
20. Brian Stelter, "A DVR Ad Eraser Causes Tremors at TV Upfronts," *The New York Times*, accessed April 2, 2014, http://www.nytimes.com.

21. Marissa McNaughton, "Orabrush for Dogs: Orapup's Viral Video Gets 4 Million Views,' *The Realtime Report*, accessed March 29, 2014, http://therealtimereport.com.
22. "Music Listeners Pump Up the Volume on Digital Radio," *eMarketer*, accessed October 23, 2014, www.emarketer.com.
23. "US Total Media Ad Spend Inches Up, Pushed by Digital," *eMarketer*, accessed March 22, 2014, www.emarketer.com.
24. Jim Conaghan, "Newspaper Digital Audience Hits New Peak," Newspaper Association of America, accessed October 23, 2014, www.naa.org.
25. Neal Lulofs, "Top 25 U.S. Consumer Magazines for June 2014," Alliance for Audited Media, accessed October 23, 2014, www.auditedmedia.com.
26. Ginger Conlon, "Outlook 2014: Marketing Spending to Rise," *Direct Marketing News*, accessed October 23, 2014, www.dmnews.com.
27. Association website, www.oaaa.org accessed October 23, 2014.
28. Association website, www.oaaa.org, accessed October 23, 2014; Larry Copeland, "Cities Snipe over Super-Bright Digital Billboards," *USA Today*, accessed March 27, 2014, www.usatoday.com.
29. Seth Rosenblatt, "Google Demolishes Financial Expectations to Close 2013," *CNET*, accessed March 27, 2014, http://news.cnet.com.
30. Mark Hoelzel, "Mobile Video Advertising Is Taking Off, As Ad Buyers Pile Billions of Dollars into Small-Screen Ads," *Business Insider*, accessed October 23, 2014, www.businessinsider.com.
31. Katherine Rosman, "Augmented Reality Finally Starts to Gain Traction," *The Wall Street Journal*, accessed March 31, 2014, http://online.wsj.com.
32. Bureau of Labor Statistics, "Public Relations and Fundraising Managers" and "Public Relations Specialists," *Occupational Outlook Handbook: 2014–2015*, accessed March 31, 2014, www.bls.gov.
33. Paul Farhi, "The Rules of the Super Bowl Ad Game," *Washington Post*, accessed March 31, 2014, www.washingtonpost.com.

Chapter 17

Personal Selling and Sales Promotion

1. Describe the role of today's salesperson.
2. Describe the four sales channels.
3. Explain the three major trends in personal selling.
4. Discuss the three basic sales tasks.
5. Outline the seven steps in the sales process.
6. Identify the seven functions of a sales manager.
7. Explain the role of ethical behavior in personal selling.
8. Describe the role of sales promotion in the promotional mix and the different types of sales promotions.

SALESFORCE.COM EXPANDS ITS MARKETING CLOUD

One of the most influential recent trends in marketing is the use of social media such as Facebook, Twitter, LinkedIn, and Google+ to reach customers, develop relationships with them, and shape their brand preferences and buying habits. Many companies need help today integrating all those social and mobile platforms with their own customer relationship management (CRM) systems, so they know, for instance, what Facebook users are saying about their goods and services and can quickly react. That's where Salesforce.com comes in. More than 150,000 companies already rely on this cloud-computing pioneer to help them tap into social media in an effective and efficient way that yields useful information.

21. Marissa McNaughton, "Orabrush for Dogs: Orapup's Viral Video Gets 4 Million Views,' *The Realtime Report*, accessed March 29, 2014, http://therealtimereport.com.
22. "Music Listeners Pump Up the Volume on Digital Radio," *eMarketer*, accessed October 23, 2014, www.emarketer.com.
23. "US Total Media Ad Spend Inches Up, Pushed by Digital," *eMarketer*, accessed March 22, 2014, www.emarketer.com.
24. Jim Conaghan, "Newspaper Digital Audience Hits New Peak," Newspaper Association of America, accessed October 23, 2014, www.naa.org.
25. Neal Lulofs, "Top 25 U.S. Consumer Magazines for June 2014," Alliance for Audited Media, accessed October 23, 2014, www.auditedmedia.com.
26. Ginger Conlon, "Outlook 2014: Marketing Spending to Rise," *Direct Marketing News*, accessed October 23, 2014, www.dmnews.com.
27. Association website, www.oaaa.org accessed October 23, 2014.
28. Association website, www.oaaa.org, accessed October 23, 2014; Larry Copeland, "Cities Snipe over Super-Bright Digital Billboards," *USA Today*, accessed March 27, 2014, www.usatoday.com.
29. Seth Rosenblatt, "Google Demolishes Financial Expectations to Close 2013," *CNET*, accessed March 27, 2014, http://news.cnet.com.
30. Mark Hoelzel, "Mobile Video Advertising Is Taking Off, As Ad Buyers Pile Billions of Dollars into Small-Screen Ads," *Business Insider*, accessed October 23, 2014, www.businessinsider.com.
31. Katherine Rosman, "Augmented Reality Finally Starts to Gain Traction," *The Wall Street Journal*, accessed March 31, 2014, http://online.wsj.com.
32. Bureau of Labor Statistics, "Public Relations and Fundraising Managers" and "Public Relations Specialists," *Occupational Outlook Handbook: 2014–2015*, accessed March 31, 2014, www.bls.gov.
33. Paul Farhi, "The Rules of the Super Bowl Ad Game," *Washington Post*, accessed March 31, 2014, www.washingtonpost.com.

Chapter 17

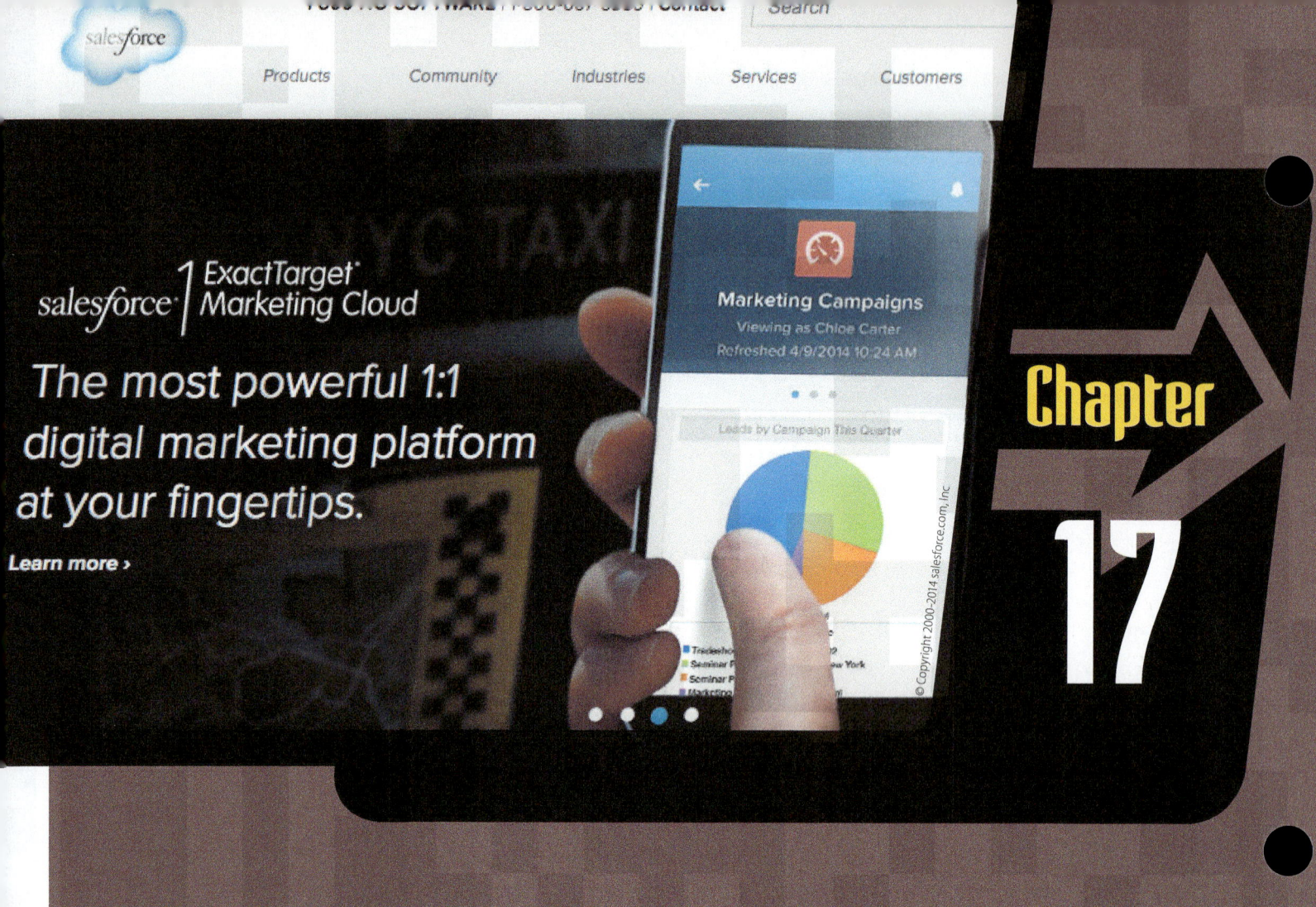

Personal Selling and Sales Promotion

1. Describe the role of today's salesperson.
2. Describe the four sales channels.
3. Explain the three major trends in personal selling.
4. Discuss the three basic sales tasks.
5. Outline the seven steps in the sales process.
6. Identify the seven functions of a sales manager.
7. Explain the role of ethical behavior in personal selling.
8. Describe the role of sales promotion in the promotional mix and the different types of sales promotions.

SALESFORCE.COM EXPANDS ITS MARKETING CLOUD

One of the most influential recent trends in marketing is the use of social media such as Facebook, Twitter, LinkedIn, and Google+ to reach customers, develop relationships with them, and shape their brand preferences and buying habits. Many companies need help today integrating all those social and mobile platforms with their own customer relationship management (CRM) systems, so they know, for instance, what Facebook users are saying about their goods and services and can quickly react. That's where Salesforce.com comes in. More than 150,000 companies already rely on this cloud-computing pioneer to help them tap into social media in an effective and efficient way that yields useful information.

Salesforce, a company based in San Francisco with more than 15,000 employees worldwide, initially focused on providing cloud-computing services for sales operations and information management. Now it has ramped up its investment in what it calls the Salesforce Marketing Cloud so it can extend its services to chief marketing officers, leading a trend that's expected to make corporate marketing departments the biggest information technology spenders in many organizations.

With acquisitions of companies such as ExactTarget, Buddy Media, Radian6, GoInstant, and RelateIQ, Salesforce has invested more than $3.5 billion in companies that focus on the analysis, management, and sharing of social media and Web information. These acquisitions put Salesforce in a strong position to offer CMOs new integrated marketing services that allow them to track and act on the "crucial insights about themselves" that social media users volunteer online. According to the CEO of Radian6, Salesforce's strategy confirms that social media has evolved to become "the central core" of most corporate marketing operations.

Salesforce operates a social network of its own, called Chatter, which serves its own clients exclusively but will now (thanks to the Radian6 acquisition) also allow them to see customers' posts on Facebook and Twitter, blogs, and more data in real time. Salesforce believes it's on track to develop a multi-billion-dollar business with the new suite of services available on its Marketing Cloud. It is so confident it can help its clients excel at multichannel CRM, in fact, that "CRM" is the symbol the company uses for its NYSE stock listing.[1]

EVOLUTION OF A BRAND

Industry observers predict that digital marketing will replace traditional marketing as the engine of business growth in the near future. Salesforce's acquisitions of ExactTarget, Radian6, Buddy Media, GoInstant, and RelateIQ reflect the firm's plans to strengthen its social marketing and Web presence across various social media channels. As companies become more experienced in using social media to market their goods and services, Salesforce's newly unified platform can make that process easier.

- What sorts of problems will traditional marketers continue to face as they adapt to the world of digital marketing?
- How can Salesforce's Marketing Cloud help its clients identify their customers' needs and meet those needs?
- Salesforce's acquisition of RelateIQ provides the company with the opportunity to capture data from email, calendars, and smartphone calls to provide real-time insights to its customers. How will this acquisition provide Salesforce with a competitive advantage in the CRM sector?

Chapter Overview

personal selling Interpersonal influence process involving a seller's promotional presentation conducted on a person-to-person basis with the buyer.

The Salesforce.com story illustrates how important it is for marketers to not simply sell products but to understand their customers and connect with them through product innovations that make life easier. In exploring personal selling strategies, this chapter gives special attention to the relationship-building opportunities that the selling situation presents.

Personal selling is the process of a seller's person-to-person promotional presentation to a buyer. The sales process is essentially interpersonal, and it is basic to any enterprise. Accounting, engineering, human resource management, production, and other organizational activities produce no benefits unless a seller matches the needs of a client or customer. The more than 16 million people employed in sales occupations in the United States testify to the importance of selling.[2] Personal selling is much more costly and time consuming than other types of promotion because of its direct contact with customers. This makes personal selling the single largest marketing expense in many firms.

Personal selling is a primary component of a firm's promotional mix when one or more of several well-defined factors are present:

1. Customers are geographically concentrated.
2. Individual orders account for large amounts of revenue.
3. The firm markets goods and services that are expensive, technically complex, or require special handling.
4. Trade-ins are involved.
5. Products move through short channels.
6. The firm markets to relatively few potential customers.

For example, personal selling is an important component of the promotional mix for a car dealer, although both dealers and manufacturers also rely heavily on advertising. Because cars and trucks are expensive, customers usually like to go to a dealership to compare models or discuss a purchase, and trade-ins are often involved. So, a dealer's salespeople provide valuable assistance to the customer.

Table 17.1 summarizes the factors that influence the importance of personal selling in the overall promotional mix based on four variables: consumer, product, price, and marketing channels. This chapter also explores *sales promotion*, which includes all marketing activities—other than personal selling, advertising, and publicity—that enhance promotional effectiveness.

TABLE 17.1 Factors Affecting the Importance of Personal Selling in the Promotional Mix

Variable	Conditions That Favor Personal Selling	Conditions That Favor Advertising
Consumer	Geographically concentrated	Geographically dispersed
	Relatively low numbers	Relatively high numbers
Product	Expensive	Inexpensive
	Technically complex	Simple to understand
	Custom made	Standardized
	Special handling requirements	No special handling requirements
	Transactions frequently involve trade-ins	Transactions seldom involve trade-ins
Price	Relatively high	Relatively low
Channels	Relatively short	Relatively long

Chapter 17 Personal Selling and Sales Promotion

THE EVOLUTION OF PERSONAL SELLING

Throughout U.S. history, selling has been a major factor in economic growth. Even during the 1700s, Yankee peddlers took their carts full of goods from village to village and farm to farm, helping expand trade among the colonies. Today, professional salespeople are problem solvers who focus on satisfying the needs of customers before, during, and after sales are made. Armed with knowledge about their firm's goods or services, those of competitors, and their customers' business needs, salespeople pursue a common goal of creating mutually beneficial long-term relationships with customers.

Personal selling is a vital, vibrant, dynamic process. As domestic and foreign competition increases the emphasis on productivity, personal selling takes on a more prominent role in the marketing mix. Salespeople must communicate the advantages of their firms' goods and services over those of competitors. They must be able to do the following:

- Focus on a customer's situation and needs and create solutions that meet those needs.
- Follow through and stay in touch before, during, and after a sale.
- Know the industry and have a firm grasp not only of their own firm's capabilities but also of their competitors' abilities.
- Work hard to exceed their customers' expectations.

Relationship marketing affects all aspects of an organization's marketing function, including personal selling. This means marketers in both internal and external relationships must develop different sales skills. Instead of working alone, many salespeople now operate in sales teams. The customer-focused firm wants its salespeople to form long-lasting relationships with buyers by providing high levels of customer service rather than going for quick sales. Even the way salespeople perform their jobs is constantly changing. Growing numbers of companies have integrated communications and computer technologies into the sales routine. These trends are covered in more detail later in the chapter.

Personal selling is an attractive career choice for today's college students. According to the Bureau of Labor Statistics, jobs in sales and related fields are expected to grow by about 7 percent over the next decade.[3] Company executives usually recognize a good salesperson as a hard worker who can solve problems, communicate clearly, and be consistent. In fact, many companies are headed by executives who began their careers in sales.

> **1** Describe the role of today's salesperson.

ASSESSMENT CHECK

1.1 What is personal selling?
1.2 What is the main focus of today's salespeople?

THE FOUR SALES CHANNELS

Personal selling occurs through several types of communication channels: over-the-counter selling, including online selling; field selling; telemarketing; and inside selling. Each of these channels includes business-to-business and direct-to-customer selling. Although telemarketing and online selling are lower-cost alternatives, their lack of personal interaction with existing or prospective customers often makes them less effective than personalized, one-to-one field selling and over-the-counter channels. In fact, many organizations use a number of different channels.

> **2** Describe the four sales channels.

OVER-THE-COUNTER SELLING

The most frequently used sales channel, **over-the-counter selling**, typically describes selling in retail and some wholesale locations. Most over-the-counter sales are direct-to-customer, although business customers are frequently served by wholesalers with over-the-counter sales reps. Customers typically

over-the-counter selling Personal selling conducted in retail and some wholesale locations in which customers come to the seller's place of business.

visit the seller's location on their own initiative to purchase desired items. Some visit their favorite stores because they enjoy shopping. Others respond to many kinds of appeals, including direct mail; personal letters of invitation from store personnel; and advertisements for sales, special events, and new-product introductions.

Marketers are getting increasingly creative in their approach to over-the-counter selling. Recently, Macy's shifted its marketing focus from attracting new customers to retaining and cultivating their existing customer base. According to the company, customer loyalty is key, and it has put the customer at the center of its decisions. To retain and grow its customer base, Macy's believes it has to personalize the in-store and online shopping experiences for its loyal customers. The retail chain's Star Rewards was recently named one of the top retail loyalty programs.[4]

Enterprise Rent-A-Car, the world's largest car-rental company, has more than 8,100 locations, annual revenues of more than $16.4 billion, and more than 78,000 employees. Enterprise has a long history of hiring former college athletes. It has an ongoing partnership with Kansas-based Career Athletes, a firm that matches former student athletes with career opportunities in the business world. These business recruits learn to work with profit and loss statements and gain experience in marketing and customer service.[5]

Clothing retailers have begun to enhance the shopping experience by expanding the capabilities of the fitting room. Ann Taylor has redesigned its fitting rooms to look like walk-in closets, complete with chandeliers. Old Navy has moved its fitting rooms from the back of the store to the center and also has "quick change" areas for its targeted customers—young mothers pressed for time. Nordstrom recently announced it was contemplating the use of iPads in its fitting rooms as a way of enhancing the customer experience. Shoppers would be able to look up product information and availability using the tablets.[6]

Regardless of a retailer's innovation, a few things remain constant in selling. For example, customers never like hearing salespeople say the following:

- "That's not my department."
- "If it's not out (on the rack or shelf), we don't have it."

Nordstrom offers customers the use of iPads in store fitting rooms as a way of enhancing their retail shopping experience.

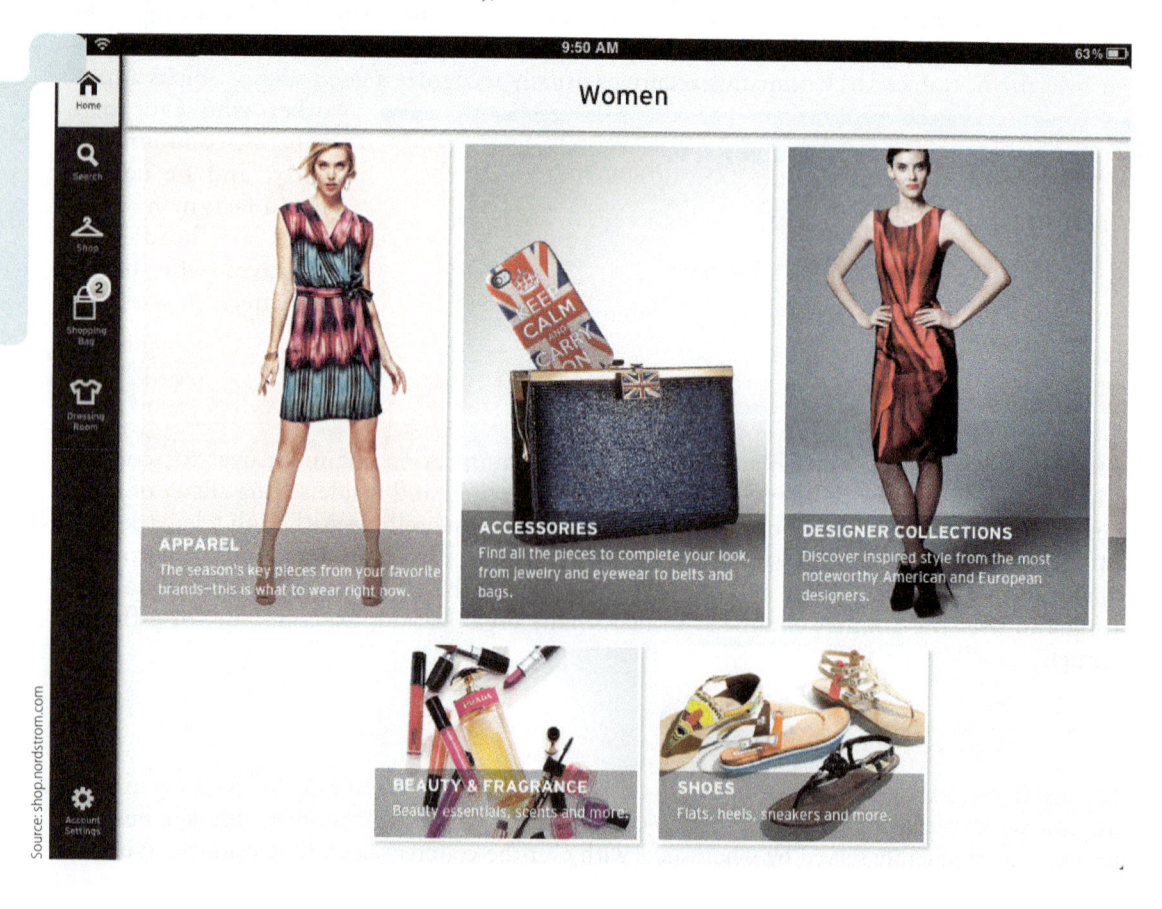

Chapter 17 Personal Selling and Sales Promotion

- "I don't know" or "I'm new."
- "I'm closing" or "I'm on a break."
- "The computer is down."

Although these quotes may seem humorous, they also ring true. You've probably heard them, and you may have said them yourself if you've worked in a retail environment. But each statement conveys the message that the salesperson is not willing or able to serve the customer—exactly the opposite of what every marketer wants to convey.

FIELD SELLING

Field selling involves making sales calls on prospective and existing customers at their businesses or homes. Some situations involve considerable creative effort, such as the sale of major computer installations. Often, the salesperson must first convince customers that they need the good or service and then that they need the particular brand the salesperson is selling. Field sales of large industrial installations, such as Airbus's A380 double-deck airliner, often require considerable technical expertise.

Largely because it involves travel, field selling is considerably more expensive than other selling options. Rising prices of fuel, airfares, car rentals, and hotel rates have increased the cost of business trips. Needing to find ways to trim costs while increasing productivity, some firms have replaced certain travel with conference calls, while others require salespeople to stay in less expensive hotels and spend less on meals.

In fairly routine field selling situations, such as calling on established customers in industries such as food, textiles, or wholesaling, the salesperson basically acts as an order-taker who processes regular customers' orders. But more complex situations may involve weeks of preparation, formal presentations, and many hours of post-sales call work. Field selling is a lifestyle that many people enjoy; they also cite some of the negatives, such as travel delays and impact on family life.

Some firms view field selling as a market in itself and have developed goods and services designed to help salespeople do their jobs. Panasonic manufactures the Toughbook series—a line of laptops,

field selling Sales presentations made at prospective customers' locations on a face-to-face basis.

Panasonic manufactures a family of Toughpad tablet devices as well as Toughbook laptop computers with field sales reps in mind.

network marketing Personal selling that relies on lists of family members and friends of a salesperson, who organizes gatherings of potential customers for an in-home presentation of selected products.

telemarketing Promotional presentation involving the use of the telephone on an outbound basis by salespeople or on an inbound basis by customers who initiate calls to obtain information and place orders.

outbound telemarketing Sales method in which sales personnel place phone calls to prospects and try to conclude the sale over the phone.

tablets, and handheld devices designed with field sales reps in mind. Each Toughbook product has a magnesium alloy case—significantly stronger than the plastic cases of standard computers—and is built for rugged handling. Some Toughbooks can withstand a six-foot drop and are rain, dust, and vibration resistant.[7]

Taking their cue from the successes of businesses such as Pampered Chef and Tupperware, many smaller businesses now rely on field selling in customers' homes. Often called **network marketing**, this type of personal selling relies on lists of family members and friends of the salesperson or "party host," who organizes a gathering of potential customers for an in-home demonstration of products. Utah-based Vault Denim buys the previous season's designer jeans from manufacturers. Its consultants then sell the jeans at home parties for about half the retail price. The company recently expanded its offerings to include skin care products also sold at home parties.[8]

TELEMARKETING

Telemarketing is a channel in which the selling process is conducted by phone and serves two general purposes—sales and service—and two general markets—business-to-business and direct-to-customer. Both inbound and outbound telemarketing are forms of direct marketing.

Outbound telemarketing involves sales personnel who rely on the telephone to contact potential buyers, reducing the substantial costs of personal visits to customers' homes or businesses. Technologies such as predictive dialers, autodialing, and random-digit dialing increase chances that telemarketers will reach people at home. *Predictive dialers* weed out busy signals and answering machines, nearly doubling the number of calls made per hour. *Autodialing* allows telemarketers to dial numbers continually; when a customer answers the phone, the call is automatically routed to a sales representative. However, the Telephone Consumer Protection Act of 1991 prohibits the use of autodialers to contact (or leave messages on) telephone devices such as answering machines.[9] *Random-digit dialing* allows telemarketers to reach unlisted numbers and block Caller ID.

A major drawback of telemarketing is that most consumers dislike the practice, and more than 220 million have signed up for the national Do Not Call Registry.[10] If an unauthorized telemarketer does call any of these numbers, the marketer is subject to a fine of up to $16,000.[11] Organizations exempt from the fine include not-for-profits, political candidates, companies that have obtained the customer's permission, marketing researchers, and firms that have an existing business relationship with the customer.

At home parties, Vault Denim consultants sell last year's jeans at about half the retail price.

Why do some firms still use telemarketing? The average call cost is low, and companies point to a significant rate of success. In a recent year, total incremental sales from telemarketing exceeded $2 trillion. According to the Direct Marketing Association, about 1.3 million people work in telemarketing jobs that support 7.9 million other jobs, for a total of 9.2 million jobs in the United States.[12]

Inbound telemarketing typically involves a toll-free number that customers can call to obtain information, make reservations, and purchase goods and services. When a customer calls a toll-free number, the caller can be identified and routed to the representatives with whom he or she has done business before, creating a human touch not possible before. This form of selling provides maximum convenience for customers who initiate the sales process. Many large catalog merchants, such as Pottery Barn, L.L.Bean, Lands' End, and Performance Bike, keep their inbound telemarketing lines open 24/7.

Some firms are taking dramatic steps to incorporate inbound telemarketing into their overall marketing strategy. JetBlue Airways, for example, keeps operating costs low by employing more than 1,800 customer support agents who work from home.[13]

Some firms use telemarketing because the average call cost is low and companies point to a significant rate of success.

INSIDE SELLING

The role of many of today's telemarketers is a combination of field selling techniques applied through inbound and outbound telemarketing channels with a strong customer orientation, called **inside selling**. Inside sales reps perform two primary jobs: They turn opportunities into actual sales, and they support technicians and purchasers with current solutions. Inside sales reps do far more than read a canned script to unwilling prospects. Their role goes beyond taking orders; they solve problems, provide customer service, and sell. A successful inside sales force relies on close working relationships with field representatives to solidify customer relationships.

The six-member inside sales force—the Client Experience Team—of the NBA's Detroit Pistons supports the team's marketing efforts, such as special events for season ticket holders, including backstage tours, tipoff parties, and privileges such as getting into games 30 minutes early. Season ticket holders are also issued the official Pistons On-Court Jacket, which comes with an embedded microchip, to get 20 percent off at concessions and 30 percent off merchandise. Pistons sales reps use online chat, telephone, and email to stay connected.[14]

inbound telemarketing Sales method in which prospects call a seller to obtain information, make reservations, and purchase goods and services.

inside selling Selling by phone, mail, and electronic commerce.

INTEGRATING THE VARIOUS SELLING CHANNELS

Figure 17.1 illustrates how firms are likely to blend alternative sales channels—from over-the-counter selling and field selling to telemarketing and inside selling—to create a successful, cost-effective sales organization. Existing customers whose business problems require complex solutions are likely best served by the traditional field sales force. Other current customers who need answers but not the same attention as the first group can be served by inside sales reps who contact them as needed. Over-the-counter sales reps serve existing customers by supplying information and advice and completing sales transactions. Telemarketers may be used to strengthen communication with customers or to reestablish relationships with customers that may have lapsed over a few months.

ASSESSMENT CHECK

2.1. What is over-the-counter selling?

2.2. What is field selling?

2.3. Distinguish between outbound and inbound telemarketing.

> **Briefly Speaking**
>
> "The way to get started is to quit talking and begin doing."
>
> —**Walt Disney**
> *American entertainment pioneer and founder of The Walt Disney Company*

FIGURE 17.1 Alternative Sales Channels for Serving Customers

Over-the-Counter Selling Customers in retail settings with typical, routine needs

Field Selling Customers who need solutions to complex problems

Telemarketing *Outbound:* Existing customers; businesses that have been contacted in the last three months; people or companies that have granted you permission to call. *Inbound:* New and existing customers and customers of competitors; previous purchasers and service personnel seeking

Inside Selling Customers who need answers to frequently asked questions

Customers

TRENDS IN PERSONAL SELLING

> **3** Explain the three major trends in personal selling.

In today's complex marketing environment, effective personal selling requires different strategies from those used by salespeople in the past. As pointed out in the discussion of *buying centers* in Chapter 7, rather than selling one-on-one, in B2B settings it is now customary to sell to teams of corporate representatives who participate in the client firm's decision-making process. In business-to-business sales situations involving technical products, customers expect salespeople to answer technical questions—or bring along someone who can. They also want representatives who understand technical jargon and can communicate using sophisticated technological tools. Patience is also a requirement because the B2B sales cycle, from initial contact to closing, may take months or even years. To address all of these concerns, companies rely on three major personal selling approaches: relationship selling, consultative selling, and team selling. Regardless of the approach, however, experts agree on a few basic guidelines for conducting successful personal selling.

RELATIONSHIP SELLING

relationship selling Regular contacts between sales representatives and customers over an extended period to establish a sustained buyer–seller relationship.

Most firms emphasize **relationship selling**, a technique for building a mutually beneficial partnership with a customer through regular contacts over an extended period. Such buyer–seller bonds become increasingly important as firms cut back on the number of suppliers and look for companies that provide high levels of customer service and satisfaction. Salespeople must also find ways to distinguish themselves and their products from competitors. To create strong, long-lasting relationships with customers, salespeople must meet buyers' expectations. Table 17.2 summarizes the results of several surveys that indicate what buyers expect of professional salespeople.

The success of tomorrow's marketers depends on the relationships they build today in both the business-to-consumer and business-to-business markets. Located throughout the Northeast, Spanish Santander Bank understands that first impressions are particularly important in relationship selling.

TABLE 17.2   What Buyers Expect from Salespeople

Buyers prefer to do business with salespeople who:

Orchestrate events and bring whatever resources are necessary to satisfy the customer

Provide counseling to the customer based on in-depth knowledge of the product, the market, and the customer's needs

Solve problems proficiently to ensure satisfactory customer service over extended time

Demonstrate high ethical standards and communicate honestly at all times

Willingly advocate the customer's cause within the selling organization

Create imaginative arrangements to meet buyers' needs

Arrive well prepared for sales calls

To allow its staff to spend more time with customers, the bank automated many sales processes and implemented sales effectiveness tools to help it become more customer focused.[15]

Relationship selling is equally important, if not more so, in business-to-business sales. Firms may invest millions of dollars in goods and services from a single firm, so creating relationships is vital. Based in Jacksonville, Florida, Barnett is a leading national distributor of plumbing, heating and air conditioning, electrical, and hardware products. It uses barcode technology to keep its contractors' trucks well stocked with all sorts of supplies—just in case they are needed on a job. After contractors finish at a site, they use a scanner to record the parts used in the job. The parts are automatically reordered at the end of the day, and Barnett replenishes the inventory.[16]

CONSULTATIVE SELLING

Field and inside sales representatives must use sales methods that satisfy today's cost-conscious, knowledgeable buyers. One such method, **consultative selling**, involves meeting customer needs by listening to customers, understanding—and caring about—their problems, paying attention to details, and following through after the sale. It works hand in hand with relationship selling in building customer loyalty.

Richardson, a sales consulting firm based in Philadelphia, recently trained staff at Sun Trust banks in consultative selling techniques. The banking industry has changed significantly over the past several years, and Sun Trust was looking for ways to re-invigorate its staff and to increase customer retention. Instead of focusing strictly on selling, the bank needed to build solid relationships through excellent customer service. Richardson developed a training program for every client-facing professional in the company. During the training, participants learned how to build relationships with clients using a consistent, service-oriented approach. As a result of the training, the employees were able to adapt to the new strategy and win more business.[17] One important aspect of consultative selling is being prepared for a sales call, including dressing professionally.

Online companies have instituted consultative selling models to create long-term customers. Particularly for complicated, high-priced products that require installation or specialized service, Web sellers must quickly communicate the benefits and features of their products. They accomplish this through consultative selling.

Cross-selling—offering multiple goods or services to the same customer—is another technique that capitalizes on a firm's strengths. It costs a bank five times as much to acquire a new customer as to cross-sell to an existing one. Moreover, research shows that the more a customer buys from an institution, the less likely that person is to leave. So, a customer who opens a checking account at a local bank may follow with a safe-deposit box, retirement savings account, and a mortgage loan. Wells Fargo relies on cross-selling to promote its broad array of banking products and services. See the "Marketing Success" feature to learn more.

consultative selling Meeting customer needs by listening to them, understanding their problems, paying attention to details, and following through after the sale.

cross-selling Selling multiple, often unrelated, goods and services to the same customer based on knowledge of that customer's needs.

MARKETING SUCCESS
Successful Cross-Selling Strategies at Wells Fargo

Background. Wells Fargo is the nation's fourth-largest bank and, like its competitors, seeks increased revenue even as low interest rates have made loans a less profitable business.

The Challenge. The company, which provides retail banking, retirement, and wealth management services among others, wants to be the "the premier provider of financial services in every one of our markets."

The Strategy. Wells Fargo has elevated the sales strategy of cross-selling to an art. Its representatives are encouraged to suggest new products and packages of time- and money-saving services to existing customers, pitching a broad array of offerings while keeping a customer-centric approach. They use information about customers' financial situations to understand their other financial needs. Wells Fargo is then able to offer personalized suggestions to increase the number of checking accounts, credit cards, debit cards, home equity loans, savings and retirement accounts, and online banking services its customers use.

The Outcome. The company's sales per household have continued to increase over the last decade, while its customer service ratings remain high. The average U.S. household uses about 16 banking products from various financial institutions. Wells Fargo sells each customer an average of six products. Other banks have begun to emulate Wells Fargo's cross-selling strategy.

Sources: Company website, www.wellsfargo.com, accessed March 30, 2014; Maria Tor and Saad Sarfraz, "Largest 100 Banks in the World," *SNL Research*, accessed March 30, 2014, www.snl.com; Jim Marous, "Banks and Credit Unions Must Improve Cross-Selling Efforts," *Bank Marketing Strategy*, accessed March 30, 2014, http://jimmarous.blogspot.com; Halah Tourhalai, "The Art of the Cross-Sell," *Forbes*, accessed March 30, 2014, www.forbes.com.

---

team selling Selling situation in which several sales associates or other members of the organization are employed to help the lead sales representative reach all those who influence the purchase decision.

virtual sales team Network of strategic partners, suppliers, and others who recommend a firm's goods or services.

> **Briefly Speaking**
>
> "Although your customers won't love you if you give bad service your competitors will."
>
> —Kate Zabriskie
> Founder of Business Training Works, Inc.

TEAM SELLING

Another development in the evolution of personal selling is **team selling**, in which a salesperson joins with specialists from other functional areas of the firm to complete the selling process. Teams can be formal and ongoing or created for a specific, short-term selling situation. Although some salespeople have hesitated to embrace the idea of team selling, preferring to work alone, a growing number believe team selling brings better results. Customers often prefer the team approach, which makes them feel well served. Consider a restaurant meal. If the host, servers, wine steward, chef, and kitchen crew are all working well together as a team, your experience at the restaurant is likely to be positive. But if the service stops and starts, your order is incorrect, the food is cold, the silverware is dirty, and the staff seems grouchy, you probably won't eat at that restaurant again.

Another advantage of team selling is the formation of relationships between companies rather than between individuals. In sales situations that call for detailed knowledge of new, complex, and ever-changing technologies, team selling offers a distinct competitive edge in meeting customers' needs. In most computer software B2B departments, a third of the sales force is made up of technically trained, nonmarketing experts such as engineers or programmers. A salesperson continues to play the lead role in most sales situations, but technical experts bring added value to the sales process. Some companies establish permanent sales-and-tech teams that conduct all sales presentations together; others have a pool of engineers or other professionals who are on call for client visits.

Some resourceful entrepreneurs are building a **virtual sales team**—a network of strategic partners, suppliers, and others qualified and willing to recommend a firm's goods or services. Michelle Marciniak and Susan Walvius, both former college basketball coaches, came up with a new use for the moisture-wicking fabric that workout clothes are made of: bed sheets. Together they founded Sheex, a South Carolina–based company that makes bed sheets and sleepwear that are cool to the touch and transfer body heat away from the sleeper. Rather than a traditional sales force, a virtual sales force of "sleep ambassadors" promotes Sheex bed sheets. Athletes, such as Super Bowl MVP Cliff Avril,

ASSESSMENT CHECK

3.1 Identify the three major personal selling approaches.

3.2 Distinguish between relationship selling and consultative selling.

golfer Nicole Smith, and free skier Jaclyn Paaso, post discount codes via Twitter or other social media. They receive commissions based on sales of Sheex. "It's kind of a virtual sales team of athletes," Walvius says.[18]

SALES TASKS

Today's salesperson is more concerned with establishing long-term buyer–seller relationships and helping customers select the correct products for meeting their needs than with simply selling whatever is available. Where repeat purchases are common, the salesperson must be certain that the buyer's purchases are in his or her best interest; otherwise, no future relationship will be possible. The seller's interests are tied to the buyer's in a mutually beneficial manner.

Although all sales activities help the customer in some manner, they are not all alike. Three basic sales tasks can be identified: (1) order processing, (2) creative selling, and (3) missionary sales. Most of today's salespeople are not limited to performing tasks in a single category. Instead, they often perform all three tasks to some extent. A sales engineer for a computer firm may do 50 percent missionary sales, 45 percent creative selling, and 5 percent order processing. Most sales positions are classified on the basis of the primary selling task performed.

Then there's the philosophy that *everyone* in the organization, regardless of what his or her job description is, should be engaged in selling. Southwest Airlines believes delivering great customer service is paramount for every employee, from the reservations agent to the baggage handler to the flight attendant. Southwest employees are trained to put the customer's needs first, and the airline relies heavily on technology to coordinate the effort.[19]

> Discuss the three basic sales tasks.

ORDER PROCESSING

Order processing, which can involve both field selling and telemarketing, is often typified by selling at the wholesale and retail levels. For instance, a Snapple route salesperson who performs this task must take the following steps:

1. *Identify customer needs.* The route salesperson determines that a store has only 7 cases of Snapple left in stock when it normally carries an inventory of 50.

2. *Point out the need to the customer.* The route salesperson informs the store manager of the inventory situation.

3. *Complete (write up) the order.* The store manager acknowledges the need for more of the product. The driver unloads 43 cases of Snapple, and the manager signs the delivery slip.

Order processing is part of most selling positions. It becomes the primary task in situations in which needs can be readily identified and are acknowledged by the customer. Even in such instances, however, salespeople whose primary responsibility involves order processing will devote some time persuading their wholesale or retail customers to carry more complete inventories of their firms' merchandise or handle additional product lines. They are also likely to try to motivate purchasers to feature some of their firms' products, increase the amount of shelf space devoted to these items, and improve product location in the stores.

Technology now streamlines order-processing tasks. Interactive store kiosks at brick-and-mortar retailers, such as New Balance and Nordstrom, provide a touchscreen that lets customers browse a store's catalog, compare brands and product features, and even place their order—all from a single, user-friendly device—eliminating endless cruising of store aisles.[20]

order processing Selling, mostly at the wholesale and retail levels, that involves identifying customer needs, pointing them out to customers, and completing orders.

creative selling
Personal selling in which salespeople use well-planned strategies to seek new customers by proposing innovative solutions to customers' needs.

When P.F. Chang's wanted to create excitement about its loyalty program, it launched a new mobile app that increases customer interaction with the Asian restaurant chain.

Source: www.pfchangs.com

CREATIVE SELLING

When a considerable amount of decision making is involved in purchasing a good or service, an effective salesperson uses **creative selling** techniques to solicit an order. In contrast to the order-processing task, which deals mainly with maintaining existing business, creative selling is generally used to develop new business either by adding new customers or introducing new goods and services. New products or upgrades to more expensive items often require creative selling. The salesperson must first identify the customer's problems and needs and then propose a solution in the form of the item offered. When attempting to expand an existing business relationship, creative selling techniques are used in over-the-counter selling, field selling, inside selling, and telemarketing.

Creative selling can generate "buzz" for a product. Digital marketing agency Rockfish, based in Rogers, Arkansas, developed a creative campaign for P.F. Chang's and its mobile app. The Asian restaurant chain's loyalty program was not satisfying its customers, so the company asked Rockfish to take a new approach with a mobile app. Upon joining the loyalty program via mobile device, customers are immediately rewarded with a free order of tasty lettuce wraps—a signature dish. Next, the marketing agency increased consumers' personal interaction with the chain by creating the Dish of Destiny—a feature that makes menu recommendations based on customers' Chinese zodiac sign. The Words of Wisdom game allows customers to create their own fortunes and share them with friends. The mobile app was recently named best restaurant mobile app by the Web Marketing Association.[21]

MISSIONARY SELLING

Missionary selling is an indirect approach to sales. Salespeople sell the firm's goodwill and educate their customers, often providing technical or operational assistance. A cosmetics company salesperson may call on retailers to demonstrate how a new product is used or check on special promotions and overall product movement, while a wholesaler takes orders and delivers merchandise. For years, large pharmaceutical companies used the most aggressive approach to missionary selling, courting doctors (the indirect customers) by providing lavish restaurant meals, educational seminars, and other incentives in the hope of persuading them to prescribe a particular brand to patients. Although the doctor is clearly the decision maker, the transaction is not complete until the patient hands the prescription over to a pharmacist, and, traditionally, pharmaceutical companies measured success in terms of number of prescriptions written for their drugs. But changes in the industry code of conduct now prohibit missionary salespeople—called detailers—from offering any incentives of value to their customers. Instead, the Pharmaceutical Research and Manufacturers of America decreed that meetings with doctors must focus exclusively on education, not freebies. Some pharmaceutical companies now ask their sales forces to change their focus to becoming resources for doctors in treating patients and providing practical support.[22]

Some missionary sales may offer **sales incentives**, such as trips, gas cards, and free product upgrades. Missionary sales may involve both field selling and telemarketing. Many aspects of team selling can also be seen as missionary sales, as when technical support salespeople help design, install, and maintain equipment; when they train customers' employees; and when they provide information or operational assistance.

ASSESSMENT CHECK

4.1 What are the three major tasks performed by salespeople?

4.2 What are the three steps of order processing?

THE SALES PROCESS

If you have worked in a retail store, or if you've sold magazine subscriptions or candy to raise money for your school or sports team, you will recognize many of the activities involved in the following list of steps in the sales process. Personal selling encompasses the following sequence of activities: (1) prospecting and qualifying, (2) approach, (3) presentation, (4) demonstration, (5) handling objections, (6) closing, and (7) follow-up.

As Figure 17.2 indicates, these steps follow the AIDA concept (attention, interest, desire, action). Once a sales prospect has been qualified, an attempt is made to secure his or her attention. The presentation and demonstration steps are designed to generate interest and desire. Successful handling of buyer objections should arouse further desire. Action occurs at the close of the sale.

Salespeople modify the steps in this process to match their customers' buying processes. A consumer who eagerly looks forward to the local symphony orchestra's new concert season each year needs no presentation except for details about scheduled performances and perhaps whether any famous musicians will be on the bill. But the same consumer would expect a demonstration from an auto dealer when looking for a new car or might appreciate a presentation of dinner specials by the server prior to ordering a meal at a restaurant.

PROSPECTING AND QUALIFYING

Prospecting—the process of identifying potential customers—may involve hours, days, or weeks of effort, but it is a necessary step. Leads about prospects come from many sources: the Internet, computerized databases, trade show exhibits, previous customers, friends, neighbors, other vendors, nonsales employees in the firm, suppliers, and social and professional contacts. Although a firm may emphasize personal selling as the primary component of its overall promotional strategy, direct mail and advertising campaigns are also effective in identifying prospective customers.

Before salespeople begin their prospecting effort, they must be clear about what their firm is selling and create a "brand story"—that is, define their product in terms of what it can do for a customer. Because customers generally look for solutions to problems or ways to make their lives better or businesses more successful, this focus on the customer is critical. Once they develop a brand story, the sales team must be consistent about telling it at every possible point of contact, whether in a face-to-face conversation with a prospect, in advertising, or in promoting the product to the media.

In addition, salespeople must be well informed about the goods and services of the industry in general. They need to find out how other goods are marketed and packaged. They can try out a service themselves to understand how the industry operates. In these ways, they will understand what prospective customers need and want—and how they can serve them.

Qualifying—determining that the prospect really is a potential customer—is another important sales task. Not all prospects are qualified to make purchase decisions. Even though an employee in a firm might like your products, he or she might not be authorized to make the purchase. A consumer who test-drives a Porsche might fall in love with it but not be able to afford the $100,000+ price tag. As a sales representative, you should determine whether a certain prospect is qualified to make a purchase. If you determine at the outset that there's no chance for a purchase, then it's best to move on.

APPROACH

Once you have identified a qualified prospect, you need to collect all relevant information and plan an **approach**—your initial contact with the prospective customer. If your

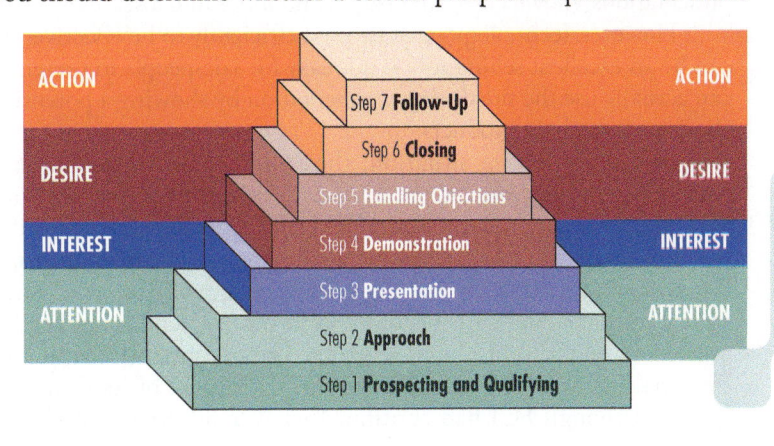

Outline the seven steps in the sales process.

missionary selling Indirect selling method in which salespeople promote goodwill for the firm by educating customers and providing technical or operational assistance.

sales incentives Programs that reward salespeople for superior performance.

prospecting Personal selling function of identifying potential customers.

qualifying Determining a prospect's needs, income, and purchase authority as a potential customer.

approach Salesperson's initial contact with a prospective customer.

FIGURE 17.2 The AIDA Concept and the Personal Selling Process

- Step 1 Prospecting and Qualifying — ATTENTION
- Step 2 Approach — ATTENTION
- Step 3 Presentation — INTEREST
- Step 4 Demonstration — INTEREST
- Step 5 Handling Objections — DESIRE
- Step 6 Closing — DESIRE
- Step 7 Follow-Up — ACTION

precall planning Use of information collected during the prospecting and qualifying stages of the sales process and during previous contacts with the prospect to tailor the approach and presentation to match the customer's needs.

firm already has a business relationship with the customer or has permission to contact the person, you may use telemarketing. But before you do so, gather as much information as you can.

Information gathering makes **precall planning** possible. As mentioned earlier, educate yourself about the industry in general, as well as goods and services offered by competitors. Read any marketing research available. Go to trade shows—you can learn a lot about many companies and their products at one location, usually in one day. Learn as much as you can about the firm you plan to approach: Browse the company's website; find online news articles and press releases about the company; and talk with other people in the industry. Know its product offerings well. Identify ways you can help the firm do better. Without invading an individual customer's privacy, see if you have anything in common—perhaps you grew up in the same state, or you both like to play tennis. All of this planning will help you make an effective approach.

As you plan your approach, try to answer the following questions:

- Who am I approaching, and what are their jobs within the company?
- What is their level of knowledge? Are they already informed about the idea I am going to present?
- What do they want or need? Should I speak in technical terms or provide general information?
- What do they need to hear? Do they need to know more about specific products or how those products can serve them? Do they need to know how the product works? Do they need to know about cost and availability?

If you are a retail salesperson, you can ask a shopper questions to learn more about his or her needs and preferences. Say you work at a large sporting goods store. You might ask a young male shopper whether he works out at home, what equipment he already has, what his fitness goals are. The answers to these questions should lead you in the direction of a sale.

PRESENTATION

presentation Personal selling function of describing a product's major features and relating them to a customer's problems or needs.

In a **presentation**, you convey your marketing message to the potential customer. You describe the product's major features, point out its strengths, and cite other customers' successes with the product. One popular form of presentation is a "features–benefits" framework, wherein you talk about the good or service in terms meaningful to the buyer. If you work for a car dealership, you might point out to a young couple safety features such as side airbags and built-in car seats.

Your presentation should be well organized, clear, and concise. If appropriate, use visual sales support materials, such as a brochure or streaming video from your tablet or laptop. If this is your first presentation to a potential customer, it will likely be more detailed than a routine call to give an existing customer some updates. Regardless of the situation, though, be attuned to your audience's response so you can modify your presentation—even on the spur of the moment—to meet their needs. Many presentations use multimedia tools that can offer everything from interactivity to current pricing information. Companies such as SlideDog enable users to combine PowerPoint presentations, movie clips, web pages, and more into a seamless viewing experience.[23]

However, technology must be used efficiently to be effective. For example, a company's website can be an excellent selling tool if it is easy for salespeople to present and buyers to use. A salesperson can actually use the site during a presentation by showing a potential customer how to use it to learn about and purchase products.

In a **cold calling** situation, the approach and presentation often take place at the same time. Cold calling means phoning or visiting the customer without a prior appointment and making a sales pitch on the spot. Cold calling requires nerve, skill, and creativity, but salespeople who are successful at it still point to the importance of preparation. See the "Career Readiness" feature for some tips on making cold calling work for you. During economic downturns, the ability to make cold calls becomes even more essential, as Tom Wood discovered. Wood is the president and CEO of Floor Coverings International (FCI) in Norcross, Georgia. FCI struggled financially during the recent recession, with some of its franchisees going out of business altogether. Although FCI had continued its Web ads and local direct mail, Wood decided that the

> **Briefly Speaking**
>
> "I still work hard to know my business. I'm continuously looking for ways to improve all my companies, and I'm always selling. Always."
>
> —Mark Cuban
> *Owner of the Dallas Mavericks NBA team and co-founder, HDNet*

cold calling Contacting a prospect without a prior appointment.

CAREER READINESS
How to Make a Successful Cold Call

Cold calling might be one of selling's biggest challenges. Here's how to tackle the process with confidence.

1. Think of the cold call as a conversation, not a sales call. Introduce yourself and ask an attention-getting question whose answer leads to an advantage of your good or service.

2. Follow up with leading questions that let the customer acknowledge the benefits of purchasing from you. This helps forestall objections later.

3. If you reach voice mail, leave a very brief but intriguing message that piques the prospect's interest and use a referral to find a common connection.

4. If you have to get past a gatekeeper, try just asking politely for help reaching the decision maker. Most people want to see themselves as helpful. Always thank the gatekeeper for putting your call through.

5. You may need to make an average of 50 calls to log one sale, but be sure you sound fresh and confident each time. Frequently changing your opening statement will help you achieve this, as well as letting you find the opening that works best.

6. If you're calling to make an appointment, sell the appointment, not the product.

7. If all else fails, ask the prospect whom else you might call.

Sources: Jane Porter, "Seven Secrets to Cold Calling Success," *Entrepreneur*, accessed March 31, 2014, www.entrepreneur.com; Chris Joseph, "Sales Techniques for Cold Calls in Marketing," *eHow.com*, accessed March 31, 2014, www.ehow.com; Carl Ruenheck, "Warming Up Those Necessary Cold Calls," *Business Know How*, accessed March 31, 2014, www.businessknowhow.com; Sean McPheat, "Tips on Cold Calling," *MTD Sales Training*, accessed March 31, 2014, www.mtdsalestraining.com; "9 Tips for Successful Cold Calling," *WAHM.com*, accessed March 31, 2014, www.wahm.com; Geoffrey James, "How to Make a Successful Cold Call," *Inc.*, accessed March 31, 2014, www.inc.com.

---

company had to do more to help the remaining franchisees find new potential customers. The company's Fast Start program turned its corporate employees loose to teach franchise owners the tried-and-true methods: knocking on doors, cold calling, and networking. Fast Start also showed the franchisees how to develop relationships with other companies, such as real estate agents, restoration and remodeling companies, and home inspectors, which could be sources of future leads.[24]

DEMONSTRATION

One of the most important advantages of personal selling is the opportunity to demonstrate a product. During a **demonstration**, the buyer gets a chance to try the product or at least see how it works. A demonstration might involve a test drive of the latest hybrid car or an in-store cooking class using pots and pans that are for sale.

Many firms use new technologies to make their demonstrations more outstanding than those of their competitors. Multimedia interactive demonstrations are common. Visitors to the Black & Decker website can click on video demonstrations of products such as the Matrix Quick Connect Tool System or post questions or tips for other do-it-yourselfers.[25] The key to an outstanding demonstration—one that gains the customer's attention, keeps his or her interest, is convincing, and stays in the customer's memory—is planning. But planning should also include time and space for free exchanges of information. During your demonstration, you should be prepared to stop and answer questions, demonstrate a certain feature again, or let the customer try the product firsthand.

demonstration Stage in the personal selling process in which the customer has the opportunity to try out or otherwise see how a good or service works before purchase.

Giving the customer the opportunity to try a product is an important advantage of personal selling.

objections Expression of sales resistance by the prospect.

closing Stage of the personal selling process in which the salesperson asks the customer to make a purchase decision.

> **Briefly Speaking**
>
> "People get caught up in wonderful eye-catching pitches, but they don't do enough to close the deal. It's no good if you don't make the sale … you don't win the deal unless you actually get them to sign on the dotted line."
>
> —Donald J. Trump
> *Chairman and president, The Trump Organization*

HANDLING OBJECTIONS

Potential customers often have legitimate questions and concerns about a good or service they are considering. **Objections** are expressions of resistance by the prospect, and it is reasonable to expect them. Objections might appear in the form of stalling or indecisiveness. "Let me call you back," your prospect might say, or "I just don't know about this." Or your buyer might focus on something negative, such as high price.

You can answer objections without being aggressive or rude. Use an objection as an opportunity to reassure your buyer about price, features, durability, availability, and the like. If the objection involves price, you might be able to suggest a less-expensive model or a payment plan. If the objection involves a comparison to competitive products, point out the obvious—and not so obvious—benefits of your own. If the objection involves a question about availability, a few clicks on your laptop should show how many items are in stock and when they can be shipped.

CLOSING

The moment of truth in selling is the **closing**—the point at which the salesperson asks the prospect for an order. If your presentation has been effective and you have handled all objections, a closing would be the natural conclusion to the meeting. But you may still find it difficult to close the sale. Closing does not have to be thought of in terms of a "hard sell." Instead, you can ask your customer, "Would you like to give this a try?" or, "Do I have your approval to proceed?"

Other methods of closing include the following:

1. Addressing the prospect's major concern about a purchase and then offering a convincing argument. *"If I can show you how the new heating system will reduce your energy costs by 25 percent, would you be willing to let us install it?"*
2. Posing choices for the prospect in which either alternative represents a sale. *"Would you prefer the pink sweater or the green one?"*
3. Advising the buyer that a product is about to be discontinued or will go up in price soon (but be completely honest about this—you don't want a customer to learn later that this was not true).
4. Remaining silent so the buyer can make a decision on his or her own.
5. Offering an extra inducement designed to motivate a favorable buyer response, such as a quantity discount, an extended service contract, or a low-interest payment plan.

Even if the meeting or phone call ends without a sale, the effort is not over. You can use a written note or an email to keep communication open, letting the buyer know you are ready and waiting to be of service.

FOLLOW-UP

The word *close* can be misleading because the point at which the prospect accepts the seller's offer is where much of the real work of selling begins. In today's competitive environment, the most successful salespeople make sure that today's customers will also be tomorrow's.

It is not enough to close the sale and move on. Relationship selling involves reinforcing the purchase decision and ensuring the company delivers the highest-quality merchandise. As a salesperson, you must also ensure that customer service needs are met and that satisfaction results from all of a customer's dealings with your company. Otherwise, some other company may get the next order.

These post-sale activities, which often determine whether a person will become a repeat customer, constitute the sales **follow-up**. Sales experts believe in a wide array of follow-up techniques, ranging from holiday cards to online greetings. Some suggest phone calls at regular intervals. Others prefer automatic email reminders when it is time to renew or reorder. At the very least, however, you should contact customers to find out if they are satisfied with their purchases. This step allows you to psychologically reinforce the customer's original decision to buy. It also gives you an opportunity to correct any problems and ensure the next sale. Follow-up helps strengthen the bond you try to build with customers in relationship selling. You have probably experienced follow-up as a customer—if your auto dealership called to see if you were satisfied with recent service or if your doctor's office phoned to find out if you were feeling better.

follow-up Post-sale activities that often determine whether an individual who has made a recent purchase will become a repeat customer.

> **ASSESSMENT CHECK**
>
> 5.1 Identify the seven steps of the sales process.
> 5.2 Why is follow-up important to the sales effort?

MANAGING THE SALES EFFORT

The overall direction and control of the personal selling effort are in the hands of a firm's sales managers. In a typical geographic sales structure, a district or divisional sales manager might report to a regional or zone manager. This manager in turn reports to a national sales manager or vice president of sales.

Currently, there are more than 359,000 sales managers in the United States.[26] The sales manager's job requires a unique blend of administrative and sales skills, depending on the specific level in the sales hierarchy. Sales skills are particularly important for first-level sales managers, because they are involved daily in the continuing process of training and directly leading the sales force. But as people rise in the sales management hierarchy, they require more managerial skills and fewer sales skills to perform well.

Sales force management links individual salespeople to general management. The sales manager performs seven basic managerial functions: (1) recruitment and selection, (2) training, (3) organization, (4) supervision, (5) motivation, (6) compensation, and (7) evaluation and control. Sales managers perform these tasks in a demanding and complex environment. They must manage an increasingly diverse sales force. Women account for slightly less than half of U.S. professional salespeople, and their numbers are growing at a faster rate than those for men.[27]

6 Identify the seven functions of a sales manager.

RECRUITMENT AND SELECTION

Recruiting and selecting successful salespeople are among the sales manager's greatest challenges. After all, these workers will collectively determine just how successful the sales manager is. New salespeople—such as you—might come from colleges and universities, trade and business schools, the military, other companies, and even the firm's current nonsales staff. A successful sales career offers satisfaction in all of the following five areas a person generally considers when deciding on a profession:

1. *Opportunity for advancement.* Studies have shown that successful sales representatives advance rapidly in most companies.

2. *Potential for high earnings.* Salespeople have the opportunity to earn a very comfortable living.

3. *Personal satisfaction.* A salesperson derives satisfaction from achieving success in a competitive environment and helping customers satisfy their wants and needs.

4. *Job security.* Selling provides a high degree of job security because there is always a need for good salespeople.

During an interview, recruiters look for enthusiasm, organizational skills, sociability, and other traits.

5. *Independence and variety.* Salespeople often work independently, calling on customers in their territory. They have the freedom to make important decisions about meeting their customers' needs and frequently report that no two workdays are the same.

Careful selection of salespeople is important for two reasons. First, a company invests a substantial amount of time and money in the selection process. Second, hiring mistakes can damage relationships with customers and overall performance and are costly to correct.

Most large firms use a specific seven-step process in selecting sales personnel: application screening, initial interview, in-depth interview, testing, reference checks, physical examination, and hiring decision. An application screening is typically followed by an initial interview. If the applicant looks promising, an in-depth interview takes place. During the interview, a sales manager looks for the person's enthusiasm, organizational skills, ambition, persuasiveness, ability to follow instructions, and sociability.

Next, the company may administer aptitude, interest, and knowledge tests. One popular testing approach is the assessment center. This technique uses situational exercises, group discussions, and various job simulations, allowing the sales manager to measure a candidate's skills, knowledge, and ability. Assessment centers enable managers to see what potential salespeople can do rather than what they say they can do. Before hiring a candidate, the firm checks references, reviews company policies, and may require a physical examination.

TRAINING

To shape new sales recruits into an efficient sales organization, managers must conduct an effective training program. The principal methods used in sales training are on-the-job training, individual instruction, in-house classes, and external seminars.

Popular training techniques include instructional videos, lectures, role-playing exercises, and interactive computer programs. Simulations can help salespeople improve their selling techniques. Many firms supplement their training by enrolling salespeople in executive development programs at local colleges and by hiring specialists to teach customized training programs. In other instances, sales reps attend courses and workshops developed by outside companies. Best Buy received some negative press for training its salespeople to push extended warranties on customers, which many felt caused customer service to suffer. See the "Solving an Ethical Controversy" feature for opposing views on this strategy.

Although sales meetings are often packed with various topics, they can be an excellent opportunity for sales training. New York–based Santinelli International, the manufacturer of lens edging equipment to the optical industry, uses its national sales meeting as a platform for training. The practical advice and give-and-take in such sessions motivates colleagues to reassess their own skills and try new techniques.[28]

Ongoing sales training is important for all salespeople, even veterans. Sales managers often conduct this type of training informally, traveling with field reps and then offering sales-related advice. Like sales meetings, classes and workshops are other ways to reinforce training. Mentoring is also a key tool in training new salespeople.

SOLVING AN ETHICAL CONTROVERSY
When the Sale Doesn't Benefit the Customer

Some reputable sources such as *Consumer Reports* say most product failures occur late in a product's life, making extended warranties a poor value for consumers. Selling such protection is so profitable that many companies push it anyway, at prices that can run up to 20 percent or more of the item's purchase price. Best Buy is one retailer that aggressively pitches warranties for electronics on the grounds that products break, customers handle them clumsily, or the plans are cheap and save time and money. Some critics insist such plans are scams.

Is it appropriate for companies to sell extended warranties that might not be in the customer's best interest?

PRO
1. Some customers want the peace of mind of knowing they can repair or replace an item in a few years at no extra charge.
2. Buyers will make up their own minds about what is a good value.

CON
1. Most product failures occur so early that repair is still covered under the manufacturer's own short-term warranty.
2. Some extended warranties are so overpriced that it's cheaper to buy a replacement item.

Summary
For consumers, there doesn't seem to be a clear-cut answer about whether to spend the extra money to buy extended warranties. In the meantime, many retailers continue to provide their salespeople with incentives to sell extended warranties because of the revenue the warranties generate for the company.

Sources: "Extended Warranty Buying Guide," *Consumer Reports*, accessed March 31, 2014, www.consumerreports.org; Rich Smith, "Are Extended Warranties Worth It? Harvard Debates Consumer Reports," *Daily Finance*, accessed March 31, 2014, www.dailyfinance.com; Regina Lewis, "Are Extended Warranties Worth It?" *USA Today*, accessed March 31, 2014, www.usatoday.com; Brendan Matthews, "How This Retailer Actually Makes Money," *Motley Fool*, accessed March 31, 2014, www.fool.com; "How to Beware of Extended Warranty Scams," *eHow.com*, accessed March 31, 2014, www.ehow.com; Damon Darlin, "Don't Worry, Be Happy: The Warranty Psychology," *The New York Times*, accessed March 31, 2014, www.nytimes.com.

ORGANIZATION

Sales managers are responsible for the organization of the field sales force. General organizational alignments—usually made by top management—may be based on geography, products, types of customers, or some combination of these factors. Figure 17.3 presents a streamlined organizational chart illustrating each of these alignments.

A product sales organization is likely to have a specialized sales force for each major category of the firm's products. This approach is common among B2B companies that market large numbers of highly technical, complex products sold through different marketing channels.

Firms that market similar products throughout large territories often use geographic specialization. Multinational corporations may have different sales divisions on different continents and in different countries. A geographic organization may also be combined with one of the other organizational methods.

However, many companies are moving away from using territorial sales reps as they adopt customer-focused sales forces. For example, a single territory that contains two major customers might be redefined so that the same sales rep covers both customers. Customer-oriented organizations use different sales force strategies for each major type of customer served. Some firms assign separate

FIGURE 17.3
Basic Approaches to Organizing the Sales Force

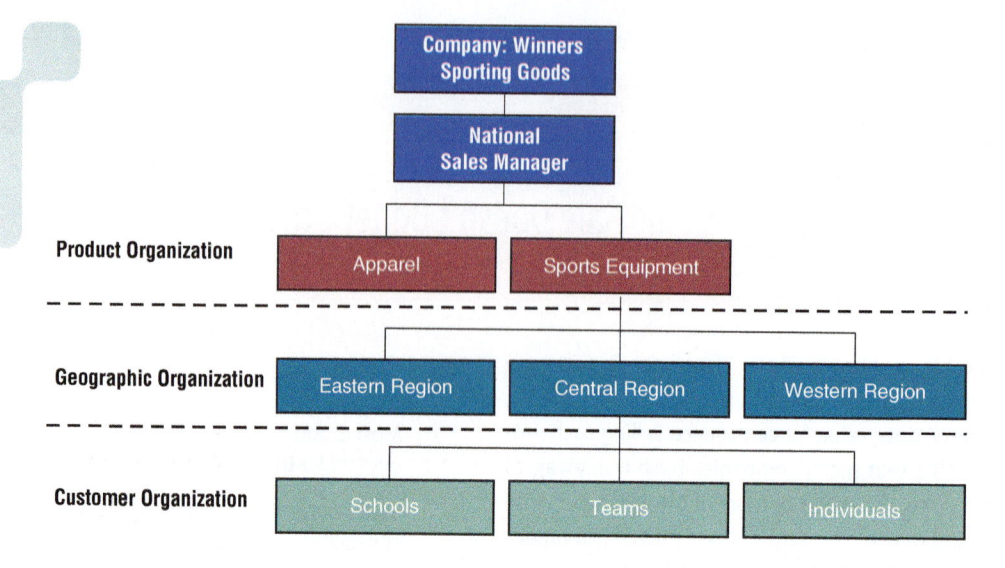

```
                    Company: Winners
                     Sporting Goods
                            |
                        National
                      Sales Manager
                            |
Product Organization    Apparel — Sports Equipment
- - - - - - - - - - - - - - - - - - - - - - - - - - -
Geographic Organization   Eastern Region — Central Region — Western Region
- - - - - - - - - - - - - - - - - - - - - - - - - - -
Customer Organization    Schools — Teams — Individuals
```

sales forces for their consumer and organizational customers. Others have sales forces for specific industries, such as financial services and publishing. Sales forces can also be organized by customer size, with a separate sales force assigned to large, medium, and small accounts.

Many firms using a customer-oriented structure adopt a **national accounts organization**. This format strengthens a firm's relationship with its largest customers by assigning senior sales personnel or sales teams to major accounts. Organizing by national accounts helps sales representatives develop cooperation among departments to meet special needs of the firm's most important customers. An example of national account selling is the relationship of Walmart and its major vendors. SC Johnson, Unilever, H.J. Heinz, Johnson & Johnson, Kimberly-Clark, Nestlé, Hormel, and Colgate Palmolive are just some of the companies that have sales offices near Walmart's headquarters in Bentonville, Arkansas.

As companies expand their market coverage across national borders, they could use a variant of national account sales teams. These global account teams may be staffed by local sales representatives in the countries in which a company is operating. In other instances, the firm selects highly trained sales executives from its domestic operations. In either case, specialized training is critical to the success of a company's global sales force.

The individual sales manager also must organize the sales territories within his or her area of responsibility. Factors such as sales potential, strengths and weaknesses of available personnel, and workloads are considered in territory allocation decisions.

national accounts organization
Promotional effort in which a dedicated sales team is assigned to a firm's major customers to provide sales and service needs.

SUPERVISION

Sales managers have differing opinions about the supervision of a sales force. Individuals and situations vary, so it is impossible to write a recipe for the exact amount of supervision needed in all cases. However, a concept known as **span of control** helps provide some general guidelines. Span of control refers to the number of sales representatives who report to first-level sales managers. The optimal span of control is affected by factors such as complexity of work activities, ability of the individual sales manager, degree of interdependence among individual salespeople, and the extent of training each salesperson receives. A 6-to-1 ratio has been suggested as the optimal span of control for first-level sales managers supervising technical or industrial salespeople. In contrast, a 10-to-1 ratio is recommended if sales representatives are calling on wholesale and retail accounts.

span of control
Number of representatives who report to first-level sales managers.

MOTIVATION

What motivates salespeople to perform their best? The sales manager is responsible for finding the answer to this question. The sales process involves problem solving, which sometimes includes frustration—particularly when a sale is delayed or falls through. Information sharing, recognition, bonuses, incentives, and benefits can all be used to help defray frustration and motivate a sales staff.

Developing an enthusiastic sales staff who are happy at their jobs is the goal of the sales manager. Motivation is an important part of a company's success.

Creating a positive, motivating environment doesn't necessarily mean instituting complex or expensive incentive programs. Monetary reward—cash—is often considered king. But sometimes simple recognition—a thank-you, a dinner, a year-end award—can go a long way. It is important for the sales manager to figure out what types of incentives will be most effective with his or her particular group of employees. Some firms go all out, dangling luxury items such as computers, digital cameras, or trips in front of the sales force as rewards. A Caribbean cruise, a trip to Disney World, or a weekend in Las Vegas could be the carrot that works, particularly if family members are included. Some firms purchase gift cards from retailers, such as L.L.Bean or Lowe's, to distribute to sales staff who perform well.

But not all incentive programs are effective at motivating employees. A program that sets unrealistic targets, that isn't publicized, or that allows only certain sales personnel to participate can actually backfire. So it is important for sales management to plan carefully for an incentive program to succeed.

Sales managers can also gain insight into the subject of motivation by studying the various theories of motivation developed over the years. One theory that has been applied effectively to sales force motivation is **expectancy theory**, which states that motivation depends on the expectations an individual has of his or her ability to perform the job and on how performance relates to attaining rewards the individual values.

expectancy theory Theory that motivation depends on an individual's expectations of his or her ability to perform a job and how that performance relates to attaining a desired reward.

Sales managers can apply the expectancy theory of motivation by following a five-step process:

1. Let each salesperson know in detail what is expected in terms of selling goals, service standards, and other areas of performance. Rather than setting goals just once a year, many firms do so semiannually, quarterly, or even monthly.

2. Make the work valuable by assessing the needs, values, and abilities of each salesperson and then assigning appropriate tasks.

3. Make the work achievable. As leaders, sales managers must inspire self-confidence in their salespeople and offer training and coaching to reassure them.

4. Provide immediate and specific feedback, guiding those who need improvement and giving positive feedback to those who do well.

5. Offer rewards each salesperson values, whether it is an incentive as described previously, opportunity for advancement, or a bonus.

COMPENSATION

Money is an important part of any person's job, and the salesperson is no exception. So deciding how best to compensate the sales force can be a critical factor in motivation. Sales compensation can be based on a commission, a straight salary, or a combination of both. Bonuses based on end-of-year results are another popular form of compensation. The increasing popularity of team selling has also forced companies to set up reward programs to recognize performance of business units and teams. Today, about 25 percent of firms reward business-unit performance.

A **commission** is a payment tied directly to the sales or profits a salesperson achieves. A salesperson might receive a 5 percent commission on all sales up to a specified quota and a 7 percent commission on sales beyond that point. This approach to sales compensation is increasingly popular. But while commissions reinforce selling incentives, they may cause some sales force members to overlook nonselling activities such as completing sales reports, delivering promotion materials, and servicing existing accounts. In addition, salespeople who operate entirely on commission may become too aggressive in their approach to potential customers, which could backfire.

commission Incentive compensation directly related to the sales or profits achieved by a sales person.

A **salary** is a fixed payment made periodically to an employee. A firm that bases compensation on salaries rather than commissions might pay a salesperson a set amount every week, twice a month, or once a month. A company must balance benefits and disadvantages in paying predetermined salaries to compensate managers and sales personnel. A straight salary plan gives management more control over how sales personnel allocate their efforts, but it may reduce the incentive to find new markets and land new accounts.

salary Fixed compensation payment made periodically to an employee.

FIGURE 17.4
Median Pay for Account Managers by Years of Experience

Source: Data from Account Manager Sales Salary, *PayScale*, accessed April 5, 2014, www.payscale.com.

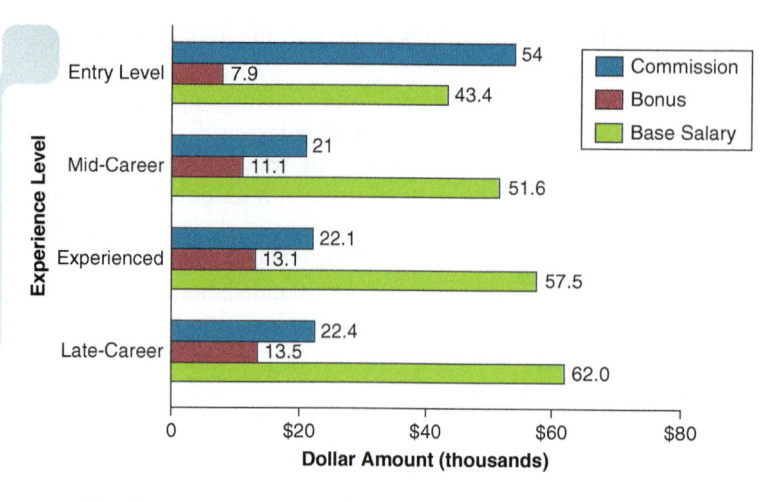

Experience Level	Commission	Bonus	Base Salary
Entry Level	54	7.9	43.4
Mid-Career	21	11.1	51.6
Experienced	22.1	13.1	57.5
Late-Career	22.4	13.5	62.0

Dollar Amount (thousands)

Many firms find it's best to develop compensation programs that combine features of both salary and commission plans. A new salesperson often receives a base salary while in training, even if he or she moves to full commission later on. If the salesperson does a lot of driving as part of the job, he or she may receive a vehicle. If the person works from home, there might be an allowance toward setting up an office there.

Total compensation packages vary according to industry, with the finance, insurance, and real estate industries coming out on top, followed closely by general services. They also vary according to years of experience in sales. Figure 17.4 reflects the findings of a recent pay survey of *account managers*—another name for a salesperson responsible for one or more customers, or *accounts*. The data shows how account managers' median base pay, bonus, and commissions vary by years of experience.

EVALUATION AND CONTROL

Perhaps the most difficult tasks required of sales managers are evaluation and control. Sales managers are responsible for setting standards and choosing the best methods for measuring sales performance. Sales volume, profitability, and changes in market share are the usual means of evaluating sales effectiveness. They typically involve the use of **sales quotas**—specified sales or profit targets that the firm expects salespeople to achieve. A particular sales representative might be expected to generate sales of $2.25 million in his or her territory during a given year. In many cases, the quota is tied to the compensation system. Technology has greatly improved the ability of sales managers to monitor the effectiveness of their sales staffs. Databases help sales managers to quickly divide revenues by salesperson, account, and geographic area.

In today's marketing environment, other measures, such as customer satisfaction, profit contribution, share of product–category sales, and customer retention, also come into play. This is the result of three factors:

1. A long-term orientation that results from emphasis on building customer relationships

2. The fact that evaluations based on sales volume alone may lead to overselling and inventory problems that may damage customer relationships

3. The need to encourage sales representatives to develop new accounts, provide customer service, and emphasize new products. Sales quotas tend to put focus on short-term selling goals rather than long-term relationships.

The sales manager must follow a formal system that includes a consistent series of decisions. This way, the manager can make fair and accurate evaluations. The system helps the sales manager answer three general questions:

1. *Where does each salesperson's performance rank relative to predetermined standards?* This comparison takes into consideration any uncontrollable variables on sales performance, such as a natural disaster or unforeseen change in the industry.

2. *What are the salesperson's strong points?* The manager might list areas of the salesperson's performance in which he or she has performed above the standard. Or strong points could be placed in categories such as technical ability, processes, and end results.

sales quotas Level of expected sales for a territory, product, customer, or salesperson against which actual results are compared.

3. *What are the salesperson's weak points?* No one likes to hear criticism, but when it is offered constructively, it can be motivation to improve performance. The manager and employee should establish specific objectives for improvement and set a timetable for judging the employee's improvement.

In completing the evaluation summary, the sales manager follows a set procedure so all employees are treated equally:

- Each aspect of sales performance for which a standard exists should be measured separately. This helps prevent the so-called halo effect, in which the rating given on one factor influences those on other performance variables.
- Each salesperson should be judged on the basis of actual sales performance rather than potential ability. This is why rankings are important in the evaluation.
- Sales managers must judge each salesperson on the basis of sales performance for the entire period under consideration, rather than for a few particular incidents.
- The evaluation should be reviewed by a third party, such as the manager's boss or a human resources manager, for completeness and objectivity.

> **ASSESSMENT CHECK**
>
> 6.1 What are the basic functions performed by a sales manager?
>
> 6.2 Define span of control.
>
> 6.3 What are the three main questions a sales manager must address as part of a salesperson's evaluation?

Once the evaluation is complete, both manager and salesperson should focus on positive action—whether it is a drive toward new goals or correcting a negative situation. An evaluation should be motivation for improved performance.

ETHICAL ISSUES IN SALES

Promotional activities can raise ethical questions, and personal selling is no exception. A difficult economy or highly competitive environment may tempt some salespeople—particularly those new to the business—to behave in ways they might later regret. They might use the company car for a family trip. They might give personal or expensive gifts to customers. They might try to sell a product they know is not right for a particular customer's needs. But today's experienced, highly professional salespeople know long-term success requires a strong code of ethics. They also know a single breach of ethics could have a devastating effect on their careers.

Sales managers and top executives can do a lot to foster a corporate culture that encourages honesty and ethical behavior. Here are some characteristics of such a culture:

- *Employees understand what is expected of them.* A written code of ethics—which should be reviewed by all employees—in addition to ethics training helps educate employees in how to conduct business ethically.
- *Open communication.* Employees who feel comfortable talking with their supervisors are more apt to ask questions if they are uncertain about situations or decisions and to report any violations they come across.
- *Managers lead by example.* Workers naturally emulate the ethical behavior of managers. A sales manager who is honest with customers and leaves the company car at home during vacation is likely to be imitated by his or her sales staff.

Regardless of corporate culture, every salesperson is responsible for his or her behavior and relationship with customers. If, as a new salesperson, you find yourself uncertain about a decision, ask yourself the questions that follow. The answers should help you make the ethical choice.

> **7** Explain the role of ethical behavior in personal selling.

ASSESSMENT CHECK

7.1 Why is it important for salespeople to maintain ethical behavior?

7.2 What are the characteristics of companies that foster corporate cultures that encourage ethical behavior?

1. Does my decision affect anyone other than myself and the bottom line?
2. Is my success based on making the sale or creating a loyal customer?
3. Are my dealings with customers in their best interest and not exploiting their trust?
4. What price will I pay for this decision?

SALES PROMOTION

8 Describe the role of sales promotion in the promotional mix and the different types of sales promotions.

sales promotion Marketing activities other than personal selling, advertising, and publicity that enhance consumer purchasing and dealer effectiveness.

Sales promotion includes marketing activities other than personal selling, advertising, and publicity designed to enhance consumer purchasing and dealer effectiveness. In the United States, companies have been giving away premiums for more than 100 years.

Sales promotion techniques were originally intended as short-term incentives aimed at producing an immediate response: a purchase. Today, however, marketers recognize sales promotion as an integral part of the overall marketing plan, and the focus has shifted from short-term goals to long-term objectives of building brand equity and maintaining continuing purchases. A frequent-flyer program enables an airline to build a base of loyal customers. A frequent-stay program allows a hotel chain to attract regular guests.

Both retailers and manufacturers use sales promotions to offer consumers extra incentives to buy. These promotions are likely to stress price advantages, giveaways, or special offerings. The general objectives of sales promotion are to speed up the sales process and increase sales volume. Promotions can also help build loyalty. Through a consumer promotion, a marketer encourages consumers to try the product, use more of it, and buy it again. The firm also hopes to foster sales of related items and increase impulse purchases. Holiday specials are one type of sales promotion.

Retailers often use sales promotions to offer consumers extra incentives to buy, especially around the holidays.

On the day after Christmas in a recent year, Macy's offered 50 percent off on women's and children's clothing as well as on holiday decorations. The store also had extended hours for shoppers.[29]

Today, consumers have many more choices among products than in the past, and, for this reason, many marketers create special programs to build loyalty among their customers. However, with loyalty programs no longer unique, marketing and sales professionals work to build loyalty among their customers by managing customer relationships and regularly evaluating those relationships to determine how they can enhance them.[30]

Because sales promotion is so important to a marketing effort, an entire promotions industry exists to offer expert assistance in its use and to design unique promotions, just as the advertising industry offers similar services for advertisers. These companies, like advertising agencies, provide other firms with assistance in promoting their goods and services. Figure 17.5 shows current spending by companies for different types of promotions, many of which are conducted by these firms.

Sales promotions often produce their best results when combined with other marketing activities. Ads create awareness, while sales promotions lead to trial or purchase. After a presentation, a salesperson may offer a potential customer a discount coupon for the good or service. Promotions encourage immediate action because they impose limited time frames. Discount coupons and rebates usually have expiration dates. In addition, sales promotions produce measurable results, making it relatively easy for marketers to evaluate their effectiveness. If more people buy shoes during a buy-one-pair-get-one-free promotion at a shoe store, its owners know the promotion was successful.

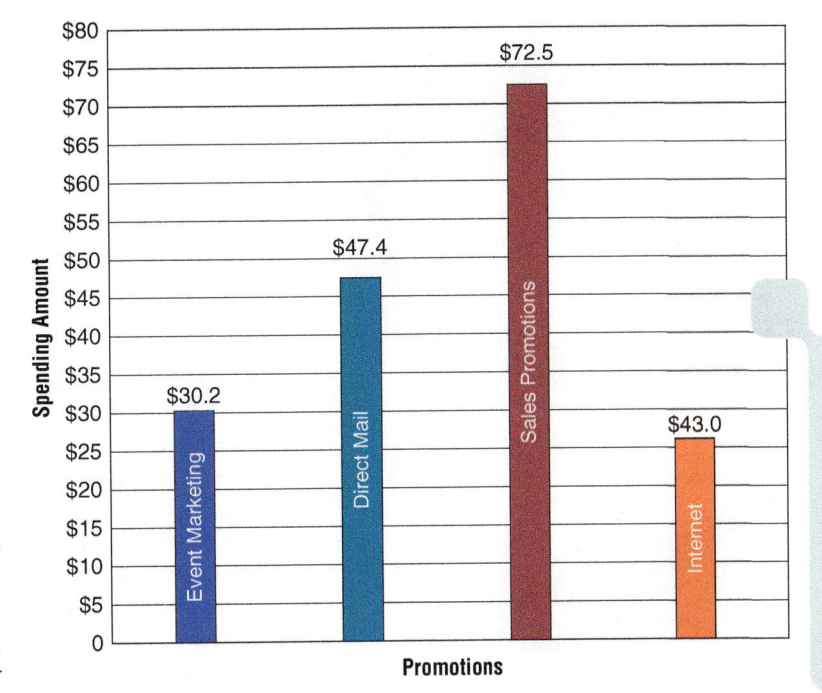

FIGURE 17.5
Current Spending by Companies for Different Types of Promotions (in billions)
Source: Data from ZenithOptimedia, "Advertising Expenditure Forecasts: Major Media and Marketing Services," *Marketing Fact Pack 2014*, accessed April 5, 2014, www.adage.com.

It is important to understand what sales promotions can and cannot do. They can encourage interest in both new and mature products, help introduce new products, encourage trial and repeat purchases, increase usage rates, neutralize competition, and reinforce advertising and personal selling efforts. On the other hand, sales promotions cannot overcome poor brand images, product deficiencies, or poor training for salespeople. While sales promotions increase volume in the short term, they may not lead to sales and profit growth in the long run.

Sales promotion techniques may serve all members of a marketing channel. In addition, manufacturers may use trade marketing methods to promote their products to resellers. Promotions are usually employed selectively. Sales promotion techniques include the following consumer-oriented promotions: coupons, refunds, samples, bonus packs, premiums, contests, sweepstakes, and specialty advertising. Trade-oriented promotions include trade allowances, point-of-purchase advertising, trade shows, dealer incentives, contests, and training programs.

CONSUMER-ORIENTED SALES PROMOTIONS

Consumer-oriented sales promotions encourage repurchases by rewarding current users, boosting sales of complementary products, and increasing impulse purchases. These promotions also attract consumer attention in the midst of advertising clutter. It's important for marketers to use sales promotions selectively; if they are overused, consumers begin to expect price discounts at all times, which ultimately diminishes brand equity. The following sections describe the various forms of consumer-oriented sales promotions.

Coupons and Refunds

Coupons, the most widely used form of sales promotion, offer discounts on the purchase price of goods and services. Consumers can redeem the coupons at retail outlets, which receive the face value of the coupon plus a handling fee from the manufacturer. The coupon industry has been challenged in recent years due to the growing clout of retailers and accounting rules that made couponing less attractive. But when the economy was weak and online coupons became

coupon Sales promotion technique that offers a discount on the purchase price of goods or services.

Mobile coupons have become common as consumers use smartphones as part of their retail shopping experience.

refund Cash given back to consumers who send in proof of purchase for one or more products.

sampling Free distribution of a product in an attempt to obtain future sales; process of selecting survey respondents or research participants.

bonus pack Specially packaged item that gives the purchaser a larger quantity at the regular price.

premium Item given free or at a reduced cost with purchases of other products.

contests Sales promotion technique that requires entrants to complete a task, such as solving a puzzle or answering questions on a quiz, for a chance to win a prize.

sweepstakes Sales promotion technique in which prize winners are selected by chance.

available, the situation changed again. In a recent year, coupon redemptions shot up 78 percent. Even so, an estimated 315 billion coupons were offered in the United States, and only 2.8 billion were redeemed. Still, consumers saved $3.5 billion.[31]

Mail, magazines, newspapers, package inserts, and the Internet are standard methods of distributing coupons. But another distribution channel for coupons has emerged: mobile phones. Thanks to advances in technology, retailers can distribute coupons digitally to mobile phone users. More than 120 million U.S. consumers use mobile coupons on their smartphones, and coupon redemption through mobile phones and tablets is expected to exceed $10 billion over the next few years.[32] **Refunds**, or rebates, offer cash back to consumers who send in proof of purchasing one or more products. Refunds help packaged-goods companies increase purchase rates, promote multiple purchases, and reward product users. Although many consumers find the refund forms too bothersome to complete, plenty still do.

Samples, Bonus Packs, and Premiums

Marketers are increasingly adopting the "try it, you'll like it" approach as an effective means of getting consumers to try and then purchase their goods and services. **Sampling** refers to the free distribution of a product in an attempt to obtain future sales. Samples may be distributed door-to-door, by mail, online, via demonstrations in stores or at events, or by including them in packages with other products.

Sampling produces a higher response rate than most other promotions. With sampling, marketers can target potential customers and be certain the product reaches them. Sampling provides an especially useful way to promote new or unusual products, because it gives the consumer a direct product experience.

A major disadvantage of traditional sampling is the high cost involved. Not only must the marketer give away small quantities of a product that might otherwise have generated revenues through regular sales, but the market is also in effect closed for the time it takes consumers to use up the samples. In addition, the marketer may encounter problems in distributing the samples.

A **bonus pack** is a specially packaged item that gives the purchaser a larger quantity at the regular price. For instance, Coppertone Tanning Oil recently offered 33 percent more sunscreen spray in a bottle for the regular price. **Premiums** are items given free or at reduced cost with purchases of other products. For example, Nexxus recently offered Humectress hair conditioner with a premium of its Therappe shampoo. Premiums have proven effective in motivating consumers to try new products or different brands. A premium should have some relationship with the product or brand it accompanies, though. For example, a home improvement center might offer free measuring tapes to its customers.

Contests and Sweepstakes

Firms often sponsor contests and sweepstakes to introduce new goods and services and attract additional customers. **Contests** require entrants to complete a task, such as solving a puzzle or answering questions in a trivia quiz, and they may also require proofs of purchase. **Sweepstakes**, on the other hand, choose winners by chance, so no product purchase is necessary. They are more popular with consumers than contests because they do not take as much effort for consumers to enter. Marketers like them, too, because they are inexpensive to run, and the number of winners is predetermined. With some contests, the sponsors cannot predict the number of people who will correctly complete the puzzles or gather the right number of symbols from scratch-off cards.

Marketers have increasingly turned to the Internet and social media sites for contests and sweepstakes because of its relatively low cost and ability to provide data immediately. Interactivity is also a key part of the online experience: As consumers become more engaged in the contest or sweepstakes event, they also build a relationship with the firm's products. Friendly Planet Travel, which conducts group tours around the world, recently held a sweepstakes as part of its "Win the World" Facebook sweepstakes. The prize was a free, all-inclusive 13-day vacation in Greece. Contestants entered a contact on Friendly Planet's Facebook page. If a contestant shared the page with a Facebook friend, his or her name was entered again for another chance at winning.[33]

Specialty Advertising

The origin of specialty advertising has been traced to the Middle Ages, when artisans gave wooden pegs bearing their names to prospects, who drove them into the walls at home to serve as convenient hangers for armor. Corporations began putting their names on various products in the late 1800s, as newspapers and print shops explored new methods to earn additional revenues from their expensive printing presses. Today, just about everyone owns a cap or T-shirt with the name or logo of a company, organization, or product displayed on it.

Specialty advertising is a sales promotion technique that places the advertiser's name, address, and advertising message on useful articles that are then distributed to target consumers. Wearable products are the most popular, accounting for nearly a third of specialty advertising sales. Pens, mugs, glassware, and calendars are other popular forms.

Advertising specialties help reinforce previous or future advertising and sales messages. Consumers like these giveaways, which generate stronger responses to direct mail, resulting in three times the dollar volume of sales compared with direct mail alone. Companies use this form of promotion to highlight store openings and new products, motivate salespeople, increase visits to trade show booths, and remind customers about their products.

specialty advertising Sales promotion technique that places the advertiser's name, address, and advertising message on useful articles that are then distributed to target consumers.

TRADE-ORIENTED PROMOTIONS

Sales promotion techniques can also contribute effectively to campaigns aimed at retailers and wholesalers. **Trade promotion** is sales promotion that appeals to marketing intermediaries rather than final consumers. Marketers use trade promotions in push strategies by encouraging resellers to stock new products, continue to carry existing ones, and promote both effectively to consumers. The typical firm spends about half of its promotional budget on trade promotion—as much money as it spends on advertising and consumer-oriented sales promotions combined. Successful trade promotions offer financial incentives. They require careful timing and attention to costs and are easy to implement by retailers.

trade promotion Sales promotion that appeals to marketing intermediaries rather than consumers.

TRADE ALLOWANCES

Among the most common trade promotion methods are **trade allowances**—special financial incentives offered to wholesalers and retailers that purchase or promote specific products. These offers take various forms. A buying allowance gives retailers a discount on goods. They include off-invoice allowances through which retailers deduct specified amounts from their invoices or receive free goods, such as one free case for every ten ordered. When a manufacturer offers a promotional allowance, it agrees to pay the reseller a certain amount to cover the costs of special promotional displays or extensive advertising that features the manufacturer's product. The goal is to increase sales to consumers by encouraging resellers to promote their products effectively.

trade allowances Financial incentive offered to wholesalers and retailers that purchase or promote specific products.

POINT-OF-PURCHASE ADVERTISING

A display or other promotion located near the site of the actual buying decision is known as **point-of-purchase (POP) advertising**. This method of sales promotion capitalizes on the fact that nearly two-thirds of shoppers make their purchase decisions as they walk through a store, so it encourages retailers to improve on-site merchandising. Product suppliers assist the vendor by creating special displays designed to stimulate sales of the promoted item.

point-of-purchase (POP) advertising Display or other promotion placed near the site of the actual buying decision.

Freestanding POP promotions often appear at the ends of shopping aisles. On a typical trip to the supermarket, you might see a POP display for Febreze air fresheners, Coppertone sunscreen, or Duracell batteries. Warehouse-style retailers, such as Home Depot and Sam's Club, along with Staples and Target, all use POP advertising displays frequently. Electronic kiosks, which allow consumers to place orders for items not available in the store, have begun to transform the POP display industry, as creators of these displays look for ways to involve consumers more actively as well as entertain them.

TRADE SHOWS

trade show Product exhibition organized by industry trade associations to showcase goods and services.

To influence resellers and other members of the distribution channel, many marketers participate in **trade shows**. These shows are often organized by industry trade associations; frequently, they are part of these associations' annual meetings or conventions. Vendors who serve the industries display and demonstrate their products for attendees. Industries that hold trade shows include manufacturers of sporting goods, medical equipment, electronics, automobiles, clothing, and home furnishings. Service industries include hair styling, health care, travel, and restaurant franchises.

Because of the expense involved in trade shows, a company must assess the value of these shows on several criteria, such as direct sales, any increase in product awareness, image building, and any contribution to the firm's marketing communications efforts. Trade shows give especially effective opportunities to introduce new products and generate sales leads. Some types of shows reach ultimate consumers as well as channel members. Home, recreation, and automobile shows, for instance, allow businesses to display and demonstrate home improvement, recreation, and other consumer products.

DEALER INCENTIVES, CONTESTS, AND TRAINING PROGRAMS

Manufacturers run dealer incentive programs and contests to reward retailers and their salespeople who increase sales and, more generally, to promote specific products. These channel members receive incentives for performing promotion-related tasks and can win contests by reaching sales goals. Manufacturers may offer major prizes to resellers, such as trips to exotic places. **Push money**—which retailers commonly refer to as *spiffs*—is another incentive that gives retail salespeople cash rewards for every unit of a product they sell. This benefit increases the likelihood that the salesperson will try to persuade a customer to buy the product rather than a competing brand.

push money Cash reward paid to retail salespeople for every unit of a product they sell.

For more expensive and highly complex products, manufacturers often provide specialized training for retail salespeople. This background helps sales personnel explain features, competitive advantages, and other information to consumers. Training can be provided in several ways: A manufacturer's sales representative can conduct training sessions during regular sales calls, or the firm can provide product information as part of a Web seminar, or webinar.

ASSESSMENT CHECK

8.1 Define sales promotion.
8.2 Identify at least four types of consumer-oriented sales promotions.
8.3 Identify at least three types of trade-oriented sales promotions.

Strategic Implications of Marketing in the 21st Century

Today's salespeople are a new breed. Richly nourished in a tradition of sales, their roles are strengthened even further through technology. Nothing can replace the power of personal selling in generating sales and building strong, loyal customer relationships.

Salespeople today are a critical link in developing relationships between the customer and the company. They communicate customer needs and wants to coworkers in various units within an organization, enabling a cooperative, companywide effort in improving product offerings and better satisfying individuals within the target market. For salespeople, the greatest benefit of electronic technologies is the ability to share knowledge when it is needed with those who need to know, including customers, suppliers, and employees.

Because buyers are now more sophisticated, demanding more rapid and lower-cost transactions, salespeople must be quick and creative as they find solutions to their customers' problems. Product lifecycles are accelerating, and customers who demand more are likely to switch from one product to another. Recognizing the long-term impact of keeping satisfied buyers—those who make repeat purchases and cross-purchases and provide referrals—versus dissatisfied buyers, organizations increasingly train their sales forces to provide superior customer service and reward them for increasing satisfaction levels.

The traditional skills of a salesperson included persuasion, selling ability, and product knowledge. But today's sales professionals are also likely to possess strong communication and problem-solving skills. Earlier generations of sales personnel tended to be self-driven; today's sales professional is more likely to be a team player as well as a customer advocate who serves his or her buyers by solving problems.

The modern professional salesperson is greatly assisted by the judicious use of both consumer- and trade-oriented sales promotions. Sales promotion is often overlooked in discussions of high-profile advertising; the typical firm allocates more promotional dollars for sales promotion than for advertising. The proven effectiveness of sales promotion makes it a widely used promotional mix component for most marketers.

Get online now for additional learning tools to help you master your marketing knowledge—visit **WWW.CENGAGEBRAIN.COM** today!

REVIEW OF CHAPTER OBJECTIVES

1 Describe the role of today's salesperson.

Today's salesperson seeks to form long-lasting relationships with customers by providing high levels of customer service rather than going for the quick sale. Firms have begun to integrate their computer and communications technologies into the sales function, so people involved in personal selling have an expanded role.

2 Describe the four sales channels.

Over-the-counter (retail) selling takes place in a retail location and usually involves providing product information and completing a sale. Field selling involves making personal sales calls on customers. Under certain circumstances, telemarketing is used to provide product information and answer questions from customers who call. Inside selling relies on phone, mail, and e-marketing to provide continuing sales and product services for customers.

3 Explain the three major trends in personal selling.

Companies are turning to relationship selling, consultative selling, and team selling. Relationship selling occurs when a salesperson builds a mutually beneficial relationship with a customer on a regular basis over an extended period. Consultative selling involves meeting customer needs by listening to customers, understanding and caring about their problems, paying attention to the details, and following through after the sale. Team selling occurs when the salesperson joins with specialists from other functional areas of the firm to complete the selling process.

4 Discuss the three basic sales tasks.

Order processing is the routine handling of an order. It characterizes a sales setting in which the need is made known and is acknowledged by the customer. Creative selling is persuasion aimed at making the prospect see the value of the good or service presented. Missionary selling is indirect selling, such as making goodwill calls and providing technical or operational assistance.

5 Outline the seven steps in the sales process.

The basic steps in the sales process are prospecting and qualifying, approach, presentation, demonstration, handling objections, closing, and follow-up.

6 Identify the seven functions of a sales manager.

The sales manager's functions are recruitment and selection, training, organization, supervision, motivation, compensation, and evaluation and control. A manager links the sales force to other aspects of the internal and external environments.

7 Explain the role of ethical behavior in personal selling.

Ethical behavior is vital to building positive, long-term relationships with customers. Although some people believe ethical problems are inevitable, employers can do much to foster a corporate culture that encourages honesty and ethical behavior. In addition, each salesperson is responsible for his or her own behavior and relationship with customers.

8 Describe the role of sales promotion in the promotional mix and the different types of sales promotions.

Sales promotion includes activities other than personal selling, advertising, and publicity designed to enhance consumer purchasing and dealer effectiveness. Sales promotion is an integral part of the overall marketing plan, intended to increase sales and build brand equity. Promotions often produce their best results when combined with other marketing activities. Consumer-oriented sales promotions include coupons, refunds, samples, bonus packs, premiums, contests and sweepstakes, and specialty advertising. Trade-oriented promotions include trade allowances, point-of-purchase (POP) advertising, trade shows, dealer incentives, contests, and training programs.

ASSESSMENT CHECK: ANSWERS

1.1 What is personal selling? Personal selling is the process of a seller's person-to-person promotional presentation to a buyer.

1.2 What is the main focus of today's salespeople? The main focus of today's salespeople is to build long-lasting relationships with customers.

2.1 What is over-the-counter selling? Over-the-counter selling describes selling in retail and some wholesale locations. Most of these transactions take place directly with customers.

2.2 What is field selling? Field selling involves making sales calls on prospective and existing customers at their businesses or homes.

2.3 Distinguish between outbound and inbound telemarketing. Outbound telemarketing takes place when a salesperson phones customers; inbound telemarketing takes place when customers call the selling firm.

3.1 Identify the three major personal selling approaches. The three major personal selling approaches are relationship selling, consultative selling, and team selling.

3.2 Distinguish between relationship selling and consultative selling. Relationship selling is a technique for building a mutually beneficial partnership with a customer. Consultative selling involves meeting customers' needs by listening to, understanding, and paying attention to their problems, then following up after a sale.

4.1 What are the three major tasks performed by salespeople? The three major tasks are order processing, creative selling, and team selling.

4.2 What are the three steps of order processing? The three steps of order processing are identifying customer needs, pointing out the need to the customer, and completing the order.

5.1 Identify the seven steps of the sales process. The seven steps of the sales process are prospecting and qualifying, approach, presentation, demonstration, handling objections, closing, and follow-up.

5.2 Why is follow-up important to the sales effort? Follow-up allows the salesperson to reinforce the customer's purchase decision, strengthen the bond, and correct any problems.

6.1 What are the basic functions performed by a sales manager? The seven basic functions of a sales manager are recruitment and selection, training, organization, supervision, motivation, compensation, and evaluation and control.

6.2 Define span of control. Span of control refers to the number of sales representatives who report to first-level sales managers.

6.3 What are the three main questions a sales manager must address as part of a salesperson's evaluation? The three main questions a sales manager must address are the following: Where does each salesperson's performance rank relative to predetermined standards? What are the salesperson's strong points? What are the salesperson's weak points?

7.1 Why is it important for salespeople to maintain ethical behavior? Salespeople need to maintain ethical behavior, because it is vital to their firm's relationships with customers, and because they represent their company. A breach of ethics could also be detrimental to an individual's career.

7.2 What are the characteristics of companies that foster corporate cultures that encourage ethical behavior? Characteristics of corporations fostering ethical behavior include the following: open communication, employees who understand what is expected of them, and managers who lead by example.

8.1 Define sales promotion. Sales promotion includes marketing activities other than personal selling, advertising, and publicity designed to enhance consumer purchasing and dealer effectiveness.

8.2 Identify at least four types of consumer-oriented sales promotions. Consumer-oriented sales promotions include coupons, refunds, samples, bonus packs, premiums, contests, sweepstakes, and specialty advertising.

8.3 Identify at least three types of trade-oriented sales promotions. Trade-oriented sales promotions include trade allowances, POP advertising, trade shows, dealer incentives, contests, and training programs.

MARKETING TERMS YOU NEED TO KNOW

personal selling 556
over-the-counter selling 557
field selling 559
network marketing 560
telemarketing 560
outbound telemarketing 560
inbound telemarketing 561
inside selling 561
relationship selling 562
consultative selling 563
cross-selling 563
team selling 564
virtual sales team 564
order processing 565
creative selling 566
missionary selling 567
sales incentives 567
prospecting 567
qualifying 567
approach 567
precall planning 568
presentation 568
cold calling 568
demonstration 569
objections 570
closing 570
follow-up 571
national accounts organization 574
span of control 574
expectancy theory 575
commission 575
salary 575
sales quotas 576
sales promotion 578
coupon 579
refund 580
sampling 580
bonus pack 580
premium 580
contests 580
sweepstakes 580
specialty advertising 581
trade promotion 581
trade allowances 581
point-of-purchase (POP) advertising 581
trade show 582
push money 582

ASSURANCE OF LEARNING REVIEW

1. How does each of the following factors affect the decision to emphasize personal selling or advertising and sales promotion?
   a. geographic market concentration
   b. length of marketing channels
   c. degree of product technical complexity
2. Which of the four sales channels is each of the following salespeople most likely to use?
   a. salesperson in a Kohl's store
   b. Century 21 real estate agent
   c. route driver for Doritos snack foods (sells and delivers to local food retailers)
   d. technical support for Xerox
3. What is team selling? Describe a situation in which you think it would be effective.
4. Why is it important for a salesperson to understand order processing—regardless of the type of selling he or she is engaged in?
5. What is the role of a sales incentive?
6. Suppose you are hired as a salesperson for a firm that offers prep courses for standardized tests. Where might you find some leads?
7. What is expectancy theory? How do sales managers use it?
8. What is the role of sales promotion in the marketing effort?
9. What are the benefits of sampling? What are the drawbacks?
10. What is trade promotion? What are its objectives?

PROJECTS AND TEAMWORK EXERCISES

1. Cross-selling can be an effective way for a firm to expand. Locate an advertisement for a firm you believe could benefit from cross-selling. List ways it could offer multiple goods or services to the same customer. Then create a new ad illustrating the multiple offerings.
2. With a partner, choose one of the following sales situations. Then take turns coming up with creative ways to close the deal, with one of you playing the customer and the other playing the salesperson. Present your closing scenarios to the class.
   a. You are a sales associate at a car dealership, and a potential customer has just test-driven one of your newest models. You have handled all the customer's objections and settled on a price. You don't want the customer to leave without agreeing to purchase the car.
   b. You operate a lawn-care business and have visited several homeowners in a new development. Three of them have already agreed to give your service a try. You are meeting with the fourth and want to close that sale, too.
3. As sales representatives for a cooperative of organic farmers, you and your team are about to make a sales presentation to a national supermarket chain. List the most important messages you wish to relate and then role-play the sales presentation.
4. On your own or with a classmate, go online and research a firm such as General Mills, Ford, or Burger King to find out what kinds of consumer-oriented promotions the company is conducting for its various brands or individual products. Which promotions seem the most appealing to you as a consumer? Why? Present your findings to the class.
5. With a classmate, design a specialty advertising item for one of the following companies or its products, or choose one of your own. Present your design sketches to the class.
   a. SeaWorld or Busch Gardens
   b. Subway
   c. Verizon Wireless
   d. FIJI bottled water
   e. Houston Astros baseball team

CRITICAL-THINKING EXERCISES

1. Since the implementation of the national Do Not Call Registry, consumers have noticed a substantial increase in emails and texts containing sales messages. As a marketer, do you think this type of selling is effective? Why or why not?
2. Green Mountain Coffee Roasters is well known for its specialty coffees, available in many retail outlets such as supermarkets and convenience stores. But visit a medical office or a car dealership, and you might find it there as well—in one-cup dispensers, ready for individuals to brew while waiting. This requires personal selling to office managers, doctors, and the like. What role does relationship selling play in this situation? What kind of training might Green Mountain sales reps receive?
3. Assume that a friend asks you to solicit donations for a local charity (you pick the charity). Outline your approach and presentation as a salesperson would.

4. Why is the recruitment and selection stage of the hiring process one of a sales manager's greatest challenges?
5. Food manufacturers often set up tables in supermarkets and offer free samples to shoppers, along with coupons for the promoted items. Sometimes restaurants offer free coffee or drink refills. What other products might lend themselves to sampling? Make a list. Pick one of the items and come up with a sampling plan for it. Where and when would you sample? To whom would you offer samples?

ETHICS EXERCISE

You have been hired by a discount sporting-goods retailer for an over-the-counter sales position. You have completed a training course that includes learning about the products, assisting customers, and cross-selling. You have made several good friends in the training course and sometimes get together after work to go running, play golf, or have dinner. You've noticed that one of your friends has really taken the training course to heart and has adopted a very aggressive attitude toward customers in the store, pushing them to buy just about anything, whether they need it or not.

1. Do you agree with your friend's actions? Why or why not?
2. Should you discuss the situation with your friend? Should you discuss it with your supervisor? Explain your response.

INTERNET EXERCISES

1. **Sales careers.** Visit the three websites listed here and review the material on careers in sales. Make a list of five interesting facts about sales careers. Did this exercise make you more or less interested in a sales career? Explain your answer.

   www.collegegrad.com/careers/marke.shtml

   http://www.forbes.com/sites/jacquelynsmith/2013/12/03/7-tips-for-landing-the-best-possible-sales-job/

   http://money.usnews.com/careers/best-jobs/sales-manager

2. **Compensation systems.** Go to the websites listed below and review the material on compensation systems. Prepare a report outlining the major issues associated with designing a sales compensation system.

   www.inc.com/guides/sales-compensation-plan.html

   www.davekahle.com/compfeature.html

   http://tecmidwest.com/2014/04/effective-sales-compensation-plan/

3. **CES.** The Consumer Electronics Show (CES) is one of the largest trade shows in the world. Visit the CES website and answer the following questions:
   a. When and where is the CES held?
   b. How many attended the most recent CES? How many firms and organizations had exhibits?
   c. What were the major new products introduced at the most recent CES?

   www.cesweb.org

Note: Internet Web addresses change frequently. If you don't find the exact site listed, you may need to access the organization's home page and search from there or use a search engine such as Google or Bing.

CASE 17.1
Shaq Promotes His Personal Brand

Shaquille O'Neal, the legendary seven-foot NBA center, veteran of many championship seasons and recipient of multiple MVP and All-Star accolades, retired from the court after 19 memorable years. But in some circles he is better known now than ever. Almost 9 million people follow him on Twitter, where he makes millions of dollars tweeting about the product brands he prefers.

O'Neal has kept tight control on his personal brand in the process. Upon retirement, he told consumer product firms eager for his endorsements that he would talk directly to fans on his own terms. Those terms are simple: Shaq wants to entertain and inspire. Determined not to become just another product spokesperson or allow his Twitter feed or Facebook page (also with millions of followers) to be scripted for him, he has focused on a strategy some call "soft power" to infuse his promotional messages with his own personality. Even his retirement announcement video was linked on Twitter.

Stunts he films to share with fans and quirky pitches that reflect his daily life are clearly catching on with his growing audience. "I never say, 'Go buy this' on my Twitter," O'Neal says. Instead, he'll ask fans how many Oreos they think he can eat in 15 seconds, and hundreds of thousands of people respond to his credibility and humor by buying Oreos. One industry observer calls O'Neal's brand one of the most authentic in social media today, praise that stems from the basketball star's commitment to project an online personality that's funny and smart, that inspires people by making them laugh, and that doesn't try to sell anything, not even himself.

Other promotional efforts with O'Neal's backing include AriZona Beverages' basketball camp scholarships, set up to coincide with the introduction of a new all-natural line of cream sodas called Soda Shaq. The partnership seems perfectly authentic for O'Neal, who credits sports with keeping him out of trouble when he was a kid.

QUESTIONS FOR CRITICAL THINKING

1. O'Neal advocates entertaining and inspiring as ways to convey a successful promotional message. What makes people take his messages seriously enough to buy products as a result of his approach?

2. One marketing communications executive says social media promotions help humans connect with other humans and not with logos. Do you agree? Why or why not?

Sources: David A. Kaplan, "Shaq Inq.," *Fortune*, accessed April 5, 2014, http://money.cnn.com; Laura Lorber, "Shaquille O'Neal on Geeks, Partnering and Winning in Business, *Entrepreneur*, accessed April 5, 2014, www.entrepreneur.com; "Twitter Athletes: $5 Million in 140 Characters," *Men's Journal*, accessed April 5, 2014, www.mensjournal.com; "Shaq on Twitter," *Twitter*, accessed April 5, 2014, https://twitter.com/shaq; "Shaquille O'Neal and AriZona Beverages Promote Healthy Lifestyles," *Yahoo Finance*, accessed April 5, 2014, http://finance.yahoo.com; Kevin Gray, "Laughing, Tweeting and Eating: The Soft Power of Shaquille O'Neal," *Smart Planet*, accessed April 5, 2014, www.smartplanet.com; Mike Adler, "Building Your Personal Brand with Shaq," *Lendio*, accessed April 5, 2014, www.lendio.com.

VIDEO CASE 17.2
Hubway Rolls Out Partners and Promotions

Commuting by subway, bus, train, or car can be expensive and inconvenient for workers trying to navigate around a city or its suburbs. Burning all that fossil fuel (or battery power) isn't the greenest way to travel, either. While it's true that these modes of transportation sometimes are the most time-efficient (and the safest way to move during bad weather), there's another method to consider for short hops and busy city streets: bicycle riding. Hubway is a bike-sharing system based in Boston that was conceived by its founders as a regional network tying together Boston, Cambridge, Brookline, and the surrounding communities. Hubway serves a greater purpose than just renting bikes to consumers. "It's not just about bikes," observes general manager Scott Mullen. "This is just another piece of the transit puzzle." The Hubway system harbors the flexibility to fill gaps left open by public transit. For example, suppose you catch a subway that deposits you four blocks from your workplace. Instead of walking, if you're a Hubway member, you can swipe your card at a designated bike station, grab a bike, and ride straight to your job.

Launching and running a bike-share system requires partners (Alta Bicycle Share and New Balance are Hubway's main partners). It also requires support from corporate members. Brogan Graham, who holds the official title of hypemaster at Hubway, is responsible for corporate sales—convincing other companies to create corporate accounts through which their employees may join the Hubway system. Corporations have the option to join at several levels, depending on whether they want to contribute 100 percent of their employees' memberships or a certain percentage. Once a company signs up, a Hubway representative visits the firm to talk with workers about bike sharing, encourage participation, and point out the benefits of commuting via bicycle as a physical fitness and green initiative. As a motivator, Hubway provides the business customer with a tally of rides, calories burned, and CO2 saved. Hubway representatives also work with other business partners, such as retailers who are willing to offer Hubway members bike helmets at low cost. For example, instead of paying $50 or $75 for a bike helmet, Hubway members may pick one up for $24.99 at locations ranging from participating CVS pharmacies to City Sports to several hospital gift shops. "Marketing is partnerships, communication, working together as a team," notes Graham.

Hubway has conducted several consumer-oriented promotions since its launch. At its initial rollout, marketers recruited students to dress as Minute Men and colonial soldiers and sent them out as the Revolutionary Riders to proclaim the coming of Hubway. After the first year of operation, Graham and his team calculated the top several men and women Hubway riders (by number of rides), dubbed them the Gold Club, and went to their homes and workplaces to present them with gold T-shirts. Other media picked up on these riders and featured them in articles and online postings. Some promotions involve short-term discounts, such as the recent "Get Hubway for the Holidays." Halfway through one December, Hubway slashed the cost of an annual membership to $60 ($25 savings)—a price good until the end of that month. As Hubway approached the kick-off of its second year in operation, members were invited to grab a bike and ride to the Boston Public Library for the festivities where, upon check-in, their use of the bike for the day would be free. The first 100 riders also received a free burrito from Boloco Burritos. New members could join at the event for a reduced membership price. Hubway spread the news about the event via Twitter and Facebook—and people came in droves.

Social media is an important part of the Hubway promotional mix. Hubway uses social media to spread the word about promotions such as the Boston Public Library event, sending targeted messages to consumers, who then become virtual ambassadors for the brand. Graham notes that a single tweet may reach 4,000 people, who not only respond to Hubway but also strike up conversations with each other about their riding experiences, including attending special events. Without a big advertising budget, explains marketing director Mary McLaughlin, Hubway relies on this type of grassroots marketing. "The one-to-one model is the best way to spread the word," says McLaughlin.

QUESTIONS FOR CRITICAL THINKING

1. Describe how Hubway can use relationship selling to build partnerships with retailers and corporations.
2. How might Hubway create sales promotions using specialty advertising?

Sources: Company website, www.thehubway.com, accessed April 5, 2014; Eric Moskowitz, "Hubway Bike-Sharing Program Is on a Roll," *The Boston Globe*, accessed April 5, 2014, www.bostonglobe.com; Jonathan Simmons, "On Biking: Learning to Love Hubway," *Boston.com*, accessed April 5, 2014, www.boston.com.

NOTES

1. Company website, www.salesforce.com, accessed October 27, 2014; Joyce Hanson, "Salesforce Acquisition of RelateIQ a CRM Game-Changer," *Investment News*, accessed October 27, 2014, www.investmentnews.com; Seth Fineberg and Alex Kantrowitz, "Who Will Win the Race for the Marketing Cloud?" *Advertising Age*, accessed March 30, 2014, http://adage.com; Phil Wainewright, "Marketing Cloud Pivotal for Salesforce Growth," *Diginomica*, accessed March 30, 2014, http://diginomica.com; Amanda Nelson, "How Social Media and CRM Work Together Successfully," *ExactTarget*, accessed March 30, 2014, www.exacttarget.com; Aimee Chanthadavong, "IT Is Now About Dealing with People: Salesforce," *ZDNet*, accessed March 30, 2014, www.zdnet.com; "100 Best Companies to Work For: 2014," *Fortune*, accessed March 30, 2014, http://money.cnn.com; "With Buddy Media Deal, Salesforce Targets CMOs," *Advertising Age*, accessed March 30, 2014, http://adage.com; Ian Schafer, "Will Salesforce's Acquisition of Buddy Media Make Social CRM Real?" *Advertising Age*, accessed March 30, 2014, http://adage.com; Lisa Arthur, "Five Years from Now, CMOs Will Spend More on IT Than CIOs Do," *Forbes*, accessed March 30, 2014, www.forbes.com; David A. Kaplan, "Salesforce's Happy Workforce," *Fortune*, accessed March 30, 2014, http://tech.fortune.cnn.com.
2. U.S. Bureau of Labor Statistics, Employment by Detailed Occupation, accessed March 31, 2014, www.bls.gov.
3. Ibid.
4. "Top 10 Retail Loyalty Programs," *Big Door*, accessed March 31, 2014, http://bigdoor.com.
5. Company website, "Factsheet," www.enterpriseholdings.com, accessed October 27, 2014; Jim Salter, "Enterprise Rental Car Brands to Hire 11, 000," *Associated Press*, accessed March 31, 2014, www.careerathletes.com.
6. Sam Lewis, "iPads in Dressing Rooms? Nordstrom Is Saying 'Yes,'" *Retail Solutions Online*, accessed March 31, 2014, www.retailsolutionsonline.com; Elizabeth Holmes and Ray A. Smith, "Why Are Fitting Rooms So Awful?" *The Wall Street Journal*, accessed March 31, 2014, http://online.wsj.com.
7. Company website, www.panasonic.com, accessed March 31, 2014.
8. Company website, "The Vault Story," https://10785.vaultdenim.com, accessed March 31, 2014.
9. Federal Communications Commission, "Unwanted Telephone Marketing Calls," accessed March 31, 2014, www.fcc.gov.
10. "How to Eliminate Annoying Robocalls," *Consumer Reports*, accessed March 31, 2014, www.consumerreports.com.
11. Lesley Fair, "Ringing in the New Year," Bureau of Consumer Protection, *Business Center Blog*, accessed March 31, 2014, http://business.ftc.gov.
12. Direct Marketing Association, "What Is the Direct Marketing Association: Overview," accessed March 31, 2014, http://thedma.org.
13. Company website, "JetBlue Opens Customer Contact Center in Orlando," http://investor.jetblue.com, accessed March 31, 2014.
14. Company website, www.nba.com, accessed March 31, 2014.
15. "Top 25 US Bank Changes Name to Santander Today," *Yahoo Finance*, accessed April 5, 2014, http://finance.yahoo.com; "Salesnet CRM Case Study—Sovereign Bank," *Salesnet*, accessed March 31, 2014, www.salesnet.com.
16. Kelly Faloon, "Vendor-Managed Truck Replenishment," *Plumbing & Mechanical* magazine, accessed March 31, 2014, www.pmmag.com.
17. Company website, "SunTrust Banks, Inc., Plays to Win, Focuses on Building Solid Relationships," www.richardson.com, accessed March 31, 2014.
18. Company website, www.sheex.com, accessed March 31, 2014; Michelle Juergen, "A Hot Business Idea—Between the Sheets," *Entrepreneur*, accessed March 31, 2014, www.entrepreneur.com.
19. Company website, www.southwest.com, accessed March 31, 2014; "Southwest Airlines Uses Big Data to Deliver Excellent Customer Service," *Big Data StartUps*, accessed March 31, 2014, www.bigdata-startups.com.
20. Graham Charlton, "11 Great Ways to Use Digital Technology in Retail Stores," *eConsultancy*, accessed March 31, 2014, http://econsultancy.com.
21. Rockfish, "P.F. Chang's Mobile: A New Approach to Loyalty," http://rockfishdigital.com, accessed April 6, 2014; organization website, "Best Restaurant Mobile Application: Razorfish and P.F. Chang's," www.iacaward.org, accessed April 6, 2014.
22. Jonathan D. Rockoff, "Drug Reps Soften Their Sales Pitches," *The Wall Street Journal*, accessed April 5, 2014, http://online.wsj.com.
23. Company website, "Features," http://slidedog.com, accessed April 4, 2014.
24. Diana Ransom, "An Old-Fashioned Approach to Finding Customers," *Entrepreneur*, accessed April 5, 2014, www.entrepreneur.com.
25. Company website, www.blackanddecker.com, accessed April 5, 2014.
26. U.S. Bureau of Labor Statistics, "Sales Managers," *Occupational Outlook Handbook, 2014–2015*, accessed April 4, 2014, www.bls.gov.
27. U.S. Bureau of Labor Statistics, "Women in the Labor Force: A Databook," accessed October 27, 2014, www.bls.gov.
28. Company website, www.santinelli.com, accessed April 4, 2014; "Santinelli Team Gathers for 40th Anniversary" (press release), www.santinelli.com, accessed April 4, 2014.
29. Andria Cheng, "Holiday 2013 Winners and Losers," *Market Watch*, accessed April 4, 2014, http://blogs.marketwatch.com.
30. "CRM Best Practices," *CRM Trends*, accessed April 4, 2014, www.crmtrends.com.
31. "Total Consumer Savings from CPG Coupons Fell Again in 2013," *Marketing Charts*, accessed April 4, 2014, www.marketingcharts.com; "Statistics and Data on Coupon Market Trends in the United States," *Statista*, accessed April 4, 2014, www.statista.com.
32. "US Mobile Users Turn to Smartphones, Tablets to Redeem Coupons," *eMarketer*, accessed October 27, 2014, www.emarketer.com; "Majority of US Internet Users Will Redeem Digital Coupons in 2013," *eMarketer*, accessed April 4, 2014, www.emarketer.com.
33. Company website, "Picture Yourself Winning Our 9-Day Athens & 4 Day Greek Isle Cruise Grand Prize," http://blog.friendlyplanet.com, accessed April 4, 2014.

Scripps Networks Interactive & Food Network

PART 6
Promotional Decisions

Generating Buzz

Scripps Networks Interactive's brands—Food Network, Cooking Channel, HGTV, DIY Network, Travel Channel, and Great American Country (GAC)—are founded on lifestyles that promote exploration, imagination, and passion within the confines of everyday life as well as the broad spectrum of adventure and global influence. The company's marketing communications strategy is a natural extension of this kind of lifestyle programming. "It's talking to people about the right things at the right times, in the right places," says Jonah Spegman, director of digital media and database marketing for Scripps Networks Interactive.

Marketers at Scripps engage in integrated marketing communications (IMC) not only within each branded television network but also across most of its programming. "A lot of our networks play in the same spaces; women age 25 to 54 is a common target audience across most of our networks," notes Spegman. Many of Scripps' cross-promotional efforts have a lot of touch points for the same audiences; it's a natural fit. For example, a single commercial might involve HGTV's speaking to the Food Network audience about an upcoming *Design Star* episode that features celebrity chef Giada De Laurentiis.

While traditional TV advertising conjures up the 30-second spot with a catchy jingle, advertising at Food Network is much more complex and interactive. Because the audience is so connected to the content of its shows, advertisers actually look to Scripps for ideas and resources that they can use. "Advertisers are very sophisticated now," observes Traci Topham, senior vice president of interactive ad sales marketing at Scripps. Advertisers approach Scripps looking to integrate with the Scripps social media space. Topham and others develop ideas that their advertising clients may run on the Food Network website or across their own mobile platforms. For example, food manufacturer Kraft might develop recipes with Food Network that consumers can access from their mobile devices.

"We're programming and selling advertising to all the screens," Topham continues. Recipes from a single episode of *Chopped* or *Iron Chef* may be driven to an advertiser's website or Food Network's site, where consumers can access them to try on their own. Nonfood advertisers participate as well. If Lexus wants to advertise its RX Hybrid on an episode of *Restaurant: Impossible*, Food Network may integrate the car into the show by having host Robert Irvine drive it—then stream that footage online at the Food Network site where Lexus ads are being shown.

Sponsors and other advertisers also want to tie Food Network talent to their own Facebook pages with celebrity testimonials. Some even develop recipes in conjunction with Food Network to post on their Facebook pages. Scripps and Food Network marketers don't see this as a competitive threat; instead they view it as co-marketing. "We try to do a 360," explains Sergei Kuharsky, senior vice president and general manager of licensing and merchandising. Food Network joins marketing assets with its partners—such as retailer Kohl's—to gain greater exposure and interaction with consumers. "Generally, in marketing you want that kind of crescendo," Kuharsky advises. He points out that one of the great advantages of being a media brand with a daily dialogue with an audience is that when the conversation focuses on a topic—such as a television show episode, a particular restaurant, or a competition—something positive happens.

Sales promotions are an important part of the Food Network promotional mix. "Promotions always have the opportunity to generate buzz and excitement around a show," says Rich Ma, manager of digital marketing for Food Network. "People love to win stuff." Ma explains that an effective sales promotion must go beyond a simple giveaway. Food Network's promotional goal is to engage viewers, so marketers tie their promotions to the TV experience. During the series *Great Food Truck Race*, Food Network marketers created an interactive promotion that allowed viewers to nominate their own local food trucks at the Food Network website, then vote for the "best" food truck in the country. The contest generated buzz for the show as well as for local food truck businesses. "That's the nature of social," says Ma. "When you have something that's hot, people start talking about it and you can add fuel to the fire by contributing to that conversation." It's also free advertising—for the network and the local businesses.

Social media is still very much in the growth stage of the product lifecycle, which means that corresponding promotional efforts are as well. Susie Fogelson, senior vice president for marketing, creative services, and public relations at Food Network, acknowledges that she has "far more questions than answers" about the most effective ways to leverage social media in an integrated marketing communications strategy. In fact, she encourages marketers to ask the most basic questions. "It's being willing to learn, explore, and be a little outside your comfort zone," Fogelson says.

QUESTIONS FOR CRITICAL THINKING

1. If you were a Food Network marketer, how would you state the network's overall marketing message?
2. Describe the types of advertising appeals that you think would be most effective with Food Network viewers.
3. In what ways do Food Network and its advertisers benefit from cross-promotion?
4. How might Food Network marketers use sales promotion techniques to build loyalty among viewers?

Part 7
Pricing Decisions

18 Pricing Concepts
19 Pricing Strategies

Chapter 18

Pricing Concepts

1. Discuss the legal constraints on pricing.
2. Identify the four major categories of pricing objectives.
3. Explain price elasticity and its determinants.
4. Describe the three practical problems involved in applying price theory concepts to actual pricing decisions.
5. Explain the two major cost-plus approaches to price setting.
6. Discuss the three shortcomings of using breakeven analysis in pricing decisions.
7. Explain the use of yield management in pricing decisions.
8. Identify the five major pricing challenges facing online and international marketers.

DOLLAR GENERAL ATTRACTS SHOPPERS ON PRICE POINTS, NOT PRICE

Dollar General, the Tennessee-based chain of discount retailers, has more than 11,000 U.S. stores and recently announced record-high sales of $17.5 billion. Like other "extreme value" chains, the fast-growing retailer is drawing many more customers than before, and these shoppers are spending more per visit than in the past. Low-income families as well as middle-class consumers are shopping at Dollar General, which recently undertook a large-scale investment and remodeling in many of its stores.

How does Dollar General earn so much with low prices on brand names like Kimberly Clark, Procter & Gamble, Kellogg, Hanes, Nabisco, and General Mills? The answer is that the company doesn't really offer low prices; by selling products in smaller sizes than other discount chains like Walmart, it actually offers low price *points*, which yield higher profit margins. In other words, although the items in the store carry nominally low prices, their smaller sizes mean customers are paying more per ounce than they might pay for the same item at Walmart. Because Dollar General shoppers may have low purchasing power at any given time, they can only afford to buy small amounts at a time and must also shop more frequently. Dollar General caters to their buying habits and financial constraints.

Dollar General calls itself "the nation's largest small-box discount retailer." The company expects sales to continue to increase, rising by as much as 10 percent over the coming year as it opens another 700 new stores. It has remodeled about 575 existing locations, spending $600 to $650 million in store openings and capital improvements. Most Dollar General outlets stock between 10,000 and 12,000 different items.

With success based on low-priced items and convenient locations, Dollar General is beginning to encroach on the market segment traditionally held by chains like Walmart, Target, and Costco. Dollar General is also taking share from grocery stores and drug chains. Operating 12 distribution centers and stores in 40 states, Dollar General believes it could profitably operate as many as 20,000 stores nationwide.[1]

EVOLUTION OF A BRAND

Extreme-value stores like Dollar General are encroaching on a target market that Walmart, Kmart, Target, Costco, and other "big-box" retailers long believed was firmly in their grasp. While stores like Dollar General were previously common in poorer regions of the country, struggling U.S. families and middle-class shoppers looking for bargains have increasingly turned to them.

- How does Dollar General's policy of carrying smaller sizes of major brand-name products appeal to its target audience? How might a big-box store attempt to regain the customers it has lost to the extreme-value stores?
- Visit Dollar General's website (www2.dollargeneral.com) and enter your ZIP code to see the specials for the store nearest you. Choose one item—a bag of potato chips, for example—and note the price—and size—of the package. Now visit the website of a big-box store like Costco and find the same product. What is the difference in the size of the package? In the price? Which store will give you a better buy for the product you chose? Why?

Chapter Overview

price Exchange value of a good or service.

One of the first questions shoppers ask is, "How much does it cost?" Marketers understand the critical role price plays in the consumer's decision-making process. For products as varied as lipstick and perfume, automobiles and gasoline, and doughnuts and coffee, marketers must develop strategies that price products to achieve their firms' objectives.

As a starting point for examining pricing strategies, consider the meaning of the term *price*. A **price** is the exchange value of a good or service; in other words, it represents whatever that product can be exchanged for in the marketplace. Price does not necessarily denote money. In earlier times, the price of an acre of land might have been 20 bushels of wheat, three head of cattle, or one boat. Even though the barter process continues to be used in some transactions, price today typically refers to the amount of funds required to purchase a product. Prices are both dynamic and difficult to set; they shift in response to a number of variables. A higher-than-average price can convey an image of prestige, while a lower-than-average price may connote good value, as the trend toward consumers' purchases of private-label store brands shows. In other instances, though, a price much lower than average may be interpreted as an indicator of inferior quality, and a higher price—like the increasing price of gasoline—may reflect both high demand and scarce supply. Pricing can also be used to modify consumer behavior.

This chapter discusses the process of determining a profitable but justifiable (or fair) price. The focus is on management of the pricing function, including pricing strategies, price–quality relationships, and pricing in various sectors of the economy. The chapter also looks at the effects of environmental conditions on price determination, including legal constraints, competitive pressures, and changes in global and online markets.

PRICING AND THE LAW

1 Discuss the legal constraints on pricing.

Pricing decisions are influenced by a variety of legal constraints imposed by federal, state, and local governments. Included in the price of products are not only the costs of the raw materials, processing and packaging, and profit for the business, but also various taxes. For instance, excise taxes are levied on a variety of products, including real-estate transfers, alcoholic beverages, and motor fuels. Sales taxes can be charged on clothing, furniture, restaurant meals, and many other purchases.

In the global marketplace, prices are directly affected by special types of taxes called *tariffs*. These taxes—levied on the sale of imported goods and services—often make it possible for firms to protect their local markets while still setting prices on domestically produced goods well above world-market levels. The average tariff on fruits and vegetables around the world is more than 50 percent, although it varies considerably from country to country. The United States levies tariffs of 10 to 20 percent on fruit and vegetable imports from European Union (EU) countries, although these two trading partners have expressed interest in eliminating tariffs on all agricultural trade. Under the North American Free Trade Agreement (NAFTA), in transactions with the United States' largest trading partners in the produce market—Mexico and Canada—tariffs for both imports and exports are zero.[2] In other instances, tariffs are levied to prevent foreign producers from engaging in a practice described in Chapter 8: *dumping* foreign-produced products in international markets at prices lower than those set in their domestic market.

The United States is not the only country that imposes tariffs to protect domestic suppliers. These tariffs raise the prices overseas consumers must pay to purchase U.S. goods. China once imposed tariffs of up to 22 percent on imported large cars and SUVs from the United States. A trade skirmish erupted when the United States charged Chinese manufacturers with illegally dumping inexpensive solar panels on the American market. The U.S. Department of Commerce imposed high tariffs on Chinese imports to protect American manufacturers.[3]

Not every "regulatory" price increase is a tax, however. Rate increases to cover costly government regulations imposed on the telecommunications industry have been appearing on Internet and cell phone bills as "regulatory cost recovery fees" or similarly named costs. These charges are not taxes, because the companies keep all the income from the fees and apply only some of it to complying with the regulations. In essence, such "recovery fees" are a source of additional revenues in an industry so price sensitive that any announced price increase is likely to send some customers fleeing to competitors.

Many people looking for a ticket to a high-demand sporting or concert event have encountered an expensive, sometimes illegal, form of pricing called *ticket scalping*. Scalpers purchase tickets they expect to resell at a higher price. Although some cities and states have enacted laws prohibiting the practice, it continues to occur in many locations.

The ticket reselling market is both highly fragmented and susceptible to fraud and distorted pricing. In response, buyers and sellers are finding that the Internet is helping to create a market in which both buyers and sellers can compare prices and seat locations. Web firms like StubHub.com and TicketsNow.com, the latter owned by Ticketmaster, are ticket clearinghouses for this secondary market. These firms have signed deals with several professional sports teams that allow season ticket holders to sell unwanted tickets and buyers to purchase them with a guarantee. NHL and NBA fans have saved up to 30 percent by buying playoff tickets from StubHub at the last minute.[4]

Pricing is also regulated by the general constraints of U.S. antitrust legislation, as outlined in Chapter 3. The following sections review some of the most important pricing laws for contemporary marketers.

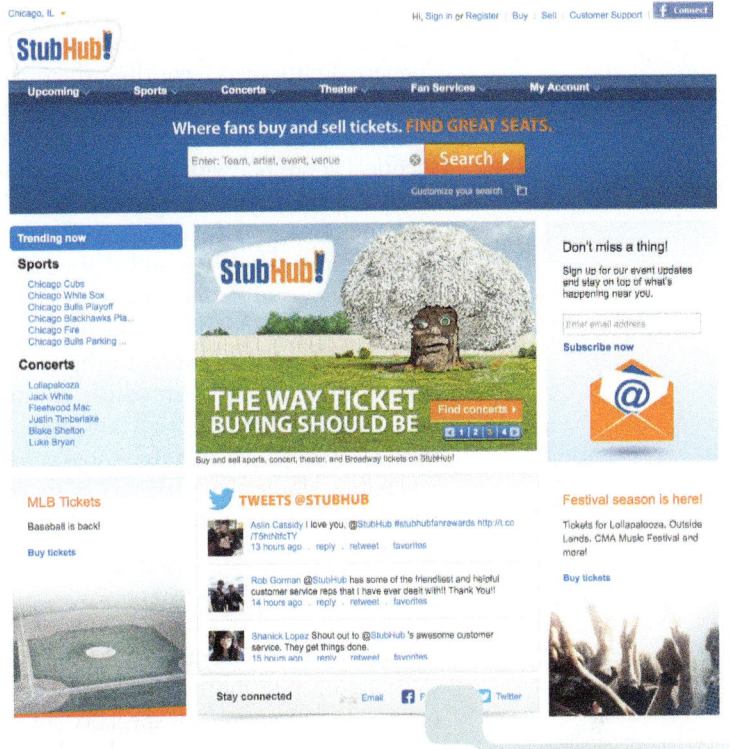

Internet company StubHub is one of several online ticket brokers that allow consumers to compare event prices and seat locations before purchasing tickets.

ROBINSON-PATMAN ACT

The **Robinson-Patman Act** (1936) typifies Depression-era legislation. Known as the Anti–A&P Act, it was inspired by price competition triggered by the rise of grocery store chains; it is said that the original draft was suggested by the U.S. Wholesale Grocers Association. Enacted in the midst of the Great Depression, when legislators viewed chain stores as a threat to employment in the traditional retail sector, this law was primarily intended to save jobs.

The Robinson-Patman Act was an amendment to the Clayton Act, enacted 22 years earlier, which had applied only to price discrimination between geographic areas, injuring local sellers. Broader in scope, Robinson-Patman prohibits price discrimination in sales to wholesalers, retailers, and other producers. It rules that differences in price must reflect cost differentials and prohibits selling at unreasonably low prices to drive competitors out of business. Supporters justified the amendment by arguing that the rapidly expanding chain stores of that era might be able to attract substantial discounts from suppliers anxious to secure their business, while small, independent stores would continue to pay regular prices.

Price discrimination, in which some customers pay more than others for the same product, dates back to the very beginnings of trade and commerce. Today, however, technology has added to the

Robinson-Patman Act Federal legislation prohibiting price discrimination not based on a cost differential; also prohibits selling at an unreasonably low price to eliminate competition.

frequency and complexity of price discrimination as well as the strategies marketers adopt to get around it. For example, marketers may encourage repeat business by inviting purchasers to become "preferred customers," entitling them to average discounts of 10 percent. As long as companies can demonstrate that their price discounts and promotional allowances do not restrict competition, they avoid penalties under the Robinson-Patman Act. Direct-mail marketers frequently send out catalogs of identical goods but with differing prices for different catalogs. ZIP code areas that traditionally consist of high spenders get the higher-price catalogs, while price-sensitive ZIP-code customers receive catalogs with lower prices. Firms accused of price discrimination often argue that they set price differentials to meet competitors' prices and that cost differences justify variations in prices. When a firm asserts it maintains price differentials as good-faith methods of competing with rivals, a logical question arises: What constitutes good faith pricing behavior? The answer depends on the particular situation.

A defense based on cost differentials works only if the price differences do not exceed the cost differences resulting from selling to various classes of buyers. Marketers must then be prepared to justify the cost differences. Many authorities consider this provision one of the most confusing areas in the Robinson-Patman Act. Courts handle most charges brought under the act as individual cases. Therefore, domestic marketers must continually evaluate their pricing actions to avoid potential Robinson-Patman violations.

UNFAIR-TRADE LAWS

unfair-trade laws State laws requiring sellers to maintain minimum prices for comparable merchandise.

Most states supplement federal legislation with their own **unfair-trade laws**, which require sellers to maintain minimum prices for comparable merchandise. Enacted in the 1930s, these laws were intended to protect small specialty shops, such as dairy stores, from so-called *loss-leader* pricing tactics in which chain stores might sell certain products below cost to attract customers. Typical state laws set retail price floors at cost plus some modest markup. Although most unfair-trade laws have remained on the books for decades, marketers had all but forgotten them until recently, when several lawsuits were brought against different warehouse clubs over their practice of loss-leader gasoline pricing. Most were found to violate no laws.

FAIR-TRADE LAWS

fair-trade laws Statutes enacted in most states that once permitted manufacturers to stipulate a minimum retail price for their product.

The concept of fair trade has affected pricing decisions for decades. **Fair-trade laws** allow manufacturers to stipulate minimum retail prices for their products and to require dealers to sign contracts agreeing to abide by these prices.

Fair-trade laws assert that a product's image, determined in part by its price, is a property right of the manufacturer. Therefore, the manufacturer should have the authority to protect its asset by requiring retailers to maintain a minimum price. Exclusivity is one method manufacturers use to achieve this. By severely restricting the number of retail outlets that carry their upscale clothing and accessories, designers can exert more control over their prices and avoid discounting, which might adversely affect their image.

Like the Robinson-Patman Act, fair-trade legislation has its roots in the Depression era. In 1931, California became the first state to enact fair-trade legislation. Most other states soon followed; only Missouri, the District of Columbia, Vermont, and Texas failed to adopt such laws. A U.S. Supreme Court decision invalidated fair-trade contracts in interstate commerce, and Congress responded by passing the Miller-Tydings Resale Price Maintenance Act (1937). This law exempted interstate fair-trade contracts from compliance with antitrust requirements, thus freeing states to keep these laws on their books if they so desired.

Over the years, fair-trade laws declined in importance as discounters emerged and price competition gained strength as a marketing strategy component. These laws became invalid with the passage of the Consumer Goods Pricing Act (1975), which halted all interstate enforcement of resale price maintenance provisions, an objective long sought by consumer groups.

ASSESSMENT CHECK

1.1 What was the purpose of the Robinson-Patman Act?

1.2 What laws require sellers to maintain minimum prices for comparable merchandise?

1.3 What laws allow manufacturers to set minimum retail prices for their products?

Chapter 18 Pricing Concepts

PRICING OBJECTIVES AND THE MARKETING MIX

The extent to which any or all of the factors of production—natural resources, capital, human resources, and entrepreneurship—are employed depends on the prices those factors command. A firm's prices and the resulting purchases by its customers determine the company's revenue, influencing the profits it earns. Overall organizational objectives and more specific marketing objectives guide the development of pricing objectives, which in turn lead to the development and implementation of more specific pricing policies and procedures.

A firm might, for instance, set an overall goal of becoming the dominant producer in its domestic market. It might then develop a marketing objective of achieving maximum sales penetration in each region, followed by a related pricing objective of setting prices at levels that maximize sales. These objectives might lead to the adoption of a low-price policy implemented by offering substantial price discounts to channel members. One start-up company's pricing strategy to signal the prestige value of its scented housecleaning products was so successful the company was snapped up by a larger firm. See the "Marketing Success" feature for the story.

Price influences and is affected by the other elements of the marketing mix. Product decisions, promotional plans, and distribution choices all affect the price of a good or service. For example, products distributed through complex channels involving several intermediaries must be priced high enough to cover the markups needed to compensate wholesalers and retailers for services they provide. Basic so-called "fighting brands" are intended to capture market share from higher-priced, options-laden competitors by offering relatively low prices. Those cheaper products are intended to entice customers to give up some options in return for a cost savings.

Identify the four major categories of pricing objectives.

MARKETING SUCCESS
The Pricey Smell of Success

Background. Caldrea and Mrs. Meyer's Clean Day are the two brands of Caldrea Company, a maker of upscale, environmentally friendly household cleaning products founded more than a decade ago in Minneapolis.

The Challenge. Caldrea's founder, Monica Nassif, wanted to create beautifully scented household cleaning and laundry products, priced higher than average, that shoppers would treat as a small indulgence.

The Strategy. "Caring for our homes should be just as luxurious as caring for our bodies," Nassif decided. She developed her company's biodegradable products in aromatherapy scents derived from essential oils and cosmetic-grade plant derivatives. The varieties, which are not tested on animals, include citrus mint, basil blue sage, lavender pine, and lemon verbena. Mrs. Meyer's products help homeowners care for surfaces ranging from wood to stainless, while Caldrea products, the more expensive of the two brands, are packaged attractively enough to display on bathroom and kitchen countertops. Their high-end pricing confers such status that they are often purchased as gifts. The company also makes a private-label line for Williams-Sonoma.

The Outcome. Caldrea and Mrs. Meyer's products are mostly sold at high-end retailers like Whole Foods; a Caldrea Essential line is also available at Target. Their luxury appeal and reliable performance command prices at least 30 percent higher than ordinary brands. The company's rapid success led to its purchase by SC Johnson, and Nassif believes partnering with SC Johnson will help the company rapidly expand its sales opportunities.

Sources: Company website, "Who We Are," www.caldrea.com, accessed April 5, 2014; company website, "Our Story," www.mrsmeyers.com, accessed April 5, 2014; Michael Burke, "SCJ to Bring Caldrea Operations to Racine," *Journal Times*, accessed April 5, 2014, http://journaltimes.com; "Mrs. Meyers Clean Day," *Bubblews*, accessed April 5, 2014, www.bubblews.com.

TABLE 18.1 Pricing Objectives

Objective	Purpose	Example
Profitability objectives	Profit maximization Target return	Samsung's initially high price for the Blu-ray disc player
Volume objectives	Sales maximization Market share	Delta's low fares in new markets
Meeting competition objectives	Value pricing	Walmart's lower prices on private house brands
Prestige objectives	Lifestyle Image	High-priced luxury autos such as Bentley
Not-for-profit objectives	Profit maximization Cost recovery Market incentives Market suppression	Reduced or zero tolls for high-occupancy vehicles to encourage carpooling

Pricing objectives vary from firm to firm, and they can be classified into four major groups: (1) profitability objectives, (2) volume objectives, (3) meeting competition objectives, and (4) prestige objectives. Not-for-profit organizations as well as for-profit companies must consider objectives of one kind or another when developing pricing strategies. Table 18.1 outlines the pricing objectives marketers rely on to meet their overall goals.

PROFITABILITY OBJECTIVES

Marketers at for-profit firms must set prices with profits in mind. Even not-for-profit organizations realize the importance of setting prices high enough to cover expenses and provide a financial cushion to cover unforeseen needs and expenses. As the Russian proverb says, "There are two fools in every market: One asks too little, one asks too much." For consumers to pay prices either above or below what they consider the going rate, they must be convinced they are receiving fair value for their money.

Economic theory is based on two major assumptions. It assumes, first, that firms will behave rationally and, second, that this rational behavior will result in an effort to maximize gains and minimize losses. Some marketers estimate profits by looking at historical sales data; others use elaborate calculations based on predicted future sales. It has been said that setting prices is an art, not a science. The talent lies in a marketer's ability to strike a balance between desired profits and the customer's perception of a product's value.

Marketers should evaluate and adjust prices continually to accommodate changes in the environment. The technological environment, for example, forces Internet marketers to respond quickly to competitors' pricing strategies. Search capabilities performed by shopping bots (described in Chapter 5) allow customers to compare prices locally, nationally, and globally in a matter of seconds.

Intense price competition, sometimes conducted even when it means forgoing profits altogether or reducing services, often results when rivals battle for leadership positions. For some years passenger airlines cut costs to compete on pricing. Computer technology allowed them to automate many services and put passengers in charge of others, such as making reservations online and checking in at electronic kiosks. Now, thanks to increased industry concentration and the high price of jet fuel, airlines struggle to cover their costs. As a result, passengers now pay sharply higher fares, and such amenities as in-flight meals have all but disappeared. Recently, some airlines have increased the number of seats reserved for frequent fliers—or passengers who are willing to pay extra. For an average fee of $50 for a round trip, passengers can get the more desirable seats next to windows, on

> **Briefly Speaking**
>
> "The bitterness of poor quality is remembered long after the sweetness of low price has faded from memory."
>
> —Aldo Gucci
> Co-owner of Gucci, an elite Italian fashion-design house

an aisle, or with more legroom. For families, this fee could add up to hundreds of dollars or more so that parents and children can sit together.⁵

Profits are a function of revenue and expenses:

Profits = Revenue − Expenses

Revenue is determined by the product's selling price and number of units sold:

Total revenue = Price × Quantity sold

Therefore, a profit-maximizing price rises to the point at which further increases will cause disproportionate decreases in the number of units sold. A 10 percent price increase that results in only an 8 percent cut in volume will add to the firm's revenue. However, a 10 percent price hike that results in an 11 percent sales decline will reduce revenue.

Economists refer to this approach as **marginal analysis**. They identify **profit maximization** as the point at which the addition to total revenue is just balanced by the increase in total cost. Marketers must resolve a basic problem of how to achieve this delicate balance when they set prices. Relatively few firms actually hit this elusive target. A significantly larger number prefer to direct their effort toward more realistic goals.

Consequently, marketers commonly set **target-return objectives**—short-run or long-run goals usually stated as percentages of sales or investment. The practice has become particularly popular among large firms in which other pressures interfere with profit-maximization objectives. In addition to resolving pricing questions, target-return objectives offer several benefits for marketers. These objectives serve as tools for evaluating performance; they also satisfy desires to generate "fair" profits as judged by management, stockholders, and the public.

VOLUME OBJECTIVES

Some economists and business executives argue that pricing behavior actually seeks to maximize sales within a given profit constraint. In other words, they set a minimum acceptable profit level and then seek to maximize sales (subject to this profit constraint) in the belief that the increased sales are more important in the long run, competitive picture than immediate high profits. As a result, companies should continue to expand sales as long as their total profits do not drop below the minimum return acceptable to management.

Sales maximization can also result from nonprice factors, such as service and quality. Stacy's Greenhouses of York, South Carolina, charges higher prices for some of its plants than for others. According to the company's president, knowing what customers value is important in setting a price, so the company tailors its prices according to the segment of the market it wants to reach. In today's economy, experienced gardeners value longer life spans in the plants they buy and therefore are willing to pay more for them.⁶

Another volume-related pricing objective is the **market-share objective**—the goal of cutting prices to get market share. Procter & Gamble experienced poor sales growth in some markets after it

marginal analysis Method of analyzing the relationship among costs, sales price, and increased sales volume.

profit maximization Point at which the additional revenue gained by increasing the price of a product equals the increase in total costs.

target-return objectives Short-run or long-run pricing objectives of achieving a specified return on either sales or investment.

market-share objective Volume-related pricing objective with the goal of controlling a portion of the market for a firm's product.

Industry consolidation and fuel prices have contributed to some airlines charging additional fees to passengers who wish to sit in a window seat or exit row.

increased prices on some products to cover its costs. In the hope of winning back some of the market share it lost, the company announced it would roll back those price increases.[7]

The PIMS Studies

Market-share objectives may prove critical to the achievement of other organizational objectives. High sales, for example, often mean more profits. The **Profit Impact of Market Strategies (PIMS) project**, an extensive and now classic study conducted by the Marketing Science Institute, analyzed more than 2,000 firms and revealed that two of the most important factors influencing profitability were product quality and market share. Companies, such as the outdoor gear maker REI, introduced their loyalty programs as a means of retaining customers and protecting their market share. However, a recent Gallup survey suggested that only a small percentage of a company's customer base actively participates in loyalty programs, but customers who are fully involved with a loyalty program tend to spend more money. One source at Gallup says the way companies can create more value is by fully engaging customers by building an emotional connection with their brand or product.[8]

The relationship between market share and profitability is evident in PIMS data that reveal an average 32 percent return on investment (ROI) for firms with market shares above 40 percent. In contrast, average ROI decreases to 24 percent for firms whose market shares are between 20 and 40 percent. Firms with a minor market share (less than 10 percent) generate average pretax investment returns less than 10 percent.[9]

The relationship also applies to a firm's individual brands. PIMS researchers compared the top four brands in each market segment they studied. Their data revealed the leading brand typically generates after-tax ROI of 18 percent, considerably higher than the second-ranked brand. Weaker brands, on average, fail to earn adequate returns.

Marketers have developed an underlying explanation of the positive relationship between profitability and market share. Firms with large shares accumulate greater operating experience and lower overall costs relative to competitors with smaller market shares. Accordingly, effective segmentation strategies might focus on obtaining larger shares of smaller markets and on avoiding smaller shares of larger ones. A firm might achieve higher financial returns by becoming a major competitor in several smaller market segments than by remaining a relatively minor player in a larger market.

Meeting Competition Objectives

A third set of pricing objectives seeks simply to meet competitors' prices. In many lines of business, firms set their own prices to match those of established industry price leaders. Price is a pivotal factor in the ongoing competition between long-distance telephone services and wireless carriers. In addition to unlimited calls to the United States and Canada for $2.99 a month, Skype, Microsoft's Internet calling company, allows unlimited calls to overseas landline phones in more than 60 other countries for $13.99 a month. The countries include most of Europe as well as Australia, New Zealand, China, Japan, Korea, Malaysia, and Taiwan.[10]

Pricing objectives tied directly to meeting prices charged by major competitors deemphasize the price element of the marketing mix and focus more strongly on nonprice variables. Pricing is a highly visible component of a firm's marketing mix and an easy and effective tool for obtaining a differential advantage over competitors. It is, however, a tool other firms can easily duplicate through price reductions of their own. Because price changes directly affect overall profitability in an industry, many firms attempt to promote stable prices by meeting competitors' prices and competing for market share by focusing on product strategies, promotional decisions, and distribution—the nonprice elements of the marketing mix.

Value Pricing

When discounts become normal elements of a competitive marketplace, other marketing mix elements gain importance in purchase decisions. In such instances, overall product value—not just price—determines product choice. In recent years, a new strategy, **value pricing**, has emerged that emphasizes the benefits a product provides in comparison to the price and quality levels of competing offerings. This strategy typically works best for relatively low-priced goods and services. Kroger, a major player in the grocery industry, offers product discounts, marked by yellow tags, in its more than 2,600 stores in 34 states. Reduced-price products include meat, produce, and health and beauty

---

Profit Impact of Market Strategies (PIMS) project Research that discovered a strong positive relationship between a firm's market share and product quality and its return on investment.

> **Briefly Speaking**
>
> "Goodwill is the one and only asset that competition cannot undersell or destroy."
>
> —**Marshall Field**
> *Founder of Marshall Field and Company department store*

value pricing Pricing strategy that emphasizes benefits derived from a product in comparison to the price and quality levels of competing offerings.

aids. On a designated day of the week, shoppers age 60 and older receive a 5 percent discount on their grocery bill, excluding alcohol, tobacco, and pharmacy prescriptions.[11]

Value-priced products generally cost less than premium brands, but marketers point out that value does not necessarily mean *inexpensive.* The challenge for those who compete on value is to convince customers that low-priced brands offer quality comparable to that of a higher-priced product. An increasing number of alternative products and private-label brands has resulted in a more competitive marketplace in recent years. Trader Joe's—a rapidly growing grocery chain that began in the Los Angeles area and has since expanded nationwide—stands out from other specialty food stores with its cedar-plank walls, nautical décor, and a captain (the store manager), first mate (the assistant manager), and the other employees (known as crew members) all attired in colorful Hawaiian shirts. The chain uses value pricing for the more than 2,000 upscale food products it develops or imports. It sells wines, cheeses, meats, fish, and other unique gourmet items at everyday closeout prices, mostly under its own brand names. If the high quality doesn't persuade customers at its more than 450 stores to buy, they can also note that Trader Joe's tuna is caught without environmentally dangerous nets, its dried apricots contain no sulfur preservatives, and its peanut butter is organic.[12]

Value pricing is perhaps best seen in the personal computer industry. In the past few years, PC prices collapsed, reducing the effectiveness of traditional pricing strategies intended to meet competition. PC sales weakened after price increases, due in part to massive flooding in Thailand, where some hard drives and other components are made. Prices have since returned to equilibrium.[13]

Kroger offers thousands of product discounts, marked by yellow tags, in its more than 2,600 stores.

Trader Joe's uses value pricing to sell upscale food products.

PRESTIGE OBJECTIVES

The final category of pricing objectives, unrelated to either profitability or sales volume, is prestige objectives. Prestige pricing establishes a relatively high price to develop and maintain an image of quality and exclusiveness that appeals to status-conscious consumers. Such objectives reflect marketers' recognition of the role of price in creating an overall image of the firm and its product offerings.

Prestige objectives affect the price tags of such products as David Yurman jewelry, Tag Heuer watches, Baccarat crystal, and Lenox china. When a perfume marketer sets a price of $400 or more per ounce, this choice reflects an emphasis on image far more than the cost of ingredients.

Analyses have shown that ingredients account for less than 5 percent of a perfume's cost. Thus, advertisements for Clive Christian's No. 1 that promote the fragrance as the "the world's most expensive perfume" use price to promote product prestige. Diamond jewelry also uses prestige pricing to convey an image of quality and timelessness.

In the business world, private jet ownership imparts an image of prestige, power, and high price tags—too high for most business travelers to consider. Most owners are worth $10 million or more, according to one industry researcher, and include those who see private ownership—enabling them to visit three cities in a day—as a business need, not a luxury. Recognizing that cost is the primary factor that makes jet ownership prohibitive, companies like NetJets have created an alternative: fractional ownership. Corporate boards of directors pressed to cut costs in a weak economy are much more willing to pay for a share in a jet than to purchase a whole aircraft.[14]

> **ASSESSMENT CHECK**
>
> 2.1 What are target-return objectives?
> 2.2 What is value pricing?
> 2.3 How do prestige objectives affect a seller's pricing strategy?

PRICING OBJECTIVES OF NOT-FOR-PROFIT ORGANIZATIONS

Pricing is also a key element of the marketing mix for not-for-profit organizations. Pricing strategy can help these groups achieve a variety of organizational goals:

1. *Profit maximization.* While not-for-profit organizations by definition do not cite profitability as a primary goal, numerous instances exist in which they try to maximize their returns on single events or a series of events. A $5,000-a-plate political fundraiser is a classic example.

2. *Cost recovery.* Some not-for-profit organizations attempt to recover only the actual cost of operating the unit. Mass transit, toll roads and bridges, and most private colleges and universities are common examples. The state of Indiana granted a 75-year lease of the its toll road to global investment firms from Australia and Spain nearly a decade ago.[15]

3. *Market incentives.* Other not-for-profit groups follow a lower-than-average pricing policy or offer a free service to encourage increased usage of the good or service. *Smithsonian* magazine

> **Briefly Speaking**
>
> "The moment you make a mistake in pricing, you're eating into your reputation or your profits."
>
> —**Katharine D. Paine**
> Founder, The Delahaye Group

Prestige objectives help market exclusive products like fractional ownership of private jets.

sponsors Museum Day Live!—free admission on a specific day to more than 1,400 museums around the country in an effort to educate the general public about art, science, and historical events.[16]

4. *Market suppression.* Price can also discourage consumption. High prices help accomplish social objectives independent of the costs of providing goods or services. Illustrations include tobacco and alcohol taxes—the so-called sin taxes—parking fines, tolls, and gasoline excise taxes. The city of Chicago recently raised its tax rate on a pack of cigarettes to more than $7.00, the largest per-pack tax in the country.[17]

METHODS FOR DETERMINING PRICES

Marketers determine prices in two basic ways: by applying the theoretical concepts of supply and demand and by completing cost-oriented analyses. During the first part of the 20th century, most discussions of price determination emphasized the classical concepts of supply and demand. During the last half of the century, however, the emphasis began to shift to a cost-oriented approach. Hindsight reveals certain flaws in both concepts.

Treatments of this subject often overlook another concept of price determination—one based on the impact of custom and tradition. **Customary prices** are retail prices consumers expect as a result of tradition and social habit. Candy makers have attempted to maintain traditional price levels by greatly reducing overall product size. Similar practices have prevailed in the marketing of soft drinks, chips, mayonnaise, soap, and ice cream as manufacturers attempt to balance consumer expectations of customary prices with the realities of rising costs. Sometimes customary prices hide a real price increase, however, when the quantity of the product has been imperceptibly reduced. After a freeze in Florida one recent winter that devastated the orange crop, Tropicana and Florida's Natural shrank their half-gallon orange juice containers by 5 ounces rather than raise the price for a full half gallon. Tropicana commented that research showed consumers are willing to pay the same price even for a little less juice. Kraft Foods' macaroni and cheese comes with two different noodle shapes, spiral and elbow. The spiral kind contains 5.5 ounces of pasta, while the elbow kind has 7.25 ounces—but both come in the same size box and sell for the same price. The company says that the manufacturing process for spiral pasta is more complicated and that it manufactures more elbow pasta.[18]

customary prices Traditional prices that customers expect to pay for certain goods and services.

> **Briefly Speaking**
>
> "Customers, I realized, don't care about functions or specific activities that occur within our organization. The end game is whether they are getting the right product at the right time at a competitive price."
>
> —Max A. Guinn
> *Senior vice president, Deere & Co*

Kraft Foods' macaroni and cheese offers two types of pasta—spiral and elbow—but the packages contain different amounts of noodles and sell for the same price. The company says the manufacturing process for the spiral pasta is costlier.

The changing price of U.S. gasoline presents another example of supply and demand. When average prices for a gallon of gas rise substantially, drivers demand to know who, if anyone, is cashing in on the price spike. Even though the United States is the world's largest refiner of gasoline, strong demand leads to an increase in oil imports. Higher gas prices have effects on other consumer costs as well. The U.S. Department of Energy counts 57 different major uses of petroleum in addition to gasoline, in products ranging from cosmetics to chewing gum. The rising costs of raw materials and energy have caused many tire manufacturers to charge more for their tires. China mines more than 90 percent of rare-earth metals, which are used in energy-efficient light bulbs and electric cars. The country has recently begun taking steps to reduce the high levels of pollution caused by the mining and processing of rare earths—steps that have driven up the price of these important metals.[19]

With fuel costs at record highs, hybrid cars are in greater demand than ever before and some dealers have had long waiting lists even at premium prices. Toyota recently unveiled a new model of its fuel-efficient Prius plug-in hybrid that promises an average of 50 miles per gallon of gas and 95 miles, on average, as an electric vehicle. Unlike other hybrids, the Prius plug-in gives drivers the choice of running on electricity alone or hybrid without draining the battery.[20]

Drivers face yet another high cost—that of traveling on the nation's bridges and roads. Their situation is complicated in the East and Northeast by the different prices set for drivers from different E-Z Pass states, which many drivers feel is unfair. See the "Solving an Ethical Controversy" feature to find out more.

ASSESSMENT CHECK

2.4 What goals does pricing strategy help a not-for-profit organization achieve?

2.5 What are the two basic ways in which marketers determine prices?

PRICE DETERMINATION IN ECONOMIC THEORY

Microeconomics suggests a way of determining prices that assumes a profit-maximization objective. This technique attempts to derive correct equilibrium prices in the marketplace by comparing supply and demand. It also requires more complete analysis than actual business firms typically conduct.

Demand refers to a schedule of the amounts of a firm's product that consumers will purchase at different prices during a specified time period. **Supply** refers to a schedule of the amounts of a good or service that will be offered for sale at different prices during a specified period. These schedules may vary for different types of market structures. Businesses operate and set prices in four types of market structures: pure competition, monopolistic competition, oligopoly, and monopoly.

Pure competition is a market structure with so many buyers and sellers that no single participant can significantly influence price. Pure competition presupposes other market conditions as well: homogeneous products and ease of entry for sellers due to low start-up costs. The agricultural sector exhibits many characteristics of a purely competitive market, making it the closest actual example. Still, many U.S. ranchers have switched their beef herds to an all-grass diet in an attempt to differentiate their product from those raised on feedlots.

Monopolistic competition typifies most retailing and features large numbers of buyers and sellers. These diverse parties exchange heterogeneous, relatively well-differentiated products, giving marketers some control over prices.

Relatively few sellers compete in an **oligopoly**. Pricing decisions by each seller are likely to affect the market, but no single seller controls it. High start-up costs form significant barriers to entry for new competitors. Each firm's demand curve in an oligopolistic market displays a unique kink at the current market price. Because of the impact of a single competitor on total industry sales, competitors usually quickly match any attempt by one firm to generate additional sales by reducing prices. Price cutting in such industries is likely to reduce total industry revenues. Oligopolies operate in the petroleum refining, automobile, tobacco, and airline industries.

Airline mergers, rising fuel prices, and a slow economy have led U.S. airlines to not only raise prices but also cut capacity, limiting flights to major cities and eliminating service to small and midsize airports. During a recent seven-year period, U.S. airlines cut scheduled domestic flights by nearly 24 percent to mid-sized airports like Pittsburgh and Milwaukee.[21]

---

demand Schedule of the amounts of a firm's product that consumers will purchase at different prices during a specified time period.

supply Schedule of the amounts of a good or service that firms will offer for sale at different prices during a specified time period.

pure competition Market structure characterized by homogeneous products in which there are so many buyers and sellers that none has a significant influence on price.

monopolistic competition Market structure involving a heterogeneous product and product differentiation among competing suppliers, allowing the marketer some degree of control over prices.

SOLVING AN ETHICAL CONTROVERSY
Differential Pricing for Highway Tolls

Some drivers are paying more to use bridges and highways in the 15 states served by the association of 26 toll agencies called E-Z Pass. The agencies set their own prices and policies, while E-Z Pass distributes transponders (more than 26 million to date) that let drivers zip through toll booths by paying electronically. Most member agencies have little known discount plans that depend on where drivers bought their E-Z Pass. Those who bought in West Virginia, Rhode Island, New York, New Hampshire, and several other states pay lower tolls in those states than other pass holders.

Should E-Z Pass agencies charge out-of-state drivers higher tolls?

PRO

1. Out-of-state drivers who travel on toll roads in New York and New Jersey should help defray the $900 million deficit faced by the region's Metropolitan Transportation Authority.
2. Differential pricing exists in many other markets, including household products.

CON

1. Higher tolls take advantage of some drivers.
2. Usually only the cash price is posted, so drivers don't even know they're paying more than others when they use the E-Z Pass.

Summary

Differential toll charges are the biggest complaint the AAA hears from its members across the country. West Virginia claims its four discount plans are too complicated to post at tollbooths. How many motorists will scour E-Z Pass members' websites to find out how to pay less?

Sources: Organizational website, E-Z Pass Group, www.e-zpassiag.com, accessed October 28, 2014; Ronan Halevy, "Updated BES10 Pricing & Free EZ Pass Migration Detailed by BlackBerry," *Berry Review*, accessed March 29, 2014, www.berryreview.com; Ariane Aramburo, "VDOT Talks about EZPass," *WAVY*, accessed March 28, 2014, http://wavy.com; "Tolls, EZ Pass Coming to Elizabeth River Tunnels Feb. 1," *News @ ODU*, accessed March 28, 2014, www.odu.edu; Kevin Bonsor, "How E-ZPass Works," *HowStuffWorks.com*, accessed March 28, 2014, www.howstuffworks.com.

A **monopoly** is a market structure in which only one seller of a product exists and for which there are no close substitutes. Antitrust legislation has nearly eliminated all but temporary monopolies, such as those created through patent protection. Regulated industries constitute another form of monopoly. The government allows regulated monopolies in markets in which competition would lead to an uneconomical duplication of services. In return for such a license, the government reserves the right to regulate the monopoly's rate of return.

The four types of market structures are compared in Table 18.2 on the following bases: number of competitors, ease of entry into the industry by new firms, similarity of competing products, degree of control over price by individual firms, and the elasticity or inelasticity of the demand curve facing the individual firm. Elasticity—the degree of consumer responsiveness to changes in price—is discussed in more detail in a later section.

COST AND REVENUE CURVES

Marketers must set a price for a product that generates sufficient revenue to cover the costs of producing and marketing it. A product's total cost is composed of total variable costs and total fixed costs. **Variable costs**, such as raw materials and labor costs, change with the level of production, and

---

oligopoly Market structure in which relatively few sellers compete and where high start-up costs form barriers to keep out new competitors.

monopoly Market structure in which a single seller dominates trade in a good or service for which buyers can find no close substitutes.

variable costs Cost that changes with the level of production (such as labor and raw materials costs).

TABLE 18.2 Distinguishing Features of the Four Market Structures

Characteristics	Type of Market Structure			
	Pure Competition	**Monopolistic Competition**	**Oligopoly**	**Monopoly**
Number of competitors	Many	Few to many	Few	No direct competitors
Ease of entry into industry by new firms	Easy	Somewhat difficult	Difficult	Regulated by government
Similarity of goods or services offered by competing firms	Similar	Different	Can be either similar or different	No directly competing goods or services
Control over prices by individual firms	None	Some	Some	Considerable
Demand curves facing individual firms	Totally elastic	Can be either elastic or inelastic	Kinked; inelastic below kink; more elastic above	Can be either elastic or inelastic
Examples	Indiana soybean farm	Best Buy stores	Verizon Wireless	Pharmaceutical company that holds patents on specific drugs

fixed costs Cost that remains stable at any production level within a certain range (such as a lease payment or insurance cost).

average total costs Cost calculated by dividing the sum of the variable and fixed costs by the number of units produced.

marginal cost Change in total cost that results from producing an additional unit of output.

fixed costs, such as lease payments or insurance costs, remain stable at any production level within a certain range. **Average total costs** are calculated by dividing the sum of the variable and fixed costs by the number of units produced. Finally, **marginal cost** is the change in total cost that results from producing an additional unit of output.

The demand side of the pricing equation focuses on revenue curves. Average revenue is calculated by dividing total revenue by the quantity associated with these revenues. Average revenue is actually the demand curve facing the firm. Marginal revenue is the change in total revenue that results from selling an additional unit of output. Figure 18.1 shows the relationships of various cost and revenue measures; the firm maximizes its profits when marginal costs equal marginal revenues.

Table 18.3 illustrates why the intersection of the marginal cost and marginal revenue curves is the logical point at which to maximize revenue for the organization. Although the firm can earn a profit at several different prices, the price at which it earns maximum profits is $22. At a price of

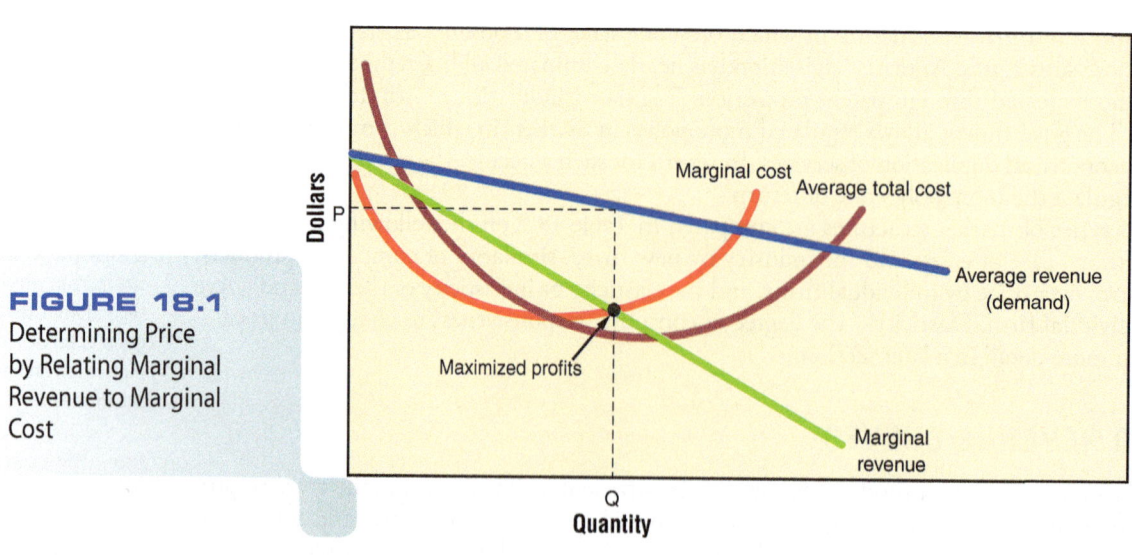

FIGURE 18.1 Determining Price by Relating Marginal Revenue to Marginal Cost

TABLE 18.3 Price Determination Using Marginal Analysis

Price	Number Sold	Total Revenue	Marginal Revenue	Total Costs	Marginal Costs	Profits (Total Revenue Minus Total Costs)
—	—	—	—	—	—	$(50)
$34	1	$34	$34	$57	$7	(23)
32	2	64	30	62	5	2
30	3	90	26	66	4	24
28	4	112	22	69	3	43
26	5	130	18	73	4	57
24	6	144	14	78	5	66
22	7	154	10	84	6	70
20	8	160	6	91	7	69
18	9	162	2	100	9	62
16	10	160	(2)	101	11	50

ASSESSMENT CHECK

2.6 What are the four types of market structures?

2.7 Identify the two types of costs that make up a product's total cost.

$24, $66 in profits is earned—$4 less than the $70 profit at the $22 price. If a price of $20 is set to attract additional sales, the marginal costs of the extra sales ($7) are greater than the marginal revenues received ($6), and total profits decline.

THE CONCEPT OF ELASTICITY IN PRICING STRATEGY

Although the intersection of the marginal cost and marginal revenue curves determines the level of output, the impact of changes in price on sales varies greatly. To understand why it fluctuates, one must understand the concept of elasticity.

Elasticity is the measure of the responsiveness of purchasers and suppliers to price changes. The price elasticity of demand (or elasticity of demand) is the percentage change in the quantity of a good or service demanded divided by the percentage change in its price. A 10 percent increase in the price of eggs that results in a 5 percent decrease in the quantity of eggs demanded yields a price elasticity of demand for eggs of 0.5. The price elasticity of supply of a product is the percentage change in the quantity of a good or service supplied divided by the percentage change in its price. A 10 percent increase in the price of shampoo that results in a 25 percent increase in the quantity supplied yields a price elasticity of supply for shampoo of 2.5.

Consider a case in which a 1 percent change in price causes more than a 1 percent change in the quantity supplied or demanded. Numerically, that means an elasticity measurement greater than 1.0. When the elasticity of demand or supply is greater than 1.0, that demand or supply is said to be elastic. If a 1 percent change in price results in less than a 1 percent change in quantity, a product's elasticity of demand or supply will be less than 1.0. In that case, the demand or supply is called *inelastic*. For example, the demand for cigarettes is relatively inelastic; research studies have shown that a 10 percent increase in cigarette prices results in only a 4 percent sales decline.

In some countries whose economies are in shambles, price levels bear little resemblance to the laws of elasticity or supply and demand. Prices in Zimbabwe once rose at unheard-of rates, the result of hyperinflation that rose to more than 7,600 percent in a *month* and estimated to be as high as 12.5 million percent a year. More recently, changes in the country's monetary policies, including the abandonment of its local currency, began to bring prices down, and the country's inflation rate continues to drop.[22]

Explain price elasticity and its determinants. 3

elasticity Measure of responsiveness of purchasers and suppliers to a change in price.

A 10 percent increase in the price of eggs, which results in a 5 percent decrease in the quantity of eggs demanded, yields a price elasticity of demand for eggs of 0.5.

Determinants of Elasticity

Why is the elasticity of supply or demand high for some products and low for others? What determines demand elasticity? One major factor influencing the elasticity of demand is the availability of substitutes or complements. If consumers can easily find close substitutes for a good or service, the product's demand tends to be elastic. A product's role as a complement to the use of another product also affects its degree of price elasticity. For example, the relatively inelastic demand for motor oil reflects its role as a complement to a more important product, gasoline. High prices for gasoline, in turn, are fueling a search for alternative energy sources like natural gas.[23]

As increasing numbers of buyers and sellers complete their business transactions online, the elasticity of a product's demand is drastically affected. Take major discounters and other price-competitive stores, for example. Small businesses and individual do-it-yourselfers shop Lowe's for tools such as wheelbarrows; parents look for birthday gifts at Toys R Us; and homeowners go to H.H. Gregg or Best Buy for new refrigerators or stoves. Today the Internet lets consumers contact many more providers directly, often giving them better selections and prices for their efforts with service sites such as Shopzilla.com for consumer goods and electronics, Net-à-Porter.com for high-fashion clothing, Kayak.com for travel bargains, and Shoebuy.com for shoes from dozens of manufacturers. The increased options available to shoppers combine to create a market characterized by demand elasticity.

Elasticity of demand also depends on whether a product is perceived as a necessity or a luxury. The Four Seasons chain of luxury hotels and resorts enjoys a strong reputation for service, comfort, and exclusivity and is a favorite among affluent individual travelers and business professionals.

Elasticity also depends on the portion of a person's budget spent on a good or service. For example, people no longer really need matches; they can easily find good substitutes. Nonetheless, the demand for matches remains very inelastic, because people spend so little on them that they hardly notice a price change. In contrast, the demand for housing or transportation is not totally inelastic, even though they are necessities, because both consume large parts of a consumer's budget.

Elasticity of demand also responds to consumers' time perspectives. Demand often shows less elasticity in the short run than in the long run. Consider the demand for home air conditioning. In the short run, people pay rising energy prices, because they find it difficult to cut back on the quantities they use. Accustomed to living with specific temperature settings and dressing in certain ways, they prefer to pay more during a few months of the year than to explore other possibilities. Over the long term, though, they may consider insulating their homes and planting shade trees to reduce cooling costs.

Elasticity and Revenue

The elasticity of demand exerts an important influence on variations in total revenue as a result of changes in the price of a good or service. Assume, for example, that Atlanta's Metropolitan Atlanta Rapid Transit Authority (MARTA) officials are considering alternative methods of raising more money for their budget. One possible method for increasing revenues would be to change rail pass fares for commuters. But should MARTA raise or lower the price of a pass? The correct answer depends on the elasticity of demand for transit rides. A 10 percent decrease in fares should attract more riders, but unless it stimulates more than a 10 percent increase in riders, total revenue will fall. A 10 percent increase in fares will bring in more money per rider, but if more than 10 percent of the riders stop using the system, total revenue will fall. A price cut will increase revenue only for a

Chapter 18 Pricing Concepts

> **ASSESSMENT CHECK**
>
> 3.1 What are the determinants of elasticity?
>
> 3.2 What is the usual relationship between elasticity and revenue?

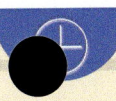

product with elastic demand, and a price increase will raise revenue only for a product with inelastic demand. MARTA officials might believe the demand for rapid rail transit is inelastic; they raise fares when they need more operating funds.

PRACTICAL PROBLEMS OF PRICE THEORY

Marketers may thoroughly understand price theory concepts but still encounter difficulty applying them in practice. What practical limitations interfere with setting prices? First, many firms do not attempt to maximize profits. Economic analysis is subject to the same limitations as the assumptions on which it is based—for example, the proposition that all firms attempt to maximize profits. Second, it is difficult to estimate demand curves. Modern accounting procedures provide managers with a clear understanding of cost structures, so managers can readily comprehend the supply side of the pricing equation. But they find it difficult to estimate demand at various price levels. Demand curves must be based on marketing research estimates that may be less exact than cost figures. Although the demand element can be identified, it is often difficult to measure in real-world settings.

> **4** Describe the three practical problems involved in applying price theory concepts to actual pricing decisions.

> **ASSESSMENT CHECK**
>
> 4.1 List the three reasons why it is difficult to put price theory into practice.

PRICE DETERMINATION IN PRACTICE

The practical limitations inherent in price theory have forced practitioners to turn to other techniques. **Cost-plus pricing**, the most popular method, uses a base-cost figure per unit and adds a markup to cover unassigned costs and to provide a profit. The only real difference among the multitude of cost-plus techniques is the relative sophistication of the costing procedures employed. For example, a local apparel shop may set prices by adding a 55 percent markup to the invoice price charged by the supplier. The markup is expected to cover all other expenses and permit the owner to earn a reasonable return on the sale of clothes. Car dealerships often rely on a markup when they set their prices; see the "Career Readiness" feature for some tips on negotiating the price of a car.

In contrast to this rather simple pricing mechanism, a large manufacturer may employ a complex pricing formula requiring several calculations. However, this method merely adds a more complicated procedure to the simpler, traditional method for calculating costs. In the end, someone must still make a decision about the markup. The apparel shop and the large manufacturer may figure costs differently, but they are remarkably similar in completing the markup side of the equation.

Cost-plus pricing often works well for a business that keeps its costs low, allowing it to set its prices lower than those of competitors and still make a profit. Walmart keeps costs low by buying most of its inventory directly from manufacturers, using a supply chain that slashes inventory costs by quickly replenishing inventory as items are sold and relying on other intermediaries only in special instances such as localized items. This strategy has played a major role in the discounter's becoming the world's largest retailer.

> **5** Explain the two major cost-plus approaches to price setting.

> **cost-plus pricing** Practice of adding a percentage of specified dollar amount—or markup—to the base cost of a product to cover unassigned costs and to provide a profit.

ALTERNATIVE PRICING PROCEDURES

The two most common cost-oriented pricing procedures are the full-cost method and the incremental-cost method. **Full-cost pricing** uses all relevant variable costs in setting a product's price. In addition, it allocates fixed costs that cannot be directly attributed to the production of the specific priced

> **full-cost pricing** Pricing method that uses all relevant variable costs in setting a product's price and allocates those fixed costs not directly attributed to the production of the priced item.

609

CAREER READINESS
Getting the Best Car Price

Making a big purchase like a car is good practice for other major decisions you may make in your career. Here's how to get the most for your money.

1. Research at least two different car makes and models. Check out the safety, fuel economy, and reliability of the cars you're considering. Do your homework before you visit a dealership.

2. Know exactly what you can afford. Find the dealer's invoice price for the car online, and be prepared to visit more than one dealer to shop for the best price.

3. The best way to test-drive the car you're interested in is by renting it for a day or two.

4. Make an offer close to the invoice price, and let the dealer know you plan to shop around.

5. Check out financing options on your own. Even if you decide on dealer financing, you'll want to be sure it's really cheaper than the rate at a bank or credit union.

6. If you have a car to trade in, find out its true value at an auto-pricing website.

7. If you can, pay cash. It reduces the dealer's administrative costs and the savings might pass on to you.

Sources: "Save Money and Avoid Scams When Buying a Car," *Car Buying Tips*, accessed April 7, 2014, www.carbuyingtips.com; Clark Howard, "The Clark Smart Steps for Buying a New Car," *ClarkHoward.com*, accessed April 5, 2014, www.clarkhoward.com; Jim Sharifi, "How to Negotiate the Best Price on a New Car," *US News*, accessed April 5, 2014, http://usnews.rankingsandreviews.com.

---

item. Under the full-cost method, if job order 515 in a printing plant amounts to 0.000127 percent of the plant's total output, then 0.000127 percent of the firm's overhead expenses are charged to that job. This approach allows the marketer to recover all costs plus the amount added as a profit margin.

The full-cost approach has two basic deficiencies. First, no consideration of competition or demand exists for the item; perhaps no one wants to pay the price the firm has calculated. Second, any method for allocating overhead (fixed expenses) is arbitrary and may be unrealistic—in manufacturing, overhead allocations are often tied to direct labor hours; in retailing, the square footage of each profit center is sometimes the factor used in computations. Regardless of the technique employed, it is difficult to show a cause–effect relationship between the allocated cost and most products.

One way to overcome the arbitrary allocation of fixed expenses is with **incremental-cost pricing**, which attempts to use only costs directly attributable to a specific output in setting prices. Consider a very small-scale manufacturer with the following income statement:

incremental-cost pricing Pricing method that attempts to use only costs directly attributable to a specific output in setting prices.

Sales (10,000 at $10)		$ 100,000
Expenses:		
Variable	$50,000	
Fixed	40,000	90,000
Net profit		$ 10,000

Suppose the firm is offered a contract for an additional 5,000 units. Because the peak season is over, these items can be produced at the same average variable cost. Assume the labor force would otherwise be working on maintenance projects. How low should the firm price its product to get the contract?

Under the full-cost approach, the lowest price would be $9 per unit. This figure is obtained by dividing the $90,000 in expenses by an output of 10,000 units. The incremental approach, on the other hand, could permit any price above $5, which would significantly increase the possibility of securing the additional contract. This price would be composed of the $5 variable cost associated with each unit of production plus, say, a $0.10-per-unit contribution to fixed expenses and overhead. With a $5.10 proposed price, the income statement now looks like this:

Sales (10,000 at $10; 5,000 at $5.10)		$ 125,500
Expenses:		
Variable	$75,000	
Fixed	40,000	$ 115,000
Net profit		$ 10,500

Profits thus increase under the incremental approach.

Admittedly, the illustration is based on two assumptions: (1) the ability to isolate markets such that selling at the lower price will not affect the price received in other markets, and (2) the absence of legal restrictions on the firm. The example, however, does illustrate that profits can sometimes be enhanced by using the incremental approach.

> **Briefly Speaking**
>
> "People want economy and they will pay any price to get it."
>
> —Lee Iacocca
> *American auto executive*

ASSESSMENT CHECK

5.1 What is full-cost pricing?

5.2 What is incremental-cost pricing?

BREAKEVEN ANALYSIS

Breakeven analysis is a means of determining the number of goods or services that must be sold at a given price to generate sufficient revenue to cover total costs. Figure 18.2 graphically depicts this process. The total cost curve includes both fixed and variable segments, and total fixed cost is represented by a horizontal line. Average variable cost is assumed to be constant per unit as it was in the example for incremental pricing.

The breakeven point is the point at which total revenue equals total cost. In the example in Figure 18.2, a selling price of $10 and an average variable cost of $5 result in a per-unit contribution

> **6** Discuss the three shortcomings of using breakeven analysis in pricing decisions.

breakeven analysis Pricing technique used to determine the number of products that must be sold at a specified price to generate enough revenue to cover total cost.

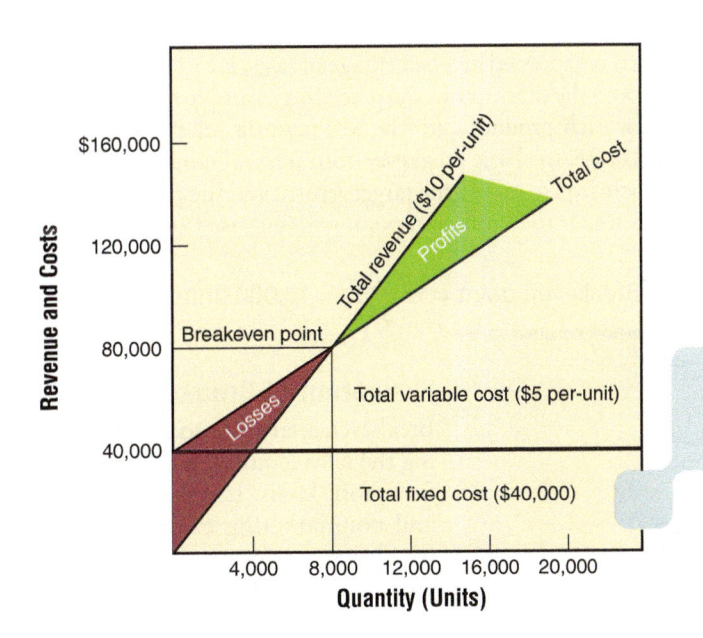

FIGURE 18.2
Breakeven Chart

to fixed cost of $5. The breakeven point in terms of units is found by using the following formula, in which the per-unit contribution equals the product's price less the variable cost per unit:

$$\text{Breakeven point (in units)} = \frac{\text{Total fixed cost}}{\text{Per-unit contribution to fixed cost}}$$

$$\text{Breakeven point (in units)} = \frac{\$40,000}{\$5} = 8,000 \text{ units}$$

The breakeven point in dollars is found with the following formula:

$$\text{Breakeven point (in dollars)} = \frac{\text{Total fixed cost}}{1 - \text{Variable cost per unit price}}$$

$$\text{Breakeven point (in dollars)} = \frac{\$40,000}{1 - (\$5/\$10)} = \frac{\$40,000}{0.5} = \$80,000$$

Sometimes breakeven is reached by reducing costs, and once it is reached, sufficient revenues will have been obtained from sales to cover all fixed costs. Any additional sales will generate per-unit profits equal to the difference between the product's selling price and the variable cost of each unit. As Figure 18.2 reveals, sales of 8,001 units (1 unit above the breakeven point) will produce net profits of $5 ($10 sales price less per-unit variable cost of $5). Once all fixed costs have been covered, the per-unit contribution will become the per-unit profit.

Target Returns

Although breakeven analysis indicates the sales level at which the firm will incur neither profits nor losses, most marketers include a targeted profit in their analyses. In some instances, management sets a desired dollar return when considering a proposed new product or other marketing strategy. A retailer may set a desired profit of $250,000 in considering whether to expand to a second location. In other instances, the target return may be expressed in percentages, such as a 15 percent return on sales. These target returns can be calculated as follows:

$$\text{Breakeven point (including specific dollar target return)} = \frac{\text{Total fixed cost} + \text{Profit objective}}{\text{Per-unit contribution}}$$

$$\text{Breakeven point (in units)} = \frac{\$40,000 + \$15,000}{\$5} = 11,000 \text{ units}$$

If the target return is expressed as a percentage of sales, it can be included in the breakeven formula as a variable cost. Suppose the marketer in the preceding example seeks a 10 percent return on sales. The desired return is $1 for each product sold (the $10 per-unit selling price multiplied by the 10 percent return on sales). In this case, the basic breakeven formula will remain unchanged, although the variable cost per unit will be increased to reflect the target return, and the per-unit contribution to fixed cost will be reduced to $4. As a result, the breakeven point will increase from 8,000 to 10,000 units:

$$\text{Breakeven point} = \frac{\$40,000}{\$4} = 10,000 \text{ units}$$

ASSESSMENT CHECK

6.1 What is the formula for finding the breakeven point in units and in dollars?

6.2 What adjustments to the basic breakeven calculation must be made to include target returns?

Evaluation of Breakeven Analysis

Breakeven analysis is an effective tool for marketers in assessing the sales required for covering costs and achieving specified profit levels. It is easily understood by both marketing and nonmarketing executives and may help them decide whether required sales levels for a certain price are realistic goals. However, breakeven analysis has its shortcomings.

First, the model assumes costs can be divided into fixed and variable categories. Some costs, such as salaries and advertising outlays, may be either fixed or variable depending on the particular situation. In addition, the model assumes per-unit variable costs do not change at different levels of operation. However, these may vary because of quantity discounts, more efficient use of the workforce, or other economies resulting from increased levels of production and sales. Finally, the basic breakeven model does not consider demand. It is a cost-based model and does not directly address the crucial question of whether consumers will purchase the product at the specified price and in the quantities required for breaking even or generating profits. The marketer's challenge is to modify the breakeven analysis and the other cost-oriented pricing approaches to incorporate demand analysis. Pricing must be examined from the buyer's perspective. Such decisions cannot be made by only considering cost factors.

> **ASSESSMENT CHECK**
>
> 6.3 What are the advantages of breakeven analysis?
>
> 6.4 What are the disadvantages of breakeven analysis?

THE MODIFIED BREAKEVEN CONCEPT

Traditional economic theory considers both costs and demand in determining an equilibrium price. The dual elements of supply and demand are balanced at the point of equilibrium. In actual practice, however, most pricing approaches are largely cost oriented. Because purely cost-oriented approaches to pricing violate the marketing concept, modifications that add demand analysis to the pricing decision are required.

Consumer research on such issues as degree of price elasticity, consumer price expectations, existence and size of specific market segments, and buyer perceptions of strengths and weaknesses of substitute products is necessary for developing sales estimates at different prices. Because much of the resulting data involves perceptions, attitudes, and future expectations of present and potential customers, such estimates are likely to be less precise than cost estimates. The breakeven analysis method illustrated in Figure 18.2 assumes a constant $10 retail price, regardless of quantity. But what happens at different retail prices? As Figure 18.3 shows, a more sophisticated approach, **modified breakeven analysis**, combines the traditional breakeven analysis model with an evaluation of consumer demand.

modified breakeven analysis Pricing technique used to evaluate consumer demand by comparing the number of products that must be sold at a variety of prices to cover total cost with estimates of expected sales at the various prices.

FIGURE 18.3
Modified Breakeven Chart: Parts A and B

(a) Five Breakeven Points for Five Different Prices

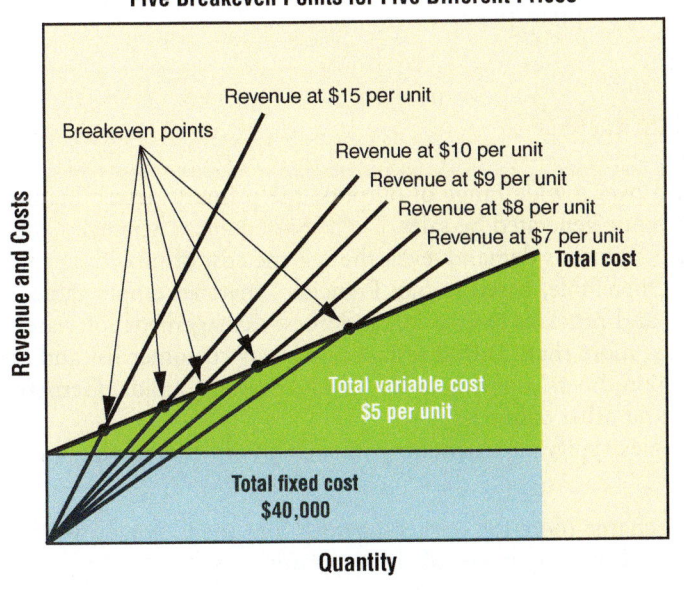

(b) Superimposing a Demand Curve on the Breakeven Chart

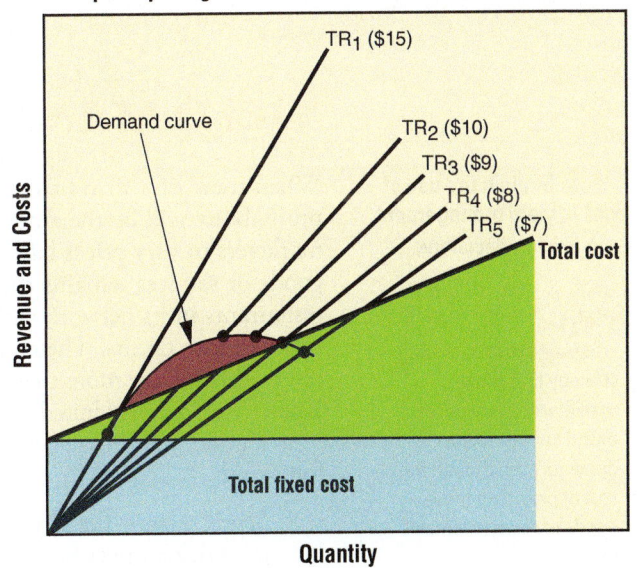

TABLE 18.4 Revenue and Cost Data for Modified Breakeven Analysis

	Revenues		Costs			Breakeven Point	
Price	Quantity Demanded	Total Revenue	Total Fixed Cost	Total Variable Cost	Total Cost	(Number of Units Required to Break Even)	Total Profit (or Loss)
$15	2,500	$37,500	$40,000	$12,500	$52,500	4,000	$(15,000)
10	10,000	100,000	40,000	50,000	90,000	8,000	10,000
9	13,000	117,000	40,000	65,000	105,000	10,000	12,000
8	14,000	112,000	40,000	70,000	110,000	13,334	2,000
7	15,000	105,000	40,000	75,000	115,000	20,000	(10,000)

Table 18.4 summarizes both the cost and revenue aspects of a number of alternative retail prices. The $5 per-unit variable cost and the $40,000 total fixed cost are based on the costs used in the basic breakeven model. The expected unit sales for each specified retail price are obtained from marketing research. The table contains the information necessary for calculating the breakeven point for each of the five retail price alternatives. These points are shown in Figure 18.3(a).

The data shown in the first two columns of Table 18.4 represent a demand schedule that indicates the number of units consumers are expected to purchase at each of a series of retail prices. As Figure 18.3(b) shows, these data can be superimposed onto a breakeven chart to identify the range of feasible prices for the marketer to charge.

Figure 18.3 reveals that the range of profitable prices exists from a low of approximately $8 (TR4) to a high of $10 (TR2), with a price of $9 (TR3) generating the greatest projected profits. Changing the retail price produces a new breakeven point. At a relatively high $15 retail price (TR1), the breakeven point is 4,000 units; at a $10 retail price, it is 8,000 units; and at the lowest price considered, $7 (TR5), it is 20,000 units.

The contribution of modified breakeven analysis is that it forces the marketer to consider whether the consumer is likely to purchase the number of units required for achieving breakeven at a given price. It demonstrates that large numbers of units sold do not necessarily produce added profits, because—other things being equal—lower prices are necessary for stimulating additional sales. Consequently, it is important to consider both costs and consumer demand in determining the most appropriate price.

ASSESSMENT CHECK

6.5 What is modified breakeven analysis?

YIELD MANAGEMENT

7 Explain the use of yield management in pricing decisions.

yield management Pricing strategy that allows marketers to vary prices based on such factors as demand, even though the cost of providing those goods or services remains the same.

When most of a firm's costs are fixed over a wide range of outputs, the primary determinant of profitability will be the amount of revenue generated by sales. **Yield management** strategies allow marketers to vary prices based on such factors as demand, even though the cost of providing those goods or services remains the same. OpenTable, based in San Francisco, matches empty tables at restaurants in its network with diners and provides reservation and guest-management software to its restaurant clients. The company has more than 31,000 restaurants on its customer list and has reserved tables for more than 620 million diners monthly in the United States, Canada, Germany, Japan, Mexico, the United Kingdom, and other countries.[24]

Similar yield management strategies typify the marketing of such goods and services as the following:

- *Sports teams*—the Chicago Cubs charge more for weekend games, and the Colorado Rockies raise ticket prices based on the crowd-pleasing power of visiting teams

- *Lodging*—lower prices in the off-season and higher prices during peak-season periods; low-priced weekend rates (except in locations such as Las Vegas, New Orleans, and Charleston, South Carolina, with high weekend-tourist visits)
- *Auto rental*—lower prices on weekends when business demand is low and higher prices during the week when business demand is higher
- *Airfares*—lower prices on nonrefundable tickets with travel restrictions such as advance purchase and Saturday-night stay requirements and penalties for flight changes and higher prices on refundable tickets that can be changed without penalty.

> **ASSESSMENT CHECK**
>
> 7.1 Explain the goal of yield management.

GLOBAL ISSUES IN PRICE DETERMINATION

It is equally important for a firm engaging in global marketing to use a pricing strategy that reflects its overall marketing strategy. Prices must support the company's broader goals, including product development, advertising and sales, customer support, competitive plans, and financial objectives.

In general, firms can use five pricing objectives to set prices in global marketing. Four of them are the same pricing objectives we discussed earlier in the chapter: profitability, volume, meeting competition, and prestige. In addition, international marketers work to achieve a fifth objective: price stability.

In the global arena, marketers may choose profitability objectives if their company is a price leader that tends to establish international prices. Profitability objectives also make sense if a firm is a low-cost supplier that can make a good profit on sales.

Volume objectives become especially important on the global stage. Both Adidas and Nike provided official outfits for multiple teams in the recent FIFA World Cup in Brazil. It is estimated the two brands control roughly 70 percent of the global soccer market. Although Nike commands 17 percent of the global sports apparel market, Adidas maintains a slight edge in the world of soccer, making $2.4 billion in a recent year.[25]

Increased competition in Europe has spurred firms to work toward the third pricing objective of meeting competitors' prices. The widespread adoption of the euro, the currency of the European Union, became a driving force in price convergence. Now more than 334 million people in 18 European countries use it. The European Commission believed that the adoption of a single currency would promote stability, low inflation, low interest rates, and increased price transparency, all of which help facilitate international trade. However, the recent recession led to a weakening of the euro and sparked financial crises in Greece and Spain, among other countries. The EU countries recapitalized failing banks, and the financial situation seems to have stabilized.[26]

Prestige is a valid pricing objective in international marketing when products are associated with intangible benefits such as high quality, exclusiveness, or attractive design. The greater a product's perceived benefits, the higher its price can be. Marketers must be aware, however, that cultural perceptions of quality can differ from one country to the next. Sometimes items that command prestige prices in the United States are considered run-of-the-mill in other nations; sometimes products that are anything but prestigious in America seem exotic to overseas consumers. American patrons, for instance, view McDonald's restaurants as affordable fast-food eateries, but in China, they are seen as fashionable and relatively expensive.

The fifth pricing objective, price stability, is desirable in international markets, although it is difficult to achieve. Wars, terrorism, economic downturns, changing governments and political parties, and shifting trade policies can alter prices. The U.S. convenience-store giant 7-Eleven, usually associated with American suburbia, faces fierce competition at home and abroad, as well

Identify the five major pricing challenges facing online and international marketers. **8**

as a backlash among consumers against its growing dominance in some urban areas. Rather than put local stores out of business, the chain has launched a Business Conversion Program to convert existing convenience stores into 7-Eleven franchises. While normally franchise fees for new 7-Elevens range from $200,000 to $400,000, under the conversion program, 7-Eleven invests an average of $280,000 in a new store while the store owner retains the space. The company also offers its franchisees access to its proprietary Retail Information System, which tracks sales data for stocking purposes. The chain hopes to convert many existing stores over the next several years but has met some resistance from residents, who prize their often quirky local stores and their contribution to neighborhood flavor.[27]

Price stability can be especially important for producers of commodities—goods and services that have easily accessible substitutes other nations can supply quickly. Countries that export international commodities, such as wood, chemicals, and agricultural crops, suffer economically when their prices fluctuate. A nation such as Nicaragua, which exports sugarcane, can find that its balance of payments changes drastically when the international price for sugar shifts. This makes it vulnerable to stiff price competition from other sugarcane producers. In contrast, countries that export value-oriented products, rather than commodities, tend to enjoy more stable prices. Prices of electronic equipment and automobiles tend to fluctuate far less than prices of crops such as sugarcane and bananas.

ASSESSMENT CHECK

8.1 What are five pricing objectives in global and online marketing?

8.2 Why is price stability difficult to achieve in online and global marketing?

STRATEGIC IMPLICATIONS OF MARKETING IN THE 21ST CENTURY

This chapter has focused on traditional pricing concepts and methods—principles critical to all marketing strategies, including e-commerce. Prices influence and can be affected by other elements of the marketing mix.

Thanks to rapid advances in technology, consumers can compare prices quickly, heightening the already intense competitive pricing environment. The Web allows for prices to be negotiated on the spot and nearly anything can be auctioned. While Internet shopping has not resulted in massive price cutting, it has increased the options available to consumers.

Electronic delivery of music, books, and other goods and services will lead to further price reductions. E-commerce has smoothed out the friction of time, which kept pricing relatively static. Microeconomics suggests a way of determining prices that assumes a profit-maximization objective. This technique attempts to derive correct equilibrium prices in the marketplace by comparing supply and demand. The current obsession with time and the ability to measure it will change the perceptions and pricing of tangible goods. A growing number of products are not made until they are ordered, and increasingly, their prices are no longer fixed. Instead, prices can shift up and down in response to changing market conditions.

Get online now for additional learning tools to help you master your marketing knowledge—visit **WWW.CENGAGEBRAIN.COM** today!

REVIEW OF CHAPTER OBJECTIVES

1 Discuss the legal constraints on pricing.

A variety of laws affect pricing decisions. Antitrust legislation provides a general set of constraints. The Robinson-Patman Act amended the Clayton Act to prohibit price discrimination in sales to other producers, wholesalers, or retailers not based on a cost differential. This law does not cover export markets or sales to the ultimate consumer. At the state level, unfair-trade laws require sellers to maintain minimum prices for comparable merchandise. These laws have been less frequently enforced in recent years. Fair-trade laws were one legal barrier to competition that was removed in the face of growing price competition. These laws permitted manufacturers to set minimum retail prices for products and require their dealers to sign contracts agreeing to abide by such prices.

2 Identify the four major categories of pricing objectives.

Pricing objectives are the natural consequence of overall organizational goals and more specific marketing goals. They can be classified into four major groups: (1) profitability objectives, including profit maximization and target returns; (2) volume objectives, including sales maximization and market share; (3) meeting competition objectives; and (4) prestige objectives.

3 Explain price elasticity and its determinants.

Elasticity is an important element in price determination. The degree of consumer responsiveness to price changes is affected by such factors as (1) availability of substitute or complementary goods, (2) the classification of a good or service as a luxury or a necessity, (3) the portion of a consumer's budget spent on an item, and (4) the time perspective.

4 Describe the three practical problems involved in applying price theory concepts to actual pricing decisions.

Three problems complicate applying price theory in actual practice. First, many firms do not attempt to maximize profits, a basic assumption of price theory. Second, it is difficult to estimate demand curves accurately. Finally, inadequate training of managers and poor communication between economists and practitioners make it difficult to apply price theory in the real world.

5 Explain the two major cost-plus approaches to price setting.

Cost-plus pricing uses a base-cost figure per unit and adds a markup to cover unassigned costs and to provide a profit. It is the most commonly used method of setting prices today. There are two primary cost-oriented pricing procedures. Full-cost pricing uses all relevant variable costs in setting a product's price and allocates those fixed costs that cannot be directly attributed to the production of the priced item. Incremental-cost pricing attempts to use only those costs directly attributable to a specific output in setting prices to overcome the arbitrary allocation of fixed expenses. The basic limitation of cost-oriented pricing is that it does not adequately account for product demand.

6 Discuss the three shortcomings of using breakeven analysis in pricing decisions.

Breakeven analysis is a means of determining the number of goods or services that must be sold at a given price to generate revenue sufficient for covering total costs. It is easily understood by marketers and may help them decide whether required sales levels for a certain price are realistic goals. Its shortcomings are as follows. First, the model assumes cost can be divided into fixed and variable categories and ignores the problems of arbitrarily making some allocations. Second, it assumes that per-unit variable costs do not change at different levels of operation, ignoring the possibility of quantity discounts, more efficient use of the workforce, and other possible economies. Third, the basic breakeven model does not consider demand. It is a cost-based model and fails to directly address the crucial question of whether consumers will actually purchase the product at the specified price and in the quantities required for breaking even or generating a profit. The modified breakeven concept combines traditional breakeven analysis with an evaluation of consumer demand. It directly addresses the key question of whether consumers will actually purchase the product at different prices and in what quantities.

7 Explain the use of yield management in pricing decisions.

Yield management pricing strategies are designed to maximize revenues in situations in which costs are fixed, such as airfares, auto rentals, and theater tickets.

8 Identify the five major pricing challenges facing online and international marketers.

In general, firms can choose from among five pricing objectives to set prices in global marketing. Four of these objectives are the same pricing objectives discussed earlier: profitability, volume, meeting competition, and prestige. The fifth objective is price stability, which is difficult to achieve because wars, border conflicts, terrorism, economic trends, changing governments and political parties, and shifting trade policies can alter prices. The same types of changes can alter pricing in online marketing.

ASSESSMENT CHECK: ANSWERS

1.1 What was the purpose of the Robinson-Patman Act? The Robinson-Patman Act amended the Clayton Act to prohibit price discrimination in sales to other producers, wholesalers, or retailers that are not based on a cost differential.

1.2 What laws require sellers to maintain minimum prices for comparable merchandise? At the state level, unfair-trade laws require sellers to maintain minimum prices for comparable merchandise.

1.3 What laws allow manufacturers to set minimum retail prices for their products? Fair-trade laws permitted manufacturers to set minimum retail prices for products and require their dealers to sign contracts agreeing to abide by such prices.

2.1 What are target-return objectives? Target-return objectives are short-run or long-run goals usually stated as percentages of sales or investment.

2.2 What is value pricing? Value pricing emphasizes the benefits a product provides in comparison to the price and quality levels of competing offerings.

2.3 How do prestige objectives affect a seller's pricing strategy? Prestige pricing establishes a relatively high price to develop and maintain an image of quality that appeals to status-conscious customers. The seller uses price to create an overall image of the firm.

2.4 What goals does pricing strategy help a not-for-profit organization achieve? Pricing strategy helps not-for-profit organizations achieve a variety of goals: profit maximization, cost recovery, market incentives, and market suppression.

2.5 What are the two basic ways in which marketers determine prices? Marketers determine prices by applying the theoretical concepts of supply and demand and by completing cost-oriented analysis.

2.6 What are the four types of market structures? The four types of market structures are pure competition, monopolistic competition, oligopoly, and monopoly.

2.7 Identify the two types of costs that make up a product's total cost. A product's total cost is composed of total variable costs and total fixed costs.

3.1 What are the determinants of elasticity? The degree of consumer responsiveness to price changes—elasticity—is affected by such factors as (1) availability of substitute or complementary goods, (2) the classification of a good or service as a luxury or a necessity, (3) the portion of a consumer's budget spent on an item, and (4) the time perspective.

3.2 What is the usual relationship between elasticity and revenue? A price cut increases revenue only for a product with elastic demand. A price increase raises revenue only for a product with inelastic demand.

4.1 List the three reasons that it is difficult to put price theory into practice. A basic assumption of price theory is all firms attempt to maximize profits. This does not always happen in practice. A second reason is demand curves can be extremely difficult to estimate. Finally, there is poor communication between economists and practitioners, making it difficult to apply price theory in the real world.

5.1 What is full-cost pricing? Full-cost pricing uses all relevant variable costs in setting a product's price.

5.2 What is incremental-cost pricing? Incremental-cost pricing attempts to use only costs directly attributable to a specific output in setting prices to overcome the arbitrary allocation of fixed expenses.

6.1 What is the formula for finding the breakeven point, in units and in dollars? Breakeven point in units = Total fixed cost/Per-unit contribution to fixed cost. Breakeven point in dollars = Total fixed cost/(1 − Variable cost per unit price).

6.2 What adjustments to the basic breakeven calculation must be made to include target returns? Breakeven point (including specific dollar target return) = (Total fixed cost + Profit objective)/Per-unit contribution.

6.3 What are the advantages of breakeven analysis? Breakeven analysis is easily understood by managers and may help them decide whether required sales levels for a certain price are realistic goals.

6.4 What are the disadvantages of breakeven analysis? First, the model assumes cost can be divided into fixed and variable categories and ignores the problems of arbitrarily making some allocations. Second, it assumes that per-unit variable costs do not change at different levels of operation, ignoring the possibility of quantity discounts, more efficient use of the workforce, and other possible economies. Third, the basic breakeven model does not consider demand.

6.5 What is modified breakeven analysis? The modified breakeven concept combines traditional breakeven analysis with an evaluation of consumer demand. It directly addresses the key question of whether consumers will actually purchase the product at different prices and in what quantities.

7.1 Explain the goal of yield management. Yield management pricing strategies are designed to maximize revenues in situations in which costs are fixed, such as airfares, auto rentals, and theater tickets.

8.1 What are five pricing objectives in global and online marketing? Five pricing objectives in global and online marketing are profitability, volume, meeting competition, prestige, and price stability.

8.2 Why is price stability difficult to achieve in online and global marketing? Price stability is difficult to achieve because wars, border conflicts, terrorism, economic trends, changing governments and political parties, and shifting trade policies can alter prices.

MARKETING TERMS YOU NEED TO KNOW

price 594
Robinson-Patman Act 595
unfair-trade laws 596
fair-trade laws 596
marginal analysis 599
profit maximization 599
target-return objective 599
market-share objective 599

Profit Impact of Market Strategies (PIMS) project 600
value pricing 600
customary prices 603
demand 604
supply 604
pure competition 604

monopolistic competition 604
oligopoly 604
monopoly 605
variable cost 605
fixed cost 606
average total cost 606
marginal cost 606

elasticity 607
cost-plus pricing 609
full-cost pricing 609
incremental-cost pricing 610
breakeven analysis 611
modified breakeven analysis 613
yield management 614

ASSURANCE OF LEARNING REVIEW

1. Distinguish between fair-trade and unfair-trade laws. As a consumer, would you support either fair-trade or unfair-trade laws? Would your answer change if you were the owner of a small store?
2. Give an example of each of the major categories of pricing objectives.
3. What are the major price implications of the PIMS studies? Suggest possible explanations for the relationships the PIMS studies reveal.
4. Identify each factor influencing elasticity and give a specific example of how it affects the degree of elasticity in a good or service.
5. What are the practical problems in applying price theory concepts to actual pricing decisions?
6. Explain the advantages and drawbacks of using incremental-cost pricing rather than full-cost pricing.
7. How can locating the breakeven point assist in price determination?
8. Explain the advantage of modified breakeven analysis over the basic breakeven formula.
9. Explain how the use of yield management can result in greater revenue than other pricing strategies.
10. How do pricing objectives for a global firm differ from those used generally?

PROJECTS AND TEAMWORK EXERCISES

1. In small teams, categorize each of the following as a specific type of pricing objective. Suggest a company or product likely to use each pricing objective. Compare your findings.
   a. 8 percent increase in profits over the previous year
   b. prices no more than 7 percent higher than prices quoted by independent dealers
   c. 10 percent increase in market share
   d. 12 percent return on investment (before taxes)
   e. setting the highest prices in the product category to maintain favorable brand image

2. How are the following prices determined and what do they have in common?
   a. admission to a local sporting event
   b. tuition at a community college
   c. local sales tax rate
   d. printing of programs for a baseball stadium
   e. lawn mowers

3. WebTech Development of Austin, Texas, is considering the possible introduction of a new product proposed by its research and development staff. The firm's marketing director estimates the product can be marketed at a price of $70. Total fixed cost is $278,000, and average variable cost is calculated at $48.
   a. What is the breakeven point in units for the proposed product?
   b. The firm's CEO has suggested a target profit return of $214,000 for the proposed product. How many units must be sold to both breakeven and achieve this target return?

4. Research the price schedule at your local movie theater multiplex. Which pricing strategy accounts for any price differentials you discover? Why don't matinee prices constitute price discrimination against those who don't qualify for the discounts?

5. How do cell-phone companies make money by charging a flat rate per month for a set number of minutes, such as $50 for 300 minutes? Can you think of a more profitable plan? Would it appeal to consumers? Why or why not?

CRITICAL-THINKING EXERCISES

1. Prices at amusement parks might rise if operators such as Disney and Universal Studios add new attractions. The parks also have to deal with high fuel prices. List as many things as you can think of that such parks offer patrons in return for their money. Which of these do you think are directly reflected in the price of admission?

2. Recording artists earn only about 9 percent in royalties per CD, using a royalty base of retail price less 25 percent for packaging costs. The rest goes to the producer and to cover recording costs, promotion, copies given away to radio stations and reviewers, and other costs such as videos. What do you think happens to the artist's royalties when a CD is marked down to sell faster? Consider two cases: (a) the marked-down CD sells more copies; and (b) it sells the same number of copies as before.

3. Some finance experts advise consumers not to worry about rising gasoline prices, the cost of which can easily be covered by forgoing one takeout meal a month, but to worry about how high energy prices will affect the rest of the economy. For example, each dollar-a-barrel price increase is equivalent to a $20 million-a-day "tax" on the economy. Explain what this means.

4. Capital Motors, a car dealership, recently announced that it will rely less on high-volume strategies such as discounts and rebates to improve its profitability. Another strategy it will employ is to sell fewer cars to rental fleets, which eventually return the cars to Capital for sale at low auction prices. How do these types of sales affect Capital's profitability?

ETHICS EXERCISE

You work for a major restaurant in your town. The manager is facing cost pressures from rising food prices and says she needs to raise revenues. She decides to reduce the size of the meal portions and use cheaper cuts of meat and fish in some entrées while holding the menu prices constant. She tells you and other staff members not to mention the changes to customers and to deflect any questions or complaints you hear. The descriptions in the menu will not be changed, she says, "because the printing costs would be too high."

1. You know the restaurant advertises the quality of its ingredients in the local media. The menu changes are not advertised, and it bothers you. What course of action would you take?

2. A customer mentions that the chicken in the sandwich he ordered is "tough and dry" and the order seems smaller than before. What would you do?

INTERNET EXERCISES

1. **Price competition.** Using a popular travel site, look up airfares for each of the following flights:

   Baltimore to Los Angeles

   Atlanta to Minneapolis

   Seattle to Dallas

   Chicago to Denver

   Charlotte to Boston

   Do some fares appear higher (on a per-mile basis) than others? Do these differences reflect how many airlines provide nonstop service between each pair of cities? What about the impact on fares of so-called discount carriers (such as Spirit Airlines)?

   www.expedia.com

   www.kayak.com

2. **Yield management.** You are planning a trip to Walt Disney World. Visit the website to price week-long stays at various times of the year. Be sure to choose similar hotels. Which weeks are the most and least expensive? Do the days of arrival and departure make any difference? Prepare a summary of your findings and bring it to class so you can participate in a discussion on yield management.

   http://disneyworld.disney.go.com/vacation-packages

3. **Airbus and Boeing subsidies.** The United States and European Union have had a long-running dispute over allegations of improper government subsidies to commercial aircraft manufacturers (the U.S. about Airbus and the EU about Boeing). Government subsidies may give the manufacturer a price advantage over its competition. Both sides have filed complaints with the World Trade Organization. Go to the WTO website and see the article link listed below. Write a report outlining the trade dispute and its current status.

   www.wto.org

   http://www.reuters.com/article/2014/05/19/us-trade-aircraft-subsidies-exclusive-idUSBREA4I03W20140519

Note: Internet Web addresses change frequently. If you don't find the exact site listed, you may need to access the organization's home page and search from there or use a search engine such as Google or Bing.

CASE 18.1
ScoreBig: Name Your Price for Live Events

If you've ever tried to get tickets for a game, show, or concert that ended up being sold out, you may be surprised to find that as many as 40 percent of seats for many such events actually go unsold. Although the live-event business earns an estimated $22 billion a year in the United States, high prices keep many people away from arenas and concert halls. Now, however, a fast-growing, Los Angeles–based company called ScoreBig lets consumers bid on hundreds of thousands of those unsold seats. Consumers can make an offer for the event of their choice in much the same way that PriceLine.com auctions hotel rooms and airline tickets.

ScoreBig operates a website through which visitors can bid on upcoming events. The company lists events with excess inventories of seats and invites customers to bid for the chance to pay at least 10 percent less and sometimes as much as 60 percent less than the original price, often within a seating area of their choice. The company provides a ballpark price for bidders. If the bid is accepted, a confirming email is sent immediately and the customer prints out the ticket. The average savings is 42 percent, and because ScoreBig deals directly with event promoters, there are no fees or handling charges.

The company's unique pricing algorithms help maximize attendance and revenues for its entertainment partners, while helping them protect their brands. ScoreBig's business strategy also helps its partners retain the integrity of its sales channel for full-price tickets while filling empty seats for live entertainment events.

QUESTIONS FOR CRITICAL THINKING

1. Critics say event promoters are to blame for the high number of unsold tickets, because they have continued to raise ticket prices to compensate for unsold seats until they rise out of range for most audiences. Yet promoters feel discounts damage their brands. Can you suggest possible answers to this pricing strategy problem?

2. Is auctioning the best way to eliminate unsold seats? Why or why not?

Sources: Company website, www.scorebig.com, accessed October 28, 2014; "ScoreBig.com Secures $18M Investment in Series D Funding Round Led by Hearst Ventures," (press release), http://blog.scorebig.com, accessed October 28, 2014; Michael Carney, "After a Year of 600% Revenue Growth, ScoreBig Bolsters Its Senior Business and Engineering Teams," *Pando Daily*, accessed April 7, 2014, http://pando.com; "ScoreBig Review: Do You Score Big Ticket Deals?" *TickPick*, accessed April 7, 2014, http://blog.tickpick.com; Darren Rovell, "Ticket Seller ScoreBig Adds Key Executive," *ESPN*, accessed April 7, 2014, http://espn.go.com; Joshua Brustein, "Are You Free Tonight? Bargains to Get You Out," *The New York Times*, accessed April 7, 2014, www.nytimes.com.

VIDEO CASE 18.2
Ski Butternut: Great Prices for Winter Fun

You might not be a skier or live anywhere near a mountain. Perhaps your idea of fun leans more toward sun, sand, and waves. But as a marketer, you can appreciate the seasonal nature of a small ski resort like Ski Butternut that's tucked away in the Berkshire Mountains of western Massachusetts How do marketers approach pricing objectives and set prices for a recreational experience that is vulnerable to the whims of weather, climate, overall economic shifts, and the cost of everything from electricity to labor—not to mention the changing incomes and lifestyles of consumers? Ski Butternut has been in business for more than 50 years, which means that its owners have solved at least some of the pricing puzzle. Matt Sawyer, director of marketing at Ski Butternut, puts it this way: "Our customers are looking for a great value. They're willing to be loyal if we treat them correctly."

Ski Butternut takes both sides of this equation—great value and loyal customers—into consideration for its pricing objectives. Sawyer readily points out that, while Ski Butternut is a for-profit company, the mountain doesn't realize a profit every winter. "Weather plays a huge role," he says. "You don't know whether you're going to be profitable until the end of February." Running a ski resort involves huge up-front costs and a lot of uncertainty. Target-return objectives for the ski school or holiday periods may melt with an early thaw. Ski Butternut managers must try to project a typical operating budget and find ways to make a profit as their customers enjoy their time on the slopes.

Plenty of ski resorts dot the New England landscape, which puts Ski Butternut in competition for consumers' recreation dollars. So Ski Butternut offers value to customers, hoping to capture market share and increase the volume of skiers on its slopes. The mountain offers value pricing to everyone, with special attention to first-time skiers, families, and season pass-holders. In order to boost the number of skiers who hit the mountain during the week (reducing gridlock on the slopes during weekends), Ski Butternut sets its Monday–Friday lift ticket price at $25. Unlike other mountains, Ski Butternut doesn't offer special deals, such as a "half-price Tuesday" or "ladies' Wednesday." Sawyer believes that customers prefer this straightforward approach to pricing. "It's easy to understand, it's predictable," he explains.

To attract more skiers and snowboarders to the mountain, Ski Butternut offers first-timers a learn-to-ski package for $75, which includes a lift ticket, lesson, and rental equipment (if purchased separately, these three items would total $135). The offer is good every day, all season—no blackout periods for weekends or holidays. "We want people to come when they can," explains Sawyer. For the second visit, skiers can purchase a $100 package ($35 off). "This price point allows people to get exposed to the sport," notes Sawyer. The mountain also offers midweek ski-and-stay packages for $45 per person/per night—a great deal especially when compared to some of the larger, more glamorous resorts.

Kids and families are a special focus for Ski Butternut, which has created several special programs for them. For example, fifth graders ski free Sunday through Friday when accompanied by a paying adult (and children who have never skied before get a free first-timers' package). Ski Butternut targets this group, because it's the optimum age to get started, experience success, and continue with a lifetime of skiing or snowboarding. Because New England is home to a number of colleges and universities, Ski Butternut offers a $20 discount to college students, giving them a reason to get outside and ski—and become loyal Butternut customers.

Sawyer points to season pass-holders as one of Ski Butternut's most important customer segments. With a $275 price tag and a breakeven point of only five visits, a Ski Butternut season pass represents huge savings to regular skiers. In return, those skiers spend dollars on food, lessons, and other mountain services. Once they've spent the money for the pass, they tend to ski at least 10 to 15 times during a season. "That's great because they are the strongest word-of-mouth advertising we're going to find," acknowledges Sawyer.

Finally, Ski Butternut boosts its volume by offering special rates to groups under its "You Serve, You Save" program, along with Boy Scouts and preregistered ski clubs. Members of the military, police officers, firefighters, and EMT professionals (and their families) receive discounted packages when they make advance reservations. "We want to give them an incentive and say thank you," explains Sawyer.

QUESTIONS FOR CRITICAL THINKING

1. Ski Butternut avoids pricing to meet the competition. Instead, it focuses on the value that it creates for customers. In your opinion, why is this a successful strategy?
2. What factors might determine demand elasticity for Ski Butternut's offerings?

Sources: Company website, www.skibutternut.com, accessed April 9, 2014; Kristen Lummis, "Ski Butternut: The Real Deal for Northeast Families," *The Brave Ski Mom*, accessed April 9, 2014, http://braveskimom.com; "New Website and Mobile Site for Ski Butternut," press release, www.skibutternut.com, accessed April 9, 2014.

NOTES

1. Company website, "Company Facts," http://newscenter.dollargeneral.com, accessed October 28, 2014; Pratik Thacker, "What Does Dollar General Have in Store for 2014?" *The Motley Fool*, accessed March 25, 2014, www.fool.com; "Dollar General to Add 700 Stores in 2014," *Nashville Business Journal*, accessed March 25, 2014, www.bizjournals.com; "Dollar General and Hostess Provide a Sweet Deal for Customers," press release, accessed March 25, 2014, http://newscenter.dollargeneral.com.
2. "Get Rid of Tariffs on Trans-Atlantic Trade," *Chicago Tribune*, accessed March 25, 2014, http://articles.chicagotribune.com.
3. Eric Justian, "China Slaps Massive Tariff on U.S. Imported Solar Materials," *Triple Pundit*, accessed March 27, 2014, www.triplepundit.com.
4. Neal Karlinsky and Bonnie McLean, "StubHub, Revolutionizing the Modern-Day Ticket Scalper," *ABC News*, accessed March 27, 2014, http://abcnews.go.com.
5. Gary Stoller, "Airline Fees Reach $400+," *USA Today*, accessed March 27, 2014, http://www.usatoday.com.
6. Richard Jones, "Plant Sales: Quality over Quantity," *Greenhouse Grower*, accessed March 25, 2014, www.greenhousegrower.com.
7. Trefis Team, "P&G Speeds Up Price Cuts to Munch More Market Share," *Forbes*, accessed March 25, 2014, www.forbes.com.
8. Angela Prilliman, "The Why and How of Choosing the Right Restaurant Loyalty Program," *FiveStars.com*, accessed March 26, 2014, http://blog.fivestars.com.
9. Robert D. Buzzell, Bradley T. Gale, and Ralph G. M. Sultan, "Market Share—A Key to Profitability," *Harvard Business Review*, January 1975, http://hbr.org.
10. Company website, www.skype.com, accessed October 28, 2014.
11. Company website, www.kroger.com, accessed October 28, 2014.
12. Company website, www.traderjoes.com, accessed October 28, 2014.
13. Tarun Iyer, "HDDs Return to Pre-Flood Prices," *Tom's Hardware*, accessed March 26, 2014, www.tomshardware.com.
14. Company website, www.netjets.com, accessed March 26, 2014.
15. Ryan Dezember and Emily Grazer, "Drop in Traffic Takes Toll on Investors in Private Roads," *The Wall Street Journal*, accessed April 2, 2014, http://online.wsj.com.
16. Megan Willett, "How to Get into 1,400 Museums for Free on National Museum Day," *Business Insider*, accessed March 27, 2014, www.businessinsider.com.
17. "Higher Tax Rates in Effect for Chicago Tobacco Consumers," *The Civic Federation*, accessed April 22, 2014, www.civicfed.org.
18. Amy Leap, "Less for Your Money," *Mail Tribune*, accessed February 26, 2014, www.mailtribune.com.
19. U.S. Energy Information Administration, "Frequently Asked Questions," www.eia.gov, accessed March 27, 2014; Chuin-Wei Yap, "China Moves to Tighten Rare-Earths Control, Pave Way for Consolidation," *The Wall Street Journal*, accessed March 27, 2014, http://online.wsj.com.
20. Company website, "Prius Plug-in Hybrid 2015," www.toyota.com, accessed October 28, 2014.
21. Justin Bachman, "Airline Mergers Bring Deep Service Cuts to Small and Midsize Airports," *Bloomberg Businessweek*, accessed October 28, 2014, www.businessweek.com.
22. "Zimbabwe Inflation Rate," *Trading Economics*, accessed October 28, 2014, www.tradingeconomics.com; Brian Hungwe, "Zimbabwe's Multi-Currency Confusion," *BBC*, accessed March 31, 2014, www.bbc.com.
23. U.S. Department of Energy, Alternative Fuels Data Center, "Fact Sheet," www.afdc.energy.gov, accessed February 27, 2014.
24. Company website, "About OpenTable," http://press.opentable.com, accessed October 28, 2014.
25. Andrew Soergel, "Adidas and Nike Face Off at World Cup," *U.S. News & World Report*, accessed October 28, 2014, www.usnews.com; Darren Heitner, "World Cup: Adidas Is All In with Argentina and Germany," *Forbes*, accessed October 28, 2014, www.forbes.com.
26. "Taking Europe's Pulse," *The Economist*, accessed April 7, 2014, www.economist.com; "The Euro," http://ec.europa.eu, accessed March 28, 2014.
27. Company website, "Store Development," http://corp.7-eleven.com, accessed March 28, 2014; Jane L. Levere, "7-Eleven Sees an Opportunity to Open Doors," *The New York Times*, accessed March 28, 2014, www.nytimes.com.

Chapter 19

Pricing Strategies

1. Describe the three alternative pricing strategies and when each strategy is most appropriate.
2. Explain how prices are quoted.
3. Identify the five pricing policy decisions marketers must make.
4. Discuss the relationship of price to consumer perceptions of quality.
5. Contrast competitive bidding and negotiated prices.
6. Explain the importance of transfer pricing.
7. Compare the three alternative global pricing strategies.
8. Relate the concepts of cannibalization, bundle pricing, and bots to online pricing strategies.

DISCOUNTS REDUCE ABANDONED E-CARTS

The volume of online shopping continues to grow, reaching more than $55 billion in one recent holiday season, up 10 percent from the year before. But another statistic, equally revealing and often overlooked, is the number of online shoppers who abandon their electronic shopping carts, purchasing nothing before moving on.

According to a recent study, about 68 percent of consumers abandon their online shopping carts, which equates to nearly $4 trillion in lost revenues for companies worldwide. Some customers simply change their minds about the purchase, while others are distracted or interrupted. A few of these may return on their own to complete their transactions. Still others balk at shipping costs on their way to the checkout page, while some aren't really shopping in the first place—they're comparing prices and may move on to buy the item elsewhere.

Marketers are increasingly aware of the large number of abandoned carts and the huge dollar value of the purchases being left on the table, but surprisingly few are doing anything about it. Industry analysts and marketing researchers urge action, however, saying that an immediate email, at the very least, can be cost effective and extremely influential in bringing customers back to close the sale. Multiple emails and even a phone call have increased sales in some cases. Yet it's believed that only about a quarter of online retailers currently send one reminder, and the number could be as low as 15 percent. Those that do include giants such as Lands' End, Best Buy, Home Depot, and Zappos.

Some smaller online retailers hesitate because they don't have the technology to follow up or because they fear customers are simply waiting to be offered a better deal. Shoppers say they are positively influenced by such offers, but some retailers fear that by using them, they may be training their customers to resist paying full price or to "game" any system to receive more or increasingly generous enticements to buy.

Systems can be put in place to prevent abuse of discount offers, such as discount codes that can be used only once. And retailers can simply ask whether the customer had difficulty checking out online and offer help. But some observers believe that reducing prices is the best way to eliminate abandoned shopping carts. Online retailers will have to decide whether it's worth offering a small discount to close the sale.[1]

EVOLUTION OF A BRAND

Successfully closing a sale is a challenge for all marketers, whether brick-and-mortar or online retailers. Some companies such as Lands' End know how to handle "unfinished" transactions, but a surprising number of e-retailers don't have pricing strategies in place for dealing with abandoned shopping carts—an omission that adds up to trillions of dollars worldwide each year.

- Have you ever abandoned a shopping cart at an online store? Did the e-retailer follow up? If so, how soon? What incentives—if any—did the e-retailer offer to persuade you to come back? Did the follow-up convince you to return to the website and complete your purchase? Why or why not?
- Imagine that you are an e-retailer trying to come up with a creative solution to the abandoned-shopping-cart problem. You'd like to offer an incentive to entice shoppers to return and complete their purchases. What are some ways to bring shoppers back—without letting them game the system?

Chapter Overview

Setting prices is neither a one-time decision nor a standard routine. Pricing is a dynamic function of the marketing mix. As illustrated by the strategies undertaken by Lands' End, Home Depot, and others, pricing is just one aspect of the overall marketing effort. While about half of all companies change prices once a year or less frequently, one in ten does so every month. Online companies may adjust prices more often, depending on what they sell. Some firms negotiate prices on the spot, as in the case of a car dealership or an antique shop.

Companies translate pricing objectives into pricing decisions in two major steps. First, someone takes responsibility for making pricing decisions and administering the resulting pricing structure. Second, someone sets the overall pricing structure—that is, basic prices and appropriate discounts for channel members, quantity purchases, and geographic and promotional considerations.

The decision to make price adjustments is directly related to demand. Most businesses slowly change the amounts they charge customers, even when they clearly recognize strong demand. Instead of raising prices, they may scale down customer service or add fees. They may also wait to raise prices until they see what their competitors do.

Few businesses want the distinction of being the first to charge higher prices. Because many firms base their prices on manufacturing costs rather than consumer demand, they may wait for increases in their own costs before responding with price changes. These increases generally emerge more slowly than changes in consumer demand. Finally, because many business executives believe steady prices help preserve long-term relationships with customers, they are reluctant to raise prices even when strong demand probably justifies the change.

Chapter 18 introduced the concept of price and its role in the economic system and marketing strategy. This chapter examines various pricing strategies and price structures, such as reductions from list prices and geographic considerations. It then looks at the primary pricing policies, including psychological pricing, price flexibility, product-line pricing, and promotional pricing, as well as price–quality relationships. Competitive and negotiated prices are discussed, and one section focuses entirely on transfer pricing. Finally, the chapter concludes by describing important factors in pricing goods and services for online and global markets.

PRICING STRATEGIES

1 Describe the three alternative pricing strategies and when each strategy is most appropriate.

The specific strategies firms use to price goods and services grow out of the marketing strategies they formulate to accomplish overall organizational objectives. One firm's marketers may price their products to attract customers across a wide range; another group of marketers may set prices to appeal to a small segment of a larger market; still another group may simply try to match competitors' price tags. In general, firms can choose from three pricing strategies: skimming, penetration, and competitive pricing. The following sections look at these choices in more detail.

SKIMMING PRICING STRATEGY

Derived from the expression "skimming the cream," **skimming pricing strategies** are also known as **market-plus pricing**. They involve intentionally setting a relatively high price compared with the prices of competing products. Although some firms continue to use a skimming strategy throughout most stages of the product lifecycle, it is more commonly used as a market-entry price for distinctive goods or services with little or no initial competition. When the supply begins to exceed demand, or when competition catches up, the initial high price is dropped.

Such was the case with high-definition televisions (HDTVs), whose average price was $19,000, including installation, when they were first introduced. The resulting sticker shock kept them out of the range of most household budgets. But more than a decade later, price cuts have brought these LCD models into the reach of mainstream consumers. At Rakuten.com (formerly Buy.com), shoppers can pick up an HP 19-inch flat-panel LCD model for about $109. On the higher end, they can purchase an LG Electronics 55-inch flat-panel LED model at Amazon.com for about $679.[2]

A company may practice a skimming strategy in setting a market-entry price when it introduces a distinctive good or service with little or no competition. When Nissan launched its all-electric car, the Leaf, the company priced the vehicle at more than $35,000. A year later, Nissan cut the price by $6,000 to spur additional sales. GM's all-electric car, the Chevrolet Volt, was introduced at an entry price close to $40,000, but the company recently dropped its price by $5,000. Contrary to Nissan and GM entries into the all-electric car sector, Tesla Motors' high-end electric car's starting price in the United States is more than $69,000.[3]

In some cases, a firm may maintain a skimming strategy throughout most stages of a product's lifecycle. The jewelry category is a good example. Although discounters, such as Costco and Home Shopping Network (HSN), offer heavier gold pieces for a few hundred dollars, firms such as Tiffany and Cartier command prices ten times that amount just for their brand names. Exclusivity justifies the pricing—and the price, once set, rarely falls.

Sometimes maintaining a high price through the product's lifecycle works, but sometimes it does not. High prices can drive away otherwise loyal customers. Baseball fans may shift from attending major league games to minor league games—if available—because of ticket, parking, and food prices. Amusement park visitors may shy away from high admission prices and head to the beach instead. If an industry or firm has been known to cut prices at certain points in the past, consumers—and retailers—will expect it. If the price cut doesn't come, consumers must decide whether to pay the higher tab or try a competitor's products.

Significant price changes in the retail gasoline and airline industries occur in the form of a **step out**, in which one firm raises prices and then waits to see if others follow suit. If competitors fail to respond by increasing their prices, the company making the step out usually reduces prices to the original level. Although airlines are prohibited by law from collectively setting prices, they can follow each other's example.

Despite the risk of backlash, a skimming strategy does offer benefits. It allows a manufacturer to quickly recover its research and development (R&D) costs. Pharmaceutical companies, fiercely protective of their patents on new drugs, justify high prices because of astronomical R&D costs: an average of 16¢ of every sales dollar, compared with 8¢ for computer makers and 4¢ in the aerospace industry. To protect their brand names from competition from lower-cost generics, drug makers frequently make small changes to their products—such as combining the original product with a complementary prescription drug that treats different aspects of the ailment.

A skimming strategy also permits marketers to control demand in the introductory stages of a product's lifecycle and then adjust productive capacity to match changing demand. A low initial price for a new

---

skimming pricing strategies Pricing strategy involving the use of a high price relative to competitive offerings.

market-plus pricing Intentionally setting a relatively high price compared with the prices of competing products; also known as *skimming pricing*.

step out Pricing practice in which one firm raises prices and then waits to see if others follow suit.

Nissan applied a skimming strategy when it first launched its all-electric Leaf model. When GM released its electric Chevrolet Volt soon after, their prices were similar. To spur additional sales, both companies recently cut prices on their electric car models.

FIGURE 19.1 Price Reductions to Increase Market Share

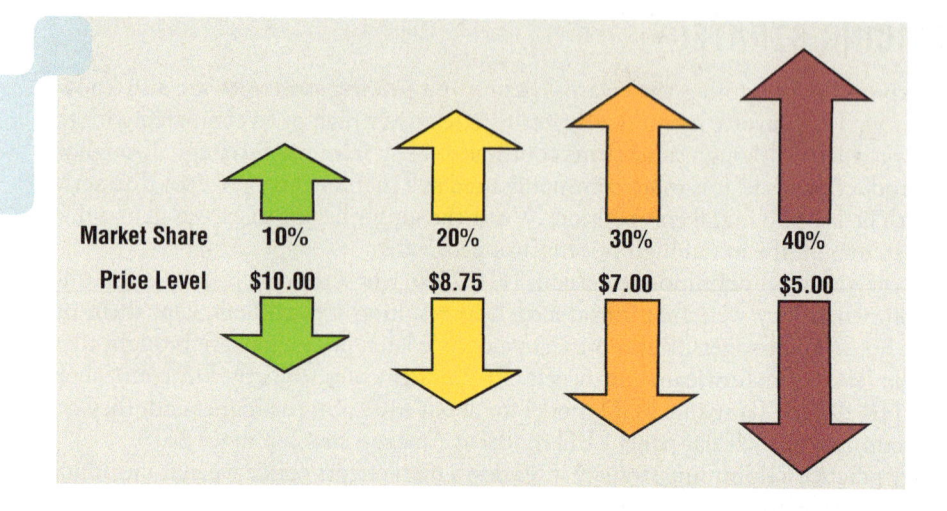

| Market Share | 10% | 20% | 30% | 40% |
| Price Level | $10.00 | $8.75 | $7.00 | $5.00 |

> **Briefly Speaking**
>
> "Never be frightened to take a profit. Better in your pocket than theirs."
>
> — Michael Levy
> British author of motivational books

product could lead to fulfillment problems and loss of shopper goodwill if demand outstrips the firm's production capacity. The result will likely be consumer and retailer complaints and possibly permanent damage to the product's image. Excess demand occasionally leads to quality issues, as the firm strives to satisfy consumer desires for the product with inadequate production facilities.

During the late growth and early maturity stages of its lifecycle, a product's price typically falls for two reasons: (1) the pressure of competition and (2) the desire to expand its market. Figure 19.1 shows that 10 percent of the market may buy Product X at $10, and another 20 percent could be added to its customer base at a price of $8.75. Successive price declines may expand the firm's market size and meet challenges posed by new competitors.

A skimming strategy has one major chief disadvantage: It attracts competition. Potential competitors see innovative firms reaping large financial returns and may decide to enter the market. This new supply may force the price of the original product even lower than its eventual level under a sequential skimming procedure. However, if patent protection or some unique proprietary ability allows a firm to exclude competitors from its market, it may extend a skimming strategy.

PENETRATION PRICING STRATEGY

penetration pricing strategy Pricing strategy involving the use of a relatively low entry price compared with competitive offerings, based on the theory that this initial low price will help secure market acceptance.

A **penetration pricing strategy** sets a low price as a major marketing weapon. Marketers often price products noticeably lower than competing offerings when they enter new markets that have dozens of competing brands. Once the product achieves some degree of recognition through consumer trial purchases stimulated by its low price, marketers may increase the price to the level of competing products. Marketers of consumer products, such as dish soap, often use this strategy. A penetration pricing strategy may also extend over several stages of the product lifecycle as the firm seeks to maintain a reputation as a low-price competitor.

A penetration pricing strategy is sometimes called *market-minus pricing* when it implements the premise that a lower-than-market price will attract buyers and move a brand from an unknown newcomer to at least the brand-recognition stage or even the brand-preference stage. Because many firms begin penetration pricing with the intention of increasing prices in the future, success depends on generating many trial purchases. Penetration pricing is common among cable and Internet providers, which typically offer low rates for a specified introductory period, then raise the rates. If competitors view the new product as a threat, marketers attempting to use a penetration strategy often discover that rivals will simply match their prices.

Retailers may use penetration pricing to lure shoppers to new stores. Strategies might take forms such as zero interest charges for credit purchases at a new furniture store, two-for-one offers for dinner at a new restaurant, or an extremely low price on a single product purchase for first-time customers.

Cable and Internet providers often use penetration pricing strategies, which offer low rates for a specified introductory period.

Penetration pricing works best for goods or services characterized by highly elastic demand. Many highly price-sensitive consumers pay close attention to this type of appeal. The strategy also suits situations in which large-scale operations and long production runs result in low production and marketing costs. Finally, penetration pricing may be appropriate in market situations in which introduction of a new product will likely attract strong competitors. Such a strategy may allow a new product to reach the mass market quickly and capture a large share prior to entry by competitors.

Some auto manufacturers have been using penetration pricing for some new models to attract customers who might not otherwise consider purchasing a vehicle during a given year or who might be looking at a more expensive competitor. India's Tata Motors launched the world's cheapest car: the Nano, which carries a price tag of $2,500 in India. Currently, the lowest-priced car in the United States is the Nissan Versa, with a sticker price of $12,800.[4]

Everyday Low Pricing

Closely related to penetration pricing is **everyday low pricing (EDLP)**, a strategy devoted to continuous low prices as opposed to relying on short-term price-cutting tactics such as cents-off coupons, rebates, and special sales. EDLP can take two forms. In the first, retailers such as Walmart and Lowe's compete by consistently offering consumers low prices on a broad range of items. Through its EDLP policy, Lowe's pledges to not only match any price the consumer sees elsewhere but to also take off an additional percentage in some cases. Walmart recently rolled out an online tool for consumers, which compares its prices on 80,000 products with those of competitors in a specific geographic region. Called "Savings Catcher," the program allows consumers to log on, input a code number from their Walmart receipt, and see if there are lower prices offered by competitors for certain products. If a lower price is found, Walmart credits the difference to the customer on an online Walmart gift card.[5] Chili's Grill & Bar is another company that has had success with everyday pricing, as well as profitable menu changes. See the "Marketing Success" feature to learn how.

The second form of the EDLP pricing strategy involves its use by the manufacturer in dealing with channel members. Manufacturers may seek to set stable wholesale prices that undercut offers competitors make to retailers, offers that typically rise and fall with the latest trade promotion deals. Many marketers reduce list prices on a number of products while simultaneously reducing promotion allowances to retailers. While reductions in allowances mean retailers may not fund in-store promotions such as shelf merchandising and end-aisle displays, the manufacturers hope stable low prices will stimulate sales instead.

Some retailers oppose EDLP strategies. Many grocery stores, for instance, operate on "high–low" strategies that set profitable regular prices to offset losses of frequent specials and promotions. Other retailers believe EDLP will ultimately benefit both sellers and buyers. Supporters of EDLP in the grocery industry point out that it already succeeds at two of the biggest competitors: Walmart and Costco.

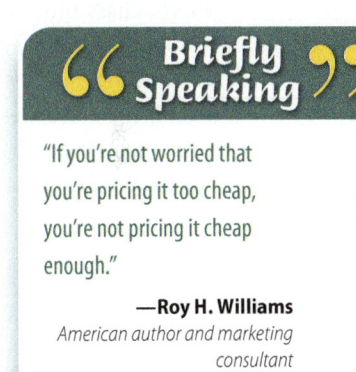

> **Briefly Speaking**
>
> "If you're not worried that you're pricing it too cheap, you're not pricing it cheap enough."
>
> —**Roy H. Williams**
> *American author and marketing consultant*

everyday low pricing (EDLP) Pricing strategy of continuously offering low prices rather than relying on short-term price cuts such as cents-off coupons, rebates, and special sales.

MARKETING SUCCESS
Chili's Serves Everyday Value

Background. Chili's Grill & Bar is a chain of about 1,600 casual-dining restaurants owned by Brinker International, based in Dallas.

The Challenge. Chili's needed to improve its profit margins, as a slow economic recovery led diners to eat out less often and order fewer drinks and desserts, which are typically high-margin items. Prices for many ingredients were also rising, including staples such as beef, cooking oil, and dairy products.

The Strategy. In addition to cost-cutting and remodeling efforts, Chili's also made profitable menu changes, extending its successful everyday value "$20 Dinner for Two" and "Lunch Combo" offerings. The company recently introduced a "Fresh Mex" menu that appeals to diners looking for better ingredients—items typically found in fast-casual chains such as Chipotle and Panera. Chili's has also focused on technology, introducing tabletop tablets that allow diners to pay for their orders and help speed up the service process. Chili's has also ramped up its "to-go" order business, which accounts for 10 percent of the chain's overall business.

The Outcome. Chili's has already experienced higher check amounts as a result of the tablets because diners add beverage and dessert purchases after their initial food order. The tablets have also helped increase consumer feedback about their Chili's experience.

Sources: Company website, www.brinker.com, accessed April 14, 2014; Monica Watrous, "Chili's Eyes Five Ways to 'Out-Fast Fast-Casual,'" *Food Business News*, accessed April 14, 2014, www.foodbusinessnews.net; Ron Ruggless, "Chili's Details Rollout of Tabletop Tablets," *Nation's Restaurant News*, accessed April 14, 2014, http://nrn.com; Ron Ruggless, "Brinker Expands Value Strategy at Chili's," *Nation's Restaurant News*, accessed April 14, 2014, http://nrn.com.

Lowe's employs everyday low pricing, a strategy devoted to continuous low prices instead of special sales and other short-term pricing tactics.

One popular pricing myth is that a low price is a sure sell. Low prices are an easy means of distinguishing the offerings of one marketer from other sellers, but such moves are easy to counter by competitors. Unless overall demand is price elastic, overall price cuts will mean less revenue for all firms in the industry. In addition, low prices may generate an image of questionable quality.

COMPETITIVE PRICING STRATEGY

Although many organizations rely heavily on price as a competitive weapon, even more implement **competitive pricing strategies**. These organizations try to reduce the emphasis on price competition by matching other firms' prices and concentrating their own marketing efforts on the product, distribution, and promotion elements of the marketing mix. As pointed out earlier, while price offers a dramatic means of achieving competitive advantage, it is also the easiest marketing variable for competitors to match. In fact, in industries with relatively homogeneous products, competitors must match each other's price reductions to maintain market share and remain competitive.

Retailers such as Home Depot and Lowe's both use price-matching strategies, assuring consumers that they will meet—and beat—competitors' prices. Grocery chains, such as Kroger's and Stop & Shop, may compete with seasonal items: soft drinks and hot dogs in the summer, hot chocolate and turkeys in the winter. As soon as one store lowers the price of an item, the rest follow suit.

Another form of competitive pricing is setting an **opening price point** within a category. Retailers often achieve this by pricing a quality private-label product below the competition. Grocery giants Publix and Kroger actively advertise their private-label goods, most of which are priced below those of manufacturers' brands. More consumers are buying private-label products, and many say the quality is comparable to that of national brands.[6]

Prices can really drop when companies continually match each other's prices, as evident in the airline and computer industries. But competitive pricing can be tricky; a price reduction affects not only the first company but also the entire industry, as other firms match the reduction. Unless lower prices can attract new customers and expand the overall market enough to offset the loss of per-unit revenue, the price cut will leave all competitors with less revenue. Research shows that nearly two-thirds of all firms set prices using competitive pricing as their primary pricing strategy.

Once competitors routinely match each other on price, marketers must turn away from price as a marketing strategy, emphasizing other variables to develop areas of distinctive competence and attract customers. That might mean offering personalized services, such as gift wrapping, or a sales associate who knows the type of clothing you like.

competitive pricing strategies Pricing strategy designed to deemphasize price as a competitive variable by pricing a good or service at the level of comparable offerings.

opening price point An opening price below that of the competition, usually on a high-quality, private-label item.

> *"Briefly Speaking"*
>
> "Price is what you pay. Value is what you get."
>
> —Warren Buffett
> CEO, Berkshire Hathaway

ASSESSMENT CHECK

1.1 What are the three major pricing strategies?
1.2 What is EDLP?

PRICE QUOTATIONS

The choice of the best method for quoting prices depends on many industry conditions, including competitive trends, cost structures, and traditional practices, along with the policies of individual firms. This section examines the reasoning and methodology behind price quotation practices.

Most price structures are built around **list prices**—the rates normally quoted to potential buyers. Marketers usually determine list prices by one or a combination of the methods discussed in Chapter 18. The sticker price on a new automobile is a good example: It shows the list price for the basic model and then adds the prices of the options. The sticker price for a new Honda Civic is $18,490. But you can add features such as push-button start, automatic climate control, and power moonroof for one price. So if you order the EX package for the Honda Civic, you'll automatically get those features, among other add-ons.[7]

The price of oil is equally important to consumers because it directly affects the list price of gasoline. Disruptions such as hurricanes and wars affect the price of oil and ultimately the price that drivers pay at the pump. Prices may also fluctuate seasonally, as demand for gasoline rises and falls. Figure 19.2 illustrates where the money from a gallon of gas goes on its journey from the oil field to your gas tank.

REDUCTIONS FROM LIST PRICE

The amount a consumer pays for a product—its **market price**—may or may not equal the list price. Discounts and allowances sometimes reduce list prices. A list price often defines a starting point from which discounts set a lower market price. Marketers offer discounts in several classifications including cash, trade, and quantity discounts.

Cash Discounts

Consumers, industrial purchasers, or channel members sometimes receive reductions in price in exchange for prompt payment of bills; these price cuts are known as **cash discounts**. Discount terms usually specify exact time periods, such as 2/10, net 30. This notation means the customer must pay

2 Explain how prices are quoted.

list prices Established price normally quoted to potential buyers.

market price Price a consumer or marketing intermediary actually pays for a product after subtracting any discounts, allowances, or rebates from the list price.

cash discounts Price reduction offered to a consumer, business user, or marketing intermediary in return for prompt payment of a bill.

within 30 days, but payment within 10 days entitles the customer to subtract 2 percent from the amount due. Consumers may receive a cash discount for immediate payment, say, paying with cash instead of a credit card at the gas pump or paying the full cash amount up front for elective health-care services such as orthodontia. Cash discounts represent a traditional pricing practice in many industries. They fulfill legal requirements provided that all customers can take the same reductions on the same terms.

In recent years, sellers have increasingly attempted to improve their own liquidity positions, reduce their bad-debt losses, and cut collection expenses by moving to a form of *negative cash discount*. Confronted with purchasers who may defer paying their bills as long as possible, another notice has begun to appear on customer statements:

> **Due on Receipt.** A FINANCE CHARGE of 1.5 percent per month (18 percent A.P.R.) is computed on and added to the unpaid balance as of the statement date.

Past-due accounts may be turned over to collection agencies.

Trade Discounts

trade discounts Payment to a channel member or buyer for performing marketing functions; also known as a *functional discount*.

Payments to channel members for performing marketing functions are known as **trade discounts**, or functional discounts. Services performed by various channel members and the related costs were discussed in Chapters 14 and 15. A manufacturer's list price must incorporate the costs incurred by channel members in performing required marketing functions and expected profit margins for each member.

Trade discounts initially reflected the operating expenses of each category, but they have become more or less customary practices in some industries. The Robinson-Patman Act, which prohibits price discrimination, allows trade discounts as long as all buyers in the same category, such as all wholesalers or all retailers, receive the same discounts.

Figure 19.3 shows how a chain of trade discounts works. In the first instance, the trade discount is "40 percent, 10 percent off list price" for wholesalers. In other words, the 40 percent discount on the $40 product is the trade discount the retailer receives to cover operating expenses and earn a profit. The wholesaler receives 10 percent of the $24 price to retailers to cover expenses and earn a profit. The manufacturer receives $21.60 from the wholesaler for each order.

In the second example in Figure 19.3, the manufacturer and retailer decide to bypass the wholesaler. The producer offers a trade discount of 45 percent to the retailer. In this instance, the retailer receives $18 for each product sold at its list price, and the manufacturer receives the remaining $22. Either the retailer or the manufacturer must assume responsibility for the services previously performed by the wholesaler, or they can share these duties between them.

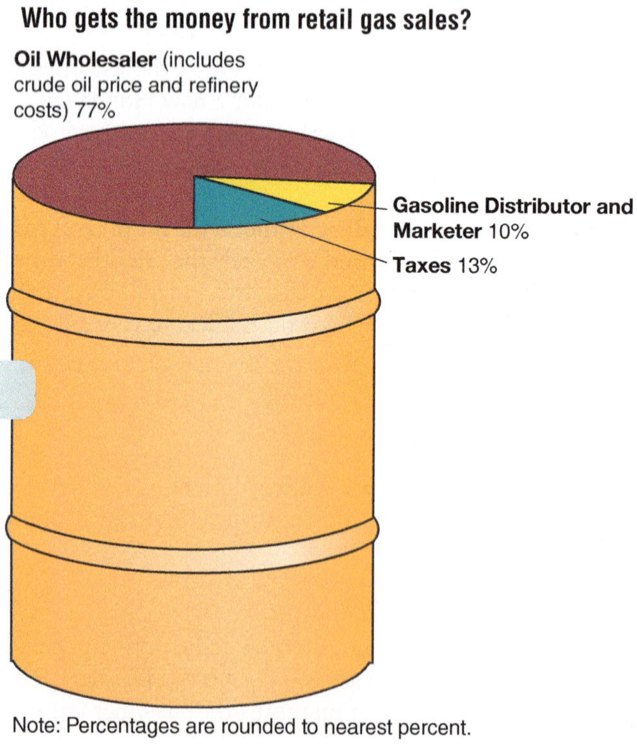

FIGURE 19.2 Components of Retail Gasoline Prices

Source: Data from U.S. Energy Information Administration, "Gasoline and Diesel Fuel Update," accessed October 30, 2014, http://eia.gov.

Who gets the money from retail gas sales?
- Oil Wholesaler (includes crude oil price and refinery costs) 77%
- Gasoline Distributor and Marketer 10%
- Taxes 13%

Note: Percentages are rounded to nearest percent.

Quantity Discounts

Price reductions granted for large-volume purchases are known as **quantity discounts**. Sellers justify these discounts on the grounds that large orders reduce selling expenses and may shift some costs for storage, transportation, and financing to buyers. The law allows quantity discounts provided they are applied on the same basis to all customers.

Quantity discounts may specify either cumulative or noncumulative terms. **Cumulative quantity discounts** reduce prices in amounts determined by purchases over stated time. Annual purchases of at least $25,000 might entitle a buyer to a 3 percent rebate, and purchases exceeding $50,000 would increase the refund to 5 percent. These reductions are considered patronage discounts because they tend to bind customers to a single supply source.

Noncumulative quantity discounts provide onetime reductions in the list price. For example, a firm might offer the following discount schedule for a product priced at $1,000 per unit:

1 unit	List: $1,000
2–5 units	List less 10 percent
6–10 units	List less 20 percent
More than 10 units	List less 25 percent

"40 PERCENT, 10 PERCENT OFF" TRADE DISCOUNT

List Price	−	Retail Trade Discount	−	Wholesale Trade Discount	=	Manufacturer Proceeds
$40	−	$16 ($40 × 40%)	−	$2.40 ($24 × 10%)	=	$21.60 ($40 − $16 − $2.40)

"45 PERCENT" TRADE DISCOUNT

List Price	−	Retail Trade Discount	=	Manufacturer Proceeds
$40	−	$18 ($40 × 45%)	=	$22 ($40 − $18)

FIGURE 19.3
Chain of Trade Discounts

quantity discounts Price reduction granted for a large-volume purchase.

Many businesses have come to expect quantity discounts from suppliers. Online photo supply retailer Shutterfly offers volume discounts for photo books and discounts of up to 40 percent on prepaid orders.[8] Marketers typically favor combinations of cash, trade, and quantity discounts. See's Candies offers a quantity discount for a minimum purchase of $700, plus continued savings throughout the year.[9]

Allowances

Allowances resemble discounts by specifying deductions from list price. The major categories of allowances are trade-ins and promotional allowances. **Trade-ins** are often used in sales of durable goods, such as automobiles. The new product's basic list price remains unchanged, but the seller accepts less money from the customer along with a used product—usually the same kind of product as the buyer purchases.

Promotional allowances reduce prices as part of an attempt to integrate promotional strategies within distribution channels. Manufacturers often return part of the prices buyers pay in the form of advertising and sales-support allowances for channel members. Automobile manufacturers frequently offer allowances to retail dealers to induce them to lower prices and stimulate sales. In an effort to alert consumers to the difference between a car's sticker price and the price the dealer actually pays to the manufacturer, *Consumer Reports* sells car and truck buyers a breakdown on dealers' wholesale costs. The information reveals undisclosed dealer profits, such as manufacturers' incentives, rebates from the dealer-invoice price, and "holdbacks"—amounts refunded to the dealer after sales are completed.[10] Dealers dislike the move to reveal their markups, arguing that no other retail sector is forced to give consumers details of their promotional allowances.

Minimum advertised pricing (MAP) occurs when a manufacturer pays a retailer not to advertise a product below a certain price. However, some electronics manufacturers are imposing **unilateral pricing policies (UPPs)** that set the same prices for some types of TVs, no matter where they are sold. Some manufacturers plan to monitor retailers' compliance; in fact, some have warned retailers that, if they sell an item in the UPP program for less than the minimum advertised price, the manufacturer will remove their authorization and stop supplying products.[11]

cumulative quantity discounts Price discount determined by amounts of purchases over stated time periods.

noncumulative quantity discounts Price reduction granted on a one-time-only basis.

allowances Specified deduction from list price, including a trade-in or promotional allowance.

trade-ins Credit allowance given for a used item when a customer purchases a new item.

promotional allowances Promotional incentive in which the manufacturer agrees to pay the reseller a certain amount to cover the costs of special promotional displays or extensive advertising.

Rebates

In still another way to reduce prices, marketers may offer a **rebate**—a refund of a portion of the purchase price. Rebates appear everywhere—on appliances, electronics, and auto promotions—by manufacturers eager to get consumers to try their merchandise or move products during periods of slow sales. The contact-lens manufacturer ACUVUE offers rebates to current and new customers who buy boxes of the company's disposable contact lenses.

Rebates can have their problems. Many consumers complain about the paperwork they have to fill out to get a rebate, particularly on larger items such as computers and kitchen appliances. Some say they fill out the paperwork only to be denied the claim on a technicality. Others report never receiving the rebate—or even a response—at all. The Better Business Bureau notes that the number of complaints filed relating to rebates has grown significantly in the past few years. Some state legislators have moved to require companies to fulfill rebate requests within a certain period of time while also requiring consumers to file their requests promptly. Yet companies argue that many consumers never even apply for their legitimate rebates.[12]

GEOGRAPHIC CONSIDERATIONS

In industries dominated by catalog and online marketers, geographic considerations weigh heavily on the firm's ability to deliver orders in a cost-effective manner at the right time and place. In other instances, geographic factors affect the marketer's ability to receive additional inventory quickly in response to demand fluctuations. And although geographic considerations strongly influence prices when costs include shipping heavy, bulky, low-unit-value products, they can also affect lightweight, lower-cost products.

Buyers and sellers can handle transportation expenses in several ways: (1) The buyer pays all transportation charges, (2) the seller pays all transportation charges, or (3) the buyer and the seller share the charges. This decision has major effects on a firm's efforts to expand its geographic coverage to distant markets. How can marketers compete with local suppliers in distant markets who are able to avoid the considerable shipping costs that their firms must pay? Sellers can implement several alternatives for handling transportation costs in their pricing policies.

FOB Pricing

FOB (free on board) plant, or **FOB origin**, prices include no shipping charges. The buyer must pay all freight charges to transport the product from the manufacturer's loading dock. The seller only pays to load the merchandise aboard the carrier selected by the buyer. Legal title and responsibility pass to the buyer after the seller's employees load the purchase and get a receipt from the representative of the common carrier. Firms such as Walmart often handle freight charges across the entire supply chain. Because Walmart sources so many products from China, "FOB China" is now common.

Many marketing intermediaries sell only on FOB plant terms to downstream channel members. These distributors believe their customers have more clout than they do in negotiating with carriers. They prefer to assign transportation costs to the channel members in the best positions to secure the most cost-effective shipping terms.

Sellers may also quote prices as **FOB origin-freight allowed**, or **freight absorbed**. These terms permit buyers to subtract transportation expenses from their bills. The amount such a seller receives for its product varies with the freight charged against the invoice. This alternative is popular among firms with high fixed costs, because it helps them expand their markets by quoting the same prices regardless of shipping expenses.

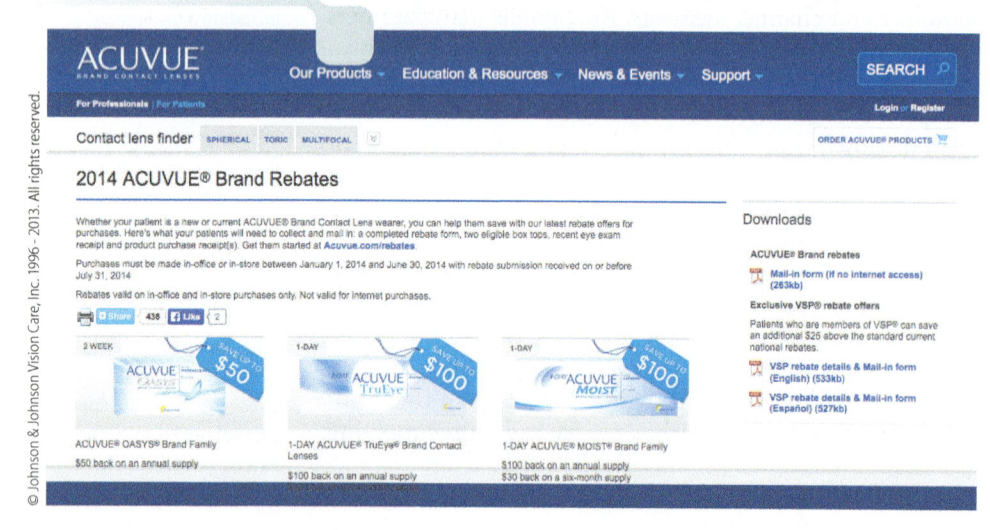

---

minimum advertised pricing (MAP) Fees paid to retailers who agree not to advertise products below set prices.

unilateral pricing policies (UPPs) Strategy that sets the same price for a specific product regardless of where it is sold.

rebate Refund of a portion of the purchase price, usually granted by the product's manufacturer.

FOB (free on board) plant (FOB origin) Price quotation that does not include shipping charges.

FOB origin-freight allowed (freight absorbed) Price quotation system that allows the buyer to deduct shipping expenses from the cost of purchases.

Rebates refund a portion of the purchase price for items such as disposable contact lenses. Marketers offer rebates as a way to reduce the price paid by customers.

Uniform-Delivered Pricing

When a firm quotes the same price, including transportation expenses, to all buyers, it adopts a **uniform-delivered pricing** policy. This method of handling transportation expenses is the exact opposite of FOB origin pricing. The uniform-delivered system resembles the pricing structure for mail service, so it is sometimes called **postage-stamp pricing**. The price quote includes a transportation charge averaged over all of the firm's customers, meaning that distant customers actually pay a smaller share of shipping costs, while nearby customers pay what is known as *phantom freight*—the amount by which the average transportation charge exceeds the actual cost of shipping.

Zone Pricing

Zone pricing modifies a uniform-delivered pricing system by dividing the overall market into zones and establishing a single price within each zone. This pricing structure incorporates average transportation costs for shipments within each zone as part of the delivered price of goods sold there; by narrowing distances, it greatly reduces but does not completely eliminate phantom freight. The primary advantage of zone pricing comes from its simplified administration that helps a seller compete in distant markets. The U.S. Postal Service's parcel rates depend on this system of pricing.

Zone pricing helps explain why gasoline can cost more in one suburb than in a neighborhood just two or three miles down the road. One way in which gasoline marketers boost profits is by mapping out areas based on formulas that factor in location, affluence, or simply what the local market will bear. Dealers are then charged different wholesale prices, which are reflected in the prices paid at the pump by customers. Some dealers argue that zone pricing should be prohibited. When drivers shop around for cheaper gas in other zones, stations in high-price zones are unable to compete.

Basing-Point Pricing

In **basing-point pricing**, the price of a product includes the list price at the factory plus freight charges from the basing-point city nearest the buyer. The basing point specifies a location from which freight charges are calculated—not necessarily the point from which the goods are actually shipped. In either case, the actual shipping point does not affect the price quotation. Such a system seeks to equalize competition between distant marketers because all competitors quote identical transportation rates. Few buyers would accept a basing-point system today, however.

For many years, the best-known basing-point system was the so-called "Pittsburgh-plus" pricing structure common in the steel industry. Steel buyers paid freight charges from Pittsburgh regardless of where the steel was produced. As the industry matured, manufacturing centers emerged in Chicago; Gary, Indiana; Cleveland; and Birmingham. Still, Pittsburgh remained the basing point for steel pricing, forcing a buyer in Atlanta who purchased steel from a Birmingham mill to pay phantom freight from Pittsburgh.

> **ASSESSMENT CHECK**
>
> 2.1 What are the three major types of discounts?
> 2.2 Identify the four alternatives for handling transportation costs in pricing policies.

uniform-delivered pricing Pricing system for handling transportation costs under which all buyers are quoted the same price, including transportation expenses. Sometimes known as *postage-stamp pricing*.

postage-stamp pricing System for handling transportation costs under which all buyers are quoted the same price, including transportation expenses; also known as *uniform-delivered price*.

zone pricing Pricing system for handling transportation costs under which the market is divided into geographic regions and a different price is set in each region.

basing-point pricing System used in some industries during the early 20th century in which the buyer paid the factory price plus freight charges from the basing-point city nearest the buyer.

PRICING POLICIES

Pricing policies contribute important information to buyers as they assess the firm's total image. A coherent policy provides an overall framework and consistency that guide day-to-day pricing decisions. Formally, a **pricing policy** is a general guideline that reflects marketing objectives and influences specific pricing decisions.

Decisions concerning price structure generally tend to focus on technical, detailed questions, but decisions concerning pricing policies cover broader issues. Price-structure decisions take the firm's pricing policy as a given, from which they specify applicable discounts. Pricing policies have important strategic effects, particularly in guiding competitive efforts. They form the basis for more practical price-structure decisions.

3 Identify the five pricing policy decisions marketers must make.

pricing policy General guideline that reflects marketing objectives and influences specific pricing decisions.

Firms implement variations of four basic types of pricing policies: psychological pricing, price flexibility, product-line pricing, and promotional pricing. Specific policies deal effectively with various competitive situations; the final choice depends on the environment within which marketers must make their pricing decisions. Regardless of the strategy selected, however, marketers sometimes must raise prices. Although it is never easy to deliver this decision to customers, if it is accomplished with honesty and tact, customers are likely to remain loyal.

PSYCHOLOGICAL PRICING

psychological pricing Pricing policy based on the belief that certain prices or price ranges make a good or service more appealing than others to buyers.

Psychological pricing applies the belief that certain prices or price ranges make products more appealing than others to buyers. No research offers a consistent foundation for such thinking, however, and studies often report mixed findings. Nevertheless, marketers practice several forms of psychological pricing. Prestige pricing, discussed in Chapter 18, sets a relatively high price to convey an image of quality and exclusiveness. Two more psychological pricing techniques are odd pricing and unit pricing.

odd pricing Pricing policy based on the belief that a price ending with an odd number just under a round number is more appealing, for instance, $9.97 rather than $10.

In **odd pricing**, marketers set prices at odd numbers just under round numbers. Many people assume that a price of $9.95 is more appealing to consumers than $10, supposedly because buyers interpret it as $9 plus change. Odd pricing originated as a way to force clerks to make change, thus serving as a cash-control device, and it remains a common feature of contemporary price quotations.

Some producers and retailers practice odd pricing but avoid prices ending in five, nine, or zero. These marketers believe customers view price tags of $5.95, $5.99, or $6 as regular retail prices, but they think of an amount such as $5.97 as a discount price. Walmart, for example, avoids using nines as ending prices for its merchandise.

unit pricing Pricing policy in which prices are stated in terms of a recognized unit of measurement or a standard numerical count.

Unit pricing states prices in terms of some recognized unit of measurement (such as grams and liters) or a standard numerical count. Unit pricing began to be widely used during the late 1960s to make price comparisons more convenient following complaints by consumer advocates about the difficulty of comparing the true prices of products packaged in different sizes. These advocates thought posting prices in terms of standard units would help shoppers make better-informed purchases. However, unit pricing has not improved consumers' shopping habits as much as supporters originally envisioned. Instead, research shows standard price quotes most often affect purchases only by relatively well-educated consumers with high earnings.

PRICE FLEXIBILITY

price flexibility Pricing policy permitting variable prices for goods and services.

Marketing executives must also set company policies that determine whether their firm will permit **price flexibility**—that is, whether or not to set one price that applies to every buyer or to permit variable prices for different customers. Generally, one-price policies suit mass-marketing programs, whereas variable pricing is more likely to be applied in marketing programs based on individual bargaining. In a large department store, customers do not expect to haggle over prices with retail salespeople. Instead, they expect to pay the amounts shown on the price tags. Usually, customers pay less only when the retailer replaces regular prices with sale prices or offers discounts on damaged merchandise. Variable pricing usually applies to larger purchases, such as automobiles, real estate, and hotel room rates. While variable pricing adds some flexibility to selling situations, it may conflict with provisions of the Robinson-Patman Act. It may also lead to retaliatory pricing by competitors and stir complaints among customers who find they paid higher prices than necessary.

Some Internet service providers have set usage caps on their customers and require subscribers who download the most content to pay the most. To help subscribers gauge how many gigabytes they use, Comcast has made a free online usage meter available in many areas in the United States. Recently the company introduced usage-based pricing, eliminating the monthly cap for its Internet subscribers and billing them for the amount of data they use.[13]

product-line pricing Practice of setting a limited number of prices for a selection of merchandise and marketing different product lines at each of these price levels.

PRODUCT-LINE PRICING

Because most firms market multiple product lines, an effective pricing strategy must consider the relationships among all of these items instead of viewing each in isolation. **Product-line pricing** is the practice of setting a limited number of prices for a selection of merchandise. For example, one well-known clothier might offer three lines of men's suits: one priced at $250, a second at $495, and the most expensive at $799. These price points help the retailer define important product characteristics that differentiate the three product lines and help the customer decide on whether to trade up or down.

Retailers practice extensive product-line pricing. In earlier days, five-and-dime variety stores exemplified this technique. It remains popular, however, because it offers advantages to both retailers and customers. Shoppers can choose desired price ranges and then concentrate on other product variables, such as colors, styles, and materials. Retailers can purchase and offer specific lines in limited price categories instead of more general assortments with dozens of different prices.

Sunglasses have become a hot fashion item in recent years, and prices for designer glasses have jumped from an average of $250 per pair to as much as $1,100 for Lioness Sunglasses at Bergdorf Goodman in New York. While sales of other luxury goods have softened, sunglass sales continue to increase. Younger consumers—teens and young women—seem to be snapping up designer shades most often. Bvlgari, Dolce & Gabbana, Prada, Alexander McQueen, and Versace all offer high-end glasses carried by luxury retailers.[14]

The price for designer sunglasses has jumped in recent years as consumer demand has increased.

A potential problem with product-line pricing is that once marketers decide on a limited number of prices to use as their price lines, they may have difficulty making price changes on individual items. Rising costs, therefore, force sellers to either change the entire price-line structure, which results in confusion, or cut costs through production adjustments. The second option opens the firm to customer complaints that its merchandise is not what it used to be.

PROMOTIONAL PRICING

In **promotional pricing**, a lower-than-normal price is used as a temporary ingredient in a firm's marketing strategy. Some promotional pricing arrangements form part of recurrent marketing initiatives, such as a shoe store's annual "buy one pair, get the second pair for one cent" sale. Another firm may introduce a promotional model or brand with a special price to begin competing in a new market. The nation's wireless providers signed up millions of customers with the promise of unlimited data access, but three of the four biggest carriers now face such capacity constraints that, instead of rationing bandwidth via price, they're reducing access speed to levels that users find frustrating. Read the "Solving an Ethical Controversy" feature for the pros and cons of this strategy.

Managing promotional pricing efforts requires marketing skill. Customers may get hooked on sales and other promotional pricing events. If they know their favorite department store has a one-day sale every month, they will likely wait to make their purchases on that day. Car shoppers have been offered so many price incentives that it is harder and harder for manufacturers and dealers to take them away—or to come up with new ones. As part of the annual Coastal Uncorked festival in Myrtle Beach, South Carolina, restaurants team up to offer promotional pricing on fixed-price dinners of three or more courses to attract new customers.[15]

promotional pricing Pricing policy in which a lower-than-normal price is used as a temporary ingredient in a firm's marketing strategy.

SOLVING AN ETHICAL CONTROVERSY
Throttling "Unlimited" Data Plans

Among wireless providers, Sprint and T-Mobile offer new subscribers unlimited data plans, while Verizon and AT&T have resorted to "throttling" the top 5 percent of unlimited data users in their areas. Unlimited plans were inaugurated when iPhones were new and fewer customers engaged heavily in video streaming and gaming activities. Now, struggling to upgrade their capacity to handle surging use, carriers are drastically slowing data speeds (or throttling) to near dial-up levels for the heaviest users, to maintain service to all without raising prices. Throttled customers are fuming, and some have gone to court.

Should wireless providers raise prices for unlimited data plans?

PRO
1. Users would be better served by the option to pay more for a better experience.
2. It's only fair for the heaviest users to pay more for what they get.

CON
1. Customers contracted for usable access at a set price and should not have to pay more for faster download speed.
2. Higher prices merely punish customers when providers should be encouraging them to use more wireless service.

Summary
Congress is expected to open more bandwidth to wireless providers, but it will take much time and money. Sprint recently announced it will begin to throttle some of its heavy data users on several prepaid plans.

Sources: Christian Brazil Bautista, "T-Mobile Launches $40 Phone Plan with Unlimited Talk and Text," *Digital Trends*, accessed April 15, 2014, www.digitaltrends.com; Phil Goldstein, "Sprint's Boost, Virgin Mobile to Throttle Heavy Data Users to Slower Speeds Starting in May," *Fierce Wireless*, accessed April 15, 2014, www.fiercewireless.com; "Compare Unlimited Cell Phone Data Plans," *Whistle Out*, accessed April 15, 2014, www.whistleout.com; Mark Davis, "Sprint Continues to Battle for T-Mobile Deal," *Kansas City Star*, accessed April 15, 2014, www.kansascity.com.

Loss Leaders and Leader Pricing

loss leaders Product offered to consumers at less than cost to attract them to stores in the hope that they will buy other merchandise at regular prices.

leader pricing Variant of loss-leader pricing in which marketers offer prices slightly above cost to avoid violating minimum-markup regulations and earn a minimal return on promotional sales.

Retailers rely most heavily on promotional pricing. In one type of technique, stores offer **loss leaders**: goods priced below cost to attract customers who, the retailer hopes, will also buy regularly priced merchandise. Loss leaders can form part of an effective marketing program, but states with unfair-trade laws limit the practice. The milk at your grocery store is likely a loss leader. Around Thanksgiving, many grocers offer the traditional turkey as a loss leader in the hope that customers will buy the trimmings there as well.[16]

Retailers frequently use a variant of loss-leader pricing called **leader pricing**. To avoid violating minimum-markup rules and earn some return on promotional sales, they offer so-called leader merchandise at prices slightly above cost. Among the most frequent practitioners of this combination pricing/promotion strategy are supermarkets and mass merchandisers, such as Walmart, Target, and Kmart. Retailers sometimes treat private-label products, such as Sam's Choice colas at Walmart stores, as leader merchandise because the store brands cost, on average, about 27 percent less than those of comparable national brands. While store brand items generate lower per-unit revenues than national brands, higher sales volume will probably offset some of the difference as will related sales of high-margin products such as toiletries and cosmetics.

Digital cameras are a good example. Although a digital point-and-shoot camera once ranged from $400 to $600, today, for the same money, shoppers can get a more technologically advanced digital SLR camera. Meanwhile, prices on the point-and-shoot models have dropped. Many of the cameras in Canon's PowerShot series are now available for less than $200.[17]

But marketers should anticipate two potential pitfalls when making a promotional pricing decision:

> **ASSESSMENT CHECK**
>
> 3.1 Define pricing policy.
> 3.2 Describe the two types of psychological pricing other than prestige pricing.
> 3.3 What is promotional pricing?

1. Some buyers may not be attracted by promotional pricing.
2. By maintaining an artificially low price, marketers may lead customers to expect it as a customary feature of the product.

PRICE–QUALITY RELATIONSHIPS

One of the most thoroughly researched aspects of pricing is its relationship to consumer perceptions of product quality. In the absence of other cues, price is an important indicator of a product's quality to prospective purchasers. Many buyers interpret high prices as signals of high-quality products. Prestige is also often associated with high prices. However, distance in time can also be a factor in people's assessment. In a recent study, participants were told that a new e-reader was not very expensive or was somewhat expensive. They were also told that it would be available in either a few days or several months. For those who were told that the e-reader would be available in a few months, price didn't seem to be much of a factor in their assessment of the reader's value. However, those who were told that the reader would be out in a few days and would be inexpensive thought it was a better buy than if it was available in a few days but would be expensive.[18]

A new type of prestige surrounds eco-friendly products. Many consumers are willing to pay more for green goods and services—those made with environmentally friendly materials and processes. These purchases make consumers feel good about what they are doing to help the environment.

Despite the appeal of prestige, nearly every consumer loves a good deal. Marketers work hard to convince consumers they are offering high-quality products at the lowest possible price. Motels were once considered both cheap and outdated. The Motel 6 chain, for example, was so named because, when it opened in 1962, a room cost $6 a night, plus tax. Today, a night at Motel 6 is still low priced—about $45 plus tax—but the chain is renovating its properties to convey a chic yet efficient look, with pedestal beds, 32-inch flat-screen TVs, granite countertops, wood-look laminate floors, and other amenities.[19]

Probably the best statement of the price–quality connection is the idea of price limits. Consumers define certain limits within which their quality perceptions vary directly with price.

> **ASSESSMENT CHECK**
>
> 4.1 Describe the price–quality connection.
> 4.2 What are price limits?

A potential buyer regards a price below the lower limit as too cheap and a price above the higher limit as too expensive. This perception holds true for both national brands and private-label products.

Discuss the relationship of price to consumer perceptions of quality.

COMPETITIVE BIDDING AND NEGOTIATED PRICES

Many government and organizational procurement departments do not pay set prices for their purchases, particularly for large purchases. Instead, they determine the lowest prices available for items that meet specifications through **competitive bidding**. This process consists of inviting potential suppliers to quote prices on proposed purchases or contracts. Detailed specifications describe the good or service the government agency or business wishes to acquire. One of the most

Contrast competitive bidding and negotiated prices.

competitive bidding Inviting potential suppliers to quote prices on proposed purchases or contracts.

important procurement tasks is to develop accurate descriptions of products the organization seeks to buy. This process generally requires the assistance of the firm's technical personnel, such as engineers, designers, and chemists.

In competing for students, colleges and universities differentiate themselves on many dimensions, including price. To keep operating costs down, institutions routinely invite competitive bids in many areas of operation, including building maintenance and janitorial services, landscaping, and food service. With costs soaring for everything related to academic life, schools look for ways to economize without diminishing their appeal in the eyes of prospective students and their parents.

A select group of state troopers test potential police cars every year to determine the best model—and price—for their organization. Although Ford's Crown Victoria Police Interceptor was the top model for many years, its production was phased out several years ago. Ford recently introduced two new Interceptors, one a conventional four-door sedan based on the Taurus, the other an SUV.[20]

In some cases, business and government purchasers negotiate contracts with favored suppliers instead of inviting competitive bids from all interested parties. The terms of such a contract emerge through offers and counteroffers between the buyer and the seller. When only one supplier offers a desired product, or when projects require extensive research and development, buyers and sellers often set purchase terms through negotiated contracts. In addition, some state and local governments permit their agencies to skip the formal bid process and negotiate product purchases under certain dollar limits—say, $500 or $1,000. This policy seeks to eliminate economic waste that would result from obtaining and processing bids for relatively minor purchases. In contrast, the city of Glendale, Arizona, requires that any services totaling $50,000 or more be subject to competitive bidding. However, with rising prices for most services, it is easy for proposals to exceed that ceiling.[21]

NEGOTIATING PRICES ONLINE

Many people see the Internet as one big auction site. Whether it's toys, furniture, or automobiles, an online auction site seems to be waiting to serve every person's needs—buyer and seller alike. Auctions are the purest form of negotiated pricing.

Ticket sales are an online auction favorite. Consumers can bid on tickets for all sorts of events: Broadway shows, professional sports, and rock concerts. Razorgator and Ticket Liquidator are two such online ticket sellers. Razorgator specializes in finding tickets to sold-out events and providing a "VIP experience." Ticket Liquidator offers low prices on tickets for thousands of events daily.[22]

Online auctions also take place at sites such as eBay and uBid.com, where consumers can snap up items as varied as diamond-and-gold cuff links or a ski vacation in Vail, Colorado. eBay reported that more than half of its transactions concern fixed-price products, and income from its Marketplace website has been overtaken by PayPal, which eBay owns. Company executives recently announced PayPal and eBay would split into separate public companies in the near future.[23]

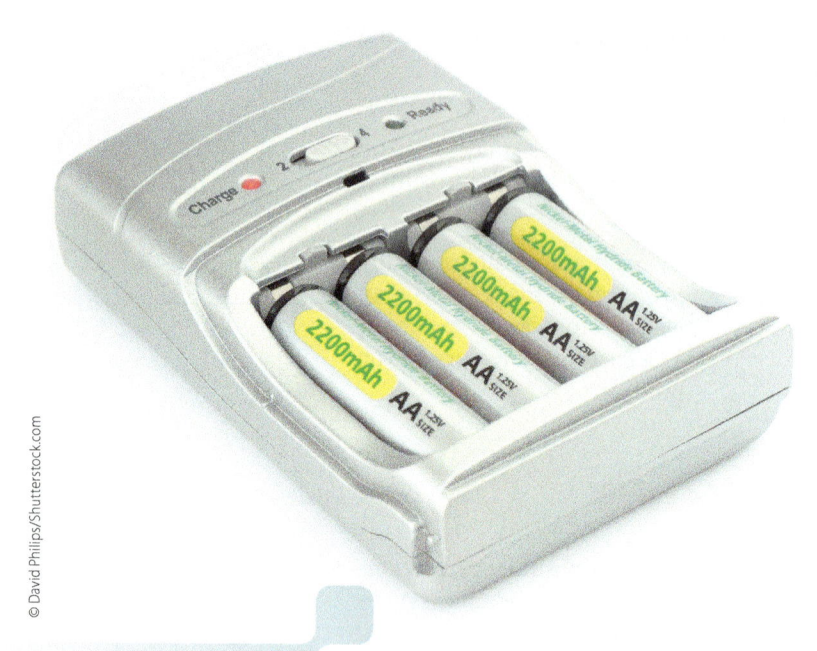

Goods made with environmentally friendly materials, such as rechargeable batteries, have a certain level of prestige. Many consumers are willing to pay more for these products.

Briefly Speaking

"You can have anything in this world you want, if you want it badly enough and you're willing to pay the price."

—Mary Kay Ash
Founder, Mary Kay Cosmetics

ASSESSMENT CHECK

5.1 What is competitive bidding?

5.2 Describe the benefits of an auction to the buyer and the seller.

Auctions are considered the purest form of negotiating prices and can occur in many places, including on the Internet. In addition to eBay, uBid.com is one of the most popular online auction sites.

THE TRANSFER PRICING DILEMMA

A pricing problem peculiar to large-scale enterprises is the determination of an internal **transfer price**—the price for moving goods between **profit centers**, which are any part of the organization to which revenue and controllable costs can be assigned, such as a department. As companies expand, they tend to decentralize management and set up profit centers as a control device in the newly decentralized operation.

In a large company, profit centers might secure many needed resources from sellers within their own organization. The pricing problem thus poses several questions: What rate should profit center A (maintenance department) charge profit center B (production department) for the cleaning compound used on B's floors? Should the price be the same as it would be if A did the work for an outside party? Should B receive a discount? The answers to these questions depend on the philosophy of the firm involved.

Transfer pricing can be complicated, especially for multinational organizations. The government closely monitors transfer-pricing practices because these exchanges offer easy ways for companies to avoid paying taxes. For example, Congress passed a bill outlawing federal contractors from hiring workers through offshore "shell"—nonexistent—companies and thus avoiding having to pay Social Security and Medicare taxes.

Figure 19.4 shows how this type of pricing manipulation might work. Suppose a South Korean manufacturer of DVD players sells its machines to its London subsidiary for distribution to dealers throughout the United Kingdom. Although each unit costs $25 to build, the manufacturer charges the distributor $75. In turn, the distributor sells the DVD players to retailers for $125 each. This arrangement gives the South Korean manufacturer a $50 profit on each machine, on which it pays taxes only in South Korea. Meanwhile, the UK distributor writes off $50 for advertising and shipping costs, leaving it with no profits—and no tax liability.

Explain the importance of transfer pricing. 6

transfer price Cost assessed when a product is moved from one profit center within a firm to another.

profit centers Any part of an organization to which revenue and controllable costs can be assigned.

ASSESSMENT CHECK

6.1 Define transfer price.
6.2 What is a profit center?

FIGURE 19.4 Transfer Pricing to Escape Taxation

Foreign Manufacturer — Cost of unit $25 — Sale price $75 — Profit $50

Foreign-Owned Distributor — Cost of unit $75, Advertising/shipping $50 — Sale price $125 — Profit $0

Retailer

GLOBAL CONSIDERATIONS AND ONLINE PRICING

7 Compare the three alternative global pricing strategies.

Throughout this course, we have seen the impact of the Internet on every component of the marketing mix. This chapter has touched on the outer edges of the Internet's influence on pricing practices. Remember: Every online marketer is inherently a global marketer that must understand the wide variety of internal and external conditions affecting global pricing strategies. Internal influences include the firm's goals and marketing strategies; the costs of developing, producing, and marketing its output; the nature of the products; and the firm's competitive strengths.

External influences include general conditions in international markets, especially those in the firm's target markets; regulatory limitations; trade restrictions; competitors' actions; economic events; and the global status of the industry.

TRADITIONAL GLOBAL PRICING STRATEGIES

In general, a company can implement one of three export pricing strategies: a standard worldwide price, dual pricing, or market-differentiated pricing. Exporters often set standard worldwide prices, regardless of their target markets. This strategy can succeed if foreign marketing costs remain low enough that they do not affect overall costs or if their prices reflect average unit costs. A company that implements a standard pricing program must monitor the international marketplace carefully, however, to make sure domestic competitors do not undercut its prices.

The dual pricing strategy distinguishes prices for domestic and export sales. Some exporters practice cost-plus pricing to establish dual prices that fully allocate their true domestic and foreign costs to product sales in those markets. These prices ensure an exporter makes a profit on any product it sells, but final prices may exceed those of competitors. Other companies opt for flexible cost-plus pricing schemes that allow marketers to grant discounts or change prices according to shifts in the competitive environment or fluctuations in the international exchange rate.

The third strategy, market-differentiated pricing, makes even more flexible arrangements to set prices according to local marketplace conditions. The dynamic global marketplace often requires frequent price changes by exporters who choose this approach. Effective market-differentiated pricing depends on access to quick, accurate market information.

ASSESSMENT CHECK

7.1 What are the three traditional global pricing strategies?

7.2 Which is the most flexible global pricing strategy?

CHARACTERISTICS OF ONLINE PRICING

8 Relate the concepts of cannibalization, bundle pricing, and bots to online pricing strategies.

To deal with the influences of the Internet on pricing policies and practices, marketers are applying old strategies in new ways, and companies are updating operations to compete with electronic technologies. Some firms offer online specials that do not appear in their stores or mail-order catalogs. These may take forms such as limited-time discounts, free shipping offers, or coupons that are good only online.

The Cannibalization Dilemma

By pricing the same products differently online, companies run the risk of **cannibalization**. The new twist on an old strategy is companies' self-inflicting price cuts by creating competition among their own products. During the first decade of e-business, marketers debated whether it was worth taking the risk of alienating customers and channel members by offering lower prices for their products online—then an unproven retail outlet. But today, marketers are savvier about integrating marketing channels, including online sites and affiliated stores—different stores owned by the same company. The trend is moving toward standardizing pricing across channels. Comparison shopping can still pay off, however. See the "Career Readiness" feature for some tips on using mobile apps to compare prices.

Walmart was one of the first brick-and-mortar retailers to introduce a "Site to Store" feature to its website so shoppers could choose how and where they want to make purchases, all at the same price. The company also offers a "Pay with Cash" program for online orders. Customers order online, pay cash at a local Walmart store for the goods, and the order is then shipped to their homes. Or, if a customer chooses "Site to Store" after paying for the order, he or she will receive a text or email when the order is ready to pick up.

Retailers are adopting this convenience feature in increasing numbers: The Container Store's "GoShop! Click & Pickup" and Lowe's "20-Minute Pick Up in Store—Free" services are two such examples. As consumers become *multichannel shoppers*, shopping their preferred retailers both online and off, they are embracing this feature and expect the retailer to recognize them as regular shoppers, regardless of the channel they choose. Research shows that multichannel retailers are more profitable than those who stick to one channel.[24]

> **cannibalization** Loss of sales of an existing product due to competition from a new product in the same line.

CAREER READINESS
Using Apps for Comparison Shopping

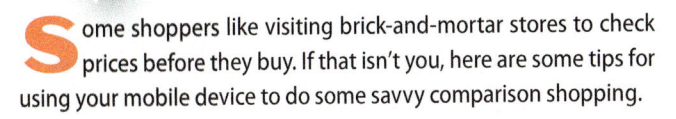

Some shoppers like visiting brick-and-mortar stores to check prices before they buy. If that isn't you, here are some tips for using your mobile device to do some savvy comparison shopping.

1. Price Check is Amazon's free iPhone and Android app for instantly checking online and in-store prices. It can compare based on pictures of the product or verbal input of its name and will show you customer reviews as well.

2. When you're shopping online, PriceBlink alerts you if there is a lower price for the item elsewhere.

3. Slickdeals is a website where users share what they know about deals, and it is also available via mobile app. You can learn about discounts on TVs, coffee makers, lawn mowers, and more. Links take you to the online retailers offering the best deals.

4. RetailMeNot is an app that collects coupon codes and sales information from a range of retailers and lets you bookmark your favorite stores so you can check for any discounts while you're shopping.

5. RedLaser reads barcodes to immediately check prices when you're in a store as well as when you make purchases directly from your phone.

Sources: Kimberly Palmer, "12 New Shopping Apps for the Best Deals," *US News*, accessed April 16, 2014, **http://money.usnews.com**; Christopher Palmeri, "Price Check! Armed with Apps, Shoppers Scour Stores for Bargains," *Bloomberg News*, accessed April 16, 2014, **www.bloomberg.com**; Joseph Pisani, "Holiday Helper: 5 Shopping Apps to Get You the Best Prices," *NBC News*, accessed April 16, 2014, **www.nbcnews.com**.

Walmart offers a "Pay with Cash" option for online orders.

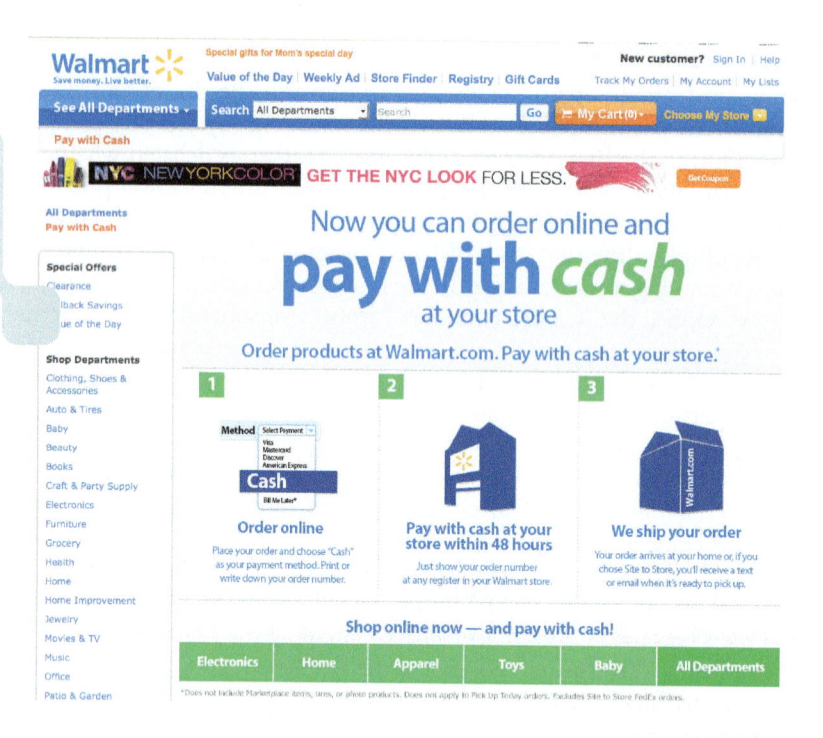

Use of Shopbots

bots (shopbots) Software program that allows online shoppers to compare prices of a particular product offered by several online retailers.

A second characteristic of online pricing is the use of search programs called **bots** or **shopbots**—derived from the word *robots*—that act as comparison shopping agents. Bots search the Web for a specific product and print a list of sites offering the best prices. In online selling, bots force marketers to keep prices low. However, marketing researchers report that most online shoppers check out several sites before buying, and price is not the only variable they consider when making a purchase decision. Service quality and support information are powerful motivators in the decision process. Also, while price is an important factor with products such as appliances, it is not as important with complex or highly differentiated products, such as real estate or financial investments. Brand image and customer service may outweigh price in these purchase decisions.

BUNDLE PRICING

bundle pricing Offering two or more complementary products and selling them for a single price.

As marketers have watched e-business weaken their control over prices, they have modified their use of the price variable in the marketing mix. Increasingly they have moved to an approach called **bundle pricing**, in which customers acquire a host of goods and services in addition to the tangible products they purchase.

Nowhere is bundle pricing more prevalent than in the telecommunications industry. Consumers are bombarded daily by advertisements for all kinds of Internet, cell phone, and cable TV packages. Verizon offers three fiber-optic service bundles that include HD TV, Internet, and digital voice services. Signing up for enhanced plans also provides access to thousands of wi-fi hot spots in the United States—a plus for businesspeople whose work takes them on the road.[25]

But sometimes consumers resist the practice of bundling, claiming they are forced to pay for services they don't want in order to receive the ones they do. This is particularly the case with cable television. Cable companies insist they have spent billions of dollars to expand their networks and technology and would be left with unused capacity if they sold only a few channels at a time to each customer. Consumer advocates argue that customers are not only forced to pay for unwanted services but also wind up paying inflated prices. The solution seems to be à la carte pricing—allowing consumers to pick and choose the shows or channels they want. However, the cable industry has not shown signs of making this type of pricing available.

ASSESSMENT CHECK

8.1 What is cannibalization?

8.2 What is bundle pricing?

Strategic Implications of Marketing in the 21st Century

Price has historically been the marketing variable least likely to be used as a source of competitive advantage. However, using price as part of a marketing program designed to meet a firm's overall organizational objectives can be a powerful strategy.

Technology has forever changed the marketplace, which affects the pricing function. Traditional geographic boundaries that allowed some businesses to operate have been broken by the Internet as well as mass merchandisers who offer a larger selection and lower prices. A customer in Wyoming might want to purchase a hand-carved walking cane from Kenya or an ornamental fan from Japan. Not a problem—the Web connects buyers and sellers around the globe.

Not only is it possible to escape the boundaries of time and space on the Internet, but price is no longer a constant in the marketing process. With the increasing number of auction sites and search technologies such as bots, customers now have more power to control the prices of goods and services. Consumers can find the lowest prices on the market, and they can also negotiate prices for many of the products they buy. To succeed, marketers will continue to offer value—fair prices for quality goods and services—and superior customer service. Those traditions will always be in style.

Get online now for additional learning tools to help you master your marketing knowledge—visit **WWW.CENGAGEBRAIN.COM** today!

REVIEW OF CHAPTER OBJECTIVES

1 Describe the three alternative pricing strategies and when each strategy is most appropriate.

The alternative pricing strategies are skimming pricing strategy, penetration pricing strategy, and competitive pricing strategy. Skimming pricing is commonly used as a market-entry price for distinctive products with little or no initial competition. Penetration pricing is used when a wide array of competing brands exists. Everyday low pricing (EDLP), a variant of penetration pricing, is used by discounters attempting to hold the line on prices without having to rely heavily on coupons, rebates, and other price concessions. Competitive pricing is employed when marketers wish to concentrate their competitive efforts on marketing variables other than price.

2 Explain how prices are quoted.

Methods for quoting prices depend on factors such as cost structures, traditional practices in a particular industry, and policies of individual firms. Price quotes can involve list prices, market prices, cash discounts, trade discounts, quantity discounts, and allowances such as trade-ins, promotional allowances, and rebates. Shipping costs often figure heavily into the pricing of goods. A number of alternatives for dealing with these costs exist: FOB plant pricing, in which the price includes no shipping charges; FOB origin-freight allowed, or freight absorbed, which allows the buyer to deduct transportation expenses from the bill; uniform-delivered price, in which the same price, including shipping expenses, is charged to all buyers; and zone pricing, in which a set price exists within each region.

3 Identify the five pricing policy decisions marketers must make.

A pricing policy is a general guideline based on pricing objectives and is intended for use in specific pricing decisions. Pricing policies include psychological pricing, unit pricing, price flexibility, product-line pricing, and promotional pricing.

4 Discuss the relationship of price to consumer perceptions of quality.

The relationship between price and consumer perceptions of quality has been the subject of considerable research. In the absence of other cues, price is an important influence on how the consumer perceives the product's quality. A well-known and accepted concept is that of price limits—limits within which the perception of product quality varies directly with price. The concept of price limits suggests that extremely low prices may be considered too cheap, thus indicating inferior quality, and prices set above an expected limit are seen as too expensive.

5 Contrast competitive bidding and negotiated prices.

Competitive bidding and negotiated prices are pricing techniques used primarily in the B2B sector and in government and organizational markets. Sometimes prices are negotiated through competitive bidding, in which several buyers quote prices on the same service or good. Buyer specifications describe the item the government or B2B firm wishes to acquire. Negotiated contracts are another possibility in many procurement situations. The terms of the contract are set through negotiations between buyer and seller.

6 Explain the importance of transfer pricing.

A phenomenon in large corporations is transfer pricing, in which a company sets prices for transferring goods or services from one company profit center to another. The term *profit center* refers to any part of the organization to which revenue and controllable costs can be assigned. In large companies whose profit centers acquire resources from other parts of the firm, the prices charged by one profit center to another directly affect both the cost and profitability of the output of both profit centers.

7 Compare the three alternative global pricing strategies.

Companies can choose from three global pricing strategies: a standard worldwide price, dual pricing, or market-differentiated pricing. A standard worldwide price may be possible if foreign marketing costs are so low that they do not affect overall costs or if the price is based on an average unit cost. The dual pricing approach establishes separate price strategies for domestic and exported products. Some exporters use cost-plus pricing methods to establish dual prices that fully allocate their true domestic and foreign costs to their product; others choose flexible cost-plus pricing. Market-differentiated pricing is the most flexible export pricing strategy, because it allows firms to price their products according to marketplace conditions. It requires easy access to quick, accurate market information.

8 Relate the concepts of cannibalization, bundle pricing, and bots to online pricing strategies.

To deal with the influences of the Internet on pricing policies and practices, marketers are applying old strategies in new ways, and companies are updating operations to compete with electronic technologies. Cannibalization secures additional sales through marginal sales gains that take sales away from the marketer's other products. Bots, also known as shopbots, act as comparison-shopping agents. Bundle pricing involves offering two or more complementary products and selling them for a single price.

ASSESSMENT CHECK: ANSWERS

1.1 What are the three major pricing strategies? The three major pricing strategies are skimming, penetration, and competitive.

1.2 What is EDLP? EDLP stands for "everyday low pricing." It is a variation of penetration pricing often used by discounters.

2.1 What are the three major types of discounts? The three major types of discounts are cash discounts, trade discounts, and quantity discounts.

2.2 Identify the four alternatives for handling transportation costs in pricing policies. The four alternatives for handling transportation costs are FOB pricing, uniform-delivered pricing, zone pricing, and basing-point pricing.

3.1 Define pricing policy. A pricing policy is a general guideline that reflects marketing objectives and influences specific pricing decisions.

3.2 Describe the two types of psychological pricing other than prestige pricing. The two additional types of psychological pricing are odd pricing, in which marketers set prices at odd numbers just under round numbers; and unit pricing, which states prices in terms of a recognized unit of measurement, such as a dozen.

3.3 What is promotional pricing? Promotional pricing is a lower-than-normal price for a set period of time.

4.1 Describe the price–quality connection. Price is an important indicator of a product's quality. However, many marketers now work hard to convince consumers they are offering high-quality products at the lowest possible price.

4.2 What are price limits? Price limits indicate certain boundaries within which consumers' product-quality perceptions vary directly with price. A price set lower than expected seems too cheap, and one set above the expected limit is seen as too expensive.

5.1 What is competitive bidding? Competitive bidding consists of inviting potential suppliers to quote prices on proposed purchases or contracts.

5.2 Describe the benefits of an auction to the buyer and seller. An auction can provide buyers with opportunities to buy goods and services at very low prices. It can also offer sellers an opportunity to sell to a wider audience (online), perhaps at a higher price than otherwise would be possible, if an item is particularly popular.

6.1 Define transfer price. A transfer price is the price for moving goods between profit centers.

6.2 What is a profit center? A profit center is any part of the organization to which revenue and controllable costs can be assigned.

7.1 What are the three traditional global pricing strategies? The three global pricing strategies are standard worldwide pricing, dual pricing, and market-differentiated pricing.

7.2 Which is the most flexible global pricing strategy? The most flexible global pricing strategy is market-differentiated pricing, which allows firms to set prices according to actual conditions.

8.1 What is cannibalization? Cannibalization involves a company's losing sales of an existing product by introducing a new product in the same selling channel.

8.2 What is bundle pricing? Bundle pricing involves combining a number of goods or services and offering them at a set price.

MARKETING TERMS YOU NEED TO KNOW

skimming pricing strategy 627
market-plus pricing 627
step out 627
penetration pricing strategy 628
everyday low pricing (EDLP) 629
competitive pricing strategy 631
opening price point 631
list price 631
market price 631
cash discount 631
trade discount 632
quantity discount 633
cumulative quantity discount 633
noncumulative quantity discount 633
allowance 633
trade-in 633
promotional allowance 633
minimum advertised pricing (MAP) 633
unilateral pricing policies (UPPs) 633
rebate 634
FOB (free on board) plant (FOB origin) 634
FOB origin-freight allowed (freight absorbed) 634
uniform-delivered pricing 635
postage-stamp pricing 635
zone pricing 635
basing-point pricing 635
pricing policy 635
psychological pricing 636
odd pricing 636
unit pricing 636
price flexibility 636
product-line pricing 636
promotional pricing 637
loss leader 638
leader pricing 638
competitive bidding 639
transfer price 641
profit center 641
cannibalization 643
bot (shopbot) 644
bundle pricing 644

ASSURANCE OF LEARNING REVIEW

1. What is the difference between a skimming price strategy and a penetration pricing strategy? Under which circumstances is each most likely to be used?
2. Why is competitive pricing risky for marketers?
3. What is the difference between a list price and a market price?
4. What are allowances? How do they work?
5. Describe the three ways buyers and sellers handle transportation expenses.
6. How is product-line pricing helpful to both retailers and their customers?

7. What is the difference between loss leader and leader pricing? Give an example of when retailers would use each of these pricing strategies.
8. What is the difference between a competitive bid and a negotiated price?
9. Describe briefly the three traditional global pricing strategies. Give an example of a firm or product that would be likely to adopt one of the three approaches, and explain why.
10. Although cannibalization generally forces price cuts, in what ways can it actually benefit a firm?

PROJECTS AND TEAMWORK EXERCISES

1. With a classmate, create two advertisements for the same product. One advertisement should feature a high price; the other advertisement should feature a low price. Present your advertisements to your classmates. Record their perceptions of the price–quality relationship. Which price do most of them seem to prefer?
2. Figure out how much it will cost to buy and own one of the following new cars from a dealership, or select another model. What is the list price? What price could you negotiate?
   a. Ford Escape hybrid
   b. Toyota Camry
   c. Dodge Challenger
   d. Chevrolet Cruze
3. Assume that a product sells for $100 per ton and that Pittsburgh is the basing-point city for calculating transportation charges. Shipping from Pittsburgh to a potential customer in Cincinnati costs $10 per ton. The actual shipping costs of suppliers in three other cities are $8 per ton for Supplier A, $11 per ton for Supplier B, and $10 per ton for Supplier C. Using this information, answer the following questions:
   a. What delivered price would a salesperson for Supplier A quote to the Cincinnati customer?
   b. What delivered price would a salesperson for Supplier B quote to the Cincinnati customer?
   c. What delivered price would a salesperson for Supplier C quote to the Cincinnati customer?
   d. How much would each supplier net (after subtracting actual shipping costs) per ton on the sale?
4. On your own or with a classmate, visit a local supermarket to find examples of promotional pricing and loss leaders. Note instances of both. Does the promotional pricing make you more likely to purchase a product? Does knowing the store uses loss-leader pricing of bananas make you more inclined to buy them? Present your findings and opinions to the class.
5. Decide on a trip you'd really like to take. Then go online to several of the travel sites—Travelocity, Priceline.com, or others—and compare prices for your trip, including airfare, hotels, and so forth. Does bundling the components give you a price break? Note any coupons or promotions for restaurants and attractions as well. Decide which trip is the best deal, and explain why.

CRITICAL-THINKING EXERCISES

1. When Chinese automakers began exporting cars, rather than focusing on developed nations in the West, they shipped autos to emerging markets in countries such as Algeria, Russia, Chile, and South Africa. In these markets, even used vehicles from multinational manufacturers are relatively scarce—and relatively expensive. The Chinese automakers, who prioritize low cost rather than design or even safety, applied a penetration-pricing strategy. A woman in Santiago, Chile, who bought a new Chery S21 explained, "The price factor is fairly decisive. I paid $5,500 new and full. Toyota with similar features costs around $12,000." Why do you think Chinese automakers chose that pricing strategy? Do you think it was successful? As Chinese regulators pressure these manufacturers to make their cars safer, do you think they will be able to keep their prices low compared with those of the international automakers? Why or why not?[26]
2. As a consumer, would you rather shop at a store that features a sale once a month or a store that practices everyday low pricing (EDLP)? Why?
3. Under Staples' "Easy Rebates" program, customers can submit most of their rebate applications online for products purchased over the Internet, through the catalog, and in Staples stores. Customers may also submit several rebates at once and receive emails about the status of their rebates at every stage.[27] Staples claims the rebates are processed much faster than those of other companies. Do you think the "Easy Rebates" program will increase the number of rebates customers actually submit? Why or why not? Do you think other firms will follow with similar programs?
4. Go online to a shopping site you use regularly and note the prices for different types of products. Does this firm use psychological pricing? Product line pricing? Note any pricing strategies you can identify. Do any of these strategies make you prefer the site over a competitor's site?
5. Why is competitive bidding an important factor in major purchase decisions such as vehicles for a police force, the construction of a bridge, or the manufacture of military uniforms?

ETHICS EXERCISE

The law allows companies in various industries to add what many refer to as "hidden" charges to customers' bills. Phone bills, airline tickets, and hotel receipts often contain charges that are difficult to identify. A traveler who stays in a hotel might be hit with a hospitality fee, a resort fee, or an automatic gratuity, to name just a few. These charges are not taxes, and although they are itemized, it is difficult for the average traveler to make sense of them. Most people either don't check their bills thoroughly or are in a hurry to check out and don't bother to dispute the charges, which may be only a few dollars. But these charges add up over the course of hundreds or thousands of visitors each year, and hotels are pocketing them—legitimately.[28]

1. Do you think adding hidden charges to hotel bills is a smart marketing strategy? Why or why not?
2. Visit the website of a hotel chain with which you are familiar to learn if it gives any information about additional surcharges. If consumers were informed about the charges ahead of time, would you feel differently about them? Why or why not?

INTERNET EXERCISES

1. **Price competition.** Using several online ticket sellers, look up prices for an event you would like to attend. Are the prices comparable? What other fees are included in the price-per-ticket? Are discounts offered for purchasing multiple tickets? Is there a loyalty program for consumers who frequent a specific ticket seller?

   www.ticketmaster.com

   www.stubhub.com

   www.livenation.com

2. **Pricing strategies.** Say you'd like to go on a Caribbean cruise. Visit the Royal Caribbean website or other cruise websites to price cruises at various times of the year—for example, summer vacation, spring break week, and Thanksgiving week. Which cruises are the most and least expensive? Prepare a summary of your findings and bring it to class so you can participate in a discussion on pricing strategies.

   www.royalcaribbean.com/findacruise

   www.carnival.com

3. **Bundle pricing.** Using online websites for several insurance companies, look up pricing for bundling different types of insurance policies—for example, auto and renter's insurance. Is there an advantage to buying two or more different policies with the same company? What are some of the disadvantages to consumers for bundling insurance coverage with one company? What are some of the other factors that impact the cost of bundling insurance policies?

   www.progressive.com

   www.geico.com

   www.statefarm.com

Note: Internet Web addresses change frequently. If you don't find the exact site listed, you may need to access the organization's home page and search from there or use a search engine such as Google or Bing.

CASE 19.1
Who Needs the U.S. Penny?

Does an object that costs more to make than it's worth have any value in today's economy? If the object is the U.S. penny, a growing consensus says "no." Canada stopped producing its penny several years ago, following the lead of Australia, Denmark, New Zealand, Brazil, Norway, Switzerland, Finland, and Britain, which all dropped their lowest-valued coins from circulation with no ill effects. And Canada's penny wasn't as big of a drain on the country's treasury as the U.S. penny. It cost only 1.6¢ to make, whereas the U.S. penny—a copper plate covered by a 99 percent zinc core—cost taxpayers 2.4¢ each. In one recent year, the U.S. Treasury lost almost $60 million minting pennies, all for coins that have no real purchasing power.

Canada's government asked citizens to bring unwanted pennies to banks to be melted down or donated to charities. Canadians who want to continue using the pennies still in circulation are free to do so. They will have fewer opportunities than before, however, since cash sales are now rounded to the nearest five cents.

The zinc industry wants to keep supplying raw material to the U.S. government, of course, but as the cost of zinc keeps rising, some people feel it's time to follow Canada's example and simply eliminate the penny, saving the government the cost of manufacturing it and diverting the metal to some other, better use.

Other people worry that, if all prices are rounded up to the nearest nickel, those most affected will be the poor. Others feel that rounded prices will acquire what economists call "stickiness" and resist further increases (which would have to be at least 5¢) for a few years, thus helping all consumers. "A 99¢ price might go down to 95¢ rather than up to $1 to avoid crossing that higher price threshold," says a senior economist at the Federal Reserve.

QUESTIONS FOR CRITICAL THINKING

1. What do you think would happen to retail prices if the United States withdrew the penny from circulation? Why?
2. Some observers suggest eliminating the nickel as well, since each one costs more than 9¢ to make and distribute. Do you agree, and why or why not? What would be the effect of such a decision on prices?

Sources: "Why Has Canada Killed Off the Penny?" *The Economist*, accessed April 16, 2014, www.economist.com; Brian Domitrovic, "Don't You Dare Eliminate the Penny," *Forbes*, accessed April 16, 2014, www.forbes.com; Christopher Ingraham, "Taxpayers Lost $105 Million on Pennies and Nickels Last Year," *The Washington Post*, accessed April 16, 2014, www.washingtonpost.com; Amy Bowen, "Is the Penny Going Away?" *USA Today*, accessed April 16, 2014, www.usatoday.com; Michael Estrin, "Is the US Getting Rid of the Penny?" *Fox Business*, accessed April 16, 2014, www.foxbusiness.com, Mike Fuljenz, "Kill the Cent and Save a Pretty Penny," *Money News*, accessed April 16, 2014, www.moneynews.com.

VIDEO CASE 19.2
BoltBus: Ride for the Right Price

It's hard to find a real bargain these days, but BoltBus is the real deal. Those black-and-orange buses you see trundling past you on the highway or along a city street could be your ticket to ride—for $1. BoltBus, owned by Greyhound Lines, operates buses along the Northeastern corridor, in California, and in the Pacific Northwest, moving more than 2 million passengers each year. The company's primary customers are those in the 18- to 34-year-old range—college students, recent grads, young professionals, and young families. These riders tend to be budget-minded, and BoltBus caters to them. Pricing is a major component of the bus line's marketing strategy.

When BoltBus launched its line in the Northeast, at least 15 other competitors already operated in the region. In addition, travelers could opt for planes or trains, or they drive their own cars. So the bus line had to offer a brand that sold tickets online, at a very competitive cost. "Pricing is really crucial because it's such a competitive environment," says William Koen, a business analyst for BoltBus. With so many other options available to consumers, BoltBus opted for penetration pricing—including its now-famous $1 ticket—relying on the buzz generated by travelers who nabbed the golden ticket as well as those who began to ride the bus line for its average $20 fare. Typically, BoltBus will sell one $1 ticket per route, selling the remainder of seats for around $20. Whoever gets the $1 ticket often posts their lucky draw on Facebook or Twitter—and the news goes viral. "The $1 ticket is meant to be fun," explains Nicole Recker, senior marketing manager, and the strategy seems to work. Everyone hopes to be the $1 ticket holder, but no one minds paying the regular fare, which is significantly lower than those of competing bus lines.

BoltBus does have to monitor its costs, particularly those of fuel and labor. When these two factors have risen, the company has increased prices in small increments to keep up, with the goal of maintaining both value and profitability. The company also continuously monitors the competition to make sure its service is priced less than its rivals while meeting its costs. BoltBus takes into account the price of gasoline, tolls, and parking for those consumers who choose to drive—and tries to offer a cheaper, more convenient service. "Generally in New York City you'll pay more in parking per day than for a one-way ticket on our buses, so having that value for our customers has driven our explosive growth," notes Koen. "It's opening up an entire new market for the bus industry."

BoltBus also takes demand into consideration when setting prices. Using historical data, marketers see how many people its buses have carried along a certain route on any given day or time period. Then they tweak certain variables—such as the frequency of runs—to maximize revenue and profitability without cutting value to customers. For example, ridership tends to increase during the weekends and holiday periods, so BoltBus offers more runs during those high-volume periods, while cutting runs during the midweek when the buses aren't filled. During low-demand periods (such as Wednesdays), BoltBus may offer a lower price to attract more volume; conversely, during high-demand periods (such as Friday evenings), ticket prices are a bit higher. This type of pricing to demand is similar to the strategy of hotels and airlines; consumers pay more to fly or stay in a hotel during popular vacation weeks. Since seats generally sell out during these high-volume periods, BoltBus doesn't need to discount the ticket price. But an empty seat represents a loss of revenue to the company, so a discounted sale is better than no sale—which is why BoltBus offers lower prices during quieter times of the week or year. "It's a high-volume business model," explains general manager David Hall. "We keep the price low and the volume high."

BoltBus' pricing policy is attractive to consumers. Prices are straightforward and easy to understand; consumers know what to expect and what they are getting for their dollar. "Transparency has been key to our success," says Recker. "It's done a lot to enhance our brand." BoltBus charges no hidden or additional fees and doesn't jack up its prices without warning. "We're very honest with our customer," says Recker.

QUESTIONS FOR CRITICAL THINKING

1. How does BoltBus use a combination of penetration pricing and everyday low pricing (EDLP) to achieve its objectives?
2. BoltBus is well known for its $1 ticket sales promotion. Though it has been successful thus far, could it ever backfire? If so, how?

Sources: Company website, www.boltbus.com, accessed April 16, 2014; Jeff Plungis, "Buses Found Cheaper Than Driving Between Largest Cities," *Bloomberg News*, accessed April 16, 2014, www.bloomberg.com; BoltBus Expands from Los Angeles; Adds Las Vegas, San Francisco Service," *PR Newswire*, accessed April 16, 2014, www.prnewswire.com; Christine Whittemore, "Travel Marketing: What the Revitalized Bus Travel Industry Can Teach You about Reinventing Your Travel Brand," *5 to 9 Branding*, accessed April 16, 2014, http://5to9branding.com.

NOTES

1. Cooper Smith, "Shopping Cart Abandonment: Online Retailers' Biggest Headache Is Actually a Huge Opportunity," *Business Insider*, accessed October 30, 2014, www.businessinsider.com; Krystina Gustafson, "Online Holiday Sales Up 10%, But Running Short of Expectations: ComScore," *CNBC*, accessed April 14, 2014, www.cnbc.com; Andrea Puhak, "Infographic: 2014 Cart Abandonment Forecast," *SaleCycle*, accessed April 14, 2014, www.salecycle.com; Mark MacDonald, "Why Online Retailers Are Losing 67.45% of Sales and What to Do About It," *Shopify*, accessed April 14, 2014, www.shopify.com; "1 in 4 Top Retailers Now Sending Cart Abandonment Emails, Most Within the First Day," *Marketing Charts*, accessed April 14, 2014, www.marketingcharts.com; Brad Tuttle, "The Passive-Aggressive Way to Haggle Online: Abandon Your Shopping Cart," *Time*, accessed April 14, 2014, http://business.time.com; Kern Lewis, "Abandoned Online Shopping Carts: How to Close Those Deals," *Forbes*, accessed April 14, 2014, www.forbes.com.
2. Company website, www.rakuten.com, accessed October 30, 2014; company website, www.amazon.com, accessed October 30, 2014.
3. Sebastian Blanco, "2014 Nissan Leaf Price Climbs $180 to $28,980, Ghosn Predicts Sales Doubling," *Green Auto Blog*, accessed April 24, 2014, http://green.autoblog.com; Mark Rogowsky, "Will Chevy's $5,000 Price Cut Charge Up Volt Sales?" *Forbes*, accessed April 24, 2014, www.forbes.com; Jason Mick, "As Sales Level in the U.S., Tesla Model S Charges Ahead in Europe, China," *Daily Tech*, accessed April 24, 2014, http://www.dailytech.com; Luke Sargeant, "Tesla Motors to Reduce Tags over the Next 3 Years," *Liberty Voice*, accessed April 24, 2014, http://guardianlv.com.
4. Saritha Rai, "Its 'World's Cheapest Car Tag' Made the Nano Undesirable in India," *Forbes*, accessed October 30, 2014, www.forbes.com; Kirk Seaman, "The 10 Cheapest New Cars Sold in America for 2014," *Car and Driver*, accessed October 30, 2014, http://blog.caranddriver.com.
5. Company website, "Savings Catcher," https://savingscatcher.walmart.com, accessed April 14, 2014; Anne D'Innocenzio, "Wal-Mart 'Savings Catcher' Tool Gives Competitors Prices," *ABC News*, accessed April 14, 2014, http://abclocal.go.com.
6. Stephanie Strom, "Groceries Are Cleaning Up in Store-Brand Aisles," *The New York Times*, accessed April 14, 2014, www.nytimes.com.
7. Company website, "2015 Honda Civic Options & Pricing," http://automobiles.honda.com, accessed October 30, 2014.
8. Company website, www.shutterfly.com, accessed April 15, 2014.
9. Company website, http://qd.sees.com, accessed April 15, 2014,.
10. Organization website, www.consumerreports.org, accessed April 15, 2014.
11. Caleb Denison, "The Sale Is Dead! Here's Why TVs Cost the Same at Every Retailer Now," *Digital Trends*, accessed April 15, 2014, www.digitaltrends.com.
12. Jill Cataldo, "Super-Couponing Tips: When Rebates Go Awry," *Lehigh Valley Live*, accessed April 15, 2014, www.lehighvalleylive.com; "Advice on Rebates and Refunds," *Better Business Bureau*, accessed April 15, 2014, http://memphis.bbb.org.
13. Reinhardt Krause, "Comcast, TWC: Broadband Usage Pricing a Key Issue?" *Investors Business Daily*, accessed April 15, 2014, http://news.investors.com.
14. Company website, www.bergdorfgoodman.com, accessed April 15, 2014.
15. Organization website, "Coastal Uncorked Festival," www.mbhospitality.org, accessed April 15, 2014,.
16. Catherine Rampell, "Turkey Economics, Annotated," *The New York Times*, accessed April 15, 2014, http://economix.blogs.nytimes.com.
17. Company website, www.usa.canon.com, accessed April 15, 2014.
18. Art Markman, "Price, Quality, and Value: How Do Shoppers Use Price to Judge Quality and Value?" *Psychology Today*, accessed April 15, 2014, www.psychologytoday.com.
19. Company website, www.motel6.com, accessed April 15, 2014.
20. Jeffrey N. Ross, "Ford Police Interceptors Win Acceleration War Against Dodge, Chevy," *Autoblog*, accessed April 15, 2014, www.autoblog.com; Edward A. Sanchez, "2014 Ford Police Interceptor Features Anti-Sneaker Safety," *Motor Trend*, accessed April 15, 2014, www.motortrend.com.
21. Paul Giblin and Craig Harris, "$513,000 No-Bid Contract to Law Firm Violated Glendale Policies," *Arizona Republic*, accessed April 15, 2014, www.azcentral.com.
22. Company website, www.razorgator.com, accessed April 15, 2014; company website, www.ticketliquidator.com, accessed April 15, 2014.
23. David Faber, " EBay and PayPal to Split into Two Separately Traded Companies," *CNBC*, accessed October 30, 2014, www.cnbc.com; company website, www.ubid.com, accessed April 16, 2014; Neal Ungerleider, "Ebay Marries Brick-and-Mortar with Connected Glass," *Fast Company*, accessed April 16, 2014, www.fastcompany.com.
24. Company website, "Pay with Cash," www.walmart.com, accessed April 16, 2014; company website, www.containerstore.com, accessed April 16, 2014; company website, www.lowes.com, accessed April 16, 2014,.
25. Company website, www.verizon.com, accessed April 16, 2014.
26. Keith Bradsher, "Chinese Cars Make Valuable Gains in Emerging Markets," *The New York Times*, accessed April 24, 2014, www.nytimes.com.
27. Company website, www.stapleseasyrebates.com, accessed April 16, 2014.
28. Dan Gillmor, "The High Price of Hidden Charges," *The Guardian*, accessed April 24, 2014, www.guardian.co.uk; Jessica Dickler, "Hotels Piling On Hidden Fees," *CNN Money*, accessed April 24, 2014, http://money.cnn.com.

Scripps Networks Interactive & Food Network

PART 7
Pricing Decisions

Good, Better, Best

How do you put a price on the experience of serving friends or family the best dinner you ever cooked? Its value is far greater than the cost of ingredients or the amount of time you spent making the meal. Instead, its value lies in your original inspiration, your goal of producing a great meal, and all the care you blended into your creation—not to mention the enjoyment of your diners. Food Network marketers face this same question when considering pricing objectives for everything from advertising to branded cookware sold by retailer Kohl's.

Although Food Network sells time to advertisers and charges cable and digital distributors for content, the network's ultimate customer is the consumer. "For us, the primary relationship is with the consumer," explains Chris Powell, executive vice president for human resources at Scripps. Food Network delivers relevant content to viewers, creating value for them that allows the network to charge advertising and distribution rates. Advertisers and distributors then have access to those consumers through various outlets—whether it's placing their products in specific episodes or tweeting about an upcoming show premier. Lexus marketers may consider paying a higher price to place a new model in Restaurant: Impossible for the privilege of having its luxury auto featured on a popular show as a worthwhile investment. Distributors may agree to rates that meet Food Network's profitability objectives.

Food Network also designs and sells tangible goods—kitchen utensils, cookware, dinnerware, table linens, and more. Creating a pricing strategy for these products involves integrating the target audience for its television shows with its choice of retailer: Kohl's. Since Food Network products are sold exclusively by Kohl's, marketers can zoom in on a target market for its pricing decisions. Using a competitive pricing strategy, Food Network positions its kitchen goods along the "good, better, best" continuum. "We try to anchor ourselves at the high end of better," observes Sergei Kuharsky, senior vice president and general manager for licensing and merchandising. "We want to be quality first, but we want to be accessible as well." If Food Network priced its kitchen goods too high, fans would view them as unaffordable—undermining sales and potentially doing damage to the lifestyle image of the network. Gabe Gordon, vice president of research for Food Network, agrees with this assessment, particularly during economically difficult times. "If you're overtly leaning toward luxury, you turn a lot of people off," he points out.

When developing its kitchen products, Food Network partners with a team of culinary experts who help design, test, and review everything from frying pans to baking dishes. If these items survive hard use in the test kitchens for four to eight weeks, they'll likely perform well in consumers' homes. Quality combined with the right price creates value for consumers. Kohl's sets the actual retail prices for these items, with product-line pricing—but the price–quality relationship is important to Food Network. "We look at our products as professionally inspired but priced for the home cook, and we want them to be as good if not better for the money than anything else out there," says Kuharsky.

Although consumers don't pay for Food Network programming (except through cable or other media subscriptions), the network takes into consideration pricing issues as it creates the lineup of shows. "I do think our programming is very aspirational," comments Gordon. "We give you the tools to make things your own." When the economy shifted downward several years ago, Food Network marketers noticed that daytime viewers responded well to shows that offered special deals or featured less-expensive menus and recipes. "When times change and money is tight, people will look for ways to cut corners in a less painful way," explains Gordon. In addition, people tend to entertain at home more—instead of dining out—so they gravitate toward shows that provide low-cost but fun or attractive ideas for social gatherings. These programs "help people live a better food life," Gordon continues. Here, price limits go to work in the minds of consumers. They establish a budget for groceries or entertaining, then shop within those limits. But they want to create the tastiest meal or trendiest party those boundaries will allow—and Food Network is there to help.

Price limits also apply to wealthier viewers who might be able to afford to buy more expensive ingredients or cookware but choose not to. If they see a certain dish featured on one of the cooking shows, they might snub it as too exotic for their family's tastes or too complicated or lengthy to make at home. "Surprisingly, you end up turning off more of the upscale people in the audience," warns Gordon. In the end, everyone must eat to live—but Food Network aspires to bring out the inner cook in all of us, upscale or not. "Food is how people express themselves," says Gordon.

QUESTIONS FOR CRITICAL THINKING

1. In your opinion, should Food Network try to attain prestige objectives through pricing? Why or why not?
2. How would you classify the market structure for Food Network's offerings (both content and tangible goods)? Explain.
3. How might Food Network and Kohl's use product-line pricing to expand their partnered offerings?
4. Describe the price–quality relationship of Food Network's programming and its cookware products at Kohl's.

Developing an Effective Marketing Plan

APPENDIX A

Overview

> "What are our mission and goals?"
> "Who are our customers?"
> "What types of products do we offer?"
> "How can we provide superior customer service?"

These are some of the questions addressed by a **marketing plan**—a detailed description of the resources and actions needed to achieve stated marketing objectives. Chapter 2 discussed **strategic planning**—the process of anticipating events and market conditions and deciding how a firm can best achieve its organizational objectives. Marketing planning encompasses all the activities devoted to achieving marketing objectives, establishing a basis for designing a marketing strategy. This appendix deals in depth with the formal marketing plan, which is part of an organization's overall business plan. At the end of this appendix, you'll see what an actual marketing plan looks like. Each plan component for a hypothetical firm called Blue Sky Clothing is presented.

marketing plan Detailed description of the resources and actions needed to achieve stated marketing objectives.

strategic planning Process of anticipating events and market conditions and deciding how a firm can best achieve its organizational objectives.

COMPONENTS OF A BUSINESS PLAN

A company's **business plan** is one of its most important documents. The business plan puts in writing what all of the firm's objectives are, how they will be met, how the business will obtain financing, and how much money the company expects to earn over a specified time period. Although business plans vary in length and format, most contain at least some form of the following components:

- An *executive summary* briefly answers the *who, what, when, where, how,* and *why* questions for the plan. Although the summary appears early in the plan, it typically is written last, after the firm's executives have worked out the details of all the other sections.
- A *competitive analysis* section focuses on the environment in which the marketing plan is to be implemented. Although this section is more closely associated with the comprehensive business plan, factors specifically influencing marketing are likely to be included here.
- The *mission statement* summarizes the organization's purpose, vision, and overall goals. This statement provides the foundation on which further planning is based.
- The overall business plan includes a series of *component* plans that present goals and strategies for each functional area of the enterprise. They typically include the following:
  - The *marketing plan*, which describes strategies for informing potential customers about the goods and services offered by the firm as well as strategies for developing long-term relationships.

business plan Formal document that outlines what a company's objectives are, how they will be met, how the business will obtain financing, and how much money the company expects to earn.

A-1

> **Briefly Speaking**
>
> "A corporation is a living organism; it has to continue to shed its skin. Methods have to change. Focus has to change. Values have to change. The sum total of those changes is transformation."
>
> —Andy Grove
> *Co-founder and former CEO, Intel Corporation*

- The *financing plan*, which presents a realistic approach for securing needed funds and managing debt and cash flows.
- The *production plan*, which describes how the organization will develop its products in the most efficient, cost-effective manner possible.
- The *facilities plan*, which describes the physical environment and equipment required to implement the production plan.
- The *human resources plan*, which estimates the firm's employment needs and the skills necessary to achieve organizational goals, including a comparison of current employees with the needs of the firm; and which establishes processes for securing adequately trained personnel if a gap exists between current employee skills and future needs.

This basic format encompasses the planning process used by nearly every successful organization. Whether a company operates in the manufacturing, wholesaling, retailing, or service sector—or a combination—the components described here are likely to appear in its overall business plan. Regardless of the size or longevity of a company, a business plan is an essential tool for a firm's owners because it helps them focus on the key elements of their business. Even small firms just starting out need a business plan to obtain financing. Figure A.1 shows the outline of a business plan for Blue Sky Clothing.

FIGURE A.1 Outline of a Business Plan

The Blue Sky Clothing Business Plan

I. Executive Summary
- Who, What, When, Where, How, and Why

II. Table of Contents

III. Introduction
- Mission Statement
- Concept and Company
- Management Team
- Product

IV. Marketing Strategy
- Demographics
- Trends
- Market Penetration
- Potential Sales Revenue

V. Financing the Business
- Cash Flow Analysis
- Pro Forma Balance Sheet
- Income Statement

VI. Facilities Plan
- Physical Environment
- Equipment

VII. Human Resources Plan
- Employment Needs and Skills
- Current Employees

VIII. Résumés of Principals

CREATING A MARKETING PLAN

Keep in mind that a marketing plan should be created in conjunction with the other elements of a firm's business plan. In addition, a marketing plan often draws from the business plan, restating the executive summary, competitive analysis, and mission statement to give its readers an overall view of the firm. The marketing plan is needed for various reasons:

- To obtain financing, because banks and most private investors require a detailed business plan—including a marketing plan component—before they even consider a loan application or a venture capital investment
- To provide direction for the firm's overall business and marketing strategies
- To support the development of long- and short-term organizational objectives
- To guide employees in achieving these objectives
- To serve as a standard against which the firm's progress can be measured and evaluated

In addition, the marketing plan is where a firm puts into writing its commitment to customers and to building long-lasting relationships. After creating and implementing the plan, marketers must reevaluate it periodically to gauge its success in moving the organization toward its goals. If changes are needed, they should be made as soon as possible.

FORMULATING AN OVERALL MARKETING STRATEGY

Before writing a marketing plan, a firm's marketers formulate an overall marketing strategy. A firm may use a number of tools in marketing planning, all of which are described in Chapter 2. These include business portfolio analysis, SWOT analysis, and the BCG matrix; executives may take advantage of a strategic window, study Porter's Five Forces model as it relates to their business, or consider adopting a first- or second-mover strategy.

In addition to the planning strategies discussed in Chapter 2, marketers are also likely to use **spreadsheet analysis**, which lays out a grid of columns and rows that organize numerical information in a standardized, easily understood format. Spreadsheet analysis helps planners answer various "what if" questions related to the firm's financing and operations. The most popular spreadsheet software is Microsoft Excel. A spreadsheet analysis helps planners anticipate marketing performance given specified sets of circumstances. For example, a spreadsheet might project the outcomes of various pricing decisions for a new product, as shown in Figure A.2.

Once general planning strategies are determined, marketers begin to flesh out the details of the marketing strategy. These include identifying the target market, studying the marketing environment, and creating a marketing mix. When marketers have identified the target market, they can develop the optimal marketing mix to reach their potential customers:

- *Product strategy.* Which goods and services should the company offer to meet its customers' needs?
- *Distribution strategy.* Through which channel(s) and physical facilities will the firm distribute its products?
- *Promotional strategy.* What mix of advertising, sales promotion, and personal selling activities will the firm use to reach its customers initially and then develop long-term relationships?
- *Pricing strategy.* At what level should the company set its prices?

> **Briefly Speaking**
>
> "A strategy delineates a territory in which a company seeks to be unique."
>
> —**Michael Porter**
> *American management theorist and writer*

spreadsheet analysis Grid that organizes numerical information in a standardized, easily understood format.

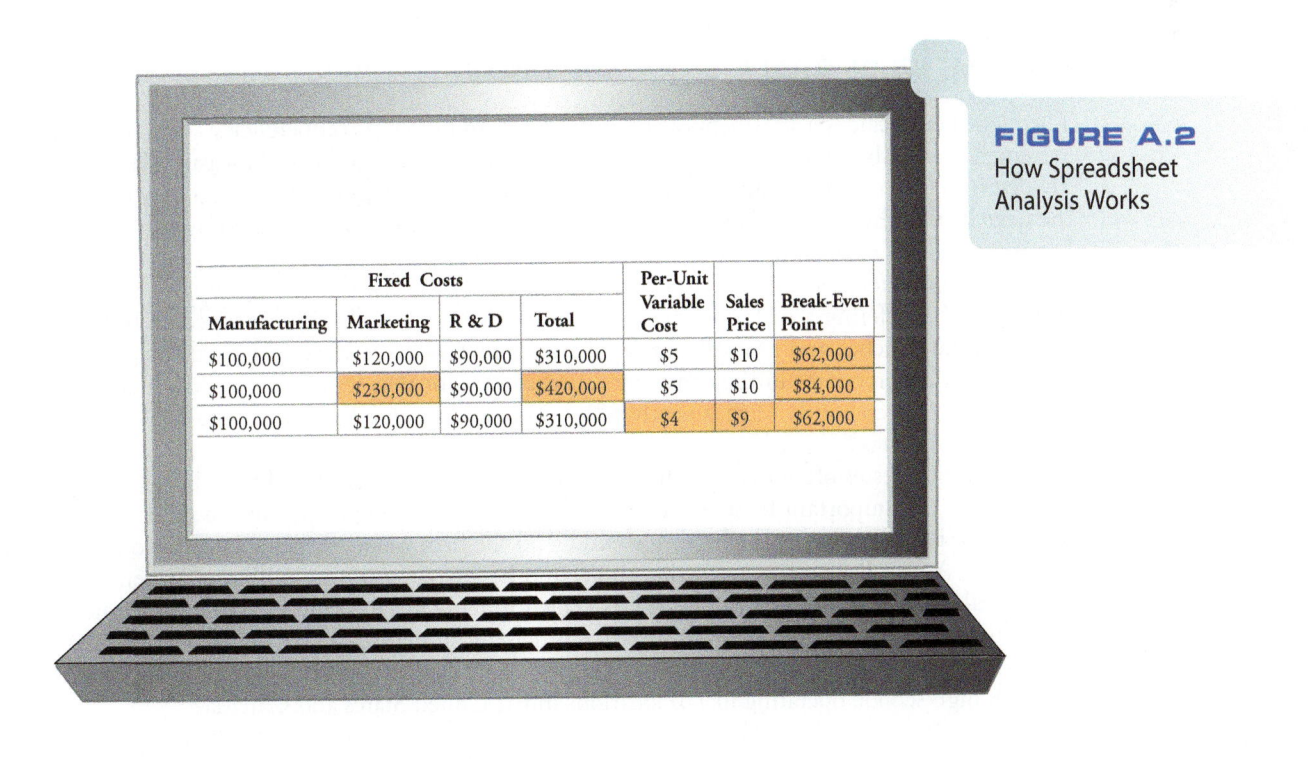

FIGURE A.2
How Spreadsheet Analysis Works

Fixed Costs				Per-Unit Variable Cost	Sales Price	Break-Even Point
Manufacturing	Marketing	R & D	Total			
$100,000	$120,000	$90,000	$310,000	$5	$10	$62,000
$100,000	$230,000	$90,000	$420,000	$5	$10	$84,000
$100,000	$120,000	$90,000	$310,000	$4	$9	$62,000

Briefly Speaking

"Failing to plan is planning to fail."

—Alan Lakein
American time management expert; author of How to Get Control of Your Time and Your Life

THE EXECUTIVE SUMMARY, COMPETITIVE ANALYSIS, AND MISSION STATEMENT

Because these three elements of the business plan often reappear in the marketing plan, it is useful to describe them here. Recall that the executive summary answers the *who, what, when, where, how,* and *why* questions for the business. In the early days of Google, the executive summary of the company's business plan included references to its strategic planning process for its search services, which involved "developing the perfect search engine … [one that] understands exactly what you mean and gives you back exactly what you want."[1] The summary also answered questions such as who was involved (key people and organizations), what length of time the plan represented, and how the goals would be met.

The competitive analysis focuses on the environment in which the marketing plan is to be implemented. Trenton, New Jersey–based TerraCycle manufactures a wide variety of products, all made from recycled materials. Believing the green movement will eventually hold sway in consumer products, TerraCycle's business goal is to become the leading eco-friendly organic brand in each of the product categories in which it competes. It doesn't attempt to overpower the category leader; instead, it aims to beat other eco-friendly competitors. For example, TerraCycle differentiates itself in the collection and reuse of nonrecyclable waste. Recently it even devised a process for recycling a commodity widely considered to be nonrecyclable: cigarette butts.[2]

The mission statement puts into words an organization's overall purpose and reason for being. According to Nintendo's corporate mission, the company is "strongly committed to producing and marketing the best products and support services available." Not only does Nintendo strive to manufacture the highest-quality video products, but it also attempts "to treat every customer with attention, consideration and respect." Nintendo is similarly committed to its employees and believes in treating them "with the same consideration and respect that we, as a company, show our customers."[3]

DESCRIPTION OF THE COMPANY

A company description is included near the beginning of the marketing plan, typically following the executive summary and before the mission statement. The company description may include a brief history or background of the firm, the types of products it offers or plans to introduce, and recent successes or achievements. In short, it consists of a few paragraphs containing the kind of information often found on the home page of a company's website.

STATEMENT OF GOALS AND CORE COMPETENCIES

The plan then includes a statement of the firm's goals and its core competencies—the things it does extremely well or better than anyone else. The goals should be specific and measurable and may be divided into financial and nonfinancial aims. A financial goal might be to add 75 new franchises in the next 12 months or to reach $200 million in revenues. A nonfinancial goal might be to enter the European market or to add a new product line every other year.

Core competencies make a firm stand out from everyone else in the marketplace. Costco's core competency is offering a wide variety of goods at low prices, including unexpected bargains like luxury-brand watches and Dom Perignon champagne. Costco leadership regards its workforce as a significant differentiator in the company's success and, for that reason, pays above-market wages. The average Costco hourly wage is nearly $21—35 percent higher than the highest minimum wage in the United States.[4]

Small businesses often begin with a single core competency and build their business and reputation on it. It is important for a new firm to identify its core competency in the marketing plan so investors or banks understand why they should lend the firm money to get started or to grow to the next stage. As a college student, David Kim found he enjoyed tutoring children. When he discovered a real demand for skilled tutoring, he decided to launch a tutoring business, which he named C2 Education. Because C2's core competency is helping students to excel, employees are hired and trained according to rigorous standards. Today, C2 Education serves students from elementary through high school, operating in 110 locations in the United States and Canada.[5]

OUTLINE OF THE MARKETING ENVIRONMENT (SITUATION ANALYSIS)

Every successful marketing plan considers the marketing environment—the competitive, economic, political–legal, technological, and social–cultural factors that affect the way a firm formulates and implements its marketing strategy. Marketing plans may address these issues in different ways, but the goal is to present information that describes the company's position or situation within the marketing environment. J. Crew, for instance, has a well-known brand name and a CEO with an impressive track record, Mickey Drexler, who previously headed The Gap. The retail environment for stores such as J. Crew is highly competitive. Merchandise that doesn't appeal to enough customers ends up on a clearance rack and hurts the bottom line. According to Drexler, the key to J. Crew's success is that it sells merchandise that cannot be sold elsewhere. Drexler pushes his buyers to "out-product" their competitors.[6] A marketing plan for J. Crew would include an evaluation of competing stores, such as The Gap and Urban Outfitters; any technological advances that would affect factors such as merchandise distribution or inventory; social–cultural issues such as fashion preferences and spending habits of customers; and economic issues affecting a pricing strategy.

One such method for outlining the marketing environment in the marketing plan is to include a SWOT analysis, described in Chapter 2. SWOT analysis identifies the firm's strengths, weaknesses, opportunities, and threats within the marketing environment. A SWOT analysis for J. Crew might include strengths such as its corporate leadership, brand name, and upscale target market. Weaknesses might include the risks inherent in the business of correctly spotting fashion trends. A major opportunity lies in the fact that J. Crew can expand almost anywhere. For example, after J. Crew acquired Madewell, a retailer that sells hip, casual clothes to an upscale audience, it expanded the chain to more than 75 stores and launched an e-commerce site. Threats for J. Crew could include competition from other trendy stores, sudden changes in customer preferences, and financial crises that affect spending. A SWOT analysis can be presented in chart format so that it is easy to read as part of the marketing plan. The sample marketing plan in this appendix includes a SWOT analysis for Blue Sky Clothing.

THE TARGET MARKET AND MARKETING MIX

The marketing plan identifies the target market for the firm's products. The Cute Overload website (www.cuteoverload.com) contains photos and videos of animals that visitors can share and about which they can post comments. But the site also offers a page-a-day desk calendar of the same name featuring images of puppies, kittens, birds, and chipmunks with humorous captions. Cute Overload targets women ages 18 to 34 who need a laugh and a brief escape from the real world. The calendars are also offered for sale on Amazon.com, and the retailer's inventory recently sold out in one day, which astonished the developer.[7] Weight Watchers has long regarded women as its primary target market and, in fact, females currently make up 90 percent of its clientele. However, as the company saw increasing interest from men, marketers for Weight Watchers began to tap into that segment, launching a men-only website and a $10 million advertising campaign directed solely at men.[8]

The marketing plan also discusses the marketing mix the firm has selected for its products. Hollywood studios are known for implementing lavish strategies for promoting their films. Not only did Walt Disney Studios use traditional means to launch its recent movie, *Frozen,* but it also ran a Disney Movie Rewards promotion. Under the promotion, moviegoers could score free admission to the movie by buying selected Disney DVDs or Blu-Rays and registering a "magic code" online at DisneyMovieRewards.com.[9]

BUDGET, SCHEDULE, AND MONITORING

Every marketing plan requires a budget, a time schedule for implementation, and a system for monitoring the plan's success or failure. At age 21, entrepreneur Joe Cirulli of Gainesville, Florida, made a to-do list of ten life goals, which included "Own a health club" and "Make it respected in the community." By age 33, Cirulli had achieved all ten of his life goals, including the opening of his Gainesville Health & Fitness Center. As Cirulli's business grew, however, he discovered a larger mission: to make Gainesville the healthiest community in America. Today, Gainesville is the first and only city to win the Gold Well City award from the Wellness Council of America, and Cirulli's

> **Briefly Speaking**
>
> "In marketing I have seen only one strategy that can't miss—and that is to market to your best customers first, your best prospects second, and the rest of the world last."
>
> —**John Romero**
> *American video game designer, programmer, and developer*

fitness center is widely regarded as one of the best in the industry. Whether or not he realized it at the time, Cirulli's life and business plan at age 21 had the makings of a marketing plan, with goals and budgets, a timeline, and measurements of progress—a formula for business success.[10]

Most long-range marketing plans encompass a two- to five-year period, although companies that do business in industries such as auto manufacturing, pharmaceuticals, or lumber may extend their marketing plans further into the future, because it typically takes longer to develop these products. However, marketers in most industries will have difficulty making estimates and predictions beyond five years because of the many uncertainties in the marketplace. Firms also may opt to develop short-term plans to cover marketing activities for a single year.

The marketing plan, whether it is long term or short term, predicts how long it will take to achieve the goals it sets out. A goal may be opening a certain number of new stores, increasing market share, or achieving an expansion of the product line. Finally, the marketing program is monitored and evaluated for its performance. Monthly, quarterly, and annual sales targets are usually tracked; the efficiency with which certain tasks are completed is determined; customer satisfaction is measured; and so forth. All of these factors contribute to the overall review of the program.

At some point, a firm may implement an *exit strategy*—a plan for the firm to leave the market. A common way for a large company to do this is to sell off a business unit. A number of these strategies have been implemented recently. For years, Sony Corporation's PC business struggled in the highly competitive industry before the company decided to exit and sharpen its focus on mobile devices, including smartphones. Sony sold its Vaio brand to Japan Industrial Partners, a Tokyo–based investment firm.[11]

SAMPLE MARKETING PLAN

The following pages contain an annotated sample marketing plan for Blue Sky Clothing. At some point in your career, you will likely be involved in writing—or at least contributing to—a marketing plan. And you'll certainly read many marketing plans throughout your business career. Keep in mind that the plan for Blue Sky is a single example; no one format is used by all companies. Also, the Blue Sky plan has been somewhat condensed to make it easier to annotate and illustrate the most vital features. The important point to remember is that the marketing plan is a document designed to present concise, cohesive information about a company's marketing objectives to managers, lending institutions, and others involved in creating and carrying out the firm's overall business strategy.

Five-Year Marketing Plan
Blue Sky Clothing, Inc.

Table of Contents

EXECUTIVE SUMMARY

This five-year marketing plan for Blue Sky Clothing has been created by its two founders to secure additional funding for growth and to inform employees of the company's current status and direction. Although Blue Sky was launched only three years ago, the firm has experienced greater-than-anticipated demand for its products, and research has shown that the target market of sports-minded consumers and sports retailers would like to buy more casual clothing than Blue Sky currently offers. As a result, Blue Sky wants to extend its current product line as well as add new product lines. In addition, the firm plans to explore opportunities for online sales. The marketing environment has been very receptive to the firm's high-quality goods—casual clothing in trendy colors with logos and slogans that reflect the interests of outdoor enthusiasts around the country. Over the next five years, Blue Sky can increase its distribution, offer new products, and win new customers.

The executive summary outlines the who, what, where, when, how, *and* why *of the marketing plan. Blue Sky is only three years old and is successful enough that it now needs a formal marketing plan to obtain additional financing from a bank or private investors for expansion and the launch of new products.*

Appendix A Developing an Effective Marketing Plan

COMPANY DESCRIPTION

Blue Sky Clothing was founded three years ago by entrepreneurs Lucy Neuman and Nick Russell. Neuman has an undergraduate degree in marketing and worked for several years in the retail clothing industry. Russell operated Go West!—an adventure business that arranged group trips to locations in Wyoming, Montana, and Idaho—which he sold to a partner. Neuman and Russell, who have been friends since college, decided to develop and market a line of clothing with a unique yet universal appeal to outdoor enthusiasts.

Blue Sky Clothing reflects Neuman's and Russell's passion for the outdoors. The company's original cotton T-shirts, baseball caps, and fleece jackets and vests bear logos of different sports, such as kayaking, mountain climbing, bicycling, skating, surfing, and horseback riding. But every item shows off the company's slogan: "Go Play Outside." Blue Sky sells clothing for both men and women, in the hottest colors with the coolest names—sunrise pink, sunset red, twilight purple, desert rose, cactus green, ocean blue, mountaintop white, and river rock gray.

Blue Sky attire is currently carried by small retail stores that specialize in outdoor clothing and gear. Most of these stores are concentrated in northern New England, California, the Northwest, and the South. The high quality, trendy colors, and unique message of the clothing have gained Blue Sky a following among consumers between ages 18 and 39. Sales have tripled in the last year alone, and Blue Sky is currently working to expand its manufacturing capabilities.

Blue Sky is also committed to giving back to the community by contributing to local conservation programs. Ultimately, the company would like to develop and fund its own environmental programs. This plan will outline how Blue Sky intends to introduce new products, expand its distribution, enter new markets, and give back to the community.

> *The company description summarizes the history of Blue Sky—how it was founded and by whom, what its products are, and why they are unique. It begins to "sell" the reader on the growth possibilities for Blue Sky.*

BLUE SKY'S MISSION AND GOALS

Blue Sky's mission is to be a leading producer and marketer of personalized, casual clothing for consumers who love the outdoors. Blue Sky wants to inspire people to get outdoors more often and enjoy family and friends while doing so. In addition, Blue Sky strives to design programs for preserving the natural environment.

During the next five years, Blue Sky seeks to achieve the following financial and nonfinancial goals:

Financial Goals

1. Obtain financing to expand manufacturing capabilities, increase distribution, and introduce two new product lines
2. Increase revenues by at least 50 percent each year
3. Donate at least $25,000 a year to conservation organizations

Nonfinancial Goals

4. Introduce two new product lines: customized logo clothing and lightweight luggage
5. Enter new geographic markets, including Southwest and Mid-Atlantic regions
6. Develop a successful Internet site, while maintaining strong relationships with retailers
7. Develop its own conservation program aimed at helping communities raise money to purchase open space

> *It is important to state a firm's mission and goals, including financial and nonfinancial goals. Blue Sky's goals include growth and profits for the company as well as the ability to contribute to society through conservation programs.*

CORE COMPETENCIES

Blue Sky seeks to use its core competencies to achieve a sustainable competitive advantage, the value of which its competitors cannot match. Already Blue Sky has developed core

> *This section reminds employees and those outside the company (such as potential lenders) exactly what Blue Sky does so well and how it plans to achieve a sustainable competitive advantage over rivals. Note here and throughout the plan: Blue Sky focuses on relationships.*

competencies in (1) offering a high-quality, branded product whose image is recognizable among consumers; (2) creating a sense of community among consumers who purchase the products; and (3) developing a reputation among retailers as a reliable manufacturer that delivers orders on schedule. The firm intends to build on these competencies through marketing efforts that increase the number of products offered as well as distribution outlets.

By forming strong relationships with consumers, retailers, and suppliers of fabric and other goods and services, Blue Sky believes it can create a sustainable competitive advantage over its rivals. No other clothing company can say to its customers with as much conviction, "Go Play Outside"!

SITUATION ANALYSIS

The marketing environment for Blue Sky represents overwhelming opportunities. It also contains some challenges the firm believes it can meet successfully. Figure A illustrates a SWOT analysis of the company conducted by its marketers to highlight Blue Sky's strengths, weaknesses, opportunities, and threats.

The SWOT analysis presents a thumbnail sketch of the company's position in the marketplace. In just three years, Blue Sky has built some impressive strengths while looking forward to new opportunities. Its dedicated founders, the growing number of brand-loyal customers, and sound financial management place the company in a good position to grow. However, as Blue Sky considers expansion of its product line and entry into new markets, the firm will have to guard against marketing myopia (the failure to recognize the scope of its business) and quality slippage. As the company finalizes plans for new products and expanded Internet sales, its management will also have to guard against competitors who attempt to duplicate

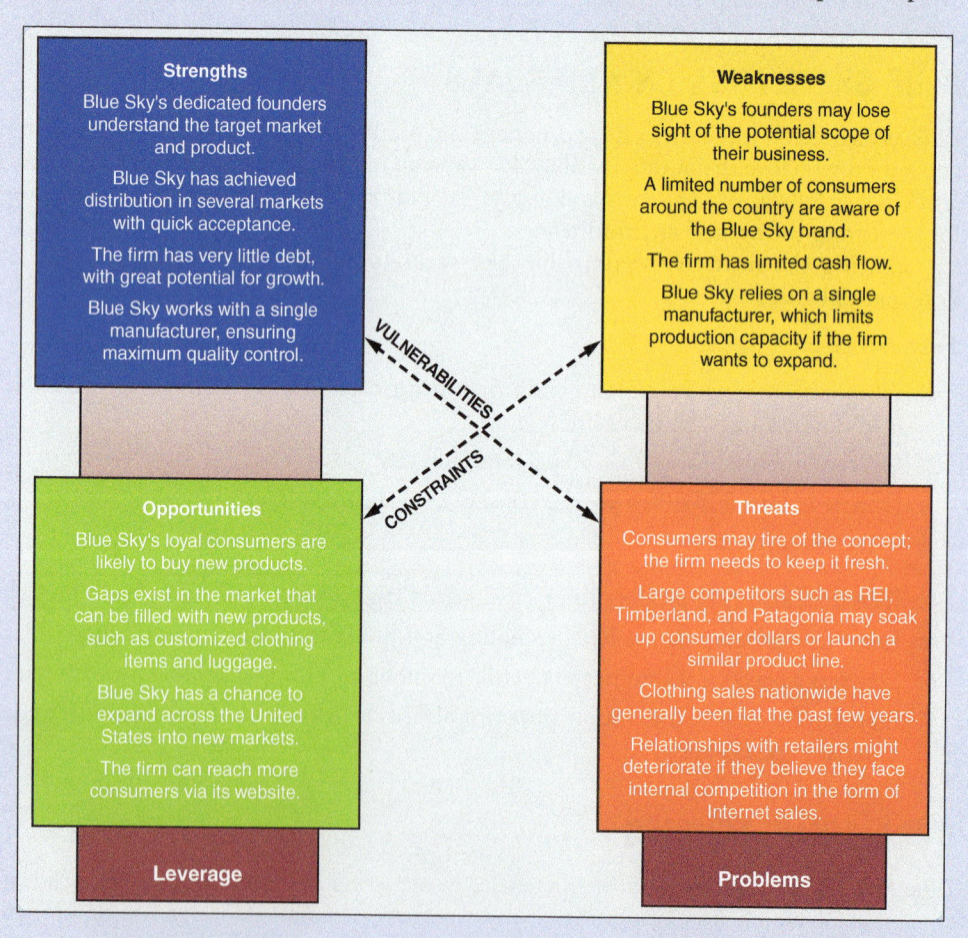

> The situation analysis provides an outline of the marketing environment. A SWOT analysis helps marketers and others identify clearly a firm's strengths, weaknesses, opportunities, and threats. Again, relationships are a focus. Blue Sky has also conducted research on the outdoor clothing market, competitors, and consumers to determine how best to attract and keep customers.

Strengths
- Blue Sky's dedicated founders understand the target market and product.
- Blue Sky has achieved distribution in several markets with quick acceptance.
- The firm has very little debt, with great potential for growth.
- Blue Sky works with a single manufacturer, ensuring maximum quality control.

Weaknesses
- Blue Sky's founders may lose sight of the potential scope of their business.
- A limited number of consumers around the country are aware of the Blue Sky brand.
- The firm has limited cash flow.
- Blue Sky relies on a single manufacturer, which limits production capacity if the firm wants to expand.

Opportunities
- Blue Sky's loyal consumers are likely to buy new products.
- Gaps exist in the market that can be filled with new products, such as customized clothing items and luggage.
- Blue Sky has a chance to expand across the United States into new markets.
- The firm can reach more consumers via its website.

Threats
- Consumers may tire of the concept; the firm needs to keep it fresh.
- Large competitors such as REI, Timberland, and Patagonia may soak up consumer dollars or launch a similar product line.
- Clothing sales nationwide have generally been flat the past few years.
- Relationships with retailers might deteriorate if they believe they face internal competition in the form of Internet sales.

Leverage | Problems
VULNERABILITIES | CONSTRAINTS

FIGURE A SWOT Analysis for Blue Sky Clothing, Inc.

the products. However, building strong relationships with consumers, retailers, and suppliers should help thwart competitors.

COMPETITORS IN THE OUTDOOR CLOTHING MARKET

The outdoor retail sales industry sells about $5 billion worth of goods annually, ranging from clothing to equipment. The outdoor apparel market has many entries. L.L. Bean, Dick's Sporting Goods, REI, Timberland, Bass Pro Shops, Cabela's, The North Face, and Patagonia are among the most recognizable companies offering these products. Smaller competitors such as Title Nine, which offers athletic clothing for women, and Ragged Mountain, which sells fleece clothing for skiers and hikers, also capture some of the market. The outlook for the industry in general—and Blue Sky in particular—is positive for several reasons. First, consumers are participating in and investing in recreational activities near their homes. Second, consumers are looking for ways to enjoy their leisure time with friends and family without overspending. Third, consumers tend to be advancing in their careers and are able to spend more.

While all of the companies listed earlier can be considered competitors, most of them sell performance apparel in high-tech manufactured fabrics. With the exception of the fleece vests and jackets, Blue Sky's clothing is made strictly of the highest-quality cotton, so it may be worn both on the hiking trail and around town. Finally, Blue Sky products are offered at moderate prices, making them affordable in multiple quantities. For instance, a Blue Sky T-shirt sells for $15.99, compared with a competing high-performance T-shirt that sells for $29.99. Consumers can easily replace a set of shirts from one season to the next, picking up the newest colors, without agonizing over the purchase.

A survey conducted by Blue Sky revealed that a high percentage of responding consumers prefer to replace their casual and active wear more often than other clothing, so they are attracted by the moderate pricing of Blue Sky products. In addition, as the trend toward health-conscious activities and concerns about the natural environment continue, consumers increasingly relate to the Blue Sky philosophy as well as the firm's future contributions to socially responsible programs.

THE TARGET MARKET

The target market for Blue Sky products is active consumers between ages 18 and 39—people who like hiking, rock climbing, bicycling, surfing, figure skating, in-line skating, horseback riding, snowboarding, skiing, kayaking, and other such activities. In short, they like to "Go Play Outside." They might not be experts at the sports they engage in, but they enjoy themselves outdoors.

These active consumers represent a demographic group of well-educated and successful individuals; they are single or married and raising families. Household incomes generally range between $60,000 and $120,000 annually. Despite their comfortable incomes, these consumers are price conscious and consistently seek value in their purchases. Regardless of their age (whether they fall at the upper or lower end of the target range), they lead active lifestyles. They are somewhat status oriented but not overly so. They like to be associated with high-quality products but are not willing to pay a premium price for a certain brand. Current Blue Sky customers tend to live in northern New England, the South, California, and the Northwest. However, one future goal is to target consumers in the Mid-Atlantic states and Southwest as well.

> Blue Sky has identified its customers as active people between ages 18 and 39. However, that doesn't mean someone who is older or prefers to read about the outdoors isn't a potential customer as well. By pinpointing where existing customers live, Blue Sky can plan for growth into new outlets.

THE MARKETING MIX

The following discussion outlines some of the details of the proposed marketing mix for Blue Sky products.

> The strongest part of the marketing mix for Blue Sky involves sales promotions, public relations, and nontraditional marketing strategies, including attending outdoor events and organizing activities such as day hikes and bike rides.

Product Strategy

Blue Sky currently offers a line of high-quality outdoor apparel items, including cotton T-shirts, caps, and fleece vests and jackets. All bear the company logo and slogan, "Go Play Outside." The firm has researched the most popular colors for its items and given them names that consumers enjoy—sunset red, sunrise pink, cactus green, desert rose, and river rock gray, among others. Over the next five years, Blue Sky plans to expand the product line to include customized clothing items. Customers may select a logo that represents their sport—say, rock climbing. Then they can add a slogan to match the logo, such as "Get Over It." A cap with a bicyclist might bear the slogan, "Take a Ride." At the beginning, there would be ten new logos and five new slogans; more would be added later. Eventually, some slogans and logos would be retired and new ones introduced. This strategy will keep the concept fresh and prevent it from becoming diluted with too many variations.

The second way in which Blue Sky plans to expand its product line is to offer lightweight luggage—two sizes of duffel bags, two sizes of tote bags, and a daypack. These items would also come in trendy and basic colors, with a choice of logos and slogans. In addition, every product would bear the Blue Sky logo.

Distribution Strategy

Currently, Blue Sky is marketed through regional and local specialty shops scattered along the California coast, into the Northwest, across the South, and in northern New England. So far, Blue Sky has not been distributed through national sporting goods and apparel chains. Climate and season tend to dictate the sales at specialty shops, which sell more T-shirts and caps during warm weather and more fleece vests and jackets during colder months. Blue Sky obtains much of its information about overall industry trends in different geographic areas and at different types of retail outlets from its trade organization, Outdoor Industry Association.

Over the next three years, Blue Sky seeks to expand distribution to retail specialty shops throughout the nation, focusing next on the Southwest and Mid-Atlantic regions. The firm has not yet determined whether it would be beneficial to sell through a major national chain, as these outlets could be considered competitors.

In addition, Blue Sky plans to expand online sales by offering the customized product line via the Internet only, thus distinguishing between Internet offerings and specialty shop offerings. Eventually, the firm may be able to place Internet kiosks at some of the more profitable store outlets so consumers could order customized products from the stores. Regardless of its expansion plans, Blue Sky fully intends to monitor and maintain strong relationships with distribution channel members.

Promotion Strategy

Blue Sky communicates with consumers and retailers about its products in various ways. Information about Blue Sky—the company as well as its products—is available via the Internet, through social media and direct mailings, and in person. The firm's promotional efforts also seek to differentiate its products from those of its competitors.

The company relies on personal contact with retailers to establish the products in their stores. This contact, whether in person or by phone, helps convey the Blue Sky message, demonstrate the products' unique qualities, and build relationships. Blue Sky sales representatives visit each store two or three times a year and offer in-store training on product features for new retailers or for those who want a refresher session. As distribution expands, Blue Sky will adjust to meet greater demand by increasing sales staff to make sure its stores are visited more frequently.

Sales promotions and public relations currently make up the bulk of Blue Sky's promotional strategy. Blue Sky staff works with retailers to offer short-term sales promotions tied to events and contests that are communicated via social media sites such as Twitter and Facebook. In addition, Nick Russell is currently working with several trip outfitters to offer

Blue Sky items on a promotional basis. Because Blue Sky also engages in cause marketing through its contribution to environmental programs, good public relations have followed.

Nontraditional marketing methods that require little cash and a lot of creativity also lend themselves perfectly to Blue Sky. Because Blue Sky is a small, flexible organization, the firm can easily implement ideas, such as distributing free water, stickers, and discount coupons at outdoor sporting events. During the next year, the company plans to engage in the following marketing efforts:

- Create a Blue Sky Tour, in which several employees take turns driving around the country to campgrounds to distribute promotional items, such as Blue Sky stickers and discount coupons.
- Attend canoe and kayak races, bicycling events, and rock-climbing competitions with our Blue Sky truck to distribute free water, stickers, and discount coupons for Blue Sky shirts or hats.
- Organize Blue Sky hikes departing from participating retailers.
- Hold a Blue Sky design contest on Facebook, selecting a winning slogan and logo to be added to the customized line.

Pricing Strategy

As discussed earlier in this plan, Blue Sky products are priced with the competition in mind. The firm is not concerned with setting high prices to signal luxury or prestige, nor is it attempting to achieve the goals of offsetting low prices by selling large quantities of products. Instead, value pricing is practiced so customers feel comfortable purchasing new clothing to replace the old, even if it is just because they like the new colors. The pricing strategy also makes Blue Sky products good gifts—for birthdays, graduations, or "just because." The customized clothing will sell for $2 to $4 more than the regular Blue Sky logo clothing. The luggage will be priced competitively.

BUDGET, SCHEDULE, AND MONITORING

Though its history is short, Blue Sky has enjoyed a steady increase in sales since its introduction three years ago. Figure B shows these three years, plus projected sales for the next three years, including the introduction of the two new product lines. Additional financial data are included in the overall business plan for the company.

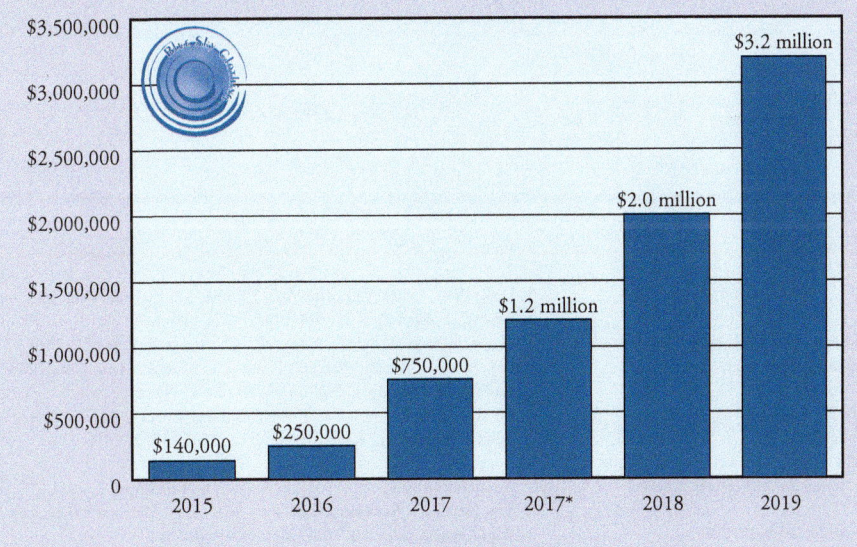

Year	Sales
2015	$140,000
2016	$250,000
2017	$750,000
2017*	$1.2 million
2018	$2.0 million
2019	$3.2 million

*Projected sales

FIGURE B Annual Sales for Blue Sky Clothing: 2015–2019

> An actual plan will include more specific financial details, which will be folded into the overall business plan. For more information, see Appendix B, "Financial Analysis in Marketing." In addition, Blue Sky states that at this stage, it does not have plans to exit the market by merging with another firm or making a public stock offering.

The timeline for expansion of outlets and introduction of the two new product lines is shown in Figure C. The implementation of each of these tasks will be monitored closely and evaluated for its performance.

Blue Sky anticipates continuing operations into the foreseeable future, with no plans to exit this market. Instead, as discussed throughout this plan, the firm plans to increase its presence in the market. At present, there are no plans to merge with another company or to make a public stock offering.

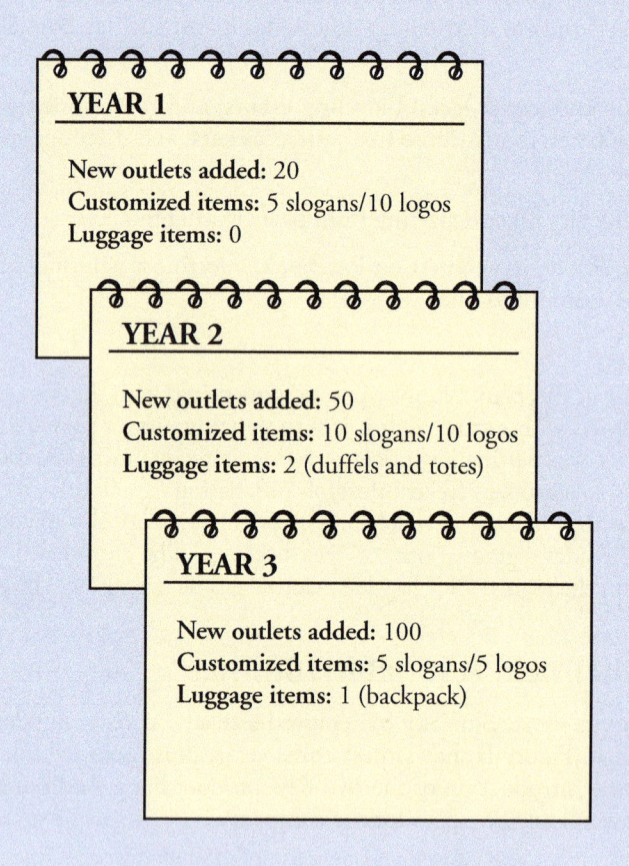

YEAR 1

New outlets added: 20
Customized items: 5 slogans/10 logos
Luggage items: 0

YEAR 2

New outlets added: 50
Customized items: 10 slogans/10 logos
Luggage items: 2 (duffels and totes)

YEAR 3

New outlets added: 100
Customized items: 5 slogans/5 logos
Luggage items: 1 (backpack)

FIGURE C
Timeline for First Three Years of Marketing Plan

NOTES

1. Company website, "Our Products and Services," www.google.com, accessed April 1, 2014.
2. Company website, www.terracycle.net, accessed April 1, 2014; "TerraCycle to Recycle Cigarette Waste," *Consumer Goods*, accessed April 1, 2014, http://consumergoods.edge.com.
3. Company website, www.nintendo.com, accessed April 1, 2014.
4. Clare O'Connor, "Red State Voters Back Minimum Wage Hike As San Francisco Approves $15," *Forbes*, accessed November 7, 2014, www.forbes.com; Aaron Taube, "Why Costco Pays Its Retail Employees $20 an Hour," *Business Insider*, accessed November 7, 2014, www.businessinsider.com.
5. Company website, http://c2educate.com, accessed November 7, 2014.
6. Leslie Price, "Mickey Drexler Vows J. Crew Will Be Less Pricey This Spring," *Racked*, accessed April 2, 2014, http://racked.com.
7. Company website, http://cuteoverload.com, accessed April 2, 2014.
8. E. J. Schultz, "Weight Watchers Picks a New Target: Men," *Crain's New York Business*, accessed April 2, 2014, www.crainsnewyork.com.
9. Eric Faulkner, "Want to See 'Frozen' for Free? Check Out This Disney Movie Reward Promotion," *Rotoscopers.com*, accessed April 2, 2014, www.rotoscopers.com.
10. Company website, http://www.ghfc.com, accessed April 2, 2014.
11. Tim Hornyak, "Sayonara, Vaio: Sony Sells off PC Business to Focus on Mobile," *PC World*, accessed April 6, 2014, www.pcworld.com.

Financial Analysis in Marketing

APPENDIX B

A number of principles from accounting and finance offer valuable tools to marketers. Understanding the contributions made by these concepts can improve the quality of marketing decisions. In addition, marketers often must be able to explain and defend their decisions in financial terms. These accounting and financial tools can be used to supply quantitative data to justify decisions made by marketing managers. In this appendix, we describe the major accounting and finance concepts that have marketing implications and explain how they help managers make informed marketing decisions.

FINANCIAL STATEMENTS

Companies prepare a set of financial statements on a regular basis. Two of the most important financial statements are the income statement and balance sheet. The analogy of photography is often used to describe an *income statement*, because it presents an overall picture of a financial record of a company's revenues, expenses, and profits over a period of time, such as a month, quarter, or year. By contrast, the *balance sheet* is a snapshot of what a company owns (called *assets*) and what it owes (called *liabilities*) at a point in time, such as at the end of the month, quarter, or year. The difference between assets and liabilities is referred to as *owner's, partners', or shareholders' equity*—the amount of funds the firm's owners have invested in its formation and continued operations. Of the two financial statements, the income statement contains more marketing-related information.

A sample income statement for Worthy Composites is shown in Figure B.1. Headquartered in Baltimore, Maryland, Worthy Composites is a B2B producer and marketer. The firm designs and manufactures various composite components for manufacturers of consumer, industrial, and government products. Total sales revenues for 2016 amounted to $675.0 million. Total expenses, including taxes, for the year were $583.1 million. The year 2016 proved profitable for Worthy Composites—the firm reported a profit, referred to as net income, of $91.9 million. While total revenue is a fairly straightforward number, several of the expenses shown on the income statement require additional explanation.

For any company that makes its own products (a manufacturer) or simply markets one or more items produced by others (an importer, retailer, or wholesaler), the largest single expense usually is a category called *cost of goods sold*. This reflects the cost, to the firm, of the goods it markets to its customers. In the case of Worthy Composites, the cost of goods sold represents the cost of components and raw materials as well as the cost of designing and manufacturing the composite panels the firm produces and markets to its business customers.

The income statement illustrates how cost of goods sold is calculated. The calculation uses the value of the firm's inventory at the beginning of 2016. Inventory is the value of raw materials, partially completed products, and finished products held by the firm at the end of some period—say, the end of the year. The cost of materials Worthy Composites purchased during the year and the direct cost of manufacturing the finished products are then added to the beginning inventory figure. The result is the cost of goods the firm has available for sale during the year. Once the firm's accountants subtract the value of inventory held at the end of 2016, they know the cost of goods sold. By simply subtracting cost of goods sold from total sales revenues generated during the year, they determine that Worthy achieved gross income of $270 million in 2016.

B-1

FIGURE B.1
Worthy Composites 2016 Income Statement

Worthy Composites, Inc.
2893 Fitzgerald Parkway
Baltimore, MD 21216

WCI

INCOME STATEMENT
For the Year Ended December 31, 2016
(in $ millions)

Sales	675.0
Cost of Goods Sold	405.0
Gross Income	270.0
Selling, Administrative, and General Expenses	82.1
Research and Development Expenses	25.4
Operating Income	162.5
Depreciation	18.6
Net Interest Expense	2.5
Before-tax Income	141.4
Provision for Income Taxes	49.5
Net Income	91.9

Cost of Goods Sold Calculation

Beginning Inventory	158.0
plus Raw Materials Purchased	200.7
plus Direct Manufacturing Expenses	226.3
Total Cost of Goods	585.0
minus Ending Inventory	(180.0)
Cost of Goods Sold	405.0

Operating expenses are another significant cost for most firms. This broad category includes marketing outlays such as sales compensation and expenses, advertising and other promotions, and the expenses involved in implementing marketing plans. Accountants typically combine these financial outlays into a single category with the label *Selling, Administrative, and General Expenses.* Other expense items included in the operating expenses section of the income statement are administrative salaries, utilities, and insurance.

Another significant expense for Worthy Composites is research and development (R&D). This category includes the cost of developing new products and modifying existing ones. Firms such as pharmaceuticals, biotechnology, and computer companies spend significant amounts of money each year on R&D. Subtracting R&D, selling, administrative, and general expenses from the gross profit equals the firm's operating income. For 2016, Worthy had operating income of $162.5 million.

Depreciation represents the systematic reduction over time in the value of certain company assets, such as production machinery or office furniture. Depreciation is an unusual expense, because it does not involve an actual cash expense. However, it does reflect the reality that equipment owned by the company is physically wearing out over time from use or from technological obsolescence. Also, charging a portion of the total cost of these long-lived items to each of the years in which they are used results in a more accurate determination of the total costs involved in the firm's operation each year.

Net interest expense is the difference between what a firm paid in interest on various loans and what it collected in interest on investments it might have made during the time period involved. Subtracting depreciation and net interest expense from the firm's operating profit reveals the firm's taxable income. Worthy had depreciation of $18.6 million and a net interest expense of $2.5 million for the year, so its 2016 taxable income was $141.4 million.

Profit-seeking firms pay taxes calculated as a percentage of their taxable income to the federal government as well as state income taxes in most states. Worthy paid $49.5 million in taxes in 2016. Subtracting taxes from taxable income gives us the firm's *net income,* $91.9 million.

PERFORMANCE RATIOS

Managers often compute various financial ratios to assess the performance of their firm. These ratios are calculated using data found on both the income statement and the balance sheet. Ratios are then compared with industry standards and with data from previous years. Several ratios are of particular interest to marketers.

A number of commonly used financial ratios focus on *profitability measures*. They are used to assess the firm's ability to generate revenues in excess of expenses and earn an adequate rate of return. Profitability measures include gross profit margin, net profit margin, and return on investment (or sales).

Gross Profit Margin

The gross profit margin equals the firm's gross profit divided by its sales revenues. In 2016, Worthy had a gross profit margin of

$$\frac{\text{Gross profit}}{\text{Sales}} = \frac{\$270.0 \text{ million}}{\$675.0 \text{ million}} = 40\%$$

The gross profit margin is the percentage of each sales dollar that can be used to pay other expenses and meet the firm's profit objectives. Ideally, businesses would like to see gross profit margins equal to or higher than those of other firms in their industry. A declining gross profit margin may indicate the firm is under some competitive price pressure.

Net Profit Margin

The net profit margin equals net income divided by sales. For 2016, Worthy had a net profit margin of

$$\frac{\text{Net income}}{\text{Sales}} = \frac{\$91.9 \text{ million}}{\$675.0 \text{ million}} = 13.6\%$$

The net profit margin is the percentage of each sales dollar the firm earns in profit or keeps after all expenses have been paid. Companies generally want to see rising, or at least stable, net profit margins.

Return on Assets (ROA)

A third profitability ratio, return on assets, measures the firm's efficiency in generating sales and profits from the total amount invested in the company. For 2016, Worthy's ROA is calculated as follows:

$$\frac{\text{Sales}}{\text{Average assets}} \times \frac{\text{Net income}}{\text{Sales}} = \frac{\text{Net income}}{\text{Average assets}}$$

$$\frac{\$675.0 \text{ million}}{\$595.0 \text{ million}} \times \frac{\$91.9 \text{ million}}{\$675.0 \text{ million}} = 1.13 \times 13.6\% = 15.4\%$$

The ROA ratio actually consists of two components. The first component, *asset turnover*, is the amount of sales generated for each dollar invested. The second component is *net profit margin*. Data for total assets are found on the firm's balance sheet.

Assume Worthy began the year with $560 million in assets and ended the year with $630 million in assets. Its average assets for the year would be $595 million. As in the other profitability ratios, Worthy's ROA should be compared with other firms in the industry and with its own previous performance to be meaningful.

Inventory Turnover

Inventory turnover typically is categorized as an activity ratio, because it evaluates the effectiveness of the firm's resource use. Specifically, it measures the number of times a firm "turns" its inventory each year. The ratio can help answer the question of whether the firm has the appropriate level of inventory. Inventory turnover equals sales divided by average inventory. From the income statement, we see Worthy Composites began 2016 with $158 million in inventory and ended the year with $180 million in inventory. Therefore, the firm's average inventory was $169 million. The firm's inventory turnover ratio equals:

$$\frac{\text{Sales}}{\text{Average inventory}} = \frac{\$675.0 \text{ million}}{\$169.0 \text{ million}} = 3.99$$

For 2016, Worthy Composites turned its inventory almost four times a year. While a faster inventory turn is usually a sign of greater efficiency, to be really meaningful, the inventory turnover ratio must be compared with historical data and appropriate peer firm averages. Different organizations can have very different inventory turnover ratios, depending on the types of products they sell. For instance, a supermarket might turn its inventory every three weeks for an annual rate of roughly 17 times per year. By contrast, a large furniture retailer is likely to average only about two turns per year. Again, the determination of a "good" or "inadequate" inventory turnover rate depends on typical rates in the industry and the firm's performance in previous years.

Accounts Receivable Turnover

Another activity ratio that may be of interest to marketers is accounts receivable turnover. This ratio measures the number of times per year a company turns its receivables. Dividing accounts receivable turnover into 365 gives us the average age of the company's receivables.

Companies make sales on the basis of either cash or credit. Credit sales allow the buyer to obtain a product now and pay for it at a specified later date. In essence, the seller is providing credit to the buyer. Credit sales are common in B2B transactions. It should be noted that sales to buyers using credit cards such as MasterCard and Visa are counted as cash sales, because the issuer of the credit card, rather than the seller, is providing credit to the buyer. Consequently, most B2C sales are counted as cash sales.

Receivables are uncollected credit sales. Measuring accounts receivable turnover and the average age of receivables are important for firms in which credit sales make up a high proportion of total sales. Accounts receivable turnover is defined as follows:

$$\text{Accounts receivable turnover} = \frac{\text{Credit sales}}{\text{Average accounts receivable}}$$

Assume all of Worthy Composites' sales are credit sales. Also, assume the firm began 2016 with $50 million in receivables and ended the year with $60 million in receivables (both numbers can be found on the balance sheet). Therefore, it had an average of $55 million in receivables. The firm's receivables turnover and average age equal:

$$\frac{\$675.0 \text{ million}}{\$55.0 \text{ million}} = 12.3 \text{ times}$$

$$\frac{365}{12.3} = 29.7 \text{ days}$$

Worthy turned its receivables slightly more than 12 times per year. The average age of its receivables was slightly less than 30 days. Because Worthy expects its customers to pay outstanding invoices within 30 days, these numbers appear appropriate. As with other ratios, however, receivables turnover and average age of receivables should also be compared with peer firms and historical data.

MARKUPS AND MARKDOWNS

The importance of pricing decisions was discussed earlier. This section expands on the prior comments by introducing two important pricing concepts: markups and markdowns. They can help establish selling prices and evaluate various pricing strategies, and they are closely tied to a firm's income statement.

Markups

The amount a marketer adds to a product's cost to set the final selling price is the markup. The amount of the markup typically results from two marketing decisions:

1. The services performed by the marketer. Other things being equal, retailers who offer more services charge larger markups to cover their costs.
2. The inventory turnover rate. Other things being equal, retailers with a higher turnover rate can cover their costs and earn a profit while charging a smaller markup.

A company's markup exerts an important influence on its image among current and potential customers. In addition, the markup affects the retailer's ability to attract shoppers. An excessive markup may drive away customers; an inadequate markup may fail to generate sufficient income to cover costs and return a profit.

Markups are typically stated as percentages of either the selling prices or the costs of the products. The formulas for calculating markups are as follows:

$$\text{Markup percentage of selling price} = \frac{\text{Amount added to cost (markup)}}{\text{Selling price}}$$

$$\text{Markup percentage on cost} = \frac{\text{Amount added to cost (markup)}}{\text{Cost}}$$

Consider a product with an invoice of 60¢ and a selling price of $1. The total markup (selling price less cost) is 40¢. The two markup percentages are calculated as follows:

$$\text{Markup percentage on selling price} = \frac{\$0.40}{\$1.00} = 40\%$$

$$\text{Markup percentage on cost} = \frac{\$0.40}{\$0.60} = 66.7\%$$

To determine the selling price knowing only the cost and markup percentage on selling price, a marketer applies the following formula:

$$\text{Price} = \frac{\text{Cost in dollars}}{(100\% - \text{Markup percentage on selling price})}$$

In the previous example, to determine the correct selling price of $1, the marketer would calculate as follows:

$$\text{Price} = \frac{\$0.60}{(100\% - 40\%)} = \$1.00$$

Similarly, you can convert the markup percentage from a specific item based on the selling price to one based on cost, and the reverse, using the following formulas:

$$\text{Markup percentage on selling price} = \frac{\text{Markup percentage on cost}}{(100\% + \text{Markup percentage on cost})}$$

$$\text{Markup percentage on cost} = \frac{\text{Markup percentage on selling price}}{(100\% - \text{Markup percentage on selling price})}$$

Again, data from the previous example give the following conversions:

$$\text{Markup percentage on selling price} = \frac{6.7\%}{(100\% + 66.7\%)} = 40\%$$

$$\text{Markup percentage on cost} = \frac{40\%}{(100\% - 40\%)} = 66.7\%$$

Marketers determine markups based partly on their judgments of the amounts consumers will pay for a given product. When buyers refuse to pay a product's stated price, however, or when improvements in other products or fashion changes reduce the appeal of the current merchandise, a producer or retailer must take a markdown.

MARKDOWNS

A markdown is a price reduction a firm takes on an item. Reasons for markdowns include sales promotions featuring price reductions on seasonal merchandise or a decision that the initial price was too high. Unlike markups, markdowns cannot be determined from the income statement, because the price reduction takes place before the sale occurs. The markdown percentage equals dollar markdowns divided by sales. For example, a retailer may decide to reduce the price of an item by $10, from $50 to $40, and sells 1,000 units. The markdown percentage equals:

$$\frac{(1{,}000 \times \$10)}{(1{,}000 \times \$40)} = \frac{\$10{,}000}{\$40{,}000} = 25\%$$

GLOSSARY

80/20 principle Generally accepted rule that 80 percent of a product's revenues come from 20 percent of its customers.

A

accessory equipment Capital items, such as desktop computers and printers, that typically cost less and last for shorter periods than installations.

administered marketing system VMS that achieves channel coordination when a dominant channel member exercises its power.

adoption process Stages consumers go through in learning about a new product, trying it, and deciding whether to purchase it again.

Advertising Paid, nonpersonal communication through various media about a business firm, not-for-profit organization, product, or idea by a sponsor identified in a message intended to inform or persuade members of a particular audience.

advertising campaign Series of different but related ads that use a single theme and appear in different media within a specified time period.

affinity marketing Marketing effort sponsored by an organization that solicits responses from individuals who share common interests and activities.

AIDA concept Steps through which an individual reaches a purchase decision: attention, interest, desire, and action.

AIO statements Items on lifestyle surveys that describe various activities, interests, and respondents' opinions.

Allowances Specified deduction from list price, including a trade-in or promotional allowance.

antitrust Laws designed to prevent restraints on trade such as business monopolies.

app Short for application, a free or purchased software download that links users to a wide range of goods and services, media and text content, social media platforms, search engines, and the like.

approach Salesperson's initial contact with a prospective customer.

atmospherics Combination of physical characteristics and amenities that contribute to a store's image.

Attitudes Person's enduring favorable or unfavorable evaluations, emotions, or action tendencies toward some object or idea.

Average total costs Cost calculated by dividing the sum of the variable and fixed costs by the number of units produced.

B

Backward integration Process through which a manufacturer attempts to gain greater control over inputs in its production process, such as raw materials.

Banner ads Strip message placed in high-visibility areas of frequently visited websites.

basing-point pricing System used in some industries during the early 20th century in which the buyer paid the factory price plus freight charges from the basing-point city nearest the buyer.

benchmarking Method of measuring quality by comparing performance against industry leaders.

big data Fueled by 21st century technological advances, the vast and unprecedented volume, speed, and array of data available for informed decision making.

blog Short for Web log, an online journal for an individual or organization.

blogging sites A platform where a host or writer posts information or opinions on various topics and followers may respond.

bonus pack Specially packaged item that gives the purchaser a larger quantity at the regular price.

Bookmarking A platform that gives users a place to save, organize, and manage links to websites and other Internet resources.

bots Software program that allows online shoppers to compare prices of a particular product offered by several online retailers.

Bots (shopbots) Software program that allows online shoppers to compare the price of a particular product offered by several online retailers.

bottom line Reference to overall company profitability.

brand Name, term, sign, symbol, design, or some combination that identifies the products of one firm while differentiating them from those of the competition.

Brand equity Added value that a respected, well-known brand name gives to a product in the marketplace.

brand extension Strategy of attaching a popular brand name to a new product in an unrelated product category.

Brand insistence Consumer refusal of alternatives and extensive search for desired merchandise.

brand licensing Practice that expands a firm's exposure in the marketplace.

brand manager Marketer responsible for a single brand.

brand mark Symbol or pictorial design that distinguishes a product.

brand name Part of a brand, consisting of letters, numbers, or words, that can be spoken and that identifies and distinguishes a firm's offerings from those of its competitors.

brand preference Consumer choice of a product on the basis of a previous experience.

Brand recognition Consumer awareness and identification of a brand.

Breakeven analysis Pricing technique used to determine the number of products that must be sold at a specified price to generate enough revenue to cover total cost.

Brokers Agent wholesaling intermediary that does not take title to or possession of goods in the course of its primary function, which is to bring together buyers and sellers.

bundle pricing Offering two or more complementary products and selling them for a single price.

G-1

business cycle Pattern of stages in the level of economic activity: prosperity, recession, depression, and recovery.

Business products Goods and services purchased for use either directly or indirectly in the production of other goods and services for resale.

business services Intangible products firms buy to facilitate their production and operating processes.

Business-to-business (B2B) e-marketing Use of the Internet for business transactions between organizations.

Business-to-business (B2B) marketing Organizational sales and purchases of goods and services to support production of other products, to facilitate daily company operations, or for resale.

business-to-business (B2B) products Product that contributes directly or indirectly to the output of other products for resale; also called industrial or organizational product.

business-to-consumer (B2C) e-marketing Selling directly to consumers over the Internet.

Business-to-consumer (B2C) products Product destined for use by ultimate consumers.

buyer Person who has the formal authority to select a supplier and to implement the procedures for securing a good or service.

buyer partnership Relationship in which a firm purchases goods and services from one or more providers.

buyer's market A market in which there are more goods and services than people willing to buy them.

buying center Participants in an organizational buying decision.

Buzz marketing Marketing that gathers volunteers to try products and then relies on them to talk about their experiences with their friends and colleagues.

C

cannibalization Loss of sales of an existing product due to competition from a new product in the same line.

cannibalization Loss of sales of an existing product due to competition from a new product in the same line.

captive brands National brand sold exclusively by a retail chain.

cash discounts Price reduction offered to a consumer, business user, or marketing intermediary in return for prompt payment of a bill.

category advisor or category captain Trade industry vendor who develops a comprehensive procurement plan for a retail buyer.

category killer Store offering huge selections and low prices in single product lines.

category management Product management system in which a category manager—with profit and loss responsibility—oversees a product line.

cause marketing Identification and marketing of a social issue, cause, or idea to selected target markets.

Central American Free Trade Agreement-DR (CAFTA-DR) Trade agreement among the United States, Central American nations, and the Dominican Republic.

channel captain Dominant and controlling member of a marketing channel.

channel conflicts Conflicts among manufacturers, wholesalers, and retailers.

channel distribution System of marketing institutions that enhances the physical flow of goods and services, along with ownership title, from producer to consumer or business user.

click-through rates Percentage of people presented with a banner ad who click on it.

closed sales territories Exclusive geographic selling region of a distributor.

closing Stage of the personal selling process in which the salesperson asks the customer to make a purchase decision.

cluster sample Probability sample in which researchers select a sample of subgroups (or clusters) from which they draw respondents; each cluster reflects the diversity of the whole population sampled.

Cobranding Cooperative arrangement in which two or more businesses team up to closely link their names on a single product.

cognitive dissonance Imbalance among knowledge, beliefs, and attitudes that occurs after an action or decision, such as a purchase.

cohort effect Tendency of members of a generation to be influenced and bound together by events occurring during their key formative years—roughly ages 17 to 22.

cold calling Contacting a prospect without a prior appointment.

collaborative planning, forecasting, and replenishment (CPFR) Planning and forecasting approach based on collaboration between buyers and sellers.

comarketing Cooperative arrangement in which two or more businesses jointly market each other's products.

commercial market Individuals and firms that acquire products to support, directly or indirectly, production of other goods and services.

commission Incentive compensation directly related to the sales or profits achieved by a salesperson.

Commission merchants Agent wholesaling intermediary that takes possession of goods shipped to a central market for sale, acts as the producer's agent, and collects an agreed-upon fee at the time of the sale.

Common carriers Businesses that provide transportation services as for-hire carriers to the general public.

common market Extension of a customs union by seeking to reconcile all government regulations affecting trade.

comparative advertising Advertising strategy that emphasizes messages with direct or indirect promotional comparisons between competing brands.

competitive bidding Inviting potential suppliers to quote prices on proposed purchases or contracts.

competitive environment Interactive process that occurs in the marketplace among marketers of directly competitive products, marketers of products that can be substituted for one another, and marketers competing for the consumer's purchasing power.

competitive pricing strategies Pricing strategy designed to deemphasize price as a competitive variable by pricing a good or service at the level of comparable offerings.

competitive strategy Methods through which a firm deals with its competitive environment.

component parts and materials Finished business products of one producer that become part of the final products of another producer.

concentrated marketing Focusing marketing efforts on satisfying a single market segment.

Concept testing Method for subjecting a product idea to additional study before actual development by involving consumers through focus groups, surveys, in-store polling, and similar strategies.

consolidated metropolitan statistical area (CMSA) Urban area that includes two or more PMSAs.

consultative selling Meeting customer needs by listening to them, understanding their problems, paying attention to details, and following through after the sale.

Consumer behavior Process through which buyers make purchase decisions.

consumer innovators Someone who purchases a new product almost as soon as the product reaches the market.

consumer orientation Business philosophy incorporating the marketing concept that emphasizes first determining unmet consumer needs and then designing a system for satisfying them.

Consumer products Products bought by ultimate consumers for personal use.

consumer rights List of legitimate consumer expectations suggested by President John F. Kennedy.

consumerism Social force within the environment that aids and protects the consumer by exerting legal, moral, and economic pressures on business and government.

containerization Process of combining several unitized loads into a single, well-protected load for shipment.

Content marketing Creating and distributing relevant and targeted material to attract and engage an audience, with the goal of driving them to a desired action.

Contests Sales promotion technique that requires entrants to complete a task, such as solving a puzzle or answering questions on a quiz, for a chance to win a prize.

Contract carriers For-hire transporters that do not offer their services to the general public.

contractual marketing system VMS that coordinates channel activities through formal agreements among participants.

controlled experiment Scientific investigation in which a researcher manipulates a test group and compares the results with those of a control group that did not receive the experimental controls or manipulations.

Convenience products Goods and services consumers want to purchase frequently, immediately, and with minimal effort.

Convenience retailers Store that appeals to customers by having an accessible location, long hours, rapid checkout, and adequate parking.

convenience sample Nonprobability sample selected from among readily available respondents.

conversion rate Percentage of visitors to a website who make a purchase.

cooperative advertising Strategy in which a retailer shares advertising costs with a manufacturer or wholesaler.

core based statistical area (CBSA) Collective term for metropolitan and micropolitan statistical areas.

core regions Region from which most major brands get 40 to 80 percent of their sales.

corporate marketing system VMS in which a single owner operates the entire marketing channel.

corporate websites Site designed to increase a firm's visibility, promote its offerings, and provide information to interested parties.

Cost-plus pricing Practice of adding a percentage of specified dollar amount—or markup—to the base cost of a product to cover unassigned costs and to provide a profit.

countertrade Form of exporting whereby goods and services are bartered rather than sold for cash.

Coupons Sales promotion technique that offers a discount on the purchase price of goods or services.

creative selling Personal selling in which salespeople use well-planned strategies to seek new customers by proposing innovative solutions to customers' needs.

cross-promotion Promotional technique in which marketing partners share the cost of a promotional campaign that meets their mutual needs.

Cross-selling Selling multiple, often unrelated, goods and services to the same customer based on knowledge of that customer's needs.

Culture Values, beliefs, preferences, and tastes handed down from one generation to the next.

Cumulative quantity discounts Price discount determined by amounts of purchases over stated time periods.

Customary prices Traditional prices that customers expect to pay for certain goods and services.

customer churn Turnover in a company's customer base.

customer relationship management (CRM) Combination of strategies and tools that drives relationship programs, reorienting the entire organization to a concentrated focus on satisfying customers.

customer relationship management (CRM) Combination of strategies and tools that drives relationship programs, reorienting the entire organization to a concentrated focus on satisfying customers.

customer satisfaction Extent to which customers are satisfied with their purchases.

customer win-back Process of rejuvenating lost relationships with customers.

Customer-based segmentation Dividing a business-to-business market into homogeneous groups based on buyers' product specifications.

customs union Establishment of a free-trade area plus a uniform tariff for trade with nonmember unions.

D

Data mining Technique in which a user employs special software to search through computerized data files to detect patterns.

database marketing Use of software to analyze marketing information, identifying and targeting messages toward specific groups of potential customers.

decider Person who chooses a good or service, although another person may have the formal authority to complete the sale.

decline stage Final stage of the product lifecycle, in which a decline in total industry sales occurs.

Delphi technique Qualitative sales forecasting method that gathers and redistributes several rounds of anonymous forecasts until the participants reach a consensus.

Demand Schedule of the amounts of a firm's product that consumers will purchase at different prices during a specified time period.

demarketing Process of reducing consumer demand for a good or service to a level that the firm can supply.

demographic segmentation Division of an overall market into homogeneous groups based on variables such as gender, age, income, occupation, education, sexual orientation, household size, and stage in the family lifecycle; also called socioeconomic segmentation.

demonstration Stage in the personal selling process in which the customer has the opportunity to try out or otherwise see how a good or service works before purchase.

department store Large store that handles a variety of merchandise, including clothing, household goods, appliances, and furniture.

Derived demand Demand for a resource that results from demand for the goods and services produced by that resource.

differentiated marketing Strategy that focuses on producing several products and pricing, promoting, and distributing them with different marketing mixes designed to satisfy smaller segments.

diffusion process Process by which new goods or services are accepted in the marketplace.

direct channel Marketing channel that moves goods directly from a producer to the business purchaser or ultimate user.

Direct marketing Direct communications, other than personal sales contacts, between buyer and seller, designed to generate sales, information requests, or store or website visits.

direct marketing Direct communications, other than personal sales contacts, between buyer and seller, designed to generate sales, information requests, or store or website visits.

direct selling Strategy designed to establish direct sales contact between producer and final user.

discount house Store that charges low prices but may not offer some services.

discretionary income Money available to spend after buying necessities such as food, clothing, and housing.

Distribution Movement of goods and services from producers to customers.

Downstream management Controlling part of the supply chain that involves finished product storage, outbound logistics, marketing and sales, and customer service.

drop shipper Limited-function merchant wholesaler that accepts orders from customers and forwards those orders to producers, which then ship directly to the buyers.

Dual distribution Network that moves products to a firm's target market through more than one marketing channel.

dumping Controversial practice of selling a product in a foreign market at a price lower than what it receives in the producer's domestic market.

E

e-business Conducting online transactions with customers by collecting and analyzing business information, carrying out the exchanges, and maintaining online relationships with customers.

economic environment Factors that influence consumer buying power and marketing strategies, including stage of the business cycle, inflation and deflation, unemployment, income, and resource availability.

Elasticity Measure of responsiveness of purchasers and suppliers to a change in price.

electronic data interchanges (EDIs) Computer-to-computer exchanges of invoices, orders, and other business documents.

electronic shopping cart File that holds items the online shopper has chosen to buy.

electronic signatures Electronic identification that allows legal contracts such as home mortgages and insurance policies to be executed online.

electronic storefronts Company websites that sell products to customers.

e-marketing Strategic process of creating, distributing, promoting, and pricing goods and services to a target market over the Internet or through digital tools.

embargo Complete ban on the import of specified products.

Emergency goods and services Products bought in response to unexpected and urgent needs.

Employee satisfaction Employee's level of satisfaction in his or her company and the extent to which that loyalty—or lack thereof—is communicated to external customers.

Encryption The process of encoding data for security purposes.

end-use application segmentation The division of a business-to-business market based on how industrial purchasers will use the product.

engagement Amount of time users spend on sites.

Engel's laws Three observations about the impact of household income on consumer spending behavior: as household income increases, a smaller percentage of expenditures goes for food; the percentage spent on housing, household operations, and clothing remains constant; and the percentage spent on other items (such as recreation and education) increases.

enterprise resource planning (ERP) system Software system that consolidates data from among a firm's various business units.

environmental management Attainment of organizational objectives by predicting and influencing the competitive, political–legal, economic, technological, and social–cultural environments.

Environmental scanning Process of collecting information about the external marketing environment to identify and interpret potential trends.

e-procurement Use of the Internet by organizations to solicit bids and purchase goods and services from suppliers.

Ethics Moral standards of behavior expected by a society.

European Union (EU) Customs union that is moving in the direction of an economic union by adopting a common currency, removing trade restrictions, and permitting free flow of goods and workers throughout the member nations.

Evaluative criteria Features a consumer considers in choosing among alternatives.

Event marketing Marketing of sporting, cultural, and charitable activities to selected target markets.

everyday low pricing (EDLP) Pricing strategy of continuously offering low prices rather than relying on short-term price cuts such as cents-off coupons, rebates, and special sales.

evoked set Number of alternatives a consumer actually considers in making a purchase decision.

Exchange control Method used to regulate international trade among importing organizations by controlling access to foreign currencies.

exchange functions Buying and selling.

exchange process Activity in which two or more parties give something of value to each other to satisfy perceived needs.

exchange rate Price of one nation's currency in terms of another country's currency.

exclusive distribution Distribution of a product through a single wholesaler or retailer in a specific geographic region.

expectancy theory Theory that motivation depends on an individual's expectations of his or her ability to perform a job and how that performance relates to attaining a desired reward.

Exploratory research Process of discussing a marketing problem with informed sources both within and outside the firm and examining information from secondary sources.

exponential smoothing Quantitative forecasting technique that assigns weights to historical sales data, giving the greatest weight to the most recent data.

exporting Marketing domestically produced goods and services in foreign countries.

external customers People or organizations that buy or use a firm's goods or services.

F

Fair-trade laws Statutes enacted in most states that once permitted manufacturers to stipulate a minimum retail price for their product.

family brand Single brand name that identifies several related products.

family lifecycle Process of family formation and dissolution.

Field selling Sales presentations made at prospective customers' locations on a face-to-face basis.

firewall Electronic barrier between a company's internal network and the Internet that limits access into and out of the network.

first mover strategy Theory advocating that the company first to offer a product in a marketplace will be the long-term market winner.

fixed costs Cost that remains stable at any production level within a certain range (such as a lease payment or insurance cost).

FOB (free on board) plant Price quotation that does not include shipping charges.

FOB origin Price quotation that does not include shipping charges.

FOB origin-freight allowed Price quotation system that allows the buyer to deduct shipping expenses from the cost of purchases.

focus group Small group of individuals brought together to discuss a specific topic.

follow-up Post-sale activities that often determine whether an individual who has made a recent purchase will become a repeat customer.

foreign licensing Agreement that grants foreign marketers the right to distribute a firm's merchandise or to use its trademark, patent, or process in a specified geographic area.

forward integration Process through which a firm attempts to control downstream distribution.

franchise Contractual arrangement in which a wholesaler or retailer agrees to meet the operating requirements of a manufacturer or other franchiser.

franchise Contractual arrangement in which a wholesaler or retailer agrees to meet the operating requirements of a manufacturer or other franchiser.

Free Trade Area of the Americas (FTAA) Proposed free-trade area stretching the length of the entire Western Hemisphere and designed to extend free trade benefits to additional nations in North, Central, and South America.

free-trade area Region in which participating nations agree to the free trade of goods among themselves, abolishing tariffs and trade restrictions.

freight absorbed Price quotation system that allows the buyer to deduct shipping expenses from the cost of purchases.

frequency marketing Frequent-buyer or -user marketing programs that reward customers with cash, rebates, merchandise, or other premiums.

friendship, commerce, and navigation (FCN) treaties International agreements that deal with many aspects of commercial relations among nations.

Full-cost pricing Pricing method that uses all relevant variable costs in setting a product's price and allocates those fixed costs not directly attributed to the production of the priced item.

full-service research supplier Marketing research organization that offers all aspects of the marketing research process.

G

Gatekeepers Person who controls the information that all buying center members will review.

General Agreement on Tariffs and Trade (GATT) International trade accord that has helped reduce world tariffs.

General merchandise retailers Store that carries a wide variety of product lines.

generic products Products characterized by plain labels, no advertising, and the absence of brand names.

geographic information systems (GISs) Software packages that assemble, store, manipulate, and display data by their location.

geographic segmentation Division of an overall market into homogeneous groups based on their locations.

global marketing strategy Standardized marketing mix with minimal modifications that a firm uses in all of its domestic and foreign markets.

global sourcing Purchasing goods and services from suppliers worldwide.

goods Tangible products customers can see, hear, smell, taste, or touch.

goods–services continuum Spectrum along which goods and services fall according to their attributes, from pure good to pure service.

Grassroots marketing Efforts that connect directly with existing and potential customers through non-mainstream channels.

gray goods Products manufactured abroad under license from a U.S. firm and then sold in the U.S. market in competition with that firm's own domestic output.

green marketing Production, promotion, and reclamation of environmentally sensitive products.

gross domestic product (GDP) Sum of all goods and services produced by a nation in a year.

growth stage Second stage of the product lifecycle that begins when a firm starts to realize substantial profits from its investment in a product.

Guerrilla marketing Unconventional, innovative, and low-cost marketing techniques designed to get consumers' attention in unusual ways.

H

high-involvement purchase decisions Purchases with high levels of potential social or economic consequences.

homeshoring Hiring workers to do jobs from their homes.

hypermarkets Giant one-stop shopping facility offering wide selections of grocery items and general merchandise at discount prices, typically filling up 200,000 or more square feet of selling space.

hypothesis Tentative explanation for a specific event.

I

Import quotas Trade restrictions limiting the number of units of certain goods that can enter a country for resale.

importing Purchasing foreign goods and services.

Impulse goods and services Products purchased on the spur of the moment.

Inbound telemarketing Sales method in which prospects call a seller to obtain information, make reservations, and purchase goods and services.

incremental-cost pricing Pricing method that attempts to use only costs directly attributable to a specific output in setting prices.

individual brand Single brand that uniquely identifies a product.

industrial distributor Channel intermediary that takes title to goods it handles and then distributes these goods to retailers, other distributors, or business or B2B customers; also called a wholesaler.

Inelastic demand Demand that, throughout an industry, will not change significantly due to a price change.

Inflation Rising prices caused by some combination of excess consumer demand and increases in the costs of one or more factors of production.

influencers Individuals with the capability of affecting the opinions or actions of others.

Influencers Typically, technical staff who affect the buying decision by supplying information to guide evaluation of alternatives or by setting buying specifications.

Informative advertising Promotion that seeks to develop initial demand for a good, service, organization, person, place, idea, or cause.

Infrastructure A nation's basic system of transportation networks, communications systems, and energy facilities.

inside selling Selling by phone, mail, and electronic commerce.

installations Major capital investments in the B2B market.

Institutional advertising Promotion of a concept, an idea, a philosophy, or the goodwill of an industry, company, organization, person, geographic location, or government agency.

integrated marketing communications (IMC) Coordination of all promotional activities to produce a unified, customer-focused promotional message.

intensive distribution Distribution of a product through all available channels.

Interactive advertising Two-way promotional messages transmitted through communication channels that induce message recipients to participate actively in the promotional effort.

Interactive marketing Buyer–seller communications in which the customer controls the amount and type of information received from a marketer through channels such as the Internet and virtual reality kiosks.

interactive marketing Buyer–seller communications in which the customer controls the amount and type of information received from a marketer through channels such as the Internet and virtual reality kiosks.

Interactive television Television service package that includes a return path for viewers to interact with programs or commercials by clicking their remote controls.

intermodal operations Combination of transport modes, such as rail and highway carriers (piggyback), air and highway carriers (birdyback), and water and air carriers (fishyback), to improve customer service and achieve cost advantages.

internal customers Employees or departments within an organization that depend on the work of another employee or department.

Internal marketing Managerial actions that help all members of the organization understand, accept, and fulfill their respective roles in implementing a marketing strategy.

internal partnerships Relationship involving customers within an organization.

interpretive research Observational research method developed by social anthropologists in which customers are observed in their natural setting and their behavior is interpreted based on an understanding of social and cultural characteristics; also known as ethnography, or "going native."

introductory stage First stage of the product lifecycle, in which a firm works to stimulate sales of a new-market entry.

ISO (International Organization for Standardization) certification Internationally recognized standards that ensure a company's goods, services, and operations meet established quality levels and its operations minimize harm to the environment.

ISO 9001:2008 Standards developed by the International Organization for Standardization based in Switzerland to ensure consistent quality management and quality assurance for goods and services throughout the European Union.

J

joint demand Demand for a product that depends on the demand for another product used in combination with it.

jury of executive opinion Qualitative sales forecasting method that assesses the sales expectations of various executives.

just-in-time (JIT) Inventory practices that seek to boost efficiency by cutting inventories to absolute minimum levels. With JIT II, suppliers' representatives work at the customer's facility.

just-in-time II (JIT II) Inventory practices that seek to boost efficiency by cutting inventories to absolute minimum levels. With JIT II, suppliers' representatives work at the customer's facility.

K

key performance indicator Quantifiable measurement, articulated in advance, that reflects an organization's goals and is critical to its success.

L

label Branding component that carries an item's brand name or symbol, the name and address of the manufacturer or distributor, information about the product, and recommended uses.

Lateral partnerships Strategic relationship that extends to external entities but involves no direct buyer–seller interactions.

leader pricing Variant of loss-leader pricing in which marketers offer prices slightly above cost to avoid violating minimum-markup regulations and earn a minimal return on promotional sales.

Learning Knowledge or skill acquired as a result of experience, which changes consumer behavior.

lifetime value of a customer Revenues and intangible benefits, such as referrals and customer feedback, a customer brings to the seller over an average lifetime of their relationship, less the amount the company must spend to acquire, market to, and service the customer.

limited-line store Retailer that offers a large assortment within a single product line or within a few related product lines.

limited-service research supplier Marketing research firm that specializes in a limited number of research activities, such as conducting field interviews or performing data processing.

line extension Development of individual offerings that appeal to different market segments while remaining closely related to the existing product line.

line extensions Development of individual offerings that appeal to different market segments while remaining closely related to the existing product line.

list prices Established price normally quoted to potential buyers.

logistics Process of coordinating the flow of information, goods, and services among members of the distribution channel.

loss leaders Product offered to consumers at less than cost to attract them to stores in the hope that they will buy other merchandise at regular prices.

low-involvement purchase decisions Routine purchases that pose little risk to the consumer.

M

mail-order wholesaler Limited-function merchant wholesaler that distributes catalogs instead of sending sales personnel to contact customers.

manufacturer's brand Brand name owned by a manufacturer or other producer.

manufacturer's representative Agents wholesaling intermediary that represents manufacturers of related but noncompeting products and receives a commission on each sale.

manufacturers' representatives Agent wholesaling intermediary who represents manufacturers of related but noncompeting products and receives a commission on each sale.

marginal analysis Method of analyzing the relationship among costs, sales price, and increased sales volume.

marginal cost Change in total cost that results from producing an additional unit of output.

markdown Amount by which a retailer reduces the original selling price of a product.

market Group of people with sufficient purchasing power, authority, and willingness to buy.

market development strategy Strategy that concentrates on finding new markets for existing products.

market penetration strategy Strategy that seeks to increase sales of existing products in existing markets.

market price Price a consumer or marketing intermediary actually pays for a product after subtracting any discounts, allowances, or rebates from the list price.

market segmentation Division of the total market into smaller, relatively homogeneous groups.

Marketing The activity, set of institutions, and processes for creating, communicating, delivering, and exchanging offerings that have value for customers, clients, partners, and society at large.

marketing channel System of marketing institutions that enhances the physical flow of goods and services, along with ownership title, from producer to consumer or business user.

marketing communications Messages that deal with buyer–seller relationships.

marketing concept Companywide consumer orientation with the objective of achieving long-run success.

marketing decision support system (MDSS) Marketing information system component that links a decision maker with relevant databases and analysis tools.

marketing ethics Marketers' standards of conduct and moral values.

marketing information system (MIS) Planned, computer-based system designed to provide managers with a continuous flow of information relevant to their specific decisions and areas of responsibility.

Marketing intelligence Sum total of information related to a firm's markets, which a firm gathers in order to better understand their customers, target customer segments, and develop long-term customer relationships.

marketing intermediary Wholesaler or retailer that operates between producers and consumers or business users.

marketing mix Blending of the four strategy elements—product, distribution, promotion, and pricing—to fit the needs and preferences of a specific target market.

marketing mix Blending of the four strategy elements—product, distribution, promotion, and price—to fit the needs and preferences of a specific target market.

marketing myopia Management's failure to recognize the scope of its business.

Marketing planning Implementing planning activities devoted to achieving marketing objectives.

Marketing research Process of collecting and using information for marketing decision making.

marketing strategy Overall, companywide program for selecting a particular target market and then satisfying consumers in that market through the marketing mix.

marketing websites Site whose main purpose is to increase purchases by visitors.

market-plus pricing Intentionally setting a relatively high price compared with the prices of competing products; also known as skimming pricing.

market-share objective Volume-related pricing objective with the goal of controlling a portion of the market for a firm's product.

markup Amount a retailer adds to the cost of a product to determine its selling price.

mass merchandiser Store that stocks a wider line of goods than a department store, usually without the same depth of assortment within each line.

materials handling system Set of activities that move production inputs and other goods within factories, warehouses, and transportation terminals.

maturity stage Third stage of the product lifecycle, in which industry sales level out.

Media research Advertising research that assesses how well a particular medium delivers an advertiser's message, where and when to place the advertisement, and the size of the audience.

media scheduling Setting the timing and sequence for a series of advertisements.

merchandisers Trade sector buyers who secure needed products at the best possible prices.

merchant wholesaler Independently owned wholesaling intermediary that takes title to the goods it handles; also known as an industrial distributor in the business goods market.

message Communication of information, advice, or a request by the sender to the receiver.

message research Advertising research that tests consumer reactions to an advertisement's creative message.

metrics Quantifiable measurements that are compared against organizational objectives to gauge overall performance.

metropolitan statistical area (MSA) Freestanding urban area with a population in the urban center of at least 50,000 and a total MSA population of 100,000 or more.

microblogs A blog posting that contains only a few words (such as on Twitter).

micromarketing Targeting potential customers at very narrow, basic levels, such as by ZIP code, specific occupation, or lifestyle—possibly even individuals themselves.

micropolitan statistical area Area with at least one town of 10,000 to 49,999 people with proportionally few of its residents commuting to outside the area.

middleman Wholesaler or retailer that operates between producers and consumers or business users.

Minimum advertised pricing (MAP) Fees paid to retailers who agree not to advertise products below set prices.

mission Essential purpose that differentiates one company from others.

Missionary selling Indirect selling method in which salespeople promote goodwill for the firm by educating customers and providing technical or operational assistance.

mobile marketing Marketing messages transmitted via wireless technology.

modified breakeven analysis Pricing technique used to evaluate consumer demand by comparing the number of products that must be sold at a variety of prices to cover total cost with estimates of expected sales at the various prices.

modified rebuy Situation in which a purchaser is willing to reevaluate available options for repurchasing a good or service.

Monopolistic competition Market structure involving a heterogeneous product and product differentiation among competing suppliers, allowing the marketer some degree of control over prices.

monopoly Market structure in which a single seller dominates trade in a good or service for which buyers can find no close substitutes.

monopoly Market structure in which a single seller dominates trade in a good or service for which buyers can find no close substitutes.

Motives Inner state that directs a person toward the goal of satisfying a need.

MRO items Business supplies that include maintenance items, repair items, and operating supplies.

multidomestic marketing strategy Application of market segmentation to foreign markets by tailoring the firm's marketing mix to match specific target markets in each nation.

multiple sourcing Purchasing from several vendors.

N

national account selling Promotional effort in which a dedicated sales team is assigned to a firm's major customers to provide sales and service.

national accounts organization Promotional effort in which a dedicated sales team is assigned to a firm's major customers to provide sales and service needs.

nearshoring Moving jobs to vendors in countries close to the business's home country.

need Imbalance between a consumer's actual and desired states.

network marketing Personal selling that relies on lists of family members and friends of a salesperson, who organizes gatherings of potential customers for an in-home presentation of selected products.

new-task buying First-time or unique purchase situation that requires considerable effort by decision makers.

niche marketing Focusing marketing efforts on satisfying a single market segment.

Noncumulative quantity discounts Price reduction granted on a one-time-only basis.

Nonpersonal selling Promotion that includes advertising, product placement, sales promotion, direct marketing, public relations, and guerrilla marketing—all conducted without being face-to-face with the buyer.

nonprobability sample Sample that involves personal judgment somewhere in the selection process.

North American Free Trade Agreement (NAFTA) Accord removing trade barriers among Canada, Mexico, and the United States.

North American Industry Classification System (NAICS) Classification used by NAFTA countries to categorize the business marketplace into detailed market segments.

O

Objections Expression of sales resistance by the prospect.

odd pricing Pricing policy based on the belief that a price ending with an odd number just under a round number is more appealing, for instance, $9.97 rather than $10.

offshoring Movement of high-cost jobs from one country to lower-cost overseas locations.

oligopoly Market structure in which relatively few sellers compete and where high start-up costs form barriers to keep out new competitors.

oligopoly Market structure in which relatively few sellers compete and where high start-up costs form barriers to keep out new competitors.

online forums A platform where users post messages and hold conversations on specified topics.

opening price point An opening price below that of the competition, usually on a high-quality, private-label item.

opinion leaders Trendsetters who purchase new products before others in a group and then influence others in their purchases.

Order processing Selling, mostly at the wholesale and retail levels, that involves identifying customer needs, pointing them out to customers, and completing orders.

Organization marketing Marketing by mutual-benefit organizations, service organizations, and government organizations intended to persuade others to accept their goals, receive their services, or contribute to them in some way.

Outbound telemarketing Sales method in which sales personnel place phone calls to prospects and try to conclude the sale over the phone.

Outsourcing Using outside vendors to provide goods and services formerly produced in-house.

over-the-counter selling Personal selling conducted in retail and some wholesale locations in which customers come to the seller's place of business.

P

partnership Affiliation of two or more companies that help each other achieve common goals.

penetration pricing strategy Pricing strategy involving the use of a relatively low entry price compared with competitive offerings, based on the theory that this initial low price will help secure market acceptance.

Perception Meaning that a person attributes to incoming stimuli gathered through the five senses.

perceptual screens Mental filtering processes through which all inputs must pass.

Person marketing Marketing efforts designed to cultivate the attention, interest, and preferences of a target market toward a person (perhaps a political candidate or celebrity).

Personal selling Interpersonal influence process involving a seller's promotional presentation conducted on a person-to-person basis with the buyer.

Personal selling Interpersonal influence process involving a seller's promotional presentation conducted on a person-to-person basis with the buyer.

Persuasive advertising Promotion that attempts to increase demand for an existing good, service, organization, person, place, idea, or cause.

phishing High-tech scam that uses authentic-looking email or pop-up messages to get unsuspecting victims to reveal personal information.

Physical distribution Broad range of activities aimed at efficient movement of finished goods from the end of the production line to the consumer.

place marketing Marketing efforts to attract people and organizations to a particular geographic area.

planned shopping center Group of retail stores planned, coordinated, and marketed as a unit.

Planning Process of anticipating future events and conditions and of determining the best way to achieve organizational objectives.

Podcasts Online audio or video file that can be downloaded to other digital devices.

point-of-purchase (POP) advertising Display or other promotion placed near the site of the actual buying decision.

political risk assessment (PRA) Units within a firm that evaluate the political risks of the marketplaces in which they operate as well as proposed new marketplaces.

political–legal environment Component of the marketing environment consisting of laws and their interpretations that require firms to operate under competitive conditions and to protect consumer rights.

population Total group that researchers want to study.

Pop-up ads Separate window that pops up with an advertising message.

Porter's Five Forces Model developed by strategy expert Michael Porter that identifies five competitive forces that influence planning strategies.

positioning Placing a product at a certain point or location within a market in the minds of prospective buyers.

positioning map Tool that helps marketers place products in a market by graphically illustrating consumers' perceptions of competing products within an industry.

postage-stamp pricing System for handling transportation costs under which all buyers are quoted the same price, including transportation expenses; also known as uniform-delivered price.

Posttesting Research that assesses advertising effectiveness after it has appeared in a print or broadcast medium.

precall planning Use of information collected during the prospecting and qualifying stages of the sales process and during previous contacts with the prospect to tailor the approach and presentation to match the customer's needs.

Predictive analytics Use of business intelligence data to model scenarios and create forecasts.

Premiums Item given free or at a reduced cost with purchases of other products.

Pre-roll video ads Brief marketing message that appears before expected video content.

presentation Personal selling function of describing a product's major features and relating them to a customer's problems or needs.

pretesting Research that evaluates an ad during its development stage.

price Exchange value of a good or service.

price flexibility Pricing policy permitting variable prices for goods and services.

pricing policy General guideline that reflects marketing objectives and influences specific pricing decisions.

Primary data Information collected for a specific investigation.

primary metropolitan statistical area (PMSA) Urbanized county or set of counties with social and economic ties to nearby areas.

private brands Brand offered by a wholesaler or retailer.

Private carriers Transporters that provide service solely for internally generated freight.

probability sample Sample that gives every member of the population a known chance of being selected.

product Bundle of physical, service, and symbolic attributes designed to satisfy a customer's wants and needs.

Product advertising Nonpersonal selling of a particular good or service.

product development Introduction of new products into identifiable or established markets.

product diversification strategy Developing entirely new products for new markets.

Product liability Responsibility of manufacturers and marketers for injuries and damages caused by their products.

product lifecycle Progression of a product through introduction, growth, maturity, and decline stages.

product line Series of related products offered by one company.

product manager Marketer responsible for an individual product or product line; also called a brand manager.

product mix Assortment of product lines and individual product offerings a company sells.

Product placement Form of promotion in which a marketer pays a motion picture or television program owner a fee to display a product prominently in the film or show.

Product positioning Consumers' perceptions of a product's attributes, uses, quality, advantages, and disadvantages relative to competing brands.

production orientation Business philosophy stressing efficiency in producing a quality product, with the attitude toward marketing that "a good product will sell itself."

Product-line pricing Practice of setting a limited number of prices for a selection of merchandise and marketing different product lines at each of these price levels.

Product-related segmentation Division of a population into homogeneous groups based on their relationships to a product.

profit centers Any part of an organization to which revenue and controllable costs can be assigned.

Profit Impact of Market Strategies (PIMS) project Research that discovered a strong positive relationship between a firm's market share and product quality and its return on investment.

profit maximization Point at which the additional revenue gained by increasing the price of a product equals the increase in total costs.

Promotion Communication link between buyers and sellers; the function of informing, persuading, and influencing a consumer's purchase decision.

Promotional allowances Promotional incentive in which the manufacturer agrees to pay the reseller a certain amount to cover the costs of special promotional displays or extensive advertising.

promotional mix Subset of the marketing mix in which marketers attempt to achieve the optimal blending of the elements of personal and nonpersonal selling to achieve promotional objectives.

promotional pricing Pricing policy in which a lower-than-normal price is used as a temporary ingredient in a firm's marketing strategy.

Prospecting Personal selling function of identifying potential customers.

Protective tariffs Taxes designed to raise the retail price of an imported product to match or exceed that of a similar domestic product.

Psychographic segmentation Division of a population into groups having similar attitudes, values, and lifestyles.

Psychological pricing Pricing policy based on the belief that certain prices or price ranges make a good or service more appealing than others to buyers.

Public relations Firm's communications and relationships with its various publics.

Pure competition Market structure characterized by homogeneous products in which there are so many buyers and sellers that none has a significant influence on price.

Push money Cash reward paid to retail salespeople for every unit of a product they sell.

Q

QR codes Short for "quick response," a two-dimensional barcode that can be read by some mobile phones with cameras.

Qualifying Determining a prospect's needs, income, and purchase authority as a potential customer.

Qualitative forecasting Use of subjective techniques to forecast sales, such as the jury of executive opinion, Delphi technique, sales force composite, and surveys of buyer intention.

Quantitative forecasting Use of statistical forecasting techniques such as trend analysis and exponential smoothing.

quantity discounts Price reduction granted for a large-volume purchase.

quick-response merchandising Just-in-time strategy that reduces the time a retailer must hold merchandise in inventory, resulting in substantial cost savings.

quota sample Nonprobability sample divided to maintain the proportion of certain characteristics among different segments or groups.

R

rack jobber Full-function merchant wholesaler that markets specialized lines of merchandise to retail stores.

radio frequency identification (RFID) Technology that uses a tiny chip with identification information that can be read by a scanner using radio waves from a distance.

raw materials Natural resources, such as farm products, coal, copper, or lumber that become part of a final product.

rebate Refund of a portion of the purchase price, usually granted by the product's manufacturer.

Reciprocity Buying from suppliers who are also customers.

reference groups People or institutions whose opinions are valued and to whom a person looks for guidance in his or her own behavior, values, and conduct, such as a spouse, family, friends, or celebrities.

Refunds Cash given back to consumers who send in proof of purchase for one or more products.

related party trade Trade by U.S. companies with their subsidiaries overseas as well as trade by U.S. subsidiaries of foreign-owned firms with their parent companies.

Relationship marketing Development and maintenance of long-term, cost-effective relationships with individual customers, suppliers, employees, and other partners for mutual benefit.

Relationship marketing Development, growth, and maintenance of long-term, cost-effective relationships with individual customers, suppliers, employees, and other partners for mutual benefit.

relationship selling Regular contacts between sales representatives and customers over an extended period to establish a sustained buyer–seller relationship.

Remanufacturing Efforts to restore older products to like-new condition.

Reminder advertising Advertising that reinforces previous promotional activity by keeping the name of a good, service, organization, person, place, idea, or cause before the public.

reposition Changing the position of a product within the minds of prospective buyers relative to the positions of competing products.

research design Master plan for conducting market research.

resellers Marketing intermediaries that operate in the trade sector.

retail advertising Advertising by stores that sell goods or services directly to the consuming public.

Retail convergence Situation in which similar merchandise is available from multiple retail outlets, resulting in the blurring of distinctions between types of retailers and merchandise offered.

retail cooperative Group of retailers that establish a shared wholesaling operation to help them compete with chains.

Retailing Activities involved in selling merchandise to ultimate consumers.

return on investment (ROI) The rate of revenues received for every dollar spent on an expense.

Revenue tariffs Taxes designed to raise funds for the importing government.

reverse channels Channel designed to return goods to their producers.

Robinson-Patman Act Federal legislation prohibiting price discrimination not based on a cost differential; also prohibits selling at an unreasonably low price to eliminate competition.

S

salary Fixed compensation payment made periodically to an employee.

sales analysis In-depth evaluation of a firm's sales.

sales force composite Qualitative sales forecasting method based on the combined sales estimates of the firm's salespeople.

sales forecast Estimate of a firm's revenue for a specified future period.

sales incentives Programs that reward salespeople for superior performance.

sales orientation Belief that consumers will resist purchasing nonessential goods and services, with the attitude toward marketing that only creative advertising and personal selling can overcome consumers' resistance and persuade them to buy.

Sales promotion Marketing activities other than personal selling, advertising, guerrilla marketing, and public relations that stimulate consumer purchasing and dealer effectiveness.

Sales promotion Marketing activities other than personal selling, advertising, and publicity that enhance consumer purchasing and dealer effectiveness.

sales quotas Level of expected sales for a territory, product, customer, or salesperson against which actual results are compared.

Sampling Process of selecting survey respondents or research participants.

Sampling Free distribution of a product in an attempt to obtain future sales; process of selecting survey respondents or research participants.

Scrambled merchandising Retailing practice of combining dissimilar product lines to boost sales volume.

search marketing Paying search engines, such as Google, a fee to make sure the company's listing appears toward the top of the search results. Also called search engine optimization (SEO).

second mover strategy Theory that advocates observing closely the innovations of first movers and then improving on them to gain advantage in the marketplace.

Secondary data Previously published information.

Secure Sockets Layer (SSL) Technology that secures a website by encrypting information and providing authentication.

selective distribution Distribution of a product through a limited number of channels.

self-concept Person's multifaceted picture of himself or herself.

Seller partnerships Relationship involving long-term exchanges of goods or services in return for cash or other valuable consideration.

seller's market A market in which there are more buyers for fewer goods and services.

selling agent Agent wholesaling intermediary for the entire marketing program of a firm's product line.

sender Source of the message communicated to the receiver.

service encounter Point at which the customer and service provider interact.

Service quality Expected and perceived quality of a service offering.

services Intangible tasks that satisfy the needs of consumer and business users.

Shaping Process of applying a series of rewards and reinforcements to permit more complex behavior to evolve.

shopbots Software program that allows online shoppers to compare prices of a particular product offered by several online retailers.

shopping products Products consumers purchase after comparing competing offerings.

simple random sample Basic type of probability sample in which every individual in the relevant universe has an equal opportunity of being selected.

skimming pricing strategies Pricing strategy involving the use of a high price relative to competitive offerings.

smishing Scam that collects personal information through cell phone text messages; stands for SMS (short message service) phishing

Social marketing The use of online social media as a communications channel for marketing messages.

Social media Different forms of electronic communication through which users can create online communities to exchange information, ideas, messages, and other content, such as videos or music.

social media analytics Tools that help marketers trace, measure, and interpret data related to social media marketing initiatives.

social media marketing (SMM) The use of social media portals to create a positive influence on consumers or business customers toward an organization's brand, products, public image, or website.

social media marketing plan A formal document that identifies and describes goals and strategies, targeted audience, budget, and implementation methods, as well as tactics for monitoring, measuring, and managing the SMM effort.

social media monitoring The process of tracking, measuring, and evaluating a firm's social media marketing initiatives.

social media platform A type of software or technology that allows users to build, integrate, or facilitate a community, interaction among users, and user-generated content.

social media tool Software (such as an app or blog) that enables users to communicate with each other online.

social news site A platform where users can post news items to links to outside articles, then vote on which postings get the most prominent display.

Social responsibility Marketing philosophies, policies, procedures, and actions that have the enhancement of society's welfare as a primary objective.

social responsibility Marketing philosophies, policies, procedures, and actions that have the enhancement of society's welfare as a primary objective.

social–cultural environment Component of the marketing environment consisting of the relationship between the marketer, society, and culture.

Social-networking sites A website that provides virtual communities through which people can share information, post opinions, and increase their circle of online friends.

sole sourcing Purchasing a firm's entire stock of an item from just one vendor.

spam Popular name for junk email.

span of control Number of representatives who report to first-level sales managers.

Specialty advertising Sales promotion technique that places the advertiser's name, address, and advertising message on useful articles that are then distributed to target consumers.

Specialty products Products with unique characteristics that cause buyers to prize those particular brands.

Specialty retailers Store that combines carefully defined product lines, services, and reputation to persuade shoppers to spend considerable shopping effort there.

Split runs Methods of testing alternate ads by dividing a cable TV audience or a publication's subscribers in two, using two different ads, and then evaluating the relative effectiveness of each.

Sponsorship Relationship in which an organization provides funds or in-kind resources to an event or activity in exchange for a direct association with that event or activity.

Staples Convenience goods and services consumers constantly replenish to maintain a ready inventory.

step out Pricing practice in which one firm raises prices and then waits to see if others follow suit.

stock-keeping unit (SKU) Offering within a product line, such as a specific size of liquid detergent.

straight rebuy Recurring purchase decision in which a customer repurchases a good or service that has performed satisfactorily in the past.

strategic alliances Partnerships in which two or more companies combine resources and capital to create competitive advantages in a new market.

strategic alliances Partnership in which two or more companies combine resources and capital to create competitive advantages in a new market.

Strategic alliances Partnership in which two or more companies combine resources and capital to create competitive advantages in a new market.

Strategic business units (SBUs) Key business units within diversified firms.

Strategic planning Process of determining an organization's primary objectives and adopting courses of action that will achieve these objectives.

strategic window Limited periods when key requirements of a market and a firm's particular competencies best fit together.

stratified sample Probability sample constructed to represent randomly selected subsamples of different groups within the total sample; each subgroup is relatively homogeneous for a certain characteristic.

subcontracting Contractual agreements that assign the production of goods or services to local or smaller firms.

subcultures Groups with their own distinct modes of behavior.

subliminal perception Subconscious receipt of incoming information.

Suboptimization Condition that results when individual operations achieve their objectives but interfere with progress toward broader organizational goals.

subsidies Government financial support of a private industry.

supercenters Large store, usually smaller than a hypermarket, that combines groceries with discount store merchandise.

Supplies Regular expenses a firm incurs in its daily operations.

Supply Schedule of the amounts of a good or service that firms will offer for sale at different prices during a specified time period.

supply chain Sequence of suppliers that contribute to the creation and delivery of a product.

supply chain Control of the activities of purchasing, processing, and delivery through which raw materials are transformed into products and made available to final consumers.

Supply chain management Complete sequence of suppliers and activities that contribute to the creation and delivery of merchandise.

survey of buyer intentions Qualitative sales forecasting method that samples opinions among groups of current and potential customers concerning their purchasing plans.

Sustainable products Products that can be produced, used, and disposed of with minimal impact on the environment.

Sweepstakes Sales promotion technique in which prize winners are selected by chance.

SWOT analysis Review that helps planners compare internal organizational strengths and weaknesses with external opportunities and threats.

syndicated service Organization that provides standardized data on a periodic basis to its subscribers.

systems integration Centralization of the procurement function within an internal division or as a service of an external supplier.

T

tactical planning Planning that guides the implementation of activities specified in the strategic plan.

target market Specific group of people a firm believes is most likely to buy its goods and services.

target-return objectives Short-run or long-run pricing objectives of achieving a specified return on either sales or investment.

tariffs Tax levied against imported goods.

team selling Selling situation in which several sales associates or other members of the organization are employed to help the lead sales representative reach all those who influence the purchase decision.

technological environment Application to marketing of knowledge based on discoveries in science, inventions, and innovations.

Telemarketing Promotional presentation involving the use of the telephone on an outbound basis by salespeople or on an inbound basis by customers who initiate calls to obtain information and place orders.

test marketing Marketing research technique that involves introducing a new product in a specific area and then measuring its degree of success.

Third-party (contract) logistics firms Company that specializes in handling logistics activities for other firms.

Time-based competition Strategy of developing and distributing goods and services more quickly than competitors.

total quality management (TQM) Continuous effort to improve products and work processes with the goal of achieving customer satisfaction and world-class performance.

trade allowances Financial incentive offered to wholesalers and retailers that purchase or promote specific products.

trade discounts Payment to a channel member or buyer for performing marketing functions; also known as a functional discount.

trade dress Visual components that contribute to the overall look of a brand.

trade industries Retailers or wholesalers that purchase products for resale to others.

trade promotion Sales promotion that appeals to marketing intermediaries rather than to consumers.

Trade promotion Sales promotion that appeals to marketing intermediaries rather than consumers.

trade shows Product exhibition organized by industry trade associations to showcase goods and services.

Trade-ins Credit allowance given for a used item when a customer purchases a new item.

trademark Brand for which the owner claims exclusive legal protection.

transaction-based marketing Buyer and seller exchanges characterized by limited communications and little or no ongoing relationships between the parties.

transaction-based marketing Buyer and seller exchanges characterized by limited communications and little or no ongoing relationship between the parties.

transfer price Cost assessed when a product is moved from one profit center within a firm to another.

Trend analysis Quantitative sales forecasting method that estimates future sales through statistical analyses of historical sales patterns.

truck wholesaler (or truck jobber) Limited-function merchant wholesaler that markets perishable food items.

tying agreements Arrangement that requires a marketing intermediary to carry items other than those they want to sell.

U

undifferentiated marketing Strategy that focuses on producing a single product and marketing it to all customers; also called mass marketing.

Unemployment Proportion of people in the economy actively seeking work that do not have jobs.

unfair-trade laws State laws requiring sellers to maintain minimum prices for comparable merchandise.

uniform-delivered pricing Pricing system for handling transportation costs under which all buyers are quoted the same price, including transportation expenses. Sometimes known as postage-stamp pricing.

unilateral pricing policies (UPPs) Strategy that sets the same price for a specific product regardless of where it is sold.

Unit pricing Pricing policy in which prices are stated in terms of a recognized unit of measurement or a standard numerical count.

universal product code (UPC) Numerical bar code system used to record product and price information.

universe Total group that researchers want to study.

unsought products Products marketed to consumers who may not yet recognize a need for them.

Upstream management Controlling part of the supply chain that involves raw materials, inbound logistics, and warehouse and storage facilities.

Users Individual or group that actually uses a business good or service.

utility Want-satisfying power of a good or service.

V

VALS Segmentation system that divides consumers into eight psychographic categories: innovators, thinkers, achievers, experiencers, believers, strivers, makers, and survivors.

Value analysis Systematic study of the components of a purchase to determine the most cost-effective approach.

value pricing Pricing strategy that emphasizes benefits derived from a product in comparison to the price and quality levels of competing offerings.

Variable costs Cost that changes with the level of production (such as labor and raw materials costs).

Vendor analysis Assessment of supplier performance in categories such as price, back orders, timely delivery, and attention to special requests.

Vendor-managed inventory (VMI) Inventory management system in which the seller—in an existing agreement with a buyer—determines how much of a product is needed.

venture team Group of personnel from different areas of an organization who work together in developing new products.

vertical marketing system (VMS) Planned channel system designed to improve distribution efficiency and cost-effectiveness by integrating various functions throughout the distribution chain.

viral marketing Efforts that allow satisfied customers to spread the word about products to other consumers.

virtual sales team Network of strategic partners, suppliers, and others who recommend a firm's goods or services.

vishing Scam that collects personal information through voice response systems; stands for voice phishing.

VoIP—Voice over Internet Protocol A phone connection through a personal computer with any type of broadband Internet connection.

W

Web services Platform-independent information exchange systems that use the Internet to allow interaction between firms.

Web-to-store shoppers Consumers who use the Internet as a tool when shopping at brick-and-mortar retailers.

wheel of retailing Hypothesis that each new type of retailer gains a competitive foothold by offering lower prices than current suppliers charge, the result of reducing or eliminating services.

wholesaler Channel intermediary that takes title to the goods it handles and then distributes these goods to retailers, other distributors, or business or B2B customers.

wholesalers Intermediaries that operate between producers and resellers.

wholesalers Channel intermediary that takes title to goods it handles and then distributes those goods to retailers, other distributors, or B2B customers.

Wholesaling intermediaries Comprehensive term that describes wholesalers as well as agents and brokers.

wikis Web page that anyone can edit.

World Trade Organization (WTO) Organization that replaces GATT, overseeing GATT agreements, making binding decisions in mediating disputes, and reducing trade barriers.

Y

Yield management Pricing strategy that allows marketers to vary prices based on such factors as demand, even though the cost of providing those goods or services remains the same.

Z

Zone pricing Pricing system for handling transportation costs under which the market is divided into geographic regions and a different price is set in each region.

NAME & COMPANY INDEX

A

AARP, 71
AARP The Magazine, 535
ABB Group, 258
ABC News, 517, 534
ABC Television Network, 527, 546
Abell, Derek F., 45, 59
Abercrombie & Fitch, 49, 244
About.com, 23, 124, 343, 521, 529, 626, 641, A-10, B-5
Abrams, Rhonda, 495
Accenture, 26
ACCO Brands, 206
Accor North America, 88
Ace Hardware, 458, 484
Activ-Flex, 394
Activia yogurt, 526
Activision, 284
ACUVUE, 634
Adams, Scott, 334
Adams, Susan, 156
AD Analytics, 487
Adelphi Theatre, 268
Adidas, 18, 254, 395, 438, 615
Adler, Lou, 519
Advance Healing Blister bandages, 394
"Adventures in Lifelong Learning", 284
Advertising Age, 96, 115, 131, 166, 199, 201, 235, 266, 306, 446, 528, 565, 567, 593, 605, A–14
Advertising Archives, 531, 637
Adweek, 31, 167, 486, 487, 605
A&E, 173
Aflac, 60–61
Airbus, 380, 385, 559
Airbus Industries, 64, 205
Air Native, 271
Akst, Daniel, B-4
Albanesius, Chloe, 59
Al.com, 342, 520
ALDI, 455

Aldwych Theatre, 268
Alixpartners.com, 33
All At Once, 283
AllBusiness.com, 505
Allegra, 13
Allison, Melissa, 286, 509
Allstate Insurance, 243
Alta Bicycle Share, 165, 588
Amazon.com, Inc., 4, 29, 145, 146, 157, 188, 199, 349, 389, 627, A-5
Amazon Prime, 145, 199, 348–349
Amber Waves, 307
American Academy of Pediatrics, 281, 539
American Airlines, 59
American Apparel, 321
American Automobile Association (AAA), 605
American Cancer Society, 15, 40, 101
American Chamber of Commerce, 8
American Council for an Energy Efficient Economy (ACEEE), 75
American Customer Satisfaction Index (ACSI), 346
American Diabetes Association, 30
American Eagle Airline, 144, 315, 494
American Eagle Outfitters, 494
American Express, 4, 14, 29, 99, 163, 210, 217, 243, 297, 356, 369, 458, 460
American Express Travel, 458
American Girl, 151, 422, 435
American Girl dolls, 151, 435
American Girl Magazine, 422
"American Idol", 422
American Indian Business Leaders, 287
American Kennel Club, 13
American Marketing Association, 31, 334, 416
American Meat Institute, 79
American Medical Association (AMA), 177
American Needle, 64
American Red Cross, 14, 16

I-1

American Trucking Association (ATA), 465
Amiti, Mary, 269
Amor Group, 143
Amtrak, 58
Amway, 503
Anderson Merchandisers, 499
Anderson, Tom, 102
Android, 50–51, 103, 109, 131, 144, 359, 418, 643, A-10
Anheuser-Busch, 84–85
Annear, Steve, 552
Ann Taylor, 102, 487, 558
Anytime Fitness, 458
Applebee's, 233
Apple Inc., 4
Aquafina, 273, 413
Aramburo, Ariane, 605
Argonne National Laboratory, 76
Arise Virtual Solutions, 379
Arm & Hammer, 293, 399, 403, 405
Armour, 408–409
Armstrong Rubber, 413
ArtTownGifts.com, 381
Asian Food Markets, 423
Asimos, Tim, 237
AskPatty.com, 276
Associated Press, 96, 97, 307
Association of American Railroads, 465
Atari, 284
Atlantic, 279, 466, 491, A-7, A-9–A-10
AT&T, 64–65, 92, 204, 243
Aunt Jemima, 413
Authors Guild, 151
Aveeno, 394
Avon, 183, 447, 503
A&W, 45

B

Baby Bells, 70
Baccarat crystal, 601
Bachman, Justin, 623
Bachman, Katy, 539
Badger, Emily, 306
Bag Borrow or Steal, 448
Balenciaga, 410
Banana Republic, 497
Band-Aid, 394
Bank of America, 350
Barbecue Addiction, 512
Barefoot Contessa, 440
Barker, Colin, 477
Barnes, Brook, 96
Barnes, Brooks, 370
Barnes-Jewish Hospital, 19
Barnes & Noble, 104, 122–123, 145, 486
Barnett, 563
Barrie, James La, 236
Barton, Dominic, 96
Bass Pro Shops, 29, A-9
Basu, Sunando, 460
Bath & Body Works, 216
Bautista, Christian Brazil, 638
Baylor College of Medicine, 19, 115
Bazaarvoice, . 314
BBH Labs, 351
Beckham, David, 254, 518
Becton, Dickinson and Company, 468
Bed, Bath & Beyond, 486, 492–493
Bedigian, Louis, 89, 197, 435, 489
Beef Products Inc., 79
Beer, Jeff, 59
The Bee's Knees, 297
Behme, Todd J., 477
Belsie, Laurent, 410, 412
Belzer, Jason, 518
Benadryl, 394
Bender, Andrew, 268
Benecol, 394
Ben & Jerry's, 8, 181, 336, 410, 413
Bennett, Shea, 31, 132
Bentley, 598
Bergdorf Goodman, 637
Berkshire Hathaway, 379
Bernard, Tara Siegel, 97
Berry, Halle, 551–552
Berry, Ken, 370–371, 551–552
Bertolli, 413
Best Aquaculture Practices, 460
Best Buy, 58, 88, 90, 490, 492, 572–573, 606, 608, 625

Best Friends Animal Society, 109
Better Business Bureau, 183, 634
Bhasin, Kim, 337
BIA/Kelsey, 102
Big Blue, 247
Big Brothers Big Sisters of America, 106
Big Lots, 485
Big Mac, 4
Billabong, 438
Bill Me Later, 147
Bilton, Nick, 489
Bing, 23, 57, 93, 107–108, 157, 164, 199, 234, 267, 304, 335, 369, 405, 436, 474, 509, 550, 587, 621, 649
Birch, Sean, 33
Biskupic, Joan, 337
Bizjak, Tony, 306
BJ's Wholesale, 399
Black & Decker, 569
Blackwood, Amy S., 33
Blair Candy, 53
Blizzard Entertainment, 324
Blomberg, Lindsey, 387
Bloomingdale's, 179, 493
Bloxham, Eleanor, 451
Blue Cross Blue Shield, 183, 299
Bluefin Labs, 345
Blue Sky Clothing, Inc. *(fictional)*, A-6, A-8
BMW, 4, 13, 144, 260, 262, 299, 353
Bobby, 372, 512
Boeing, 46, 64, 205, 234, 241, 385, 397
The Bold and the Beautiful, 417
Boloco Burritos, 589
Bolshoi Ballet, 58
BoltBus, 406, 650–651
Bonsor, Kevin, 605
Booshaka app, 104
Bosch, 385
Bose Corporation, 430
Boston Consulting Group (BCG), 52, 290
Boston Public Library, 588–589
Boudway, Ira, 552
Bounty, 416
Bowen, Amy, 650
Bowen, Brent D., 337

BrandAsset Valuator, 414
Brandwatch, 119, 127
Bravo, 372
Brazen Careerist, 125
Brettman, Allan, 267
Breyers, 336
Bridges, Judi Atkins, 336, 510
Brinker International, 630
Bristol-Myers Squibb, 50
Broadway Direct, 305
Brohan, Mark, 476
Brooks Brothers, 312
Brounstein, Marty, 428
Brustein, Joshua, 621
Buddy Media, 355
Budweiser, 417, 512
Buffet, Warren, 3
Buitoni, 270
Bullock, Jungmiwha, 307
BUNN, 200
Burden Melissa, 96
Bureau of Economic Analysis, 74, 320
Burger King, 79, 212, 214, 293, 347, 586
Burke, Michael, 597
Burlington Industries, 275
Burt's Bees, 425
Busch Stadium, 89
Business Conversion Program, 616
Business Marketing Management:, 221
Business Trip, 121, 559
BusinessWeek, 48, 436
Buss, Dale, 201
Buy.com, 608, 627
Buzzell, Robert D., 623
Bvlgari, 637
Byro, Ellen, 325

C

Cabbage Patch dolls, 151
Cabela's, A-9
Cablevision, 78
Cadbury, 44
Cadillac, 242, 353, 386
Caldrea Company, 597

Calnan, Christopher, 153
Calvin Klein, 102, 424, 430
Campaign for a Commercial-Free Childhood, 84
Campbell Soup Company, 45, 324
Canon's PowerShot series, 639
Canyon Ranch, 183, 391
Capital One, 520
Captura Group, 285
Cardwell Diane, 477
Career Athletes, 558
Cargill, 386
Carney, John, 59
Carney, Michael, 621
Carr, Austin, 149, 405
Cartier, 627
Casacchia, Chris, 132
Cascade, 414
Casella, Brett, 201
Casserly, Meghan, 33
Catalog of U.S. Government Publications (CGP), 320
Caterpillar, 205, 241, 304
CBS Television Network, 423, 446, 527, 546
CDW, 213, 391
CDW Supplier Diversity Program, 213
C2 Education, A-4
Census.gov, 280
Census of Retailing and Wholesaling, 212
Centers for Disease Control and Prevention (CDCP), 57, 82, 539
CHANEL, 448
Chang, Gordon G., 249
Channick, Robert, 482
Charles Schwab, 144
Chase Sapphire card, 188
Chattanooga State Community College, 212
Chatter, 555
Cheer, 414
Cheerios, 94, 260, 399
Cheetos, 411
Chevron, 242
Chevy Tahoe, 8
Chick-fil-A, 419, 450
Children's Advertising Review Unit (CARU), 198
Children's Miracle Network, 213
Chili's Grill & Bar, 629–630

China Arts and Entertainment Group (CAEG), 268
Chittum, Ryan, 201
Chmielewski, Dawn C., 337
Choi, Candice, 387
Chopped, 372, 440, 590
Christie, Les, 307
Chrysler Group, 261
CIA World Factbook, 267
Cinnabon, 293
Circuit City, 481
Cisco Systems, 388–389
Citibank, 51, 149
Citigroup, 243
City Sports, 588
CK Free, 424
CK One, 424
Clark, Hannah, 132
Clark, Patrick, 237
Clean & Clear, 394
ClearRx, 420
Cleveland Indians, 89
Client Experience Team, 561
Clinton Presidential Library, 19
Clive Christian's No.1, 602
Clorox Company, 286
CNBC, 259
Cnet.com, 139, 164
CNN, 259
Coalition for Fire-Safe Cigarettes, 71
Coca-Cola, 4, 45, 110, 144, 185, 198, 213–214, 260, 272–273, 306, 350, 379, 411, 414, 415, 417–418, 461, 521, 528, 533
Cocilova, Alex, 190
Coelho, Ana Livia, 552
Cohen, Arianne, 244
Coke, 185, 272, 303, 417, 535
Coke Zero, 303, 532
Coleman, Rebecca, 482
Colgate, 26, 183, 410, 416
Colgate-Palmolive, 26, 33
Colonel Sanders, 411
Colorado Rockies, 614
Comcast, 57, 113–114, 347, 526, 636
Comfort-Flex, 394

Commercial Aircraft Corporation of China, 64
Commodore, 284
Commute Greener, 74
comScore, 107
Conaghan, Jim, 553
Conlin, Brian, 306
Conlon, Ginger, 553
Conner Prairie, 14
Conner, Tim, 447
Consumer Product Safety Commission (CPSC), 63, 69, 70, 80, 431–432
Consumer Reports, 573, 633
Container Store, 643
Content Marketing Institute, 116
Converse, 440
Cooking Channel, 168, 372, 440, 448, 590, 606
The Cool People, 438
Coppertone, 580, 582
Corona beer, 550
Cortesi, Sandra, 201
Costco, 64, 244, 399, 455, 494, 509, 593, 629, A-4
Costill, Albert, 132
COTTM website, 266
Council of Better Business Bureaus, 71
County and City Data Book, 320
Coverity, 242
Covert, Adrian, 33
Coy, Peter, 33
Craftsman, 411, 474
Craigslist, 194
Cramer, Maria, 41
Crandell, Christine, 354
Crane's, 299
Crate & Barrel, 459, 502, 512
Crayons to Classrooms, 100
Create Jobs for USA, 22
Crunch Time, 297
CSN Stores, 134–135
CSO Security and Risk, 149
CSX, 385
Cuddington, Danielle, 201
Cupcake Champions, 440
Cupcake Wars, 440
Curves, 293, 605–607, 609, 617–618
Cussen, Mark P., 96

Cute Overload, A-5
Cutrone, Carolyn, 201
CVS, 76, 103, 481, 495, 518
"Cyber Monday", 144

D

Dallas International Film Festival, 487
Dallas Mavericks, 568
Darden Restaurants, 460
Dark Chocolate Dreams, 297
Daro, Ishmael N., 412
Dasani, 491
Datalliance, 469
Datamonitor, 322
Davenport, Reid, 337
David, Leonard, 33
David Yurman Jewelry, 601
Davis, Josh, 476
Davis, Mark, 638
Day, Paul, 96
Deere & Co., 603
Defense Logistics Agency (DLA), 227
DeForge, Jeanette, 200
de Gortari, Carlos Salinas, 243
De La Merced, Michael J., 460
De Laurentiis, Giada, 372, 413, 512, 590
Delivery Information Acquisition Device (DIAD V), 222
Dell Inc., 37, 461
Dell, Michael, 461
Delo, Cotton, 132
Deloitte, 335
Delta Airlines, 46, 58
Demeritt, Laurie, 108
Denny's, 347
DennysListens.com, 347
DePuy, 393, 431
Derschowitz, Jessica, 337
Design Basics, 276
Design Star, 590
Detroit Pistons, 561
Deveau, Denise, 475
Dezember Ryan, 623
DHL XML Services, 465

Diablo III, 324
Dick's Sporting Goods, 14, 233, 452, A-9
Diet Pepsi, 16
Dillard's, 358, 491, 507
Dimensions Games Corporation, 55
Diners, Drive-ins, and Dives, 440
Dion, Celine, 58
Direct Marketing Association (DMA), 71
DIRECTV, 70, 78
Discovery Communications, 456
DISH Network, 70, 78, 533, 534, 546
Disney, 65, 76, 144, 178, 243, 257, 274, 277, 369, 370, 379, 391, 414, 517, 539, 561, 575, 620, 621, A-5
Disney Institute, 369, 370
Disney, Walt, 379, 391, 561, 621, A-5
Disney World, 65, 274, 277, 575, 621
DIY Network, 168, 590, 606
Dobkin, Jenna, 133
Dodge Challenger, 8, 648
Dodrill, Tara, 387
DogSmith, 177
Dokoupil, Tony, 477
Dolan, Brian, 165
Dolce & Gabbana, 637
Dollar General, 299, 483, 508, 592, 593
Dollar Stores, 49, 197, 455, 504, 508
Dollar Tree, 483, 508, 608
Dominion Theatre, 268
Domino's Pizza, 51
Dom Perignon, A-4
Do Not Call Registry, 68, 69, 83, 325, 560, 586
Do Not Track, 148
Doritos, 413, 419, 586
Dorsey, Jack, 103, 149
Dos Equis, 526
Doucette, Kitt, 96
Dove (ice cream), 416, 461
Dove (soap), 461
Dow Chemical, 7
The Downtown Project, 95
Doyle, Alison, 519
Dreams Resorts, 180
Drexler, Mickey, A-5
Dr Pepper, 44, 45, 304, 411, 422

Drucker, Peter F., 6
DSW, 483
DuBois, Shelley, 59
Duggan, Maeve, 201
Duhigg, Charles, 325
"The Duke", 205
Dun & Bradstreet, 212, 313
Dunkin' Donuts, 40, 42, 43, 48, 116, 347, 403, 458
DuPont, 56, 205, 550
Duracell, 582
Durisin, Megan, 437
Duroni, Lance, 96
Duryee, Tricia, 438
Dyer, Pam, 59
Dyson, 528

E

Eastern Michigan University, . 349
eBay, 20
eBillme, 147
Eclipse Aviation, 430
Ecomagination website, 203
The Economist, 515
Edelstein, Stephen, 132
EDI Solutions, 466
Eha, Brian Patrick, 33
E-Lab, 324
Elderhostel, 284
Electronic Arts, 256, 257, 284
Eli Lilly, 236
Elle magazine, 145
Ellement, John R., 41
Ellett, John, 96
Elliott, Stuart, 343, 405, 460
Ellyatt, Holly, 477
Elsevier, 86
Emily Bryson York, 31
Encyclopaedia Britannica, 299
Encyclopedia of Associations, 321
ENERGY STAR, 65, 173
Enron, 24
Enterprise Rent-A-Car, 558
Entertainment, 5, 58, 59, 64, 72, 83, 105, 106, 135, 136, 140, 142, 151, 168, 181, 183, 242–243, 256, 266, 268, 281, 284–285, 288, 305, 308–309, 324, 369,

372, 376, 449, 456, 486–487, 495, 499, 515, 532, 534, 536, 539, 621
Entrepreneur, 62, 76, 320, 410, 492
Entwine Wine, 270
eProcurement Scotland Service, 143
Equifax, 71
Ernoult, Emeric, 132
Escape, 530 642, 645, 648
ESPN, 209, 517
ESPN.com, 155
ESPN Insider, 515
Estée Lauder, 493
Estrin, Michael, 650
Etcharren, Elena, 201
Eternity, 349, 424
Ethicon, 394
Euphoria, 424
European Commission, 148, 615
Everyday Lives, 270, 514
Expedia.com, 621
Experian, 71, 292
Experian Simmons, 292
Export.gov, 50, 329
E-Z Pass, 604–605
E-Z Washing Machines, 418

F

Facebook, 4, 6, 11, 12, 14, 20, 21, 22, 27, 29, 35, 44, 51, 57, 58, 61, 74, 77, 100, 101, 102, 103, 104, 105, 106, 107, 108, 109, 110, 111–120, 123–125, 129, 130, 131, 136, 137, 147, 148, 156, 158, 165, 168, 173, 178, 185, 187, 190, 202, 203, 210, 260, 266, 270, 284, 286, 296, 298, 310, 313, 314, 316, 319, 327, 343, 345, 350, 360, 370, 372, 382, 387, 440, 451, 482, 495, 512, 518, 533, 534, 552, 554, 555, 581, 587, 589, 590, 650, A-10, A-11
Facebook Places, 278
Fage, 437
Fairmont Hotels & Resorts, 89
FAO Schwartz, 205
Farber, Barry, 447
Farhi, Paul, 553
Farmers Insurance, 343
Fashion Mall at Keystone, 486

Fast Start program, 569
Febreze, 324, 325, 582
Federal Acquisition Regulation (FAR), 227
Federal Bureau of Investigation (FBI), 149
Federal Communications Commission (FCC), 207
Federal Power Commission, 70
Federal Reserve, 650
Federal Trade Commission (FTC), 67, 207, 381
FedEx, 7, 30, 92, 142, 378, 379, 463, 464, 467
Fehrenbacher, Katie, 33, 407
Ferdman, Roberto A., 59
Fernau, Karen, 306
Ferrero USA Inc., 412
Fetch Dog, 502
Fiat, 261, 396
Fiat 500 Abarth, 261
Fidelity Investments, 182
Field, Marshall, 600
Finger-Care Tough Strips, 394
Fishman, Charles, 407
Flanagan, Graham, 552
Flay, Bobby, 372, 512
Flickr, 103, 112
Floor Coverings International (FCI), 568
Florida's Natural, 603
Fogelson, Susie, 168, 270, 372, 590
Food Network, 14, 131, 168, 270, 372, 440, 512, 517, 590, 652
Food Network Star, 168, 270, 372, 440, 512
Foot Locker, 244, 492
Forbes, 16, 111, 180, 288, 374
Forbes, Moira, 201
Ford Fiesta, 105
Ford Focus, 11
Ford, Henry, 9, 42, 275, 390
Ford Motor Company, 21, 22, 275
Ford's Crown Victoria Police Interceptor, 640
Forrester Research, 101
Fortune, 339, 344
Fortune 500 corporations, 210
Fortune magazine, 61, 339, 344
Fortune's World's Most Admired Companies, 61
Foster, Dean, 246
Four Seasons Hotels and Resorts, 183, 197
Foursquare, 100, 102, 104, 125, 208, 209, 280, 440

Foxconn, 249
Fox News.com, 40, A-4
Fred Meyer, 493
Freeman & Liedtka, 86
Free, Sean, 305
Freid, Justin, 552
French's, 413
Fresh Express, 183
Fresh Healthy Vending, 504
Friendly Planet Travel, 581
Friendster, 102
Frisbees, 426
Frito-Lay, 186, 326, 413
Frohlich, Thomas C., 237
Fruit & Nut Oatmeal, 296
Fuljenz, Mike, 650
Fusion, 275, 411

G

GaGa SherBetter, 336, 510
Gainesville Health & Fitness Center, A-5
Gale, Bradley T., 623
Gallo, Carmine, 370
Gap.com, 144
Garbett Homes, 173
Garmin, 474
Gasser, Urs, 201
Gates, Bill, 7, 152, 178
Gatorade, 273, 303
Gazzaniga, Marin, 282
Geely Holding Group, 432
GEICO Insurance, 411
GE Intelligent Platforms, 76
General Electric (GE), 258
General Mills, 50, 84, 94, 100, 233, 260, 346, 368, 381, 385, 399, 428, 435, 443, 586, 592
General Motors, 242
General Services Administration (GSA), 227, 234
George Foreman Grill, 503
Geox, 394, 395
Gerstner, Lou, 278
Giada At Home, 440
Gibbons, Barry, 173
Gillette, 414

Gillin, Paul, 220
Glassman, Barry, 407
Gleeson, Brent, 31
Global Aquaculture Alliance, 460
Gloria Jean's Coffees, 492
GNC, 183
Godiva, 184
Goel, Vindu, 249
Golden, Fran, 282
Gold, Kate, 372, 440
Goldman, David, 307
Goldstein, Phil, 638
Gold Well City award, A-5
Gonzalez-Barrera, Ana, 201
"Good Neighbors Nights", 552
Goodyear, 457
Google, 4, 31, 34, 35, 42, 55, 59, 95, 101, 102, 104, 105, 107, 108, 113, 119, 130, 145, 146, 148, 151, 154, 155, 157, 158, 160, 236, 267, 280, 313, 314, 322, 350, 359, 369, 378, 379, 394, 396, 414, 417, 436, A-4
Google+, 58, 102, 104, 105, 107, 113, 296, 350, 440, 482, 554, 568
Google Analytics, 119, 158, 322
Google Earth, 280
Google Offers, 145
Gordon, Gabe, 372, 652
Gordon, Jon, 428
Gordon, Whitson, 59
Gothelf, Andrew, 33
Gottschalks, 481
Goudreau, Jenna, 31
Graham, Brogan, 165, 588
Granderson, L. Z., 460
Grazer, Emily, 623
Great American Country (GAC), 168, 590
Great Depression, 10, 67, 73, 74, 370, 595
Great Food Truck Race, 168, 590
Green Book, 75
Green Giant Vegetables, 94, 416
Green Mountain Coffee Roasters, 399, 586
Greenpeace, 118
Gregoire, Jerry, 37
Greyhound Lines, 406, 650
Group M Search, 107

Groupon, 335, 346
Grove, Andy, A-2
Gruley, Bryan, 437
GSA Advantage, 227, 228, 235
Gucci, Aldo, 598
Gucci Group, 410
güd, 425
Guess, 438
Guiltinan, Joseph P., 33
Gustafson, Katherine, 236

H

Häagen-Dazs International, 94, 336, 339, 369
Habitat for Humanity, 8, 30
Hachman, Mark, 237
Hackett, Robert, 452
Halevy, Ronan, 605
Hall, David, 406, 651
Halligan, Brian, 503
Hallmark, 10, 303, 317, 340, 350, 415
Hamilton, Scott, 14
Hanes, 592–593
Hanna Andersson, 179
Hanna, Brad, 605
Harley-Davidson, 277
Harper, Ben, 495
Harrison, J. D., 437
The Hartman Group, 108
Harvard Business Review, 495
Harvey, Will, 320
Hasselt, Caroline Van, 59
HCA Healthcare, 229
HDNet, 568
Headley, Dean E., 337
Healey, James R., 407
Healthy Choice, 84, 303, 416
Hechinger, John, 96
Hegeman, Roxana, 477
Heilmich, Nanci, 282
Heine, Christopher, 133
Heller, Laura, 518
Helm, Burt, 551
Hennessy-Fiske, Molly, 351
Henschen, Doug, 21

Herman Miller, 385
Hermès, 382, 452, 485
Hermes, Amanda, 280
Hernandez, Aaron, 41
Herrin, Jessica, 448
Hertneky, Dana, 33
Hess, Alexander E.M., 237
Hewlett-Packard (HP), 249, 313, 413
HGTV, 168, 590
Hill, Steve, 437
Hill, Toby, 200
Hilton Hotels, 233, 369
Hindustan Lever, 261
Hispanic Nurses Network, 286
History Channel, 517
H. J. Heinz Co., 419, 574
H&M, 11, 507, 518
Hoak, Amy, 307
Hoelzel, Mark, 553
Holiday Inns, 400
Home Depot, 159, . 483, 485, 492, 503, 507, 582, 625, 626, 630
Home Shopping Network (HSN), 627
Honda, 15, 48, 49, 65, 66, 97, 235, 260, 262, 353, 415, 421, 484, 551, 567, 631
Honda Civic, 631
Hoover, 417
Hormel, 574
Horovitz, Bruce, 33, 307
Horsefeathers Restaurant, 117
Houghton, Stuart, 407
Howard, Clark, 610
Howell, Elizabeth, 59
Hsieh, Tony, 95
Hsu, Tiffany, 307
Hsu, Tiffany, HTC, 403
The Hub, 143, 268, 394
Hubspot, 125, 212, 503
Hubway, 165–166, 165–166, 588, 589
Huggies, 358, 414, 420
Hulu, 455, 487, 534
Hulu Plus, 534
Hunger Games, 100
Hypponen, Mikko, 149
Hyundai, 4, 92, 185, 262, 353, 404, 416, 423, 521

I

Iams, 416
IBM, 26, 43, 44, 51, 86, 144, 152, 154, 247, 249, 258
IdeaStorm site, 139
IKEA, 255, 256, 492
IMAN Cosmetics, 488
IMDb, 104
Improvements, 81, 94, 318, 358, 365, 390, 426, 432, 465, 479, 485, 502, 516, 593, B-6
Inbound Marketing, 125
Indiana Wesleyan University, 40
Infineon Raceway, 382
Infiniti, 40, 386, 414
Information Resources, 227
Ingraham, Christopher, 650
Ingram Micro, 497
In Search of Excellence, 82, 310
InSight, 107, 109, 126, 131, 164, 235, 236, 244, 285, 291, 315, 323, 324, 326, 329, 362, 372, 384, 463, 464, 479, 555, 575
Instagram, 58, 102, 105, 116, 130, 316, 391, 440, 482
Intel, 30, 205, 206, 214, 215, 358, A-2
Interbrand, 414
InterContinental Hotels Group, 400
International Consumer Electronics Show (CES), 498
International Monetary Fund, 76, 248
International Organization for Standardization, 248, 265, 390
Internet Crime Complaint Center (IC3), 149
Interstate Commerce Commission (ICC), 464
"In the Kitchen" app, 440
Intuit, 165, 236
iPad, 4, 51, 56, 103, 144, 235, 249, 281, 295, 370, 374, 375, 385, 396, 404, 416, 504, 558
iPhone, 10, 11, 21, 50, 51, 52, 56, 62, 109, 131, 144, 249, 295, 330, 374, 375, 456, 489, 515, 638, 643
iPod, 62, 374, 375, 479
iPod touch, 62, 479
Ipsos, 318
Iron Chef, 590
iTunes Connect, 158
Iyer, Tarun, 623

J

Jacobs, Breanna, 133
Jaguar, 197, 436, 457
James, Geoffrey, 354
James, LeBron, 16, 33, 100, 528, 552
Jan-Pro, 205, 458
JCPenney, 289
J. Crew, 102, 129, 398, A-5
JC Watts Companies, 83
J.D. Power and Associates, 223, 312
Jeep, 8, 158
Jeep Cherokee, 8
Jell-O, 31
Jennifer LeClaire, 96
Jimmy John's Gourmet Sandwich Shops, 458
Johnson, Jack, 306
Johnson & Johnson, 31, 56, 394, 404, 413, 414, 469, 521, 574, 634
Johnson, Lance, 387
Johnson, Lauren, 306
Johnson's Baby Shampoo, 394
Jolly Green Giant, 416
Jonas Brothers, 14
Jones, Nicholas A., 307
Jones, Richard, 623
Jones, Ron, 133
Jose Cuervo International, 418
JPMorgan Chase, 52
Just Host, 157
Justian, 623
Juvenile Diabetes Research Foundation, 7

K

Kansara, Vikram Alexei, 476
Karlinsky Neal, 623
Kar, Saroj, 133
Kaste, Martin, 187
Kate Spade, 382
Kauffman Stadium, 89
Kaufman, Phil, 307
Kayak.com, 145, 608, 621
KB Toys, 481
K-Cup, 48, 222, 223, 399
Kearney, Laila, 25

Kellogg Company, 84, 592–593
Kelly, Jennifer, 370
Kent, Chuck, 201
Kenya Airways, 385
Keurig Incorporated, 221
KFC, 22, 244, 245, 411
Kia, 92, 262, 353, 530
Kia Spectra, 13
Kierland Commons, 487
Kimberley-Clark Corporation, 359, 366, 375, 420, 427, 446, 588, 592–593, 608
Kincaid, Jason, 33
Kindle, 4, 47, 152, 153, 199, 456, 464, 487, 645, B-5
Kish, Matthew, 405
Kitamura, Makiko, 165
Klara, Robert, 407
Klass, Perry, 539
Kleenex, 358, 411, 417, 420
Klout, 118, 119, 178, 382
Kmart, 48, 304, 483, 593, 638
The Kno, 297
Knoll Furniture, 206
Knorr, 419
Knowledge@Wharton, 438
Kodak, 418
Koen, William, 650
Koeppel, David, 201
Kohl's, 46, 48, 270, 299, 315, 357, 413, 474, 482, 486, 494, 509, 512, 586, 590, 652
Koons, Cynthia, 165
Kooser, Amanda, 33
Kossman, Sienna, 244
Kovach, Steve, 178
Kraft Foods, 31, 46, 56, 116, 117, 303, 356, 357, 443, 603
Kraft Foods Group, 31
Krauss, Clifford, 477
Krishna, R. Jai, 33
Kroc, Ray, 347
Kroger, 50, 79, 339, 455, 491, 508, 600, 601, 631
Krogstad, Jens Manuel, 306
Krumboltz, Mike, 187
K-Swiss, 193, 293
Kuharsky, Sergei, 270, 440, 512, 590, 652

Kumcu, Aylin, 307
Kurtz, Annalyn, 307

L

Lacoste, 438
Lactaid, 394
Lady Foot Locker, 492
Lady Gaga, 111, 336
Laird, Sam, 132
Lamborghini, 384
Lanai Luau, 452
Lands' End, 491, 561, 625, 626
Lankford, Lo, 97
Lapowsky, Issie, 133
Las Vegas City Hall, 95
Las Vegas Sun, 95
Lauby, Sharlyn, 133
Laura Ashley, 483
Lay's, 410, 512
Leadership Group, 83
Lean Cuisine, 418, 419
Leap, Amy, 623
Le Cirque, 378
LEED program, 468
Leggatt, Helen, 307
Lego, 6 444, 458
Leibowitz, Ben, 552
Lenhart, Amanda, 201
Lenovo, 249
Lenox china, 601
LensCrafters, 378
Lerman, Pete, 551
Leslie, Katie, 21
LexisNexis, 139
Lexus, 353, 380, 412, 414, 590, 652
LG Electronics, 262, 627
Liberty Tax Service, 458
Lichtenstein, Roy, 487
LifeScan, 393, 394
Lillian Vernon, 503
Lilypond, 132
Limited Brands, 216
Lincoln automobiles, 183
LinkedIn, 12, 77, 98, 99, 101, 102, 107, 117, 124, 125, 129, 202, 203, 260, 296, 482, 533, 554

Linn, Allison, 307
Lion Air, 385, 386
Lipton, 273, 413
Listerine, 394
Livability at a Glance, 276
Liz Lange, 413
L.L. Bean, 48, 49, 56, 105, 392, 393, 403, 481, 494, 561, 575, A-9
LoBianco, Jim, 351
Logistics Management, 461
Logo, 18, 84, 148, 400, 423, 483, 488, 581, A-7, A-10, A-11
Lolly Wolly Doodle, 20
Lombardo, John, 370
The Long Tail, 298
Lopez, Mark Hugo, 201
Lord, Joanna, 354
L'Oréal Paris, 183
Los Angeles Times, 155
Louisiana Tourism Coastal Coalition, 112
Lowe's, 183, 346, 358, 483, 484, 575, 608, 629, 630, 643
Loyd, Linda, 96
Luckerson, Victor, 337
Lucky Brand Jeans, 11
Luk, Lorraine, 249, 476
Lulofs, Neal, 553
LuLuLemon Athletica, 282
Lummis, Kristen, 622
Luna, Taryn, 306
Lunchables, 296
Lutz, Ashley, 201

M

MacKenzie, Jacqui, 482
MACTEC, 227
Macy's, 48, 140, 299, 347, 478, 479, 486, 491
Madden, Mary, 201
Madrid, Carolina, 339
Maersk Line, 465
Magnavox, 284
Magoon, Christopher, 489
Maine Hunting Shoes, 393
Major League Baseball (MBL), 3, 89, 211
Make-A-Wish Foundation, 23, 116
Maker's Mark, 418
Makower, Joel, 405
Malcolm Baldrige National Quality Award, 390
March of Dimes, 16
Marketing Science Institute, 600
Marous, Jim, 564
Marriott, 50, 57–58, 304
Marshall Field, 600
Marshall, Rick, 489
Martin, Katie, 489
Martin, Ricky, 282
Martin, Steve W., 447
Mary Kay Cosmetics, 640
MasterCard, 13, 29, 120, 163, 460, .B-4
Matchbox cars, 151
Mattel, 151, 205, 432
Maui Luau, 452
Mayer, Marissa, 34–35
Mays, Kelsey, 31
McCarty, Dawn, 451
McClain, Erica, 460
McCracken, Sam, 271
McDonald's, 212, 256, 420, 528
McKesson, 457
McLean, Bonnie, 623
McNaughton, Marissa, 553
McNevin, Ambrose, 59
McPheat, Sean, 305
Mead, Sue, 201
Meltzer, Marisa, 486
Mercedes-Benz, 262, 290, 346, 353
Mercedes-Benz C-class models, 288
Merchandise Mart, 498
Merchandising Matters, 521, 605
Merck, 50, 64
Merrill Lynch, 418
Merritt, Chris, 475
Merry Maids, 377
Metro AG, 460
Metropolitan Atlanta Rapid Transit Authority (MARTA), 608
Metropolitan Transportation Authority, 605
MGM, 17

Michael Graves, 419
Micrositezdigital.com, 132
Microsoft Business, 343
Microsoft Internet Explorer, 147
Microsoft Office, 573
Microsoft's Xbox, 284
Mighty Maple, 297
Milford, Phil, 451
Miller, Mark J., 33
Millicom International, 8
Miniard, Paul W., 191
Mini Cooper, 403
Minute Men, 588
Mitsubishi, 258
Mitzeliotis, Katrina, 518
M&Ms, 184, 417, 523
Mohney, Gillian, 552
Mok, Clement, 143
Monsanto, 24
Monster.com, 61
Moore, Stefany, 235
Mordock, Jeff, 451
Moskin, Julia, 325
Moskowitz, Eric, 166, 589
MossimoGiannulli, 419
Mossler, Fred, 437
The Most Interesting Man in the World campaign, 526
Motel, 95, 342–343, 550, 639. 88
Motorcycle Industry Council, 93
Motorola, 241, 390
Motrin, 393–394
Mountain Dew, 273
Mountain Hardwear, 438
Mountz, Mick, 451
Mourdoukoutas, Pano, 489
Mourdoukoutas, Panos, 489
MovieTickets.com, 209
MP3 players, 396
Mrs. Meyer's Clean Day, 597
MSN.com, 282
MTN, 8
MTV, 102, 259
Mui, Ylan Q., 96
Mullen, Scott, 165, 588

Mullett, Kevin, 172
Munroe Dairy, 336, 510
Murphy, David, 254, 267
Murray, Katherine, 2
Murray, Matthew, 2, 573
Music Unlimited, 123
Mylanta, 394
MySpace, 44, 102

N

Nabisco, 592
Nagourney, Adam, 33
Naked Cowboy, 417
NASCAR, 11, 280, 301, 525
NASDAQ, 83
Naslund, Amber, 113
Nassauer, Sarah, 419
Nassif, Monica, 597
National Advertising Division (NAD), 71
National Advertising Review Board, 71
National Aeronautics and Space Administration (NASA), 233
National Biodiesel Board, A–14
National Breast Cancer Awareness Month, 15
National Business Aviation Association, 14
National Center for American Indian Enterprise Development, 285–286
National Football League (NFL), 15, 64, 205, 345
National Geographic, 474
National Highway Traffic Safety Administration (NHTSA), 29, 70
National Hockey League (NHL), 3
National Institute of Standards and Technology (NIST), 390
National White Collar Crime Center, 149
National Wildlife Federation, 100
Nation's Restaurant News, 460, 630
Natural Resources Defense Council, 89
The Nature Conservancy, 89
Nautica, 317, 601
Navy Pier, 487
NCAA basketball, 525
Necco Wafers, 53

Nederlander, David T., 58
Nederlander, James L., 58
Nederlander Organization, 59, 268, 305
Nederlander Producing Company, 58, 268, 305
Nederlander, Robert, Jr., 58, 138
Nederlander Worldwide Entertainment, 268
Neff, Jack, 283, 286
Nelson, Jennifer K., 282
Nelson, Willie, 282
The Nest, 297
Nestlé, 51, 52, 143, 418, 574
Nestlé USA Prepared Foods, 418
Net-α-Porter.com, 608
Netflix, 56, 308–309, 319, 457, 464, 486, 308, 309
NetJets, 602
Netscape, 67
Network Solutions.com, 67
Neuman, Judy, 437
Neuman, Lucy (fictitious), A-7
Neuman, William, 437
Neutrogena, 394
Newark Police Department, 19
New Balance, 165, 565
Newegg.com, 139
Newman, Andrew Adam, 94, 280
Newman, Andy, 280
Newman, Mark, 280
New Mexico Spaceport Authority, 17
News Corporation, 66, 102
Newton, James, 102, 486
New York Giants, 102
New York Stock Exchange, 243
New York Times, 21, 25, 58, 94, 187, 512, 515, 535, 539
Nexus One, 359
Ngak, Chenda, 96
Nichols, Chris, 307
Nickisch, Curt, 336, 510
Nielsen Company, 312, 333. 350
Nielsen, Jakob, 143, 543
Nielsen/Net Ratings, 158
Nielsen Norman Group, 143
Nike, 23, 50, 95, 146, 178, 254, 259, 356, 405, 416, 438, 449, 528, 615

Nike's Reuse-A-Shoe program, 449
Nintendo, 30, 284, 444–445, 449, A-4
Nintendo DS, 284
Nintendo Wii, 444
99¢ Only, 483
Nisen, Max, 153
Nissan, 8, 627, 629
Nissan Versa, 384, 629
Nivea, 129
Nivea for Men, 129
NJ.com, 31
Nokia, 8
Nordstrom, 56, 146, 150, 199, 346, 449, 480, 490–491, 502, 558, 565
The North Face, 425
NorthPark Center, 487
Northwestern Mutual, 391
Nutella, 411

O

Oakley, 430
Obsession, 616
Occupational Outlook Handbook, 447
O'Connor, Clare, 96
Office Depot, 206, 244, 413
Office Depot Green, 413
Olay, 183, 281
Old Navy, 558
Olenski, Steve, 33, 132
Olmsted, Larry, 244
Olson, Lindsay, 519
Olympic Games, 349
O'Malley, Gavin, 306
O'Malley, Julia, 325
Omega watches, 298
O'Neill, Megan, 132
OneNet Service, 204
Orabrush, 103, 534
Oracle, 352
Oreskovic, Alexei, 59
Orville Redenbacher, 410
Orvis, 473, 502
Oscar de la Renta, 102
Oscar Mayer, 296

Ouellet, Megan, B-5
Outdoor Discovery Schools, 393
Outdoor Industry Association, A-10
Overstock.com, 7
Owens Corning, 418

P

Pajamagram, 502
Pajama Jeans, 503
Palmeri, Christopher, 643
Palmer, Kimberly, 643
Palmieri, Jean E., 201
Pampered Chef, 447, 503, 560
Pampers, 242
Panasonic, 559
Pandora, 182, 183
Parker, Tammy, 96
Parker, Whitney, 133
Patriots Pro Shop, 41
Paul, Gordon W., 33
PawsChoice, 452
PayPal, 147, 285, 640
PBS, 243
PCMag.com, 164
PCWorld.com, 164
Pearanormal Activity, 425
Peek, 372
Peneycad, Matthew, 132, 133
Pennington, 527
PennLive.com, 459
Pentagon, 227
Pepe's Pizzeria, 370
Pepperidge Farm, 413
Pepsi, 6, 16, 413, 424, 436
PepsiCo, 103, 170, 171, 199, 259, 262, 272–273, 306, 419, 424, 430, 436, 447, 524, 534
Perez, Sarah, 165
Perfect Pasta Pot, 503
Performance Bike, 561
Perlut, Aaron, 552
Perry Ellis, 317
Perry, Tacoma, 407
Pet Center, 442
Petco, 341

PetroChina, 242
Petropics, 452
PetsHotel, 422
PetSmart, 422
Pettijohn, Sarah L., 33
Pew Research Center, 243, 283
Pfizer, 50, 64
P&G, 37, 592–593
Pham, Alex, 639
Pharmaceutical Research and Manufacturers of America, 566
Philips, 267, 304
Phoenix Opportunity System, 227
Pichler, Josh, 307
Pier 1, 459, 461
Pike Place Market, 515
Pinkerton, 385
Pinterest, 12, 20, 31, 100–102, 105, 113, 116, 123, 129, 168, 190, 203, 316, 350, 417–418, 440, 482, 512
Pisani, Joseph, 643
Pistons On-Court Jacket, 561
Pizza Hut, 244–245, 256, 378, 458
Plank, Kevin, 408–409
PlantBottle, 411
Plato's Closet, 45, 50
Play N Trade Video Games, 55
PlayStation, 123, 284
PlayStation Network, 123
Plungis, Jeff, 651
Poggi, Jeanine, 407
Polaris missile, 429
Polyvore, 139
Pong game, 284
Popcorn Factory, 502
Porsche, 384, 386, 414–415, 567
Positioning: The Battle for Your Mind, 376
Pottery Barn, 244, 404, 459, 487, 561
Prada, 448
Prater, Connie, 96
Pratt Institute, 551
Praxair, 211
Precious Moments, 422
Press Ganey, 325
PriceGrabber.com, 145

Priceline.com, 621
Prilliman, Angela, 623
Pring, Cara, 33
Pringles, 259
Procter & Gamble, 14, 37, 110, 143, 242–243, 259, 285–286, 324, 329, 351, 357, 414, 415, 420, 428, 443, 445, 446, 460, 526, 592, 599
Product Red brand, 350
Progressive Field, 89
Progressive Insurance, 183
Progresso, 411
Prudential Financial, 416
Publix, 338–339
Puget Sound Business Journal, 412, B-5
Pull-Ups, 414
"Pure Michigan" campaign, 185
Purex, 411
Purina, 281
Purple Heart Veterans, 45
Pursche, Oliver, 437

Q

Qantas, 385
"Queen of Infomercials", 503
Quick, Becky, 96
Quick Test/Heakin, 312
Quinton, Brian, 165
Quiznos, 474

R

Rabeler, Katrina, 451
Rabkin, Eugene, 32
Radian6, 555
Ragan.com, 167
Ragged Mountain, A-9
RAID, 411
Rainforest Alliance, 113
Rainforest Cafés, 488
Ralph Lauren, 144
Rancero-Menendez, Sara, 133
Randa Luggage, 317
Rapoza, Kenneth, 33
Ravindranath, Mohana, 337
Razor Gator, A-7

RC Cola, 45
Really Simple Syndication (RSS), 2
Rector, Sylvia, 9
Redbox, 404
Red Cross, 7
RedLaser, 643
Red Lobster, 460
Reebok, 50, 64, 254, 274
Reed, Brad, 96
Reese's Pieces, 523
Regus Group, 389
Reid, Ben, 489
Relay for Life, 101
Rembrandt, 394
Restaurant: Impossible, 440, 512, 590, 652
Restaurant Source, 208
Restoration Hardware, 487
Retailer Reporting Model, 432
Reuters, 621
Revlon, 16
Revolutionary Riders, 588
Reynolds, Pat, 419
RFID Journal, 474
Rice-a-Roni, 413
Rice, Tim, 266
The Richards Group, 550
Richards, Stan, 565
Riddell, Roger, 552
Riley, Amber, 131
Rio Olympics, 266
Rite Aid Corporation, 358
Ritz-Carlton, 382
RoadRUNNER Motorcycle Touring & Travel, 306
RoadRunnerSports.com, 463
Road Scholar, 284
Road Scholar Travel Assistance Plan, 284
Rock of Gibraltar, 416
Roeger, Katie L, 33
Rolex, 16, 183, 250, 259, 412, 452
Rolls-Royce, 414
R8 One-Day program, 382
Rosenblatt, Seth, 553
Rosenblum, Emma, 407
Rosman, Katherine, 21, 553
Ross, 494

Rovell, Darren, 621
Royal Dutch/Shell Group, 143
Rozwell, Carol, 133
Ruffles, 413
Ruggless, Ron, 630
Ruhlin, Claire, 476
Ruiz, Manny, 96
Ryder, 385

S

Saba, Jennifer, 59
S. Abraham & Sons, 499
Sacramento Fire Department, 19
Safeco Field, 89
Safeway, 455
Sagee Manor vacation homes, 180
Saks Fifth Avenue, 180, 488
Salesforce.com, 352, 354, 554–556
Salesforce Marketing Cloud, 555
The Sales Hunter.com, 219
Sales & Marketing Management, 318
Salesnet.com, 352
Salup, Marni, 167
Sambo's, 349
Sam's Choice colas, 638
Sam's Club, 178, 213, 455, 473, 493–494, 538, 582
Samsung, 16, 26, 30, 56, 88, 130, 144, 267, 303, 335, 418, 490, 528, 598?
Samsung Galaxy, 5, 385
Sandals Resorts, 13, 29
Santana Row, 467
Santinelli International, 572
SAP, 66, 205, 352, 461, 520
Sarfraz, Saad, 564
The Saturday Evening Post, 324
Sauer, Abe, 489
Sauter, Michael B., 237
Save-A-Lot, 455
Savitz, Erik, 407
Savored Restaurant, 114
Scandalios, Nick, 268, 305
Schawbel, Dan, 38
Schelmetic, Tracey, 235
Schoettle, Anthony, 370

Schultz, E.J., 59
Science Diet, 26
Scism, Leslie, 59
ScoreBig, 621
Scott, Mark, 165
Scotts Miracle-Gro, 430
Scott-Thomas, Caroline, 133, 412
Scott toilet tissue, 358
Scripps Networks Interactive, 168, 270, 372, 440, 512, 590, 652
Seabrook, Teisha, 33
The Seam, 208, 389
Sears, 241, 335, 379, 411, 493
Seattle Seahawks, 349
See's Candies, 633
Sega, 284
Seiko, 258
Sephora, 349, 403
Service Employees International Union, 19
7-Eleven, 95, 458, 490, 615–616
Sevlakovs.com, 167
Shared Vision program, 213
Sharifi, Jim, 610
Sharma, Asit, 482
Sharper Image, 481
Shaw's, 336
Sheex, 564–565
Sheinin, Dave, 33
Shell, 418, 641
Shepardson, David, 96
Sherwood, Stacy, 327
Shih, Gerry, 149
Shine, 85, 281
Shoebuy.com, 608
Shopzilla.com, 608
Shutterfly, 633
Shuttleworth, 37
Siemens, 258
Sierra Club, 297
Sierra Mist, 273, 413
Silver-Greenberg, Jessica, 97
Simmons, Jonathan, 166, 589
Simply Measured, 119
Singer, Natasha, 187
Singh, Namrata, 59

Sinopec-China Petroleum, 242
"Site to Store" feature, 643
SixDegrees.com, 102
Six Flags, 30
Ski Butternut, 200, 622
SkipIt, 154
Skittles, 451
Skype, 77, 404, 600
Slager, Brad, 552
Small, Geoffrey B., 32, 476
Smartfood popcorn, 413
SmartOrg, 313
SmartPULL, 421
SmartSignal, 76
Smith, Brian, 437
Smith, Chris, 33
Smith, Craig, 96, 337
Smithfield Herald, 487
Smith, Jacky, 371
Smith, Jacquelyn, 190
Smith, Matt, 59
Smith, Ray A., 605
Smith, Robert, 59
Smith, Steve, 579
Smooth Operator, 297
Snapple, 44–45, 565
Snaptell app, 104
Snickers, 260
Snider, Nike, 165
Snyder, Eric, 487
Sobe juices, 413
Social Media Explorer, 109
SocMetrics, 114
Soergel, Andrew, 623
Sofitel, 88
Sokolowsky, Jennifer, 406
Solaris Collection, 173
Solomon, Micah, 354
Somer, Jeff, B-4
SongKick, 209
Sony, 8, 56, 123, 139, 142, 267, 397, 399, 413, 456, 504, 532, A-6
Sony.com, 142, 267
Sorabol Korean BBQ & Asian Noodles, 176
Southwest Airlines, 120, 151, 157, 379, 406, 565

Spaceport America, 17
Special Olympics, 110
Specific Media, 102
Splenda, 394
Sponsored Links, 154
Sport Clips, 458
Sports Authority, 56, 452, 486
SpotXchange, 154
Springer, Jon, 237
Sprinkles Cupcakes, 451
Sprouts Farmers Market, 482
Square, 7, 104, 486, 494, 610
Sreenivasan, Sree, 33
SRI International, 291
Srivistava, Mandira, 413
Stacy's Greenhouses, 599
Staples, 18, 143, 151, 380–381, 412, 503, 582, 630, 648
Starbucks, 43, 48, 50, 118, 158, 199, 273, 292, 379, 399, 479, 486, 494, 514–515
Starch Readership Report, 544
State Farm, 528–529
Staubach, Roger, 22
Stein Mart, 494
Stella & Dot, 448
Stella McCartney, 410, 438
Stelter, Brian, 552
Stelzner, Michael A., 133
Stenman, Jim, 187
Steve Madden, 438
Steyer, James, 539
St. John's Town Center, 487
St. Joseph's baby aspirin, 281
St. Jude Children's Research Hospital, 14, 16
Stoller, Gary, 623
Stop & Shop, 631
Straight Talk Wireless, 23
Strange, Adario, 477
Streampix, 455
Streetwise.org, 631
StubHub.com, 595, 649
Studio 6, 88
Subway, 23, 165, 245, 333, 458, 475, 525, 528, 536, 586, 588
SuccessFactors, 66

Sullivan, Danny, 33
Sultan, Ralph G. M., 623
SunChips, 451
Sunkist, 416
Sunkist Growers, 416
Sun Life Financial of Canada, 8
Super Bowl, 18, 518, 521, 525, 537, 541, 550, 564
SuperValu, 413, 455
Supplier Diversity Corporate Plan, 226
Supply House Times, 501
Survey of Current Business, 320
Susse, Tatyana, 428
Sussman, Anna Louie, 475
Sustainability Consortium, 88
Suzuki, 64
Symantec, 147
Sysco, 510

T

Tagged, 106
Tag Heuer watches, 197
Tampa Bay Rays, 349
Target, 13–16, 18, 22, 27, 29, 36, 42, 44, 51, 349, 350, 361, 372, 376, 380, 397, 406, 413, 415, 420, 422–425, 430, 449, 453, 455, 476, 478–479, 481–484, 486, 488, 492, 494–495, 502, 505–507, 510, 516–519, 521
Tastefully Simple, 447
Tata Motors, 629
Tauck Bridges, 297
Tazo, 399
Team, Trefis, 623
TelePresence, 388, 389
10 Crosby by Derek Lam, 438
Ten Dollar Dinners, 512
Terdiman Daniel, 358
Terdiman, Daniel, 351
TerraCycl, A-4
Tetra Tech, 210, 442
Tetra Tech EC, 213
Texaco, 418
Texas Instruments, 258
Thompson, Scott, 34

Thorn, Bret, 460
Ticket Liquidator, 640
Ticketmaster, 595
TicketsNow.com, 595
Tico Times.net, 487
Tide, 236
Tiffany & Company, 383
Timberland, A-8–A-9
Time, 243, 246, 251–253, 254–256
Times Square, 417
Time Warner Cable, 78
Time Warner Cable's TV Essentials, A-11
Timex, 258
Title Nine, A-9
T.J. Maxx, 478, 494
TLC, 372
T-Mobile, 64, 276, 345, 348, 638
Togo-Figa, Rochelle, 447
Tom's of Maine, 394
Topham, Traci, 590
Tor, Maria, 564
Tory Burch, 180, 380, 411, 492
Toshiba, 30, 88, 249, 399
Tostitos, 413
Tour de Cure, 16
Tourhalai, Halah, 564
Toyota, 71, 75, 242, 262, 353, 385, 436, 524, 604, 648
Toyota Camry, 648
Toyota Prius, 75
Toys "R" Us, 48, 151
Trader Joe's, 379, 601
Training magazine, 61
Transportation Security Administration (TSA), 66, 461
TransUnion, 71
Travel Channel, 168, 590
Travelocity, 73, 648
Trejos, Nancy, 407, 476
Trendrr, 119, 127
Troianovski, Anton, 96
Trump, Donald J., 570
TRUSTe, 148
Tuesday Morning, 485
Tumblr, 100, 102, 107, 129, 168, 440
Tupperware, 448, 503, 560

TweetWall, 132
Twitter, 11, 12, 14, 20, 21, 22, 27, 28, 29 51, 58, 100–109, 101, 102, 103, 104, 105, 107, 108, 110, 112, 113, 114, 115, 116, 117, 118, 119, 120, 123–125, 124, 125, 131–168, 132, 137, 165, 173, 185, 190, 202, 260, 270, 284, 296, 298, 316, 319, 322, 335, 345, 347, 350, 360, 370, 372, 382, 406, 440, 482, 495, 512, 518, 552 554, 555, 565, 587, 588, 589, 650, A-10
Tyco, 24
Tylenol, 394

U

uBid.com, 640, 641
UEFA EURO
U-Haul, 378
Ulukaya, Hamdi, 437
Uncle Ben's, 114
Under Armour, 23, 57, 407, 408, 409, 452
UNICEF, 119, 120
Uniform Commercial Code, 540
Unilever, 8, 119, 261, 304, 405, 413, 443, 574
United Airlines, 58, 139, 369
United's Mileage Plus, 349
United Stationers, 497
United Way, 15
Universal Studios Amusement Park, 64
University of Chicago, 76
University of Florida, 349
University of Notre Dame, 409
University of Phoenix, 183
University of Texas, 19
Univision, 78, 286
Unleashed, 341
UPS, 5, 13, 92, 222, 243, 463, 466, 467
Urban Outfitters, 57, A-5
USA Network, 335
U.S. Army, 17
USA Today, 155, 515, 535
U.S. Census Bureau, 47, 93, 174, 175, 180, 290, 320
U.S. Centers for Disease Control and Prevention, 539
U.S. Coast Guard, 19
U.S. Department of Agriculture (USDA), 426
U.S. Department of Commerce, 50, 74, 240, 288, 595

U.S. Department of Defense, 76, 211
U.S. Department of Energy (DOE), 93, 604
U.S. Department of Justice, 67, 70
U.S. Department of Labor, 378, 447
U.S. Environmental Protection Agency (EPA), 65
U.S. Federal Sentencing Guidelines for Organizations, 81
U.S. Food and Drug Administration (FDA), 64
U.S. Green Building Council, 88
U.S. Navy, 429, 517, 518
U.S. Olympic Committee, 349
U.S. Olympic teams, 409
U.S. Postal Service, 7, 19, 92, 226, 243, 267, 635
U.S. Secret Service, 149
U.S. Supreme Court, 314, 454, 596
U.S. Transportation Security Administration (TSA), 461
U.S. Treasury Department, 87
U.S. Wholesale Grocers Association, 595

V

Valu-Rite Pharmacies, 491
Vanguard Cleaning Systems, 458
VantageScore, 71
Variety, 492, 572
Varvil, Dustin, 479
Vault Denim, 560
Vend Natural, 514
Vente-privée.com, 494
Venture for America, 95
Vergara, Sofia, 16
Veridex, 394
Verismo, 399
Verizon Wireless, 211, 335, 586, 606
Versace, 637
Viactiv, 394
Victoria's Secret, 216, 415, 531
Vineyard Vines, 2–3
Vintage Plantations, 113
ViralHeat, 119
Virgin Galactic, 17, 36, 37, 43
Virtuosity, 484
Visa, 29, 92, 149, 163, 281, B-4
Visine, 393
Vitelli, Romeo, 539

Vocalpoint, 351
Volkswagen, 4, 112, 118, 133, 212, 242, 262, 404, 436
Volpe, Mark, 212
Volvo, 74, 432
Vonage, 155
Von Maur, 66

W

Walgreens, 103, 164, 164–165, 165, 479, 492, 495
Walker, Mason, 405
Wall, Robert, 59
Wall Street Journal, 48, 66, 515
Walmart, 14, 16, 23, 25, 28, 35, 40, 44, 45, 46, 48, 49, 50, 73, 88, 92, 101, 112, 143, 150, 151, 159, 213, 238–239, 241, 242, 299, 339, 356, 357, 413, 432, 436, 455, 460, 461, 483, 484, 486, 487, 492, 494, 499, 507, 508, 509, 574, 592, 593, 609, 629, 634, 636, 638, 643, 644
Walmart Supercenter, 494
Walter Landor & Associates, 417
Wang, Jasmine, 96
Warner Brothers, 335
Warner, Gary A., 343
Watrous, Monica, 630
Watson, Elaine, 419, 437
Wawa, 491
Weather Channel, 20, 21
Weather.com, 21
Webkinz, 6, 398
Wegmans, 336
Weight Watchers, 114, 115, 266, A-5
Welsh Rugby Union, 409
Wendy's, 49, 141, 212, 214, 419
Wente Vineyards, 270
Wentz, Laurel, 552
West Elm, 483
Westinghouse, 413, 538
Westinghouse, George, 538
Westminster Kennel Club, 31
Weston Solutions, 27
Weyerhaeuser, 385
White, Annie, 382
Whitehead, Thomas, 476
White, Martha C, 201

White Sands Missile Range, 17
White, Shaun, 14, 413
Whittaker, Zack, 407
Whittemore, Christine, 406, 651
Whole Foods Market, 455, 487
Widder, Brandon, 132
Wii, 284, 444, 445, 449
Wikipedia, 104
Wildfox Jewelry, 132
Wilhelm, Alex, 149
Wille Megan, 623
Williams, Roy H., 629
Williams-Sonoma, 151, 474, 486, 494, 502, 597
Wilson, Michael, 489
Wilson Sporting Goods, 205
Wilton Products, 106
Winfrey, Oprah, 111
Winter Olympics, 18
Wired, 298
WNET, 349
Wohl, Jessica, 482
Woodruff, Mandi, 244
Word of Mouth Marketing Association (WOMMA), 351
Wordpress, 100, 102
World Cup, 18, 409, 521, 525, 615
World Environment Center, 86
World Retail Banking Report, 348
World Series, 18
World Shoe Accessories show, 437
World Wide Web, 156
Wortham, Jenna, 351
Worthy Composites, B–1–B–4
"WOW" service, 236
Wright Investors, 321

X

Xerox Corporation, 417

Y

Yahoo, 34–35
Yahoo!, 107, 108
Yahoo! Answers, 107
Yahoo! Voices, Yammer, 335

Yang, Brian, 31
Yo Chicago.com, 567
York, Emily Bryson, 419
Young & Rubicam (Y&R), 414
YourCause.com, 14
"You Serve, You Save" program, 622
YouTube, 12, 31, 58, 79, 100, 102, 103, 104, 105, 106, 107, 108, 110, 112, 114, 116, 120, 125, 138, 154, 168, 296, 316, 322, 343, 382, 417, 482, 518, 534
Yo-yo, 417
YRC Freight, 445
Yue, Lorene, 31
Yum! Brands, 242, 244, 245

Z

Zabriskie, Kate, 564
Zagnut Candy Bars, 53
Zapin, Marni, 327
Zappos.com, 391, 463
Zappos Insights, 235, 236
Zawadzki, Sabina, 475
Ziglar, Zig, 19
Zmuda, Natalie, 48
Zoe, Rachel, 111
Zorlu Property Group, 268
Zuckerberg, Mark, 102
Zwiebach, Elliot, 509

SUBJECT INDEX

A

accessory equipment, **386**
accounts receivable turnover, B-4
achievers, 291
administered marketing system, **457**
adoption process, **424**–425
adoption/rejection stage, 425
advergames, 532
advertising, **522**. *See also* marketing; strategy
   advergames, 532
   banner ad, **153**–**154**, 532–533
   billboards, 184, 537
   celebrity sponsorship, 14, 42, 518, 527–528, 527–528, 590
   clutter, 528
   comparative, **527**
   cooperative, 453, **528**
   corporate, 526
   creating ads, 531–532
   developing ads, 529
   direct mail, 502, 536, 578
   fear-based appeals, 530
   for gamers, 532
   humorous appeals, 531
   informative, **526**
   interactive ads, 529, 532–533
   interactive media, 536–537, 544–545
   Internet, 516, 519, 529, 532–533
   keyword ads, 532
   location-based, 526
   magazines, 535–536
   media scheduling, 537
   media selection, 533–537
   message, **520**, 529
   message research for, **543**–544
   mobile, 515, 537
   newspapers, **535**
   objectives, 526–527
   outdoor, 536
   out-of-home, 518, 536
   persuasive, **526**
   planning, 518, 529, 543, 544
   pop-unders, 532
   pop-ups, **154**, 532, 548
   product, **526**
   product lifecycle and, 396, 526
   radio, 534–535
   reminder, **526**
   retail, 299, **528**–529
   sex-based appeals, 531
   soft drink, 541
   specialty, **581**
   sponsorship *vs.*, **525**
   television, 533–534
   translating objectives into plans, 529–530
   truth in, 84
   types, 526
   words to use, 529
advertising agency, 550
advertising campaign, **530**
advocates, 20–22
affinity marketing, **349**
African Americans, 47, 175–176
   population growth, 285
age
   baby boomers, 283
   boomerang (grownup living with parents), 288
   child labor/trafficking, 451
   Children's Online Privacy Protection Act, 68, 69
   customer needing child care service, 484
   demographic segmentation by, 281–285
   empty nesters, 288
   family purchasing, 181
   Generation X, 282–283
   marketing to children, 198, 281
   Millennial Generation, 57–58
   seniors, 181, 283–284
   social media preferences, 372

age (*continued*)
   tweens/teens, 281–282
   underage drinking, 84–85
AIDA concept, **520**–521, 567
AIO statements, **291**
air bags, auto, 76
aircraft manufacturers, 624
air freight, 466
Airline Deregulation Act, 69
airline industry
   boarding passes, 66
   setbacks in, 404
airplane manufacturers, 64
Alaska Natives, 176
allowances, price quotation, **633**
allowances, trade, 581
amusement parks, 620
animal rights, 93
Annual Survey of Manufactures (ASM), 212
Anti-cybersquatting Consumer Protection Act, 69
antitrust regulations, **64**, 67–68, 248
app, **103**–104
approach, **567**–568
Asch phenomenon, 177–178
Asian Americans, 176
   population growth, 285
ASPs. *See* application service providers
atmospherics, **488**–490
attention, interest, desire, action (AIDA) concept, **520**–521, 567
attitude, **186**
   changing, 186–187
   cognitive components, 186–187
   in consumer behavior, 186–187, 270
   favorable/unfavorable, 186
   modifying components, 187–188
   social media tapping into, 270
attitude-scaling devices, 186
auctions, 207–208, 500
   online, 640–641
auto industry
   air bags, 76
   encouraging commuting, 74–75
   international distribution strategy, 261
   list price, 633

   penetration pricing, 628–629
   price determination, 609
   promotional allowance, **633**
   purchasing by gender, 181
   recalls, 80, 542
   retrieving lost customers, 353–364
   safety and liability, 431
automated warehouse technology, 468
average total cost, **606**
awareness stage, of adoption process, **425**

B

B2B. *See* business-to-business marketing
B2C. *See* business-to-consumer marketing
baby boomers, 57, 283
backward integration, **457**
banner ad, **153**–154, 532–533
basic planners, 292
basing-point pricing, **635**
BCG matrix. *See* Boston Consulting Group matrix
bed sheets, 564
beef products, 79
believers, 291
belongingness needs, 182
benchmarking, **390**
big-box retailer, 593
big data, 310
bike-sharing system, 165–166
billboards, 184, 537
blog, 21, 103, **152**, 351, 476, 651
   career readiness, 12
   micro-, 102–103
blogging forum, **102**
blogging site, **102**
board of directors, 38, 39
bonus packs, **580**
bookmarking site, **102**
boomerang (grownup living with parents), 288
bot (shopbot), **145**, **644**
bottom line, **14**
brain imaging, 186
brand(s), **410**. *See also* product identification
   captive, **413**
   cobranding, **356**–357

equity, **414**–415
evolution of, 5
family, 270, **413**–414
flanker, 424
focusing on tradition, 437
launching of, 409–410
loyalty, 411–412
manufacturer's, **413**
preferences, 411
private, **413**
role of, 415–416
selected brand names and brand marks, 411
truth in advertising claims, 412
types of, 412–414
brand equity, **415**–415
brand extensions, **421**–422
brand insistence, **412**
brand licensing, **422**–423
brand manager, **415**
brand mark, **416**–417
brand name, **416**–417
brand preference, **411**
brand recognition, **411**
breakeven analysis, **611**–612
modified, **613**–614
broadband streaming services, 494
broker, **500**–501
budget, sample of, A-5–A-6
budget, marketing plan, A-5
bundle pricing, **644**
buses, 650–651
business cycle, **72**–73
business plan, **A-1**. *See also* marketing plan; marketing planning
business portfolio analysis, 51
business products, **275**
accessory equipment, **386**
business services, **388**–389
classification, 394
component parts/materials, **386**
installations, 385–386
raw materials, **386**–387
supplies, 387–388
types of, 385–389
business services, **388**–389

business-to-business (B2B) marketing. *See also* buyer–seller relationships
analysis tools, 224
B2C marketing compared to, 205
buyer–seller, 213, 355–357
buyer sizes/numbers, 212
buying centers, **225**
buying situations classification, 223–224
cell phone discounts, 211
characteristics of, 212–214
commercial market, **206**
components, 206–208
customer type segmentation, 210–211
defined, **142, 204, 355**
demographic characteristics segmentation, 210
end-use application segmentation, **211**
e-procurement on open exchanges, 143
evaluating international, 213–214
foreign business markets, 208–209
geographic market concentration, 212
government agencies as market, 207
improving buyer–seller relationships, 357–358
influences on purchase decisions, 218–221
institutional markets, 227–229
international markets, 229
Internet connection, 208
limited-buyer markets, 212, 213
make/buy/lease decision, 216–218
market demand, 214–216
NAICS, **210**–211
offshoring, **217**
organizational buying process model, 221–223
outsourcing, 217–218
partnerships, 22–23, 209, 212, 213, 270
proprietary transactions, 142–143
purchase categories segmentation, 211
purchase decision process, 218–220
relationship marketing and, 213
resellers, **206**, 208
resource-producing industries, 206
social media initiative for, 202–203
trade industries, **206**
21st century marketing, 230

business-to-business (B2B) product, **380**
business-to-consumer (B2C) marketing, **143**
   access and convenience of, 145–146
   B2B marketing compared to, 205
   bots, **145**
   competitive pricing of, 144–145
   conversations via social media, 372
   Cyber Monday events using, 143
   electronic shopping carts, **144**, 624–625
   electronic storefronts in, **144**
   online buyers and sellers, 146–147
   personalized service in, 146–147
business-to-consumer (B2C) product, **382**
bus travel/companies, 406
buyer, 213, **225**
buyer partnerships, **356**
buyer–seller relationships
   in B2B marketing, 213, 355–357
   building loyalty, 354
   databases, 358
   electronic data interchange and Web services, **142**, 358
   improving, 357–358
   relationship marketing, 348–351
   vendor-managed inventory, 358–360
buyer's market, **10**
buying center, **225**–226
buying process, model of organizational, 221–223
buzz marketing, **351**, 524

C

cameras, 638–639
cannibalization, **424**, **643**
captive brand, **413**
career, marketing
   closing sales, 447, **570**, 625
   cold calling, **568**
   comparison shopping, 643
   distractions at work, 190
   first real job, 37
   green technology and environmental causes, 75
   international travel, 244
   knowing your competition, 495
   negotiating with customers, 219
   networking, 519

   in SMM, 123–125
   in social media, 125
   social media and target markets, 295
   social media marketing manager, 12
   surveys for mobile devices, 327
car rental, 558
carriers, 463–464
cash-and-carry wholesaler, 499, 500
cash discounts, **631**–632
catalogs, 596
category advisor (category captain), 220–**221**
category killer, **492**
category management, **415**
cause marketing, 16, **18**
CBSA. *See* core based statistical area
c-business, 143
celebrity sponsorship, 42, 527–528, 527, 528, 590
cell phone
   B2B discounts, 211
   Consumer Telephone Records Act, 69
   Do-Not-Call Improvement Act, 69
   mobirati, 292
Central American Free Trade Agreement-DR (CAFTA-DR), **253**
CEO. *See* chief executive officer
cereal manufacturers, 50, 84
CFO. *See* chief financial officer
chain of trade discounts, 632
channel captain, **455**
channel conflicts, **151**
   gray goods, 456
   horizontal, 455
   vertical, 455–456
channels, sales, 520–521
   alternative, 562
personal selling *vs.* advertising, 556
channel strategies
   market factors, 450, 452
   organizational and competitive factors, 451–452
   product factors, 450–451
   selection of, 450–452
chief executive officer (CEO), 38–39
chief financial officer (CFO), 39

chief operating officer (COO), 38–39
child care service, 484
child labor/trafficking, 451
children
   family purchasing, 181
   marketing to, 198, 281
   tweens/teens, 281–282
Children's Online Privacy Protection Act, 68, 69
cigarettes, 67, 71, 82
Clayton Act, 67, 68, 454
click-through rate, **158**
closed sales territory, **454**
closing, 447, **570**
   abandoned shopping cart *vs.*, 625
closure concept, 184
clothing industry, 475, 558
cloud-computing services, 554–555
cluster sample, **323**
clutter, 528
CMSA. *See* consolidated metropolitan statistical area
cobranding, **356**–357
cocoa, 450
coffee, 586
cognitive dissonance, **193**
cohort effect, **284**
cold calling, **568**
collaborative planning, forecasting, and replenishment (CPFR), **358**
colleges, 640
college towns, 482
comarketing, **356**–357
commercial airplane manufacturers, 64
commercial market, **206**
commercial organizations. *See* for-profit organizations
commercials, television, 60–61, 270, 521
commission, **575**
commission merchant, **500**, 501
common carriers, **463**
common market, **252**
communication. *See also* integrated marketing communications
   industry infrastructure, 246
   marketing communications, **516**

process, 520–522
technology, 4
Community Trademark (CTM), 254
commuting, 74
company description, A-4
   in sample marketing plan, A-6
comparative advertising, **527**
competition
   objectives, 600
   Omnibus Trade and Competitiveness Act, 250
   types, 64–65
competitive analysis, A-4
competitive bidding, **639**–641
competitive environment, 62, **64**
competitive pricing strategy, **630**–631
competitive strategy, **65**–66
complaint handling, 347
component parts/materials, **386**
computer technology, 76–77
   business intelligence, 331
   data mining, **331**
   MDSSs, **331**
   MISs, 331
concentrated (or niche) marketing, **297**
concepts
   AIDA, **520**–521, 567
   closure, 184
   marketing, 10–11
   pricing, 603–609, 616
   self-concept, **189**–**190**
   self-concept theory, 189–190
concept testing, **430**
consolidated metropolitan statistical area (CMSA), **279**
constraints, 44
   catering to financial, 592–593
consultative selling, **563**
consumer(s)
   laws protecting, 69
   middle-class, 179–180, 239
   multichannel shoppers, 643
   personal selling *vs.* advertising, 556
   product recalls website for, 80
   social media and marketing to, 372

consumer behavior, **172**, 199. *See also* needs
   attitude, 186–187, 270
   cultural influences, 173–177, 270
   decision process, 190–191
   family influences, 181–182
   interpersonal determinants of, 173–181
   motives, 182–184
   perception, **184**–186
   personal determinants of, 182–190
   problem or opportunity recognition,191
   routinized response behavior, 194
   self-concept theory, 189–190
   social influences, 176–180
   21st century, 195
consumer durable, 242
consumer electronics, 242, 249, 262
Consumer Goods Pricing Act (1975), 596
consumer innovator, **425**
consumerism, **78**–79
consumer orientation, **10**
consumer products, **275**
   applying classification system, 384
   classification, 383–384
   convenience, 381
   shopping, 381–382
   specialty, **382**–383
   types of, 380
   unsought, **380**
consumer product safety, 63, 431
Consumer Product Safety Act (1972), 69, 431
consumer rights, **79**–80
Consumer Telephone Records Act, 69
containerization, **469**
content marketing, **116**
contest, **580**. *See also* sales promotion
contract carriers, **464**
contracts, 226, 231
contractual agreements, 256–257
contractual marketing system, **457**
control, degree of, 255–256
controlled experiment, **328**
convenience product, **380**
convenience retailer, **491**
convenience sample, **323**
convergence, scrambled merchandising and, **494**–495

conversion rate, **158**
COO. *See* chief operating officer
cookies, 148, 187, 540
cookware, 140
cooperative advertising, **453**, **528**–529
copyright disputes, 68, 151
core based statistical area (CBSA), **278**
core competencies, A-4
   in sample marketing plan, A-8–A-9
core region, **279**
corporate advertising, 526
corporate marketing system, **457**
corporate social responsibility (CSR)
   career in, 74
corporate websites, **141**
corporations, transnational, 240
cost per impression, 545, 545
cost per response, 545
cost per thousand (CPM) rate, 542
cost-plus pricing, **609**
cost-reimbursement contracts, 226
counterfeit products, 489
countertrade, **262**
coupon
   dollar-off, 520
   Internet, 155
   sales promotion, **578**–579
CPFR. *See* collaborative planning, forecasting, and replenishment
CPM. *See* cost per thousand rate
creative selling, **566**
creativity
   ad agency's, 550
credit card
   Identity Theft Enforcement and Restitution Act, 67
   lobbying about, 63
   subprime, 85
Credit Card Accountability, Responsibility and Disclosure Act, 69, 85
CRM. *See* customer relationship management
cross-promotion, **538**–540
cross-selling, **563**, 564
cruise vacations, 304
CSR. *See* corporate social responsibility
CTM. *See* Community Trademark

cultural diversity, 78
cultural influences
   on consumer behavior, 173–176, 270
   social–cultural environment, 62, 77–80, 246–247, 270
culture, **173**
   international product and promotional strategy, 260–261
   products adapted to local, 243
   subcultures, **174–176**
cumulative quantity discount, **633**
customary prices, **603**
customer(s)
   attitude, 186–187, 270
   as boss, 16
   converted to advocates, 20–22
   creation, 6
   CRM, **211**, **352**, 353–355
   external customers, **342**
   feedback, 347, 521
   increasingly complex, 263
   internal, **342**
   Internet usage caps on, 636
   keeping, 348–349
   lifetime value of, 5, 19, 360
   loyalty, 20
   Maslow's hierarchy of needs, 182–184
   need and satisfaction, 346–347
   needs, 6, 6–7, 10, 24
   objections from, **570**
   preferred, 596
   retrieving lost, 353–355
customer-based segmentation, **210**
customer churn, **348**
customer relationship management (CRM), **211**, **352**
   benefits of, 352–353
   problems with, 353
   retrieving lost customers, 353–355
customer satisfaction, **346**
   as art/science, 2–12, 23–24
   customer needs, 6, 6–7, 10, 24, 182–184, 346–347
   enhancing, 11, 25
   ensuring, 23
customer service
   e-business, 150–151
   as retailing strategy, 481–482
   standards, 463
customer service standards, 463
customer-to-business (C2B) conversations, 372
customer win-back, **353**
customs union, **252**
cyber-attack, 148
Cyber Monday, 143

D

data analysis companies, 312
database marketing, **349**–350
   electronic data interchange and Web services, 142, 358
   social media use in, 270, 372
data collection, 319–323
data interpretation/presentation, 319. *See also* secondary data
data mining, **313**, 331
deception, puffery and, 540
decider, **225**
decline stage, **397**–398
decoding, 521
deflation, 73–74
Delphi technique, **362**
demand, **604**
   derived, **215**
   inelastic, **215**, 605, 607
   joint, **215**
   market, 214–216
demarketing, **74**
demographic characteristics segmentation, 210
demographic segmentation, **280**
   abroad, 290
   age, 281–285
   cohort effect, **284**
   ethnic groups, 285–287
   family lifecycle, **288**
   gender, 281
   household type, 288–289
   income/expenditure patterns, 289–290
demonstration, **569**
department store, **492–493**
Depression era, 595–596

deregulation, 64, 69–70
derived demand, **214**
detailers, 566
developing ads, 529
differentiated marketing, **296**–297, 642, 644
diffusion process, **426**
digital consumers, 199
Digital Millennium Copyright Act, 68
direct channel, **447**
direct mail, 502, 536
   spending for, 579
direct marketing, **502**, **523**
   automatic merchandising, 504
   direct mail, 502, 536, 578
   direct-response retailing, 503
   direct selling, **447**–448, 502
   Internet, 503
   promotional mix, 523, 525
   telemarketing, 68, 503, 561–561, 561
director of marketing research, 39
direct selling, **447**–448, 503
disaster plan, 264
discount codes, 565
discount coupons, 579
discount house, **493**
discount offers, 625
discounts. *See also* price quotations
   B2B, 211
   cash discounts, **630**–631
   chain of trade, 633
   discount houses, **493**
   for government, 211, 229
   noncumulative quantity, **633**
   small-box discount retailer, 593
   trade, **632**
discretionary income, **7**
disease, outbreak, 266
dish soap marketers, 628
distribution, **444**. *See also* marketing (distribution) channels; physical distribution
   B2C compared to B2B marketing, 205
   dual, **449**
   exclusive distribution, **454**, 475
   global marketing strategy, **259**, A-10
   intensive, **453**
   international distribution strategy, 261
   in marketing environment, 62
   marketing mix, 47–48
   in retailing strategy, 486–487
diversity. *See also* market segmentation
   cultural, 78
   ethnic, 174
   household type, 288–289
   product diversification strategy, **424**
doctors, 566
Do-Not-Call Improvement Act, 69
downstream management, **589**
drop shipper, 499, **500**
dual adaptation, 260
dual distribution, **449**
due on receipt, 632
dumping, **251**

E

e-business, **136**. *See also* e-marketing; Internet
   assessing site effectiveness, 157–158
   channel conflicts, **151**, 455–456
   copyright disputes, 68, 151
   customer service, 150–151
   implementation of website goals, 156–157
   online payment safety, 147–148
   payment systems, 147–148
   pricing and maintenance/promotion costs, 157
   privacy issues, 148–149, 138
   promotional pricing, **637**
   site design, 141, 150
   21st century, 159
   Web business models, 140–142
   website development, 155
   website goals, 156–157
eco-friendly products, 639
e-commerce, 164
economic environment, **72**
   business cycle, **72**–73
   deflation, 73–74
   discretionary income, **74**
   global marketing and, 245
   income, **74**
   inflation, 73–74

international, 75–76
in marketing environment, 62
resource availability, 74–75
unemployment, **74**
economics, multinational economic integration, 251–254
economic theory
cost/revenue curves, 605–607
elasticity, **604**–605
practical problems, 609
price determination, 604–605
EDIs. *See* electronic data interchanges
EDLP. *See* everyday low pricing
80/20 principle, **293**
elasticity, **607**. *See also* inelastic demand
determinants of, 608
revenue and, 608–609
electronic boarding pass, 66
electronic data interchanges (EDIs), **142**, **358**
electronic shopping cart, **144**, 624–625
Electronic Signature Act, 69
electronic signatures, **148**
electronic storefronts, **144**
e-marketing, **138**. *See also* advertising
capabilities, 139
global reach, 139
integrated marketing, 139–140
interactive marketing, 139, 140
opportunities, 139–141
personalization, 139
right-time marketing, 139–140
21st century, 159
embargo, **250**
emergency goods/services, **381**
employee satisfaction, **343**
empty nesters, 288
encoding, 521
encryption, 83, **147**
end-use application segmentation, **211**
engagement, **158**
Engel's laws, **289**–290
enterprise resource planning (ERP) system, **461**
entertainment industry, 65, 243, 266
environment. *See also* marketing environment; political–legal environment; social–cultural environment; sustainability

competitive, 62, **64**
risks/opportunities of, in marketing planning, 40, 44
technological, 62, 76–77, 247–248
environmental management, **63**
environmental scanning, **63**
e-procurement, **143**
on open exchanges, 143
equity brand, **414**–415
ERP. *See* enterprise resource planning
esteem, 182
ETC. *See* export trading company
ethics, **24**. *See also* marketing ethics
airline industry, 404
copyright disputes, 68, 151
fake online reviews, 153
hidden charges, 649
highway tolls, 605
marketing planning and celebrity endorsements, 42
mobile crime, 207
online news content, 198
phishing, **149**
piracy, 474
pop-ups, 548
pricing, 605
promotional strategies, 539–540
in public relations, 539–540
RFID and privacy concerns, 436
safety and liability, 431
sales process, 578
social media, 121–123
social responsibility and, 24–26
truth in advertising claims, 412
unlimited data plan, 638
vishing, **150**
ethnic groups, 285–287
ethnographic studies, 329–330
evaluation, in developing ads, 529
evaluation stage, of adoption process, **425**
evaluative criteria, **193**
event marketing, 16, **18**–19
spending for, 578
everyday low pricing (EDLP), **629**–630
evoked set, **192**
exchange control, **251**

exchange functions, **24**
exchange process, **8**
exchange rate, **246**
exclusive distribution, **454**, 475
executive summary, 110
   sample of, A-4, A-6
experiencers, 291
exploratory research, **316**–317
exponential smoothing, 362–**364**
export broker, 501
exporting, **240**
   Export Trading Company Act (1982), 248
   global market, 255–256
   political–legal environment, 248–249
   service/retail, in global market, 242–244
export-trading company (ETC), 255
Export Trading Company Act (1982), 248
extended problem solving, 194
external customers, **342**
extranets, 142–143
extreme sports fans, 517
extreme value store, 593

F

facial recognition technology, 186
Fair Packaging and Labeling Act (1966), 431
fair-trade laws, **596**
fake stores, 489
family brand, 270, **413**
family lifecycle, **288**
FAR. *See* Federal Acquisition Regulation
fast food restaurants
   fast-casual market positioning, 298
   as limited-buyer market, 214
   world's largest, 257
favorable attitude, 186
FCN. *See* friendship, commerce and navigation treaties
fear-based advertising appeals, 530
Federal Acquisition Regulation (FAR), 227
Federal Food and Drug Act, 67, 69
federal regulation
   Airline Deregulation Act, 69
   Anti-cybersquatting Consumer Protection Act, 69
   Children's Online Privacy Protection Act, 68, 69
   Clayton Act, 67, 68, 454
   Consumer Goods Pricing Act (1975), 596
   Consumer Product Safety Act (1972), 69, 431
   consumer protection, 69
   Consumer Telephone Records Act, 69
   Credit Card Accountability, Responsibility and Disclosure Act, 69, 85
   Digital Millennium Copyright Act, 68
   Do-Not-Call Improvement Act, 69
   Electronic Signature Act, 69
   Export Trading Company Act (1982), 248
   Fair Packaging and Labeling Act (1966), 431
   Federal Food and Drug Act, 67, 69
   Federal Trade Commission Act, 67, 68, 454
   Fee Extension Act, 69
   Flammable Fabrics Act (1953), 431
   Food Allergen Labeling and Consumer Protection Act, 431
   Foreign Corrupt Practices Act, 248
   Fraud Enforcement and Recovery Act, 69
   Helping Families Save Their Homes Act, 69
   Identity Theft Enforcement and Restitution Act, 67
   Miller-Tydings Resale Price Maintenance Act (1937), 596
   Motor Carrier Act, 69
   National Environmental Policy Act, 69
   Nutrition Labeling and Education Act (1990), 421
   Omnibus Trade and Competitiveness Act, 250
   Poison Prevention Packaging Act (1970), 431
   in political–legal environment, 67–68
   Public Health Cigarette Smoking Act, 69
   Real ID Act, 69
   Robinson-Patman Act, 67, 68, **595**–596
   Sherman Antitrust Act, 67, 68, 454
   Staggers Rail Act, 69
   Telecommunications Act, 69, 70
   Trade Act (1998), 248
   Wheeler-Lea Act, 68
Federal Sentencing Guidelines for Organizations, 81
Federal Trade Commission Act, 67, 68, 454
feedback
   customer, 347, 521
   in marketing planning, 39–40
   role in developing ads, 529

Fee Extension Act, 69
field selling, **559**–560, 561
finance charge, 632
financial analysis
   financial statements, B-1–B-2
   markdowns, **485**, B-6
   markups, B-4–B-5
   performance ratios, B-2–B-4
financial statements, B-1–B-2
firewall, **149**
first mover strategy, **43**
fixed costs, **606**
fixed-price contracts, 225
fixed pricing, 614
Flammable Fabrics Act (1953), 431
flanker brand, 424
FOB. *See* free on board
FOB origin, **634**
FOB origin-freight allowed (freight absorbed), **634**
FOB (free on board) plant, or FOB origin, **634**
focus group, **326**
foie gras, 93
follow-up, 570–**571**
Food Allergen Labeling and Consumer Protection Act, 431
food industry, 64
   beverages, 83
   childhood obesity and, 84
   GMOs, 247–248
   interactive buyers and sellers, 270
   social media strategy of, 270, 372
   supermarket chains, 423
Foreign Corrupt Practices Act, 248
foreign licensing, **256**
foreign manufacturer, 642
foreign-owned distributor, 642
form utility, 5
for-profit organizations, 213
forward integration, **457**
franchise, **256**, **458**, 616
Fraud Enforcement and Recovery Act, 69
free on board (FOB), **634**
free-trade area, **251**
Free Trade Area of the Americas (FTAA), **253**
freight forwarders/supplemental carriers, 467

frequency marketing, **348**
friendship, commerce and navigation treaties (FCN), **248**
FTAA. *See* Free Trade Area of the Americas
full-cost pricing, **609**–610
full-service research suppliers, **312**
fun seekers, 424
furniture
   manufacturers, 255
   retailers, 242

G

garage parties, 277
gatekeeper, **225**
GATT. *See* General Agreement on Tariffs and Trade
GDP. *See* gross domestic product
gender, 281
   auto purchasing by, 181
   extreme sports fans, 517
   opinion leaders, **180**
   social media interactions by, 372
   women on motorcycles, 277
General Agreement on Tariffs and Trade (GATT), 249, **252**
general merchandise retailer, **492**
general sales manager, 39
Generation X, 282–283
generic products, **412**
genetically modified organisms (GMOs), 247–248
geographic information systems (GISs), **280**
geographic market concentration, 212
geographic segmentation, **277**, 279
   migration, 278
   population, 277, 278
   urbanization, 278–279
GISs. *See* geographic information systems
global economic crisis, 73
globalization. *See also* global marketing strategy; Internet
   e-marketing, 139
   marketing strategy, 615
global marketing, 238–239
   benefits of, 244–245
   categories of, 240
   contractual agreements, 256–257

global marketing, (continued)
  developing global marketing strategy, 259–262
  direct investment, 257–258
  dumping, **251**
  economic environment, 245–246
  employment and, 240, 250
  factors creating today's, 7–8
  globalization and, 254
  importing and exporting, 255–256
  language's role in, 247
  marketing mix, 259–260
  from multinational corporations, 258
  multinational economic integration, 251–254
  political–legal environment, 71, 74–76, 248–249
  service/retail exports, 242–244
  social–cultural influences in, 62, 77–80, 246–247
  technological environment, 62, **76–77**, 247–248
  trade barriers, 249–251
global marketing strategy, **259**. *See also* strategy
  countertrade, **262**
  developing, 259–262
  distribution strategy, 261, A-10
  multidomestic marketing strategy, 259–**260**
  pricing strategy, 261, 615
  product/promotion strategy, 260–261
global marketplace, 7–8
global sourcing, **214**
GMOs. *See* genetically modified organisms
goals, marketing plan, A-4
"good for you" products, 424
goods, **377**
  classifying, 380–384
  Consumer Goods Pricing Act (1975), 596
  gray, **456**
  impulse, **381**
  luxury, 179–180
  services *vs.*, 377–378
goods-services continuum, **377**
government
  as category of business market, 207
  discounts for, 211, 229
  product recalls information website, 80
  purchasing procedures, 227
  regulatory agencies, 70
  as research and technology source, 76–77

government regulation. *See also* federal regulation
  in political–legal environment, 67–68
grassroots marketing, **350**
gray goods, **456**
Great Depression, 67
Green Book, 75
green marketing, 74, **88**
  eco-friendly products, 639
grocery industry, 482
gross domestic product (GDP), **72**, 262
  U. S. compared to China and India, 246
  United States, 240
gross profit margin, B-3
growth stage, **396**–397
guerrilla marketing, **524**

H

hackers, 148
health. *See also* federal regulation
  doctors, 566
  Flammable Fabrics Act (1953), 431
  Food Allergen Labeling and Consumer Protection Act, 431
  GMOs issue, 247–248
  obesity *vs.*, 83
  organic foods, 482
  Public Health Cigarette Smoking Act, 69
Helping Families Save Their Homes Act, 69
hidden charges, 649
high-definition television, 627
high-involvement purchase decisions, **190**
high-speed broadband connections, 258
highway tolls, 605
Hispanic Americans, 47, 175, 176
  population growth, 285
historical eras, 8–12
hits, 544
homeshoring, **379**
horizontal channel conflicts, 455
hotels, 649
household cleaning products, 597
household type, 288–289
housing, 608

humorous appeals, 531
hypermarkets, **494**
hypothesis, **317**

I

Identity Theft Enforcement and Restitution Act, 67
IMC. *See* integrated marketing communications
importing, **240**
    global marketing, 255–256
import quotas, **250**
impressions, 544
impulse goods/services, **381**
IMS. *See* Internet Protocol Multimedia Subsystem
inbound telemarketing, **561**
income, **74**
income/expenditure patterns, 289–290
incremental-cost pricing, **610**
independent wholesaling intermediary, 498–502
individual brand, **413**–414
industrial distributor, **386**, 499
inelastic demand, **215**, 608, 608
inflation, 73–74
influencer, **111**, **225**
infomercial, 503
informative advertising, **526**
infrastructure, **246**
innovators/innovation, 291
inside selling, **561**
installations, **385**–386
institutional advertising, **526**
institutional markets, 227–229
integrated marketing communications (IMC), 48, **516**
    components, 516
    databases in, 519–520
    one-to-one, 515
    optimal marketing mix, 517
    overview, 517
    teamwork, 518–519
intensive distribution, **453**
interactive advertising, **529**, 529
interactive buyers and sellers, 270
interactive marketing, 17, **20**, 139, **140**
interactive media, 536–537, 544–545
interactive television, **350**

interdependent partnership, 346, 346
interest stage, of adoption process, **425**
intermodal operations, **464**
internal customers, **342**
internal marketing, 342–344, **343**
internal partnerships, **356**
international distribution strategy, 261
international economic environment, 75–76
international joint ventures, 258
international market research, 328–329
international markets, 229. *See also* globalization
International Organization for Standardization (ISO), 248, **390**
international product and promotional strategy, 260–261
Internet, 516, 519, 529, 533–544. *See also* blog; cookies; e-business; e-marketing
    auctions, 640–641
    for B2B marketing, 208
    banking services, 243
    buyers and sellers, 146–147
    children and, 68, 69
    Children's Online Privacy Protection Act, 68, 69
    coupons, 154
    cyber-attack, 148
    Electronic Signature Act, 69
    government censorship of, 248
    Identity Theft Enforcement and Restitution Act, 67
    online communities, 152
    online forum, **102**
    online price negotiation, 640–641
    online pricing, 642–644
    payment safety, 142–143, 147–148
    Porter's Five Forces and, **42**–43
    privacy, 148–149
    Real ID Act, 69
    secondary data sources, 322
    shopping carts, 144, 624–625
    spending for sales promotion on, 578
    techniques for measuring use of, 327
    usage caps on customers, 636
    user characteristics, 146
    Voice over Internet Protocol, **77**
    as way of life, 504
    Web services, 142, **358**

Internet, (*continued*)
   Web-to-store shoppers, **158**
   wiki, **152**
   worldwide penetration of, 137
Internet Protocol Multimedia Subsystem (IMS), 77
interpretive research, **325**, 329
   ethnographic studies, 329–330
introductory stage, **395**–396
introductory stage, in product lifecycle, **395**–396
inventory control systems, 469
inventory turnover, B-3–B-4
ISO. *See* International Organization for Standardization
ISO 1400 series, 248
ISO 9000 series, 248
ISO 9001:2008, **390**

J

JIT. *See* just-in-time
JITII. *See* just-in-time II
jobs. *See also* career, marketing
   first day at, 37
joint demand, **215**
joint ventures, international, 258
jury of executive opinion, **362**
just-in-time (JIT), **216**
just-in-time II (JITII), **216**

K

key performance indicator, 314
keyword ads, 532

L

labeling
   Food Allergen Labeling and Consumer Protection Act, 431
   Nutrition Labeling and Education Act (1990), 421
labels, **421**
language
   global advertising outlets, 259
   global marketing role of, 246
   international product and promotional strategy, 260–261
   most spoken, 247
   Spanish-language programs, 78
lateral partnerships, **356**
law(s), 67–71, 248–249, 454. *See also* federal regulation; political–legal environment
   consumer protection, 67
   consumer rights, **79**–80
   Engel's laws, **289**–290
   hidden charges, 649
   pricing and, 594–596
   unfair trade, **56**
leader pricing, 596, 615, **638**
learning, **188**
learning theory, 188–189
legal environment, 248–249, 454
lifetime value of a customer, 5, 19, **360**
limited-buyer markets, 212, 214
limited-function wholesaler, 499, 500
limited-line store, **492**
limited problem solving, 194
limited-service research supplier, **312**
line extension, **394**, **421**
liquor, 68
listening, 222
list price, **631**
live events, 621, 640
location, retailer by, 494
location-based advertising, 526
logistics, **444**. *See also* physical distribution
   channel development and, 470
   reverse, 150
   RFID, 436, **460**–461
   supply chain management and, 470
   third-party, **440**–441
logos, college, 84
long channels, 451, 452
loss leader, 596, 614, **638**–**639**
low-involvement purchase decisions, **190**
loyalty
   brand, 411–412
   building, 354
   customer, 20
   IMC and, 516
luxury goods, 179–180
luxury pricing, 597, 608

M

magazines, 535–536
mail-order wholesaler, **500**
managerial levels, 36
manufacturer's brand, **413**
manufacturers' representative, **448**, **501**
MAP. *See* minimum-advertised pricing
marginal analysis, **599**, 607
marginal cost, **606**
markdown, **485**, B-6
market(s), **274**. *See also* target markets
   buyer's, **10**
   commercial, **206**
   demand, 214–216
   factors, in marketing channels, 450, 452
   foreign business, 262
   geographic market concentration, 212
   share, 294–295, **599**
   supermarkets, 50
market development strategy, **423**
marketing, 6–7. *See also* direct marketing; e-marketing; global marketing; relationship marketing
   concentrated (or niche), **297**
   differentiated, **296**–297, 642
   nontraditional, 15–19
   overall marketing strategy, A-3
   21st century, 26
   undifferentiated, **295**–296
marketing career. *See* career, marketing
marketing (distribution) channels, **444**
   alternative, 447
   cooperation, 456
   direct selling, **447**–448, 503
   distribution intensity, 453–454
   dual distribution, **449**
   intermediaries, 448–449
   management/leadership, 455–456
   market factors, 450, 452
   organizational/competitive factors, 452
   performing functions, 454
   product factors, 452
   reverse, **449**–450
   role of, 444–445
   sorting, 445
   strategies, 450–454
   types, 445–447
marketing communications, **516**. *See also* integrated marketing communications
marketing concept, **10**
marketing decision support systems (MDSSs), **331**
marketing environment. *See also* political–legal environment
   marketing mix elements within, 62
   sample outline, A-5
   social–cultural environment, 62, 77–80, 246–247, 270
   technological environment, 62, **76**–77, 247–248
marketing environment outline (situation analysis), A-5
marketing era, 10–11
marketing ethics, **81**. *See also* ethics
   creating program, 81
   distribution, 84
   ethics officers, 81
   marketing research, 82–83
   pricing, 85
   product strategy, 83
   promotions, 84–85
   questions/issues in, 82
   standards, 81, 84
   stick-and-carrot approach, 81
   workplace questionnaire, 82
marketing history
   converting wants to needs, 11–12
   historical eras, 8–12
   marketing era, 40–11
   production era, 9
   relationship era, 8, 11
   sales era, 9
marketing information systems (MISs), **331**
marketing intelligence, 310
marketing intermediary (middleman), **445**. *See also* wholesaling intermediary
   producer to agent to business user, 449
   producer to agent to wholesaler to retailer to consumer, 448
   producer to wholesaler to business user, 448
   producer to wholesaler to retailer to consumer, 448

marketing mix, **47, 376**
  in distribution strategy, 47–48
  elements within environmental framework, 62
  global, 258–260
  IMC and optimal, 517
  pricing objectives, 597–598
  pricing strategy, 49
  promotion strategy, 48–49
  in sample marketing plan, A-5–A-6
  strategic, 47–49
marketing myopia, **12**–13
marketing plan
  budget, schedule, and monitoring, A-5–A-6
  company description, A-4
  components, A-1–A-2
  creating, A-2–A-3
  executive summary, competitive analysis, and mission statement, A-4
  goals and core competencies, A-4
  marketing environment outline (situation analysis), A-5
  overall marketing strategy, A-3
  sample, A-6
  target market and marketing mix, A-5
marketing planning, **37**. *See also* marketing strategy
  business plan, **A-1**
  business portfolio analysis, 51
  case study 1: hotel chains, 57–58
  case study 2: theaters, 58–59
  defining mission, **40**
  at different managerial levels, 39
  elements of, 45–51
  environmental characteristics and, 50–51
  environmental risks/opportunities, 40, 44
  first mover strategy, **43**
  formulating, implementing, and monitoring strategy, 41–42
  marketing mix variables, 47–49
  methods, 51–53
  overview, 36
  process steps, 39–40
  second mover strategy, **44**
  target market description, 46–47
  tools and techniques, 42–45
  in 21st century, 53
marketing public relations (MPR), **522**
marketing research, **310**
  data interpretation/presentation, 319
  defining problem, 316
  development, 311
  director, 39
  example of product reformulation, 325
  exploratory research, **316**–317
  hypothesis, **317**
  international, 328–329
  interpretive, **325**, 329–330
  message research, **543**–544
  primary research methods, 323–324
  process, 315–319
  research design, **317**–318
  sampling techniques, **322**–323
  secondary data collection, 320–322
  survey methods, 325–328
  21st century, 364
marketing strategy, **41**. *See also* marketing planning
  Porter's Five Forces, **42**–43
  second mover strategy, **44**
market-minus pricing, **628**
market penetration strategy, **423**
market-plus pricing, **627**
market potential forecast, 294
market price, **631**
market segmentation, **275**
  abroad, 290
  for auto manufacturers, 275
  by brand loyalty, 293–294
  in consumer markets, 277
  customer-based, **210**
  demographic segmentation, **280**–290
  effective, 276–277
  Engel's laws, **289**–290
  geographic segmentation, **277**–280
  GISs, **280**
  market potential forecast, 294
  process, 294–295
  product-related segmentation, **292**–294
  profile development, 294

psychographic segmentation, **291**
   selection and execution of strategies, 298–299
   strategies, 295–298
   21st century, 300
   urban marketplace, 278
   by usage rates, 293
market share/market growth matrix. *See* Boston Consulting Group matrix
market-share objective, **600**
markup, **485**
   in financial analysis, B-4–B-5
Maslow's hierarchy of needs, 182–184
mass marketing, 636
mass merchandiser, **493**–494
materials handling system, **469**
maturity stage, **397**
MDSSs. *See* marketing decision support systems
meat products, 296
media. *See also* Internet
   interactive, 536–537, 544–545
   newspapers, 535
   radio, 534–535
   television, 258, 521, 533–534, 627
media research, **553**–554. *See also* marketing research
   posttesting, **554**
   pretesting, **543**
media scheduling, **537**
media selection, 533–537
media sharing, 103
men
   as extreme sports fans, 517
merchandise mart, 498
merchandisers, **220**–221
   quick-response merchandising, **358**
   wheel of retailing, **481**
merchant wholesaler, **499**
   types of, 500
mergers, 70
message, **520**, 529
message research, **553**–554
metrics, 313
metropolitan statistical area (MSA), **278**
microblog, **102**–103
micromarketing, **297**
micropolitan statistical area, **279**

middle-class consumers, 179–180
middleman. *See* marketing intermediary
middle management, 39
migration, 278
military, as technology source, 76
Millennial Generation, 57–58
Miller-Tydings Resale Price Maintenance Act (1937), 596
minimum-advertised pricing (MAP), **633**
MISs. *See* marketing information systems
mission, **40**
missionary selling, **566**
mission statement, A-4
mixed race Americans, 287
mobile advertising, 515, 536
mobile crime, 207
mobile devices, surveys about, 327
mobile marketing, **20**
mobile payment system, 147–148
mobile professionals, 292
mobirati (mobile phone user population), 292
modified breakeven analysis, **613**–614
modified rebuy, **223**–224
monitoring, in marketing plan, sample of, A-11–A-12
monopolistic competition, **604**
monopoly, **64**, **605**. *See also* antitrust
motive, **182**
Motor Carrier Act, 69
motor carriers, 464
motorcycles, 277
MPR. *See* marketing public relations
MRO items, **388**
MSA. *See* metropolitan statistical area
multichannel shoppers, 643
multidomestic marketing strategy, 259–**260**
multinational economic integration, 251–254
multiple sourcing, 219
music stores, 508

N

NAICS. *See* North American Industry Classification System
national account selling, **357**–358
national accounts organization, **574**

National Environmental Policy Act, 69
Native Americans, 176, 287
  population growth, 287
Native Hawaiians, 176
natural disaster, 266, 576
nearshoring, **217**
needs, **182**–184
  converting to wants, 11–12
  customer, 4, 6–7, 10, 24, 182–184, 346–347
  Maslow's hierarchy, 182–184
  physiological, 182
  safety, 182
  self-actualization, 182–184
  social/belongingness, 182
net profit margin, B-3
network marketing, **560**
new customers, converted to advocates, 20–22
newspapers, 535
new-task buying, **224**
noise, 521–522
noncumulative quantity discount, **633**
nonpersonal selling, **522**, 526
nonprobability sample, **323**
nonstore retailing, **502**
  automatic merchandising, 504
  direct mail, 502–503, 536, 568
  direct-response retailing, 503
  direct selling, **447**–448, 503
  Internet, 503
  telemarketing, 68, 69, 503, **560**–561, 561
nontraditional marketing, 15
  categories, 16
  cause marketing, 16, **18**
  event marketing, 16, **18**–19, 579
  organization marketing, 16, **19**
  person marketing, **16**
  place marketing, 16, **17**
North American Free Trade Agreement (NAFTA), 8, 68, 210, 213, **252**, 594
North American Industry Classification System (NAICS), **210**–211
not-for-profit organizations
  examples of, 14
  marketing, 13–14
  marketing characteristics, 14–15
  pricing objectives, 602–603
  relationship marketing and, 213
  social media use by, 109–110
  strategic alliances for, 23
Nutrition Labeling and Education Act (1990), 421

O

obesity, 83–84
objection, **570**
objectives, 526–527
odd pricing, **636**
off-price retailer, 493
offshoring, **217**
oil industry, retail gas sales, 627
oligopoly, **64**, **605**
OMMA. *See* Online Media Marketing and Advertising Awards
Omnibus Trade and Competitiveness Act, 250
online auctions, 640–641
online banking services, 243
online buyers and sellers, 146–147
online communities, 152
online coupons, 154
online forum, **102**
online payment safety, 147–148
online price negotiation, 640–641
online pricing, 644, 646
online shopping carts, **144**, 624–625
OPEC. *See* Organization of Petroleum Exporting Countries
opening price point, **631**
operational planning, 39
opinion leader, **180**
opportunity recognition, 191–194
order processing, 469, **565**
organizational model of buying process
  1: anticipate problem/need/opportunity/solution, 221
  2: determine characteristics/quantity of good/service, 221
  3: describe characteristics/quantity of goods/service, 222
  4: search/qualify sources, 222

5: acquire/analyze proposals, 222
6: evaluate proposals/select suppliers, 222
7: select order routine, 223
8: feedback/evaluation, 223
organization marketing, 16, **19**
Organization of Petroleum Exporting Countries (OPEC), 261
outdoor, 536
out-of-home, 518, 536
outsourcing, **217**–218. *See also* nearshoring; offshoring
overall marketing strategy, A-3
over-the-counter selling, **557**–559, 561
ownership, form of, 490–491
ownership (possession) utility, 5–6

P

Pacific Islanders, 176
packaging, 184, 186, 418
    cost-effective, 420–421
    damage, spoilage, pilferage protection, 419–420
    Fair Packaging and Labeling Act (1966), 431
    labels, **421**
    Poison Prevention Packaging Act (1970), 431
    as promotional tool, 420
    protective, in physical distribution, 469
partnership, **355**
    B2B marketing, 22, 209, 212, 270
    buyer partnerships, **356**
    choosing partners, 356
    cobranding and comarketing, **356**–357
    custom deals and rewards within, 209
    interdependent, 346
    internal, **356**
    international joint ventures, 258
    lateral partnerships, **356**
    not-for-profit organizations, 23
    relationship marketing and, 22, 213
    seller, **356**
    top U. S. trade, 240
    types, 356
party plan, 448
patents, 44
payment fraud, 150

payment systems, 147–148
pay with cash, 643, 644
peanuts, 297
penetration pricing strategy, **628**–629
    market-minus pricing, **628**
people of mixed race, 287
perception, **184**
    in consumer behavior, 184–186
    individual factors, 184
    perceptual screens, **184**–185
    stimulus factors, 184
    subliminal, **185**–186
perceptual screens, **184**–185
performance ratios, B-2
    accounts receivable turnover, B-4
    gross profit margin, B-3
    inventory turnover, B-3–B-4
    net profit margin, B-3
    return on assets, B-3
perfumes, 423
personalization., 139
personal selling, **522, 556**
    advertising *vs.*, 556
    AIDA concept, **520**–521, 567
    consultative selling, **563**
    cross-selling, **563**, 564
    relationship selling, **562**–563
    role of, 557
    social media as new corporate homepage, 554–555
    team selling, **564**–565
    trends, 562–565
person marketing, **16**
persuasive advertising, **526**
pets, 177, 288, 341, 452
pharmaceutical companies, 50, 566
    temporary monopolies, 64
philanthropy, 85–86
phishing, **149**
physical distribution, **444**. *See also* transportation
    carriers, 463–464
    customer service standards, 463
    elements, 462
    freight forwarders/supplemental carriers, 467
    intermodal coordination, 467–468

physical distribution, (*continued*)
    inventory control systems, 469
    materials handling system, **469**
    order processing, 469, **565**
    protective packaging, 469
    suboptimization, **462**
    transportation and, 463–464
    warehousing, 468
physiological needs, 182
PIMS. *See* Profit Impact of Market Strategies
PIMS studies, **600**
pink slime, 79
pipelines, 466
piracy, 474
pizza, 259–260, 370–371, 551
place marketing, 16, **17**
place utility, 6
planned shopping center, **486**
planning, **36**, 518, 529, 543, 544. *See also* marketing planning
    CPFaR, **358**
    ERP system, **461**
    levels, 39
    precall, **568**
    strategic, 37–**38**
plastic shopping bags, 78
PMSA. *See* primary metropolitan statistical area
podcast, **152**–153
point-of-purchase (POP) advertising, **581**–582
Poison Prevention Packaging Act (1970), 431
political–legal environment, **67**–71
    controlling, 71
    federal regulation, 67–68
    global marketing, 74, 78, 248–249
    interest groups, 71
    international, 248–249
    legal problems of exclusive distribution, **453**–**454**, 475
    in marketing environment, 62
    regulatory agencies, 70
    regulatory forces, 71
    self-regulation, 71
political risk assessment (PRA), **248**
POP adverting. *See* point-of-purchase advertising
population (universe), **322**
population, geographic segmentation by, 277, 278

pop-unders, 532
pop-ups, **154**, 532, 548
Porter's Five Forces, **42**–43
positioning, **298**–299. *See also* product positioning
    re-, 299
positioning map, **299**
postage-stamp pricing, **635**
postpurchase evaluation, 193–194
posttesting, **544**
PRA. *See* political risk assessment
pragmatic adopters, 292
precall planning, **568**
predictive analytics, 313
preferred customer, 596
premiums, **580**
presentation, **568**–569. *See also* data interpretation/presentation
prestige objectives, 601–602, 639
pretesting, **543**
pre-roll video, 154
price, **594**. *See also* price quotations; pricing; pricing policies; pricing strategies
    B2C compared to B2B marketing, 205
    control, 261
    customary prices, **603**
    determination, cost and revenue curves, 605–607
    determination, marginal analysis, **599**, 607
    determination in economic theory, 604–605
    determination methods, 603–604
    discrimination, 595
    level of relationship marketing, 345
    market price, **631**
    off-price retailer, 493
    online price negotiation, 640–641
    personal selling *vs.* advertising, 556
    value and, 600–601
price quotations
    allowances, **633**
    basing-point pricing, **635**
    cash discounts, **631**–632
    FOB pricing, 634
    geographic considerations, 634–635
    list price, **631**–634
    quantity discounts, **633**
    rebates, 579, **634**

trade discounts, **632**
uniform-delivered pricing, **635**
zone pricing, **635**
pricing
  alternative procedures, 609–611
  basing-point, **635**
  breakeven analysis, **611**–612
  bundle, **644**
  cannibalization dilemma, **424**, **643**
  characteristics of online, 642–644
  comparison shopping tips, 643
  competition objectives, 600
  concepts, 604–609, 616
  EDLP, **629**–630
  ethics, 605
  fixed, 614
  full-cost method of, **609**–610
  global issues, 594
  global marketing strategy, 615
  housing, 608
  increase, 608
  incremental-cost, **610**
  law and, 594–596
  leader, 600, 615, **638**
  live events, 621
  luxury, 597, 608
  in marketing environment, 62
  marketing mix and objectives for, 596–597
  market-minus, **628**
  market-plus, **627**
  modified breakeven analysis, **613**–614
  objectives, not-for-profit organizations, 602–603
  odd, **636**
  PIMS studies, **600**
  postage-stamp, **635**
  prestige objectives, 601–602
  profitability objectives, 598–599
  psychological, 636
  shopbot, **145**, **644**
  traditional global pricing strategies, 642
  unit price, 599, 606, 610–611, 633
  value, **600**–601
  volume objectives, 600
  yield management, **614**–615
  zone, 635

pricing leader, 600, 615, **638**
pricing policies, **636**
  flexibility, **636**
  loss leaders and leader pricing, 596, 615, **638**–639
  price-quality relationships, 639
  product-line pricing, **636**–637
  promotional pricing, **637**–639
  psychological pricing, **636**
pricing strategies, 626
  auctions, 207, 500, 640–641
  competitive, 630–631
  everyday value, 629–630
  foreign market, 261
  penetration, **628**–630
  sample, A-11
  skimming, **627**–628
primary data, **318**
primary metropolitan statistical area (PMSA), **279**
primary research methods
  controlled experiments, **328**
  observation, 323–324
  surveys, 321
privacy
  Children's Online Privacy Protection Act, 68, 69
  e-business, 148–149
  facial recognition technology, 186
  Internet, 82–83
  RFID and, 436
private brand, **413**
private carriers, **464**
private data, 321
private exchange, 143
probability sample, **323**
product(s), 376, **377**. *See also* business products; consumer products; goods; product development; product identification; product lifecycle; product-line
  advertising, **526**
  B2C compared to B2B marketing, 205
  innovative, 375–376
  in marketing environment, 62
  personal selling *vs.* advertising, 556
  recalls, 80, 544
  reformulation, 325
  safety and liability, 63, **431**
  specialty, **382**–383

product adaptation, as international distribution strategy, 260
product advertising, **526**. *See also* advertising
product development, **424**
   adopter categories, 425–426
   adoption process, **424**–425
   business analysis step in, 430
   commercialization, 431
   early adopter identification, 426–427
   idea generation, 429
   new-product committees, 427
   new product departments, 427
   organizing for, 427–429
   process of, 429–431
   product managers, **427**–**428**
   rate of adoption determinants, 426–427
   screening step in, 430
   strategies, 423–424
   test marketing, 431
   venture teams, **428**–429
product diversification strategy, **424**
product identification
   brand extensions, **421**–422
   brand licensing, **422**–423
   brand marks, **416**–417
   brand names, **416**–417
   global, 418
   packaging, 418–421
   trade dress, **418**
   trademarks, 417–418
product invention, 260
production era, 9
production orientation, **9**
product liability, **431**
product lifecycle, **395**
   decline stage, **397**–398
   extending, 398
   fads, 398
   finding new uses, 399
   growth stage, **396**–397
   increasing use frequency, 398
   increasing users, 398
   introductory stage, **395**–396
   making physical changes, 399
   maturity stage, **397**
   in promotional mix, 393–395
   stages, 395–398, 541
product-line, 393
   deletion decisions, 399
   growing, 392–393
   line extension, 394
   market position enhanced by, 393
product-line pricing, **636**–637
product manager, **427**–428
product mix, **393**
   decisions, 394–395
   depth, 394
   length, 394
   line extension, 394
   width, 394
product placement, **523**
product positioning, **298**–299, **423**
product-related segmentation, **292**–294
product strategy sample, A-10
profile development, 294
profitability, pricing objective, 598–599
profit center, **641**
Profit Impact of Market Strategies (PIMS), **600**
profit maximization, **599**
promotion, **516**. *See also* promotional mix; sales promotion
   B2C compared to B2B marketing, 205
   cross-, **538**
   in marketing environment, 64
promotional allowance, **633**
promotional mix, **522**
   advantages/disadvantages, 524–525
   advertising, **522**–523, 525
   direct marketing, 525
   elements, 522–525
   elements comparison, 525
   factors influencing, 540
   fixed-sum-per-unit method for budgeting, 541–542
   funding, 541–542
   guerrilla marketing, **524**
   Internet and social media impact, 545
   meeting competition method for budgeting, 542
   nature of market, 540

nature of product, 540–551
nonpersonal selling, **522**, 526
optimal, 522
percentage-of-sales method for budgeting, 542
personal selling, **522**, 526
pricing, 541
product lifecycle stages, 395–398, 541
product placement, **523**
public relations, **523**–524, 525
sales promotion, **523**, 525
task-objective method for budgeting, 542
promotional pricing, **637**–639
promotional strategy
   ethics, 539–540
   sample, A-10–A-11
proprietary transactions, 142–143
prospecting, **567**
protective packaging, 469
protective tariffs, **250**
psychographic segmentation, **291**
psychological pricing, **636**
Public Health Cigarette Smoking Act, 69
public companies, 242
publicity. *See also* advertising
   nonpersonal selling, **522**, 526
   public relations and, **523**–524
public relations, **523**–524
   buzz about pizza, 551
   ethics, 539–540
   measuring effectiveness, 542–543
   nonpersonal selling, **522**, 526
   promotional mix, 523
   publicity and, 524, 538
   sales promotion, 523
puffery, 540
purchase categories segmentation, 211
purchase decision/act, 193
   environmental factors, 218–219
   interpersonal factors, 219–220
   organizational factors, 219
   role of merchandisers and category advisors, 220–**221**
pure competition, **604**
"pure-play" dot-com retailers, 150
push money, **582**

Q

QR code, **104**
qualifying, **567**
qualitative forecasting, **362**–363
quality
   benchmarking method of measuring, **390**
   perceived, 299
   as product strategy, 376, 380
   service, 390–392
   TQM, **380**
   worldwide programs, 390
quantitative forecasting, **362**, 363–364
quantity discounts, **633**
quick-response merchandising, **358**
quota sample, **323**

R

radio, 534–535
radio-frequency identification (RFID), 436, **460**–461
railroads, 464–465
raw materials, **386**–387
Real ID Act, 69
rebate, 579, **634**
rebuy, straight or modified, **223**–224
recalls, 80, 544
recession, 76
reciprocity, **224**
reference groups, **178**–179
refund, **580**
regional sales manager, 39
regular purchaser, converting new customers to, 20
related party trade, **240**
relationship era, 8, 11
relationship marketing, **11**, 37, 213, **340**. *See also* customer satisfaction
   B2B marketing and, 213
   buyer–seller relationship, 348–351
   customers as advocates, 350–351
   elements, 342
   evaluating, 360–361
   example of, 343
   internal marketing, 342–344
   levels, 344–346
   not-for-profit organizations, 213

relationship marketing, (*continued*)
   partnership and, 22, 213
   pricing and level of, 345
   transaction-based marketing shift to, 19–20, 340–344
   21st century, 364
relationship selling, **562**–565
remanufacturing, **229**
reminder advertising, **526**
remote service center, 258
repositioning, 299
research design, **317**–318. *See also* marketing research
resellers, **206**, 208
resource availability, 75–75
resource-producing industries, 206
response, 521
restaurant business, 510
   Asian American, 177
   equipment, 208
   global marketing, 245
   improved profit margin, 630
retail advertising, **528**–529
   perceived quality, 299
retail convergence, **494**–495
retail cooperative, **457**–458, 502
retailer, 641–642
   convergence and scrambled merchandising, **494**–495
   department stores, **492**–493
   discount houses, **493**
   by form of ownership, 490–491
   general merchandise, **492**
   hypermarkets and supercenters, **494**
   limited-line, 492
   by location, 494
   mass merchandisers, **493**–494
   off-price, 493
   retailer-owned cooperatives/buying offices, 502
   by services provided, 491
   by shopping effort, 491
   showroom/warehouse retailers, 493
   specialty retailer, **491**
   third-largest U. S., 509
   variety stores, 492
retailing, 243, **480**. *See also* nonstore retailing
   evolution of, 481
   wheel of, **481**

retailing strategy
   atmospherics, 488–490
   components, 482
   customer service, 484–485
   location/distribution, 486–487
   merchandising strategy, 483–484
   pricing, 485
   promotional, 487–488
retrieving lost customers, 353–355
return on assets (ROA), B-3
return on investment (ROI), **119**
revenue
   elasticity and, 608–609
   price determination and revenue curves, 604–605
   profit maximization, **599**
revenue tariffs, **250**
reverse channel, **449**–450
reverse logistics, 150
rewards program, 515
RFID. *See* radio-frequency identification
right-time marketing, 139–140
ROA. *See* return on assets
Robinson-Patman Act, 67, 68, **595**–596
ROI. *See* return on investment
routinized response behavior, 194
royalties, 620

S

safety and liability, auto industry, 63, 431
safety needs, 182
salary, **575**
sales analysis, **317**
sales branches, 498
sales channels, 557
   field selling, **559**–560
   inside selling, 561
   integration of, 561–562
   over-the-counter, 557–579
   telemarketing, 68, 503, **560**–561, 565
sales era, 9
sales force composite, **362**
sales forecast, **361**
   Delphi technique, **362**
   exponential smoothing, 364

jury of executive opinion, **362**
in marketing plan, 335
qualitative forecasting, **362**–363
quantitative forecasting, **362**, 363–364
sales force composite, **362**
survey of buyer intentions, 362–363
test market, 363
trend analysis, **363**–364
21st century, 335
sales incentives, **566**
sales manager, 571
   compensating function of, 575–576
   evaluating and controlling functions of, 576–577
   motivating function of, 574–575
   organizing function of, 573–574
   recruiting and selecting function of, 571–572
   supervising function of, 574
   training function of, 572
sales office, 498
sales orientation, **9**
salespeople, 557
   buyers' expectations of, 562
sales process
   AIDA concept, **520**–521, 567
   approach, 567
   closing, 447, **570**, 625
   demonstration, **569**
   ethical issues, 578
   follow-up, 570–**571**
   handling objections, **570**
   presentation, **568**
   prospecting, **567**
   qualifying, **567**
sales promotion, **523**, **578**–579
   cash rewards, 582
   consumer-oriented, 579–581
   contests and sweepstakes, 270, 580–581
   coupons and refunds, **579**–580
   cross-promotion, **538**
   dealer incentives, contests, and training programs, 582
   point-of-purchase advertising, **581**–582
   samples, bonus packs, and premiums, **580**
   specialty advertising, 581
   spending for types of, 579
   trade allowances, **581**
   trade-oriented, 581
   trade shows, **582**, 587
sales quota, **576**
sales tasks
   creative selling, **566**
   missionary selling, **566**
   order processing, 469, **565**
same-sex couples, 289
sample marketing plan
   budget, schedule, and monitoring, A-11–A-12
   core competencies, A-7–A-8
   executive summary, company description, A-6
   goals, A-7
   marketing environment outline (situation analysis), A-8–A-9
   mission statement, A-4
   target market and marketing mix, A-5, A-9
sampling, **580**
   stratified sample, **323**
   techniques, **322**
SBUs. *See* strategic business units
scalping, ticket, 595
schedule, in sample marketing plan, A-11–A-12
scrambled merchandising, **494**–495
search marketing, **154**
secondary data, **318**
   collection, 320–322
   government data, 320
   online sources, 322
   private data, 321
   2010 U. S. Census, 320
second mover strategy, **44**
Secure Sockets Layer (SSL), **147**
segmentation. *See* market segmentation
selective distribution, **453**
self-actualization needs, 182–184
self-concept, **189**
self-concept theory, 189–190
seller partnerships, **356**
seller's market, **10**
selling agent, **501**
sender, **520**
seniors, 181, 283–284
Sentencing Commission, U. S., 81

service encounter, **390**
service gaps, 347
service industry, 242
service quality, **391**
services, **377**, 491
   classifying, 383–384
   customer service, 150–151, 463, 484–485
   impulse, **381**
   types of business, 388–389
   Web services, 142, **358**
service sector
   emergency goods/services, **381**
   goods *vs.*, 377–378
   importance of, 378–379
sex-based advertising appeals, 531
shaping, **188**
sherbet, 510
Sherman Antitrust Act, 67, 68, 454
shopping carts, online, 144, 624–625
shopping effort, 491
shopping products, **381**–382
short channels, 452
simple random sample, **323**
single-person household, 289
skimming pricing strategy, **627**–628. *See also* market-plus pricing
ski resorts, 622
SKU. *See* stock-keeping unit
small-box discount retailer, 593
SMM. *See* social media marketing
social/belongingness needs, 182
social classes, 179–180
social connectors, 292
social credit score, 178
social–cultural environment, **77**, 246–247
   consumerism influenced by, 77–80
   in marketing environment, 62
social interactions level, of relationship marketing, 345–346
social marketing, 19, **20**
social media, **100**. *See also* social media platform; social media tool
   B2B outreach via, 203–204
   business use of, 108–109
   consumer use of, 107–110

   customer attitude conveyed via, 270
   database marketing using, 372
   entry-level job in, 125
   ethics, 121–123
   IMC and, 515
   marketing presence in, 98–100, 104–107
   as new corporate homepage, 554–555
   not-for-profit organizations use of, 109–110
   promotional mix and, 542
   reaching target markets, 295
   SMM, **111**–125
   in 21st century, 126
   workplace ethics and, 121–123
social media analytics, **118**
social media marketing (SMM), **111**–125
social media marketing plan, **111**
social media monitoring, **118**–121
social media platform, **100**–**101**
   blogging sites and forums, 102
   bookmarking sites, **102**
   microblogs, 102–103
   social networking sites, 101–102
   social news sites, **102**
social media tool, **100**–**101**
   apps, 103–104
   blog and microblog postings, 103
   media sharing, 103
   QR codes, **104**
social networking
   career in marketing, 519
   network marketing, **560**
social networking sites, **101**–**102**
social news sites, **102**
social responsibility, **24**–**26**, **85**
soft currencies, 246
soft drinks, 541
solar panels, 37
sole sourcing, **216**
sorting, 445
sound systems, 430
spaceship, commercial travel by, 36–37
spam, **152**
Spanish-language programs, 78
span of control, **574**

special rate, 463
specialty advertising, **581**
specialty products, **382**–383
specialty retailer, **491**
specialty stores, 492
split runs, **544**
sponsored links, 154
sponsorship, **525**
   advertising *vs.*, 525
    celebrity, 16, 42, 527, 527, 528, 590
sports apparel manufacturers, 64
sports eyewear, 430
spreadsheet analysis, **A-3**
spyware, 148
SSL. *See* Secure Sockets Layer
Staggers Rail Act, 69
staples, **381**
"staycations," 36
step out, **627**
stick-and-carrot approach, 81stimulus factors, 184
stock-keeping unit (SKU), **484**
straight extension, 260
straight rebuy, **223**
strategic alliance, **23**, **63**, **359**–360
   not-for-profit organization, 23
strategic business units (SBUs), **51**
strategic planning, 37–**38**
strategic window, **45**
strategy, 37. *See also* marketing planning
   channel, 450–452
   competitive, **65**
   competitive pricing, **630**–631
   customer service as retailing strategy, 481–482
   distribution, 260, A-10
   ethics in promotional strategies, 539–540
   first mover, **43**
   food industry use of social media, 372
   formulating, implementing, and monitoring, 41–42
   global marketing, 259–262, 615
   international distribution, 261
   international product and promotional, 260–261
   market development, **423**
   marketing, **41**
   marketing (distribution) channels, 450–454
   marketing mix, 47–49

   overall marketing, A-3
   Porter's Five Forces, 42–43
   product, and marketing ethics, 82–83
   product diversification, 423
   second mover, **44**
   skimming pricing, **627**–628
stratified sample, **323**
strengths, weaknesses, opportunities, and threats (SWOT), **44**–45
strivers, 291
subcontracting, **257**
subcultures, **174**–176
subliminal perception, **185**–186
suboptimization, **462**
subprime credit cards, 85
subsidies, **250**
sunglasses, 637
Super 301 provisions, 250
supercenter, **494**
supermarkets, 50
supervisory management, 39
supplemental carriers, freight forwarders and, 467
supplies, **387**–388
supply, **604**
supply chain, **358**, **459**
supply chain management, **444**, 459–462
   logistics, 470
   21st century marketing and, 470
   vendor-managed inventory and, 358–359
survey, 325
   experimental method, 328
   focus groups, **326**
   internet-based methods, 327–328
   methods, 325–328
   personal interviews, 326
   telephone interviews, 325
sustainability
   green marketing, 74, **88**
   marketplace, 27
   myopic thinking *vs.*, 13
   as social responsibility, 24–26
sustainable products, **26**
sweepstakes, 270, **580**–581
SWOT. *See* strengths, weaknesses, opportunities, and threats

SWOT analysis, **44**–45
syndicated services, **312**
systems integration, **220**

T

tactical execution, in ad development, 529
tactical planning, **38**
target markets, **274**, A-5
   marketing plan, A-5
   in marketing planning, 46–47
   social media reaching, 295
target-return objective, **599**
tariffs, **249**. *See also* General Agreement on Tariffs and Trade
team leader, 39
team selling, **564**–565
teamwork, 518–519
technological environment, **76**, 77
   marketing environment and, 62, 247–248
technology. *See also* Internet; *specific application*; *specific product*
   addressing social concerns, 76
   automated warehouse, 468
   business intelligence, 331
   communication, 4
   data mining, **331**
   facial recognition, 186
   government sources, 76
   green, 74
   MDSSs, **331**
   military, 76
   MISs, 331
   revolution, 4
   RFID, 436, **460**–461
Telecommunications Act, 69, 70
telemarketing, 68, 503, **560**–561, 565
Telemarketing Sales Rule Amendments, 69
telephone. *See also* cell phone
   B2B cell phone discounts, 211
   Consumer Telephone Records Act, 69
   Do-Not-Call Improvement Act, 69
   interviews, 346
television
   ads, 533–534
   bundle pricing for, **644**
   commercials, 60–61, 270, 521
   high-definition, 627
   high-speed broadband connections, 258
   interactive, **350**
television services, 258
temporary monopoly, 64
test marketing, **328**, **363**
theater-goers, 58–59
   market segmentation for, 304
thinkers, 291
third-party (contract) logistics firm, **460**–461
ticket scalping, 595
time-based competition, **66**
time utility, 6
tobacco industry, 82
top management, 39
total quality management (TQM), **380**
TQM. *See* total quality management
Trade Act (1998), 248
trade allowance, **581**
trade associations, 212
trade discounts, **632**
trade dress, **418**
trade fair, 498
trade-in, **633**
trade industries, **206**
trademark, **417**–418
   Community Trademark, 254
trade promotion, **523**, **581**
trade shows, **582**, 587
transaction-based marketing, **19**, **340**
   converting new customers, 20–22
   interactive marketing, 17, **20**, **139**–140
   mobile marketing, **20**
   relationship marketing shift, 19–20, 340–344
   social marketing to build relationships, 20
   strategic alliances, 23
transfer price, **641**
transfer pricing dilemma, 642
transportation. *See also* physical distribution
   air freight, 466
   carriers, 463–464
   comparing modes, 466–467
   major modes, 464–467
   motor carriers, 465

pipelines, 466
railroads, 464–465
supplemental carriers and freight forwarders, 467
water carriers, 465–466
trend analysis, sales forecast from, **363**–364
trial stage, of adoption process, **425**
truck jobber, **499**
truck wholesaler, **499**, 500
truth, in advertising, 84
tweens and teens, 281–282
brand extension strategy, **421**
extreme sports, 517
underage drinking, 84–85
tweeting, 370
21st century marketing, 26
B2B, 230
channel development, logistics, and supply chain management, 470
consumer behavior, 195
Digital Millennium Copyright Act, 68
e-business, 159
Internet and social media in, 126, 545
marketing planning, 53
marketing research, 364
pricing concepts, 616
pricing strategies, 645
relationship marketing, 364
retail sector, 504
sales forecasting, 364
salespeople in, 583
2010 U. S. Census, 176, 320
tying agreement, **454**

U

unaided recall tests, 544
underage drinking, 84–85
undifferentiated marketing, **295**–296
unemployment, **74**
unfair trade laws, **596**
unfavorable attitude, 186
uniform-delivered pricing, **635**
unitized pallets, 469
unit price, 599, 604, 610–611, 633
unit pricing, **636**

universal product code (UPC), **421**
universities, 640
unlimited data plan, 637
unsought products, **380**
UPC. *See* universal product code
upstream management, **459**
urbanization, 277
CMSA, **279**
MSA, **278**
PMSA, **279**
urban marketplace, 278
user, **225**. *See also* marketing intermediary (middleman)
increasing product users, 398
Internet-user characteristics, 146
mobile phone user population, 292
utilities providers, 64
utility, **5**
form, 5
ownership, 5, 23
place, 5–6
time, 5–6
types, 5

V

vacation
cruises, 304
hotels, 649
"staycations," 36
VALS™, **291**–292
value
of customer lifetime, 5, 19, 360
everyday, 630
price and, 600–601
value analysis, **224**
value pricing, **600**–601
variable costs, **605**
variety stores, 492
vending machines, 504
vendor analysis, **224**
vendor-managed inventory (VMI), **358**
strategic alliances, 359–360
supply chain management, 358–359
venture team, **428**–429
vertical channel conflicts, 455–456

vertical marketing systems (VMS), **457**–458
view-through rates, 544
viral marketing, **350**
virtual conferences, 37
virtual sales team, **564**
vishing, **150**
VMI. *See* vendor-managed inventory
VMS. *See* vertical marketing systems
vodka, 262
Voice over Internet Protocol (VoIP), **77**
volume objectives, 599–600
vulnerabilities, 44

W

warehouse clubs, 493
warehousing, 468
water carriers, 465–466
Web services, 142, **358**. *See also* Internet
Web-to-store shoppers, **158**
Wheeler-Lea Act, 68
wheel of retailing, **481**
wholesaler, **23**–24, **445**, **495**
wholesaler-sponsored voluntary chain, 457
wholesaling intermediary, **495**
   creating utility, 496
     functions, 496–497

independent, 498–502
lowering costs, 497
services, 496–497
types, 498–502
widgets, 296
wiki, **152**
wireless fidelity (Wi-Fi), 65
wireless providers, 637
wireless technology
   RFID, 436, **460**–461
   services, 247
women
   auto purchasing, 181
   on motorcycles, 277
   opinion leader, **180**
   social media interactions among, 370
World Trade Organization (WTO), 7, 250, **252**, 621
WTO. *See* World Trade Organization

Y

yield management, **614**–615
yogurt, 437

Z

zone pricing, **635**

INTERNATIONAL INDEX

A

Africa, 241
   African Americans, 174, 175
   cocoa farmers, 451
   evaluating purchasing patterns in, 214
   Internet use, 137
   political–legal environment, 248
   technological environment, 247
   walmart, 238
Algeria, 648
Arabic, 247
Argentina
   FTAA, **253**
   U.S. outsourcing to, 214
Asia, 8, 50, 76
   Asian-Americans, 75, 76
   counterfeit electronics, 489
   international marketing in, 229–230
   Internet use, 137
   technological environment, 247
   U.S. businesses purchased by Asians, 258
Australia, 174, 208, 245, 248, 257
   global marketing in, 245
   Internet use, 137
   technological environment, 247
Austria, 17, 253, 254
   GMOs banned, 248
   marketing research in, 333

B

backshoring, 379
Belgium, 253, 254
   marketing research in, 333
Brazil
   FTAA, **253**
   Olympic Games, 18
   outsourcing to, 214
   soccer's World Cup, 409
   top U.S. trading partner, 241–242
Bulgaria, 214, 253
   GMOs banned, 247

C

Canada, 8, 17, 41–42, 71, 252
   battery roundup, 449
   census, 290
   direct investment in U.S., 256
   EU trade with, 254
   FTAA, **253**
   international direct investments, 256
   NAFTA, 7, 68, 210, 213, 252, 594–595
   penny eliminated in, 649
   plastic shopping bags, 78–79
   product labeling, 421
   strategic windows, 45
   U.S. direct investment in, 256
   U.S. trading partner, 241–242, 594–595
Caribbean, 247, 250, 292
   Caribbean Americans, 175
   technological environment, 247
Central America, 241
   Americans from, 176
   FTAA, **253**
   U.S. outsourcing to, 214
Central American Free Trade Agreement-DR (CAFTA-DR), **253**
Chile, 214, 239, 258
   Chinese autos imports, 648
   FTAA, **253**
   outsourcing to, 214
China
   auto market, 648
   Chinese Americans, 176, 424
   counterfeit products, 489
   currency policy, 267
   evaluating purchasing patterns in, 214
   exports to United States, 75–76
   FOB, 634
   GDP, 246
   GDP compared to U.S. and India, 262
   global e-commerce sales, 239
   global IT sourcing in, 214
   government data for, 290
   gray market, 456
   Hong Kong business operations in, 258

China (*continued*)
   importing technology and foreign capital, 246
   international direct investments, 257
   Internet use, 137
   MP3 player manufacturing, 4
   pizza, 174
   political–legal environment, 248, 249
   rare earth metals, 604
   strategic business alliances with, 63
   strategic partnership agreement with, 268
   Sweden collaboration with, 432
   top U.S. trading partner, 241–242
   tourism, 243
   U.S. brand launching in, 414
   U.S. businesses purchased by Chinese, 258
   U.S. trading partner, 595
   Walmart, 239
   among world's largest marketers, 241
   world's second-largest market, 8
Colombia, 175
   FTAA, **253**
   outsourcing to, 214
common market, **252**
Community Trademark (CTM), **254**
Consumer products, 275
contractual agreements, 256–257
Costa Rica, U.S. outsourcing to, 214
countertrade, **262**
Croatia, 253, 254
Cuban Americans, 175
customs union, **252**
Cyprus, 253, 254
Czech Republic, 253, 254

D

Denmark, 253, 254
Dominican Republic, 175
Dubai, 244
   retailer operates stores in, 244
dumping, **251**

E

eastern Europe, political–legal environment, 248
Ecuador, 175
   FTAA, **253**
Egypt, 8
embargo, **250**
England. *See* Great Britain
English language, 246
Estonia, 253, 254

Eurasia, 213
euro, 7, 174, 253–254
   economic recession, 245, 615
Europe, 8, 75, 174
   direct investment in U.S., 257
   global marketing in, 244
   history of marketing, 10–11
   international direct investments, 257
   Internet use, 137
   ISO standardization, **248**, 390
   political–legal environment, 248
   U.S. brand launching in, 409, 414
European Commission, 148
European Union (EU), 7, **253**, 254, 390
   bankruptcy and bailouts within, 76
   Canada trade with, 254
   consolidation of buying centers, 226
   CTM, **254**
   cultural differences within, 173
   economic environment, 245
   economic recession and, 615
   GMOs issue, 247
   members, 253–254
   U.S. tariffs on imports, 594
exchange control, **251**
exchange rate, **246**
exporting, **240**
   Chinese exports to U.S., 75–76
   countertrade, 262
   Export Trading Company Act (1982), 248
   global market, 255–256
   OPEC, 261
   political–legal environment for, 248–249
   service/retail exports, 242–243
   top U.S. trading partners, 241–242
   U.S. service and retail exports, 242–244
   WTO monitoring of, 7, 249–251, **252**, 621

F

fake stores, 489
Finland, 253, 254
   marketing research in, 333
foreign licensing, **256**–257
foreign market entrance strategies
   contractual agreements, 256–257
   foreign licensing, 256–257
   franchising, **256**
   importing and exporting, 255–256
   international direct investment, 257
   subcontracting, **257**

International Index

France
   copyright laws, 151
   cosmetics and beauty product development, 430
   GMOs banned, 247
   keeping customers in, 348
   marketing research in, 333
   segmentation data for, 290
   socio-cultural environment, 246
   top U.S. trading partner, 241–242
   U.S. franchise in, 256, 333
franchise, **256**
free-trade area, **251**
Free Trade Area of the Americas (FTAA), **253**
friendship, commerce, and navigation (FCN) treaties, **248**

G

General Agreement on Tariffs and Trade (GATT), 249, **252**
Germany, 17, 253, 254
   census, 290
   copyright laws, 151
   data for, 290
   footwear company, 254
   GMOs banned, 247
   government data for, 290
   keeping customers in, 348
   marketing research in, 333
   new global market, 239
   top U.S. trading partner, 241–242
   among world's largest marketers, 241
global marketing
   benefits, 244–245
   categories, 240
   contractual agreements, 256–257
   countertrade exports, 262
   developing global marketing strategy, 259–262
   developing strategy for, 259–260
   direct investment, 257
   dumping, 251
   economic environment, 245
   employment and, 240, 250
   factors creating today's, 7–8
   globalization and, 254
   international distribution strategy, 261
   international product and promotional strategies, 260
   language's role in, 246
   marketing mix and, 259–260
   multinational corporations evolving to, 258
   multinational economic integration, 251–254

   political–legal environment, 73, 74–76, 87–88, 248–249
   pricing strategy, 261
   service/retail exports, 242–243
   social–cultural influences in, 62, 77–81, 246
   technological environment, 62, 247–248
   trade barriers to, **249–251**
   world's largest marketers, 241
Great Britain, 44, 173, 409
   keeping customers, 348
   Olympic Games in, 18
   segmentation data for, 290
Greece, 76, 253, 254, 581
   economic recession and, 615
   political–legal environment, 248
Gross Domestic Product (GDP), 72
   U.S., 240
   U.S. compared to China and India, 262
Guatemala
   FTAA, **253**
   Guatemalan Americans, 175

H

Hindi, 247
homeshoring, **379**
Honduras, 175
Hong Kong, 258, 259
   data for, 290
   gray market, 456
   operations in China, 258
   radio in, 534
Hungary, 253, 254
   GMOs banned, 247

I

Iceland, 254, 255
importing, **240**
   dumping and, **251**
   GATT tariff negotiations, 249, **252**
   global market, 255–256
   import quotas, **250**
   technology and foreign capital, 246
   top U.S. trade partners, 241–242
   WTO monitoring of, 7, 249–251, **252**, 621
import tariffs, **251**
India, 8, 20, 174
   auto industry, 629
   GDP, 246
   GDP compared to U.S. and China, 262
   global IT sourcing in, 214

India, (continued)
    global marketing in, 245
    importing technology and foreign capital, 246
    Indo-Americans, 175
    international direct investment in, 257
    Internet use, 137
    U.S. cash-and-carry stores in, 257
    Western influences, 47
Indonesia, 260
    outsourcing to, 214
international contractual agreements, 256–257
international direct investment, 257
international distribution strategy, 261
international economic environment, 75–76
international franchising, 256
international joint ventures, 257
international market research, 328–329
International Organization for Standardization (ISO), **248**, 390
international political–legal environment, 248
international subcontracting, 257
international travel, 244
Internet use, comparison of countries, 137
Ireland, 76, 253, 254
Israel, 409
Italy, 76, 253, 254
    marketing research in, 333
    segmentation data for, 290

J

Japan, 8, 17, 522
    celebrity sponsorship in, 527
    census, 290
    direct investment in U.S., 257
    global marketing in, 244
    government data for, 290
    international direct investments, 256
    international product and promotional strategies, 260
    Internet use, 137
    Japanese Americans, 176, 424
    keeping customers in, 348
    segmentation data for, 290
    top U.S. trading partner, 241–242
    U.S. brand launching in, 414
    among world's largest marketers, 241

K

Kenya, purchasing patterns in, 213
key performance indicator, 314

Korea. *See also* South Korea
    internet service, 137
    Korean Americans, 176–177, 424
    winter games, 18
Kraft Foods Group, 31
Kuwait, 244

L

Latin America, 8, 238
    Internet use, 137
    Spanish language, 247
    technological environment, 247
Latvia, 253, 254
Libya, 76
Lithuania, 137, 253, 254
Luxembourg, 8, 253, 254

M

Macedonia, 253, 254
Malaysia
    evaluating purchasing patterns in, 214
    outsourcing to, 214
Malta, 253, 254
Mandarin (Chinese), 247
Market segmentation, 275
Metrcis, 313
Mexico, 4
    EU trade with, 254
    FTAA, **253**
    NAFTA, 7, 68, 210, 213, 252, 594–595
    outsourcing to, 214
    U.S. trading partner, 241–242, 594–595
Middle East, 8, 76, 213
    Internet use, 137
    political–legal environment, 248
    technological environment, 247
    U.S. fast food in, 333
Montenegro, 253, 254
multidomestic marketing strategy, **260**
multinational corporations, 258

N

Netherlands, 226, 253–254
    international direct investments, 257
    marketing research in, 333
    U.S. direct investment in, 257
    among world's largest marketers, 241
New Zealand, 245

Nicaragua, 616
North America, 9, 88, 243
   FTAA, **253**
   Internet data traffic, 309
   Internet use, 137
   NAFTA, 7, 68, 210, 213, **252**, 594–595
   NAICS, **210**
   segmentation by customer type, 210, 291–292
   technological environment, 247
   transportation, 463
North American Free Trade Agreement (NAFTA), 7, 68, 210, 213, **252**
   on tariffs, 594–595
North American Industry Classification System (NAICS), **210**

O

Oceania, 247
offshoring, 217
Organization of Petroleum Exporting Countries (OPEC), 261
outsourcing, 214

P

Peru
   FTAA, **253**
   outsourcing to, 214
   Peruvian Americans, 175
Philippines
   outsourcing to, 214
   Philippino Americans, 175, 424
Poland, 253, 254
political risk assessment (PRA), **248**
Portugal, 76, 253, 254
protective tariffs, **250**
Puerto Rico, 175

R

related party trade, **240**
revenue tariffs, **250**
Romania, 50, 253, 254
   Internet use, 137
Russia, 18, 213
   Chinese autos imports, 648
   evaluating purchasing patterns in, 213
   global marketing in, 244
   international product and promotional strategies, 260
   WTO membership, 252

S

satellite radio, 534
Scandinavia, 17
Serbia, 253, 254
Singapore, 260
Slovakia, 253, 254
Slovenia, 253, 254
South Africa, 8
   Chinese autos imports, 648
   purchasing patterns in, 214
   walmart stores, 239
South America, 22, 241
   Americans from, 175
   FTAA, **253**
   Internet use, 137
   outsourcing to, 214
   political–legal environment, 248
   technological environment, 247
South Korea, 4
   auto industry, 423
   Internet use, 137
   top U.S. trading partner, 241–242
Spain, 76, 253, 254
   economic recession, 615
   international marketing in, 229–230
   political–legal environment, 248
   segmentation data for, 290
Spanish language, 247
Sri Lanka, 214
subcontracting, **257**
subsidies, **250**
Sweden, 253, 254, 518
   automaker, 431
   multinational engineering company, 258
Switzerland, 137, 248, 390

T

Taiwan, 174
   Taiwanese Americans, 423
   top U.S. trading partner, 241–242
tariffs, **249**
   GATT, 249, **242**
   import, **250**
   NAFTA on, 594–595
   U.S. tariffs on EU imports, 594
technological environment, global marketing and, 62, 247–248

Thailand, 260
  economic environment in, 245
  natural disaster, 601
  outsourcing to, 214
trade barriers
  embargo, **250**
  exchange control, **251**
  import tariffs, **251**
  protective tariffs, **250**
  revenue tariffs, **250**
  subsidies, **250**
Tunisia, 522
Turkey, 254
  purchasing patterns in, 214

U

United Kingdom, 17, 253, 254
  government data for, 290
  marketing research in, 333
  plastic shopping bags, 78–79
  social media use, 104
  top U.S. trading partner, 241–242
  U.S. direct investment in, 257
  among world's largest marketers, 241
United Nations, 241–242
United States (U.S.), 17, 26, 45
  antitrust laws, 64
  armour sponsors, 409
  Arvind brands, 258
  businesses purchased by Asian companies, 258
  Canada trading partner, 594–595
  consumer protection, 63
  culture, 173
  Department of Commerce, 50
  direct investment abroad, 257
  ethnic populations, 47
  foreign direct investment in, 257
  foreign trade partners, 241–242
  FTAA, **253**
  GDP, 240
  GDP compared to China and India, 262
  geographic segmentation, 277–280
  government data for, 290
  history of marketing, 10–11
  international brand launching, 414
  in international legal environment, 248–249
  Internet use, 137, 146
  keeping customers in, 348
  largest retailer in, 509
  NAFTA, 7, 68, 210, 213, 252, 595–595
  opinion leaders, 180
  outsourcing to Argentina, 214
  outsourcing to Central America, 214
  outsourcing to Costa Rica, 214
  outsourcing to Vietnam, 214
  penny eliminated, 649
  plastic shopping bags, 78–79
  segmentation by customer type, 210, 291–292
  segmentation by demographics, 209, 280–290
  service and retail exports, 242–243
  service sector, 378–379
  social class hierarchy, 179–180
  social media job titles, 123
  social media use, 105
  soda consumption, 45
  sports leagues, 254, 267
  strategic windows, 45
  streamline inventory, 443
  subcultures, 174–176
  as target for international auto industry, 262
  as target for international marketers, 262
  tech-savvy consumers, 52
  top trading partners, 241–242
  trade deficit, 378
  2014Census, 176, 320–321
  UK trading partner, 241–242
  volunteers, 13–14
  world's largest market, 8
  among world's largest marketers, 241
Uruguay, 252

V

Venezuela, 175, 253
Vietnam
  U.S. outsourcing to, 214
  Vietnamese Americans, 176

W

West Africa, 451
western Europe, 9–10
World Trade Organization (WTO), 7, 249–251, **252**, 621